Lecture Notes in Artificial Intelligence 8467

Subseries of Lecture Notes in Computer Science

Lecture Notes in Artificial Intelligence   8467

Subseries of Lecture Notes in Computer Science

LNAI Series Editors

Randy Goebel
University of Alberta, Edmonton, Canada
Yuzuru Tanaka
Hokkaido University, Sapporo, Japan
Wolfgang Wahlster
DFKI and Saarland University, Saarbrücken, Germany

LNAI Founding Series Editor

Jörg Siekmann
DFKI and Saarland University, Saarbrücken, Germany

Leszek Rutkowski   Marcin Korytkowski
Rafał Scherer   Ryszard Tadeusiewicz
Lotfi A. Zadeh   Jacek M. Zurada (Eds.)

Artificial Intelligence and Soft Computing

13th International Conference, ICAISC 2014
Zakopane, Poland, June 1-5, 2014
Proceedings, Part I

 Springer

Volume Editors

Leszek Rutkowski
Marcin Korytkowski
Rafał Scherer
Częstochowa University of Technology
42-200 Częstochowa, Poland
E-mail: {leszek.rutkowski, marcin.korytkowski, rafal.scherer}@iisi.pcz.pl

Ryszard Tadeusiewicz
AGH University of Science and Technology
30-059 Kraków, Poland
E-mail: rtad@agh.edu.pl

Lotfi A. Zadeh
University of California Berkeley
Department of Electrical Engineering and Computer Sciences
Berkeley, CA 94720-1776, USA
E-mail: zadeh@cs.berkeley.edu

Jacek M. Zurada
University of Louisville
Computational Intelligence Laboratory
Louisville, KY 40292, USA
E-mail: jacek.zurada@louisville.edu

ISSN 0302-9743   e-ISSN 1611-3349
ISBN 978-3-319-07172-5   e-ISBN 978-3-319-07173-2
DOI 10.1007/978-3-319-07173-2
Springer Cham Heidelberg New York Dordrecht London

Library of Congress Control Number: 2014938247

LNCS Sublibrary: SL 7 – Artificial Intelligence

Typesetting: Camera-ready by author, data conversion by Scientific Publishing Services, Chennai, India

Printed on acid-free paper

Springer is part of Springer Science+Business Media (www.springer.com)

Preface

This volume constitutes the proceedings of the 13th International Conference on Artificial Intelligence and Soft Computing, ICAISC 2014, held in Zakopane, Poland, during June 1–5, 2014. The conference was organized by the Polish Neural Network Society in cooperation with the University of Social Sciences in Łódź, the Institute of Computational Intelligence at the Częstochowa University of Technology, and the IEEE Computational Intelligence Society, Poland Chapter. Previous conferences took place in Kule (1994), Szczyrk (1996), Kule (1997) and Zakopane (1999, 2000, 2002, 2004, 2006, 2008, 2010, 2012, and 2013) and attracted a large number of papers and internationally recognized speakers: Lotfi A. Zadeh, Igor Aizenberg, Shun-ichi Amari, Daniel Amit, Piero P. Bonissone, Jim Bezdek, Zdzisław Bubnicki, Andrzej Cichocki, Włodzisław Duch, Pablo A. Estévez, Jerzy Grzymala-Busse, Martin Hagan, Yoichi Hayashi, Akira Hirose, Kaoru Hirota, Er Meng Joo, Janusz Kacprzyk, Jim Keller, Laszlo T. Koczy, Soo-Young Lee, Robert Marks, Evangelia Micheli-Tzanakou, Kaisa Miettinen, Ngoc Thanh Nguyen, Erkki Oja, Witold Pedrycz, Marios M. Polycarpou, José C. Príncipe, Jagath C. Rajapakse, Šarunas Raudys, Enrique Ruspini, Jörg Siekmann, Roman Slowiński, Igor Spiridonov, Ponnuthurai Nagaratnam Suganthan, Ryszard Tadeusiewicz, Shiro Usui, Fei-Yue Wang, Jun Wang, Bogdan M. Wilamowski, Ronald Y. Yager, Syozo Yasui, and Jacek Zurada. The aim of this conference is to build a bridge between traditional artificial intelligence techniques and so-called soft computing techniques. It was pointed out by Lotfi A. Zadeh that "soft computing (SC) is a coalition of methodologies which are oriented toward the conception and design of information/intelligent systems. The principal members of the coalition are: fuzzy logic (FL), neurocomputing (NC), evolutionary computing (EC), probabilistic computing (PC), chaotic computing (CC), and machine learning (ML). The constituent methodologies of SC are, for the most part, complementary and synergistic rather than competitive." These proceedings present both traditional artificial intelligence methods and soft computing techniques. Our goal is to bring together scientists representing both areas of research. This volume is divided into six parts:

- Neural Networks and Their Applications
- Fuzzy Systems and Their Applications
- Evolutionary Algorithms and Their Applications
- Classification and Estimation
- Computer Vision, Image and Speech Analysis
- Special Session 3: Intelligent Methods in Databases

The conference attracted 331 submissions from 29 countries, and after the review process, 139 papers were accepted for publication. ICAISC 2014 hosted three special sessions:

Special Session 1: "Machine Learning for Visual Information Analysis and Security" organized by:

- Rafał Scherer, Częstochowa University of Technology, Poland
- Svyatoslav Voloshynovskiy, University of Geneva, Switzerland

The session was supported by the project "New Perspectives on Intelligent Multimedia Management with Applications in Medicine and Privacy Protecting Systems" co-financed by a grant from Switzerland through the Swiss Contribution to the Enlarged European Union.

Special Session 2: "Applications and Properties of Fuzzy Reasoning and Calculus", organized by:

- Witold Kosiński, Polish-Japanese Institute of Information Technology, Poland

Special Session 3: "Intelligent Methods in Databases" organized by:

- Rafał A. Angryk, Georgia State University, USA
- Marcin Gabryel, Częstochowa University of Technology, Poland
- Marcin Korytkowski, Częstochowa University of Technology, Poland

The session was supported by the project "Innovative Methods of Retrieval and Indexing Multimedia Data Using Computational Intelligence Techniques" funded by the National Science Centre.

I would like to thank our participants, invited speakers, and reviewers of the papers for their scientific and personal contribution to the conference. The following reviewers were very helpful in reviewing the papers:

R. Adamczak	M. Choraś	I. Fister
T. Babczyński	K. Choros	M. Fraś
M. Baczyński	P. Cichosz	M. Gabryel
M. Białko	R. Cierniak	A. Gawęda
A. Bielskis	P. Ciskowski	M. Giergiel
M. Blachnik	C. CoelloCoello	F. Gomide
L. Bobrowski	B. Cyganek	Z. Gomółka
L. Borzemski	J. Cytowski	M. Gorgoń
J. Brest	I. Czarnowski	M. Gorzałczany
T. Burczyński	J. de la Rosa	D. Grabowski
R. Burduk	W. Duch	E. Grabska
B. Butkiewicz	L. Dutkiewicz	K. Grąbczewski
C. Castro	L. Dymowa	P. Grzegorzewski
K. Cetnarowicz	A. Dzieliński	J. Grzymala-Busse
J. Chang	P. Dziwiński	H. Haberdar
M. Chis	D. Elizondo	R. Hampel
W. Cholewa	A. Fanea	Y. Hayashi

Z. Hendzel

Z. Hippe

A. Horzyk

E. Hrynkiewicz

D. Jakóbczak

A. Janczak

D. Kacprzak

O. Kahm

W. Kamiński

T. Kaplon

A. Kasperski

V. Kecman

E. Kerre

F. Klawonn

J. Kluska

L. Koczy

A. Kołakowska

J. Konopacki

J. Korbicz

M. Kordos

P. Korohoda

J. Koronacki

M. Korzeń

W. Kosiński

J. Kościelny

M. Korytkowski

L. Kotulski

Z. Kowalczuk

J. Kozlak

M. Kraft

M. Kretowska

M. Kretowski

D. Krol

A. Kubiak

P. Kudová

J. Kulikowski

O. Kurasova

V. Kurkova

M. Kurzyński

J. Kusiak

N. Labroche

J. Lampinen

A. Ligęza

H. Liu

M. Ławryńczuk

J. Łęski

B. Macukow

K. Madani

W. Malina

J. Mańdziuk

U. Markowska-Kaczmar

M. Marques

A. Marszałek

A. Martin

A. Materka

R. Matuk Herrera

J. Mazurkiewicz

V. Medvedev

J. Mendel

M. Mernik

J. Michalkiewicz

Z. Mikrut

S. Misina

W. Mitkowski

W. Moczulski

W. Mokrzycki

M. Morzy

T. Munakata

G. Nalepa

L. Nassif

A. Nawrat

M. Nieniewski

A. Niewiadomski

R. Nowicki

A. Obuchowicz

E. Oja

S. Osowski

M. Pacholczyk

F. Pappalardo

K. Patan

M. Pawlak

A. Piegat

Z. Pietrzykowski

V. Piuri

P. Prokopowicz

A. Przybył

R. Ptak

E. Rafajłowicz

E. Rakus-Andersson

M. Rane

Š. Raudys

R. Rojas

L. Rolka

I. Rudas

F. Rudziński

A. Rusiecki

H. Safari

S. Sakurai

N. Sano

J. Sas

a. Sashima

R. Scherer

M. SepesyMaucec

P. Sevastjanov

A. Sędziwy

A. Skowron

E. Skubalska-
Rafajłowicz

K. Slot

D. Słota

A. Słowik

J. Smoląg

C. Smutnicki

A. Sokołowski

T. Sołtysiński

J. Starczewski

J. Stefanowski

E. Straszecka

V. Struc

P. Strumiłło

M. Studniarski

P. Suganthan

R. Sulej

V. Sumati

J. Swacha

P. Szczepaniak

E. Szmidt

M. Szpyrka

J. Świątek

R. Tadeusiewicz

H. Takagi

Y. Tiumentsev

A. Tomczyk

V. Torra

B. Trawinski

E. Volna	S. Wiak	S. Zadrożny
R. Vorobel	B. Wilamowski	D. Zaharie
M. Wagenknecht	M. Witczak	D. Zakrzewska
T. Walkowiak	M. Wojciechowski	A. Zamuda
L. Wang	M. Wozniak	R. Zdunek
Y. Wang	M. Wygralak	
J. Wąs	J. Zabrodzki	

Finally, I thank my co-workers Łukasz Bartczuk, Piotr Dziwiński, Marcin Gabryel, Marcin Korytkowski, and the conference secretary Rafał Scherer for their enormous efforts to make the conference a very successful event. Moreover, I would like to acknowledge the work of Marcin Korytkowski, who designed the Internet submission system.

The conference volumes are devoted to the memory of Prof. Witold Kosiński, co-founder of the Polish Neural Network Society, who passed away on March 14, 2014.

June 2014   Leszek Rutkowski

Organization

ICAISC 2014 was organized by the Polish Neural Network Society in cooperation with the University of Social Sciences in Łódź, the Institute of Computational Intelligence at Częstochowa University of Technology, and the IEEE Computational Intelligence Society, Poland Chapter and with technical sponsorship from the IEEE Computational Intelligence Society.

ICAISC Chairs

Honorary chairs

Lotfi Zadeh (USA)
Jacek Żurada (USA)

General chair

Leszek Rutkowski (Poland)

Co-chairs

Włodzisław Duch (Poland)   Józef Korbicz (Poland)
Janusz Kacprzyk (Poland)   Ryszard Tadeusiewicz (Poland)

ICAISC Program Committee

Rafał Adamczak - Poland
Cesare Alippi - Italy
Shun-ichi Amari - Japan
Rafal A. Angryk - USA
Jarosław Arabas - Poland
Robert Babuska - The Netherlands
Ildar Z. Batyrshin - Russia
James C. Bezdek - USA
Marco Block-Berlitz - Germany
Leon Bobrowski - Poland
Piero P. Bonissone - USA
Bernadette Bouchon-Meunier - France
James Buckley - Poland
Tadeusz Burczynski - Poland

Andrzej Cader - Poland
Juan Luis Castro - Spain
Yen-Wei Chen - Japan
Wojciech Cholewa - Poland
Fahmida N. Chowdhury - USA
Andrzej Cichocki - Japan
Paweł Cichosz - Poland
Krzysztof Cios - USA
Ian Cloete - Germany
Oscar Cordón - Spain
Bernard De Baets - Belgium
Nabil Derbel - Tunisia
Ewa Dudek-Dyduch - Poland
Ludmiła Dymowa - Poland

Andrzej Dzieliński - Poland
David Elizondo - UK
Meng Joo Er - Singapore
Pablo Estevez - Chile
János Fodor - Hungary
David B. Fogel - USA
Roman Galar - Poland
Alexander I. Galushkin - Russia
Adam Gaweda - USA
Joydeep Ghosh - USA
Juan Jose Gonzalez de la Rosa - Spain
Marian Bolesław Gorzałczany - Poland
Krzysztof Grąbczewski - Poland
Garrison Greenwood - USA
Jerzy W. Grzymala-Busse - USA
Hani Hagras - UK
Saman Halgamuge - Australia
Rainer Hampel - Germany
Zygmunt Hasiewicz - Poland
Yoichi Hayashi - Japan
Tim Hendtlass - Australia
Francisco Herrera - Spain
Kaoru Hirota - Japan
Adrian Horzyk - Poland
Tingwen Huang - USA
Hisao Ishibuchi - Japan
Mo Jamshidi - USA
Andrzej Janczak - Poland
Norbert Jankowski - Poland
Ali Jannatpour - Canada
Robert John - UK
Jerzy Józefczyk - Poland
Tadeusz Kaczorek - Poland
Władysław Kamiński - Poland
Nikola Kasabov - New Zealand
Okyay Kaynak - Turkey
Vojislav Kecman - New Zealand
James M. Keller - USA
Etienne Kerre - Belgium
Frank Klawonn - Germany
Jacek Kluska - Poland
Leonid Kompanets - Poland
Przemysław Korohoda - Poland
Jacek Koronacki - Poland
Witold Kosiński - Poland

Jan M. Kościelny - Poland
Zdzisław Kowalczuk - Poland
Robert Kozma - USA
László Kóczy - Hungary
Rudolf Kruse - Germany
Boris V. Kryzhanovsky - Russia
Adam Krzyzak - Canada
Juliusz Kulikowski - Poland
Roman Kulikowski - Poland
Věra Kůrková - Czech Republic
Marek Kurzyński - Poland
Halina Kwaśnicka - Poland
Soo-Young Lee - Korea
George Lendaris - USA
Antoni Ligęza - Poland
Sławomir Litwiński - Poland
Zhi-Qiang Liu - Hong Kong
Simon M. Lucas - UK
Jacek Łęski - Poland
Bohdan Macukow - Poland
Kurosh Madani - France
Luis Magdalena - Spain
Witold Malina - Poland
Krzysztof Malinowski - Poland
Jacek Mańdziuk - Poland
Antonino Marvuglia - Ireland
Andrzej Materka - Poland
Jaroslaw Meller - Poland
Jerry M. Mendel - USA
Radko Mesiar - Slovakia
Zbigniew Michalewicz - Australia
Zbigniew Mikrut - Poland
Sudip Misra - USA
Wojciech Moczulski - Poland
Javier Montero - Spain
Eduard Montseny - Spain
Kazumi Nakamatsu - Japan
Detlef D. Nauck - Germany
Antoine Naud - Poland
Edward Nawarecki - Poland
Ngoc Thanh Nguyen - Poland
Antoni Niederliński - Poland
Robert Nowicki - Poland
Andrzej Obuchowicz - Poland
Marek Ogiela - Poland

Erkki Oja - Finland
Stanisław Osowski - Poland
Nikhil R. Pal - India
Maciej Patan - Poland
Witold Pedrycz - Canada
Leonid Perlovsky - USA
Andrzej Pieczyński - Poland
Andrzej Piegat - Poland
Vincenzo Piuri - Italy
Lech Polkowski - Poland
Marios M. Polycarpou - Cyprus
Danil Prokhorov - USA
Anna Radzikowska - Poland
Ewaryst Rafajłowicz - Poland
Sarunas Raudys - Lithuania
Olga Rebrova - Russia
Vladimir Red'ko - Russia
Raúl Rojas - Germany
Imre J. Rudas - Hungary
Enrique H. Ruspini - USA
Khalid Saeed - Poland
Dominik Sankowski - Poland
Norihide Sano - Japan
Robert Schaefer - Poland
Rudy Setiono - Singapore
Paweł Sewastianow - Poland
Jennie Si - USA
Peter Sincak - Slovakia
Andrzej Skowron - Poland
Ewa Skubalska-Rafajłowicz - Poland
Roman Słowiński - Poland
Tomasz G. Smolinski - USA
Czesław Smutnicki - Poland
Pilar Sobrevilla - Spain
Janusz Starzyk - USA
Jerzy Stefanowski - Poland

Pawel Strumillo - Poland
Ron Sun - USA
Johan Suykens Suykens - Belgium
Piotr Szczepaniak - Poland
Eulalia J. Szmidt - Poland
Przemysław Śliwiński - Poland
Adam Słowik - Poland
Jerzy Świątek - Poland
Hideyuki Takagi - Japan
Yury Tiumentsev - Russia
Vicenç Torra - Spain
Burhan Turksen - Canada
Shiro Usui - Japan
Michael Wagenknecht - Germany
Tomasz Walkowiak - Poland
Deliang Wang - USA
Jun Wang - Hong Kong
Lipo Wang - Singapore
Zenon Waszczyszyn - Poland
Paul Werbos - USA
Slawo Wesolkowski - Canada
Sławomir Wiak - Poland
Bernard Widrow - USA
Kay C. Wiese - Canada
Bogdan M. Wilamowski - USA
Donald C. Wunsch - USA
Maciej Wygralak - Poland
Roman Wyrzykowski - Poland
Ronald R. Yager - USA
Xin-She Yang - UK
Gary Yen - USA
John Yen - USA
Sławomir Zadrożny - Poland
Ali M. Ș. Zalzala - United Arab
  Emirates

ICAISC Organizing Committee

Rafał Scherer, Secretary
Łukasz Bartczuk, Organizing Committee Member
Piotr Dziwiński, Organizing Committee Member
Marcin Gabryel, Finance Chair
Marcin Korytkowski, Databases and Internet Submissions

Table of Contents – Part I

Neural Networks and Their Applications

Fuzzy Systems and Their Applications

Evolutionary Algorithms and Their Applications

Classification and Estimation

Computer Vision, Image and Speech Analysis

Intelligent Methods in Databases

Table of Contents – Part II

Data Mining

Bioinformatics, Biometrics and Medical Applications

Agent Systems, Robotics and Control

Artificial Intelligence in Modeling and Simulation

Various Problems of Artificial Intelligence

Machine Learning for Visual Information Analysis and Security

Applications and Properties of Fuzzy Reasoning and Calculus

Clustering

Neural Networks and Their Applications

Hybrid System of ART and RBF Neural Networks for Classification of Vibration Signals and Operational States of Wind Turbines

Andrzej Bielecki[1], Tomasz Barszcz[2], Mateusz Wójcik[3], and Marzena Bielecka[4]

[1] AGH University of Science and Technology,
Faculty of Electrical Engineering, Automatics, Computer Science and Biomedical Engineering, Chair of Applied Computer Science
Al. Mickiewicza 30, 30-059 Cracow, Poland
azbielecki@gmail.com

[2] AGH University of Science and Technology,
Faculty of Mechanical Engineering and Robotics, Chair of Robotics and Mechatronics, Al. Mickiewicza 30, 30-059 Cracow, Poland
tbarszcz@agh.edu.pl

[3] Jagiellonian University,
Faculty of Physics, Astronomy and Applied Computer Science,
Reymonta 4, 30-059 Cracow, Poland
mateusz.wojcik@uj.edu.pl

[4] AGH University of Science and Technology,
Faculty of Geology, Geophysics and Environmental Protection,
Chair of Geoinformatics and Applied Computer Science,
Al. Mickiewicza 30, 30-059 Cracow, Poland
bielecka@agh.edu.pl

Abstract. In recent years wind energy has been the fastest growing branch of the power generation industry. Maintenance of the wind turbine generates its the largest cost. A remote monitoring is a common method to reduce this cost. Growing number of monitored turbines requires an automatized way of support for diagnostic experts. Early fault detection and identification is still a very challenging task. A tool, which can alert an engineer about potentially dangerous cases, is required to work in real-time. The goal of this paper is to show an efficient system to online classification of operational states of the wind turbines and to detecting their early fault cases. The proposed system was designed as a hybrid of ART-2 and RBF networks. It had been proved before that the ART-type ANNs can successfully recognize operational states of a wind turbine during the diagnostic process. There are some difficulties, however, when classification is done in real-time. The disadvantages of using a classic ART-2 network are pointed and it is explained why the RBF unit of the hybrid system is needed to have a proper classification of turbine operational states.

Keywords: wind turbines, monitoring, hybrid system, ART neural network.

L. Rutkowski et al. (Eds.): ICAISC 2014, Part I, LNAI 8467, pp. 3–11, 2014.
© Springer International Publishing Switzerland 2014

1   Introduction

Determining the operational state of the wind turbine, which works under variable load, is a complex task. Nowadays it is done by an expert. There are various kinds of data which are collected when a turbine works - see [5] for wind turbine machine and data description. The number of operating data (such as wind speed, rotational speed, power) and vibration signals of a gear and bearing elements is very large, and therefore their constant analysis by experts is unrealistic. Methods and systems for automatic determining of the current operational states are necessary. They would support the work of experts.

The problem of classification of the wind turbine data had been investigated by several authors beforehand. The research by Shuhui et al. [17], who compared classification techniques for the wind curve estimation, was one of the first works on this subject. It should be mentioned, however, that the works describe only multilayered feed-forward types of networks. Another important contribution was given by Kim [12], who compared several classification methods. His experiments showed that unless the number of independent variables in the system is low, ANNs work better than other methods. Nevertheless, the multi-layer feed-forward network, trained by the back-propagation algorithm, was the investigated one.

The research concerning possibilities of ART neural networks, carried out, so far, by the authors, were innovative and gave positive results [3,4,5]. The systems based on ART-2 networks were able to perform classification of the operational states of a wind turbine. ART-2 networks are capable of performing efficient classification and identification of new classes of states. The experiments that had been done beforehand did not simulate fully the real-time processing. The simulations had time steps which triggered diagnostic checks. Every time all the data between steps had to be processed. The data could be passed to ANN with different order to improve the classification. Large number of the data, which should be calculated during every step, was the disadvantage of this solution. In this paper a new type of a system based on ANNs is proposed in order to do real-time monitoring which can detect a fault on its early stage.

2   Characteristics of the Proposed System

The new hybrid system contains two units: a classical ART-2 network, which will be briefly recalled in next subsection, and a structure of RBF networks with specified operations which were done on ART-2 network (see subsection 2.2).

2.1   ART-2 Unit

The ART-2 is an unsupervised neural network, based on the adaptive resonance theory (ART). A typical ART-2 architecture, introduced by Carpenter and Grossberg [7,8], is presented as the left part of Fig.1 (only one unit of each type is shown here). In the considered subsystem, an input pattern s is the first, presented to the F_1 layer, which consists of six kinds of units - the W, X, U, V, P and Q cells. It then undergoes a process of activation, including normalization, noise suppression and updating. This result in an output pattern p from the F_1 layer. An activation is produced across F_2 layer through bottom-up weights b_{ij} as a response to this output pattern. As the F_2 layer is a competitive layer with a winner-takes-all mode, only one stored pattern is a winner. It also represents the best matching pattern for the input pattern at the F_1 layer. Furthermore, the pattern of activation on the F_2 layer brings about an output pattern that is sent back to the F_1 layer via top-down weights t_{ji}. For the orienting sub-system, it contains a reset mechanism r and a vigilance parameter ρ to check the similarity between the output pattern from the F_2 layer and the original input pattern from the F_1 layer. If both patterns are concordant, the neural network enters a resonant state where the adaptation of the stored pattern is conducted. Otherwise, the neural network assigns an uncommitted (inhibitory) node on the F_2 layer for this input pattern, and thereafter, learns and transforms it into a new stored pattern.

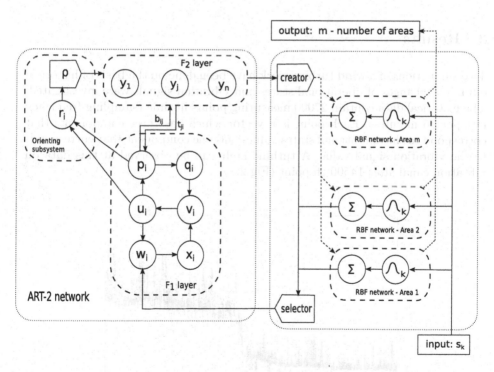

Fig. 1. Architecture of hybrid system of ART and RBF

2.2 New RBF Unit

The new unit in the proposed system is designed to better control over the work of ART-2 network. Creating the internal areas, determined by RBF networks, in the analyzed space, is the main idea of the introduced system. The mapping between ART-2 clusters (F_2 layer) and that areas is introduced. Each cluster, after its creation, is paired with the specified area. At the starting point there is only one area and only one area is modified at the same time. The RBF unit observes the number of clusters in F_2 layer. It waits every c_{time} after each cluster is added to F_2 layer. When the number of clusters is stable then it "closes" the current area and "opens" a new one. For every point from the data set, which is put as an input signal, one area is selected. If that area is open, all the data points are saved. The area which is being closed, has its borders determined. An RBF network is specified to set the borders. The Mixture of Gaussians method (see [19] - mog_dd function) is applied to create RBF network and to learn it by using all the saved points. Initially RBF unit waits s_{time} before making decision of closing first area. The architecture of new hybrid system is presented as whole Fig.1.

3 Results

Two simulations of a wind turbine work have been done on the basis of historical data. The changes of operational states and vibration signals were investigated. The historical data contain 27000 measuring points in time (sampling frequency is 1 per 15 minutes). Each point is a vector which has three components that correspond to the operational states values and one component that corresponds to the vibration signal value. A turbine fault can be observed at this data on vibration canal after 14500-th point (Fig.2).

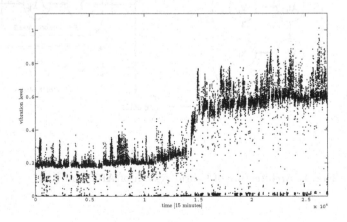

Fig. 2. Vibration signals for all measuring points

First simulation used classical ART-2 network as it was used in [3,4,5]. The second one used a hybrid system, fully described in section 2. Each simulation expressed the real-time actions done by an online classifier. Each data point was put into the system once in the same order as it had been recorded. It means that the failure should have been observed during simulation, not at the end of the simulation or only at the end of some parts of simulation data. The ART part of the hybrid system had all parameters set as the network in the first simulation (vigilance parameter $\rho = 0.978$). The hybrid system has also the parameters c_{time} and s_{time} set to values 1000 and 2000. The wind turbine states classification after 3000 simulation time points is shown in Fig.3. To this point both simulations gave the same results.

After that time point, the first simulation - the ART-2 network - continued working with a classical algorithm. It gave some unwanted results at the end of the simulation as it was shown in Fig.4. The mentioned disadvantage was manifested by the fact that there was one cluster (a green one in Fig.4) with both low and high values of vibrations whereas it should be divided into two separated clusters. Similar phenomena was observed many times during the simulation.

Table 1. Details of simulation process using the proposed hybrid system

Time	Observed actions
1	1-st class-neuron was added to new opened area 1
50	2-nd class-neuron was added to area 1
71	3-td class-neuron was added to area 1
91	4-rh class-neuron was added to area 1
214	5-th class-neuron was added to area 1
743	6-th class-neuron was added to area 1
747	7-th class-neuron was added to area 1
977	8-th class-neuron was added to area 1
3000	Borders of area 1 were determined and area 2 was opened
5869	1-st class-neuron was added to area 2
6253	2-nd class-neuron was added to area 2
11158	3-td class-neuron was added to area 2
14382	4-th class-neuron was added to area 2
16385	Borders of area 2 were determined and area 3 was opened
16797	1-st class-neuron was added to area 3
22429	2-nd class-neuron was added to area 3
24493	Borders of area 3 were determined and area 4 was opened
26266	1-st class-neuron was added to area 4

The second simulation - the hybrid system - determined borders of the system internal areas. Table 1 presents the moments when some new classes and areas were created during the simulation (see also Fig.5 and Fig.6). If there are the points which were not fitted to the first area, then it means that a potential fault

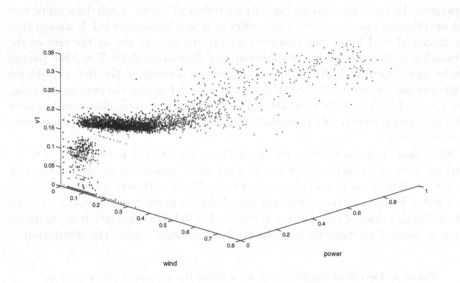

Fig. 3. The operational states (wind, power) and vibration signal classified by both classical ART-2 network and hybrid system using first 3000 points

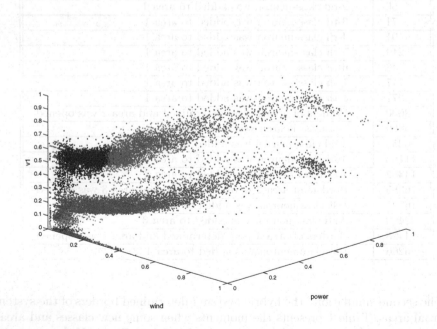

Fig. 4. The operational states (wind, power) and vibration signal classified by classical ART-2 network using all measuring points

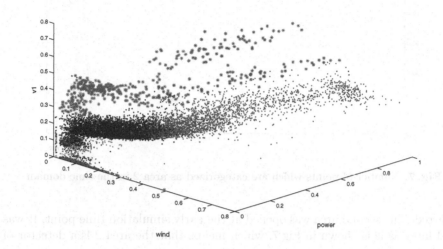

Fig. 5. The operational states (wind, power) and vibration signal classified by classical ART-2 network using first 15000 points

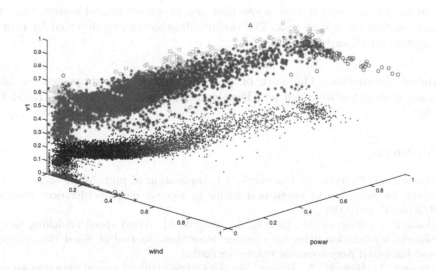

Fig. 6. The operational states (wind, power) and vibration signal classified by hybrid system using all measuring points

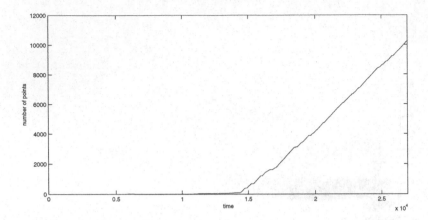

Fig. 7. Number of points which are categorized as area 2 in the time domain

occurred. The second area was opened at the early simulation time point. It was filled later as it is shown in Fig.7, which means that the area 2 is a detector of a turbine failure.

4   Concluding Remarks

It has been stressed that monitoring is crucial in wind turbines exploitation. There are few attempts to create systems for intelligent monitoring, based on artificial intelligence - see [9] and references given there. The simulations, described in the previous section, show that the proposed hybrid system can be a good solution for a such task. The turbine damage can be detected by using that system on an early stage.

Acknowledgements. The work of Andrzej Bielecki was supported by the National Centre for Research and Development grant number WND-DEM-1-153/01.

References

1. Barszcz, T., Bielecki, A., Romaniuk, T.: Application of probabilistic neural networks for detection of mechanical faults in electric motors. Electrical Review 8/2009, 37-41 (2009)
2. Barszcz, T., Bielecka, M., Bielecki, A., Wójcik, M.: Wind speed modelling using Weierstrass function fitted by a genetic algorithm. Journal of Wind Engineering and Industrial Aerodynamics 109, 68–78 (2012)
3. Barszcz, T., Bielecki, A., Wójcik, M.: ART-type artificial neural networks applications for classification of operational states in wind turbines. In: Rutkowski, L., Scherer, R., Tadeusiewicz, R., Zadeh, L.A., Zurada, J.M. (eds.) ICAISC 2010, Part II. LNCS (LNAI), vol. 6114, pp. 11–18. Springer, Heidelberg (2010)

4. Bielecka, M., Barszcz, T., Bielecki, A., Wójcik, M.: Fractal modelling of various wind characteristics for application in a cybernetic model of a wind turbine. In: Rutkowski, L., Korytkowski, M., Scherer, R., Tadeusiewicz, R., Zadeh, L.A., Zurada, J.M. (eds.) ICAISC 2012, Part II. LNCS, vol. 7268, pp. 531–538. Springer, Heidelberg (2012)
5. Barszcz, T., Bielecki, A., Wójcik, M.: ART-2 artificial neural networks applications for classification of vibration signals and operational states of wind turbines for intelligent monitoring. In: Advances in Condition Monitoring of Machinery in Non-Stationary Operations. Lecture Notes in Mechanical Engineering, pp. 679–688 (2014)
6. Barszcz, T., Randall, R.B.: Application of spectral kurtosis for detection of a tooth crack in the planetary gear of a wind turbine. Mechanical Systems and Signal Processing 23, 1352–1365 (2009)
7. Carpenter, G.A., Grossberg, S.: A massively parallel architecture for a self-organizing neural pattern recognition machine. Computer Vision, Graphics, and Image Processing 37, 54–115 (1987)
8. Carpenter, G.A., Grossberg, S.: ART2: self-organization of stable category recognition codes for analog input pattern. Applied Optics 26, 4919–4930 (1987)
9. Hameeda, Z., Honga, Y.S., Choa, T.M., Ahnb, S.H., Son, C.K.: Condition monitoring and fault detection of wind turbines and related algorithms: A review. Renewable and Sustainable Energy Reviews, 13, 1–39 (2009)
10. Jabłoński, A., Barszcz, T.: Procedure for data acquisition for machinery working under non-stationary operational conditions. In: The Ninth International Conference on Condition Monitoring and Machinery Failure Prevention Technologies, London, June 12-14 (2012)
11. Jabłoński, A., Barszcz, T., Bielecka, M.: Automatic validation of vibration signals in wind farm distributed monitoring systems. Measurement 44, 1954–1967 (2011)
12. Kim, Y.S.: Performance evaluation for classification methods: A comparative simulation study
13. Korbicz, J., Obuchowicz, A., Uciński, D.: Artificial Neural Networks - Foundations and Applications. Academic Press PLJ, Warsaw (1994) (in Polish)
14. Kusiak, A., Li, W.: The prediction and diagnosis of wind turbine faults. Renewable Energy 36, 16–23 (2011)
15. Rutkowski, L.: Neural Networks and Neurocomputers. Technical University in Częstochowa Press, Częstochowa (1996) (in Polish)
16. Shieh, M.D., Yan, W., Chen, C.H.: Soliciting customer requirements for product redesign based on picture sorts and ART2 neural network. Expert Systems with Applications 34, 194–204 (2008)
17. Shuhui, L., Wunsch, D.C., O'Hair, E., Giesselmann, M.G.: Comparative analysis of regression and artificial neural network models for wind turbine power curve estimation. Journal of Solar Energy Engineering 123, 327–332 (2001)
18. Tadeusiewicz, R.: Neural Networks. Academic Press, Warsaw (1993) (in Polish)
19. Tax, D.M.J.: DDtools, the Data Description Toolbox for Matlab (2013)

The Parallel Approach to the Conjugate Gradient Learning Algorithm for the Feedforward Neural Networks

Jarosław Bilski[1], Jacek Smoląg[1], and Alexander I. Galushkin[2]

[1] Institute of Computational Intelligence, Częstochowa University of Technology,
Częstochowa, Poland
{Jaroslaw.Bilski,Jacek.Smolag}@iisi.pcz.pl
[2] Moscow Institute of Physics and Technology, Russia
neurocomputer@yandex.ru

Abstract. This paper presents the parallel architecture of the conjugate gradient learning algorithm for the feedforward neural networks. The proposed solution is based on the high parallel structures to speed up learning performance. Detailed parallel neural network structures are explicitly shown.

1 Introduction

The feedforward neural networks have been investigated by many scientists e.g. [1], [17], [27], [29], [30]. To train the feedforward networks the gradient methods were often used, see e.g. [8], [12], [16], [28]. The conjugate gradient algorithm is one of these learning methods [7], [9], [10], [14], [15]. In the classical case the neural networks learning algorithms are implemented on serial computer. Unfortunately, this approach is very slow because the learning algorithm requires high computational load. Therefore, high performance dedicated parallel structure is a suitable solution, see eg. [2] - [6], [24], [25]. This paper presents a new concept of the parallel realisation of the conjugate gradient learning algorithm. A single iteration of the parallel architecture requires much less computation cycles than a serial implementation. The efficiency of this new architecture is very satisfying and is explained in the last part of the paper.

The structure of the feedforward network is shown in Fig. 1. The network has L layers, N_l neurons in each $l - th$ layer and N_L outputs. The input vector contains N_0 input signals. In the recall phase the network is described by

$$s_i^{(l)} = \sum_{j=0}^{N_{l-1}} w_{ij}^{(l)} x_i^{(l)}$$
$$y_i^{(l)}(t) = f(s_i^{(l)}(t))$$

(1)

The parallel realisation of the recall phase algorithm uses architecture which requires many simple processing elements. The parallel realisation of the feedforward network in recall phase (1) is depicted in Fig. 2a and its processing

L. Rutkowski et al. (Eds.): ICAISC 2014, Part I, LNAI 8467, pp. 12–21, 2014.
© Springer International Publishing Switzerland 2014

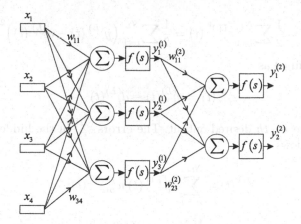

Fig. 1. Sample structure of the feedforward neural network

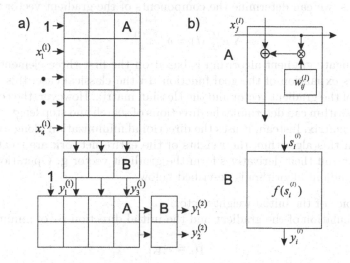

Fig. 2. Recal phase of the feedforward network and the structures of processing elements

elements (PE) in Fig. 2b. Two kinds of functional processing elements are used in the proposed solution. The aim of the processing elements A is to create matrices which contain values of weights in all layers. The input signals are entered for rows elements parallel, multiplied by weights and received results are summed in columns. The activation function for each neuron in the $l-th$ layer is calculated after determination of product $\mathbf{w}_i^{(l)}\mathbf{x}^{(l)}$ in processing element of type B. The outputs of neurons in the previous layer are simultaneously inputs to the next layer. The output $\mathbf{y}^{(L)}$ for the last layer is the output of the whole network.

The conjugate gradient method [14] is used to train the feedforward network. We minimize the following goal criterion

$$J(t) = \frac{1}{2} \sum_{i=1}^{N_L} \varepsilon_i^{(L)^2}(t) = \frac{1}{2} \sum_{i=1}^{N_L} \left(y_i^{(L)}(t) - d_i^{(L)}(t) \right)^2 \tag{2}$$

where $\varepsilon_i^{(L)}$ is defined as

$$\varepsilon_i^{(L)}(t) = y_i^{(L)}(t) - d_i^{(L)}(t) \tag{3}$$

and $d_i^{(L)}(t)$ is the $i - th$ desired output. The errors $\varepsilon_i^{(l)}$ in the hidden layers are calculated as follows

$$\varepsilon_i^{(l)}(t) \triangleq \sum_{m=1}^{N_{l+1}} \delta_i^{(l+1)}(t) w_{mi}^{(l+1)}(t) \tag{4}$$

$$\delta_i^{(l)}(t) = \varepsilon_i^{(l)}(t) f'\left(s_i^{(l)}(t) \right) \tag{5}$$

On this basis, we can determine the components of the gradient vector for each weight

$$\nabla w_{ij}^{(l)}(t) = \delta_i^{(l)} x_j^{(l)} \tag{6}$$

The conjugate gradient algorithm is based on the first three elements of the Taylor series expansion of the goal function. In the classical case, this requires knowledge of the gradient vector and the Hessian matrix. However, the conjugate gradient algorithm can determine the directions of search and step length without the Hessian matrix. Instead, it uses the directional minimization along a selected direction. In this algorithm, the weights of the entire network are treated as a single vector and their derivatives form the gradient vector **g**. Operation of the conjugate gradient algorithm is described below.

1. The choice of the initial weight vector.
2. The calculation of the gradient and the initial direction $\mathbf{p}_1$ of minimization

$$\mathbf{p}_1 = -\mathbf{g}_1 \tag{7}$$

3. The linear minimization along the selected direction

$$\mathbf{w}_{t+1} = \mathbf{w}_t + \alpha^* \mathbf{p}_t \tag{8}$$

where α^* is the factor which minimizes the vector $\mathbf{w}_t$ in direction $\mathbf{p}_t$.
4. Calculate the new values of weights.
5. Calculate the new gradient.
6. Calculate the new direction of minimization

$$\mathbf{p}_{t+1} = -\mathbf{g}_{t+1} + \beta_t \mathbf{p}_t \tag{9}$$

where β_t is given by (10), (11) or (12).
7. If the network has not been learned return to step 3

In practice, there are 3 different methods to calculate β_t.

– Hestenes-Stiefel

$$\beta_t = \frac{\mathbf{g}_{t+1}^T(\mathbf{g}_{t|1} - \mathbf{g}_t)}{\mathbf{p}_t^T(\mathbf{g}_{t+1} - \mathbf{g}_t)} \tag{10}$$

– Polak-Ribiere

$$\beta_t = \frac{\mathbf{g}_{t+1}^T(\mathbf{g}_{t+1} - \mathbf{g}_t)}{\mathbf{g}_t^T\mathbf{g}_t} \tag{11}$$

– Fletcher-Reeves

$$\beta_t = \frac{\mathbf{g}_{t+1}^T\mathbf{g}_{t+1}}{\mathbf{g}_t^T\mathbf{g}_t} \tag{12}$$

This paper used the method of calculating β_t proposed by Fletcher and Reeves. The task of suggested parallel structure will be realisation of all calculations described by equations (1) - (9) and (12).

2 Parallel Realisation

First, we calculate the errors in all neurons using backpropagation and determine the gradient vector. This is accomplished by the structure shown in Fig. 3. Its processing elements are shown in Fig. 4. The A processing elements are used to calculate the error $\varepsilon_i^{(L)}$ (3) in the output layer. The elements B transfer the errors to the linear part of neurons (5), and the processing elements C compute errors $\varepsilon_i^{(l)}$ in the hidden layers (4).

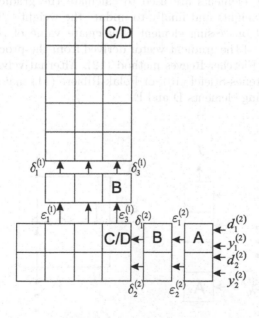

Fig. 3. The structure showing how to propagate error back and compute the gradient vector

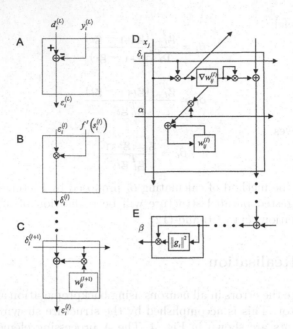

Fig. 4. The processing elements for propagating error back and computing the gradient vector

The D processing elements are used to calculate the gradient vector components (6) for all weights and finally to update the weights (9) of the neural network. Additional processing element E calculate value of β_t based on the square of the length of the gradient vector derived from the processing elements D according to the Fletcher-Reeves method (12). Alternatively, one can apply the methods of Hestenes-Stiefel (10), or Polak-Ribiere (11) making minor modifications in processing elements D and E.

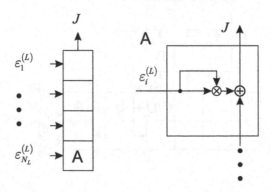

Fig. 5. The structure for computing the goal function and its processing element

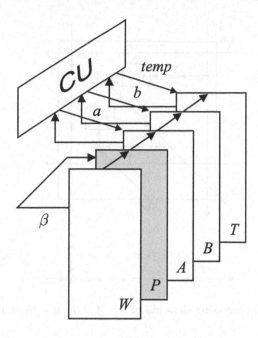

Fig. 6. The general structure for parallelization of the conjugate gradient learning algorithm

Figure 5 shows the structure of the goal function calculation and its processing element. Figure 6 shows the general structure of the parallel conjugate gradient learning algorithm. It consists of several layers. The layer W contains the parallel structures of the recall phase, the error backpropagation, the performing of the gradient of the goal function and the coefficient β_t. The P layer is used to determine the current direction vector of search on the basis of the gradient vector, the previous direction vector of search and factor β_t (12). The

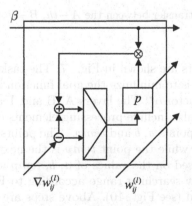

Fig. 7. The processing element of the $P - th$ layer

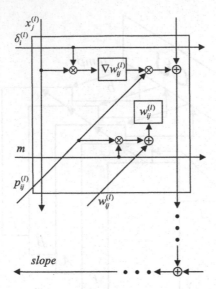

Fig. 8. Additional processing elements in the $A - th$, $B - th$ and $T - th$ layers

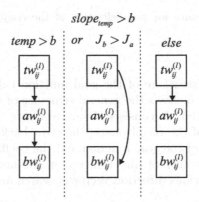

Fig. 9. Idea of the weight transfer between the $A - th$, $B - th$ and $T - th$ layers during searching the α^*

layers processing elements are shown in Fig. 7. The task of the layers A, B, T, and the control unit CU is to minimize the goal function in the direction $\mathbf{p_t}$ and determine the value of factor α^*. The layers A, B and T are analogous in structure to the W layer but also include processing elements calculating the slope of the goal function at the points a, b and $temp$. The points a and b determine the current range searching, while the point $temp$ is the next approximation of α^*. The control unit CU based on the values of a, b, $temp$ and the slopes at these points, determines a new searching range according to Fig. 9. Then, the new $temp$ point is determined (see Fig. 10). Above steps are repeated until we find the α^* minimizing the goal function in the direction $\mathbf{p_t}$ [7].

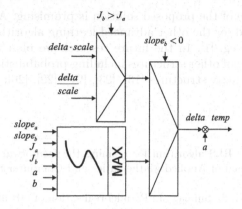

Fig. 10. The method of determining a temporary solution during searching the α^*

3   Conclusion

In this paper the parallel realisation of the conjugate gradient learning algorithm for the feedforward neural network was proposed. We assume that all multiplications and additions operations take the same time unit. For simplicity of the result presentation we show graphs for only one layer. We can compare computational performance of the parallel implementation of the conjugate gradient learning algorithm with sequential solution up to $N_{l-1} = 100$ inputs and up to $N_l = 100$ outputs of neural network. Computational complexity of the serial conjugate gradient learning algorithm is of order $\mathcal{O}(K^2)$ and equals $TS_l = 11N_lN_{l-1}-2N_l-2N_{l-1}+m(11N_lN_{l-1}-2N_l-2N_{l-1}+29)$. In the presented parallel architecture each iteration requires only $TP_l = N_l+2N_{l-1}+m(N_l+2N_{l-1}+21)$ time units (see Fig. 11) The factor m is the number of steps required to reach the directional minimum and to obtain the α^*. Assuming $m = 10$ performance factor $(PF = TS_l/TP_l)$ of parallel realisation of the conjugate gradient learning algorithm achieves nearly 350 for $N_{l-1} = 100$ inputs, $N_l = 100$ outputs in the $l-th$ layer and it grows fast when these numbers grow, see Fig. 11. We observed

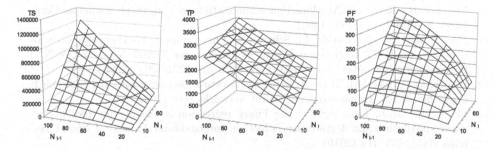

Fig. 11. Number of times cycles in a) classical (serial), b) parallel implementation and c) performance factor

that the performance of the proposed solution is promising. Analogous parallel approach can be used for the other advanced learning algorithm of feedforward neural networks, see eg. [1]. In the future research we plan to design parallel realisation of learning of other structures including probabilistic neural networks [18]-[20] and various fuzzy structures [13], [23], [21], [22], [26].

References

1. Bilski, J.: The UD RLS algorithm for training the feedforward neural networks. International Journal of Applied Mathematics and Computer Science 15(1), 101–109 (2005)
2. Bilski, J., Litwiński, S., Smoląg, J.: Parallel realisation of QR algorithm for neural networks learning. In: Rutkowski, L., Siekmann, J.H., Tadeusiewicz, R., Zadeh, L.A. (eds.) ICAISC 2004. LNCS (LNAI), vol. 3070, pp. 158–165. Springer, Heidelberg (2004)
3. Bilski, J., Smoląg, J.: Parallel realisation of the RTRN neural network learning. In: Rutkowski, L., Tadeusiewicz, R., Zadeh, L.A., Zurada, J.M. (eds.) ICAISC 2008. LNCS (LNAI), vol. 5097, pp. 11–16. Springer, Heidelberg (2008)
4. Bilski, J., Smoląg, J.: Parallel realisation of the recurrent Elman neural network learning. In: Rutkowski, L., Scherer, R., Tadeusiewicz, R., Zadeh, L.A., Zurada, J.M. (eds.) ICAISC 2010, Part II. LNCS (LNAI), vol. 6114, pp. 19–25. Springer, Heidelberg (2010)
5. Bilski, J., Smoląg, J.: Parallel realisation of the recurrent multi layer perceptron learning. In: Rutkowski, L., Korytkowski, M., Scherer, R., Tadeusiewicz, R., Zadeh, L.A., Zurada, J.M. (eds.) ICAISC 2012, Part I. LNCS (LNAI), vol. 7267, pp. 12–20. Springer, Heidelberg (2012)
6. Bilski, J., Smoląg, J.: Parallel approach to learning of the recurrent Jordan neural network. In: Rutkowski, L., Korytkowski, M., Scherer, R., Tadeusiewicz, R., Zadeh, L.A., Zurada, J.M. (eds.) ICAISC 2013, Part I. LNCS (LNAI), vol. 7894, pp. 32–40. Springer, Heidelberg (2013)
7. Charalambous, C.: Conjugate gradient algorithm for efficient training of artificial neural networks. IEE Proc.-G 139(3), 301–310 (1992)
8. Fahlman, S.: Faster learning variations on backpropagation: An empirical study. In: Proceedings of Connectionist Models Summer School, Los Atos (1988)
9. Fletcher, R., Powell, M.J.D.: A rapidly convergent descent method for minimization. Computer Journal 6, 163–168 (1963)
10. Fletcher, R., Reeves, C.M.: Function minimization by conjugate gradients. Computer Journal 7, 149–154 (1964)
11. Korytkowski, M., Rutkowski, L., Scherer, R.: On combining backpropagation with boosting. In: IEEE International Joint Conference on Neural Network (IJCNN) Proceedings, Vancouver, July 16-21, vols. 1-10, pp. 1274–1277 (2006)
12. Hagan, M.T., Menhaj, M.B.: Training feedforward networks with the Marquardt algorithm. IEEE Transactions on Neural Networks 5(6) (1994)
13. Li, X., Er, M.J., Lim, B.S., et al.: Fuzzy regression modelling for tool performance prediction and degradation detection. International Journal of Neural Systems 20(5), 405–419 (2010)
14. Nocedal, J., Wright, S.J.: Conjugate Gradient Methods in Numerical Optimization, pp. 497–528. Springer, New York (2006)

15. Polak, E.: Computational methods in optimization: a unified approach. Academic Press, New York (1971)
16. Riedmiller, M., Braun, H.: A direct method for faster backpropagation learning: The RPROP Algorithm. In: IEEE International Conference on Neural Networks, San Francisco (1993)
17. Rumelhart, D.E., Hinton, G.E., Williams, R.J.: Learning internal representations by error propagation. In: Rumelhart, D.E., McCelland, J. (ed.) Parallel Distributed Processing, vol. 1, ch. 8. The MIT Press, Cambridge (1986)
18. Rutkowski, L.: Multiple Fourier series procedures for extraction of nonlinear regressions from noisy data. IEEE Transactions on Signal Processing 41(10), 3062–3065 (1993)
19. Rutkowski, L.: Non-parametric learning algorithms in the time-varying environments. Signal Processing 18(2), 129–137 (1989)
20. Rutkowski, L.: Generalized regression neural networks in time-varying environment. IEEE Trans. Neural Networks 15, 576–596 (2004)
21. Rutkowski, L., Cpałka, K.: Compromise approach to neuro-fuzzy systems. In: Sincak, P., Vascak, J., Kvasnicka, V., Pospichal, J. (eds.) Intelligent Technologies - Theory and Applications, vol. 76, pp. 85–90. IOS Press (2002)
22. Rutkowski, L., Cpałka, K.: Neuro-fuzzy systems derived from quasi-triangular norms. In: Proceedings of the IEEE International Conference on Fuzzy Systems, Budapest, July 26-29, vol. 2, pp. 1031–1036 (2004)
23. Rutkowski, L., Przybył, A., Cpałka, K.: Novel Online Speed Profile Generation for industrial machine tool based on flexible neuro-fuzzy approximation. IEEE Transactions on Industrial Electronics 59(2), 1238–1247 (2012)
24. Smoląg, J., Bilski, J.: A systolic array for fast learning of neural networks. In: Proc. of V Conf. Neural Networks and Soft Computing, Zakopane, pp. 754–758 (2000)
25. Smoląg, J., Rutkowski, L., Bilski, J.: Systolic array for neural networks. In: Proc. of IV Conf. Neural Networks and Their Applications, Zakopane, pp. 487–497 (1999)
26. Starczewski, J.T.: A type-1 approximation of interval type-2 FLS. In: Di Gesù, V., Pal, S.K., Petrosino, A. (eds.) WILF 2009. LNCS, vol. 5571, pp. 287–294. Springer, Heidelberg (2009)
27. Tadeusiewicz, R.: Neural Networks, AOW RM (1993) (in Polish)
28. Werbos, J.: Backpropagation through time: What it does and how to do it. Proceedings of the IEEE 78(10) (1990)
29. Wilamowski, B.M., Yo, H.: Neural network learning without backpropagation. IEEE Transactions on Neural Networks 21(11), 1793–1803 (2010)
30. Żurada, J.: Introduction to Artificial Neural Systems. West Publishing Company (1992)

A Cascade Neural Network Architecture Investigating Surface Plasmon Polaritons Propagation for Thin Metals in OpenMP*

Francesco Bonanno[1], Giacomo Capizzi[1], Grazia Lo Sciuto[2], Christian Napoli[3], Giuseppe Pappalardo[3], and Emiliano Tramontana[3]

[1] Dpt. of Electric, Electronic and Informatics Eng., University of Catania, Italy
gcapizzi@diees.unict.it
[2] Department of Industrial Engineering, University of Catania, Italy
glosciuto@dii.unict.it
[3] Department of Mathematics and Informatics, University of Catania, Italy
{napoli,pappalardo,tramontana}@dmi.unict.it

Abstract. Surface plasmon polaritons (SPPs) confined along metal-dielectric interface have attracted a relevant interest in the area of ultra-compact photonic circuits, photovoltaic devices and other applications due to their strong field confinement and enhancement. This paper investigates a novel cascade neural network (NN) architecture to find the dependance of metal thickness on the SPP propagation. Additionally, a novel training procedure for the proposed cascade NN has been developed using an OpenMP-based framework to strongly reduce the training time. The performed experiments confirm the effectiveness of the proposed NN architecture for the problem at hand.

Keywords: Cascade neural network architectures, Surface plasmon polaritons, Plasmonics, Plasmon structure.

1 Introduction

Surface Plasmon Polaritons (SPPs) are quantized charge density oscillations occurring at the interface between a metal and a dielectric when a photon couples to the free electron gas of the metal. The emerging field of surface plasmonics has applied SPP coupling to a number of new and interesting applications [1],[2],[3], such as Surface Enhanced Raman Spectroscopy (SERS), photovoltaic devices optimisation, optical filters, photonic band gap structures, biological and chemical sensing, and SPP enhanced photodetectors.

Some papers appeared in literature simulate and analyse the excitation and propagation of SPPs on sinusoidal metallic gratings in conical mounting. Researchers working in the emerging field of plasmonics have shown the significant contribution of SPPs for applications in sensing and optical communication.

---

* This work was supported by the Miur project "Energetic" (PON02_00355_3391233 IT).

L. Rutkowski et al. (Eds.): ICAISC 2014, Part I, LNAI 8467, pp. 22–33, 2014.

One promising solution is to fabricate optical systems at metal-dielectric interfaces, where electromagnetic modes called SPPs offer unique opportunities to confine and control light at length scales below $100\,nm$ [4],[5].

The studies and experiences conducted on SPPs are well assessed and show that the propagation phenomena are well established by the involved materials in the plasmon structure at large thickness, conversely when it becomes smaller than the wavelength of the exciting wave, investigations are required due to the actual poor understanding [6].

This paper proposes a novel neural netwok (NN) topology to study of the problems of a SPP propagating at a metal flat interface separating dielectric medium. Currently, we are using NNs to study the inner relation between SPPs exciting wavelength, metal thickness and SPP wavelength and propagation length. The focus of this paper is on the determination of the dependance of the SPP propagation of the metal thickness employing suitable NN schematics. Due to the high sensitivity of the neural model to data oscillations a novel training procedure has been devised in order to avoid polarisations and miscorrections of some NN weights. Moreover, since such a training procedure could be expensive in terms of computational power and wall-clock time, a parallel version using an OpenMP environment, with shared memory, has been developed and optimised to obtain maximum advantage from the available parallel hardware. A big amount of data has been put into proper use for the investigated NN topology. Such data have been made available by solving 3D Maxwell equations with relative boundary conditions by COMSOL Multiphysics, which is an efficient and powerful software package to simulate the characteristics of SPPs.

2   Basics of Surface Plasmon Polaritons

The field of plasmonics is witnessing a growing interest with an emerging rapid development due to the studies and researches about the behaviour of light at the nanometer scale. Light absorption by solar cells patterned with metallic nanogratings has been recently investigated, however we consider light-excited SPPs at the metal surface. The outcomes of our investigation can be used to improve efficient capturing of light in solar energy conversion cells [1]. Therefore, our main research interests are toward the properties of SPPs.

SPPs are electromagnetic waves propagating along metal-dielectric interfaces and exist over a wide range of frequencies, evanescently decaying in the perpendicular direction. Such electromagnetic surface waves arise via the coupling of the electromagnetic fields to oscillations of the conductor electron's plasma [7]. SPP is the fundamental excitation mode at a metal-dielectric interface that is coupled to an electromagnetic wave as described in [7]. The most simple geometry sustaining SPPs is that of a single, flat interface (see Fig. 1) between a dielectric, non-absorbing half space ($z > 0$) with positive real dielectric constant ε_2 and an adjacent conducting half space ($z < 0$) described via a dielectric function $\varepsilon_1(\omega)$. The requirement of metallic character implies that $Re[\varepsilon_1] < 0$. As shown in [7], for metals this condition is fulfilled at frequencies below the bulk plasmon frequency ω_p. We look for propagating wave solutions confined to the interface, i.e. with evanescent decay in the perpendicular z-direction [7].

The electromagnetic field of a SPP at the dielectric-metal interface is obtained by solving Maxwell's equations in each medium with the associated boundary conditions. The adopted structure is a metal-dielectric interface composed by Molybdenum and air as shown in Fig. 1. This structure is the most simple in order to reduce computational effort, as the main purpose of the paper is to investigate the important relation between dispersion and thickness of the metal by means of a proper novel NN architecture. It should be noted that this relation is not affected by the complexity of the structure.

The basic mathematical equations describing the electromagnetic phenomena concerning SPP propagation are listed below:

$$\begin{aligned}
\mathbf{H}_d &= (0, H_{yd}, 0)\, e^{i(k_{xd}\, x + k_{zd}\, z - \omega t)} \\
\mathbf{E}_d &= (E_{xd}, 0, E_{zd})\, e^{i(k_{xd}\, x + k_{zd}\, z - \omega t)} \\
\mathbf{H}_m &= (0, H_{ym}, 0)\, e^{i(k_{xm}\, x - k_{zm}\, z - \omega t)} \\
\mathbf{E}_m &= (E_{xm}, 0, E_{zm})\, e^{i(k_{xm}\, x - k_{zm}\, z - \omega t)}
\end{aligned} \tag{1}$$

with boundary condition at $z = 0$

$$\begin{aligned}
E_{xm} &= E_{xd} \\
H_{ym} &= H_{yd} \\
\varepsilon_m\, E_{zm} &= \varepsilon_d\, E_{zd}
\end{aligned} \tag{2}$$

as a consequence of the previous equation we have

$$k_{xm} = k_{xd} \tag{3}$$

We consider a system consisting of a dielectric material, characterised by an isotropic, real, positive dielectric constant ε_d, and a metal characterised by an isotropic, frequency dependent, complex dielectric function $\varepsilon_m = \varepsilon_r + i\varepsilon_i$. In order to introduce the main parameters characterising SPPs assuming the interface is normal to z-axis and the SPPs propagate along the x direction (i.e., $k_y = 0$), the SPP wavevector k_x or β is related to the optical frequency ω through the dispersion relation.

$$k_x = k_0 \sqrt{\frac{\varepsilon_d\, \varepsilon_m}{\varepsilon_d + \varepsilon_m}} \tag{4}$$

$$\beta = \frac{\omega}{c} \sqrt{\frac{\varepsilon_d\, \varepsilon_m}{\varepsilon_d + \varepsilon_m}} \tag{5}$$

We take ω to be real and allow k_x to be complex, since our main interest is in stationary monochromatic SPP fields in a finite area, where

$$k_0 = \frac{\omega}{c} \tag{6}$$

is the wavevector in free space, and $\lambda_0 = \frac{c}{\omega}$ is the wavelength in vacuum. For metals, the permittivity is complex, which leads to k_x being complex. The imaginary part of k_x defines the SPPs damping and as it propagates along the surface. The real part of k_x is connected to the plasmons wavelength, λ_{SPP}:

$$\lambda_{SPP} = \frac{2\pi}{Re[\beta]} \tag{7}$$

L_{SPP} is the SPP propagation length, physically the energy dissipated through the metal heating and it is the propagation distance. L_{SPP} is defined as follows:

$$L_{SPP} = \frac{1}{Im[\beta]} \tag{8}$$

Finally, the following reports the expression of the electric field of plasmon wave:

$$\mathbf{E}_{SPP} = \mathbf{E}_0^{\pm}\, e^{i(k_x x \pm k_z z - \omega t)} \tag{9}$$

where

$$k_x = k_x' + ik_x''$$
$$k_x' = \frac{2\pi}{\lambda_{SPP}}$$

3 Input Data for the Proposed Cascade NN Architecture

By solving the full wave 3D Maxwell equations in the simple geometry shown in Fig. 2, which separates two media as metal and dielectric, using the finite element method-based software package COMSOL Multiphysics, we have obtained the L_{SPP} and λ_{SPP} data values for different thickness values. The perfectly matched layer boundary condition was chosen for the external surface of the plasmon structure. The exciting wave was monochromatic on the visible spectra and ranging from $400\,nm$ to $700\,nm$.

We have performed many numerical simulations while varying the exciting wavelengths for each investigated thickness, hence obtaining the corresponding SPP waves. A SPP propagates at the interface dielectric-metal decaying into the metal.

The values of L_{SPP} and λ_{SPP} were computed for the all visible range of wavelength at the following different thickness values t of the metal: $36\,nm$, $42\,nm$, $48\,nm$, $54\,nm$, $60\,nm$, $72\,nm$, $84\,nm$, $96\,nm$ and $128\,nm$.

4 The Proposed Neural Network Architecture

The prediction of λ_{SPP} and L_{SPP} from the set of values λ_0 and t is related to the problem of the dependence of L_{SPP} from λ_{SPP}. To obtain a correct prediction of λ_{SPP} by a neural network-based approach a value of λ_{SPP} is needed. Although this can be obtained by a cascade process, the traditional means have that the cascade NN is accommodated by separate training sessions for each different

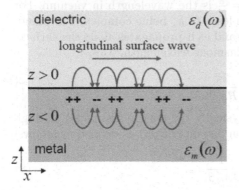

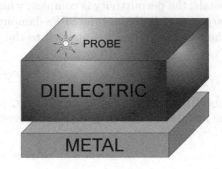

Fig. 1. Geometry for SPP propagation at a single interface between metal and dielectric

Fig. 2. Implemented geometry in COMSOL

dedicated NN. Unfortunately, such training sessions would result in very time-consuming computation.

In order to overcome the above mentioned problem, this paper proposes a novel parallel paradigm for training that manages to run a single comprehensive training for the cascade NN as a whole, thus avoiding separate training phases. This novel solution has been used for the problem at hand, described in Section 2.

Essentially, the adopted topology has been derived from a pair of common two-layer feed-forward neural networks (FFNNs) [8], used to separately predict λ_{SPP} and L_{SPP}, respectively. The comprehensive structure is similar to a cascade feed-forward, whereby the output of the first neuroprocessing stage is connected with the input of the second stage and form a new extended input vector for the second stage. On the other hand, the vector provided as input to the second neuroprocessing stage depends on the predicted values obtained from the first stage, hence it propagates a prediction error.

Moreover, during the training phase, while some outputs can be validated for the first neuroprocessing stage, the localised deviation from the correct frequency spectrum could corrupt the training of the second stage. The behaviour of this novel topology is as a two step processing of the data signal that is comprehensive also of a so called *second validation* or *ω-validation*, described in the following, aiming at avoiding such an error propagation, which would otherwise endanger the correct training of the second neuroprocessing stage.

A given output from the first stage has to be validated on the frequencies domain, by a validation module, before it can be used. This validation module performs the ω-validation by means of the Fourier computation on a delayed Gaussian window of the output and training signal.

An intermediate level of data processing requires the implementation of a module performing the Fourier transform of the data. Its relative parameters are not *a priori* established, however are on-line determined by the novel NN topology and then by its training procedure.

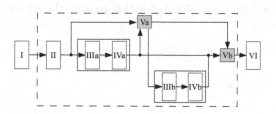

Fig. 3. The proposed cascade NN architecture

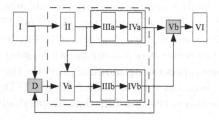

Fig. 4. An equivalent recurrent schema

Fig. 3 represents the proposed architecture, which will be detailed in the following. It is possible to recognise two groups of modules, the first comprising IIIa and IVa, whereas the second IIIb and IVb, each acting as a FFNN. The proposed novel topology behaves as a cascade FFNN topology [9]. Fig. 4 depicts a more complex novel topology that performs the prediction as a Nonlinear AutoRecoursive with exogenous inputs (NARX) recurrent neural network topology [10]. Such figure shows the implemented delay lines to the blocks performing the neural processing. It should be noted that we have implemented one neuron as a *purelin* while the remaining neurons in the first hidden layer process the input signal. The performed simulations have shown an increased computational effort, for this recurrent scheme, while the corresponding results have not significantly improved the accuracy on the predicted data. Even though this is a novel recurrent cascade topology this paper fully investigates the scheme shown in Fig. 3. The following provides the details of the proposed NN cascade.

Input data analysis. The input layer (I) does not directly provide the input vector (**u**) to the first FFNN hidden layer (IIIa), being it firstly processed by an intermediate layer (II) that is trained to extrapolate a set of parameters necessary to perform the ω-validation, i.e. the σ for the Gaussian window Fourier analysis. This layer (II) is also provided with ad adjunct *purelin* neuron acting as a transmission line for the following layer (IIIa).

The main purpose of II is to characterise the frequency peaks windows on the data spectrum in order to associate, after the training phase, an optimum σ value to perform gaussian-window Fourier analysis on the output data from the second FFNN hidden layer (IVa). For this reason, the input to the following layers are provided as

$$\mathbf{x}^{\text{Va}} = \mathbf{y}^{\text{II}}(\mathbf{x}^{\text{I}}) = [\tau, \Delta_\tau, \sigma | \mathbf{x}^{\text{I}}]$$

$$\mathbf{x}^{\text{IIIa}} = \mathbf{x}^{\text{I}}$$

(10)

where $\mathbf{x}^{\text{Va}}$ retains the discrete sample number τ and both the window size Δ_τ and σ for the described Fourier analysis.

FFNNs hidden layers The first neuroprocessing module acts as a fully connected FFNN and consists of two hidden layers, i.e. IIIa and IVa. The first hidden layer (IIIa) embeds 10 neurons with *tansig* activation function, whereas the second hidden layer (IVa) consists of 7 neurons with *logsig* activation function. Similarly, the second neuroprocessing module provides the functionalities of a fully connected FFNN, however its two hidden layers, IIIb and IVb, consist of 8 and 5 neurons with *tansig* activation function, respectively.

FFNN training and validation The implemented FFNN neuroprocessing modules are trained by the Levenberg-Marquardt algorithm with a gradient descent method. Hence, for the τ-esime discrete time step, the variation introduced to the weights are given by

$$w_{ij}^{\mu\nu}(\tau) = w_{ij}^{\mu\nu}(\tau - 1) - \eta e(\tau) \frac{\partial e(\tau)}{\partial w_{ij}^{\mu\nu}(\tau)}$$

$$e^\mu(\tau) = \tilde{\mathbf{y}}^\mu(\tau) - \mathbf{y}^\mu(\tau)$$

(11)

where $w_{ij}^{\mu\nu}(\tau)$ represents the value for the τ-esime step of the connection weight from the i-esime neuron of the μ layer to the j-esime neuron of the ν layer, η is the learning rate parameter, $\tilde{\mathbf{y}}^\mu(\tau)$ and $\mathbf{y}^\mu(\tau)$ are respectively the training and output signal from the μ layer.

ω-validation The output of the first neuroprocessing module comes from the second FFNN hidden layer (IVa) and is sent, as valid output, to the last layer of the network and also as input to the validation module (Va). The validation module consists of a functional unit performing the fast Fourier transform on a selected window of the input signals. Moreover, the validation module uses a dynamically allocated buffer to implement a size-varying delay line.

The latter is used to enable real-time online resizing of the Fourier window to suit the properties of the investigated signal. These adjustments are performed starting from the parameters contained in $\mathbf{x}^{\text{Va}}$ as (10). Once the gaussian windowed Fourier transform has been computed, the following values are determined

$$M(\tau, \Delta_\tau, \sigma) = \max_{[\tau:\tau+\Delta_\tau]} \left\{ \left| \hat{F}_\sigma[\mathbf{y}^{\tilde{\text{IVa}}}] - \hat{F}_\sigma[\mathbf{y}^{\text{IVa}}] \right| \right\}$$

$$m(\tau, \Delta_\tau, \sigma) = \min_{[\tau:\tau+\Delta_\tau]} \left\{ \left| \hat{F}_\sigma[\mathbf{y}^{\tilde{\text{IVa}}}] - \hat{F}_\sigma[\mathbf{y}^{\text{IVa}}] \right| \right\}$$

(12)

then the module is trained to admit only certain regions of the (M, m) pairs plan which validate the output signal of the layer IVa.

If the output signal results validated, it is then sent as input for the layer IIIb as

$$\mathbf{x}^{\text{IIIb}} = [\mathbf{x}^{\text{I}} | \mathbf{y}^{\text{IVa}}] \tag{13}$$

The first neuroprocessing module takes $\mathbf{x}^{\text{I}}$ as input and is trained by all the available patterns, while the second module is trained only by the allowed sequences selected according to the validation procedure. In the other case, i.e. if the ω-validation is negative, the second module skips the data during the training process and gives a NaN flagging, being the relative data for the second variable unavailable.

Final output Finally, the implemented topology gives a global output with a layer consisting of two neurons *purelin*.

5   Training Procedure on OpenMP

The neural network architecture proposed above has introduced a sequential validation phase for the results of the first neuroprocessing module. Validation has to be performed before the first module results can be sent as input for the second module. Unfortunately, such sequential operations make the training process expensive in terms of CPU time. In order to shorten training time in this section is described a parallel implementation of the same neural network architecture, using OpenMP, that manages to obtain asynchronous training and validation.

Generally, when parallelising an application using OpenMP, processes are forked, joined and synchronised (e.g. by means of a barrier). Such mechanisms, however, introduce a runtime overhead, e.g. when the processes having produced and communicated their results have to wait until the synchronisation barrier is over. This is often the case when the computation times of processes are not perfectly balanced [11]. Therefore, our parallel version aims at reducing such an overhead by avoiding, as much as possible, the fork-join-barrier constructs, and by introducing instead processes that produce and consume data. The main reason for using OpenMP is that, by means of a shared memory, communication overhead among processes can be avoided, however, on the other hand, shared memory requires a complex handling of semaphores and locks before accessing some parts of the memory itself. We have handled the synchronisation concern in such a way that overhead is minimised [12].

Mainly, the proposed parallel solution is based on the continuous execution of different processes to care for the different phases of training for the above cascade NN. In our experiments a multi-core processor has been used, however any kind of shared memory system supporting OpenMP directives can be employed.

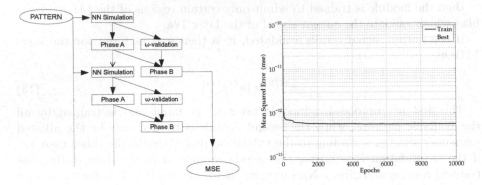

Fig. 5. The proposed OpenMP training asynchronous stream

Fig. 6. Global performance graph of the implemented NN architecture

The proposed cascade NN has been trained to predict the values of λ_{SPP} and L_{SPP} starting from an input vector.

$$\mathbf{u}(\tau) = [\lambda_0, t] \tag{14}$$

To evaluate the performance of the cascade NN, two different kinds of error were considered. We define two *local errors* e^a and e^b, as well as a *global error* e^* as follows:

$$
\begin{aligned}
e^a &= \tilde{\mathbf{y}}^{IVa} - \mathbf{y}^{IVa} \\
e^b &= \tilde{\mathbf{y}}^{IVb} - \mathbf{y}^{IVb} \\
e^* &= \max\{e^a, e^b\} \geq |\tilde{\mathbf{y}}^{VI} - \mathbf{y}^{VI}|
\end{aligned}
\tag{15}
$$

where $\tilde{\mathbf{y}}$ indicates the training value.

For each training epoch, the outputs from layers IVa, IVb and VI (see Fig. 3.) were used to compute the errors e^a, e^b and e^* as in (15). The training has been organised in four different activities, executed on an OpenMP environment (see Fig. 5).

The first activity, named NN Simulation, provides as input to the whole cascade neural network with a training pattern, which has been previously generated.

The second activity, named Phase A, and started once the first activity has terminated, uses a gradient descent algorithm to adjust the neural weights of the intermediate layer II and the first neuroprocessing (layers IIIa and IVa).

The third activity is the ω-validation and is started concurrently with Phase A, hence after NN Simulation has finished, since the results produced by IVa are needed. The ω-validation activity performs the gaussian windowed fast Fourier transform of the training set and the predicted signal resulting as output of IVa, then M and m defined in (12) are computed. Eventually, the values of M and m are used to decide if the pattern data are usable to train the second neuro-processing module (IIIb and IVb).

Finally, the fourth activity is **Phase B** performing a further training that adjusts the output weights of layer VI. For the proposed schema (see Fig. 3), module Vb acts as a controller determining whether it is appropriate to merge data from IVa and IVb before they can be given as input to VI. The merge is enabled when the ω-validation has given a positive result, otherwise only data resulting from IVa are used. Moreover, all the weights in layer VI are adjusted when the result of ω-validation is positive, otherwise only the synaptic weights of the first neuron in VI is adjusted.

The four activities above are started each as a process (see Fig. 5). Process NN Simulation feeds data and triggers the execution of processes **Phase A** and ω-validation. The latter two processes give their outputs to process **Phase B**, and then *wait* for new data, till the training stops. Process **Phase B** starts as soon as input data are available. At the end of the training epoch the global network performances are stored for further analysis. All the measures of performance involved in the training process are given by the Mean Squared Error (MSE), though for the global network performances, the formula is adjusted by using the global error e^* of (15).

Fig. 5 shows in two vertical tiers some rectangles. Each rectangle corresponds to a process that can execute in parallel with another that is on the same row. In the picture, the time evolves while going down. The arrows with continuous lines represent a flow of data from a producer to a consumer process, whereas the dotted line the communication of an event. Ellipses show repositories of data. The said interactions among processes are iterated until the training session stops.

While having devised a parallel solution, our effort has been to optimise the use of computational resources, hence autonomous processes needing as less synchronisation as possible have been implemented as described above. Our proposed solution manages to greatly reduce the wall-clock timeframe needed for the training.

6   Results and Conclusions

The proposed NN cascade has been mainly derived from a couple of common two-layer feed-forward neural networks used to separately predict λ_{SPP} and L_{SPP}. The comprehensive structure is similar to a cascade feed-forward, where the output of the first neuroprocessing stage has been connected with the inputs for the second stage to form a new extended input vector.

For training and evaluation we have used the global error e^* to compute the mean square error (MSE) of the network. Fig. 6 shows the performance of the proposed and implemented novel cascade NN architecture in terms of such metrics. Fig. 7 reports the values of the computed and predicted λ_{SPP} and L_{SPP}. The obtained results confirm the good predictions obtained by the novel NN schema.

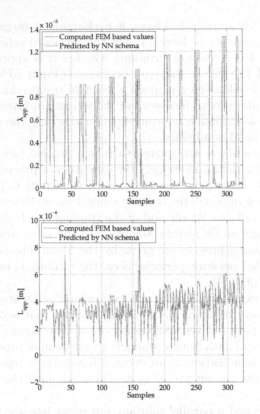

Fig. 7. The computed and predicted λ_{SPP} and L_{spp}

Simulation results for the NN cascade confirm the effectiveness of the developed novel architecture whose performance during the training and evaluation phases show a very low MSE. Other complex NN architectures such as pure NARX model or advanced Wavelet Recurrent Neural Networks [13] could not be used because of the prediction instability for the data at hand.

Acknowledgment. This work was supported by the Miur projects "Energetic" (PON02 00355 3391233 IT) and "PRISMA" PON04a2 A/F within PON 2007-2013 framework.

References

1. Franken, R.H., Stolk, R.L., Li, H., Van der Werf, C.H.M., Rath, J.K., Schropp, R.E.I.: Understanding light trapping by light scattering textured back electrodes in thin film n-i-p-type silicon solar cells. Journal of Applied Physics 102(1), 14503–14509 (2007)
2. Atwater, H.A., Polman, A.: Plasmonics for improved photovoltaic devices. Nature Materials 9(3), 205–213 (2010)

3. Fahr, S., Rockstuhl, C., Lederer, F.: Metallic nanoparticles as intermediate reflectors in tandem solar cells. Appl. Phys. Lett. 95(12), 121105–121107 (2009)
4. Walters, R.J., van Loon, R.V.A., Brunets, I., Schmitz, J., Polman, A.: A silicon-based electrical source of surface plasmon polaritons. Nature Materials 9(3), 21–25 (2010)
5. De Waele, R., Burgos, S.P., Polman, A., Atwater, H.A.: Plasmon dispersion in coaxial waveguides from single-cavity optical transmission measurements. Nano Lett. 9, 2832–2837 (2009)
6. Shah, A., Torres, P., Tscharner, R., Wyrsch, N., Keppner, H.: Photovoltaic technology: the case for thin-film solar cells. Science 285(5428), 692–698 (1999)
7. Maier, S.A.: Plasmonic: Fundamentals and Applications. Springer (2007)
8. Mandic, D.P., Chambers, J.: Recurrent neural networks for prediction: learning algorithms, architectures and stability. John Wiley & Sons, Inc. (2001)
9. Schetinin, V.: A learning algorithm for evolving cascade neural networks. Neural Processing Letters 17(1), 21–23 (2003)
10. Williams, R.J., Zipser, D.: A learning algorithm for continually running fully recurrent neural networks. Neural Computation 1(2), 270–280 (1989)
11. Dagum, L., Menon, R.: OpenMP: an industry standard API for shared-memory programming. IEEE Computational Science & Engineering 5(1), 46–55 (1998)
12. Chapman, B., Jost, G., Van Der Pas, R.: Using OpenMP: portable shared memory parallel programming, vol. 10. The MIT Press (2008)
13. Capizzi, G., Napoli, C., Paternò, L.: An innovative hybrid neuro-wavelet method for reconstruction of missing data in astronomical photometric surveys. In: Rutkowski, L., Korytkowski, M., Scherer, R., Tadeusiewicz, R., Zadeh, L.A., Zurada, J.M. (eds.) ICAISC 2012, Part I. LNCS, vol. 7267, pp. 21–29. Springer, Heidelberg (2012)

Application of Support Vector Machines, Convolutional Neural Networks and Deep Belief Networks to Recognition of Partially Occluded Objects

Joseph Lin Chu and Adam Krzyżak

Department of Computer Science and Software Engineering
Concordia University
1455 de Maisonneuve Blvd. West, Montreal, Quebec, Canada H3G 1M8
jo_chu@encs.concordia.ca, krzyzak@cs.concordia.ca

Abstract. Artificial neural networks have been widely used for machine learning tasks such as object recognition. Recent developments have made use of biologically inspired architectures, such as the Convolutional Neural Network, and the Deep Belief Network. We test the hypothesis that generative models such as the Deep Belief Network should perform better on occluded object recognition tasks than purely discriminative models such as Convolutional Neural Networks. We find that the data does not support this hypothesis when the generative models are run in a partially discriminative manner. We also find that the use of Gaussian visible units in a Deep Belief Network trained on occluded image data allows it to also learn to classify non-occluded images.[1]

1 Introduction

Partially occluded object recognition has historically been a challenging task. Most methods of solving this problem rely on complex preprocessing and feature extraction algorithms, often involving image segmentation and other extra processing [16] [22] [23] [24]. More recently, techniques involving the use of generative model reconstructions have been proposed [18].

Convolutional Neural Networks (CNNs) are feed-forward Artificial Neural Networks (ANNs), while Deep Belief Networks (DBNs) make use of Restricted Boltzmann Machines (RBMs) that use recurrent connections. The fundamental difference between these networks then, is that the DBN is capable of functioning as a generative model, whereas a CNN is merely a discriminative model. A generative model is able to model all variables probabilistically and therefore to generate values for any of these variables. In that sense it can do things like reproduce samples of the original input. A discriminative model on the other hand models only the dependence of an unobserved variable on an observed variable,

---

[1] This research was supported by the Natural Sciences and Engineering Research Council of Canada.

L. Rutkowski et al. (Eds.): ICAISC 2014, Part I, LNAI 8467, pp. 34–46, 2014.

which is sufficient to perform classification or prediction tasks, but which cannot reproduce samples like a generative model can. This suggests that DBNs should perform better on the task of partially occluded object recognition, as they ought to be able to use their generative effects to partially reconstruct the image to aid in classification. This hypothesis is what we wish to test in our work comparing CNNs, and DBNs.

2 Learning Algorithms

In order to contrast the effectiveness of generative models with discriminative models on the occluded object recognition task, we compared several models of Artificial Neural Network (ANN), as well as other machine learning algorithms, including: the Support Vector Machine (SVM), the CNN, (two discriminative models) and the DBN, (one generative model). Although the SVM is not a proper ANN strictly speaking, its popularity as a discriminative classifier means that it deserves inclusion as a control.

2.1 Support Vector Machine

The SVM is a powerful discriminant classifier first developed by Cortes & Vapnik [4]. Although technically not considered to be an ANN, Collobert & Bengio [3] showed that they had many similarities to Perceptrons with the obvious exception of learning algorithm.

2.2 Convolutional Neural Networks

The earliest of the hierarchical ANNs based on the visual cortex's architecture was the Neocognitron, first proposed by Fukushima & Miyake [6]. This network was based on the work of neuroscientists Hubel & Wiesel [13], who showed the existence of Simple and Complex Cells in the visual cortex. Fukushima took the notion of Simple and Complex Cells to create the Neocognitron, which implemented layers of such neurons in a hierarchical architecture [5].

Then LeCun et al [14] developed the CNN, which made use of multiple Convolutional and Subsampling layers, while also using stochastic gradient descent and backpropagation to create a feed-forward network that performed exceptionally well on image recognition tasks such as the MNIST. The Convolutional Layer of the CNN is equivalent to the Simple Cell Layer of the Neocognitron, while the Subsampling Layer of the CNN is equivalent to the Complex Cell Layer of the Neocognitron. Essentially they delocalize features from the visual receptive field, allowing such features to be identified with a degree of shift invariance. This unique structure allows the CNN to have two important advantages over a fully-connected ANN. First, is the use of the local receptive field, and second is weight-sharing. Both of these advantages have the effect of decreasing the number of weight parameters in the network, thereby making computation of these networks easier.

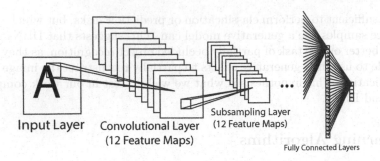

Input Layer   Convolutional Layer   Subsampling Layer
(12 Feature Maps)   (12 Feature Maps)

Fully Connected Layers

Fig. 1. The basic architecture of the CNN

2.3 Deep Belief Networks

One of the more recent developments in machine learning research has been the Deep Belief Network (DBN). The DBN is a recurrent ANN with undirected connections. Structurally, it is made up of multiple layers of RBMs, such that it can be seen as a 'deep' architecture. To understand how this is an effective structure, we must first understand the basic nature of a recurrent ANN.

Recurrent ANNs differ from feed-forward ANNs in that their connections can form cycles. The advantage of recurrent ANNs is that they can possess associative memory-like behaviour. Early Recurrent ANNs, such as the Hopfield network [11], showed promise in this regard, but were limited. The Hopfield network was only a single layer architecture that could only learn very limited problems due to limited memory capacity. A multi-layer generalization of the Hopfield Network was developed known as the Boltzmann Machine [1], which while able to store considerably more memory, suffered from being overly slow to train.

A variant of the Boltzmann Machine was first known as a Harmonium [21], but later called a RBM, which initially saw little use. Then Hinton [7] developed a fast learning algorithm for RBMs called Contrastive Divergence, which uses Gibbs sampling within a gradient descent process. The RBM is primarily different from a regular Boltzmann Machine by the simple fact that it lacks the lateral or sideways connections within layers.

By stacking RBMs together, Hinton, Osindero, & Teh, [9] created the DBN. The DBN is trained in a greedy, layer-wise fashion. This generally involves pre-training each RBM separately starting at the bottom layer and working up to the top layer. All layers have their weights initialized using unsupervised learning in the pre-training phase, after which fine-tuning using Backpropagation is performed using the labeled data, training in a supervised manner.

When introduced, the DBN produced then state of the art performance on such tasks as the MNIST. Later DBNs were also applied to 3D object recognition [17]. Ranzato, Susskind, Mnih, & Hinton [18] also showed how effective DBNs could be on occluded facial images.

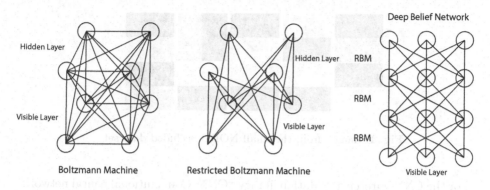

Fig. 2. The structure of the general Boltzmann Machine, the RBM, and the DBN

3 Methodology

For the object/image dataset, the small NORB [15] was used. The small NORB consists of 5 object categories and several thousand images per category, for a total of 24300 images each in the training and test sets. The small NORB proper includes a pair of stereo images for each training example, but we chose to only use one of the images in the pair. Normal, non-occluded images with the object fully visible in the image are seen in Figure 3. Occluded images were created by occluding a random half of each image in the test set with zeroes (black) as shown in Figure 4.

Fig. 3. Images from the small NORB non-occluded data set

For the SVMs we tested various parameters from the literature, such as Huang & LeCun [12] and Ranzato et al. [19] and eventually settled on a Gamma value of 0.0005, and a C value of 40. Gamma is how far a single training example affects things, with low values being "far" and high values being "close". C is the tradeoff between misclassifying as few training samples as possible (high C) and a smooth decision surface (low C). For code for the SVMs, we used the library "LIBSVM" by Chih-Chung Chang and Chih-Jen Lin from the National Taiwan University [2].

Fig. 4. Images from the small NORB occluded data set

For the CNN, Sirotenko's Matlab library "CNN Convolutional neural network class" (http://www.mathworks.com/matlabcentral/fileexchange/24291-cnn-convolutional-neural-network-class) was used and modified extensively to serve our purposes. Determining the architecture of a CNN requires special considerations. To calculate the reasonable dimensions of a square layer from either its previous layer (or next layer) in the hierarchy requires at least some of the following variables to be assigned. Let x be the width of the previous (or current) square layer. Let y be the width of the current (or next) square layer. Let r be the width of the square receptive field of nodes in the previous (or current) layer to each current (or next) layer node, and f be the offset distance between the receptive fields of adjacent nodes in the current (or next) layer. The relationship between these variables is best described by

$$y = \frac{x - (r - f)}{f} \tag{1}$$

where, $x \geq y$, $x \geq r \geq f$, and $f > 0$.
For convolutional layers $f = 1$ and (1) generalizes to

$$y = x - r + 1 \tag{2}$$

For subsampling layers $r = f$, and thus (1) generalizes to

$$y = \frac{x}{f} \tag{3}$$

From this we can determine the dimensions of each layer. The architecture for the CNN on the NORB dataset is shown in Table 1, where S, C and F represent convolutional, subsampling and fully connected layers, respectively.

Various parameters for the CNN were also experimented with to determine the optimal parameters to use in our experiments. We eventually settled on 100 epochs of training. The CNN learning rate and learning rate decrement parameters were determined by using Huang and LeCun's recommendations [12]. That is to say, the learning rate was initially set to 2.00E-05, and gradually decremented to approximately 2.00E-07.

For the DBN we used Stansbury's Matlab library "Matlab Environment for Deep Architecture Learning (MEDAL)" (https://github.com/dustinstansbury/medal). Experiments were also conducted on the parameters

Table 1. The architecture of the CNN used on the NORB dataset, based on Huang & LeCun [12]

CNN			
Layer	Nodes	k or r	Feature Maps
S1	96x96		
C2	92x92	5	8
S3	23x23	4	8
C4	18x18	6	24
S5	6x6	3	24
C6	1x1	6	24
F1	100	1	
F2	5	1	

for the DBN. By default, DBNs use binary visible units. A modification has been suggested to use Gaussian visible units for image data [10]. DBNs using both binary and Gaussian visible units were tested.

Two different amounts of hidden nodes were used, 2000 and 4000 respectively for the binary units. This was because prior experiments used to determine the effectiveness of various parameter configurations found that the binary units in combination with 2000 hidden nodes seemed to actually perform better than the combination of binary units and 4000 hidden nodes, which was different than expected. Gaussian units on the other hand, showed greater effectiveness at 4000 hidden nodes, than at 2000 hidden nodes, which was expected. For this reason, we tested multiple configurations. Eventually, through systematic efforts involving testing various parameters at different values and looking at the change in performance, we settled on the Layer, Learning Rate, and Epoch parameters for the Visible and Hidden Node cases shown in Table 2. Hinton also provided some suggested values that we took into consideration [8].

Table 2. The parameters chosen as an optimal configuration for the DBNs

Parameters - DBN						
Parameters			Learning Rate		Epochs	
Visible	Layers	Hidden	Pre-Training	Fine-Tune	Pre-Training	Fine-Tune
Binary	2	2000	0.1	0.01	200	50
Binary	2	4000	0.1	0.01	200	50
Gaussian	2	4000	0.001	0.001	200	50

Some more parameters we settled on are shown in Table 3, some of which were based on experimentation, while others were simply default settings that worked well. Details about the various parameters are described by Hinton [8].

Finally, experiments were performed with the optimized parameters for SVMs, CNNs, and DBNs on the small NORB image dataset. Each of the training and testing sets consisted of 24300 images. These experiments consisted of three

Table 3. The parameters chosen as an optimal configuration for the DBNs

Parameters - DBN	
Momentum	0.5
Weight Penalty	2.00E-04
Batch Size	100
Begin Simulated Annealing At	50
Number of Gibbs Sampling	1
Sparsity	0.01
Start to Vary Learning Rate At	50

different methods of training: one which consisted of training exclusively on the non-occluded training set, followed by testing on both a non-occluded test set and an occluded test set; one which consisted of training exclusively on the occluded training set, followed by testing on both a non-occluded test set and an occluded test set; and finally one which consisted of training on a mixture of non-occluded and occluded images, followed by testing on both a non-occluded test set and an occluded test set. Three replicates were performed for each experimental setup and averaged.

4   Results

4.1   Support Vector Machines

Table 4 provides a direct comparison of the non-occluded, occluded, and mixed trained SVMs.

Table 4. A comparison of the accuracy results of the non-occluded, occluded, and mixed trained SVMs

SVM - NORB				
Training	Training Test	Mixed Test	Non-Occluded Test	Occluded Test
Non-Occluded	**0.999 ± 0.003**	0.513 ± 0.001	**0.825 ± 0.007**	0.200 ± 0.003
Occluded	0.994 ± 0.0001	0.446 ± 0.0002	0.200 ± 0.0001	0.692 ± 0.0005
Mixed	0.973 ± 0.0003	**0.754 ± 0.001**	0.813 ± 0.001	**0.694 ± 0.0005**

Note: Mean of 3 replicates ± standard error.

4.2   Convolutional Neural Networks

Table 5 provides a direct comparison of the non-occluded, occluded, and mixed trained CNNs.

Table 5. A comparison of the accuracy results of the non-occluded, occluded, and mixed trained CNNs

CNN - NORB				
Training	Training Test	Mixed Test	Non-Occluded Test	Occluded Test
Non-Occluded	**0.955 ± 0.000**	0.515 ± 0.000	**0.831 ± 0.000**	0.199 ± 0.000
Occluded	0.693 ± 0.003	0.444 ± 0.017	0.304 ± 0.031	0.585 ± 0.002
Mixed	0.832 ± 0.002	**0.717 ± 0.003**	0.769 ± 0.009	**0.665 ± 0.010**

Note: Mean of 3 replicates ± standard error.

4.3   Deep Belief Networks

Tables 6-8 provide a direct comparison of the non-occluded, occluded, and mixed trained DBNs, with the differences between each table resulting from the effects of choosing different visible units and number of hidden units in the ANN.

Table 6 shows specifically the performance of the DBNs using binary visible units and having 2000 hidden nodes.

Table 6. A comparison of the accuracy results of the non-occluded, occluded, and mixed trained DBNs using binary visible units with 2000 hidden nodes

DBN - Binary Visible Unit w/ 2000 Hidden Nodes				
Training	Training Test	Mixed Test	Non-Occluded Test	Occluded Test
Non-Occluded	**0.993 ± 0.0002**	0.545 ± 0.000	**0.873 ± 0.007**	0.214 ± 0.004
Occluded	0.847 ± 0.007	0.451 ± 0.026	0.193 ± 0.044	**0.708 ± 0.009**
Mixed	0.832 ± 0.013	**0.680 ± 0.013**	0.676 ± 0.037	0.684 ± 0.020

Note: Mean of 3 replicates ± standard error.

Table 7 shows specifically the performance of the DBNs using binary visible units and having 4000 hidden nodes.

Table 7. A comparison of the accuracy results of the non-occluded, occluded, and mixed trained DBNs using binary visible units with 4000 hidden nodes

DBN - Binary Visible Unit w/ 4000 Hidden Nodes				
Training	Training Test	Mixed Test	Non-Occluded Test	Occluded Test
Non-Occluded	**0.989 ± 0.002**	0.520 ± 0.008	**0.841 ± 0.014**	0.203 ± 0.002
Occluded	0.852 ± 0.007	0.458 ± 0.014	0.208 ± 0.022	**0.708 ± 0.006**
Mixed	0.866 ± 0.008	**0.673 ± 0.001**	0.653 ± 0.004	0.693 ± 0.004

Note: Mean of 3 replicates ± standard error.

Table 8 shows specifically the performance of the DBNs using Gaussian visible units and having 4000 hidden nodes.

Table 8. A comparison of the accuracy results of the non-occluded, occluded, and mixed trained DBNs using Gaussian visible units with 4000 hidden nodes

DBN - Gaussian Visible Unit w/ 4000 Hidden Nodes				
Training	Training Test	Mixed Test	Non-Occluded Test	Occluded Test
Non-Occluded	**0.981 ± 0.003**	0.550 ± 0.002	**0.832 ± 0.006**	0.258 ± 0.013
Occluded	0.786 ± 0.001	0.673 ± 0.002	0.693 ± 0.006	0.652 ± 0.005
Mixed	0.860 ± 0.016	**0.697 ± 0.023**	0.714 ± 0.044	**0.679 ± 0.006**

Note: Mean of 3 replicates ± standard error.

5 Discussion

The experiments performed have shown that when training a classifier on only the non-occluded training set, the occluded task is a particularly challenging one for both the discriminative models, such as SVMs and CNNs, and the generative models, namely the DBNs. In general, training on the non-occluded images tends to lead to good performance on the non-occluded test set, but poor performance on the occluded test set, while in most cases, training on the occluded images leads to good performance on the occluded test set, and poorer performance on the non-occluded test set.

However, it appears that training on the occluded training set only, for DBNs using Gaussian visible units at least, produces a highly unusual result of good performance on the non-occluded test set (69% accuracy). This behaviour is not apparent with the DBN using binary visible units (19-21% accuracy). A much less pronounced but similar effect is also visible with the CNN (30% accuracy), which is not seen at all with SVM, which performs at chance (20% accuracy). It may be that this is because the SVM is a purely discriminative model. The CNN while also a discriminative model, is also an ANN, which gives it some similarity to the DBN. Nevertheless, the unexpectedly good performance of the Gaussian visible unit based DBN on the dataset type it wasn't trained on is something perhaps worth looking into for future research. Though this seems to come at a cost to performance on occluded test set, as it is the only classifier that performs better on the dataset type it wasn't trained on (69% accuracy), than on the type it was trained on (65% accuracy).

Training the SVM, the CNN, and the DBN with Gaussian visible units on a mixed training set containing both non-occluded and occluded images leads to slightly worse performance on the non-occluded test set than an exclusively non-occluded trained classifier, and slightly better performance on the occluded test set than an exclusively occluded trained classifier. This result suggests that mixed training actually improves performance on the occluded problem. It is possible that these classifiers are benefiting from the more complete images in the non-occluded part of the training set.

Training a DBN with binary visible units on a mixed training set containing both non-occluded and occluded images performs worse on the non-occluded test set than a pure non-occluded training set, and is worse but is very close in performance on the occluded test set to that trained on a pure occluded training set. This is expected, as a mixed training set should yield mediocre performance on both test sets compared to classifiers trained exclusively on the non-occluded or the occluded training sets.

While training a SVM, CNN, and a DBN with Gaussian visible units on a mixed training set leads to better relative performance on the non-occluded test image set than on the occluded test image set, the reverse appears to be the case with DBNs with binary visible units, which had better relative performance on the occluded test image set than on the non-occluded test image set. This is somewhat curious, and may be indicative of the differences between binary and Gaussian visible units.

In comparison to other work in the literature, the experiments performed on the SVM and CNN did not exceed the performance of the results from Huang and LeCun [12]. Huang and LeCun were able to achieve 88.4% accuracy with their SVM on the small NORB dataset, and 93.8% accuracy with their CNN on the small NORB dataset [12]. The SVM in our experiments, with the same parameters as Huang and LeCun [12], achieved 82.5% ± 0.7% accuracy, while our CNN achieved 83.1% accuracy. Our best performing algorithm was actually a DBN using binary visible units and 2000 hidden nodes, which achieved 87% accuracy. In comparison, Nair and Hinton [17], achieved 93.5% accuracy with their DBN on the standard small NORB dataset, and 94.8% accuracy with their DBN using extra unlabeled data. Thus, on the non-occluded images, we did not achieve quite as good results as the best in the literature.

A major reason for our relatively inferior performance was that we chose to only take one of the two stereo images in the NORB dataset to be used by our algorithms. The top performing results in the literature on the other hand, generally made use of both of the stereo images. We chose not to use the stereo pair images primarily because of limitations on our part, namely that it would double the size of the dataset in memory, and that in the case of the CNN it would require a considerable modification to the architecture of the network. Thus, we chose to save both memory and time by using only the single image. This was an important choice, because we were limited in the amount of RAM available on our computers, and the amount of time to required to train with even this limited version of the NORB was quite substantial. Also, in reality it often difficult to obtain stereo images without resorting to some special robotic vision setup. Conversely, single images are readily available in many datasets, CCTV cameras, and Internet searches.

As far as occluded images are concerned, there is a lack of results in the literature that are directly comparable to our work. Probably the most similar work done so far would be Ranzato et al. [18]. Their work on classifying facial expressions includes some use of occlusion. Rather than using NORB, they used the Cohn-Kanade (CK) dataset, and the Toronto Face Database (TFD), classifying 7 different facial expressions, rather than 5 objects. Their Type 3 - right half, Type 4 - bottom half, and Type 5 - top half occlusions are most similar to the occlusions we used in our experiments. Unlike our experiments, their deep generative model actually attempts to reconstruct the image first before classifying.

This takes full advantage of the unique properties of generative models. As such, they achieve fairly impressive results.

Overall their results in combination with our own results appear to show that the advantage of using a generative model comes from the reconstruction process that Ranzato et al. [18] were able to use, and is not simply a result of classification using a generative model discriminatively as we did. Further research naturally could involve actually implementing some kind of reconstruction process similar to what Ranzato et al. [18] used, except on the small NORB dataset, to see whether or not this conjecture actually holds.

A further possible reason why the performance of the generative DBN did not exceed the discriminative models could be because the DBNs were fine-tuned with Backpropagation. As this process is inherently discriminative rather than generative, the final resulting network perhaps behaves more like a discriminative model than a generative model. If this is the case, we should be able to see some difference in the accuracy of the model when it has only been pre-trained, and not yet fine-tuned with Backpropagation. To truly test this possibility, we may need to find a generative model that is fully generative through and through, such as a Deep Boltzmann Machine (DBM) [20].

6   Conclusions

It thus appears that the original hypothesis that the generative models would perform significantly better on the occluded task than the discriminative models is not well supported by the results of the experiments performed. Rather, when run in a discriminative manner, the generative model, in our case, the DBN appears to perform close to equally well to the discriminative models, the SVM and the CNN. This suggests that, with regards to other findings in the literature which use generative models and are able to show a difference, that this difference is primarily due to the additional use of reconstruction processes, and is not due to merely the architecture and training algorithm itself.

On the other hand, with regards to DBNs using Gaussian visible units, when trained on the occluded training set and tested on the non-occluded dataset, show remarkable performance that perhaps warrants further research. In fact, this may suggest that intentionally occluding data sets may allow for good performance on both the non-occluded and occluded tasks, at least when using this particular variant of DBN. Such could prove useful in tasks in which the original training set is non-occluded, but the real-world test data may well be occluded, such as in the case of real-world face recognition from CCTV cameras.

References

1. Ackley, D.H., Hinton, G.E., Sejnowski, T.J.: A learning algorithm for boltzmann machines. Cognitive Science 9, 147–169 (1985)
2. Chang, C.C., Lin, C.J.: LIBSVM: A library for support vector machines. ACM Transactions on Intelligent Systems and Technology 2, 27:1–27:27 (2011), software available at http://www.csie.ntu.edu.tw/~cjlin/libsvm

3. Collobert, R., Bengio, S.: Links between perceptrons, mlps and svms. In: Proceedings of the 21st International Conference on Machine Learning (ICML), p. 23 (2004)
4. Cortes, C., Vapnik, V.N.: Support-vector networks. Machine Learning 20, 273–297 (1995)
5. Fukushima, K.: Neocognitron for handwritten digit recognition. Neurocomputing 51, 161–180 (2003)
6. Fukushima, K., Miyake, S.: Neocognitron: A new algorithm for pattern recognition tolerant of deformations and shifts in position. Pattern Recognition 15(6), 455–469 (1982)
7. Hinton, G.E.: Training products of experts by minimizing contrastive divergence. Neural Computation 14(8), 1771–1800 (2002)
8. Hinton, G.E.: A practical guide to training restricted boltzmann machines. Momentum 9(1), 599–619 (2010)
9. Hinton, G.E., Osindero, S., Teh, Y.W.: A fast learning algorithm for deep belief nets. Neural Computation 18, 1527–1554 (2006)
10. Hinton, G.E., Salakhutdinov, R.R.: Reducing the dimensionality of data with neural networks. Science 313, 504–507 (2006)
11. Hopfield, J.J.: Neural networks and physical systems with emergent collective computational abilities. Proceedings of the National Academy of Sciences of the USA 79(8), 2554–2558 (1982)
12. Huang, F.J., LeCun, Y.: Large-scale learning with svm and convolutional nets for generic object categorization. In: Proceedings of the 2006 IEEE Computer Society Conference on Computer Vision and Pattern Recognition (CVPR), vol. 1, pp. 284–291 (2006)
13. Hubel, D.H., Wiesel, T.N.: Receptive fields, binocular interaction and functional architecture in a cat's visual cortex. Journal of Physiology 160, 106–154 (1962)
14. LeCun, Y., Bottou, L., Bengio, Y., Haffner, P.: Gradient-based learning applied to document recognition. Proceedings of the IEEE 86(11), 2278–2324 (1998)
15. LeCun, Y., Huang, F., Bottou, L.: Learning methods for generic object recognition with invariance to pose and lighting. In: IEEE Computer Society Conference on Computer Vision and Pattern Recognition (CVPR), vol. 2, pp. 97–104 (2004)
16. Martinez, A.M.: Recognizing imprecisely localized, partially occluded, and expression variant faces from a single sample per class. IEEE Transactions on Pattern Analysis and Machine Intelligence 24(6), 748–763 (2002)
17. Nair, V., Hinton, G.E.: 3d object recognition with deep belief nets. In: Advances in Neural Information Processing Systems (NIPS), pp. 1339–1347 (2009)
18. Ranzato, M., Susskind, J., Mnih, V., Hinton, G.: On deep generative models with applications to recognition. In: 2011 IEEE Conference on Computer Vision and Pattern Recognition (CVPR), pp. 2857–2864 (2011)
19. Ranzato, M.A., Huang, F.J., Boureau, Y.L., LeCun, Y.: Unsupervised learning of invariant feature hierarchies with applications to object recognition. In: 2007 IEEE Conference on Computer Vision and Pattern Recognition (CVPR), pp. 1–8 (2007)
20. Salakhutdinov, R., Hinton, G.E.: Deep boltzmann machines. In: International Conference on Artificial Intelligence and Statistics (AISTATS), pp. 448–455 (2009)
21. Smolensky, P.: Information processing in dynamical systems: Foundations of harmony theory. In: Rumelhart, D.E., McLelland, J.L. (eds.) Parallel Distributed Processing: Explorations in the Microstructure of Cognition, vol. 1, ch. 6, pp. 194–281. MIT Press (1986)

22. Tsang, P.W.M., Yuen, P.C.: Recognition of partially occluded objects. IEEE Transactions on Systems, Man and Cybernetics 23(1), 228–236 (1993)
23. Winn, J., Shotton, J.: The layout consistent random field for recognizing and segmenting partially occluded objects. In: 2006 IEEE Computer Society Conference on Computer Vision and Pattern Recognition (CVPR), vol. 1, pp. 37–44 (2006)
24. Wiskott, L., Malsburg, C.V.D.: A neural system for the recognition of partially occluded objects in cluttered scenes: A pilot study. International Journal of Pattern Recognition and Artificial Intelligence 7(4), 935–948 (1993)

A New Multilayer Perceptron Initialisation Method with Selection of Weights on the Basis of the Function Variability

Krzysztof Halawa

Wrocław University of Technology
Wyb. Wyspiańskiego 27, 50-370 Wrocław, Poland
krzysztof.halawa@pwr.wroc.pl

Abstract. Learning results of multilayer perceptrons highly depend on the initial weight values. The proper selection of weights may improve network performance and reduce time of the learning process. In the paper, a new multilayer perceptron weight selection algorithm based on determination of the variability of the approximated function, within various fragments of its domain, has been proposed. This algorithm has a low computational complexity. Results of numerical experiments have been presented for many learning sets. The comparison of cost function values for neural networks initialized with the applying of the proposed algorithm and for networks initialised by the popular Nguyen-Widrow algorithm has been shown. Independently of the epoch number, the use of the proposed algorithm made it possible to achieve better results for a vast majority of the learning sets.

Keywords: neural network, multilayer perceptron, initialisation.

1 Introduction

The multilayer perceptron MLP is one of the most common neural network architectures because it has some significant advantages. A predisposition for operation with multi-dimensional data is one of them [1]. MLP consists of an input layer including the network inputs, one or more hidden layers and one output layer. MLPs with one hidden layer are frequently applied. The output value of neurons is equal to $f\left(w_0 + \sum_{l=1}^{q} w_l u_l\right)$, where f denotes the activation function, q is the number of the neuron inputs, $w_1, \ldots, w_q$ are the weights, w_0 is called the bias or the threshold value, $u_1, \ldots, u_q$ are the neuron inputs. The activation functions of neurons in the hidden layers are the most often sigmoidal. These functions may be bipolar or unipolar. One of the bipolar activation functions is given by the formula

$$f_b(x) = \frac{2}{1 + \exp(-2x)} - 1. \tag{1}$$

The shape of this function is similar to $\tanh(x)$, where $\tanh$ denotes the hyperbolic tangent. For determination of the function (1), a lower number of processor

L. Rutkowski et al. (Eds.): ICAISC 2014, Part I, LNAI 8467, pp. 47–58, 2014.

operations is required than for the calculation of the $\tanh(x)$ value. If a MLP is applied in microcontrollers, that have a low computational power, the function $\tanh(x)$ may be interpolated with the use of the look-up tables or approximated with piecewise continuous polynomial models [2].

In Figure 1, the $R^2 \rightarrowtail R$ transformation has been presented, which is done by the neuron with two inputs and the activation function given by the formula (1). The middle of the slope is marked with the bold line. The middle of the q-dimensional hyper-slope is the straight line described by the equation

$$w_0 + \sum_{l=1}^{q} w_l u_l = 0. \tag{2}$$

The Euclidean norm of the neuron weight vector $\| [w_1, \ldots, w_q]^T \|$ determines the slope width. The bias w_0 shifts the slope and has no influence on its width.

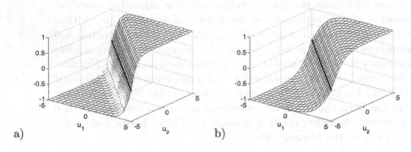

a)   b)

Fig. 1. Neuron output described by the function $f_b(w_1 u_1 + w_2 u_2 + w_0)$ for a) $w_1 = w_2 = 1$ and $w_0 = 0$ b) $w_1 = w_2 = 0.5$ and $w_0 = 0$. The middles of the slopes are marked with the bold lines.

The proper selection of the initial weight values is very significant for the speed and results of the MLP learning, that is usually carried out with the first or second order gradient algorithms. The appropriate initialisation of the weight values decreases the probability of getting stuck at a shallow local minimum of the cost function. This makes it possible to avoid the case that a part of the neurons is unused. Too low weight values may significantly slow down the learning process. Too high weight values result in neuron saturation and increase the probability of quickly getting stuck at a lousy local minimum. Besides the proper slope width, their proper placement in the hyperspace is very important. The serious problems with proper selection of initial values of the weights result often in that the learning is repeated multiple times, beginning each time, from a different starting point. This is so called multistart.

A significant influence of initial weight values on learning results was the reason of some trials to make use of various initialisation methods, most of which is applied very rarely. A part of them is time consuming and complicated in usage. In [3], the application of the genetic algorithms for selection of the weights and choosing the MLP topology is described. In [4] the sensitivity analysis based initialization method for two-layer MLP is proposed. First, random values are assigned to output layer weights. After that, these values are updated based on sensitivity formulas, and finally the weights are calculated using an appropriate linear system of equations. Authors of [5] considered a method depending on the weight fluctuation analysis and matching to various data. The paper [6] presents the algorithm using the least squares method LSM for optimising weights of neurons with the linear activation functions in the last layer. After LSM, the weight optimisation in the previous layers with the gradient methods is applied. A method with using prototypes for selection of weights for MLP intended for modeling of mechanical forces is described in [7]. The use of straight linear approximation to analytically determine a minimum of the sum of squared errors is presented in [8].

The Nguyen-Widrow algorithm [9] is commonly used for selection of the initial weight values in the hidden layers. This algorithm may be used only with neurons having a bias and which activation function is bounded. The concept of the Nguyen-Widrow algorithm relies on the selection of the weight values in such a way that the slopes are close to evenly distributed in the input space. In [9], an application of this algorithm with MLPs having only one hidden layer has been proposed, but this algorithm may be used for initialisation of a higher number of the hidden layers. The first step of the Nguyen-Widrow algorithm consists of association pseudorandom numbers uniformly distributed on the interval of $[-1, 1]$ for all weights in the hidden layer. In this way, the hyper-slope directions are random. If the neuron input values are included in the interval of $[-1, 1]$, then the neuron weight vectors are normalised so that their Euclidean norms are equal to $0.7\varphi^{1/q}$, where φ is the number of neurons in the initialised layer. Next, the biases are generated utilising the pseudorandom number generator, of the uniform distribution on the interval $[-0.7\varphi^{1/q}, 0.7\varphi^{1/q}]$, which results in a close to even distribution of the slopes. In [9], it has been shown that the Nguyen-Widrow algorithm makes it possible to significantly shorten the learning time and to achieve much better results than in the case that the weight and bias values are pseudorandom numbers of the uniform distribution on the interval $[-0.5, 0.5]$. Superiority of the Nguyen-Widrow algorithm is also shown in [10]. Simplicity, good performance, low computational complexity and task independence are reasons why Nguyen-Widrow initialisation algorithm is available in many sophisticated software for neural networks computing. For example, this is the default initialisation method in Matlab Neural Network Toolbox.

The algorithm proposed by the author of the present paper evenly arranges in the input space, only a part of the slopes. Most of the slopes are located in those areas of the space wherein the function being approximated changes most and to which the biggest data number belongs to. In order to determine the function variability, standard deviations of the approximated function values are calculated, but other variability measures may also be used.

Numerous experiments with MLPs initialised with the use of the proposed algorithm and with MLPs initialised according to the Nguyen-Widrow algorithm have been conducted. These experiments confirmed the reasonability of the application of the algorithm proposed in this paper. The reason for comparing the results of the application of the proposed algorithm only with the results obtained from Nguyen-Widrow algorithm, was the eagerness to conduct as many number of the time consuming computer simulations as possible and the fact of the exceptional popularity of the Nguyen-Widrow algorithm.

The further part of this article is organised as follows. In Section 2, the proposed initialisation algorithm is presented and its computational complexity is explained. In Section 3, the way in which the computer simulations were conducted is described and the obtained results are shown. The conclusions are at the end of the paper.

2   Proposed Method

For the sake of a concise notation, it is assumed, in this section, that the network input values belong to the interval $[-1, 1]$ and that the network has only one output. In such case, the learning set consists of the pairs $\{\mathbf{X}_i, d_i\}_{i=1}^N$ where d_i denotes the desirable network output value when its inputs are equal to the elements of the vector $\mathbf{X}_i = [x_{i,1}, x_{i,2}, \ldots, x_{i,S}]^T$, S is the number of the network inputs. MLP maps the S-dimensional hyperspace $\mathcal{H} = [-1, 1]^S$ into the set of real numbers.

The first step of the proposed algorithm relies on division of the hyperspace $\mathcal{H}$ into lower disjoint fragments of the equal size. In Fig. 2, an exemplary division of $\mathcal{H}$ for MLPs which have 1, 2 and 3 inputs is shown. Let n denote the number of the space fragments, obtained after the division of $\mathcal{H}$, and let v be the number of neurons in the hidden layer which is located closest to the input layer. The algorithm is designed to initialise this layer. The division of $\mathcal{H}$ should be performed in such way that $n < v$ and $n \ll N$, where the symbol $\ll$ denotes much less. Let $h_1, h_2, \ldots, h_n$ denote the fragments obtained after the division of $\mathcal{H}$.

For each fragment h_a, $a = 1, 2, \ldots, n$, the standard deviation σ_a is calculated from all values d_i assigned with the vectors $\mathbf{X}_i$ belonging to h_a. If no vector $\mathbf{X}_i$ belongs to h_a, then $\sigma_a = 0$ is assumed.

In the next step, for each fragment h_a, the number of slopes, intentionally located to pass through h_a, is calculated. This number is denoted by λ_a. It is given by the formula

$$\lambda_a = \left\lfloor \frac{\sigma_a \cdot \#_a}{\sum_{a=1}^n \sigma_a \cdot \#_a} \cdot \frac{v}{2} \right\rfloor, \tag{3}$$

where $\#_a$ is the number of the vectors $\mathbf{X}_i$ belonging to h_a, $\lfloor \cdot \rfloor$ denotes the floor function which value is equal to the largest integer not greater than the argument.

Let us note that $0 \leq \lambda_a \leq \frac{v}{2}$ except of the very rare probable case that $\sum_{a=1}^n \sigma_a \#_a = 0$, wherein the proposed algorithm cannot be applied. Such case may only happen when the function being approximated does not change in all fragments.

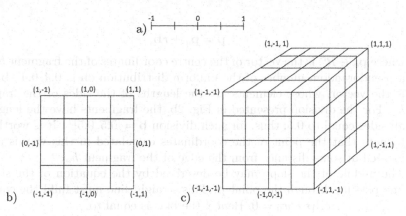

Fig. 2. Exemplary division of the data space $\mathcal{H}$ into smaller fragments, for a) MLP with one input, b) MLP with two inputs, c) MLP with three inputs

Most of the slopes are placed in the fragments where the values of the products $\sigma_a \# a$ are the highest, i.e. where the variability of the approximated function is considerable and where is a lot of data. It is often reasonable to expect that more measuring data is in the significant fragments. If it is not the case, then, instead of determining λ_a from the relationship (3), one may calculate λ_a using the formula

$$\lambda_a = \left\lfloor \frac{\sigma_a}{\sum_{a=1}^{n} \sigma_a} \cdot \frac{v}{2} \right\rfloor. \tag{4}$$

Each neuron produces one slope. The number of neurons whose weights are selected so that the middles of the slopes created by them passes through the relevant h_a amounts to

$$\beta = \sum_{a=1}^{n} \lambda_a. \tag{5}$$

The number of the other neurons in the hidden layer is equal to

$$\delta = v - \beta \geq \frac{v}{2}. \tag{6}$$

After determining the number of slopes located in respective fragments $h_1, h_2, \ldots, h_n$, the weights and the biases of the neurons forming those slopes should be calculated. For each fragment h_a, for which $\lambda_a > 0$, the following procedure is repeated λ_a times

a) The weight values $w_1, w_2, \ldots, w_s$ are selected as random numbers uniformly distributed on the interval $[-1, 1]$.
b) The weight vectors are normalised so that their Euclidean norm is equal to $0.7\delta^{1/s}$, i.e. $\left\| [w_1, w_2, \ldots, w_s]^T \right\| = 0.7\delta^{1/s}$.
c) Is determining the point by which the middle of the slope is passing through. This point is positioned within the fragment h_a. The coordinates **p** of this point are generated on the basis of the relationship

$$\mathbf{p} = \mathbf{p}_a + r\mathbf{b}, \tag{7}$$

where $\mathbf{p}_a \in R^S$ is the vector of the centre coordinates of the fragment h_a, r is a pseudorandom number of the uniform distribution on $[-0.4, 0.4]$, $\mathbf{b} \in R^S$ is the vector, whose elements are the lengths of the sides of the fragment h_a. For the division presented in Fig. 2b, the fragments have the lengths of all sides equal to 0.5; thus, for such division $\mathbf{b} = [0.5, 0.5]^T$. It is worthwhile to note that the point of the coordinates calculated in this way is always located at some distance from the edge of the fragment h_a.

d) The middle of the slope may be described by the equation of the straight line passing through the point $\mathbf{p}$. This straight line must fulfil the equation $[w_1, w_2, \ldots, w_s]\mathbf{p} + w_0 = 0$. Hence, the bias is equal to

$$w_0 = -[w_1, w_2, \ldots, w_s]\mathbf{p}. \tag{8}$$

In this way, the weights and biases for β of the neurons have been determined. The weights of the other δ neurons in the same layer are selected with the use of the Nguyen-Widrow algorithm. The Euclidean norm of the weight vectors for all neurons is equal to $0.7\delta^{1/s}$.

Figure 2 depicts an exemplary division of the space into smaller fragments that, for $s = 2$, are squares and, for $s = 3$ - cubes. Obviously, the side lengths may be different within various dimensions and, for $s = 2$, the space $\mathcal{H}$ may be divided into rectangles and, for $s = 3$, into rectangular prisms, while for $s = 4$, into hyper-rectangular prisms. Together with the increasing network input number, the dimension of the space $\mathcal{H}$ will increase which will result in the exponential increase of the number of fragments obtained after the division. If $s = 7$ and the fragments are hyper-cubes with the side length of 0.5, then the number of those hyper-cubes amounts to as much as $4^7 = 16384$ and the condition $n < v$ is not satisfied. For $s > 3$, it is possible to use the a priori knowledge to chose the two most significant inputs and, in those two dimensions only, make the division into squares or rectangles. If we do not dispose the a priori knowledge on the process being modelled by the network, then one of the methods described in [11] may be used for the selection of the two or three most significant inputs.

If MLP has several outputs, then σ_a may be assumed as the sum of the standard deviations of the desired values of all network outputs. This is the only necessary change for entering in the algorithm.

In spite of the rather long description, the proposed initialisation algorithm is simple and may be briefly summarized in the following steps:
- division of the space $\mathcal{H}$ into n smaller disjoint fragments $h_1, h_2, \ldots, h_n$ and calculation of standard deviations $\sigma_1, \sigma_2, \ldots, \sigma_n$
- calculation of the numbers of the slopes arranged intentionally in the fragments $h_1, h_2, \ldots, h_n$
- determination of the weights of β neurons according to steps **a** and **b** from page 51
- calculation of these neurons biases from the equation (8)

- determination of the weights and biases of the other δ neurons, with the use of the Nguyen-Widrow algorithm

Computation complexity of Steps 1-5 can be easily determined. The numbers of operations required for steps 1-5 are presented in Tab. 1. Since $\beta \leq v$, $v \geq \delta \geq v/2$ and $n << N$, the total computational complexity is $O(N + v)$.

Table 1. Computational complexity of Steps 1-5

Step	1	2	3	4	5
Comp. Complexity	$O(N)$	$O(n)$	$O(\beta)$	$O(\beta)$	$O(\delta)$

3 Numerical Experiments

The proposed algorithm was tested on MLPs having one hidden layer which contained 30 or 45 neurons. The activation function of these neurons is described by the equation (1). In the output layer was one neuron with the linear activation function $f(x) = x$. The cost function minimized during learning was the mean squared normalised error, given by the formula

$$E = \frac{1}{N} \sum_{i=1}^{N} (d_i - y(\mathbf{X}_i))^2 , \qquad (9)$$

where $y(\mathbf{X}_i)$ denotes the network output value, when the network inputs are equal to the elements of the vector $\mathbf{X}_i$, d_i is the desirable value of the output. For learning of MLPs, 6 various learning sets were used, which will be described in a further part of this section. The Levenberg-Marquardt algorithm was used to learn both MLPs with the hidden layer initialised according to the Nguyen-Widrow algorithm and MLPs with the hidden layer initialised by applying the proposed algorithm. The weights and the biases in the output layer were pseudorandom numbers of the uniform distribution on $[-2, 2]$. After 200 epochs, the learning was interrupted due to very insignificant changes in the cost function value. The initialisations and learning were repeated 100 times for each data set in order to obtain consistent results. In Table 3 and Table 5, the results obtained from calculating the mean of 100 cost function values after 50, 100, 150 and 200 learning epochs are presented. There are also shown, the averaged values of the 100 best results obtained from all learning epochs (independently in which of the 200 epochs the cost function had the lowest value). Due to the huge number of operations to be conducted, all simulations were run on Supernova cluster which is in the Wrocław Network and Supercomputer Centre. Two-hundred learning epochs for $2 \cdot 2 \cdot 6 \cdot 100 = 2400$ networks were performed in total. The experiments were conducted using Matlab R2011b.

In Tables 2 and 4, the number of the intentionally arranged slopes is presented, which are sorted in the descending order of the products $\sigma_a \#_a$ values.

Prior to network learning, all data set was rescaled so that the values of the MLP inputs belonged to the interval $[-1, 1]$.

Fig. 3. Map of a South America piece terrain

The first learning set included the altitudes of a piece of South American surface, presented in Fig. 3. The data used to create this set was downloaded from the U.S. Geological Survey server, where a raster-type numerical model of the whole world, called GTOPO30 (30 arc second resolution, approx. 1 km) is freely available. The name of downloaded file is w100s10. The data description is in [12]. Half of the data was used for learning the network to model the terrain located between the geographic coordinates 80°West, 10°South and 60°West, 60°South. In the downloaded file, the altitudes are specified at the points on the grid of size 1km x 1km. In order to decrease the instance number in the learning set to 9000, MLP was trained to model the terrain on the basis of the averaged data on the areas of 40km x 40km. The altitudes in the created learning set were given in kilometres.

MLP was also learned to approximate various functions on the area $[-2, 2]$ x $[-2, 2]$. These functions were described by the equations:

$f_1(x, y) = \text{sinc}\left(\sqrt{x^2 + y^2}\right)$, where $\text{sinc}(x) = \frac{\sin(x)}{x}$,

$f_2(x, y) = x^2 - y^2 + 1$,

$f_3(x, y) = \sin(xy)$,

$f_4(x, y) = \tanh\left(x + y^2\right)$.

The functions f_1, f_2, f_3, f_4 have been presented in Fig. 4. The learning sets included 10000 function values arranged uniformly in the area of $[-2, 2]$ x $[-2, 2]$.

A next learning set was a common UCI benchmark [13] with the real-world data. It included the information on the forest fires in Portugal, described in [14]. The applied input values were:

1. x-axis spatial coordinate within the Montesinho park map: 1 to 9
2. y-axis spatial coordinate within the Montesinho park map: 2 to 9
3. FFMC index from the FWI system: 18.7 to 96.20
4. DMC index from the FWI system: 1.1 to 291.3
5. DC index from the FWI system: 7.9 to 860.6
6. ISI index from the FWI system: 0.0 to 56.10
7. temperature in Celsius degrees: 2.2 to 33.30
8. relative humidity in %: 15.0 to 100
9. wind speed in km/h: 0.40 to 9.40
10. rain in mm/m^2: 0.0 to 6.4

The networks were trained to model the number of forest hectares burned in fires. Since the burned areas are very skewed towards 0.0 according to a suggestion of the author of [14], the logarithmic transformation was applied and,

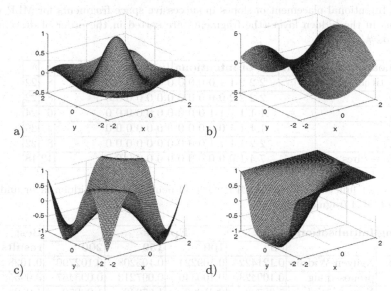

Fig. 4. Plots of functions: a) f_1 b) f_2 c) f_3 d) f_4

due to that, the desirable values of the output were the values of the natural logarithm of the burned down surface. After rejection of the incomplete data from the learning set, 683 instances remained therein.

For networks containing 30 neurons in the hidden layer, a division into 4x4 fragments has been applied, while for networks with 45 neurons in the hidden layer, a division into 5x5 fragments has been used.

Two-input networks were trained with the use of first five learning sets. The MLP for modelling the forest fires had 10 inputs. For this learning set, two dimensions were selected, for which the absolute value of the tau-Kendall's correlation coefficient has the highest value. Though, the coefficient is considerable less suitable for selecting important dimensions, then the methods described in [11], still, the application of the proposed algorithm has made it possible to achieve a lower cost function value, independently of the number of neurons in the hidden layer and of the learning epoch number.

In each experiment, λ_a was calculated on the basis of the relationship (3). For the first five learning sets, it is of no importance if λ_a has been determined from (3), or from (4), since the learning data is distributed uniformly.

For all learning sets except one, better cost function values were achieved for the networks initiated with the proposed algorithm. Only for MLP with 45 neurons in the hidden layer, a worse result was achieved solely for f_2 approximation after 200 epochs. The reason probably was the very fast increase of the function value near the area edge $[-2, 2]$ x $[-2, 2]$. For the other learning sets, better results were obtained using the proposed initialisation method, independently from the number of the neurons in the hidden layer and of the number of epochs.

Table 2. Intentional placement of slopes in successive space fragments for MLP with 30 neurons in the hidden layer (the fragments are sorted in the order of descending products $\sigma_a \# a$)

Learning set	Numbers of intentionally arranged slopes	β	δ
altitudes	2 2 2 1 1 0 0 0 0 0 0 0 0 0 0 0	8	22
f_1	2 2 2 2 0 0 0 0 0 0 0 0 0 0 0 0	8	22
f_2	1 1 1 1 1 1 0 0 0 0 0 0 0 0 0 0	6	24
f_3	1 1 1 1 0 0 0 0 0 0 0 0 0 0 0 0	4	26
f_4	2 2 1 1 1 1 0 0 0 0 0 0 0 0 0 0	8	22
forestfires	7 4 1 0 0 0 0 0 0 0 0 0 0 0 0 0	12	18

Table 3. Cost function values for MLP with 30 neurons in the hidden layer and the division into 4x4 fragments

Learning set	Initialisation	Epochs				Best results
		50	100	150	200	
altitudes	Nguyen-Widrow	0.121422	0.109224	0.105208	0.102790	0.1028
	proposed alg.	0.109423	0.100346	0.097213	0.095467	0.0955
f_1	Nguyen-Widrow	5.38733 $\cdot 10^{-5}$	2.35098 $\cdot 10^{-5}$	1.67948 $\cdot 10^{-5}$	1.26850 $\cdot 10^{-5}$	1.2593 $\cdot 10^{-5}$
	proposed alg.	4.04619 $\cdot 10^{-5}$	2.00634 $\cdot 10^{-5}$	1.48935 $\cdot 10^{-5}$	1.14843 $\cdot 10^{-5}$	1.1484 $\cdot 10^{-5}$
f_2	Nguyen-Widrow	2.04380 $\cdot 10^{-5}$	1.78020 $\cdot 10^{-6}$	6.40758 $\cdot 10^{-7}$	2.67063 $\cdot 10^{-7}$	2.6634 $\cdot 10^{-7}$
	proposed alg.	1.03015 $\cdot 10^{-5}$	1.49403 $\cdot 10^{-6}$	4.74928 $\cdot 10^{-7}$	2.28305 $\cdot 10^{-7}$	1.9308 $\cdot 10^{-7}$
f_3	Nguyen-Widrow	0.000216	6.07932 $\cdot 10^{-5}$	3.27470 $\cdot 10^{-5}$	2.20635 $\cdot 10^{-5}$	2.2064 $\cdot 10^{-5}$
	proposed alg.	0.000162	4.18492 $\cdot 10^{-5}$	2.09658 $\cdot 10^{-5}$	1.48085 $\cdot 10^{-5}$	1.4809 $\cdot 10^{-5}$
f_4	Nguyen-Widrow	5.64910 $\cdot 10^{-5}$	1.75280 $\cdot 10^{-5}$	1.04108 10^{-5}	$\cdot 7.77503$ $\cdot 10^{-6}$	7.5759 $\cdot 10^{-6}$
	proposed alg.	4.07863 $\cdot 10^{-5}$	1.46316 $\cdot 10^{-5}$	8.21932 $\cdot 10^{-6}$	5.60217 $\cdot 10^{-6}$	5.5904 $\cdot 10^{-6}$
forestfires	Nguyen-Widrow	0.332333	0.223907	0.199884	0.188826	0.1888
	proposed alg.	0.319951	0.221115	0.197248	0.187231	0.1872

Table 4. Intentional placement of slopes in successive space fragments for MLP with 45 neurons in the hidden layer (the fragments are sorted in the order of descending products $\sigma_a \# a$)

Learning set	Numbers of intentionally arranged slopes	β	δ
altitudes	3 3 3 2 2 1 1 0 0 0 0 0 0 0 0 0 0 0 0 0 0 0 0 0	15	30
f_1	1 1 1 1 1 1 1 1 0 0 0 0 0 0 0 0 0 0 0 0 0 0 0 0	8	37
f_2	1 1 1 1 1 1 1 1 1 1 1 1 0 0 0 0 0 0 0 0 0 0 0 0	12	33
f_3	1 1 1 1 1 1 1 1 0 0 0 0 0 0 0 0 0 0 0 0 0 0 0 0	8	37
f_4	2 2 2 1 1 1 1 1 0 0 0 0 0 0 0 0 0 0 0 0 0 0 0 0	12	33
forestfires	9 6 2 1 1 0 0 0 0 0 0 0 0 0 0 0 0 0 0 0 0 0 0 0	19	26

Table 5. Cost function values for MLP with 45 neurons in the hidden layer and the division into 5x5 fragments

Learning set	Initialisation	Epochs				Best results
		50	100	150	200	
altitudes	Nguyen-Widrow	0.092335	0.084083	0.080648	0.078118	0.0781
	proposed alg.	0.084756	0.075429	0.071347	0.069773	0.0698
f_1	Nguyen-Widrow	1.77273 $\cdot 10^{-5}$	8.13942 $\cdot 10^{-6}$	4.87171 $\cdot 10^{-6}$	3.11094 $\cdot 10^{-6}$	3.1066 $\cdot 10^{-6}$
	proposed alg.	1.14645 $\cdot 10^{-5}$	5.08797 $\cdot 10^{-6}$	3.46884 $\cdot 10^{-6}$	2.60112 $\cdot 10^{-6}$	2.4441 $\cdot 10^{-6}$
f_2	Nguyen-Widrow	8.79198 $\cdot 10^{-6}$	1.71116 $\cdot 10^{-6}$	6.34263 $\cdot 10^{-7}$	2.64994 $\cdot 10^{-7}$	2.2113 $\cdot 10^{-7}$
	proposed alg.	7.43586 $\cdot 10^{-6}$	1.27823 $\cdot 10^{-6}$	6.00127 $\cdot 10^{-7}$	3.46263 $\cdot 10^{-7}$	2.4405 $\cdot 10^{-7}$
f_3	Nguyen-Widrow	0.000152	2.49260 $\cdot 10^{-5}$	1.10722 $\cdot 10^{-5}$	6.83138 $\cdot 10^{-6}$	6.7847 $\cdot 10^{-6}$
	proposed alg.	5.22798 $\cdot 10^{-5}$	1.54230 $\cdot 10^{-5}$	8.01098 $\cdot 10^{-6}$	5.46735 $\cdot 10^{-6}$	5.4662 $\cdot 10^{-6}$
f_4	Nguyen-Widrow	2.72470 $\cdot 10^{-5}$	8.45098 $\cdot 10^{-6}$	4.37114 10^{-6}	$\cdot 2.71129$ $\cdot 10^{-6}$	2.6623 $\cdot 10^{-6}$
	proposed alg.	1.46324 $\cdot 10^{-5}$	4.55952 $\cdot 10^{-6}$	2.28194 $\cdot 10^{-6}$	1.47283 $\cdot 10^{-6}$	1.4486 $\cdot 10^{-6}$
forestfires	Nguyen-Widrow	0.100030	0.029168	0.020253	0.017022	0.0170
	proposed alg.	0.090955	0.026000	0.018777	0.016336	0.0163

4   Conclusions

The proposed method is quite simple for implementation and has a low linear computational complexity. For all used learning sets, the time of initialisation with the described algorithm does not exceed 0.4% of one epoch of the Levenberg-Marquardt algorithm. The conducted experiments confirm the efficiency of the proposed method and the reasonability of selection of the fragment number slightly lower than the number of neurons in the hidden layer.

The presented method may be recommended, in particular, for networks with a low number of inputs or when it is known, before processing the learning, which network inputs are the most important ones. If the network input number is high and it is not a priori known which dimensions are particularly significant, then the methods for determining the most significant inputs, described in [11], may be applied. The author suggests considering to accept of lower lengths of the sides $h_1, \ldots, h_n$ in the dimensions assigned to more important inputs.

After simple modifications, the proposed method may also be used for minimizing other cost functions. For instance, it is only necessary to modify (3) or (4) to minimize a weighted sum of squared errors in which the squared errors are multiplied by the biggest values in those fragments of the domain in which the function or the process being modelled should be mapped at the highest accuracy.

References

1. Nelles, O.: Summary of 11th chapter. In: Nelles, O. (ed.) Nonlinear System Identification: From Classical Approaches to Neural Networks and Fuzzy Models, pp. 296–297. Springer, Berlin (2001)
2. Ebert, T., Bänfer, O., Nelles, O.: Multilayer Perceptron Network with Modified Sigmoid Activation Functions. In: Wang, F.L., Deng, H., Gao, Y., Lei, J. (eds.) AICI 2010. LNCS, vol. 6319, pp. 414–421. Springer, Heidelberg (2010)
3. Maniezzo, V.: Genetic evolution of the topology and weight distribution of the neural networks. Neural Networks 5(1), 39–53 (1994)
4. Guijarro-Berdiñas, B., Fontenla-Romero, O., Pérez-Sánchez, B., Alonso-Betanzos, A.: A new initialization method for neural networks using sensitivity analysis. In: Proceedings of the International Conference on Mathematical and Statistical Modeling in Honor of Enrique Castillo, San Diego (2006)
5. Wei, X., Xiu-Tao, Y.: The application of optimal weights initialization algorithm based on information amount in multi-layer perceptron networks. In: Proceedings of the 3rd IEEE International Conference on Computer Science and Information Technology (ICCSIT), vol. 6, pp. 196–198 (2010)
6. Cho, S., Chow, T.W.S.: Training multilayer neural networks using fast global learning algorithm - least-squares and penalized optimization methods. Proceedings of Neurocomputing 25, 115–131 (1999)
7. Jin-Song, P., Mai, E.C., Wright, J.P., Smyth, A.W.: Neural network initialization with prototypes - function approximation in engineering mechanics applications. In: Proceedings of the International Joint Conference on Neural Networks, Orlando, pp. 2110–2116 (2007)
8. Erdogmus, D., Fontenla-Romero, O., Principe, J.C., Alonso-Betanzos, A., Castillo, E.: Linear-least-squares initialization of multilayer perceptrons through backpropagation of the desired response. IEEE Transactions on Neural Networks 16(2), 325–327 (2005)
9. Nguyen, D., Widrow, B.: Improving the learning speed of 2-Layer neural networks by choosing initial values of the adaptive weights. In: Proceedings of the International Joint Conference on Neural Networks, vol. 3, pp. 21–26 (1990)
10. Pavelka, A., Procházka: Algorithms for Initialization of Neural Network Weights, Sbornik prispevku 11. In: Konference MATLAB, vol. 2, pp. 453–459 (2004)
11. van de Laar, P., Heskes, T., Gielen, S.: Partial retraining: a new approach to input relevance determination. International Journal of Neural Systems 9(1), 75–85 (1999)
12. Online documentation of GTOPO30 data (2012), http://eros.usgs.gov/#/Find_Data/Products_and_Data_Available/gtopo30/README
13. UCI Machine Learning Repository, http://archive.ics.uci.edu/ml
14. Cortez, P., Morais, A.: A data mining approach to predict forest fires using meteorological data. In: Neves, J., Santos, M.F., Machado, J. (eds.) New Trends in Artificial Intelligence, Proceedings of the 13th EPIA - Portuguese Conference on Artificial Intelligence, pp. 512–523. APPIA, Guimarães (2007)

Soft Committee Machine Using Simple Derivative Term

Kazuyuki Hara[1] and Kentaro Katahira[2]

[1] College of Industrial Technology, Nihon University,
1-2-1 Izumi-cho, Narashino-shi, Chiba 275-8575, Japan
[2] Graduate School of Environmental Studies, Nagoya University,
Furo-cho, Chikusa-ku, Nagoya, 464-8601, Japan

Abstract. In on-line gradient descent learning, the local property of the derivative of the output function can cause slow convergence. This phenomenon, called a *plateau*, occurs in the learning process of the multilayer network. Improving the derivative term, we employ the proposed method replacing the derivative term with a constant that greatly increases the relaxation speed. Moreover, we replace the derivative term with the 2nd order of expansion of the derivative, and it beaks a plateau faster than the original method.

Keywords: soft committee machine, derivative, Taylor expansion, relaxation speed, residual error, statistical mechanics.

1 Introduction

Learning in neural networks can be formulated as the optimization of an objective function that quantifies the system's performance. An important property of feed-forward networks is their ability to learn a rule from examples. Statistical mechanics has been successfully used to study this property[1, 2]. A compact description of learning dynamics can be obtained by using statistical mechanics, which uses a large input dimension N and provides an accurate model of mean behavior for a realistic N[1, 2].

Several studies have investigated ways to accelerate the learning process[3–5]. For example, slow convergence due to *plateaus* occurs in learning processes that use a gradient descent algorithm. In gradient descent learning, the parameters are updated in the direction of the steepest descent of the objective function and the derivative of the output is taken into account. Falhman [6] proposed a learning method in which the derivative term is replaced with a constant and empirically showed that their method could speed up the convergence. We refer to this learning method as the simple method in this paper. We supplied the theoretical support for the simple method for a simple perceptron [7].

In this paper, we use the simple method to train a soft committee machine and investigate how it solves a credit assign problem. We theoretically analyze the behavior of the simple method using statistical mechanics methods and derive coupled differential equations of the order parameters that depict its learning

L. Rutkowski et al. (Eds.): ICAISC 2014, Part I, LNAI 8467, pp. 59–66, 2014.

behavior. We validate the analytical solutions by comparing them with those of a simulation. We then compare the behaviors of the simple method with those of the original method.

2 Model

In this work, we employ a teacher-student formulation and assume the existence of a teacher network that produces the desired output for the student network. First we formulate a teacher network and a student network and then we introduce the gradient descent algorithm.

The student is a soft committee machine with weight vectors between input and two hidden units, $J_i^{(m)} = (J_{i1}^{(m)}, ..., J_{iN}^{(m)})$, $i = 1, 2$, where m denotes learning iterations. The soft committee machine is a two-layer fully connected network consisting of non-linear hidden units and a linear output unit. The weight values between the hidden units and the output unit are fixed to $+1$. This network calculates the majority vote of hidden unit outputs. The teacher is a simple perceptron with weight vectors $\boldsymbol{B} = (B_1, ..., B_N)$ for simplicity [1].

We assume that the teacher and student receive N-dimensional input $\boldsymbol{\xi}^{(m)} = (\xi_1^m, ..., \xi_N^{(m)})$, that the teacher outputs $t^{(m)} = g(y^{(m)})$, and that the student outputs $s^{(m)} = \sum_{i=1}^{2} s_i^{(m)} = \sum_{i=1}^{2} g(x_i^{(m)})$. Here, $g(\cdot)$ is the output function, $y^{(m)}$ is the inner potential of the teacher calculated using $y^{(m)} = \sum_{j=1}^{N} B_j \xi_j^{(m)}$, and $x_i^{(m)}$ is the inner potential of the ith hidden unit of the student calculated using $x_i^{(m)} = \sum_{j=1}^{N} J_{ij}^{(m)} \xi_j^{(m)}$.

We assume that the elements $\xi_j^{(m)}$ of the independently drawn input $\boldsymbol{\xi}^{(m)}$ are uncorrelated random variables with zero mean and unit variance; that is, the jth element of the input is drawn from a probability distribution $P(\xi_j)$. The thermodynamic limit of $N \to \infty$ is also assumed. The statistics of the inputs in the thermodynamic limit are $\langle \xi_j^{(m)} \rangle = 0$, $\langle (\xi_j^{(m)})^2 \rangle = 1$, and $\|\boldsymbol{\xi}^{(m)}\| = \sqrt{N}$, where $\langle \cdots \rangle$ denotes the average and $\| \cdot \|$ denotes the norm of a vector. Each element B_j, $j = 1 \sim N$, is drawn from a probability distribution with zero mean and $1/N$ variance. With the assumption of the thermodynamic limit, the statistics of the teacher weight vector are $\langle B_j \rangle = 0, \langle (B_j)^2 \rangle = 1/N$, and $\|\boldsymbol{B}\| = 1$. The distribution of inner potential $y^{(m)}$ follows a Gaussian distribution with zero mean and unit variance in the thermodynamic limit. For the sake of analysis, we assume that each element of $J_{ij}^{(0)}$, which is the initial value of the student vector $J_i^{(0)}$, is drawn from a probability distribution with zero mean and $1/N$ variance. The statistics of the ith hidden weight vector of student are $\langle J_{ij}^{(0)} \rangle = 0, \langle (J_{ij}^{(0)})^2 \rangle = 1/N$, and $\|J_i^{(0)}\| = 1$ in the thermodynamic limit. The output function of hidden units of the student $g(\cdot)$ is the same as that of the teacher. The distribution of the inner potential $x_i^{(m)}$ follows a Gaussian distribution with zero mean and $(Q_{ii}^{(m)})^2$ variance in the thermodynamic limit. Here, $(Q_{ii}^{(m)})^2 = J_i^m \cdot J_i^m$. These assumptions are used for the theoretical analysis.

Next, we introduce the gradient descent algorithm. For the possible inputs $\{\boldsymbol{\xi}\}$, we want to train the student network to produce the desired outputs $t = s$. The generalization error is defined as

$$\epsilon_g^{(m)} = \left\langle \frac{1}{2}(t^{(m)} - s^{(m)})^2 \right\rangle = \left\langle \frac{1}{2}\left(g(y^{(m)}) - g(x_1^{(m)}) - g(x_2^{(m)}) \right)^2 \right\rangle, \quad (1)$$

where angle brackets $\langle \cdot \rangle$ denote the average over possible inputs. At each learning step m, a new uncorrelated input $\boldsymbol{\xi}^m$ is presented, and the current hidden weight vector of student $\boldsymbol{J}_i^m$ is updated using

$$\boldsymbol{J}_i^{(m+1)} = \boldsymbol{J}_i^{(m)} + \frac{\eta}{N}\left(g(y^{(m)}) - g(x_1^{(m)}) - g(x_2^{(m)}) \right) g'(x_i^{(m)})\boldsymbol{\xi}^{(m)}, \quad (2)$$

where η is the learning step size and $g'(x)$ is the derivative of the output function $g(x)$.

3   Theory

The sigmoid function is used as the output of the teacher and that of the hidden unit of the student: $g(x) = \mathrm{erf}(x/\sqrt{2})$. The derivative of the function is $g'(x) = \sqrt{2/\pi}\exp(-x^2/2)$. The learning equation of the soft committee machine[1] is then

$$\boldsymbol{J}_i^{(m+1)} = \boldsymbol{J}_i^{(m)} + \frac{\eta}{N}\left(\mathrm{erf}(\frac{y^{(m)}}{\sqrt{2}}) - \mathrm{erf}(\frac{x_1^{(m)}}{\sqrt{2}}) - \mathrm{erf}(\frac{x_2^{(m)}}{\sqrt{2}}) \right) \sqrt{\frac{2}{\pi}}\exp(\frac{(x_i^{(m)})^2}{2})\boldsymbol{\xi}^{(m)}. \quad (3)$$

By using $g(x) = \mathrm{erf}(x/\sqrt{2})$ in Eq. (1), the generalization error of the soft committee machine[1] with two hidden units can be obtained by

$$\epsilon_g = \frac{1}{\pi}\left[\sum_{i=1}^{2}\left\{ \sin^{-1}\left(\frac{Q_{ii}^2}{1 + Q_{ii}^2} \right) - 2\sin^{-1}\left(\frac{R_i}{\sqrt{2(1 + Q_{ii}^2)}} \right) \right\} \right.$$
$$\left. + 2\sin^{-1}\left(\frac{Q_{12}^2}{\sqrt{1 + Q_{11}^2}\sqrt{1 + Q_{22}^2}} \right) + \sin^{-1}\left(\frac{1}{2} \right) \right] \quad (4)$$

Here, $R_i = \boldsymbol{B} \cdot \boldsymbol{J}_i$ and $Q_{12}^2 = \boldsymbol{J}_1 \cdot \boldsymbol{J}_2$. We omit m for simplicity. From this equation, we can calculate the generalization error by substituting Q_{ii}^2, Q_{12}^2, and R_i at each time step m into Eq. (4) .

In this paper, as mentioned above, we use the simple method to train a soft committee machine. We expand $g'(x) = \sqrt{2/\pi}\exp(x^2/2) \sim \sqrt{2/\pi}(1 + x^2/2 + x^4/8\cdots)$ and use the first term. We thus modify learning Eq. (3) to include a constant term:

$$J_i^{(m+1)} = J_i^{(m)} + \frac{\eta}{N}\left(\mathrm{erf}(\frac{y^{(m)}}{\sqrt{2}}) - \mathrm{erf}(\frac{x_1^{(m)}}{\sqrt{2}}) - \mathrm{erf}(\frac{x_2^{(m)}}{\sqrt{2}})\right)\sqrt{\frac{2}{\pi}}\boldsymbol{\xi}^{(m)}$$

$$= J_i^{(m)} + \frac{\eta}{N}\delta_i\boldsymbol{\xi}^{(m)}. \tag{5}$$

The general forms of the differential equations of Q_{ii}^2, Q_{12}^2, and R_i are given by

$$\frac{dR_i}{dt} = \eta\langle\delta_i y\rangle, \tag{6}$$

$$\frac{dQ_{ii}^2}{dt} = 2\eta\langle\delta_i x_i\rangle + \eta^2\langle\delta_i^2\rangle, \tag{7}$$

$$\frac{dQ_{12}^2}{dt} = \eta(\langle\delta_2 x_1\rangle + \langle\delta_1 x_2\rangle) + \eta^2\langle\delta_1\delta_2\rangle. \tag{8}$$

Here, we define t as $t = m/N$, and represent the learning process using continuous time t in the thermodynamic limit of $N \to \infty$. By calculating $\langle\delta_i y\rangle$, $\langle\delta_i x_i\rangle$, $\langle\delta_i x_j\rangle$, $\langle\delta_i^2\rangle$, and $\langle\delta_1\delta_2\rangle$, we can obtain the differential equations of the simple method:

$$\frac{dR_i}{dt} = \frac{\sqrt{2}\eta}{\pi}\left(1 - \sum_{k=1}^{2}\frac{2R_i}{\sqrt{2(1+Q_{ii}^2)}}\right) \tag{9}$$

$$\frac{dQ_{ii}^2}{dt} = \frac{2\sqrt{2}\eta}{\pi}\left(R_i - \frac{2Q_{ii}^2}{\sqrt{2(1+Q_{ii}^2)}} - \frac{2Q_{12}^2}{\sqrt{2(1+Q_{ll}^2)}}\right)$$
$$+ \frac{4\eta^2}{\pi^2}\left[\sum_{k=1}^{2}\left\{\sin^{-1}\left(\frac{Q_{kk}^2}{1+Q_{kk}^2}\right) - 2\sin^{-1}\left(\frac{R_k}{\sqrt{2(1+Q_{kk}^2)}}\right)\right\}\right.$$
$$\left. + 2\sin^{-1}\left(\frac{Q_{12}^2}{\sqrt{1+Q_{11}^2}\sqrt{1+Q_{22}^2}}\right) + \sin^{-1}\left(\frac{1}{2}\right)\right] \tag{10}$$

$$\frac{dQ_{12}^2}{dt} = \frac{\sqrt{2}\eta}{\pi}\left\{\sum_{k=1}^{2}\left(R_i - \frac{2Q_{ii}^2}{\sqrt{2(1+Q_{ii}^2)}} - \frac{2Q_{12}^2}{\sqrt{2(1+Q_{ll}^2)}}\right)\right\}$$
$$+ \frac{4\eta^2}{\pi^2}\left[\sum_{k=1}^{2}\left\{\sin^{-1}\left(\frac{Q_{kk}^2}{1+Q_{kk}^2}\right) - 2\sin^{-1}\left(\frac{R_k}{\sqrt{2(1+Q_{kk}^2)}}\right)\right\}\right.$$
$$\left. + 2\sin^{-1}\left(\frac{Q_{12}^2}{\sqrt{1+Q_{11}^2}\sqrt{1+Q_{22}^2}}\right) + \sin^{-1}\left(\frac{1}{2}\right)\right] \tag{11}$$

Here, $i \neq l$.

4   Results

Figure 1 shows the numerical calculation of the theoretical results and the simulation results. The horizontal axis indicates time $t = m/N$, where m is the learning iteration. The vertical axis for theoretical results shows the generalization error. As written in Sec. 2, the element of the Input $\boldsymbol{\xi}^{(m)}$ is generated by uncorrelated random variables with zero mean and unit variance. The vertical axis for simulation results shows the square mean error for N inputs. Initial conditions were $R_1^{(0)} = R_2^{(0)} = 0$, $(Q_{11}^{(0)})^2 = (Q_{22}^{(0)})^2 = 1$, and $(Q_{12}^{(0)})^2 = 0$. For the simulation results, $N = 1000$, and each point was obtained by averaging over 10 trials. The learning step size η was set to $0.1, 0.5, 1$, or 2.0. Theoretical results are labeled 'th' and are shown by the solid line. Simulation results using the simple method are labeled "sim" and are shown by the broken line. Simulation results of the original method are labeled 'original' and shown by the dotted line.

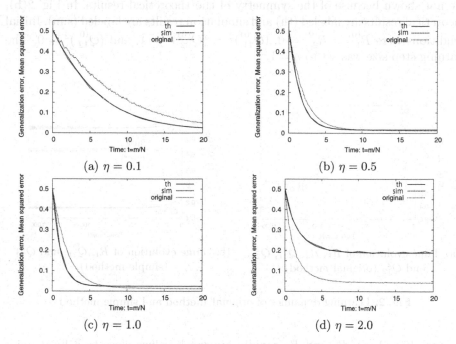

Fig. 1. Time evolution of mean squared error. Learning step size of $\eta = 0.1, 0.5, 1.0$, or 2.0 is used.

First, we compare the numerical calculations of the theoretical results with the simulation results using the simple method to determine the validity of the theoretical results. From the figures, the numerical calculations of the theoretical results (solid line) agreed with those of the simulation results (broken line).

Next, we compare the relaxation speed for the simple method with that of the original method. From Fig. 1 (a)-(c), we can see that the relaxation speed of the simple method is faster than that of the original method when the learning step size is less than 1.0. However, it slows down and the residual error becomes large when the learning step size is 2.0 (Fig. 1 (d)).

4.1 Learning Dynamics of the Simple Method

As shown in Fig. 1, residual errors become large when the simple method is used. We therefore investigate the learning dynamics of the simple method and compare them with those of the original method.

Figure 2 show the learning dynamics of the original method (Fig. 2 (a)) and those of the simple method (Fig. 2(b)). The vertical axis shows R_i, Q_{ii}^2, and Q_{12}^2. Figure 2 (a) shows the simulation results obtained using the original method and Fig. 2 (b) shows the results obtained by numerical calculation of the theoretical results and by simulations using the simple method. R_2 and Q_{22}^2 in Fig. 2(b) are not shown because of the symmetry of the theoretical results. In Fig. 2(b), theoretical results are labeled (th) and simulation results are labeled (sim). Initial conditions were $R_1^{(0)} = R_2^{(0)} = 0$, $(Q_{11}^{(0)})^2 = (Q_{22}^{(0)})^2 = 1$, and $(Q_{12}^{(0)})^2 = 0$. The learning step size was set to $\eta = 1$.

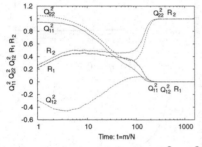 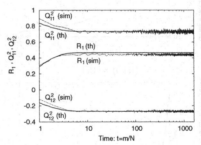

(a) Time evolution of R_1, R_2, Q_{11}^2, Q_{22}^2, and Q_{12}^2 (original method).   (b) Time evolution of R_1, Q_{11}^2, and Q_{12}^2 (simple method).

Fig. 2. Learning dynamics of original method and simple method

From Fig. 2 (a), R_1 and R_2 rapidly approach values close to a fixed point that is stable within the symmetric subspace. However, when $t > 200$, R_1 and R_2 eventually approach values $R_1 = 0$ and $R_2 = 1$. These are the optimum fixed points that break the symmetry between hidden units. Q_{11}^2 and Q_{22}^2 are also almost 1 at the early stage of learning, but at $t > 200$, Q_{11}^2 and Q_{22}^2 eventually approach values $Q_{11}^2 = 0$ and $Q_{22}^2 = 1$, which are the optimum fixed points. This means that J_2 converges into B, and J_1 completely disappears when $t > 300$. Q_{12}^2 converges into zero, indicating that J_1 and J_2 are orthogonal to each other. Figure 2(b) shows that by using the simple method, Q_{11}^2, Q_{22}^2, R_1, R_2, and Q_{12}^2 stay close to a fixed point that is stable within the symmetry subspace.

Next, we consider using the 2nd or 4th orders of expansion of $\exp(x/\sqrt{2})$ whereby $R_1, R_2, Q_{11}^2, Q_{22}^2$, and Q_{12}^2 behave independently. The learning equation using the 0th order, 2nd order, and 4th order is

$$J_i^{(m+1)} = J_i^{(m)} + \frac{\eta}{N}(t^{(m)} - s_1^{(m)} - s_2^{(m)})\sqrt{\frac{2}{\pi}}\left(1 - \frac{(x_i^{(m)})^2}{2} + \frac{(x_i^{(m)})^4}{8}\right)\xi^{(m)}.$$

(12)

If $|x_i| < \sqrt{2}$, we don't update J_i.

Figure 3 shows the results obtained by using the simulation results. The vertical axis shows the mean squared error. Each figure includes the mean square error obtained by the original method labeled 'original', that of using 0th and 2nd orders labeled '2nd', and that of using 0th, 2nd, and 4th orders labeled '4th'. Figure 3(a) shows the results when the learning step size is $\eta = 0.1$, (b) shows those of $\eta = 0.5$, (c) shows those of $\eta = 1$, and (d) shows those of $\eta = 2$. Each point was obtained by averaging over 10 trials.

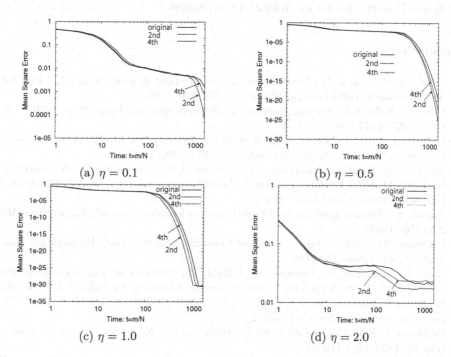

(a) $\eta = 0.1$ (b) $\eta = 0.5$

(c) $\eta = 1.0$ (d) $\eta = 2.0$

Fig. 3. Time evolution of mean squared error. Original method, 2nd order approximation, and 4th order approximation are used. Learning step size is set to $\eta = 0.1, 0.5, 1.0,$ or 2.0.

From these figures, it is shown that using the 0th and 2nd orders helped the mean squared error break out of the *plateau* faster than the other two methods, including the original method.

5   Conclusion

In this paper, we applied a simple method that replaces the derivative with a constant to a soft committee machine. We first built the theory of the soft committee machine with a simple method using the statistical mechanical method. We then demonstrated the validity of the theoretical results by comparing them with those of the simulation results. We found that the relaxation speed of the simple method was faster than that of the original method until the learning step size reached $\eta \geq 1$; at $\eta = 2$, the residual error became larger than that of the original method. It was also found that the simple method stayed close to a fixed point that is stable within the symmetry subspace. To overcome this problem, we added the 2nd order expansion of the derivative, and this modification resulted in the eventual approach to the optimum fixed point that broke the symmetry between hidden units.

Acknowledgments. The authors thank Professor Masato Okada and Associate Professor Hayaru Shouno for insightful discussions.

References

1. Biehl, M., Schwarze, H.: Learning by on-line gradient descent. Journal of Physics A: Mathematical and General Physics 28, 643–656 (1995)
2. Saad, D., Solla, S.A.: On-line learning in soft-committee machines. Physical Review E 52, 4225–4243 (1995)
3. Fukumizu, K.: A Regularity Condition of the Information Matrix of a Multilayer Perceptron Network. Neural Networks 9(5), 871–879 (1996)
4. Rattray, M., Saad, D.: Incorporating Curvature Information into On-line learning. In: Saad, D. (ed.) On-line Learning in Neural Networks, pp. 183–207. Cambridge University Press, Cambridge (1998)
5. Amari, S.: Natural gradient works efficiently in learning. Neural Computation 10, 251–276 (1998)
6. Fahlman, S.E.: An Empirical Study of Learning Speed in Back-Propagation Networks, CMU-CS-88-162 (1988)
7. Hara, K., Katahira, K., Okanoya, K., Okada, M.: Theoretical Analysis of Function of Derivative Term in On-Line Gradient Descent Learning. In: Villa, A.E.P., Duch, W., Érdi, P., Masulli, F., Palm, G. (eds.) ICANN 2012, Part II. LNCS, vol. 7553, pp. 9–16. Springer, Heidelberg (2012)
8. Williams, C.K.I.: Computation with Infinite Neural Networks. Neural Computation 10, 1203–1216 (1998)

Representations of Highly-Varying Functions by One-Hidden-Layer Networks

Věra Kůrková

Institute of Computer Science, Academy of Sciences of the Czech Republic
Pod Vodárenskou věží 2, 18207 Prague, Czech Republic
vera@cs.cas.cz

Abstract. Limitations of capabilities of one-hidden-layer networks are investigated. It is shown that for networks with Heaviside perceptrons as well as for networks with kernel units used in SVM, there exist large sets of d-variable functions which cannot be tractably represented by these networks, i.e., their representations require numbers of units or sizes of weighs depending on d exponentially. Our results are derived using the concept of variational norm from nonlinear approximation theory and the concentration of measure property of high dimensional Euclidean spaces.

Keywords: model complexity of neural networks, one-hidden-layer networks, highly-varying functions, tractability of representations of multivariable functions by neural networks.

1 Introduction

Originally, biologically inspired neural networks were modeled as as multilayer distributed computational systems. Later, one-hidden-layer architectures became dominant in applications due to relatively simple optimization procedures needed for adjustment of their parameters (see, e.g., [1, 2] and the references therein). In some literature, one-hidden-layer networks are called shallow networks to distinguish them from deep ones containing more hidden layers.

In addition to a variety of successful applications of one-hidden-layer networks, also theoretical confirmation of their capabilities has been obtained. Shallow networks with many types of computational units are known to be universal approximators, i.e., they can approximate up to any desired accuracy all continuous functions on compact subsets of $\mathbb{R}^d$. In particular, the universal approximation property holds for shallow networks with perceptrons having any non-polynomial activation function [3, 4] and with radial and kernel units satisfying mild conditions [5–7], [8, p.153]). Moreover, all functions defined on finite subsets of $\mathbb{R}^d$ can be represented exactly by one-hidden-layer networks with either sigmoidal perceptrons [9] or with Gaussian radial units [10].

Proofs of the universal approximation capability of shallow networks require potentially unlimited numbers of hidden units. These numbers representing model complexities are critical factors for practical implementations. Dependence of

L. Rutkowski et al. (Eds.): ICAISC 2014, Part I, LNAI 8467, pp. 67–76, 2014.

model complexities of shallow networks on their input dimensions, types of units, functions to be approximated, and accuracies of approximation have been studied using tools from nonlinear approximation theory (see, e.g., [11] and references therein). Inspection of upper bounds on rates of approximation by shallow networks led to descriptions of various families of functions that can be well approximated by shallow networks with reasonably small numbers of computational units of various types. On the other hand, cases when numbers of networks units are untractably large are less understood. Only few lower bounds on rates of approximations by shallow networks are known and the estimates are mostly non constructive and hold for types of computational units that are not commonly used [12, 13]. Moreover, in some cases, sizes of weights can be more critical factors for successful learning than numbers of network units [14].

Recently, new hybrid learning algorithms were developed for deep networks [15, 16]. Training networks with more than one hidden layer involves complicated nonlinear optimization procedures and thus generally it is more difficult than training shallow ones. Hence, it is desirable to develop some theoretical background for characterization of tasks whose computations by networks with shallow architectures would require networks with considerably higher complexities than computations by deep networks. Bengio et al. [17] suggested that a cause of difficulties in representing functions by shallow networks tractably can be their "amount of variations". As a class of function with high-variations they considered the parities on d-dimensional Boolean cubes $\{0, 1\}^d$. They proved that a classification of points in $\{0, 1\}^d$ according to their parities by support vector machine (SVM) with Gaussian kernel units cannot accomplish this task with less than $2^{d/2}$ units.

On the other hand, it is well-known and easy to verify that for any d, the d-dimensional parity can be represented by a one-hidden-layer Heaviside perceptron network with d units. Indeed, parity can be visualized as a plane wave orthogonal to the diagonal of the cube in the direction of the vector $(1, \ldots, 1)$ (see, e.g.,[18, 19]). So some functions are highly-varying with respect to one type of computational units, while they are "varying" much less with respect to another type of units. Thus it is reasonable to consider the notion of a highly-varying function with respect to a type of computational units.

In this paper, we propose to formalize this concept in terms of a norm called variation with respect to a set of functions. This norm has been studied in nonlinear approximation theory and plays an important role in estimates of rates of approximation by neural networks (see, e.g., [11] and the references therein). We show that the size of the variational norm of a function with respect to a dictionary of computational units reflects both the number of hidden units and sizes of output weights in a shallow network with units from the dictionary representing such function. Using the concept of variational norm, we describe classes of d-variable functions whose representations by networks with a given type of units with increasing numbers of inputs d are not tractable in the sense that representations of such functions by these network require numbers of units or some of sizes of output weights to grow exponentially with d. Using concentration of measure property in high-dimensional Euclidean spaces we estimate probability distributions of sizes of variations. We show that for popular dictionaries (such as dictionaries formed by SVM and by Heaviside perceptrons) with increasing dimension d almost any randomly chosen Boolean function has large variational norm (depending on d exponentially). Our results imply that for large d, in sets of functions with constant Euclidean norms most Boolean real valued functions cannot be tractably represented by Heaviside perceptron networks or by SVMs. We illustrate general existential results by an example of a concrete class of non tractable functions. Some preliminary results from this paper appeared as work in progress in local conference proceedings [20].

The paper is organized as follows. Section 2 contains basic concepts on shallow networks, dictionaries of computational units and Boolean functions. Section 3 presents a mathematical formalization of the concept of a "highly-varying function", shows that it is related to large sizes of networks representing such functions or large output weights of these networks. In Section 4 estimates of probabilistic measures of sets of functions with variations depending on d exponentially are derived and illustrated by an example of a class of functions which cannot be tractably represented by one-hidden-layer Heaviside perceptron networks. Section 5 is a brief disussion.

2 Preliminaries

One-hidden-layer networks with single linear outputs, compute input-output functions from sets of the form

$$\operatorname{span}_n G := \left\{ \sum_{i=1}^n w_i g_i \mid w_i \in \mathbb{R},\ g_i \in G \right\},$$

where G, called a *dictionary*, is a set of functions computable by a given type of units, the coefficients w_i are output weights, and n is the number of hidden units. This number can be interpreted as a measure of *model complexity*. In this paper we use the term *shallow network* meaning one-hidden-layer network with a single linear output. By

$$\operatorname{span} G := \bigcup_{n \in \mathbb{N}} \operatorname{span}_n G$$

is denoted the set of functions computable by one-hidden-layer networks with units from the dictionary G with any number of hidden units.

We investigate growth of complexities of networks representing functions of increasing numbers of variables d. Let D be an infinite subset of the set of positive integers, $\mathcal{F} = \{ f_d \mid d \in D \}$ a class of functions and $\{ G_d \mid d \in D \}$ a class of dictionaries, such that for every $d \in D$, f_d is a function of d variables and G_d is formed by functions of d variables. We call the problem of representing the set $\mathcal{F}$ by networks from $\{ \operatorname{span} G_d \mid d \in D \}$ *tractable* if for every $d \in D$, there exists a network in $\operatorname{span}_{n_d} G$ representing f_d as its input-output function such that n_d and absolute values of all output weights in the network grow with d polynomially. Note that different concepts of tractability were used in other contexts (see, e.g., [11]).

In this paper, we focus on representations of real-valued functions on finite subsets of $\mathbb{R}^d$ by shallow networks with units from several dictionaries. We denote by $H_d(X)$ the dictionary of functions on $X \subset \mathbb{R}^d$ computable by *Heaviside perceptrons*, i.e.,

$$H_d(X) := \{\vartheta(v \cdot . + b) : X \to \{0,1\} \mid v \in \mathbb{R}^d, b \in \mathbb{R}\},$$

where ϑ denotes the *Heaviside activation function* defined as

$$\vartheta(t) := 0 \text{ for } t < 0 \text{ and } \vartheta(t) := 1 \text{ for } t \geq 0.$$

Note that H_d is the *set of characteristic functions of half-spaces*. The dictionary $S_d(X)$ is formed by functions on X computable by perceptrons with *signum activation function* $\mathrm{sgn} : \mathbb{R} \to \{-1, 1\}$ defined as

$$\mathrm{sgn}(t) := -1 \text{ for } t < 0 \text{ and } \mathrm{sign}(t) := 1 \text{ for } t \geq 0.$$

We denote

$$P_d(X) := \{\mathrm{sgn}(v \cdot . + b) : X \to \{-1, 1\} \mid v \in \mathbb{R}^d, b \in \mathbb{R}\}.$$

For a kernel $K_d : \mathbb{R}^d \times \mathbb{R}^d \to \mathbb{R}$, we denote by $F_{K_d}(X)$ the dictionary of kernel units, i.e.,

$$F_{K_d}(X) := \{K_d(., x) : X \to \mathbb{R} \mid x \in X\}.$$

The set of real-valued functions on the *d-dimensional Boolean cube* $\{0,1\}^d$ is denoted

$$\mathcal{B}(\{0,1\}^d) := \{f \mid f : \{0,1\}^d \to \mathbb{R}\}.$$

It is a linear space isomorphic to the Euclidean space $\mathbb{R}^{2^d}$. Thus on $\mathcal{B}(\{0,1\}^d)$ we have the *Euclidean inner product* defined as

$$\langle f, g \rangle := \sum_{u \in \{0,1\}^d} f(u)g(u)$$

and the *Euclidean norm* $\|f\|_2 := \sqrt{\langle f, f \rangle}$. By $\cdot$ is denoted the inner product on $\{0,1\}^d$, defined as $u \cdot v := \sum_{i=1}^{d} u_i v_i$.

3   Highly-Varying Functions

In this section, we investigate a mathematical formalization of the observation of Bengio et al. [17] that representations of highly-varying functions might require large networks. We show that the concept of a variational norm from approximation theory can play a role of a measure of tractability of representations of classes of functions by shallow networks.

For a subset G of a normed linear space $(\mathcal{X}, \|.\|_{\mathcal{X}})$, G-*variation (variation with respect to the set G)*, denoted by $\|.\|_G$, is defined as

$$\|f\|_G := \inf \{c \in \mathbb{R}_+ \mid f/c \in \mathrm{cl}_{\mathcal{X}} \,\mathrm{conv}\,(G \cup -G)\},$$

where $-G := \{-g \mid g \in G\}$, $\mathrm{cl}_{\mathcal{X}}$ denotes the closure with respect to the norm $\|\cdot\|_{\mathcal{X}}$ on $\mathcal{X}$, and $\mathrm{conv}\,G := \left\{\sum_{i=1}^k a_i g_i \mid a_i \in [0,1], \sum_{i=1}^k a_i = 1, g_i \in G, k \in \mathbb{N}\right\}$ is the convex hull of G.

Variation with respect to a set of functions was introduced by Kůrková [21] as an extension of Barron's [22] concept of variation with respect to sets of characteristic functions. Barron investigated the set of characteristic functions of half-spaces, which corresponds to the dictionary of functions computable by Heaviside perceptrons. For $d = 1$, variation with respect to half-spaces coincides up to a constant with the concept of total variation from integration theory. Variational norms play an important role in estimates of approximation rates by one-hidden-layer networks (see, e.g., [11, 23, 24] and the references therein).

The following straightforward consequence of the definition of G-variation shows that in all representations of a function with large G-variation by networks with units from the dictionary G, the number of units must be large or some absolute values of output weights must be large.

Proposition 1. *Let G be a bounded subset of a normed linear space $(\mathcal{X}, \|.\|)$, then for every $f \in \mathcal{X}$,*
(i) $\|f\|_G \leq \left\{\sum_{i=1}^k |w_i| \,\Big|\, f = \sum_{i=1}^k w_i \, g_i, \, w_i \in \mathbb{R}, \, g_i \in G, k \in \mathbb{N}\right\}$;
(ii) *for G finite with* $\mathrm{card}\, G = k$,
$$\|f\|_G = \min \left\{\sum_{i=1}^k |w_i| \,\Big|\, f = \sum_{i=1}^k w_i \, g_i, \, w_i \in \mathbb{R}, \, g_i \in G\right\}.$$

Proposition 1 implies that families of sets of d-variable functions $\{F_d \mid d \in D\}$ with G_d-variations growing with d exponentially cannot be tractably represented by networks with units from G_d.

Note that G-variation is a norm and thus by multiplying f by suitable constants we can obtain functions with arbitrarily large or small variations. However, in neurocomputing we are interested in computation of functions with similar sizes as computational units. For example, in dictionaries $H_d(X)$ and $P_d(X)$ $F_{K_d}(X)$ formed by functions on a finite subset X of $\mathbb{R}^d$, the supremum of l_2-norms of their elements is $2^{\mathrm{card}\,X/2}$. Thus we explore variational norms of functions in the spheres of radii $2^{\mathrm{card}(X)/2}$ in the Euclidean spaces $\mathcal{B}(X)$.

To describe classes of functions with large variations, we use the following lower bound on variational norm from [19] (see also [25, 26]). By $G^{\perp}$ is denoted the *orthogonal complement of G*.

Theorem 1. *Let $(\mathcal{X}, \|.\|_{\mathcal{X}})$ be a Hilbert space and G its bounded subset. Then for every $f \in \mathcal{X} \setminus G^{\perp}$, $\|f\|_G \geq \dfrac{\|f\|^2}{\sup_{g \in G} |g \cdot f|}$.*

Theorem 1 implies that functions which are "almost orthogonal" to G have large variations. To take advantage of this theorem, we use the *angular pseudometrics* δ on the unit sphere S^{m-1} in $\mathbb{R}^m$ defined as

$$\delta(f,g) = \arccos |f \cdot g|.$$

Note that this pseudometrics defines the distance as the minimum of the two angles between f and g and between f and $-g$ (it is a pseudometrics as the distance of antipodal vectors is zero).

The next corollary of Theorem 1 states that functions which have large distances measured by an angular pseudometrics δ from the set G have large G-variations.

Corollary 1. *Let m be a positive integer, $G \subset S^{m-1}$, and $f \in S^{m-1}$ such that has for some $\alpha \in (0, \pi/2)$ and all $g \in G$, the angular distance $\delta(f,g) \geq \alpha$. Then $\|f\|_G \geq \frac{1}{\cos \alpha}$.*

4 Sets of Functions with Large Variations

In this section we show that for reasonably "small" dictionaries G formed by functions on finite subsets X of $\mathbb{R}^d$ with card $X = m$ there exist "large subsets" of spheres in $\mathbb{R}^m$ consisting of functions with "large" G-variations. The following theorem estimates probability that a randomly chosen vector $f \in S^{m-1}$ has G-variation larger than $\frac{1}{\cos \alpha}$. Its proof is based on a geometrical property of high-dimensional Euclidean spaces called "concentration of measure". This property implies that for large dimensions m, most of the areas of spheres S^{m-1} in m-dimensional spaces $\mathbb{R}^m$ lie "close" to the equators of these spheres (see, e.g., [27]).

Theorem 2. *Let m be a positive integer, μ a uniform measure on S^{m-1} such that $\mu(S^{m-1}) = 1$, G a finite subset of S^{m-1} with card $G = k$, $\alpha \in (0, \pi/2)$, and $V_\alpha = \{f \in S^m \mid \|f\|_G \geq \frac{1}{\cos \alpha}\}$. Then $\mu(V_\alpha) \geq 1 - k\, e^{-\frac{m(\cos \alpha)^2}{2}}$.*

Proof. By Corollary 1, V_α contains all $f \in S^{m-1}$ satisfying for all $g \in G$, $|f \cdot g| \leq \cos \alpha$, i.e., all f with $\delta(f,g) = \arccos |f \cdot g| \geq \alpha$. Let $C(g, \varepsilon)$ denotes the spherical cap with a center $g \in G$ and the angle $\alpha = \arccos \varepsilon$ defined as $C(g, \varepsilon) = \{h \in S^{m-1} \mid h \cdot g \geq \varepsilon\}$. So f is not contained in any of the spherical caps $C(g, \varepsilon)$ with a center $g \in G$. With d increasing, the normalized measures of the spherical caps are decreasing exponentially fast: $\mu(C(g, \varepsilon)) \leq e^{-\frac{m\varepsilon^2}{2}}$ (see, e.g., [28, p.11]). Thus $\mu(V_\alpha) \geq 1 - k\, e^{-\frac{m(\cos \alpha)^2}{2}}$.

Combining Theorem 2 with "relatively small"sizes of the dictionaries $H_d(\{0,1\}^d)$, $P_d(\{0,1\}^d)$, and $F_{K_d}(\{0,1\}^d)$, induced by a bounded kernel $K_d : \{0,1\}^d \times \{0,1\}^d \to \mathbb{R}$ (such as the Gaussian), we obtain an estimate of the fraction of the area of the sphere of radius $2^{d/2}$ in the space $\mathcal{B}(\{0,1\}^d) \simeq \mathbb{R}^{2^d}$ which contains functions with variations depending on d exponentially. By S_r^{m-1} we denote the sphere of radius r in $\mathbb{R}^m$.

Theorem 3. *Let d be a positive integer, μ a uniform measure on $S_{2^{d/2}}^{2^d-1}$ such that $\mu(S_{2^{d/2}}^{2^d-1}) = 1$, G a dictionary formed by functions on $\{0,1\}^d$ such that for all $g \in G$, $\|g\|_2 \leq 2^{d/2}$, $\alpha \in (0, \pi/2)$, and $V_\alpha(G) = \{f \in S^{2^d-1} \mid \|f\|_G \geq \frac{1}{\cos \alpha}\}$.*

(i) If $G = H_d(\{0,1\}^d)$, then $\mu(V_\alpha(H_d(\{0,1\}^d))) \geq 1 - 2^{d^2} e^{-\frac{2^d(\cos \alpha)^2}{2}}$;

(ii) if $G = P_d(\{0,1\}^d)$, then $\mu(V_\alpha(H_d(\{0,1\}^d))) \geq 1 - 2^{d^2} e^{-\frac{2^d(\cos \alpha)^2}{2}}$;

(iii) if $G_{K_d}(\{0,1\}^d)$, where $K : \{0,1\}^d \times \{0,1\}^d$ is a kernel such that $\sup_{x \in \{0,1\}^d} |K(x,x)| \leq 1$, then $\mu(V_\alpha(G_{K_d}(\{0,1\}^d))) \geq 1 - 2^d e^{-\frac{2^d(\cos \alpha)^2}{2}}$.

Proof. (i) and (ii) follow from Theorem 2 and an upper bound $2^{d^2 - d \log_2 d + \mathcal{O}(d)}$ on the dictionary card $H_d(\{0,1\}^d)$ [29, 30]. Thus cardinalities of both dictionaries $H_d(\{0,1\}^d)$ and $P_d(\{0,1\}^d)$ are smaller than 2^{d^2}, which is much smaller than the cardinality 2^{2^d} of the whole space $\mathcal{B}(\{0,1\}^d)$. The Euclidean norm of all elements of $P_d(\{0,1\}^d)$ is $2^{d/2}$, which is the maximal value of the Euclidean norms of elements of $H_d(\{0,1\}^d)$.

(iii) follows from Theorem 2 and the cardinality 2^d of the dictionary $G_{K_d}(\{0,1\}^d)$ formed by kernel units centered at the vertices of the Boolean cube $\{0,1\}^d$.

Theorem 3 holds for any kernel with $\sup_{x \in \{0,1\}^d} |K(x,x)| = 1$ and implies that representations of most functions from $\mathcal{B}(\{0,1\}^d)$ having their Euclidean norms equal to $2^{d/2}$ by SVM induced by the kernel K are not tractable, i.e., their representations require exponentially large numbers of units or exponentially large sizes of output weights.

Setting $\cos \alpha = 2^{-d/4}$, we obtain from Theorem 3 the lower bound

$$1 - e^{-\frac{2^{d/2} - 2d^2}{2}}$$

on the relative size of the subset of the ball of radius $2^{d/2}$ in $\mathcal{B}(\{0,1\}^d)$ containing functions with variations with respect to half-spaces larger or equal to $2^{d/4}$. So by Proposition 1, for large d almost any randomly chosen real-valued Boolean function with the norm $2^{d/2}$ cannot be tractably represented by a shallow Heaviside perceptron network.

Theorem 3 showing that for large d, almost any function on the sphere of radius $2^{\text{card} X}$ has variation depending on d exponentially is existential. However, to construct concrete examples of such functions is not easy. The only example of which we are aware is the function "inner product mod 2" which serves in theory of circuit complexity as ana example of a function which does not belong to the class $\widehat{LT_2}$ of depth-2 polynomial-size threshold gate circuits with weights being polynomially bounded integers (see, e.g., [18]). For every even positive integer d, let $\beta_d : \{0,1\}^d \to \{-1,1\}$ be defined for all $x \in \{0,1\}^d$ as

$$\beta_d := (-1)^{l(x) \cdot r(x)}$$

where $l(x), r(x) \in \{0,1\}^{d/2}$ are defined for every $i = 1, \ldots \frac{d}{2}$ as $l(x)_i := x_i$ and $r(x)_i := x_{\frac{d}{2}+i}$. When the range $\{-1,1\}$ is replaced with $\{1,0\}$, functions computing inner products of $l(x)$ with $r(x)$ mod 2 are obtained.

The following theorem is a corollary of a lower bound on the variational norm from [19, Theorem 3.7]. Recall the $h = \Omega(g(d))$ for two functions $g, h : \mathbb{N} \to \mathbb{R}$ meaning that there exist a positive constant c and $n_0 \in \mathbb{N}$ such that for all $n \geq n_o$ one has $h(n) \geq c\,g(n)$ [31].

Theorem 4. *Let d be an even integer, then* $\|\beta_d\|_{H_d(\{0,1\}^d)} \geq \|f\|_{P_d(\{0,1\}^d)} = \Omega(2^{d/6})$.

By Theorem 4 and Proposition 1 we get the following corollary.

Corollary 2. *Let d be an even integer and $\beta_d(x) = \sum_{i=1}^m w_i \vartheta(v_i \cdot x + b_i)$ be a representations of the function $\beta_d : \{0,1\}^d \to \{-1,1\}$ by a one-hidden-layer Heaviside perceptron network. Then $\sum_{i=1}^m |w_i| = \Omega(2^{2d/6})$.*

Corollary 2 implies that a representation of a class of d-variable Boolean functions $\{\beta_d \mid d \text{ even}\}$ by one-hidden-layer Heaviside perceptron networks is not tractable. These functions cannot be represented by Heaviside perceptron networks with both numbers of units and sums of absolute values of output weights polynomially bounded.

5 Discussion

We investigated model complexities of one-hidden-layer networks representing high-dimensional functions. We showed that the concept of variational norm with respect to a dictionary studied on approximation theory reflects both numbers of units and sizes of output weights in representing networks with units from the dictionary. Using properties of high-dimensional spaces, we proved that for networks with common units (such as perceptrons and SVM kernel units) with increasing input dimension d most of the functions require networks with number of units or sizes of output weights depending on d exponentially. An essential condition in our arguments is a relatively small size of these dictionaries. The upper bound $2^{d^2 - d \log_2 d + \mathcal{O}(d)}$ on the dictionary of Heaviside perceptrons on the Boolean cube was derived already in 19th century by one of the founders of high-dimensional geometry [29].

Our results hold for functions of comparable norms as network units. Note that also in theory of circuit complexity (see, e.g., [18]), there are studied representations of functions of fixed Euclidean norms by networks with gates computing functions with the same norms by networks with constrains on both numbers of units and their output weights. In particular, in this theory there are studied representations of Boolean functions with values in $\{-1,1\}$ by networks composed from signum perceptrons. All these functions have Euclidean norms equal to $2^{d/2}$.

Acknowledgments. This work was partially supported by grant COST LD13002 of the Ministry of Education of the Czech Republic and institutional support of the Institute of Computer Science RVO 67985807.

References

1. Fine, T.L.: Feedforward Neural Network Methodology. Springer, Heidelberg (1999)
2. Chow, T.W.S., Cho, S.Y.: Neural Networks and Computing: Learning Algorithms and Applications. World Scientific (2007)
3. Leshno, M., Lin, V.Y., Pinkus, A., Schocken, S.: Multilayer feedforward networks with a nonpolynomial activation function can approximate any function. Neural Networks 6, 861–867 (1993)
4. Pinkus, A.: Approximation theory of the MLP model in neural networks. Acta Numerica 8, 143–195 (1999)
5. Park, J., Sandberg, I.: Approximation and radial-basis-function networks. Neural Computation 5, 305–316 (1993)
6. Mhaskar, H.N.: Versatile Gaussian networks. In: Proc. of IEEE Workshop of Nonlinear Image Processing, pp. 70–73 (1995)
7. Kůrková, V.: Some comparisons of networks with radial and kernel units. In: Villa, A.E.P., Duch, W., Érdi, P., Masulli, F., Palm, G. (eds.) ICANN 2012, Part II. LNCS, vol. 7553, pp. 17–24. Springer, Heidelberg (2012)
8. Steinwart, I., Christmann, A.: Support Vector Machines. Springer, New York (2008)
9. Ito, Y.: Finite mapping by neural networks and truth functions. Mathematical Scientist 17, 69–77 (1992)
10. Micchelli, C.A.: Interpolation of scattered data: Distance matrices and conditionally positive definite functions. Constructive Approximation 2, 11–22 (1986)
11. Kainen, P.C., Kůrková, V., Sanguineti, M.: Dependence of computational models on input dimension: Tractability of approximation and optimization tasks. IEEE Transactions on Information Theory 58, 1203–1214 (2012)
12. Maiorov, V.: On best approximation by ridge functions. J. of Approximation Theory 99, 68–94 (1999)
13. Maiorov, V., Pinkus, A.: Lower bounds for approximation by MLP neural networks. Neurocomputing 25, 81–91 (1999)
14. Bartlett, P.L.: The sample complexity of pattern classification with neural networks: The size of the weights is more important than the size of the network. IEEE Trans. on Information Theory 44, 525–536 (1998)
15. Hinton, G.E., Osindero, S., Teh, Y.W.: A fast learning algorithm for deep belief nets. Neural Computation 18, 1527–1554 (2006)
16. Bengio, Y.: Learning deep architectures for AI. Foundations and Trends in Machine Learning 2, 1–127 (2009)
17. Bengio, Y., Delalleau, O., Roux, N.L.: The curse of highly variable functions for local kernel machines. In: Advances in Neural Information Processing Systems 18, pp. 107–114. MIT Press (2006)
18. Roychowdhury, V., Siu, K., Orlitsky, A.: Neural models and spectral methods. In: Roychowdhury, V., Siu, K., Orlitsky, A. (eds.) Theorertical Advances in Neural Computation and Learning, pp. 3–36. Kluwer Academic Press (1997)
19. Kůrková, V., Savický, P., Hlaváčková, K.: Representations and rates of approximation of real-valued Boolean functions by neural networks. Neural Networks 11, 651–659 (1998)
20. Kůrková, V.: Representations of highly-varying functions by perceptron networks. In: Informačné Technológie - Aplikácie a Teória - ITAT 2013, Košice, UPJŠ (2013)

21. Kůrková, V.: Dimension-independent rates of approximation by neural networks. In: Warwick, K., Kárný, M. (eds.) Computer-Intensive Methods in Control and Signal Processing. The Curse of Dimensionality, pp. 261–270. Birkhäuser, Boston (1997)

22. Barron, A.R.: Neural net approximation. In: Narendra, K. (ed.) Proc. 7th Yale Workshop on Adaptive and Learning Systems, pp. 69–72. Yale University Press (1992)

23. Barron, A.R.: Universal approximation bounds for superpositions of a sigmoidal function. IEEE Trans. on Information Theory 39, 930–945 (1993)

24. Kůrková, V., Sanguineti, M.: Comparison of worst-case errors in linear and neural network approximation. IEEE Transactions on Information Theory 48, 264–275 (2002)

25. Kůrková, V.: Minimization of error functionals over perceptron networks. Neural Computation 20, 250–270 (2008)

26. Kůrková, V.: Complexity estimates based on integral transforms induced by computational units. Neural Networks 33, 160–167 (2012)

27. Matoušek, J.: Lectures on Discrete Geometry. Springer, New York (2002)

28. Ball, K.: An elementary introduction to modern convex geometry. In: Levy, S. (ed.) Falvors of Geometry, pp. 1–58. Cambridge University Press (1997)

29. Schläfli, L.: Theorie der vielfachen Kontinuität. Zürcher & Furrer, Zürich (1901)

30. Schläfli, L.: Gesamelte Mathematische Abhandlungen, Band 1. Birkhäuser, Basel (1950)

31. Knuth, D.E.: Big omicron and big omega and big theta. SIGACT News 8, 18–24 (1976)

Non-euclidean Principal Component Analysis for Matrices by Hebbian Learning

Mandy Lange, David Nebel*, and Thomas Villmann

Computational Intelligence Group,
University of Applied Sciences Mittweida, 09648 Mittweida, Germany

Abstract. Modern image data analysis is apparently based on matrix norms. The calculation of those norms is frequently time consuming as well as matrix calculations in general. For this reason, complexity reduction is a key feature in image analysis. In this paper we investigate Schatten-p-norms as matrix norms based on the matrix trace operator, such that the mathematical vector space of matrices becomes a Banach space. As the first main result we develop a semi-inner product for these Banach spaces which generate the respective norms. Then we explain a mathematical theory of eigen-matrices for this scenario and give as the second main result an online learning scheme for the iterative determination of those eigen-matrices with respect to a covariance operator defined for datasets of matrices/images, which can be used for complexity reduction.

1 Introduction

Analysis of image data is still an promising subject due to the images size. Further, image data can be compared by Schatten-$p$norms [7, 17], which seem to be more appropriate for similarity descriptions[5, 13]. However, calculation of matrix norms or distance measure thereof frequently require expansive calculations. Therefore, a low-dimensional feature representation is demanded. This is frequently done either by explicit feature extraction based on image processing tools or by handling the data matrices as vectors equipped with respective l_p-norms and subsequent principal component analysis in both cases [1, 10, 11, 18]. However, both approaches are accompanied with an information loss [2].

In this paper we consider matrix norms as an alternative way, in particular we focus on Schatten-p-norms. We explain the concept of eigen-matrices and principal components for this scenario. For this purpose, we develop a semi-inner product (SIP) assigned to Schatten-p-norms and present an online learning algorithm for determination of the principal components for a given matrix data set, which make use of the SIP. We mathematically proof these concepts and give illustrative examples to demonstrate the approach.

---

* D.N. is supported by a grant of the European Social Foundation (ESF), Saxony.

L. Rutkowski et al. (Eds.): ICAISC 2014, Part I, LNAI 8467, pp. 77–88, 2014.

2   Banach Vector Spaces and Semi-inner Products

Banach spaces have gained popularity in machine learning, recently [3, 6, 8, 9, 19, 20]. Prominent n-dimensional examples are the l_p-spaces with the Minkowski-p-norm

$$\|\mathbf{x}\|_p = \sqrt[p]{\sum_{i=1}^{n} |x_i|^p} \tag{2.1}$$

for $1 \leq p \leq \infty$. In particular, the frequently applied l_1-norm $\|\bullet\|_1$ constitutes a Banach space but does not form a Hilbert space. Thus, an inner product generating $\|\bullet\|_1$ does not exist.

2.1   Semi-inner Products for Vector Spaces

In the following, we briefly introduce basic concepts and properties of semi-inner products, which are important for Hebbian PCA learning in Banach spaces, neglecting details for better reading. The details are explained in the Appendix.

Semi-inner products, introduced by G. LUMER in 1961, can be seen as a generalization of inner products [12]:

Definition 1. *A semi-inner product (SIP) $[\bullet, \bullet]$ of a general vector space V is a map*

$$[\bullet, \bullet] : V \times V \longrightarrow \mathbb{C} \tag{2.2}$$

with the following properties:

1. *positive semi-definite*

$$[\mathbf{x}, \mathbf{x}] \geq 0 \tag{2.3}$$

   and $[\mathbf{x}, \mathbf{x}] = 0$ iff $\mathbf{x} = \mathbf{0}$
2. *linear with respect to the first argument for $\xi \in \mathbb{C}$*

$$\xi \cdot [\mathbf{x}, \mathbf{z}] + [\mathbf{y}, \mathbf{z}] = [\xi \cdot \mathbf{x} + \mathbf{y}, \mathbf{z}] \tag{2.4}$$

3. *Cauchy-Schwarz inequality*

$$|[\mathbf{x}, \mathbf{y}]|^2 \leq [\mathbf{x}, \mathbf{x}] [\mathbf{y}, \mathbf{y}] \tag{2.5}$$

We emphasize that, in contradiction to inner products, SIPs may violate the symmetry condition, i.e. we generally have $[\mathbf{x}, \mathbf{y}] \neq \overline{[\mathbf{y}, \mathbf{x}]}$.

G. LUMER has proven that an arbitrary Banach space $\mathbb{B}$ with norm $\|\mathbf{x}\|_{\mathbb{B}}$ can be equipped with a SIP $[\bullet, \bullet]_{\mathbb{B}}$ such that

$$\|\mathbf{x}\|_{\mathbb{B}} = \sqrt{[\mathbf{x}, \mathbf{x}]_{\mathbb{B}}} \tag{2.6}$$

is valid [12]. Although this SIP maybe not unique, we can always find a SIP such that

$$[\mathbf{x}, \lambda \cdot \mathbf{y}] = \overline{\lambda} \cdot [\mathbf{x}, \mathbf{y}] \tag{2.7}$$

holds whereas uniqueness is achieved when the SIP is continuous with respect to the second argument [4].

The SIPs for the above mentioned (complex) l_p-spaces are given as

$$[\mathbf{x}, \mathbf{y}]_p = \frac{1}{\left(\|\mathbf{y}\|_p\right)^{p-2}} \sum_{i=1}^{n} x_i \cdot \bar{y}_i \cdot |y_i|^{p-2} \tag{2.8}$$

with the real counterpart

$$[\mathbf{x}, \mathbf{y}]_p = \frac{1}{\left(\|\mathbf{y}\|_p\right)^{p-2}} \sum_{i=1}^{n} x_i |y_i|^{p-1} \, sgn\,(y_i) \tag{2.9}$$

as explained in [10].

2.2 Hebbian Learning of Principal Components Using SIPs

Suppose the space $\mathbb{C}^n$ equipped with the SIP $[\bullet, \bullet]_p$ and a dataset $V = \{\mathbf{v}_k | k = 1 \ldots N\} \subset \mathbb{C}^n$ of centered vectors is given. Let further $W = \{\mathbf{w}_k | k = 1 \ldots K\}$ be a set of vectors with $K = \min(n, N)$ randomly initialized. Recently, it has been shown that the iterative process

$$\mathbf{w}_k = \mathbf{w}_k + \varepsilon \cdot [\mathbf{v}_l, \mathbf{w}_k]_p \cdot \left(\mathbf{v}_l - \sum_{j=1}^{k} [\mathbf{v}_l, \mathbf{w}_j]_p \cdot \mathbf{w}_j \right) \tag{2.10}$$

for a randomly chosen vectors $\mathbf{v}_l \in V$ and a learning rate $0 < \varepsilon \ll 1$ converges to the K eigenvectors of the covariance matrix C_V of V corresponding to the K largest eigenvalues [10]. If $p = 2$, this algorithm is the well-known Hebbian Principle Component Analysis (HPCA) algorithm introduced by OJA and SANGER [14–16].

3 Schatten-Norms and Semi-inner Products

In the following we assume matrices $A, B \in \mathbb{C}^{m \times n}$. We emphasize a this point that $\mathbb{C}^{m \times n}$ is a mathematical vector space. The Schatten-p-norm $s_p(A)$ of a matrix A is defined as

$$s_p(A) = \sqrt[p]{\sum_{k=1}^{n} (\sigma_k)^p} \tag{3.1}$$

with the $\sigma_k(A)$ are the singular values of A, i.e. the squared singular values $(\sigma_k(A))^2$ are the eigenvalues of $\Omega = A^* A$ and where A^* denotes the conjugate complex of A [17]. With this matrix norm[1] the vector space $\mathbb{C}^{m \times n}$ becomes a

---

[1] Matrix norms (operator norms) differ from usual norms that the submultiplicativity $\|A \cdot B\| \leq \|A\| \cdot \|B\|$ is additionally required. Thus, matrix norms become compliant with the matrix multiplication. For a detailed description and properties compared to usual norms we refer to [7].

Banach space $\mathfrak{B}_{m,n}$ of matrices. In the following we will develop a SIP for this Banach space. For this purpose, first we review basic properties of the norm s_p. Thereafter we present the respective SIP and investigate its utilization in Hebbian Oja-learning.

3.1 Basic Properties of Schatten-p-Norms

In this section we summarize some basic properties, which are useful in the following investigations. Let $|A|$ denote the absolute value of $A \in \mathfrak{B}_{m,n}$ to be the positive square root of $\Omega = A^*A$. Then the Schatten-p-norm can be written as

$$s_p\left(A\right) = \sqrt[p]{trace(|A|^p)} \tag{3.2}$$

with the matrix trace operator $trace\,(\bullet)$ [7].

Remark 1. We remark at this point that the trace operator is a linear operator and it is cyclic, i.e. $s_p\left(\lambda \cdot A + \gamma B\right) = \lambda \cdot s_p\left(A\right) + \gamma \cdot s_p\left(B\right)$ and

$$s_p\left(ABC\right) = s_p\left(CAB\right) \tag{3.3}$$

are valid, the latter using the usual matrix product based on the Euclidean inner product.

The Schatten-p-norm $s_p\left(A\right)$ belongs to the class of sub-multiplicative matrix norms, i.e. $s_p\left(AB\right) \leq s_p\left(A\right) \cdot s_p\left(B\right)$. Further, it is unitarily-invariant such that $s_p\left(A\right) = s_p\left(PA\right)$ with P being an unitar matrix. Because of the trace property (3.2) it follows that $s_p\left(A\right)$ is also invariant with respect to any basis transformation: $s_p\left(A\right) = s_p\left(BAB^{-1}\right)$. By definition, it is also self-adjoint such that $s_p\left(A\right) = s_p\left(A^*\right)$ is valid.

Important cases are $p = 1$ and $p = \infty$, which correspond to the nuclear or trace norm and the spectral norm, respectively. The value $p = 2$ defines the Frobenius-norm, which is consistent with the vector norm $\|\bullet\|_2$. It is also known as Hilbert-Schmidt-norm $s_2\left(A\right) = \sqrt{trace\left(A^*A\right)}$. The dual of $s_p\left(A\right)$ is the norm $s_q\left(A\right)$ with $\frac{1}{p} + \frac{1}{q} = 1$.

3.2 Semi-inner Products for Schatten-p-Norms

According to the definition (3.1), the Schatten-p-norm $s_p\left(A\right)$ can be seen as the Minkowski-p-norm (2.1) of the vector σ of the singular values of the matrix A. It is already known that the Frobenius-norm is induced by an inner product given as

$$\langle A, B \rangle_F = trace\left(A^*B\right) \tag{3.4}$$

making the space of the matrices to a Hilbert space [7]. According to the Cauchy-Schwarz-inequality we have $|\langle A, B \rangle_F|^2 \leq |\langle A, A \rangle_F| \cdot |\langle B, B \rangle_F|$. Using this observation and keeping in mind that Schatten-p-norms correspond to Banach spaces we can state the following lemma:

Theorem 1. *The Banach space $\mathfrak{B}_{m,n}$ of matrices $A, B \in \mathbb{C}^{m\times n}$ equipped with the Schatten-p-norm $s_p(A) = \sqrt[p]{\sum_{k=1}^{n}(\sigma_k)^p}$ from (3.1) corresponds to the SIP $[A, B]_p : \mathfrak{B}_{m,n} \times \mathfrak{B}_{m,n} \to \mathbb{C}$ defined as*

$$[A, B]_p = \frac{1}{(s_p(B))^{p-2}} trace\left(AB^*\left(|B|_m\right)^{p-2}\right) \tag{3.5}$$

with $|B|_m = \sqrt{BB^*}$ or, equivalently,

$$[A, B]_p = \frac{1}{(s_p(B))^{p-2}} trace\left(A^*B\left(|B|_n\right)^{p-2}\right) \tag{3.6}$$

is valid with $|B|_n = \sqrt{B^*B}$.

The proof of the theorem is given in the Appendix.

We remark that the real SIP $[A, B]_p^\circ : \mathfrak{B}_{m,n}^\circ \times \mathfrak{B}_{m,n}^\circ \to \mathbb{R}$ for the Banach space $\mathfrak{B}_{m,n}^\circ = \mathbb{R}^{m\times n}$ is also linear in the second argument and, hence, it generates a linear operator

$$\mathscr{F}_A[B] = [A, B]_p^\circ \cdot A \tag{3.7}$$

in $\mathfrak{B}_{m,n}^\circ$ according to [10].

4 Principal Components in $\mathfrak{B}_{m,n}$

In this section we explain the concept of eigen-matrices and principal components for the Banach space of matrices and present a respective online learning algorithm.

4.1 Principal Components

Let $\mathfrak{B}(n \cdot m) = \{\mathfrak{b}_k\}_{k=1,\ldots,n\cdot m}$ be a basis in the vector space $\mathfrak{B}_{m,n}$. We consider a linear projection operator $\mathbf{P}_{m,n}^{l,p} : \mathfrak{B}_{m,n} \to \mathbb{C}^l$ defined by

$$\mathbf{P}_{\mathfrak{B}(n\cdot m)}^{l,p}[A] = \left([A, \mathfrak{b}_1]_p, \ldots, [A, \mathfrak{b}_l]_p\right)^\top \tag{4.1}$$

with $1 \leq l \leq n \cdot m$. Further, assuming a set $\mathcal{S} = \{S_1, S_2, \ldots | S_k \in \mathfrak{B}_{m,n}\}$ we define the linear covariance operators $\mathbf{C}_\mathcal{S} \in \mathfrak{B}^{[m,n]\times[m,n]}$ as the expectation $\mathbf{C}_\mathcal{S} = E[S_k \odot S_k^*]$. The set $\mathfrak{B}^{[m,n]\times[m,n]}$ is the space of block matrices of size $m \times n$ where each element is itself a matrix of size $m \times n$. Each operator $\mathbf{O}$ generates a linear mapping $\mathbf{O} : \mathfrak{B}_{m,n} \to \mathfrak{B}_{m,n}$ by

$$\mathbf{O}[A] = \begin{pmatrix} [O_{11}, A]_p & \cdots & [O_{1n}, A]_p \\ \vdots & & \vdots \\ [O_{m1}, A]_p & \cdots & [O_{m,n}, A]_p \end{pmatrix} \tag{4.2}$$

and a matrix $X \in \mathfrak{B}_{m,n}$, $X \neq 0$, is called an eigen-matrix of the operator $\mathbf{O}$ if

$$\mathbf{O}[X] = \lambda X \tag{4.3}$$

is valid. The scalar λ is the eigenvalue assigned to X. The set $\Lambda = \{\lambda_k | k = 1, \ldots, n \cdot m\}$ of all eigenvalues forms the spectrum of $\mathbf{O}$. If the operator is regular, i.e. $\mathbf{O}^{-1}$ exists, then the respective eigen-matrices X_k generate a basis in $\mathfrak{B}_{m,n}$, because $\mathfrak{B}_{m,n}$ is a vector space itself. If $\mathbf{O} = \mathbf{C}_S$ the eigen-matrices are also denotes as principal components.

4.2   Hebbian Learning of Principal Components

In this section we extend the Oja-Sanger-learning of principal compo-
nents of the $\mathbb{R}^n$ to the Banach space $\mathfrak{B}_{m,n}^{\circ}$. We suppose a dataset $\mathcal{V} = \{V_k | k = 1 \ldots N, V_k \in \mathfrak{B}_{m,n}^{\circ}\}$ of centered matrices and a set $\mathcal{W} = \{W_k | k = 1 \ldots K, W_k \in \mathfrak{B}_{m,n}^{\circ}\}$ randomly initialized with $K = \min(n \cdot m, N)$. We consider the iterative process

$$\triangle W_k = \varepsilon \cdot [V_l, W_k]_p^{\circ} \cdot \left(V_l - \sum_{j=1}^{k} [V_l, W_j]_p^{\circ} \cdot W_j \right) \tag{4.4}$$

for a randomly chosen matrices $V_l \in \mathcal{V}$ and a learning rate $0 < \varepsilon \ll 1$. We can state the following lemma:

Lemma 1. *The algorithm defined in* (4.4) *converges such that the matrices* W_k *are the eigen-matrices according to the eigen-matrix equation* (4.3) *corresponding to the* K *largest eigenvalues of the covariance operator* $\mathbf{C}_{\mathcal{V}}$ *of the dataset* $\mathcal{V}$.

Proof. Since $\mathfrak{B}_{m,n}$ is a Banach space with the SIP $[\bullet, \bullet]_p$ generating the norm $s_p(\bullet)$, the convergence follows by the same arguments as for the Banach space considerations in [10], i.e. like in the original proof only the norm properties are required to show convergence. Now we restrict ourself two the case of only one principal component, i.e. $K = 1$ and set $W = W_1$. The stationary state is given by $\triangle W = 0$. Because of $0 < \varepsilon \ll 1$ we can consider the expectation and obtain for this state

$$E[\mathscr{F}_V[W]] = \gamma \cdot W, \tag{4.5}$$

which is again an eigenvalue equation with $\gamma = E\left[[V, W]_p^{\circ} \cdot [V, W]_p^{\circ}\right]$. Further, we know from (3.7) that $\mathscr{F}_V[W] = [V, W]_p^{\circ} \cdot V$ is a linear operator for each $V \in \mathcal{V}$. We have

$$E[\mathscr{F}_V[W]] = E\left[V \cdot [V, W]_p^{\circ}\right]$$
$$= E[V \odot V^*][W]$$
$$= \mathbf{C}_{\mathcal{V}}[W]$$

in complete analogy to [10]. The generalization to $K > 1$ is straightforward following the argumentation in [16]. This completes the proof.

5   Illustrative Example

We illustrate the above considerations by the following experiment. We consider a database of gray-scale images from handwritten digits $'0' \ldots '9'$ consisting of images of size 16×16 pixels. We determined the first two principal components for several Schatten-p-norms and compare them with the respective vectorial counterpart. The results for the l_2-, l_1-, and l_5-norms are depicted in Fig.'s 1, 2, and 3, respectively.

As we can observe from the exemplary simulations, clear differences between the matrix and the vectorial approach are apparently. Thus, the different mathematical treatment leads to diverse guise also depending on the parameter p. However, the consequences of this different behavior for applications is not yet clear so far, i.e. whether principal components in the matrix space can be contribute to better performance in applications. However, this is not the focus of this contribution, which is dedicated to provide the mathematical theory.

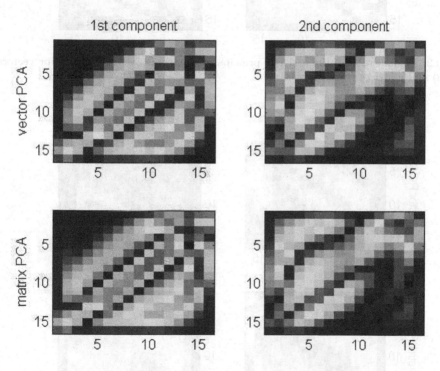

Fig. 1. Visualization of the first two principal components for the l_2-norm for vectors (top) and matrices (bottom)

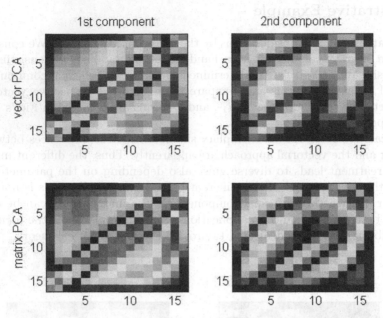

Fig. 2. Visualization of the first two principal components for the l_1-norm for vectors (top) and matrices (bottom)

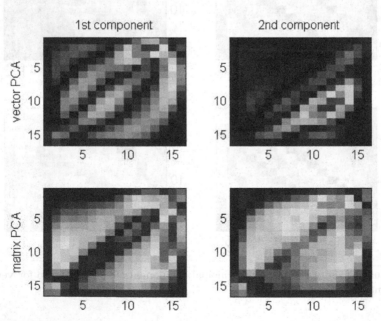

Fig. 3. Visualization of the first two principal components for the l_5-norm for vectors (top) and matrices (bottom)

6 Concluding Remarks and Future Work

In this paper we investigated the mathematical theory of Schatten-p-norms for matrices and considered principal component analysis in the respective Banach space of matrices. For this purpose we present a semi-inner product inducing the norm and adapt the Oja-Sanger algorithm for vectorial principal component analysis to this matrix case. For both new aspects we provide the mathematical theory and proof mathematically the required properties. After verification of the mathematical concepts we illustrated the different behavior of the matrix approach compared to the vectorial ansatz for an illustrative example. In future work we will investigate the properties of this matrix approach in deeper detail in applications like image classification or time-dissolved spectra. For this purpose, we can use Schatten-p-norms directly in vector quantization methods like self-organizing maps or learning vector quantization. An alternative offered by this paper is to transfer the original data in the coordinate space of the principal matrices and handling the classification problem in that transformed data space.

References

[1] Biehl, M., Kästner, M., Lange, M., Villmann, T.: Non-Euclidean principal component analysis and Oja's learning rule – theoretical aspects. In: Estevez, P.A., Principe, J.C., Zegers, P. (eds.) Advances in Self-Organizing Maps. AISC, vol. 198, pp. 23–34. Springer, Heidelberg (2013)

[2] Bishop, C.: Pattern Recognition and Machine Learning. Springer Science+Business Media, LLC, New York (2006)

[3] Der, R., Lee, D.: Large-margin classification in Banach spaces. In: JMLR Workshop and Conference Proceedings. AISTATS, vol. 2, pp. 91–98 (2007)

[4] Giles, J.: Classes of semi-inner-product spaces. Transactions of the American Mathematical Society 129, 436–446 (1967)

[5] Gu, Z., Shao, M., Li, L., Fu, Y.: Discriminative metric: Schatten norms vs. vector norm. In: Proc. of The 21st International Conference on Pattern Recognition (ICPR 2012), pp. 1213–1216 (2012)

[6] Hein, M., Bousquet, O., Schölkopf, B.: Maximal margin classification for metric spaces. Journal of Computer Systems Sciences 71, 333–359 (2005)

[7] Horn, R., Johnson, C.: Matrix Analysis, 2nd edn. Cambridge University Press (2013)

[8] Kaden, M., Lange, M., Nebel, D., Riedel, M., Geweniger, T., Villmann, T.: Aspects in classification learning - Review of recent developments in Learning Vector Quantization. In: Foundations of Computing and Decision Sciences (page accepted, 2014)

[9] Lange, M., Biehl, M., Villmann, T.: Non-Euclidean independent component analysis and Ojaś learning. In: Verleysen, M. (ed.) Proc. of European Symposium on Artificial Neural Networks, Computational Intelligence and Machine Learning (ESANN 2013), Louvain-La-Neuve, Belgium, pp. 125–130 (2013), i6doc.com

[10] Lange, M., Biehl, M., Villmann, T.: Non-Euclidean principal component analysis by Hebbian learning. Neurocomputing (page in press, 2014)

[11] Lange, M., Villmann, T.: Derivatives of l_p-norms and their approximations. Machine Learning Reports 7(MLR-04-2013), 43–59 (2013) ISSN:1865-3960, http://www.techfak.uni-bielefeld.de/~fschleif/mlr/mlr_04_2013.pdf

[12] Lumer, G.: Semi-inner-product spaces. Transactions of the American Mathematical Society 100, 29–43 (1961)

[13] Nie, F., Wang, H., Cai, X., Huang, H., Ding, C.: Robust matrix completiition via joint Schattenen p-norm and l_p-norm minimization. In: Zaki, M., Siebes, A., Yu, J., Goethals, B., Webb, G., Wu, X. (eds.) Proc. of the 12th IEEE International Conference on Data Mining (ICDM), Brussels, pp. 566–574. IEEE Press (2012)

[14] Oja, E.: Neural networks, principle components and subspaces. International Journal of Neural Systems 1, 61–68 (1989)

[15] Oja, E.: Nonlinear PCA: Algorithms and applications. In: Proc. of the World Congress on Neural Networks, Portland, pp. 396–400 (1993)

[16] Sanger, T.: Optimal unsupervised learning in a single-layer linear feedforward neural network. Neural Networks 12, 459–473 (1989)

[17] Schatten, R.: A Theory of Cross-Spaces. Annals of Mathematics Studies, vol. 26. Princeton University Press (1950)

[18] Sonka, M., Hlavac, V., Boyle, R.: Image Processing, Analysis and Machine Vision, 2nd edn. Brooks Publishing (1998)

[19] von Luxburg, U., Bousquet, O.: Distance-based classification with Lipschitz functions. Journal of Machine Learning Research 5, 669–695 (2004)

[20] Zhang, H., Xu, Y., Zhang, J.: Reproducing kernel banach spaces for machine learning. Journal of Machine Learning Research 10, 2741–2775 (2009)

Appendix

In this Appendix we proof the Theorem (1):

Proof. We start the proof considering (3.5). It is clear that (3.6) holds, iff (3.5) is valid, because A and A^* have the same singular values as well as B and B^*, and, additionally paying attention to the properties of the *trace* operator for matrices. Thus it remains to proof the SIP-properties:

1. **Linearity:** We observe that $[A, B]_p$ is linear in the first argument because of the linearity of the trace operator.

2. **Scalar multiplication in the second argument:** The relation $s_p(\lambda \cdot B) = |\lambda| \cdot s_p(B)$ is valid because of the norm properties and $|\lambda \cdot B|_m = |\lambda| \cdot |B|_m$ such that

$$(\lambda \cdot B)^* \left(|\lambda \cdot B|_m\right)^{p-2} = \overline{\lambda} \cdot |\lambda|^{p-2} \cdot B^* \cdot \left(|B|_m\right)^{p-2}$$

is valid. Using the cyclic property (3.3) and, again, the linearity we obtain $[A, \lambda \cdot B]_p = \overline{\lambda} \cdot [A, B]_p$.

3. **Positive semi-definiteness:** We consider

$$[A, A]_p = \frac{1}{(s_p(A))^{p-2}} trace \left(AA^* \left(|A|_m\right)^{p-2}\right).$$

Because, AA^* and $|A|_m$ are both positive semi-definite, $trace \left(AA^* \left(|A|_m\right)^{p-2}\right) \geq 0$ is valid and, hence, $[A, A]_p \geq 0$. The equality holds only for $A = 0$.

4. **Cauchy-Schwarz-inequality:** Last we proof the Cauchy-Schwarz inequality. For this purpose, we suppose two matrices $A, B \in \mathfrak{B}_{m,n}$ and β_i are the eigenvalues of

B. We consider

$$\left|trace\left(A \cdot B^* \cdot \left(|B|_m\right)^{p-2}\right)\right| \leq \left|trace\left(A \cdot B_+^* \cdot \left(|B_+|_m\right)^{p-2}\right)\right|$$
$$= \left|trace\left(A \cdot B_+ \cdot (B_+)^{p-2}\right)\right|$$
$$= \left|trace\left(A \cdot (B_+)^{p-1}\right)\right|$$

whereby B_+ is a matrix $B_+ \in \mathbb{R}^{m \times n}$ is a real matrix with the eigenvalues $\beta_i^+ = |\beta_i|$. We observe at this point that for the singular values of B and B_+ the equality

$$\sigma_i(B) = \sigma_i(B_+)$$

holds. Further, using the Neumann-inequality

$$trace\left(A \cdot \hat{B}\right) \leq \sum_{i=1}^{n^*} \sigma_i(A) \cdot \sigma_i\left(\hat{B}\right)$$

with $n^* = \min(m, n)$ for arbitrary matrices $A, \hat{B} \in \mathfrak{B}_{m,n}$ with the respective singular values $\sigma_i(A)$ and $\sigma_i\left(\hat{B}\right)$, we can conclude that

$$trace\left(A \cdot (B_+)^{p-1}\right) < \sum_{i=1}^{n^*} \sigma_i(A) \cdot (\sigma_i(B_+))^{p-1}$$

holds. Thus,

$$\left|[A, B]_p\right| = \left|\frac{1}{(s_p(B))^{p-2}} trace\left(AB^*\left(|B|_m\right)^{p-2}\right)\right|$$
$$\leq \frac{1}{(s_p(B))^{p-2}} \sum_{i=1}^{n^*} \sigma_i(A) \cdot (\sigma_i(B_+))^{p-1}$$
$$= \frac{1}{(s_p(B_+))^{p-2}} \sum_{i=1}^{n^*} \sigma_i(A) \cdot (\sigma_i(B_+))^{p-1}$$

whereby we used the equality

$$s_p(B) = s_p(B_+)$$

because of the same singular values. We consider the respective (real) SIP (2.9) in l_p-spaces

$$[\sigma(A), \sigma(B_+)]_p = \frac{1}{\left(\|\sigma(B_+)\|_p\right)^{p-2}} \sum_{i=1}^{n^*} \sigma_i(A) |\sigma_i(B_+)|^{p-1} \cdot sgn(\sigma_i(B_+))$$

for the singular value vectors $\sigma(A)$ and $\sigma(B_+)$, which can be simplified to

$$[\sigma(A), \sigma(B_+)]_p = \frac{1}{\left(\|\sigma(B_+)\|_p\right)^{p-2}} \sum_{i=1}^{n^*} \sigma_i(A) \cdot (\sigma_i(B_+))^{p-1}$$

paying attention to $\sigma_i(B_+) \geq 0$ such that $sgn(\sigma_i(B^+)) = 1$. For this SIP, the Cauchy-Schwarz-inequality

$$\left|[\sigma(A), \sigma(B_+)]_p\right| \leq \|\sigma(A)\|_p \cdot \|\sigma(B_+)\|_p$$

for the singular value vectors is valid in l_p-spaces.

Keeping in mind that $\|\sigma(A)\|_p = s_p(A)$ as well as $\|\sigma(B_+)\|_p = s_p(B_+)$ we can collect the pieces and finally obtain

$$\left|[A, B]_p\right| \leq s_p(A) \cdot s_p(B)$$

which is the required Cauchy-Schwarz-inequality for the SIP $[A, B]_p$ from (3.5) related to the Schatten-p-norm $s_p(A)$ from (3.1).

This concludes the proof of the theorem.

Spin-glass Implementation
of a Hopfield Neural Structure

Łukasz Laskowski[1,2], Magdalena Laskowska[2], Jerzy Jelonkiewicz[1],
and Arnaud Boullanger[3]

[1] Czestochowa University of Technology, Department of Computer Engineering,
Al. A.K. 36, 42-200 Czestochowa, Poland
[2] Czestochowa University of Technology, Institute of Physics, Al. Armii Krajowej 19,
PL-42-200 Czestochowa, Poland
[3] Université Montpellier II, Chimie Moléculaire et Organisation du Solide,
Institut Charles Gerhardt, UMR 5253 CC 1701, 2 Place E. Bataillon,
F-34095 Montpellier Cedex 5, France

Abstract. Paper presents the hardware implementation of the Hopfield
continuous neural network. We propose a molecular realization of a spin
glass model. In particular, we consider a spin glass like structure that
allows interconnection strengths change and neuron state test. Proposed
device is based on SBA-15 mesoporous silica thin film, activated by Mn_{12}
molecular magnets. Our idea seems to be feasible from the technological
point of view.

Keywords: Hopfield neural network, artificial neuron, spin-glass.

1 Introduction

Neural network hardware has been a subject of rapid development during the
last decade. Unlike the conventional von-Neumann architecture that is sequential in nature, hardware implementation of artificial neural networks (ANNs)
profits from massively parallel processing. A large variety of hardware has been
designed to exploit the inherent parallelism of the neural network models. Despite the tremendous growth in the digital computing power of general-purpose
processors, neural network hardware has been found to be promising in some
specialized applications, such as image processing, speech synthesis and analysis, pattern recognition, high energy physics and so on [1–4]. Due to limited
space it is not intention of the paper to present the state of the art in neural network hardware architectures nor provide a broad view of principles and
practice of hardware implementation of neural networks. On the other hand it
is quite natural to find relationship to the closest and existing competitors of
the proposed solution. These are digital and analog neurochips. Digital Neural
ASICs are the most powerful and mature neurochips. Digital techniques offer
high computational precision, high reliability, and high programmability. Furthermore, powerful design tools are available for digital full- and semi-custom
design. Disadvantages are the relatively large circuit size compared to analog

L. Rutkowski et al. (Eds.): ICAISC 2014, Part I, LNAI 8467, pp. 89–96, 2014.

implementations. Synaptic weights can be stored on or off chip. This choice is determined by the trade-off between speed and size. There are two well-known digital Neurochips, CNAPS [5] and SYNAPSE-1 [6].The standard CNAPS system consists of a common sequencer chip and four processor chips. Its die measures about one square inch with more than 13 million transistors integrated. Unlike CNAPS and the SYNAPSE which were designed for a wide range of neural network algorithms, the NESPINN (Neurocomputer for Spiking Neural Networks), designed at the Institute of Microelectronics of the Technical University of Berlin, is optimized more strictly to a certain class of neural networks: spiking neural networks. Spiking neural networks model neurons on a level relating more closely to biology. They do not only incorporate synaptic weighting, postsynaptic summation, static threshold and saturation, but also computation of membrane potentials, synaptic time delays and dynamical thresholds. One NESPINN-Board is designed to compute about 105 programmable neurons in real-time [7]. Analog electronics have some interesting characteristics that can directly be used for neural network implementation. Operational amplifiers, for instance, are easily built from single transistors and automatically perform neuron-like functions, such as integration and sigmoid transfer. These otherwise computationally intensive calculations are automatically performed by physical processes such as summing of currents or charges. Analog electronics are very compact and offer high speed at low energy dissipation. With current state-of-the-art micro electronics, simple neural (non-learning) associative memory chips with more than 1000 neurons and 1000 inputs each can be integrated on a single chip performing about 100 GCPS. Disadvantages of analog technology are the susceptibility to noise and process-parameter variations that limit computational precision and make it harder to understand what exactly is computed. Chips built according to the same design will never function in exactly the same way. Apart from the difficulties involved in designing analog circuits, the problem of representing adaptable weights is limiting the applicability of analog circuits. Weights can for instance be represented by resistors, but these are not adaptable after the production of the chips. Chips with fixed weights can only be used in the recall phase. Implementation techniques that do allow for adaptable weights are: capacitors, floating gate transistors, charge coupled devices (CCDs), etc [8]. The main problems with these techniques arise from process-parameter variations across the chip, limited storage times (volatility), and lack of compatibility with standard VLSI processing technology. The weight sets for these train-able chips are obtained by training on a remote system (PC or workstation) and are then downloaded onto the chip. Then another short learning phase can be carried out in the chip used for the forward phase, and the remote system updates the weights until the network stabilizes. This yields a weight matrix that is adjusted to compensate for the inevitable disparities in analog computations due to process variance. This method has been used for Intel's analog ETANN chip [9]. It should be clear that these chips are suited for many different applications, but do not allow for on-board training. Although analog chips will never reach the flexibility attainable with digital chips, their speed and compactness make them very attractive for neural network research, especially when they adopt the adaptive properties of the original neural network paradigms. A final promising advantage is that they more directly interface with the real, analog world, whereas digital implementations will always require fast analog-to-digital converters to read in world information and digital-to-analog converters to put their data back into the world. Advances in lithographic techniques and our understanding of solid-state systems have brought us to a point where we are interested in the electronic transport properties of organic molecules that are a few nanometers in size. One reason for this study is that simply the fact that such studies have not been performed before. Moreover successful implementation of molecular transistor has turned our attention to using it as a single artificial neuron [10]. The purpose of this paper is to present completely new hardware implementation of the artificial neuron based on molecular technique. We describe the idea of a spin-glass like hardware implementation of a Hopfield neural structure. This approach recalls the original Hopfield model of a continuous neural network. The Hopfield continuous neural network has come up as a projection of a physical spin-glass model[11, 12] into an artificial neural networks domain. Spin-glasses are unique kinds of structures that consist of paramagnetic atoms arranged in a rigid lattice (solid). Opposite to the ferromagnetic and anti ferromagnetic solids, the spin glasses are not lasting long structures. Their main properties are: disorder and rivalry of spin-spin interactions [13]. The later can be either ferromagnetic or anti ferromagnetic with the same probability. This disorder can originate from structural properties of a sample or atoms type in the crystalline lattice. This leads to the phenomenon called frustration - there is no configuration of spins that satisfies all bonds between lattice points. The schematic representation of a spin-glass can be seen in fig.1.

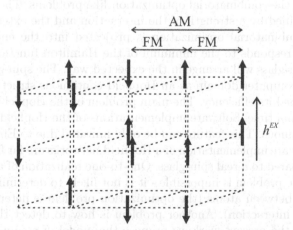

Fig. 1. The schematic representation of a spin-glass. In the picture FM means ferromagnetic interaction, while AM means anti ferromagnetic interaction, h^{EX} is an external magnetic field. Arrows mean spins directions of atoms.

For those systems quenched randomness of spin-spin interactions can be observed [14].Characteristic property of solids in spin-glass state is their reaction to the external magnetic field. Opposite to the ferromagnetic solids (external magnetic field is removed from the substance) and a paramagnetic substance (magnetic moments of atoms rapidly set up along the magnetic field), in the spin-glass a slow upward drift occurs toward the minimum in the sense of the Hamilton function minimum. This process has been induced by the external field. A single spin senses the magnetic field either as externally applied or from other spins. The magnetic field affecting on a single spin can be expressed in equation:

$$h_i = \sum_{j=1}^{N} w_{ij} S_j + h^{EX}. \tag{1}$$

In equation (1) h_i is a magnetic field affecting on atom i, S_j is a j-atom spin, h^{EX} is an external magnetic field, $w_{ij} > 0$ measures the strength of the interaction.

The system like this has a few ground states - the total energy function has more than one minimum. The ground state of a spin glass is its configuration that minimizes the frustration. According to the total minimum of the potential energy principle, the system is drifting towards configuration corresponding to its minimum energy. In the Ising spin glass model the Hamilton function of the total energy can be expressed by equation (2).

$$H = \sum_{i=1}^{N} \sum_{j=1}^{N} w_{ij} S_i S_j + h^{EX} \sum_{i=1}^{N} S_i. \tag{2}$$

As Hopfield noticed [15], [16], finding the ground state of a spin glass is equivalent to solving the combinatorial optimization like problems. The energy landscape is determined by a strength of the interaction and the external magnetic field. If the combinatorial optimization is projected into the energy function the solution corresponds to the minimum of the Hamilton function. Therefore, spins in the spin-glass will arrange in the expected way. The spin-glass has been projected into computer domain as an Hopfield continuous structure. The simulations confirmed its efficiency. The main problem of the Hopfield structures is the computational time. Software implementations of the Hopfield networks are not really continuous. This feature can be only imitated due to Euler discretization. Also hardware implementation of a Hopfield networks are far from ideal and cannot be compared to a real spin-glass. One-to-one realization of a spin-glass to solving a specific problem is impossible - it is not likely to determine strength of the interaction between atoms (the optimization problem is determined by the strength of the interaction). Another problem is how to detect the spin of the atom states. In the present work we propose the model of a spin-glass realized by a molecular neurons localized in a thin film of a hexagonally arranged mesoporous silica SBA-15. Our approach offers full control of the interaction strength (corresponding to the interconnection strength in the neural network).

2 The Idea

Authors propose using of SBA-15 mesoporous silica thin film, activated by Mn_{12} molecular magnets. Silica SBA-15 has a form of thin and long rods with walls built with amorphous silica (SiO_2). The rods arrangement is regular, in this case hexagonal. The structure of this species was depicted in fig. 2.

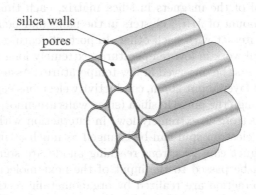

silica walls

pores

Fig. 2. The structure of SBA-15 type mesoporous silica

This material can be deposed as a thin films on a substrate (e.g. silicon wafers). Interesting feature of this layout is that it is possible to obtain 2D hexagonal structure (mesopores arranged vertically to the substrate's surface)[17], what was depicted in figure 3.

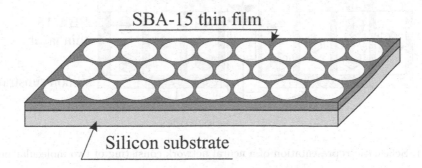

SBA-15 thin film

Silicon substrate

Fig. 3. 2D hexagonally arranged SBA-15 thin film on a silicon wafer substrate

Silica SBA-15can be activated by Mn_{12} molecular magnets [18]. Magnetic crystals Mn_{12} exhibit unusual magnetic ground states, with high electron spin, S = 10. In this case the most important thing is to obtain homogenous distribution of doping agent inside silica matrix and maintain such a distance between active units, so they do not interact with each other. As authors mastered the method of doping SBA-15 silica pores by Mn12 molecular magnets (bounded by propyl-carbonate units), the distribution control of the doping agents and distance between active centres was possible [19], [20]. Having this done we can construct single-molecule-magnet based neuron, the core of the spin-glass like neural network. The critical point of this idea is the thin film from SBA-15 silica grafted by Mn_{12} molecular magnets, deposed between two electrodes. Due to distribution control of the magnets in silica matrix, each time we are able to obtain the same amount of Mn_{12} clusters in the molecular neuron and be sure, that they do not interact with each other. Important feature of the molecular neuron is that it will work in low temperature (extremely long time of magnetic relaxation of Mn_{12} can be observed in low temperature). Assuming thickness of a active silica based layer about 20nm, conductivity electrons can tunnel between electrodes only through the pores in silica (silica walls are amorphous so a chance of passing it by electrons is extremely low) in interaction with Mn_{12} magnets located there. The electron spin can be changed as much as magnetic moment of a molecular magnet can. Electrons reaching anode are spin-polarized. This output current can be passed to the input of the next molecular neuron. The strength of the interaction are realized by organometalic rectifier-resistor (polianiline based system). The tuning of the resistance enables the adjustment of the electron mean free path and therefore probability of electron spin relaxation. The schematic representation of the network consist of two molecular neurons was depicted in figure 4.

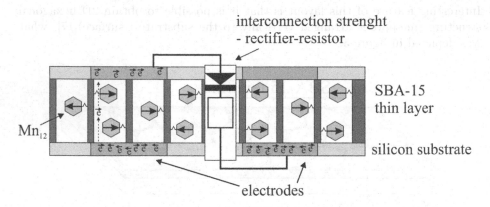

Fig. 4. Schematic representation of a neural network consisting of two molecular neurons

As it was mentioned before, there is no possibility of checking the atoms spin state in the lattice of the spin glass. In the case of proposed system, the state of each molecular neuron can be defined by measuring the current of polarized electrons (source of polarized electrons can be e.g. a ferromagnetic electrode).

3 Conclusion

In the paper we have presented completely novel hardware implementation of an artificial neuron - single-molecule-magnet based neuron. Our idea seems to be feasible from the technological point of view. Authors mastered the technology of the thin SBA-15 film deposition on the silicon substrate. The geometrical properties of these layers were confirmed by TEM microscope imaging and X-Ray scattering. The physical-chemistry properties were checked by Raman spectroscopy supported by DFT simulations, SQUID magnetometry and EPR spectroscopy. Considering the current status of research it is our belief a successful realization of a molecular neuron is only a matter of time.

Aknowledgement. Financial support for this investigation has been provided by the National Centre of Science (Grant-No: 2011/03/D/ST5/05996).

References

1. Bartczuk, Ł., Przybył, A., Dziwiński, P.: Hybrid state variables - fuzzy logic modelling of nonlinear objects. In: Rutkowski, L., Korytkowski, M., Scherer, R., Tadeusiewicz, R., Zadeh, L.A., Zurada, J.M. (eds.) ICAISC 2013, Part I. LNCS, vol. 7894, pp. 227–234. Springer, Heidelberg (2013)
2. Sherer, R.: Neuro-Fuzzy Relational Systems for Nonlinear Approximation and Prediction. Nonlinear Analysis 71, 1420–1425 (2009)
3. Cierniak, R.: A new approach to image reconstruction from projections problem using a recurrent neural network. Applied Mathematics and Computer Science 18, 147–157 (2008)
4. Cierniak, R.: New neural network algorithm for image reconstruction from fan-beam projections. Neurocomputing 72, 3238–3244 (2009)
5. McCartor, H.: A Highly Parallel Digital Architecture for Neural Network Emulation. In: VLSI for Artificial Intelligence and Neural Networks, pp. 357–366 (1991)
6. Ramacher, U., Raab, W., Anlauf, J., Hachmann, U., Beichter, J., Bruls, N., Webeling, M., Sicheneder, E.: Multiprocessor and Memory Architecture of the Neurocomputers SYNAPSE-1. In: Proceedings of the 3rd International Conference on Microelectronics for Neural Networks (Micro Neuro), pp. 227–231 (1993)
7. Jahnke, A., Roth, U., Klar, H.: A SIMD/Dataflow Architecture for a Neurocomputer for Spike-Processing Neural Networks (NESPINN). In: Proceedings of the 6th International Conference on Microelectronics for Neural Networks (Micro Neuro), pp. 232–237 (1996)
8. Schwartz, T.J.: A Neural Chips Survey. AI Expert 5(12), 34–39 (1990)
9. Tam, S., Gupta, B., Castro, H., Holler, M.: Learning on an Analog VLSI Neural Network Chip. In: Proceedings of the IEEE International Conference on Systems, Man and Cybernetics (1990)
10. Rutkowski, L., Cpalka, K.: Neuro-fuzzy systems derived from quasi-triangular norms. In: Proceedings of the IEEE International Conference on Fuzzy Systems, vol. 2, pp. 1031–1036 (2004)
11. Fischer, K.H., Hertz, J.A.: Spin Glasses. Cambridge University Press (1991)
12. Prampero, P., Attux, R.: Magnetic particle swarm optimization. Journal of Artificial Intelligence and Soft Computing Research 2(1), 59–72 (2012)

13. Binder, K., Young, A.P.: Spin glasses: Experimental facts, theoretical concepts, and open questions. Review of Modern Physics 58, 801–976 (1986)
14. Palmer, R.G.: Broken ergodicity in spin-glasses. Lecture Notes in Physics, vol. 192, pp. 234–251 (1983)
15. Hopfield, J.J., Tank, D.W.: "Neural" computation of decisions in optimization problems. Biological Cybernetics 52, 141–152 (1985)
16. Hopfield, J.J., Tank, D.W.: Artificial neural networks. IEEE Circuits and Devices Magazine 8, 3–10 (1988)
17. Kataoka, S., Endo, A., Harada, A., Ohmori, T.: Fabrication of mesoporous silica thin films inside microreactors. Materials Letters 62, 723–726 (2008)
18. Naitabdi, A., Bucher, J.P., Gerbier, P., Rabu, P., Drillon, M.: Self-assembly and magnetism of Mn12 nanomagnets on native and functionalized gold surfaces. Adv. Materials 17, 1612–1616 (2005)
19. Laskowski, L., Kassiba, A., Makowska-Janusik, M., Mehdi, A., Gibaud, A., Errien, N., Swiatek, J.: Magnetic behaviour of nickel-cyclam complexes in mesoporous silica: EPR investigations. J. Phys.: Condens. Matter 21, 076004 (2009)
20. Laskowska, M., Laskowski, L., Dzilinski, K.: Mesoporous silica functionalized by Nickel-cyclam molecules: preparation and Raman investigations. Current Topics in Biophysics 35, 11–18 (2012)

Neural-Network Based Robust FTC: Application to Wind Turbines

Marcel Luzar, Marcin Witczak, Józef Korbicz, and Piotr Witczak

Institute of Control and Computation Engineering, University of Zielona Góra,
ul. Pogórna 50, 65-246 Zielona Góra, Poland
{m.luzar,m.witczak,j.korbicz}@issi.uz.zgora.pl,
p.witczak@weit.uz.zgora.pl

Abstract. The paper deals with the problem of a robust fault diagnosis of a wind turbine. The preliminary part of the paper describes the Linear Parameter-Varying model derivation with a Recurrent Neural Network. The subsequent part of the paper describes a robust fault detection, isolation and identification scheme, which is based on the observer and $\mathcal{H}_\infty$ framework for a class of non-linear systems. The proposed approach is designed in such a way that a prescribed disturbance attenuation level is achieved with respect to the actuator fault estimation error while guaranteeing the convergence of the observer. Moreover, the controller parameters selection method of the considered system is presented. Final part of the paper shows the experimental results regarding wind turbines, which confirms the effectiveness of proposed approach.

Keywords: Fault diagnosis, fault identification, robust control, fault-tolerant control, neural networks.

1 Introduction

The problem of fault diagnosis (FD) of non-linear industrial systems ([3,5,6,10,11]) has received considerable attention during the last three decades. Indeed, it developed from the art of designing a satisfactory performing systems into the modern theory and practice that it is today. Within the usual framework, the system being diagnosed is divided into three main components, i.e. plant (or system dynamics ([10])), actuators and sensors. The paper deals with the problem of full fault diagnosis of actuator, i.e. apart from the usual two steps consisting of fault detection and isolation (FDI), the fault identification is also performed. This last step is especially important from the viewpoint of Fault-Tolerant Control (FTC) ([1,8]), which is possible if and only if there is an information about the size of the fault being a result of fault identification (or fault estimation). In this paper a robust fault estimation approach is proposed, which can be efficiently applied to realise the above-mentioned three-step procedure. The proposed approach is designed in such a way that a prescribed disturbance attenuation level is achieved with respect to the fault estimation error while guaranteeing the convergence of the observer. While the fault-tolerant control scheme is based on replacing the faulty actuator and feeding them into the robust controller.

L. Rutkowski et al. (Eds.): ICAISC 2014, Part I, LNAI 8467, pp. 97–108, 2014.

The paper is organized as follows. Section 2 presents a method for transforming a neural state-space model into a discrete-time polytopic LPV model. Section 3 describes the proposed actuator observer. Whilst section 4 describes the robust controller and an integration procedure with the observer based strategy. The final part of the paper presents a comprehensive case study regarding the wind turbine, which clearly indicate the performance of the proposed approach.

2   Derivation of a LPV Model in Polytopic Form from a Neural-Network Model

The goal of this section is to present a neural state-space model that can represent a general class of state-space models and can be easily transformed into a LPV one.

Let us consider the following discrete-time LPV model:

$$x_{k+1} = A(\theta_k)x_k + B(\theta_k)u_k, \tag{1}$$

$$y_{k+1} = C(\theta_k)x_{k+1}, \tag{2}$$

where $A(\theta_k)$, $B(\theta_k)$, $C(\theta_k)$ are continuous mappings and θ_k is a time-varying parameter. Matrices A,B,C are θ_k dependent and represents a general LPV model.

A general form of state-space neural network model proposed within the framework of the paper is

$$x_{k+1} = Ax_k + Bu_k + A_1\sigma(E_1x_k), \tag{3}$$

$$y_{k+1} = Cx_{k+1}, \tag{4}$$

where $x \in \mathbb{R}^n$ denotes the state vector, $y \in \mathbb{R}^p$ the output and $u \in \mathbb{R}^m$ the input vector. A, A_1, B, C, E_1 are real-valued matrices of appropriate dimensions and represent the weights which will be adjusted during the training stage of the Recurrent Neural Network (RNN). The non-linear activation function $\sigma(\cdot)$, which is applied elementwise in (3)–(4) is taken as a continuous, differentiable and bounded function.

For stability and identifiability proofs of the proposed RNN the reader is refereed to ([4]). Practical implementation RNN is shown in Fig. 1: the outputs instead of the states are taken as input to sigmoidal layer. This modification facilities the implementation of LPV controllers designed based on this model. The subsequent section shows how to use the derived neural network for robust fault diagnosis and how to transform it into an LPV form.

3   Actuator Fault Diagnosis

The main objective of this section is to provide a detailed design procedure of the robust observer, which can be used for actuator fault diagnosis. In other words, the main role of this observer is to provide the information about the actuator

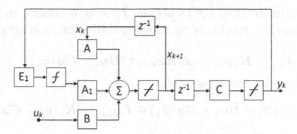

Fig. 1. State-space recurrent neural network

fault. Indeed, apart from serving as a usual residual generator (see, e.g.,([10])), the observer should be designed in such a way that a prescribed disturbance attenuation level is achieved with respect to the actuator fault estimation error while guaranteeing the convergence of the observer.

Let us consider to following non-linear system:

$$x_{k+1} = Ax_k + Bu_k + g(x_k) + L_a f_{a,k} + W_1 w_k, \tag{5}$$

$$y_{k+1} = Cx_{k+1} + W_2 w_{k+1}, \tag{6}$$

where $x_k \in X \subset \mathbb{R}^n$ is the state vector, $u_k \in \mathbb{R}^r$ stands for the input, $y_k \in \mathbb{R}^m$ denotes the output, $f_{a,k} \in \mathbb{R}^m$ stands for the actuator fault. While $w_k \in l_2$ is a an exogenous disturbance vector with $W_1 \in \mathbb{R}^{n \times n}$, $W_2 \in \mathbb{R}^{m \times n}$ being its distribution matrices while

$$l_2 = \{ \mathbf{w} \in \mathbb{R}^n |\ \|\mathbf{w}\|_{l_2} < +\infty \}, \|\mathbf{w}\|_{l_2} = \left(\sum_{k=0}^{\infty} \|w_k\|^2 \right)^{\frac{1}{2}}. \tag{7}$$

Following ([2,10]), let us assume that the system is observable and the following rank condition is satisfied:

$$\text{rank}(CL_a) = \text{rank}(L_a) = s \tag{8}$$

Under the assumption (8) it is possible to calculate

$$H = (CL_a)^+ = \left[(CL_a)^T CL_a \right]^{-1} (CL_a)^T. \tag{9}$$

Multiplying (6) by H, and then substituting (5), it can be shown that

$$f_{a,k} = H(y_{k+1} - CAx_k - CBu_k - Cg(x_k) - CW_1 w_k - W_2 w_{k+1}). \tag{10}$$

Finally, by substituting (10) into (5), it can be shown that:

$$x_{k+1} = \bar{A}x_k + \bar{B}u_k + Gg(x_k) + \bar{L}y_{k+1} + GW_1 w_k - \bar{L}W_2 w_{k+1}, \tag{11}$$

where $G = (I_n - L_a HC)$, $\bar{A} = GA$, $\bar{B} = GB$, $\bar{L} = L_a H$.

In order to estimate (10), i.e. to obtain $\hat{f}_k$ it is necessary to estimate the state of the system, i.e. to obtain $\hat{x}_k$. Consequently, the fault estimate is given as follows

$$\hat{f}_{a,k} = H(y_{k+1} - CA\hat{x}_k - CBu_k - Cg(\hat{x}_k)). \tag{12}$$

The corresponding observer structure is

$$\hat{x}_{k+1} = \bar{A}\hat{x}_k + \bar{B}u_k + Gg(\hat{x}_k) + \bar{L}y_{k+1} + K_o(y_k - C\hat{x}_k), \tag{13}$$

while the state estimation error is given by

$$
\begin{aligned}
e_{k+1} &= (\bar{A} - K_oC)\,e_k + Gs_k + (GW_1 - K_oW_2)w_k - \bar{L}W_2w_{k+1} = \\
&= A_1e_k + Gs_k + \bar{W}_1w_k + \bar{W}_2w_{k+1},
\end{aligned} \tag{14}
$$

where

$$s_k = g(x_k) - g(\hat{x}_k). \tag{15}$$

Similarly, the fault estimation error $\varepsilon_{f_a,k}$ can be defined

$$\varepsilon_{f_a,k} = f_{a,k} - \hat{f}_{a,k} = -HC(Ae_k + s_k + W_1w_k) - HW_2w_{k+1}. \tag{16}$$

Noth that both e_k and $\varepsilon_{f_a,k}$ are non-linear with respect to e_k. To settle this problem within the framework of this paper, the following solution is proposed.

Using the Differential Mean Value Theorem (DMVT) ([13]), it can be shown that

$$g(a) - g(b) = M_x(a - b), \tag{17}$$

with

$$M_x = \begin{bmatrix} \dfrac{\partial g_1}{\partial x}(c_1) \\ \vdots \\ \dfrac{\partial g_n}{\partial x}(c_n) \end{bmatrix}, \tag{18}$$

where $c_1, \ldots, c_n \in \mathrm{Co}(a, b)$, $c_i \neq a$, $c_i \neq b$, $i = 1, \ldots, n$. Assuming that

$$\bar{a}_{i,j} \geq \frac{\partial g_i}{\partial x_j} \geq \underline{a}_{i,j}, \quad i = 1, \ldots, n, \quad j = 1, \ldots, n, \tag{19}$$

it is clear that:

$$\mathbb{M}_x = \left\{ M \in \mathbb{R}^{n \times n} | \bar{a}_{i,j} \geq m_{x,i,j} \geq \underline{a}_{i,j}, \; i,j = 1, \ldots, n, \right\} \tag{20}$$

Thus, using (17), the term $A_1e_k + Gs_k$ in (14) can be written as

$$A_1e_k + Gs_k = (\bar{A} + GM_{x,k} - K_oC)e_k \tag{21}$$

where $M_{x,k} \in \mathbb{M}_x$. From (21), it can be deduced that the state estimation error can be converted into an equivalent form

$$e_{k+1} = A_2(\alpha)e_k + \bar{W}_1w_k + \bar{W}_2w_{k+1}, \tag{22}$$
$$A_2(\alpha) = \tilde{A}(\alpha) - K_oC,$$

which defines an LPV polytopic system ([7]) with

$$\tilde{\mathbb{A}} = \left\{ \tilde{A}(\alpha) : \quad \tilde{A}(\alpha) = \sum_{i=1}^{N} \alpha_i \tilde{A}_i, \sum_{i=1}^{N} \alpha_i = 1, \alpha_i \geq 0 \right\}, \tag{23}$$

where $N = 2^{n^2}$. Note that this is a general description, which does not take into account that some elements of $M_{x,k}$ maybe constant. In such cases, N is given by $N = 2^{(n-c)^2}$ where c stands for the number of constant elements of $M_{x,k}$.

In a similar fashion, (16) can be converted into

$$\varepsilon_{fa,k} = -HC \left(A_3(\alpha)e_k + W_1 w_k \right) - HW_2 w_{k+1}, \tag{24}$$

with

$$\mathbb{A}_3 = \left\{ A_3(\alpha) : \quad A_3(\alpha) = \sum_{i=1}^{N} \alpha_i A_{3,i}, \sum_{i=1}^{N} \alpha_i = 1, \alpha_i \geq 0 \right\}. \tag{25}$$

The objective of further deliberations is to design the observer (13) in such a way that the state estimation error e_k is asymptotically convergent and the following upper bound is guaranteed

$$\|\varepsilon_f\|_{l_2} \leq \omega \|\mathbf{w}\|_{l_2} \tag{26}$$

where $\omega > 0$ is a prescribed disturbance attenuation level. Thus, on the contrary to the approaches presented in the literature, ω should be achieved with respect to the fault estimation error but not the state estimation error.

Thus, the problem of $\mathcal{H}_\infty$ observer design ([14]) is to determine the gain matrix K_o such that

$$\lim_{k \to \infty} e_k = 0 \quad \text{for } w_k = 0, \tag{27}$$

$$\|\varepsilon_f\|_{l_2} \leq \omega \|\mathbf{w}\|_{l_2} \quad \text{for } w_k \neq 0, \, e_0 = 0. \tag{28}$$

In order to settle the above problem it is sufficient to find a Lyapunov function V_k such that:

$$\Delta V_k + \varepsilon_{fa,k}^T \varepsilon_{fa,k} - \mu^2 w_k^T w_k - \mu^2 w_{k+1}^T w_{k+1} < 0, k = 0, \ldots \infty, \tag{29}$$

where $\Delta V_k = V_{k+1} - V_k$, $\mu > 0$.

Indeed, if $w_k = 0$, $(k = 0, \ldots, \infty)$ then (29) boils down to

$$\Delta V_k + \varepsilon_{fa,k}^T \varepsilon_{fa,k} < 0, \, k = 0, \ldots \infty, \tag{30}$$

and hence $\Delta V_k < 0$, which leads to (27). If $w_k \neq 0$ $(k = 0, \ldots, \infty)$ then (29) yields

$$J = \sum_{k=0}^{\infty} \left(\Delta V_k + \varepsilon_{fa,k}^T \varepsilon_{fa,k} - \mu^2 w_k^T w_k - \mu^2 w_{k+1}^T w_{k+1} \right) < 0, \tag{31}$$

which can be written as

$$J = -V_0 + \sum_{k=0}^{\infty} \varepsilon_{f_a,k}^T \varepsilon_{f_a,k} - \mu^2 \sum_{k=0}^{\infty} w_k^T w_k - \mu^2 \sum_{k=0}^{\infty} w_{k+1}^T w_{k+1} < 0. \qquad (32)$$

Bearing in mind that

$$\mu^2 \sum_{k=0}^{\infty} w_{k+1}^T w_{k+1} = \mu^2 \sum_{k=0}^{\infty} w_k^T w_k - \mu^2 w_0^T w_0, \qquad (33)$$

inequality (32) can be written as

$$J = -V_0 + \sum_{k=0}^{\infty} \varepsilon_{f_a,k}^T \varepsilon_{f_a,k} - 2\mu^2 \sum_{k=0}^{\infty} w_k^T w_k + \mu^2 w_0^T w_0 < 0. \qquad (34)$$

Knowing that $V_0 = 0$ for $e_0 = 0$, (34) leads to (28) with $\omega = \sqrt{2}\mu$.

Since the general framework for designing the robust observer is given, then the following form of the Lyapunov function is proposed ([13]):

$$V_k = e_k^T P(\alpha) e_k, \qquad (35)$$

where $P(\alpha) \succ 0$. On the contrary to the design approach presented in the literature (see, e.g. ([14])) and the references therein) it is not assumed that $P(\alpha) = P$ is constant. Indeed, $P(\alpha)$ can be perceived as a parameter-depended matrix of the form (cf. ([7]))

$$P(\alpha) = \sum_{i=1}^{N} \alpha_i P_i. \qquad (36)$$

As a consequence:

$$\Delta V_k + \varepsilon_{f_a,k}^T \varepsilon_{f_a,k} - \mu^2 w_k^T w_k - \mu^2 w_{k+1}^T w_{k+1} =$$
$$e_k^T \left(A_2(\alpha)^T P(\alpha) A_2(\alpha) + A_3(\alpha)^T H_1 A_3(\alpha) - P(\alpha) \right) e_k +$$
$$e_k^T \left(A_2(\alpha)^T P(\alpha) \bar{W}_1 + A_3(\alpha)^T H_1 W_1 \right) w_k +$$
$$e_k^T \left(A_2(\alpha)^T P(\alpha) \bar{W}_2 + A_3(\alpha)^T H_2 \right) w_{k+1} +$$
$$w_k^T \left(\bar{W}_1^T P(\alpha) A_2(\alpha) + W_1^T H_1 A_3(\alpha) \right) e_k +$$
$$w_k^T \left(\bar{W}_1^T P(\alpha) \bar{W}_1 + W_1^T H_1 W_1 - \mu^2 I \right) w_k +$$
$$w_k^T \left(\bar{W}_1^T P(\alpha) W_2 + W_1^T H_2 \right) w_{k+1} +$$
$$w_{k+1}^T \left(\bar{W}_2^T P(\alpha) A_{2,k} + H_2^T A_3(\alpha) \right) e_k +$$
$$w_{k+1}^T \left(\bar{W}_2^T P(\alpha) W_1 + H_2^T W_1 \right) w_k +$$
$$w_{k+1}^T \left(\bar{W}_2^T P(\alpha) \bar{W}_2 + W_2^T H^T H W_2 - \mu^2 I \right) w_{k+1} < 0.$$

with $H_1 = C^T H^T HC$ and $H_2 = C^T H^T HW_2$.

By defining

$$v_k = \left[e_k^T, w_k^T, w_{k+1}^T \right]^T \tag{37}$$

inequality (37) becomes

$$\Delta V_k + \varepsilon_{f_a,k}^T \varepsilon_{f_a,k} - \mu^2 w_k^T w_k - \mu^2 w_{k+1}^T w_{k+1} = v_k^T M_V v_k < 0, \tag{38}$$

where M_V is given by (39).

$$M_V = \begin{bmatrix} A_2(\alpha)^T P(\alpha) A_2(\alpha) + A_3(\alpha)^T H_1 A_3(\alpha) - P(\alpha) & A_2(\alpha)^T P(\alpha) \bar{W}_1 + A_3(\alpha)^T H_1 W_1 \\ \bar{W}_1^T P(\alpha) A_2(\alpha) + W_1^T H_1 A_3(\alpha) & \bar{W}_1^T P(\alpha) \bar{W}_1 + W_1^T H_1 W_1 - \mu^2 I \\ \bar{W}_2^T P(\alpha) A_2(\alpha) + H_2^T A_3(\alpha) & \bar{W}_2^T P(\alpha) W_1 + H_2^T W_1 \end{bmatrix}$$
$$\begin{bmatrix} A_2(\alpha)^T P(\alpha) \bar{W}_2 + A_3(\alpha)^T H_2 \\ \bar{W}_1^T P(\alpha) W_2 + W_1^T H_2 \\ \bar{W}_2^T P(\alpha) \bar{W}_2 + W_2^T H^T HW_2 - \mu^2 I \end{bmatrix}. \tag{39}$$

The following theorem constitutes the main result of this section:

Theorem 1. *For a prescribed disturbance attenuation level $\mu > 0$ for the fault estimation error (16), the $\mathcal{H}_\infty$ observer design problem for the system (5)–(6) and the observer (13) is solvable if there exists matrices $P_i \succ 0$ $(i = 1, \ldots, N)$, U and N such that the following LMIs are satisfied:*

$$\begin{bmatrix} A_{3,i}^T H_1 A_{3,i} - P_i & A_{3,i}^T H_1 W_1 & A_{3,i}^T H_3 & A_{2,i} U^T \\ W_1^T H_1 A_{3,i} & W_1^T H_1 W_1 - \mu^2 I & W_1^T H_2 & \bar{W}_1^T U^T \\ H_2^T A_{3,i} & H_2^T W_1 & W_2^T H^T HW_2 - \mu^2 I & \bar{W}_2^T U^T \\ U A_{2,i} & U \bar{W}_1 & U \bar{W}_2 & P_i - U - U^T \end{bmatrix} \prec 0,$$
$$i = 1, \ldots, N. \tag{40}$$

where (cf. (23) and (14))

$$U A_{2,i} = U(\tilde{A}_i - K_o C) = U \tilde{A}_i - NC, \tag{41}$$
$$U \bar{W}_1 = U(GW_1 - K_o W_2) = UGW_1 - NW_2. \tag{42}$$

Proof. The following lemma can be perceived as the generalisation of this presented in ([7]).

Lemma 1. *The following statements are equivalent*

i) *There exists $X(\alpha) \succ 0$ such that*

$$V(\alpha)^T X(\alpha) V(\alpha) - W(\alpha) \prec 0, \tag{43}$$

ii) *There exists $X(\alpha) \succ 0$ such that*

$$\begin{bmatrix} -W(\alpha) & V(\alpha)^T U^T \\ UV(\alpha) & X(\alpha) - U - U^T \end{bmatrix} \prec 0. \tag{44}$$

Proof. For proof, see [12].

It is easy to show that (44) is satisfied if there exist matrices $\boldsymbol{X}_i \succ \boldsymbol{0}$ such that

$$
\begin{bmatrix} -\boldsymbol{W}_i & \boldsymbol{V}_i^T \boldsymbol{U}^T \\ \boldsymbol{U}\boldsymbol{V}_i & \boldsymbol{X}_i - \boldsymbol{U} - \boldsymbol{U}^T \end{bmatrix} \prec \boldsymbol{0}, \quad i = 1, \ldots, N. \tag{45}
$$

Subsequently, observing that the matrix (39) must be negative definite and writing it as

$$
\begin{bmatrix} \boldsymbol{A}_2(\alpha)^T \\ \bar{\boldsymbol{W}}_1^T \\ \bar{\boldsymbol{W}}_2^T \end{bmatrix} \boldsymbol{P}(\alpha) \begin{bmatrix} \boldsymbol{A}_2(\alpha) & \bar{\boldsymbol{W}}_1 & \bar{\boldsymbol{W}}_2 \end{bmatrix} + \tag{46}
$$

$$
\begin{bmatrix} \boldsymbol{A}_3(\alpha)^T \boldsymbol{H}_1 \boldsymbol{A}_3(\alpha) - \boldsymbol{P}(\alpha) & \boldsymbol{A}_3(\alpha)^T \boldsymbol{H}_1 \boldsymbol{W}_1 & \boldsymbol{A}_3(\alpha)^T \boldsymbol{H}_3 \\ \boldsymbol{W}_1^T \boldsymbol{H}_1 \boldsymbol{A}_3(\alpha) & \boldsymbol{W}_1^T \boldsymbol{H}_1 \boldsymbol{W}_1 - \mu^2 \boldsymbol{I} & \boldsymbol{W}_1^T \boldsymbol{H}_2 \\ \boldsymbol{H}_2^T \boldsymbol{A}_3(\alpha) & \boldsymbol{H}_2^T \boldsymbol{W}_1 & \boldsymbol{W}_2^T \boldsymbol{H}^T \boldsymbol{H} \boldsymbol{W}_2 - \mu^2 \boldsymbol{I} \end{bmatrix} \prec 0. \tag{47}
$$

and then applying Lemma 1 and (45) leads to (40), which completes the proof.

Finally, the design procedure boils down to solving LMIs (40) and then (cf. (41)–(42)) $\boldsymbol{K}_o = \boldsymbol{U}^{-1} \boldsymbol{N}$.

It can be also observed that the observer design problem can be treated as an minimization task, i.e.

$$
\mu^* = \min_{\mu > 0, \boldsymbol{P}_1 \succ \boldsymbol{0}, \boldsymbol{U}, \boldsymbol{N}} \mu \tag{48}
$$

under (40).

4   Controller Design

The objective of this section is to design the control strategy $\boldsymbol{u}_{f,k}$ for (5)–(6) the tracking error

$$
\boldsymbol{e}_k = \boldsymbol{x}_k - \boldsymbol{x}_{f,k}, \tag{49}
$$

will be asymptotically convergent with guaranteeing the prescribed disturbance attenuation level. To achieve this goal, the following control strategy is proposed:

$$
\boldsymbol{u}_{f,k} = -\hat{\boldsymbol{f}}_{k-1} + \boldsymbol{K}_c(\boldsymbol{x}_k - \hat{\boldsymbol{x}}_{f,k}) + \boldsymbol{K}_2 \boldsymbol{\gamma}_k + \boldsymbol{u}_k. \tag{50}
$$

Taking into account the problems with one-step fault prediction, the following assumption is imposed

$$
\hat{\boldsymbol{f}}_k = \hat{\boldsymbol{f}}_{k-1} + \bar{\boldsymbol{v}}_k, \quad \bar{\boldsymbol{v}}_k \in l_2. \tag{51}
$$

Bearing in mind that all faults present in the real systems have a finite value, such an assumption is fully justified. Thus, for the convergence analysis, the following form of the FTC control is used

$$
\boldsymbol{u}_{f,k} = -\hat{\boldsymbol{f}}_{k-1} - \bar{\boldsymbol{v}}_k + \boldsymbol{K}_c(\boldsymbol{x}_k - \hat{\boldsymbol{x}}_{f,k}) + \boldsymbol{K}_2 \boldsymbol{\gamma}_k + \boldsymbol{u}_k, \tag{52}
$$

where

$$\gamma_k = g\left(x_k\right) - g\left(\hat{x}_{f,k}\right). \tag{53}$$

Using a similar approach as in Section 3 and setting $K_2 = HC$, the tracking error becomes:

$$e_k = A_1 e_k + \left(BHCA - BK_c\right)e_{f,k} + G\omega_k + \tilde{W}\bar{w}_k, \tag{54}$$

with $K_2 = HC$, $A_1 = A - BK_c$ and $H = (CB)^+$, where

$$\tilde{W} = [B, \ [BHC - I]\,W], \quad \bar{w}_k = \begin{bmatrix} \bar{v}_k \\ w_k \end{bmatrix}, \quad \omega_k = g\left(x_k\right) - g\left(x_{f,k}\right).$$

Using the same arguments as in Sec. 3, the convergence analysis can be relaxed to the following form of the tracking error

$$e_{k+1} = A_1 e_k + Gs_k + \bar{W}_1 w_k + \bar{W}_2 w_{k+1}, \tag{55}$$

Similarly as in Sec. 3, (55) can be expressed as:

$$e_{k+1} = A_2(\alpha)e_k + \bar{W}_1 w_k + \bar{W}_2 w_{k+1}, \tag{56}$$

$$A_2(\alpha) = \left(A(\alpha) - BK_c\right)e_k, \tag{57}$$

with

$$\mathbb{A} = \left\{ A(\alpha): \quad A(\alpha) = \sum_{i=1}^{N} \alpha_i A_i, \ \sum_{i=1}^{N} \alpha_i = 1, \ \alpha_i \geq 0 \right\}. \tag{58}$$

The following theorem constitutes the main result of the present section.

Theorem 2. *For a prescribed disturbance attenuation level $\mu > 0$ for the tracking error (55), the $\mathcal{H}_\infty$ controller design problem (52) for the system (5)–(6) is solvable if there exist $P \succ 0$, U, V such that the following LMIs are satisfied:*

$$\begin{bmatrix} I - P_i & 0 & 0 & A_{2,i}U \\ 0 & -\mu^2 I & 0 & \tilde{W}_1 U \\ 0 & 0 & \mu^2 I & \tilde{W}_2 U \\ U^T A_{2,i}^T & U^T \tilde{W}_1^T & U^T \tilde{W}_2^T & P_i - U - U^T \end{bmatrix} \prec 0,, \quad i = 1,\ldots,N.$$

with

$$A_{2,i}U = \left(\tilde{A}_i - BK_c\right)U = \tilde{A}_i U - BV. \tag{59}$$

Proof. The proof is similar to the one of Theorem 1.

Thus, the final design procedure is: given a prescribed disturbance attenuation level μ, obtain $P \succ 0$, U, V by solving (59). Finally, the gain matrix of the FTC controller is:

$$K_c = VU^{-1}. \tag{60}$$

5   Illustrative Example

The objective of this section is to provide an illustrative example regarding the proposed robust FTC. The presented example is based on the wind turbine collected data provided in [9]. Note that the analytical model given in [9] is not used. The model was obtained using the artificial neural network, presented in Section 2. The proposed neural network was trained using Levenberg-Marquardt backpropagation algorithm. 70% of the data set gathered from the system was taken as a training set, 15% as validation set and 15% as testing set. Figure 2 presents the performance of the neural network. The training process stops after 12 iterations which confirms, that prescribed Mean Squared Error level is reached. In figure 3 the result of neural network modelling is presented. It is clear, that the neural model reflects real system satisfactorily.

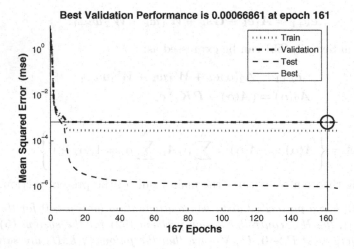

Fig. 2. Neural network performance

The considered fault is the 30% reduced pressure in hydraulic pitch system.

The simulation results of the fault-tolerant controller are compared to the results of the reference controller in figure 4. The FTC is designed to manage low pressure in the pitch system, which is not the case for the reference controller that performs poorly in the fault case, showing the oscillations in the control signal. It is clear, that the LPV controller performs significantly better than the reference controller in the fault case. The pitch usage is higher for reference controller than for fault-tolerant controller.

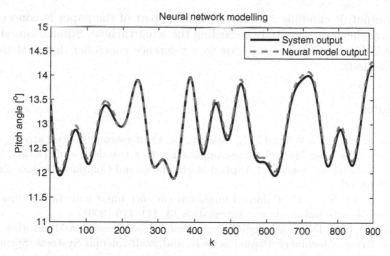

Fig. 3. System and neural model output for the pitch angle (validation set)

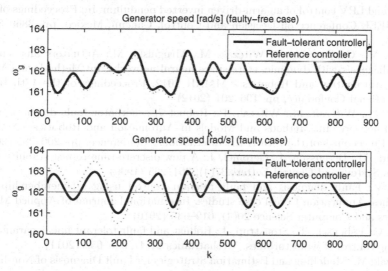

Fig. 4. Simulation results of the fault-tolerant controller (solid line) and the reference controller (dotted line) at both normal and low pressure in the hydraulic pitch system

6 Conclusions

The paper deals with the problem of robust FTC for a class on non-linear systems. In particular, a combination of the celebrated generalised observer scheme with the robust $\mathcal{H}_\infty$ approach is proposed to settle the problem of robust fault diagnosis. The proposed approach is designed in such a way that a prescribed disturbance attenuation level is achieved with respect to the actuator fault estimation error while guaranteeing the convergence of the observer. Moreover, the controller design, which realises the switching strategy between observer and real actuator output, is carefully analysed. The final part of the paper is concerned with a comprehensive case study regarding the wind turbine. Simulations show that the LPV controllers are superior to a reference controller designed using classical methods.

References

1. De Oca, S., Puig, V., Witczak, M., Dziekan, L.: Fault-tolerant control strategy for actuator faults using lpv techniques: application to a two degree of freedom helicopter. International Journal of Applied Mathematics and Computer Science 22(1), 161–171 (2012)
2. Gillijns, S., De Moor, B.: Unbiased minimum-variance input and state estimation for linear discrete-time systems. Automatica 43, 111–116 (2007)
3. Iserman, R.: Fault Diagnosis Applications: Model Based Condition Monitoring, Actuators, Drives, Machinery, Plants, Sensors, and Fault-tolerant Systems. Springer, Berlin (2011)
4. Lachhab, N., Abbas, H., Werner, H.: A neural-network based technique for modelling and LPV control of an arm-driven inverted pendulum. In: Proceedings of the 47th IEEE Conference on Decision and Control, Cancun, Mexico, pp. 3860–3865 (2008)
5. Luzar, M., Czajkowski, A., Witczak, M., Mrugalski, M.: Actuators ans sensors fault diagnosis with dynamic, state-space neural networks. In: Methods and Models in Automation and Robotics - MMAR 2012: Proceedings of the 17th IEEE International Conference, pp. 196–201 (2012)
6. Luzar, M., Witczak, M., Witczak, P.: Robust $\mathcal{H}_\infty$ actuator fault diagnosis with neural network. In: Methods and Models in Automation and Robotics - MMAR 2013: Proceedings of the 18th IEEE International Conference, pp. 200–205 (2013)
7. Oliveira, M., Bernussou, J., Geromel, J.: A new discrete-time robust stability condition. System and Control Letters 37(4), 261–265 (1999)
8. Puig, V.: Fault diagnosis and fault tolerant control using set-membership approaches: Application to real case studies. International Journal of Applied Mathematics and Computer Science 20(4), 619–635 (2010)
9. Sloth, C., Esbensen, T., Stoustrup, J.: Robust and fault-tolerant linear parameter-varying control of wind turbines. Mechatronics 21(4), 645–659 (2011)
10. Witczak, M.: Modelling and Estimation Strategies for Fault Diagnosis of Non-linear Systems. Springer, Berlin (2007)
11. Witczak, M., Puig, V., Montes De Oca, S.: A fault-tolerant control strategy for non-linear discrete-time systems: application to the twin-rotor system. International Journal of Control 86(10), 1788–1799 (2013)
12. Witczak, M.: Fault Diagnosis and Fault-Tolerant Control Strategies for Non-Linear Systems. Springer, Berlin (2014)
13. Zemouche, A., Boutayeb, M.: Observer design for Lipschitz non-linear systems: the discrete time case. IEEE Trans. Circuits and Systems - II: Express Briefs 53(8), 777–781 (2006)
14. Zemouche, A., Boutayeb, M., Iulia Bara, G.: Observer for a class of Lipschitz systems with extension to $\mathcal{H}_\infty$ performance analysis. Systems and Control Letters 57(1), 18–27 (2008)

An Improved Adaptive Self-Organizing Map

Dominik Olszewski

Faculty of Electrical Engineering,
Warsaw University of Technology, Poland
dominik.olszewski@ee.pw.edu.pl

Abstract. We propose a novel adaptive Self-Organizing Map (SOM). In the introduced approach, the SOM neurons' neighborhood widths are computed adaptively using the information about the frequencies of occurrences of input patterns in the input space. The neighborhood widths are determined differently for each neuron in the SOM grid. In this way, the proposed SOM properly visualizes the input data, especially, when there are significant differences in frequencies of occurrences of input patterns. The experimental study on real data, on three different datasets, confirms the effectiveness of the proposed adaptive SOM.

Keywords: Self-Organizing Map, adaptive Self-Organizing Map, neighborhood width, Gaussian kernel, visualization.

1 Introduction

The Self-Organizing Map (SOM) [1] is an example of the artificial neural network architecture. It can be also interpreted as a visualization technique, since the algorithm performs a projection from multidimensional space to 2-dimensional space, this way creating a map structure. The location of points in 2-dimensional grid aims to reflect the similarities between the corresponding objects in multidimensional space. Therefore, the SOM algorithm allows for visualization of relationships between objects in multidimensional space.

The SOM technique is an unsupervised data analysis approach, i.e., there is no additional training data required. Although the method consists of two substantial phases, i.e., the training phase and the testing phase, both of the phases proceed using the same testing dataset. During the training phase, the weights corresponding to each neuron in the SOM grid are being computed. An important step during this process is updating of the neurons in the neighborhood of the Best Matching Unit (BMU) – the closest neuron to the currently matched input pattern. Usually, the neighborhood of the BMU is selected using the Gaussian kernel (see [1] for other choices of neighborhood functions). However, the choice of the neighborhood function parameters, and the choice of the function itself is always to some extent arbitrary, because there are no strict guidelines, and resulting optimal solutions in this matter. Therefore, any justified proposals regarding the neighborhood size of the BMU are desirable, because that choice strongly affects the quality of the final SOM visualization, and consequently, the performance of the entire analysis.

L. Rutkowski et al. (Eds.): ICAISC 2014, Part I, LNAI 8467, pp. 109–120, 2014.

1.1 Our Proposal

In this paper, we propose a method for the SOM neurons' neighborhood widths adaptive computation. The neighborhood widths are determined differently for each neuron in the SOM grid. The introduced method is based on the measurement of the frequencies of occurrences of patterns in the input space. The Gaussian kernel is employed as the neurons' neighborhood function, and the Gaussian standard deviation determining the neurons' neighborhood width is calculated adaptively on the basis of the mentioned frequency. Therefore, the whole considered SOM is an adaptive enhancement to the traditional approach. In case of input patterns appearing frequently in the input space, the corresponding BMU's neighborhood is wider than in case of input patterns occurring rarely in the input space. Consequently, the proposed adaptive SOM reserves larger area for frequent input patterns, and smaller area for rare input patterns. In this way, the novel SOM properly visualizes input data, especially, when there are significant differences in frequencies of occurrences of input patterns in the input space. As a result, the entire visualization comprising the final result will reflect the input data more accurately.

2 Related Work

The SOM visualization technique has been extensively studied, and numerous improvements and extensions have been developed, including the Growing Hierarchical SOM (GHSOM) [2], the asymmetric SOM [3, 4], the supervised SOM [5], and the adaptive SOM [6–11], to name a few. Naturally, the adaptive SOM versions are of particular interest for the purposes of our research.

In the paper [11], a statistical iterative Gaussian kernel smoothing problem is considered. The authors propose a batch SOM algorithm consisting of two steps. In the first step, the training data are partitioned according to the Voronoi regions of the map unit locations. In the second step, the units are updated by taking weighted centroids of the data falling into the Voronoi regions, with the weighing function given by the neighborhood. The neighborhood width is decreased in each iteration of the algorithm. The difference between the approach from the work [11] and the method developed in our paper is that in [11], the neighborhood width is being constantly decreased exponentially according to the adaptation rule (4) introduced in [11], while in our work, the neighborhood width is adapted to a given dataset depending on the dataset's specific properties.

In the paper [10], an Adaptive Double SOM (ADSOM) is proposed. The constructed map is designed for subsequent clustering analysis without requiring of a priori knowledge about the number of clusters. ADSOM updates its free parameters and allows convergence of its position vectors to a fairly consistent number of clusters provided its initial number of nodes is greater than the expected number of clusters.

The paper [9] proposes a Time Adaptive SOM (TASOM). The work, together with the paper [11], is especially important in the context of our research, because it also introduces a method of neurons neighborhood size adaptive computation.

In the approach proposed in [9], every neuron has its own learning rate and neighborhood size. The difference between the solution from [9] and our method is following. In [9], the adaptation of the neighborhood size results from the "closed-loop" learning of the parameter, i.e., the neighborhood size is updated on the basis of the final quality of visualization (so as to minimize an appropriate error function). Consequently, a learning process is a necessary stage of that analysis. On the other hand, in case of our approach, the neighborhood size is computed in the "open-loop" system, only on the basis of the input dataset analysis (i.e., measurement of frequencies of occurrences of input patterns). No learning process is required, and the method does not rely on the final results of the visualization. Consequently, no additional error function is necessary.

In the work [8], an adaptive hierarchical structure called "Binary Tree TASOM" (BTASOM) is introduced. The considered SOM enhancement resembles a binary natural tree having nodes composed of TASOM networks. The BTASOM is proposed to make TASOM fast and adaptive in the number of its neurons.

The paper [7] proposes an adaptive incremental learning algorithm of the SOM weights. According to the algorithm, the SOM weights are updated incrementally using a higher-order difference equation, which implements a low-pass digital filter.

Finally, in the paper [6], an adaptive GHSOM-based approach (A-GHSOM) is introduced as an effective technique to deal with the anomaly detection problem. As the authors claim, their GHSOM enhancement can adapt on-line to the ever-changing anomaly detection. Consequently, according to the authors, A-GHSOM is superior over the standard GHSOM-based methods, and it provides higher accuracy in identifying intrusions, particularly "unknown" attacks.

3   Traditional Self-Organizing Map

The SOM algorithm provides a non-linear mapping between a high-dimensional original data space and a 2-dimensional map of neurons. The neurons are arranged according to a regular grid, in such a way that the similar vectors in input space are represented by the neurons close in the grid. Therefore, the SOM technique visualizes the data associations in the input high-dimensional space.

It was shown in [12] that the results obtained by the SOM method are equivalent to the results obtained by optimizing the following error function:

$$e\left(\mathcal{W}\right) = \sum_r \sum_{x_\mu \in V_r} \sum_s h_{rs} D\left(x_\mu, \, w_s\right) \tag{1}$$

$$\approx \sum_r \sum_{x_\mu \in V_r} D\left(x_\mu, \, w_r\right) + K \sum_r \sum_{s \neq r} h_{rs} D\left(w_r, \, w_s\right), \tag{2}$$

where x_μ are the objects in high-dimensional space, w_r and w_s are the prototypes of objects in the grid, h_{rs} is a neighborhood function (e.g., the Gaussian kernel) that transforms non-linearly the neuron distances (see [1] for other choices of neighborhood functions), $D(\cdot,\cdot)$ is the squared Euclidean distance, and V_r is the Voronoi region corresponding to prototype w_r. The number of prototypes is sufficiently large so that $D(x_\mu, w_s) \approx D(x_\mu, w_r) + D(w_r, w_s)$.

According to (2), the SOM error function can be decomposed as the sum of the quantization error and the topological error. The first one minimizes the loss of information, when the input patterns are represented by a set of prototypes. By minimizing the second one, we assure the maximal correlation between the prototype dissimilarities and the corresponding neuron distances, this way assuring the visualization of the data relationships in the input space.

The SOM error function can be optimized by an iterative algorithm consisting of two steps (discussed in [12]). First, a quantization algorithm is executed. This algorithm represents each input pattern by the nearest neighbor prototype. This operation minimizes the first component in (2). Next, the prototypes are arranged along the grid of neurons by minimizing the second component in the error function. This optimization problem can be solved explicitly using the following adaptation rule for each prototype [1]:

$$w_s = \frac{\sum_{r=1}^{M}\sum_{x_\mu \in V_r} h_{rs} x_\mu}{\sum_{r=1}^{M}\sum_{x_\mu \in V_r} h_{rs}}, \tag{3}$$

where M is the number of neurons, and h_{rs} is a neighborhood function (for example, the Gaussian kernel of width $\sigma(t)$). The width of the kernel is adapted in each iteration of the algorithm using the rule proposed by [11], i.e.,

$$\sigma(t) = \sigma_m (\sigma_f/\sigma_m)^{t/N_{iter}}, \tag{4}$$

where $\sigma_m \approx M/2$ is typically assumed in the literature (for example, in [1]), and σ_f is the parameter that determines the smoothing degree of the principal curve generated by the SOM algorithm [11].

4   A Novel Adaptive Self-Organizing Map

In this paper, we propose a novel adaptation rule of the SOM neurons' neighborhood widths. The neighborhood widths are determined differently for each neuron in the SOM grid. The proposed rule employs the exponential update (4) from the work [11], includes the information about the frequencies of occurrences of all input patterns, and consequently, provides a more accurate and effective adaptation process than the rule (4) itself.

The SOM neurons' neighborhood widths are adapted in our research using the Gaussian kernels of the following standard deviation:

$$\sigma_i(|x_i|, t) = \frac{|x_i|}{\max_j(|x_j|)}\sigma_m (\sigma_f/\sigma_m)^{t/N_{iter}}, \tag{5}$$

where x_i, $i = 1, \ldots, n$ is a vector of features representing the ith object in analyzed dataset, $j = 1, \ldots, n$, n is the total number of objects, $|\cdot|$ is the L_1-norm meaning the number of objects given as the argument, and the rest of the notation is explained in (4).

By utilizing the information about the frequencies of occurrences of input patterns, the method proposed in this paper exploits the specific nature and character of a given dataset, and this way, it visualizes the dataset in the SOM grid more accurately by better adjusting to the dataset features and properties.

If the Gaussian kernels specifying the SOM neurons' neighborhood width are fitted to the frequencies of occurrences of input patterns, then the resulting SOM will assign the wider neighborhoods (i.e., the larger area in the SOM grid) to the neurons corresponding to the input patterns appearing more frequently in the input space, and likewise, the obtained SOM will assign the narrower neighborhoods (i.e., the smaller area in the SOM grid) to the neurons corresponding to the input patterns appearing less frequently in the input space.

The desirable consequence of this phenomenon is that the proposed improved adaptive SOM is dataset-dependent, and therefore, it reflects properly the relationships between input patterns, especially if the input dataset is highly diverse with respect to the input patterns' frequencies of occurrences.

5   Experiments

In our experimental study, we have evaluated effectiveness of the proposed improved adaptive SOM technique by conducting the clustering process in the SOM grid obtained using the proposed approach and in the SOM grid returned by a reference method. As the reference method, we have used the traditional time adaptive SOM technique. As the clustering method, we have employed the standard well-known k-means clustering algorithm with the correct number of clusters provided a priori as the input data. Clustering process has been carried out in the 2-dimensional space of the SOM grid. The experimental research aims to ascertain the superiority of the introduced adaptive SOM on the basis of the comparison of the clustering results obtained using the proposed SOM and the classical one. The experiments have been conducted on real data in the three different research fields: in the field of words clustering, in the field of sound signals clustering, and in the field of human heart rhythm signals clustering. The first part of the experimental study has been carried out on the large dataset of high-dimensionality (Subsection 5.3), while the remaining two experimental parts have been conducted on smaller datasets, but also of high-dimensionality (Subsection 5.4 and Subsection 5.5). In this way, one can assess the performance of the investigated methods operating on datasets of different size and nature, and consequently, one can better evaluate the effectiveness of the proposed approach.

The sound signals visualization and clustering was carried out on the piano music recordings, and the human heart rhythm signals analysis was conducted using the ECG recordings derived from the MIT-BIH ECG Databases [13].

In case of the piano music dataset and the ECG recordings dataset, a graphical illustration of the U-matrices generated by SOM is provided, while in case of the "Bag of Words" dataset no such illustration is given, because of the high number of instances in that dataset, which would make such images unreadable.

5.1 Evaluation Criteria

As the basis of the comparisons between the investigated methods, i.e., as the clustering evaluation criteria, we have used the accuracy rate [4, 14] and the uncertainty degree [4]:

1. **Accuracy rate.** This evaluation criterion determines the number of correctly assigned objects divided by the total number of objects.
   Hence, for the entire dataset, the accuracy rate is determined as follows:

$$q = \frac{m}{n}, \tag{6}$$

   where m is the number of correctly assigned objects, and n is the total number of objects in the entire dataset.
   The accuracy rates q_i and the accuracy rate q assume values in the interval $\langle 0, 1 \rangle$, and naturally, greater values are preferred.
   The accuracy rate q was used in our experimental study as the main basis of the clustering accuracy comparison of the three investigated approaches.

2. **Uncertainty degree.** This evaluation criterion determines the number of overlapping objects divided by the total number of objects in a dataset. This means, the number of objects, which are in the overlapping area between clusters, divided by the total number of objects. The objects belonging to the overlapping area are determined on the basis of the ratio of dissimilarities between them and the two nearest clusters centroids. If this ratio is in the interval $\langle 0.9, 1.1 \rangle$, then the corresponding object is said to be in the overlapping area.
   The uncertainty degree is determined as follows:

$$U_d = \frac{\mu}{n}, \tag{7}$$

   where μ is the number of overlapping objects in the dataset, and n is the total number of objects in the dataset.
   The uncertainty degree assumes values in the interval $\langle 0, 1 \rangle$, and, smaller values are desired.

5.2 Feature Extraction

Features of the time series considered in Subsection 5.4 and Subsection 5.5 have been extracted using a method based on the discrete Fourier transform (DFT), which is described in details in [15].

5.3   Words Visualization and Clustering

In the first part of our experimental study, we have utilized excerpts from the "Bag of Words" dataset from the UCI Machine Learning Repository [16]. It is a high-dimensional dataset of strongly asymmetric nature, especially useful in case of the asymmetric data relationships analysis. It is so, because significant differences in frequencies of occurrences of different words in the entire dataset. Therefore, the experimental investigation on the "Bag of Words" dataset clearly shows the superiority of the proposed asymmetric approach over its traditional symmetric counterpart.

Dataset Description. The "Bag of Words" dataset consists of five text collections: Enron E-mail Collection, Neural Information Processing Systems (NIPS) full papers, Daily KOS Blog Entries, New York Times News Articles, PubMed Abstracts. The total number of analyzed words was approximately 10,868,000. In the SOM grids generated by the investigated methods, five clusters representing those five text collections in the "Bag of Words" dataset were formed.

Text Feature Extraction. Feature extraction of the textual data investigated in this part of our experimental study was carried out using the term frequency – inverse document frequency (tf-idf) approach. The Vector Space Model (VSM) constructed in this way is particularly useful in our research, because it implicitly captures the terms frequency (both: local – document-dependent and global – collection-dependent), which are the source of the hierarchy-based asymmetric relationships in analyzed data (i.e., in this case, between words).

The dimensionality of the analyzed VSM model (i.e., the number of features) was chosen as the minimal length of the vocabularies in the five considered text collections. Consequently, the number of features utilized in this part of our experimental study was 6,906. It was necessary to truncate the longer vocabularies in order to build the data matrix comprising the analyzed VSM model. As a result, not all of the words in the remaining four text collections have been taken into account. Nevertheless, the considered experimental problem remains a high-dimensionality issue, and the number and variety of the words in the analyzed vocabularies makes the problem complex and challenging. Of course, also the highly-asymmetric nature of the investigated dataset is preserved.

Experimental Results. The results of this part of our experiments are reported in Tables 1 and 2, where the accuracy rates corresponding to each investigated approach are presented.

The average (arithmetic average) numbers of words assigned to correct clusters reported in Table 1 and words located in the overlapping areas in Table 2 (in numerators of the ratio fractions) were rounded to the nearest integer values.

The results of this part of our experimental study show that clustering of the SOM grid obtained using the introduced adaptive method outperforms clustering of the SOM grid returned by the standard adaptive approach. The proposed approach leads to the higher clustering accuracy measured on the basis of the

Table 1. Accuracy rates of the words clustering

	q
Traditional adaptive SOM	$8,389,009/10,868,000 = 0.7719$
Proposed adaptive SOM	$9,183,822/10,868,000 = 0.8450$

Table 2. Uncertainty degrees of the words clustering

	U_d
Traditional adaptive SOM	$2,304,016/10,868,000 = 0.2120$
Proposed adaptive SOM	$1,523,182/10,868,000 = 0.1402$

accuracy rate, and also to the lower clustering uncertainty measured on the basis of the uncertainty degree.

5.4   Piano Music Composer Visualization and Clustering

In this part of our experiments, we considered three clusters representing three piano music composers: Johann Sebastian Bach, Ludwig van Beethoven, and Fryderyk Chopin.

Dataset Description. Each music piece was represented by a 30-seconds sound signal sampled with the 44100 Hz frequency. The entire dataset consisted of 70 sound signals. Feature extraction process was carried out according to the Discrete-Fourier-Transform-based (DFT-based) method described in Subsection 5.2.

Experimental Results. The results of this part of our experiments are demonstrated in Fig. 1, and in Tables 3 and 4. Figure 1 presents the maps (U-matrices) generated by the symmetric (Fig. 1(a)) and asymmetric (Fig. 1(b)) SOM techniques. The U-matrix is a graphical presentation of SOM. Each entry of the U-matrix corresponds to a neuron in the SOM grid, while value of that entry is the average dissimilarity between the neuron and its neighbors. Table 3, in turn, presents the accuracy rates, while Table 4 reports the uncertainty degrees corresponding to each of the examined approaches.

The average (arithmetic average) numbers of signals assigned to correct clusters reported in Table 3 and signals located in the overlapping areas in Table 4 (in numerators of the ratio fractions) were rounded to the nearest integer values.

Also in this part of our experiments, the proposal of this paper appeared to be superior over the other examined adaptive visualization technique.

5.5   Human Heart Rhythms Visualization and Clustering

The human heart rhythm signals clustering experiment was carried out on the dataset of ECG recordings derived from the MIT-BIH ECG Databases [13].

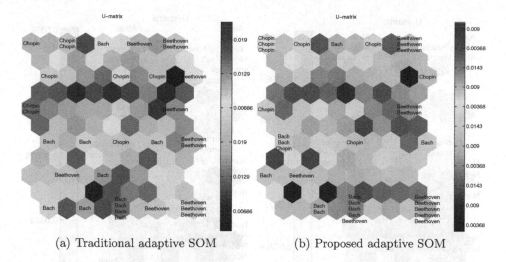

(a) Traditional adaptive SOM   (b) Proposed adaptive SOM

Fig. 1. Piano Music Composers Maps (U-matrices)

Table 3. Accuracy rates of the piano music composer clustering

	q
Traditional adaptive SOM	$27/32 = 0.8438$
Proposed adaptive SOM	$31/32 = 0.9688$

In this part of our experiments, we considered three clusters representing three types of human heart rhythms: normal sinus rhythm, atrial arrhythmia, and ventricular arrhythmia. This kind of clustering can be interpreted as the cardiac arrhythmia detection and recognition based on the ECG recordings.

Dataset Description. Our clustering recognizes the normal rhythm, and also, recognizes arrhythmias originating in the atria, and in the ventricles.

We analyzed 20-minutes ECG holter recordings sampled with the 250 Hz frequency. The entire dataset consisted of 63 ECG signals. Feature extraction was carried out according to the DFT-based method described in Subsection 5.2.

Table 4. Uncertainty degrees of the piano music composer clustering

	U_d
Traditional adaptive SOM	$8/32 = 0.2500$
Proposed adaptive SOM	$1/32 = 0.0313$

Experimental Results. The results of this part of our experiments are presented in Fig. 2, and in Tables 5 and 6, which are constructed in the same way as in Subsection 5.4.

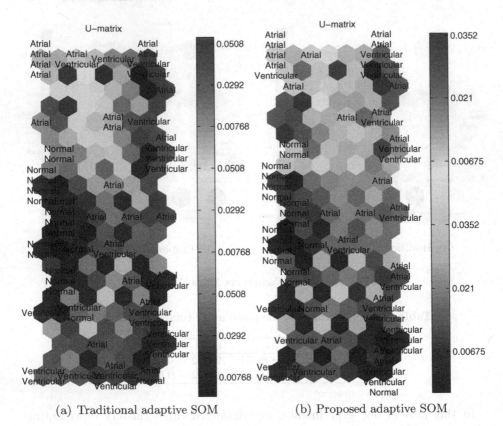

(a) Traditional adaptive SOM   (b) Proposed adaptive SOM

Fig. 2. Human Heart Rhythms Maps (U-matrices)

Table 5. Accuracy rates of the human heart rhythms clustering

	q
Traditional adaptive SOM	$45/63 = 0.7143$
Proposed adaptive SOM	$58/63 = 0.9206$

Table 6. Uncertainty degrees of the human heart rhythms clustering

	U_d
Traditional adaptive SOM	$18/63 = 0.2857$
Proposed adaptive SOM	$7/63 = 0.1111$

Finally, in the last part of our empirical study, the proposed adaptive SOM clustered by the k-means clustering algorithm produced results superior over the results returned by the reference method clustered using the same algorithm, confirming the usefulness and effectiveness of the proposed solution.

6 Summary

In this paper, a novel adaptive SOM version was proposed. In the introduced approach, the neurons' neighborhood widths are determined using the information about the frequencies of occurrences of input patterns in the input space. The neighborhood widths are determined differently for each neuron in the SOM grid. In case of input patterns appearing frequently in the input space, the neighborhood of the corresponding BMU is wider than in case of the input patterns occurring rarely in the input space. Consequently, the patterns frequent in the input space will receive larger area for their prototypes in the SOM grid, in contrast to the patterns rare in the input space, which will get less place for their prototypes in the grid. In this way, the proposed method provides a proper visualization of the input data, especially, when there are significant differences in the frequencies of occurrences of input patterns, and consequently, our proposal can be regarded as superior over the traditional adaptive SOM technique.

Acknowledgment. This work was prepared as a part of the statutory jobs.

References

1. Kohonen, T.: Self-Organizing Maps, 3rd edn. Springer (2001)
2. Rauber, A., Merkl, D., Dittenbach, M.: The Growing Hierarchical Self-Organizing Map: Exploratory Analysis of High-Dimensional Data. IEEE Transactions on Neural Networks 13(6), 1331–1341 (2002)
3. Olszewski, D., Kacprzyk, J., Zadrożny, S.: Time Series Visualization Using Asymmetric Self-Organizing Map. In: Tomassini, M., Antonioni, A., Daolio, F., Buesser, P. (eds.) ICANNGA 2013. LNCS, vol. 7824, pp. 40–49. Springer, Heidelberg (2013)
4. Olszewski, D.: An Experimental Study on Asymmetric Self-Organizing Map. In: Yin, H., Wang, W., Rayward-Smith, V. (eds.) IDEAL 2011. LNCS, vol. 6936, pp. 42–49. Springer, Heidelberg (2011)
5. Płoński, P., Zaremba, K.: Self-Organising Maps for Classification with Metropolis-Hastings Algorithm for Supervision. In: Huang, T., Zeng, Z., Li, C., Leung, C.S. (eds.) ICONIP 2012, Part III. LNCS, vol. 7665, pp. 149–156. Springer, Heidelberg (2012)
6. Ippoliti, D., Zhou, X.: A-GHSOM: An Adaptive Growing Hierarchical Self Organizing Map for Network Anomaly Detection. Journal of Parallel and Distributed Computing 72(12), 1576–1590 (2012)
7. Tucci, M., Raugi, M.: A Filter Based Neuron Model for Adaptive Incremental Learning of Self-Organizing Maps. Neurocomputing 74(11), 1815–1822 (2011)
8. Shah-Hosseini, H.: Binary Tree Time Adaptive Self-Organizing Map. Neurocomputing 74(11), 1823–1839 (2011)
9. Shah-Hosseini, H., Safabakhsh, R.: TASOM: A New Time Adaptive Self-Organizing Map. IEEE Transactions on Systems, Man, and Cybernetics, Part B: Cybernetics 33(2), 271–282 (2003)
10. Ressom, H., Wang, D., Natarajan, P.: Adaptive Double Self-Organizing Maps for Clustering Gene Expression Profiles. Neural Networks 16(5-6), 633–640 (2003)

11. Mulier, F., Cherkassky, V.: Self-Organization as an Iterative Kernel Smoothing Process. Neural Computation 7(6), 1165–1177 (1995)
12. Heskes, T.: Self-Organizing Maps, Vector Quantization, and Mixture Modeling. IEEE Transactions on Neural Networks 12(6), 1299–1305 (2001)
13. Goldberger, A.L., Amaral, L.A.N., Glass, L., Hausdorff, J.M., Ivanov, P.C., Mark, R.G., Mietus, J.E., Moody, G.B., Peng, C.K., Stanley, H.E.: PhysioBank, PhysioToolkit, and PhysioNet: Components of a new research resource for complex physiologic signals. Circulation 101(23), e215–e220 (2000), Circulation Electronic Pages, http://circ.ahajournals.org/cgi/content/full/101/23/e215
14. Olszewski, D.: Asymmetric k-Means Algorithm. In: Dobnikar, A., Lotrič, U., Šter, B. (eds.) ICANNGA 2011, Part II. LNCS, vol. 6594, pp. 1–10. Springer, Heidelberg (2011)
15. Olszewski, D.: k-Means Clustering of Asymmetric Data. In: Corchado, E., Snášel, V., Abraham, A., Woźniak, M., Graña, M., Cho, S.-B. (eds.) HAIS 2012, Part I. LNCS, vol. 7208, pp. 243–254. Springer, Heidelberg (2012)
16. Frank, A., Asuncion, A.: UCI machine learning repository (2010), http://archive.ics.uci.edu/ml

Usage of the TRACO Compiler
for Neural Network Parallelization

Marek Palkowski and Wlodzimierz Bielecki

West Pomeranian University of Technology in Szczecin
Faculty of Computer Science and Information Systems
Zolnierska 49, 71210 Szczecin, Poland
{mpalkowski,wbielecki}@wi.zut.edu.pl
http://www.wi.zut.edu.pl

Abstract. Artificial neural networks (ANNs) are used often to solve a
wide variety of problems using high performance computing. The paper
presents automatic loop parallelization for selected ANNs programs by
means of the TRACO compiler that permits us to extract loop dependences and produce synchronization-free slices including loop statement
instances. Coarse-grained parallelism of nested program loops is obtained
by creating a thread of computations on each processor to be executed independently. Program loops of recurrent and back-propagation networks
are analysed. The speed-up and efficiency of parallel programs produced
by means of TRACO are studied. Related compilers and ANNs parallelization techniques are considered. Future work is outlined.

Keywords: artificial neural networks, automatic loop parallelization,
iteration space slicing, multi-core processing.

1 Introduction

Artificial neural networks (ANNs) are tools for non-linear statistical data modelling. They are designed much like biological neural networks. Both comprise
a series of simple information processing units that operate in parallel. ANNs
can be used to solve a wide variety of problems while being robust to error in
training data. They have been successfully applied to pattern recognition and
classification tasks, time series prediction, data mining, function approximation,
data clustering and filtering, as well as data compression [1].

Parallel processing of neural network algorithms is an important research
issue since neural networks are large networks in practice, and they are used in
real-time applications.

The lack of automated tools permitting for exposing parallelism for multi-
core and multiprocessor systems decreases the productivity of programmers and
increases the time and cost of producing the parallel program. Because most
computations are contained in program loops, automatic extraction of parallelism from loops is extremely important, allowing us to produce parallel code
from existing sequential applications and to create multiple threads that can be
easily scheduled to achieve high program performance.

L. Rutkowski et al. (Eds.): ICAISC 2014, Part I, LNAI 8467, pp. 121–130, 2014.
© Springer International Publishing Switzerland 2014

Different techniques have been developed to extract coarse-grained parallelism that is represented with synchronization-free slices of computations available in loops, for example, those presented in papers [2, 3]. Unfortunately, these techniques very often fail to parallelize loops exposing storage-related dependences, and as consequence potential parallelism is left unexploited in some cases [4].

In this paper, we demonstrate automatic loop parallelization by means of Iteration Space Slicing (ISS) [4] implemented in the TRACO compiler. It permits for extracting coarse-grained parallelism in neural network applications. Program loops of recurrent and back-propagation networks are studied. Experimental results, exposing speed-up and efficiency of parallel programs generated by TRACO, are presented.

2   Parallelism Extraction

Iteration Space Slicing (ISS) techniques are implemented in the source-to-source TRACO compiler which applies also other techniques for loop parallelization: free-scheduling, variable privatization and parallel reduction. Output C-like code, produced by TRACO, is compilable and contains OpenMP directives [5]. TRACO is available at the website http://traco.sourceforge.net.

ISS was introduced by Pugh and Rosser [6]. It takes dependence information as input to find all statement instances that must be executed to produce the correct values for the specified array elements. Dependences of a loop nest are described by dependence relations with constraints presented by means of the Presburger arithmetic (PA) that is the first-order theory of the integers in the language L having 0, 1 as constants, $+,-$ as binary operations, and equality $=$, order $<$ and congruences $\equiv_n$ modulo all integers $n \geq 1$ as binary relations.

Coarse-grained code is presented with synchronization-free slices or with slices requiring occasional synchronization. Let us remind the basics of ISS. An (iteration-space) slice is defined as follows.

Definition 1. Given a dependence graph defined by a set of dependence relations, a slice S is a weakly connected component of this graph, i.e., a maximal subgraph such that for each pair of vertices in the subgraph there exists a forward or reverse path.

ISS requires an exact representation of loop-carried dependences and consequently an exact dependence analysis which detects a dependence if and only if it actually exists. TRACO uses the dependence analysis [7] proposed by Pugh and Wonnacott where dependences are represented by dependence relations. This analysis is implemented in Petit [8].

A dependence relation is a tuple relation of the form [*input list*]→[*output list*]: *formula*, where *input list* and *output list* are the lists of variables and/or expressions used to describe input and output tuples and *formula* describes the constraints imposed upon *input list* and *output list* and it is a Presburger formula built of constraints represented with algebraic expressions and using logical and existential operators.

Standard operations on relations and sets are used, such as intersection ($\cap$), union ($\cup$), difference (-), domain (dom R), range (ran R), relation application ($S' = R(S)$: $e' \in S'$ iff exists e s.t. $e \to e' \in R, e \in S$), positive transitive closure of relation R, $R+ = \{[e] \to [e'] : e \to e' \in R \vee \exists \ e \ '', e \to e'' \in R \wedge e'' \to e' \in R+\}$, transitive closure $R^* = R+ \cup I$. In detail, the description of these operations is presented in papers [7, 9].

Definition 2. An ultimate dependence source is a source that is not the destination of another dependence. Given a relation R, describing all dependences in a loop, a set, S_{UDS}, containing ultimate dependence sources, can be calculated as follows S_{UDS}=domain(R)-range(R).

Definition 3. The set of ultimate dependence sources of a slice forms the set of its sources.

Definition 4. The representative source of a slice is its lexicographically minimal source.

The approach to extract synchronization-free slices [4] relies on the transitive closure of an affine dependence relation describing all dependences in a loop and consists of two steps. First, representatives of slices are found in such a manner that each slice is represented with its lexicographically minimal statement instance. Next, slices are reconstructed from their representatives and code scanning these slices is generated.

In order to find the elements of set S_{UDS} that are representatives of slices, we build a relation, R_{USC}, that describes all pairs of the ultimate dependence sources that are transitively connected in a slice, as follows:

$$R_{USC} = \{[e] \to [e'] : e, e' \in S_{UDS}, e \neq e', (R^*(e) \cap R^*(e') \neq \varnothing)\}, \qquad (1)$$

where the dependence relation R describes all the dependences in a loop. Relation R_{USC} binds elements e and e' that are transitively connected, i.e., they are the sources of the same slice.

To reconstruct slices, set S_{repr} containing representatives of each slice is found as

$$S_{repr} = S_{UDS} - range(R_{USC}). \qquad (2)$$

If e is the representative of a slice with multiple sources, then the remaining sources of this slice can be found applying relation $(R_{USC})^*$ to e, i.e., $(R_{USC})^*(e)$. If a slice has the only source, then $(R_{USC})^*(e)=e$. The elements of a slice represented with e can be found applying relation R^* to the set of sources of this slice:

$$S_{slice} = R^*((R_{USC})^*(e). \qquad (3)$$

The parallel code is generated by means of a loop generator for scanning polyhedra, for example, CLOOG [10] or the *codegen* function of the Omega project [11] can be applied.

The presented technique is illustrated by means of the following parametrized loop.

Example 1.

```
for(i=1; i<=n; i++)
  for(j=1; j<=n; j++)
    a[i][j] = a[i+1][j+1] + a[i+1][j-1];
```

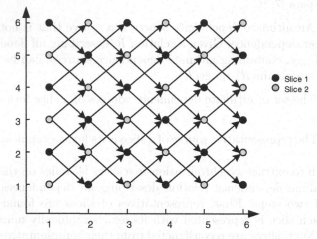

Fig. 1. Dependences for the loop example, n=6

For this loop, there are the two dependence relations returned by Petit [8].
$R_1 = \{[i,j] \rightarrow [i+1,j+1] : 1 \leqslant i < n \;\&\&\; 1 \leqslant j < n\}$,
$R_2 = \{[i,j] \rightarrow [i+1,j-1] : 1 \leqslant i < n\text{-}2 \;\&\&\; 2 \leqslant j < n\}$.
Dependences are illustrated in Figure 1.

Relation R_{USC} calculated by means of the Omega calculator [9] is empty, i.e.,
$R_{USC} = \varnothing$. The following set including sources of slices are produced by means
of the Omega calculator.
$S_{repr} = \{[i,j] : i = 1 \;\&\&\; 1 \leqslant j \leqslant 2\}$.

Applying the *Gen_affine* algorithm for independent slices extraction [4], the
following parallel code with OpenMP pragmas [5] is generated:

```
#pragma omp parallel for private(k,i,j) default(shared)
for(k=1; k<=min(n,2); k++)
  for(i=1; i<=n; i++)
    for(j=1+(-i-k)%2; j<=n; j+=2)
      a[i][j] = a[i+1][j+1]+a[i+1][j-1];
```

3   Neural Networks Parallelization

Source code samples of the following neural networks have been analysed and
multi-threaded by means of TRACO.

– *Boltzmann Machine* - is a network of symmetrically coupled stochastic binary
   units. A studied application is a rendition of the classic Travelling Salesman
   Problem [12], where the shortest tour needs to be found among all cites

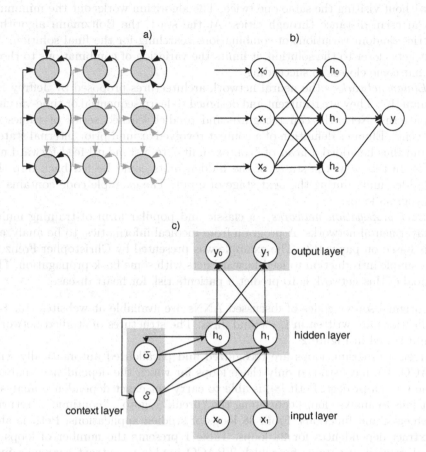

Fig. 2. a) Boltzmann Machine with a simple matrix architecture, b) common structure of a multilayer backpropagation network, c) common structure of the Elman network [14]

Table 1. Effectiveness and compilation time (in seconds) for TRACO, CETUS, and PLUTO

ANN	All loops	TRACO			CETUS			PLUTO		
		Loops	%	Time	Loops	%	Time	Loops	%	Time
boltzmann	16	5	31	1,35	4	25	3,1	2	12	0,58
back propagation	9	7	77	1,45	7	77	5,92	4	44	1,49
elman	18	16	88	0,90	16	88	4,00	13	72	0,63
total	43	28	65	3,71	27	62	13,03	19	44	2,71

without visiting the same one twice. The algorithm works out the minimum Cartesian distance through cities. At the start, the Boltzmann algorithm tries random variations of combinations searching for the final solution. As it gets closer to the solution, it limits the variation of combinations to those that come closest to succeeding.

- *Elman networks* - the neural network architectures proposed by Jeffrey Elman [15]. They are recurrent and designed to learn sequential or time-varying patterns. Networks can recognize and predict learned series of values or events. Elman's definition of a context revolved around prior internal states, and thus he added a layer of "context units" to a standard feed-forward net [1]. In this way, the states of the hidden units could be fed back into the hidden units during the next stage of input. The example code contains 18 program loops.
- *Back-propagation networks* - a classic and popular form of training multi-layer neural networks. A program from medical informatics, to be analyzed, is based on paper [13]. The example was presented by Christopher Frenz as a simple introduction to feed-forward nets with some back-propagation. The goal of this network is to predict a patients risk for heart disease.

The original source codes of discussed ANNs are available at websites [13, 14]. Applications are written in C++ and Java. The structures of studied networks are illustrated in Figure 2.

Given a program, loops are recognized and parallelized automatically with TRACO. We have studied only those loops for which the dependence analyser of the Omega project, Petit [8], is able to carry out exact dependence analysis. Petit fails to analyse loops containing the "break", "goto", "continue", "return" statements, and functions. From 38 loops of studied applications, Petit is able to extract dependences for 28 loops. Table 1 presents the number of loops in neural network programs for which TRACO is able to extract coarse-grained parallelism, percentage of these loops, and compilation time for them (columns 3, 4, and 5).

4   Experiments

In this section, we present the performance of the following computatively heavy ANNs loops:

- the Boltzman Machine - initialize and update weight loops,
- Elman networks - loops of feed forward and back-propagation functions,
- Back-propagation - initialize and update hidden layer loops.

Speed-up is a ratio of sequential and parallel program time execution, $S = T(1)/T(P)$, where P is the number of processors. Efficiency, $E = S/P$, tells us about usage of available processors while parallel code is executed. Table 2 shows time (in seconds), speed-up, and efficiency for loops produced with TRACO for 2, 6, and 12 processors. The experiments were carried out on an Intel Xeon Processor E5645, 12 Threads, 2.4 GHz, 12MB Cache and 16GB RAM.

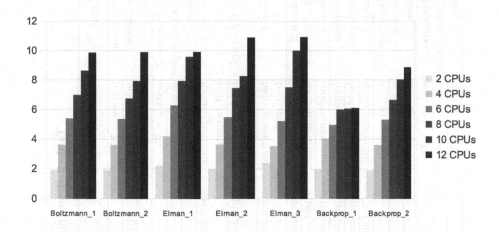

Fig. 3. Speed-up of program loops for the various numbers of CPUs

Analysing data in Table 2, we may conclude that for all parallel loops produced with TRACO, positive speed-up is achieved. Efficiency depends on the problem size defined by loop index upper bounds and the number of CPUs used for parallel program execution. For most cases, efficiency increases with increasing the problem size. Figure 3 illustrates the positive speed-up presented in Table 2 in a graphical way.

5   Related Work

Various techniques have been developed to parallelize neural network algorithms, for example, those presented in papers [16–18]. Many algorithms are dedicated to parallel training and parallel back-propagation [19, 20]. Although the efficiency of these solutions is satisfactory for many cases, parallel program development is usually manual and time- consuming. TRACO allows developers to automatically parallelize existing serial code without any modifications of sources.

The results of the paper are within the ISS framework introduced by Pugh and Rosser [6]. That paper examines one of possible uses of ISS, namely how to optimize interprocessor communication. However, the authors did not propose how to find synchronization-free slices.

Different compilers based on the polyhedral model [21] have been developed to extract coarse-grained parallelism available in loops. The affine transformation framework (ATF), considered in papers [2, 3] unifies a large number of previously proposed loop transformations. ATF is implemented in the PLUTO project [21], which transforms C programs from source to source for coarse-grained parallelism and data locality simultaneously. The core transformation framework mainly works by finding affine transformations for efficient tiling and fusion, but not limited to those.

Table 2. Time (in seconds), speed-up, and efficiency for loops produced with TRACO

Loop	Parameters	1 CPU	2 CPUs			6 CPUs			12 CPUs		
		Time	Time	S	E	Time	S	E	Time	S	E
boltzmann_1	ncities = 75	0.152	0.081	1.877	0.938	0.031	4.903	0.817	0.019	8.000	0.667
initialize	ncities = 100	0.613	0.321	1.910	0.955	0.107	5.729	0.955	0.060	10.217	0.851
loop	ncities = 125	1.241	0.649	1.912	0.956	0.230	5.396	0.899	0.126	9.849	0.821
boltzmann_2	ncities = 75	0.145	0.078	1.859	0.929	0.035	4.143	0.690	0.021	6.905	0.575
update weights	ncities = 100	0.420	0.231	1.818	0.909	0.083	5.060	0.843	0.046	9.130	0.761
loop	ncities = 125	0.998	0.525	1.901	0.950	0.186	5.366	0.894	0.101	9.881	0.823
elman_1	hidden_neurons = input_neurons = context_neurons = 2000	0.083	0.043	1.930	0.965	0.016	5.188	0.865	0.009	9.222	0.769
loop 1	hidden_neurons = input_neurons = context_neurons = 5000	1.474	0.664	2.220	1.110	0.235	6.272	1.045	0.149	9.893	0.824
loop 2	hidden_neurons = input_neurons = context_neurons = 8000	0.490	0.237	2.068	1.034	0.091	5.385	0.897	0.049	10.000	0.833
feed forward	hidden_neurons = output_neurons = 2000	0.048	0.024	2.000	1.000	0.010	4.800	0.800	0.005	9.600	0.800
loop 1	hidden_neurons = output_neurons = 5000	0.226	0.117	1.932	0.966	0.053	4.264	0.711	0.026	8.692	0.724
loop 2	hidden_neurons = output_neurons = 8000	0.685	0.345	1.986	0.993	0.125	5.480	0.913	0.063	10.873	0.906
elman_2	hidden_neurons = output_neurons = 2000	0.012	0.007	1.714	0.857	0.003	4.000	0.667	0.001	12.000	1.000
elman_3	hidden_neurons = output_neurons = 5000	0.054	0.021	2.571	1.286	0.008	6.750	1.125	0.005	10.800	0.900
back prop. loop 1	hidden_neurons = output_neurons = 8000	0.120	0.050	2.400	1.200	0.023	5.217	0.870	0.011	10.909	0.909
backprop_1	n = m = 2000	0.184	0.094	1.957	0.979	0.037	4.973	0.829	0.026	7.077	0.590
initialize	n = m = 4000	0.722	0.334	2.162	1.081	0.118	6.119	1.020	0.105	6.876	0.573
loop	n = m = 6000	1.571	0.786	1.999	0.999	0.317	4.956	0.826	0.261	6.019	0.502
backprop_2	n = m = 2000	0.041	0.021	1.952	0.976	0.010	4.100	0.683	0.008	5.125	0.427
update hidden	n = m = 4000	0.140	0.074	1.892	0.946	0.033	4.242	0.707	0.016	8.750	0.729
loop	n = m = 6000	0.345	0.182	1.896	0.948	0.065	5.308	0.885	0.039	8.846	0.737

The CETUS tool provides an infrastructure for research on multi-core compiler optimizations that emphasizes automatic parallelization [22]. The compiler targets C programs and supports source-to-source transformations. It performs loop dependence analysis and generates parallel loop annotations. However CETUS transformations are limited only to induction variable substitution, reduction recognition, and array privatization.

Table 1 presents the comparison of the TRACO, CETUS and PLUTO effectiveness for studied ANNs loops. Although PLUTO produces parallel code in the shortest period of time, it parallelizes only 44 % of loops. CETUS extracts parallelism for 62 % of program loops and takes more than 13 seconds to produce parallel code for all ANNs. TRACO parallelizes 65 % of program loops and takes in sum 3,71 seconds.

6   Conclusion

The paper presents applying Iteration Space Slicing implemented in TRACO for automatic producing parallel code for tasks of neural network programming. Loops computation are divided into multiple slices which are mapped to processors as threads. TRACO allows users to achieve significant speed-up of parallel ANNs programs on shared memory machines with multi-core processors. The effectiveness of applying TRACO is better or comparable with that demonstrated by the optimizing compilers CETUS and PLUTO.

In the future, we indent to study the parallelization of other ANNs applications, such as Kohonen Self-Organizing Maps, Adaptive Resonance Theory, and Probabilistic Neural Networks. We consider also the implementation of source-to-source locality optimization techniques in TRACO.

References

1. Fausett, L.: Fundamentals of neural networks: Architectures, algorithms, and applications, pp. 169–175. Prentice Hall, New Jersey (1994)
2. Lim, A., Lam, M., Cheong, G.: An affine partitioning algorithm to maximize parallelism and minimize communication. In: ICS 1999, pp. 228–237. ACM Press (1999)
3. Feautrier, P.: Some efficient solutions to the affine scheduling problem, part I and II, one and multidimensional time. International Journal of Parallel Programming 21, 313–348, 389–420 (1992)
4. Beletska, A., Bielecki, W., Cohen, A., Palkowski, M., Siedlecki, K.: Coarse-grained loop parallelization: Iteration space slicing vs affine transformations. Parallel Computing 37, 479–497 (2011)
5. OpenMP Specification, version 3.1 (2011), http://www.openmp.org
6. Pugh, W., Rosser, E.: Iteration space slicing and its application to communication optimization. In: International Conference on Supercomputing, pp. 221–228 (1997)
7. Pugh, W., Wonnacott, D.: An exact method for analysis of value-based array data dependences. In: Banerjee, U., Gelernter, D., Nicolau, A., Padua, D.A. (eds.) LCPC 1993. LNCS, vol. 768, pp. 546–566. Springer, Heidelberg (1994)
8. Kelly, W., Pugh, W., Rosser, E., Maslov, V., Shpeisman, T., Wonnacott, D.: New User Interface for Petit and Other Extensions. User Guide (1996)

9. Kelly, W., Maslov, V., Pugh, W., Rosser, E., Shpeisman, T., Wonnacott, D.: The omega library interface guide. Technical report, College Park, MD, USA (1995)
10. Bastoul, C.: Code Generation in the Polyhedral Model Is Easier Than You Think. In: PACT'13 IEEE International Conference on Parallel Architecture and Compilation Techniques, Juan-les-Pins, France, pp. 7–16 (2004)
11. Wonnacott, D.: A Retrospective of the Omega Project, Haverford College Computer Science Tech Report (2010)
12. Aarts, E.: Boltzmann machines for travelling salesman problems. European Journal of Operational Research 39(1), 79–95 (1989)
13. Frenz, C.: Give Your .NET App Brains and Brawn with the Intelligence of Neural Networks. MSDN Magazine 5/2005 (2005), http://msdn.microsoft.com/msdnmag/issues/05/05/NeuralNetworks/default.aspx
14. McCullock, J.: Mnemosyne Studio - Neural Network Programming (2011), http://mnemstudio.org
15. Elman, J.L.: Finding structure in time. Cognitive Science 14, 179–211 (1990)
16. Seiffert, U.: Artificial Neural Networks on Massively Parallel Computer Hardware. In: ESANN 2002 Proceedings - European Symposium on Artificial Neural Networks, Bruges (Belgium), pp. 319–330. d-side publi. (2002) ISBN 2-930307-02-1
17. Dahl, G., McAvinney, A., Newhall, T.: Parallelizing neural network training for cluster systems. In: PDCN 2008 Proceedings of the IASTED International Conference on Parallel and Distributed Computing and Networks, pp. 220–225 (2008)
18. Long, L., Gupta, A.: Scalable Massively Parallel Artificial Neural Networks. Journal of Aerospace Computing, Information and Communication 5(1) (2008)
19. Beyon, T.: A parallel implementation of the back-propagation algorithm on a network of transputers. In: Proc. First IEEE Int. Neural Network Conf. (1987)
20. Tsaregorodtsev, V.G.: Parallel Implementation of Back-Propagation Neural Network Software on SMP Computers. In: Malyshkin, V.E. (ed.) PaCT 2005. LNCS, vol. 3606, pp. 186–192. Springer, Heidelberg (2005)
21. Bondhugula, U., Hartono, A., Ramanujan, J., Sadayappan, P.: A practical automatic polyhedral parallelizer and locality optimizer. In: ACM SIGPLAN Programming Languages Design and Implementation, PLDI 2008 (2008)
22. Chirag, D., Hansang, B., Seung-Jai, M., Seyong, L., Eigenmann, R., Midkiff, S.: CETUS: A Source-to-Source Compiler Infrastructure for Multicores. IEEE Computer, 36–42 (2009)

Training Neural Networks on Noisy Data

Andrzej Rusiecki[1], Mirosław Kordos[2], Tomasz Kamiński[2], and Krzysztof Greń[2]

[1] Wroclaw University of Technology, Institute of Computer Engineering, Control and Robotics,
Wrocław, Wybrzeże Wyspiańskiego 27, Poland
andrzej.rusiecki@pwr.wroc.pl
[2] University of Bielsko-Biala, Department of Mathematics and Computer Science,
Bielsko-Biała, Willowa 2, Poland
mkordos@ath.bielsko.pl

Abstract. This paper discusses approaches to noise-resistant training of MLP neural networks. We present various aspects of the issue and the ways of obtaining that goal by using two groups of approaches and combinations of them. The first group is based on a different processing of each vector depending of the likelihood of the vector being an outlier. The likelihood is determined by instance selection and outlier detection. The second group is based on training MLP neural networks with non-differentiable robust objective functions. We evaluate the performance of particular methods with different level of noise in the data for regression problems.

1 Introduction

Multilayer perceptrons (MLP) are among the most popular approaches used to build data-based models for various applications. They are usually considered as reliable and easy-to-use tools. However, their performance strongly depends on the quality of the training data [3, 18]. In this paper we present and test some state of the art methods, which allows training the MLPs on contaminated datasets.

MLP networks are trained by minimizing an error function on the training set, to make the network map the input data distribution to output space variables, which in case of regression are real numbers. However, since the error is minimized to make the network output for each vector as close as possible to the real vector output, it is crucial that the training data is of a good quality. Good quality means that the data reflects the underlying problem. If the data contains a lot of faulty measurements, other errors and outliers it obviously does not match the problem well, so also the neural network trained on that data will not.

In this paper we take into account two groups of methods to deal with the noisy data problem. The first group of methods makes some adjustment to other neural network itself, such as the error function, the neuron transfer functions and others to make the network to process differently data points of different properties in such a way that it is less sensitive to outliers. These methods are presented in section 2.

The second group uses outlier reduction methods, which are applied to the data prior to the network training. Thus, the data is modified and a typical MLP network is then trained on that data. This is discussed in section 3.

L. Rutkowski et al. (Eds.): ICAISC 2014, Part I, LNAI 8467, pp. 131–142, 2014.

Finally we discuss the possibilities of joining the two groups of methods together. The section 4 presents the experimental comparison of nine different methods from all the three groups on seven regression tasks performed with various amount of noise added to the data. Finally the section 5 concludes this work.

2   Data with Outliers and Robust Learning

An outlier can be defined as an observation distant from the bulk of the data. Such observations may be caused by human mistakes, measurement or rounding errors, long-tailed noise, etc. This is why outliers are usually considered as gross errors but they can be also potentially meaningful. In typical raw data, the quantity of outliers ranges from 1% to 10% [11], however it is hard to predict how much outliers the data contain.

The feedfoward neural network trained to minimize MSE (mean squared error) builds a model based on fitting training patterns as close as possible (according to the MSE measure). Such approach is indeed optimal for data contaminated by errors generated from zero-mean Gaussian distribution but when outliers appear in the training set, the network model becomes unreliable [3, 18, 19]. This is why several robust learning algorithms, to train neural networks on the data with outliers, have been proposed [3–5, 18, 25]. Such methods, usually based on the robust statistical estimators, should be reliable also when the training data quality is unknown.

One of the basic approaches to make a learning algorithm more robust to outliers is to replace the MSE performance measure by another function. In this approach, the robustness to outliers is achieved by reducing the impact of large training residuals, potentially caused by outlying data points. Many such functions derived from robust statistical estimators can be found in the literature. New LMLS (Least Mean Log Squares) error function was proposed by Liano [18]. Chen and Jain [3] applied the Hampel's hyperbolic tangent with scale estimator β, determining residuals suspected to be caused by outliers, Chunag and Su [4] added the annealing scheme to decrease the value of β. Error functions based on the tau-estimators [19] and the MCD (Minimum Covariance Determinant) [24] were also proposed. El-Melegy *et al.* presented the Simulated Annealing for Least Median of Squares (SA-LMedS) algorithm [5], while Rusiecki proposed the LTS (Least Trimmed Squares) [23] and LTA (Least Trimmed Absolute Values) [26] algorithms. The RANSAC (random sample consensus) framework, known from the area of image processing, was applied to the MLPs learning by El-Melegy [6–8].

2.1   Trimmed and Median-Based Error Measures

In the previous research many modified performance functions have been examined and the best results have been obtained with the quantile-based and trimmed performance measures [5, 17, 25, 26]. Trimmed and quantile-based robust estimators are proved to be outlier-resistant, so it is not surprising that they perform well also in network training.

The main problem is that such measures are not continuous and some approximations of their derivatives in gradient-based learning must be used. An alternative approach is to train the network with non-gradient methods. In this paper we use the Variable Step

Search (VSS) Algorithm [14] to train the network with robust non-differentiable error measures. The main idea of the VSS algorithm is to guess the optimal modifications of single weights at each iteration based on their changes in previos iterations and then to adjust the changes. Since change of a single weight does not change signal propagations in the entire network, the signals (unlike in gradient-based methoods) are propagated each time only through the recently changed fragments of the network. However, we do not focus on the learning algorithm itself and use VSS with the same parameters through all the tests. It is also not crucial to use VSS and it can be replaced with several other MLP training methods.

3 LTA and ILMedS Algorithms

One of the desired properties of robust estimators is a high breakdown point. It is defined as the smallest percentage ϵ^* of contaminated data that can cause the estimator to take on aberrant values [11]. Theoretically, for the least squares method the breakdown point $\epsilon^* = 0$. The least trimmed absolute value (LTA) and the least median of squares (LMedS) are known in the robust statistics to be the classical high breakdown point robust estimators (breakdown point close to $\epsilon^* = 0.5$). In fact, the breakdown point $\epsilon^* = 0.5$ is the best that can be expected from any estimator [22]. Unlike robust M-estimators, the LTA and LMedS do not change operations performed on single residuals (such as squaring or taking absolute value), but replace the sum of residuals with a trimmed sum or a certain statistical value as median. Hence, the LMedS estimator is based on the Chebyshev (L_∞) norm and the LTA is a trimmed version of L_1 norm.

3.1 Least Trimmed Absolute Values

The least trimmed absolute value estimator (LTA) is one of the well-known robust location estimators. Similarly to the least trimmed squares (LTS) [22] it does not change operations performed on residuals. Hence, in this case, residuals are not squared but their absolute values are taken. Then the summation is replaced with a trimmed sum.

Let us consider the general nonlinear regression model:

$$y_i = \eta(x_i, \theta) + \epsilon_i, \quad i = 1, \ldots, n, \tag{1}$$

where y_i denotes the dependent variable, $x_i = (x_{i1}, \ldots, x_{ik})$ the independent input vector, $\theta \in R^p$ is the underlying parameter vector, and ϵ_i denotes independent and identically distributed (iid) random errors with a continuous distribution function. Now we can define the least trimmed absolute value estimator:

$$\hat{\theta} = \arg \min_{\theta \in R^p} \sum_{i=1}^{h} (|r|)_{i:n}, \tag{2}$$

where $(|r|)_{1:n} \leq \cdots \leq (|r|)_{n:n}$ are the absolute residuals $|r_i(\theta)| = |y_i - \eta(x_i, \theta)|$ sorted in ascending order. In the summation only h smallest absolute values of the residuals are used. Setting the trimming constant h as $n/2 < h \leq n$ we can decide what percentage of largest residuals will not affect the estimator.

LTA Error Criterion. The new robust error criterion based on the LTA estimator was introduced in [26] as:

$$E_{LTA} = \sum_{i=1}^{h} (|r|)_{i:n},\qquad(3)$$

where $(|r|)_{1:n} \leq \cdots \leq (|r|)_{n:n}$ are ordered absolute network output residuals for each training pattern.

This error measure should provide robustness to outliers excluding from the training process patterns causing largest errors (assuming that these patterns are outliers). The trimming constant h can be set empirically but in [26] a simple approach to estimate the scaling factor was proposed. Calculation of h is based on a robust measure of scale, namely the median of all absolute deviations from the median (MAD)[13]:

$$\text{MAD}\,(r_i) = 1.483 \, \text{median}|r_i - median(r_i)|.\qquad(4)$$

The trimming parameter is then calculated as:

$$h = \|\{r_i : |r_i| < 3 * \text{MAD}(|r_i|), i = 1\ldots n\}\|.\qquad(5)$$

To determine h, errors obtained after initial training phase should be used.

3.2 Iterative Least Median of Squares

LMedS Estimator. The least median of squares estimator (LMedS) was originally proposed by Rousseeuw [22] but it was informally used even earlier [13]. The LMedS estimator acts on the squared residuals, replacing sum by the robust median, so it can be defined as follows:

$$\hat{\theta} = \arg \min_i \text{med } r_i^2.\qquad(6)$$

Iterative LMedS. In the domain of robust neural network learning algorithms, the LMedS error criterion was proposed by El-Melegy in [5], where simulated annealing was employed to minimize the median error. The LMedS performance is defined as:

$$E_{med} = \text{med } r_i^2.\qquad(7)$$

For the error criterion given by 7, the following additional training procedure was proposed [5, 25]. After an initial training phase, the robust standard deviation (RSD)[21] is calculated as:

$$\sigma_r = 1.4826 * (1 + \frac{5}{(N-p)})\sqrt{E_{med}^*},\qquad(8)$$

where E_{med}^* is the best achieved LMedS error value (N and p are the size of the training set and the dimension of the input vector). Then all the training patterns associated with residuals exceeding a threshold should be removed from the training set:

$$r_i^2 \geq 2.5 * \sigma_r^2.\qquad(9)$$

These steps should be repeated iteratively several times. A detailed explanation of the chosen threshold and methodology can be found in [5, 21, 25].

To train the network with LTA and ILMedS approaches we decided to use non-gradient VSS algorithm [14] to cope with the problem of the performance function non-differentiability.

4   Outlier Reduction

4.1   Instance Selection

Using instance selection, the most of the outliers get removed from the training dataset and the noise in the data is reduced. In general there may by also other reasons for instance selection, as reducing the data size or improving generalization, but these topics are out of scope of this work. A large survey of about 70 different instance selection algorithms for classification tasks can be found in [27]. So far there were very few approaches in the literature to instance selection for regression problems. Moreover, the approaches were verified only on artificial datasets generated especially for the purpose of testing the algorithms. Zhang [31] presented a method to select the input vectors while calculating the output with k-NN. Tolvi [28] presented a genetic algorithm to perform feature and instance selection for linear regression models. In their works Guillen et al. [10] discussed the concept of mutual information used for selection of prototypes in regression problems.

Instance selection for regression problems is a more complex issue for two reasons. First, in classification it is enough to determine the border between two classes, while in regression the values in each point of the data are important. This results in a much weaker data compression that can be achieved in regression tasks. And second, in classification we must only decide if a certain points belong to a given class or not. Thus most of the instance selection algorithms are based on k-NN classification, where the result of the classification determines if the given instance is preserved or rejected. In regression problems, while comparing two instances, we consider the distance between them, according to some (usually Euclidean) distance measure. Thus, the criterion to decide whether a given instance should be rejected is some distance threshold. There are a lot of options of how the threshold can be determined. It can be constant or proportional to the local density of the data. In general the threshold should be determined experimentally, but our experiments showed that in the regENN algorithm [15], the rejection threshold θ can be set to 2-8 standard deviations of the data for a broad range of regression problems. The higher value can be used for a better quality data and the lower for highly contaminated data.The reason for this is that in more contaminated data there are more outliers that should be removed and there is a higher probability that the some of the neighbors of the considered instance are also outliers. While in a better quality data even the points that are far from their neighbors do not necessary require rejection, as they may not contain any wrong values. Using θ proportional to the standard deviation of k nearest neighbors of the instance x_i, instead of proportional to a standard deviation of the entire data allows, as the experiments showed, for obtaining higher compression of the dataset while preserving the same prediction accuracy. We developed the regENN algorithm from the ENN (Edited Nearest Neighbor) algorithm [30] and presented it in [15]. The main idea of the regENN algorithm is to reject instances if their output differs more than θ from a value predicted by the weighted k-NN with $k = 9$, where the weight w_i exponentially decreases with the distance d_i between the given instance and its i-th neighbor x_i. The predicted output y is expressed by the following equation:

$$y = \frac{\sum_{i=1}^{k} w_i y_i}{\sum_{i=1}^{k} w_i} \tag{10}$$

where $w_i = 2^{-0.2d_i}$. As the regression model to predict the output $Y(x_i)$ we use k-NN with $k = 9$ as the Model(T,x_i) we also use k-NN with $k = 9$, although also other methods can be used here, as neural network, regression trees, etc. ($k = 9$ was evaluated experimentally to be a good choice for a broad range of problems [16]).

Algorithm 1. regENN algorithm

Require: T
  $m \leftarrow sizeof(\mathbf{T})$;
  for $i = 1 \ldots m$ **do**
    $\bar{Y}(\mathbf{x}_i) =$ Model$((\mathbf{T} \setminus \mathbf{x}_i), \mathbf{x}_i)$;
    $S \leftarrow$ k-NN$(\mathbf{T}, \mathbf{x}_i)$
    $\theta = \alpha \cdot std(Y(\mathbf{X}_S))$
    if $|Y(\mathbf{x}_i) - \bar{Y}(\mathbf{x}_i)| > \theta$ **then**
      $\mathbf{T} \leftarrow \mathbf{T} \setminus \mathbf{x}_i$
    end if
  end for
  $\mathbf{P} \leftarrow \mathbf{T}$
  return P

4.2 Anomaly Detection

Anomaly detection deals with the outliers in a different way than instance selection; it does not reject or keep them but it assigns an anomaly score to each instance. The higher the score, the bigger outlier is the instance. There is a bunch of anomaly detection methods and a survey of them can be found in [2]. For the purpose of this work we modified the k-NN Global Anomaly Score algorithm (k-NN GAS). The k-NN GAS assigns the anomaly scores prior to the network training and then the MLP error function divides the error the network makes on the instance by the instance anomaly score. In this way the more outstanding instances have weaker influence on the network training. The advantage of anomaly detection over instance selection is that we do not have to make a crisp decision about the instance. The k-NN GAS calculates the anomaly score based on the k-NN algorithm. The outlier score of an instance is the average distance between the instance and its k nearest neighbors (again we use $k = 9$ and Euclidean distance measure). However, for the purpose of labeled data, we had to modify the k-NN GAS, including both distances: in the input space d_x and in the output space d_y. We define the modified anomaly score A_{sc} as:

$$A_{sc} = d_y/d_x \tag{11}$$

5   Experimental Evaluation

5.1   Datasets

We performed the experiments on two groups of regression problems: the real-world datasets and artificial datasets. We used the real-world datasets, which were first standardized so that the mean value of each attribute is zero and the standard deviation is one to make result comparison easier. We started from the original datasets ($\delta=0$ in the tables 5-7) and gradually were adding some random noise to outputs only to the training subsets in the crossvalidation. $\delta=0.1$ represents $v=0.5$ and $f=0.20$, $\delta=0.2$: $v=1.0$ and $f=0.25$, $\delta=0.3$: $v=1.5$ and $f=0.30$, $\delta=0.4$: $v=2.0$ and $f=0.35$, $\delta=0.5$: $v=2.5$ and $f=0.40$. The noise was added to outputs with random frequency f and amplitude $v(2 - r * r)$, where $0 < r < 1$ is a random number. The artificial datasets (Function A, Function B and Function C) and Building Benchmark were contaminated with so-called Gross Error Model [3, 4, 18, 23] with additive noise: $F = (1 - \delta)G + \delta H$, where F denotes the error distribution, $G \sim N(0.0, 10.0)$ models small Gaussian noise, and $H \sim N(0.0, 0.1)$ represents high value outliers. Hence, the probability of outliers is δ. The datasets are available from [32].

Function A. The 1-D function to be approximated was proposed by Liano in [18] and used to test many robust learning algorithms [3–5, 19, 26]. It is defined as:

$$y = |x|^{-2/3}. \tag{12}$$

A training set was prepared by sampling independent variable in the range $[-2, 2]$ with a step 0.01.

Function B. The second 1-D function was previously used in [3, 4] and defined as:

$$y = \frac{\sin(x)}{x}. \tag{13}$$

For a training set, the independent variable was sampled in the range $[-7.5, 7.5]$ with a step of 0.1.

Function C. Another function was a two-dimensional spiral defined as:

$$\begin{cases} x = \sin y \\ z = \cos y \end{cases} \tag{14}$$

Training data were generated by sampling the dependent variable y in the range $[0, \pi]$ with a step $\pi/100$. The network was trained to model y as a function of x and z (for the given range it is a function).

Building. The first real-world training task was taken from the PROBEN 1 benchmark collection [20]. The task was to predict building energy consumption based on 14 input variables, such as the date, time, and weather conditions. Following [1], we trained a network on the first 3156 observations to predict dependent variable over the next 1052 time steps of the test set.

Table 1. MSE on training subset for Function A, 10 hidden neurons, 12 training epochs

δ	0.0	0.1	0.2	0.3	0.4	0.5
MSE	0.0038±0.002	0.11±0.006	0.44±0.008	0.49±0.08	0.59±0.09	0.81±0.09
ILMedS	0.0045±0.001	0.0057±0.003	0.0076±0.003	0.0059±0.002	0.015±0.005	0.021±0.01
LTA	0.0065±0.001	0.0041±0.001	0.011±0.005	0.0046±0.002	0.0063±0.002	0.0073±0.002
ENN-MSE	0.0039±0.002	0.0055±0.002	0.0077±0.003	0.013±0.030	0.014±0.033	0.018±0.028
ENN-ILMedS	0.0048±0.001	0.0061±0.002	0.0070±0.002	0.0071±0.002	0.0092±0.003	0.014±0.023
ENN-LTA	0.0039±0.001	0.0039±0.001	0.0048±0.002	0.0055±0.002	0.0059±0.002	0.0067±0.002
GAS-MSE	0.0033±0.002	0.0044±0.002	0.0048±0.002	0.0061±0.002	0.0087±0.002	0.017±0.004
GAS-ILMedS	0.0037±0.001	0.0042±0.002	0.0056±0.002	0.0088±0.002	0.021±0.005	0.067±0.019
GAS-LTA	0.0021±0.001	0.0020±0.001	0.0023±0.001	0.0027±0.001	0.0035±0.001	0.0068±0.002

Table 2. MSE on training subset for Function B, 10 hidden neurons, 12 training epochs

δ	0.0	0.1	0.2	0.3	0.4	0.5
MSE	0.0044±0.002	0.67±0.12	0.45±0.05	0.45±0.03	1.90±0.09	4.66±0.10
ILMedS	0.0045±0.002	0.046±0.017	0.024±0.011	0.056±0.035	0.11±0.03	0.15±0.09
LTA	0.0072±0.002	0.0056±0.002	0.0091±0.002	0.010±0.005	0.021±0.007	0.15±0.04
ENN-MSE	0.0034±0.001	0.0038±0.001	0.0055±0.002	0.0053±0.002	0.0081±0.002	0.027±0.007
ENN-ILMedS	0.0030±0.001	0.0040±0.003	0.0049±0.003	0.0056±0.002	0.0066±0.003	0.018±0.005
ENN-LTA	0.0038±0.001	0.0036±0.001	0.0040±0.002	0.0048±0.002	0.0076±0.003	0.015±0.004
GAS-MSE	0.0031±0.001	0.0049±0.002	0.0068±0.003	0.011±0.003	0.023±0.006	0.082±0.031
GAS-ILMedS	0.0042±0.001	0.0051±0.002	0.0067±0.003	0.013±0.003	0.034±0.011	0.18±0.06
GAS-LTA	0.0040±0.002	0.0043±0.002	0.0045±0.002	0.0045±0.002	0.0062±0.003	0.021±0.006

Table 3. MSE on training subset for Function C, 10 hidden neurons, 12 training epochs

δ	0.0	0.1	0.2	0.3	0.4	0.5
MSE	0.0025±0.001	0.19±0.02	0.60±0.05	1.62±1.77	2.58±0.48	4.16±0.30
ILMedS	0.0021±0.001	0.015±0.012	0.081±0.039	1.74±0.94	1.14±0.78	1.62±1.77
LTA	0.0008±0.001	0.0041±0.002	0.0045±0.002	0.014±0.009	0.011±0.004	0.057±0.031
ENN-MSE	0.0025±0.001	0.0041±0.002	0.0061±0.002	0.014±0.005	0.023±0.008	0.044±0.012
ENN-ILMedS	0.0020±0.001	0.0043±0.002	0.0087±0.003	0.017±0.006	0.022±0.005	0.039±0.01
ENN-LTA	0.0008±0.001	0.0018±0.001	0.0044±0.002	0.010±0.003	0.021±0.002	0.039±0.002
GAS-MSE	0.0022±0.001	0.0039±0.002	0.0056±0.008	0.015±0.004	0.044±0.009	0.1415±0.09
GAS-ILMedS	0.0024±0.001	0.0065±0.003	0.0077±0.003	0.013±0.003	0.092±0.035	0.34±0.01
GAS-LTA	0.0014±0.001	0.0035±0.001	0.0048±0.005	0.0042±0.002	0.0046±0.002	0.054±0.018

Concrete Compression Strength. There are 1030 instances with 7 input attributes in the dataset reflecting the amount of particular substances in the concrete mixture, such as cement, slag, water, etc. [29]. The task is to predict the concrete compressive strength. There are 1030 instances in the database.

Crime and Communities. There are 318 instances with originally 120 input attributes in the data set, describing various social, economical and criminal factors [29].

Table 4. MSE on training subset for Building dataset, 10 hidden neurons, 12 training epochs

δ	0.0	0.1	0.2	0.3	0.4	0.5
MSE	0.0018±0.0003	1.013±0.030	3.85±0.06	8.29±0.13	15.6±0.2	24.3±2.2
ILMeds	0.0017±0.0003	0.036±0.019	0.16±0.06	0.25±0.13	0.41±0.18	15.2±1.5
LTA	0.0020±0.0004	0.0032±0.0006	0.0048±0.001	0.013±0.003	0.026±0.004	2.15±3.9
ENN-MSE	0.0018±0.0003	0.0039±0.0006	0.0060±0.012	0.018±0.004	0.034±0.006	0.24±0.05
ENN-ILMedS	0.0017±0.0003	0.0035±0.0006	0.0056±0.001	0.015±0.002	0.040±0.008	0.17±0.04
ENN-LTA	0.0020±0.0004	0.0035±0.0005	0.0081±0.002	0.014±0.002	0.029±0.005	0.21±0.05

However, after preliminary feature selection we used only 7 attributes. The value to predict is per capita violent crime.

SteelC14. The dataset contains 2384 instances with 18 input attributes. The task is to predict the amount of carbon that must be added in the steel-making process, given various chemical and physical properties of the liquid steel in the furnace.

5.2 Experimental Setup

We implemented the algorithms in C#. The source code can be downloaded from the SVN repository at [32]. The whole process in different configurations was run in 10-fold crossvalidation loops. To be able to compare the results, we always measure and report in the tables 1-7 the MSE error on the test sets, no matter which error function was used for the network training. Also the MLP architecture was constant (the same for each training method) for a given dataset (the numbers of hidden neurons are given in the result tables). We run the tests on several forms of the datasets: the original datasets and the datasets with various amount of random noise (see section 5.1) added to the output variables. However, the noise was added only to the training data, while the test data were left unchanged. That allowed us to determine how the methods can deal with various noise levels.

5.3 Results

The results in the tables show MSE on the test subsets (always MSE on the test subset is compared for any training method and any error function used during the training). Analyzing results of the experiments, one may notice that the traditional method, minimizing MSE criterion perform well only for clean datasets without outliers. When the data contains outlying patterns, the method breaks down. More interesting phenomenon is that even for clean training data, different modified algorithms always obtained better results (e.g. GAS methods in Table 1, or ENN and GAS methods in Table 2).

For contaminated training sets, all the enhanced algorithms performed better than the traditional one. Only pure ILMedS method for several datasets (Tables 5, 6, 7) obtained lager errors than the MSE. In general, the best performance was achieved for hybrid algorithms combining ILMedS and LTA with ENN, or GAS approaches.

Table 5. MSE on training subsets for Concrete dataset, 6 hidden neurons, 12 training epochs

δ	0.0	0.1	0.2	0.3	0.4	0.5
MSE	0.79±0.25	0.84±0.21	1.01±0.19	1.47±0.22	2.26±0.19	3.80±0.33
ILMedS	0.91±0.25	1.05±0.36	1.14±0.34	2.01±0.46	2.80±0.85	4.01±1.30
LTA	1.06±0.33	0.96±0.39	0.94±0.35	0.94±0.32	1.07±0.29	1.60±0.35
ENN-MSE	0.79±0.25	0.82±0.21	0.89±0.20	1.02±0.14	1.05±0.15	1.15±0.18
ENN-ILMedS	0.85±0.09	0.86±0.11	0.89±0.11	0.88±0.15	0.98±0.21	1.09±0.17
ENN-LTA	1.05±0.20	0.95±0.16	0.94±0.09	1.00±0.18	1.13±0.25	1.21±0.18
GAS-MSE	0.78±0.32	0.87±0.36	0.94±0.29	1.13±0.28	1.41±0.25	2.16±0.39
GAS-ILMedS	0.76±0.26	0.97±0.38	1.08±0.30	1.21±0.43	1.64±0.34	2.80±0.81
GAS-LTA	1.10±0.30	1.09±0.44	1.03±0.40	0.96±0.33	1.00±0.34	1.05±0.33

Table 6. MSE on training subsets for Crime dataset, 5 hidden neurons, 12 training epochs

δ	0.0	0.1	0.2	0.3	0.4	0.5
MSE	0.34±0.07	0.37±0.10	0.56±0.17	1.17±0.41	2.23±0.42	3.31±0.71
ILMedS	0.37±0.12	0.43±0.10	0.63±0.13	1.37±0.44	2.70±1.11	4.09±1.33
LTA	0.39±0.11	0.39±0.10	0.48±0.13	0.56±0.18	0.88±0.24	1.96±0.92
ENN-MSE	0.34±0.07	0.34±0.10	0.40±0.07	0.61±0.19	0.70±0.49	1.58±1.38
ENN-ILMedS	0.37±0.11	0.36±0.09	0.46±0.15	0.53±0.11	0.69±0.21	0.77±0.35
ENN-LTA	0.38±0.13	0.38±0.12	0.45±0.12	0.54±0.14	0.64±0.40	0.81±0.30
GAS-MSE	0.34±0.09	0.39±0.12	0.47±0.13	0.61±0.18	1.22±0.47	2.43±0.83
GAS-ILMedS	0.34±0.10	0.37±0.11	0.47±0.10	0.86±0.62	1.51±0.72	2.99±1.23
GAS-LTA	0.37±0.11	0.39±0.10	0.46±0.12	0.47±0.14	0.61±0.16	1.08±0.63

Table 7. MSE on training subsets for SteelC14, 5 hidden neurons, 12 training epochs

δ	0.0	0.1	0.2	0.3	0.4	0.5
MSE	0.071±0.018	0.10±0.03	0.27±0.02	0.70±0.08	1.61±0.12	3.14±0.16
ILMedS	0.082±0.035	0.17±0.04	0.55±0.14	1.07±0.41	2.06±0.86	2.58±1.05
LTA	0.071±0.045	0.069±0.038	0.093±0.034	0.11±0.05	0.15±0.04	0.27±0.07
ENN-MSE	0.069±0.016	0.072±0.031	0.92±0.10	0.10±0.04	0.14±0.04	0.22±0.06
ENN-ILMedS	0.070±0.014	0.098±0.023	0.21±0.03	0.55±0.02	0.78±0.18	1.13±0.56
ENN-LTA	0.068±0.015	0.111±0.029	0.24±0.03	0.60±0.02	0.12±0.03	0.21±0.07
GAS-MSE	0.073±0.045	0.084±0.021	0.121±0.010	0.27±0.05	0.69±0.08	1.30±0.32
GAS-ILMedS	0.071±0.034	0.110±0.050	0.221±0.140	0.60±0.25	0.68±0.20	1.31±0.41
GAS-LTA	0.073±0.054	0.074±0.036	0.074±0.043	0.078±0.04	0.09±0.04	0.15±0.05

6 Conclusions

We described briefly some modifications of learning methods designed to deal with the problem of noisy data for regression tasks. It is clearly evident that all the presented approaches can be considered as more reliable than the traditional learning algorithms minimizing the MSE criterion. This is particularly important when the quality of training data is unknown. Even for clean training patterns some of the modified methods performed better than the MSE. For different testing problems and different amounts of outliers the observed performances varied between tested methods. However, in most cases, especially for the noisy data, ENN with LTA performed best. The future efforts can be then directed at defining and choosing optimal algorithms for given conditions (types of problems and quantities of outlying points).

References

1. Beliakov, G., Kelarev, A., Yearwood, J.: Derivative-free optimization and neural networks for robust regression. Optimization 61(12), 1467–1490 (2012)
2. Ben-Gal, I.: Outlier detection. Kluwer Academic Publishers (2005)
3. Chen, D., Jain, R.: A robust backpropagation learning algorithm for function approximation. IEEE Transactions on Neural Networks 5(3), 467–479 (1994)
4. Chuang, C.C., Su, S.F., Hsiao, C.C.: The annealing robust backpropagation (arbp) learning algorithm. IEEE Transactions on Neural Networks 11(5), 1067–1077 (2000)
5. El-Melegy, M.T., Essai, M.H., Ali, A.A.: Robust training of artificial feedforward neural networks. In: Hassanien, A.-E., Abraham, A., Vasilakos, A.V., Pedrycz, W. (eds.) Foundations of Computational, Intelligence Volume 1. SCI, vol. 201, pp. 217–242. Springer, Heidelberg (2009)
6. El-Melegy, M.: Random sampler m-estimator algorithm for robust function approximation via feed-forward neural networks. In: The 2011 International Joint Conference on Neural Networks (IJCNN), pp. 3134–3140 (2011)
7. El-Melegy, M.: Ransac algorithm with sequential probability ratio test for robust training of feed-forward neural networks. In: The 2011 International Joint Conference on Neural Networks (IJCNN), pp. 3256–3263 (2011)
8. El-Melegy, M.: Random sampler m-estimator algorithm with sequential probability ratio test for robust function approximation via feed-forward neural networks. IEEE Transactions on Neural Networks and Learning Systems 24(7), 1074–1085 (2013)
9. Golak, S., Burchart-Korol, D., Czaplicka-Kolarz, K., Wieczorek, T.: Application of neural network for the prediction of eco-efficiency. In: Liu, D., Zhang, H., Polycarpou, M., Alippi, C., He, H. (eds.) ISNN 2011, Part III. LNCS, vol. 6677, pp. 380–387. Springer, Heidelberg (2011)
10. Guillen, A.: Applying mutual information for prototype or instance selection in regression problems. In: ESANN 2009 (2009)
11. Hampel, F.R., Ronchetti, E.M., Rousseeuw, P.J., Stahel, W.A.: Robust Statistics: The Approach Based on Influence Functions (Wiley Series in Probability and Statistics), revised edn. Wiley-Interscience, New York (2005)
12. Hart, P.: The condensed nearest neighbor rule (corresp.). IEEE Transactions on Information Theory 14(3), 515–516 (1968)
13. Huber, P.J.: Robust Statistics. Wiley Series in Probability and Statistics. Wiley-Interscience (1981)

14. Kordos, M., Duch, W.: Variable Step Search Algorithm for Feedforward Networks. Neurocomputing 71(13-15), 2470–2480 (2008)
15. Kordos, M., Białka, S., Blachnik, M.: Instance selection in logical rule extraction for regression problems. In: Rutkowski, L., Korytkowski, M., Scherer, R., Tadeusiewicz, R., Zadeh, L.A., Zurada, J.M. (eds.) ICAISC 2013, Part II. LNCS, vol. 7895, pp. 167–175. Springer, Heidelberg (2013)
16. Kordos, M., Blachnik, M., Strzempa, D.: Do We Need Whatever More Than k-NN? In: Rutkowski, L., Scherer, R., Tadeusiewicz, R., Zadeh, L.A., Zurada, J.M. (eds.) ICAISC 2010, Part I. LNCS (LNAI), vol. 6113, pp. 414–421. Springer, Heidelberg (2010)
17. Kordos, M., Rusiecki, A.: Improving MLP Neural Network Performance by Noise Reduction. In: Dediu, A.-H., Martín-Vide, C., Truthe, B., Vega-Rodríguez, M.A. (eds.) TPNC 2013. LNCS, vol. 8273, pp. 133–144. Springer, Heidelberg (2013)
18. Liano, K.: Robust error measure for supervised neural network learning with outliers. IEEE Transactions on Neural Networks 7(1), 246–250 (1996)
19. Pernia-Espinoza, A.V., Ordieres-Mere, J.B., de Pison, F.J.M., Gonzalez-Marcos, A.: Tao-robust backpropagation learning algorithm. Neural Networks 18(2), 191–204 (2005)
20. Prechelt, L.: Proben1 – a set of neural network benchmark problems and benchmarking rules. Tech. rep. (1994)
21. Rousseeuw, P.J., Leroy, A.M.: Robust Regression and Outlier Detection. John Wiley & Sons, Inc., New York (1987)
22. Rousseeuw, P.J.: Least median of squares regression. Journal of the American Statistical Association 79(388), 871–880 (1984)
23. Rusiecki, A.: Robust LTS backpropagation learning algorithm. In: Sandoval, F., Prieto, A., Cabestany, J., Graña, M. (eds.) IWANN 2007. LNCS, vol. 4507, pp. 102–109. Springer, Heidelberg (2007)
24. Rusiecki, A.: Robust MCD-based backpropagation learning algorithm. In: Rutkowski, L., Tadeusiewicz, R., Zadeh, L.A., Zurada, J.M. (eds.) ICAISC 2008. LNCS (LNAI), vol. 5097, pp. 154–163. Springer, Heidelberg (2008)
25. Rusiecki, A.: Robust learning algorithm based on iterative least median of squares. Neural Processing Letters 36(2), 145–160 (2012)
26. Rusiecki, A.: Robust learning algorithm based on LTA estimator. Neurocomputing 120, 624–632 (2013)
27. Salvador, G., Derrac, J., Ramon, C.: Prototype selection for nearest neighbor classification: Taxonomy and empirical study. IEEE Transactions on Pattern Analysis and Machine Intelligence 34, 417–435 (2012)
28. Tolvi, J.: Genetic algorithms for outlier detection and variable selection in linear regression models. Soft Computing 8, 527–533 (2004)
29. Merz, C., Murphy, P.: Uci repository of machine learning databases (2013), http://www.ics.uci.edu/mlearn/MLRepository.html
30. Wilson, D.L.: Asymptotic properties of nearest neighbor rules using edited data. IEEE Transactions on Systems, Man and Cybernetics SMC-2(3), 408–421 (1972)
31. Zhang, J.: Intelligent selection of instances for prediction functions in lazy learning algorithms. Artifcial Intelligence Review 11, 175–191 (1997)
32. Source code and datasets used in the paper, https://code.google.com/p/mlp2013/

Principal Component Analysis to Reduce Forecasting Error of Industrial Energy Consumption in Models Based on Neural Networks

Isaac Santos Sacramento[1], Gueibi Peres Souza[2], and Raul Sidnei Wazlawick[1]

[1] Federal University of Santa Catarina, Informatic and Statistic Institute,
Trindade, Florianpolis, Brazil
[2] Federal University of Santa Catarina, Department of Economics and International
Relations, Trindade, Florianpolis, Brazil

Abstract. Industrial energy consumption depends on social and economic variables, and the way in which variables are selected is an important issue in causal forecasting. In this paper, we have developed a method to select the input variables for the monthly forecasting of energy consumption by artificial neural networks. The method consists of applying principal component analysis to reduce the dimensionality of data. The forecasts obtained by applying the principal component analysis were combined by a neural network and compared to the ones obtained by selecting variables using a correlation analysis. An important contribution of this work is the evidence that principal component analysis reduces the number of variables in the input set and, consequently, the error rate of neural networks in energy forecasting. The Mean Absolute Percentage Error (MAPE) and Theil's U statistic were used to provide evidence of the predictive capability of the proposed method. The neural network with variables selected via the first principal component analysis obtained out of sample errors of that were approximately 15.4% lower than the neural nets with input variables selected by correlation analysis. In addition, the performance of the neural net, the input of which was selected in the second principal component, has demonstrated a MAPE that was 10.65% lower than the neural net fed with variables selected using a correlation analysis. Completing the analysis, the combination of forecasts exhibited errors that were approximately 0.93% lower than the error obtained by selecting variables using a correlation analysis. The neural net that was fed with variables selected in the third principal component did not reach errors lower than the naive method. However, the nets results were relevant to the combination of forecasts.

Keywords: Principal Component Analysis, Correlation Analysis, Neural Network, Electricity Energy Forecasting, Time Series.

1 Introduction

The energy consumption is usually assessed based on historical series and its relation to other relevant variables, such as economic, demographic and climatic

L. Rutkowski et al. (Eds.): ICAISC 2014, Part I, LNAI 8467, pp. 143–154, 2014.

indexes, as well as the energy price [8]. Variable selection, which is often the initial step in the application of causal forecasting methods, is commonly used empirically when it should occur as widely and unrestrictedly as possible. Correlation analysis is used to select the variables for forecasting energy demand and consumption [7][15][19][20]. However, this method can be an expensive activity when handling a database with many variables.

Tsekouras, Elias, Kavatza and Contaxis [20] studied energy forecasting for industrial and residential classes. They assessed a regressive nonlinear multivariate method that included a correlation analysis to select the input data. This selection method was even used by Tsekouras, Dyalinas, Hatziargyriou and Kavatza [19] to limit the input variables to nonlinear functions on energy prediction in Greece. The authors found adequate models for forecasting in small metropolitan areas. Mohamed and Bodger [13] applied a correlation analysis to select the demographic and economic variables for multiple linear regressions to predict the energy consumption in New Zeland. The authors concluded that the accuracy of their models would strongly depend on forecasting the input variables via a simple regression. In addition to this study, correlation analyses were applied to select the variables in energy prediction as previously shown [22].

According to Armstrong [2], the accuracy of the forecasting combining forecasts derived from different methods can be improved. The combination of forecasts was applied by Wichard [23] to build a method consisting of three types of individual models: a nearest neighbor/trajectory ensemble model, the one-year-cycle, including the Easter correction, and a neural network ensemble. This approach was used to cope with the different seasonal features of a time series.

Several recent papers have addressed the selection of appropriate input variables for forecasts. Earlier research [6] has demonstrated that Principal Component Analysis can reduce the errors in the forecasting with real data when applied to the definition of a dynamic regression model. Muoz and Czernichow [14] studied the degree of significance in a subset of input variables based on the statistical study of the output of the forecast method. According to the authors, the standardized inputs that are not used by the model to estimate its outputs are considered to have a low significance. The authors concluded that the inputs of the model are the estimations of the input of the process if the inputs of a process are an estimation from a set of samples of the training set. Magalhes and Wazlawick [5] defined a model for short-term load forecasting in which the input variables are optimized via genetic algorithms. The authors demonstrated that the forecasting errors could be reduced in a variety of nodes of an electrical system using the genetic algorithm to support the definition of a neural network's input layer and parameters. Souza, Samohyl and Pereira [17] introduced an approach related to the selection of input variables. The authors showed that the Principal Component Analysis (PCA) for the selection of explanatory variables could improve the prediction by combining regressive models compared to a simple correlation analysis. The authors discussed the accuracy of two methodologies, PCA or correlation analysis, to estimate the number of parameters that are larger than the size of the sample. In this sense, this argument may be equally efficient when applied to studies involving models based on Neural Networks (NN). We have noticed that the impact of PCA on the results of neural network forecasts has not been fully analyzed, even though PCA is a well-known technique and NN is widely applied to solve forecasting problems.

Neural Networks (NN) are a class of non-linear prediction models that have attracted the interest of the research community for forecasting [1, 3, 4, 9–11, 18, 21]. This interest is justified because the NN is a universal approximator in certain conditions [16]. Specifically, neural networks with a single hidden layer that contain a finite number of hidden neurons and an arbitrary activation function can approximate any function that is continuous on R^m.

2   Data Analysis

The time series were used in this study consisted of real data from the state of Santa Catarina, Brazil from 2004 to 2011. Principal component analysis, correlation analysis and neural networks were applied to the industrial energy consumption historical data, including the economic and industrial indices.

Industrial processes are responsible for 40% of the total electrical energy consumption in the State of Santa Catarina, and the time series were measured monthly in Megawatt-Hour (MW h). The economical and industrial indices were obtained from a public website (Time Series Management System (SGS)) maintained by the Central Bank of Brazil. We used all time series that met the study period, which comprised a total of 30 variables, each with 90 steps. Despite the relatively short size of the time series, 12 observations were separated for performance analysis. These data were used as part of the process of setting the weights of neural networks. The other 78 observations were used to train and validate the models.

The data set was scaled by Eq. (1). In this normalization X_{ij} represents the observation j of the variable i. Each observation was subtracted from the mean μ_i of the temporal series and devided by its standard deviation σ_i, resulting in a newer observation Z_{ij}. This procedure avoids distortion in results of principal component analysis.

$$Z_{ij} = \frac{X_{ij} - \mu_i}{\sigma_i} \qquad (1)$$

3   Principal Component Analysis Background

The Principal Component Analysis (PCA) is a mathematic method that transforms a set of variables into a set of principal components with the same dimension as the original data. The principal components have the following features: each component is a linear combination of the variables, the components are orthogonal and they maintain a maximum amount of information related to the variance of the original data ordered by estimate. The PCA proceeds via a dimensional reduction on a database with many variables to transform them into a new coordinate system by rotating the axis of the original data.

The analysis is based on the total variance of the data set. Specifically, a set of p variables $X_1, X_2, \ldots, X_p$, which are represented in the matrix **S**. Each variable, with n observations, will result in $Z_1, Z_2, \ldots, Z_p$ non-correlated indices. The non-correlation of the indices implies the measurement of different dimensions in the variance of the principal components, such that $Var(Z_1) \geq Var(Z_2) \geq \ldots \geq Var(Z_p)$.

The principal components are obtained by solving the equation of the covariance matrix **S**, $det[S - \lambda I] = 0$. Where I is the identity matrix and λ is the vector of eigenvalues[1].

$$S = \begin{pmatrix} Var(X_1) & Cov(X_1, X_2) & \ldots & Cov(X_1, X_p) \\ Cov(X_2, X_1) & Var(X_2) & \ldots & Cov(X_2, X_p) \\ \vdots & \vdots & \ddots & \vdots \\ Cov(X_p, X_1) & Cov(X_n, X_2) & \ldots & Var(X_p) \end{pmatrix}$$

Let $\lambda_1, \lambda_2, \ldots, \lambda_p$ be the eigenvalues that solve the matrix **S**. Each of the eigenvalues λ_i is related to an eigenvector $\tilde{\alpha}_i$, which is ortogonal to the others. Let α_i be the eigenvector related to the eigenvalue λ_i. the first principal component Z_1 represents the largest possible variability in the data. The first principal component is given by the linear combination of Eq. (2), and its eigenvector is given by $\tilde{\alpha}_1 = [\alpha_{11}\alpha_{12} \ldots \alpha_{1p}]$

$$Z_1 = \alpha_{11}X_1 + \alpha_{12}X_2 + \ldots + \alpha_{1p}X_p \tag{2}$$

The calculation is analogous until the p-th principal component, which is calculated as follows (3):

$$Z_p = \alpha_{p1}X_1 + \alpha_{p2}X_2 + \ldots + \alpha_{pp}X_p \tag{3}$$

The application of PCA may be summarized as the following steps:

1. Standardization of variables.
2. Calculation of the covariance matrix.
3. Calculation of eigenvalues and eigenvectors.
4. Discard the components that explain a small proportion of the variability of the data.

The first three steps were performed in an automated application developed in MatLab, and the last step was considered part of the interpretation in the principal component analysis.

4   Forecast Consumption Industrial Electricity

We selected the most suitable set of variables to forecast the industrial consumption electricity in the State of Santa Catarina using a principal component

---

[1] Let $T : V \to V$ be a linear operation. If exists $v \in V$, $v \neq 0$ and $\lambda \in \mathbf{R}$ such that $T(v) = \lambda \times v$, λ is said to be an eingenvalue of T and v is an eigenvector of T related to λ.

analysis. The study period ranged from April 2004 to November 2010, and the forecasting horizon was one year ahead, from December 2010 to November 2011.

A Pearson correlation analysis and principal component analysis were applied to the data. Through the correlation was extracted a set of variables which were used as the input set to the neural networks. The PCA was applied in two steps: first, three principal components were chosen and from each of them we selected a set of variables to be used individually as input for neural networks. Second, the obtained forecasts were used as the input variables in a new neural network model. Fig. 1 illustrates the proposed method.

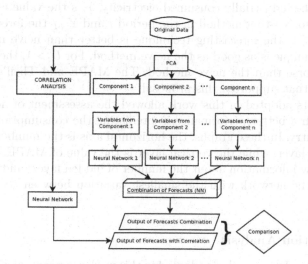

Fig. 1. Forecasting method of industrial energy consumption by combining neural networks

The neural networks (NN) adopted in this work are of the feed-forward class. Aiming to improve the forecasting performance, the NN models were implemented by varying the number of hidden layers between 1 and 2, each one varying its number of neurons from 1 to 30. The training set consisted of monthly data between April of 2004 to June of 2009, and the validation set consisted of data from July of 2009 to September of 2010. The forecasting was performed in terms of the adhesion test to one year ahead, i.e., to September of 2011.

To evaluate the performance of NN with input selected by PCA and compare it with results of NN with input selected by correlation, we employed the Mean Absolute Percent Error (MAPE) (4). n is the number of forecasting observations, Y_i is the real value of industrially consumed electricity for period i and $\hat{Y}_i$ is the forecast by the respective forecasting method in the period i.

$$MAPE = 100 \times \frac{1}{n} \sum_{k=1}^{n} \frac{\left| Y_i - \hat{Y}_i \right|}{\hat{Y}_i} \tag{4}$$

We also adopted the use of Theil's U, which allows the evaluation of the heuristics used in the forecast compared with the accuracy of the naive method. Eq. (5) expresses Theil's U, with which the method with the biggest errors can be disregarded.

$$U = \sqrt[2]{\frac{\sum_{k=1}^{n-1}(\frac{\hat{Y}_{i+1}-Y_i}{Y_i} - \frac{Y_{i+1}-Y_i}{Y_i})^2}{\sum_{k=1}^{n-1}(\frac{Y_{i+1}-Y_i}{Y_i})^2}} \tag{5}$$

where n is the number of observations forecasted with the proposed method, Y_i the actual value of industral consumption electricity for period i, Y_{i+1} is the next value of the industrially consumed electricity, $\hat{Y}_i$ s the value estimated by the respective forecasting method in the period i and $\hat{Y}_{i+1}$ the forecast in time $i + 1$. For $U < 1$, the forecasting technique is better than neive method. For $U = 1$, the technique is as good as the neive method. For $U > 1$, the forecasting technique is worse than the neive method. The MAPE and Theil's U enabled benchmarking that supported this proposal.

The box-plots adopted in this work allowed the assessment of network configurations with a better performance in predicting the consumption of electric power by industry. In these graphs, the horizontal axis is the number of neurons in each hidden layer, while the vertical layer is the value of MAPE. The tops of the graphs show information about the number of hidden layers and the number of neurons of the network with the smallest variation between the lowest and highest MAPE.

4.1   Correlation Analysis

The Pearson correlation analysis adopted in this work represents the linear correlation degree between two variables. The correlation index, r, is a dimensionless measure that varies over the interval $[-1, 1]$. When $r = 1$, the two variables are perfectly correlated. When $r = 0$ both variables are not correlated. $r = -1$ indicates a perfect yet inverse correlation. Thus, the closer to 1 or -1 the correlation index is, the more correlated the variables are.

The variables were selected based on the critical correlation coefficient to samples with 90 observations. The statistical meaning of the correlation index was verified with Students t-test. Let H_0 be the null hypothesis, in which the variables X_i and the industrial electricity are not correlated, and let H_1 be the alternative hypotesis. H_0 is rejected when the correlation coefficient between these parameters is larger than the critical correlation t, for $N - 2$ degrees of freedom and 99% of confidence.

For the samples with 90 observations and 99% of confidence, the critical correlation is $t = 0.2702$. The variables correlated with the Industrial Consumption (IC), and their correlation indices r are presented in Tab. 1. The acronyms IVVV and ICMS refer to the Index of Retail Sail in the State of Santa Catarina and the Tax on Goods, respectively.

The variables selected by the correlation analysis were used to build forecasting models of the industrial electricity consumption by neural networks. The

Table 1. Table of varibles correlated to Industrial Energy Consumption

Variables	Correlation
100 Industrial Consumption (IC)	1.000
102 Capacity Utilization	0.6019
1477 IVVV - Total	0.5327
1492 IVVV - Fuels	0.5085
1505 IVVV - Food, Beverages and Tabacco	0.4887
1518 IVVV - Tissues	0.4461
1531 IVVV - Furniture and Appliances	0.3248
1557 IVVV - Automobiles	0.7801
1570 IVVV - Hipermarkets	0.4817
4348 ICMS Collection	0.6767
4375 Revenue of States	0.4910
7646 ICMS - Primary Sector	0.6420
14025 Financial System Credits (PF)	0.7382
14052 Financial System Credits (PJ)	0.7107
14079 Financial System Credits (Total)	0.7247
15383 Economic Activity - Previews Methodology	0.8018
15884 Default of the Financial System (PF)	0.3601
17742 Regional Economic Activity	0.7888
20199 Retail Sale Amount- Expanded	0.6952
20200 Retail Sale - Pharmaceutical Goods	0.7213
20202 Retail Sale - Office Supplies	0.6283
20203 Retail Sale - Other Goods	0.4931
20204 Retail Sale - Building Material	0.7553
20442 Regional Economic Activity - Index	0.7321
20455 Regional Economic Activity - Sazonal Adjust	0.7873

relevant results showed MAPE and Theil's U values below 1. The graphic in Fig. 2 shows the change in the error reported by different architectures of neural networks. This graphic shows the MAPE variability as a function of the number of neurons in the hidden layer. The upper and lower values as well as the outliers above three standard deviation are presented, which are represented by the symbol +.

For the prediction (tests in the sample), the network with 1 hidden layer and 12 neurons showed a lowest MAPE value of 0.7506% and highest value equal to 4.4350%. One outlier equal to 10.6780% was observed, and all values of Theil's U were below 1. The neural network performance out of the sample remained between 1.1045 and 8.2199, and Theil's U varied between 0.2097 and 1.4594.

4.2   Principal Component Analysis

The data scaled by Eq. 1 were applied to a PCA. The analysis resulted in the eigenvalues of each principal component and an explanatory percentage, i.e., the degree to which the variance of the original data can explain each component and the cumulative percentage, which is the sum of explanatory percentage

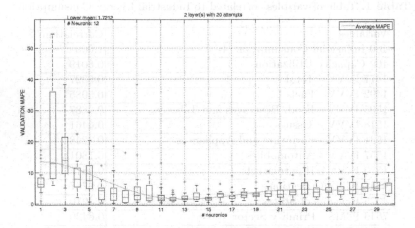

Fig. 2. Prediction errors in the correlation analysis

Table 2. Values obtained with application of PCA

Component	Eigenvalues	Explanatory Percentage	Cumulative
1	19.1991	63.9970	63.9970
2	2.7375	9.1250	73.12
3	2.1558	7.1858	80.31

until such a component. These data are introduced in Tab. 2 for the three first components. The first three principal components are responsible for 80.30% of the total variance of the data, which justifies the use of these components from which the input sets to the neural models were selected. This approach was adopted by Mardia [12], who used the principal components that accumulate at least 70% of the total variance.

The first principal component explains 63.9970% of the variability of data, the second principal component is responsible for 9.1250% and the third principal component represents 7.1858% of the remaining variance of data.

Once the relevant principal components were observed, the next step was the selection of the variables with the strongest influence on the variability of the component via the mean of each eigenvector according to Souza, Samohyl and Pereira [17]. The variables whose contribution to the component was above the mean of the eigenvectors were selected. Thus, we selected 21 variables in the first component, 19 variables in the second principal component and 11 retained variables in the third. These selected variables composed the input set to the neural networks.

The variable sets obtained with the principal components were tested in different architectures of the neural network. The neural nets tended to be less accurate when we used variables of the components beyond the last retained component. Thus, the predictive ability of neural networks decreased with the variance, which is explained by the last principal component retained. Three

Table 3. Table of results obtained by PCA and Neural Networks

CP	Conf.	MAPE Pred.	U Pred.	MAPE Forec.	U Forec.
1	1-15	0.4257%	0.1367	0.9343%	0.2121
2	1-11	0.3564%	0.0707	0.9868%	0.1366
3	1-1	2.5634%	0.6704	3.7482%	0.6927

neural architectures could be highlighted that had the lowest MAPE and Theil's U values below 1 using the variables obtained in each of the three first principal components.

We achieved an in-sample performance with a lower and upper MAPEs equal to 0.4257% and 3.0897% in the architecture, respectively with the variables retained in the first principal component [1 - 15]. This finding indicates 1 hidden layer and 15 neurons in this layer. The performance out of the sample reached a minimal MAPE equal to 0.9343% and maximum MAPE equal 6.7426%. No outliers were observed.

The variables from the second principal component resulted in a smaller variability of the neural network [1 - 11] (1 hidden layer and 11 neurons) in the sample. The minimal in-sample MAPE was 0.3564%, while the minimal MAPE out of the sample was 0.9868%. Three outliers equal to 5.7797%, 6.5429% and 6.7126% were observed in this configuration. The values for the Theil's U were equal to 0.0707 and 1.0281. Comparing this result to those of the first principal component, the values for the MAPE and Theil's U were lower. This is a particularly interesting result because these neural nets had a bigger predictive capability and the variables from the second principal component had a bigger explanatory capability than the first one even though the second principal component had fewer retained variables than the first principal component.

The third principal component explained 7.1858% of the variability of the data. This component retained 11 variables. The network with configuration [1 - 1] reached a 2.5635% and 3.7482% minimal MAPE for the prediction and forecasting, respectively. The values for Theil's U of this neural network were 0.6704 in prediction and 0.6927 in forecasting.

The simplest configuration showed the lowest variability, because of that we omited the graphic for third principal component. However, its predictive capacity did not exceed the performance of the neural networks with the variables from the correlation analysis, first or second principal component. Nevertheless, its predictions in-sample and forecasts were essential to the results of the combination of forecasts, shown in the next section. Tab. 3 shows the values of the MAPEs and Theil's U discussed earlier.

4.3   Combination of Energy Consumption Forecasts

The results reached by the three principal components motivated the investigation of the electricity consumption via the combination of forecasts. We believe that the neural networks can generate the predictive potential with variables of each principal component via the combination of forecasts. The combination was the method that reached the smallest MAPEs in the estimation of industrial energy consumption in and out of the sample because each component adds relevant information to the neural networks.

The data used as input to the combination model were the predictions and forecasts obtained from variables selected through the principal components, as illustrated in Fig.. A new neural network model was trained, validated and tested while respecting the same proportion of data established in previous models and its results were compared to results obtained with correction analyses. Fig. 3 shows the performance of the neural nets for the combination of forecasts.

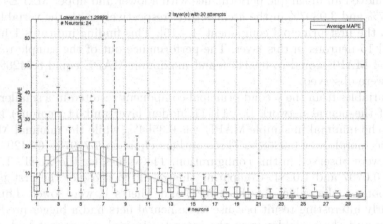

Fig. 3. Prediction errors with combination of forecasts

The combination of forecasts was more precise than the selection of variables by the correlation analysis. The neural network of the combination had a MAPE equal to 0.3584% for the in-sample test and 1.0942% for the tests out of the sample. These values are smaller than those achieved by the correlation analysis, which were 0.45478% in-sample and 1.1045% out of sample. An expressive gain in comparison to the lowest MAPE values with the principal component was not observed, for which the best result was 0.3564% in the sample and 0.9868% out of the sample. The values of the Theil's U for combined forecasts were below 1 in and out of the sample, which indicates that the combination is a better predictor than the naive model.

5 Conclusion

This report describes a method to predict the industrial energy consumption in the State of Santa Catarina that considers the dimensional reduction of the input data via a principal component analysis, which was compared to the Pearson Correlation Analysis. The principal component analysis allowed the selection of a set of appropriate variables to perform the prediction by neural networks. The industrial energy consumption was forecast by submitting these variables to different neural networks. Neural networks fed with data from the first and second principal component were demonstrated to be more accurate compared to those trained with variables selected by correlation analysis. These results motivated the combination of forecasts. As such, we used the forecasts obtained by the first three principal components. The model generated by the combination of forecasts was more accurate than the models with input variables from the individual principal component, which suggested that the method is an alternative solution for variable selection in forecasting problems. Future studies related to this study include assessing the performance via the application of the method with competition data, such as NNG-C.

References

1. Adya, M., Collopy, F.: How effective are neural networks at forecasting and prediction? A review and evaluation. Journal of Forecasting (17), 481–495 (1998)
2. Armstrong, J.: Combining forecasts. In: Principles of Forecasting: A Handbook for Researchers and Practitioners, pp. 417–439. Kluwer Academic Publishing (2001)
3. Balkin, S.D., Ord, J.K.: Automatic neural network modeling for univariate time series. International Journal of Forecasting 16(4), 509–515 (2000)
4. da Silva, A.P.A., Ferreira, V.H., Velasquez, R.M.: Input space to neural network based load forecasters. International Journal of Forecasting 24(4), 616–629 (2008)
5. de Oliveira, C.M., Wazlawick, R.S.: Electrical reallocation of transformers in distribution systems using genetic algorithms. International Journal of Engineering Intelligent Systems for Electrical Engineering and Communications 12(1), 21–28 (2004)
6. del Moral, M.J., Valderrama, M.J.: A principal component approach to dynamic regression models. Journal of Forecasting (13), 237–244 (1997)
7. Duan, L., Niu, D., Gu, Z.: Long and medium term power load forecasting with multi-level recursive regression analysis. In: International Symposium on Intelligent Information Technology Application, vol. 1, pp. 514–518 (December 2008)
8. Elias, C.N., Hatziargyriou, N.D.: An annual midterm energy forecasting model using fuzzy logic. IEEE Transactions on Power Systems 24(1), 469–478 (2009)
9. Farahat, M.A.: Long term industrial load forecasting and planning using Neural Networks technique and fuzzy inference method. In: 39th International Conference on Power Engineering, vol. 1, p. 4 (September 2004)
10. Kahoa, T.Q.D., Phuong, L.M., Binh, P.T.T., Lien, N.T.H.: Application of wavelet and neural network to long-term load forecasting. In: International Conference on Power System Technology, vol. 1, pp. 840–844 (November 2004)
11. Liu, H., Cai, L., Wu, X.: Grey-RBF neural network prediction model for city electricity demand forecasting. In: International Conference on Wireless Comunications, Network and Mobile Computing, pp. 1–5 (October 2008)
12. Mardia, K.V., Kent, J.T., Bibby, J.M.: Multivariate analysis. Academic, London (1979)
13. Mohamed, Z., Bodger, P.: Forecasting electricity consumption in the New Zealand using economic and demographic variables. Energy 30(10), 1833–1843 (2005)
14. Muñoz, A., Czernichow, T.: Variable selection using feedforward and recurrent neural networks. Engineering Intelligent Systems for Electrical Engineering and Communications 6(2), 91–102 (1998)

15. Pao, H.: Comparing linear and non-linear forecast for Taiwan' electricity consumption. Energy 31(12), 2129–2141 (2006)
16. Rubio, G., Pomares, H., Rojas, I., Herrera, L.J.: A heuristic method for parameter selection in LS-SVM: Application to time series prediction. International Journal of Forecasting 27(3), 725–739 (2011)
17. Souza, G.P., Samohyl, R.W., Pereira, R.C.: Assessing preliminar applicability of Principal Component Analysis to a big dataset to build linear regression models. In: Brazilisan Simposium of Probability ans Statistics-SINAPE, Caxambu-MG, Brasil (2006)
18. Terasvirta, T., Medeiros, M.C., Rech, G.: Building neural network models for time series: a statistical approach. Journal of Forecasting (25(1)), 49–75 (2006)
19. Tsekouras, G.J., Dyalinas, G.J., Hatziargyriou, N.D., Kavatza, S.: A non-linear multivariable regression model for midterm energy forecasting of power system. Electric Power System Research 77(12), 1560–1568 (2007)
20. Tsekouras, G.J., Elias, C.N., Kavatza, S., Contaxis, G.C.: A hybrid non-linear regression midterm energy forecasting method using data mining. In: Power Tech Conference Proceedings, vol. 1, p. 6 (June 2003)
21. Zhang, G., Patuwo, B.E., Hu, M.Y.: Forecasting with artificial neural networks: the state of the art. International Journal of Forecasting 14(1), 35–62 (1998)
22. Zhao, H., Liu, R., Zhao, Z., Fan, C.: Analysis of Energy Consumption Prediction Model Based on Genetic Algorithm and Wavelet Neural Network. In: 3rd International Workshop on Intelligent Systems and Applications (ISA), pp. 1–4 (May 2011)
23. Wichard, J.D.: Forecasting the NN5 time series with hybrid models. International Journal of Forecasting 27(3), 700–707 (2011)

Boundedness of Weight Elimination
for BP Neural Networks

Jian Wang[1,2,3], Jacek M. Zurada[2,4],
Yanjiang Wang[3], Jing Wang[1], and Guofang Xie[5]

[1] Dalian University of Technology, Dalian, Liaoning 116024, China
[2] University of Louisville, Louisville, KY 40292, USA
[3] China University of Petroleum, Qingdao, Shandong 266580, China
[4] Information Technology Institute, University of Social Sciences,
90-113 Lodz, Poland
[5] Freelance Translator and Amateur Mathematician, China

Abstract. Weight elimination can be usefully interpreted as an assumption about the prior distribution of the weights trained in the backpropagation neural networks (BPNN). Weight elimination based on different scaling of weight parameters is of a general form, with the weight decay and subset selection methods as special cases. The applications of this method have been well developed, however, only few references provides more comprehensive theoretical analysis. To address this issue, we investigate the uniform boundedness of the trained weights based on a descriptive proof.

Keywords: backpropagation, neural networks, weight decay, weight elimination, boundedness.

1 Introduction

The multilayer perceptron network trained by the backpropagation (BP) algorithm is currently the most widely used neural network architecture. BP is a specific training technique for implementing the gradient descent in weight space. The first description of this algorithm was presented in 1974 [1]. It was rediscovered independently in [2, 3] and then widely publicized. However, the problem of perceptron network generalization has proven more challenging.

Penalization (or regularization) method is often used to achieve better generalization in perceptron networks [4]. The error on the training set can become very small, but when the test set is presented, the error is still large, thus indicating poor generalization. Insofar as the network design is statistical in nature, the tradeoff between the fitting of the training data and the goodness of the model for test data can be achieved by minimizing the total error with regularization method. In the context of BP learning, or similar supervised learning procedures, a common regularization strategy is to add an extra constraint (penalty term) based on the complexity of samples and weights. The cost function for the penalization inductive principle is expressed as follows

$$R_{pen}(\mathbf{w}) = R_{emp}(\mathbf{w}) + \lambda \Phi[f(\mathbf{x}, \mathbf{w})]. \tag{1}$$

L. Rutkowski et al. (Eds.): ICAISC 2014, Part I, LNAI 8467, pp. 155–165, 2014.
© Springer International Publishing Switzerland 2014

The first term $R_{emp}(\mathbf{w})$ of the total risk $R_{pen}(\mathbf{w})$ is the standard performance metric, which depends on the network model and the input samples. The second term $\Phi[f(\mathbf{x}, \mathbf{w})]$ is the complexity penalty, which is measured in terms of the weights.

Two different classes of penalty functionals are used for peceptron networks: nonparametric and parametric penalties [4]. Nonparametric penalties attempt to evaluate the smoothness by using a differential operator, where the smoothness can be defined in terms of the wiggliness of function measured in the frequency domain [5]. In contrast, parametric penalties measure the complexity indirectly by imposing constraints on the parameters of cost function. A general form is as follows

$$\Phi[f(\mathbf{x}, \mathbf{w})] = \Phi(\mathbf{w}). \tag{2}$$

Two popular examples of penalty functions of this type are

$$\Phi_r(\mathbf{w}) = \sum_{i=1} w_i^2, \qquad \text{"ridge" or "weight decay"} \tag{3}$$

$$\Phi_s(\mathbf{w}) = \sum_{i=1} I(w_i \neq 0), \qquad \text{"subset selection"} \tag{4}$$

where $I(\cdot)$ denotes the indicator function.

Due to the discontinuous property of the above indicator function, combinational optimization is required to minimize (4). To effectively circumvent this NP hard problem, the discontinuous penalty can be approximated by a continuous one [6]. In the sequel, the following two complexity regularizations are presented.

$$\Phi_p(\mathbf{w}) = \sum_{i=1} |w_i|^p, \qquad \text{"bridge"} \tag{5}$$

$$\Phi_q(\mathbf{w}) = \sum_{i=1} \frac{(w_i/q)^2}{1 + (w_i/q)^2} \triangleq \Phi(\mathbf{w}), \qquad \text{"weight elimination"} \tag{6}$$

In this paper, we focus on the theoretical analysis of "weight elimination" (6), where q is the scale parameter of the weights. $\Phi(\mathbf{w})$ is used instead of $\Phi_q(\mathbf{w})$ throughout this paper for simplicity. For weight elimination, it approaches the weight decay penalty as $q \to \infty$ and approaches the subset selection penalty as $q \to 0$. The concept of weight elimination was first presented in [7]. More variants and applications have been demonstrated in [8–13].

Boundedness of weights plays an important role in preventing divergence when training and poor generalization after the training. In real applications, as in all modeling problems, the smaller sized network is preferred when it can adequately represent the training data. To the best of our knowledge, the boundedness analyses for neural networks are mainly focused on weight decay (cf. (3)) under some conditions [14–17]. The penalty term is defined as the squared norm of the weight vector. Additionally, the convergence analyses (asymptotic and deterministic) are discussed for different training modes such as batch and incremental modes.

To the best of our knowledge, there is no reference that discusses the boundedness of the weight sequence for weight elimination. The main contribution of this paper is in analysis of the property from mathematical view. On the basis of the analytic procedure, we show the best choice for parameter q in (6) which means the maximum interval of initial weights that can be chosen to guarantee the bounded weight sequence during training.

2 Weight Elimination Procedure

Denote the numbers of the neurons of the input, hidden and output layers of BP neural networks are p, n and 1, respectively. We do not consider the biases in this network model since it does not influence the theoretical analysis in this paper. Suppose that the training sample set is $\{\mathbf{x}^j, O^j\}_{j=0}^{J-1} \subset \mathbb{R}^p \times \mathbb{R}$, where $\mathbf{x}^j$ and O^j are the input and the corresponding target output of the j-th sample, respectively. Let $\mathbf{w} = (w_1, w_2, \cdots, w_r) \in \mathbb{R}^r$ be the weight vector, where $r = p(n+1)$. Let $f : \mathbb{R} \to \mathbb{R}$ be the activation function for the neural network. For any given input $\mathbf{x} \in \mathbb{R}^p$, the actual output is

$$y = f(\mathbf{w}, \mathbf{x}). \tag{7}$$

For fixed weights $\mathbf{w}$, the output error is defined as

$$E(\mathbf{w}) = \frac{1}{2} \sum_{j=0}^{J-1} (O^j - f(\mathbf{w}, \mathbf{x}^j))^2 + \lambda \Phi(\mathbf{w})$$
$$= F(\mathbf{w}, \mathbf{x}^j) + \lambda \Phi(\mathbf{w}), \tag{8}$$

where $F(\mathbf{w}, \mathbf{x}^j) = \frac{1}{2} \sum_{j=0}^{J-1} (O^j - f(\mathbf{w}, \mathbf{x}^j))^2$ and $\lambda > 0$ is the penalty coefficient. The gradients of the error function with respect to $w_i (i = 1, \cdots, p(n+1))$ is as follows

$$E_{w_i}(\mathbf{w}) = F_{w_i}(\mathbf{w}, \mathbf{x}^j) + \lambda \Phi_{w_i}(\mathbf{w})$$
$$= F_{w_i}(\mathbf{w}, \mathbf{x}^j) + \lambda \frac{2w_i q^2}{(q^2 + w_i^2)^2}. \tag{9}$$

Given an initial weight $\mathbf{w}^0 \in \mathbb{R}^{p(n+1)}$, the learning procedure with penalty term (6) updates the weights iteratively by

$$w_i^{m+1} = w_i^m - \eta E_{w_i}(\mathbf{w}^m), \tag{10}$$

where $\eta > 0$ is the constant learning rate,

$$E_{w_i}(\mathbf{w}^m) = F_{w_i}(\mathbf{w}^m, \mathbf{x}^j) + \lambda \frac{2q^2 w_i^m}{(q^2 + (w_i^m)^2)^2}, \tag{11}$$

where $m \in \mathbb{N}$; $i = 1, \cdots, p(n+1)$; $j = 0, 1, \cdots, J-1$.

The concept of this algorithm is to add a novel penalty term to the usual cost function and minimize the sum by BP [7]. The parameter q is the scaling coefficient of the trained weights. λ represents the relative importance of the penalty term with respect to the error $F(\mathbf{w}, \mathbf{x}^j)$.

3　Boundedness of Weights

To analyze the boundedness of the trained weights, the following assumptions are needed:

(A1) The function f satisfies that f and f' are uniformly bounded on $\mathbb{R}$;

(A2) The learning rate η satisfies that $0 < \eta < \frac{q^2}{2\lambda}$.

By (8) and (9), it is easy to prove that $F_{w_i}\left(\mathbf{w}^m, \mathbf{x}^j\right)$ is uniformly bounded on $\mathbb{R}$. That is, there exists a positive constant β subject to

$$F_{w_i}\left(\mathbf{w}^m, \mathbf{x}^j\right) \leq \beta. \tag{12}$$

Lemma 1. *[18] Given the general quartic equation*

$$ax^4 + 4bx^3 + 6cx^2 + 4dx + e = 0 \tag{13}$$

with real coefficients and $a \neq 0$, the nature of its roots is mainly determined by its discriminant

$$\Delta = I^3 - 27K^2, \tag{14}$$

where

$$H = b^2 - ac, \tag{15}$$
$$I = ae - 4bd + 3c^2, \tag{16}$$
$$G = a^2 d - 3abc + 2b^3, \tag{17}$$
$$K = \frac{4H^3 - a^2 HI - G^2}{a^3}, \tag{18}$$

Then, if $\Delta < 0$, the equation has two real distinct roots and two complex conjugate roots. In addition, the roots of this equation under this condition are as follows

$$x_{1,2} = \frac{1}{a}\left(-b - \mathrm{sgn}\,(G)\sqrt{t} \pm \sqrt{\frac{|G|}{\sqrt{t}} - t + 3H}\right), \tag{19}$$

$$x_{3,4} = \frac{1}{a}\left(-b + \mathrm{sgn}\,(G)\sqrt{t} \pm i\sqrt{\frac{|G|}{\sqrt{t}} + t - 3H}\right) \tag{20}$$

where $\mathrm{sgn}(\cdot)$ *stands for a sign function,*

$$\mathrm{sgn}\,(G) = \begin{cases} 1, & (G > 0). \\ -1, & (G < 0). \end{cases} \tag{21}$$

$$t = \frac{a}{2}\left(\sqrt[3]{-K + \sqrt{\frac{-\Delta}{27}}} + \sqrt[3]{-K - \sqrt{\frac{-\Delta}{27}}}\right) + H. \tag{22}$$

Remark: To analyze the boundedness of weight sequence in the training procedure, it is necessary to discuss the relationship among the parameters q, λ and β. Based on the training process of weight elimination, we need to solve a quartic equation in the following Lemma, where the parameters q, λ and β are its coefficients. This Lemma demonstrates the solutions under some specific conditions.

Lemma 2. *Consider the function* $P(x) = x^4 + 2q^2x^2 - 2\frac{\lambda}{\beta}q^2x + q^4$, $(x > 0)$, *where* λ, β, q *are the learning parameters of weight elimination. If* $q < \frac{3\sqrt{3}\lambda}{8\beta}$, *then the equation*

$$P(x) = 0 \tag{23}$$

has two real distinct roots, x_1, x_2, *where* x_1 *and* x_2 *are the functions of parameter* q *for fixed* λ, β. *In addition,* x_1 *is strictly concave function with the maximum* $\frac{\lambda}{2\beta}$ *when* $q = \frac{\lambda}{2\beta}$, *while* x_2 *is strictly convex function with respect to variable* q.

Proof. By Lemma 1, we know that the coefficients of equation (23) corresponding to (13) are $a = 1$, $b = 0$, $c = \frac{q^2}{3}$, $d = -\frac{\lambda}{2\beta}q^2$, $e = q^4$, separately. Then we have

$$H = -\frac{q^2}{3}, \tag{24}$$

$$I = \frac{4q^4}{3}, \tag{25}$$

$$G = -\frac{q^2}{2}\frac{\lambda}{\beta}, \tag{26}$$

$$K = \frac{8q^6}{27} - \frac{q^4}{4}\left(\frac{\lambda}{\beta}\right)^2, \tag{27}$$

$$\Delta = I^3 - 27K^2 = \frac{\lambda^2 q^8}{16\beta^4}\left(64q^2\beta^2 - 27\lambda^2\right). \tag{28}$$

Since $P''(x) = 12x^2 + 4q^2 > 0$, then $P(x)$ is a strict convex function. Applying the discriminant rule of Lemma 1, there are two distinct roots when $\Delta < 0$, that is,

$$0 < q < \frac{3\sqrt{3}}{8}\frac{\lambda}{\beta}. \tag{29}$$

For brevity, we first consider the special case with respect to $\frac{\lambda}{\beta} = 1$. Then we extend the discussion on the general cases of parameter $\frac{\lambda}{\beta}$. In addition, the two real distinct roots based on the formula (19) and (22) are as follows

$$x_1 = \sqrt{t} - \sqrt{\frac{q^2}{2\sqrt{t}} - t - q^2}, \tag{30}$$

$$x_2 = \sqrt{t} + \sqrt{\frac{q^2}{2\sqrt{t}} - t - q^2}, \tag{31}$$

where $t = \frac{1}{2}\left(\sqrt[3]{-K + \sqrt{\frac{-\Delta}{27}}}\right) - \frac{q^2}{3}$. We note that the real roots x_1 and x_2 of
Eq. (23) depend on the parameter q, that is, $x_1(q)$ and $x_2(q)$ are functions with
respect to variable q.

In fact, the parameters λ, β and q here are identical to those of the weight
elimination algorithm (10), (11) and (12). Generally, the parameters λ and β are
fixed in the training. It is then essential to study the parameter q in discussing
the boundedness of weight sequence for weight elimination. The relationships
between the real roots of Eq. (23) and parameter q are as follows.

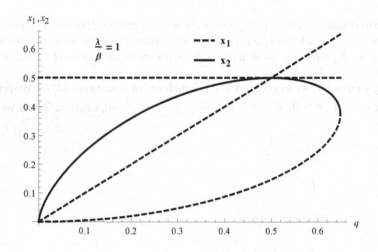

Fig. 1. Two real distinct roots of Eq. (23) for different q when $\frac{\lambda}{\beta} = 1$

It can be seen from Fig. 1 that the two real roots function curves of Eq. (23)
varying with the parameter q. For each q, there are two corresponding real roots,
the continuous curve represents the bigger real ones $x_2(q)$, while the dashed curve
is the smaller ones $x_1(q)$. That is, the vertical axis of Fig. 1 shows the changing
values of the real roots of Eq. (23). Furthermore, Fig. 1 shows that the smaller
roots $x_1(q)$ of Eq. (23) are strictly monotone increasing, while the bigger ones
$x_2(q)$ are first monotone increasing and then monotone decreasing after reaching
the maximum, 0.5. We note that here $\frac{\lambda}{2\beta} = \frac{1}{2}$, and $q = \frac{1}{2}$ (we consider the case
$\frac{\lambda}{\beta} = 1$ here).

Similarly, we can analyze the Fig. 2 with roots of Eq. (23) with different ratio
of $\frac{\lambda}{\beta}$, $\frac{\lambda}{\beta} = 2$ (cf. Fig. 2 a)) and $\frac{\lambda}{\beta} = \frac{1}{2}$ (cf. Fig. 2 b)), separately. Comparing
Fig. 1 and Fig. 2, an intuitive observation is that the variation tendency of the
real roots is to have the same properties with respect to a different $\frac{\lambda}{\beta}$. Another
important property is that the maximum of the bigger roots is equal to $\frac{\lambda}{2\beta}$, and
$q = \frac{\lambda}{2\beta}$.

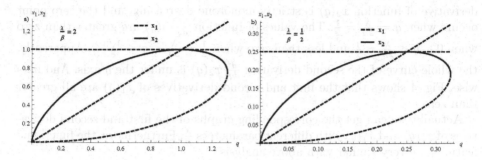

Fig. 2. Two real distinct roots of Eq. (23) for different q, a) $\frac{\lambda}{\beta} = 2$ and b) $\frac{\lambda}{\beta} = \frac{1}{2}$

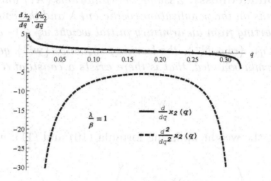

Fig. 3. The first and second derivatives of $x_2(q)$ when $\frac{\lambda}{\beta} = 1$

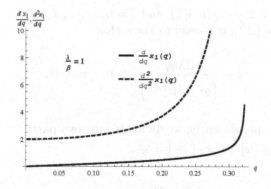

Fig. 4. The first and second derivatives of $x_1(q)$ when $\frac{\lambda}{\beta} = 1$

To verify this supposition, Fig. 3 and Fig. 4 show the first and second derivatives of the functions $x_2(q)$ and $x_1(q)$ for parameter $\frac{\lambda}{\beta} = 1$. We note that the vertical axes represent the corresponding function values $\frac{d}{dq}\mathbf{x}_2(q)$, $\frac{d^2}{dq^2}\mathbf{x}_2(q)$ and $\frac{d}{dq}\mathbf{x}_1(q)$, $\frac{d^2}{dq^2}\mathbf{x}_1(q)$, separately. For Fig. 3, it is interesting to note that the first derivative of function $x_2(q)$ is strictly monotone decreasing, and the zero point occurs when $q = \frac{\lambda}{2\beta} = \frac{1}{2}$. The values of function $\frac{d}{dq}x_2(q)$ are greater than zero when $0 < q < \frac{\lambda}{2\beta} = \frac{1}{2}$ and less than zero when $\frac{1}{2} = \frac{\lambda}{2\beta} < q < \frac{3\sqrt{3}}{8}\frac{\lambda}{\beta}$. Apparently, the whole curve of the second derivative $\frac{d^2}{dq^2}x_2(q)$ is under the q axis. And likewise, Fig. 4 shows that the first and second derivatives of $x_1(q)$ are all greater than zero.

Actually, we can get the corresponding graphs of the first and second derivatives of $x_2(q)$ and $x_1(q)$ with different parameters $\frac{\lambda}{\beta}$. Furthermore, the functional features are very similar with above analysis.

Theorem 1 (Boundedness). *Assume the conditions $(A1)$ and $(A2)$ are valid, parameter q depends on the penalization coefficient λ and the constant β in (12). If $q = \frac{\lambda}{2\beta}$, then starting from an arbitrary initial weight $w_i^0 \in (-q, q)$ or the m-th weight $w_i^m \in (-q, q)$, $(m \in \mathbb{N}^+)$, the learning sequence $\{\mathbf{w}^m\}$ generated by (10) and (11) is uniformly bounded, that is there exists a constant $\alpha > 0$ such that*

$$\|\mathbf{w}^m\| < \alpha. \tag{32}$$

Proof. Employing the weight updating formula (10) and (11), we have

$$w_i^{m+1} = \left(1 - \frac{2\lambda\eta q^2}{\left(q^2 + (w_i^m)^2\right)^2}\right) w_i^m - \eta F_{w_i}\left(\mathbf{w}^m, \mathbf{x}^j\right), \tag{33}$$

where $m \in \mathbb{N}$, $i = 1, 2, \cdots, p(n+1)$, and $j = 0, 1, \cdots, J-1$.
By the assumption $(A2)$, it is easy to know that

$$1 - \frac{2\lambda\eta q^2}{\left(q^2 + (w_i^m)^2\right)^2} > 0, \quad m \in \mathbb{N}. \tag{34}$$

To show the whole proof clearly, we divide it into two parts:
Case 1. $x_1\left(\frac{\lambda}{2\beta}\right) \leq |w_i^m| \leq x_2\left(\frac{\lambda}{2\beta}\right) = \frac{\lambda}{2\beta}$.
let

$$\bar{A} = \frac{\left(q^2 + A^2\right)^2}{2\lambda q^2} F_{w_i}\left(\mathbf{w}^m, \mathbf{x}^j\right), \tag{35}$$

where $A = |w_i^m|$.
By Lemma 2 and (12), we have

$$\bar{A} \leq \frac{\left(q^2 + A^2\right)^2}{2\lambda q^2}\beta \leq A. \tag{36}$$

By (33) and (36), we obtain that

$$\left|w_i^{m+1}\right| \leq \left(1 - \frac{2\lambda\eta q^2}{(q^2 + A^2)^2}\right) A + \eta \frac{2\lambda q^2 \bar{A}}{(q^2 + A^2)^2}$$
$$\leq A + \eta \frac{2\lambda q^2}{(q^2 + A^2)^2} \left(\bar{A} - A\right) \tag{37}$$
$$\leq A.$$

Case 2. $\left|w_i^m\right| < x_1\left(\frac{\lambda}{2\beta}\right)$.

On the basis of the above analysis, the boundedness of weight sequence can be

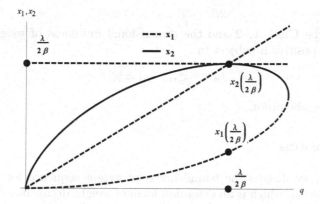

Fig. 5. Two real distinct roots of Eq. (23) for different q when $\frac{\lambda}{\beta} = 1$.

guaranteed once (See Fig. 5)

$$\left|w_i^{m+1} - w_i^m\right| \leq x_2\left(\frac{\lambda}{2\beta}\right) - x_1\left(\frac{\lambda}{2\beta}\right). \tag{38}$$

By Lemma 2, we get the smaller root when $q = \frac{\lambda}{2\beta}$

$$x_1\left(\frac{\lambda}{2\beta}\right) = \frac{\sqrt{2(-2 + u + v)} - \sqrt{-8 - 2(u + v) + 12\sqrt{\frac{6}{-2+u+v}}}}{4\sqrt{3}} \frac{\lambda}{\beta}, \tag{39}$$

$u = \left(19 - 3\sqrt{33}\right)^{\frac{1}{3}}$ and $v = \left(19 + 3\sqrt{33}\right)^{\frac{1}{3}}$. It is easy to compute that $x_1\left(\frac{\lambda}{2\beta}\right) \approx 0.1478\frac{\lambda}{\beta} < \frac{3}{16}\frac{\lambda}{\beta}$.

$$\left| w_i^{m+1} - w_i^m \right| \leq \eta \left| F_{w_i} \left(\mathbf{w}^m, \mathbf{x}^j \right) \right| + \eta \frac{2\lambda \left| w_i^m \right|}{q^2}$$

$$\leq \frac{\lambda}{8\beta} + \left| w_i^m \right| \leq \frac{\lambda}{8\beta} + x_1 \left(\frac{\lambda}{2\beta} \right) \tag{40}$$

$$\leq x_2 \left(\frac{\lambda}{2\beta} \right) - x_1 \left(\frac{\lambda}{2\beta} \right).$$

Then we have

$$\left| w_i^{m+1} \right| \leq \left| w_i^m \right| + \left| w_i^{m+1} - w_i^m \right|$$

$$\leq \frac{\lambda}{8\beta} + 2 \left| w_i^m \right| \leq \frac{\lambda}{8\beta} + 2x_1 \left(\frac{\lambda}{2\beta} \right) \tag{41}$$

$$\leq \frac{\lambda}{2\beta}.$$

Considering the **Case 1, 2** and the dimensional finiteness of weight vectors, there exists a positive α subject to

$$\left\| \mathbf{w}^m \right\| \leq \alpha. \quad m \in \mathbb{N}. \tag{42}$$

This completes the proof.

4   Conclusions

In this paper, we discuss the boundedness of weight sequence for the case of weight elimination, which is an extension form of weight decay and subset selection. We show that the training parameters such as learning rate and penalty coefficient play an essential role in determining the initial interval of weights, which can control the magnitude of weights in a bounded region. We show the novel relationships among these parameters. Theorem 1 gives the best suggestion for choosing the weight scaling coefficient q, which depends on the ratio between the penalty coefficient λ and β, that is, $q = \frac{\lambda}{2\beta}$. It shows that the initial weights can be randomized in a maximum bounded interval. There are still some open questions to investigate in the future: the convergence analysis of this algorithm, the strict theoretical proof of weights boundedness and how to choose the scaling parameter q for numerical experiments.

Acknowledgments. The authors wish to thank the anonymous reviewers for careful error proofing of the manuscript and many insightful comments and suggestions which greatly improved this work.

This project was supported in part by the National Natural Science Foundation of China (No. 61305075, 61271407), the China Postdoctoral Science Foundation (No. 2012M520624), the Natural Science Foundation of Shandong Province (No. ZR2013FQ004), the Specialized Research Fund for the Doctoral Program of Higher Education of China (No. 20130133120014) and the Fundamental Research Funds for the Central Universities (No. 13CX02009A).

References

1. Werbos, P.J.: Beyond regression: new tools for prediction and analysis in the behavioral sciences. Ph.D. thesis. Harvard University, Cambridge, MA (1974)
2. Parker, D.B.: Learning-logic, invention report. Stanford University, Stanford (1982)
3. Rumelhart, D.E., Hinton, G.E., Williams, R.J.: Learning representations by back-propagation errors. Nature 323, 533–536 (1986)
4. Cherkassky, V., Mulier, F.M.: Learning from data: Concepts, Theory, and Methods. IEEE Press (2007)
5. Girosi, F., Jones, M., Poggio, T.: Regularization theory and neural networks architectures. Neural Computation 7, 219–269 (1995)
6. Friedman, J.: An Overview of Predictive Learning and Function Approximation. In: From Statistics to Neural Networks, vol. 136, pp. 1–61. Springer, Heidelberg (1994)
7. Weigend, A.S., Rumelhart, D.E., Huberman, B.A.: Generalization by weight-elimination applied to currency exchange rate prediction. In: IJCNN 1991-Seattle International Joint Conference on Neural Networks, vol. 1, pp. 837–841 (1991)
8. Bebis, G., Georgiopoulos, M., Kaspalris, T.: Coupling weight elimination and genetic algorithms. In: IEEE International Conference on Neural Networks, vol. 2, pp. 1115–1120 (1996)
9. Gupta, A., Lam, M.: The weight decay backpropagation for generalizations with missing values. Annals of Operations Research 78, 165–187 (1998)
10. Leung, C.-S., Tsoi, A.-C., Chan, L.-W.: Two regularizers for recursive least squared algorithms in feedforward multilayered neural networks. IEEE Transactions on Neural Networks 12, 1314–1332 (2001)
11. Kuo, R.J., Wu, P., Wang, C.P.: An intelligent sales forecasting system through integration of artificial neural networks and fuzzy neural networks with fuzzy weight elimination. Neural Networks 15, 909–925 (2002)
12. Ennett, C.M., Frize, M.: Weight-elimination neural networks applied to coronary surgery mortality prediction. IEEE Transactions on Information Technology in Biomedicine 7, 86–92 (2003)
13. May, P., Zhou, E., Lee, C.W.: A Comprehensive Evaluation of Weight Growth and Weight Elimination Methods Using the Tangent Plane Algorithm. International Journal of Advanced Computer Sciences and Applications 4, 149–156 (2013)
14. Zhang, H., Wu, W., Liu, F., Yao, M.: Boundedness and Convergence of Online Gradient Method With Penalty for Feedforward Neural Networks. IEEE Transactions on Neural Networks 20, 1050–1054 (2009)
15. Shao, H., Zheng, G.: Boundedness and convergence of online gradient method with penalty and momentum. Neurocomputing 74, 765–770 (2011)
16. Wang, J., Wu, W., Zurada, J.M.: Boundedness and convergence of MPN for cyclic and almost cyclic learning with penalty. In: The 2011 International Joint Conference on Neural Networks (IJCNN), pp. 125–132 (2011)
17. Wang, J., Wu, W., Zurada, J.M.: Computational properties and convergence analysis of BPNN for cyclic and almost cyclic learning with penalty. Neural Networks 33, 127–135 (2012)
18. http://www.xieguofang.cn/Maths/Quartic/Quartic_Xie_Method_of_Determining_Root_Configuration.htm

Fuzzy Systems and Their Applications

New Method for Nonlinear Fuzzy
Correction Modelling of Dynamic Objects

Łukasz Bartczuk[1], Andrzej Przybył[1], and Petia Koprinkova-Hristova[2]

[1]Częstochowa University of Technology,
Institute of Computational Intelligence, Poland
{lukasz.bartczuk,andrzej.przybyl}@iisi.pcz.pl
[2]Bulgarian Academy of Sciences, Institute of Control and System Research, Bulgaria
proprinkova@icsr.bas.bg

Abstract. In the paper a method to use the equivalent linearization technique of the nonlinear state equation with the coefficients generated by the fuzzy rules for current operating point is proposed. On the basis of the evolutionary strategy and properly defined identification procedure, the fuzzy rules are automatically designed to maximize the accuracy of the resulting linear model.

1 Introduction

Nonlinear fuzzy correction modelling is an important issue from scientific and practical point of view (see e.g. [56]-[57]). Models of various physical phenomena are often used in practice. It is because a model is very useful in development of the control system to build a failure detection and to extract knowledge concerning intrinsic behaviour of the modelled dynamic objects. In daily practice the physical dynamic systems, which are nonlinear in a typical case, are treated as linear systems. This method offers several advantages, for example the ability to use well developed methods of the control theory, which refer to the linear models. Let's consider the nonlinear state equation:

$$\frac{dx}{dt} = f(\mathbf{x}, \mathbf{u}) = \mathbf{A}\mathbf{x} + \mathbf{B}\mathbf{u} + \eta g(\mathbf{x}, \mathbf{u}), \tag{1}$$

where $g(\mathbf{x}, \mathbf{u})$ is a separate nonlinear part of the system and η is the influence factor of the nonlinearities of the whole system. If we assume that η is small and the system is weakly nonlinear then the linear approximation about an equilibrium point will be useful in some strictly defined range. However, it should be noted that such a model is often unsuitable for many practical applications because of too low accuracy. This is especially true if the actual operating point goes beyond the defined boundaries.

In this paper we propose the solution to increase accuracy of the method described above by the method based on equivalent linearization technique [1]. In such a case the state equation (1) can be shown as follows:

$$\frac{dx}{dt} = f(\mathbf{x}, \mathbf{u}) = \mathbf{A_{eq}}\mathbf{x} + \mathbf{B_{eq}}\mathbf{u} + e(\mathbf{x}, \mathbf{u}), \tag{2}$$

L. Rutkowski et al. (Eds.): ICAISC 2014, Part I, LNAI 8467, pp. 169–180, 2014.

where $\mathbf{A_{eq}} = \mathbf{A} + \mathbf{P_A}$, $\mathbf{B_{eq}} = \mathbf{B} + \mathbf{P_B}$ and $e(\mathbf{x}, \mathbf{u})$ is an error term. The correction matrices $\mathbf{P_A}, \mathbf{P_B}$ are estimated for current operating point. When we analyse a small area around current operating point and the error term is small (i.e. it can be neglected) then the state equation (2) can be treated as linear. To solve the problem of a loss of accuracy when operating point is changing, in the paper it is proposed to calculate the new values of the correction matrices $\mathbf{P_A}, \mathbf{P_B}$ for each new point of work. Moreover, instead of the complicated analytical calculation it is proposed to estimate the values of matrices $\mathbf{P_A}, \mathbf{P_B}$ coefficients with the help of evolutionary strategy in a properly planned identification process. To enable the adjustment of the state equation (2) to the current operating point $(\mathbf{x}, \mathbf{u})$, the coefficients of correction matrices are generated by the fuzzy rules for each new point of work.

Summing up, the expected result of the proposed solution is to achieve high accuracy of the models with a simple description (e.g. by using a small number of fuzzy rules). This paper is a continuation of our earlier works [3,47], except that this time we focused to receive fuzzy rules characterized by a high degree of interpretability.

2   Intelligent System for Nonlinear Modelling

In the proposed method the coefficients of the correction matrix $\mathbf{P_A}(k)$ are generated by multi-input, multi-output neuro-fuzzy system. Neuro-fuzzy systems (see e.g. [32], [39], [48]-[55], [58]-[62]) combine the learning properties of neural networks and the natural language description of fuzzy systems (see e.g. [4]-[9], [18]-[21], [37]-[38]).

Each of the systems has a collection of N fuzzy IF $-$ THEN rules in the form:

$$\mathcal{R}^r : \text{IF } x_1 \text{ is } A_1^r \text{ AND} \ldots \text{AND} x_n \text{ is } A_n^r \text{ THEN } y_1 \text{ is } B_1^r \text{ AND} \ldots \text{AND } y_m \text{ is } B_m^r,$$
(3)

where $\mathbf{x} = [x_1, \ldots, x_n] \in \mathbf{X} \subset \mathbf{R}^n$ is a vector of input signals, $y = [y_1, \cdots, y_m] \in \mathbf{Y} \subset \mathbf{R}^m$ is a vector of output values. $A_1^r, \ldots, A_n^r, B_1^r, \ldots, B_m^r, r = 1, \ldots, N$ are fuzzy sets characterized by the membership functions $\mu_{A_i^r}(x_i), \mu_{B_j^r}(y_j), i = 1, \ldots, n; j = 1, \ldots, m; r = 1, \ldots, N$. Each fuzzy rule (3) determines fuzzy set $\overline{B}_j^r \subset \mathbf{R}^m$ whose membership function is given by following formula:

$$\mu_{\overline{B}_j^r}(y_j) = \mu_{\mathbf{A}^r \to B_j^r}(\overline{\mathbf{x}}, y_j) = T \left\{ \underset{i=1}{\overset{n}{T^*}} \left(\mu_{A_i^r}(x_i) \right), \mu_{B_j^r}(y_j) \right\},$$
(4)

where T and T^* are t-norms operators (not necessarily the same) [48]. When we used singletons as the membership functions for output fuzzy sets then the above formula can be simplified as follows:

$$\mu_{\overline{B}_j^r}(\overline{y}_j^r) = \mu_{\mathbf{A}^r \to B_j^r}(\overline{\mathbf{x}}, \overline{y}_j^r) = \underset{i=1}{\overset{n}{T^*}} \left(\mu_{A_i^r}(x_i) \right).$$
(5)

Assuming that the defuzzification is realized using the dependency:

$$\overline{y}_j = \frac{\sum\limits_{r=1}^{N} \overline{y}_j^r \cdot \mu_{\overline{B}_j^r}(\overline{y}^r)}{\sum\limits_{r=1}^{N} \mu_{\overline{B}_j^r}(\overline{y}_j^r)} \tag{6}$$

and substituting (5) to formula (6) we finally get:

$$\overline{y} = \frac{\sum\limits_{r=1}^{N} \overline{y}_j^r \cdot T^{*n}_{i=1} \left(\mu_{A_i^r}(x_i) \right)}{\sum\limits_{r=1}^{N} T^{*n}_{i=1} \left(\mu_{A_i^r}(x_i) \right)}. \tag{7}$$

Using fuzzy systems (see e.g. [24], [27], [36], [44]-[45]) to modelling real systems we want to meet two objectives: **(a)** achieving a high degree of accuracy and **(b)** achieving a high degree of interpretability. The accuracy can be defined as a similarity of the responses of the real systems and fuzzy systems. It can be measured with root mean square error (RMSE). In a case of interpretability it is difficult to find unambiguous definition what it means. We assume that interpretability is the ease of understanding the operations of the actual system through analysis of its model. Practice shows that these two objectives are contradictory and combination of their fulfilment is very difficult. For this reason, in creation of the fuzzy model we seek to achieve a compromise between accuracy and interpretability (see e.g. [17], [26], [42]-[43]). As shown in [26] interpretability can be analysed at various levels. In this paper we assumed that obtained fuzzy model should be as accurate and simple as possible. We also assumed that membership functions should be easily distinguishable. In order to fulfilled the last condition we assumed that in a point of intersection of two membership functions their membership should not be greater than 0.6.

3   Evolutionary Construction of the Fuzzy System

In order to create the interpretable fuzzy model of the dynamic nonlinear processes we use the evolutionary algorithm (see e.g. [22], [40], [41], [46]). In particular we use the evolutionary strategy $(\mu + \lambda)$ see e.g. [11], [13], [25]. The purpose of this is to obtain the parameters of the fuzzy system described in the previous section. In the process of evolution we assumed that:

- In a single chromosome $\mathbf{X}$ all parameters of the fuzzy system are encoded in a following way:

$$\mathbf{X} = \begin{pmatrix} \overline{x}_{1,1}^A, \sigma_{1,1}^A, \cdots, \overline{x}_{1,n}^A, \sigma_{1,n}^A, \overline{y}_{1,1}^B, \cdots, \overline{y}_{1,m}^B, \\ \cdots, \\ \overline{x}_{N,1}^A, \sigma_{N,1}^A, \cdots, \overline{x}_{N,n}^A, \sigma_{N,n}^A, \overline{y}_{N,1}^B, \cdots, \overline{y}_{N,m}^B \end{pmatrix}, \tag{8}$$

where $\overline{x}_{r,i}^A$ and $\sigma_{r,i}^A$ are parameters of the input fuzzy sets A_i^r, $r = 1, \ldots, N; i = 1, \ldots, n$, and $\overline{y}_{r,j}^B$ is parameter of the output singleton fuzzy sets B_j^r, $j = 1, \ldots, M$.

- The goal of evolutionary strategy is to minimize the following fitness function:

$$fitness(\mathbf{X}) = fAcc(\mathbf{X}) + w \cdot fInter(\mathbf{X}), \tag{9}$$

where: $fAcc(\mathbf{X})$ is a function of determining the difference between output signals $\hat{x}_1$ and $\hat{x}_2$ generated by the model created in the step $k + 1$ and corresponding reference x_1, x_2 values:

$$fAcc(\mathbf{X}) = \sqrt{\frac{1}{2 \cdot K} \sum_{k=1}^{K} \left(\begin{array}{c} (x_1(k+1) - \hat{x}_1(k+1))^2 + \\ (x_2(k+1) - \hat{x}_2(k+1))^2 \end{array} \right)}, \tag{10}$$

where K is a number of the reference values; w - is a scaling factor of the interpretability component of the fitness function (in out experiments set as 0.1) and $fInter(\mathbf{X})$ is a function of determining the interpretability condition:

$$fInter(\mathbf{X}) = \sum_{i=1}^{n} \sum_{j=1}^{n_i-1} \begin{cases} I_{(A_j^i, A_{j+1}^i)} - max_\mu & \text{when} I_{(A_j^i, A_{j+1}^i)} > max_\mu \\ 0 & \text{in other cases,} \end{cases} \tag{11}$$

where $I_{(A_j^i, A_{j+1}^i)}$ is a membership degree of the fuzzy sets A_j^i, A_{j+1}^i in intersection point of their membership functions and is defined as $I_{(A_j^i, A_{j+1}^i)} = \max\min(\mu_{A_j^i}(x), \mu_{A_{j+1}^i}(x))$, and max_μ is a maximal membership value at intersection point.
- Genes in chromosomes $\mathbf{X}$ were initialized according with the method described in [13].

Detailed description of the evolutionary strategy $(\mu + \lambda)$, used to train neuro-fuzzy systems (see e.g. [12]-[16], [23], [33]-[35]), can be found in [11], [13].

4   Experimental Results

The usefulness of our method will be demonstrated with two modelling problems (1) well-known harmonic oscillator and (2) nonlinear electric circuit with a DC motor supplied by a solar generator [2], [29]. The harmonic oscillator can be defined by the following formula:

$$\frac{d^2x}{dt^2} + 2\zeta\frac{dx}{dt} + \omega^2 x = 0, \tag{12}$$

where ζ, ω are oscillator parameters and $x(t)$ is a reference value of the modelled process as function of time. We used the following state variables $x_1(t) = dx(t)/dt$ and $x_2(t) = x(t)$. In such a case the system matrix $\mathbf{A}$ and the matrix of corrections coefficients $\mathbf{P_A}$ is described as follows:

$$\mathbf{A} = \begin{bmatrix} 0 & \omega \\ -\omega & 0 \end{bmatrix} \qquad \mathbf{P_A} = \begin{bmatrix} 0 & p_{12}(\mathbf{x}) \\ p_{21}(\mathbf{x}) & 0 \end{bmatrix}.$$

In our experiments the parameter ω was modified in simulation according with a formula:

$$\omega(x) = 2\pi - \frac{\pi}{(1 + |2 \cdot x|^6)} \tag{13}$$

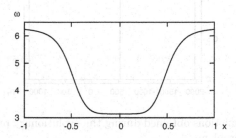

Fig. 1. The value of ω parameter as a function of $x(t)$

to make the object nonlinear. The changes of ω as a function of x is presented in Fig. 1.

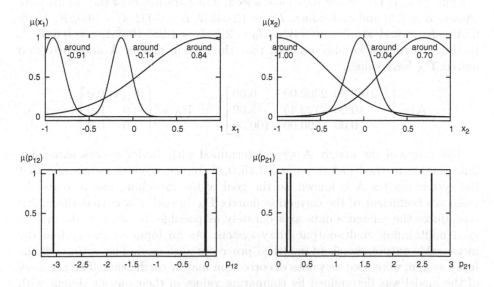

Fig. 2. Membership functions obtained during evolutionary process for harmonic oscillator problem

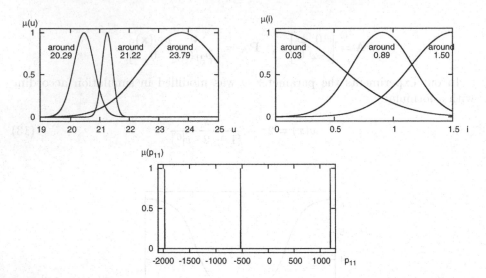

Fig. 3. Membership functions obtained during the evolutionary process for the nonlinear electrical circuit problem

In the second experiment the nonlinear electrical circuit with solar generator and DC drive system was modelled. In this case the following state variables were used: $x_1(k) = -\frac{I_s}{C}e^{-au(k)} - \frac{1}{C}i(k) + \frac{I_s+I_0}{C}$, $x_2(k) = \frac{1}{L}i(k) - \frac{R_m}{L}u(k) - \frac{K_x}{L}\Omega(k)$, $x_3(k) = \frac{K_x}{L}u(k) - \frac{K_r}{J}\Omega(k)$, where: $u(k)$ is the generator voltage, $i(k)$ is the rotor current, $\Omega(k)$ is DC motor rotational speed. The parameters of the circuit were chosen as in [29] and had values: $R_m = 12.045\Omega$, $L = 0.1H$, $C = 500\mu F$, $K_x = 0.5Vs$, $K_r = 0.1Vs^2$, $J = 10^{-3}Ws^3$, $I_0 = 2A$, $I_s = 1.28 \cdot 10^{-5}A$, $a = 0.54V^{-1}$. In this experiment we also assumed that the system matrix $\mathbf{A}$ and correction matrix $\mathbf{P_A}$ have values:

$$\mathbf{A} = \begin{bmatrix} -2163.86 & 2000.00 & 0.00 \\ 10.00 & -120.45 & -5.00 \\ 0.00 & 500.00 & -100.00 \end{bmatrix} \quad \mathbf{P_A} = \begin{bmatrix} p_{11}(\mathbf{x}) & 0 & 0 \\ 0 & 0 & 0 \\ 0 & 0 & 0 \end{bmatrix}.$$

The values of the matrix $\mathbf{A}$ were determined with Taylor's series expansion linearization method [30] in point $[22.15, 0, 0]$. In out method we assume that the system matrix $\mathbf{A}$ is known, so the goal of the modelling was recreate the unknown coefficient of the correction matrix $\mathbf{P_A}$ in such a way that the model reproduces the reference data as accurately as possible. In order to do this we used multi-input, multi-output fuzzy system. As an input of the system the measurable output signals of modelled processes were used. The outputs of the fuzzy system were used as values of correction matrix coefficients. The accuracy of the model was determined by comparing values of their output signals with referenced values. The error was computed according to the formula (10).

In both experimental problems the correction matrix $\mathbf{P_B}$ was not considered and its coefficients were equal to 0.0. For both modelling problems the neuro-

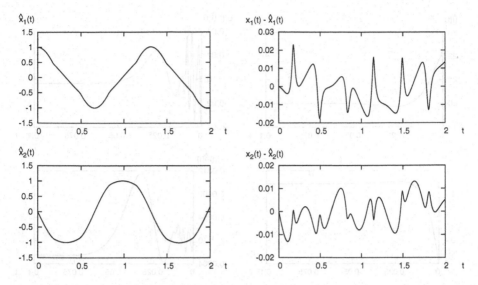

Fig. 4. Comparison between the reference and estimated data for the harmonic oscillator problem

fuzzy systems with Gaussian and singleton membership functions for antecedents and descendant of rules were used. In order to determine membership function parameters we used evolutionary strategy (μ, λ) which is characterized by the following parameters: $\mu = 50$, $\lambda = 300$, $p_c = 0.7$ and the number of generations = 2000. The results of the simulations are presented in Fig. 4 - 3 and can be summarized as follows:

- Neuro-fuzzy systems obtained as the results of evolutionary process are characterized - in both cases - by 3 rules, 2 inputs ($\hat{x}_1(k)$ and $\hat{x}_2(k)$) and two outputs $p_{12}(k)$ and $p_{21}(k)$ in harmonic oscillator problem and two inputs $\hat{u}(k)$ and $\hat{i}(k)$ and one output $p_{11}(k)$ in nonlinear electrical circuit problem.
- The rules in obtained systems for harmonic oscillator problem can be written as follows

$$R^1 : \text{IF } x_1 \text{ is around}(-0.91) \text{ AND } x_2 \text{ is around}(0.7)$$
$$\text{THEN } p_{12} = -0.014 \text{ AND } p_{21} = 0.16$$
$$R^2 : \text{IF } x_1 \text{ is around}(-0.14) \text{ AND } x_2 \text{ is around}(-1)$$
$$\text{THEN } p_{12} = -3.06 \text{ AND } p_{21} = 0.268$$
$$R^3 : \text{IF } x_1 \text{ is around}(0.84) \text{ AND } x_2 \text{ is around}(-0.04)$$
$$\text{THEN } p_{12} = -0.0 \text{ AND } p_{21} = 0.23$$

- The rules in obtained systems for nonlinear electrical problem can be written as follows

$$R^1 : \text{IF } u \text{ is around}(20.29) \text{ AND } i \text{ is around}(0.89) \text{ THEN } p_{11} = 1199.99$$
$$R^2 : \text{IF } u \text{ is around}(21.22) \text{ AND } i \text{ is around}(0.03) \text{ THEN } p_{11} = -515.03$$
$$R^3 : \text{IF } u \text{ is around}(23.79) \text{ AND } i \text{ is around}(1.5) \text{ THEN } p_{11} = -1973.18$$

- The corresponding fuzzy sets are shown respectively in Fig. 2 and 3.

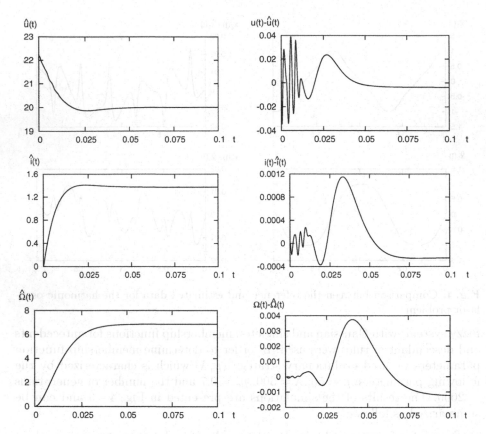

Fig. 5. Comparison between the reference and estimated data for the nonlinear electrical circuit problem

- The accuracy of nonlinear modelling obtained in our simulations are depicted in Fig. 4 and 5. The average root mean square error has a value 0.007655 and 0.007616 respectively for harmonic oscillator problem and nonlinear electrical circuit problem. It should be noted that better accuracy could be obtained when we use more complicated fuzzy system structure or we abandon the interpretability issues.

5   Conclusions

In the paper the method to create the linear model of the nonlinear phenomena was proposed. To provide of high accuracy of the model in a wide range of operating points the correction coefficients are generated by fuzzy rules. Moreover, the evolutionary strategy and properly defined identification procedure is used to automatically design the fuzzy rules. The presented experimental results proved the validity of the proposed method.

Acknowledgment. The project was financed by the National Science Center on the basis of the decision number DEC-2012/05/B/ST7/02138.

References

1. Caughey, T.K.: Equivalent Linearization Techniques. The Journal of the Acoustical Society of America 35(11), 1706–1711 (1963)
2. Barland, M., et al.: Commende optimal d'un systeme generateur photovoltaique converisseur statique - receptur. Revue Phys. Appl. 19, 905–915 (1984)
3. Bartczuk, Ł., Przybył, A., Dziwiński, P.: Hybrid State Variables - Fuzzy Logic Modelling of Nonlinear Objects. In: Rutkowski, L., Korytkowski, M., Scherer, R., Tadeusiewicz, R., Zadeh, L.A., Zurada, J.M. (eds.) ICAISC 2013, Part I. LNCS (LNAI), vol. 7894, pp. 227–234. Springer, Heidelberg (2013)
4. Bilski, J., Litwiński, S., Smoląg, J.: Parallel Realisation of QR Algorithm for Neural Networks Learning. In: Rutkowski, L., Siekmann, J.H., Tadeusiewicz, R., Zadeh, L.A. (eds.) ICAISC 2004. LNCS (LNAI), vol. 3070, pp. 158–165. Springer, Heidelberg (2004)
5. Bilski, J., Rutkowski, L.: Numerically Robust Learning Algorithms for Feed Forward Neural Networks. In: Neural Networks and Soft Computing. Advances in Soft Computing, pp. 149–154. Physica-Verlag, A Springer-Verlag Company (2003)
6. Bilski, J., Smoląg, J.: Parallel Approach to Learning of the Recurrent Jordan Neural Network. In: Rutkowski, L., Korytkowski, M., Scherer, R., Tadeusiewicz, R., Zadeh, L.A., Zurada, J.M. (eds.) ICAISC 2013, Part I. LNCS (LNAI), vol. 7894, pp. 32–40. Springer, Heidelberg (2013)
7. Bilski, J., Smoląg, J.: Parallel Realisation of the Recurrent Elman Neural Network Learning. In: Rutkowski, L., Scherer, R., Tadeusiewicz, R., Zadeh, L.A., Zurada, J.M. (eds.) ICAISC 2010, Part II. LNCS (LNAI), vol. 6114, pp. 19–25. Springer, Heidelberg (2010)
8. Bilski, J., Smoląg, J.: Parallel Realisation of the Recurrent Multi Layer Perceptron Learning. In: Rutkowski, L., Korytkowski, M., Scherer, R., Tadeusiewicz, R., Zadeh, L.A., Zurada, J.M. (eds.) ICAISC 2012, Part I. LNCS (LNAI), vol. 7267, pp. 12–20. Springer, Heidelberg (2012)
9. Bilski, J., Smoląg, J.: Parallel Realisation of the Recurrent RTRN Neural Network Learning. In: Rutkowski, L., Tadeusiewicz, R., Zadeh, L.A., Zurada, J.M. (eds.) ICAISC 2008. LNCS (LNAI), vol. 5097, pp. 11–16. Springer, Heidelberg (2008)
10. Chang, W.-J., Chang, W., Liu, H.-H.: Model-based fuzzy modeling and control for autonomous underwater vehicles in the horizontal plane. Journal of Marine Science and Technology 11(3), 155–163 (2003)
11. Cordon, O., Herrera, F., Hoffmann, F., Magdalena, L.: Genetic Fuzzy Systems: Evolutionary tuning and learning of fuzzy knowledge bases. World Scientific (2001)
12. Cpalka, K.: A Method for Designing Flexible Neuro-fuzzy Systems. In: Rutkowski, L., Tadeusiewicz, R., Zadeh, L.A., Żurada, J.M. (eds.) ICAISC 2006. LNCS (LNAI), vol. 4029, pp. 212–219. Springer, Heidelberg (2006)
13. Cpałka, K.: On evolutionary designing and learning of flexible neuro-fuzzy structures for nonlinear classification. In: Nonlinear Analysis Series A: Theory, Methods and Applications, vol. 71, pp. 1659–1672. Elsevier (2009)
14. Cpałka, K., Rutkowski, L.: A New Method for Designing and Reduction of Neurofuzzy Systems. In: Proceedings of the 2006 IEEE International Conference on Fuzzy Systems (IEEE World Congress on Computational Intelligence, WCCI 2006), Vancouver, BC, Canada, pp. 8510–8516 (2006)
15. Cpałka, K., Rutkowski, L.: Flexible Takagi-Sugeno Fuzzy Systems. In: Proceedings of the International Joint Conference on Neural Networks 2005, Montreal, pp. 1764–1769 (2005)
16. Cpałka, K., Rutkowski, L.: Flexible Takagi Sugeno Neuro-fuzzy Structures for Nonlinear Approximation. WSEAS Transactions on Systems 4(9), 1450–1458 (2005)

17. Cpałka, K., Łapa, K., Przybył, A., Zalasiński, M.: A new method for designing neuro-fuzzy systems for nonlinear modelling with interpretability aspects. Neurocomputing (in print, 2014), http://dx.doi.org/10.1016/j.neucom.2013.12.031

18. Dziwiński, P., Bartczuk, Ł., Starczewski, J.T.: Fully controllable ant colony system for text data clustering. In: Rutkowski, L., Korytkowski, M., Scherer, R., Tadeusiewicz, R., Zadeh, L.A., Zurada, J.M. (eds.) SIDE 2012 and EC 2012. LNCS, vol. 7269, pp. 199–205. Springer, Heidelberg (2012)

19. Dziwiński, P., Rutkowska, D.: Algorithm for generating fuzzy rules for WWW document classification. In: Rutkowski, L., Tadeusiewicz, R., Zadeh, L.A., Żurada, J.M. (eds.) ICAISC 2006. LNCS (LNAI), vol. 4029, pp. 1111–1119. Springer, Heidelberg (2006)

20. Dziwiński, P., Rutkowska, D.: Ant focused crawling algorithm. In: Rutkowski, L., Tadeusiewicz, R., Zadeh, L.A., Zurada, J.M. (eds.) ICAISC 2008. LNCS (LNAI), vol. 5097, pp. 1018–1028. Springer, Heidelberg (2008)

21. Dziwiński, P., Starczewski, J.T., Bartczuk, Ł.: New linguistic hedges in construction of interval type-2 FLS. In: Rutkowski, L., Scherer, R., Tadeusiewicz, R., Zadeh, L.A., Zurada, J.M. (eds.) ICAISC 2010, Part II. LNCS, vol. 6114, pp. 445–450. Springer, Heidelberg (2010)

22. El-Abd, M.: On the hybridization on the artificial bee colony and particle swarm optimization algorithms. Journal of Artificial Intelligence and Soft Computing Research 2(2), 147–155 (2012)

23. Gabryel, M., Cpałka, K., Rutkowski, L.: Evolutionary strategies for learning of neuro-fuzzy systems. In: Proceedings of the I Workshop on Genetic Fuzzy Systems, Granada, pp. 119–123 (2005)

24. Gabryel, M., Korytkowski, M., Scherer, R., Rutkowski, L.: Object Detection by Simple Fuzzy Classifiers Generated by Boosting. In: Rutkowski, L., Korytkowski, M., Scherer, R., Tadeusiewicz, R., Zadeh, L.A., Zurada, J.M. (eds.) ICAISC 2013, Part I. LNCS, vol. 7894, pp. 540–547. Springer, Heidelberg (2013)

25. Gabryel, M., Woźniak, M., Nowicki, R.K.: Creating Learning Sets for Control Systems Using an Evolutionary Method. In: Rutkowski, L., Korytkowski, M., Scherer, R., Tadeusiewicz, R., Zadeh, L.A., Zurada, J.M. (eds.) SIDE 2012 and EC 2012. LNCS, vol. 7269, pp. 206–213. Springer, Heidelberg (2012)

26. Gacto, M.J., Alcala, R., Herrera, F.: Interpretability of linguistic fuzzy rule-based systems: An overview of interpretability measures. Information Sciences 181, 4340–4360 (2011)

27. Greenfield, S., Chiclana, F.: Type-reduction of the discretized interval type-2 fuzzy set: approaching the continuous case through progressively finer discretization. Journal of Artificial Intelligence and Soft Computing Research 1(3), 183–193 (2011)

28. Johansen, T.A., Shorten, R., Murray-Smith, R.: On the Interpretation and Identification of Dynamic Takagi–Sugeno Fuzzy Models. IEEE Transactions on Fuzzy Systems 8(3) (2000)

29. Jordan, A.J.: Linearization of non-linear state equation. Bulletin of the Polish Academy of Science. Technical Science 54(1), 63–73 (2006)

30. Kaczorek, T., Dzieliński, A., Dąbrowski, L., Łopatka, R.: The Basis of Control Theory. WNT, Warsaw (2006) (in Polish)

31. Kamyar, M.: Takagi-Sugeno Fuzzy Modeling for Process Control. In: Industrial Automation, Robotics and Artificial Intelligence (EEE8005), School of Electrical, Electronic and Computer Engineering, vol. 8 (2008)

32. Koprinkova-Hristova, P.: Backpropagation through time training of a neuro-fuzzy controller. International Journal of Neural Systems 20(5), 421–428 (2010)

33. Korytkowski, M., Nowicki, R., Rutkowski, L., Scherer, R.: AdaBoost Ensemble of DCOG Rough–Neuro–Fuzzy Systems. In: Jędrzejowicz, P., Nguyen, N.T., Hoang, K. (eds.) ICCCI 2011, Part I. LNCS, vol. 6922, pp. 62–71. Springer, Heidelberg (2011)
34. Korytkowski, M., Rutkowski, L., Scherer, R.: On combining backpropagation with boosting. In: Proceedings of the IEEE International Joint Conference on Neural Network (IJCNN), vols. 1-10, pp. 1274–1277 (2006)
35. Korytkowski, M., Rutkowski, L., Scherer, R.: From Ensemble of Fuzzy Classifiers to Single Fuzzy Rule Base Classifier. In: Rutkowski, L., Tadeusiewicz, R., Zadeh, L.A., Zurada, J.M. (eds.) ICAISC 2008. LNCS (LNAI), vol. 5097, pp. 265–272. Springer, Heidelberg (2008)
36. Kroll, A.: On choosing the fuzziness parameter for identifying TS models with multidimensional membership functions. Journal of Artificial Intelligence and Soft Computing Research 1(4), 283–300 (2011)
37. Laskowski, Ł.: A Novel Continuous Dual Mode Neural Network in Stereo-Matching Process. In: Diamantaras, K., Duch, W., Iliadis, L.S. (eds.) ICANN 2010, Part III. LNCS, vol. 6354, pp. 294–297. Springer, Heidelberg (2010)
38. Laskowski, Ł.: Hybrid-Maximum Neural Network for Depth Analysis from Stereo-Image. In: Rutkowski, L., Scherer, R., Tadeusiewicz, R., Zadeh, L.A., Zurada, J.M. (eds.) ICAISC 2010, Part II. LNCS, vol. 6114, pp. 47–55. Springer, Heidelberg (2010)
39. Li, X., Er, M.J., Lim, B.S., Zhou, J.H., Gan, O.P., Rutkowski, L.: Fuzzy Regression Modeling for Tool Performance Prediction and Degradation Detection. International Journal of Neural Systems 20(5), 405–419 (2010)
40. Lobato, F.S., Steffen Jr., V.: A new multi-objective optimization algorithm based on differential evolution and neighborhood exploring evolution strategy. Journal of Artificial Intelligence and Soft Computing Research 1(4), 259–267 (2011)
41. Lobato, F.S., Steffen Jr., V., Silva Neto, A.J.: Solution of singular optimal control problems using the improved differential evolution algorithm. Journal of Artificial Intelligence and Soft Computing Research 1(3), 195–206 (2011)
42. Łapa, K., Przybył, A., Cpałka, K.: A new approach to designing interpretable models of dynamic systems. In: Rutkowski, L., Korytkowski, M., Scherer, R., Tadeusiewicz, R., Zadeh, L.A., Zurada, J.M. (eds.) ICAISC 2013, Part II. LNCS (LNAI), vol. 7895, pp. 523–534. Springer, Heidelberg (2013)
43. Łapa, K., Zalasiński, M., Cpałka, K.: A new method for designing and complexity reduction of neuro-fuzzy systems for nonlinear modelling. In: Rutkowski, L., Korytkowski, M., Scherer, R., Tadeusiewicz, R., Zadeh, L.A., Zurada, J.M. (eds.) ICAISC 2013, Part I. LNCS (LNAI), vol. 7894, pp. 329–344. Springer, Heidelberg (2013)
44. Patan, K., Patan, M.: Optimal Training strategies for locally recurrent neural networks. Journal of Artificial Intelligence and Soft Computing Research 1(2), 103–114 (2011)
45. Peteiro-Barral, D., Bardinas, B.G., Perez-Sanchez, B.: Learning from heterogeneously distributed data sets using artificial neural networks and genetic algorithms. Journal of Artificial Intelligence and Soft Computing Research 2(1), 5–20 (2012)
46. Prampero, P.S., Attux, R.: Magnetic particle swarm optimization. Journal of Artificial Intelligence and Soft Computing Research 2(1), 59–72 (2012)
47. Przybył, A., Cpałka, K.: A new method to construct of interpretable models of dynamic systems. In: Rutkowski, L., Korytkowski, M., Scherer, R., Tadeusiewicz, R., Zadeh, L.A., Zurada, J.M. (eds.) ICAISC 2012, Part II. LNCS (LNAI), vol. 7268, pp. 697–705. Springer, Heidelberg (2012)

48. Rutkowski, L.: Computational Intelligence: Methods and Techniques. Springer (2008)
49. Rutkowski, L., Cpałka, K.: Compromise approach to neuro-fuzzy systems. In: Sincak, P., Vascak, J., Kvasnicka, V., Pospichal, J. (eds.) Intelligent Technologies - Theory and Applications, vol. 76, pp. 85–90. IOS Press (2002)
50. Rutkowski, L., Cpałka, K.: Flexible weighted neuro-fuzzy systems. In: Proceedings of the 9th International Conference on Neural Information Processing (ICONIP 2002), Orchid Country Club, Singapore, CD, November 18-22 (2002)
51. Rutkowski, L., Cpałka, K.: Neuro-fuzzy systems derived from quasi-triangular norms. In: Proceedings of the IEEE International Conference on Fuzzy Systems, Budapest, July 26-29, vol. 2, pp. 1031–1036 (2004)
52. Rutkowski, L., Przybył, A., Cpałka, K.: Novel on-line speed profile generation for industrial machine tool based on flexible neuro-fuzzy approximation. IEEE Transactions on Industrial Electronics 59, 1238–1247 (2012)
53. Rutkowski, L., Przybył, A., Cpałka, K., Er, M.J.: Online Speed Profile Generation for Industrial Machine Tool Based on Neuro-fuzzy Approach. In: Rutkowski, L., Scherer, R., Tadeusiewicz, R., Zadeh, L.A., Zurada, J.M. (eds.) ICAISC 2010, Part II. LNCS (LNAI), vol. 6114, pp. 645–650. Springer, Heidelberg (2010)
54. Starczewski, J., Rutkowski, L.: Connectionist Structures of Type 2 Fuzzy Inference Systems. In: Wyrzykowski, R., Dongarra, J., Paprzycki, M., Waśniewski, J. (eds.) PPAM 2001. LNCS, vol. 2328, pp. 634–642. Springer, Heidelberg (2002)
55. Starczewski, J., Scherer, R., Korytkowski, M., Nowicki, R.: Modular Type-2 Neuro-fuzzy Systems. In: Wyrzykowski, R., Dongarra, J., Karczewski, K., Wasniewski, J. (eds.) PPAM 2007. LNCS, vol. 4967, pp. 570–578. Springer, Heidelberg (2008)
56. Theodoridis, D.C., Boutalis, Y.S., Christodoulou, M.A.: Robustifying analysis of the direct adaptive control of unknown multivariable nonlinear systems based on a new neuro-fuzzy method. Journal of Artificial Intelligence and Soft Computing Research 1(1), 59–79 (2011)
57. Tran, V.N., Brdys, M.A.: Optimizing control by robustly feasible model predictive control and application to drinking water distribution systems. Journal of Artificial Intelligence and Soft Computing Research 1(1), 43–57 (2011)
58. Zalasiński, M., Cpałka, K.: A new method of on-line signature verification using a flexible fuzzy one-class classifier, pp. 38–53. Academic Publishing House EXIT (2011)
59. Zalasiński, M., Cpałka, K.: New Approach for the On-Line Signature Verification Based on Method of Horizontal Partitioning. In: Rutkowski, L., Korytkowski, M., Scherer, R., Tadeusiewicz, R., Zadeh, L.A., Zurada, J.M. (eds.) ICAISC 2013, Part II. LNCS, vol. 7895, pp. 342–350. Springer, Heidelberg (2013)
60. Zalasiński, M., Cpałka, K.: Novel algorithm for the on-line signature verification. In: Rutkowski, L., Korytkowski, M., Scherer, R., Tadeusiewicz, R., Zadeh, L.A., Zurada, J.M. (eds.) ICAISC 2012, Part II. LNCS, vol. 7268, pp. 362–367. Springer, Heidelberg (2012)
61. Zalasiński, M., Cpałka, K.: Novel Algorithm for the On-Line Signature Verification Using Selected Discretization Points Groups. In: Rutkowski, L., Korytkowski, M., Scherer, R., Tadeusiewicz, R., Zadeh, L.A., Zurada, J.M. (eds.) ICAISC 2013, Part I. LNCS (LNAI), vol. 7894, pp. 493–502. Springer, Heidelberg (2013)
62. Zalasiński, M., Łapa, K., Cpałka, K.: New Algorithm for Evolutionary Selection of the Dynamic Signature Global Features. In: Rutkowski, L., Korytkowski, M., Scherer, R., Tadeusiewicz, R., Zadeh, L.A., Zurada, J.M. (eds.) ICAISC 2013, Part II. LNCS (LNAI), vol. 7895, pp. 113–121. Springer, Heidelberg (2013)

Intuitionistic Fuzzy Decision Trees - A New Approach

Paweł Bujnowski, Eulalia Szmidt, and Janusz Kacprzyk

Systems Research Institute, Polish Academy of Sciences,
ul. Newelska 6, 01–447 Warsaw, Poland
Warsaw School of Information Technology, ul. Newelska 6, 01-447 Warsaw, Poland
pbujno@gmail.com, {szmidt,kacprzyk}@ibspan.waw.pl

Abstract. We present here a new classifier called an intuitionistic fuzzy decision tree. The performance of the new algorithm is illustrated by providing an analysis of well known benchmark data. The results are compared to some other well known classification algorithms.

1 Introduction

Decision trees, with their well known advantages, are very popular classifiers which recursively partition a space of instances (observations). Following the source Quinlan the ID3 algorithm [21], many other approaches have been developed along that line (cf. [25]).

Classical (crisp) decision trees were extended to fuzzy decision trees which turned out to be more stable, and effective method to extract knowledge in uncertain classification problems (Janikow [16], Olaru et al. [20], Yuan and Shaw [38], Marsala [18], [19]).

The next natural step is to take advantages of the intuitionistic fuzzy sets introduced by Atanassov [1], [2], [3] (A-IFSs for short) while building the trees.

In this paper we propose a new intuitionistic fuzzy decision tree classifier. The data is expressed by means of intuitionistic fuzzy sets. Also the measures constructed for the intuitionistic fuzzy sets are applied while making decisions how to split a node while expanding the tree. The intuitionistic fuzzy tree proposed here is an extension of the fuzzy ID3 algorithm [6].

The potential of the new algorithm is illustrated by providing an analysis of well known benchmark data. The results are compared to other commonly used algorithms.

2 A Brief Introduction to A-IFSs

One of the possible generalizations of a fuzzy set in X (Zadeh [39]) given by

$$A' = \{< x, \mu_{A'}(x) > | x \in X\} \tag{1}$$

where $\mu_{A'}(x) \in [0,1]$ is the membership function of the fuzzy set A', is an A-IFS (Atanassov [1], [2], [3]) A is given by

$$A = \{< x, \mu_A(x), \nu_A(x) > | x \in X\} \tag{2}$$

L. Rutkowski et al. (Eds.): ICAISC 2014, Part I, LNAI 8467, pp. 181–192, 2014.
© Springer International Publishing Switzerland 2014

where: $\mu_A : X \to [0,1]$ and $\nu_A : X \to [0,1]$ such that

$$0 \leq \mu_A(x) + \nu_A(x) \leq 1 \qquad (3)$$

and $\mu_A(x)$, $\nu_A(x) \in [0,1]$ denote a degree of membership and a degree of non-membership of $x \in A$, respectively. (An approach to the assigning memberships and non-memberships for A-IFSs from data is proposed by Szmidt and Baldwin [26]).

Obviously, each fuzzy set may be represented by the following A-IFS:
$A = \{< x, \mu_{A'}(x), 1 - \mu_{A'}(x) > | x \in X\}$.

An additional concept for each A-IFS in X, that is not only an obvious result of (2) and (3) but which is also relevant for applications, we will call (Atanasov [2])

$$\pi_A(x) = 1 - \mu_A(x) - \nu_A(x) \qquad (4)$$

a *hesitation margin* of $x \in A$ which expresses a lack of knowledge of whether x belongs to A or not (cf. Atanassov [2]). It is obvious that $0 \leq \pi_A(x) \leq 1$, for each $x \in X$.

The hesitation margin turns out to be important while considering the distances (Szmidt and Kacprzyk [27], [28], [30], entropy (Szmidt and Kacprzyk [29], [31]), similarity (Szmidt and Kacprzyk [32]) for the A-IFSs, etc. i.e., the measures that play a crucial role in virtually all information processing tasks.

Hesitation margins turn out to be relevant for applications - in image processing (cf. Bustince et al. [14], [13]) and classification of imbalanced and overlapping classes (cf. Szmidt and Kukier [33], [34], [35]), group decision making, negotiations, voting and other situations (cf. Szmidt and Kacprzyk papers).

3 Intuitionistic Fuzzy Decision Tree - New Algorithm Description

The intuitionistic fuzzy decision tree proposed here has its roots in the soft decision tree introduced by Baldwin et al. [6] which follow the source *ID3* tree introduced by Quinlan [21].

We consider numeric attributes but the methods presented here can be also easily applied to the nominal attributes (the algorithm is even simpler then). We use here intuitionistic fuzzy sets for data representation. More, the new idea of deriving intuitionistic fuzzy sets in each node was applied as potentially giving the most accurate results.

Splitting the nodes is the most important step in generating a decision tree. The step demands to point out the best attributes for splitting. Proper picking up the attributes influences accuracy of a decision tree, and its interpretation properties. In the tree presented here intuitionistic fuzzy entropy was used (Szmidt and Kacprzyk[29]) as a counterpart of "information gain" [21].

In the next sections the most important components of the algorithm are described.

3.1 Fuzzy Partitions of the Attribute Values (granulation)

The idea of a universe partition (granulation), i.e., replacing a continuous domain with a discrete one has been extended to fuzzy sets by Ruspini [23]. The idea was used here

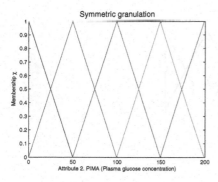
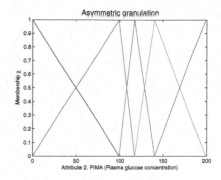

Fig. 1. Illustration of symmetric fuzzy partitioning, and asymmetric fuzzy partitioning (on attribute 2 "Plasma glucose concentration" of benchmark "Pima Diabetes" with 5 fuzzy sets)

to partition a universe of each attribute by introducing a set of triangular fuzzy sets such that for any attribute value the sum of memberships of the partitioning fuzzy sets is 1.

More formally, the membership $\chi_{j,k}(o_{ij})$ of the i-th observation (instance) o_{ij} in respect to the j-th attribute to the triangular fuzzy sets k and $k+1$ (where $k = 1, \ldots, p$) is:

$$\chi_{j,k}(o_{ij}) + \chi_{j,k+1}(o_{ij}) = 1, \quad k = 1, \ldots, p-1, \tag{5}$$

and for the j-th attribute A_j we have $o_{ij} \in A_j$, $i = 1, \ldots, n$, $j = 1, \ldots, m$.
In other words, the sum of the membership values for an observation o_{ij} is one (the sum results from only two neighboring fuzzy sets).

Remark. Here, for the purpose of granulation we use symbol χ for the membership values so to make a difference between membership values resulting from the attribute granulation (χ) and the membership values of the intuitionistic fuzzy sets μ.

We use here symmetric, evenly spaced triangular fuzzy sets (symmetric fuzzy partitions), and asymmetric, unevenly spaced triangular fuzzy sets (asymmetric fuzzy partitions such that each partition contains equal number of data points) [4,23]. In Fig. 1 an example is shown of symmetric fuzzy partitioning (symmetric granulation), and asymmetric fuzzy partitioning (asymmetric granulation). The two kinds of partitioning are illustrated on attribute 2 of the "PIMA Diabetes" problem with 5 fuzzy sets. Fuzzy partitioning (triangular fuzzy sets) is a starting point to assign nodes in a soft ID3 decision tree - cf. Fig. 2.

3.2 Fuzzy *ID3* Algorithm

In this section we present a fuzzy generalization of *ID3* algorithm [6].
Consider the following database

$$T = \{o_i = <o_{i,1}, \ldots, o_{i,m}> \mid i = 1, \ldots, n\}, \tag{6}$$

where $o_{i,j}$ is a value of the j-th attribute A_j, $j = 1, \ldots, m$, for the i-th instance. We assume that $o_{i,j}$ are crisp.

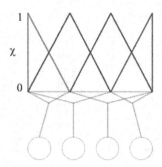

Fig. 2. Fuzzy partitioning as a starting point to constructing nodes in a soft ID3 tree

At the beginning of generating a fuzzy *ID3* decision tree from data, its root contains all the instances (top down approach). Each node is split by partitioning its instances. A node becomes a leaf if all the attributes are used in the path considered or if all its instances are from a unique class.

Splitting the nodes in a decision tree can be represented by the rules. Assume that P_j is a partition set of the attribute space Ω_j ($j = 1, \ldots, m$), and that partition of each attribute is via triangular fuzzy sets. Let $P_{\chi_{j,k}} \in P_j$ be the k-th partitioning fuzzy set expressed by a triangle membership function $\chi_{j,k}$ being a component of the partition of the j-th attribute. The following rule expresses conjunction of the fuzzy conditions along the path from the root to a tree node

$$B \equiv P_{\chi_{j_1}} \wedge \cdots \wedge P_{\chi_{j_N}} \qquad (7)$$

where $P_{\chi_{j_r}}$ are triangular fuzzy sets, and its set of indexes represented by the subsequence (j_r) is in a considered rule a result of pointing up a pair: (1) a unique attribute numbers j, and (2) one from the k triangle fuzzy sets for each attribute partitioning. Formula (7) expresses a conjunction of the conditions which are to be fulfilled for an instance o_i so that it were present in a considered node. Database $T = \{o_i, i = 1, \ldots, n\}$ generates a *support* for B (7) given as:

$$w(B) = \sum_{i=1}^{n} \prod_{j_r} Prob(P_{\chi_{j_r}} | o_i) \qquad (8)$$

where $Prob(P_{\chi_{j_r}} | o_i)$ is a probability defined on the fuzzy set $P_{\chi_{j_r}}$ provided the observation o_i. It is easily calculated using the membership function $\chi_{j_r(o_i)}$.

Let $\{C_l, l = 1, \ldots, h\}$ denotes a set of decision classes. Formula (8) is also used for generating support for a given decision class, e.g., C_x in a given node, namely

$$Prob(C_x | B) = \frac{w(C_x \wedge B)}{\sum_{l=1}^{h} w(C_l \wedge B)} = \frac{w(C_x \wedge B)}{w(B)}. \qquad (9)$$

Splitting a node (starting from a root) is related to the attributes' abilities evaluation to generate a next level with the child nodes. A potential possibility of an attribute A for producing child nodes A_s, $s = 1, \ldots p$ is tested by calculating its classical entropy:

$$I(A_s) = - \sum_{l=1}^{h} Prob(C_l|A_s) \, log(Prob(C_l|A_s)), \; s = 1, \ldots p., \qquad (10)$$

The common entropy for an attribute A is the following weighted mean value:

$$I(A) = \frac{\sum_{s=1}^{p} w(A_s) \cdot I(A_s)}{\sum_{s=1}^{p} w(A_s)} \qquad (11)$$

In (10) and (11) it has been assumed that A_s represents a rule from the root to the s-th child node.

Using the presented above formulas makes it possible to generate the nodes in a fuzzy *ID3* tree [6].

3.3 Deriving Intuitionistic Fuzzy Sets from Data

We will present now a modification of the soft *ID3* approach (Section 3.2) by using intuitionistic fuzzy sets.

Let assume that an attribute A, splitting a node into the child nodes $A_s, s = 1, \ldots p$, is tested. For simplicity we assume that only two decision classes C^+ and C^- are considered. Support for these classes in each node is

$$\begin{aligned} for \; class \; C^+ &: w(C^+ \wedge A_1), \, w(C^+ \wedge A_2), \cdots, w(C^+ \wedge A_p) \\ for \; class \; C^- &: w(C^- \wedge A_1), \, w(C^- \wedge A_2), \cdots, w(C^- \wedge A_p). \end{aligned} \qquad (12)$$

Independently for each class their frequencies for the verified splitting are calculated (proportions between support of a class in the child nodes and its cardinality in the parent node)

$$\begin{aligned} p(C^+|A_s) &: \frac{w(C^+ \wedge A_1)}{w(C^+ \wedge A)}, \, \frac{w(C^+ \wedge A_2)}{w(C^+ \wedge A)}, \cdots, \frac{w(C^+ \wedge A_p)}{w(C^+ \wedge A)} \\ p(C^-|A_s) &: \frac{w(C^- \wedge A_1)}{w(C^- \wedge A)}, \, \frac{w(C^- \wedge A_2)}{w(C^- \wedge A)}, \cdots, \frac{w(C^- \wedge A_p)}{w(C^- \wedge A)}. \end{aligned} \qquad (13)$$

Having the relative frequencies $p(C^+|A_i)$ and $p(C^-|A_i)$ (13), we use the algorithm given in [5,6] to construct independently fuzzy sets representing the classes C^+, and C^-. The fuzzy sets obtained for C^+, and C^- are abbreviated Pos^+ and Pos^-, respectively. In the fuzzy *ID3* tree [6] the fuzzy sets $Pos^+(A_s)$ and $Pos^-(A_s)$, $s = 1, \ldots, p$ are tested by a classical entropy (10) - (11) to assess the attributes.

In the algorithm proposed here we use the fuzzy model (expressed by Pos^+ and Pos^-) to construct intuitionistic fuzzy model (details are presented in Szmidt and Baldwin [26]). Intuitionistic fuzzy model of the data in the child nodes A_s, $s = 1, \ldots p$ (due to the algorithm in [26]) is expressed by the following intuitionistic fuzzy terms

$$\begin{aligned} \pi(A_s) &= Pos^+(A_s) + Pos^-(A_s) - 1 \\ \mu(A_s) &= Pos^+(A_s) - \pi(A_s) \\ \nu(A_s) &= Pos^-(A_s) - \pi(A_s). \end{aligned} \qquad (14)$$

This way each child node s is described by the following intuitionistic fuzzy set

$$< A_s, \mu(A_s), \nu(A_s), \pi(A_s) >, \; s = 1, \ldots, p \qquad (15)$$

where μ describes support for the class C^+; ν describes support for the class C^-; π expresses lack of knowledge concerning μ and ν.

An instance o_i characteristic at node A_s can be expressed as well in terms of intuitionistic fuzzy sets

$$\chi_{A_s}(o_i) \cdot < \mu(A_s), \nu(A_s), \pi(A_s) >, \; i = 1, \ldots, n,$$

where χ_{A_s} is a membership function at node A_s expressed by the product in (8). Having in mind the property (5) we can obtain full information value of an instance o_i while partitioning A and obtaining in result the child nodes $\{A_s, \; s = 1, \ldots, p\}$:

$$\chi_{A_s}(o_i) \cdot < \mu(A_s), \nu(A_s), \pi(A_s) > +\chi_{A_{s+1}}(o_i) \cdot < \mu(A_{s+1}), \nu(A_{s+1}), \pi(A_{s+1}) > .$$
(16)

Both (15) and (16) may be used (alternatively) in the algorithm proposed for assessing and choosing the attributes while splitting the nodes in the intuitionistic fuzzy decision tree.

3.4   Selection of an Attribute to Split a Node

In the process of expanding a tree – a crisp, fuzzy or intuitionistic fuzzy tree, the crucial step is splitting a node into children nodes. To split a node an attribute is selected on the basis of its "information gain". Different measures may be used to assess "information gain". We use here an intuitionistic fuzzy measure – intuitionistic fuzzy entropy [29].

Intuitionistic fuzzy entropy $E(x)$ of an intuitionistic fuzzy element $x \in A$ is given as [29]:

$$E(x) = \frac{min\{l_{IFS}(x, M), l_{IFS}(x, N)\}}{max\{l_{IFS}(x, M), l_{IFS}(x, N)\}},$$
(17)

where M, N are the intuitionistic fuzzy elements ($< \mu, \nu, \pi >$) fully belonging (M) or fully not belonging (N) to a set considered

$$M = < 1, 0, 0 >$$
$$N = < 0, 1, 0 >,$$

$l_{IFS}(\cdot, \cdot)$ is the normalized Hamming distance [28,30]:

$$l_{IFS}(x, M) = \tfrac{1}{2}(|\mu_x - 1| + |\nu_x - 0| + |\pi_x - 0|)$$

$$l_{IFS}(x, N) = \tfrac{1}{2}(|\mu_x - 0| + |\nu_x - 1| + |\pi_x - 0|).$$

It is also possible to use other intuitionistic fuzzy measures to evaluate the attributes (cf. [36], [37]) but due to the space limitation here we discuss entropy only.

Intuitionistic fuzzy entropy of an intuitionistic fuzzy set with n elements: $X = \{x_1, \ldots, x_n\}$ is [29]:

$$E(X) = \frac{1}{n} \sum_{i=1}^{n} E(x_i).$$
(18)

To compute intuitionistic fuzzy entropy $E(A_s)$ (17) in a child node A_s, $s = 1, \ldots, p$, we make use of the intuitionistic fuzzy representations (12)–(15) of the possible child nodes derived while testing attribute A.

Total intuitionistic fuzzy entropy of an attribute A is abbreviated $E(W_A)$ whereas entropy of a child node – $E(A_s)$. Total intuitionistic fuzzy entropy of A is a sum of the weighted intuitionistic fuzzy entropy measures of all the child nodes A_s, $s = 1, \ldots, p$, with the weights reflecting supports (cardinalities) of the nodes:

$$E(W_A) = \frac{\sum_{s=1}^{p} w(A_s)E(A_s)}{\sum_{s=1}^{p} w(A_s)}. \tag{19}$$

Instead of using (19) we may calculate $E(W_A)$ by applying a weighted intuitionistic fuzzy representation of each instance o_i (16) while partitioning an attribute A. Next, using (18), a total intuitionistic fuzzy entropy is calculated for a chosen attribute. This method was applied in the numerical experiments (cf. Section 4).

An attribute for which total intuitionistic fuzzy entropy is minimal is selected for splitting a node.

A flowchart representing a process of generating intuitionistic fuzzy decision tree is in Fig. 3.

3.5   Classification of the Instances

A leaf in a soft tree is described by a proportion of the classes considered. A single instance usually belongs to several leaves. In result we need aggregated information about total degree of membership of a single observation to each class.

To classify the instances we use here measure SUM which is a sum of the products of the instance membership values at leafs and support for a class considered in these leafs [6]. Total support of the observation o_i, $i = 1, \ldots, n$, for a class C is:

$$supp(C|o_i)_{SUM} = \sum_{j=1}^{L} supp(C|T_j) \cdot \chi(T_j|o_i), \tag{20}$$

where $\{T_j : j = 1, \ldots, L\}$ is a set of the leafs; L is the number of the leafs; $supp(C|T_j)$ is a support of the classes considered in the j-th leaf; $\chi(T_j|o_i)$ is a membership value of the observation o_i (it is a result of the partitioning of the universe attributes), different for each leaf, fulfilling: $\sum_{j=1}^{L} \chi(T_j|o_i) = 1$.

4   Results of the Numerical Experiments

We have verified classification abilities of the new intuitionistic fuzzy decision tree with other well known algorithms.

The following measures were used to compare the behavior of the classifiers compared:
– total proper identification of the instances belonging to the classes considered,
– the area under ROC curve [15].

Behavior of the intuitionistic fuzzy decision tree proposed here was compared especially with other decision trees, namely:

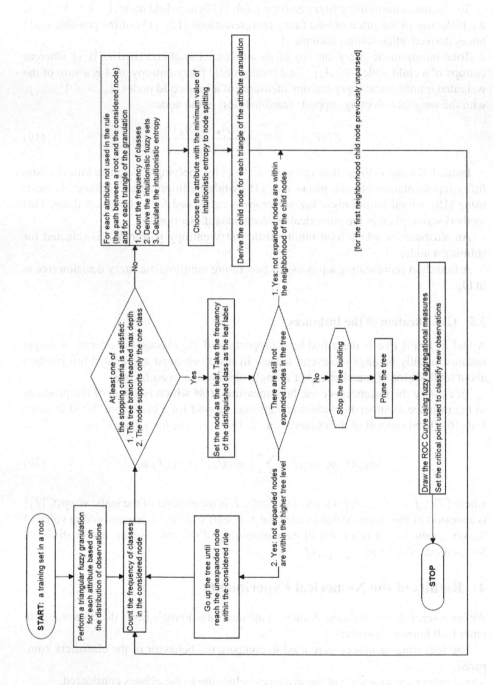

Fig. 3. A flowchart representing a process of generating intuitionistic fuzzy tree

Table 1. "Sonar" benchmark data – comparison of the intuitionistic fuzzy decision tree and other classifiers

Algorithm	Classification accuracy ($\bar{x} \pm \sigma$) [%]	
	for both classes	AUC ROC
intuitionistic fuzzy tree (asym)	80.80 ± 7.76 (∗)	89.81 ± 5.66 (∗)
Random Forest	80.41 ± 8.80	89.53 ± 7.58
Multilayer Perceptron	81.61 ± 8.66	88.48 ± 7.31
pruned intuitionistic fuzzy tree (asym)	78.63 ± 7.89	86.92 ± 6.29 (−)
LMT	76.27 ± 9.62 (−)	84.15 ± 8.55 (−)
NBTree	77.07 ± 9.65 (−)	83.10 ± 9.89 (−)
SDT (refitting)	73.28 ± b.d. (b.d.)	b.d.
SDT (backfitting)	72.56 ± b.d. (b.d.)	b.d.
Logistic	72.47 ± 8.90 (−−)	80.02 ± 8.78 (−−)
*J*48 (*unpruned C*4.5)	73.42 ± 9.36 (−)	79.37 ± 10.83 (−−)
*J*48 (*pruned C*4.5)	73.61 ± 9.34 (−)	79.31 ± 10.80 (−−)

- **J48** – implementation of the crisp tree proposed by Quinlan *C4.5* ([22]),
- **LMT** (*Logistic Model Tree*) – a hybrid tree building the logistic models at the leaves ([17]),
- **NBTree** – hybrid decision tree building the Bayes classifiers at the leaves,
- **RandomForest** – here consisting of 10 decision trees which nodes are generated on the basis of a random set of attributes ([10]).

Besides the trees, also neural networks (**MultilayerPerceptron**), and logistic regression (**Logistic**) were used for the evaluation. The evaluation of the above algorithms was performed using WEKA (http://www.cs.waikato.ac.nz/ml/weka/). Next, the results obtained by Olaru and Wehenkel [20] using *Soft Decision Trees (SDT)* are compared.

We present here the results obtained by intuitionistic fuzzy decision tree for "Sonar" benchmark data (http://archive.ics.uci.edu/ml/datasets.html). The dataset contains 208 instances, 60 numerical attributes, 2 classes (111 – metal cylinder, and 97 instances – rocks). We use simple cross validation method with 10 experiments of 10-fold cross validation (giving 100 trees). For each experiment an average value of the accuracy measures, and of their standard deviations were calculated. So to compare an average accuracy of the new intuitionistic fuzzy decision tree with other classifiers, *t-Student* test was used (Table 1). One minus in Table 1 means that the (worse) result was obtained by a classifier while using classical *t-Student* test, two minuses mean using corrected *t-Student* test (for cross validation).

Results obtained (Table 1 – accuracy, and Fig. 4 – ROC curves) show that the intuitionistic fuzzy decision tree is the best concerning the area under ROC curve, and the second one in respect of accuracy (a little worse than *Multilayer Perceptron*). In other words, the new intuitionistic fuzzy decision tree turned out a better classifier for "Sonar" benchmark data than other crisp and soft decision trees, even slightly better than *Random Forest*, and almost as effective as *Multilayer Perceptron*.

Surprisingly enough, just for the "Sonar" benchmark data, the proposed classifier turned out to be worse than the simplest k-nearest neighbor classifier. Due to space

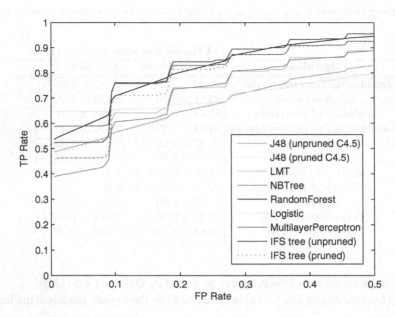

Fig. 4. "Sonar" benchmark data – comparison of the areas under ROC curves for the intuitionistic fuzzy decision tree and other classifiers (TP – True Positive, FP – False Positive rates [15])

Table 2. Comparison of the accuracy of k-NN classifier, trees.J48 and the intuitionistic fuzzy decision tree for chosen benchmark data

| Data set | Classification accuracy ($\bar{x} \pm \sigma$) [%] | | | |
	k-NN for k=1	k-NN for k=3	trees.J48 (pruned)	IFS tree
PIMA	70.62 ± 4.67	73.86 ± 4.55	74.49 ± 5.27	$\mathbf{75.72 \pm 4.37}$
Sonar	$\mathbf{86.17 \pm 8.45}$	83.76 ± 8.51	73.61 ± 9.34	80.80 ± 7.76
Ionosphere	87.10 ± 5.12	86.02 ± 4.31	89.74 ± 4.38	$\mathbf{90.36 \pm 4.50}$
Wine	95.12 ± 4.34	95.85 ± 4.19	93.20 ± 5.90	$\mathbf{97.88 \pm 3.53}$
Glass	70.30 ± 8.96	69.84 ± 8.61	67.61 ± 9.26	$\mathbf{75.16 \pm 6.21}$
Iris	95.40 ± 4.80	95.20 ± 5.11	94.73 ± 5.30	$\mathbf{96.20 \pm 4.37}$

limitation we do not present a detailed comparison of the proposed classifier for other data sets (as for the "Sonar" data – Table 1), but results of the experiments with the k-nearest neighbor classifier (Table 2) are added for several other benchmark data sets, namely: "PIMA", "Ionosphere", "Wine", "Glass", "Iris" (http://archive.ics.uci.edu/ml/datasets.html). It is easy to notice that the proposed classifier produces more accurate results than the k-nearest neighbor classifier (the "Sonar" benchmark data is an exception). In other words, the proposed classifier may be not the best solution for all possible data sets, but no other classifier can be, for obvious reasons! However, for the data sets presented in Table 2 it turned out to be usually better, and certainly not worse than the classifiers presented in Table 1. In addition, as a tree type classifier, it can be a properer, if not the best choice, in many applications when comprehensibility and transparency to the human being is relevant.

5 Conclusions

We have proposed a new intuitionistic fuzzy decision tree which is an extension of the fuzzy ID3 decision tree algorithm. The tree proposed was tested on a well known benchmark examples. The results are very encouraging.

References

1. Atanassov, K.: Intuitionistic Fuzzy Sets. VII ITKR Session. Sofia (June 1983) (Deposed in Central Sci.-Techn. Library of Bulgarian Academy of Sciences, 1697/84)
2. Atanassov, K.: Intuitionistic Fuzzy Sets: Theory and Applications. Springer (1999)
3. Atanassov, K.: On Intuitionistic Fuzzy Sets Theory. Springer (2012)
4. Baldwin, J.F., Karale, S.B.: Asymmetric Triangular Fuzzy Sets for Classification Models. In: Palade, V., Howlett, R.J., Jain, L.C. (eds.) KES 2003. LNCS (LNAI), vol. 2773, pp. 364–370. Springer, Heidelberg (2003)
5. Baldwin, J.F., Lawry, J., Martin, T.P.: A mass assignment theory of the probability of fuzzy events. Fuzzy Sets and Systems 83, 353–367 (1996)
6. Baldwin, J.F., Lawry, J., Martin, T.P.: Mass Assignment Fuzzy ID3 with Applications. In: Unicom Workshop on Fuzzy Logic Applications and Future Directions, London (1997)
7. Bartczuk, Ł., Rutkowska, D.: A New Version of the Fuzzy-ID3 Algorithm. In: Rutkowski, L., Tadeusiewicz, R., Zadeh, L.A., Żurada, J.M. (eds.) ICAISC 2006. LNCS (LNAI), vol. 4029, pp. 1060–1070. Springer, Heidelberg (2006)
8. Benbrahim, H., Bensaid, A.: A comparative study of pruned decision trees and fuzzy decision trees. In: NAFIPS 2000, pp. 227–231 (2000)
9. Bezdek, J.C.: Pattern Recognition with Fuzzy Objective Function Algorithms. Kluwer Academic Publishers, Norwell (1981)
10. Breiman, L.: Random Forests. Machine Learning 45(1), 5–32 (2001)
11. Breiman, L., Friedman, J.H., Olsen, R.A., Stone, C.J.: Classification and Regression Trees. Wadsworth, Belmont (1984)
12. Bujnowski, P.: Using intuitionistic fuzzy sets for constructing decision trees in classification tasks. PhD dissertation, IBS PAN, Warsaw (2013) (in Polish)
13. Bustince, H., Mohedano, V., Barrenechea, E., Pagola, M.: Image thresholding using intuitionistic fuzzy sets. In: Atanassov, K., Kacprzyk, J., Krawczak, M., Szmidt, E. (eds.) Issues in the Representation and Processing of Uncertain and Imprecise Information. Fuzzy Sets, Intuitionistic Fuzzy Sets, Generalized Nets, and Related Topics. EXIT, Warsaw (2005)
14. Bustince, H., Mohedano, V., Barrenechea, E., Pagola, M.: An algorithm for calculating the threshold of an image representing uncertainty through A-IFSs. In: IPMU 2006, pp. 2383–2390 (2006)
15. Hand, D.J., Till, R.J.: A simple generalization of the area under the ROC curve for multiple class classification problems. Machine Learning 45, 171–186 (2001)
16. Janikow, C.Z.: Fuzzy Decision Trees: Issues and Methods. IEEE Transactions on Systems, Man, and Cybernetics 28(1), 1–14 (1998)
17. Landwehr, N., Hall, M., Frank, E.: Logistic Model Trees. Machine Learning 95(1-2), 161–205 (2005)
18. Marsala, C.: Fuzzy decision trees to help flexible querying. Kybernetika 36(6), 689–705 (2000)
19. Marsala, C., Bouchon-Meunier, B.: An adaptable system to construct fuzzy decision tree. In: NAFIPS 1999, pp. 223–227 (1999)

20. Olaru, C., Wehenkel, L.: A complete fuzzy decision tree technique. Fuzzy Sets and Systems, 221–254 (2003)
21. Quinlan, J.R.: Induction of decision trees. Machine Learning 1, 81–106 (1986)
22. Quinlan, J.R.: C4.5: Programs for Machine Learning. Morgan Kaufman Publishers, Inc., San Mateo (1993)
23. Ruspini, E.H.: A New Approach to Clustering. Information and Control 15, 22–32 (1969)
24. Rutkowski, L.: Artificial intelligence methods and techniques, pp. 237–307. PWN, Warszawa (2009) (in Polish)
25. Safavian, S.R., Landgrebe, D.: A survey of decision tree classifier methodology. IEEE Trans. Systems Man Cybernet. 21, 660–674 (1991)
26. Szmidt, E., Baldwin, J.: Intuitionistic Fuzzy Set Functions, Mass Assignment Theory, Possibility Theory and Histograms. In: 2006 IEEE WCCI, pp. 237–243 (2006)
27. Szmidt, E., Kacprzyk, J.: On measuring distances between intuitionistic fuzzy sets. Notes on IFS 3(4), 1–13 (1997)
28. Szmidt, E., Kacprzyk, J.: Distances between intuitionistic fuzzy sets. Fuzzy Sets and Systems 114(3), 505–518 (2000)
29. Szmidt, E., Kacprzyk, J.: Entropy for intuitionistic fuzzy sets. Fuzzy Sets and Systems 118, 467–477 (2001)
30. Szmidt, E., Kacprzyk, J.: Distances Between Intuitionistic Fuzzy Sets: Straightforward Approaches may not work. In: 3rd International IEEE Conference Intelligent Systems, IEEE IS 2006, London, pp. 716–721 (2006)
31. Szmidt, E., Kacprzyk, J.: Some problems with entropy measures for the Atanassov intuitionistic fuzzy sets. In: Masulli, F., Mitra, S., Pasi, G. (eds.) WILF 2007. LNCS (LNAI), vol. 4578, pp. 291–297. Springer, Heidelberg (2007)
32. Szmidt, E., Kacprzyk, J.: A New Similarity Measure for Intuitionistic Fuzzy Sets: Straightforward Approaches may not work. In: 2007 IEEE Conf. on Fuzzy Systems, pp. 481–486 (2007a)
33. Szmidt, E., Kukier, M.: Classification of Imbalanced and Overlapping Classes using Intuitionistic Fuzzy Sets. In: IEEE IS 2006, London, pp. 722–727 (2006)
34. Szmidt, E., Kukier, M.: A New Approach to Classification of Imbalanced Classes via Atanassov's Intuitionistic Fuzzy Sets. In: Wang, H.-F. (ed.) Intelligent Data Analysis: Developing New Methodologies Through Pattern Discovery and Recovery, pp. 85–101. Idea Group (2008)
35. Szmidt, E., Kukier, M.: Atanassov's intuitionistic fuzzy sets in classification of imbalanced and overlapping classes. In: Chountas, P., Petrounias, I., Kacprzyk, J. (eds.) Intelligent Techniques and Tools for Novel System Architectures. SCI, vol. 109, pp. 455–471. Springer, Heidelberg (2008)
36. Szmidt, E., Kacprzyk, J., Bujnowski, P.: Measuring the Amount of Knowledge for Atanassov's Intuitionistic Fuzzy Sets. In: Petrosino, A. (ed.) WILF 2011. LNCS, vol. 6857, pp. 17–24. Springer, Heidelberg (2011)
37. Szmidt, E., Kacprzyk, J., Bujnowski, P.: How to measure the amount of knowledge conveyed by Atanassov's intuitionistic fuzzy sets. Information Sciences 257, 276–285 (2014)
38. Yuan, Y., Shaw, M.J.: Induction of fuzzy decision trees. Fuzzy Sets and Systems 69, 125–139 (1996)
39. Zadeh, L.A.: Fuzzy sets. Information and Control 8, 338–353 (1965)

An Industrial Fuzzy PID Autotuner
Based on the Relay Method

Sławomir Jaszczak and Joanna Kołodziejczyk

Westpomeranian University of Technology in Szczecin,
Department of Computer Science, Poland
{sjaszczak,jkolodziejczyk}@wi.zut.edu.pl

Abstract. The article analyses a auto-tuning method for a fuzzy PID
controller based on the relay experiment. The algorithm was implemented and tested on a real plant for redox agent stabilisation in a
paper mill. Experiments have discovered some unsolved, practical problems which were discussed in the paper i.e. determination of the ON-OFF
parameters, the non-shocked switching from the ON-OFF tuning algorithm into a continues fuzzy PID algorithm.

Keywords: Control Systems, Fuzzy Control, PID Algorithm, Auto-
tuning, Relay method.

1 Introduction

One of the major problem in control systems is the tuning process of the specific
control algorithm. Tuning should optimise the performance of a control algorithm
for a given process. Plants incorrectly tuned become unstable, what is potentially
dangerous. A common reason for instability is exceeding the very narrow range
of acceptable values of adjustable parameters of control algorithms. It is difficult to perform tuning manually or semiautomatically (by an operator) mainly
according to non linearity of the controlled plant. From the plant's operator
point of view the most convenient way of tuning is an "one push button" solution. Fully automatic tuning methods are proposed in control literature for some
time now [6]. PLC and PAC controllers' producers such as GE, Siemens, Ber-
necker&Reiner and others allow creating control systems with automatic tuning
(usually by using a functional block). The problem is that in most cases tuning
algorithms are so-called "mixtures" base on one of the method given below and
heuristic algorithms, which usually aren't given at all. There are two kinds of
experiments in the auto-tuning techniques [6]:

1. open-loop methods:
    - Ziegler-Nichols' Process Reaction Curve method (or the Ziegler-Nichols'
      Open-Loop method) *Ziegler and Nichols (1942)*
    - Hagglund and Åström's Robust tuning method *Hägglund and Åström
      (2002)*

L. Rutkowski et al. (Eds.): ICAISC 2014, Part I, LNAI 8467, pp. 193–204, 2014.

  - Skogestad's Model-based method (or: the SIMC method (Simple Internal Model Control) *Skogestad (2003, 2004)*
2. closed-loop methods:
  - Ziegler-Nichols' Ultimate Gain method (or the Ziegler-Nichols' Closed-Loop method) *Ziegler and Nichols (1942)*
  - Relay method (using a relay function to obtain the sustained oscillations as in the Ziegler-Nichols' method), *Åström and Hägglund (1995)*
  - Tyreus-Luyben's method (which is based on the Ziegler-Nichols' method, but with more conservative tuning), *Luyben and Luyben (1997)*
  - Setpoint Overshoot method, *Shamsuzzoha et al. (2010)*
  - Good Gain method; *Haugen (2010)*

Unfortunately applying them into a real time control system isn't an easy task because of several facts : a sophisticated methodology of the tuning preparation - an process engineer has to establish many numerical factors, what demands a detailed knowledge about a controlled process; there isn't an universal method for every plant i.e. every type of plant's dynamic; usually a tuning process is a long term experiment; some of those method aren't suitable to apply them in a real time control mainly because the fact, that calculation need more time than one program cycle; some of those methods are to sensitive in case of disturbances influence. As a result of those remarks we try to develop and implement a method which is able to overcome those disadvantages. Most of these solutions are suitable for classic PID algorithms but not fuzzy PID algorithms, which have become popular in practical applications. The fuzzy PID controller develops a nonlinear control surface which is more suitable for nonlinear plants. Some problems might occur in applications of fuzzy PID algorithms in industrial implementation [7]. The tuning process is more complex due to qualitative synthesis i.e. the rule construction, deciding on inference and defuzzification methods and quantitative synthesis i.e. input and output scaling factors setting and membership functions selection for both fuzzification and defuzzification. In the article a methodology of fuzzy PID controller automatic tuning for scaling factors (equivalent to classic PID algorithm parameters) is proposed.

The main idea is based on the relay experiment [2] that is an ON-OFF control algorithm. The conversion from the Åström algorithm to a fuzzy PID algorithm was proposed in [5]. The article analyses practical aspects of fuzzy PID algorithm tuning using a PAC controller. Experiments on a real control plant for redox agent stabilisation show that relay tuning for fuzzy PID algorithms needs to be modified. Some ideas of relay tuning methodology are proposed.

2   State of the Art

The fundamental specifications of the tuning algorithm set by the authors are minimum computation time and the ability to work on-line during normal operations of the system. Using the original idea presented in [5] had to be preceded by overcoming a variety of implementing problems arising from practical phenomena existing in real time control systems like dynamic and static nonlinearities, measuring noise and nonstationarity etc. Dynamic nonlinearities of real control plants result in changing the given SP value while the operational point is transformed and can negatively influence control quality. Changing the SP value actually brings the system out of equilibrium into the intermediate state. This situation is critical to a real installation as it can destabilize the control system. That is why when the operating point changes the control algorithm needs to be tuned. Signal noise creates computing difficulties in creating the signal derivative or determining its minimum or maximum etc. Nonstationarity of the system and automation devices (actuators) along with dynamic nonlinearities result in operating condition changes, while these alterations arise from changing physical properties of the system and actuators (i.e. aging process).

The relay method being safe and easy is often used when tuning PID algorithms of the ISA and IND structure. This is especially important in industrial practice where downtime and retooling time has to be minimized and stable functioning is essential. More arguments for the relay method are connected with technology parameters in process control systems:

1. a process in safe plant's shutdown mode is controlled using the ON-OFF method i.e. stabilizing the redox agent in paper mills, reactor temperature etc. in this time the control signal amplitudes do not need to perfectly obey technological requirements. It is usually sufficient to remain within a predefined variability range. This perfectly matches initial tuning conditions of the control algorithm for the tuning happens when the system is in shutdown mode.
2. the tuning process needs to work online because in most cases production capabilities and performance has to be kept up
3. the algorithm shall not require complicated preparatory activities like initial manual parameter setup etc.

For many industrial installations a ON-OFF algorithm being the fundament of the relay method, can be used only to tune settings of the proper PID controller and be turned on when production performance could be low i.e when a production is suspended but installation should be controlled. The information gathered while operating in this mode can be used to gain settings for the PID controller.

3 How the Autotuner Works

A novel digital controller uses auto-tuning algorithms for immediate controller factors adjustment as a response to a dynamically changing process. The auto-tuning procedure can be run automatically each time the amplitude of the given value is changed. A proposed auto-tuning procedure based on the relay experiment works as follows:

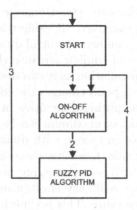

Fig. 1. The tuning procedure of the fuzzy PID algorithm

The procedure runs as a state machine with the following states (Fig. 1):

Start — waiting for an action
ON-OFF algorithm — tuning ON-OFF algorithm, relay experiment conduction and factors calculation for a continuous algorithm.
Fuzzy PID algorithm — run the continuous algorithm (fuzzy PID algorithm in this case)

and following transitions:

1 — launch the relay experiment – operator function
2 — launch the continuous algorithm – non-shock transition from the ON-OFF algorithm to the continuous algorithm
3 — stop the continuous algorithm – a safe plant shutdown
4 — relaunch the relay experiment with changed operating point.

The tuning algorithm analyzes the control value (Fig. 2) that is obtained in the closed-loop control system employing a ON-OFF algorithm (Fig. 3). The key points are the amplitude of the oscillation (A) and the oscillation period (T_{osc}) of the control signal. Based on them settings for the PID and PID-like algorithms (e.g. a fuzzy PID algorithm) are calculated by using formulas presented in [6]. The main idea is to bring the control system to the quasi-critical state, as in the Ziegler-Nichols method, but not to the limit of stability, which in general is not safe.

The ON-OFF algorithm executes a periodic generation of a control value $u(t)$ composed of two values: CV_{max} and CV_{min} to the controlled plant causing the controlled value $y(t)$ to oscillate within given limits: form $minError$ to $maxError$. Switching the $u(t)$ signal to a CV_{max} is performed when the controlled error $e(t)$ is lower than $maxError$ and the process is continued until the $e(t)$ amplitude will be equal to $minError$. Then the $u(t)$ signal is switched to the CV_{min} amplitude and is unchanged until the error $e(t)$ is equal to $maxError$.

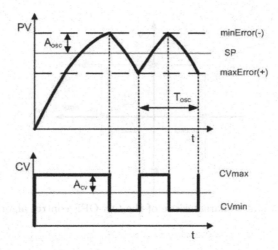

Fig. 2. Control value (CV) and process value (PV) signals in the control system with ON-OFF algorithm

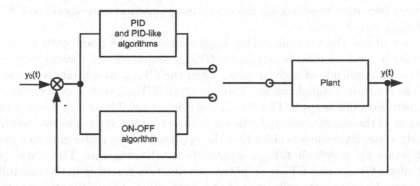

Fig. 3. An idea of the autotuner in the control system with PID and PID-like algorithms [3]

The cycle of switching is repeated as shown in Fig. 2. The switching frequency and oscillation amplitude are dependent on the inner dynamic of the process and the $u(t)$ amplitudes in ON and OFF states.

The main problem with a practical implementation of the ON-OFF algorithm (static characteristic of the algorithm: 4) is to specify the control value (CV) amplitudes for ON (CV_{max}) and OFF (CV_{min}) states guaranteeing safe operation of the controlled plant. Safety is ensured when the controlled signal (PV) does not exceed the range between $minError$ and $maxError$. Error values are technological plant limitations and are given by a technologist. In the literature the only given method for setting CV_{max} and CV_{min} amplitudes is setting them arbitrarily. If those values are incorrect in real implementations then the

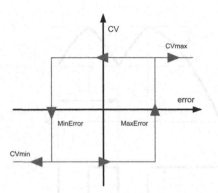

Fig. 4. A static characteristic of the ON-OFF control algorithm

upper range value i.e. $minError$ never is reached or is exceeded. Moreover the controlled value PV should spread symmetrically around the SP. The selection of CV_{max} and CV_{min} amplitudes for a plant with given requirements is a non trivial task. Unlike a system described in [5] real systems are highly dynamically nonlinear (sensitive to switching the operating point that correspond to CV_{max} and CV_{min} amplitudes).

In case of the ON-OFF algorithm implemented on the plant with unknown dynamics a good solution is setting an CV_{max} amplitude to a small value e.g. equal to an amplitude of a given value. Then the CV_{max} amplitude is increased until the controlled signal reaches a steady state (CV_{min} state). A derivative of the controlled value is applied for steady state detection. The derivative expresses a tangent of the signal angle and when it is close to 0 the system begins to reach a steady state. Experiments show that the application of a static gain to a given steady-state for a default CV_{max} amplitude is advantageous. The static gain value allows CV_{max} and CV_{min} amplitudes estimation resulting in the controlled value spreading symmetrically around the given value. This estimation assumes system linearity (Fig. 5).

When the ON-OFF algorithm is correctly tuned the next problem is to precisely specify the oscillation amplitude (A_{osc}) and the oscillation period (T_{osc}) (Fig 2) for the controlled value that is generally mixed with a measurement noise. The measurement noise might be a source of fault tuning in the presented method and this aspect was omitted in [5]. Signal filtering (e.g. Kalman filtering) used before the scaling factors of the continuous algorithm are set, can be a solution to the problem.

A gain K_u and a period of time T_u can be calculated from A_{osc} and T_{osc} [5], which are used to compute factors for the continuous algorithm:

$$K_u = \frac{4A_{cv}}{\pi A_{osc}},$$

$$T_u = \frac{2\pi}{\omega_{osc}},$$

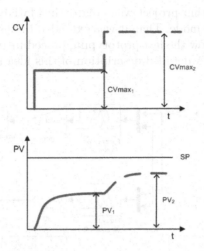

Fig. 5. Estimation of amplitudes CV_{max} and CV_{min} based on a static gain

where A_{osc} — oscillation amplitude, A_{cv} — relay element hysteresis, ω_{osc} — oscillation frequency.

Formulas for the fuzzy PID scaling factors calculus [3] are presented in Table 1.

Table 1. Formulas for the fuzzy PID scaling factors calculus [3]

Base	GE	GCE	GU	GCU
K_u, T_u	1	$\frac{1}{4}T_u$	$0.3gK_u$	$1.2g\frac{k_u}{T_u}$

The non-shocked switching to the continuous algorithm should be performed after the scaling factors calculation. The control system with an ON-OFF algorithm is in transition mode that makes the switching complicated. It is easy to lead the system to a steady state when experiments start in initial conditions i.e. all variables are equal to zero. Avoiding overshooting during switching is a technological problem. Non shocked switching in the tuning algorithms is an interesting area for further research.

4   FuzzyPID Algorithm Synthesis

The first idea for a fuzzyPID algorithm was a three input system. The consequence was a three-dimensional rule base that is non intuitive and difficult to define for a human expert. Li and Gatland (1996) proposed a solution that is a combination of fuzzy PI and fuzzy PD. There are two separate parts for PI and PD with a two inputs rule base each. One more advantage is that both rule bases share the same inputs.

The fuzzyPID algorithm project was created in Matlab-Simulink and tested in the model in the loop mode. Than it was extended by the embedded functions from B&R library to allow the fast prototyping procedure on the PAC controller from B&R [4] (Fig. 6). A detailed description of this idea is given in [7].

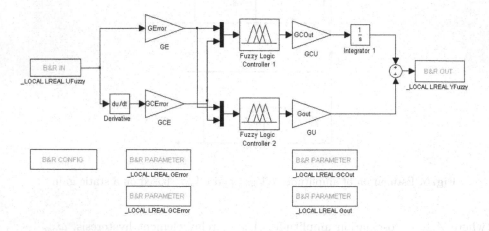

Fig. 6. Model of the fuzzy PID algorithm with embedded functions

A fuzzification was performed on inputs using triangular membership functions (Fig. 7 (a)). Before fuzzification input signals were scaled to the range $[-1, 1]$ using blocks GE and GCE. A center of gravity deffuzification method is performed using triangular membership functions (Fig. 7 (b)).

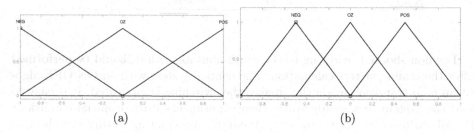

(a)   (b)

Fig. 7. (a) Membership functions in the fuzzy PID algorithm, (b) a defuzzification function in the fuzzy PID algorithm

Rules are presented in the Table 2 where e — error, ce — error derivative.

5   Experiments on Auto-tuned FuzzyPID

5.1   Control Plant Description

The presented tuning algorithm was verified in the redox agent stabilizing system i.e. dispensing of hypochlorite to the the circulating water tank intended for

Table 2. Rules in fuzzy PID algorithm: inputs: e — error, ce — error derivative, output: U

e/ce	NEG	OZ	POS
NEG	NEG	NEG	OZ
OZ	NEG	OZ	POS
POS	OZ	POS	POS

paper machines. The redox factor is the degree of circulating water oxidation. Large quantities of water are consumed in wood and wood-free paper production. Water is transported using pumps and the piping goes through a paper machine. Kilometers of pipes, closed water circuits, high temperature and cellulose pulp creates ideal conditions for either bacteria or fungal rapid growth. Some of these organisms are neutral and do not affect the quality of the final product, however, some of these can impair the quality of production, and even cause failures, gaps and breaks in production. To limit the growth of bacteria it is necessary to use strong oxidizing agents i.e. toxic biocides. Neutralization is particularly important in closed water circuits.

Hypochlorites are very strong oxidizing agents. They react with many organic and inorganic compounds. The reaction removes clots and microbial organisms. The redox agent stabilizer consists of the following components (Fig. 8), according to [1]:

1. redox sensor (QE),
2. redox converter (QT)
3. automatic control unit (FC),
4. controlled device (pump).

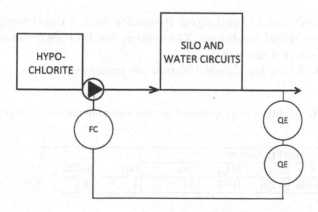

Fig. 8. A simplified diagram of the redox stabilization system with P&ID symbols

5.2   Experimental Results

The maim experiment first tunes the fuzzy PID algorithm based on the methodology given in the article for a given set value SP and then tests the controlled system with another set value SP. This approach should confirm the resistance of the controlled system to changing dynamic plant properties via an operating point switch. Fig. 9 shows that the tuning process lasts for about 10 minutes. The reason is the large inertia of the process. It is worth noticing that at the moment of switching form ON-OFF control to a continues fuzzy PID control the Redox_PV controlled signal amplitude drops significantly. The problem of non-shocked switching is a handicap that should be taken into account in multi-control systems.

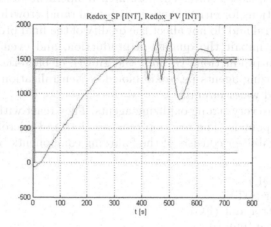

Fig. 9. A tuning process of the fuzzy PID control agorithm

Fig. 10 presents a controlled signal Redox_PV with a tuned fuzzy PID algorithm with zero initial conditions. The system can be considered as recovered after approximately 4 minutes.

In the Table 3 measured quality factors are presented.

Table 3. Quality factors gathered during experiments on the real plant

quality factors					GE	GCE	GU	GCU
T_n	T_r	M_p	M_{pp}	eu				
48.3871	218.145	0.197	19.7	0	1	4.08	0.76	0.19

The next experiment tests the resistance of the controlled system to stochastic disturbances. The PV signal disappearance was examined. Such a PV change can simulate a sensor damage.

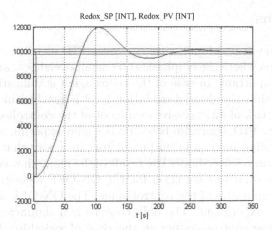

Fig. 10. A step response of the real time plant in the control system with the fuzzy PID algorithm

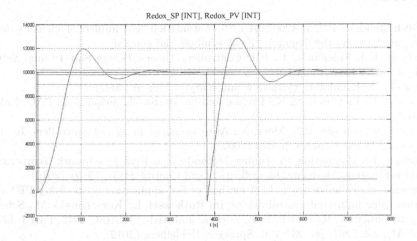

Fig. 11. A robustness test related to the introduction of a stochastic disturbance in the control system with a fuzzy PID controller

After the Redox_PV signal disappears for a short time the fuzzy PID algorithm brings it again to the Redox_SP set point. Summarizing it can be stated that the fuzzy PID algorithm tuning based on the relay experiment allows for a factor selection resulting in the controlled plant being stable.

6   Conclusions

Based on the survey it was found that the fuzzy PID algorithm is an excellent solution for systems where the emphasis is on small overshoot, and the recovery time is not very important. In case of the redox agent stabilization it is a good solution ensuring that the desired oxidation level is reached in the circulating water without the risk of an excessive overshoot of the controlled signal.

The tuning fuzzy PID algorithm based on the relay experiment allows factors adjustment i.e. scaling input and output factors in a way that ensures stable operation and minimizes overshoot. The result of the research was a development of an automated parameters selection for the ON-OFF algorithm i.e. the ON and OFF states amplitudes of the control value. The ON-OFF algorithm is the basis for the relay experiment. The only concern is a significant disruption in the operation of the control system at the time of switching from tuning to continuous control.

References

1. Polish standard PN/M-42007/01:1989, automation and industrial measurements. The markings on the diagrams. Basic symbols and general
2. Åström, K.J., Hägglund, T.: PID Controllers Theory, Design and Tuning. Setting the standard for automation
3. Brzozka, J.: Regulatory cyfrowe w automatyce. Mikom (2002)
4. Dworak, P., Pietrusewicz, K.: Programowalne sterowniki automatyki PAC. Nakom (2007)
5. Escamilla-Ambrosio, P.J., Mort, N.: Auto tuning of fuzzy pid controllers. In: 15th Triennial World Congres, p. 679 (2002)
6. Haugen, F.: Comparing PI Tuning Methods in a Real Benchmark Temperature Control System. Modeling, Identification and Control 31(3), 79–91 (2010)
7. Jaszczak, S., Kołodziejczyk, J.: A method of fast application of the fuzzy PID algorithm using industrial control device. In: Rutkowski, L., Korytkowski, M., Scherer, R., Tadeusiewicz, R., Zadeh, L.A., Zurada, J.M. (eds.) ICAISC 2012, Part I. LNCS (LNAI), vol. 7267, pp. 237–246. Springer, Heidelberg (2012)

A New Pseudo-metric for Fuzzy Sets

Laszlo Kovacs[1] and Joel Ratsaby[2],*

[1] Department of Information Technology, University of Miskolc, HUNGARY. H-3515,
Miskolc-Egyetemvaros
kovacs@iit.uni-miskolc.hu
[2] Department of Electrical and Electronics Engineering, Ariel University of Samaria,
Ariel 40700, Israel
ratsaby@ariel.ac.il
http://www.ariel.ac.il/sites/ratsaby/

Abstract. A new distance function for fuzzy sets is introduced. It is
based on the descriptive complexity, that is, the number of bits (on average) that are needed to describe an element in the symmetric difference
of the two sets. The value of the distance gives the amount of additional
information needed to describe either one of the two sets when the other
is known. We prove that the distance function is a pseudo-metric, namely,
it is non-negative, symmetric, it equals zero if the sets are identical and
it satisfies the triangle inequality.

Keywords: Fuzzy sets, descriptive complexity, entropy, distance,
triangle-inequality.

1 Introduction

The notion of distance between two objects is very general. Distance metrics and
distance functions have now become essential tools in many areas of mathematics and its applications including geometry, probability, statistics, coding/graph
theory, data analysis, pattern recognition. For a comprehensive source on this
subject see [1]. A fuzzy set is a class of objects with continuous values of membership and hence extends the classical definition of a set. To distinguish a set
from a fuzzy set we refer to the former as a crisp set. Formally, a fuzzy set
is a pair (E, m) where E is a set of objects and m is a membership function
$m : E \to [0, 1]$. A crisp set A has for all $x \in A$, $m_A(x) \in \{0, 1\}$. Fuzzy set theory
can be used in a wide range of domains in which information is incomplete or
imprecise, such as pattern recognition, decision theory. The concept of distance
and similarity is important in the area of fuzzy logic and sets. We now review
a few common ways of defining distance functions on fuzzy sets (see [2] and
references therein). We note in passing that this is by no means an exhaustive
review of all the different distance functions on fuzzy sets.

Classical distance functions measure how far two points are in Euclidean
space. For instance, the Minkowski distance between two points x and y in
$\mathbb{R}^n$ is defined as

* Corresponding author.

L. Rutkowski et al. (Eds.): ICAISC 2014, Part I, LNAI 8467, pp. 205–216, 2014.

$$d_r(x, y) := \left(\sum_{i=1}^{n} |x_i - y_i|^r \right)^{1/r}, \quad r \geq 1. \tag{1}$$

Let E be a finite set and let $\Phi(E)$ be the set of all fuzzy subsets of E. Consider two fuzzy subsets $A, B \in \Phi(E)$ with membership functions $m_A, m_B : E \to [0, 1]$. Then (1) can be extended to the following distance function,

$$d_r(A, B) := \left(\sum_{x \in E} |m_A(x) - m_B(x)|^r \right)^{1/r}, \quad r \geq 1.$$

Based on (1) with $r = 2$, the Hausdorff distance between two non-empty compact crisp sets $U, V \subset \mathbb{R}$, is defined as

$$q(U, V) := \max \left\{ \sup_{v \in V} \inf_{u \in U} d_2(u, v), \sup_{u \in U} \inf_{v \in V} d_2(u, v) \right\}. \tag{2}$$

This can be extended to fuzzy sets as follows: let $A \in \Phi(E)$ be a fuzzy set and denote by A_α the α-level set of the fuzzy set A which is defined as $A_\alpha = \{x \in E : m_A(x) \geq \alpha\}$. Then for two fuzzy subsets $A, B \in \Phi(E)$ the distance in (2) can be extended to the following distance between A and B,

$$q(A, B) := \int_0^1 q(A_\alpha, B_\alpha) d\alpha.$$

Another approach is based on set-theoretic distance functions. For a fuzzy set $A \in \Phi(E)$ define the cardinality of A as $|A| = \sum_{x \in E} m_A(x)$. Extend the intersection and union operations by defining the membership functions as is done in [3],

$$m_{A \cap B}(x) := \min \{m_A(x), m_B(x)\} \tag{3}$$

and

$$m_{A \cup B}(x) := \max \{m_A(x), m_B(x)\}. \tag{4}$$

Then for fuzzy sets $A, B \in \Phi(E)$ we may define the distance function

$$D_1(A, B) := 1 - \frac{|A \cap B|}{|A \cup B|} = 1 - \frac{\sum_{x \in E} m_{A \cap B}(x)}{\sum_{x \in E} m_{A \cup B}(x)}.$$

A generalization and detailed analysis of cardinality-based similarity measures for crisp and fuzzy sets is done in [4, 5]. The authors analyze similarity measures which are formulated as rational expressions that involve set-cardinalities. The general form for a similarity measure for fuzzy sets A and B in $\Phi(E)$ is given by

$$S(A, B) := \frac{\alpha(a + b - 2u) + \beta u + \gamma(|E| - a - b + u)}{\alpha'(a + b - 2u) + \beta' u + \gamma'(|E| - a - b + u)}$$

where α, α', β, β', γ, γ' are fixed at the value 0 or 1 and

$$a := |A| = \sum_{x \in E} m_A(x), \quad b := |B| = \sum_{x \in E} m_B(x), \quad u = \left| A \bigcap B \right| = \sum_{x \in E} m'_{A \cap B}(x)$$

where $m'_{A \cap B}(x) = I(m_A(x), m_B(x))$ and $I : [0,1]^2 \to [0,1]$ is a generalization of Boolean conjunction. They show that such similarity measures satisfy the same transitivity properties as their crisp counterparts.

Another distance function is based on four features of a fuzzy set. Let the domain of interest be $\mathbb{R}$ and consider a fuzzy set A in $\varPhi(\mathbb{R})$. The power of A (which extends the notion of cardinality) is defined as

$$\text{power}(A) := \int_{-\infty}^{\infty} m_A(x)dx.$$

Let $h(x) = -x \ln x - (1-x) \ln(1-x)$ then define the entropy of A as

$$\text{entropy}(A) := \int_{-\infty}^{\infty} h(m_A(x))dx.$$

Define the centroid as

$$c(A) := \frac{\int_{-\infty}^{\infty} x m_A(x)dx}{\text{power}(A)}$$

and the skewness as

$$\text{skew}(A) := \int_{-\infty}^{\infty} (x - c(A))^3 m_A(x)dx.$$

Let $v(A) = [\text{power}(A), \text{entropy}(A), c(A), \text{skew}(A)]$ then [6] defines the distance between two fuzzy sets A, $B \in \varPhi(\mathbb{R})$ as the Euclidean distance $\|v(A) - v(B)\|$.

A more recent work [7] investigates relationships between distance functions [8], proximity measures [9] and entropy for fuzzy sets [10]. In [9] it is shown that distances on fuzzy sets are equal to the negation of their proximity.

We now proceed to discuss the notion of distances that are based on descriptive complexity of sets.

2   Information Based Distance Functions

A good distance function is one which picks out only the 'true' dissimilarities and ignores factors that arise from irrelevant variables or are due to unimportant random fluctuations that enter the measurements. In most applications the design of a good distance function requires inside information about the domain. An example of this lies in the field of information retrieval [11], where the distance between two documents is influenced largely by words that appear less frequently since the words which appear more frequently are less informative.

Typically, different domains require the design of different distance functions which take such specific prior knowledge into account. It can therefore be an expensive process to acquire expertise in order to formulate a good distance. Recently, a new distance function for sets was introduced [12] which is based on the concept of descriptional complexity (or discrete entropy). A description of an object in a finite set can be represented as a finite binary string which provides a unique index of the object in the set. The description complexity of the object is the minimal length of a string that describes the object. The distance function of [12, 13] is based on the idea that two sets should be considered similar if given the knowledge of one the additional complexity in describing an element of the other set is small (this is also referred to as the conditional combinatorial entropy, see [14] and references therein). The advantage in this formulation of distance is its universality; it can be applied without any prior knowledge or assumption about the domain of interest, that is, about the elements that the sets contain. Such distance functions can be viewed as information-based, since the conditional descriptional complexity is essentially the amount of information needed to describe an element in one set given that we know the other set (for more on the notion of combinatorial information and entropy see [14]). This idea has been recently used to define a universal distance for images [15, 16].

In the current paper we introduce a distance measure between two general sets, in particular, sets that can be crisp or fuzzy. Following the information-based approach of [12, 13] we use entropy as the main operator that gives the measure of dissimilarity between two sets. We use the membership of the symmetric difference of two sets as the probability of a Bernoulli random variable whose entropy is the expected description complexity of an element that belongs to only one of the two sets. Thus the distance function measures how many bits (on average) are needed to describe an element in the symmetric difference of the two sets. In other words, it is the amount of additional information needed to describe any one of the two sets given knowledge of the other.

On account of its being a description-complexity based distance, it is bestowed with certain characteristics. For instance, the distance between a crisp set A and its complement $\overline{A}$ is zero since there is no need for additional information in order to describe one of these two sets when knowing the other. Knowledge of a set A automatically implies knowing the set $\overline{A}$ and vice versa. They are clearly not equal, but our distance function cleverly renders them as similar to each other as any two sets can be (zero distance apart).

Unlike many of the measures of dissimilarity referenced in [17] which satisfy the axioms of Liu [8], our distance satisfies a triangle inequality. This is a central point of our paper. It is mathematically significant and we devote the majority of the proof of the main theorem (Theorem 3) to it. A distance function for fuzzy sets for which the triangle inequality is satisfied is not only important as a mathematical fact in that it embeds any space of sets (fuzzy and crisp) with a proper metric, but also from a practical perspective in many applications.

An important application area for a distance function that satisfies the triangle inequality over sets is machine learning over spaces of concepts. A concept

[18] is a subset of objects or events defined over a domain, for example, the subset of 'people' that constitute 'teachers'. Concepts that can be represented in crisp sets are essentially boolean-functions over the domain. Concepts that can be represented in fuzzy sets have an associated uncertainty, for instance, the concept of 'beautiful' over the domain of 'living beings'. Some living beings belong to the concept 'beautiful' only with a certain level of certainty. Learning classification over such concepts means to be able to infer a fuzzy set from training examples, e.g., $\{bird, 0.2\}, \{dog, 0.8\}, \ldots$, consists of living beings with the values of membership in the set 'beautiful'. The importance of the triangle inequality for machine learning comes from the fact that many machine-learning algorithms learn by searching over a space of concepts. A proper metric enables a more efficient searching strategy (see for instance [19]). Because fuzzy sets are a natural way of describing concepts with uncertainty, our distance function is applicable also for conceptual clustering [20, 21] which is useful for fields as diverse as knowledge management, information retrieval, data mining [22, 23, 24].

The next section formally introduces the distance function and in Theorem 3 we prove its metric properties.

3   New Distance Function

We write w.p. for "with probability". Let $[N] = \{1, \ldots, N\}$ be a domain of interest. Let $A \in \Phi([N])$ be a set with membership function $m_A : [N] \to [0, 1]$. We use x to denote a value in $[N]$. Given two fuzzy subsets $A, B \in \Phi([N])$ with membership functions $m_A(x), m_B(x)$, as mentioned in section 1 we denote by

$$m_{A \cup B}(x) := \max \{m_A(x), m_B(x)\}$$

and

$$m_{A \cap B}(x) := \min \{m_A(x), m_B(x)\}.$$

Define by $A \triangle B = (A \bigcup B) \setminus (A \bigcap B)$ the symmetric difference between crisp sets A,B. For fuzzy sets $A, B \in \Phi([N])$ we define it as

$$m_{A \triangle B}(x) := m_{A \cup B}(x) - m_{A \cap B}(x). \tag{5}$$

Define a sequence of Bernoulli random variables $X_A(x)$ for $x \in [N]$ taking the value 1 w.p. $m_A(x)$ and the value 0 w.p. $1 - m_A(x)$. Define by $H(X_A(x))$ the Shannon entropy of $X_A(x)$,

$$H(X_A(x)) := -m_A(x) \log m_A(x) - (1 - m_A(x)) \log(1 - m_A(x)). \tag{6}$$

Other works on fuzzy sets [10] also use (6) to define a notion of entropy. Let

$$X_{A \triangle B}(x) := \begin{cases} 1 \ w.p. & m_{A \triangle B}(x) \\ 0 \ w.p. & 1 - m_{A \triangle B}(x), \end{cases}$$

then we define a new distance function between $A, B \in \Phi([N])$ as

$$\text{dist}(A, B) := \frac{1}{N} \sum_{x=1}^{N} H(X_{A \triangle B}(x)). \tag{7}$$

Remark 1. This definition can easily be extended to the case of an infinite domain, for instance, a subset of the real line. In that case, the distance function can be defined as the expected value of $\mathbb{E}H(X_{A \triangle B}(\xi))$ where ξ is a random variable with some probability distribution $P(\xi)$ with respect to which the expectation is computed.

The next theorem shows that the distance function satisfies the metric properties.

Theorem. *The distance function dist(A, B) is a pseudo-metric on $\Phi([N])$, i.e., it is non-negative, symmetric, it equals zero if $A = B$ and it satisfies the triangle inequality.*

Remark 2. Note that the function dist(A, B) may equal zero even when $A \neq B$.
We now prove Theorem 3.

Proof. Since the entropy function is non-negative (see for instance, [25]) then for any two subsets $A, B \in \Phi([N])$ we have dist$(A, B) \geq 0$. It is easy to see that the symmetry property is satisfied since for every $x \in [N]$ we have $X_{A \triangle B}(x) = X_{B \triangle A}(x)$. For every subset A the value dist$(A, A) = 0$ since $m_{A \triangle A}(x) = 0$ hence $H(X_{A \triangle A}(x)) = 0$ for all x.

Let us now show that the triangle inequality holds. Let A, B, C be any three elements of $\Phi([N])$. Fix any point $x \in [N]$ and without loss of generality suppose that $m_A(x) \leq m_B(x) \leq m_C(x)$. Denote by $p = m_B(x) - m_A(x)$ and $q = m_C(x) - m_B(x)$. Without loss of generality assume that $p \leq q$. Then we have $m_{A \triangle C}(x) = p + q$. Denote by $H(p), H(q)$ and $H(p+q)$ the entropies $H(X_{A \triangle B}(x)), H(X_{B \triangle C}(x))$ and $H(X_{A \triangle C}(x))$ respectively. We aim to show that $H(p+q) \leq H(p) + H(q)$. This will imply that for every $x \in [N]$, $H(X_{A \triangle C}(x)) \leq H(X_{A \triangle B}(x)) + H(X_{B \triangle C}(x))$ and hence it holds for the average $\frac{1}{N} \sum_x H(X_{A \triangle C}(x)) \leq \frac{1}{N} \sum_x H(X_{A \triangle B}(x)) + \frac{1}{N} \sum_x H(X_{B \triangle C}(x))$.

We start by considering the straight line function $\ell : [0, 1] \to [0, 1]$ defined as:

$$\ell(z) := \frac{H(q) - H(p)}{q - p} z + H(p) - \frac{H(q) - H(p)}{q - p} p$$

which cuts through the points $(z, \ell(z)) = (p, H(p))$ and $(z, \ell(z)) = (q, H(q))$. For a function f let f' denote its derivative. We claim the following,

Claim 1. $H'(z) \leq \ell'(z)$ for all $z \in [q, 1]$.

Proof: The derivative of $H(z)$ is $H'(z) = \log\left(\frac{1-z}{z}\right)$. This is a decreasing function on $[0, 1]$ hence it suffices to show that $H'(q) \leq \ell'(z)$ for all $z \in [q, 1]$. The derivative of $\ell(z)$ is $\frac{H(q) - H(p)}{q - p}$. So it suffices to show that

$$\log\left(\frac{1-q}{q}\right) \leq \frac{H(q) - H(p)}{q - p}.$$

This is equivalent to

$$(q - p) \log \left(\frac{1 - q}{q} \right) \leq H(q) - H(p). \tag{8}$$

The left hand side of (8) can be reduced to,

$$q \log(1 - q) - q \log q - p \log(1 - q) + p \log q. \tag{9}$$

Adding and subtracting the term $(1 - q) \log(1 - q)$ and using $H(q) = -q \log q - (1 - q) \log(1 - q)$ makes (9) be expressed as

$$H(q) + p \log q + (1 - p) \log(1 - q).$$

Substituting this for the left hand side of (8) and canceling $H(q)$ on both sides, gives the following inequality which we need to prove

$$p \log q + (1 - p) \log(1 - q) \leq p \log p + (1 - p) \log(1 - p).$$

It suffices to show that,

$$p \log \left(\frac{p}{q} \right) + (1 - p) \log \left(\frac{1 - p}{1 - q} \right) \geq 0. \tag{10}$$

That (10) holds, follows from the information inequality (see Theorem 2.6.3 of [25]) which lower bounds the divergence $D(P \| Q) \geq 0$ where P, Q are two probability functions and $D(P \| Q) = \sum_x P(x) \log \frac{P(x)}{Q(x)}$. Hence the claim is proved. ∎

Next we claim the following:

Claim 2. $H(p + q) \leq \ell(p + q)$.

Proof: Consider the case that $p \leq q \leq \frac{1}{2}$. Since $q \leq \frac{1}{2}$ then $H'(z)$ evaluated at $z = q$ is non-negative. Hence both $H(z)$ and $\ell(z)$ are monotone increasing on $q \leq z \leq \frac{1}{2}$ and $H(q) = \ell(q)$. By Claim 1, ℓ increases faster than H on $[q, 1]$, in particular on the interval $q \leq z \leq \frac{1}{2}$. Hence, for all $z \in [q, \frac{1}{2}]$ we have $H(z) \leq \ell(z)$. Now, if $p + q \in [q, \frac{1}{2}]$ then it follows that $H(p + q) \leq \ell(p + q)$. Otherwise it must hold that $p + q \in (\frac{1}{2}, 1]$. But H is decreasing and ℓ is increasing over this interval. Hence we have $\ell(z) > \ell(\frac{1}{2}) \geq H(\frac{1}{2}) > H(z)$ for $z \in (\frac{1}{2}, 1]$, in particular for $z = p + q$ hence $\ell(p + q) \geq H(p + q)$. This proves the claim. ∎

From Claim 2 it follows that

$$H(p + q) \leq \frac{H(q) - H(p)}{q - p}(p + q) + H(p) - \frac{H(q) - H(p)}{q - p}p$$
$$= H(p) + q \frac{H(q) - H(p)}{q - p}. \tag{11}$$

It suffices to show that

$$q \frac{H(q) - H(p)}{q - p} \leq H(q)$$

its equivalent being,

$$\frac{H(q)}{q} \leq \frac{H(p)}{p}. \tag{12}$$

Letting $f(z) = \frac{H(z)}{z}$ and differentiating we obtain

$$f'(z) = \frac{\log(1-z)}{z^2}$$

which is non-positive for $z \in [0,1]$. Hence f is non-increasing over this interval. Since by assumption $q \geq p$ then it follows that $f(q) \leq f(p)$ and (12) holds. This completes the proof of the theorem. $\qquad\square$

4   Properties of the Distance Function

Let E be a finite set and let $\Phi(E)$ be the set of all fuzzy subsets of E and denote by $\mathbb{R}_+ := [0,\infty)$. In [8] a set of axioms for a distance function on fuzzy sets are defined as follows: let $d : \Phi^2(E) \to \mathbb{R}_+$ be a distance function then the following axioms must hold in order for d to be a Liu-distance:

1. $d(A,B) = d(B,A)$, for any A, $B \in \Phi(E)$
2. $d(A,A) = 0$ for all $A \in \Phi(E)$
3. $d(D,D^c) = \max_{A,B \in \Phi(E)} d(A,B)$, for all crisp sets $D \subseteq E$
4. For all A, B and $C \in \Phi(E)$, if $A \subset B \subset C$ then $d(A,B) \leq d(A,C)$ and $d(B,C) \leq d(A,C)$.

We now show that our proposed distance function (7) is not a Liu-distance. First, it does not satisfy axiom 3. To see that consider two sets A and its complement $\overline{A}$. Their membership functions satisfy the relation:

$$m_{\overline{A}}(x) = 1 - m_A(x)$$

hence the membership function for the symmetric difference is

$$m_{A \triangle \overline{A}}(x) = \max\{m_A(x), (1 - m_A(x))\} - \min\{m_A(x), (1 - m_A(x))\}.$$

Note that for any $x \in [N]$ with a crisp membership value, i.e., $m_A(x) = 1$, or $m_A(x) = 0$, we have $m_{A \triangle \overline{A}}(x) = 1$ and hence in this case $H(X_{A \triangle \overline{A}}(x)) = 0$. This means that for a crisp set A our distance function has the following property (we call this the *complement-property*):

$$\mathrm{dist}(A, \overline{A}) = 0 \tag{13}$$

which is the 'opposite' of axiom 3 in [8] since Liu's axiom demands that the distance between a crisp set and its complement be maximal over all possible pairs of fuzzy sets.

From an information theoretic perspective, the property of (13) is expected since the knowledge of a set A must provide full knowledge of its complement set. That is, there is *no* additional description necessary to describe $\overline{A}$ given the knowledge of A and this is what dist$(A, \overline{A}) = 0$ means.

Secondly, our distance does not satisfy axiom 4 as we now show. Consider the sets A, B, and C with corresponding membership functions $m_A(x) = 0.1$, $m_B(x) = 0.5$ and $m_C(x) = 0.9$. Clearly, by definition of containment of fuzzy sets [3] we have $A \subset B \subset C$ however in this example dist$(A, B) > $ dist(A, C) and dist$(B, C) > $ dist(A, C) which violates axiom 4.

Recalling the definition of fuzzy set intersection (3) and union (4) then in [8] a σ-distance for fuzzy sets is defined as a distance function d such that for any $A, B \in \Phi(E)$ and any crisp set $D \subseteq E$ the following is satisfied, $d(A, B) = d(A \cap D, B \cap D) + d(A \cap D^c, B \cap D^c)$. We claim that our distance function (7) is a σ-distance as is now show: we have,

$$
\text{dist}(A \cap D, B \cap D) + \text{dist}(A \cap D^c, B \cap D^c)
$$
$$
= \frac{1}{N} \sum_{x \in D} \left[H\left(X_{(A \cap D) \triangle (B \cap D)}(x) \right) + H\left(X_{(A \cap D^c) \triangle (B \cap D^c)}(x) \right) \right]
$$
$$
+ \frac{1}{N} \sum_{x \in D^c} \left[H\left(X_{(A \cap D) \triangle (B \cap D)}(x) \right) + H\left(X_{(A \cap D^c) \triangle (B \cap D^c)}(x) \right) \right]. \quad (14)
$$

For any $x \in E$,

$$
m_{(A \cap D) \triangle (B \cap D)}(x) = m_{(A \cap D) \cup (B \cap D)}(x) - m_{(A \cap D) \cap (B \cap D)}(x)
$$
$$
= m_{(A \cup B) \cap D}(x) - m_{(A \cap B) \cap D}(x) \quad (15)
$$

and

$$
m_{(A \cap D^c) \triangle (B \cap D^c)}(x) = m_{(A \cap D^c) \cup (B \cap D^c)}(x) - m_{(A \cap D^c) \cap (B \cap D^c)}(x)
$$
$$
= m_{(A \cup B) \cap D^c}(x) - m_{(A \cap B) \cap D^c}(x). \quad (16)
$$

Now, for all $x \in D$ we have $D(x) = 1$ hence (15) equals $m_{(A \cup B)}(x) - m_{(A \cap B)}(x) = m_{A \triangle B}(x)$ and (16) equals 0 and hence for $x \in D$ the following holds,

$$
H\left(X_{(A \cap D) \triangle (B \cap D)}(x) \right) + H\left(X_{(A \cap D^c) \triangle (B \cap D^c)}(x) \right) = H\left(X_{A \triangle B}(x) \right). \quad (17)
$$

Similarly, for all $x \in D^c$ we have $D^c(x) = 1$ and $D(x) = 0$ hence (15) equals 0 and (16) equals $m_{(A \cup B)}(x) - m_{(A \cap B)}(x) = m_{A \triangle B}(x)$ and therefore (17) also holds for $x \in D^c$. Therefore (14) equals

$$
\frac{1}{N} \sum_{x \in E} H(X_{A \triangle B}(x)) = \text{dist}(A, B)
$$

which proves the claim. While our distance function does not satisfy axiom 4 of [8] it satisfies a *bona fide* triangle inequality as shown in the proof of Theorem 3.

In the proof of Theorem 3 we assumed that $m_{A \triangle B}(x)$, which when viewed as a function $g(m_A(x), m_B(x)) = \max\{m_A(x), m_B(x)\} - \min\{m_A(x), m_B(x)\}$, is a metric; in particular, for any real z, $g(z, z) = 0$ and for any real numbers $z \leq r \leq w$, g satisfies the triangle inequality, $g(z, w) \leq g(z, r) + g(r, w)$. If we replace the min and max with any t-norm T and t-conorm S, respectively, then we obtain a generalized expression for $m_{A \triangle B}(x)$, which we denote as

$$g(m_A(x), m_B(x)) = S(m_A(x), m_B(x)) - T(m_A(x), m_B(x)) \qquad (18)$$

and which may not be a metric. For instance, let T be the Lukasiewicz t-norm $T(x, y) = \max\{0, x + y - 1\}$ then using the DeMorgan's formula $S(x, y) = N(T(N(x), N(y)))$ with N the strict negation $N(x) = 1 - x$ we obtain $S(x, y) = \min\{1, x + y\}$. In this case the generalized form of (18) is $\min\{1, m_A(x) + m_B(x)\} - \max\{0, m_A(x) + m_B(x) - 1\}$ which for $A = B$ gives $\min\{1, 2m_A(x)\} - \max\{0, 2m_A(x) - 1\}$ and can differ from zero for some values of $m_A(x)$. Therefore the generalized form is not a metric in this case.

With respect to the axioms of [17], our distance function satisfies axiom D3 which states that $A = B$ implies $\text{dist}(A, B) = 0$ (this follows from Theorem 3). It does not satisfy axiom D2, D3 of [17] which are axioms 3,4 of [8] (as shown above). It satisfies the symmetry axiom G2 of [17].

5   Conclusion

This paper introduces a new distance function for fuzzy sets based on their descriptive complexity. The distance function is shown to be a pseudo-metric and as such it satisfies the triangle inequality. This fact makes it applicable to machine learning applications which rely on search strategies in high dimensional spaces and many of which require an input space with a proper metric in order for the search to be efficient. In particular, our distance function is applicable in the area of conceptual clustering as fuzzy sets are a natural way to represent concepts that are less certain in nature. This is not the case for many other dissimilarity measures on fuzzy sets. In fact, the triangle inequality is missing from the list of axioms of [17] that most dissimilarity measures aim to satisfy. In comparison to other existing distance-functions for fuzzy sets, our new distance function gives a value which is proportional to the additional amount of information needed to describe a fuzzy set A when fuzzy set B is known, or vice versa. It thus has a natural information theoretic interpretation.

References

[1] Deza, E., Deza, M.: Encyclopedia of Distances. Series in Computer Science, vol. 15. Springer (2009)
[2] Zwick, R., Carlstein, E., Budescu, D.V.: Measures of similarity among fuzzy concepts: A comparative analysis. International Journal of Approximate Reasoning 1, 221–242 (1987)
[3] Zadeh, L.A.: Fuzzy sets. Information Control 8, 338–353 (1965)

[4] De Baets, B., De Meyer, H., Naessens, II.: A class of rational cardinality-based similarity measures. Journal of Computational and Applied Mathematics 132(1), 51–69 (2001)

[5] De Baets, B., Janssens, S., De Meyer, H.: On the transitivity of a parametric family of cardinality-based similarity measures. International Journal of Approximate Reasoning 50(1), 104–116 (2009)

[6] Bonissone, P.P.: A pattern recognition approach to the problem of linguistic approximation in system analysis. In: Proceeding of the International Conference on Cybernetics and Society, pp. 793–798 (1979)

[7] Bustince, H., Barrenechea, E., Pagola, M.: Relationship between restricted dissimilarity functions, restricted equivalence functions and normal en-functions: Image thresholding invariant. Pattern Recognition Letters 29(4), 525–536 (2008)

[8] Liu, X.: Entropy, distance measure and similarity measure of fuzzy sets and their relations. Fuzzy Sets Syst. 52(3), 305–318 (1992)

[9] Fan, J., Xie, W.: Some notes on similarity measure and proximity measure. Fuzzy Sets and Systems 101(3), 403–412 (1999)

[10] De Luca, A., Termini, S.: A definition of a nonprobabilistic entropy in the setting of fuzzy sets theory. Information and Control 20(4), 301–312 (1972)

[11] Baeza-Yates, R., Ribeiro-Neto, B.: Modern Information Retrieval. Addison-Wesley (1999)

[12] Ratsaby, J.: Information set distance. In: Proceedings of the Mini-Conference on Applied Theoretical Computer Science (MATCOS 2010), Koper, Slovenia, October 13-14, pp. 61–64. University of Primorska Press (2011)

[13] Ratsaby, J.: Combinatorial information distance. In: Enchescu, C., Filip, F.G., Iantovics, B. (eds.) Advanced Computational Technologies, pp. 201–207. Romanian Academy Publishing House (2012)

[14] Ratsaby, J.: Information efficiency. In: van Leeuwen, J., Italiano, G.F., van der Hoek, W., Meinel, C., Sack, H., Plášil, F. (eds.) SOFSEM 2007. LNCS, vol. 4362, pp. 475–487. Springer, Heidelberg (2007)

[15] Chester, U., Ratsaby, J.: Universal distance measure for images. In: Proceedings of the 27th IEEE Convention of Electrical Electronics Engineers in Israel (IEEEI 2012), Eilat, Israel, November 14-17, pp. 1–4 (2012)

[16] Chester, U., Ratsaby, J.: Machine learning for image classification and clustering using a universal distance measure. In: Brisaboa, N., Pedreira, O., Zezula, P. (eds.) SISAP 2013. LNCS, vol. 8199, pp. 59–72. Springer, Heidelberg (2013)

[17] Couso, I., Garrido, L., Sánchez, L.: Similarity and dissimilarity measures between fuzzy sets: A formal relational study. Information Sciences 229, 122–141 (2013)

[18] Mitchell, T.: Machine Learning. McGraw Hill (1997)

[19] Giraud-Carrier, C., Martinez, T.: An efficient metric for heterogeneous inductive learning applications in the attribute-value language. In: Yfantis, E.A. (ed.) Intelligent Systems Third Golden West International Conference (Proceedings of GWIC 1994), pp. 341–350. Springer (1995) ISBN 978-0-7923-3422-4

[20] Fisher, D.H.: Knowledge acquisition via incremental conceptual clustering. Machine Learning 2(2), 139–172 (1987)

[21] Gennari, J.H., Langley, P., Fisher, D.: Models of incremental concept formation. Artificial Intelligence 40(1-3), 11–61 (1989)

[22] Cheng, Y., Fu, K.: Conceptual clustering in knowledge organization. IEEE Transactions on Pattern Analysis and Machine Intelligence PAMI-7(5), 592–598 (1985)

[23] Bhatia, S.K., Deogun, J.S.: Conceptual clustering in information retrieval. IEEE Transactions on Systems, Man, and Cybernetics, Part B: Cybernetics 28(3), 427–436 (1998)

[24] Talavera, L., Bejar, J.: Generality-based conceptual clustering with probabilistic concepts. IEEE Transactions on Pattern Analysis and Machine Intelligence 23(2), 196–206 (2001)

[25] Cover, T.M., Thomas, J.A.: Elements of information theory. Wiley-Interscience, New York (2006)

New Method for Design of Fuzzy Systems for Nonlinear Modelling Using Different Criteria of Interpretability

Krystian Łapa[1], Krzysztof Cpałka[1], and Lipo Wang[2]

[1] Częstochowa University of Technology,
Institute of Computational Intelligence, Poland
{krystian.lapa,krzysztof.cpalka}@iisi.pcz.pl
[2] Nanyang Technological University,
School of Electrical & Electronic Engineering, Singapore
elpwang@ntu.edu.sg

Abstract. In this paper a new method for designing neuro-fuzzy systems for nonlinear modelling is proposed. This method contains a complex weighted fitness function with interpretability criteria and new enhanced tuning process for selecting parameters and structure of the system based on a hybrid population-based algorithm (composed of evolutionary strategy, genetic algorithm and bees algorithm). To evaluate this method, we used a well-known dynamic nonlinear modelling problem.

1 Introduction

The analysis of technical issues aims at finding and understanding the essence of the problem, it tries to create a model. The reason for this is the willingness to ensure predictability, which guarantees safety, decreases costs and ensures control. In the literature the following approaches to modelling are considered: **(a) White-box model.** This approach uses phenomenological (theoretical) description of physical phenomena. For more details, see e.g. [9], [40]. **(b) Black-box model.** In this approach the behaviour of the object is recreated on the basis of observations of cause and effect of dependencies. For more details, see e.g. [19]-[20], [25]-[26], [35]-[36], [51], [56]. **(c) Grey-box model.** This approach is based on model structure derived from some laws and parameters tuned to the data defining behaviour of the object. These methods include, among others, multivariable non-stationary systems, hybrid solutions and systems of computational intelligence such as fuzzy systems, neuro-fuzzy systems etc. For more details, see e.g. [6], [18], [21], [32]-[34], [40]-[41], [43]-[44].

There is still a search for such nonlinear modelling methods which will be characterized by a good accuracy and possibility to interpret the knowledge accumulated within it. The interpretability issue in the context of nonlinear modelling is much harder than in case of classification (in the system the exact value of the output signal is important). Each limitation put upon system structure (used to increase the interpretability) has pronounced negative effect

L. Rutkowski et al. (Eds.): ICAISC 2014, Part I, LNAI 8467, pp. 217–232, 2014.

on the accuracy (and vice versa). In the literature there are different approaches to increase the interpretability of fuzzy systems. It can be noted that these approaches are mainly based on a suitable structure of the fuzzy system (e.g. [1]-[5], [10]-[13], [22]-[23], [27], [48], [52]-[55]) or on the use of specific training algorithm (e.g. methods in the field of multiobjective optimization or evolutionary optimization) (see e.g. [14], [17], [28]-[29], [38], [57]). In this paper we propose a new method for designing neuro-fuzzy systems for nonlinear modelling (see e.g. [30]). This method can be described as follows: (1) the parameters and also the structure of the neuro-fuzzy systems are obtained in the learning process, (2) the learning process takes into consideration accuracy of the system, complexity of the system, and interpretability criteria, (3) presented criteria allow to obtain clear and well-spread semantic of the rules of the system, (4) learning process was based on hybrid population algorithm composed of evolutionary strategy (μ, λ) (see e.g. [15]) and bees algorithm (see e.g. [37]). To evaluate performance of our method we used well-known dynamic nonlinear modelling problem - Van der Pol oscillator problem.

This paper is organized into 5 sections. Section 2 contains description of the fuzzy system for nonlinear modelling. Description of the new method for designing our system is given in Section 3. Simulation results are presented in Section 4. Conclusions are drawn in Section 5.

2   Description of the Fuzzy System for Nonlinear Modelling

In our previous works we considered a new class of the neuro-fuzzy systems (see e.g. [24], [47], [49]-[50]) - the flexible neuro-fuzzy systems (see [42], [59]-[62]). Those systems have very high accuracy in the field on classification and approximation problems. We consider multi-input, multi-output neuro-fuzzy system mapping $\mathbf{X} \rightarrow \mathbf{Y}$, where $\mathbf{X} \subset \mathbf{R}^n$ and $\mathbf{Y} \subset \mathbf{R}^m$. The flexible fuzzy rule base consists of a collection of N fuzzy IF-THEN rules in the form

$$R^k : \left[\left(\begin{array}{c} \text{IF } \left(\bar{x}_1 \text{ is } A_1^k\right) \left| w_{k,1}^A \text{ AND} \ldots \text{AND} \left(\bar{x}_n \text{ is } A_n^k\right) \left| w_{k,n}^A \right. \right. \\ \text{THEN } \left(y_1 \text{ is } B_1^k\right), \ldots, \left(y_m \text{ is } B_m^k\right) \end{array} \right) \left| w_k^{\text{rule}} \right. \right], \quad (1)$$

where $\bar{\mathbf{x}} = [\bar{x}_1, \ldots, \bar{x}_n] \in \mathbf{X}$, $\mathbf{y} = [y_1, \ldots, y_m] \in \mathbf{Y}$, $A_1^k, \ldots, A_n^k$ are fuzzy sets characterized by membership functions $\mu_{A_i^k}(x_i)$, $i = 1, \ldots, n$, $k = 1, \ldots, N$, $B_1^k, \ldots, B_m^k$ are fuzzy sets characterized by membership functions $\mu_{B_j^k}(y_j)$, $j = 1, \ldots, m$, $k = 1, \ldots, N$, $w_{k,i}^A \in [0,1]$, $i = 1, \ldots, n$, $k = 1, \ldots, N$, are weights of antecedents, $w_k^{\text{rule}} \in [0,1]$, $k = 1, \ldots, N$, are weights of rules. In Mamdani approach output signal $\bar{y}_j$, $j = 1, \ldots, m$ of the neuro-fuzzy system is described by the formula (for more details see our previous papers, e.g. [45]-[46])

$$\bar{y}_j = \frac{\sum_{r=1}^{R} \bar{y}_{j,r}^{\text{def}} \cdot \overset{N}{\underset{k=1}{S^*}} \left\{ T \left\{ \overset{n}{\underset{i=1}{T^*}} \left\{ \mu_{A_i^k} (\bar{x}_i) ; w_{k,i}^A \right\}, \mu_{B_j^k} \left(\bar{y}_{j,r}^{\text{def}} \right) \right\} ; w_k^{\text{rule}} \right\}}{\sum_{r=1}^{R} \overset{N}{\underset{k=1}{S^*}} \left\{ T \left\{ \overset{n}{\underset{i=1}{T^*}} \left\{ \mu_{A_i^k} (\bar{x}_i) ; w_{k,i}^A \right\}, \mu_{B_j^k} \left(\bar{y}_{j,r}^{\text{def}} \right) \right\} ; w_k^{\text{rule}} \right\}}, \tag{2}$$

where $\bar{y}_{j,r}^{\text{def}}$, $j = 1, \ldots, m$, $r = 1, \ldots, R$, are discretization points, R is a number of discretization points.

In the next section a new learning algorithm for evolution of flexible neuro-fuzzy system (2) is proposed. The aim of the algorithm is the selection of the parameters and structure of the neuro-fuzzy system for nonlinear modelling described by equation (2) with the accuracy and interpretability taken into consideration. In the process of evolution (evolution of parameters) we will find all parameters of the neuro-fuzzy system (2). Moreover, in the process of evolution (evolution of the structure) we will find number of inputs n, number of rules N, number of antecedents and consequents (number of fuzzy sets) and number of discretization points R.

In the next section we are going to show the use of a new population based algorithm used to select the structure and parameters of system (2) with the accuracy and interpretability taken into consideration.

3 Description of the New Evolutionary Approach to Choice of the System Structure and Parameters for Nonlinear Modelling

As mentioned before, for selection of structure and parameters of system (2) we have proposed a new evolutionary algorithm. The algorithm is based on the Pittsburgh approach ([31], [42]), on the evolutionary strategy (μ, λ) for selecting parameters of system (2), on the classical genetic algorithm for choosing structure of system (2) and on the bees algorithm for fixing parameters of reduced systems (2). The evolutionary strategy (μ, λ) starts with a random generation of the initial parents population $\mathbf{P}$ containing μ individuals. Next, a temporary population $\mathbf{T}$ is created by means of reproduction, whose population contains λ individuals, while $\lambda \geq \mu$. Reproduction consists in a multiple random selection of λ individuals out of the population $\mathbf{P}$ (multiple sampling) and placing the selected ones in temporary population $\mathbf{T}$. Individuals of the population $\mathbf{T}$ undergo crossover and mutation operations as a result of which an offspring population $\mathbf{O}$ is created, which also has size λ. The purpose of the repair procedure of the population $\mathbf{O}$ is to correct the parameters if they reach inadmissible values. The new population $\mathbf{P}$ containing μ individuals is selected only out of the best λ individuals of the population $\mathbf{O}$. The bees algorithm mimics the food foraging behaviour of honey bee colonies and it is used to tuning parameters of system (2). The aim of using this algorithm is to tune the parameters of the systems with recently reduced structure and to repair damaged accuracy. The behaviour of the bees can be described as follows: (1) For every μ population chromosomes of **P** and μ chromosomes are generated (scout bees), (2) For every chromosome of **B** a search territory area is calculated (as an area of solution explorations coded in the population **P**). For every iteration of the algorithm the area of exploration is decreased, (3) After this modification, chromosomes from **B** are repaired and evaluated (analogically to evolutionary strategy (μ, λ)), (4) In the last step one solution (with best fitness function value) is picked from each group of scout bees and moved into the population **P**. More details about bees algorithm can be seen in [37].

3.1   Coding of Parameters and Structure

The parameters of system (2) were coded in the following chromosome (Pittsburgh approach)

$$
\mathbf{X}_{ch}^{par} = \left\{ \begin{array}{c} \bar{x}_{1,1}^A, \sigma_{1,1}^A, \ldots, \bar{x}_{n,1}^A, \sigma_{n,1}^A, \ldots \\ \bar{x}_{1,Nmax}^A, \sigma_{1,Nmax}^A, \ldots, \bar{x}_{n,Nmax}^A, \sigma_{n,Nmax}^A, \\ \bar{y}_{1,1}^B, \sigma_{1,1}^B, \ldots, \bar{y}_{m,1}^B, \sigma_{m,1}^B, \ldots \\ \bar{y}_{1,Nmax}^B, \sigma_{1,Nmax}^B, \ldots, \bar{y}_{m,Nmax}^B, \sigma_{m,Nmax}^B, \\ w_{1,1}^A, \ldots, w_{n,1}^A, \ldots, w_{1,Nmax}^A, \ldots, w_{n,Nmax}^A, \\ w_1^{rule}, \ldots, w_{Nmax}^{rule}, \\ \bar{y}_{1,1}^{def}, \ldots, \bar{y}_{1,Rmax}^{def}, \ldots, \bar{y}_{m,1}^{def}, \ldots, \bar{y}_{m,Rmax}^{def} \end{array} \right\} = \left\{ X_{ch,1}^{par}, \ldots, X_{ch,L}^{par} \right\},
$$

$$(3)$$

where $L = Nmax \cdot (3 \cdot n + 2 \cdot m + 1) + Rmax$, $ch = 1, \ldots, \mu$ for the parent population or $ch = 1, \ldots, \lambda$ for the temporary population, $Nmax$ is the maximum number of rules, $Rmax$ is the maximum number of discretization points. The maximum number of rules $Nmax$ should be selected individually to the problem from the range $[1, Nmax]$. Analogously, the maximum number of discretization points $Rmax$ should also be selected to the problem individually from the range $[1, Rmax]$ ([7]). The purpose of the algorithm is also to select the number of antecedents (from the range $[1, n]$) and consequents (from the range $[1, m]$) within each rule from rule base. The reduction of the system is done with the use of additional chromosome $\mathbf{X}_{ch}^{red}$. Its genes take binary values and indicate which rules, antecedents, consequents, inputs, and discretization points are selected. The chromosome $\mathbf{X}_{ch}^{red}$ is given by

$$
\mathbf{X}_{ch}^{red} = \left\{ \begin{array}{c} x_1, \ldots, x_n, \\ A_1^1, \ldots, A_n^1, \ldots, A_1^{Nmax}, \ldots, A_n^{Nmax}, \\ B_1^1, \ldots, B_m^1, \ldots, B_1^{Nmax}, \ldots, B_m^{Nmax}, \\ rule_1, \ldots, rule_{Nmax}, \\ \bar{y}_{1,1}^{def}, \ldots, \bar{y}_{1,Rmax}^{def}, \ldots, \bar{y}_{m,1}^{def}, \ldots, \bar{y}_{m,Rmax}^{def} \end{array} \right\} = \left\{ X_{ch,1}^{red}, \ldots, X_{ch,L^{red}}^{red} \right\}, \quad (4)
$$

where $L^{red} = Nmax \cdot (n + m + 1) + n + m \cdot Rmax$ is the length of the chromosome $\mathbf{X}_{ch}^{red}$, $ch = 1, \ldots, \mu$, for the parent population or $ch = 1, \ldots, \lambda$, for the temporary population. Its genes indicate which rules ($rule_k$, $k = 1, \ldots, Nmax$), antecedents (A_i^k, $i - 1, \ldots, n$, $k - 1, \ldots, Nmax$), consequents (D_j^k, $j -$ $1, \ldots, m$, $k = 1, \ldots, Nmax$), inputs ($\bar{x}_i$, $i = 1, \ldots, n$), and discretization points ($\bar{y}^r$, $r = 1, \ldots, Rmax$) are taken to the system. We can easily notice that the number of inputs used in the system encoded in the chromosome ch can be determined as follows

$$n_{ch} = \sum_{i=1}^{n} \mathbf{X}_{ch}^{red}\{x_i\},\tag{5}$$

where $\mathbf{X}_{ch}^{red}\{x_i\}$ means gene of the chromosome $\mathbf{X}_{ch}^{red}$ associated with the input x_i (as previously mentioned, if the value of the gene is 1, the associated input is taken into account during work of the system). The number of rules (N_{ch}) used in the system encoded in the chromosome ch may be determined analogously. Implementation of the strategy (μ, λ) uses an additional chromosome

$$\sigma_{ch}^{par} = \left(\sigma_{ch,1}^{par}, \ldots, \sigma_{ch,L}^{par}\right),\tag{6}$$

where $ch = 1, \ldots, \mu$ for the parent population or $ch = 1, \ldots, \lambda$ for the temporary population. This allows the implementation of the mechanism of self-adaptive range of mutation. At the beginning of the operation of evolutionary strategy the range is large, while during the convergence its gradual reduction is observed. This results in a smooth transition from exploration (occurring at the beginning of the algorithm) to exploitation of the promising areas.

3.2 Evolution of Parameters and Structure

This hybrid population-based method allows for tuning both structure and parameters of system (2) with interpretability criteria. It is worth mentioning that: **(a)** An evolutionary strategy (μ, λ) was used for tuning the parameters of system (2). It processes chromosomes $\mathbf{X}_{ch}^{par}$ i σ_{ch}^{par} from the population $\mathbf{P}$, $\mathbf{T}$ and $\mathbf{O}$. The details about crossover and mutation operators from this strategy can be found in [42]. **(b)** For the structure evolution of system (2), a classic genetic algorithm was chosen. It processes chromosomes $\mathbf{X}_{ch}^{red}$ from the population $\mathbf{P}$, $\mathbf{T}$ and $\mathbf{O}$. The details about crossover and mutation operators from this strategy can be found in [31]. It is important to mention that genetic algorithm works together with evolutionary strategy (μ, λ), and it allows to reduce any element of the system structure, such like antecedence, consequences, inputs, rules and discretization points. **(c)** For tuning parameters of system (2), a bees algorithm was additionally used. It processes chromosomes $\mathbf{X}_{ch}^{par}$ from the population $\mathbf{B}$. The purpose of use the bees algorithm is to search neighbourhood around chromosomes from population $\mathbf{B}$ (chromosomes with reduced structure of the system) and replace them with fitter solutions. The details about bees algorithm can be found in [37]. **(d)** The important mechanism of our method is a process of evaluation of the chromosomes from the populations $\mathbf{P}$, $\mathbf{T}$, $\mathbf{O}$ and $\mathbf{B}$ described in Section 3.3. It takes into consideration an accuracy-interpretability trade-off and allows to obtain a balanced dependent from weights of the fitness function components solutions (see e.g. [16], [58]).

3.3   Chromosome Population Evaluation

Each individual $\mathbf{X}_{ch}$ of the parental and temporary populations is represented by sequence of chromosomes $\langle \mathbf{X}_{ch}^{\text{par}}, \sigma_{ch}^{\text{par}}, \mathbf{X}_{ch}^{\text{red}} \rangle$, given by formulas (3), (4) and (6). The genes of the two first chromosomes take real values, whereas the genes of the last chromosome takes integer values from the set $\{0, 1\}$. The system aims to minimize the following fitness function

$$\text{ff}\,(\mathbf{X}_{ch}) = T^* \left\{ \begin{array}{c} \text{ffaccuracy}\,(\mathbf{X}_{ch})\,, \text{ffcomplexity}\,(\mathbf{X}_{ch})\,, \text{ffinterpretability}\,(\mathbf{X}_{ch})\,; \\ w_{\text{ffaccuracy}}, w_{\text{ffcomplexity}}, w_{\text{ffinterpretability}} \end{array} \right\},$$
$$(7)$$

where $T^* \{\cdot\}$ is the algebraic weighted t-norm (see e.g. [8]), $w_{\text{ffaccuracy}} \in (0, 1]$ denoted weight of the component $\text{ffaccuracy}\,(\mathbf{X}_{ch})$ etc. The individual components of the $\text{ff}\,(\mathbf{X}_{ch})$ are defined as follows:

The component $\text{ffaccuracy}\,(\mathbf{X}_{ch})$ determines the accuracy of system (2) i.e. average normalized system error for all outputs and all data from learning sequence

$$\text{ffaccuracy}\,(\mathbf{X}_{ch}) = \frac{1}{m_{ch}} \sum_{j=1}^{m_{ch}} \frac{\frac{1}{Z} \sum_{z=1}^{Z} |d_{z,j} - \bar{y}_{z,j}|}{\max\limits_{z=1,\dots,Z} \{d_{z,j}\} - \min\limits_{z=1,\dots,Z} \{d_{z,j}\}}, \qquad (8)$$

where m_{ch} is a number of outputs encoded in the chromosome ch, Z is the number of samples of learning sequence, $d_{z,j}$ is desired value of output signal $j = 1, ..., m$ for input vector $z = 1, ..., Z$, $\bar{y}_{z,j}$ is real value of the output signal $j = 1, ..., m$ for input vector $z = 1, ..., Z$. The purpose of the normalization of the component $\text{ffaccuracy}\,(\mathbf{X}_{ch})$ was to ensure an influence on every component of the function (7).

The component $\text{ffcomplexity}\,(\mathbf{X}_{ch})$ determines complexity of system (2) i.e. a number of reduced elements of the system (rules, antecedents- input fuzzy sets, consequents- output fuzzy sets, inputs, and discretization points) in relation to length of the chromosome $\mathbf{X}_{ch}^{\text{red}}$ (it allows to increase complexity-based interpretability)

$$\text{ffcomplexity}\,(\mathbf{X}_{ch}) = \frac{\left(\begin{array}{c} \sum\limits_{i=1}^{n} \mathbf{X}_{ch}^{\text{red}} \{x_i\} \cdot \sum\limits_{k=1}^{Nmax} \mathbf{X}_{ch}^{\text{red}} \{\text{rule}_k\} \cdot \mathbf{X}_{ch}^{\text{red}} \{A_i^k\} + \\ + \sum\limits_{j=1}^{m} \sum\limits_{k=1}^{Nmax} \mathbf{X}_{ch}^{\text{red}} \{\text{rule}_k\} \cdot \mathbf{X}_{ch}^{\text{red}} \{B_j^k\} + \\ + \sum\limits_{j=1}^{m} \sum\limits_{r=1}^{Rmax} \mathbf{X}_{ch}^{\text{red}} \{\bar{y}_{m,r}^{\text{def}}\} \end{array} \right)}{N_{ch} \cdot (n_{ch} + m) + m \cdot Rmax}, \qquad (9)$$

where n is a number of inputs, m is a number of outputs, $Rmax$ is maximum number of discretization points, $Nmax$ is maximum number of rules, $\mathbf{X}_{ch}^{\text{red}} \{x_i\}$ means a gene of the chromosome $\mathbf{X}_{ch}^{\text{red}}$ associated with the input x_i, etc.

The component ffinterpretability $(\mathbf{X}_{ch})$ determines the semantic interpretability of system (2) encoded in the tested chromosome (it allows to increase semantic-based interpretability)

$$\text{ffinterpretability}\,(\mathbf{X}_{ch}) = T^* \left\{ \begin{array}{l} \text{ffint}_A\,(\mathbf{X}_{ch}),\text{ffint}_B\,(\mathbf{X}_{ch}),\text{ffint}_C\,(\mathbf{X}_{ch}),\\ \text{ffint}_D\,(\mathbf{X}_{ch}),\text{ffint}_E\,(\mathbf{X}_{ch}),\text{ffint}_F\,(\mathbf{X}_{ch});\\ w_{\text{ffintA}},w_{\text{ffintB}},w_{\text{ffintC}},w_{\text{ffintD}},w_{\text{ffintE}},w_{\text{ffintF}} \end{array} \right\},$$
(10)

where $w_{\text{ffintA}} \in (0,1]$ denotes weight of the component $\text{ffint}_A\,(\mathbf{X}_{ch})$, etc. The individual components of the formula (10) are defined as follows:

(a) The component $\text{ffint}_A\,(\mathbf{X}_{ch})$ minimizes number of rules fired at the same time in system (2) for the fuzzy sets

$$\text{ffint}_A\,(\mathbf{X}_{ch}) = 1 - \frac{1}{Z}\sum_{z=1}^{Z}\frac{\left(\max\limits_{k=1,\ldots,Nmax}\left\{\mathbf{X}_{ch}^{\text{red}}\{\text{rule}_k\}\cdot\tau_k\,(\bar{\mathbf{x}}_z)\right\}\right)^2}{\sum\limits_{k=1}^{Nmax}\mathbf{X}_{ch}^{\text{red}}\{\text{rule}_k\}\cdot\tau_k\,(\bar{\mathbf{x}}_z)},$$
(11)

where $\tau_k\,(\bar{\mathbf{x}}_z)$ is the flexible firing strength of the k-th rule, $\bar{\mathbf{x}}_z$ is a vector of input signals learning sequence $(z = 1,\ldots,Z)$.

(b) The component $\text{ffint}_B\,(\mathbf{X}_{ch})$ maximizes the fit to the training data of input fuzzy sets of system (2) encoded in the tested chromosome

$$\text{ffint}_B\,(\mathbf{X}_{ch}) = \frac{\sum\limits_{z=1}^{Z}\sum\limits_{i=1}^{n}\mathbf{X}_{ch}^{\text{red}}\{x_i\}\cdot\left(1-\max\limits_{k=1,\ldots,Nmax}\left\{\mathbf{X}_{ch}^{\text{red}}\{\text{rule}_k\}\cdot\mu_{A_i^k}\,(\bar{x}_{z,i})\right\}\right)}{Z\cdot n_{ch}},$$
(12)

where $\mu_{A_i^k}\,(\bar{x}_{z,i})$ is a membership function of the input fuzzy set A_i^k, $\bar{x}_{z,i}$ is a real value of the input signal $i = 1,\ldots,n$ of the input vector $\bar{\mathbf{x}}_z$, $z = 1,\ldots,Z$.

(c) The component $\text{ffint}_C\,(\mathbf{X}_{ch})$ reduces the overlapping of the input and output fuzzy sets of system (2) encoded in the tested chromosome

$$\text{ffint}_C\,(\mathbf{X}_{ch}) =$$

$$\frac{1}{4}\cdot\left(\frac{\sum\limits_{i=1}^{n_{ch}}\sum\limits_{k=1}^{\text{noifs}(i)-1}\left(\left|c_{\text{ffintc}}-\exp\left(-\left(\frac{\mathbf{X}_{ch}^{\text{supp}}\{\bar{x}_{i,k}^{A}\}-\mathbf{X}_{ch}^{\text{supp}}\{\bar{x}_{i,k+1}^{A}\}}{\mathbf{X}_{ch}^{\text{supp}}\{\sigma_{i,k}^{A}\}+\mathbf{X}_{ch}^{\text{supp}}\{\sigma_{i,k+1}^{A}\}}\right)^2\right)\right|+\left|-\exp\left(-\left(\frac{\mathbf{X}_{ch}^{\text{supp}}\{\bar{x}_{i,k}^{A}\}-\mathbf{X}_{ch}^{\text{supp}}\{\bar{x}_{i,k+1}^{A}\}}{\mathbf{X}_{ch}^{\text{supp}}\{\sigma_{i,k}^{A}\}-\mathbf{X}_{ch}^{\text{supp}}\{\sigma_{i,k+1}^{A}\}}\right)^2\right)\right|\right)}{\sum\limits_{i=1}^{n_{ch}}(\text{noifs}(i)-1)}\right.$$
$$\left.+\frac{\sum\limits_{j=1}^{m}\sum\limits_{k=1}^{\text{noofs}(j)-1}\left(\left|c_{\text{ffintc}}-\exp\left(-\left(\frac{\mathbf{X}_{ch}^{\text{supp}}\{\bar{y}_{j,k}^{B}\}-\mathbf{X}_{ch}^{\text{supp}}\{\bar{y}_{j,k+1}^{B}\}}{\mathbf{X}_{ch}^{\text{supp}}\{\sigma_{j,k}^{B}\}+\mathbf{X}_{ch}^{\text{supp}}\{\sigma_{j,k+1}^{B}\}}\right)^2\right)\right|+\left|-\exp\left(-\left(\frac{\mathbf{X}_{ch}^{\text{supp}}\{\bar{y}_{j,k}^{B}\}-\mathbf{X}_{ch}^{\text{supp}}\{\bar{y}_{j,k+1}^{B}\}}{\mathbf{X}_{ch}^{\text{supp}}\{\sigma_{j,k}^{B}\}-\mathbf{X}_{ch}^{\text{supp}}\{\sigma_{j,k+1}^{B}\}}\right)^2\right)\right|\right)}{\sum\limits_{j=1}^{m}(\text{noofs}(j)-1)}\right),$$
(13)

where $\mathbf{X}_{ch}^{\mathrm{supp}}$ stands for additional chromosome with list of non-reduced fuzzy sets

$$\mathbf{X}_{ch}^{\mathrm{supp}} = \left\{ \begin{array}{l} \bar{x}_{1,1}^{A}, \sigma_{1,1}^{A}, \bar{x}_{1,2}^{A}, \sigma_{1,2}^{A}, \ldots, \\ \bar{x}_{n_{ch},1}^{A}, \sigma_{n_{ch},1}^{A}, \bar{x}_{n_{ch},2}^{A}, \sigma_{n_{ch},2}^{A}, \ldots, \\ \bar{y}_{1,1}^{B}, \sigma_{1,1}^{B}, \bar{y}_{2,N_{ch}}^{B}, \sigma_{2,N_{ch}}^{B}, \ldots, \\ \bar{y}_{m,N_{ch}}^{B}, \sigma_{m,N_{ch}}^{B}, \bar{y}_{2,N_{ch}}^{B}, \sigma_{2,N_{ch}}^{B}, \ldots \end{array} \right\} = \left\{ X_{ch,1}^{\mathrm{supp}}, \ldots, X_{ch,L^{\mathrm{supp}}}^{\mathrm{supp}} \right\}, \quad (14)$$

where $L^{\mathrm{supp}} = 2 \cdot \left(\sum_{i=1}^{n_{ch}} \mathrm{noifs}\,(i) + \sum_{j=1}^{m} \mathrm{noofs}\,(j) \right)$, stands for length of the chromosome $\mathbf{X}_{ch}^{\mathrm{supp}}$, n_{ch} stands for the number of system inputs coded in the chromosome ch (see formula (5)). Moreover, a number of i input fuzzy sets from equation (13) can be reached using function noifs (i) defined as follows

$$\mathrm{noifs}\,(i) = \sum_{k=1}^{N_{ch}} \mathbf{X}_{ch}^{\mathrm{red}}\,\{\mathrm{rule}_k\} \cdot \mathbf{X}_{ch}^{\mathrm{red}}\,\{A_i^k\}, \quad (15)$$

where N_{ch} stand for number of rules of the system encoded in chromosome ch. Analogically a number of j output fuzzy sets can be calculated.

The lists of parameters encoded in chromosome $\mathbf{X}_{ch}^{\mathrm{supp}}$ does not have specified final elements - their amount depends on the structure of the chromosome $\mathbf{X}_{ch}^{\mathrm{red}}$. It is worth to mention that the lists of parameters are sorted by the centres of the fuzzy sets. Single rows from the $\mathbf{X}_{ch}^{\mathrm{supp}}$ contain parameters connected with specified input and output fuzzy sets. Due to that this approach is different than in case of approach using chromosome $\mathbf{X}_{ch}^{\mathrm{red}}$.

(d) The component $\mathrm{ffint}_D\,(\mathbf{X}_{ch})$ increases the integrity of the shape of the input and output fuzzy sets associated with the inputs and outputs of system (2) encoded in the tested chromosome

$$\mathrm{ffint}_D\,(\mathbf{X}_{ch}) =$$

$$\left(\begin{array}{c} \sum_{i=1}^{n} \mathbf{X}_{ch}^{\mathrm{red}}\{x_i\} \cdot \sqrt{\sum_{k1=1}^{Nmax} \dfrac{\mathbf{X}_{ch}^{\mathrm{red}}\{\mathrm{rule}_{k1}\} \cdot \left(\begin{array}{c} \mathbf{X}_{ch}^{\mathrm{par}}\left\{\sigma_{i,k1}^{A}\right\} + \\ -\dfrac{\sum_{k2=1}^{Nmax} \mathbf{X}_{ch}^{\mathrm{red}}\{\mathrm{rule}_{k2}\} \cdot \mathbf{X}_{ch}^{\mathrm{par}}\left\{\sigma_{i,k2}^{A}\right\}}{N_{ch}} \end{array} \right)^2}{N_{ch}}}}{n_{ch}} + \\ + \sum_{j=1}^{m} \sqrt{\sum_{k1=1}^{Nmax} \dfrac{\mathbf{X}_{ch}^{\mathrm{red}}\{\mathrm{rule}_{k1}\} \cdot \left(\begin{array}{c} \mathbf{X}_{ch}^{\mathrm{par}}\left\{\sigma_{j,k1}^{B}\right\} + \\ -\dfrac{\sum_{k2=1}^{Nmax} \mathbf{X}_{ch}^{\mathrm{red}}\{\mathrm{rule}_{k2}\} \cdot \mathbf{X}_{ch}^{\mathrm{par}}\left\{\sigma_{j,k2}^{B}\right\}}{N_{ch}} \end{array} \right)^2}{N_{ch}}}}{m} \end{array} \right), \quad (16)$$

where $\mathbf{X}_{ch}^{\mathrm{par}}\left\{\sigma_{i,k}^{A}\right\}$ stands for a gene of the chromosome $\mathbf{X}_{ch}^{\mathrm{par}}$ associated with the parameter $\sigma_{i,k}^{A}$ (width of input Gaussian-type fuzzy set A_i^k used in simulations),

$\mathbf{X}_{ch}^{par} \left\{ \sigma_{j,k}^{B} \right\}$ means gene of the chromosome $\mathbf{X}_{ch}^{par}$ associated with the parameter $\sigma_{j,k}^{B}$.

(e) The component $\mathrm{ffint}_E \left(\mathbf{X}_{ch} \right)$ increases complementarity of the input fuzzy sets of system (2) encoded in the tested chromosome

$$\mathrm{ffint}_E \left(\mathbf{X}_{ch} \right) = \frac{\sum_{z=1}^{Z} \sum_{i=1}^{n} \left(\cdot \max \left(1, \left| 1 - \sum_{k=1}^{Nmax} \mathbf{X}_{ch}^{red} \{ \mathrm{rule}_k \} \cdot \mu_{A_i^k} \left(\bar{x}_{z,i} \right) \right| \right) \right)}{Z \cdot n_{ch}}. \tag{17}$$

(f) The component $\mathrm{ffint}_F \left(\mathbf{X}_{ch} \right)$ increases readability of the antecedents and weights of rules of system (2) encoded in the tested chromosome

$$\mathrm{ffint}_F \left(\mathbf{X}_{ch} \right) = 1 - \frac{\left(\sum_{k=1}^{Nmax} \mathbf{X}_{ch}^{red} \{ \mathrm{rule}_k \} \cdot \left(\frac{\sum_{i=1}^{n} \mathbf{X}_{ch}^{red} \{ x_i \} \cdot \mu_w \left(w_{i,k}^{A} \right)}{n_{ch}} \right) + \sum_{k=1}^{Nmax} \mathbf{X}_{ch}^{red} \{ \mathrm{rule}_k \} \cdot \mu_w \left(w_k^{rule} \right) \right)}{2 \cdot N_{ch}}, \tag{18}$$

where $\mu_w \left(w_{i,k}^{A} \right)$ is a function defining congeries around values 0, 0.5 and 1 (in simulations we assumed that $a = 0.25$, $b = 0.50$ i $c = 0.75$). This function is described as follows

$$\mu_w \left(x \right) = \begin{cases} \frac{a-x}{a} & \text{for } x \geq 0 \text{ and } x \leq a \\ \frac{x-a}{b-a} & \text{for } x \geq a \text{ and } x \leq b \\ \frac{c-x}{c-b} & \text{for } x \geq b \text{ and } x \leq c \\ \frac{x-c}{1-c} & \text{for } x \geq c \text{ and } x \leq 1 \end{cases}. \tag{19}$$

4   Simulation Results

In our paper we considered the van der Pol oscillator ([63]) which is used in the medicine as the model of the heartbeat. In our simulations three approaches were assumed. In each of them different weights of fitness function (7) were chosen. It is worth to mention that the function (7) is very elastic due to weights, and allows to obtain solutions with different accuracy-interpretability trade-off. Owing to the fact that we choose three specified cases (see Table 1): **(a)** "high accuracy" case, where most important part of the (7) takes responsibility for accuracy of system (2) (see column (a) in Table 1). **(b)** "high interpretability" case, where the most important part of the (7) takes responsibility for interpretability of system (2) (see column (b) in Table 1). **(c)** "good accuracy and good interpretability" (balanced), where both accuracy component and interpretability component weights in the function (7) were set to high values (2) (see column (c) in Table 1). Supplemental properties of our simulations can be

Table 1. Components of fitness function (7) and reduction level of system (2) for different weights of (7) (for the best chromosomes): a) high accuracy case, b) high interpretability case, c) high accuracy and interpretability case

Name of the component	Case (a)	Case (b)	Case (c)
$w_{\text{ffaccuracy}}$	1.00	0.50	0.75
$w_{\text{ffinterpretability}}$	0.50	1.00	0.75
$w_{\text{ffcomplexity}}$	0.50	0.50	0.50
$w_{\text{ffintA}} = w_{\text{ffintB}} = w_{\text{ffintE}}$	0.20	0.20	0.20
$w_{\text{ffintC}} = w_{\text{ffintD}}$	1.00	1.00	1.00
w_{ffintF}	0.50	0.50	0.50
ffaccuracy $(\mathbf{X}_{ch})$	0.0092	0.1531	0.0482
ffinterpretability $(\mathbf{X}_{ch})$	0.3936	0.0001	0.0007
ffcomplexity $(\mathbf{X}_{ch})$	0.5526	0.5789	0.9211
ff $(\mathbf{X}_{ch})$	0.0050	0.0001	0.0688
$RMSE$	0.2212	0.7883	0.5218
Name of the reduced elements	Case (a)	Case (b)	Case (c)
inputs	0/2	0/2	0/2
antecedents	2/6	2/6	3/6
consequences	7/12	6/12	7/12
rules	1/3	1/3	1/3
discretization points	12/20	14/20	13/20

summed up as follows: **(1)** For modelling dynamic objects the method presented in our previous work [39] was used. In this method, every output of system (2) generates one element of variable state matrix. **(2)** For system (2) a Gaussian functions with algebraic triangular norms were used. **(3)** The following properties of evolutionary algorithm was assumed: the number of chromosomes in the population was set to 100, the algorithm performs 10 000 steps (generations), the crossover probability was set as $p_c = 0.8$, the mutation probability was set as $p_m = 0.2$, the mutation intensity was set as $\sigma = 0.3$. **(4)** In interpretability component (10) of the fitness function (7) following weights was set: ffint$_C$ $(\mathbf{X}_{ch})$ $(w_{\text{ffintC}} = 1.0)$, ffint$_D$ $(\mathbf{X}_{ch})$ $(w_{\text{ffintD}} = 1.0)$ i ffint$_F$ $(\mathbf{X}_{ch})$ $(w_{\text{ffintF}} = 0.5)$. Weights of remaining components of function (10) was set as 0.2.

The conclusions from simulations can be summarized as follows: **(1)** Example (a) allowed to obtain a system with very high accuracy and quite acceptable interpretability. **(2)** Example (b) and (c) allowed obtain high readability of fuzzy sets (see Fig. 1), high readability of weights of fuzzy sets and rules (see Fig. 2) and good accuracy of the system (see Fig. 3). **(3)** Example (c) (as predicted) allowed obtain better accuracy of the system than example b (b) with acceptable compromise between semantic interpretability and complex-based interpretability (see Table 1).

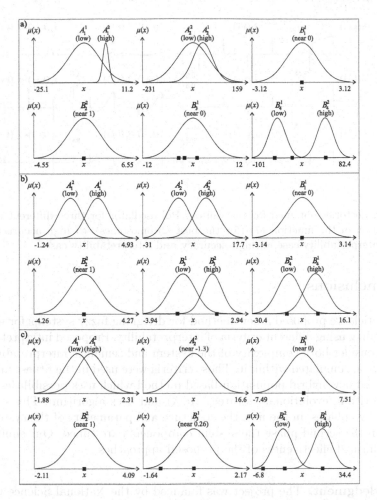

Fig. 1. Inputs and outputs fuzzy sets of the neuro-fuzzy system (2) for the van der Pol oscillator problem for three various settings of the function (7) (for the best chromosomes): a) high accuracy case, b) high interpretability case, c) high accuracy and interpretability case

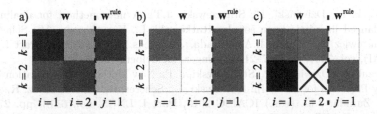

Fig. 2. Weights representation in the neuro-fuzzy system (2) (dark areas correspond to low values of weights and vice versa) for the van der Pol oscillator problem for different weights configuration of the function (7) (for the best chromosomes): a) high accuracy case, b) high interpretability case, c) high accuracy and interpretability case

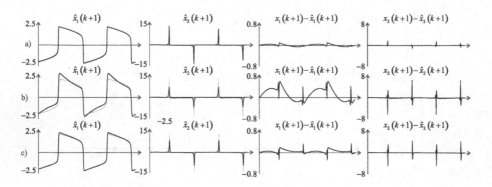

Fig. 3. Trajectories obtained for the van der Pol oscillator for three different weights configuration of the function (7) (for the best chromosomes): a) high accuracy case, b) high interpretability case, c) high accuracy and interpretability case

5 Conclusions

In this article we proposed a new method for designing fuzzy systems for nonlinear modelling using different criteria of interpretability. Proposed interpretability criteria consider both complexity of the system and semantic interpretability of knowledge accumulated within it. Those criteria were used in the fitness function of presented new hybrid population-based method which uses possibilities of genetic algorithm, evolutionary strategy (μ, λ) and bees algorithm. This method works in two phases, in the first the structure and parameters of the system are chosen, in the second phase the system components are tuned. Our simulation results affirmed effectiveness of the proposed approaches.

Acknowledgment. The project was financed by the National Science Centre (Poland) on the basis of the decision number DEC-2012/05/B/ST7/02138.

References

1. Bartczuk, Ł., Dziwiński, P., Starczewski, J.T.: A new method for dealing with unbalanced linguistic term set. In: Rutkowski, L., Korytkowski, M., Scherer, R., Tadeusiewicz, R., Zadeh, L.A., Zurada, J.M. (eds.) ICAISC 2012, Part I. LNCS (LNAI), vol. 7267, pp. 207–212. Springer, Heidelberg (2012)
2. Bartczuk, Ł., Dziwiński, P., Starczewski, J.T.: New Method for Generation Type-2 Fuzzy Partition for FDT. In: Rutkowski, L., Scherer, R., Tadeusiewicz, R., Zadeh, L.A., Zurada, J.M. (eds.) ICAISC 2010, Part I. LNCS, vol. 6113, pp. 275–280. Springer, Heidelberg (2010)
3. Bartczuk, Ł., Przybył, A., Dziwiński, P.: Hybrid state variables - fuzzy logic modelling of nonlinear objects. In: Rutkowski, L., Korytkowski, M., Scherer, R., Tadeusiewicz, R., Zadeh, L.A., Zurada, J.M. (eds.) ICAISC 2013, Part I. LNCS, vol. 7894, pp. 227–234. Springer, Heidelberg (2013)

4. Bartczuk, Ł., Rutkowska, D.: A New Version of the Fuzzy-ID3 Algorithm. In: Rutkowski, L., Tadeusiewicz, R., Zadeh, L.A., Żurada, J.M. (eds.) ICAISC 2006. LNCS (LNAI), vol. 4029, pp. 1060–1070. Springer, Heidelberg (2006)
5. Bartczuk, Ł., Rutkowska, D.: Medical Diagnosis with Type-2 Fuzzy Decision Trees. In: Kącki, E., Rudnicki, M., Stempczyńska, J. (eds.) Computers in Medical Activity. AISC, vol. 65, pp. 11–21. Springer, Heidelberg (2009)
6. Bilski, J., Rutkowski, L.: Numerically Robust Learning Algorithms for Feed Forward Neural Networks. In: Advances in Soft Computing - Neural Networks and Soft Computing, pp. 149–154. Physica-Verlag, A Springer-Verlag Company (2003)
7. Cpalka, K.: A Method for Designing Flexible Neuro-fuzzy Systems. In: Rutkowski, L., Tadeusiewicz, R., Zadeh, L.A., Żurada, J.M. (eds.) ICAISC 2006. LNCS (LNAI), vol. 4029, pp. 212–219. Springer, Heidelberg (2006)
8. Cpałka, K., Rutkowski, L.: Flexible Takagi Sugeno Neuro-fuzzy Structures for Nonlinear Approximation. WSEAS Transactions on Systems 4(9), 1450–1458 (2005)
9. Dekker, M.: Advanced Process Identification and Control, Incorporated, ch. 1 (2002)
10. Dziwiński, P., Bartczuk, Ł., Starczewski, J.T.: Fully controllable ant colony system for text data clustering. In: Rutkowski, L., Korytkowski, M., Scherer, R., Tadeusiewicz, R., Zadeh, L.A., Zurada, J.M. (eds.) SIDE 2012 and EC 2012. LNCS, vol. 7269, pp. 199–205. Springer, Heidelberg (2012)
11. Dziwiński, P., Rutkowska, D.: Algorithm for generating fuzzy rules for WWW document classification. In: Rutkowski, L., Tadeusiewicz, R., Zadeh, L.A., Żurada, J.M. (eds.) ICAISC 2006. LNCS (LNAI), vol. 4029, pp. 1111–1119. Springer, Heidelberg (2006)
12. Dziwiński, P., Rutkowska, D.: Ant focused crawling algorithm. In: Rutkowski, L., Tadeusiewicz, R., Zadeh, L.A., Zurada, J.M. (eds.) ICAISC 2008. LNCS (LNAI), vol. 5097, pp. 1018–1028. Springer, Heidelberg (2008)
13. Dziwiński, P., Starczewski, J.T., Bartczuk, Ł.: New linguistic hedges in construction of interval type-2 FLS. In: Rutkowski, L., Scherer, R., Tadeusiewicz, R., Zadeh, L.A., Zurada, J.M. (eds.) ICAISC 2010, Part II. LNCS, vol. 6114, pp. 445–450. Springer, Heidelberg (2010)
14. El-Abd, M.: On the hybridization on the artificial bee colony and particle swarm optimization algorithms. Journal of Artificial Intelligence and Soft Computing Research 2(2), 147–155 (2012)
15. Gabryel, M., Cpałka, K., Rutkowski, L.: Evolutionary strategies for learning of neuro-fuzzy systems. In: Proceedings of the I Workshop on Genetic Fuzzy Systems, Granada, pp. 119–123 (2005)
16. Gacto, M.J., Alcala, R., Herrera, F.: Interpretability of linguistic fuzzy rule-based systems: An overview of interpretability measures. Information Sciences 181, 4340–4360 (2011)
17. Ghandar, A., Michalewicz, Z.: An experimental study of Multi-Objective Evolutionary Algorithms for balancing interpretability and accuracy in fuzzy rule base classifiers for financial prediction. In: 2011 IEEE Symposium on Computational Intelligence for Financial Engineering and Economics, pp. 1–6 (2011)
18. Greblicki, W., Rutkowska, D., Rutkowski, L.: An orthogonal series estimate of time-varying regression. Annals of the Institute of Statistical Mathematics 35(2), 215–228 (1983)
19. Horzyk, A., Tadeusiewicz, R.: Self-Optimizing Neural Networks. In: Yin, F.-L., Wang, J., Guo, C. (eds.) ISNN 2004. LNCS, vol. 3173, pp. 150–155. Springer, Heidelberg (2004)

20. Jelonkiewicz, J., Przybył, A.: Accuracy improvement of neural network state variable estimator in induction motor drive. In: Rutkowski, L., Tadeusiewicz, R., Zadeh, L.A., Zurada, J.M. (eds.) ICAISC 2008. LNCS (LNAI), vol. 5097, pp. 71–77. Springer, Heidelberg (2008)

21. Kamyar, M.: Takagi-Sugeno Fuzzy Modeling for Process Control. In: Industrial Automation Robotics and Artificial Intelligence (EEE8005), School of Electrical, Electronic and Computer Engineering (2008)

22. Korytkowski, M., Nowicki, R., Rutkowski, L., Scherer, R.: AdaBoost Ensemble of DCOG Rough–Neuro–Fuzzy Systems. In: Jędrzejowicz, P., Nguyen, N.T., Hoang, K. (eds.) ICCCI 2011, Part I. LNCS, vol. 6922, pp. 62–71. Springer, Heidelberg (2011)

23. Korytkowski, M., Rutkowski, L., Scherer, R.: On combining backpropagation with boosting. In: Proceedings of the IEEE International Joint Conference on Neural Network (IJCNN), vols. 1-10, pp. 1274–1277 (2006)

24. Korytkowski, M., Rutkowski, L., Scherer, R.: From Ensemble of Fuzzy Classifiers to Single Fuzzy Rule Base Classifier. In: Rutkowski, L., Tadeusiewicz, R., Zadeh, L.A., Zurada, J.M. (eds.) ICAISC 2008. LNCS (LNAI), vol. 5097, pp. 265–272. Springer, Heidelberg (2008)

25. Laskowski, Ł.: A novel hybrid-maximum neural network in stereo-matching process. Neural Comput. & Applic. 23, 2435–2450 (2013)

26. Laskowski, Ł.: Objects auto-selection from stereo-images realised by self-correcting neural network. In: Rutkowski, L., Korytkowski, M., Scherer, R., Tadeusiewicz, R., Zadeh, L.A., Zurada, J.M. (eds.) ICAISC 2012, Part I. LNCS, vol. 7267, pp. 119–125. Springer, Heidelberg (2012)

27. Li, X., Er, M.J., Lim, B.S., Zhou, J.H., Gan, O.P., Rutkowski, L.: Fuzzy Regression Modeling for Tool Performance Prediction and Degradation Detection. International Journal of Neural Systems 20(5), 405–419 (2010)

28. Lobato, F.S., Steffen Jr., V.: A new multi-objective optimization algorithm based on differential evolution and neighborhood exploring evolution strategy. Journal of Artificial Intelligence and Soft Computing Research 1(4), 259–267 (2011)

29. Lobato, F.S., Steffen Jr., V., Silva Neto, A.J.: Solution of singular optimal control problems using the improved differential evolution algorithm. Journal of Artificial Intelligence and Soft Computing Research 1(3), 195–206 (2011)

30. Łapa, K., Zalasiński, M., Cpałka, K.: A new method for designing and complexity reduction of neuro-fuzzy systems for nonlinear modelling. In: Rutkowski, L., Korytkowski, M., Scherer, R., Tadeusiewicz, R., Zadeh, L.A., Zurada, J.M. (eds.) ICAISC 2013, Part I. LNCS, vol. 7894, pp. 329–344. Springer, Heidelberg (2013)

31. Michalewicz, Z.: Genetic Algorithms + Data Structures = Evolution Programs. Springer (1999)

32. Nowicki, R.: On classification with missing data using rough-neuro-fuzzy systems. International Journal of Applied Mathematics and Computer Science 20(1), 55–67 (2010)

33. Nowicki, R., Rutkowski, R.: Soft Techniques for Bayesian Classification. In: Rutkowski, L., Kacprzyk, J. (eds.) Neural Networks and Soft Computing. Advances in Soft Computing, pp. 537–544. Springer Physica-Verlag (2003)

34. Nowicki, R., Scherer, R., Rutkowski, L.: A method for learning of hierarchical fuzzy systems. In: Sincak, P., Vascak, J., Kvasnicka, V., Pospichal, J. (eds.) Intelligent Technologies - Theory and Applications, pp. 124–129. IOS Press (2002)

35. Patan, K., Korbicz, J.: Nonlinear model predictive control of a boiler unit: A fault tolerant control study. Applied Mathematics and Computer Science 22(1), 225–237 (2012)

36. Pławiak, P., Tadeusiewicz, R.: Approximation of phenol concentration using novel hybrid computational intelligence methods. Applied Mathematics and Computer Science 24(1) (in print, 2014)
37. Pham, D.T., Ghanbarzadeh, A., Koc, E., Otri, S., Rahim, S., Zaidi, M.: The Bees Algorithm, A Novel Tool for Complex Optimisation Problems. In: Proceedings of the 2nd International Virtual Conference on Intelligent Production Machines and Systems, pp. 454–459 (2006)
38. Prampero, P.S., Attux, R.: Magnetic particle swarm optimization. Journal of Artificial Intelligence and Soft Computing Research 2(1), 59–72 (2012)
39. Przybył, A., Cpałka, K.: A new method to construct of interpretable models of dynamic systems. In: Rutkowski, L., Korytkowski, M., Scherer, R., Tadeusiewicz, R., Zadeh, L.A., Zurada, J.M. (eds.) ICAISC 2012, Part II. LNCS, vol. 7268, pp. 697–705. Springer, Heidelberg (2012)
40. Przybył, A., Jelonkiewicz, J.: Genetic algorithm for observer parameters tuning in sensorless induction motor drive. In: Rutkowski, L., Kacprzyk, J. (eds.) Networks and Soft Computing (6th International Conference on Neural Networks and Soft Computing 2002), Zakopane, Poland, pp. 376–381 (2003)
41. Przybył, A., Smoląg, J., Kimla, P.: Distributed Control System Based on Real Time Ethernet for Computer Numerical Controlled Machine Tool (in Polish). Przeglad Elektrotechniczny 86(2), 342–346 (2010)
42. Rutkowski, L.: Computational Intelligence. Springer (2008)
43. Rutkowski, L.: An application of multiple Fourier series to identification of multivariable nonstationary systems. International Journal of Systems Science 20(10), 1993–2002 (1989)
44. Rutkowski, L.: The real-time identification of time-varying systems by nonparametric algorithms based on the Parzen kernels. International Journal of Systems Science 16, 1123–1130 (1985)
45. Rutkowski, L.: Flexible structures of neuro-fuzzy systems. In: Sincak, P., Vascak, J. (eds.) Quo Vadis Computational Intelligence. STUDFUZZ, vol. 54, pp. 479–484. Springer, Heidelberg (2000)
46. Rutkowski, L., Cpałka, K.: Flexible weighted neuro-fuzzy systems. In: Proceedings of the 9th International Conference on Neural Information Processing (ICONIP 2002), Orchid Country Club, Singapore, CD, November 18-22 (2002)
47. Rutkowski, L., Przybył, A., Cpałka, K., Er, M.J.: Online Speed Profile Generation for Industrial Machine Tool Based on Neuro-fuzzy Approach. In: Rutkowski, L., Scherer, R., Tadeusiewicz, R., Zadeh, L.A., Zurada, J.M. (eds.) ICAISC 2010, Part II. LNCS (LNAI), vol. 6114, pp. 645–650. Springer, Heidelberg (2010)
48. Rutkowski, L., Przybył, A., Cpałka, K.: Novel on-line speed profile generation for industrial machine tool based on flexible neuro-fuzzy approximation. IEEE Transactions on Industrial Electronics 59, 1238–1247 (2012)
49. Scherer, R.: Neuro-fuzzy relational systems for nonlinear approximation and prediction. Nonlinear Analysis Series A: Theory, Methods and Applications 71(12), e1420–e1425 (2009)
50. Scherer, R., Rutkowski, L.: Connectionist fuzzy relational systems. In: Halgamuge, S.K., Wang, L. (eds.) Computational Intelligence for Modelling and Prediction. SCI, vol. 2, pp. 35–47. Springer, Heidelberg (2005)
51. Siwek, K., Osowski, S., Szupiluk, R.: Ensemble neural network approach for accurate load forecasting in a power system. Applied Mathematics and Computer Science 19(2), 303–315 (2009)

52. Starczewski, J.T.: A Type-1 Approximation of Interval Type-2 FLS. In: Di Gesù, V., Pal, S.K., Petrosino, A. (eds.) WILF 2009. LNCS, vol. 5571, pp. 287–294. Springer, Heidelberg (2009)
53. Starczewski, J.T., Rutkowski, L.: Connectionist Structures of Type 2 Fuzzy Inference Systems. In: Wyrzykowski, R., Dongarra, J., Paprzycki, M., Waśniewski, J. (eds.) PPAM 2001. LNCS, vol. 2328, pp. 634–642. Springer, Heidelberg (2002)
54. Starczewski, J.T., Rutkowski, L.: Interval type 2 neuro-fuzzy systems based on interval consequents. In: Rutkowski, L., Kacprzyk, J. (eds.) Neural Networks and Soft Computing. Advances in Soft Computing, pp. 570–577. Springer, Heidelberg (2003)
55. Starczewski, J.T., Scherer, R., Korytkowski, M., Nowicki, R.: Modular type-2 neuro-fuzzy systems. In: Wyrzykowski, R., Dongarra, J., Karczewski, K., Wasniewski, J. (eds.) PPAM 2007. LNCS, vol. 4967, pp. 570–578. Springer, Heidelberg (2008)
56. Szaleniec, M., Goclon, J., Witko, M., Tadeusiewicz, R.: Application of artificial neural networks and DFT-based parameters for prediction of reaction kinetics of ethylbenzene dehydrogenase. Journal of Computer-Aided Molecular Design 20(3), 145–157 (2006)
57. Zhou, S.M., Gan, J.Q.: Low-level interpretability and high-level interpretability: a unified view of data-driven interpretable fuzzy system modelling. Fuzzy Sets and Systems 159, 3091–3131 (2008)
58. Zalasiński, M., Łapa, K., Cpałka, K.: New Algorithm for Evolutionary Selection of the Dynamic Signature Global Features. In: Rutkowski, L., Korytkowski, M., Scherer, R., Tadeusiewicz, R., Zadeh, L.A., Zurada, J.M. (eds.) ICAISC 2013, Part II. LNCS (LNAI), vol. 7895, pp. 113–121. Springer, Heidelberg (2013)
59. Zalasiński, M., Cpałka, K.: A new method of on-line signature verification using a flexible fuzzy one-class classifier, pp. 38–53. Academic Publishing House EXIT (2011)
60. Zalasiński, M., Cpałka, K.: New Approach for the On-Line Signature Verification Based on Method of Horizontal Partitioning. In: Rutkowski, L., Korytkowski, M., Scherer, R., Tadeusiewicz, R., Zadeh, L.A., Zurada, J.M. (eds.) ICAISC 2013, Part II. LNCS (LNAI), vol. 7895, pp. 342–350. Springer, Heidelberg (2013)
61. Zalasiński, M., Cpałka, K.: Novel algorithm for the on-line signature verification. In: Rutkowski, L., Korytkowski, M., Scherer, R., Tadeusiewicz, R., Zadeh, L.A., Zurada, J.M. (eds.) ICAISC 2012, Part II. LNCS (LNAI), vol. 7268, pp. 362–367. Springer, Heidelberg (2012)
62. Zalasiński, M., Cpałka, K.: Novel Algorithm for the On-Line Signature Verification Using Selected Discretization Points Groups. In: Rutkowski, L., Korytkowski, M., Scherer, R., Tadeusiewicz, R., Zadeh, L.A., Zurada, J.M. (eds.) ICAISC 2013, Part I. LNCS (LNAI), vol. 7894, pp. 493–502. Springer, Heidelberg (2013)
63. Żebrowski, J., Grudziński, K.: Observations and modelling of unusual patterns in human heart rate variability. Acta Physica Polonica B 36, 1881–1894 (2005)

Fuzzy Reinforcement Learning for Dynamic Power Control in Cognitive Radio Networks

Jerzy Martyna

Institute of Computer Science, Faculty of Mathematics and Computer Science
Jagiellonian University, ul. Prof. S. Lojasiewicza 6, 30-348 Cracow, Poland

Abstract. Intelligent and flexible spectrum access procedures and resource allocation methods are needed to build cognitive radio (CR) networks. Apart from the major objective to maximise spectra efficiency, the
goal of the CR network design is to rationalise the distribution of radio
resources and the cost of their usage. This paper proposes a new fuzzy
reinforcement learning method that allows for learning the best transmit
power control strategy that in turn enables cognitive secondary users
to achieve its required transmission rate and quality whilst minimising
interference. An example is presented to illustrate the performance and
applicability of the proposed method.

1 Introduction

Traditional spectrum management policies are challenged by increasing demand
for spectrum resources. The Federal Communications Commission (FCC) has
reported that spectrum shortage is caused by the current inefficiency of spectrum
usage rather than the physical spectrum scarcity. The report shows that "for
the measurement period, typical channel occupancy was less than 15%, while
the peak usage was close to 85%," [4]. Cognitive radio (CR) systems [14], [8]
have emerged as a potential technology to revolutionise spectrum utilisation.
Cognitive radio is defined as a radio system that continuously performs spectrum
sensing, dynamically identifying unused spectra and then operating in those
spectrum holes.

The main challenge to dynamic spectrum access (DSA) in the CR systems lies
in finding a balance with the conflicting goal of satisfying performance requirements for secondary (unlicensed) users (SUs), while minimising interference to
primary (licensed) users (PUs) and other secondary users. In particular, concurrent transmissions of PUs and SUs may occur only if the aggregate interference
caused by the SUs at the PUs is maintained below some acceptable threshold.
Thus, in order to achieve these tasks, SUs are required to recognise PUs, determine environmental characteristics and adapt their system parameters to flexible
radio channel changes over time and space according to the presence of PUs and
SUs as well as the infrastructure costs of the secondary networks.

Power control in CR networks has been analysed in various research studies.
In the paper by Hoang [9], a CR network is treated as a set of base stations

L. Rutkowski et al. (Eds.): ICAISC 2014, Part I, LNAI 8467, pp. 233–242, 2014.

that make opportunistic spectrum accesses to support fixed-location wireless subscribers. A downlink power allocation scheme that maximises the number of supported subscribers is obtained by solving a mixed-integer linear programming problem. However, the solution proposed in Hoang [9] is not applicable to cases where the PUs employ spread transmissions over multiple carriers. In the paper by Wang et al. [15], the optimal power control in a CR network is modelled as a concave maximisation, and an improved branch and bound algorithm is proposed. Gatsis [7] suggests a utility function-based approach to the power control problem in peer-to-peer CR networks. In the paper by Gao [6], the energy efficiency maximisation is considered. Given the data rate requirements and maximal power limits, a constrained optimisation problem is formulated for each secondary user to minimise the energy consumption per bit over all selected subcarriers, while avoiding interference to the existing users. However, none of the above-mentioned papers have dealt with radio channel changes over time and space according to the presence/absence of PUs or SUs.

Fuzzy logic system is one of the most effective methods that is able to simultaneously handle numerical data and linguistic knowledge. It can be also used in partial-state systems. Therefore, fuzzy logic is often used in many research problems in CR networks. Among others, in the paper by Matinmikko et al. [13], a fuzzy logic system is proposed for cooperative spectrum sensing in CR networks. In the model given by Le et al. [11], fuzzy logic is used for power control schemes in the CR network, in which some SUs transmitting simultaneously as the PUs on the same band was modelled. A fuzzy logic to select the most suitable SU to access the spectrum in the CR network was also studied by Le et al. [12]. Recently, the problem of spectrum sharing in multi-service cognitive networks has been studied using reinforcement learning by Alsarhan [1]. In this paper, the machine-learning paradigm is presented as a means for extracting an optimal control policy for spectrum sharing.

The main goal of this paper is to introduce a new method of power control in CR networks based on the fuzzy reinforcement-learning algorithm. It allows us to achieve its required transmission rate and quality, while minimising interference to primary and secondary users. The proposed technique guarantees the balance of the two requirements for the maximum acceptable SU transmission power to satisfy interference constraints and the minimum transit power required by SUs to satisfy a determined level of service. Moreover, the main possibility for the proposed method lies in dynamic frequency selection and adaptive power control.

This paper is organised as follows. Section 2 presents system model for the CR network. Section 3 formulates the fuzzy reinforcement learning approach for power control in the CR network. In section 4, we present the results of the simulation experiments. The conclusion and future research are summarised in the last section.

2   Model System

In this section, we consider a system model based on the distributed power control scheme.

We assume that the distributed power control scheme requires local link gain, an estimated signal-to-interference plus noise ratio (SINR), a bit error rate, etc. The presented scheme is based on the distributed power control model presented by Foschini et al. [5]. According to this approach to the presented scheme, distributed power control is based on satisfying certain SINR thresholds in the network [5]. Thus, the transmission power of the i-th link in the t-th time slot is given by:

$$P_i(t+1) = \frac{\gamma_i}{SINR_i(t)} P_i(t) \tag{1}$$

where γ_i is the threshold of a lower SINR for each link i and $SINR_i(t)$ can be defined as follows:

$$SINR_i(t) = \frac{G_{ii} P_i(t)}{\sum_{j \neq i} G_{ij} P_j(t) + N_i} \tag{2}$$

where G_{ij} is the channel response from transmitter of the i-th link to the receiver of the j-th link, and N_i is the power of the additive white gaussian noise (AWGN). In the distributed manner, each user measures its current $SINR_i(t)$ autonomously and makes its power decision for the next step in order to achieve its target γ_i. This scheme is the standard distributed power control and it convergences to the Pareto optimal, which is the minimal operational power point for the network of links.

The proposed power control strategy is based on balancing the SU transmission power level with the required minimum value and the acceptable maximum degree. The required minimum transmit power is established by adjusting it to the demanded SINR by the SU receiver. The acceptable transmission power is obtained by considering the admitted interference at the primary user's receiver. Thus, each cognitive SU tries to obtain the required SINR whilst minimising interference to the PUs. We can indicate three possible cases in determining the transmit power interferences:

a) If the sensing power is bellow the PU threshold level, the licensed PU cannot be detected by the SU. Then, the SU can reduce its transmit power in order to avoid interference to the PU receiver at unknown location.
b) If the sensing power is above the PU threshold level, the SU is not able to transmit its data in the same area. Therefore, the transmission should be delayed or the SU must stand some metres away from the PU coverage zone.
c) If the sensing power is well above the PU threshold level, the SU can transmit with a lower power level without causing measurable disturbing interference to the PU receiver. This situation allows for the realisation of short communications between the SU transmitter and a receiver distant from PU receiver.

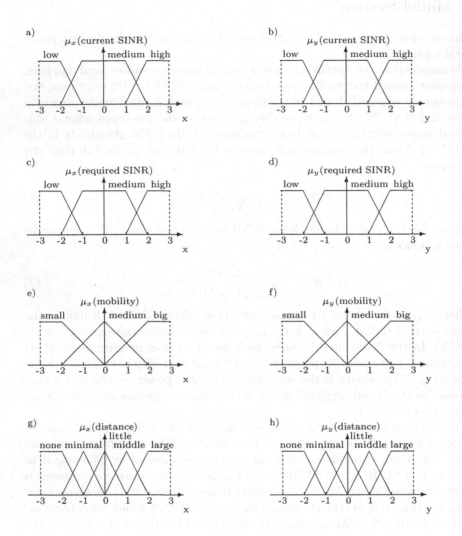

Fig. 1. Fuzzy sets for two-dimensional environment defining membership functions of *current SINR* (a, b), *required SINR* (c, d), *mobility* (e, f); *distance* with respect to nearest PU (g, h)

3   Fuzzy Reinforcement Learning Method for Power Control in the CR Network

We assume that a single SU station is equipped in three sensors: one to detect SINR, the second to indicate mobility degree, and the third to find the distance between the SU and the nearest PU. For a two-dimensional environment, all the information obtained by the *j*-th SU about the current SINR is defined by the membership functions μ_x, μ_y (see Figs. 1(a) and Fig. 1(b)). The required SINRs at the SU are described by the membership functions given in Fig. 1(c) and Fig. 1(d). The mobility degrees are defined by the membership functions presented in Fig. 1(e) and Fig. 1(f). The data from third sensor allows us to find the distance to nearest PU. The membership functions are given in Fig. 1(g) and Fig. 1(h).

A membership value defining the fuzzy state of the j-th SU with reference to the SINR and in respect to the k-th nearest PU is given by:

$$\mu_{state}^{(j)}(current \ SINR^{(k)}) = \mu_x^{(j)}(current \ SINR^{(k)}) \cdot \mu_y^{(j)}(current \ SINR^{(k)})$$
(3)

A membership function defining the fuzzy state of the j-th SU in respect of the k-th required SINR for a two-dimensional environment is as follows:

$$\mu_{state}^{(j)}(required \ SINR^{(k)}) = \mu_x^{(j)}(required \ SINR^{(k)}) \cdot \mu_y^{(j)}(required \ SINR^{(k)})$$
(4)

A membership function defining the fuzzy state of the j-th SU defining its mobility degree with respect to k-th nearest PU for a two-dimensional environment is as follows:

$$\mu_{state}^{(j)}(mobility^{(k)}) = \mu_x^{(j)}(mobility^{(k)}) \cdot \mu_y^{(j)}(mobility^{(k)})$$
(5)

Similarly, the distance of j-th SU to the nearest k-th PU which also defines the fuzzy state for a two-dimensional environment is computed as:

$$\mu_{state}^{(j)}(distance^{(k)} = \mu_x^{(j)}(distance^{(k)}) \cdot \mu_y^{(j)}(distance^{(k)})$$
(6)

The system model is described by the multidimensional membership function, which can be treated as a multidimensional hypercube. The fuzzy state for the j-th SU can be defined by the fuzzy pair (s_n, a_n) for the n-th fuzzy variable, where s and a are the state and action respectively. Using the aggregation of the fuzzy state, we can achieve:

$$Q_{state}^{(j)}(s, a) \leftarrow Q_{state}^{(j)}(s, a) + \sum_{n=1}^{N} \alpha_n^{(j)} \cdot \mu_{state}^{(j)}(s_n, a_n)$$
(7)

where N is the total number of fuzzy variables.

For the four exemplary fuzzy variables we have the Q-function for j-th SU, namely

$$Q_{state}^{(j)} \leftarrow Q_{state}^{(j)}(s, a)$$
$$+ \sum_{k=1}^{K} (\alpha_k^{(j)} \mu_{state}^{(j)}(current \ SINR^{(k)}) + \alpha_k^{(j)} \mu_{state}^{(j)}(required \ SINR^{(k)}))$$
$$+ \sum_{l=1}^{L} (\alpha_l^{(j)} \mu_{state}^{(l)}(mobility^{(l)}) + \alpha_l^{(j)} \mu_{state}^{(l)}(distance^{(l)}))$$
(8)

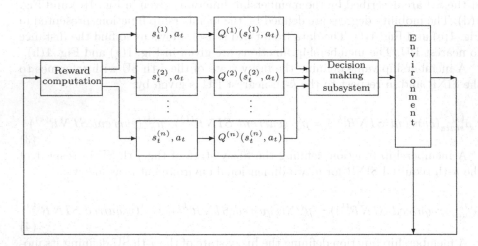

Fig. 2. A block diagram for an agent system architecture in the case of data mining

where $\alpha_n^{(j)}$ is the learning rate for SU j with respect to n-th fuzzy variable, K is the total number of SUs, L is the total number of PU.

Let the radio transmitting range of the SU be equal to R. Thus, we can again define the Q-function value as follows:

$$Q_{state}^{(j)}(s_{t+1}, a_{t+1}) \leftarrow \begin{cases} 0 & \text{if } j \notin \{J\} \\ Q_{state}^{(j)}(s_t, a_t) + \alpha_{state}^{(j)}(s_t, a_t) & \text{if } j \in \{J_{0<r\leq0.5R}\} \\ Q_{state}^{(j)}(s_t, a_t) + \beta^{(j)} Q_{state}^{(j)}(s_t, a_t) & \text{if } j \in \{J_{0.5R<r\leq R}\} \end{cases}$$

$$(9)$$

where $\{J\}$ is the set of SUs and PUs in the range of the PU observation with the radius equal to R, $\{J_{0<r\leq0.5\cdot R}\}$ and $\{J_{0.5\cdot R<r\leq R}\}$ are the sets of SUs and PUs in the range of the SU observation with the radius equal to $0 < r \leq 0.5 \cdot R$ and $0.5 \cdot R < r \leq R$, respectively. $\beta^{(j)}$ are learning rate factors.

The state space in reinforcement learning can be treated as a stochastic problem. In the standard approach, we can generalise the Q-value across states using the function approximation $Q(s, a, f)$ for approximating $Q(s, a)$, where f is the set of all learned fuzzy logic mechanisms [2], [3]. To handle all the information, we can use the data mining approach.

Fig. 2 presents the system architecture used for the data mining process of a single SU station in the CR network. The data mining process referring to a single SU is given by the following procedure:

Procedure 1

1) The SU by use its sensors fixes the current values of all the membership functions. Further, it defines the actual value of state-action pair.

2) The SU computes the learning rate α, which for the j-th SU is given as follows:

$$\alpha^{(j)} = \frac{1}{\sum_{n=1}^{N} \mu_{state}^{(n)}} \tag{10}$$

where N is the total number of fuzzy variables. Above equation shows that by increase of the number of fuzzy variables the learning rate becomes smaller.

3) The SU computes the Q-function for each fuzzy parameter. We applied the selection procedure based on Kóczy-Hirot method presented a.o. by Joó [10]. This method computes a conclusion as a weighted sum of vague consequent values b_n, which is given by

$$C(b_h) = \frac{\sum_{h=1}^{H} w_h \cdot dist(y_0, b_h)}{\sum_{h=1}^{H} w_h} \tag{11}$$

where w_h is the weight inverse proportional to the vague distance of the observation x from action a. For the h-th rule the weight is defined as

$$w_h = \frac{1}{dist(x, a)} \tag{12}$$

5) After the choice of the action by the SU the reward function $r_t(s_t, a_t)$ is computed. Further, it upgrades the ΔQ_t and computes $Q_t(s_t, a_t)$.

6) The computation goes to step 1. ∎

The function Q is computed by the Q-learning algorithm; this algorithm was first introduced by Watkins [16], and Watkins and Dayan [17]. We recall that the Q-function is given by:

$$Q_t(s_t, a_t) = (1 - \alpha)Q_t(s_t, a_t) + \alpha(r_t + \gamma \max_{a_t \in A} Q_t(s_t', a_t')) \tag{13}$$

where A is the set of all the possible actions, α $(0 \leq \alpha < 1)$ and γ $(0 \leq \gamma \leq 1)$ denote the learning rate and the discount parameter, $Q_t(s_t', a_t')$ is the value of the Q function after the execution of action a_t'. Fig. 3 shows the raw form of the

---

initialization $t = 0$, $r_T = (s_t, a_t) = 0$;
for $\forall$ $s_t \in S$ **and** $a_t \in A$ **do**
    begin
        $t := t + 1$; *access the current state* s_t;
        $a_t \leftarrow$ *choose_action*(s_t, Q_t);
        perform_action a_t;
        compute: $r_t(s_t, a_t)$, s_{t+1};
        $\Delta Q_t \leftarrow (r_t + \gamma \max_{a_t}(Q_t(s_{t+1}, a_t))) - Q_t(s_t, a_t)$;
        $Q_t(s_t, a_t) \leftarrow (1 - \alpha)Q_t(s_t, a_t) + \alpha \Delta Q_t$;
    end;

Fig. 3. Q-learning algorithm estimates new state obtained by performing the chosen action at each time step

Q-learning algorithm. It can be seen that the Q-learning algorithm is an incremental reinforcement learning method. The choice of the action does not show how to obtain it. Therefore, the Q-learning algorithm can use other strategies that it learns, irrespective of the assumed strategy. This means that it does not need actions that would maximise the reward function.

4   Simulation Results

In this section, we give some simulation results of the proposed reinforcement method.

In our simulation, we used an arrangement of 20 SU transmitter and receiver pairs in an area equal 1 km × 1 km. We simulated 3000 samples of Rayleigh faded received signals for each pair. In order to evaluate transmission power control, the maximum power of the PU transmitter was equal to 30 dBm and maximum power of the SU transmitter was set to 20 dBm. We assumed two PU transmitters. The obtained transmit control power is obtained here as the difference of the observed SINR value at SU receiver and the required SINR. For the simulation, we generated 3000 randomly distributed Rayleigh faded signal samples for the PU transmitter.

12 rules have been defined for the decision system of each SU, namely:

Each rule was associated with a weight. The rules concerning the SINR values have a weight equal to 3. All rules concerned with SU mobility were assigned a weight of 2. The weight equal to 1 used only for the distance to the nearest PU. Initially, all the values of Q were the same and were equal to 0.5. The learning

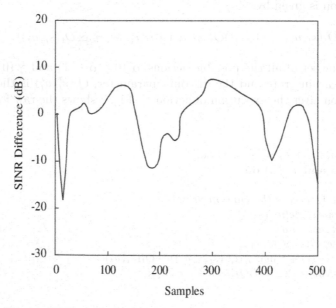

Fig. 4. SINR difference in dependence on number of samples

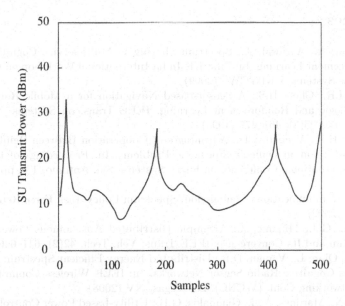

Fig. 5. SU transmit power in dependence on number of samples

rates are $\alpha = 0.1$ and $\beta = 0.06$. We assumed that the radio transmitting range of the SU was equal to 50 m.

Fig. 4 shows the obtained average difference between the required SINR and the measured SINR at the SU for 500 samples. We assumed that in the simulation, a Brownian-like mobility model is used.

Fig. 5 presents the obtained average transmit power at the transmitter of the SU. We can see that the SU power is reduced for the smaller value of frequency. It is caused by the lower degree of interferences from the other SU transmitters.

5   Conclusions

In this paper, we presented a fuzzy reinforcement learning for power control in CR networks. A learning scheme based on the Q-learning algorithm, which combines fuzzy sets for two-dimensional environments was developed for this model. The proposed model introduces a multidimensional membership function into the fuzzy logic system and provides a generalisation of the Q-value across states on the system. As a result, we achieved a power control method allowing us to obtain the required transmission rate by the secondary users. An example was presented to demonstrate the application of the proposed technique. Future research will focus on incorporating more system parameters, such as QoS provisioning transmission and energy consumption.

References

[1] Alsarhan, A., Agrawal, A.: Spectrum Sharing in Multi-service Cognitive Using Reinforcement Learning. In: First UK India International Workshop on Cognitive Wireless Systems, UKIWCWS (2009)

[2] Beon, H.R., Chen, H.S.: A Sensor-based Navigation for a Mobile Robot Using Fuzzy-Logic and Reinforcement Learning. IEEE Trans. on Systems, Man, and Cybernetics 25(3), 467–477 (1995)

[3] Berenji, H.R., Vengerov, D.: Advantages of Cooperation Between Reinforcement Learning Agent in Difficult Stochastic Problems. In: Proceedings of the Ninth IEEE International Conference on Fuzzy Systems, San Antonio, TX, pp. 871–876 (2000)

[4] Federal Communications Commission, Spectrum Policy Task Force Report, FCC 02 -155 (2002)

[5] Foschini, G.J., Miljanic, Z.: A Simple Distributed Autonomous Power Control Algorithm and Its Convergence. IEEE Trans. Veh. Tech. 42(2), 641–646 (1993)

[6] Gao, S., Qian, L., Vaman, D.R.: Distributed Energy Efficient Spectrum Access in Wireless Cognitive Radio Sensor Networks. In: IEEE Wireless Communications and Networking Conf. (WCNC), Las Vegas, NV (2008)

[7] Gatsis, N., Marques, A.G., Giannakis, G.B.: Utility-based Power Control for Peer-to-Peer Cognitive Radio Networks with Heterogeneous QoS Constraints. In: IEEE Int. Conf. on Acoustics, Speech and Signal Processing (ICASSP), Las Vegas, NV (2008)

[8] Haykin, S.: Cognitive Radio: Brain-empowered Wireless Communications. IEEE Journal on Selected Areas in Communications 23(2), 201–220 (2005)

[9] Hoang, A., Liang, Y.: Downlink Channel Assignment and Power Control for Cognitive Radio Networks. IEEE Trans. on Wireless Communications 7(8), 3106–3117 (2008)

[10] Joó, L., Kóczy, L.T., Tikk, D., Varlaki, P.: On a Stable Interpretation Method. In: Proceedings of the 7th International Fuzzy System Association World Congress, Prague, Czech Republic, pp. 133–137 (1997)

[11] Le, H.-S.T., Liang, Q.: An Efficient Power Control Scheme for Cognitive Radios. In: Proc. IEEE Wireless Communications and Networking Conference (WCNC), pp. 2559–2563 (2007)

[12] Le, H.-S.T., Ly, H.D.: Opportunistic Spectrum Access Using Fuzzy Logic for Cognitive Radio Networks. In: Proc. Second Int. Conf. on Electronics (ICCE), pp. 240–245 (2008)

[13] Matinmikko, M., Rauma, T., Mustonen, M., Harjula, I., Sarvanko, H., Mämmela, A.: Application of Fuzzy Logic to Cognitive Radio Systems. IEICE Trans. on Comm. E92-B(12), 3572–3580 (2009)

[14] Mitola III, J.: Cognitive Radio for Flexible Mobile Multimedia Conference, San Diego, CA, pp. 3–10 (1999)

[15] Wang, X., Zhu, Q.: Power Control for Cognitive Radio Base on Game Theory. In: Int. Conf. on Wireless Communications, China (2007)

[16] Watkins, C.J.C.H.: Learning from Delayed Rewards, Ph. D. thesis King's College, Cambridge (1989)

[17] Watkins, C.J.C.H., Dayan, P.: Technical Note: Q-learning. Machine Learning 8, 279–292 (1992)

On Multi-subjectivity in Linguistic Summarization of Relational Databases

Adam Niewiadomski and Izabela Superson

Institute of Information Technology, Lodz University of Technology
Adam.Niewiadomski@p.lodz.pl, 143104@edu.p.lodz.pl

Abstract. In this paper, we focus on one of the most powerful computing methods for natural-language-driven representation of data, i.e. on Yager's concept of a *linguistic summary of a relational database* (1982). In particular, we introduce an original extension of that concept: new forms of linguistic summaries. The new forms are named "Multi-Subject" linguistic summaries, because they can handle more than one table or more than one set of records/objects collected in a database, e.g. *More boys than girls play football well*. Thanks to that, the generated linguistic summaries – quasi-natural language sentences – are more interesting and human-oriented. Finally, they new method is applied to a computer system that generates natural language description of numeric data, that makes them possible to be clearly presented to an end-user.

Keywords: Multi-Subjectivity in relational databases, linguistic summaries of databases, Multi-Subject linguistic summaries, fuzzy sets.

1 Linguistic Summaries of Relational Databases: A Brief Overview on Ideas and Related Literature

More than thirty years ago, R. R. Yager proposed the idea of *a linguistic summary of a (relational) database* [1], e.g. *More than half of basketball players are very tall*. This simple concept appeared to be a direct answer to people's needs for quick and friendly receiving of large amounts of data and/or information. What is the most important, the idea does not refer to any of terse statistical method for aggregating data (the mean, variation, standard deviation, etc.) but on fuzzy models of natural language expressions. Even if these expressions are less precise than numbers, e.g. *more than half of objects* instead of 55.6% *of objects* or *a very tall boy* instead of 195 *cm-tall-boy*, they are commonly understood and provide knowledge on what the summarized data mean.

To be more precise, the concept of a linguistic summary is based on Zadeh's calculus of linguistically quantified propositions (statements) [2]. There are two basic forms of linguistic summaries (based on two forms of linguistically quantified propositions, respectively) presented in the literature [1, 3–7]:

$$Q \ P \ \text{are/have} \ S \ [T] \tag{1}$$

L. Rutkowski et al. (Eds.): ICAISC 2014, Part I, LNAI 8467, pp. 243–255, 2014.
© Springer International Publishing Switzerland 2014

e.g. *Many boys are tall* [0.83], and

$$Q \ P \text{ being } W \text{ are/have } S \ [T] \tag{2}$$

e.g. *Many boys who are teenagers, are tall* [0.63]. In both forms (1) and (2), Q is a *quantity in agreement*, e.g. *Many, More than 900*, represented by an aggregation operator, e.g. fuzzy quantifier or an OWA operator [8], P is the subject of the summary, e.g. men, cars, or any other objects described in the summarized database, and S is a *summarizer* – a linguistic expression for properties of the objects, represented by a fuzzy set. The W symbol, appearing only in form (2), is *a qualifier*, represented by a fuzzy set, that determines additional and/or specific properties of the objects that the summary deals with. $T \in [0,1]$ is *a degree of truth* and it determines how good (how informative, how true) the summary is; values of T are evaluated according to the Zadeh calculus of linguistically quantified propositions and/or to another different methods of evaluating [5, 9].

Obviously, this paper is too short to present or even mention all methods and applications of linguistic summarization of relational databases, e.g. [10–12]. Moreover, we are not able to enumerate all the concepts for data summarization that are based on fuzzy sets but take into account assumptions different than the Yager originals, e.g. [13–16]. What is to be done here is to introduce a *Multi-Subject Linguistic Summary* of a relational database. That means that a summary contains more than one subject P_1, e.g. P_1 and P_2, and models of imprecise linguistic expressions (summarizers, quantifiers, etc.) are built using fuzzy sets.

Hence, the rest of the paper is organized as follows: in Section 3, the new concept called a *Multi-Subject Linguistic Summary* of a relational database is presented. We intend to construct and evaluate summaries related to more than one subject P that is represented by tuples in the summarized database $\mathbb{D}$, e.g. to P_1 *and* P_2 or to P_1 *in comparison to* P_2. These two or more subjects are represented by non-fuzzy sets of tuples collected in separated tables in $\mathbb{D}$, or can be, if necessary, results of some other selecting, querying and/or filtering tuples, with respect to chosen values and/or attributes, e.g. male and female. Obviously, these general explanations are explained in details and exemplified in Section 3.

Section 4 contains a brief description of the experiment (developing and exploring software) that helped us to present, determine and evaluate usefulness and performance of Multi-Subject Linguistic Summaries of relational databases. We show sample outputs of the program produced for a chosen database, and how users (intermediate and advanced) may affect on summaries that are generated by the software.

Finally, there are conclusions on the usefulness of the concepts and the methods presented, drawn in Section 5.

2   Multi-subjectivity in Relational Databases: New Possibilities of Data Linguistic Summarization

We refer to the traditional model of relational databases by Codd [17]. We assume that a database consists of tables being sets of tuples (usually called "records"), and one tuple is a representation of one real object (a child, person, car, trans-action, etc.). Table $\mathbb{D}$ consists of tuples d_i, $i = 1, 2, \ldots, m$, and $m \in \mathbb{N}$ is the number of tuples in $\mathbb{D}$. Each tuple d_i consists of $n \in \mathbb{N}$ values of attributes $V_1, \ldots, V_n$ and the domains of the attributes are $\mathbb{X}_1, \ldots, \mathbb{X}_n$, respectively. The values of attributes express properties of objects, e.g. height, salary, price, date, etc. and they are treated as "columns" of the table. The value of attribute V_j for object y_i, is denoted as $V_j(y_i) \in \mathbb{X}_j$, $i \in \{1, 2, \ldots, m\}$, $j \in \{1, 2, \ldots, n\}$. Hence, the database D collecting information on elements from $\mathbb{Y} = \{y_1, \ldots, y_m\}$ is in the form of:

$$\mathbb{D} = [d_1, d_2, \ldots, d_m]^T \tag{3}$$

where $d_i = \langle V_1(y_i), V_2(y_i), \ldots, V_n(y_i) \rangle$.

It is important to note here that objects $\{y_1, \ldots, y_m\}$ from set $\mathbb{Y}$ are the subject of a linguistic summary, see (1) and (2). The introduced concept of a multi-subject linguistic summary is based on **possible splitting set $\mathbb{Y}$ into two or more subsets** but elements in these subsets are still described by the same attributes (columns). So it is possible to make comparisons between subjects on the base of linguistically expressed values of other attributes, e.g. splitting set "children into subsets "boys" and "girls" makes it possible to compare height or weight for these two subjects.

The process of "splitting" dataset into two or more subsets representing se-lected subjects is described as follows:

FOR $i := 1$ TO m

1. Select attribute V_j, $j = 1, 2, \ldots, n$ in $\mathbb{D}$. This attribute determines whether a given object is a member of one of subjects that are to be distinguished.
2. Get object y_i
3. Get $V_j(y_i)$ and add object y_i to the corresponding subset.

A sample database $\mathbb{D}$ in the form of (3) is shown in Table 1. It is a part of a larger database, then summarized in the example presented in Section 4. The table illustrates the possibility of extracting two sets of subjects for multi-subject summaries; in this case, it is attribute "Gender" and its two values: "boy" and "girl", that allow us to "split" the set of data into two subsets, exemplified by Table 2 and Table 3, respectively:

It must be underlined that Table 2 and 3 do not represent real database ta-bles stored separately in a database management system; such a storage could be inefficient and non-optimal, especially, with respect to normal forms of re-lational database tables, popular optimisation criteria for databases. The pre-sented tables are only results of filtering operations performed on $\mathbb{D}$ (represented by Table 1) with respect to values of a chosen attribute, here: "Gender", for both "boys" and "girls" values.

What is crucial for the main idea of the paper, i.e. for multi-subject linguistic summaries, is that **(at least) two separated sets of objects**, previously stored as one set in $\mathbb{D}$, are now distinguished. These sets represent **different subjects** P_1, P_2, **... of multi-subject linguistic summaries** that are now presented in Section 3.

Table 1. A sample database $\mathbb{D}$ collecting information on children in school age

ID	Gender	Age	Height
1.	girl	7	130
2.	boy	8	120
3.	boy	13	150
4.	girl	8	140
5.	girl	18	160

Table 2. The part of dataset $\mathbb{D}$ presented in Table 1, filtered for attribute "Gender"="boy"

ID	Gender	Age	Height
2.	boy	8	120
3.	boy	13	150

Table 3. The part of dataset $\mathbb{D}$ presented in Table 1, filtered for attribute "Gender"="girl"

ID	Gender	Age	Height
1.	girl	7	130
4.	girl	8	140
5.	girl	18	160

3   New Forms of Summaries: Multi-subject Linguistic Summaries

Note that none of the older forms of linguistic summaries, i.e. (1) and (2), is able to represent the relations or associations between different groups of objects and/or their properties, e.g. between boys and girls in relation to their height, age, etc. For those non-multi-subject methods, the only opportunity is to generate summaries that includes the pre-selected set of objects, e.g. boys or girls, as qualifier W, see (2), e.g. *About half of BOYS are tall*, where *BOYS* is a qualifier.

On the other hand, these relations can be easily discovered and expressed in an interesting way using multi-subject linguistic summaries. Four forms of expressions that are linked to more than one subject (in the sense of "subset of objects/records/tuples") are now presented.

3.1   The First form of a Multi-subject Linguistic Summary

The first form of a multi-subject linguistic summary is proposed:

$$Q \; P_1 \; relatively \; to \; P_2 \; are \; S_1[T] \tag{4}$$

where Q is a fuzzy quantifier, P_1 and P_2 are the subjects of the summary and S_1 is a summarizer, represented by a fuzzy set. The degree of truth of summary (4) for is evaluated with formula (5):

$$T(Q\ P_1\ relatively\ to\ P_2\ are\ S_1) =$$

$$= \mu_Q \left(\frac{\frac{1}{M_{P_1}} \Sigma\text{-}count(S_{1_{P_1}})}{\frac{1}{M_{P_1}} \Sigma\text{-}count(S_{1_{P_1}}) + \frac{1}{M_{P_2}} \Sigma\text{-}count(S_{1_{P_2}})} \right) \tag{5}$$

where:

$$\Sigma\text{-}count(S_{1_{P_1}}) = \sum_{i=1}^{m} \{u_{S_1}(d_i) : d_i \in^* P_1\} \tag{6}$$

and $\Sigma\text{-}count(S_{1_{P_2}})$ – analogously. The notation $d_i \in^* P_1$ means that d_i is a tuple representing P_1 subject. M_{P_1} and M_{P_2} are numbers of tuples representing subjects P_1 and P_2, respectively:

$$M_{P_1} = \sum_{i=1}^{m} t_{i_{P_1}} \tag{7}$$

where:

$$t_{i_{P_1}} = \begin{cases} 1, & \text{if } d_i \in^* P_1 \\ 0, & \text{otherwise} \end{cases} \tag{8}$$

For instance:

$$t_{i_{\text{boys}}} = \begin{cases} 1, & \text{if } V_j(d_i) = "boy" \\ 0, & \text{if } V_j(d_i) = "girls" \end{cases} \tag{9}$$

and $V_j = Gender$.

An example of a summary in the form of (4) is now given:

$$\textit{Most of boys relatively to girls are tall} \ [0.456] \tag{10}$$

where $Q = most\ of$, $P_1 = boys$, $P_2 = girls$, $S_1 = tall$.

3.2 The Second Form of a Multi-subject Linguistic Summary

The second form of a multi-subject summary proposed here is given:

$$Q\ P_1\ relatively\ to\ P_2\ being\ S_2\ are\ S_1[T] \tag{11}$$

where S_2 is a qualifier, cf. (2). The degree of truth of the summary is evaluated via formula (12):

$$T(Q\ P_1\ relatively\ to\ P_2\ being\ S_2\ are\ S_1) =$$

$$= \mu_Q \left(\frac{\frac{1}{M_{P_1}} \Sigma\text{-}count(S_{1_{P_1}} \cap S_{2_{P_1}})}{\frac{1}{M_{P_1}} \Sigma\text{-}count(S_{1_{P_1}} \cap S_{2_{P_1}}) + \frac{1}{M_{P_2}} \Sigma\text{-}count(S_{1_{P_2}} \cap S_{2_{P_2}})} \right) \tag{12}$$

where Q is a relative quantifier, P_1 and P_2 are the subjects of the summary, S_2 is a qualifier related to both P_1 and P_2 subjects, S_1 is a summarizer,

$$\Sigma\text{-}count(S_{1_{P_1}} \cap S_{2_{P_1}}) =$$

$$= \sum_{i=1}^{m} \min\{\mu_{S_1}(d_i), \mu_{S_2}(d_i)\}, \ d_i \in^* P_1 \tag{13}$$

and $\Sigma\text{-}count(S_{2_{P_1}})$, $\Sigma\text{-}count(S_{2_{P_2}})$, $d_i \in^* P_1$ – analogously to (4).

An example of a summary in the form of (11) is now presented:

About two-third of boys relatively to girls being teenagers, are tall $[0.390]$ (14)

where Q =*about two-third*, P_1 =*boys*, P_2 =*girls*, S_1 =*tall*, S_2 =*teenagers*.

Summaries in form (11) allow us to retrieve information about selected subjects' features S_1, according to other subjects conditions (specific features that both subjects must posses). It means that in this case, the tuples taken into account represent boys and girls who are qualified by S_2 as teenagers.

3.3   The Third Form of a Multi-subject Linguistic Summary

The third form of a multi-subject linguistic summary is proposed as:

$$Q \ P_1 \ being \ S_2 \ relatively \ to \ P_2 \ are \ S_1[T] \tag{15}$$

and its degree of truth is evaluated with formula (16).

$$T(Q \ P_1 \ being \ S_2 \ relatively \ to \ P_2 \ is \ S_1) =$$

$$= \mu_{\widetilde{Q}} \left(\frac{\frac{1}{M_{P_1}} \Sigma\text{-}count(S_{1_{P_1}} \cap S_{2_{P_1}})}{\frac{1}{M_{P_1}} \Sigma\text{-}count(S_{1_{P_1}}) + \frac{1}{M_{P_2}} \Sigma\text{-}count(S_{1_{P_2}})} \right) \tag{16}$$

where Q is a relative quantifier, P_1 and P_2 are the subjects of the summary, S_2 is a qualifier referring only to subject P_1 and S_1 is a summarizer.

An example of such a summary is given (15):

About half of boys being teenagers relatively to girls, are tall $[0.256]$ (17)

where Q =*about half*, P_1 =*boys*, P_2 =*girls*, S_1 =*tall*, S_2 =*teenagers*.

Summaries in the form of (15) allows users to retrieve information on some selected features of subjects, according to chosen conditions given for subject P_1 only (i.e. some specific features that only subject P_1 must fulfill). It means that tuples taken into account by the summary represent both P_1 and P_2 subjects, i.e. boys and girls, but only P_1 is additionally qualified by S_2 (here: as teenagers).

3.4   The Fourth Form of a Multi-subject Linguistic Summary

The fourth form of a multi-subject summary is proposed:

$$More\ P_1\ than\ P_2\ are\ S_1[T] \tag{18}$$

This form does not involve any quantifier. The degree of truth of the summary is given by formula (19):

$$T(More\ P_1\ than\ P_2\ are\ S_1) = \frac{\Sigma\text{-}count(S_{1_{P_1}})}{\Sigma\text{-}count(S_{1_{P_1}}) + \Sigma\text{-}count(S_{1_{P_2}})} \tag{19}$$

where P_1 and P_2 are the subjects of the summary, M_{P_1} and M_{P_2} are the numbers of tuples representing subjects P_1 and P_2, $d_{i_{P_1}} : d_i \in^* P_1 \wedge d_{i_{P_2}} : d_i \in^* P_2$.

An example of such a summary is given:

$$More\ boys\ than\ girls\ are\ tall\ [0.756] \tag{20}$$

where $P_1 =boys$, $P_2 =girls$ and $S_1 =tall$.

Summaries in the form of (18) allow users to compare two different subjects without using any additional measures or fuzzy models, e.g. quantifiers. This method is useful for generating simple, quick and very intuitive summaries.

3.5   A Note on Differences between Multi-subject Forms and Classic Forms of Linguistic Summaries

Note that none of the older forms of linguistic summaries, i.e. (1) and (2), is able to represent the relations between different groups of objects and their properties, e.g. boys and girls, and their height, age, etc. On the other hand, these relations can be easily discovered and expressed in an interesting way using multi-subject linguistic summaries. For older, non-multi-subject methods, the only opportunity is to generate summaries that includes the pre-selected set of objects, e.g. boys or girls, as qualifier W, see (2), e.g. *About half of BOYS are tall*, where *BOYS* is a qualifier.

Now, in Section 4, we show results of an experiment: a database containing information on children medical examination is summarized using newly proposed forms of linguistic summaries. The results are finally related to those obtained via non-multi-subject forms, cf. (1) and (2) summaries.

4   Describing and Summarizing Databases Linguistically via Multi-subject Summaries: An Application Example

4.1   Goals and Methods of the Application

The application created for testing purposes is based on the Java 1.7 SE Platform. The database used in the experiment contains data of children in the age of 7 up to 18 years old. The data describes e.g. children height, mass, date of birth,

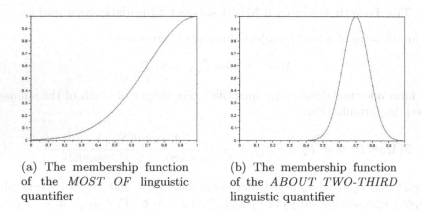

(a) The membership function of the *MOST OF* linguistic quantifier

(b) The membership function of the *ABOUT TWO-THIRD* linguistic quantifier

Fig. 1. Fuzzy sets representing selected quantifiers

living conditions such as number of rooms in flat, number of people in family, family financial situation, etc. The database contain data on 13 956 children, including 6 991 boys and 6 965 girls.

In the experiment, generated summaries are assumed to discover how children's age and gender is related to their height. Two subjects taken into account in multi-subject summaries are boys and girls. The process of logical splitting the database into two separated sets of data describing boys and girls, respectively, is exemplified by Table 1, 2 and 3, on Page 246). The relative quantifiers are used in the experiment called *most of, about two-third* and *about half* to represent the quantities in agreement for selected subjects, and to evaluate degrees of truth of the multi-subject summaries. The proposed membership functions for the quantifiers *most of* and *about two-third* are presented in Figure 1a and 1b.

The generated summaries are based on qualifiers and summarizers represented by fuzzy sets. Sample summarizers and qualifiers are:

- tall (height)
- short (height)
- in early school age (age)
- teenager (age)

The label *tall* is represented by fuzzy set $TALL$

$$TALL = \{\langle x, \mu_{TALL}(x) \rangle : x \in [150, 195], \mu_{TALL}(x) \in [0, 1]\} \qquad (21)$$

where

$$\mu_{TALL}(x) = \begin{cases} \frac{2(x-150)}{45}, & \text{if } 150 \leq x \leq \frac{150+195}{2} \\ \frac{2(195-x)}{45}, & \text{if } \frac{150+195}{2} \leq x \leq 195 \\ 0, & \text{if } x \leq 150 \text{ or } x \geq 195 \end{cases} \qquad (22)$$

the label *short* is represented by fuzzy set

$$SHORT = \{\langle x, \mu_{SHORT}(x) \rangle : x \in [103, 150], \mu_{SHORT}(x) \in [0, 1]\} \qquad (23)$$

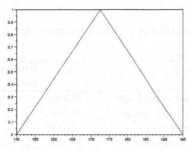

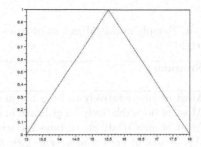

(a) The membership function of the *TALL* fuzzy set

(b) The membership function of the *TEENAGE* fuzzy set

Fig. 2. Fuzzy sets representing selected summarizers

where

$$\mu_{SHORT}(x) = \begin{cases} \frac{2(x-103)}{47}, & \text{if } 103 \leq x \leq \frac{103+150}{2} \\ \frac{2(150-x)}{47}, & \text{if } \frac{103+150}{2} \leq x \leq 150 \\ 0, & \text{if } x \leq 103 \text{ or } x \geq 150 \end{cases} \tag{24}$$

Analogously, the label *teenage* is represented by fuzzy set

$$TEENAGE = \{\langle x, \mu_{TEENAGE}(x)\rangle : x \in [13, 18], \mu_{TEENAGE}(x) \in [0, 1]\} \tag{25}$$

where

$$\mu_{TEENAGE}(x) = \begin{cases} \frac{2(x-13)}{5}, & \text{if } 13 \leq x \leq \frac{13+18}{2} \\ \frac{2(18-x)}{5}, & \text{if } \frac{13+18}{2} \leq x \leq 18 \\ 0, & \text{if } x \leq 13 \text{ or } x \geq 18 \end{cases} \tag{26}$$

and the label *early school age* is represented by fuzzy set

$$EARLY\ SCHOOL\ AGE =$$
$$\{\langle x, \mu_{EARLY\ SCHOOL\ AGE}(x)\rangle : x \in [7, 12], \mu_{EARLY\ SCHOOL\ AGE}(x) \in [0, 1]\} \tag{27}$$

where

$$\mu_{EARLY\ SCHOOL\ AGE}(x) = \begin{cases} \frac{2(x-7)}{5}, & \text{if } 7 \leq x \leq \frac{7+12}{2} \\ \frac{2(12-x)}{5}, & \text{if } \frac{7+12}{2} \leq x \leq 12 \\ 0, & \text{if } x \leq 7 \text{ or } x \geq 12 \end{cases} \tag{28}$$

The plots of the membership functions of fuzzy sets *TALL* and *TEENAGE* are presented in Figure 2a and 2b.

4.2   Results and Their Interpretation

The output of the experimental software, i.e. the generated summaries, are collected in Table 4. For each summary, the evaluated degree of truth (column T)

Table 4. Sample multi-subject summaries illustrating relations between children age and height

No. Summary	$[T]$	Summary form
1. Most of girls relatively to boys are in early school age	0.495	
2. Most of boys relatively to girls are in early school age	0.505	
3. Most of girls relatively to boys are teenagers	0.511	
4. About half of boys relatively to girls are teenagers	0.994	(4)
5. Most of girls relatively to boys are tall	0.206	
6. Most of boys relatively to girls are tall	0.298	
7. Most of girls relatively to boys are short	0.249	
8. About two-thirds of boys relatively to girls are short	0.043	
9. Most of boys relatively to girls being in early school age, are tall	0.004	
10. Most of boys relatively to girls being teenagers, are tall	0.129	(11)
11. Most of girls relatively to boys being in early school age, are short	0.124	
12. About half of girls relatively to boys being teenagers, are short	0	
13. Most of girls being in early school age, relatively to boys are short	0.101	
14. Most of girls being teenagers, relatively to boys are short	0.004	(15)
15. Most of boys being teenagers, relatively to girls are tall	0.098	
16. About two-thirds of boys in early school age relatively to girls, are tall	0	
17. More boys than girls are tall	0.534	
18. More girls than boys are short	0.5	
19. More boys than girls are teenagers	0.49	(18)
20. More girls than boys are teenagers	0.510	
21. More boys than girls are in early school age	0.506	
22. About half of children are girls	1	
23. Most of children are in early school age	0.32	(1)
24. About two-thirds of boys are tall	0	
25. Most of boys being tall are teenagers	0.031	(2)

and the form of the summary (column "Summary form"), are provided. The "Summary form" refers to the number of equation in this paper, that means (4), (11), (15), (18) refer to the first, the second, the third and the fourth form of a multi-subject linguistic summary given in Section 3, respectively, and (1) and (2) refer to the older forms of linguistic summaries.

According to expert' opinion, the results are intuitively correct. The first eight summaries 1.-8. are constructed according to the first form of a multi-subject linguistic summary (4). Analysing their degrees of truth we can see that there is no disproportion between information on boys or girls, e.g. summaries 1. and 2. are of very similar degree of truth.

The next summaries, 9.-16., lead us to the conclusion that there are more tall girls than tall boys in early school age: e.g. summary 9. contains the opposite statement, i.e. boys relatively to girls in the early school age are tall, and it is of the very low degree of truth. The situation changes for teenagers: there are more tall teenager boys than teenager girls, summary 10. Also, it cannot be said that in comparison to boys, major part of teenager girls are short, because it would mean that there are many teenager girls from 103cm to 150cm height summary 10. (the reader must take into consideration that children in the dataset was from 103cm to 195cm tall, so in this circumstances, a short child is more or less between 103cm and 150cm tall).

Summaries from 17. to 20. confirm lack of substantial disproportion between number of tall boys and tall girls and teenager boys and teenager girls. There are not many more tall boys than tall girls, according to summaries 17. and 18 and there is only a few more teenager girls than teenagres boys, according to summaries 19. and 20.. Summary 21. confirms that there are more teenager girls (the number of early school aged boys is slightly bigger than early school aged girls).

Using the older forms of the linguistic summaries, i.e. (1) and (2), provides us with extensive information about the analysed dataset. Extending summarizations set from Table 4 with summaries in known forms, 22.-25., completes our knowledge on the summarized database. For example, information on proportions between boys and girls, amount of tall boys, tall girls, teenager boys, teenager girls, teenage boys which are tall, early school aged girl which are short, are provided. The dedicated algorithm can evaluate degrees of truth, select the best (the most informative) summaries and present tham in clear and intuitive forms, e.g. *About half of children are girls. Most of boys relatively to girls are all. About two-third of girls being in early school age, relatively to boys are tall.* The last conclusion shows in particular, that newly proposed multi-subject summaries of databases do not exclude the older forms, but can be used together with them, to extend and improve the process of extracting and representing knowledge from large datasets.

5   Conclusions

The goal of the research is to develop fuzzy-based methods that make it possible to describe provided data in as human-friendly manner as possible, preferably: with natural or quasi-natural language. In this paper, we present an original concept that extends the known methods of data linguistic summarization and representation: Multi-Subject Linguistic Summaries of relational databases. In particular, we put emphasis on new and more interesting forms of linguistic summaries, that were based on describing one subject P only, until now (for bibliographical references, see Section 1). The new forms of linguistic summaries are given by Equations (4), (11), (15), and (18), in Section 3. The details of evaluating degrees of truth of the new forms are presented in Section 3, too. From the point of view of an average user, the most important detail of the

Multi-Subject Linguistic Summaries is that the output of the proposed method remains texts/messages composed by a human. Sample application of Multi-Subject Linguistic Summaries to a system providing users with natural-language-information on a chosen set of data, is described in Section 4. We believe the proposals here introduced, i.e. describing more than one subject by a summary, may have potential to extend the summarization methods already known in the scientific literature.

References

1. Yager, R.R.: A new approach to the summarization of data. Information Sciences 28, 69–86 (1982)
2. Zadeh, L.A.: A computational approach to fuzzy quantifiers in natural languages. Computers and Maths with Applications 9, 149–184 (1983)
3. Yager, R.R., Ford, M., Canas, A.J.: An approach to the linguistic summarization of data. In: Proceedings of 3rd International Conference, Information Processing and Management of Uncertainty in Knowledge-Based System, Paris, France, pp. 456–468 (1990)
4. George, R., Srikanth, R.: Data summarization using genetic algorithms and fuzzy logic. In: Herrera, F., Verdegay, J.L. (eds.) Genetic Algorithms and Soft Computing, pp. 599–611. Physica–Verlag, Heidelberg (1996)
5. Kacprzyk, J., Yager, R.R.: Linguistic summaries of data using fuzzy logic. International Journal of General Systems 30, 133–154 (2001)
6. Kacprzyk, J., Yager, R.R., Zadrożny, S.: A fuzzy logic based approach to linguistic summaries of databases. International Journal of Applied Mathematics and Computer Sciences 10, 813–834 (2000)
7. Kacprzyk, J., Yager, R.R., Zadrożny, S.: Fuzzy linguistic summaries of databases for an efficient business data analysis and decision support. In: Abramowicz, W., Żurada, J. (eds.) Knowledge Discovery for Business Information Systems, pp. 129–152. Kluwer Academic Publisher, B. V., Boston (2001)
8. Yager, R.R.: On ordered weighted averaging operators in multicriteria decision making. IEEE Transactions on Systems, Man, and Cybernetics 18, 183–190 (1988)
9. Niewiadomski, A.: Six new informativeness indices of data linguistic summaries. In: Szczepaniak, P.S., Wgrzyn Wolska, K. (eds.) Advances in Intelligent Web Mastering, pp. 254–259. Springer (2007)
10. Kacprzyk, J., Zadrożny, S.: Flexible querying using fuzzy logic: An implementation for Microsoft Access. In: Andreasen, T., Christiansen, H., Larsen, H.L. (eds.) Flexible Query Answering System, pp. 247–275. Kluwer, Boston (1997)
11. Niewiadomski, A.: News Generating Via Fuzzy Summarization of Databases. In: Wiedermann, J., Tel, G., Pokorný, J., Bieliková, M., Štuller, J. (eds.) SOFSEM 2006. LNCS, vol. 3831, pp. 419–429. Springer, Heidelberg (2006)
12. Zadrożny, S.: Imprecise queries and linguistic summaries of databases. Academic Publishing House EXIT, Warsaw (2006) (in Polish)
13. Bosc, P., Pivert, O.: Fuzzy querying in conventional databases. In: Zadeh, L.A., Kacprzyk, J. (eds.) Fuzzy Logic for the Management of Uncertainty, pp. 645–671. Wiley, New York (1992)

14. Raschia, G., Mouaddib, N.: SAINTETIQ: a fuzzy set-based approach to database summarization. Fuzzy Sets and Systems 129, 137–162 (2002)
15. Rasmussen, D., Yager, R.R.: A fuzzy SQL summary language for data discovery. In: Dubois, D., Prade, H., Yager, R.R. (eds.) Fuzzy Information Engineering: A Guided Tour of Application's, pp. 253–264. Wiley, New York (1997)
16. Srikanth, R., Agrawal, R.: Mining quantitative association rules in large relational databases. In: The 1996 ACM SIGMOD International Conference on Management of Data, pp. 1–12 (1996)
17. Codd, E.F.: A relational model of data for large shared data banks. Communications of the ACM 13(6), 377–387 (1970)

The Learning of Neuro-Fuzzy Classifier with Fuzzy Rough Sets for Imprecise Datasets

Bartosz A. Nowak[1], Robert K. Nowicki[1], Janusz T. Starczewski[1], and Antonino Marvuglia[2]

[1] Institute of Computational Intelligence, Czestochowa University of Technology, Al. Armii Krajowej 36, 42-200 Czestochowa, Poland
{bartosz.nowak,robert.nowicki,janusz.starczewski}@iisi.pcz.pl
http://www.iisi.pcz.pl
[2] Public Research Centre Henri Tudor (CRPHT)
Resource Centre for Environmental Technologies (CRTE)
6A, avenue des Hauts-Fourneaux, L-4362 Esch-sur-Alzette, Luxembourg
antonino.marvuglia@tudor.lu
http://www.tudor.lu

Abstract. The paper concerns the architecture of a neuro-fuzzy classifier with fuzzy rough sets which has been developed to process imprecise data. A raw output of such system is an interval which has to be interpreted in terms of classification afterwards. To obtain a credible answer, the interval should be as narrow as possible; however, its width cannot be zero as long as input values are imprecise. In the paper, we discuss the determination of classifier parameters using the standard gradient learning technique. The effectiveness of the proposed method is confirmed by several simulation experiments.

Keywords: fuzzy systems, rough sets, rough-fuzzy hybrid systems, imprecise data, gradient learning.

1 Introduction

The fuzzy systems are frequently used for classification task, see eg. [23]. The imperfection of processed data is a problem in any real application. In general, data might be unavailable, imprezise and uncertain. Fuzzy systems can handle this problem since they comprise the fuzzifier before the fuzzy inference mechanism. Our aim is to apply a non-singleton fuzzification in order to enrich the structure of typical neuro-fuzzy systems, see eg. [16,26,28,45]. The motivation for this fuzzification arises in the rough sets theory by taking into account the imprecision of the measurements. The application of the non-singleton fuzzification affects the reduction of sensitivity to changes of input values.

In our approach, the fuzzification is a mapping from the input space to a fuzzy set. When we obtain, as a result of fuzzification, a fuzzy set A' defined on some set V rather than a membership grade at single point x, we mean the non-singleton fuzzification. Our approach regards the non-singleton fuzzification as the mapping to a generalized membership function $\mu_{A'}(v, \bar{v})$ in order to analyze the whole spectrum of fuzzified $\bar{v}$ values

L. Rutkowski et al. (Eds.): ICAISC 2014, Part I, LNAI 8467, pp. 256–266, 2014.

ahead of time of reasoning. A need of an a'priori knowledge about the imprecision of inputs is crucial to determine an adequate fuzzification of membership functions.

In this paper, we will extend the idea of fuzzification in two dimensions. Firstly, we generalize fuzzification of non-singleton types with the use of rough sets. Secondly, we equip neuro-fuzzy systems with genuine implications to achieve neuro-fuzzy classifiers.

Although, fuzzy sets [46] and the rough sets [21] are quite different techniques for representation of uncertain data, they can be used together in two known forms: of rough fuzzy sets [3,18,19,40], and of fuzzy rough sets [8,10,12,13,25,41].

We will make the extensive use of fuzzy rough sets defined as follows [4,5]. If Φ is a fuzzy partitioning of a universe U, fuzzy sets F_i are its partitions, and A is a fuzzy subset of U, i.e., $A \subseteq U$. The fuzzy rough set is defined as a pair $(\Phi_* A, \Phi^* A)$, where the set $\Phi_* A$ is a Φ–lower approximation of the fuzzy set A, and the set $\Phi^* A$ is its Φ–upper approximation. Then, membership functions of fuzzy sets $\Phi_* A$ and $\Phi^* A$ are defined as follows:

$$\mu_{\Phi^* A}(F_i) = \sup_{v \in U} \min\left(\mu_{F_i}(v), \mu_A(v)\right), \tag{1}$$

$$\mu_{\Phi_* A}(F_i) = \inf_{v \in U} \max\left(1 - \mu_{F_i}(v), \mu_A(v)\right). \tag{2}$$

Eqs. (1) and (2) describe the widest and narrowest fuzzy sets as a composition of fuzzification and a fuzzy antecedent set with respect to the marginal t-norm and conorm, i.e. min and max. Thus the first of these expressions is a particular case of non-singleton fuzzification applied to Mamdani fuzzy logic systems. Surprisingly, the second equation realizes the non-singleton fuzzification in logical-type fuzzy systems. Consequently, the fuzzy rough set can be viewed as an extension to non-singleton fuzzification. Actually, this approach may be considered as a new generation method for type-2 fuzzy sets in fuzzy logic systems [44].

2 Fuzzy Rough Systems

In [20], we proposed a method to embed non-singleton fuzzification into the antecedent part of a fuzzy logic system. Now, we can apply this result to the fuzzy rough approximation of an antecedent fuzzy set A^k by assuming that the fuzzy partitioning Φ is determined by imprecision of input data. This imprecision may be induced by a non-singleton fuzzification, such that a premise fuzzy set A' plays a role of a fuzzy partition set F_i in the definition of the fuzzy rough set given by (1) and (2).

The shape of the membership function of A' is known a priori depending on the fuzzification method. Emphasizing that A' is also an explicit function of $\bar{v}$, we can involve the information about fuzzification by substituting Φ–upper and Φ–lower approximations of A^k, denoted by A^{*k} and A^k_*, for a conventional compatibility between a fuzzy premise A' and a fuzzy antecedent A^k, i.e.,

$$\mu_{A^{*k}}(\bar{\mathbf{v}}) = \sup_{\mathbf{v} \in \mathbf{V}} \min\left(\mu_{A'}(\mathbf{v}, \bar{\mathbf{v}}), \mu_{A^k}(\mathbf{v})\right). \tag{3}$$

$$\mu_{A^k_*}(\bar{\mathbf{v}}) = \inf_{\mathbf{v} \in \mathbf{V}} \max\left(1 - \mu_{A'}(\mathbf{v}, \bar{\mathbf{v}}), \mu_{A^k}(\mathbf{v})\right). \tag{4}$$

Consequently, the upper approximation together with the lower approximation may be regarded as an extension of the conventional non-singleton fuzzification in conjunction-type (Mamdani) fuzzy systems.

Let us assume that $\bar{\mathbf{v}}$ is independent of $\mathbf{v}$. In order to find all the supreme minima in equation (3), we have to vary $\mu_{A'}(\mathbf{v}, \bar{\mathbf{v}})$ in the whole spectrum of possible $\bar{\mathbf{v}}$ values. For each $\bar{\mathbf{v}}$, an upper fuzzy rough grade is produced. Similarly, in order to find all the lowest maxima in equation (4), we have to vary the fuzzy complement of $\mu_{A'}(\mathbf{v}, \bar{\mathbf{v}})$ in the whole spectrum of possible $\bar{\mathbf{v}}$ values.

Gaussian Fuzzification of Gaussian Antecedents. Suppose we have two Gaussian membership functions, $\mu_{A'_i}$ and $\mu_{A_{k,i}}$, and assume an aggregating t-norm to be the algebraic product. The antecedent membership function embedding Gaussian fuzzification by $\mu_{A'_i}(\mathbf{v})$ can be evaluated as follows:

$$
\begin{aligned}
\mu_{\tilde{A}_k}(\bar{v}_i) &= \sup_{v_i \in V_i} \left(\mu_{A'_i}(\bar{v}_i, v_i) \mu_{A_{k,i}}(v_i) \right) \\
&= \sup_{v_i \in V_i} \left(\exp\left(-\frac{1}{2}\left(\frac{v_i - \bar{v}_i}{\sigma_i}\right)^2\right) \exp\left(-\frac{1}{2}\left(\frac{v_i - c_{k,i}}{\sigma_{k,i}}\right)^2\right) \right) \\
&= \sup_{v_i \in V_i} \exp\left(-\frac{1}{2}\left(\frac{v_i - \bar{v}_i}{\sigma_i}\right)^2 - \frac{1}{2}\left(\frac{v_i - c_{k,i}}{\sigma_{k,i}}\right)^2\right),
\end{aligned}
\tag{5}
$$

where $c_{k,i}, \sigma_{k,i}$ are center and spread of Gaussian-type fuzzy set in antecedent of k-th rule and i-th input, σ_i defines imprecision of i-th input.

Using differentiation, $\mu_{A'_i}(v_i, \bar{v}_i)\mu_{A_{k,i}}(v_i)$ attains its supremum at

$$
v^*_{k,i} = \frac{(\sigma_i)^2 c_{k,i} + (\sigma_{k,i})^2 \bar{v}_i}{(\sigma_i)^2 + (\sigma_{k,i})^2}.
\tag{6}
$$

We obtain the following membership function which remains Gaussian, i.e.,

$$
\mu_{\tilde{A}_i}(\bar{v}_i) = \exp\left(-\frac{1}{2}\left(\frac{\bar{v}_i - c_{k,i}}{\tilde{\sigma}_{k,i}}\right)^2\right),
\tag{7}
$$

where

$$
\tilde{\sigma}_{k,i} = \sqrt{(\sigma_i)^2 + (\sigma_{k,i})^2}.
\tag{8}
$$

The lower membership function then can be approximated by two pieces of Gaussian functions interpolated at points $(c_{k,i} - \tilde{\sigma}_{k,i}, c_{k,i}, c_{k,i} + \tilde{\sigma}_{k,i})$, i.e.,

$$
\mu_{\underset{\sim}{A}_k}(\bar{v}_i) =
\begin{cases}
\exp\left(-\frac{1}{2}\left(\frac{v_i - \mathcal{M}_{k,i}}{\tilde{\sigma}_{k,i}}\right)^2\right) & \text{if } \bar{v}_i < c_{k,i} \\
\exp\left(-\frac{1}{2}\left(\frac{v_i - \mathcal{N}_{k,i}}{\tilde{\sigma}_{k,i}}\right)^2\right) & \text{otherwise,}
\end{cases}
$$

where

$$\mathcal{M}_{k,i} = c_{k,i} + \tilde{\sigma}_{k,i} \sqrt{-2 \ln \left(1 - \frac{\frac{\sigma_i^2}{\sigma_{k,i}^2}}{\left(1 + \frac{\sigma_i^2}{\sigma_{k,i}^2}\right)^{\left(\frac{\sigma_{k,i}}{\sigma_i}\right)^2 + 1}} \right)}, \tag{9}$$

$$\mathcal{N}_{k,i} = c_{k,i} - \tilde{\sigma}_{k,i} \sqrt{-2 \ln \left(1 - \frac{\frac{\sigma_i^2}{\sigma_{k,i}^2}}{\left(1 + \frac{\sigma_i^2}{\sigma_{k,i}^2}\right)^{\left(\frac{\sigma_{k,i}}{\sigma_i}\right)^2 + 1}} \right)}. \tag{10}$$

2.1 Fuzzy Rough Classifier

The membership of an object x to a class ω_j (specified by the corresponding conse-quent) is fuzzy ($\bar{z}_j^k = \mu_{\omega_j}(x)$). Consequently, rules can be rewritten as

$$R^k: \text{IF } v_1 \text{ is } A_1^k \text{ AND } v_2 \text{ is } A_2^k \text{ AND} \dots$$
$$\dots \text{ AND } v_n \text{ is } A_n^k \text{ THEN } x \in \omega_1(\bar{z}_1^k), x \in \omega_2(\bar{z}_2^k), \dots \tag{11}$$
$$\dots, x \in \omega_m(\bar{z}_m^k),$$

where observations v_i of the object x are independent variables, $k = 1, \dots, N$ is the number of N rules, and $\bar{z}_j^k$ is the membership degree of the object x to the j–th class (ω_j) according to rule k.

An optimization procedure to obtain the maximum and minimum centroids for a rough (or interval-valued) fuzzy set on the assumption that crisp memberships of ob-jects to classes are given, i.e., the k-th rule consequent that object either belongs to the j-th class or not is binary, $\bar{z}_j^k \in \{0, 1\}$, was given in [18,19].

If we consider the neuro-fuzzy classifier defined by the equation

$$z_j = \frac{\sum_{\substack{k=1 \\ k: \bar{z}_j^k = 1}}^{N} \widetilde{A}^k}{\sum_{k=1}^{N} \widetilde{A}^k}, \tag{12}$$

where $\widetilde{A}^k$ is a rough approximation of a fuzzy set A^k given by its upper and lower approximations, A_*^k and A^{k*}, respectively, and the single-rule membership of object to the j-th class is binary

$$\bar{z}_j^k = \begin{cases} 1 & \text{if } \mathbf{x} \in \omega_j \\ 0 & \text{if } \mathbf{x} \notin \omega_j \end{cases} \tag{13}$$

for all rules $k = 1, \dots, N$ and all classes $\omega_j, j = 1, \dots, m$. Then, the lower and upper approximations of the membership of object $\mathbf{x}$ to class ω_j is given by

$$\bar{z}_{j*} = \frac{\sum_{\substack{k=1 \\ k: \bar{z}_j^k = 1}}^{N} \mu_{A_L^k}(\bar{\mathbf{v}})}{\sum_{k=1}^{N} \mu_{A_L^k}(\bar{\mathbf{v}})} \tag{14}$$

and

$$\overline{z}_j^* = \frac{\sum_{\substack{k=1 \\ k:\, \overline{z}_j^k=1}}^{N} \mu_{A_U^k}(\overline{\mathbf{v}})}{\sum_{k=1}^{N} \mu_{A_U^k}(\overline{\mathbf{v}})}, \tag{15}$$

where A_L^k and A_U^k are defined as follows

$$A_L^k = \begin{cases} A_*^k & \text{if } \overline{z}_j^k = 1 \\ A^{k*} & \text{if } \overline{z}_j^k = 0 \end{cases} \tag{16}$$

and

$$A_U^k = \begin{cases} A^{k*} & \text{if } \overline{z}_j^k = 1 \\ A_*^k & \text{if } \overline{z}_j^k = 0\,. \end{cases} \tag{17}$$

In the case of binary memberships of objects to classes, this result does not require any arrangement of $\overline{z}_j^k$ [18,44]. Having rough approximations, the upper A_{j*}^k and the lower A_j^{k*}, of a binary set $\overline{z}_j^k \in \{0,1\}$ representing the single-rule class membership (13), where k is the index for rules $k = 1,\ldots,N$ and j is the index for classes $j = 1,\ldots m$, the lower and upper approximations of the membership of an object to class ω_j is given by

$$\overline{z}_{j*} = \frac{\sum_{k=1}^{N} A_{j*}^k \overline{z}_j^k}{\sum_{k=1}^{N} A_{j*}^k \overline{z}_j^k + \sum_{k=1}^{N} A_j^{k*} \neg \overline{z}_j^k}, \tag{18}$$

$$\overline{z}_j^* = \frac{\sum_{k=1}^{N} A_j^{k*} \overline{z}_j^k}{\sum_{k=1}^{N} A_{j*}^k \neg \overline{z}_j^k + \sum_{k=1}^{N} A_j^{k*} \overline{z}_j^k}\,. \tag{19}$$

The resulting neuro-fuzzy rough classifier architecture is presented in Figure 1.

Interpretation of Defuzzified Values. Let $\overline{z}_{j*}$ be a lower membership grade of an object x to a class ω_j and $\overline{z}_j^*$ be its upper membership grade in the form of equations (14) and (15), respectively. In this case, we may fix two numbers (thresholds) z_{IN} and z_{OUT} such that $1 > z_{IN} \geq z_{OUT} > 0$. Consequently, the crisp decision can be made in the following way

$$\begin{cases} x \in \omega_j & \text{if } \overline{z}_{j*} \geq z_{IN} \text{ and } \overline{z}_j^* > z_{IN} \\ x \notin \omega_j & \text{if } \overline{z}_{j*} < z_{OUT} \text{ and } \overline{z}_j^* \leq z_{OUT} \\ \text{Perhaps } x \in \omega_j & \text{if } z_{IN} > \overline{z}_{j*} \geq z_{OUT} \text{ and } \overline{z}_j^* > z_{IN} \\ \text{Perhaps } x \notin \omega_j & \text{if } \overline{z}_{j*} < z_{OUT} \text{ and } z_{OUT} < \overline{z}_j^* \leq z_{IN} \\ \text{undefined} & \text{otherwise.} \end{cases} \tag{20}$$

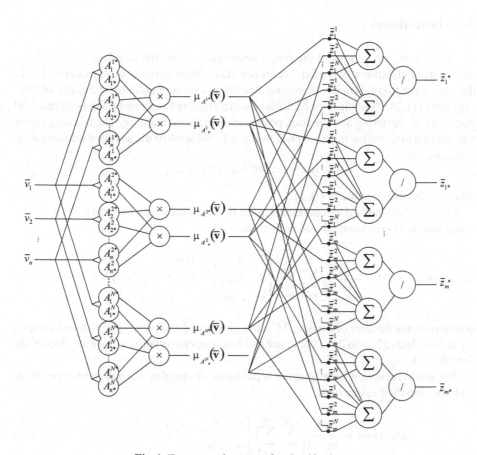

Fig. 1. Fuzzy rough system for classifcation

If we assume for convinience that $z_{\text{IN}} = z_{\text{OUT}} = \frac{1}{2}$, formula (20) takes the following form

$$
\begin{cases}
x \in \omega_j & \text{if } \overline{z}_{j*} \geq \frac{1}{2} \text{ and } \overline{z}_j^* > \frac{1}{2} \\
x \notin \omega_j & \text{if } \overline{z}_{j*} < \frac{1}{2} \text{ and } \overline{z}_j^* \leq \frac{1}{2} \\
\text{undefined} & \text{otherwise.}
\end{cases}
\tag{21}
$$

Potentially, other type reduction methods may be adapted [9].

3   Simulations

In simulations, we compared the rough neuro-fuzzy with the standard non-singleton neuro-fuzzy classifiers. We used 3 rules per class. Both systems were initialized with the use of the fuzzy c-means clustering algorithm, omitting potential existence of concept drift [11,24]. Samples, for each class, were clustered separately. We performed 50 iterations of clustering and the back propagation gradient learning. The learning factor was set to 0.001 and the momentum factor to 0.1. We applied the standard minimization criterion, i.e.,

$$
Q = 0.5 \left(z_d - \overline{z}^* \right)^2 + 0.5 \left(z_d - \overline{z}_* \right)^2,
\tag{22}
$$

where z_d is desired value in $\{0, 1\}$.

The proposed method was evaluated using two measures. The first one describes how often sample is misclassified into each class.

$$
\textit{misclassified} = 1 - \frac{1}{m * M} \sum_{s=1}^{M} \sum_{j=1}^{m}
\begin{cases}
1 & \text{if } \overline{z}_{s,j}^* > 0.5 \wedge \overline{z}_{s,j*} > 0.5 \wedge x_s \in \omega_j \\
1 & \text{if } \overline{z}_{s,j}^* < 0.5 \wedge \overline{z}_{s,j*} < 0.5 \wedge x_s \notin \omega_j \\
0 & \text{else,}
\end{cases}
\tag{23}
$$

where m is the number of classes, M is the number of samples, x_s is s-th test sample, ω_j is j-th class, $\overline{z}_{s,j}^*$ and $\overline{z}_{s,j*}$ are upper and lower approximation of membership of the sample x_s to ω_j.

The second criterion for evaluation is the mean of samples that was neither unclassified nor classified to any class,

$$
\textit{uncertain} = \frac{1}{m * M} \sum_{s=1}^{M} \sum_{j=1}^{m}
\begin{cases}
1 & \text{if } \overline{z}_{s,j}^* \leq 0.5 \wedge \overline{z}_{s,j*} \geq 0.5 \\
0 & \text{else.}
\end{cases}
\tag{24}
$$

The proposed solution was evaluated using different spreads for input values

$$
\sigma_i = \textit{spread\_of\_input\_values} * (v_{i,max} - v_{i,min}) * (2 \log(2))^{-0.5},
\tag{25}
$$

where $\textit{spread\_of\_input\_values}$ is a constant coefficient, $v_{i,max}, v_{i,min}$ are respectively maximal and minimal values of attribute v_i. It is worth to mention that $e^{-0.5 \left(\frac{1}{(2 \log(2)) - 0.5} \right)^2} = 0.5$.

Note that the rate of misclassification in most of cases is close or equal to 0. This is the advantage of our approach to derive a more reliable fuzzy classifier.

Table 1. Classification rates

data base	network	measure	spread of input values			
			0	1.25%	3.75%	12.5%
dermatology	NF	misclassified	0.001	0.004	0.004	0.005
	RNF	misclassified	0.001	0.000	0.000	0.000
		uncertain	0.000	0.326	0.617	10.000
glass (2 classes)	NF	misclassified	0.066	0.047	0.038	0.023
	RNF	misclassified	0.066	0.047	0.061	0.018
		uncertain	0.000	0.005	0.014	0.126
ionosphere	NF	misclassified	0.034	0.046	0.031	0.029
	RNF	misclassified	0.034	0.023	0.017	0.011
		uncertain	0.000	0.658	0.644	0.649
iris	NF	misclassified	0.004	0.004	0.009	0.013
	RNF	misclassified	0.004	0.004	0.004	0.000
		uncertain	0.000	0.000	0.027	0.284
optdigits	NF	misclassified	0.014	0.014	0.012	0.010
	RNF	misclassified	0.014	0.000	0.000	0.000
		uncertain	0.000	0.848	0.961	10.000
page-blocks	NF	misclassified	0.033	0.036	0.052	0.066
	RNF	misclassified	0.033	0.020	0.019	0.019
		uncertain	0.000	0.425	0.529	0.578
parkinsons	NF	misclassified	0.391	0.281	0.205	0.160
	RNF	misclassified	0.391	0.602	0.226	0.036
		uncertain	0.000	0.000	0.056	0.456
pendigits	NF	misclassified	0.004	0.004	0.005	0.006
	RNF	misclassified	0.004	0.003	0.002	0.004
		uncertain	0.000	0.025	0.032	0.143
PID	NF	misclassified	0.236	0.236	0.217	0.236
	RNF	misclassified	0.236	0.169	0.087	0.010
		uncertain	0.000	0.138	0.392	0.861
vowel	NF	misclassified	0.011	0.011	0.012	0.028
	RNF	misclassified	0.011	0.008	0.005	0.016
		uncertain	0.000	0.007	0.051	0.295
wisconsin	NF	misclassified	0.043	0.043	0.043	0.037
	RNF	misclassified	0.043	0.039	0.039	0.024
		uncertain	0.000	0.020	0.027	0.085

4   Conclusions

In the paper, the neuro-fuzzy classifier with rough sets has been used. For research purposes, input values were non-singleton, namely Gaussian type, which resulted in rough answer of the classifier. Obviously, other types of non-singleton fuzzy sets for inputs values can be used. In the other papers (eg. [17,18]) concerning this type of classifiers, the interval-type of input values were used for expression of missing values, and in [44] — the triangle type of fuzzy sets. In these results, the use of non-sigleton inputs in most of cases decreased the rate of improperly classified samples at the cost of uncertainty.

The effectiveness of our classifier can be probably increased with the use of methods reducing the base of rules. Presented simulations were performed using Neuro-fuzzy classifier with rough sets, Mamdani-type reasoning and CA defuzzification; however, similar tests can be directly performed for other types of networks, such as logical-type fuzzy systems [18,27], modular fuzzy logic systems [14,15,43], flexible fuzzy systems [1,2,33,37,39] or relational systems [42] or even systems with non-parametric defuzzification [7,29,36]. Moreover, nonparametric approaches to pattern classification has been presented in [6,30,34,35]. The proposed idea of learning can be adopted also to genetic and evolutionary algorithms [22]. They can also be applied as a source of initial rules as well as c-mean algorithm and decision trees [31,32,38].

Acknowledgments. The project was funded by the National Science Centre under decision number DEC-2012/05/B/ST6/03620.

References

1. Cpałka, K.: A new method for design and reduction of neuro-fuzzy classification systems. IEEE Transactions on Neural Networks 20(4), 701–714 (2009)
2. Cpałka, K., Rutkowski, L.: Flexible Takagi-Sugeno neuro-fuzzy structures for nonlinear approximation. WSEAS Transactions on Systems 4(9), 1450–1458 (2005)
3. Czogala, E., Roderer, H.: On the control of allpass components using conventional, fuzzy and rough fuzzy controllers. In: Proceedings of IEEE International Conference on Fuzzy Systems, International Joint Conference of the Fourth IEEE International Conference on Fuzzy Systems and the Second International Fuzzy Engineering Symposium, vol. 3, pp. 1405–1412 (1995)
4. Dubois, D., Prade, H.: Rough fuzzy sets and fuzzy rough sets. International Journal of General Systems 17(2-3), 191–209 (1990)
5. Dubois, D., Prade, H.: Putting rough sets and fuzzy sets together. In: Sowiski, R. (ed.) Intelligent Decision Support: Handbook of Applications and Advances of the Rough Sets Theory, pp. 203–232. Kluwer, Dordrecht (1992)
6. Greblicki, W., Rutkowski, L.: Density-free bayes risk consistency of nonparametric pattern recognition procedures. Proceedings of the IEEE 69(4), 482–483 (1981)
7. Greblicki, W., Rutkowska, D., Rutkowski, L.: An orthogonal series estimate of time-varying regression. Annals of the Institute of Statistical Mathematics 35(1), 215–228 (1983)
8. Greco, S., Inuiguchi, M., Słowiński, R.: Fuzzy rough sets and multiple-premise gradual decision rules. International Journal of Approximate Reasoning 41(2), 179–211 (2006)
9. Greenfield, S., Chiclana, F.: Type-reduction of the discretized interval type-2 fuzzy set: approaching the continuous case through progressively finer discretization. Journal of Artificial Intelligence and Soft Computing Research 1(3), 193 (2011)
10. Inuiguchi, M., Tanino, T.: New fuzzy rough sets based on certainty qualification. In: Pal, S.K., Polkowski, L., Skowron, A. (eds.) Rough-Neural Computing: Techniques for Computing with Words, pp. 277–296. Springer, Heidelberg (2004)
11. Jaworski, M., Duda, P., Pietruczuk, L.: On fuzzy clustering of data streams with concept drift. In: Rutkowski, L., Korytkowski, M., Scherer, R., Tadeusiewicz, R., Zadeh, L.A., Zurada, J.M. (eds.) ICAISC 2012, Part II. LNCS, vol. 7268, pp. 82–91. Springer, Heidelberg (2012)
12. Jensen, R., Shen, Q.: Semantics-preserving dimensionality reduction: rough and fuzzy-rough-based approaches. IEEE Transactions on Knowledge and Data Engineering 16, 1457–1471 (2004)

13. Jensen, R., Shen, Q.: Fuzzy-rough sets assisted attribute selection. IEEE Trans. Fuzzy Syst. 15(1), 73–89 (2007)
14. Korytkowski, M., Rutkowski, L., Scherer, R.: From ensemble of fuzzy classifiers to single fuzzy rule base classifier. In: Rutkowski, L., Tadeusiewicz, R., Zadeh, L.A., Zurada, J.M. (eds.) ICAISC 2008. LNCS (LNAI), vol. 5097, pp. 265–272. Springer, Heidelberg (2008)
15. Korytkowski, M., Scherer, R., Rutkowski, L.: On combining backpropagation with boosting. In: 2006 International Joint Conference on Neural Networks, IEEE World Congress on Computational Intelligence, Vancouver, BC, Canada, pp. 1274–1277 (2006)
16. Mouzouris, G.C., Mendel, J.M.: Nonsingleton fuzzy logic systems: theory and application. IEEE Transactions on Fuzzy Systems 5(1), 56–71 (1997)
17. Nowak, B.A., Nowicki, R.K.: Learning in rough-neuro-fuzzy system for data with missing values. In: Wyrzykowski, R., Dongarra, J., Karczewski, K., Waśniewski, J. (eds.) PPAM 2011, Part I. LNCS, vol. 7203, pp. 501–510. Springer, Heidelberg (2012)
18. Nowicki, R.: On combining neuro-fuzzy architectures with the rough set theory to solve classification problems with incomplete data. IEEE Trans. Knowl. Data Eng. 20(9), 1239–1253 (2008)
19. Nowicki, R.: Rough-neuro-fuzzy structures for classification with missing data. IEEE Trans. Syst., Man, Cybern. B 39 (2009)
20. Nowicki, R.K., Starczewski, J.T.: On non-singleton fuzzification with DCOG defuzzification. In: Rutkowski, L., Scherer, R., Tadeusiewicz, R., Zadeh, L.A., Zurada, J.M. (eds.) ICAISC 2010, Part I. LNCS (LNAI), vol. 6113, pp. 168–174. Springer, Heidelberg (2010)
21. Pawlak, Z.: Rough sets. International Journal of Computer and Information Science 11, 341–356 (1982)
22. Peteiro-Barral, D., Guijarro-Bardinas, B., Perez-Sanchez, B.: Learning from heterogeneously distributed data sets using artificial neural networks and genetic algorithms. Journal of Artificial Intelligence and Soft Computing Research 2(1), 5–20 (2012)
23. Pietruczuk, L., Duda, P., Jaworski, M.: A new fuzzy classifier for data streams. In: Rutkowski, L., Korytkowski, M., Scherer, R., Tadeusiewicz, R., Zadeh, L.A., Zurada, J.M. (eds.) ICAISC 2012, Part I. LNCS (LNAI), vol. 7267, pp. 318–324. Springer, Heidelberg (2012)
24. Pietruczuk, L., Duda, P., Jaworski, M.: Adaptation of decision trees for handling concept drift. In: Rutkowski, L., Korytkowski, M., Scherer, R., Tadeusiewicz, R., Zadeh, L.A., Zurada, J.M. (eds.) ICAISC 2013, Part I. LNCS (LNAI), vol. 7894, pp. 459–473. Springer, Heidelberg (2013)
25. Radzikowska, A.M., Kerre, E.E.: A comparative study of fuzzy rough sets. Fuzzy Sets and Systems 126, 137–155 (2002)
26. Rutkowska, D., Nowicki, R., Rutkowski, L.: Singleton and non-singleton fuzzy systems with nonparametric defuzzification. In: Strumillo, P., kaminski, W., Skrzypski, J. (eds.) Computational Intelligence and Application. STUDFUZZ, vol. 23, pp. 292–301. Springer, Heidelberg (1999)
27. Rutkowska, D., Nowicki, R.: Implication-based neuro–fuzzy architectures. International Journal of Applied Mathematics and Computer Science 10(4), 675–701 (2000)
28. Rutkowska, D., Rutkowski, L., Nowicki, R.: On processing of noisy data by fuzzy inference neural networks. In: Proceedings of the IASTED International Conference, Signal and Image Processing, Nassau, Bahamas, pp. 314–318 (October 1999)
29. Rutkowski, L.: A general approach for nonparametric fitting of functions and their derivatives with applications to linear circuits identification. IEEE Transactions on Circuits and Systems 33(8), 812–818 (1986)
30. Rutkowski, L.: Adaptive probabilistic neural networks for pattern classification in time-varying environment. IEEE Transactions on Neural Networks 15(4), 811–827 (2004)

31. Rutkowski, L., Jaworski, M., Pietruczuk, L., Duda, P.: Decision trees for mining data streams based on the gaussian approximation. IEEE Transactions on Knowledge and Data Engineering 26(1), 108–119 (2014)
32. Rutkowski, L., Pietruczuk, L., Duda, P., Jaworski, M.: Decision trees for mining data streams based on the mcdiarmid's bound. IEEE Transactions on Knowledge and Data Engineering 25(6), 1272–1279 (2013)
33. Rutkowski, L., Przybył, A., Cpałka, K.: Novel online speed profile generation for industrial machine tool based on flexible neuro-fuzzy approximation. IEEE Transactions on Industrial Electronics 59(2), 1238–1247 (2012)
34. Rutkowski, L.: On bayes risk consistent pattern recognition procedures in a quasi-stationary environment. IEEE Transactions on Pattern Analysis and Machine Intelligence PAMI-4(1), 84–87 (1982)
35. Rutkowski, L.: Sequential pattern recognition procedures derived from multiple fourier series. Pattern Recognition Letters 8(4), 213–216 (1988)
36. Rutkowski, L.: Non-parametric learning algorithms in time-varying environments. Signal Processing 18(2), 129–137 (1989)
37. Rutkowski, L., Cpałka, K.: Compromise approach to neuro-fuzzy systems. In: Sincak, P., Vascak, J., Kvasnicka, V., Pospichal, J. (eds.) Intelligent Technologies - Theory and Applications, vol. 76, pp. 85–90. IOS Press (2002)
38. Rutkowski, L., Jaworski, M., Pietruczuk, L., Duda, P.: The CART decision tree for mining data streams. Information Sciences 266, 1–15 (2014)
39. Rutkowski, L., Przybył, A., Cpałka, K., Er, M.J.: Online speed profile generation for industrial machine tool based on neuro-fuzzy approach. In: Rutkowski, L., Scherer, R., Tadeusiewicz, R., Zadeh, L.A., Zurada, J.M. (eds.) ICAISC 2010, Part II. LNCS (LNAI), vol. 6114, pp. 645–650. Springer, Heidelberg (2010)
40. Sarkar, M.: Rough fuzzy functions in classification. Fuzzy Sets and Systems 132(2), 353–369 (2002)
41. Sarkar, M., Yegnanarayana, B.: Rough fuzzy set theoretic approach to evaluate the importance of input features in classification. In: Proceedings of International Conference on Neural Networks — ICNN 1997, Texas, USA, June 9-12, pp. 1590–1595 (1997)
42. Scherer, R.: Neuro-fuzzy relational systems for nonlinear approximation and prediction. Nonlinear Analysis 71, e1420–e1425 (2009)
43. Scherer, R., Rutkowski, L.: Connectionist fuzzy relational systems. In: Hagamuge, S., Wang, L. (eds.) Computational Intelligence for Modelling and Control. SCI, vol. 2, pp. 35–47. Springer, Heidelberg (2005)
44. Starczewski, J.T.: Generalized uncertain fuzzy logic systems. In: Starczewski, J.T. (ed.) Advanced Concepts in Fuzzy Logic and Systems with Membership Uncertainty. STUDFUZZ, vol. 284, pp. 137–179. Springer, Heidelberg (2013)
45. Theodoridis, D.C., Boutalis, Y.S., Christodoulou, M.A.: Robustifying analysis of the direct adaptive control of unknown multivariable nonlinear systems based on a new neuro-fuzzy method. Journal of Artificial Intelligence and Soft Computing Research 1(1), 59–79 (2011)
46. Zadeh, L.: Fuzzy sets. Information and Control 8, 338–353 (1965)

Aggregation Operator for Ordered Fuzzy Numbers Concerning the Direction

Piotr Prokopowicz[1] and Samira Malek Mohamadi Golsefid[2]

[1] Institute of Mechanics and Applied Computer Science
Kazimierz Wielki University, Bydgoszcz, Poland
[2] Amirkabir University of Technology
Department of Industrial Engineering,Tehran, Iran
piotrekp@ukw.edu.pl
http://www.imis.ukw.edu.pl

Abstract. Ordered Fuzzy Numbers (OFN) were proposed about 10 years ago [7, 8] as a tool for the calculations of imprecise values represented by fuzzy numbers. Calculation methods based on this model shall retain properties of operations known from real numbers. In addition, in contrast to the classic operations on convex fuzzy numbers, making a series of operations in accordance with the OFN model is not doomed to greater and greater imprecision of the results.

Apart from good computational properties, OFNs also offer new possibilities for imprecise information processing by using fuzzy systems. [13, 14, 18] show examples of systems and the various proposals for methods based on the new model. There is a range of work [20, 21, 23], which focus on implications or inference operators. In the works [10, 23, 24, 29] various aspects of defuzzification were analyzed. Little attention has been paid to aggregation of premises of rules based on OFN so far. Therefore, the aim of this paper is to propose effective aggregation operator which will generate good results as well as being intuitively consistent with the idea of the new model. Moreover, the proposed solution maintains the expected properties of the aggregate functions [6, 16], it takes into account key idea of OFN the direction of components.

Keywords: aggregation operator, Ordered Fuzzy Numbers, direction in aggregation, fuzzy system with Ordered Fuzzy Numbers.

1 Introduction

The theory of fuzzy sets [1, 2] is one of the popular and useful tools for the processing of imprecise information. For example, it enables creating a precise description of the situation modeled linguistically by using the general and imprecise concepts. That may be due to the incomplete knowledge of the subject as well as inaccuracy of the obtained data. An important part of the effective use of such data is a tool for proper and intuitive representation. When inaccurate quantitative data are processed fuzzy numbers are used (usually convex fuzzy numbers). Unfortunately, common calculation mechanisms here are based

L. Rutkowski et al. (Eds.): ICAISC 2014, Part I, LNAI 8467, pp. 267–278, 2014.

on interval arithmetic and cause that the already small number of basic arithmetic operations can easily lead to a drastic increase of the imprecise of results. Therefore, its practical usefulness is lost.

The model of the Ordered Fuzzy Numbers is helpful here, as it introduces convenient and flexible computing mechanisms eliminating main calculations defect based on interval arithmetic. The new model takes into account the order of the characteristic parts of a fuzzy number (hence the name contains the word 'Ordered') giving the fuzzy number an additional feature - direction. Thanks to the consideration of order when performing operations, we get the opportunity to reduce the imprecision of the following operations. The new model has a number of properties that were presented in the publications [7, 15, 25].

2   Ordered Fuzzy Numbers (OFN)

In the series of papers [7, 8, 14, 15, 17–19] were introduced and developed main concepts of the idea of Ordered Fuzzy Numbers. Following these papers fuzzy number will be identified with the pair of functions defined on the interval [0, 1].

Definition 1. *The Ordered Fuzzy Number (OFN in short) A is an ordered pair of two continuous functions*

$$A = (f_A, g_A) \tag{1}$$

f_A and g_A are called the up-part and the down-part, respectively, both defined on the closed interval [0, 1] with values in R.

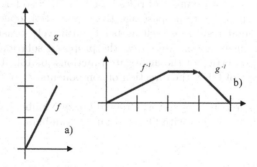

Fig. 1. a)Ordered Fuzzy Number from definition, b)Ordered Fuzzy Number as convex fuzzy number with an arrow

If the both functions f and g are monotonic (Fig.1a), they are also invertible and possess the corresponding inverse functions defined on a real axis with the values in [0, 1]. Now, if these two opposite functions are not connected, we linking them with constant function (with the value 1). In this case, we receive an object which directly represents the classical fuzzy number. For the finalization of transformation, we need to mark an order of f and g with an arrow on the graph (see Fig.1b). Notice that pairs (f,g) and (g,f) are the two different Ordered Fuzzy Numbers, unless $f = g$. They differ by their direction (or orientation). The interpretations for this direction and its relations with the real world problems are explained in the [17, 19]. It is worth to point out that a class of Ordered Fuzzy Numbers (OFNs) represents the whole class of convex fuzzy numbers with continuous membership functions (about classical convex fuzzy numbers see [3, 5, 12]). Calculations on Ordered Fuzzy Numbers were analyzed and discussed among others in the papers [11, 15, 25].

By adding direction to fuzzy numbers, the OFN model is slightly more general than convex fuzzy numbers. An example of practical interpretation of the new property is presented in [17, 19]. OFNs are considered there as the results of observation in time, and the elapsed time is the natural interpretation of direction, which is still independent from the value of membership degrees of the fuzzy number. Introducing direction, however, has also other consequences. A kind of discrepancy with the classical model of convex fuzzy numbers appears. To some extent it is natural, because OFNs are becoming a specific extension of the classical proposal and thus unprecedented elements appear - improper OFNs. This element has been commented in [7, 8, 25]. However, thanks to the new property, also new potential for the practical use of OFN appears. We get a new quality associated with the direction. The work [26, 27] present the practical use of orientation of OFN in modeling financial data, and [28] in modeling diversity of opinions in social networks.

3   Premise Part of Rule in the Fuzzy System

A popular and practical application of fuzzy set theory [1, 2] is rule-based fuzzy system. A special feature of this system is the form of rules defining the system, which can be described linguistically. This allows to describe the modeled values by the use of everyday imprecise language. However, the imprecise information processing using the fuzzy systems is not so intuitive. It is divided into several phases, that involve the use of specific operations. There are many publications such as [4, 9, 12] which discuss further how fuzzy systems work. In this study, only aggregation of premises of the rules is introduced which is directly related to the purpose of the study.

In the fuzzy systems *if-then* rules are often used, and a premise is as follows:

$$\textbf{IF } A_1 \text{ } is \text{ } P_1 \text{ } AND \text{ } A_2 \text{ } is \text{ } P_2 \text{ } AND \text{ } ... \text{ } AND \text{ } A_n \text{ } isP_n \text{ } \textbf{THEN}... \quad (2)$$

where A_i - fuzzy input, P_i - OFN from premise of rule, $i = 1..n$ - the number of input variables in the rule. The statement A_i *is* P_i means a fuzzy fact (sometimes also called a fuzzy proposition), to which the truth value resulting from the degree of compatibility of the two fuzzy sets should be assigned. The calculation of these values is the goal of the first phase of the fuzzy system - the so-called *fuzzification* (see more in [4, 9, 12]). The fuzzification of the popular *singleton* type is a trivial task, because the input data are treated as crisp values and then instead of A_i set we have a_i number, which is calculated as the value of membership function of set P_i - just $\mu_{P_i}(a_i)$. In the following discussion we assume that this level of compatibility of i-th elementary premise A_i is P_i, is denoted as S_i, and s_i is the argument of the i-th linguistic variable for which S_i is found. Indicatively, we can write it as

$$\mathbf{Truth}(A_i \text{ is } P_i) = S_i = \mu_{P_i}(a_i) \tag{3}$$

In case of premise part (2) which consists of a number of fuzzy facts, as a result of fuzzification phase we receive a number of truth values. The next step is their aggregation.

4   Basic Properties of Aggregations

Generally speaking, aggregation operation is used in situations where a number of data link to each other and we need to find a single value to represent all of them. There are specifications various application areas which need aggregation [16], such as, making decisions based on multiple criteria, or determining one result from a variety of peer evaluations. Another important area of application is the aggregation of rule premise in rule-based fuzzy system, where we have a lot of input variables. Aggregation operation is a function that converts a number of input data into a single value. Transformation depends on the chosen method, but it is expected that in the process of determination of the result all of the input data have been used in some way. Typically, aggregations where the number of the input data is greater than one are considered. Moreover, in order to be able to call the function an aggregation, it should have two elementary properties [6].

1. Boundary conditions. If all input data are minimal (or maximal), the result will also the minimal (maximal) value. In the case of aggregation of the fuzzy sets the interval $[0, 1]$ is used as range of values. That is, when all the arguments are equal to 1, the result of aggregation is equal to 1 and similarly for zeros. For aggregation A:

$$A(0, 0, ..., 0) = 0 \text{ and } A(1, 1, ..., 1) = 1 \tag{4}$$

2. Nondecreasing - function is nondecreasing against each input variable. This means that the growth of any of the input data cannot cause a decrease of the result of aggregation A.

$$\forall_{i=2..n} x_i \leq y_i \wedge (x_1, ..., x_n) \neq (y_1..., y_n) \Rightarrow A(x_1, ..., x_n) < A(y_1, ..., y_n) \tag{5}$$

Apart from these two elementary properties a number of other important properties such as continuity, symmetry (anonymity) and idempotency are pointed out [6, 16, 22].

Continuity means that a small change in one input argument implies small change of the result. In the context of engineering applications, continuity corresponds intuition which is related to the fact that a small error in the entry cannot cause a large error in the output.

Symmetry means the independence of result from the sequence of input data. This property is also called anonymity, because based on the output it is not possible to determine the values of input variables.

Idempotency means that if, for each independent input have the same value, the particular value will be the result of aggregation. It may be noted that the boundary conditions are really idempotency for the maximal and minimal values.

There are many different properties which can characterize an aggregation operator [6, 16, 22]. However, those above-mentioned are the most essential and desirable in practical applications.

5   Direction Parametrization in OFN

The key element of the new model of fuzzy numbers is the order between up-part and down-part, which is independent from the real numbers. This can be also called the direction or order. It is taken into account in the definitions of arithmetic operations and their extensions, which make the calculations flexible and unified and more importantly, their properties and relationships are consistent with calculations on real numbers [25]. Therefore, it seems natural that information processing methods based on OFNs also take into account the direction. In this publication aggregation operator of rule premises of a fuzzy system that meets this assumption will be proposed. To accomplish this, supporting structures facilitating the analysis and understanding of the problem will be useful.

5.1   Part Function

The PART function is a tool allowing to read the information about what part of OFN the considered argument belongs to.

Definition 2. *Let A is an OFN defined on the X. The $PART_A : X \rightarrow Y$ function is determined as follows:*

$$PART_A(x) = y \Leftrightarrow \mu_A(x) \in y, \tag{6}$$

where $x \in X$, $y \in Y = \{CONST_A, UP_A, DOWN_A, NONE_A\}$, $\mu_A(x)$ – membership function of OFN A, $CONST_A$ – a subset of X for which the membership function of A number takes the values of 1, UP_A – a subset of X for which the inverse of the up-part has values, $DOWN_A$ – a subset of X for which the inverse of the down-part has values, $NONE_A$ – a subset of X for which the membership function of A number is 0.

To illustrate the effect of $PART$ better, you can take a look at the drawing shown in figure 2, we have the following results: $PART(x_1) = DOWN$, $PART(x_2) = UP$, $PART(x_3) = CONST$, $PART(x_4) = UP$, $PART(x_5) = NONE$

Since fuzzy numbers are considered over the space (or subspace) of real numbers, the sets UP, CONST and DOWN can be treated as numerical intervals. Let's assume the following denotations of their boundaries:

$$UP = (s, 1^-) , \quad CONST = [1^-, 1^+) , \quad DOWN = [1^+, e). \tag{7}$$

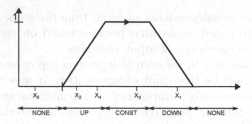

Fig. 2. Parts of the support of OFN

5.2   Direction Determinant

It is worth noting that the direction of the OFN is an additional property opposed to the classical fuzzy numbers and has a different meaning than the degree of membership. Thus, if we want to aggregate all the information contained in the OFN, a suggestion appears that the result of the aggregation should be something more than just a level of activation. Here, the new parameter to facilitate consideration of direction in information processing will be introduced. It is related to the support values of a given OFN and it is named the **direction determinant**. The purpose of this parameter is to represent a kind of order 'intensity' of the argument. It is also used as a tool to communicate the aggregated information about the order of individual components of premise part of rule. The direction determinant is connected with a particular OFN and is defined only for its support.

Definition 3. *Let A denote the OFN, and x is an element of the support.* **Proportional direction determinant** *of x in relation to A marked as dir_x^A is calculated as a the result of directional function $D : suppA \to (-1; 1)$ for the argument x in the following way:*

$$dir_x^A = D_A(x) = \begin{cases} 0 & : for \;\; PART(x) = CONST \\ \frac{(x-1^-)}{(1^--s)} & : for \;\; PART(x) = UP \\ \frac{(x-1^+)}{(e-1^+)} & : for \;\; PART(x) = DOWN \end{cases} \qquad (8)$$

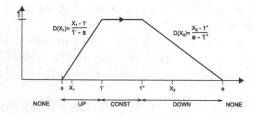

Fig. 3. Proportional direction determinant calculations

The above-mentioned determinant is called proportional, because it is calculated from the ratio of the position of support of the considered the argument in relation to the whole fuzzy boundary of OFN, to which this argument belongs. It is well illustrated on Fig.3. Such approach is justified in one of the useful interpretations of the order [17]. It can be considered as a direction of passing time. Then, the direction of a number depends on whether with the passage of time, the values were decreased or increased.

At the same time partial membership at the fuzzy boundaries is connected with determining the imprecise concept of "now". This imprecision usually is intuitively symmetrical, which means that our fuzzy "now" in the context includes as much time forward as backwards. Hence, in this regard, UP and $DOWN$ in the scale of time (independently of the arguments) are equal. Thus, there is reason for calculating the determinant of the element situated on UP or $DOWN$ to the proportion of the respective intervals and not only to the value.

It is worth noting that, if the degree of membership is equal to zero, the direction determinant is undefined, because the argument is not a part of function domain D (the value is outside the support OFN). It should also be noted that for the arguments in the $CONST$ interval, we have the direction determinant that is equal to zero, what is justified, as these are the values about which we have no doubt - their membership is full (equal to 1). According to this intuition we should also expect (and this is taken into account) that, the closer the arguments are to the kernel of fuzzy number, their direction 'intensity' (that is the direction determinant) is smaller.

5.3 Directed Aggregation Operator

In view of the previously adopted designations (8) we can now take a look at the definition of aggregation operator OFN, which we will call Directed Averaging Aggregation Operator - **DAAO**. The idea of averaging aggregation operator had already been used for classical fuzzy sets (for example see [4]). The new proposal, beside the level of activation, also generates the direction determinant dir.

Definition 4. *Let's assume the premise part of rule R is specified in (2).*

$$\textbf{IF } A_1 \text{ is } P_1 \textbf{ AND } A_2 \text{ is } P_2 \textbf{ AND } ... \textbf{ AND } A_n \text{ is} P_n \textbf{ THEN}... \qquad (9)$$

where A_i - fuzzy input data, P_i - OFN from premise rule, $i = 1..n$ - the number of input variables in the rule. Let's also assume that S_i denotes a degree of compatibility of the elementary premise A_i is P_i, while s_i denotes argument of the i-th linguistic variable for which a level of S_i compatibility was found. Calculation the **Directed Averaging Aggregation Operator** *proceeds as follows:*

1. *If any degree of compatibility is zero, the degree of activation of the rule is equal to zero. We consider this rule as inactivated, and the direction determinant is undefined.*

2. *Otherwise, the level of activation of the rule L_R is calculated as the arithmetic mean of degrees of compatibility for all basic premises (elementary) in the rule.*

$$L_R = \Sigma_{i=1}^n \frac{S_i}{n} \tag{10}$$

3. *In addition, the direction determinant dir_R is calculated as the arithmetic mean of the determinants D_P for the s_i – arguments of degrees of compatibility S_i for the rule premises.*

$$dir_R = \Sigma_{i=1}^n \frac{D_{P_{S_i}}(s_i)}{n} \tag{11}$$

The relationship between the S_i and s_i is as follows:

$$S_i = \mu_{P_i}(s_i) \tag{12}$$

where μ_{P_i} is a membership function of a fuzzy number P_i which is a model for the i-th elementary premise.

In the case where the fuzzification of a singleton type is applied, a degree of compatibility is calculated directly from the membership function. Then s_i is simply an input data for the i-th input variable.

The proposed aggregation operator for OFN generates a result with two components. For the calculation of each of them the arithmetic mean is used. Since the arithmetic mean is a function meeting the above-mentioned basic criteria of aggregation operators (see [6, 16, 22]), the Directed Averaging Aggregation Operator also meets them. However, we are dealing with two different parameters: the degree of membership and the direction determinant. Therefore, it is worth having a look at some important dependencies between them. The result of zero indicates that the activation is not moved in any direction. Note that this happens only in two cases:

1. when all degree of satisfaction of the premises will be equal to one, the degree of rule activation will be equal to one,
2. when the resultant of degrees of compatibility of components on the UP side will be precisely balanced with the resultant on the DOWN side, then degree of activation will be greater than zero, and less than one.

Let's take a closer look at the first case. The level of activation may be only equal to one when the determinant is equal to zero. This means that in the case of complete compatibility of premises the given data do not represent any direction. This is especially important if we want to combine the concept of OFN with the idea of classical fuzzy sets. Thanks to this the fundamental meaning of full membership (also the full non-membership) coincides in both solutions.

To illustrate the effect of aggregation operator better, let's take a look at a specific example. The Fig.4 shows two convex fuzzy numbers, which will be aggregated for the following values of their supports. For the calculations discretization of the arguments with the steps of 0.1 was used.

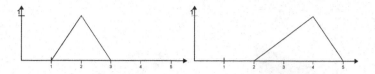

Fig. 4. Fuzzy numbers for the aggregation

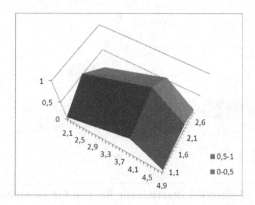

Fig. 5. Results of arithmetic mean aggregation

The fig.5 shows the result of the arithmetic mean as the degree of membership of aggregation operator.

If we want to analyze the operation of DAAO we need to replace numbers from Fig.4 with the OFNs. If the direction compatible with values of the argument axis we call "positive" and the opposite direction – "negative", then we have four possible options:

a) both numbers are directed positively,
b) both number are directed negatively,
c) first is directed positively, the other - negatively,
d) first is directed negatively, the other - positively.

Results of the aggregation of degree of membership for each of the above variants are identical to the results of convex fuzzy numbers as on Fig.5. The Fig.6 shows the results when we aggregate the direction determinant. As you can see, each has a different character, however, it is clear, that all results retain continuity and that they are nondecreasing.

6   Summary

OFNs have a good mechanism for implementation of the calculations, allowing the conversion of non-precision quantitative information in the same way as the calculations on the real numbers. With this freedom of computing, a number of new methods of processing imprecise information by using fuzzy system can be proposed. There is a number of works covering different aspects of imprecise information processing based on OFNs: inference operators, accumulation

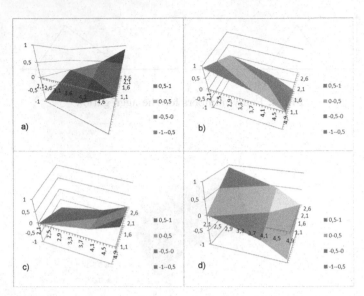

Fig. 6. Aggregation of direction determinant for two OFNs a)both positive, b)both negative, c)positive-negative d)negative positive

of results of rules, and defuzzification. These include methods which take into account the direction and also which ignore it. In this publication, aggregation operator for OFN is proposed. An important element is the consideration of direction. This is achieved by introducing an additional parameter - the direction determinant. Its important advantage is that it is defined generally. Its usefulness does not only need to be limited to the aggregation operations. It is a convenient tool to include direction in other methods as well. The introduction of an additional parameter has one more important advantage . It is connected to compatibility with the processing methods based on classical fuzzy sets. If after using the methods based on OFN, there is a need for using any of the conventional methods, we can focus only on processing degrees of membership of fuzzy numbers. We would lose the additional information represented by the direction, but keep compatibility with conventional methods. What is also important, we will maintain good computational properties since these do not depend directly on the direction determinant.

Proposed method of aggregation for OFNs, certainly does not cover the topic. Calculating the direction determinant based on the proportion of the argument distance from the fuzzy number core to the relevant part of the support is the exact solution only for the linear up-part and down-part. In the case of non-linear parts of OFN, the current proposal is only an estimation of the expected outcome, because it only regards the interval boundaries without considering all degrees of membership. Thus, the direction determinant for two different OFNs can be identical. In future, the direction determinant modification (increasing the precision) is needed. It will be one of the next steps in research on aggregation operators respecting direction.

The next step in the study of fuzzy systems based on the OFNs leads to developing a complete and coherent fuzzy system. Such system should respect the direction in processing both rules premises and conclusions. Furthermore, it should meet the expected properties such as continuity and monotonicity.

References

1. Zadeh, L.A.: Fuzzy sets. Information and Control 8, 338–353 (1965)
2. Zadeh, L.A.: The concept of a linguistic variable and its application to approximate reasoning, Part I, II, III. Information Sciences 8, 199–249 (1975)
3. Nguyen, H.T.: A note on the extension principle for fuzzy sets. J. Math. Anal. Appl. 64, 369–380 (1978)
4. Driankov, D., Hellendoorn, H., Reinfrank, M.: An Introduction to fuzzy control. Springer, Heidelberg (1996)
5. Wagenknecht, M., Hampel, R., Schneider, V.: Computational aspects of fuzzy arithmetic based on archimedean t-norms. Fuzzy Sets and Systems 123(1), 49–62 (2001)
6. Calvo, T., Kolesarova, A., Komornikova, M., Mesiar, R.: Aggregation operators: properties, classes and construction methods. In: Aggregation Operators: New Trends and Applications, pp. 3–104. Physica, Heidelberg (2002)
7. Kosiński, W., Prokopowicz, P., Ślęzak, D.: Ordered fuzzy numbers. Bulletin of the Polish Academy of Sciences, Ser. Sci. Math. 51(3), 327–338 (2003)
8. Kosiński, W., Prokopowicz, P., Ślęzak, D.: On algebraic operations on fuzzy numbers. In: Intelligent Information Processing and Web Mining. ASC, vol. 22, pp. 353–362. Springer (2003)
9. Ross, T.J.: Fuzzy Logic for Engineering Applications-, 2nd edn. John Wiley and Sons, UK (2004)
10. Kosiński, W.: On defuzzyfication of ordered fuzzy numbers. In: Rutkowski, L., Siekmann, J.H., Tadeusiewicz, R., Zadeh, L.A. (eds.) ICAISC 2004. LNCS (LNAI), vol. 3070, pp. 326–331. Springer, Heidelberg (2004)
11. Koleśnik, R., Prokopowicz, P., Kosiński, W.: Fuzzy calculator – useful tool for programming with fuzzy algebra. In: Rutkowski, L., Siekmann, J.H., Tadeusiewicz, R., Zadeh, L.A. (eds.) ICAISC 2004. LNCS (LNAI), vol. 3070, pp. 320–325. Springer, Heidelberg (2004)
12. Buckley James, J., Eslami, E.: An Introduction to Fuzzy Logic and Fuzzy Sets. Physica-Verlag, A Springer-Verlag Company, Heidelberg (2005)
13. Prokopowicz, P.: Methods based on the ordered fuzzy numbers used in fuzzy control. In: Proc. of the Fifth International Workshop on Robot Motion and Control – RoMoCo 2005, Dymaczewo, Poland, pp. 349–354 (June 2005)
14. Prokopowicz, P.: Using Ordered Fuzzy Numbers Arithmetic in Fuzzy Control. In: Artificial Intelligence and Soft Computing Proc. of the 8th ICAISC, Poland, pp. 156–162. Academic Publishing House EXIT, Warsaw (2006)
15. Kosiński, W.: On fuzzy number calculus. International Journal of Applied Mathematics and Computer Science 16(1), 51–57 (2006)
16. Beliakov, G., Pradera, A., Calvo, T.: Aggregation functions: a guide for practitioners. STUDFUZZ, vol. 221. Springer, Berlin (2007)
17. Kosiński, W., Prokopowicz, P.: Fuzziness - Representation of Dynamic Changes, Using Ordered Fuzzy Numbers Arithmetic, New Dimensions in Fuzzy Logic nd Related Technologies. In: Proc. of the 5th EUSFLAT, Ostrava, Czech Republic, vol. I, pp. 449–456. University of Ostrava (2007)

18. Prokopowicz, P.: Adaptation of Rules in the Fuzzy Control System Using the Arithmetic of Ordered Fuzzy Numbers. In: Rutkowski, L., Tadeusiewicz, R., Zadeh, L.A., Zurada, J.M. (eds.) ICAISC 2008. LNCS (LNAI), vol. 5097, pp. 306–316. Springer, Heidelberg (2008)
19. Kosiński, W., Prokopowicz, P., Kacprzak, D.: Fuzziness – representation of dynamic changes by ordered fuzzy numbers. In: Seising, R. (ed.) Views on Fuzzy Sets and Systems from Different Perspectives. STUDFUZZ, vol. 243, pp. 485–508. Springer, Heidelberg (2009)
20. Kosiński, W., Wilczyńska-Sztyma, D.: Defuzzification and implication within ordered fuzzy numbers. In: 2010 IEEE World Congress on Computational Intelligence, WCCI 2010 (2010)
21. Kacprzak, M., Kosiński, W.: On lattice structure and implications on ordered fuzzy numbers. In: Proc. of the 7th EUSFLAT Conference, EUSFLAT 2011 and French Days on Fuzzy Logic and Applications, LFA 2011 (2011)
22. Grabisch, M., Marichal, J.-L., Mesiar, R., Pap, E.: Aggregation functions: Means. Information Sciences 181(1), 1–22 (2011)
23. Kacprzak, M., Kosiński, W., Prokopowicz, P.: Implications on Ordered Fuzzy Numbers and Fuzzy Sets of Type Two. In: Rutkowski, L., Korytkowski, M., Scherer, R., Tadeusiewicz, R., Zadeh, L.A., Zurada, J.M. (eds.) ICAISC 2012, Part I. LNCS (LNAI), vol. 7267, pp. 247–255. Springer, Heidelberg (2012)
24. Kosiński, W., Rosa, A., Cendrowska, D., Węgrzyn-Wolska, K.: Defuzzification Functionals Are Homogeneous, Restrictive Additive and Normalized Functions. In: Rutkowski, L., Korytkowski, M., Scherer, R., Tadeusiewicz, R., Zadeh, L.A., Zurada, J.M. (eds.) ICAISC 2012, Part I. LNCS (LNAI), vol. 7267, pp. 274–282. Springer, Heidelberg (2012)
25. Prokopowicz, P.: Flexible and Simple Methods of Calculations on Fuzzy Numbers with the Ordered Fuzzy Numbers Model. In: Rutkowski, L., Korytkowski, M., Scherer, R., Tadeusiewicz, R., Zadeh, L.A., Zurada, J.M. (eds.) ICAISC 2013, Part I. LNCS (LNAI), vol. 7894, pp. 365–375. Springer, Heidelberg (2013)
26. Marszałek, A., Burczyński, T.: Modelling Financial High Frequency Data Using Ordered Fuzzy Numbers. In: Rutkowski, L., Korytkowski, M., Scherer, R., Tadeusiewicz, R., Zadeh, L.A., Zurada, J.M. (eds.) ICAISC 2013, Part I. LNCS, vol. 7894, pp. 345–352. Springer, Heidelberg (2013)
27. Kacprzak, D., Kosiński, W., Kosiński, W.K.: Financial Stock Data and Ordered Fuzzy Numbers. In: Rutkowski, L., Korytkowski, M., Scherer, R., Tadeusiewicz, R., Zadeh, L.A., Zurada, J.M. (eds.) ICAISC 2013, Part I. LNCS (LNAI), vol. 7894, pp. 259–270. Springer, Heidelberg (2013)
28. Kacprzak, M., Kosiński, W., Węgrzyn-Wolska, K.: Diversity of opinion evaluated by ordered fuzzy numbers. In: Rutkowski, L., Korytkowski, M., Scherer, R., Tadeusiewicz, R., Zadeh, L.A., Zurada, J.M. (eds.) ICAISC 2013, Part I. LNCS (LNAI), vol. 7894, pp. 271–281. Springer, Heidelberg (2013)
29. Kosiński, W., Prokopowicz, P., Rosa, A.: Defuzzification Functionals of Ordered Fuzzy Numbers. IEEE Transactions on Fuzzy Systems 21(6), 1163–1169 (2013), doi:10.1109/TFUZZ.2013.2243456

The Idea for the Integration of Neuro-Fuzzy Hardware Emulators with Real-Time Network

Andrzej Przybył[1] and Meng Joo Er[2]

[1] Częstochowa University of Technology,
Institute of Computational Intelligence, Poland
andrzej.przybyl@iisi.pcz.pl
[2] Nanyang Technological University,
School of Electrical & Electronic Engineering, Singapore
emjer@ntu.edu.sg

Abstract. In modern industry a real-time Ethernet-based control systems are typically used instead of a centralized solution. This is due to the economical reason and to allow easy expansion and modernization of the machines. The distributed architecture enables i.a. the use of hardware emulators instead of the real control object, in a manner transparent to the whole system. This is an advantage because it can be useful for the development of the control system. It will make that cheap and safe testing of complex control systems will be available. The testing process might be performed in a working control system in which part of it (e.g. a control object) has been temporarily replaced by an emulator. However, emulators typically need an increased performance of the real-time communication interface to transfer a large amounts of the service data. In this paper we propose a new method to create high performance real-time, Ethernet-based communication solution which will be suitable for the most demanding applications, for example for the development process and connection with hardware emulators.

1 Introduction

Todays in the industry, the real-time Ethernet (RTE) based systems are commonly used because of their higher performance when compared to existing field-buses. Unfortunately, at present there is not defined one common RTE standard and many different and non-compatible solutions are used. It seems that the full standardization in this area is not yet possible in the near future [26] and research on real-time communication over Ethernet is still ongoing. In a real-time communication the most important goal is to deliver messages from their source to the destination in a deterministic time. Moreover, the delivery time must be also as short as possible to meet the requirements of the control system. Different systems have different requirements, so currently three basic categories of the real-time systems (RT Class 1-3) are defined [42]. The standardization of the RTE is especially hard to achieve [40] in the most demanded RT class 3 area. This is mainly because of the non-typical methods that are used in different solutions to improve their real-time performance. On the other hand the

L. Rutkowski et al. (Eds.): ICAISC 2014, Part I, LNAI 8467, pp. 279–294, 2014.

communication solutions based on a typical methods (in hardware and software) allow usually easier standardization but unfortunately at the cost of quality indicators [1]. As a result there is currently no existing one solution that will be good enough for all types of applications. It seems likely that different RTE systems will coexist side by side at the factory level [61], connected via gateways (Fig. 1). One of the possible future scenario is that an attempt to standardize the communication between different RTE standards and/or the factory network through the gateways will be undertaken. Next possible scenario is the existence of universal multi-protocol network devices, which will be able to automatically change the currently used protocol. Such versatility is possible, especially when network devices are based on a field programmable gate array (FPGA) chips.

In this paper we propose a novel hard real-time Ethernet-based solution for industrial control systems with a master-slave control hierarchy. Proposed method uses FPGA chip to process some data on the fly. It allows very efficient real-time communication and better network efficiency than offered by competitive solutions. It is designed to use as a hard real-time backplane bus for machine or process control, however it is not fully compatible with the Ethernet standard. In the presented system, the hard real-time domain is separated from the other machines/processes in the factory. It is connected to the factory network (soft real-time domain) through the gateway (Fig. 1). This enables to use different (i.e. non-compatible) communication solutions in the factory. However, it is possible to synchronize them when needed. Moreover, in such an approach the human to machine interface is also built in the soft real-time domain, which allows to use popular (and well known) operating systems like Windows, Linux etc. for these purposes. In this paper, only some general information about the requirements of interface to the neuro-fuzzy (see e.g. [14]-[19], [27]) emulator will be presented. Neuro-fuzzy systems (see e.g. [36]-[38], [51]-[55]) combine the natural language description of fuzzy systems (see e.g. [2]-[6], [21]-[24], [28]-[29], [62]-[64]) and the learning properties of neural networks (see e.g. [8]-[13], [30], [35], [48], [56]). The design and implementation of the emulator in the FPGA is an independent work, undertaken in the context of other research. In this paper we propose to embed the emulator, based on neuro-fuzzy and state variables theories [47], into the FPGA. When the emulator is properly designed and implemented in the FPGA, it is able to work in a real-time. Integration of such hardware emulator with the real-time industrial network allows quite easily (and non-invasive to the rest of the system) to replace the real control object by the emulator (Fig. 2). However, the hardware emulator (typically used in a development process of a complex controller of machine or industrial process) needs a large amount of data to be transmitted synchronously to the controlled process, but without affecting it. These data are in a typical case the inputs, state variables and outputs of the model of the controlled object. For the development purposes these data must be recorded in an local buffer of the emulator with very short sampling time. The sampling time value depends on the physical phenomena modelled with the emulator. In a typical case the sampling time (i.e. simulation time) has value in a range from tens of μs to hundreds of ns or even less. Typical microprocessor

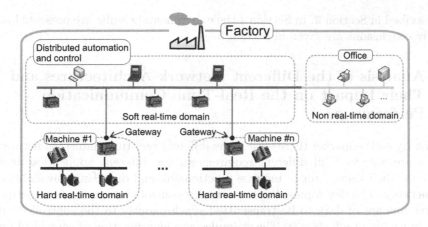

Fig. 1. Coexistence of different communication standards at the factory level

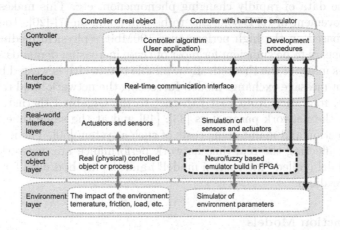

Fig. 2. Idea for the control system a) with the real object, and b) with the object emulator

system is not able to implement emulator, record sampling data and transmit it through the real-time network (in a packets) in such a case. However, due to the reasons listed above, the FPGA is well suited for this purpose, i.e. to implement the emulator and to integrate it with the hard real-time industrial network. Especially two novel methods are proposed in this work: **(a)** Special (asymmetric) node structure together with a proposed queuing technique to allow very efficient full-duplex communication. **(b)** Bandwidth management to maximize the efficiency of the non-real-time communication, which will be useful for the less time-critical tasks, such as: monitoring, inspection, management, supervision, fault-detection, servicing and development.

This paper is organized as follows: Section 2 presents an analysis of different network architectures and their impact on communication performance. The idea of a new method for the hard real-time full-duplex communication system is described in Section 3. In Section 4 the experimental results are presented and finally conclusions are given in Section 5.

2 Analysis of the Different Network Architectures and Their Impact on the Real-Time Communication Performance

Currently on the market there exist many different real-time industrial networks which are able to fulfil different requirements for different application areas. However, their users want to increase functionality and diagnostics available for the network. The development of the complex control systems needs sometimes a large amount of data to be transmitted synchronously to the controlled process, but without affecting it. The examples are: identification of controlled process, connecting to hardware emulators, development new controller structure, recording the data of rapidly changing phenomenon, etc. This makes research on the improvement of RTE solutions to be still going on [7]-[20]. Todays RTE is typically based on the high performance 100Mbit/s physical medium, which currently appears to be sufficient for most of these increasing demands. However, in some cases many of the theoretically available bandwidth is wasted because of the inefficient message exchange model. Increasing the network baud rates to the 1 Gbit/s, i.e. migration from Fast Ethernet to the Gigabit Ethernet, improves only part of the network parameters [33], [49] and at the same time generates higher production and maintaining costs of such a system [50]. The most important factors affecting the real-time network performance are: network message exchange model (called "interaction model") and the method used for accessing the shared medium.

2.1 Interaction Models

The main interaction models, i.e. the way in which the devices communicate within the network, are: client-server, peer-to-peer, producer- consumer and publisher-subscriber. Their basic properties are summarized as follows: **(a) The client-server model** It is a traditional data exchange mechanism available in most systems, where a client makes a request and waits for the response. The server fulfils the request and sends a response. **(b) Peer-to-peer** It is the most flexible network model. All devices (peers) are at the same logical level and can communicate independently with any others. Each network node may responds to the request of any other. However, a special attention must be paid to avoid collisions because each device can initiate a transaction to any other at any time. The efficient collision avoidance mechanism is necessary in order to ensure determinism of the communication system. **(c) Producer-consumer** In this case one (or more) network device is the producer. It produces the data and equips/encapsulates it with the identifier indicating the data content. Such data are not addressed to specified network devices, but they are transmitted via broadcast on the whole network system. Other (anonymous) network devices (called consumers) listen for the incoming data packets and if they recognize the data identifier, they will consume the data. For many control systems, there are some parameters which must be delivered to a number of network devices. That data have to be transmitted only once and are consumed by multiple nodes at the same time. This allows a more precise synchronization and more efficient use of network bandwidth [34]. **(d) Publisher-subscriber** Similarly to the producer-consumer; this is also the data oriented exchange model [41]. In this case there are many subscribers who communicate with a publisher and request a data identified by content. The publisher has a list of the requests of the subscribers and disseminate the requested data via multicast addressing to the groups of subscribers.

The producer-consumer, as well as the publisher-subscriber network model, is characterized by high performance and efficient utilization of available bandwidth. It is particularly well visible in the systems where the same real-time control data have to be available to many devices in the same time. These models are preferable to be used in distributed control. On the other hand, the explicit messaging used in other network models (i.e. the messages are not data-oriented but they have their source and destination device address instead of data identifier) is more appropriate for configuration of the network devices, uploading and downloading firmware, etc. In the real-time networks there are two types of real-time data transport: synchronous (periodic) and asynchronous (aperiodic). The periodic data transport is used for most critical real-time control (i.e. motion control) while aperiodic data transport is used for slightly less demanding tasks like automation. Some real-time networks also support a non real-time communication mode which can be useful for secondary and non-time-critical tasks, like configuration, monitoring and servicing.

2.2 Media Access Methods

The communication solutions are built on the basis of the shared or switched medium. Moreover, there are also specialized network solutions, such as for example EtherCAT, Sercos III and Profinet IRT which are based on the dedicated network devices [31], [50].

Switched Media Networks. Networks based on switched medium, which utilizes multi-port switching devices (switches) offer great flexibility with respect to the network topology. They allow to full-duplex communication and prevents collisions. However, this solution does not offer the highest performance for real-time communication. One of the main reason is the relatively long delay (latency time) introduced by the switch. In the switched Ethernet, collisions do not occur because of the used full-duplex communication and data queuing ability of the switch device. Unfortunately, if too many network devices sent their data to the same recipient at the same time, then part of them is lost. This is due to overflow of the switch memory buffer (queue). As a result the switched network have poor real-time performance when there is a heavy traffic [39]-[45].

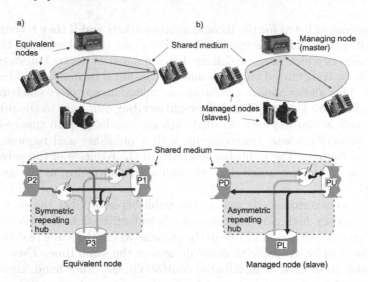

Fig. 3. The illustration of the a) network structure typically used in the real-time communication with shared medium, three ports network device capable for the daisy-chaining and b) the proposed asymmetric architecture of the devices, well fitted for the master-slave control hierarchy

Shared Media Networks. A second group are shared networks, which are based on repeaters or hubs. Although in this case it is generally also possible to build any network topology, for practical reasons a linear structure is mostly used (Fig. 3a). This is because the repeating hubs are typically embedded into each network device and are equipped with only three ports. Because all devices in the network are working on a shared medium, the network can operate only in half-duplex mode. Therefore the network bandwidth is used at most half, for example 100Mbit/s instead of 2x100Mbit/s if we consider Fast Ethernet.

Popular technique for collisionless access to shared medium is master-slave pooling mechanism. In such a solution the subordinate devices (slaves) one-time gain access to the network in response to commands coming from the device manager (master). The exchange of messages is divided into communication cycles and synchronized by a special frame coming from the master device. Master-slave pooling mechanism is used for example in the EPL v2 and in the VARAN Bus solutions. The disadvantage of the master-slave pooling mechanism is the introduction of additional delays resulting from the slave response time for request and response preparation time. If the slave functionality is provided by the software, the delay can has a significant effect on overall network performance degradation. The another aspect is that any network which is operating on the basis of standardized Ethernet, has a major drawback: it adds a large overhead for communication for small data packets. This overhead is related to the minimum frame length equal to 64 bytes plus 8 bytes of preamble and start frame delimiter (SFD) plus 12 bytes length of inter frame gap (IFG) defined by the IEEE 802.3, while typical message in the distributed control systems has, for example, about 8 bytes of even less. As a result, available bandwidth (i.e. 100Mbit/s for Fast Ethernet) is used very inefficiently and it is equal to about ten percent. It should be noted that in the Gigabit Ethernet the minimum frame length has been increased to 512 bytes. In such a case the effective bandwidth utilization in a standard Gigabit Ethernet will be about 1.5% only. The minimum frame length, as well as required IFG, results from the slot time used for collision detection mechanism CSMA/CD in the standardized Ethernet. It is important to note that if the CSMA/CD mechanism is not used (because some other mechanism is used to avoid collisions) then the limitation to minimum frame length and IFG are not necessary, however they are still required by the standard. The very low efficiency when using standard Ethernet frames is the reason, why some of the RTE solutions do not meet standard Ethernet frame limitation. One of the example is the VARAN Bus [57] which does not use the standard MAC format and the minimum frame length is not maintained. Moreover the length of the Preamble, SFD and the IFG is greatly reduced. Thanks to that the important increase in the network efficiency is obtained.

Networks with Dedicated Media Access. A effective method to handle short messages in standardized Ethernet is to use so-called summation frames and "on the fly processing" mechanism introduced by Beckhoff and used in EtherCAT and Sercos III. Another very efficient method for a treatment of short messages is used in Profinet IRT [46]. This method is called dynamic frame packing (DFP). EtherCAT and Sercos III are a master-slave systems, where the master device generates Ethernet frame (or frames) at a predetermined rate. These frames are then used by all slaves for the data transport. Data are read from and updated to a specified part of the long frame (summation frame) on the fly by subsequent slaves. The frames are processed on-line fully in hardware via FPGA or ASIC chip. Consequently, both of these two solutions needs specialized hardware. Choosing the right part of the frame is made on the basis of a proper mapping of logical addresses. As a result, this network allows full-duplex communication, and short messages are not burdened with high overhead. Summing up, the analysis presented above shows that existing solutions do not fully exploit the possibilities offered by the Ethernet medium. It is possible to develop new, more effective methods of communication, tailored to the requirements of distributed real-time control systems.

3   A New Hard Real-Time Ethernet-Based Solution for Master-Slave Control System

In this paper there is proposed novel, powerful hard real-time Ethernet-based solution for a systems, which are based on a master-slave control hierarchy. Master-slave structure is typical for the vast majority of applications. In presented solution the master device serves as a management unit both for process

control and communication. As a result only master device can initiate an aperiodic, real-time asynchronous (RTA) transaction on a communication network.
While periodic, real-time synchronous messages (RTS) can be generated independently by slaves or by a master at predefined communication cycles. Moreover, the non-real-time (NRT) messages can be generated by any device at every
communication cycles, however, only within defined time windows (i.e. based on
TDMA paradigm). Details of these mechanisms will be explained in the next
part of the paper. In the proposed system the master device generates the RTA
command (request) and sends it, via the network, to the slaves (distributed
nodes). An answer from the specified slave device is generated and comes back
to the master. This a priori knowledge about the messages flow and their size
(in the real-time communication) together with a proposed queuing technique
gives the possibility to very effective use of the full-duplex communication. This
results from the fact that the network device can be built with an asymmetric
structure (Fig. 3b) adapted to the presented model of the control hierarchy.

3.1   The Idea of the Asymmetric Network Structure

If we look at the proposed structure of the network device (Fig. 3b) we can see
that the number of collision points is reduced from three to only one, when compared to the typically used structure shown in (Fig. 3a). Additionally, the proposed structure allows for communication in the full-duplex mode. Thus formed
network structure is asymmetrical. A downstream communication (from master
down in hierarchy to the slave) is performed by repeating incoming data from
port PU to ports PD and PL. Communication in this direction is therefore collisionless. An upstream communication (response from the slave up in hierarchy
to the master) is performed with the use of special queuing technique, which
prevents collisions (Fig. 4). This method is somewhat similar to that used in the
Profinet IRT solution [43], [46]. The queuing technique mentioned above, as well
as the next method of bandwidth management proposed in this paper, will be
presented now.

3.2   The Proposed Bandwidth Management Method

The upstream communication is done through fifo buffers (Fig. 4). However, the
appropriate bandwidth management controlled by the master device ensures that
there will never be a buffer overflow. It follows from the fact that for each transmission cycle T_C there is assigned a limited number of transmitted RTS, RTA
and NRT data. The TDMA mechanism is used to divide the upstream communication cycle into three stages: real-time synchronous T_U, real-time asynchronous
T_R and non-real-time T_A (see Fig. 5).

We can see that the whole communication cycle T_C is a sum of the three
values, as follows $T_C = T_U + T_P + T_D$, where T_U is a time to deliver all periodic
messages (generated at the beginning of the cycle by active slaves) to the master.
While T_P is processing time of received data in the master device. Furthermore
T_D is a time to deliver all periodic messages generated by the master to all

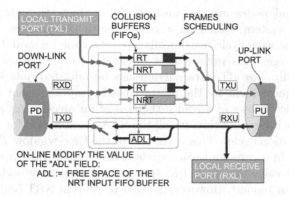

Fig. 4. Proposed architecture of managed node

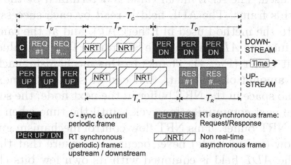

Fig. 5. Proposed media access mechanism and communication model

Fig. 6. Format of the proposed sync & control periodic frame

nodes. It is important to note that proposed communication procedure allows to receive data from slaves, process it in a master device and then send processed data back to the slaves (i.e. close the controllers loop through the network) in one communication cycle. This significantly expands the applicability of such an interface, because the controller cycle time of many practical control systems must be as short as possible. Many of the competitive communication solutions need at least two cycles for this purpose.

The values that define the time slices for two stages (T_U and T_R) are included in the special sync/control (SC) frame (Fig. 6). The time slice for the third (NRT) stage is calculated in each node as follows $T_A = T_C - T_U - T_R$. Because the communication cycle time is constant, this calculation can be easily done.

The idea of high performance communication, proposed in this paper, is based on the assumption that the slave devices can send upstream their RTS data at the start of the communication cycle (see Fig. 5). The number of data to be sent by individual nodes are designed on the configuration stage of the distributed control system. Based on a knowledge of the number of frames and data bytes sent at each cycle, master allocates the time interval T_U for the first (synchronous) stage. This value is then inserted into SC frame as a value of a field TU. Secondly, any RTA transaction can be initiated only by the master device. Each request (sent by the master) needs response (sent by the slave). The master device knows in advance the size of an answer. As a result it can allocate a proper interval of time for all the RTA answers (i.e. for all requests in given communication cycle). This is the size of the time window T_R, i.e. the size of the last stage in a communication cycle. This value is then inserted into the SC frame as the value of a field TR. In the third stage any node can send its NRT data without request. However, in order to prevent NRT buffer overflow (if many nodes send their data at the same time), the special filed ADL in the SC frame (Fig. 6) is used. The ADL initial value is determined by the master and it is inserted into this frame. The ADL field is read by each successive nodes (on the fly - similar to the method used in EtherCAT), and at the same time a new value is inserted into the ADL field in the SC frame. This is a value of free space of the NRT input buffer (Fig. 4). Thanks to this mechanism, each node knows the limitation of amount of NRT data that can be sent to the next (upstream) node. If there is no space in the NRT buffer in the next node, the sending process is delayed (to the next communication cycle) until the time when it is adequate free space in the NRT buffer. This NRT flow control mechanism guarantees that the buffer overflow (in any node) never occurs. To ensure that the whole ADL field is correct the ADL field is equipped with its own few bits checksum. The on-line processing of the ADL field is done fully in the hardware, so there is only a small latency time for process of repeating data from the port RXU to TXD. The frames scheduling is used in each node (Fig. 4) to transmits NRT data from both (local an input) buffer to the outgoing port TXU (upstream) based on the rule of First-Come-First-Serve (FCFS). This gives a similar latencies for NRT communication for all devices in the network.

4   Experimental Results

In this section a very approximate calculation will be done to confirm the effectiveness of the presented method. Exact calculations are omitted, due to the size limitations of the paper. In the presented example it was assumed that eight distributed nodes (servo drives) have been connected through the real-time (Fast Ethernet-based) network to the master device (reference trajectory generator in the CNC machine tool). The control algorithm requires 12 bytes of data from each servos at each control cycle. The control cycle and the communication cycle have the same values equals to $T_C = 125\mu s$. After the processing time T_P is completed, the results are sent back to the servos. In this example each servo receives back 8 bytes of data. This scenario is executed in every communication cycle. One of the distributed node was the neuro-fuzzy (see e.g. [59]-[60]) based hardware emulator implemented in the FPGA. The electronic board derived

Table 1. Performance of proposed real-time communication solutions

No. of nodes	Cyclic data bytes I/O (control algorithm)	Comm. cycle time	Emulation cycle time	Cyclic data bytes I/O (emulator)
8	96/64	$125\mu s$	$10\ \mu s$	384/0

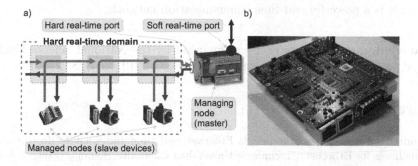

Fig. 7. Distributed computer numerical controlled machine control system

from the existing servo-drive with an Xilinx XC3ADSP3400 FPGA was used as the hardware platform (Fig. 7). As it was indicated in the Introduction, the design and implementation of the emulator in the FPGA is an independent work, undertaken in the context of other research. Moreover, as it was mentioned at the beginning of this paper a maximum possible bandwidth is required to observe and control the emulator. In the experiment at each communication cycle almost four hundred of data bytes were received from the emulator, independently to data received from- and transmitted to- the other distributed nodes. These periodic real-time data were required to record the exact state of the emulator (being under development) at each emulation cycle. The received data were pre-processed in the master device and saved in a memory for future use in off-line mode, for the development purposes. The requirements of distributed control system with the emulator and the performance of the proposed method were presented in Table 1.

Tests confirmed that the performance of the proposed solution allows to communicate with the hardware emulator and transmit a large amount of the data in each cycle. Additionally, the efficient non real-time communication channel was used for management and diagnostic of the emulated object. Particularly, the ambient conditions were controlled fully independently (i.e. without interfering with the action) from the ongoing control process of HSM machine tool. The features of the proposed solution enables to control system development in an convenient way. This allows to greatly improve the whole control system in future and gives great versatility and the new possibilities for designing of complex control systems.

5   Conclusions

This paper presented a new solution for hard real-time communication over the Ethernet, which offers great flexibility and high throughput (i.e. effective bandwidth capacity) and is adequate for the most demanding applications. The two most important features that distinguish this solution from other are: the ability to work very effectively in a full-duplex mode (which allows the use of very short communication cycle times) and the efficient non real-time communication. The result is a powerful real-time communication network.

Acknowledgment. The project was financed by the National Science Centre (Poland) on the basis of the decision number DEC-2012/05/B/ST7/02138.

References

1. Andre, R.: Real-Time Ethernet. Is Ethernet real time and what to do to ensure timeliness for Ethernet?, Technische Universitat Chemnitz, Seminar transportation Systems, pp. 1–21 (2009)
2. Bartczuk, Ł., Dziwiński, P., Starczewski, J.: A new method for dealing with unbalanced linguistic term set. In: Rutkowski, L., Korytkowski, M., Scherer, R., Tadeusiewicz, R., Zadeh, L.A., Zurada, J.M. (eds.) ICAISC 2012, Part I. LNCS (LNAI), vol. 7267, pp. 207–212. Springer, Heidelberg (2012)
3. Bartczuk, Ł., Dziwiński, P., Starczewski, J.T.: New Method for Generation Type-2 Fuzzy Partition for FDT. In: Rutkowski, L., Scherer, R., Tadeusiewicz, R., Zadeh, L.A., Zurada, J.M. (eds.) ICAISC 2010, Part I. LNCS (LNAI), vol. 6113, pp. 275–280. Springer, Heidelberg (2010)
4. Bartczuk, Ł., Przybył, A., Dziwiński, P.: Hybrid state variables - fuzzy logic modelling of nonlinear objects. In: Rutkowski, L., Korytkowski, M., Scherer, R., Tadeusiewicz, R., Zadeh, L.A., Zurada, J.M. (eds.) ICAISC 2013, Part I. LNCS (LNAI), vol. 7894, pp. 227–234. Springer, Heidelberg (2013)
5. Bartczuk, Ł., Rutkowska, D.: A New Version of the Fuzzy-ID3 Algorithm. In: Rutkowski, L., Tadeusiewicz, R., Zadeh, L.A., Żurada, J.M. (eds.) ICAISC 2006. LNCS (LNAI), vol. 4029, pp. 1060–1070. Springer, Heidelberg (2006)
6. Bartczuk, Ł., Rutkowska, D.: Medical Diagnosis with Type-2 Fuzzy Decision Trees. In: Kącki, E., Rudnicki, M., Stempczyńska, J. (eds.) Computers in Medical Activity. AISC, vol. 65, pp. 11–21. Springer, Heidelberg (2009)
7. Beran, J., Zezulka, F.: Evaluation of Real-Time Behaviour in Virtual Automation Networks. In: Proceedings of the 17th World Congress the International Federation of Automatic Control, pp. 13970–13975 (2008)
8. Bilski, J., Litwiński, S., Smoląg, J.: Parallel Realization of QR Algorithm for Neural Networks Learning. In: Rutkowski, L., Siekmann, J.H., Tadeusiewicz, R., Zadeh, L.A. (eds.) ICAISC 2004. LNCS (LNAI), vol. 3070, pp. 158–165. Springer, Heidelberg (2004)
9. Bilski, J., Rutkowski, L.: Numerically Robust Learning Algorithms for Feed Forward Neural Networks. In: Neural Networks and Soft Computing. Advances in Soft Computing, pp. 149–154. Physica-Verlag, A Springer-Verlag Company (2003)

10. Bilski, J., Smoląg, J.: Parallel Approach to Learning of the Recurrent Jordan Neural Network. In: Rutkowski, L., Korytkowski, M., Scherer, R., Tadeusiewicz, R., Zadeh, L.A., Zurada, J.M. (eds.) ICAISC 2013, Part I. LNCS (LNAI), vol. 7894, pp. 32–40. Springer, Heidelberg (2013)
11. Bilski, J., Smoląg, J.: Parallel Realisation of the Recurrent Elman Neural Network Learning. In: Rutkowski, L., Scherer, R., Tadeusiewicz, R., Zadeh, L.A., Zurada, J.M. (eds.) ICAISC 2010, Part II. LNCS (LNAI), vol. 6114, pp. 19–25. Springer, Heidelberg (2010)
12. Bilski, J., Smoląg, J.: Parallel Realisation of the Recurrent Multi Layer Perceptron Learning. In: Rutkowski, L., Korytkowski, M., Scherer, R., Tadeusiewicz, R., Zadeh, L.A., Zurada, J.M. (eds.) ICAISC 2012, Part I. LNCS (LNAI), vol. 7267, pp. 12–20. Springer, Heidelberg (2012)
13. Bilski, J., Smoląg, J.: Parallel Realisation of the Recurrent RTRN Neural Network Learning. In: Rutkowski, L., Tadeusiewicz, R., Zadeh, L.A., Zurada, J.M. (eds.) ICAISC 2008. LNCS (LNAI), vol. 5097, pp. 11–16. Springer, Heidelberg (2008)
14. Cpałka, K.: A Method for Designing Flexible Neuro-fuzzy Systems. In: Rutkowski, L., Tadeusiewicz, R., Zadeh, L.A., Żurada, J.M. (eds.) ICAISC 2006. LNCS (LNAI), vol. 4029, pp. 212–219. Springer, Heidelberg (2006)
15. Cpałka, K.: On evolutionary designing and learning of flexible neuro-fuzzy structures for nonlinear classification. In: Nonlinear Analysis Series A: Theory, Methods and Applications, vol. 71, pp. 1659–1672. Elsevier (2009)
16. Cpałka, K., Łapa, K., Przybył, A., Zalasiński, M.: A new method for designing neuro-fuzzy systems for nonlinear modelling with interpretability aspects. Neurocomputing (in print, 2014), http://dx.doi.org/10.1016/j.neucom.2013.12.031
17. Cpałka K., Rutkowski L, A New Method for Designing and Reduction of Neuro-fuzzy Systems. In: Proceedings of the 2006 IEEE International Conference on Fuzzy Systems (IEEE World Congress on Computational Intelligence, WCCI 2006), Vancouver, BC, Canada, pp. 8510–8516 (2006)
18. Cpałka, K., Rutkowski, L.: Flexible Takagi-Sugeno Fuzzy Systems. In: Proceedings of the International Joint Conference on Neural Networks 2005, Montreal, pp. 1764–1769 (2005)
19. Cpałka, K., Rutkowski, L.: Flexible Takagi Sugeno Neuro-fuzzy Structures for Nonlinear Approximation. WSEAS Transactions on Systems 4(9), 1450–1458 (2005)
20. Decotignie, J.D.: Ethernet-Based Real-Time and Industrial Communications. Proceedings of the IEEE 93(6), 1102–1117 (2005)
21. Dziwiński, P., Bartczuk, Ł., Starczewski, J.T.: Fully controllable ant colony system for text data clustering. In: Rutkowski, L., Korytkowski, M., Scherer, R., Tadeusiewicz, R., Zadeh, L.A., Zurada, J.M. (eds.) EC 2012 and SIDE 2012. LNCS, vol. 7269, pp. 199–205. Springer, Heidelberg (2012)
22. Dziwiński, P., Rutkowska, D.: Algorithm for generating fuzzy rules for WWW document classification. In: Rutkowski, L., Tadeusiewicz, R., Zadeh, L.A., Żurada, J.M. (eds.) ICAISC 2006. LNCS (LNAI), vol. 4029, pp. 1111–1119. Springer, Heidelberg (2006)
23. Dziwiński, P., Rutkowska, D.: Ant focused crawling algorithm. In: Rutkowski, L., Tadeusiewicz, R., Zadeh, L.A., Zurada, J.M. (eds.) ICAISC 2008. LNCS (LNAI), vol. 5097, pp. 1018–1028. Springer, Heidelberg (2008)
24. Dziwiński, P., Starczewski, J.T., Bartczuk, Ł.: New linguistic hedges in construction of interval type-2 FLS. In: Rutkowski, L., Scherer, R., Tadeusiewicz, R., Zadeh, L.A., Zurada, J.M. (eds.) ICAISC 2010, Part II. LNCS (LNAI), vol. 6114, pp. 445–450. Springer, Heidelberg (2010)

25. Fan, X., Jonsson, M., Jonsson, J.: Guaranteed real-time communication in packet-switched networks with FCFS queuing. Computer Networks 53, 400–417 (2009)
26. Felser, M.: Real Time Ethernet: standardization and implementations. In: IEEE International Symposium on Industrial Electronics (ISIE 2010), Invited paper (2010)
27. Gabryel, M., Cpałka, K., Rutkowski, L.: Evolutionary strategies for learning of neuro-fuzzy systems. In: Proceedings of the I Workshop on Genetic Fuzzy Systems, Granada, pp. 119–123 (2005)
28. Gabryel, M., Korytkowski, M., Scherer, R., Rutkowski, L.: Object Detection by Simple Fuzzy Classifiers Generated by Boosting. In: Rutkowski, L., Korytkowski, M., Scherer, R., Tadeusiewicz, R., Zadeh, L.A., Zurada, J.M. (eds.) ICAISC 2013, Part I. LNCS (LNAI), vol. 7894, pp. 540–547. Springer, Heidelberg (2013)
29. Gabryel, M., Woźniak, M., Nowicki, R.K.: Creating Learning Sets for Control Systems Using an Evolutionary Method. In: Rutkowski, L., Korytkowski, M., Scherer, R., Tadeusiewicz, R., Zadeh, L.A., Zurada, J.M. (eds.) SIDE 2012 and EC 2012. LNCS, vol. 7269, pp. 206–213. Springer, Heidelberg (2012)
30. Horzyk, A., Tadeusiewicz, R.: Self-Optimizing Neural Networks. In: Yin, F.-L., Wang, J., Guo, C. (eds.) ISNN 2004. LNCS, vol. 3173, pp. 150–155. Springer, Heidelberg (2004)
31. Jansen, D., Buttner, H.: Real-Time Ethernet the EtherCAT solution. Computing & Control Engineering Journal 15, 16–21 (2004)
32. Jasperneite, J., Imtiaz, J., Schumacher, M., Weber, K.: A Proposal for a Generic Real-Time Ethernet System. IEEE Transactions on Industrial Informatics 5(2), 75–85 (2009)
33. Jasperneite, J., Schumacher, M., Weber, K.: Limits of Increasing the Performance of Industrial Ethernet Protocols. In: IEEE Conference on Emerging Technologies and Factory Automation, ETFA, pp. 17–24 (2007)
34. Kandemir, M., Choudhary, A., Banerjee, P., Ramanujam, J., Shenoy, N.: Minimizing data and synchronization costs in one-way communication. IEEE Transactions on Parallel and Distributed Systems 11(12), 1232–1251 (2000)
35. Korytkowski, M., Rutkowski, L., Scherer, R.: On combining backpropagation with boosting. In: Proceedings of the IEEE International Joint Conference on Neural Network (IJCNN), vols. 1-10, pp. 1274–1277 (2006)
36. Korytkowski, M., Rutkowski, L., Scherer, R.: From Ensemble of Fuzzy Classifiers to Single Fuzzy Rule Base Classifier. In: Rutkowski, L., Tadeusiewicz, R., Zadeh, L.A., Zurada, J.M. (eds.) ICAISC 2008. LNCS (LNAI), vol. 5097, pp. 265–272. Springer, Heidelberg (2008)
37. Łapa, K., Przybył, A., Cpałka, K.: A new approach to designing interpretable models of dynamic systems. In: Rutkowski, L., Korytkowski, M., Scherer, R., Tadeusiewicz, R., Zadeh, L.A., Zurada, J.M. (eds.) ICAISC 2013, Part II. LNCS (LNAI), vol. 7895, pp. 523–534. Springer, Heidelberg (2013)
38. Łapa, K., Zalasiński, M., Cpałka, K.: A new method for designing and complexity reduction of neuro-fuzzy systems for nonlinear modelling. In: Rutkowski, L., Korytkowski, M., Scherer, R., Tadeusiewicz, R., Zadeh, L.A., Zurada, J.M. (eds.) ICAISC 2013, Part I. LNCS (LNAI), vol. 7894, pp. 329–344. Springer, Heidelberg (2013)
39. Mifdaoui, A., Frances, F., Fraboul, C.: Performance analysis of a Master/Slave switched Ethernet for military embedded applications. IEEE Transactions on Industrial Informatics 6(4), 534–547 (2010)
40. Moraes, R.: Survey of Real-Time Communication in CSMA-Based Networks. Network Protocols and Algorithms 2(1), 158–183 (2010)

41. Murphy, P.A.: The Next Generation Networking Paradigm: Producer-Consumer Model. In: Dedicated Systems Magazine. Networks. 2000-Q1, pp. 26–28 (2000)
42. Neumann, P.: Communication in industrial automation - What is going on? Control Engineering Practice 15, 1332–1347 (2007)
43. Neumann, P., Pöschmann, A.: Ethernet-based Real-Time Communications with PROFINET IO. WSEAS Transactions on Communications 5(5), 235–245 (2005)
44. Neumann, P., Pöschmann, A., Messerschmidt, R.: Architectural Concept of Virtual Automation Networks. In: Proceedings of the 17th World Congress The International Federation of Automatic Control, pp. 13964–13969 (2008)
45. Pedreiras, P., Leite, R., Almeida, L.: Characterizing the Real-Time Behavior of Prioritized Switched-Ethernet. In: RTLIA 2003, 2nd Workshop on RealTime LANs in the Internet Age (Satellite of ECRTS 2003), Porto, Portugal, pp. 59–62 (2003)
46. Profinet IRT, Profinet Industrial Ethernet protocol, PI organization, http://www.profibus.com
47. Przybył, A., Cpałka, K.: A new method to construct of interpretable models of dynamic systems. In: Rutkowski, L., Korytkowski, M., Scherer, R., Tadeusiewicz, R., Zadeh, L.A., Zurada, J.M. (eds.) ICAISC 2012, Part II. LNCS, vol. 7268, pp. 697–705. Springer, Heidelberg (2012)
48. Pławiak, P., Tadeusiewicz, R.: Approximation of phenol concentration using novel hybrid computational intelligence methods. Applied Mathematics and Computer Science 24(1) (in print, 2014)
49. Robert, J., Georges, J.P., Rondeau, E., Divoux, T.: Minimum Cycle Time Analysis of Ethernet-Based Real-Time Protocols. International Journal of Computers, Communications and Control 7(4), 743–757 (2012)
50. Rostan, M.: Industrial Ethernet technologies: Overiew. EtherCAT Technology Group, pp. 1–114 (January 2011)
51. Rutkowski, L., Cpałka, K.: Compromise approach to neuro-fuzzy systems. In: Sincak, P., Vascak, J., Kvasnicka, V., Pospichal, J. (eds.) Intelligent Technologies - Theory and Applications, vol. 76, pp. 85–90. IOS Press (2002)
52. Rutkowski, L., Cpałka, K.: Flexible weighted neuro-fuzzy systems. In: Proceedings of the 9th International Conference on Neural Information Processing (ICONIP 2002), Orchid Country Club, Singapore, CD, November 18-22 (2002)
53. Rutkowski, L., Cpałka, K.: Neuro-fuzzy systems derived from quasi-triangular norms. In: Proceedings of the IEEE International Conference on Fuzzy Systems, Budapest, July 26-29, vol. 2, pp. 1031–1036 (2004)
54. Rutkowski, L., Przybył, A., Cpałka, K.: Novel on-line speed profile generation for industrial machine tool based on flexible neuro-fuzzy approximation. IEEE Transactions on Industrial Electronics 59, 1238–1247 (2012)
55. Rutkowski, L., Przybył, A., Cpałka, K., Er, M.J.: Online Speed Profile Generation for Industrial Machine Tool Based on Neuro-fuzzy Approach. In: Rutkowski, L., Scherer, R., Tadeusiewicz, R., Zadeh, L.A., Zurada, J.M. (eds.) ICAISC 2010, Part II. LNCS (LNAI), vol. 6114, pp. 645–650. Springer, Heidelberg (2010)
56. Szaleniec, M., Goclon, J., Witko, M., Tadeusiewicz, R.: Application of artificial neural networks and DFT-based parameters for prediction of reaction kinetics of ethylbenzene dehydrogenase. Journal of Computer-Aided Molecular Design 20(3), 145–157 (2006)
57. The VARAN Bus, the Real-Time Ethernet Bus System, VARAN-BUS-USER-ORGANISATION, http://www.varan-bus.net
58. Vitturi, S., Peretti, L., Seno, L., Zigliotto, M., Zunino, C.: Real-time Ethernet networks for motion control. Computer Standards & Interfaces 33(5), 465–476 (2011)

59. Zalasiński, M., Cpałka, K.: A new method of on-line signature verification using a flexible fuzzy one-class classifier, pp. 38–53. Academic Publishing House EXIT (2011)
60. Zalasiński, M., Cpałka, K.: Novel algorithm for the on-line signature verification. In: Rutkowski, L., Korytkowski, M., Scherer, R., Tadeusiewicz, R., Zadeh, L.A., Zurada, J.M. (eds.) ICAISC 2012, Part II. LNCS (LNAI), vol. 7268, pp. 362–367. Springer, Heidelberg (2012)
61. Zhang, X.L., Tang, X.Q., Chen, J.H., Zhou, H.C., Wu, T.: Hierarchical real-time networked CNC system based on the transparent model of industrial Ethernet. International Journal on Advanced Manufacturing Technology 34, 161–167 (2007)
62. Zalasiński, M., Łapa, K., Cpałka, K.: New Algorithm for Evolutionary Selection of the Dynamic Signature Global Features. In: Rutkowski, L., Korytkowski, M., Scherer, R., Tadeusiewicz, R., Zadeh, L.A., Zurada, J.M. (eds.) ICAISC 2013, Part II. LNCS (LNAI), vol. 7895, pp. 113–121. Springer, Heidelberg (2013)
63. Zalasiński, M., Cpałka, K.: New Approach for the On-Line Signature Verification Based on Method of Horizontal Partitioning. In: Rutkowski, L., Korytkowski, M., Scherer, R., Tadeusiewicz, R., Zadeh, L.A., Zurada, J.M. (eds.) ICAISC 2013, Part II. LNCS (LNAI), vol. 7895, pp. 342–350. Springer, Heidelberg (2013)
64. Zalasiński, M., Cpałka, K.: Novel Algorithm for the On-Line Signature Verification Using Selected Discretization Points Groups. In: Rutkowski, L., Korytkowski, M., Scherer, R., Tadeusiewicz, R., Zadeh, L.A., Zurada, J.M. (eds.) ICAISC 2013, Part I. LNCS (LNAI), vol. 7894, pp. 493–502. Springer, Heidelberg (2013)

Hierarchical Fuzzy Logic Systems: Current Research and Perspectives

Krzysztof Renkas and Adam Niewiadomski

Institute of Information Technology
Lodz University of Technology
215 Wolczanska St., 90-924 Lodz, Poland
Krzysztof.Renkas@gmail.com, Adam.Niewiadomski@p.lodz.pl

Abstract. This paper presents possible application of hierarchical fuzzy logic systems to control vehicles in computer games. The main idea is presented in two ways, a *current research* referring to paper [14] and concerning the new architecture of a fuzzy logic system as *Hierarchical Fuzzy Logic Systems (HFLS)*, and a brief look at the application of higher order fuzzy sets to these systems. "Hierarchical" means that fuzzy sets produced as output of one of fuzzy controllers are then processed as an input of another fuzzy controller. The use of such a controller significantly enhances the possibilities of computational intelligence methods in single-player games, i.e. where the "enemy" is controlled by agents simulating some real behaviour. The original proposal takes into account type-1 fuzzy sets which are not able to model uncertainties. The proposal presented in this paper models a type-2 hierarchical fuzzy logic system with uncertainties support, built with fuzzy controllers (in the sense of Mamdani). The advantages and disadvantages of HFLS in comparison to classical fuzzy systems with preliminary discussion about type-2 hierarchical fuzzy logic system are enumerated and commented on.

Keywords: fuzzy logic systems, hierarchical fuzzy logic systems, type-2 hierarchical fuzzy logic systems, hierarchical fuzzy controller, type-2 fuzzy sets, type-2 hierarchical fuzzy controller, simulation in computer games.

1 Introduction

This paper addresses issues of simulations in computer games. In particular, we are interested in computational intelligence methods based on fuzzy logic systems that make it possible to simulate an enemy in single-player games. The new solution proposed here is to replace *Type-1 Hierarchical Fuzzy Logic Systems* (T1HFLS) with *Type-2 Hierarchical Fuzzy Logic Systems* (T2HFLS). The main idea of this solution is to provide uncertainties to our system, extending the currently used type-1 to type-2 fuzzy sets. The main concept of the system is not changed with respect to [14] and the general structure looks the same (see Figure 3). This concept says that outputs of one type-2 fuzzy controller (fuzzy or defuzzified) are then considered as input of another type-2 fuzzy controller and is discussed in detail in Section 3 and 4. Please note that not each of the controlers used in T2HFLS must be the *Type-2 Fuzzy Controller (T2FC)*, which

L. Rutkowski et al. (Eds.): ICAISC 2014, Part I, LNAI 8467, pp. 295–306, 2014.
© Springer International Publishing Switzerland 2014

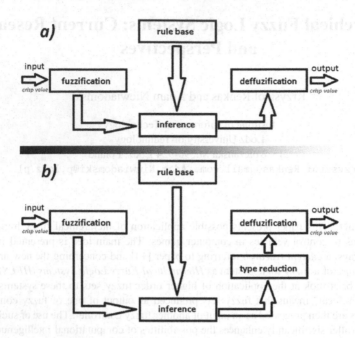

Fig. 1. Example of two fuzzy controllers, based on type-1 fuzzy sets (a) and type-2 fuzzy sets (b)

means that T2HFLS could be consist of T2FC and *Type-1 Fuzzy Controller (T1FC)*. Also the mode of action is quite the same, except for some new mechanisms dedicated for T2FC such as the type reduction block.

In general, fuzzy logic systems or fuzzy controllers are useful in case when a controlled process is not linear and the use of traditional controllers may appear inefficient. Type-2 fuzzy logic systems or type-2 fuzzy controllers are useful in case when additionally we want to model uncertainty in our system or controller. *Fuzzy controller (FC)* is a control unit based on fuzzy logic [18], which makes decisions based on knowledge containing the rules like *IF ... THEN ...;* with unspecified predicates [17]. Fuzzy controlling based on type-1 FS includes three stages: fuzzification, inference and defuzzification. Using type-2 FS we get a fourth stage as a type of reduction placed before the defuzzification block. Figure 1 shows schemes of those two controllers. There are two general models of fuzzy controllers: Mamdani model and Takagi-Sugeno-Kanga model (TSK) [17]. In this paper we refer only to the Mamdani model which operates on fuzzy antecedents and fuzzy consequents using defuzzification of a fuzzy output to get crisp value while TSK uses a bit different construction of rules to evaluate crisp output [9].

Moreover, we concentrate on proposals of architecture of *Hierarchical Fuzzy Controllers (HFC)*. The main difference between HFC and FC is that HFC is built of several traditional FCs, and is one complex inference system. Figure 2 shows examples of two controllers. The first one is a traditional fuzzy controller (A), and the other is sample structure of a HFC (B). As it is shown in case of B, output of one of FCs becomes input of another one in the HFC structure. This structure may contain traditional fuzzy controllers of both Mamdani and TSK types.

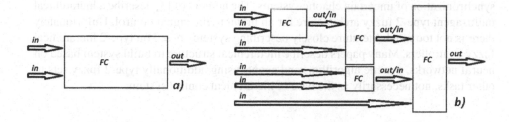

Fig. 2. Examples of two fuzzy controllers, simple (a) and hierarchical as HFLS (b)

In this paper we still operate on HFLS because it is a helpful tool for controlling. Hierarchical structure allows us to significantly decrease the number of rules in the inference block of the system and simplify the process of modelling and simulating the behaviours of vehicles in comparison to classic FC. This proposal was firstly described in [13] and then in [14]. Experiments were conducted on the basis of a game entitled *Tank 1990*, in particular, its newer version, *Tank 1990-2012*, developed by the author. The main new value added in this article is proposal of adjusting this system to work on type-2 FS which gives us much more capabilities during designing and creating hierarchical fuzzy logic systems.

The rest of the paper is organized as follows: Section 2 contains some literature references about type-1 and type-2 HFLS. The main concepts of architecture of original hierarchical fuzzy logic system for game purposes are given in Subsection 3.1 in detail. Subsection 3.2 describes application of our HFLS to our specific problem and 4 contains introduction to type-2 fuzzy sets and controlling with general perspectives about our system extensions. In Section 5, tests of the designed system with tests proposals for T2HFLS; and the results with preliminary discussion are described. The last Section 6 contains conclusions and some future directions of the research.

2   Literature References

At the start to better understand the HFC based on type-1 FS we could recall to [6,15,10,16,5]. The authors of those papers introduce HFC for many different problems such as controlling agricultural robots in a natural environment, truck backer-upper system, grouping cars into platoons and controlling the velocity and the gap between cars in single lane platoons, controlling mobile robots moving from point A to point B avoiding obstacles and controlling an urban traffic network in rush hours.

Much less information can be found about type-2 HFC and their applications. The author of [7] uses a hierarchical type-2 fuzzy logic control architecture for autonomous robots, where the problem was modeled as two layered architecture. The first level (low level) contains four interval type-2 FC responsible for different robot behaviours such as avoidance, goal seeking, left and right edge following. The second level (high level) contains an interval type-2 FC responsible for the coordination of low level controllers. Paper [12] presents application of hierarchical interval type-2 fuzzy neural network to synchronization of uncertain chaotic systems. The authors of [3] describe a hierarchical multi-agent type-2 fuzzy architecture for an urban traffic signal control. Unfortunately there is not too much literature closely describing systems based on type-2 hierarchical fuzzy controllers. Many papers describe hierarchical structure to build system based on neural networks, genetic algorithms and agents using additionally type-2 fuzzy sets to other tasks, not necessarily as the base of hierarchical control system.

3 Type-2 Hierarchical Fuzzy Logic System and 2D Vehicle Simulation

3.1 The Architecture of Hierarchical Fuzzy Logic System

During the analysis of different problems solutions based on multistage inference we could note that applied controllers usually do not use the hierarchical structure. Outputs of such FCs are returned as independent values, without any connections between them during inference.

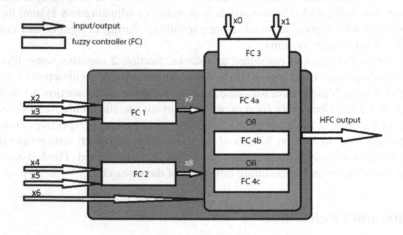

Fig. 3. General diagram of designed HFLS structure

In contrast to them during last research, we proposed the newly HFLS structure. This structure combines all of FCs into one system, where the output of one FC becomes the input of another one. The final output of this system is one crisp value. Furthermore, not each of combined controllers works during each iteration of inference. Figure 3 shows the discussed structure.

We can see different locations of unit controllers, communicating with each other in different ways in Figure 3. Application of this HFLS to a specific case is described in Subsection 3.2 in detail. To maintain a certain level of abstraction, we can assume that the system has 7 inputs denoted as $x_0, \ldots, x_6$ assigned to different internal drivers, which can additionally take other outputs as inputs, e.g. x_7 and x_8. The system could be started many times, for example $m \in \mathbb{N}$ times, i.e. we consider m iterations. In each iteration, system can be started n times for different data sets. For example, controlling a pluton of cars, inclusive n cars includes m iterations that has common elements for each car. In each iteration, one can call the inference for each car (data set), that is to say n times. FCs on a blue background (see Fig. 3) are run in each iteration for each data set, so this is $m \cdot n$ times. FCs on the salmon background, Fig. 3, are some kind of "sub-controllers" managed by FC no. 3. For each m iterations FC 3 is running once, making decision which of the FCs marked as $4a, \ldots, 4c$ will be running for n next data sets in actual iteration.

By using the proposed structure of HFLS, we can simplify tank control problem in a computer game. In this game, HFLS manages a battalion of tanks. In this case we can treat iteration as inference for the entire battalion. A single set of data concerns a specific tank in this battalion. At the start of iteration, FC 3 selects the strategy on the basis of the game (available strategies: defensive, offensive and mixed). FC $4a, \ldots, 4c$ correspond to the mentioned strategies chosen by FC 3. In the next step for each tank, controllers No. 1 and 2 are activated, and one of next controller, 4a, 4b, or 4c, returns the final system decision about action for a given tank.

3.2 Hierarchical Fuzzy Logic System in Controlling Tank Activity: Current Research

The chosen issue to solve has been defined as controlling military vehicles during clashes in computer games. General rules of the game were drawn from *Tank 1990*[1] developed by *Namco* [1].

Applying this HFLS has to show the simplicity of the proposed solution for controlling tanks by a HFLS in comparison to typical FC.

Input data and controller knowledge Input data for inference come from the simulator and they are expressed by the following linguistic variables:

- opponent tanks count (x_0)
- average force of opponent tanks (x_1)
- distance to the nearest opponent tank (x_2)
- force difference between our tank and nearest opponent tank (x_3)
- number of allies – tanks that belong to our battalion (x_4)
- average force of allies (x_5)
- tank is being attacked (x_6)

The fuzzy controllers are based on Mamdani's model with fuzzy antecedents and fuzzy consequents. To represent linguistic information in current state we used type-1 FS. Controller based on type-1 FS is much more simple to design, implement and is much more effective during inference, but does not provide support for uncertainty. In section 4 we describe our proposition of extending the current solution from type-1 to type-2. Examples of rules are listed below.

---

[1] Basic information about game *Battle City*, an earlier version of the game *Tank 1990*. [2]

– strategy controller rules

```
RULE 1 : IF TANKS_COUNT IS SMALL AND AVERAGE_TANKS_FORCE IS SMALL
    THEN STRATEGY IS DEFENSIVE;
...
```

– support controller rules

```
...
RULE 6 : IF ALLIES_COUNT IS BIG AND AVERAGE_ALLIES_FORCE IS MEDIUM
    THEN SUPPORT IS BIG;
...
```

– action controller rules (offensive strategy)

```
RULE 0 : IF TANK_IS_BEING_ATTACKED IS YES THEN ACTION IS ATTACK;
RULE 1 : IF RISK IS ZERO AND SUPPORT IS ZERO
    THEN ACTION IS PATROL;
...
```

The Simulator and The Use of HFLS Game *Tank 1990-2012* was created as a simulator for testing and demonstrating designed controller and rule base. This simulator has been implemented in Java. Figure 4 shows two screenshots of this game.

Fig. 4. Screenshots of game *Tank 1990-2012*. Home page (on the left) and first stage during battle (on the right).

The structure of used HFLS is shown in Figure 3. Inputs of this HFLS are described in section 3.2. FCs 1 and 2 correspond to the controllers computing the level of risk x_7 and support x_8. These variables are transferred as an input to the tank action controller $4a, \ldots, 4c$. Only one of these FCs is activated in the current iteration depending on the strategy chosen by the FC 3. Offensive, defensive and mixed strategies are allowed. The controlling system selects actions for each tank in battalion. Final decision allows to escape, attack, stay at the current position and to patrol the immediate surroundings.

4   Type-2 Hierarchical Fuzzy Logic System: Perspectives

Tests and results obtained during solving problem using type-1 HFLS are satisfying. The most interesting results and conclusions are presented in section 5, for more please see [13,14]. Furthermore, we decided to extend our solution to type-2 HFLS. The first reason is that type-2 HFLS is not popular in the literature. The second reason is that fuzzy controllers based on type-2 FS make our solution much more realistic and flexible.

Mendel in [11] enumerates four sources of uncertainties in type-1 fuzzy logic systems:

- „words mean different things to different people" – the meanings of the words that are used in the rules can be uncertain
- when knowledge is extracted from a group of experts who do not all agree, consequents may have a histogram of values associated with them
- measurements that activate a type-1 fuzzy logic systems may be noisy and therefore uncertain
- the data that are used to tune the parameters of a type-1 may also be noisy

Those four points are the best reason to modernize current HFLS to type-2 HFLS, except for the fact that using type-2 FS computationals is more complicated than using type-1 FS. In subsection 3.2 we described inputs as linguistic variables which are uncertain words, which could mean different things to different experts and that is one of reaffirmations that our case belongs to problem group, that should be solved using type-2 FS.

At the beginning, we present some basic notations for type-2 FS.

Definition 1 ([11]). *A type-2 fuzzy set, denoted as $\tilde{A}$, is characterized by a type-2 membership function $\mu_{\tilde{A}}(x, u)$, where $x \in X$ and $u \in J_x \subseteq [0, 1]$, i.e.,*

$$\tilde{A} = ((x, u), \mu_{\tilde{A}}(x, u)) \mid \forall x \in X, \forall u \in J_x \subseteq [0, 1] \ . \tag{1}$$

in which $0 \leq \mu_{\tilde{A}}(x, u) \leq 1$.

x is primary variable, J_x is the primary membership of x. Simplifying we could say that membership functions of type-2 fuzzy sets are themselves fuzzy and operate on domain in $[0, 1]$.

Definition 2 ([11]). *Footprint of uncertainty (FOU) is the union of all primary memberships, i.e.,*

$$FOU(\tilde{A}) = \cup_{x \in X} J_x \ . \tag{2}$$

FOU in the primary memberships of a type-2 fuzzy set, $\tilde{A}$, consists of a bounded region, see Figure 5.

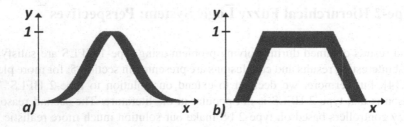

Fig. 5. FOUs with Gaussian membership function (a) and an interval type-2 fuzzy set (b)

Adjusting Hierarchical Fuzzy Logic System to Work With Type-2 Fuzzy Sets. Subsection 3.2 shows some example rules created for type-1 HFLS, to adjust our controller to operate on type-2 FS we do not need to modify the prepared rules. This is because the distinction between type-1 and type-2 fuzzy sets is about the nature of membership function and is not related with the form of rules. The first thing that should be done is to evaluate the type-1 FS to type-2 FS. We should modify actual fuzzy sets descriptions, to get type-2 FS and choose the best class of those sets to our problem. The main domain of those class contains *Gaussian type-2 FS, interval type-2 FS, sigmoidal type-2 FS, trapezoidal type-2 FS* and *triangular type-2 fuzzy set.*

Moving on to the inference process we must say that in the type-2 case, our inference looks quite the same. In a T1FC inputs are fuzzified to type-1 FS and then they are mapped to type-1 fuzzy output. Antecedents in rules are connected by the t-norm and multiple rules may be combined using t-conorm operations to get one fuzzy output. Using type-2 FS all we need is to do unions and intersection (t-norms and t-conorms) of type-2 fuzzy sets. The union of $\tilde{A}$ and $\tilde{B}$ could be expressed as:

$$\mu_{\tilde{A} \cup \tilde{B}}(x) = \Sigma_{u \in J_x^u} \Sigma_{w \in J_x^w} f_x(u) \star g_x(w)/u \vee w \equiv \mu_{\tilde{A}}(x) \sqcup \mu_{\tilde{B}}(x) \text{ where } x \in X \ . \tag{3}$$

Symbol $\sqcup$ denotes the *join* operation, $\star$ denotes a t-norm (e.g., minimum, product, etc.). The intersection could be expressed as:

$$\mu_{\tilde{A} \cap \tilde{B}}(x) = \Sigma_{u \in J_x^u} \Sigma_{w \in J_x^w} f_x(u) \star g_x(w)/u \star w \equiv \mu_{\tilde{A}}(x) \sqcap \mu_{\tilde{B}}(x) \text{ where } x \in X \ . \tag{4}$$

Symbol $\sqcap$ denotes the *meet* operation and the $\vee$ represents the *max* t-conorm. [11,8]

During the inference process we get type-2 FS as output. Before the last stage as defuzzification we need to do type reduction. General process of working T2FC is shown on figure 1, scheme *b*. During type reduction process we get type-1 FS from type-2 FS, and then this set could be defuzzified to obtain a crisp value as the output of our single T2FC. This value could be the final output of our type-2 HFLS if it is produced by the final controller in our system or could be an input to another T2FC. Type reduction method could be called a defuzzification method [4]. Original defuzzification gives us a crisp value which we could call type 0 (crisp) value from type-1 set. Type reduction gives us a type-1 set from type-2 set. To type reduction we could use *height type reduction, centroid type reduction, center of sums type reduction, center of sets type reduction* or many others.

5   Tests and Results

"Tank 1990-2012": a Current State. Tests The experiment is conducted on the basis of the computer game entitled *Tank 1990-2012* created by the author, and it is a newer version of classic *Tank 1990*. Especially, the main difference is the use of HFLS, and the rule base accessible to everyone, so it allows to do own tests[2]

Other tests must be done for the proposed extension of the current solution. Those tests should be connected with the application of type-2 FS. The basic tests should test different configurations of new controller in terms of different type-2 FS class, different t-norms and t-conorms used during inference process and different reduction type methods. The best configuration should be chosen and compared to current HFLS. This comparison could be based on efficiency, time-consuming, speed and complexity of computationals, general behaviours of tanks during the battle and playability, assessed by players.

Current Results Table 1 shows results of the first test described in the paragraph above. As it is shown in Table 1 it is quite easy to win playing *Tank 1990* (43 losses, 59.7%). On the other hand, this is almost impossible to win in newer *Tank 1990-2012* (100.0% losses); this is because the latter version of the game is equipped with much more intelligent method of controlling tanks.

Table 1. Summary of losses during played games *Tank 1990-2012* and *Tank 1990* during 72 tests

	Tank 1990-2012	Tank 1990
defeat	72 (100%)	43 (59.2%)
victory	0 (0%)	29 (20.3%)

The second test concerns time periods needed to achieve victory. Different configurations of HFLS are tested and the best are minimum *t-norm*, Łukasiewicz *s-norm* and the middle of maximum (MOM) as defuzzification method. *Tank 1990* was tested in *NES* console simulator. Average results are shown in the Table 2. As we can see, almost identical results are achieved, and the difference is only 0.4 seconds.

[2] We want to refer to the most interesting tests. The first one applies to general behaviour of game and tanks controlled by HFLS. In this test case games *Tank 1990* and *Tank 1990-2012* were launched 72 times, counting losses in subsequent stages taking stage 11 as the last one. The second test is more detailed comparing efficiency of different controller configurations. *Tank 1990-2012* was launched 50 times for each configuration and the best configuration was selected. The same test was done with *Tank 1990*, launching the game 50 times and comparing the average time with the time of the best configuration from *Tank 1990-2012*. During this test user could not do any moves with the tank. Please note that test conditions were not the same, for example the speed of vehicles in the original game was much higher. The last one we want to mention is summary of HFLS rule base which has been made in comparison to single FC rule base doing the same task. This comparison shows simpler and more efficient solution.

Table 2. Average times necessary to win in *Tank 1990-2012* and *Tank 1990* [s]

Tank 1990-2012	Tank 1990
29.8s	29.4s

Table 3. Number of fired rules needed to infer for four battalions of 1, 5, 10 and 20 tanks in HFLS and FC

number of tanks in battalion	fired rules in HFLS	fired rules in FC
1	44	1 458
5	184	7 290
10	359	14 580
20	709	29 160

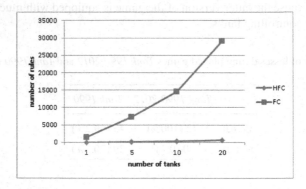

Fig. 6. Number of fired rules during one inference for battalion of 1, 5, 10 and 20 tanks during inference in HFLS and simple FC

Summarizing HFLS rule base, we count $7 + 2 = 9$ linguistic variables (7 as input and 2 as auxiliary). Counting created rules we get $9 + 9 + 9 + 3 \cdot 17 = 78$. During the inference process, 9 rules decide about strategy, 9 rules about support, 9 rules about risk, and 17 rules about the tanks action (each strategy uses a different set of rules to select tank action, so that is why we have $3 \cdot 17 = 51$ rules). For example to do one iteration of inference for battalion of 5 tanks, we must select strategy (9 rules) at the start of iteration, then for each tank we must get risk and support value ($9 + 9 = 18$ rules) and at the end choose the final tank action (17 rules). So to do this task we must fire $9 + 5 \cdot (18 + 17) = 184$ rules. The complexity of these rules is low: two antecedents and one consequent.

To solve this problem using single layered FC, we should have to include all combinations of those 7 input variables into this FC. In this case we need to create $9 \cdot 9 \cdot 9 \cdot 2 =$

1458 rules (strategy, support, risk and info that tank is being attacked). Using this FC to our sample battalion we need to fire $5 \cdot 1458 = 7290$ rules with 7 antecedents. Sample forecasts are presented in Table 3.

The summary of this comparison is depicted by the graph shown in Figure 6.

6   Conclusions and Future Work

The tests run prove some positive effects of applying HFLS to control virtual vehicles in games. The results of the first test, presented in Table 1, determine much higher game difficulty, i.e. more intelligent behaviour of enemy tanks, controlled by HFLS, with respect to the *Tank 1990*. The results of the second test, see Table 2, inform us that the more time-consuming computations (mostly inferences) in case of HFLS do not decrease the speed of the game; the lack of a negative effect is really important observation here, mostly because of higher computational complexity of HFLS. We also note that the use of HFLS has a positive impact on the tank control in the newer version of the tested game, i.e. *Tank 1990-2012*. The vehicles move intelligently and try to achieve clearly defined goals, while tanks in the older version, i.e. *Tank 1990*, move chaotically and make irrational decisions.

From the point of view of a programmer/developer, HFLS make it possible to adapt controllers easily to specific problems appearing in software, not necessarily in games. The modular and hierarchical design of such a controller makes a problem easy to understand and allows to find a simple solution to this problem. For instance, the HFLS described in Section 3 requires only 78 unique inference rules, while the analogous FC for the same purposes requires 1 458 (!). Furthermore, the rules of FC are more complex, because of using 7 linguistic variables, while the HFLS uses only 2.

Using type-2 FS to describe antecedents and consequents should provide support for uncertainty without any interference into rule base and general structure of current HFLS. The negative aspect of application of type-2 FS is that we need to implement more complicated unions and intersection methods and implement new block to provide type reduction. Those new and modified methods will decrease the performance of the controller which could have a negative impact to the speed of the game.

During feature research at the start we will implement the perspectives described in this paper. All of the mentioned methods and solutions should be implemented, tested which could let us give the first opinion about ratio of benefits of application type-2 FS to negative impact and cost of additional work during implementation. Apart from the positive or negative results we want to continue research focused on other classes of type-2 FS and methods used during inference and defuzzification, to make our solution much more powerful and flexible for different problems.

Our future research may also direct towards combining genetic and/or evolutionary algorithms or artificial neural networks with HFLS. Other different direction of development is the use of multi-agent systems to present type-2 HFLS with distributed architecture. Genetic and evolutionary algorithms, as optimisation methods, can be used to find optimal route to the specified destination or object. Neural networks can be useful in dynamic tuning knowledge bases of HFLS. Multi-agent systems seem to be perfect tool to apply type-2 fuzzy controller with hierarchical structure to many problems in unspecified and uncertain environment.

References

1. American web page of namco, http://www.namcoamerica.com [access: 10 XII 2013]
2. Game description battle city, http://pl.wikipedia.org/wiki/Battle_City [access: 10 XII 2013]
3. Balaji, P.G., Srinivasan, D.: Distributed multi-agent type-2 fuzzy architecture for urban traffic signal control. In: IEEE International Conference on Fuzzy Systems, FUZZ-IEEE 2009, pp. 1627–1632 (2009)
4. Dubois, D., Prade, H.: Fuzzy Sets and Systems: Theory and Applications. Mathematics in science and engineering. Academic Press (1980)
5. Gegov, A.E., Frank, P.M.: Hierarchical fuzzy control of multivariable systems. Fuzzy Sets and Systems 72, 299–310 (1995)
6. Hagras, H., Callaghan, V., Colley, M., Carr-West, M.: A behaviour based hierarchical fuzzy control architecture for agricultural autonomous mobile robots. Journal of Autonomous Robots 13, 37–52 (2002)
7. Hagras, H.: A hierarchical type-2 fuzzy logic control architecture for autonomous mobile robots. IEEE Transactions on Fuzzy Systems 12(4), 524–539 (2004)
8. Karnik, N.N., Mendel, J.M.: Operations on type-2 fuzzy sets. Fuzzy Sets and Systems 122(2), 327–348 (2001)
9. Kaur, A., Kaur, A.: Comparison of mamdani-type and sugeno-type fuzzy inference systems for air conditioning system. International Journal of Soft Computing and Engineering (IJSCE) 2 (May 2012)
10. Kim, H.M., Dickerson, J., Kosko, B.: Fuzzy throttle and brake control for platoons of smart cars. Fuzzy Sets and Systems 84, 209–234 (1996)
11. Mendel, J., John, R.: Type-2 fuzzy sets made simple. IEEE Transactions on Fuzzy Systems 10(2), 117–127 (2002)
12. Mohammadzadeh, A., Kaynak, O., Teshnehlab, M.: Two-mode indirect adaptive control approach for synchronization of uncertain chaotic systems by the use of a hierarchical interval type-2 fuzzy neural network (2013)
13. Renkas, K.: Hierarchical fuzzy system and controlling military vehicles in computer games. Master's thesis, Lodz University of Technology, 116 Stefana Zeromskiego St., Lodz, Poland (September 2012)
14. Renkas, K., Niewiadomski, A.: Hierarchical fuzzy logic systems and controlling vehicles in computer games. Journal of Applied Computer Science (JACS) 21(2) (2013) (in print)
15. Riid, A., Rstern, E.: Fuzzy hierarchical control of truck and trailer. In: BEC 2002: Proceedings of the 8th Biennial Baltic Electronics Conference, October 6-9, pp. 141–144 (2002)
16. Wang, L.X.: Modeling and control of hierarchical systems with fuzzy systems. Automatica 33(6), 1041–1053 (1997)
17. Yager, R.R., Filev, D.P.: Essentials of Fuzzy Modeling and Control. A Wiley-Interscience publication, John Wiley & Sons (1994)
18. Zadeh, L.A.: The concept of a linguistic variable and its applications to approximate reasoning (i). Information Sciences 8, 199–249 (1975)

Application of Models
of Relational Fuzzy Cognitive Maps
for Prediction of Work of Complex Systems

Grzegorz Słoń

Kielce University of Technology,
al. Tysiaclecia P. P. 7, 25-314 Kielce, Poland
g.slon@tu.kielce.pl

Abstract. The paper presents certain aspects of application of model
of the Relational Fuzzy Cognitive Map (RFCM) for advanced analysis
of activity of complex dynamic systems. Intelligent models, including
various types of cognitive maps, are commonly used to study the effect
of the selected parameter on the others or to classification of objects
described by many parameters. RFCM model characteristics, in addition
to the above uses, allows to use it also for modeling the work of systems
with the internal dynamics. It follows that such a model can be used to
predict the state of the system in the future steps of a discrete time. In
the paper, selected results of testing just such a use of the RFCM model
are described.

Keywords: relational fuzzy cognitive map, intelligent modeling, fuzzy
relations, fuzzy numbers, arithmetic of fuzzy numbers, prediction.

1 Introduction

Modeling the work of the complex systems, characterized by uncertainty and
imprecision of the information has always been a difficult task. Uncertainty of
the information is associated with inaccurate knowledge of the structure of a
modeled system, which results that such a structure is difficult to describe with
the use of the system of equations (usually it is not possible). Imprecision of
the information stems from the way of obtaining data on the values of selected
parameters of the system. In many fields (such as economics, medicine, politics,
sociology, meteorology, and even some technical issues) the values are estimated
or recognized subjectively, may therefore be dependent on the observer (expert).
On the other hand, it is hard to resign from modeling, which is necessary process for understanding many phenomena, and also significantly reduces the costs
of design and exploitation research. For many years, research continues on the
creation of methods which allow to skip a negative impact of both the uncertainty and imprecision of the information. Uncertainty can be, to some extent,
mitigated by using so-called "intelligent" modeling using neural or neural-like
structures (such as an artificial neural network). As for the imprecision, the answer is to introduce into a model the fuzzy algebra [4, 7, 8, 13, 14].

L. Rutkowski et al. (Eds.): ICAISC 2014, Part I, LNAI 8467, pp. 307–318, 2014.

In this sense, special attention should be devoted to developed since 1986 [3] structures called Fuzzy Cognitive Maps (FCM), because, in addition to the basic tasks of classification, they allow to consider the dynamic internal structure of the modeled object. A model, constructed using the FCM technique, is a digraph, in vertices of which the main quantities of the object (called concepts), selected by the expert, are placed, while the arches reproduce causal relations between concepts. So it can be said that such a model is characterized by a following pair:

$$< \mathbf{C}, \mathbf{E} > \tag{1}$$

where: $\mathbf{C} = \{c_1, ..., c_n\}$ – set of concepts; $\mathbf{E} = \{e_{i,j}\}_{i,j=1,...,n;i\neq j}$ – set of causal relations between concepts; n – number of concepts.

In the basic form both concepts and links between them are linguistic quantities, and their values are expressed as the linguistic values [1–3, 9]. Such a form, however, makes the model difficult to learn (which is an essential element of the design process of intelligent model), and therefore in the majority of applications found in the literature (e.g. [5]) the following form of the FCM description occurs:

$$< \mathbf{x}, \mathbf{w} > \tag{2}$$

where: $\mathbf{x} = \{x_1, ..., x_n\}$ – set of normalized values of concepts expressed numerically; $\mathbf{w} = \{w_{i,j}\}_{i,j=1,...,n;i\neq j}$ – the set of weights of causal connections between concepts, expressed as numbers from the range $[-1, 1]$; n – number of concepts.

Form (2) facilitates the model learning (for this purpose mainly various population-based methods [5] are used) and its application, but it is de facto departure from the basic advantage of the classical FCM, which is the fuzzification of values. For this reason, since 2008, the works are conducted on developing such a method of modeling uncertain and imprecise systems, in which the fuzzification of parameters would be kept at all stages of the design and operation of the model. Developed, as a result, method is based on the model of so-called Relational Fuzzy Cognitive Map (RFCM) [10–12], which is in a sense an extension of the existing approach to FCM. Model of RFCM is also digraph with concepts and connections, but values of the concepts are represented by fuzzy numbers, and the connections between them – by fuzzy relations. Such a model can be, in general, described as follows:

$$< \mathbf{X}, \mathbf{R} > \tag{3}$$

where: $\mathbf{X} = \{X_1, ..., X_n\}$ – set of fuzzy values of concepts expressed by fuzzy numbers; $\mathbf{R} = \{R_{i,j}\}_{i,j=1,...,n;i\neq j}$ – set (matrix) of fuzzy relations between concepts; n – number of concepts.

Graphical visualizations of models (1), (2) and (3) are similar each other and have a form like in Fig. 1.

The differences result from the way of the description of the model concepts and from the way in which the model is taught and used. The object of this paper is the RFCM model.

The fundamental task of any kind of a cognitive map is to identify the impact, which a single, selected concept can exert on the others. Various attempts are

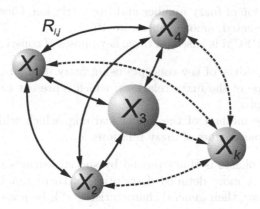

Fig. 1. Visualization of general form of RFCM. X_k – general representation of fuzzy values of concepts X_5-X_n; $R_{i,j}$ – general representation of fuzzy relations; n – number of concepts of RFCM.

made to apply cognitive maps to predict future states of systems (such as in [6]), but they relate to the standard FCM constructions that are based de facto on the processing of real numbers. Moreover, in such approaches time waveforms of selected parameters are not specially studied. The introduction of dynamic structure of the RFCM extends the scope of applications of the cognitive models with additional functionalities related to the direct modeling of system behavior in transient states, including forecasting the waveforms of the selected concepts of the system. In this paper, there is presented an example of just such a use of RFCM.

2 The Design and Operation of the RFCM Model

There are various possible approaches to the construction of the RFCM models, however, in the case of modeling systems with dynamic internal structure, it seems to be the best the model that accounts a non-linear rate of change of values of the concepts [10, 11]:

$$X_j(t+1) = X_j(t) \oplus \bigoplus_{\substack{i=1 \\ i \neq j}}^{n} [(X_i(t) \ominus X_i(t-1)) \circ R_{i,j}] \tag{4}$$

where: $X_j(t)$ – fuzzy value of the considered (j-th) concept in a step t of discrete time (represented by the fuzzy number); $R_{i,j}$ – fuzzy relation between concepts i-th and j-th; $i, j = 1, ..., n$; n – number of concepts; $t = 0, 1, 2, ..., T$ – consecutive steps of discrete time; T – considered interval (number of steps) of discrete time.

Exploitation of model (4) consists in calculating the fuzzy values of each concept in the subsequent steps of discrete time. Operators occurring in (4) mean: $\oplus$ – fuzzy addition of fuzzy numbers; $\ominus$ – fuzzy subtraction of fuzzy numbers;

∘ – fuzzy composition of fuzzy number and fuzzy relation. Closer description of their actions is presented, among others, in [10].

Modeling using RFCM is based on three key phases of constructing the model:

– fuzzification of values of key concepts using fuzzy numbers,
– selection of type of the fuzzy relations, which represent causal connections between concepts,
– selection of the method of the model learning, which will be used to the adaptation of parameters of fuzzy relations.

Each of the above phases is characterized by special features unprecedented in other approaches. A more detailed description of them can be found, among others, in [10]. Below, their general characteristics will be presented.

2.1   Fuzzification of Values of the Concepts

The first step for fuzzifying the concepts is to determine the span of the support and the number of linguistic values k, describing the concept. In the elaborated method [10–12] it is assumed that the number of linguistic values is constant for the entire model (for all concepts), and the support should provide sufficient symmetry of membership functions associated with the individual concepts. Experiments have shown that the sufficient span of the support is the range of $[-2, 2]$. Then the general form of membership functions of fuzzy numbers representing fuzzy values of concepts should be selected. They should have a symmetrical character (according to the class of Λ, π or $\mathbf{G}$ [10]). For example, the membership function of class $\mathbf{G}$ of fuzzy value of the concept has a form:

$$\mu_{X_i}(s) = e^{-\left(\frac{s - \overline{X}_i}{\sigma_i}\right)^2} \tag{5}$$

where: X_i – fuzzy value of the i-th concept; s – support; $\overline{X}_i$ – center (normalized real value) of the i-th concept; σ_i – fuzziness coefficient of the i-th concept; $i = 1, ..., n$; n – number of concepts.

On the support k evenly spaced sample points should be deposited. Fuzzification consists in the determination of the center and then define a membership function according to (5).

Another problem is the initial normalization of the real values of concepts. It is always used in intelligent models to ensure even distribution of influence of individual concepts and independence from the different scales used for measuring the parameters. A commonly used max-min method converts input values (irrespective of their original character) into normalized values falling within the range $[0, 1]$. In dynamic systems signs of the processed values may be important, and therefore for the needs of RFCM models there was developed a modified method of normalization [10], described by the following equation:

$$x(t) = \text{Sgn}(x^*(t)) \frac{|x^*(t)|}{max(|x^*|)} \tag{6}$$

where: t – selected step of a discrete time, in which normalization is performed; $x^*(t)$ – real (input) value in step t of a discrete time; $x(t)$ – normalized (output) value in step t of a discrete time.

Values of concepts, normalized with the use of (6), are fallen within the range $[-1, 1]$.

2.2   Designing Fuzzy Relations

The method for creating RFCM is based on the assumption of a high degree of automation of the process of building individual elements. It determines the shape of the relations between the concepts. In essence the choice of the fuzzy relations is crucial for the proper functioning of the model. Numerous studies and trials have led to the development of a certain general functional form (membership function) [10, 11], on the basis of which all the fuzzy relations of the model can be designed:

$$\mu_R(a, b) = f_R\left(\frac{p_1 \cdot b - p_2 \cdot r(a)}{p_3 \cdot \sigma}\right) \tag{7}$$

where: a, b – adequate points of supports of fuzzy numbers A and B connected with the relation R (in the RFCM models these supports are identical); f_R – the base function dependent on the selected membership function; σ – fuzziness coefficient (dispersion); $r(a)$ – functional coefficient of power of the fuzzy relation R; p_1, p_2, p_3 – coefficients dependent on the selected class of the membership function.

For building fuzzy relations in RFCM models the best suitable functions are of classes Λ, Π, π or G [4, 10]. The membership function of class G can be defined in the following way:

$$\mu_{R_{i,j}}(s_i, s_j) = e^{-f^2} \tag{8}$$

where: $f = \frac{s_j - r_{i,j}(s_i)}{\sigma_{i,j}}$; $\mu_{R_{i,j}}$ – the membership function of the fuzzy relation $R_{i,j}$ between concepts i-th and j-th; s_i, s_j – supports of fuzzy values of concepts i-th and j-th; $r_{i,j}(s_i)$ – coefficient of power of the fuzzy relation $R_{i,j}$ (in a functional form); $\sigma_{i,j}$ – fuzziness coefficient of the fuzzy relation $R_{i,j}$.

The coefficient of power of relation $r_{i,j}(s_i)$, occurring in equation (8), is a function of a support, and supports s_i and s_j are sets of the same k points, so: $s_i = \{s_{i(1)}, s_{i(2)}, ..., s_{i(k)}\} = s_j = \{s_{j(1)}, s_{j(2)}, ..., s_{j(k)}\}$, where k – the number of the sampling points of the support.

The simplest form of the $r_{i,j}$ is a linear form (9):

$$r_{i,j}(s_i) = \overline{r}_{i,j} \cdot s_i \tag{9}$$

where: $\overline{r}_{i,j}$ – direction number of function of power of fuzzy relation between concepts i-th and j-th.

2.3   The Model Learning

Learning of the RFCM model is a supervised process, which requires the use of a certain number of complete historical data. As mentioned earlier, in classical FCM models there is used a method consisting in the conversion of values of all fuzzy quantities into a numerical form, and then the population-based adaptation of such arisen parameters of the map. In the RFCM model all operations, including learning, are made on fuzzy quantities. Each relation is described with several parameters, which means that the direct application of population-based methods is impossible. So, therefore it has been developed an approach using "algorithm of successive approximations with variable step of parameter changes" [10, 11]. Generally, the method is similar to conventional ones, i.e. it consists in successive making minor changes of parameters of individual fuzzy relations and, after each such change, analysis a certain criterion – the closeness coefficient:

$$J(Q) = \Phi\left(\|\overline{X}_i(t) - Z_i(t)\|\right) \Rightarrow \min_Q \tag{10}$$

where: $\Phi()$ – selected optimization function (e.g. quadratic); $\overline{X}_i(t)$, $Z_i(t)$ – defuzzified and crisp (reference) trajectories of changes of values of the i-th concept; $\| \ \|$ – selected norm; t - discrete time.

Quantity Q, appearing in equation (10), is a vector of changed parameters. For relations of type **G** it can take a form:

$$Q = [\{\overline{r}_{i,j}\}, \{\sigma_{i,j}\}, k]^T \tag{11}$$

where: k – number of the support sampling points; $\{\overline{r}_{i,j}\}$ – directional numbers of functional coefficients of powers of fuzzy relations $R_{i,j}$; $\{\sigma_{i,j}\}$ – fuzziness coefficients of fuzzy relations $R_{i,j}$; $i, j = 1, ..., n$; n – number of concepts in the model.

In the algorithm of successive approximations with variable step of parameter changes the randomness is abandoned in favor of planned changes of individual parameters – with concomitant use of time-varying increments. All fuzzy relations are successively modified in accordance with the algorithm, which general idea (for a single relation) is shown in Fig. 2.

Fig. 2 shows subsequent stages of a single adaptation step for a single fuzzy relation. At each stage, the value of the closeness coefficient is verified. If it is less than the current one, the change of the parameter ($\Delta\overline{r}$ or $\Delta\sigma$) is accepted, if not, the change is withdrawn. Individual adaptation steps are repeated successively for all relations until the "Stop" condition is satisfied.

3   The Use of RFCM Model to Prediction Purposes

Prediction process involves designating the future, unknown states of the system basing on the knowledge of its current behavior. Intelligent models, thanks to various supervised learning techniques, work well in classification tasks. In addition, the models of RFCM kind, due to its multi-directional structure, may be

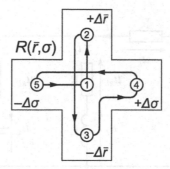

Fig. 2. General idea of the algorithm of adaptation of a single fuzzy relation of class G with linear function of power of the relation. $+\Delta\bar{r}$, $-\Delta\bar{r}$, $+\Delta\sigma$, $-\Delta\sigma$ – changes of values of the key parameters in the subsequent stages of the algorithm.

used to reproduce the operation of the dynamic system in certain circumstances and to analyze the effect of changes of the selected concept on the other ones. As it turns out, they are not all the possible applications. In certain circumstances, such a model can be used for prediction. The rest of the paper will be devoted to presentation of the results of tests of such a model work.

Predictive application of the RFCM model requires some modification to the procedure of normalization of concept values. Into the method shown in (6) there is introduced an additional scale coefficient, which takes into account the possible values higher than those observed in the historical data. Then equation (6), for selected, the i-th concept, takes the form (12):

$$x_i(t) = \varphi_i \cdot \mathrm{Sgn}(x_i^*(t)) \frac{|x_i^*(t)|}{max(|x_i^*|)} \tag{12}$$

where: $\varphi_i \in [0, 1]$ – scale coefficient for the normalization of the i-th concept.

Normalization according to (12) is used at the stage of the model learning. The model learns on chronologically earlier part of complete historical data, while it's tested on the full set of this data.

3.1   Modeled Object

For the purposes of test modeling there was chosen the object giving the ability to easily obtaining reference data for various operating conditions. This object is a simple RLC circuit shown in Fig. 3.

By using a system of differential equations a situation was modeled, in which in the circuit from Fig. 3 the voltage E is turning on. Time courses of values of individual quantities of the circuit were used as a source of historical data, which was assumed that one step of a discrete time corresponds to 50ms of a real time. The waveforms, obtained in this way, have been normalized according to (12), with a scale coefficient $\varphi = 0.8$ equal for all concepts. Reference waveforms, for 30 consecutive steps of a discrete time, are shown in Fig. 4.

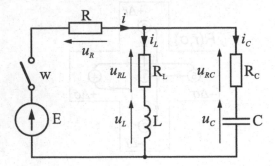

Fig. 3. Diagram of the RLC circuit, which was a source of the reference data. $R = 10\Omega$, $R_L = R_C = 0.01\Omega$, $L = 0.08H$, $C = 0.05F$, $E = 10V$.

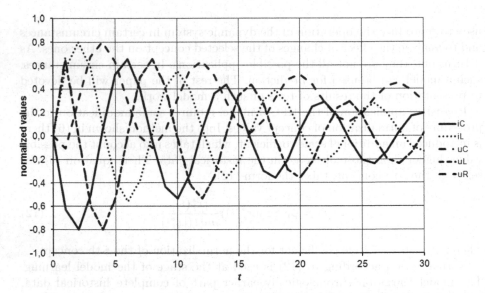

Fig. 4. Reference waveforms – normalized historical data. t – discrete time.

Then, a model in the form of RFCM with a construction as in Fig. 1 was built, which contains $n = 7$ concepts whose fuzzy values were denoted as follows: X_1 – E, X_2 – i, X_3 – i_C, X_4 – i_L, X_5 – u_C, X_6 – u_L, X_7 – u_R. It was assumed that values of concepts will be fuzzified basing on the membership functions of type (5), and fuzzy relations will be built according to equation (8). It was also assumed common, for all concepts, fuzziness coefficient $\sigma_i = 0.6$. With regard to the fuzzy relations there were assumed initial values of direction numbers of power functions $\bar{r}_{i,j} = 0$ and fuzziness coefficients $\sigma_{i,j} = 0.4$.

The main problem during the RFCM learning is the duration of this process (which results from the nature of discrete arithmetic operations on fuzzy numbers and fuzzy relations). In this connection, it should be taking into consideration possible low number of the support sampling points (linguistic values). It was assumed that on the support with a range $[-2, 2]$ only 9 sample points will be evenly spaced. Thus, the fuzzy value of each concept is represented by the fuzzy number (fuzzy set) consisting of 9 fuzzy singletons. An exemplary form of such a number (with a center equal to 0.5) is shown in Fig. 5.

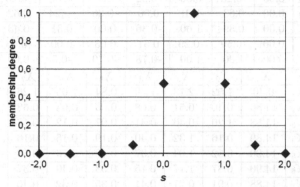

Fig. 5. Graphical representation of a number fuzzyfied around the center = 0.5, represented by 9 fuzzy singletons on the support $[-2, 2]$. s – support.

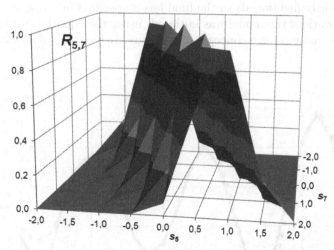

Fig. 6. Graphical representation of the fuzzy relation between concepts 5 and 7, with parameters: $\bar{r} = 0.43$, $\sigma = 0.53$. s_5 – the support of concept 5; s_7 – the support of concept 7 ($s_5 \equiv s_7$).

Fuzzy relation corresponding to such a support is of the shape shown in Fig. 6. So designed structure of RFCM has been learning using the algorithm of successive approximations with variable step of parameter changes, but, for the learning purposes only the first 20 records from the reference set was used. The result is a model with the parameters given in Table 1:

Table 1. Final results of the RFCM learning process

$\bar{r}$	X_1	X_2	X_3	X_4	X_5	X_6	X_7
X_1	0.00	1.00	1.00	1.00	1.00	1.00	1.00
X_2	0.00	0.00	1.00	0.65	0.04	-0.62	1.00
X_3	0.00	-0.25	0.00	-0.32	0.7	0.71	-0.13
X_4	0.00	0.63	-0.18	0.00	-0.36	-0.24	0.62
X_5	0.00	0.39	1.00	-0.36	0.00	0.31	0.43
X_6	0.00	-0.59	-0.29	0.51	0.03	0.00	-0.43
X_7	0.00	1.00	1.00	-0.78	-0.79	-0.5	0.00

σ	X_1	X_2	X_3	X_4	X_5	X_6	X_7
X_1	0.40	1.52	2.13	1.49	0.84	1.05	1.26
X_2	14.86	0.40	0.51	0.68	0.06	0.63	0.68
X_3	14.88	1.20	0.40	0.31	0.07	0.12	0.17
X_4	14.89	0.16	1.32	0.40	0.19	0.15	0.16
X_5	14.90	0.52	1.04	0.37	0.40	0.76	0.53
X_6	14.90	0.87	1.17	0.15	0.53	0.40	0.37
X_7	14.88	0.91	0.21	0.41	0.35	0.32	0.40

It is worth to note that the quantities $\bar{r}$ and σ were the main object of the model learning. During this process, their values have been converted from the initial (previously mentioned) to the final levels specified in Table 1.

Next, the work of the model was initiated, using the equations of type (4) to determine the values of the concepts in the consecutive steps of a discrete time.

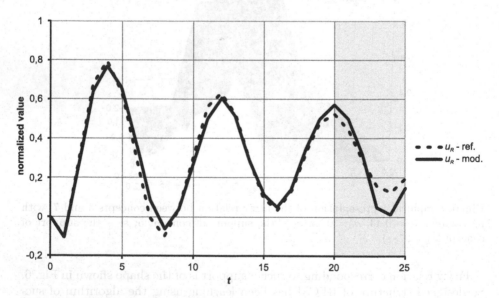

Fig. 7. Comparison of time courses of quantity u_R: real one (reference) and obtained by the RFCM model working in prediction mode. "u_R - ref." – the reference waveform; "u_R - mod." – the waveform calculated by the model.

These values have been defuzzified (with weighted average method). The effect of the model work for one selected quantity (u_R), is shown in Fig. 7.

The area marked in gray in Fig. 7 is a prediction zone. The values in this area have not been the subject of learning – they have been calculated by the model. The waveforms for only one quantity are presented – to ensure clarity of the image (for other quantities the results are similar).

As it is shown in Fig. 7, within the scope of direct learning (the model learning was carried out on a data set covering the first 20 steps of a discrete time), the model gives a very good representation of the reference values and such effects were already shown in previous works (among others in [10–12]). However, as also seen in Fig. 7, well-trained model can "predict" the next values (gray area on the chart). As the "distancing" from the end of "learning zone" the gap between the results of prediction, and the behavior of the real object is growing, but even then the model retains the trends in changes of concepts.

4   Conclusions

Relational Fuzzy Cognitive Map is a structure that meets several important conditions. Firstly, the model created with the use of it retains fully fuzzy form. Secondly, with its help one can get a good representation of the real time courses of selected quantities of a complex dynamic system. Thirdly, for dynamic system it is enough to have a knowledge of the part (the beginning) of time waveforms of selected quantities and, on this basis, it is possible to predict (in a certain time interval) the continuation of these waveforms. The results presented in this paper have to some extent preliminary character, because the research on the issue of prediction using RFCM is still conducted. However, even these incomplete results confirm the potential of proposed method.

References

1. Carvalho, J.P., Tom, J.A.: Rule-based fuzzy cognitive maps - Expressing Time in Qualitative System Dynamics. In: Proc. of the FUZZ-IEEE 2001, Melbourne, Australia, pp. 280–283 (2001)
2. Dickerson, J.A., Kosko, B.: Virtual worlds as fuzzy cognitive maps. Presence 3(2), 173–189 (1994)
3. Kosko, B.: Fuzzy cognitive maps. Int. Journal of Man-Machine Studies 24, 65–75 (1986)
4. Lachwa, A.: Fuzzy world of sets, numbers, relations, facts, rules and decisions. Akademicka Oficyna Wydawnicza EXIT, Warsaw (2001) (in Polish)
5. Papageorgiou, E.I.: Learning Algorithms for Fuzzy Cognitive Maps - A Review Study. IEEE Transactions on Systems, Man and Cybernetics, Part C: Applications and Reviews 42(2), 150–163 (2012)
6. Papageorgiou, E.I., Froelich, W.: Multi-step prediction of pulmonary infection with the use of evolutionary fuzzy cognitive maps. Neurocomputing (92/2012), 28–35 (2012)

7. Rutkowska, D., Piliński, M., Rutkowski, L.: Neural networks, genetic algorithms and fuzzy systems. PWN, Warsaw (1997) (in Polish)
8. Rutkowski, L.: Methods and techniques of artificial intelligence. PWN, Warsaw (2005) (in Polish)
9. Siraj, A., Bridges, S.M., Vaughn, R.B.: Fuzzy Cognitive Maps for Decision Support in an Intelligent Intrusion Detection System. In: IFSA World Congress and 20th NAFIPS International Conference, Vancouver, Canada, pp. 2165–2170 (2001)
10. Słoń, G.: Relational Fuzzy Cognitive Maps in Complex Systems Modeling. Wydawnictwo Politechniki Świetokrzyskiej, Kielce (2013) (in Polish)
11. Słoń, G.: The Use of Fuzzy Numbers in the Process of Designing Relational Fuzzy Cognitive Maps. In: Rutkowski, L., Korytkowski, M., Scherer, R., Tadeusiewicz, R., Zadeh, L.A., Zurada, J.M. (eds.) ICAISC 2013, Part I. LNCS (LNAI), vol. 7894, pp. 376–387. Springer, Heidelberg (2013)
12. Słoń, G., Yastrebov, A.: Optimization and Adaptation of Dynamic Models of Fuzzy Relational Cognitive Maps. In: Kuznetsov, S.O., Ślęzak, D., Hepting, D.H., Mirkin, B.G. (eds.) RSFDGrC 2011. LNCS, vol. 6743, pp. 95–102. Springer, Heidelberg (2011)
13. Stylios, C.D., Groumpos, P.P.: Fuzzy cognitive maps in modeling supervisory control systems. Journal of Intelligent & Fuzzy Systems 8(2), 83–98 (2000)
14. Takagi, H., Sugeno, M.: Fuzzy Identification of Systems and Its Application to Modeling and Control. IEEE Transactions on Systems, Man and Cybernetics SMC-15(1), 116–132 (1985)

Color Digital Picture Recognition Based on Fuzzy Granulation Approach

Krzysztof Wiaderek[1], Danuta Rutkowska[1,2], and Elisabeth Rakus-Andersson[3]

[1] Institute of Computer and Information Sciences,
Czestochowa University of Technology, 42-201 Czestochowa, Poland
krzys@icis.pcz.pl, drutko@kik.pcz.pl
[2] Information Technology Institute, University of Social Sciences,
90-113 Lodz, Poland
[3] Department of Mathematics and Natural Sciences,
Blekinge Institute of Technology, S-37179 Karlskrona, Sweden
elisabeth.andersson@bth.se

Abstract. The paper concerns specific problems of color digital picture recognition by use of the concept of fuzzy granulation, and in addition rough information granulation. This idea employs information granules that contain pieces of knowledge about digital pictures such as location of objects as well as their size and color. Each of those attributes is described by means of linguistic values of fuzzy sets, and the shape attribute is also considered with regard to the rough sets. The picture recognition approach is focused on retrieving a picture (or pictures) from a large collection of color digital pictures (images) - based on the linguistic description of a specific object included in the picture to be recognized.

1 Introduction

The main idea of the fuzzy granulation approach to color digital picture recognition - developed and employed in this paper - is based on the concept introduced by the authors in [15]. Some problems mentioned in the last section of [15], within the context of further research, are considered in this paper. In particular, the third dimension of the CIE chromaticity triangle (color model) - that is the luminance - is included in our approach. Besides, in addition to the size attribute, approximate shape of an object located in the picture to be recognized is taken into account, and - apart from the fuzzy granules - application of the rough granulation is proposed.

Nowadays we collect a lot of various color digital pictures, and the number of such pictures are still growing. Moreover, the picture resolution increases, so we need new methods for searching, recognition, and retrieving a particular picture from a large collection of them. Let us imagine a problem of searching for a picture based on a piece of knowlegde about a particular object that we remember as located in this picture. Let us assume that we may roughly describe the location as well as shape, size, and color of that object. In such a case, we can employ the approach proposed in this paper, and it seems to be very useful.

L. Rutkowski et al. (Eds.): ICAISC 2014, Part I, LNAI 8467, pp. 319–332, 2014.

Two main attributes, considered in the linguistic fuzzy description of the specific object included in the picture, are color and location. Other attributes, such as shape and size are strictly related with the location, and concern the same 2-dimensional space of pixels. The color attribute may refer to different space of the color spaces, e.g. the following color models: the CIE chromaticity triangle, RGB three-dimensional space, HSL (hue, saturation, lightness), and similar HSV. More information about various color models can be found in [15] and many other publications, including [3].

Color is a very important attribute of digital pictures. It carries significant information that helps to distinguish, recognize, compare, and classify different pictures or objects presented on various pictures. We can use only this attribute in the case when we do not have any information about the specific object except its color. Of course, with less knowledge, it is more difficult to find the proper picture (or pictures).

In this paper, and in [15], the concept of fuzzy granulation, originally introduced by Zadeh [17], is proposed to describe fuzzy location of pixels as well as fuzziness of their color. In consequence, we can consider a color digital picture as a fuzzy set of pixels or groups of pixels that we call macropixels, according to the fuzzy set theory [16]. The attributes of the shape and size may be considered within the framework of the rough sets (also called Pawlak sets) [4]. However, we can apply fuzzy sets represented by various types of membership functions; for details, see e.g. [10]. In particular, specific shapes of functions defined on two-dimensional space, expressed by proper mathematical formulas are very useful as the membership functions, with regard to both the location space and CIE color space.

It should be mentioned that some other authors combine fuzzy set and rough set theories [2], [9] in different applications, e.g. [8]. Granulation approaches have been developed within the framework of both fuzzy granulation [17] and rough granulation [5]. Information granules are applied in pattern recognition and image processing, e.g. [5] and [12], with fuzzy and rough granulation, respectively.

This paper develops the approach, introduced in [15], for solving the problems of picture recognition based on the vague knowlegde about a specific object (or any detail) included in the picture to be recognized and retrieved. The bigger is the knowledge the easier to find the proper solution, however the algorithm is more complicated because of processing more information. Thus, the special algorithm depends on the knowledge about the picture we want to recognize and retrieve.

The paper is organized as follows. The next section describes the concept of fuzzy granulation. In Section 3, a new algorithm is proposed and employed for granulating a color digital picture (pixel space) into the so-called "macropixels". Section 4 presents a new method for color space granulation. This is fuzzy granulation of the CIE chromaticity triangle with the third dimension, i.e. luminance. In Section 5, results from two previous sections are combined in order to obtain fuzzy information granules concerning the color digital pictures. Moreover, rough granules are also considered. Section 6 illustrates the problem of color digital picture recognition based on the information granules. Conclusions and final remarks are included in Section 7.

2   Fuzzy Granulation

As emphasized at the beginning of Section 1, the idea of fuzzy granulation in application to the color digital picture recognition, presented in [15], is considered in this paper.

Image processing is one of examples where information granulation may be applied and play an important role in pattern recognition [7]. In this case, the similarity of objects that are candidats for grouping into a granule usually refers to the closeness of pixels located spatially close to each other. In the concept of information granulation, the granules can take a form of sets, fuzzy sets, rough sets, etc., but most often are concentrated on the use of fuzzy sets. In this paper, we also apply fuzzy granulation to digital color pictures. This is presented in Sections 3 and 4. However, in Section 5, we propose to apply rough granulation.

The idea of macropixels, introduced in [15] and developed in Section 3, is strictly related to the fuzzy granulation approach. As a matter of fact, the algorithm proposed in Section 3, for creating the macropixels, realizes granulation of the pixel space. In this case, the granules refer to the closeness of pixels located spatially close to each other, and previously take a form of sets. Then, fuzzy membership functions are defined, so the macropixels are viewed as fuzzy sets.

The fuzzy color areas of the CIE diagram, discussed in [15], are combined with the luminance in Section 4, and considered as color space granulation. It is worth emphasizing that in this way we granulate the 3D color space (CIE chromaticity triangle with the luminance) that is the color model representing colors as perceived by humans, unlike the RGB. The fuzzy regions of the CIE chromaticity triangle are viewed as fuzzy sets, as well as the luminance intervals. In [15], the granules as groups of points with similar pure color (hue) are applied to the fuzzy granulation approach. In this paper, the luminance enriches the information granules.

Both the fuzzy location of pixels and fuzzy color, considered in Sections 3 and 4, respectively, are considered in the framework of the fuzzy granulation. When pixels of the same (or similar) color are located within a macropixel, we have a granule of the same color and location. In addition, as mentioned in [15], the third attribute, i.e. the size of the macropixels may be taken into account. Thus, we can see a digital color picture as a collection of macropixels associated with corresponding granules that carry information about color, location, and size. This concept is especially useful with regard to the problem of color digital picture recognition discribed in Section 6. In this paper, we also introduce another attribute, that is shape of an object to be recognized, and in this context we propose to employ the rough granulation (see Section 5).

3   Algorithm of Pixel Space Granulation

As explained in Section 1, the shape and size attributes are strictly related with the location that is considered in the 2-dimensional space of pixels. The color digital pictures are composed of pixels belonging to this pixel space. The location of an object in a picture can be pointed by means of the "macropixels" defined as groups of pixels. The idea of the macropixels is introduced in [15]. As a matter of fact, the macropixels can be treated as fuzzy granules, and the algorithm - proposed to determine the macropixels - granulates the pixel space, i.e. the digital picture area of pixels (smallest picture elements).

The algorithm that creates the macropixels - dividing the width and height of the picture into intervals (what is a proces of granulation) - is introduced in this section and illustrated in Fig. 1.

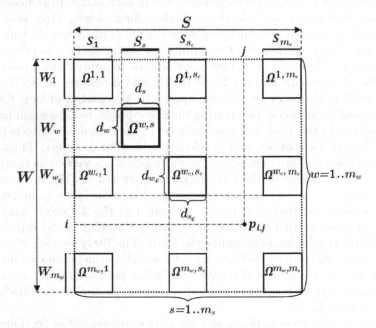

Fig. 1. Illustration of picture granulation into macropixels

Let Ω denotes a digital picture, composed of pixels, $p_{i,j}$, for $i = 1, ..., M_w$, and $j = 1, ..., M_s$. Thus, the number of pixels in the picture Ω equals $M = M_w M_s$ where M_w and M_s determine height W and width S of the picture, respectively.

Figure 1 shows the digital picture, Ω, of size WS, with pixels $p_{i,j} \in \Omega$. In addition, the macropixels, denoted as $\Omega^{w,s}$, where $w = 1, ..., m_w$ and $s = 1, ..., m_s$ are depicted. This means that $m_w m_s$ is the number of macropixels $\Omega^{w,s}$ in the picture Ω, and the following equation fullfils

$$\Omega = \bigcup_{\substack{w=1,...,m_w \\ s=1,...,m_s}} \Omega^{w,s} \qquad (1)$$

To create the macropixels, the height W and width S of the picture Ω are divided into intervals, denoted as W_w and S_s, for the macropixel's height and width, respectively:

$$W = \cup_{w=1}^{m_w} W_w \qquad (2)$$

and

$$S = \cup_{s=1}^{m_s} S_s \tag{3}$$

The central intervals, denoted as W_{w_c} and S_{s_c}, may be of different sizes than the rest ones that are intervals of the same height W_w and width S_s. This is important and must be taken into account in the algorithm of creating the macropixels. The central macropixel is denoted as Ω^{w_c, s_c} in Fig. 1.

With regard to all the macropixels, for $w = 1, ..., w_{c-1}, w_c, w_{c+1}, ..., m_w$ and $s = 1, ..., s_{c-1}, s_c, s_{c+1}, ..., m_s$, where m_w and m_s are the number of intervals W_w and S_s in the height W and width S of the picture, respectively, we have:

$$p_{i,j} \in \Omega^{w,s} \Leftrightarrow i \in W_w, \; j \in S_s \tag{4}$$

Formally, we define the macropixels as Cartesian products of their heigth and width:

$$\Omega^{w,s} = W_w \times S_s \tag{5}$$

The intervals W_w and S_s can be expressed as follows:

$$W_w = [b_{W_w}, ..., e_{W_w}] \tag{6}$$

$$S_s = [b_{S_s}, ..., e_{S_s}] \tag{7}$$

where b_{W_w}, e_{W_w}, and b_{S_s}, e_{S_s}, denote the begin and end of the intervals, respectively.

Each macropixel $\Omega^{w,s}$ forms the granule (5), and may be vieved in the same way as the picture Ω. The number of pixels (4) in the macropixel $\Omega^{w,s}$ equals:

$$M_{w,s} = M_W^{w,s} M_S^{w,s} \tag{8}$$

where $M_W^{w,s}$ and $M_S^{w,s}$ define the number o pixels corresponding to the height W_w and width S_s of the macropixel, given by (6) and (7), respectively, according to the following formulas:

$$M_W^{w,s} = e_{W_w} - b_{W_w} + 1 \tag{9}$$

$$M_S^{w,s} = e_{S_s} - b_{S_s} + 1 \tag{10}$$

As mentioned earlier, all makropixels in Fig.1, except the central ones, are of the same height and width that we denote d_w and d_s, respectively, and determine as follows:

$$d_w = M_w \; div \; m_w \tag{11}$$

$$d_s = M_s \; div \; m_s \tag{12}$$

The width and height of central intervals, denoted as d_{w_c} and d_{s_c}, respectively, are determined according to the following formulas:

$$d_{w_c} = M_w \; div \; m_w \; + \; M_w \; mod \; m_w \tag{13}$$

$$d_{s_c} = M_s \; div \; m_s \; + \; M_s \; mod \; m_s \tag{14}$$

and
$$w_c = m_w \ div \ 2 + 1, \quad s_c = m_s \ div \ 2 + 1 \tag{15}$$

Now, let us present the algorithm that allows to obtain all the intervals W_w and S_s that determine the height and width of the macropixels, respectively, for $w = 1, ..., w_{c-1}, w_c, w_{c+1}, ..., m_w$ and $s = 1, ..., s_{c-1}, s_c, s_{c+1}, ..., m_s$.

This algorithm is based on Equations (6) and (7), as well as (11) - (14); in order to get the begin and end values of the W_w and S_s intervals, denoted as b_{W_w}, e_{W_w}, and b_{S_s}, e_{S_s}, respectively.

For the first, W_1 and S_1, intervals, we have:

$$W_1: \quad b_{W_1} = 1, \quad e_{W_1} = b_{W_1} + d_w - 1 \tag{16}$$

$$S_1: \quad b_{S_1} = 1, \quad e_{S_1} = b_{S_1} + d_s - 1 \tag{17}$$

Then, because of the fact that the size of central macropixels may differ from others, we consider two cases:

I - Let us notice, from (11) and (13), that if $M_w \ mod \ m_w = 0$ then $d_w = d_{w_c}$. Analogously, from (12) and (14), if $M_s \ mod \ m_s = 0$ then $d_s = d_{s_c}$.

II - Otherwise, if $M_w \ mod \ m_w \neq 0$ then $d_w \neq d_{w_c}$, and if $M_s \ mod \ m_s \neq 0$ then $d_s \neq d_{s_c}$; from (11), (13), and (12), (14), respectively.

In case I,
  for $w = 2, ..., m_w$

$$W_w: \quad b_{W_w} = e_{W_{w-1}} + 1, \quad e_{W_w} = b_{W_w} + d_w - 1 \tag{18}$$

for $s = 2, ..., m_s$

$$S_s: \quad b_{S_s} = e_{S_{s-1}} + 1, \quad e_{S_s} = b_{S_s} + d_s - 1 \tag{19}$$

In case II,
  for $w = 2, ..., w_{c-1}, w_{c+1}, ..., m_w$ use formula (18)
  and for $w = w_c$ determine the central interval as follows:

$$W_{w_c}: \quad b_{W_{w_c}} = e_{W_{w_c-1}} + 1, \quad e_{W_{w_c}} = b_{W_{w_c}} + d_{w_c} - 1 \tag{20}$$

Analogously, for $s = 2, ..., s_{c-1}, s_{c+1}, ..., m_s$ use formula (19) and for $s = s_c$ determine the central interval as follows:

$$S_{s_c}: \quad b_{S_{s_c}} = e_{S_{s_c-1}} + 1, \quad e_{S_{s_c}} = b_{S_{s_c}} + d_{s_c} - 1 \tag{21}$$

In this way, we obtain $m_w m_s$ macropixels that may be viewed as the granules within the pixel space. These granules include information about location of pixels in a digital picture.

As mentioned earlier, we can treat each makropixel $\Omega^{w,s}$ like the picture Ω, then implement the presented algorithm to the macropixels, and get more but smaller ones. The number of the makropixels at first level of recursion equals $m_s m_w$, and generally at level g, we get $(m_s m_w)^g$ macropixels. Of course, we can modify the algorithm to obtain different number of the macropixels.

The algorithm proposed in this section performs crisp granulation. However, the results may be viewed as the granulation with fuzzy boundaries between the macropixels, so appropriate membership functions can be introduced for the fuzzy granules (see [15] and Section 5).

4   Color Space Granulation

As mentioned in Section 1, we consider two main attributes: location and color. The location attribute concerns the pixel space that is granulated according to the algorithm proposed in Section 3. Now, we are interested in the color attribute and color space granulation.

Color digital pictures are composed of pixels. In computers, the color attribute associated with each pixel, is expressed as an RGB triplet (r, g, b). Every component (RGB coordinate), in the RGB color model, can vary from zero to a defined maximum value (e.g. 1 or 255). An RGB triplet (r, g, b) represents the 3-dimensional coordinate of the point of the given color within the cube created by 3 axes (red, blue, and green). The triplets (r, g, b) are viewed as ordinary Cartesian coordinates in the Euclidean space. The (r, g, b) coordinates can be transformed into the CIE chromaticity triangle, i.e. to the color areas located on the 2-dimensional space (of the CIE diagram) with (x, y) coordinates.

Mathematical formulas describing transformations between different color spaces can be found in many publications, e.g. [3]. The transformation from the RGB to CIE is also explained and the mathematical equations are included in [14]. For considerations in this paper, it is sufficient to express the transformation in the following, general form:

$$x = f_1(r, g, b), \quad y = f_2(r, g, b), \quad Y = f_3(r, g, b) \tag{22}$$

where (x, y) denotes 2-dimensional coordinates in the CIE triangle, and Y is the additional coordinate corresponding the luminance. Knowing the functions (22), we can transform each (r, g, b) triplet assigned to particular pixels of a digital color picture to the CIE chromaticity triangle, and also to the third dimension that is the luminance. In this way, we can determine the proper color area of the CIE diagram (that represents a pure color called hue) and the luminance to every pixel of the digital picture. The hue with the luminance constitutes the color that people perceive and recognize.

Now, let us denote, like in Section 3:

Ω – digital color picture,

M – number of pixels in the picture Ω,

but unlike in Section 3:

p_j – j-th pixel in the picture Ω, where $j = 1, ..., M$,

and additionally:

$h_j = (x_j, y_j)$ calculated from (22) for triplet $(r_j, g_j, b_j) = p_j$, where $j = 1, ..., M$

l_j – luminance of the pixel p_j, for $j = 1, ..., M$.
$c_j = (h_j, l_j)$ – full color attribute of the pixel p_j, for $j = 1, ..., M$.

Let Δ_{CIE} denotes the CIE chromaticity triangle, and $\{H_1, H_2, ..., H_N\}$ - crisp color areas (regions with sharp boundaries) of the Δ_{CIE}. Hence, we have the following equation:

$$\Delta_{CIE} = \bigcup_{n=1}^{N} H_n \qquad (23)$$

The color areas (regions) of the CIE chromaticity triangle, $\{H_1, H_2, ..., H_N\}$, may be treated as fuzzy regions, with fuzzy boundaries between them. This means that the fuzzy color areas are fuzzy sets of points (x, y) belonging to these regions with membership grades expressed by a value from the interval $[0.1]$. The membership functions of the fuzzy sets may be defined in different ways. An algorithm for creating such membership functions for the fuzzy color areas of the CIE triangle is proposed in [14]. Like in [15], let us denote the fuzzy regions of the CIE diagram as $\{\tilde{H}_1, \tilde{H}_2, ..., \tilde{H}_N\}$. Other types of membership functions, for the fuzzy CIE areas, may also be employed.

Table TP in Table 1 contains values of the membership functions concerning the hue attribute of the pixels. This refer to the fuzzy sets $\{\tilde{H}_1, \tilde{H}_2, ..., \tilde{H}_N\}$. Table TL in Table 1 includes values of membership functions that define fuzzy sets in the luminance space. The fuzzy sets $\{\tilde{L}_1, \tilde{L}_2, ..., \tilde{L}_{m_L}\}$ can be represented by triangular or trapezoidal membership functions, with the meaning, e.g. "small", "medium", "large", with regard to the luminance. Both the hue and luminance attribute produce the color attribute of the pixels p_j, for $j = 1, ..., M$. Fuzzy granules are created, as the Cartesian product of corresponding fuzzy sets $\{\tilde{H}_1, \tilde{H}_2, ..., \tilde{H}_N\}$ and $\{\tilde{L}_1, \tilde{L}_2, ..., \tilde{L}_{m_L}\}$. These granules contain information about the color as the combination of the hue and luminance.

The luminance l_j, for $j = 1, ..., M$, and the fuzzy sets $\{\tilde{L}_1, \tilde{L}_2, ..., \tilde{L}_{m_L}\}$, are defined in the luminance space $L = [0, ..., 255]$. By use of formulas (22), the (r_j, g_j, b_j) values of every pixel, p_j, for $j = 1, ..., M$, in the digital color picture Ω, can easily be transformed to the corresponding point (x_j, y_j) in the Δ_{CIE} space defined by Equation (23). In addition, values of the luminance attribute can be obtained as $l_j = Y_j$, for $j = 1, ..., M$. Hence, we can determine membership values of h_j to the fuzzy sets $\{\tilde{H}_n\}$, for $n = 1, ..., N$, as $\mu_{\tilde{H}_n}(h_j) = \mu_{\tilde{H}_n}(x_j, y_j)$, and membership values of luminance l_j to fuzzy sets $\tilde{L}_t$, for $t = 1, ..., m_L$. In this paper, we employ trapezoidal membership functions, $\mu_{\tilde{L}_t}(l_j)$, defined in the range of the luminance that is different for each CIE region H_n, for $n = 1, ..., N$. However, as mentioned earlier, other types of the membership functions $\mu_{\tilde{L}_t}(l_j)$ can be applied. Assuming that m_n denotes the number of the fuzzy sets (fuzzy luminance intervals) associated with H_n, we have $m_L = \sum_{n=1}^{N} m_n$ fuzzy sets $\tilde{L}_t$ in Table TL. For example, if we consider three fuzzy sets, defining "small", "medium", and "big" luminance, respectively, for each CIE region H_n, then $m_L = 3N$.

Table 1. Membership table of color of pixels; hue (TP) and luminance (TL)

TP	h_1	h_2	...	...	h_j	...	...	h_M
$\tilde{H}_1$	$\mu_{\tilde{H}_1}(h_1)$	$\mu_{\tilde{H}_1}(h_2)$	...	...	$\mu_{\tilde{H}_1}(h_j)$	...	...	$\mu_{\tilde{H}_1}(h_M)$
$\tilde{H}_2$	$\mu_{\tilde{H}_2}(h_1)$	$\mu_{\tilde{H}_2}(h_2)$	...	...	$\mu_{\tilde{H}_2}(h_j)$	...	...	$\mu_{\tilde{H}_2}(h_1)$
...								
$\tilde{H}_n$	$\mu_{\tilde{H}_n}(h_1)$	$\mu_{\tilde{H}_n}(h_2)$	...	...	$\mu_{\tilde{H}_n}(h_j)$	...	...	$\mu_{\tilde{H}_n}(h_M)$
...								
$\tilde{H}_N$	$\mu_{\tilde{H}_1}(h_1)$	$\mu_{\tilde{H}_N}(h_2)$	...		...	$\mu_{\tilde{H}_N}(h_j)$	...		$\mu_{\tilde{H}_N}(h_M)$

TL	l_1	l_2			l_j			l_M
$\tilde{L}_1$	$\mu_{\tilde{L}_1}(l_1)$	$\mu_{\tilde{L}_1}(l_2)$	...	...	$\mu_{\tilde{L}_1}(l_j)$	...	...	$\mu_{\tilde{L}_1}(l_M)$
...								
$\tilde{L}_t$	$\mu_{\tilde{L}_t}(l_1)$	$\mu_{\tilde{L}_t}(l_2)$	...	...	$\mu_{\tilde{L}_t}(l_j)$	...	...	$\mu_{\tilde{L}_t}(l_M)$
...								
$\tilde{L}_{m_L}$	$\mu_{\tilde{L}_{m_L}}(l_1)$	$\mu_{\tilde{L}_{m_L}}(l_2)$	...		...	$\mu_{\tilde{L}_{m_L}}(l_j)$	...		$\mu_{L_{m_L}}(l_M)$

5   Fuzzy and Rough Information Granulation

In the previous sections, new methods for fuzzy granulation of both pixel and color spaces are presented. Now, we can use the granules produced by these methods in order to obtain information granules about the color digital picture. These granules may carry information concerning the location, size, shape, and color of a specific object located on the picture. We can consider the fuzzy information granules as well as rough granules.

The pixel and color space granulation, presented in Sections 3 and 4, respectively, allows to create fuzzy granules that carry information about location, size, and color of the granules.

With regard to the color, we obtain the following fuzzy granules:

- For the pure color (hue) — fuzzy CIE color areas, $\{\tilde{H}_n\}$, for $n = 1, ..., N$, where e.g. $N = 23$, with the membership functions $\mu_{\tilde{H}_n}(h_j)$, for $j = 1, ..., M$; see Table TP in Table 1
- For the luminance — $\{\tilde{L}_t\}$, for $t = 1, ..., m_L$, where m_L equals to the number of fuzzy luminance intervals (fuzzy sets) defined for every CIE region H_n, for $n = 1, ..., N$; see Table TL in Table 1

Thus, for both the hue and luminance, we constract granules as the Cartesian product of corresponding fuzzy sets $\{\tilde{H}_n\}$, and $\{\tilde{L}_t\}$, for $n = 1, ..., N$, and $t = 1, ..., m_L$, where t is appropriate for H_n, what means that the number of the fuzzy luminance granules associated with H_n equals to m_n. It should be explained that the crisp granules H_n, for $n = 1, ..., N$, are viewed as $\alpha - cuts$, i.e. crisp $\alpha - level$ sets (see e.g. [11]) of the fuzzy sets $\tilde{H}_n$, respectively, where $\alpha - level$ equals 0.5. The color granules are fuzzy sets, defined according to the definition of the Cartesian product of fuzzy sets ((see e.g. [11]), as follows:

$$\mu_{\widetilde{C}_t}(c_j) = \mu_{\widetilde{H}_n \times \widetilde{L}_t}(h_j, l_j) = \min[\mu_{\widetilde{H}_n}(h_j), \mu_{\widetilde{L}_t}(l_j)] \tag{24}$$

for $j = 1, ..., M$, where $c_j = (h_j, l_j)$, and $\widetilde{C}_t = \widetilde{H}_n \times \widetilde{L}_t$ is the Cartesian product of fuzzy sets $\widetilde{H}_n$ and $\widetilde{L}_t$, represented by membership functions $\mu_{\widetilde{H}_n}(h_j)$ and $\mu_{\widetilde{L}_t}(l_j)$, respectively. Let us notice that the number of the color granules, $\widetilde{C}_t$, equals to the number of the luminance granules, $\widetilde{L}_t$, that is m_L; see Table 1. The color granules are defined in the 3D color space, where every $c_j = (h_j, l_j)$, for $j = 1, ..., M$, corresponds to a point given by formula (22).

Referring to the location, we consider granules as the fuzzy macropixels, taking into account both their size and location in the color digital picture:

- For the location — Fig.1 shows the macropixels $\Omega^{w,s}$, for $w = 1, ..., m_w$ and $s = 1, ..., m_s$, located in the picture Ω; the location is determined by the intervals W_w and S_s, defining the macropixel's height and width. As mentioned at the end of Section 3, fuzzy boundaries between the macropixels may be expressed by appropriate membership functions. Hence, the macropixels are viewed as fuzzy sets (fuzzy granules) defined e.g. by trapezoidal membership functions as presented in [15].
- For the size — fuzzy sets with membership functions that describe size of the macropixels $\Omega^{w,s}$, for $w = 1, ..., m_w$ and $s = 1, ..., m_s$ as e.g. "small", "medium", "big" (3 fuzzy sets) or "very small", "small", "medium", "big", "very big" (5 fuzzy sets), may be created as trapezoidal functions. The size of macropixels obtained by use of the algorithm proposed in Section 3 may be evaluated according to these membership functions.

In this way, we can construct fuzzy information granules, as the Cartesian products of fuzzy sets corresponding to the location and size of the macropixels, analogously to the color granules created according to formula (24). Thus, the location attribute can be viewed in a wider sense, including both the location and size - and information about this attribute is carried in the fuzzy granules.

Combining the location and color, in the same way, i.e. as the Cartesian product of fuzzy sets, we may obtain fuzzy information granules that contain information concerning fuzzy values of all the attributes considered with regard to the location and color.

Now, let us focus our attention on another, additional attribut that can be included into the information granules. With regard to color digital pictures, we may be interested in shape of an object located in a picture (see Section 6).

Figure 2 illustrates a hat shape object located in the picture Ω. Its size and location can easily be described by use of the fuzzy information granules above discussed. This additional attribute - shape - may also be defined by a membership function in the 2-dimensional pixel space. The object's shape can be approximated by specific mathematical functions, similarly to the membership functions of the CIE pure color regions.

However, with regard to the shape attribute, we propose to apply rough granulation, based on the rough set theory introduced by Pawlak [4], in addition to the fuzzy approach. As we see in Fig.2, the shape of the object can easily be determined by the lower and upper approximations of the group of macropixels corresponding to the object in the picture. The rough granularity, developed e.g. in [5] and [8], may be employed in the problem of color digital picture recognition considered in this paper (Section 6). According to Zadeh [17], the rough set theory is one of the approaches that use crisp granulation. Thus, we apply the rough granulation to the crisp granules (macropixels) obtained by use of the algorithm presented in Section 3. Then, we create the information granules that contain both the fuzzy and rough information about the color, location (including size), and shape attributes.

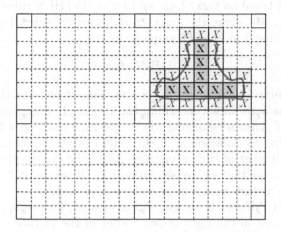

Fig. 2. Rough localisation of shape of an object in a digital picture

6   Picture Recognition

Now, let us consider two problems of color digital picture recognition based on the information granules described in Section 5.

Problem 1: Having a large collection of the pictures, we would like to find a picture (or pictures) presenting an object characterized by three attributes – size, color, and location – with fuzzy values (e.g. a big object of a color close to red, located somewhere in the center). In order to recognize such a picture (or a group of similar pictures), we can employ the idea of macropixels (created by use of the algoritm proposed in Section 3), considered with regard to the fuzzy location and size (Section 5), along with the fuzzy approach to the color granulation (Section 4). The fuzzy granulation, considered in Section 5, with the information granules that contain information about size, color, and location, is especially useful with regard to this problem. Macropixels of different sizes and the same (or similar) color and location may form the information granules.

Problem 2: Having a large collection of the pictures, we would like to find a picture (or pictures) presenting an object characterized by the same three attributes as in Problem 1 – size, color, location – but with the additional attribute i.e. shape. In this case, the rough aproach is proposed to be applied, as described in Section 5. The rough granulation with regard to the shape, combined with the fuzzy approach to the other attributes, may be employed to this problem.

The fuzzy granules discussed in Section 5 are multidimensional fuzzy sets that represent fuzzy relations between color, location, and size (attributes of the macropixels). In the fuzzy granulation approach, a digital color picture is viewed as a composition of the fuzzy granules that carry information about the color, location, and size, as well as interactions between them (expressed by the fuzziness that results in overlapping of the granules).

Both classification problems can be solved by use of a fuzzy system with the inference method based on fuzzy logic and fuzzy IF-THEN rules; for details see e.g. [11], and also [15] where the fuzzy granules are considered. In general, the rules of the following form may be employed:

$$\text{IF } G \text{ THEN class } D \tag{25}$$

where G is the fuzzy granule, and D is the class of pictures that suit to the description of the attributes concerning the object. In this way, we expect to obtain a group of pictures belonging to the specific class (e.g. with a big object of a color close to red, somewhere in the center of the picture). Then, having relatively small number of such a pictures (after the classification), it is much easier to find this one that we are searching for. Of course, it is possible to get just the only one picture from a large collection of others.

With regard to Problem 2, we may be interested, for example, in an object of hat shape located in the right upper corner of the picture (as presented in Fig.2), in addition to other attributes like size and color. Concerning the shape, a user of the system can indicate these macropixels that fully belong to the shape, and those that may belong (which means - belong partially); as Fig.2 shows. The former corresponds to the lower approximation while the latter to upper approximation, referring to the rough set terminology. However, the hat shape object can be viewed as a fuzzy set, and we can define the membership function of this set as follows: it equals 1 for the lower approximation area (inside the hat shape), and 0.5 for the area of macropixels included the boundary of the hat shape, and 0 for other area of the picture; see Fig.2. Thus, all the attributes may be considered within a fuzzy granule. Hence, the fuzzy system based on the rules of the form (25) can be employed.

7   Conclusions and Final Remarks

This paper concerns the concept of fuzzy granulation, and also combined with the rough granulation, in application to digital color pictures. In particulary, we consider a problem of picture recognition based on information granules that contain a piece of knowledge about the specifc picture to be recognized.

Fuzzy granulation approach, as mentioned in Section 1, has been introduced by Zadeh [17]. Some information one also can find in e.g. [11]. New ideas concerning the fuzzy granulation approach have been developed by Pedrycz, especially with regard to neural networks (see e.g. [6]) but also to pattern recognition [7]. Rough granulation is presented and developed e.g. in [5] and [8].

In this paper, as well as in [15], we consider problems of color digital pictures recognition that can be viewed as a special case of image processing and image recognition. However, we are interested in a large collection of the color digital pictures that are images, of course, but typical, taken by popular digital cameras, not e.g. medical images. Therefore, we use the name "picture" rather that "image", in order to focus our attention on the application to usual photos. Moreover, the important issue is that we are now not going to recognize the exact image presented in the picture but only its specific part described by an approximate color, location, and also shape.

It should be emphasized that the main idea concerning the problems considered in this paper is to describe a picture by linguistic terms that refer to color, location, and size, i.e. the attributes of macropixels. Then, our task is to recognize (and e.g. classify) pictures with specific features, expressed by the linguistic description, such as "a big object of a color close to red, located somewhere in the center of the picture". Thus, our aim is not to recognize details of the image but only selected features characterized by approximate (fuzzy) values.

Further research on this subject may concern very interesting problems of image understanding (see e.g.[13]), based on the fuzzy granulation approach, also combined with the rough information granules discussed in Section 5.

Color and shape attributes may also be considered with regard to the content-based image retrieval (see e.g. [1]), where shape representation techniques are usually boundary-based and region-based.

It is important to note that our approach to image recognition does not require to process every pixel in particular pictures but only the area of selected macropixels. Furthermore, we do not need to realize segmentation with crisp boundaries, so we do not have to employ any algorithm for edge detection.

Of course, more practical experiments will be realized to illustrate performance of the system proposed in this paper to solve the digital picture recognition problems. In this way, we will be able to compare results of the picture recognition depending on the information about attributes of the object presented in the picture to be recognized. It seems to be obvious, as mentioned in Section 1, that the more information we have the better recognition results.

References

1. Bazarganigilani, M.: Optimized image feature selection using pairwise classifiers. J. Artificial Intelligence and Soft Computing Research 1(2), 147–153 (2011)
2. Dubois, D., Prade, H.: Rough fuzzy sets and fuzzy rough sets. Intern. Journal of General Systems 17(2-3), 191–209 (1990)
3. Fortner, B., Meyer, T.E.: Number by Color. A Guide to Using Color to Undersdand Technical Data. Springer (1997)
4. Pawlak, Z.: Rough Sets. Theoretical Aspects of Reasoning about Data. Kluwer Academic Publishers, Dordrecht (1991)

5. Pawlak, Z.: Granularity of knowledge, indiscernibility and rough sets. In: Fuzzy Systems, Proc. IEEE World Congress on Computational Intelligence, vol. 1, pp. 106–110 (1998)
6. Pedrycz, W.: Neural networks in the framework of granular computing. Intern. Journal of Applied Mathematics and Computer Science 10(4), 723–745 (2000)
7. Pedrycz, W., Vukovich, G.: Granular computing in pattern recognition. In: Bunke, H., Kandel, A. (eds.) Neuro-Fuzzy Pattern Recognition, pp. 125–143. World Scientific (2000)
8. Peters, J.F., Skowron, A., Synak, P., Ramanna, S.: Rough sets and information granulation. In: De Baets, B., Kaynak, O., Bilgiç, T. (eds.) IFSA 2003. LNCS (LNAI), vol. 2715, pp. 370–377. Springer, Heidelberg (2003)
9. Rakus-Andersson, E.: Fuzzy and Rough Techniques in Medical Diagnosis and Medication. Springer (2007)
10. Rakus-Andersson, E.: Approximation and rough classification of letter-like polygon shapes. In: Skowron, A., Suraj, Z. (eds.) Rough Sets and Intelligent Systems - Professor Zdzisław Pawlak in Memoriam. ISRL, vol. 43, pp. 455–474. Springer, Heidelberg (2013)
11. Rutkowska, D.: Neuro-Fuzzy Architectures and Hybrid Learning. Springer (2002)
12. Senthilkumaran, N., Rajesh, R.: Brain image segmentation using granular rough sets. International Journal of Arts and Sciences 3(1), 69–78 (2009)
13. Tadeusiewicz, R., Ogiela, M.R.: Why Automatic Understanding? In: Beliczynski, B., Dzielinski, A., Iwanowski, M., Ribeiro, B. (eds.) ICANNGA 2007. LNCS, vol. 4432, pp. 477–491. Springer, Heidelberg (2007)
14. Wiaderek, K.: Fuzzy sets in colour image processing based on the CIE chromaticity triangle. In: Rutkowska, D., Cader, A., Przybyszewski, K. (eds.) Selected Topics in Computer Science Applications, pp. 3–26. Academic Publishing House EXIT, Warsaw (2011)
15. Wiaderek, K., Rutkowska, D.: Fuzzy granulation approach to color digital picture recognition. In: Rutkowski, L., Korytkowski, M., Scherer, R., Tadeusiewicz, R., Zadeh, L.A., Zurada, J.M. (eds.) ICAISC 2013, Part I. LNCS (LNAI), vol. 7894, pp. 412–425. Springer, Heidelberg (2013)
16. Zadeh, L.A.: Fuzzy sets. Information and Control 8, 338–353 (1965)
17. Zadeh, L.A.: Toward a theory of fuzzy information granulation and its centrality in human reasoning and fuzzy logic. Fuzzy Sets and Systems 90, 111–127 (1997)

Evolutionary Algorithms
and Their Applications

Clustering of Vehicle Usage Behavior
by Means of Artificial Bee Colony

Cosimo Birtolo, Davide Ronca, Giovanni Capasso, and Gennaro Sorrentino

Poste Italiane – Information Technology
S - FSTII - RSI – Piazza Matteotti 3 – 80133 Naples, Italy
{birtoloc,roncadav,capass56,sorre137}@posteitaliane.it

Abstract. This paper proposes a new formulation of Artificial Bee Colony (ABC) in order to address clustering problems. The proposed algorithm models the inspector bee within the colony. It is tested for some benchmarks and is adopted to a real-world problem in Transportation System domain. In particular, we propose a clustering problem for the identification of vehicle usage in Poste Italiane by grouping together those vehicles with same features as fuel economies, frequency and value of refueling activities.

Keywords: Artificial Bee Colony, Soft Computing, Clustering, Intelligent Transportation Systems.

1 Introduction

Reducing operational costs in industry is always a great challenge. In transportation domain, annual costs are expressed by fuel consumption, vehicle maintenance, insurance policy and vehicle management. A significant part of these costs is highly influenced by working conditions, followed routes, conditions found in urban cycle (stop-start traffic), and which type of vehicle (e.g., Fiat Panda, Fiat Punto, Fiat Doblò) is chosen for each delivery task. In order to implement a cost reduction strategy, it is possible to adopt several solutions. We can choose to decrease the use of expensive vehicles; to replace the old vehicles or to improve the performance of high-cost vehicles; to increase the number of tasks associated to top-ranked vehicles. Considering a huge vehicle fleet, it is difficult to detect the best strategy.

Clustering vehicles on the basis of their performance can help to identify the most suitable solution.

In this paper, we address the vehicle's clustering task by means of a meta-heuristic approach. In detail, we model an Artificial Bee Colony (ABC) with a new bee role in the colony, performed by inspector bee. This model conforms with real honey bee colony; indeed, in nature some bees among the foraging ones are called inspectors because they preserve the colony's history and historical information related to food sources.

The proposed algorithm is adopted in order to opportunely define clusters of vehicle according to their performance.

L. Rutkowski et al. (Eds.): ICAISC 2014, Part I, LNAI 8467, pp. 335–346, 2014.

The remainder of this paper is organized as follows: Section 2 describes Bee Colony algorithm; Section 3 depicts the proposed formulation of ABC and describes the algorithm structure, Section 4 provides experimental results; Section 5 experiments the proposed algorithm for real-world clustering problems and Section 6 outlines conclusions and future directions.

2 Artificial Bee Colony

Bee Colony optimization algorithm is a meta-heuristic approach that belongs to the swarm intelligence algorithms. This approach has been recently adopted in order to solve several combinatorial optimization problems [1]. Bee colony optimization-based algorithms are inspired by the behavior of the real honey bee colony.

Honey bees are social insects and live in large organized communities. The provision of the food is one of the major activities within a colony. This activity involves specific bees which collaborate among each other: the "employed bees", which research and communicate where the food sources are; the "onlooker bees" which extract and carry the food.

The main task of an employed bee is to look for food. When the food source has been found, the bee memorizes the spatial coordinates and communicates the position and the quality of the source through a dance around the hive. The main task of an onlooker bee is observing the employed bees dance outside the hive. On the basis of the message expressed by the dance, the onlooker bee chooses the food source that best fits its needs.

Inspired by nature, Karaboga [2] models three bee behaviors in the colony and define Artificial Bee Colony (ABC) Algorithm, where the solutions represent the food sources and the quantity of the nectar of the food sources corresponds to the fitness of the associated solution. Employed bees whose solutions is not improved after a fixed number of trials, defined *limit*, become scouts (i.e., the bees which look for food sources in a random way) and their solutions are abandoned.

In other words, the general formulation of the ABC algorithm can be described by the following phases: (i) Bee Initialization, (ii) Employed Bee Phase, (iii) Onlooker Bee Phase, (iv) Scout Bee Phase, (v) Memorization of the best solution found. These last four phases are iterated until the stop criteria is met. Commonly the algorithm stops when a fixed maximum number of cycles is reached. In recent years the literature has investigated different real world applications of ABC algorithm [3].

2.1 Clustering and ABC

Clustering algorithms aim at grouping data into a number of clusters. Data in the same cluster share a high degree of similarity while they are very dissimilar from data of other clusters. Clustering algorithms aim at partitioning the population into a fixed number k of classes, each of those being represented by an average item named centroid.

The clustering problem can be stated as the minimization of the sum of Euclidean squared distance between each object x_j and the center of the cluster c_j to which it belongs (i.e., centroids). The traditional clustering algorithm is K-means [4] which has been applied to a wide range of problems in different domains. However, K-means is sensitive to the initial states and can converge to the local optimum solution. Recently, many methods have been proposed in order to overcome this drawback [5,6]. Among them, evolutionary approaches are adopted in different clustering problems (i.e., fixed or variable number of clusters, centroid-based, medoid-based, label-based, tree-based or graph-based representation) as described by Hruschka et al.[7]. Furthermore, some ABC techniques are recently proposed [8,9].

In particular, Karaboga and Ozturk [8] firstly introduced ABC for clustering tasks, showing how ABC formulation outperformed Particle Swarm Optimization (PSO) algorithm. Moreover the authors experimented ABC in classification tasks, comparing it with traditional classification algorithms such as Neural Networks (Multi Layer Perceptron), Bayesian Network, Radial Basis Function (RBF) proving the benefits for a bee colony. A first hybrid approach is proposed by Yan et al. [9] who present a Hybrid Artificial Bee Colony algorithm. The authors consider a social learning between bees by means of cross-over operators of Genetic Algorithm and apply the proposed algorithm to some classification tasks proving some benefits in respect to traditional k-means, ABC and PSO algorithm.

3   ABC with Inspector Bee

Our proposed algorithm is inspired by the Simple ABC given by Karaboga [2], but it extends the colony modeling a fourth bee behavior, i.e., Inspector Bee.

In a real bee colony, inspection role was modeled by Biesmeijer and de Vries [10], who introduced additional behavioral states for forager bees. In their work they define the inspectors as foragers that retire from an unprofitable food source but continue to make occasional trips to it, while reactivated foragers are bees that stop inspecting after a certain period of time and return to wait for dances to follow at the nest.

Granovskiy et al [11] studied the role of inspector bees. Their experiments show that a bee colony is able to successfully reallocate its foraging resources in dynamic environments even when dance language information is limited. According to the authors, it remains unclear in what foraging situations reactivation and inspection are important and in what cases the dance language is the primary mechanism for communicating memory. The ability of the colony to react to rapid changes in their environment can be justified by the inspector bees that act as the colony's short-term memory [10]. So that, these bees allow the colony to quickly begin utilizing previously abandoned food sources once they become profitable again.

Inspection can be considered an important mechanism for reallocating foragers when food sources are hard to find: for these reasons we introduce inspector in

---

Algorithm 1. ABCi: algorithm's pseudo-code

1: Load training samples
2: Set the number of employed bees and onlooker bees
3: Generate the initial population z_s, $s = 1..SN$ with trial counter $t_s = 0$
4: Evaluate the nectar amount (fitness function) of the food sources ($\forall s$)
5: Inspector bee moves to the best food source
6: Set cycle to 1
7: **repeat**
8:    **for all** employed bee assigned to solution s **do**
9:        Produce new solution v_s with $t_s = 0$
10:       Evaluate the fitness of the new solution v_s
11:       Apply greedy selection process for the identification of new population z_s
12:   **end for**
13:   Calculate the probability values p_s for the solutions z_s, $s = 1..SN$
14:   **for all** onlooker bee **do**
15:       Select a solution z_s depending on p_s
16:       Produce new solution v_s with $t_s = 0$
17:       Evaluate the fitness of the new solution v_s
18:       Apply greedy selection process for the identification of new population z_s
19:       **if** greedy selection process preserves old solution **then**
20:           Increment the trial counter t_s associated to the solution z_s
21:       **end if**
22:   **end for**
23:   Inspector bee moves to the best food source and memorize it
24:   **if** there is a solution with $t > limit$ (scout bee) **then**
25:       Generate a new solution according a randomized process
26:       Memorize the new solution, replacing the abandoned one
27:   **end if**
28:   $cycle = cycle + 1$
29: **until** cycle = MCN

---

the proposed Artificial Bee Colony. In our model, the Inspector Bee memorizes the best solution across the different cycles, so that if a solution is abandoned by bees and is not considered as the best solution for the next cycle, the inspector preserves this information.

3.1   Algorithm Structure and Fitness Function

Pseudo-code of our Artificial Bee Colony with Inspector behavior (ABCi) is outlined by Algorithm 1. The parameters of the proposed ABC algorithm as well as Karaboga's formulation are: the number of food sources (i.e., K), the number of employed and onlooker bees, the value of the *limit*, and the maximum cycle number (MCN).

In clustering problem the food sources are the cluster centroids, while the solution is the position of food source which maximizes the nectar amount (the position of centroids which minimizes the fitness function).

In the initialization phase, the algorithm randomly generates a group of food sources corresponding to the solutions in the search space. According to Eq.1, the fitness of food sources is evaluated and for each food source a counter, which stores each bee number of trials, is set to 0 in this phase.

$$fitness(s) = \sum_{i=1}^{N} \sum_{j=1}^{K} w_{i,j} \left\| x_i - c_j \right\|^2 \tag{1}$$

where K is the number of clusters, N is the number of objects, x_i is a generic input to be clustered, c_j is the jth centroid, and s is the solution (the position of K centroids).

In the employed bees' phase (see lines 8-13 in algorithm's pseudo-code), each employed bee is sent to the food source and finds a neighboring food source. The neighboring food source is provided according to Eq.2 as follows:

$$v_{i,j} = z_{i,j} + \phi \left(z_{i,j} - z_{k,j} \right) \tag{2}$$

where k is a randomly selected food source different from i, j is a randomly chosen centroid. ϕ is a random number between [-1,1]. The new food source v is determined by changing randomly one dimension on jth centroid. If the produced value exceeds its predetermined boundary, it will set to be equal to the boundary. Then the new food source is evaluated. Therefore, a greedy selection is applied. In other words, the employed bee produces a modification in the position (i.e. solution) and checks the nectar amount (fitness value) of that source (solution). The employed bee evaluates this nectar information (fitness value) and then assigns to the food source a probability related to its fitness value according to the Eq.3.

$$p(s) = f(s) \bigg/ \sum_{j=1}^{S} Nf(j) \tag{3}$$

where SN is the number of food sources and $f(s) = \frac{1}{1+fitness(s)}$, where fitness is defined in Eq.1.

In the onlooker bees' phase (see lines 14-23 in algorithm's pseudo-code), the onlooker bee selects a food source based on a probability of a source explored by employed bees. Once the food sources have been selected, each onlooker bee finds a new food source similarly to the employed bee (see Eq.2) and the greedy selection process selects the new source. If this process preserves old solution, the value of counter, which is associated to the employed bee, increases.

In scout bees' phase (see lines 24-27 in algorithm's pseudo-code), when the value of the counter t of a food source is greater than *limit*, the food source is abandoned, the inspector bee memorizes the source and the employed bee becomes a scout. The scout bee generates a new solution according to Eq.4 and sets the value of counter equal to 0, hence the bee memorizes the new solution replacing the abandoned one.

$$z_{j,d} = \min_{i=1}^{N} (x_{i,d}) + rand(0,1) \cdot \left(\max_{i=1}^{N} (x_{i,d}) - \min_{i=1}^{N} (x_{i,d}) \right) \qquad (4)$$

where $j = 1, 2, ...K$ and $d = 1, 2, ..., D$. N is the number of objects, K is the number of clusters, and D is the number of features. $x_{i,d}$ represents the d-th feature of the input data x_i.

4   Experimentation

In this section we experiment the ABC algorithm for clustering problem.

In order to evaluate the performance of the proposed ABC approach, we compare the results of the K-means, ABC, and the proposed ABCi for a clustering task by comparing some datasets selected from the UCI machine learning repository [12]. In particular we consider Credit Approval dataset containing 690 samples, which are different credit card applications, with 15 attributes and Dermatology dataset consisting of 366 samples characterized by 34 features which are 12 patient clinical attributes and 22 histopathological features. These datasets have a good mix of attributes (continuous, nominal with small numbers of values, and nominal with larger numbers of values) and data can be grouped into two (approved or not approved transactions) and six class (according to the specific disease) respectively.

Finally, our clustering problem consists in 11765 cars, 1700 vans and 825 trucks (14290 vehicles) and data refers to vehicle route, fuel consumption and fuel transactions performed from January 1, 2013 to September 30, 2013.

4.1   Experimental Results

First of all, we run the algorithm 20 times with different limit values (i.e., 0, 5, 10, 20, 50, 100, 1000) in order to study quantitatively the convergence of the two different ABC formulations. Each run considers 1000 cycles with a colony of 10 employer bees and from 10 to 100 onlookers.

Best solutions occur when limit value increases, as the exploitation behavior becomes more relevant. However, we can notice how ABCi's convergence is not heavily affected by limit value if they range between 20 and 100, thus the algorithm to be robust to this situation.

As depicted in Fig.1 and in Fig.2, limit value equals to 50 (black curve) could be a good tradeoff, even if the optimal parameter value depends on the particular problem. Indeed, the Dermatology dataset is more complex and needs a greater colony size (110 bees) and seems not to converge with limit value equal to 0, 5 and 1000.

Investigating these results more deeply, we consider Mann-Whitney-Wilcoxon test and we report results in Tab.1, where the average value of best fitness of 20 different trials per technique (i.e., ABC, ABC with inspector, k-Means) is considered. The null hypothesis is: the investigated techniques provide solutions which

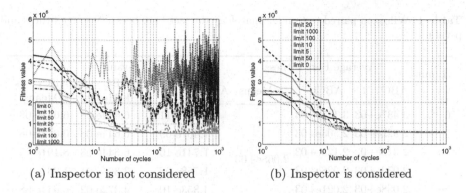

(a) Inspector is not considered   (b) Inspector is considered

Fig. 1. Credit Approval dataset: Average fitness behavior by varying the limit

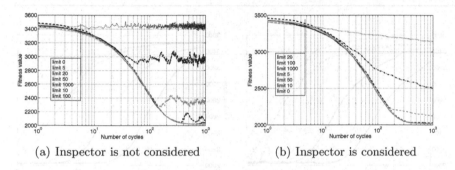

(a) Inspector is not considered   (b) Inspector is considered

Fig. 2. Dermatology dataset: Average fitness behavior by varying the limit

belong to the same population entailing a comparable clustering performance; while the alternative hypothesis is: the provided solutions differ statistically.

Assuming 0.05 as upper limit to reject the null hypothesis, we can affirm that there is statistical difference between ABC and ABCi. We prove that ABCi outperforms ABC because it provides a lower fitness value in most of the cases. We cannot reject the null hypothesis with higher values of limit (i.e., limit equals to 100 entails a p-value of 0.157 and 0.583 for Credit Approval and Dermatology database respectively) and ABC and ABCi performance are comparable. Indeed, considering a higher value of limit, the abandonment behavior of an employed bee decreases and the benefit of an inspector bee is not estimable.

Instead, comparing k-means with ABC approach, we prove how a bee colony can outperform when we consider a limit value greater than 50 for Dermatology dataset and in all the cases for Credit Approval dataset.

Moreover, in order to study the effect of the number of onlookers for algorithm's convergence speed, we show in Fig.3 the average fitness behavior of 20 different runs. As we expected, the more the number of onlookers increases, the more quickly the algorithm converges.

Table 1. Wilcoxon paired test on Dermatology dataset (110 bees): Average fitness and p-values

| Limit | Average Best Fitness | | | p-value | | |
	ABC	ABCi	k-Means	ABC vs. ABCi	ABC vs. k-Means	ABCi vs. k-Means
0	3.437e+03	3.145e+03		1.451e-11	6.644e-08	6.644e-08
5	2.922e+03	2.503e+03		1.407e-09	6.644e-08	6.644e-08
10	2.322e+03	2.125e+03	2.068e+03	1.741e-10	6.644e-08	8.191e-05
20	2.079e+03	2.028e+03		1.758e-08	3.366e-01	1.938e-03
50	2.038e+03	2.021e+03		4.353e-10	4.372e-02	6.644e-08
100	2.020e+03	2.020e+03		5.831e-01	6.644e-08	6.644e-08
1000	2.020e+03	2.020e+03		6.715e-03	6.644e-08	6.644e-08

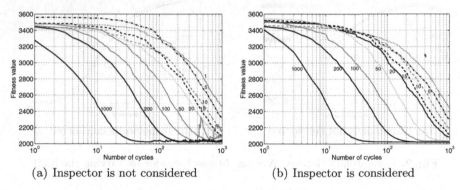

(a) Inspector is not considered   (b) Inspector is considered

Fig. 3. Dermatology dataset: Average fitness behavior by varying the number of on-lookers (10 employers)

Finally, we experimented the vehicle clustering problem with ABCi. As depicted in Fig. 4, 50 onlookers within a colony size of 61 bees (10 employers and an inspector bee) could represents a good trade-off between quality and algorithm performance.

Indeed, considering these parameters we obtain an average best fitness after 100 cycles equals to 1037.53, while it is equal to 1057.33 when 20 onlookers are considered. Performing the Mann-Whitney-Wilcoxon test, we prove a statistical difference between these two configurations ($p - value = 0.0038$).

5   Assessing and Forecasting Vehicle Performance

Vehicle clustering aims at grouping together Poste Italiane vehicles with the same behavior in terms of cost and fuel consumption. In this section we propose two predictive indicator (i.e., *Vehicle Value* and *Refueling Activities*) and a retrospective index (i.e., *Average Fuel Consumption Index*) in order to typify

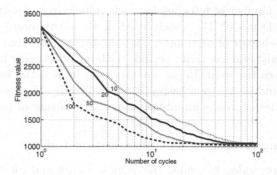

Fig. 4. Poste Italiane dataset: Average fitness behavior

vehicle usage behaviors. In the last paragraph, we adopt these indicators for the clustering task.

5.1   Estimating Vehicle Value

LifeTime Value is a dynamic financial indicator which is adopted in e-Commerce domain, and it depends on the customer's behavior. This indicator represents an attractive metrics for the definition of marketing strategies because it provides a forecast on future costs and revenues generated by the customer [13]. It represents the user value over its entire lifecycle and can be defined like the sum of the retrospective value V_R and the prospective value V_P as expressed in Eq.5.

$$LV(u) = V_R(u) + V_P(u) \tag{5}$$

where u is a customer; V_R is the current value of the customer (calculated using historical data); while V_P is the future value that a customer will have, namely the future earnings the customer will provide to the merchant; this is based on the prediction of future purchases made by the customer through Sequential Minimal Optimization (SMO), an iterative algorithm based on support vector regression adopted for solving some optimization problems [14].

We apply lifetime value to Transportation System and define *Vehicle Value* as the forecasting of the fuel amount for each vehicle. Comparing to e-Commerce definition, the customer are replaced by vehicles and the purchasing by refueling. The aim is to predict the future fuel cost of a vehicle according to its history.

5.2   Predicting Refueling Activities

We define an index called *Refueling Activities* which allows to assess the vehicle's usage by measuring the frequency and the number of refueling.

Knowing future activities of vehicles allow to plan a correct cost strategy and support the outlier detection process (i.e., a low number of real refueling respect to the predicted value, could indicate a misuse of the vehicle). In our approach we consider the number of refueling for each vehicle in a certain period of time. We use BG/NBD model [15], widely used in the e-commerce domain in order to predict the behavior of customers. This model assumes that after a purchase process, there exists an inactivity period (without purchasing activity) in which the customer uses the item. In our domain, the item is the fuel, the customer is the vehicle, and so the purchasing is the refueling. High value of predicted refueling activities expresses an intense usage or a misuse of refueling process.

5.3   Measuring Average Fuel Consumption Index

Fuel consumption index measures the vehicle's cost and identify at the same time the vehicle's performance. Indeed, it considers the fuel demand related to the followed route.

$$c\left(T\right) = \frac{\sum\limits_{t=1}^{T} L\left(t\right) - \sum\limits_{s} \frac{route(s)}{fc_n(s)}}{\sum\limits_{s} \frac{route(s)}{fc_n(s)}} \tag{6}$$

where T is the time interval, L is the number of liters in a refueling occurred at time t, $route$ expresses the number of km covered in a specified fuel consumption figures s which are expressed as urban, extra-urban, highway, and combined. Fuel consumption figures are measured in km/l and fc_n indicates the type-approval fuel consumption which differs for each vehicle according to the EC Whole Vehicle Type Approval (ECWVTA).

5.4   Vehicle Clustering

We consider three different datasets: (i) car, (ii) van, and (iii) truck. For each dataset we identify 9 clusters and adopt ABCi clustering in order to group together in a same cluster those vehicles with the same delivery behavior. According to our experimentation in Section 4.1, the ABCi algorithm is setup with the following parameters: MCN = 100, colony size = 61 (50 onlooker bees, 10 employed bees and 1 inspector), limit = 100.

For each dataset, we consider three features for clustering purpose: (i) average monthly fuel consumption index which is evaluated as the mean of fuel consumption index defined in Eq. 6, (ii) predicted Refueling Activities which are evaluated considering 9 months for training and predict the usage of vehicle, and (iii) predicted Refueling Value which expresses the future fuel cost of the vehicle.

The proposed algorithm outperforms k-Means with an average fitness of 1398.70 and 1417.05 respectively (three features are considered).

In Fig. 5, we report a scatter plot with average monthly fuel consumption index, predicted Refueling Activities, and predicted Refueling Value. We can detect those vehicles with the highest predicted value and the highest fuel consumption index. These cars are properly grouped in clusters which are suitable for knowledge extraction processes and are useful to understand the reason of the provided cars' performances.

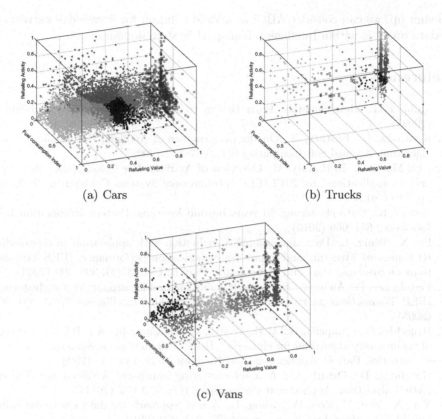

(a) Cars   (b) Trucks

(c) Vans

Fig. 5. Vehicle Clustering Problem with ABC algorithm

6   Conclusions and Future Work

In this paper we presented a bee colony algorithm for clustering problems and experimented a real-world dataset which consists of 14,290 Poste Italiane vehicles and about 329,855 refueling transactions.

Our preliminary experimentation showed the impact in adopting inspector bee within the colony, and the benefit is proved. Then, the algorithm is tested for different clustering tasks and experimentation proves the ability of ABCi algorithm in converging towards solutions with high fitness. Moreover, the algorithm proved to provide better results as long as the colony size increases; furthermore exploration and exploitation behavior is investigated as long as the limit value changes. Then, we modeled the vehicle clustering problem by three features which are Vehicle Value, Refueling Activities, and Fuel Consumption Index and we addressed this problem by ABCi approach. As qualitative experimentation shows, the algorithm is able to group together vehicles with the same real fuel consumption behavior.

In future, we aim to extend the clustering problem in a wider time interval and we want to evaluate how each vehicle changes performances through the year.

To sum up, we can consider ABCi as a valid solution for knowledge extraction in data analysis within Intelligent Transport System domain.

References

1. Talbi, E.G.: Metaheuristics: From Design to Implementation. Wiley Publishing (2009)
2. Karaboga, D., Basturk, B.: On the performance of Artificial Bee Colony (ABC) algorithm. Applied Soft Computing 8(1), 687–697 (2008)
3. Abu-Mouti, F., El-Hawary, M.: Overview of Artificial Bee Colony (abc) algorithm and its applications. In: 2012 IEEE International Systems Conference (SysCon), pp. 1–6 (2012)
4. Jain, A.K.: Data clustering: 50 years beyond k-means. Pattern Recognition Letters 31(8), 651–666 (2010)
5. Fu, X., Wang, L.: Data dimensionality reduction with application to simplifying RBF network structure and improving classification performance. IEEE Transactions on Systems, Man, and Cybernetics, Part B: Cyb. 33(3), 399–409 (2003)
6. Lee, J., Lee, D.: An improved cluster labeling method for support vector clustering. IEEE Transactions on Pattern Analysis and Machine Intelligence 27(3), 461–464 (2005)
7. Hruschka, E., Campello, R.J.G.B., Freitas, A., De Carvalho, A.C.P.L.F.: A survey of evolutionary algorithms for clustering. IEEE Transactions on Systems, Man, and Cybernetics, Part C: Applications and Reviews 39(2), 133–155 (2009)
8. Karaboga, D., Ozturk, C.: A novel clustering approach: Artificial Bee Colony (ABC) algorithm. Applied Soft Computing 11(1), 652–657 (2011)
9. Yan, X., Zhu, Y., Zou, W., Wang, L.: A new approach for data clustering using hybrid ABC algorithm. Neurocomput. 97, 241–250 (2012)
10. Biesmeijer, J.C., de Vries, H.: Exploration and exploitation of food sources by social insect colonies: a revision of the scout-recruit concept. Behavioral Ecology and Sociobiology 49(2-3), 89–99 (2001)
11. Granovskiy, B., Latty, T., Duncan, M., Sumpter, D.J.T., Beekman, M.: How dancing honey bees keep track of changes: the role of inspector bees. Behavioral Ecology 23(3), 588–596 (2012)
12. Bache, K., Lichman, M.: UCI machine learning repository (2013)
13. Birtolo, C., Diessa, V., De Chiara, D., Ritrovato, P.: Customer churn detection system: Identifying customers who wish to leave a merchant. In: Ali, M., Bosse, T., Hindriks, K.V., Hoogendoorn, M., Jonker, C.M., Treur, J. (eds.) IEA/AIE 2013. LNCS, vol. 7906, pp. 411–420. Springer, Heidelberg (2013)
14. Shevade, S., Keerthi, S., Bhattacharyya, C., Murthy, K.: Improvements to SMO algorithm for SVM Regression. Technical report, National University of Singapore, Control Division Dept of Mechanical and Production Engineering, National University of Singapore, Technical Report CD-99-16 (1999)
15. Fader, P.S., Hardie, B.G.S., Lee, K.L.: "Counting your Customers" the easy way: An alternative to the Pareto/NBD Model. Marketing Science 24(2), 275–284 (2005)

Search Space Analysis for the Combined Mathematical Model (Linear and Nonlinear) of the Water Distribution Network Design Problem

Marco Antonio Cruz-Chávez[1,*], Érika Yesenia Ávila-Melgar[1],
Martín Heriberlo Cruz-Rosales[2],
Beatriz Martínez-Bahena[1], and Guillermo Flores-Sánchez

[1] Research in Engineering and Applied Sciences Center
Av. Universidad 1001, Chamilpa, C.P.62209, Cuernavaca, Morelos, México
[2] Science Faculty, Autonomous University of Morelos State
Av. Universidad 1001, Chamilpa, C.P.62209, Cuernavaca, Morelos, México
{mcruz,erikay,mcr}@uaem.mx

Abstract. This paper presents an experimental study of the solutions space generated by the mathematical model of the Water Distribution Network Design Problem by using Two-Looped network benchmarks to find the feasible solutions space. It shows how the performance of a typical Evolutionary Algorithm (EA) can be improved by considering the importance of working with a feasible population and carrying out repetitive mutations and crossovers to generate new feasible offspring with better fitness. The replacement of parents represents the mortality index of a population at each generation of EA. Aiming to compensate the mortality index, EA is forced to maintain a constant population size by increasing the number of descendants with the crossover operator. The experimental results show both the feasible solutions space and the results of the algorithm when using feasible solutions and varying population size.

Key words: EPANET Solver, Genetic Algorithm, feasible/unfeasible solution.

1 Introduction

In life, there are problems with several solutions and one must be chosen. This is the case for combinatory optimization problems[1].

An optimization problem has some important characteristics; it has an objective function to be optimized, a search space, and a subset of the search space. The feasible solutions space for combinatory optimization problems is a discrete set, or it can be reduced to a discrete set.

The Water Distribution Network Design problem (WDND) is an optimization problem. It consists of finding the most efficient way to supply water to consumers, within given constraints. For example pressure requirements must

---

* Corresponding author.

L. Rutkowski et al. (Eds.): ICAISC 2014, Part I, LNAI 8467, pp. 347–359, 2014.
© Springer International Publishing Switzerland 2014

be reached to offer users an adequate service when satisfying their water requirements. The WDND Problem has been widely studied by many researchers. The first attempts to solve the problem were based on Lineal Programming techniques. Alperovits and Shamir [2] proposed a linear programming gradient method which has been adapted and improved by Quindry [3], Goulter et al. [4], Fujiwara et al. [5], and Kessler et al. [6], among others. It is noteworthy that the previously cited works present similarities in their mathematical formulation, decision variables, and methods used to solve the problem. The mathematical formulation was based on lineal programming models, the decision variables was based on continuous variables, and the solution method for the problem was primarily based on lineal programming methods. The design of the network tended to be a branched layout. In the last decade, the WDND problem has gradually been modified. It has been formulated as a non linear programming problem and pipe diameters have been stated as discrete decision variables. The solution method for the problem has generally been based on heuristic methods like Evolutionary Algorithms (EAs), Simulated Annealing and others. The design of the network has been a looped layout, and the network technique to supply water to consumers has been gravity. Even though the problem has been referred to as the WDND problem for three decades, there are some important differences between the first two decades and last decade. These differences alter the problem slightly, and do not allow for direct comparison. They include mathematical formulation, decision variables, topology (branched or looped), solution method, and technique to feed the network (pumping or gravity).

According to the computational complexity theory, WDND is verified as an NP-Complete problem by mapping it to the well-known Job Shop Scheduling Problem [7]. It is classified in the set of NP-Hard problems [8], and has been widely studied over 30 years by many researchers due to its practical application. In order to solve this problem, several approaches have been applied. When trying to solve the WDND problem, global optimization [9, 10], linear programming [2, 3], non-linear programming [4, 5, 6, 11, 12] and many other heuristics have been applied [13, 14, 15, 16]. When attempts are made to solve this problem for real instances, it is extremely complex to find the optimum solution. Even for small benchmarks of NP-Complete problems, finding the global optimum solution by using an exact method would take years [17]. A good alternative is the use of heuristic methods. One of the most promising and commonly used methods is the well-known EAs. These methods are stochastic search procedures, based on evolution and natural selection [18, 19]. They suggest a satisfactory success rate for identifying good solutions. They have successfully handled NP-Complete problems [20, 21] for different fields, including the WDND problem [22, 23]. An EA consists of 5 main components: 1) Solution Representation, 2) Initial Population, 3) Evaluation Function, 4) Genetic Operators and 5) Parametric values for population size, crossover and mutation probabilities, and number of generations. Recently, many works have focused on developing EAs. When working with an EA to solve the WDND problem, some questions related to the components of the EA arise: What percentage of the feasible solutions is included in the complete search space? How many solutions should be generated to find a feasible solution? What must the size of the feasible initial population be in order to have a representative sample of the search space? What method is used to create an initial population?

In order to find the global optimal solution, it is important to know the size of the feasible solutions space. The goal is to know if the size and characteristics of the initial population help the Evolutionary Algorithm to converge earlier to a better solution. These questions are addressed in this article.

In this paper, an EA, called EA-WDND, is presented. EA-WDND differs from traditional EAs in four important aspects: 1) Initial population creation. It is a subset of a feasible solutions space, all the individuals of the population can be selected to generate offspring. 2) The population size of offspring generated is bigger than the population size of parents. 3) For each generation, the population is created by the best offspring; parents are combined to produce offspring and then they die. Unfeasible individuals cannot survive. 4) EA-WDND algorithm solves two models: the constraints satisfaction model by using Epanet Solver, and the optimization model by evaluating the objective function.

The principal contribution of this work is the experimental study of the search space of the WDND Problem. It helps determine how many solutions should be generated, and the time needed to obtain different sizes of feasible populations. The study shows the difficulty of finding a feasible solution in the complete solutions space. An experimental study of an evolutionary algorithm, EA-WDND, presented here, shows convergence by using different sizes of initial feasible populations.

This paper is organized as follows: Section 2 explains the combined Mathematical Model for the WDND Problem. Section 3 presents a description of the Evolutionary Algorithm. Section 4 defines the Solutions Space for the WDND Problem. Section 5 describes the experimental results of the solutions space. Section 6 presents the conclusions and future investigations to provide continuity to this work.

2   Water Distribution Network Design Problem (WDND)

The optimization of the looped water distribution networks is an important and complex problem with applications in urban, industrial and irrigation water supply. It consists of minimizing the network investment cost with pipe diameters as decision variables, while link layout, connectivity, and demands are imposed as constraints [24]. The solution to the problem is the least cost optimum configuration, which is a sequence of the necessary pipe diameters to convey water from sources to all the network water users, satisfying their requirements.

Recently, the model that represents the WDND problem has been stated as a non-programming lineal model, and hydraulic restrictions have been managed as implicit restrictions [12]. In this work, the mathematical model represents looped networks and has been divided into two models to classify design restrictions, independent of operation restrictions: 1) the model of lineal programming includes network design restrictions which can be stated mathematically in terms of the cost of a pipeline and unit length for each pipeline (Table 1 and 2). The constraints satisfaction model includes network operation restrictions.

Table 1. Model of lineal programming

$$\min T_c = \sum_{i=1}^{n} \sum_{j=1}^{n} \sum_{d_k=d_1}^{d_n} C_{ijd_k} L_{ijd_k} X_{ijd_k} \qquad (1)$$

Subject to:

$$\sum_{i=1}^{n} \sum_{j=1}^{n} X_{ijd_k} \geq 0 \qquad \forall (d_k = d_1,...,d_n) \qquad (2)$$

$$\sum_{i=1}^{n} \sum_{d_k=d_1}^{d_n} X_{ijd_k} \geq 1 \qquad \forall (j = 1,...,n) \qquad (3)$$

$$\sum_{i=1}^{n} \sum_{j=1}^{n} \sum_{d_k=d_1}^{d_n} X_{ijd_k} = 1 \qquad (4)$$

$$X_{ijd_k} \in \{0,1\} \qquad \forall (i, j, k) \qquad (5)$$

Table 2. Constraints Satisfaction Model

$$\sum_{i} Q_{in} - \sum_{i} Q_{out} = Q_e \qquad \forall\ i \in n \qquad (6)$$

$$\sum_{m} h_f - \sum_{m} E_p = 0 \qquad \forall m \qquad (7)$$

$$H_{min} \leq H_i \leq H_{max} \qquad \forall\ i \in n \qquad (8)$$

$$V_{min} \leq V_{L_{ij}} \leq V_{max} \qquad \forall L_{ij} \qquad (9)$$

Equation (1) is the objective function. It consists of minimizing the total cost, T_c, of the water distribution network configuration, where n is the number of pipes in the network. T_c is based on the sum of the costs of each pipe of length L_{ijd_k}. Cost C_{ijd_k} is taken from a commercial diameters list and it depends directly of the diameter of pipe used. The cost of a pipeline is assumed to be linearly proportional to its length. The objective function is subject to constraints set. Constraints in (2) indicate that one or more pipes L_{ijd_k} in the network can have the same diameter d_k. At the same time, it indicates when a diameter included in the set D of commercial diameters, is not being used for a pipe in the network. D is the set of commercial diameters available for the water

network design, $D = d_1, d_2, , d_n$. Constraints in (3) indicate that each node i in
the network can be connected to pipes of length L_{ijd_k} with the same or different commercial diameter sizes. Constraints in (4) indicate that for each pipe,
of length, a single pipe diameter of the list of commercially available diameters
must be used. Restrictions in (5) define values that can be assigned to the set of
variables X. For example, when considering reference to (1), if a pipe connected
from node i to node j uses a diameter d_k then $X_{ijd_k} = 1$, otherwise $X_{ijd_k} = 0$.

The constraints satisfaction model (Table 2) includes network operation restrictions. They refer to the necessary restrictions to operate a looped water
network properly. Constraint (6) represents the physical law of mass conservation on each of n nodes of the network, where Qin are the pipe flows into the
loop, $Qout$ are the pipe flows away from the loop, and Qe is positive if it is an
external demand and negative if it is a supply. The flow entering a node must be
equal to the flow leaving the node. Constraint (7) refers to the law of conservation of energy in a mesh m; in this case m is a loop in the network. It indicates
that the sum of the frictional energy losses along pipe lengths belonging to the
hydraulic mesh should be zero if there are not power pumps in m. Constraint (8)
refers to the minimum and maximum pressure requirements to satisfy the users
water requirements while guaranteeing appropriate network operation. Pressure
requirements are verified at each demand node i of the network. Finally, constraint (9) is related to the limitation of flow velocity V in pipes. The minimum
velocity requirement is defined to avoid reducing the diameter of pipes because of
sediments. The maximum velocity requirement helps to reach required pressures.

3 Evolutionary Algorithm

Evolutionary Algorithms (EAs) are adaptive methods which attempt to imitate
the biological and genetic processes and can successfully be applied to optimization problems. The main fields of application of EAs include problems such as
Water Distribution Networks, with high complexity, non-linear behavior, and
a high number of decision variables [25]. EAs are stochastic numerical search
procedures inspired by biological evolution allowing the individuals with better
fitness to survive and propagate their genes to successive generations. EAs deal
with a population of individuals, which experience constant changes by means
of genetic operators like reproduction, crossover, and mutation. EAs are gaining
popularity due to their capabilities in handling several real world problems involving complexity, noisy environments, imprecision, uncertainty, and vagueness
[26].

In this work, for the WDND problem, the individuals of a population are
represented by a set of parameters (commercial diameters and lengths of pipes)
that describe a solution. Each solution is codified into a chromosome structure
to represent the analogy with the characters strings. They are evaluated with
respect to the objective function in (1) and ranked according to their fitness. The
best individuals for the problem are those individuals with least-cost. Generally,
the best individuals are more likely to be candidate solutions to reproduce,
having offspring that compose the next generation.

Figure 1 shows the solution methodology used to solve the WDND problem by using an evolutionary algorithm. The proposed algorithm in this work, called EA-WDND, works in Linux platforms. It uses the well-known Epanet Solver [27] version 2.0 [28] to verify hydraulic constraints, Table 2.

The solutions space SS, also known in the literature as search space, includes all possible solutions to the problem. The size of the SS depends directly on the input instance analyzed. Hence, for two-looped network instances, the search space would include 1,875,000,000 possible solutions. SS includes feasible and unfeasible solutions. Feasible solutions are those solutions that obey restrictions of the lineal programming model and restrictions of the hydraulic model at the same time (section 2). Unfeasible solutions are those solutions that do not obey all constraints included in both models.

An instance of a WDND problem is defined by the function $f : SS \rightarrow R$, where SS is the finite set of solutions that defines the problem instance, R is the set of real values that defines each solution in SS, and f is the objective function. In a problem instance, it is necessary to find the solution $s \in SS$ for which $f(s) \leq f(y), \forall y \in SS$, where s is feasible. The set R includes decision variables which are discrete values; specifically it refers to pipe diameters. In Fig. 1, $FU = \{\}s|s \in SS, FU \subseteq SS()$ is a subset taken from SS. FU can contain feasible and unfeasible solutions because restrictions of the hydraulic model are not considered at this point. The set of feasible solutions space is represented by $FS = \{s|s$ is feasible, $FS \subseteq FU, FS \neq FU\}$. The set FS considers both the constraints of the lineal and the hydraulic model. FS is created by taking solutions from FU and verifying them to determine whether they obey hydraulic constraints. The verification is done using the EPANET Solver. Therefore, FS can only include feasible solutions.

It is known that the initial feasible population, which is not necessarily the best one, allows good individuals in next generations of the genetic algorithm to be obtained. When generating the initial population, a question arises regarding its optimal size. The selection operator used is "the best" (elitist) [29]. It consists of taking the best individuals of the population FS. According to their fitness, the operator the best selects an average of the best individual values from a population. Then individuals are combined producing offspring that will compose the next generation, called the Feasible Solutions Subset FSS, see Fig. (1), $FSS = \{s|s \in FS, FSS \subseteq FS, FSS \neq FS\}$. FSS has the same definition for the feasible solutions space FS. The difference between FS and FSS is that FS, in the first generation of the algorithm, contains feasible individuals randomly generated. FSS contains offspring of individuals included into the FS set. For the next generations, FS is created by replacing its individuals with offspring that result from applying crossover and mutation operators. It is important to mention that the number of crossover or mutations is directly related to the population size. For each individual of the population, a crossover or mutation is applied. Consequently, the number of feasible offspring individuals included in FS is slightly larger than the size of FSS. Some descendants are eliminated because they are not feasible when Epanet evaluates them. The feasible individ-

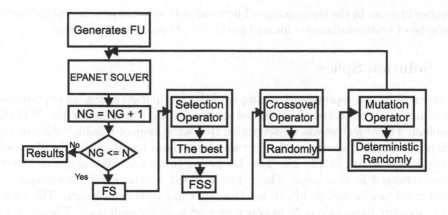

Fig. 1. Solution methodology for the WDND problem

uals are kept in a temporary list and they are ranked according to their fitness. The fittest offspring replace parents at each generation to constitute a new feasible population set, FSS. The FSS set is used at each generation to carry out crossover or mutation on its individuals.

The crossover operator is a function $C_r(s_1, s_2) \overrightarrow{\sigma}(s_1', s_2')$, it consists of exchanging σ chromosome information from the two parents s_1, s_2 to produce an offspring pair (s_1', s_2') who inherits characteristics from the parents, then $FS = \{(s_1, s_2) | (s_1', s_2') \in FS, (s_1', s_2') \in SS\}$. The crossover σ refers to the combination of two feasible solutions, s_1 and s_2, to generate two new individuals, s_1' and s_2. These new individuals are then verified in Epanet to determine whether they are feasible solutions. The crossing strategy implemented in this work is called one point cross-over [24]. It generates two offspring, the s_1' and s_2 chromosomes. To determine whether the offspring chromosomes are better than their parents, their fitness has to be computed with the objective function, see (1). In the EA-WDND algorithm, the parents are removed and replaced by the best offspring to keep a stable population size. The result is a new generation, usually with better fitness.

The mutation operator [24] involves randomly replacing a targeted gene. The mutation operator is a function $M(s) \overrightarrow{\alpha}(s')$. The mutation α, implemented in the mutation module, consists of randomly replacing the targeted gene using a random number $K \in [1, n]$, where n is the total number of genes in the chromosome. Each gene represents a pipe diameter. It is replaced with a random integer $K[d_1, d_n]$, where n is the total number of commercial diameters. For each individual mutated, an offspring chromosome is generated and a deterministic mutation α is carried out. The mutation operator α involves randomly selecting a gene to be mutated, using a random number $K \in [1, n]$, where n is the total number of genes in the chromosome. It is replaced with the gene of greatest diameter that is located in the next position of the array $(i + 1)$. Another variation consists of randomly selecting a gene to be mutated, using a random number $K \in [1, n]$, where n is the total number of genes in the chromosome. The randomly selected gene is replaced with the gene of smallest diameter located in the $(i - 1)$ position of the array.

4 Solution Space

In order to have a representative sample of the population space, an experimental study was conducted. It consisted of generating solutions for the WDND problem. The objective was to determine the percentage of feasible solutions for this problem. The experimental study was carried out based on the Two-Looped network benchmark [2, 12]. The Two-Looped network has seven nodes and eight pipes arranged in two loops. The network is fed by the gravity technique. It has a fixed head reservoir of 210 m. The pipes are 1000 m in length. The minimum pressure limitation is 30 m above ground level for each node. There are 14 commercial diameters which can be selected. The nodal head and demands, the cost per meter for each size of pipe, and other data are widely reported in many previous works [2, 30, 31, 3, 32].

In the literature, information on how to define the size of initial population for the WDND problem was not found. Some researches use various population sizes, Table 3.

Table 3. Population size

(a) Before

Date	Researchers	Population Size
1997	Savic et al.	50
1999	Montesinos et al.	300
2003	Matias et al.	100-1000
2006	Reca et al.	500

(b) After

Sample	Feasible Individuals	Time (sec.)
15,000	144	12
30,000	293	24
60,000	589	63
120,000	1188	98
240,000	2374	186
480,000	4752	383
960,000	9509	720
1,920,00	19355	1500

5 Experimental Results

The experimental study for the WDND problem involved the generation of different population sizes to know the number of feasible individuals (verified in Epanet) that can be obtained for each sample. Additionally, for each sample, the time required to obtain feasible populations was measured. To generate a feasible population, the algorithm was executed 30 times for each defined sample population. Table 3, shows the results obtained from the executions of the algorithm. After 30 executions were carried out, the average for a sample of 15,000 individuals was 144 feasible individuals generated in 12 seconds.

According to the obtained results, it can be noted that the feasible solutions space is 0.01% of the complete solutions space for the benchmark Two-Looped network, Fig. 2a. Based on the experimental results, it can be deduced that the time needed to generate the complete solutions space (1,475,800,000) should be approximately 521 hours, Fig. 2b. The required time increases according to the input instance, so the algorithm could spend years generating all possible solutions for larger instances.

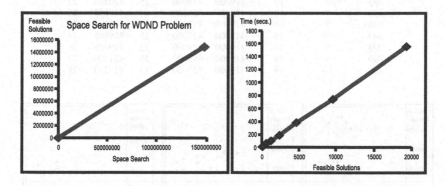

Fig. 2. Feasible solution space and time to generate feasible solutions

The EA-WDND algorithm was tested using different sized feasible populations. It was executed 30 times for each generated population. On each execution, EA-WDND carried out 20 iterations (generations), labeled 0 to 19. At each generation, the EA-WDND applied the crossover and mutation operators with a probability of 70% and 30% respectively. The population size was kept constant, even when crossover and mutation operators generated more descendants than the population size. Whatever the number of resulting offspring, the population size was the same for all the generations. This was achieved by removing parents and replacing them with the fittest offspring. The offspring were ranked according to their fitness. The best individuals were selected at each generation and they became parents. In some cases, mutations were carried out on them, so they produced new feasible offspring (verified by Epanet) that composed the next generation. It can be said that for each generation the population was created, it was combined to produce feasible offspring (verified in Epanet), and then it was replaced. Table 4 shows the experimental results obtained with EA-WDND after carrying out 30 executions.

"Max. Iteration of Min Cost" refers to the iteration for which the algorithm, in the worst case, would find the minimum solution for the network cost. For the first row, it means that in the worst case the algorithm would find the minimum solution in iteration 19. Min. Cost is the least-cost value for the benchmark. The best cost reported in the literature, for two-looped networks, is 419000. It is the lowest value found in 20 iterations and 30 executions of the algorithm. Max. Costs refers to the highest-cost value found in 20 iterations and 30 executions of the algorithm. Media Iteration refers to the iterations in which the EA-WDND algorithm finds the best values. It is the average for the iterations of 30 executions. Media Cost refers to the average obtained from 30 executions

Table 4. Experimental study of WDND feasible solution space

Population Size	Min. Iteration of Min Cost	Max. Iteration of Min Cost	Min. Cost	Max. Cost	Media Iteration	Media Cost	Number of Times
100	9	19	419000	450000	13	429400	9
200	7	19	419000	449000	14	422500	17
300	7	19	419000	437000	15	420566	22
400	9	10	419000	426000	14	419533	25
500	9	19	419000	437000	15	419966	23
600	10	19	419000	437000	15	419866	27
700	5	18	419000	428000	13	419666	26
800	8	19	419000	483000	15	421300	27
900	10	19	419000	423000	16	419233	28

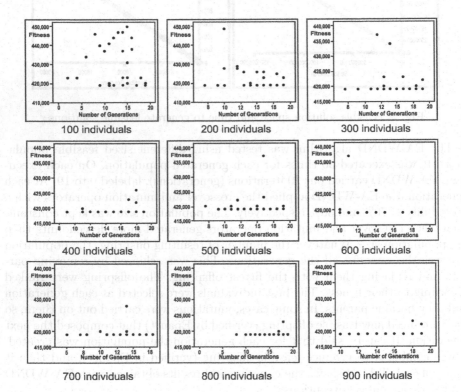

Fig. 3. Best values found using different population sizes

of the algorithm; it is the cost for the network. Number of times refers to the occurrences in which the algorithm finds the best solution. For the first row, it means that the algorithm finds the Min. Cost (419000) in 9 executions. It can be seen that for populations of 900 individuals, the Min. Cost was obtained 28 times. This means that the algorithm failed to find the Min. Cost in only 2 executions, as shown in Table 4. For the best case, the minimum cost was found on iteration number 10, which demonstrates the good convergence of the algorithm.

Also, it can be seen that when working with populations of 700 individuals, the EA-WDND algorithm found the minimum cost for the network, for the best case on iteration number 5 and for the worst case on iteration number 18. It can be seen that the media costs were 419666 and the media iterations was 13.

Figure 3 shows the experimental results obtained by the EA-WDND algorithm. It can be seen that, as the population size increased, better solutions were obtained. Most times, for populations of 900 individuals, the best value known in the literature was obtained. It is important to point out that convergence for this algorithm was reached quite quickly. The best solution known in the literature was found approximately in 80% of the executions, except in the case of populations of 100 individuals.

6   Conclusions and Future Works

This paper shows how the performance of a typical evolutionary algorithm can be improved by considering the importance of the population size taken from the feasible solutions space. It shows the experimental results obtained in the solutions space for WDND Problem using a Two-Looped network benchmark. The behavior of the EA is the same as in optimization problems. According to the obtained results, it can be observed that the feasible solutions space for the WDND problem is 0.01% of the complete solutions space for the benchmark Two-Looped network. For each generation, the population was created, combined to produce offspring, and then died (unfeasible solutions). It was replaced by the best offspring (feasible solutions with Epanet). It was observed that the removal of parents that had died and their replacement with the fittest offspring helped the EA-WDND converge. It also helped to obtain the best values known in the literature, in iteration number 5 in the best case and iteration number 20 in the worst case. It can be said that the convergence rate and speed was superior for this algorithm. Continuation of this work includes tests in parallel environments, using larger instances such as the Hanoi and Balerma network.

References

[1] Baños Navarro, R.: Hybrid Metaheuristics for Mono-objective and Multi-objective Optimization. PhD. Tesis, Almería, Spain (December 2006) (in Spanish), http://www.ace.ual.es/~rbanos/CV.html (last date of access May 12, 2009)

[2] Alperovits, E., Shamir, U.: Design of optimal water distribution systems. Water Resources Research 13(6), 885–900 (1977)

[3] Fujiwara, O., Jenchimahakoon, B.: A modified linear programming gradient method for optimal design of looped. Water Resources Research 23(6), 977–982 (1987)

[4] Savic, D., Walters, G.A.: Genetic algorithms for least-cost design of water distribution networks. Journal of Water Resources Planning and Management 123(2), 67–77 (1997)

[5] Abebe, A.J., Solomatine, D.P.: Application of global optimization to the design of pipe networks. In: Proceedings of the International Conference on Hydroinformatics, pp. 989–996. A. A. Balkema, Brookfield (1998)

[6] Montesinos, P., Garcia-Guzman, A., Ayuso, J.L.: Water distribution network optimization using modified genetic algorithm. Water Resources Research 35(11), 3467–3473 (1999)

[7] Cruz-Chávez, M.A., Ávila Melgar, E.Y., Juárez-Pérez, F., Torres-Sánchez, W.G.: Empirical Transformation of Job Shop Scheduling Problem to the Hydraulic Networks Problem in a Water Distribution System. In: Electronics Robotics and Automotive Mechanics Conference, CERMA 2009, pp. 76–81. IEEE-Computer Society, México (2009) ISBN 978-0-7695-3799-3

[8] Gupta, I., Bassin, J., Gupta, A., Khanna, P.: Optimization of water distribution system. Environmental Software 8, 101–113 (1993)

[9] Sherali, H.D., Totlani, R., Loganathan, G.: Enhanced lower bounds for the global optimization of water distribution networks. Water Resources Research 34(7), 1831–1841 (1998)

[10] Costa, A.L., De-Medeiros, J., Pessoa, F.: Global optimization of water distribution networks through a reduced space branch-and-bound search. Water Resources Research 37(4), 1083–1090 (2000)

[11] Loganathan, V., Greene, J.J., Ahn, T.J.: Design heuristic for globally minimum cost water distribution systems. Water Resources Research 121(2), 182–192 (1995)

[12] Reca, J., Martínez, J.: Genetic algorithms for the design of looped irrigation water distribution networks. Water Resources Research 42 (2006)

[13] Gil, C., Baños, R., Ortega, J., Márquez, A.L., Fernández, A., Montoya, M.G.: Ant colony optimization for water distribution network design: A comparative study. In: Cabestany, J., Rojas, I., Joya, G. (eds.) IWANN 2011, Part II. LNCS, vol. 6692, pp. 300–307. Springer, Heidelberg (2011)

[14] Liberatore, S., Sechi, G.M., Zuddas, P.: Water distribution systems optimization by metaheuristic approach, advances in water supply management, pp. 265–272. Balkema Publisher, Lisse (2003)

[15] López-Ibáñez, M., Devi-Prasad, T., Paechter, B.: Representations and evolutionary operators for the scheduling of pump operations in water distribution, networks. Evolutionary Computation 19(3), 429–467 (2011)

[16] Baños, R., Gil, C., Reca, J., Montoya, F.: A memetic algorithm applied to the design of water distribution networks. Applied Soft Computing 10(1), 261–266 (2010)

[17] Papadimitriou, C., Steiglitz, K.: Combinatorial Optimization: Algorithms and Complexity. Dover Publications (1998) ISBN-10: 0486402584

[18] Holland, J.H.: Adaptation in natural and artificial systems. MIT Press, Cambridge (1975)

[19] Goldberg, D.: Genetic algorithms in search, optimization and machine learning. Addison-Wesley Publishing Co., Inc., Reading (1989) ISBN: 0201157675

[20] Adenso-Díaz, B., Ghaziri, H., Glover, F., González, J.L., Laguna, M., Moscazo, P., Tseng, F.T.: Optimization heuristic and neural networks in the direction of operatios and engineering, Madrid, Spain (1996) (in Spanish), Paraninfo, S.A. (ed.) ISBN: 84-283-2269-4

[21] Glover, F.: Future paths for integer programming and links to artificial intelligence. Computers and Operations Research 13, 533–549 (1986)

[22] Cruz-Chávez, M.A., Rodríguez-León, A., Ávila-Melgar, E.Y., Juárez-Pérez, F., Cruz-Rosales, M.H., Rivera-López, R.: Genetic-annealing algorithm in grid environment for scheduling problems. In: Kim, T., Stoica, A., Chang, R.-S. (eds.) SUComS 2010. CCIS, vol. 78, pp. 1–9. Springer, Heidelberg (2010)

[23] Cruz-Chávez, M.A., Rodríguez-León, A., Ávila Melgar, E.Y., Juárez-Pérez, F., Zavala-Díaz, J.C., Rivera-López, R.: Parallel hybrid evolutionary algorithm in a grid environment for the job shop scheduling problem. In: Proceedings of the Second EELA-2 Conference, CIEMAT, pp. 227–234 (2009) ISBN 978-84-7834-627-1

[24] Baños, R., Fonseca, C., Gil, C., Márquez, A., Ávila Melgar, E., Montoya, F.: Design and evaluation of evolutionary operators for water distribution network optimisation. In: International Conference on Metaheuristics and Nature Inspired Computing, META 2010, Djerba, Tunisia (October 2010)

[25] Nazif, S., Karamouz, M., Tabesh, M., Moridi, A.: Pressure management model for urban water distribution. Networks, Water Resources Management (February 01, 2010) 0920-4741

[26] Abraham, A., Grosan, C., Ishibuchi, H.: Hybrid Evolutionary Algorithms. SCI, vol. 75, XVI, 404 p. 207 illus. Springer, Heidelberg (2007)

[27] Official site, E.: http://www.epa.gov/nrmrl/wswrd/dw/epanet.html#downloads

[28] Rossman, L.: Epanet 2 user's manual. epa/600/r-00/057 (2000)

[29] Al-Jadaan, O., Rajamani, L., Rao, C.R.: Improved selection operator for ga. Journal of Theoretical and Applied Information Technology, 269–277 (2008) ISSN 1992-8645

[30] Quindry, G., Brill, E., Liebman, J.: Optimization of looped water distribution systems. J. Environ. Eng., ASCE 107(4), 665–679 (1981)

[31] Goulter, I.C., Lussier, B.M., Morgan, D.R.: Implications of head loss path choice in the optimization of water distribution networks. Water Resources Research 22(5), 819–822 (1986)

[32] Kessler, A., Shamir, U.: Analysis of the linear programming gradient method for optimal design of water supply networks. Water Resources Research 25(7), 1469–1480 (1989)

Archive Management in Interactive Evolutionary Computation with Minimum Requirement for Human User's Fitness Evaluation Ability

Hisao Ishibuchi, Takahiko Sudo, and Yusuke Nojima

Department of Computer Science and Intelligent Systems,
Graduate School of Engineering, Osaka Prefecture University,
1-1 Gakuen-cho, Naka-ku, Sakai, Osaka 599-8531, Japan
{hisao,nojima}@cs.osakafu-u.ac.jp, takahiko.sudo@ci.cs.osakafu-u.ac.jp
http://www.cs.osakafu-u.ac.jp/ci/

Abstract. Interactive evolutionary computation (IEC) has a large potential ability as a personalized optimization technique to search for preferred solutions. In IEC, evolution of a population is driven by human user's preference through his/her subjective fitness evaluation. As a result, different solutions are obtained by different users for the same problem. One important challenge in the design of an efficient IEC algorithm is to decrease the human user's burden in fitness evaluation. We have proposed an idea of a (1+1)ES model of IEC with the minimum requirement for human user's fitness evaluation ability under the following assumptions: (i) human users can evaluate only a single solution at a time, (ii) human users can remember only the previously examined single solution, (iii) the evaluation result is whether the current solution is better than the previous one or not, and (iv) human users can perform a prespecified number of evaluations in total. This model always has a single archive solution, which is used as the final solution when its execution is terminated. In this paper, we generalize the (1+1)ES model of IEC to a general (μ+1)ES model where μ is not a constant but a variable control parameter. More specifically, the value of μ is controlled so that only a single solution is obtained after the final generation (i.e., $\mu=1$ at the final generation whereas μ can be more than one in the other generations). We show how we can derive the upper bound on the value of μ at each generation from the requirement of $\mu=1$ at the final generation and the above-mentioned four assumptions. We also examine the search behavior of the (μ+1)ES model for various values of μ.

Keywords: Evolutionary algorithms, interactive evolutionary computation, human users, fitness evaluation, archive solutions, archive management.

1 Introduction

Since a well-known "Biomorph" simulation in "The Blind Watchmaker" by Dawkins [1] in the 1980s, interactive evolutionary computation (IEC) has been

L. Rutkowski et al. (Eds.): ICAISC 2014, Part I, LNAI 8467, pp. 360–371, 2014.

actively studied to efficiently utilize human user's subjective fitness evaluation in the field of evolutionary computation (EC). In IEC, each solution is evaluated by a human user based on his/her subjective preference. Thus IEC can be viewed as a personalized optimization technique. Different solutions are obtained by different human users for the same problem using the same IEC algorithm. This is because the same solution is evaluated differently by different human users. Such subjectivity in fitness evaluation is a clear characteristic feature of IEC in comparison with many other EC algorithms. According to Takagi [2], IEC is used in the following two meanings:

(1) EC based on subjective fitness evaluation by a human user.
(2) EC with an interactive human-computer interface.

The first meaning is narrow while the second one is broad. The second broad meaning includes the first narrow one. Various applications of IEC in the narrow meaning have been reported in the literature [3–9]. The second broad meaning is usually related to decision making where "interactive" means the utilization of the decision maker's preference in decision making. It is interesting to note that "interaction" is often used in the first narrow meaning in evolutionary single-objective optimization whereas it is almost always used in the second broad meaning in evolutionary multiobjective optimization [10–13]. In this paper, we use IEC in the first narrow meaning. One advantage of IEC is its high applicability to a wide variety of optimization tasks with no explicit objective functions such as music composition and computer graphics in evolutionary art. Another advantage is its personalized optimization ability. A population of solutions in IEC is driven by a human user through his/her subjective fitness evaluation. Whereas IEC can be viewed as a flexible personalized optimization technique with high applicability to a wide variety of optimization tasks, its application to real-world problems is not easy due to various limitations in human user's fitness evaluation (e.g., it is unrealistic to ask a human user to evaluate tens of thousands of solutions). The execution of IEC is terminated after a small number of fitness evaluations (e.g., 400 evaluations in 20 generations with 20 solutions [7]). Thus it is important to decrease the burden of human users in the fitness evaluation in IEC [14]. In some application tasks such as music composition, human users can evaluate only a single solution at a time. It is impossible to evaluate multiple pieces of music by listening to them simultaneously. We have a number of similar situations in our everyday life such as choosing a pair of glasses by wearing them and looking around. In almost all trial-and-error processes, we can examine a single setting at a time. For example, before starting to drive a rental car, we adjust the position of the seat and the angle of each mirror by examining a single combination of mirror angles and a seat position at a time. In such a trial-and-error process, we can compare the current setting (e.g., the current combination of mirror angles and a seat position) only with the previously examined one or two settings. As a result, some settings are re-examined before a single setting is chosen. Based on these discussions, we formulated a (1+1)ES model of IEC to search for the most preferred solution under the following assumptions in our former study [15]:

(i) Human users can evaluate only a single solution at a time.

(ii) Human users can remember only the previously examined single solution.

(iii) The evaluation result is whether "The current solution is better" or "The previously examined solution is better" between them.

(iv) Human users can perform a prespecified number of evaluations in total.

The (1+1)ES model of IEC had a single archive solution as a candidate for the single final solution. A new solution was generated by applying a mutation operator to the archive solution. This means that no crossover was used in our (1+1)ES model of IEC. In this paper, we generalize the (1+1)ES model of IEC to a $(\mu+1)$ES model where μ is the number of archive solutions, which are candidates for the final single solution. The value of μ should be one at the final generation whereas μ can be more than one in the other generations. The upper bound on the value of μ at each generation is derived from the requirement of $\mu=1$ at the final generation and the above-mentioned four assumptions. This paper is organized as follows: First we explain solution comparison under the above-mentioned four assumptions in Section 2. Next we explain our (1+1)ES model of IEC in our former study [15] in Section 3. Then we generalize the (1+1)ES model to a $(\mu+1)$ES model in Section 4. The behavior of each model is illustrated by computational experiments in Section 5. Finally we conclude this paper in Section 6.

2   Solution Comparison

Our four assumptions make it impossible to use almost all IEC algorithms due to severely limited fitness evaluation ability of decision makers. For example, decision makers in our four assumptions cannot give any fitness value to each solution. They cannot choose good solutions from the current population, either. They cannot perform even pair-wise comparison [16, 17] since they cannot evaluate two solutions simultaneously. A comparison of two solutions is performed sequentially under our four assumptions as follows. First one solution (say x_1) is evaluated. Then the other solution (say x_2) is evaluated. After the second evaluation, we know whether "x_1 is better" or "x_2 is better" between x_1 and x_2. This implementation looks the same as pair-wise comparison. However, we need two evaluations whereas pair-wise comparison is usually viewed as being a single evaluation in IEC. Moreover, decision makers remember only x_2 after the second evaluation. This means that further two evaluations are needed to compare x_1 with another solution (say x_3) whereas x_2 can be compared with x_3 by an additional single evaluation (i.e., by evaluating x_3 after x_2).

Let us further explain our four assumptions using a simple task to choose the best solution among four candidates x_1, x_2, x_3 and x_4. For explanation purposes, we assume that x_4 is the best, x_3 is the second best, x_2 is the third best and x_1 is the worst (i.e., $x_1 \prec x_2 \prec x_3 \prec x_4$ where $x_1 \prec x_2$ means "x_2 is better than x_1"). If we can use the standard pair-wise comparison, we can find the best solution x_4 after three evaluations. That is, the best solution x_4 is found by performing the standard pair-wise comparison three times independent of the order of comparisons. For example, if we start with the comparison between x_3 and x_4 and then between x_1 and x_2, the best solution x_4 is found by the third comparison between x_4 and x_2. In the second comparison, it is possible to compare x_4 (the winner of the first comparison) with x_2 instead of the comparison between x_1 and x_2. In this case, the best solution x_4 is found from the third comparison between x_4 and x_1.

However, the number of required evaluations to find the best solution x_4 depends on the presentation order of solutions to decision makers under our four assumptions. Let us consider the presentation order "x_1, x_2, x_3, x_4". First x_1 is evaluated. No evaluation result is available because no solution is evaluated before x_1. Next x_2 is evaluated. The evaluation result of the second evaluation is "x_2 is better than x_1". Then x_3 is evaluated. The evaluation result is "x_3 is better than x_2". Finally x_4 is evaluated. The evaluation result is "x_4 is better than x_3". The best solution x_4 is found after these four evaluations. We can also find the best solution x_4 after four evaluations when the presentation order is "x_4, x_3, x_2, x_1". In this case, we obtain the following evaluation results: "x_4 is better than x_3", "x_3 is better than x_2", and "x_2 is better than x_1". Thus we can see that x_4 is the best solution. However, we need six evaluations when the presentation order is "x_4, x_2, x_3, x_1". In this case, we obtain the following evaluation results: "x_4 is better than x_2", "x_3 is better than x_2", and "x_3 is better than x_1". From these results, we cannot say which is better between x_3 and x_4. Since the decision maker remembers only x_1 after the fourth evaluation on x_1 is completed, x_3 and x_4 are evaluated again. As a result, the total number of evaluations is six. The presentation order is "x_4, x_2, x_3, x_1, x_3, x_4" or "x_4, x_2, x_3, x_1, x_4, x_3". The number of evaluations can be decreased from six to five by examining x_4 (instead of x_1) in the fourth evaluation. That is, five evaluations are needed to find the best solution x_4 when the presentation order is "x_4, x_2, x_3, x_4, x_1".

3 Our (1+1)ES Model of IEC

Before explaining our (1+1)ES model of IEC in our previous work [15], we explain the concept of archive solutions. In this paper, we mean candidate solutions by archive solutions. Let us examine the solution comparison in the presentation order "x_4, x_2, x_3, x_1" again. When the first solution x_4 is evaluated, only x_4 is a candidate solution. Thus an archive includes only x_4. After x_2 is evaluated, the archive still includes only x_4 as a candidate solution because the evaluation result is "x_4 is better than x_2". After x_3 is evaluated as "x_3 is better than x_2", both x_4 and x_3 are included in the archive as candidate solutions. After x_1 is evaluated as "x_3 is better than x_1", the archive includes both x_3 and x_4. That is, both x_3 and x_4 are candidates for the best solution. This is not a good situation since we need additional two evaluations to compare them with each other. Such an undesirable situation can be avoided by evaluating x_4 instead of x_1 in the fourth evaluation. After the evaluation of x_4 in the fourth evaluation, the archive includes only x_4 since the evaluation result is "x_4 is better than x_3".

Our (1+1)ES model of IEC has only a single archive solution. In its simplest version [15], the archive solution is presented to the decision maker to be examined again if the archive solution is not the previously examined solution. In this manner, the current best solution is always kept in the memory of the decision maker as the previously examined solution. If the archive solution is the same as the previously examined solution, a new solution is evaluated. Let us check the examination order "x_4, x_2, x_3, x_1" using this simplest version of our (1+1)ES model. In the third evaluation, the previously examined solution x_2 is not the same as the archive solution x_4. Thus x_4 is examined in the third evaluation again (whereas we know that x_4 is better than x_2). Then x_3 is evaluated in the fourth evaluation as "x_4 is better than x_3". After the fourth evaluation, the archive solution x_4 is not the same as the previously examined solution x_3, x_4 is presented to the decision maker again to examine it in the fifth evaluation. After that, x_1 is examined. As a result, the examination order becomes "x_4, x_2, x_4, x_3, x_4, x_1".

As this example shows, the simplest version looks inefficient since the same archive solution is repeatedly presented to the decision maker. In the modified version [15] of our (1+1)ES model of IEC, the archive solution is presented to the decision maker only when a new archive solution is added to the archive. That is, when the size of the archive becomes two, the older archive solution is presented to the decision maker. In this case, the new archive solution is the same as the previously examined solution. Thus one of the two archive solutions is removed after the comparison of the current solution (i.e., the older archive solution) with the previously examined one (i.e., the new added archive solution). In this manner, the archive size is decreased from two to one whenever it becomes two. Let us use the examination order "x_4, x_2, x_3, x_1" again to illustrate the modified version. After the second evaluation (i.e., evaluation of x_2), the archive solution x_4 is not the same as the previously examined solution x_2. However, x_4 is not presented to the decision maker since the archive includes only x_4. Thus x_3 is examined in the third evaluation. After the examination of x_3, the number of solutions in the archive increases from one to two (i.e., x_4 and x_3). Thus the older archive solution x_4 is presented to the decision maker to compare it with the previously examined solution x_3 which is also the newly added archive solution. Since the evaluation result of x_4 is "x_4 is better than x_3", x_3 is removed from the archive. That is, the archive includes only x_4. Then x_1 is examined (i.e., x_1 is compared with the previously examined x_4). As a result, the presentation order becomes "x_4, x_2, x_3, x_4, x_1", which is more efficient than "x_4, x_2, x_4, x_3, x_4, x_1" in the simplest version.

4   Proposed (μ+1)ES Model

Before generalizing our (1+1)ES model to a (μ+1)ES model, let us describe the archive management mechanisms in the two versions of our (1+1)ES model of IEC in a more formal manner. Let x_{t-1} and x_t be the solutions presented at the $(t\text{-}1)$th evaluation and the t-th evaluation, respectively. We also denote the archive (i.e., the set of archive solutions) by S. The archive S is updated in the following manner after x_t is evaluated.

Update Rules of Archive S: If x_t is evaluated as being better than x_{t-1} (i.e., $x_{t-1} \prec x_t$), x_t is added to S if x_t is not in S. In this case (i.e., $x_{t-1} \prec x_t$), x_{t-1} is removed from S if x_{t-1} is in S. If the evaluation result of x_t is "x_{t-1} is better than x_t" (i.e., $x_t \prec x_{t-1}$), no solution is added to S. In this case (i.e., $x_t \prec x_{t-1}$), x_t is removed from S if x_t is in S.

From these archive update rules, we can see that the size of the archive S increases only if the following three conditions hold:

(a) x_t is evaluated as being better than x_{t-1},
(b) x_t is not in S (i.e., x_t is a newly generated solution),
(c) x_{t-1} is not in S (otherwise x_{t-1} is removed from S if (a) holds).

This means that S does not increase when x_{t-1} is in S (i.e., when the previously examined solution is the archive solution). Thus a new solution is generated in the simplest version when x_{t-1} is the archive solution. Otherwise, x_t is selected from S to prevent the increase of the archive size. In this manner, the archive size is maintained as one in the simplest version. From these discussions, the archive management mechanism in the simplest version of our (1+1)ES model of IEC can be written as follows:

Archive Management in the Simplest Version: If x_{t-1} is in the archive S, a new solution is generated as the current solution x_t. If x_{t-1} is not in the archive S, an archive solution in S is presented to the decision maker as the current solution x_t.

From the above-mentioned archive update rules, the size of the archive S decreases when the following three conditions hold:

(d) x_t is evaluated as being better than x_{t-1},
(e) x_t is in S (otherwise x_t is added to S if (d) hold),
(f) x_{t-1} is in S (otherwise x_{t-1} cannot removed from S even if (d) holds).

or the following two conditions hold:

(g) x_{t-1} is evaluated as being better than x_t,
(h) x_t is in S (otherwise x_t cannot be removed from S).

This means that the archive size does not decrease when x_t is a newly generated solution. In other words, the selection of x_t from S is needed to decrease its size. We can also see from (d)-(f) that the size of S always decreases when both x_{t-1} and x_t are included in S at the time of the evaluation of x_t.

From these discussions, the archive management mechanism in the modified version of our (1+1)ES model of IEC can be written as follows:

Archive Management in the Modified Version: If S includes only a single archive solution after the evaluation of x_{t-1}, a new solution is generated as the current solution x_t. If the number of archive solutions in S increases from one to two after the evaluation of x_{t-1}, the older archive solution (which is not the newly added archive solution $\mathbf{x}_{t-1}$) is presented to the decision maker as the current solution $\mathbf{x}_t$.

This archive management mechanism can be generalized to a $(\mu+1)$ES model as follows:

Archive Management in Our $(\mu+1)$ES Model: If the number of archive solutions in S is smaller than μ (i.e., $|S| < \mu$) after the evaluation of $\mathbf{x}_{t-1}$, a new solution is generated as the current solution $\mathbf{x}_i$. If the number of archive solutions in S is equal to or larger than μ (i.e., $|S| \geq \mu$) after the evaluation of $\mathbf{x}_{t-1}$, a solution in S except for $\mathbf{x}_{t-1}$ is randomly selected from S as the current solution $\mathbf{x}_t$.

The modified version of the $(1+1)$ES model is the same as our $(\mu+1)$ES model with $\mu=2$. In this paper, we refer to the simplest version and the modified version of the $(1+1)$ES model in our former study [15] as the $(1+1)$ES model and the $(2+1)$ES model, respectively.

Let us denote a prespecified number of evaluations as N. We also denote the value of μ, the presented solution and the archive at the t-th evaluation (before the t-th solution evaluation) as $\mu(t)$, $\mathbf{x}_t$ and S_t, respectively. An important requirement in our $(\mu+1)$ES model is that the archive includes only a single solution after N evaluations. This requirement is written as $|S_{N+1}| = 1$. The point in our $(\mu+1)$ES model is to specify $\mu(t)$ so that $|S_{N+1}| = 1$ holds after N evaluations.

Since the size of the archive can be decreased by choosing solutions from the archive for two evaluations in a row (as we have already discussed in this section), the size of the archive at the t-th evaluation (i.e., $|S_t|$) can be decreased to $|S_{N+1}| = 1$ if the following relation holds:

$$2(|S_t| - 1) \leq N - t. \tag{1}$$

From this relation, we have

$$|S_t| \leq 1 + (N - t)/2. \tag{2}$$

Thus $\mu(t)$, which is the allowable size of the archive, is specified by

$$\mu(t) \leq 1 + (N - t)/2. \tag{3}$$

We also introduce the upper limit μ_{Max} of $\mu(t)$ as a pre-specified constant parameter. The role of μ_{Max} is illustrated in computational experiments in the next section. Using μ_{Max} and Eq.(3), we define $\mu(t)$ as follows:

$$\mu(t) = \min\{\mu_{\text{Max}}, 1 + (N - t)/2\}. \tag{4}$$

5   Computational Experiments

We perform computational experiments using an artificially generated test problem. So our computational experiments are not directly related to IEC applications. The aim of our computational experiments is to illustrate our $(\mu+1)$ES model of IEC and the effect of $\mu(t)$ in Eq.(4) on the search behavior of our $(\mu+1)$ES model.

As a test problem, we use a 500-item knapsack problem with two constraint conditions. This problem was generated from the following well-known two-objective 500-item 0/1 knapsack problem of Zitzler & Thiele [18]:

$$\text{Maximize } \mathbf{f}(\mathbf{x}) = (f_1(\mathbf{x}),\ f_2(\mathbf{x})), \tag{5}$$

$$\text{subject to } \sum_{j=1}^{500} w_{ij}x_j \leq c_i,\ i = 1, 2, \tag{6}$$

$$x_j = 0 \text{ or } 1,\ j = 1, 2, ..., 500, \tag{7}$$

$$\text{where } f_i(\mathbf{x}) = \sum_{j=1}^{500} p_{ij}x_j,\ i = 1, 2. \tag{8}$$

In this formulation, $\mathbf{x}$ is a 500-dimensional binary vector, p_{ij} is the profit of item j according to knapsack i, w_{ij} is the weight of item j according to knapsack i, and c_i is the capacity of knapsack i. Each profit p_{ij} and each weight w_{ij} are random integers in the interval [10, 100]. For details of the formulation, see Zitzler & Thiele [18].

We generated a test problem using the sum of the two objectives in (5) as follows:

$$f(\mathbf{x}) = f_1(\mathbf{x}) + f_2(\mathbf{x}). \tag{9}$$

We can use any test problem for examining the behavior of our $(\mu+1)$ES model. The use of the single-objective problem with (9) is to visually examine the behavior in the original two-dimensional objective space and the future possible extension of our $(\mu+1)$ES model to multi-objective interactive evolutionary computation.

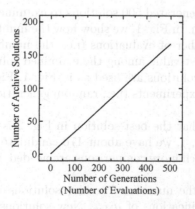

Fig. 1. The number of archive solutions for randomly generated 500 solutions

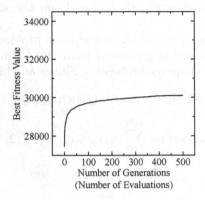

Fig. 2. The best objective value for randomly generated 500 solutions

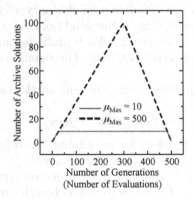

Fig. 3. The number of archive solutions when we used our $(\mu+1)$ES model

First, we randomly generated 500 solutions to examine the characteristic feature of this test problem. In Fig. 1, we show how the number of archive solutions increases with the number of evaluations (i.e., the number of randomly generated solutions). The best value among the examined solutions is shown in Fig. 2 where the same 500 solutions are used as in Fig. 1. Fig. 1 and Fig. 2 are average results over 100 experiments (i.e., random generation of 500 solutions was iterated 100 times).

It should be noted that the best solution in Fig. 2 is not identified. For example, as shown in Fig. 1, we have about 170 candidate solutions at the 500th generation. That is, much more comparisons are needed in Fig. 2 to find a single solution.

In Fig. 3, we show the number of archive solutions in our $(\mu+1)$ES model for some different specifications of μ_{Max}. New solutions in our computational experiments are generated by mutation from archive solutions. As shown in Fig. 3, the number of archive solutions is well-controlled by μ_{Max} and $\mu(t)$ in Eq.(4). The best objective value among examined solutions is shown in Figs. 4-5.

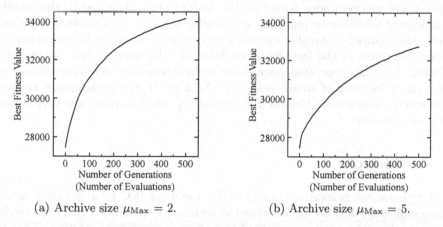

(a) Archive size $\mu_{\text{Max}} = 2$.   (b) Archive size $\mu_{\text{Max}} = 5$.

Fig. 4. The best objective value among the examined solutions at each generation ($\mu_{\text{Max}} = 2$ and $\mu_{\text{Max}} = 5$)

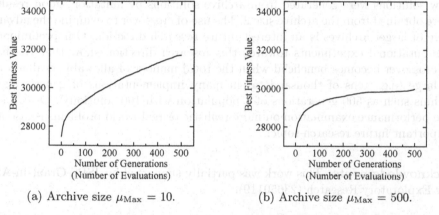

(a) Archive size $\mu_{\text{Max}} = 10$.   (b) Archive size $\mu_{\text{Max}} = 500$.

Fig. 5. The best objective value among the examined solutions at each generation ($\mu_{\text{Max}} = 10$ and $\mu_{\text{Max}} = 500$)

From these figures, we can see that good results were obtained from a very small archive size. By increasing the archive size, the performance of our (μ+1)ES model was degraded. When the archive size was specified between 2 and 10, much better results were obtained from our model in Figs. 4-5 than those from random sampling in Fig. 2.

However, when the archive size was actually unbounded (i.e., $\mu_{\text{Max}} = 500$) in Fig. 5 (b), experimental results from our model were similar to those from random sampling in Fig. 2. As shown by the dashed line in Fig. 3, the number of archive solutions was increased by generating new solutions through mutation in the first 300 evaluations. In this search phase, the quality of archive solutions was not significantly improved because no strong selection pressure was given (since there was no upper bound on the archive size). As a result, the quality of generated solutions by mutation was similar to the case of random sampling. Then, the number of archive solutions was decreased to one by re-examining archive solutions in the last 200 evaluations. In this search phase, many new solutions were not generated since many archive solutions were re-examined to decrease the number of archive solutions. As a result, the performance was not significantly improved in the last 200 evaluations whereas there was very strong selection pressure.

6   Conclusions

In this paper, we generalized our $(1+1)$ES model of IEC to a $(\mu+1)$ES model where multiple solutions can be stored as archive solutions. Our $(\mu+1)$ES model has an archive management mechanism to find a single final solution. That is, the archive size is controlled by a variable control parameter so that the archive size becomes one after all evaluations are completed. Through computational experiments, we examined the effect of the upper limit on the archive size. When new solutions were generated from archive solutions by mutation, good results were obtained from the archive size 2. The use of crossover to examine the advantage of larger archives is an interest future research direction. Our preliminary computational experiments towards this research direction show that the use of crossover becomes beneficial when the total number of allowable evaluations is large (e.g., tens of thousands as in many implementations of genetic algorithms such as 500 generations of a population with 100 solutions). Of course, the performance examination on more realistic or real-world problems is also an important future research topic.

Acknowledgments. This work was partially supported by JSPS Grant-in-Aid for Exploratory Research (23650119).

References

1. Dawkins, R.: The Blind Watchmaker. Norton, New York (1986)
2. Takagi, H.: Interactive Evolutionary Computation: Fusion of the Capabilities of EC Optimization and Human Evaluation. Proceedings of the IEEE 89(9), 1275–1296 (2001)
3. Kim, H.S., Cho, S.B.: Application of Interactive Genetic Algorithm to Fashion Design. Engineering Applications of Artificial Intelligence 13(6), 635–644 (2000)
4. Cho, S.B.: Towards Creative Evolutionary Systems with Interactive Genetic Algorithm. Applied Intelligence 16(2), 129–138 (2002)
5. Cho, S.B.: Emotional Image and Musical Information Retrieval with Interactive Genetic Algorithm. Proceedings of the IEEE 92(4), 702–711 (2004)
6. Lameijer, E.W., Kok, J.N., Bäck, T., Ijzerman, A.P.: The Molecule Evoluator. An Interactive Evolutionary Algorithm for the Design of Drug-like Molecules. Journal of Chemical Information and Modeling 46(2), 545–552 (2006)

7. Takagi, H., Ohsaki, M.: Interactive Evolutionary Computation-based Hearing Aid Fitting. IEEE Trans. on Evolutionary Computation 11(3), 414–427 (2007)
8. Arevalillo-Herráez, M., Ferri, F.J., Moreno-Picot, S.: Distance-based Relevance Feedback using a Hybrid Interactive Genetic Algorithm for Image Retrieval. Applied Soft Computing 11(2), 1782–1791 (2011)
9. Lai, C.C., Chen, Y.C.: A User-oriented Image Retrieval System based on Interactive Genetic Algorithm. IEEE Trans. on Instrumentation and Measurement 60(10), 3318–3325 (2011)
10. Avigad, G., Moshaiov, A.: Interactive Evolutionary Multiobjective Search and Optimization of Set-based Concepts. IEEE Trans. on Systems, Man, and Cybernetics - Part B: Cybernetics 39(4), 1013–1027 (2009)
11. Chaudhuri, S., Deb, K.: An Interactive Evolutionary Multi-objective Optimization and Decision Making Procedure. Applied Soft Computing 10(2), 496–511 (2010)
12. Deb, K., Sinha, A., Korhonen, P.J., Wallenius, J.: An Interactive Evolutionary Multiobjective Optimization Method based on Progressively Approximated Value Functions. IEEE Trans. on Evolutionary Computation 14(5), 723–739 (2010)
13. Kaliszewski, I., Miroforidis, J., Podkopaev, D.: Interactive Multiple Criteria Decision Making based on Preference Driven Evolutionary Multiobjective Optimization with Controllable Accuracy. European Journal of Operational Research 216(1), 188–199 (2012)
14. Sun, X., Gong, D., Zhang, W.: Interactive Genetic Algorithms with Large Population and Semi-supervised Learning. Applied Soft Computing 12(9), 3004–3013 (2012)
15. Ishibuchi, H., Hoshino, K., Nojima, Y.: Problem Formulation of Interactive Evolutionary Computation with Minimum Requirement for Human User's Fitness Evaluation Ability. In: Proc. of 16th Asia Pacific Symposium on Intelligent and Evolutionary Systems, Kyoto, Japan, December 12-14, pp. 52–57 (2012)
16. Takagi, H., Pallez, D.: Paired Comparisons-based Interactive Differential Evolution. In: Proc. of NaBIC 2009, Coimbatore, India, December 9-11, pp. 475–480 (2009)
17. Fukumoto, M., Inoue, M., Imai, J.: User's Favorite Scent Design using Paired Comparison-based Interactive Differential Evolution. In: Proc. of CEC 2010, Barcelona, Spain, July 18-23, pp. 4519–4524 (2010)
18. Zitzler, E., Thiele, L.: Multiobjective Evolutionary Algorithms: A Comparative Case Study and the Strength Pareto Approach. IEEE Trans. on Evolutionary Computation 3(4), 257–271 (1999)

Investigation of Mutation Strategies
in Differential Evolution
for Solving Global Optimization Problems

Miguel Leon and Ning Xiong

Mälardalen University, Västerås, Sweden

Abstract. Differential evolution (DE) is one competitive form of evolutionary algorithms. It heavily relies on mutating solutions using scaled differences of randomly selected individuals from the population to create new solutions. The choice of a proper mutation strategy is important for the success of an DE algorithm. This paper presents an empirical investigation to examine and compare the different mutation strategies for global optimization problems. Both solution quality and computational expense of DE variants were evaluated with experiments conducted on a set of benchmark problems. The results of such comparative study would offer valuable insight and information to develop optimal or adaptive mutation strategies for future DE researches and applications.

Keywords: Evolutionary Algorithm, Differential Evolution, Mutation Strategies, Global Optimization Problem.

1 Introduction

Evolutionary algorithms (EAs) have been proved to be powerful means to solve various optimization problems[1], [2], [3]. Generally, EAs are superior to traditional optimization techniques in two aspects. First, they require no derivative information of the objective function in deciding the search direction. Second, they perform parallel population-based search and thereby exhibiting more chance to find the global optimum in high dimensional problem spaces [4].

Differential evolution (DE) [5] presents one competitive class of evolutionary algorithms. Unlike other EAs, DE modifies solutions by using the difference of parameter vectors of pair(s) of randomly selected individuals from the population. The locations of the selected solutions decide the direction and magnitude of the search. Therefore the mutation in DE is performed based on the distribution of solutions in the population rather than a pre-specified probability density function.

Indeed there are quite a few alternative strategies to implement the mutation operation in DE [6]. One specific mutation strategy specifies which solution to modify (disturb) and how many difference vectors to use to create the disturbance. If the disturbance is made to a randomly selected solution, it implies that the search direction is decided at random without bias. In contrast, when the disturbance is executed on the best individual in the population, exploitation is more favored in the search process. Hence different strategies of mutation can

L. Rutkowski et al. (Eds.): ICAISC 2014, Part I, LNAI 8467, pp. 372–383, 2014.

reflect different attitudes towards exploration and exploitation. More detailed explanation of the various mutation strategies is given in Sections 2 and 3.

However, there is a lack of knowledge about the comparative performance of the various mutation strategies for solving global optimization problems. In practice it is most common to use a difference vector to mutate a random solution (termed as DE/rand/1 strategy) or the best individual from the population (termed as DE/best/1 strategy). The DE/rand/1 strategy was accepted in previous works as starting point for improved mutation operators. The enhanced mutation approach [7] assumed the usage of the DE/rand/1 strategy and suggested a way to strategically select the three random individuals from the entire space. The paper [8] proposed neighborhood-based mutation for multi-modal optimization tasks. It is realized by employing the DE/rand/1 strategy in local subgroups of the population. Moreover, the DE/rand/1 strategy was also combined with many local search methods for further performance improvement, see examples in [9], [10], [11]. More recently, random local search has been coupled into DE using both DE/rand/1 and DE/best/1 strategies [12]. Nevertheless none of the above mentioned works considered other mutation strategies than DE/rand/1 and DE/best/1 for DE improvement.

This paper presents an empirical investigation to examine and compare the different mutation strategies for global optimization problems. Both solution quality and computational expense of DE variants were evaluated with experiments conducted on a set of benchmark functions. The results of experiments enable us to compare the relative performance of the alternative mutation methods, thereby acquiring valuable insight and information to develop optimal or adaptive strategy for future DE researches and applications.

The remaining of the paper is organized as follows. Section 2 outlines the general DE paradigm. Section 3 explains the alternative mutation strategies. In Section 4 we discuss and compare the experiment results. Finally, Section 5 gives the concluding remarks.

2   Basic Differential Evolution Algorithm

DE is a stochastic algorithm maintaining a population with N_p individuals. Every individual in the population stands for a possible solution to the problem. One individual in the population is represented by vector $X_{i,g}$ with $i = 1, 2, \ldots, N_p$ and g referring to the index of the generation. A cycle in DE consists of three consecutive steps: mutation, crossover and selection which are described as follows:

MUTATION. Inspired from biological evolution, mutation is carried out in DE to facilitate random perturbations on the population. For each population member, a mutant vector is generated. In the basic version of DE, the mutant vector is obtained by randomly selecting three different individuals in the population and then adding a scaled difference of any two of the three vectors to the third one. More precisely, this mutant vector is created according to Eq. 1

$$V_{i,g} = X_{r_1,g} + F \times (X_{r_2,g} - X_{r_3,g}) \tag{1}$$

where $V_{i,g}$ represents the mutant vector, i stands for the index of the vector, g stands for the generation, $r_1, r_2, r_3 \in \{ 1,2,\ldots,N_p\}$ are random integers and F is the scaling factor in the interval $[0, 2]$.

Fig. 1 shows how this mutation strategy works. All the variables in the figure appear in Eq. 1 with the same meaning, and d is the difference vector between $X_{r_2,g}$ and $X_{r_3,g}$.

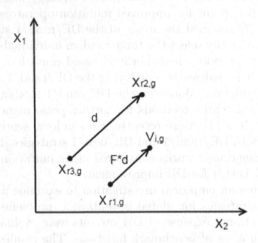

Fig. 1. Random mutation with one difference vector

CROSSOVER. This operation combines every individual in the actual population with the corresponding mutant vector created in the mutation stage. These new solutions created are called trial vectors and we use $T_{i,g}$ to represent the trial vector corresponding to individual i in generation g. Every parameter in the trial vector are decided in terms of Eq. 2

$$T_{i,g}[j] = \begin{cases} V_{i,g}[j] & \text{if } rand[0, 1] < CR \quad \text{or} \quad j = j_{rand} \\ X_{i,g}[j] & \text{otherwise} \end{cases} \qquad (2)$$

where j stands for the index of every parameter in a vector, J_{rand} is a randomly selected integer between 1 and N_p to ensure that at least one parameter from mutant vector will enter the trial vector and CR is the probability of recombination.

SELECTION. This operation compares a trial vector and its parent solution in the current population to decide the winner to survive into the next generation. Therefore, if the problem of interest is minimization, the individuals in the new generation are chosen using Eq. 3

$$X_{i,g+1} = \begin{cases} T_{i,g} & \text{if } f(T_{i,g}) < f(X_{i,g}) \\ X_{i,g} & \text{otherwise} \end{cases} \qquad (3)$$

where $T_{i,g}$ is the trial vector, $X_{i,g}$ is an individual in the population, $X_{i,g+1}$ is the individual in the next generation, $f(T_{i,g})$ represents the fitness value of the trial vector and $f(X_{i,g})$ stands for the fitness value of the individual in the population.

The pseudocode for the basic DE is given in Fig. 2. First we create the initial population with randomly generated individuals. Every individual in the population is then evaluated with a pre-specified fitness function. After that we create the mutant vectors using Eq. 1 and then we recombine such mutant vectors with their respective parents to obtain a set of offspring. Finally we compare the parents and offspring to select superior ones into a new, updated population. This procedure with steps from 4 to 7 is repeated until the termination condition is satisfied.

---

1. Initialize the population with randomly created individuals.

2. Calculate the fitness values of all individuals in the population

3. While the termination condition is not satisfied do

4.   Create mutant vectors using a mutation strategy in Eq. 1

5.   Create trial vectors by recombining noisy vectors with parents vectors according to Eq. 2

6.   Evaluate trial vectors with their fitness values

7.   Select winning vectors according to Eq. 3 as individuals in the new generation

8. End While

Fig. 2. Pseudocode Differential Evolution

3   Variants of Mutation in Differential Evolution

Various approaches have been proposed to implement mutation in DE [6]. The mutation strategy introduced in the preceding section is termed as random mutation, which is often used in classic DE. In order to distinguish different variants of mutation strategies, the following notation is commonly used in the literature:

$$DE/x/y/z,$$

where x represents the vector to be mutated, y is the number of difference vectors used in mutation and z denotes the crossover operator employed. We will skip z here because we always use the binominal crossover which has been explained in Section 2. Hence the random mutation strategy is notated as DE/rand/1. The five other well Known approaches of mutation will be outlined in the following subsections.

3.1   Best Mutation Strategy with One Difference Vector

Best mutation strategy [13] attempts to mutate the best individual in the population. When only one difference vector is employed in mutation, the approach is represented by DE/best/1. A new, mutated vector is created according to Eq. 4

$$V_{i,g} = X_{best,g} + F \times (X_{r_1,g} - X_{r_2,g}) \tag{4}$$

where $V_{i,g}$ represents the mutant vector, i is the index of the vector, g stands for the generation, $r_1, r_2, r_3 \in \{1,2,\ldots,N_p\}$ are randomly created integers, $X_{best,g}$ represents the best solution in the population and F is the scaling factor in the interval $[0, 2]$.

The main idea of this mutation strategy (notated as DE/best/1) is to use the scaled difference between two randomly selected vectors to mutate the best individual in the population. Fig. 3 shows how a new mutant vector is generated according to this strategy, where d is the difference vector between vectors $X_{r_1,g}$ and $X_{r_2,g}$.

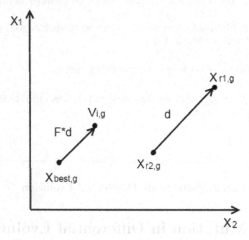

Fig. 3. Best mutation with one difference vector

3.2   Random Mutation Strategy with Two Difference Vectors

Random mutation with two difference vectors [14] is similar to the DE/rand/1 strategy, but it uses two difference vectors and it is notated as DE/rand/2. A mutant vector is created using 5 randomly selected vectors as follows:

$$V_{i,g} = X_{r_1,g} + F1 \times (X_{r_2,g} - X_{r_3,g}) + F2 \times (X_{r_4,g} - X_{r_5,g}) \tag{5}$$

where $F1$, $F2$ are the scaling factors in the interval $[0, 2]$ and $r_1, r_2, r_3, r_4, r_5 \in \{1,2,\ldots,N_p\}$ are randomly created integers, and $V_{i,g}$ stands for the mutant vector i for generation g.

3.3   Best Mutation Strategy with Two Difference Vectors

The strategy of best mutation with two difference vectors [5] is denoted as DE/best/2. It uses two difference vectors in mutation of the best individual of the population. The mutant vector is created in terms of Eq. 6 in the following:

$$V_{i,g} = X_{best,g} + F1 \times (X_{r_1,g} - X_{r_2,g}) + F2 \times (X_{r_3,g} - X_{r_4,g}) \qquad (6)$$

where $V_{i,g}$ stands for the the mutant vector, i is the index of the vector, g stands for the generation, $F1$ and $F2$ are the two scaling factors in the interval $[0, 2]$ and $r_1, r_2, r_3, r_4 \in \{ 1,2,\ldots,N_p\}$ are randomly created integers.

3.4   Current to Random Mutation Strategy

The current to rand mutation strategy is referred to as DE/current-to-rand/1. It moves the current individual towards a random vector before being disturbed with a scaled difference of two randomly selected individuals. Thus the mutant vector is created according to Eq. 7 as follows

$$V_{i,g} = X_{i,g} + F1 \times (X_{r_1,g} - X_{i,g}) + F2 \times (X_{r_2,g} - X_{r_3,g}) \qquad (7)$$

where $X_{i,g}$ represents the current individual, $V_{i,g}$ stands for the mutant vector, g stands for the generation, i is the index of the vector, $F1$ and $F2$ are the scaling factors in the interval $[0, 2]$ and $r1, r2, r3 \in \{ 1,2,\ldots,N_p\}$ are randomly created integers.

Fig. 4 explains how the DE/current-to-rand/1 strategy works to produce a mutant vector, where $d1$ is the difference vector between the current individual, $X_{i,g}$, and $X_{r_1,g}$, and $d2$ is the difference vector between $X_{r_3,g}$ and $X_{r_2,g}$.

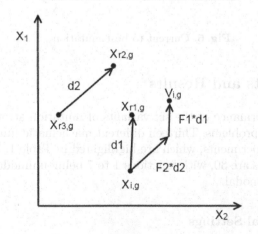

Fig. 4. Current to random mutation

3.5 Current to Best Mutation Strategy

The current to best mutation strategy [14] is referred as DE/current-to-best/1. It moves the current individual towards the best individual in the population before being disturbed with a scaled difference of two randomly selected vectors. Hence the mutant vector is created by

$$V_{i,g} = X_{i,g} + F1 \times (X_{best,g} - X_{i,g}) + F2 \times (X_{r_1,g} - X_{r_2,g}) \qquad (8)$$

where $V_{i,g}$ stands for the mutant vector, $X_{i,g}$ and $X_{best,g}$ represent the current individual and the best individual in the population respectively, $F1$ and $F2$ are the scaling factors in the interval $[0, 2]$ and $r_1, r_2 \in \{1,2,\ldots,N_p\}$ are randomly created integers.

Fig. 5 shows how the DE/current-to-best/1 strategy works to produce a mutant vector, where $d1$ denotes the difference vector between the current individual $X_{i,g}$ and $X_{best,g}$, $d2$ is the difference vector between $X_{r_1,g}$ and $X_{r_2,g}$.

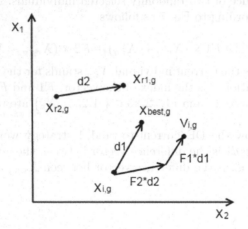

Fig. 5. Current to best mutation

4   Experiments and Results

We tested the performance of the six variants of mutation strategies in DE on a set of benchmark problems. Thirteen different mathematic functions from [15] were used in our experiments, which are highlighted in Table 1. The dimensions of all these functions are 30, with functions 1 to 7 being unimodal and functions 8 to 13 being multimodal.

4.1 Experimental Settings

The three control parameters for DE are: population size (Np), crossover rate (CR) and the scaling factor (F) for mutation. These parameters used in our experiments were specified as follows: $Np = 60$, $CR = 0.85$ and $F = 0.9$ when

Table 1. The thirteen functions used in the experiments

FUNCTION

$f1(x) = \sum_{i=1}^{n} x_i^2$

$f2(x) = \sum_{i=1}^{n} |x_i| + \prod_{i=1}^{n} |x_i|$

$f3(x) = \sum_{i=1}^{n} (\sum_{j=1}^{i} x_j)^2$

$f4(x) = max_i\{|x_i|, 1 \leq i \leq n\}$

$f5(x) = \sum_{i=1}^{n-1} [100 \times (x_{i+1} - x_i^2)^2 + (x_i - 1)^2]$

$f6(x) = \sum_{i=1}^{n} (x_i + 0.5)^2$

$f7(x) = \sum_{i=1}^{n} i \times x_i^4 + random[0, 1)$

$f8(x) = \sum_{i=1}^{n} -x_i \times sin(\sqrt{|x_i|})$

$f9(x) = \sum_{i=1}^{n} [x_i^2 - 10 \times cos(2 \times \pi \times x_i) + 10]$

$f10(x) = -20 \times exp(-0.2 \times \sqrt{\frac{1}{n} \times \sum_{i=1}^{n} x_i^2}) - exp(\frac{1}{n} \times \sum_{i=1}^{n} cos(2\pi x_i)) + 20 + e$

$f11(x) = \frac{1}{4000} \times \sum_{i=1}^{n} x_i^2 - \prod_{i=1}^{n} cos(\frac{x_i}{\sqrt{i}}) + 1$

$f12(x) = \frac{\pi}{n} \times \{10sin^2(\pi y_i) + \sum_{i=1}^{n-1}((y_i - 1)^2[1 + 10sin^2(\pi y_{i+1})]) + (y_n - 1)^2\} + $
$\quad + \sum_{i=1}^{n} u(x_i, 10, 100, 4)$, where $y_i = 1 + \frac{1}{4}(x_i + 1)$

$$u(x_i, a, k, m) = \begin{cases} k(x_i - a)^m, & x_i > a \\ 0, & -a \leq x_i \leq a \\ k(x_i - a)^m, & x_i < -a \end{cases}$$

$f13(x) = 0.1 \times \{sin^2(3\pi x_1) + \sum_{i=1}^{n-1}((x_i - 1)^2[1 + sin^2(3\pi x_{i+1})]) + $
$\quad + (x_n - 1)[1 + sin^2(2\pi x_n)^2]\} + \sum_{i=1}^{n} u(x_i, 5, 100, 4)$

only one difference vector is used and $F1 = 0.3$ and $F2 = 0.7$ when two difference vectors are involved (as in DE/rand/2 and DE/Best/2). The DE variants (with different mutation strategies) were applied and tested on the benchmark functions in attempts to find the best solutions for them. Every DE variant was executed for each function 20 times to get a fair result for the comparison. The terminate condition for the execution of the DE programs is that the error with respect to the global optimum is below $10e$-8 or the number of fitness evaluations has exceeded $300,000$.

The results of experiments will be demonstrated in the following. First we compare the performance (the quality of acquired solutions) of the DE variants in the benchmark functions, and secondly we compare the convergence speed of the DE variants in finding their optima solutions.

4.2 Comparison of the Quality of Solutions

First we consider the quality of solutions obtained by the DE variants. The results obtained on the thirteen benchmark functions are showed in Table 2. The first column corresponds to the test functions used for evaluation. All the other columns are used to present the average error of the results obtained for a certain function with respect to its global optimal value. A figure in boldface means the lowest average error among those achieved by the DE variants.

We compare the quality of solutions on unimodal and multimodal functions respectively. It can be seen from Table 2 that, in unimodal functions (functions

Table 2. Average error of the found solutions

FUNCTION	DE/rand/1	DE/best/1	DE/rand/2	DE/best/2	DE/ctor/1	DE/ctob/1
f1	**0.00E+00**	**0.00E+00**	**0.00E+00**	**0.00E+00**	**0.00E+00**	**0.00E+00**
f2	1.58E-08	4.70E-05	**0.00E+00**	5.00E-01	**0.00E+00**	**0.00E+00**
f3	5.81E+01	2.50E+02	1.69E-01	2.32E-07	8.73E-06	**0.00E+00**
f4	5.81E+00	1.58E-02	1.10E-02	9.08E-06	3.11E-02	**2.35E-08**
f5	2.66E+01	6.54E+00	6.86E-04	7.98E-01	**0.00E+00**	2.00E-01
f6	**0.00E+00**	**0.00E+00**	**0.00E+00**	**0.00E+00**	**0.00E+00**	**0.00E+00**
f7	1.12E-02	9.58E-03	5.73E-03	5.14E-03	**2.63E-03**	2.65E-03
f8	**2.47E+03**	3.24E+03	6.62E+03	3.29E+03	6.94E+03	2.59E+03
f9	**1.09E+01**	4.24E+01	1.72E+02	4.51E+01	1.53E+02	2.57E+01
f10	1.88E+01	1.40E+01	**0.00E+00**	2.05E+00	**0.00E+00**	**0.00E+00**
f11	**0.00E+00**	**0.00E+00**	**0.00E+00**	**0.00E+00**	**0.00E+00**	**0.00E+00**
f12	**0.00E+00**	9.85E-02	**0.00E+00**	5.71E-02	**0.00E+00**	**0.00E+00**
f13	**0.00E+00**	3.83E-03	**0.00E+00**	5.47E-03	**0.00E+00**	**0.00E+00**

1-7), DE/current-to-rand/1 and DE/current-to-best/1 appeared as the strongest alternative sine they reached the global optimum in four of the seven functions. DE/best/2 and DE/rand/2 were also very good in the 7 unimodal functions, with results very similar to those of the strongest candidates. The weakest approaches here were DE/rand/1 and DE/best/1, as they produced significant error in some cases such as function 3, 4, and 5, as shown in the table.

In multimodal functions (functions 8-13), DE/current-to-best/1 appeared as the best choice, as it found the results similar to the best ones on functions 8 and 9 and the global optima on all the other functions. DE/rand/1 was also attractive, as it found the best solutions on functions 8 and 9. In function 10, DE/rand/1 and DE/best/1 got the worst performance with large error, while all the other candidates acquired the optimum or near optimal solutions. Finally, on functions 11, 12 and 13 all the approaches behaved equally well with optimal or close to optimal results.

Based on the above analysis, we can point out that, for unimodal functions, it is better to use DE/current-to-best/1 or DE/current-to-rand/1. But good results can be achieved with DE/best/2 and DE/rand/2 as well. DE/rand/1 and DE/best/1 are very weak in unimodal functions. In multimodal functions the best results can be achieved with DE/current-to-best/1 and DE/rand/1, except in function 10 for which the performance of DE/rand/1 is not good. DE/current-to-rand/1 and DE/rand/2 can have very poor performance occasionally, such as in functions 8 and 9.

4.3   Comparison of the Computational Cost

In this subsection we compare the numbers of fitness evaluations that were done by the DE variants before the global optima were reached. We did this in the following way: First we recorded the number of DE executions from which the global optimum was reached. These numbers are given in Table 3. Then we calculated the average number of evaluations for every DE variant on each test function, as listed in Table 4.

Table 3. Number of executions with acquired optimum

FUNCTION	DE/rand/1	DE/best/1	DE/rand/2	DE/best/2	DE/ctr/1	DE/ctb/1
f1	20	20	20	20	20	20
f2	6	18	20	19	20	20
f3	0	0	0	0	0	18
f4	0	0	0	0	0	6
f5	0	0	0	16	19	19
f6	20	20	20	20	20	20
f10	0	6	20	17	20	20
f11	20	20	20	20	20	20
f12	20	15	20	17	20	20
f13	20	16	20	17	20	20

In Table 3 we can observe that DE/current-to-best/1 always got the highest success rate. DE/current-to-rand/1 and DE/rand/2 got success rate similar to that of DE/current-to-best/1 in many cases. No comparison was made on functions 7, 8 and 9 since the DE variants never reached the global optima on these functions. The worst algorithm in this comparison was DE/rand/1 because it never found an optimum in seven functions and on function 2 its success rate was very low.

Table 4. Mean number of evaluations conducted

FUNCTION	DE/rand/1	DE/best/1	DE/rand/2	DE/best/2	DE/ctr/1	DE/ctb/1
f1	211008	103353	96315	57720	64494	**54132**
f2	299013	158205	166530	99303	115071	**94536**
f3	300000	300000	300000	300000	300000	**287898**
f4	300000	300000	300000	300000	300000	**294825**
f5	300000	300000	300000	240870	287796	**206241**
f6	212178	108045	96369	57819	64962	**54189**
f10	300000	260661	153717	132552	102117	**86028**
f11	177993	90879	81240	48219	54213	**45786**
f12	185953	157440	97425	132786	61422	**51192**
f13	208842	147054	104472	95055	67845	**55629**

From Table 4 it is clear that DE/current-to-best/1 was the fastest algorithm on all the functions. Then we attempt to identify the second fastest alternative from DE/current-to-rand/1 and DE/best/2. For this purpose we do comparison on unimodal functions (functions 1 to 7) and multimodal functions (functions 8 to 13) respectively. On unimodal functions, DE/best/2 was better in all of the four functions for comparison, but the difference was not so large. On multimodal functions, DE/current-to-rand/1 was better in three of the four functions with large differences. Overall the worst algorithm was DE/rand/1 because it took the most evaluations in all the 8 unimodal and multimodal functions (functions 3 and 4 are excluded in this comparison). Based on these results we can point out that DE/current-to-best/1 is a faster DE variant while DE/rand/1 is a slower one.

5   Conclusions

This paper presents an empirical study to compare six different mutation strategies in optimization problems. All these mutation approaches have been tested in a set of benchmark problems in terms of both the quality of solutions and the computational expense, i.e. the number of fitness evaluations required. The results of experiments have led to the recommendation of the DE/current-to-best/1 strategy, which is not only computationally efficient but also superior in guaranteeing the quality of solutions in a diversity of problems.

It is important to be aware of the relative performance of distinct mutation strategies to develop competent DE algorithms. In future we will exploit the information acquired in this paper for construction of optimal or adaptive strategies of mutation to tackle more complex and larger scale optimization tasks. Moreover, we will also apply and test our new computing algorithms in real industrial scenarios.

Acknowledgment. The work is funded by the Swedish Knowledge Foundation (KKS) grant (project no 16317). The authors are also grateful to ABB FACTS, Prevas and VG Power for their co-financing of the project.

References

1. Herrera, F., Lozano, M., Verdegay, J.: Tackling real-coded genetic algorithms: Operators and tools for the behavioral analysis. Artificial Intelligence Review 12, 265–319 (1998)
2. Beyer, H., Schwefel, H.: Evolution strategies: A comprehensive introduction. Natural Computing 1, 3–52 (2002)
3. Lee, C., Yao, X.: Evolutionary programming using mutations based on the levy probability distribution. IEEE Transactions on Evolutionary Computation 8, 1–13 (2004)
4. Xiong, N., Leon, M.: Principles and state-of-the-art of engineering optimization techniques. In: Proc. The Seventh International Conference on Advanced Engineering Computing and Applications in Sciences, ADVCOMP 2013, Porto, Portugal, pp. 36–42 (2013)
5. Storn, R., Price, K.: Differential evolution - a simple and efficient heuristic for global optimization over continuous spaces. Journal of Global Optimization 11(4), 341–359 (1997)
6. Price, K., Storn, Lampinen, J.: Differential evolution a practical approach to global optimization. Springer Natural Computing Series (2005)

7. Kumar, P., Pant, M.: Enhanced mutation strategy for differential evolution. In: IEEE Congress on Evolutionary Computation (CEC), pp. 1–6 (2012)

8. Qu, B., Suganthan, P., Liang, J.: Differential evolution with neighborhood mutation for multimodal optimization. IEEE Transactions on Evolutionary Computation 16, 601–614 (2012)

9. Noman, N., Iba, N.: Enhancing differential evolution performance with local search for high dimensional function optimization. In: Proceedings of the 2005 Conference on Genetic and Evolutionary Computation, GECCO 2005, pp. 967–974 (2005)

10. Dai, Z., Zhou, A.: A differential evolution with an orthogonal local search. In: Proc. 2013 IEEE Congress on Evolutionary Computation (CEC), Cancun, Mexico, pp. 2329–2336 (2013)

11. Poikolainen, I., Neri, F.: Differential evolution with concurrent fitness based local search. In: Proc. 2013 IEEE Congress on Evolutionary Computation (CEC), Cancun, Mexico, pp. 384–391 (2013)

12. Leon, M., Xiong, N.: Using random local search helps in avoiding local optimum in differential evolution. In: Proc. Artificial Intelligence and Applications, AIA 2014, Innsbruck, Austria, pp. 413–420 (2014)

13. Xu, H., Wen, J.: Differential evolution algorithm for the optimization of the vehicle routing problem in logistics. In: Proc. 2012 Eighth International Conference on Computational Intelligence and Security (CIS), Guangzhou, China, pp. 48–51 (2012)

14. Gong, W., Cai, Z.: Differential evolution with ranking-based mutation operators. IEEE Transactions on Cybernetics PP, 1–16 (2013)

15. Yao, X., Liu, Y., Lin, G.: Evolutionary programming made faster. Proc. IEEE Transactions on Evolutionary Computation 3, 82–102 (1999)

Robust Consensus: A New Measure for Multicriteria Robust Group Decision Making Problems Using Evolutionary Approach

Kaustuv Nag[1], Tandra Pal[2], and Nikhil R. Pal[3]

[1] Department of Instrumentation and Electronics Engineering,
Jadavpur University, Kolkata, India
kaustuv.nag@gmail.com
[2] Department of Computer Science and Engineering,
National Institute of Technology, Durgapur, India
tandra.pal@gmail.com
[3] Electronics and Communication Sciences Unit (ECSU),
Indian Statistical Institute, Calcutta, India
nikhil@isical.ac.in

Abstract. In fuzzy group decision making problems, we often use multi-objective evolutionary optimization. The optimizers search through the whole search space and provide a set of nondominated solutions. But, sometimes the decision makers express their prior preferences using fuzzy numbers. In this case, the optimizers search in the preferred *soft* region and provide solutions with higher *consensus*. If perturbation in the decision variable space is unavoidable, we also need to search for *robust* solutions. Again, this perturbation affects the degree of consensus of the solutions. This leads to search for solutions those are robust to their degree of consensus. In this work, we address these issues by redefining consensus and proposing a new measure called *robust consensus*. We also provide a reformulation mechanism for multiobjective optimization problems. Our experimental results show that the proposed method is capable of finding robust solutions having robust consensus in the specified soft region.

Keywords: Consensus, evolutionary algorithms, fuzzy group decision making, multiobjective optimization, robustness.

1 Introduction

Most of the real world optimization problems have multiple conflicting objectives. That is why, in the last few decades multiobjective optimization (MOO) has drawn a lot of research interests. Multiobjective optimizers, e.g., genetic algorithms (GAs), after completion of their search process, usually provide a set of nondominated solutions, such that, without additional knowledge further reduction of the solution set is not possible. It is left to decision makers' (DMs') choice to pick the right solution from the solution set.

L. Rutkowski et al. (Eds.): ICAISC 2014, Part I, LNAI 8467, pp. 384–394, 2014.

It is hard from DMs' point of view to find the appropriate solution from a set of nondominated solutions. Besides, we cannot rely on a single DM due to her lack of knowledge about all the objectives. As an example, in an interview board, a set of experts from different knowledge domains makes a consensus decision. Another example is how a decision is made by an organization - here the board of directors makes the decision. Group decision making (GDM), thus, is a point of interest. In most cases, the DMs cannot express their specific choices a priori. Rather they provide a rough idea about their choices. Fuzzy group decision making (FGDM) is one of the popular ways to address this issue. A popular FGDM strategy is that each DM expresses her approximate prior opinion by providing a fuzzy reference point for each objective. Again, the weights of all the DMs may not necessarily be the same. In this case, a suitable aggregation operator is used to find the optimal solution.

In the above mentioned FGDM strategy, a problem associated with the DMs is that their opinions often change. For example, the board of directors of a company may change. Even, individual DM's choice evolves depending on her past experiences. In this case, it becomes important to find solutions, which will be acceptable by the DMs even if some of DMs change their individual preference. *Consensus* is a measure to address this issue. In FGDM, usually consensus is used to find the closeness among the DMs' choices [3], [18]. It is expected that the set of solutions chosen finally should be as close as possible to the collective decision.

There are several unavoidable circumstances when the solutions perturb in decision variable space. In those cases, we prefer the solutions which are *robust* to such perturbations. In the literature, there are several definitions of *robustness* [4], [2] in multiobjective optimization. Robustness is defined either in objective space or in variable space. In this work, we find solutions which are robust to their perturbation in the variable space. Again, when a solution gets perturbed in the variable space, it is likely to be shifted in the objective space. As a consequence, the consensus of the solution also changes. So, we want to find solutions which will be robust with respect to its consensus.

In this work, we assume that the DMs provide some *soft constraints* to the multiobjective optimizer to restrict the search process to a set of specific regions of the search space, and the optimizer provides *robust* solutions from this *roughly* specified preference regions. We reformulate the optimization problem to obtain robust solutions from these specified regions, and find solutions which are robust with respect to their degree of consensus. For this purpose we define a new measure called *robust consensus*.

2   Preliminary Concepts

2.1   Multiobjective Optimization

In a multiobjective optimization problem (MOP), we intend to optimize more than one conflicting objectives, sometimes trying to satisfy also a set of equality and inequality constraints. In this work, however, we consider only unconstrained

MOPs (UMOPs). An UMOP can always be restated as an unconstrained multiobjective minimization problem (UMMP) and throughout this paper, unless mentioned specifically, we always consider UMMPs. To be more specific about UMMPs, below we formally define several basics of it.

Definition 1. Formally an UMMP can be defined as in (1).

$$\text{minimize } \mathbf{f}(\mathbf{x}) = (f_1(\mathbf{x}), f_2(\mathbf{x}), \cdots, f_m(\mathbf{x})), \ \mathbf{x} \in \Omega, \tag{1}$$

where $\Omega \subset \mathcal{R}^n$ is the variable space, $\mathbf{f} : \mathcal{R}^n \to \mathcal{R}^m$, and the functions $f_i(i = 1, 2, \cdots, m)$ are called objective functions.

Definition 2. A solution $\mathbf{f}(\mathbf{x_1}), \mathbf{x_1} \in \Omega$, is said to *dominate* another solution $\mathbf{f}(\mathbf{x_2}), \mathbf{x_2} \in \Omega$, denoted by $\mathbf{f}(\mathbf{x_1}) \preceq \mathbf{f}(\mathbf{x_2})$, if $\forall i, f_i(\mathbf{x_1}) \leq f_i(\mathbf{x_2})$, and $\exists j$, s.t., $f_j(\mathbf{x_1}) < f_j(\mathbf{x_2})$.

Definition 3. A solution $\mathbf{f}(\mathbf{x^*}), \mathbf{x^*} \in \Omega$ is called a *Pareto optimal solution*, if $\nexists \mathbf{x} \in \Omega$, s.t., $\mathbf{f}(\mathbf{x}) \preceq \mathbf{f}(\mathbf{x^*})$. A set of all such solutions in the objective space is called *Pareto front*. The corresponding set of points in the decision variable space is called the *Pareto Set*.

Definition 4. A set of solutions $\mathcal{S}$ is called a *nondominated* set of solutions, if $\forall \mathbf{u} \in \mathcal{S}, \nexists \mathbf{v} \in \mathcal{S}$, s.t., $\mathbf{v} \preceq \mathbf{u}$.

There are many multiobjective evolutionary algorithms (MOEAs) in the literature to solve MOPs. SPEA2 [21], NSGA-II [5] etc. are some of the popular MOEAs. The default goal of these algorithms is to provide the DMs a set of nondominated solutions, which is close to, and well spread along the Pareto front. If the DMs want to provide some prior *hard* preferences, they represent them as constraints. In many cases, however, the DMs want to search in a particular region of the search space corresponding to some particular area of the Pareto front. Sometimes, they want to stop searching much before the Pareto front is reached. Again, DMs may like to search in *robust* regions, as well as the regions where they have experiences. In these cases, the searching needs to be guided to those specific regions. In our work, we address this issue by embedding consensus in the search process.

2.2   Fuzzy Group Decision Making

Group Decision Making (GDM) has been proven to be useful in many disciplines, like emergency management [20], situation assessment [16], product development [15], and accident evaluation [14]. In most cases, GDM is performed in two steps (processes): *consensus process* and *selection process* [18]. In consensus process, the target is to find the maximum degree of agreement among the DMs. The selection process is used to obtain the solution set of alternatives in accordance with the collective opinions of DMs. For this model it is desirable to obtain the maximum degree of consensus before applying the selection process. In our work, however, we propose an *embedded* model, where these two processes are considered in an integrated manner.

The DMs often prefer to provide some prior *soft* preferences regarding their choices. In fuzzy group decision making (FGDM), one way to represent DM's choices is to express their preferences by fuzzy numbers. Often these numbers are far away from the Pareto front. In that case we need to restrict the search in that specified region. Again, if there are perturbations in the decision variable space, it is possible that though a solution is robust in objective space, its degree of consensus varies highly. In this case, we want to get solutions those are robust with respect to their consensus.

2.3 Related Works

There are few works on FGDM problems with consensus and/or robustness. However, there is no work, as per our knowledge, that have incorporated robustness and consensus in an integrated manner in the FGDM using MOOs. Works on robustness in MOEAs can be found in [2], [4]. Some works related to consensus are there in [9], [10], [12], [13]. A work, somewhat similar to us, can be found in [18]. Nevertheless, the authors, in [18], did not deal with *robust consensus*. They used another definition of robustness. At first their search procedure would reach the Pareto front, and then, a solution selection scheme based on robustness and consensus is used. It makes their system always trying to provide some solutions from the Pareto front, which may not be the desirable solutions with respect to consensus as DMs' preferences may be far away from it. So, essentially they select consensus solution from the Pareto front. In our work, we evolve solutions from the *soft* regions expressed by the DMs as their preferred region in the objective space. In [18], the authors have worked on preference robustness, which is defined by the minimum transition cost in the decision space when a solution is perturbed in the objective space.

3   Problem Formulation

Let there be d DMs, denoted as D_j $(j = 1, 2, \cdots, d)$. The weight vector associated with the DMs is represented as $\mathbf{w} = (w_1, w_2, \cdots, w_d)$, s.t. $\sum_{j=1}^{d} w_j = 1$. To express their preferences, DMs provide reference points in the objective space, denoted by $R_j = (r_{j1}, r_{j2}, \cdots, r_{jm})$, where r_{ji} $(i = 1, 2, \cdots, m)$ is the reference value of the ith objective provided by j^{th} DM. In this work, we consider that the DMs provide reference values as triangular fuzzy numbers [19], where each value is represented as triplet, $r_{ji} = (r_{ji}^{lower}, r_{ji}^{most}, r_{ji}^{upper})$. The membership value of a point r is defined in (2).

$$\mu_{r_{ji}}(r) = \begin{cases} \dfrac{\left(r - r_{ji}^{\text{lower}}\right)}{\left(r_{ji}^{\text{most}} - r_{ji}^{\text{lower}}\right)}, r_{ji}^{\text{lower}} \leq r \leq r_{ji}^{\text{most}} \\ \dfrac{\left(r_{ji}^{\text{upper}} - r\right)}{\left(r_{ji}^{\text{upper}} - r_{ji}^{\text{most}}\right)}, r_{ji}^{\text{most}} \leq r \leq r_{ji}^{\text{upper}} \\ 0, \text{otherwise}. \end{cases} \tag{2}$$

Here r_{ji}^{lower}, r_{ji}^{most}, and r_{ji}^{upper} are respectively the lower bound, most desirable value, and the upper bound of the DM's preference fuzzy number r_{ji}.

4   Robustness, Consensus, and Problem Reformulation

4.1   Robustness

In the literature, robustness has been defined in many ways according to the application areas, such as life science, engineering, mathematics, statistics, optimization, and decision science [2]. In multiobjective optimization, two of the major contributions on robustness can be found in [2], [4]. Among the several definitions of robustness, in this work, we use the one defined in [18].

Definition 5. A solution $\mathbf{x}^{\circledast}$ is called a multiobjective robust solution, if it is a Pareto optimal solution to the multiobjective minimization problem as defined in (3).

$$\text{minimize } \mathbf{f}^e(\mathbf{x}) = (f_1^e(\mathbf{x}), f_2^e(\mathbf{x}), \cdots, f_m^e(\mathbf{x})), \mathbf{x} \in \mathbf{\Omega},$$

$$\text{subject to } f_j^e(\mathbf{x}) = \frac{1}{|\mathcal{B}_\delta(\mathbf{x})|} \int_{\mathbf{y} \in \mathcal{B}_\delta(\mathbf{x})} f_j(\mathbf{y}) d\mathbf{y}, j = 1, \cdots, m. \tag{3}$$

The above formulation is defined with respect to a δ-neighborhood $\mathcal{B}_\delta(\mathbf{x})$ of a solution $\mathbf{x}$. A solution which is robust as per the above definition, according to the literature, is called *multiobjective robust solution of type-I* [4].

4.2   Consensus

There are several definitions of consensus in the literature [9], [11], [18]. The drawback in the definition of consensus presented in [18] is that even if the value of the objective function $f_i(\mathbf{x})$ matches exactly with r_{ji}^{most}, the peak of the membership function $\forall i$ and $\forall j$, then also there will be a substantial value of d_{ji} (fuzzy distance between the solution and the reference point of the jth DM on i^{th} objective [18]) suggesting a mismatch between the computed solution and preferred solution and thereby reducing the consensus. To overcome this drawback, we define consensus in the following way.

Definition 6. Let $\mathbf{w} = (w_1, w_2, \cdots, w_d)$ be the weight vector associated with d DMs. Then *consensus* of a solution $\mathbf{x} \in \Omega$ is defined in (4) as follows.

$$consensus(\mathbf{x}) = \sum_{j=1}^{d} w_j \hat{\mu}_j(\mathbf{x}), \tag{4}$$

where $\hat{\mu}_j(\mathbf{x})$ is defined in (5).

$$\hat{\mu}_j(\mathbf{x}) = \phi(\mu_{r_{j1}}(f_1(\mathbf{x})), \ \mu_{r_{j2}}(f_2(\mathbf{x})), \cdots, \ \mu_{r_{jm}}(f_m(\mathbf{x}))). \tag{5}$$

Here, $\hat{\mu}_j(\cdot)$ is basically a multidimensional membership function; m is the number of objectives; $\mu_{r_{ji}}(\cdot)$, $i = 1, 2, \cdots, m$, is already defined in (2); $f_i(\cdot)$, $i = 1, 2, \cdots, m$, is the ith objective function; and $\phi(\cdot)$ is a t-norm aggregation operator which in this work is taken as the $min(\cdot)$.

There is a problem with this definition of consensus: it assumes that a robust solution will always be robust to its degree of consensus. But, this may not always be true. To demonstrate this scenario with an example, let us consider Fig. 1. In this figure, a robust solution $\mathbf{x} \in \Omega$ in the variable space and its mapping $\mathbf{f}(\mathbf{x})$ in the objective space are shown respectively in the left panel and in the right panel. The preference points in the objective space provided by two DMs, D_1 and D_2, are shown by + symbol. Let, the weights of the DMs be w_1 and w_2 respectively, and $w_1 > w_2$. Since $w_1 > w_2$ and $\mathbf{f}(\mathbf{x})$ is closer to D_1, the robust solution $\mathbf{x}$ is also a solution with good consensus. But when $\mathbf{x}$ is perturbed, $\mathbf{f}(\mathbf{x})$ no longer is a solution with good consensus. Note that the degree of consensus is not only dependent on the weights but also on membership functions. The δ neighborhood of $\mathbf{x}$ is shown in the left panel and the corresponding perturbation in the objective space is shown in the right panel by the shaded regions. Due to the perturbation of $\mathbf{x}$ the objectives get shifted towards D_2's reference point. In this case, the consensus should decrease. In other words, although $\mathbf{x}$ is a robust solution, it is not robust to its degree of consensus. To overcome this problem, we need to find solutions which are robust to their degree of consensus. To address this issue, we define a new measure, *robust consensus*, bellow in (6).

Definition 7. Robust consensus of a solution is defined in (6).

$$robust\ consensus(\mathbf{x}) = \frac{1}{|\mathcal{B}_\delta(\mathbf{x})|} \int_{\mathbf{z} \in \mathcal{B}_\delta(\mathbf{x})} consensus(\mathbf{z}) d\mathbf{z} \tag{6}$$

The above formulation is defined with respect to a δ-neighborhood $(\mathcal{B}_\delta(\mathbf{x}))$ of a solution $\mathbf{x}$. Higher value of this measure indicates higher *robust consensus* of the solution.

4.3   Problem Reformulation for MOEA-FGDM

We could use any multiobjective evolutionary algorithm (MOEA) [5], [6], [17], [21], [22] for this task. We have, however, used NSGA-II [5] as the multiobjective

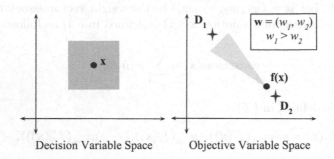

Fig. 1. Showing a solution x, its δ neighborhood, its mapping (perturbed) in objective space, and two DMs' preferred reference points D_1 and D_2

optimizer. To find robust solutions, which are also robust consensus, we reformulate the m objective UMMP defined in (1) as an $(m+1)$ objective UMMP as described in (7).

$$\text{minimize } \hat{\mathbf{f}}^e(\mathbf{x}) = (f_1^e(\mathbf{x}), f_2^e(\mathbf{x}), \cdots, f_m^e(\mathbf{x}), - \text{ robust consensus}(\mathbf{x})), \tag{7}$$
$$\text{subject to } \mathbf{x} \in \mathbf{\Omega},$$

where $f_j^e(\mathbf{x})$s are the same as in (3).

By solving this problem, we can obtain the desired robust solutions. There is, however, a concern: how to computationally integrate the consensus over a region? We address this problem in the following way. Let, $\mathbf{x} \in \mathbf{\Omega}$ be a solution. A set of H random points $\mathbf{x}_k$ $(k = 1, 2, \cdots, H)$ is chosen such that $\forall k$ $(k = 1, 2, \cdots, H), \forall i(i = 1, 2, \cdots, n), (\mathbf{x}^{(i)} - \delta^{(i)}) \leq \mathbf{x}_k^{(i)} \leq (\mathbf{x}^{(i)} + \delta^{(i)})$, where, $x_k^{(i)}$ is the ith component of x_k, $\delta^{(i)} \geq 0$ is the maximum allowed perturbation along i^{th} variable, and n is the number of variables. For simplicity, we consider $\forall i, \delta^{(i)} = \tilde{\delta}$. However, one can use different values of $\delta^{(i)}$s, and that may be more appropriate for real life problems. For all randomly chosen points we compute the objective (or consensus) values and find their arithmetic mean. With an increase in H the accuracy level increases. To decrease computational cost, nonetheless, one can choose smaller value of H. The $\delta^{(i)}$s are very important parameters. The results vary significantly with the choice of this parameter value. When $\tilde{\delta} = 0$, the proposed robust consensus reduces to consensus, and this problem formulation will not provide robust solutions.

5   Test Problem, Experimentation, and Discussions

5.1   Test Problem

BINH [1] is a well known UMMP test problem defined in (8).

$$\text{minimize } f_1(x_1, x_2) = x_1^2 + x_2^2,$$
$$\text{minimize } f_2(x_1, x_2) = (x_1 - 5)^2 + (x_2 - 5)^2, \tag{8}$$

Table 1. DMs' fuzzy reference points for modified M-BINH problem

Decision Maker (D_j)	r_{j1}	r_{j2}
D1	(10.0, 15.0, 20.0)	(16.0, 21.0, 26.0)
D2	(8.5, 14.0, 19.5)	(16.0, 22.0, 28.0)
D3	(11.0, 16.0, 21.0)	(13.0, 20.0, 27.0)
D4	(8.0, 13.0, 18.0)	(15.0, 19.0, 23.0)
D5	(9.0, 17.0, 25.0)	(14.0, 18.0, 22.0)

where $-5 \leq x_1, x_2 \leq 10$. The authors [18] have modified this problem to make it suitable for the robustness-consensus FGDM problem. They call it M-BINH. We use the same modified formulation. It is described in (9).

$$x_p^c = \frac{x_p^{max} + x_p^{min}}{2}, \quad r_{1,p} = 0.2, \quad r_{2,p} = \frac{x_p}{x_p^{max}},$$

$$x_p = \begin{cases} x_p, & \text{if } x_p \leq 1 \\ x_p^{min} + \text{floor}\left(\dfrac{x_p - x_p^{min}}{r_{1,p}}\right) r_{1,p}, & \text{if } x_p < x_p^c \\ x_p^c + \text{floor}\left(\dfrac{x_p - x_p^c}{r_{2,p}}\right) r_{2,p}, & \text{else,} \end{cases} \tag{9}$$

$$p = 1, 2,$$

$$\text{minimize } f_1(x_1, x_2) = x_1^2 + x_2^2,$$

$$\text{minimize } f_2(x_1, x_2) = (x_1 - 5)^2 + (x_2 - 5)^2,$$

where $0 \leq x_1, x_2 \leq 5$, x_p^{min} and $x_p^{max}(p = 1, 2)$ indicate respectively the lower and upper bounds of the variable space.

We assume that there are five DMs and the corresponding weight vector is $\mathbf{w} = (0.20, 0.20, 0.20, 0.20, 0.20)$, i.e., all the DMs are equally important. Their fuzzy preference points are presented in Table 1. These parameters are not the same as in [18]. We have changed them to make the problem more suitable to show the effectiveness of our approach.

We reformulate the M-BINH problem in (10).

$$\text{minimize } \mathbf{f}_{\text{M-BINH}}^{\text{robust}}(\mathbf{x}) = (f_1^e(\mathbf{x}), f_2^e(\mathbf{x}), -\text{ robust consensus}(\mathbf{x})),$$

$$\text{where } f_1^e(\mathbf{x}) = \frac{1}{|\mathcal{B}_\delta(\mathbf{x})|} \int_{\mathbf{y} \in \mathcal{B}_\delta(\mathbf{x})} f_1(\mathbf{y}) d\mathbf{y}, \tag{10}$$

$$f_2^e(\mathbf{x}) = \frac{1}{|\mathcal{B}_\delta(\mathbf{x})|} \int_{\mathbf{y} \in \mathcal{B}_\delta(\mathbf{x})} f_2(\mathbf{y}) d\mathbf{y}.$$

Here $f_1(\mathbf{x})$ and $f_2(\mathbf{x})$ are defined as in (9), and *robust consensus* is defined in (6).

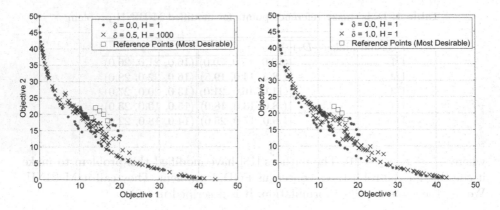

Fig. 2. Showing nondominated sets $\mathcal{S}_1^0$, $\mathcal{S}_{1000}^{0.5}$, and $\mathcal{S}_{1000}^1$

5.2   Common Parameter Settings

We have set population size to 100. Simulated binary crossover (SBX) has been used, where crossover probability $p_c = 0.95$ and distribution index for crossover $\eta_c = 20$. We have used polynomial mutation where mutation probability $p_m = 1/n$ and distribution index for mutation $\eta_m = 10$. Here $n(=2)$ is the number of variables. We have executed NSGA-II for 1000 generations. The reason for choosing such a high number of generations is to allow the searching algorithm enough chance to converge. We have used jMetal 4.4 [7], [8] for the simulation purpose.

5.3   Experiments, Results, and Discussions

At first we execute the algorithm for three pairs of $(H, \tilde{\delta})$ parameter sets: $(1, 0)$, $(1000, 0.5)$, and $(1000, 1)$. Let us denote the sets of nondominated solutions obtained for these three parameter sets by $\mathcal{S}_1^0$, $\mathcal{S}_{1000}^{0.5}$, and $\mathcal{S}_{1000}^1$ respectively. When $H = 1$, and $\tilde{\delta} = 0$, our problem searches for solutions which are not robust both in terms of the objectives and the consensus. To reduce the error in computing robustness, we have used a high value of H. It is worth mentioning that for the parameter pair $(1, 0)$, our problem formulation reduces to simple consensus optimization problem, i.e., in that specific case, we are searching for consensus solutions which may not be robust in terms of their objectives. However, to observe how the output changes with the change of $\tilde{\delta}$, we plot the objective values of $\mathcal{S}_1^0$ and $\mathcal{S}_{1000}^{0.5}$ in the left panel, and the objective values of $\mathcal{S}_1^0$ and $\mathcal{S}_{1000}^1$ in the right panel in Fig. 2.

From Fig. 2, we observe that when $\tilde{\delta}$ increases, the obtained set of solutions moves away from the set $\mathcal{S}_1^0$. Basically, with the increase of $\tilde{\delta}$, i.e., when we search for more robust solutions, the robust consensus of the solutions decreases. In Fig. 2, we have also shown the most desirable points suggested by each DM. Around the coordinate $(15, 15)$ in the objective space, there is a region with more crowded solutions which is close to the region where most of the desirable points suggested by the DMs lie. We observe that with the increase of $\tilde{\delta}$, this region becomes wider as well as one of the end points of the solution set gets drifted towards the middle region. With the increase of $\tilde{\delta}$, the system stops in a region which is preferred by the *soft* choices of the DMs and the obtained solutions are away from the Pareto front of the unaltered UMMP. When δ changes the t-norm operator $\phi(\cdot)$ and the weight vector $\mathbf{w}$ also play important roles on the direction of the drift of the solution sets.

6 Conclusions

In this work, we redefine consensus and define a new measure called *robust consensus*, which indicates the robustness of a multiobjective solution with respect to its consensus among the preferences provided by a set of DMs. We have also shown a reformulation mechanism for multiobjective fuzzy decision making problems. It provides the DMs a set of solutions from their preferred search regions. The DMs express their prior preferences by providing reference points for each objective. Using the multiobjective genetic algorithm NSGA-II, we have successfully solved a modified test problem, M-BINH and shown that the proposed method is capable of providing solutions from the region desired by the DMs. Further, we have shown that the proposed definition of *robust consensus* is sensitive to its parameter δ. The effect of the formulation for different aggregation operators is not studied in this work. We intend to do this in our future work.

Acknowledgments. Kaustuv Nag is grateful to the Department of Science and Technology (DST), India for providing financial support in the form of INSPIRE Fellowship (code no. IF120686).

References

1. Binh, T.T., Korn, U.: An evolution strategy for the multiobjective optimization. In: Proceedings of the Second International Conference on Genetic Algorithms (Mendel 1996), Brno, Czech Republic, pp. 23–28. Citeseer (1996)
2. Bui, L.T., Abbass, H.A., Barlow, M., Bender, A.: Robustness against the decision-maker's attitude to risk in problems with conflicting objectives. IEEE Transactions on Evolutionary Computation 16(1), 1–19 (2012)
3. Cabrerizo, F.J., Moreno, J.M., Pérez, I.J., Herrera-Viedma, E.: Analyzing consensus approaches in fuzzy group decision making: advantages and drawbacks. Soft Computing 14(5), 451–463 (2010)
4. Deb, K., Gupta, H.: Introducing robustness in multi-objective optimization. Evolutionary Computation 14(4), 463–494 (2006)
5. Deb, K., Pratap, A., Agarwal, S., Meyarivan, T.: A fast and elitist multiobjective genetic algorithm: NSGA-II. IEEE Transactions on Evolutionary Computation 6(2), 182–197 (2002)
6. Deb, K., et al.: Multi-objective optimization using evolutionary algorithms, vol. 2012. John Wiley & Sons, Chichester (2001)

7. Durillo, J., Nebro, A., Alba, E.: The jmetal framework for multi-objective optimization: Design and architecture. In: CEC 2010, Barcelona, Spain, pp. 4138–4325 (July 2010)
8. Durillo, J.J., Nebro, A.J.: jmetal: A java framework for multi-objective optimization. Advances in Engineering Software 42, 760–771 (2011), http://www.sciencedirect.com/science/article/pii/S0965997811001219
9. Herrera, F., Herrera-Viedma, E., Verdegay, J.L.: A model of consensus in group decision making under linguistic assessments. Fuzzy Sets and Systems 78(1), 73–87 (1996)
10. Herrera, F., Herrera-Viedma, E., Verdegay, J.L.: Linguistic measures based on fuzzy coincidence for reaching consensus in group decision making. International Journal of Approximate Reasoning 16(3), 309–334 (1997)
11. Herrera-Viedma, E., Herrera, F., Chiclana, F.: A consensus model for multiperson decision making with different preference structures. IEEE Transactions on Systems, Man and Cybernetics, Part A: Systems and Humans 32(3), 394–402 (2002)
12. Herrera-Viedma, E., Martinez, L., Mata, F., Chiclana, F.: A consensus support system model for group decision-making problems with multigranular linguistic preference relations. IEEE Transactions on Fuzzy Systems 13(5), 644–658 (2005)
13. Hsu, H.M., Chen, C.T.: Aggregation of fuzzy opinions under group decision making. Fuzzy Sets and Systems 79(3), 279–285 (1996)
14. Krohling, R.A., Campanharo, V.C.: Fuzzy TOPSIS for group decision making: A case study for accidents with oil spill in the sea. Expert Systems with Applications 38(4), 4190–4197 (2011)
15. Lu, J., Ma, J., Zhang, G., Zhu, Y., Zeng, X., Koehl, L.: Theme-based comprehensive evaluation in new product development using fuzzy hierarchical criteria group decision-making method. IEEE Transactions on Industrial Electronics 58(6), 2236–2246 (2011)
16. Lu, J., Zhang, G., Ruan, D.: Intelligent multi-criteria fuzzy group decision-making for situation assessments. Soft Computing 12(3), 289–299 (2008)
17. Nag, K., Pal, T.: A new archive based steady state genetic algorithm. In: 2012 IEEE Congress on Evolutionary Computation (CEC), pp. 1–7. IEEE (2012)
18. Xiong, J., Tan, X., Yang, K.W., Chen, Y.W.: Fuzzy group decision making for multiobjective problems: Tradeoff between consensus and robustness. Journal of Applied Mathematics 2013 (2013)
19. Zadeh, L.A.: Fuzzy sets. Information and Control 8(3), 338–353 (1965)
20. Zhang, G., Ma, J., Lu, J.: Emergency management evaluation by a fuzzy multi-criteria group decision support system. Stochastic Environmental Research and Risk Assessment 23(4), 517–527 (2009)
21. Zitzler, E., Laumanns, M., Thiele, L.: SPEA2: Improving the strength pareto evolutionary algorithm. In: Giannakoglou, K., Tsahalis, D., Periaux, J., Papailou, P., Fogarty, T. (eds.) Evolutionary Methods for Design, Optimization and Control with Applications to Industrial Problems, EUROGEN 2001, Athens, Greece, pp. 95–100 (2002)
22. Zitzler, E., Thiele, L.: Multiobjective evolutionary algorithms: A comparative case study and the strength pareto approach. IEEE Transactions on Evolutionary Computation 3(4), 257–271 (1999)

Preliminary Study on the Particle Swarm Optimization with the Particle Performance Evaluation

Michal Pluhacek*, Roman Senkerik, and Ivan Zelinka

Tomas Bata University in Zlin, Faculty of Applied Informatics,
Nam T.G. Masaryka 5555, 760 01 Zlin, Czech Republic
{pluhacek,senkerik,zelinka}@fai.utb.cz

Abstract. In this paper, the novel concept of particle performance evaluation within the particle swarm optimization algorithm (PSO) is introduced. In this method the contribution of each particle to the process of obtaining the global best solution is investigated periodically. For the particle with no contribution to the global best solution over a given number of iterations the velocity calculation is changed; in the case of this presented research, in order to improve its performance towards the global trend.

Keywords: PSO, Swarm intelligence, Performance evaluation, Optimization.

1 Introduction

Since it has been introduced [1], the original PSO algorithm [1], [2] has been repeatedly studied in details (e.g. in [3]) and variously modified. [4] – [8]. The "swarm intelligence" [2] employed within the algorithm has been becoming more complex [4], [5], [7] and the behavior of the swarm as a whole has been analyzed in the various learning and adaptive processes.

This preliminary study investigates on a different approach where the performance of the each particle within the the swarm is analyzed separately and the particles are treated with more individual approach. The swarm as a whole maintains its basic initial settings during the whole optimization. The goal of this study is to show some of the advantages, further to show a potential of such approach and finally to prepare the new open tasks for the future research.

* This work was supported by Grant Agency of the Czech Republic - GACR P103/13/08195S, partially supported by Grant of SGS No. SP2014/42, VSB - Technical University of Ostrava, Czech Republic, by the Development of human resources in research and development of latest soft computing methods and their application in practice project, reg. no. CZ.1.07/2.3.00/20.0072 funded by Operational Programme Education for Competitiveness, co-financed by ESF and state budget of the Czech Republic, further was supported by European Regional Development Fund under the project CEBIA-Tech No. CZ.1.05/2.1.00/03.0089 and by Internal Grant Agency of Tomas Bata University under the project No. IGA/FAI/2014/010.

L. Rutkowski et al. (Eds.): ICAISC 2014, Part I, LNAI 8467, pp. 395–405, 2014.
© Springer International Publishing Switzerland 2014

2   Particle Swarm Optimization Algorithm

The original PSO algorithm was proposed in 1995 by Eberhart and Kennedy [1]. The inspiration came from the natural behavior of fish and birds. The basic principle is that each particle in the swarm is defined by "position", which is in general the combination of cost function (CF) parameters, and "velocity". The new position of the particle in the next generation is then obtained as a sum of actual position and velocity. The velocity calculation follows two natural tendencies of the particle: To move to the best solution found so far by the particular particle (known in the literature as personal best: *pBest* or local best: *lBest*). And to move to the overall best solution found in the swarm or defined sub-swarm (known as global best: *gBest*).

According to the method of selection of the swarm or subswarm for *gBest* information spreading, the PSO algorithms are noted as global PSO (GPSO) [8] or local PSO (LPSO) [9]. Within this research the PSO algorithm with global topology (GPSO) [8] was utilized.

In the original GPSO the new position of particle is altered by the velocity given by (1):

$$v_{ij}^{t+1} = w \cdot v_{ij}^t + c_1 \cdot Rand \cdot (pBest_{ij} - x_{ij}^t) + c_2 \cdot Rand \cdot (gBest_j - x_{ij}^t) \qquad (1)$$

Where:
v_i^{t+1} - New velocity of the ith particle in iteration $t+1$.
w – Inertia weight value.
v_i^t - Current velocity of the ith particle in iteration t.
c_1, c_2 - Priority factors (set to the typical value = 2).
$pBest_i$ – Local (personal) best solution found by the ith particle.
$gBest$ - Best solution found in a population.
x_{ij}^t - Current position of the ith particle (component j of the dimension D) in iteration t.
$Rand$ – Pseudo random number, interval (0, 1).

The maximum velocity of particles in the GPSO is typically limited to 0.2 times the range of the optimization problem and this pattern was followed in this study. The new position of a particle is then given by (2), where x_i^{t+1} is the new particle position:

$$x_i^{t+1} = x_i^t + v_i^{t+1} \qquad (2)$$

Finally the linear decreasing inertia weight [6], [8] is used in the GPSO here. Its purpose is to slow the particles over time thus to improve the local search capability in the later phase of the optimization. The inertia weight has two control parameters w_{start} and w_{end}. A new w for each iteration is given by (3), where t stands for current iteration number and n stands for the total number of iterations. The values used for the GPSO in this study were $w_{start} = 0.9$ and $w_{end}=0.4$.

$$w = w_{start} - \frac{((w_{start} - w_{end}) \cdot t)}{n} \qquad (3)$$

3   PSO with Particle Performance Evaluation (PSO with PPE)

The novel approach proposed in this study is based on the simple premise that all particles should take part in the process of finding and improving of the final solution. The only way of communication among the particles in the GPSO design [1], [8] represents the shared knowledge of the position of the best globally found solution (*gBest*). In other words: To be beneficial for the swarm, the particle has to update the *gBest*. Therefore the first step in the particle performance evaluation (PPE) is the exact monitoring of the *gBest* updaters. A counter is allocated to the each particle. Each iteration the counter is incremented by 1 and is set to 0 when the particle triggers a *gBest* update. In this way, it is possible to measure the number of iterations since the last *gBest* was found by particular particle. The second step in the PPE approach is to alter the performance of the particular particle when it has not triggered the *gBest* update for a given maximum number of iterations.

In this initial research the simple constant c_1 (1) is modified to vector (see (4)).

$$v_{ij}^{t+1} = w \cdot v_{ij}^t + c_{1i} \cdot Rand \cdot (pBest_{ij} - x_{ij}^t) + c_2 \cdot Rand \cdot (gBest_j - x_{ij}^t) \quad (4)$$

Where:
c_{1i} – Priority factor 1 for the ith particle.

Subsequently when the particular particle does not trigger a *gBest* update for 1/10 of the total number of iterations, the c_1 value for that particle is set to 0.05. The value of c_1 is set back to 2 when the particle reaches the *gBest* update.

Through utilization of this very simple pattern it is possible to reduce the number of particles with no *gBest* updates (triggers), further to reduce the number of iteration between *gBest* updates for the each particle and to improve the overall performance of the PSO algorithm in some cases as it is presented in the following sections. Furthermore in this modification the saturation of maximum velocity is no longer required and the inertia weight can be set to a constant. Thus the number of necessary variables and controlling parameters has been decreased.

4   Test Functions

Following test functions were used in this preliminary study to represent the simple and more complex optimization problems.

The Sphere function is given by (5).

$$f(x) = \sum_{i=1}^{\text{dim}} x_i^2 \quad (5)$$

Optimum position for E_n: $(x_1, x_2 \ldots x_n) = (0,0,\ldots, 0)$
Optimum value for E_n: $y = 0$

Schwefel's function is given by (6).

$$f(x) = \sum_{i=1}^{\dim} -x_i \sin(\sqrt{|x|}) \tag{6}$$

Optimum position for E_n: $(x_1, x_2 \ldots x_n) = (420.969, 420.969, \ldots, 420.969)$
Optimum value for E_n: $y = -418.983 \cdot dimension$

5   Experiment Setup

Within all performance testing the two PSO versions were utilized. The first one was the original canonical global PSO with linear decreasing inertia weight (as described in the section 2), noted GPSO. The second version was the proposed PSO with PPE, as described in the section 3 (noted PSO with PPE).

Within the performance tests, the benchmark functions, which are described in the section 6, were used for both aforementioned versions of PSO algorithm. For each version, totally 20 separate runs were performed and statistically analyzed.

Control parameters were set up based on the previous numerous experiments and literature sources [1], [6], [8] as follows:

Population size: 30
Generations: 1000
Dimension: 40
Runs: 20
For GPSO:
$v_{max} = 0.2 \cdot \text{Range}$
$w_{start} = 0.9$
$w_{end} = 0.4$
For GPSO with PPE:
$v_{max} = 1 \cdot \text{Range}$
$w = 0.5$

6   Experiment 1

Within the first experiment, totally 20 independent runs of each algorithm (PSO version) for the Sphere function were analyzed. Statistical overview is given in Table 1. The mean *gBest* history is depicted in Figures 1 and 2. Subsequently an extensive analysis of a single run of both algorithms was carried out. The Fig. 3 depicts the number of iterations since the last *gBest* update for each particle. Please note that the bar chart is sorted. In order not to confuse with indexes of particles in the population the "individual" term is used. The first "individual" is the particle with the last *gBest* update and vice versa. Finally the Figures 4 and 5 depict the history of the personal best (*pBest*) for each particle in the single run of the algorithm.

Table 1. Results for the Sphere function (dim = 40)

Dim: 40	GPSO	PSO with PPE
Mean CF Value:	2.052E-04	**1.996E-09**
Std. Dev.:	2.108E-04	3.833E-09
CF Value Median:	1.342E-04	1.032E-09
Max. CF Value:	7.250E-04	1.654E-08
Min. CF Value:	2.513E-05	8.521E-11

gBest Value

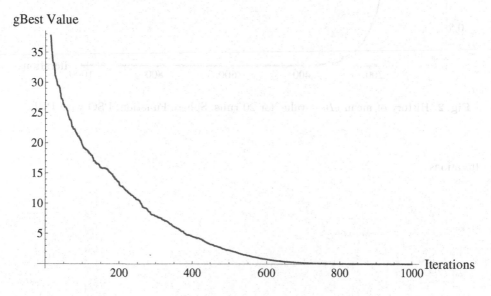

Fig. 1. History of mean *gBest* value for 20 runs. Sphere Function. GPSO.

7   Experiment 2

In the second experiment the Schwefel's benchmark function (6) represented the example of more complex optimization problem. The presentation of results follows the similar pattern as in the previous section. Table 2 contains the statistical overview of the results for 20 independent runs of both algorithms. Mean *gBest* history is depicted in Figures 6 and 7. The analysis of number of iterations since the last *gBest* update within the single run is depicted in Fig. 8. The histories of *pBest* for all individuals and for both GPSO and PSO with PPE are depicted in Figures 9 and 10. The discussion of results follows in the next section.

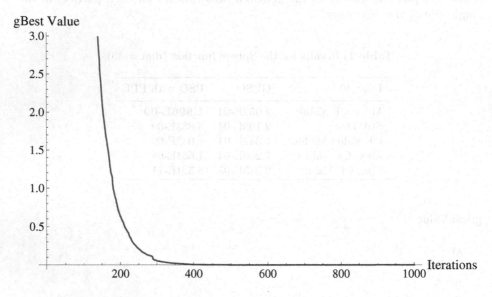

Fig. 2. History of mean *gBest* value for 20 runs. Sphere Function. PSO with PPE.

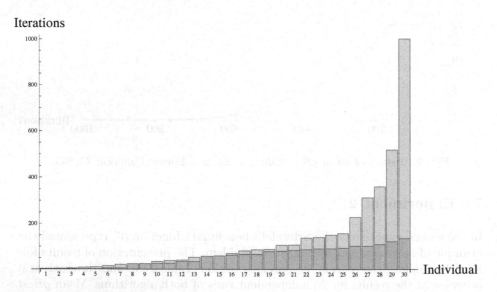

Fig. 3. Number of iterations since last *gBest* update for each particle (sorted). Sphere Function – comparison. GPSO – blue, PSO with PPE - red.

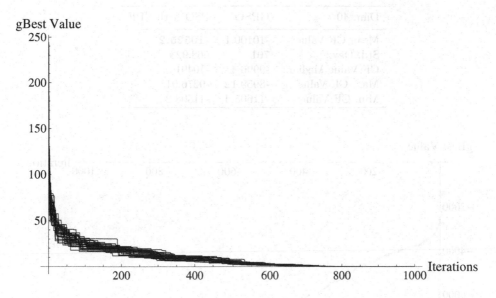

Fig. 4. History of *pBest* value for all individuals. Sphere function. GPSO.

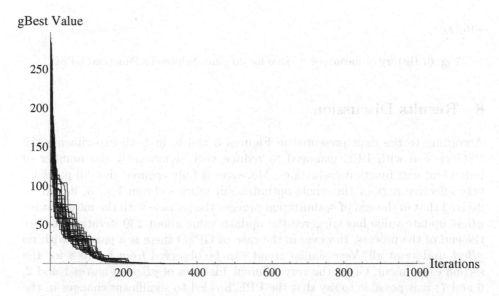

Fig. 5. History of *pBest* value for all individuals. Sphere function. PSO with PPE.

Table 2. Results for the Schwefel's function (dim = 40)

Dim: 40	GPSO	PSO with PPE
Mean CF Value:	-10100.1	**-10525.2**
Std. Dev.:	701	668.923
CF Value Median:	-9996.4	-10491
Max. CF Value:	-8959.12	-9276.91
Min. CF Value:	-11605.4	-11508.2

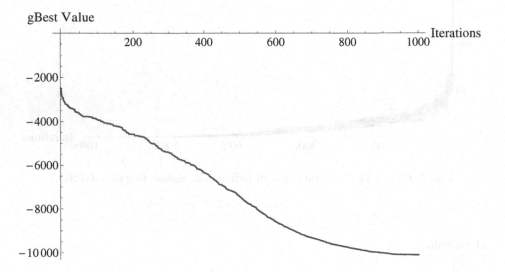

Fig. 6. History of mean *gBest* value for 20 runs. Schwefel's Function. GPSO.

8   Results Discussion

According to the data presented in Figures 3 and 8, in both experiments the PSO version with PPE managed to reduce very significantly the number of redundant cost function evaluations. Moreover it fully ensured that all particles take effective part in the whole optimization process. From Fig. 3, it can be derived that in the end of optimization process the particle with the most distant *gBest* update value has triggered the update value about 130 iterations before the end of the process. However in the case of GPSO there is a particle with no *gBest* update at all. Very similar trend can be observed from figure 8 for the second experiment. Given the very different histories of *gBest* (Figures 1 and 2, 6 and 7) it is possible to say that the PPE has led to significant changes in the behavior of the whole swarm and the process of *gBest* updating.

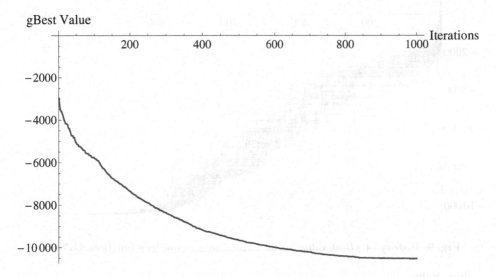

Fig. 7. History of mean *gBest* value for 20 runs. Schwefel's Function. PSO with PPE.

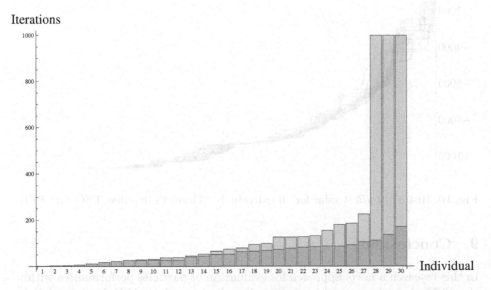

Fig. 8. Number of iterations since last *gBest* update for each particle (sorted). Schwefel's Function – comparison. GPSO – blue, PSO with PPE - red.

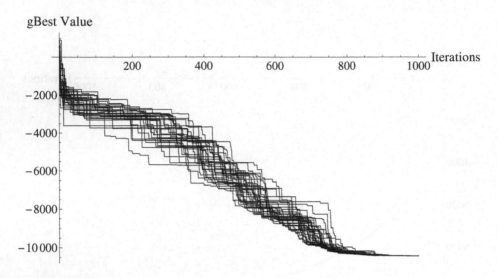

Fig. 9. History of *pBest* value for all individuals. Schwefel's function. GPSO.

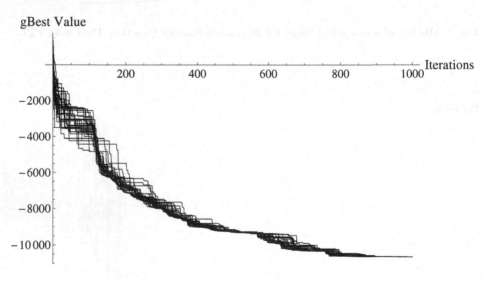

Fig. 10. History of *pBest* value for all individuals. Schwefel's function. PSO with PPE.

9   Conclusions

In this research a novel approach for evaluation of particles performances within the PSO algorithm was described and preliminary tested. Data presented in Table 1 and 2 show mild improvement in the quality of solution finding. The PPE approach seems to be a valid design and it is our belief that with more sophisticated behavior changes of the particles, the significant improvements of the performance can be achieved and the future research will focus mainly in this direction. The first goal of reducing the number of redundant cost function evaluation was achieved. The main purpose of this study was to inform about this approach and to highlight the main ideas.

References

1. Kennedy, J., Eberhart, R.: Particle swarm optimization. In: IEEE International Conference on Neural Networks, pp. 1942–1948 (1995)
2. Kennedy, J., Eberhart, R.C., Shi, Y.: Swarm Intelligence. Morgan Kaufmann Publishers (2001)
3. van den Bergh, F., Engelbrecht, A.P.: A study of particle swarm optimization particle trajectories. Information Sciences 176(8), 937–971 (2006)
4. Liang, J., Suganthan, P.N.: Dynamic multi-swarm particle swarm optimizer. In: Swarm Intelligence Symposium, SIS 2005, pp. 124–129 (2005)
5. Liang, J.J., Qin, A.K., Suganthan, P.N., Baskar, S.: Comprehensive learning particle swarm optimizer for global optimization of multimodal functions. IEEE Transactions on Evolutionary Computation 10(3), 281–295 (2006)
6. Nickabadi, A., Ebadzadeh, M.M., Safabakhsh, R.: A novel particle swarm optimization algorithm with adaptive inertia weight. Applied Soft Computing 11(4), 3658–3670 (2011)
7. Zhi-Hui, Z., Jun, Z., Yun, L., Yu-hui, S.: Orthogonal Learning Particle Swarm Optimization. IEEE Transactions on Evolutionary Computation 15(6), 832–847 (2011)
8. Yuhui, S., Eberhart, R.: A modified particle swarm optimizer. In: IEEE World Congress on Computational Intelligence, May 4-9, pp. 69–73 (1998)
9. Kennedy, J., Mendes, R.: Population structure and particle swarm performance. In: Proceedings of the 2002 Congress on Evolutionary Computation, CEC 2002, pp. 1671–1676 (2002)

Numerical Optimal Control of Integral-Algebraic Equations Using Differential Evolution with Fletcher's Filter

Wojciech Rafajłowicz

Wojciech Rafajłowicz is with the Institute of Computer Engineering,
Control and Robotics, Wrocław University of Technology,
Wybrzeże Wyspiańskiego 27, 50 370 Wrocław, Poland
wojciech.rafajlowicz@pwr.wroc.pl

Abstract. Integral-algebraic equations are an interesting method of modeling real world problems with not too severe assumptions. We proposed a simple numerical method of using differential evolution. Constraints in optimal control problems are handled using a method based on the works of Fletcher and his co-workers' filter.

Numerical results for typical benchmark problems are provided. The efficiency of the proposed method occurred to be satisfactory.

1 Introduction

In [22] the method of solving constrained optimization problems using differential evolution with Fletcher's filter has been proposed. Our aim in this paper is to propose an extension of this approach to optimal control problems and to test the extended version on difficult problems of time-optimal control of systems described by integral equations with additional state constraints.

Integral equations considered in this paper are confined to Volterra type II equations. Other formulations are possible, like mixed Volterra equations or Fredholm equations. The only difference is in the equations solving method. Proposed methodology can be used as well for differential equations with one remark. The right-hand side of ODE should be differentiable. When it is necessary to use piecewise constant control this assumption does not hold. We can try to overcome this by using differential equations also piecewise but integral equations do not have such limitations.

An optimal control problem can be very generally formulated as follows

$$\min_u J = \min_u \int \mathcal{J}(t, y, u) \tag{1}$$

additional constraints can be imposed on system control and state. The problem will be stated in section 2.

L. Rutkowski et al. (Eds.): ICAISC 2014, Part I, LNAI 8467, pp. 406–415, 2014.
© Springer International Publishing Switzerland 2014

1.1 Differential Evolution

Differential evolution is a method proposed by Kenneth Price and Reiner Stron in a technical report [17] in 1995 and later published in papers and books. From that time the method has become increasingly popular as one of the most efficient methods that retain evolutionary methods abilities to search for non-local solutions while providing better results. However, in this paper we deal with problems with constraints and for this reason we need to extend a differential evolution by a method of handling constraints. Following [22] we consider here the DE method in conjunction with Fletcher's filter methodology.

Evolutionary computing methods are widely used in control problems like in [24],[25].

1.2 Filter

The filter was proposed by Fletcher and his co-workers in 2001, firstly for sequential linear programming and then for sequential quadratic programming in [4],[5],[6]. Today the Filter SQP method is considered as a state-of-the-art method in classical constrained optimization.

We are convinced that the combined methodology of differential evolution and the filter is much wider and can be useful in solving optimal control problems.

The filter, as a method of solving constrained optimization problems was proposed in artificial inteligence field for evolutionary computing in [21] and as a method supplementing differential evolution in [22]. Some modifications of filter method were proposed in [20]. Differential evolution without constraints was previously used for example in [26] or [13], methods using rudimentary constraints handling techniques were investigated in [2]

2 Optimal Control Problem Formulation

After discretization, regardless of a result from a previously described method or much more complicated one like those described in [1], [11] we obtain a system of nonlinear equations. Now we can choose one of two ways of solving the control problem. We decide to use nonlinear equations solver separetly from the optimization method. This ensures that our results are correct in the sense that resulting controls would provide exactly the same result when used directly on the system without the optimization method. This does not compromise the abilty to constrain a system state on selected points.

Typical, useful and still difficult is the problem of time optimal control. In this problem we want the system to reach a desired state (usually 0) in the shortest possible time. Commonly the fact that this point should be stable is omitted.

$$\min t_k$$
$$y(t_k) = 0 \tag{2}$$

Usually control is constrained in some way.

$$H(y, u) = 0$$
$$|u(t)| \leq 1 \tag{3}$$

The simplest example can be a problem of stopping a pendulum or mass on the spring. In this case $y = [y_1, y_2]$ is a vector where y_1 is speed and y_2 is the resulting position. We want both of them to be 0 which is the stable point for this problem.

For this problem a theoretical solution does exist, so we add additional constraints like

$$y(t_\xi) = y_\xi \tag{4}$$

can be added. We still use some part of analytical result, for example the fact that control would be in a switched form so we can use only a few steps (we do not expect and try to approximate continuous control function).

3   Integral Equations

3.1   Definition

Integral equations have been investigated for a long time. Their general classification is as Volterra and Fredholm with two type each.

$$Ay(t) = y_0 + \int_a^b \mathcal{F}(y, t, \tau) d\tau \tag{5}$$

Voltera equations have time t as an upper integral limit $b = t$ and usually zero as the lower one $a = 0$.

If $A = 0$ then an equation is of type I. In any other case $A \neq 0$ is of type II.

Integral equations arise in many fields and problems. As is well known integral equations can be obtained from differential equations by integrating them. This fact is used in one of the proofs of existence and uniqueness of the ODE solution.

Integral equations can also occur as a natural description of a problem in many cases e.g. when conservation laws are applied. One of the first cases of integral equations was stated by Abel in 1823 when he was considering the problem of tautochrone. In this problem we are looking for a curve that allows material points sliding from it to arrive at the lowest point in the same time regardless of said points' starting position along the curve.

This equation is of the Volterra type and has the form

$$f(y) = \int_0^y \frac{\Phi(y)}{\sqrt{y - \Upsilon}} d\Upsilon \tag{6}$$

Fredholm type integral equations arises for example in a case of boundary value problem.

3.2   Solution Methods

Some integral equations can be solved in an analytic way but it is usually difficult. Many numerical methods have been proposed. Most of them are based on quadratures used for integration and are called the Nystrom method. Others use collocation which can require solving systems of algebraic equations. In case of linear integral equations we get a system of linear equations. Some other techniques can be combined like polynomial spline collocation.

3.3   Integro-algebraic Case

Collocation methods resulting in algebraic equations are suited to expansion into integro-algebraic equations.

4   Differential Evolution with a Fletcher Filter

Differential evolution is a meta-heuristic method of optimization. Instead of computing gradient, two random agents from the population are selected and their difference is used with some coeficient (F) in lieu of gradient. The method could be easily modified for different problems and using modern computational power with parallelization. This method is called evolutionary. However it is different then a typical biologically inspired evolution presented for example in [7], [8]. Previously, in [22] we have proposed a method of using the filter to handle constraints.Here, we review it briefly.

Other method of contrained optimization using differential evolution were proposed [9], [10], [14], [15], [16], [23]

In a typical case differential evolution requires a population consisting of vectors from R^n which is the domain of goal function $f(x)$. Function $h(g(x))$ informs us how much constraints are violated – 0 if none. In our case additional agents are stored in the filter. The method require two parameters $CR \in [0,1]$, $F \in [0,2]$.

In this approach the differentiated elements come from the population and the modified element from the filter, so the method is as follows.

– Choose parameters: for differential evolution $CR \in [0,1]$, $F \in [0,2]$ and for the filter: size of population and (possibly) maximal size of the filter. Initialize initial population and insert at least one element in the filter, possibly with small constraint violation h.
– Until reaching a stop criterion, for each element in the population x
   Step 1. Choose at random an element from the filter and denote it by a. Choose two elements from the population b and c such that $b \neq c$. Choose a random number R from $1 \ldots n$ (the current working dimension for all vectors).
   Step 2. For each dimension $k = 1 \ldots n$
      1. Choose random r from $[0,1]$
      2. If $r < CR$ or $k = R$ then $y_k = a_k + F \cdot (b_k - c_k)$
      3. else $y_k = x_k$

Step 3. For resulting y calculate $f(y)$ and $h(g(y))$. If pair (f, h) is acceptable to the filter replace element x by y. Add triple (f, h, y) to the filter. Otherwise do not change the population

5 Numerical Results

5.1 Problem Formulation

Let us consider a simple second order non-damped oscillating object with $\omega = 1$ in form of an integral equations. As stated, using this form reduces complications regarding nonsmoothness of controls that could result from optimization.

$$x_1 = x_{01} + \int_0^t x_2(t)dt \tag{7}$$

$$x_2 = x_{02} + \int_0^t [-x_1(t) + u(t)]dt$$

We use typical constraints

$$|u(t)| \leq 1$$

Here we propose a new method of control parametrization – generally

$$u(t) = \sum_{i=1}^n u_i \cdot s_i(t) \tag{8}$$

where $s_i(t)$ is a step. These steps can be of different length. For the sake of making the optimization problem simpler we choose the following scheme

$$s_1(t) = \begin{cases} 1 \ for \ t \in [0, t_1] \\ 0 \ for \ t > t_1 \end{cases} \tag{9}$$

$$s_2(t) = \begin{cases} 1 \ for \ t \in (t_1, t_1 + t_2] \\ 0 \quad otherwise \end{cases} \tag{10}$$

$$s_n(t) = \begin{cases} 1 \ for \ t \in [\sum_{i=1}^{n-1} t_i, \sum_{i=1}^n t_i] \\ 0 \quad otherwise \end{cases} \tag{11}$$

This kind of formulation has the following advantages:

− simple calculation of goal function
− simple constraints

So our problem is formulated as follows

$$J = \int_0^{t_k} u(\tau)d\tau = \sum_{i=1}^n u_i = T_k$$

constraints regarding control

$$\forall u_i \in [-1, 1],$$

constraints regarding time

$$\forall t_i \geq 0,$$

and required result (system stops at stable point)

$$y_1(T_k) = 0,$$

$$y_2(T_k) = 0.$$

As we perceive final points as more important so we multiply them by factor M which results in the following equations

$$\begin{aligned} M \cdot y_1(T_k) &\leq 0 \\ -M \cdot y_1(T_k) &\leq 0 \\ M \cdot y_2(T_k) &\leq 0 \\ -M \cdot y_2(T_k) &\leq 0 \end{aligned} \tag{12}$$

In order to get y_1 and y_2 integral equations 7 must be solved. As a method of solving them a simple Nystrom method with trapezoid rule was chosen.

The ethod of problem parametrization that was chosen means that calculations time is variable but in most cases it is irrelevant. In more complicated cases polynomial spline collocation can be used. It is well-suited here due to existing subdivisions of interval.

Differential evolution has two general parameters F and CR. Their selection is crucial to success in finding good solution.

5.2 No State Constraints Results

Firstly a typical time-optimal problem was investgated. Simulations were carried out for different parameters.

Generally smaller values of both F and CR are preferred and lead to better results. They do not differ then those used for typical constrained optimization benchmarks. The additional, problem related, parameter M has a huge impact on results. It changes constraints violation function $h(g)$ so results are not easily comparable. Generally best results were achieved for $M = 5$ or not much bigger. Results can be seen on fig. 1 and resulting contron on fig, 2

Calculation time was about 50 seconds for 300 iterations and 35 elements in population.

5.3 Additional State Constraints

A much more complicated case is when we add additional constraints. For example we can add constraint

$$y_1(0.2) = 1.2 \tag{13}$$

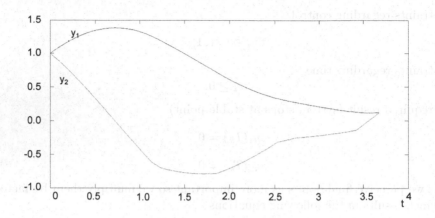

Fig. 1. State trajectory for $M = 5$

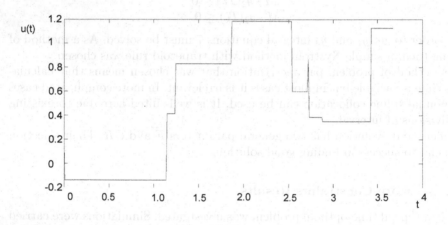

Fig. 2. Control function for $M = 5$

It should be noted that trying to force a state to get closer to the desired state is futile but we can try making the change slower by constraining point which require trajectory change.

On the fig. 3 we can clearly see that the required point is nearly reached but we are far from the desired final point resulting in further oscillations.

5.4   Pareto Front

Typically in multiobjective optimization, a Pareto front forms showing tradeoffs between goal function and possible constraints violation (fig. 4). Previously (in [21] it was discovered that for benchmark problems the Pareto front is forming inside the filter. The filter ensures that only the front stays in the filter

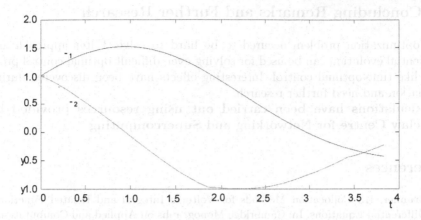

Fig. 3. System state trajectory and point constraint

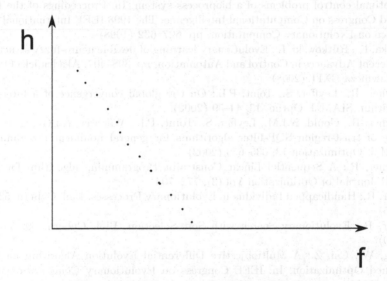

Fig. 4. Typical situation possible in the filter

(all elements are good in some sense: either smaller goal function or smaller constraints violation).

In this optimal control case only one element exists in the filter. These results come from simulations for different size of populations and it is consistent from the beginning of calculations. The possible reason is that solutions are so difficult to find that only one is found and then slightly improved.

6   Concluding Remarks and Further Research

The optimization problem occured to be hard to solve. Filter approach and differential evolution can be used for solving even difficult optimal control problems like time-optimal control. Interesting effects have been discovered during simulation and need further research.

Calculations have been carried out using resources provided by Wroclaw Centre for Networking and Supercomputing

References

1. Brunner, H.: Collocation Methods for Volterra Integral and Related Functional Differential Equations. In: Cambridge Monographs on Applied and Computational Mathematics. Cambridge University Press (2004)
2. Chiou, J.-P., Wang, F.: A hybrid method of differential evolution with application to optimal control problems of a bioprocess system. In: Proceedings of the IEEE World Congress on Computational Intelligence, The 1998 IEEE International Conference on Evolutionary Computation, pp. 627–632 (1998)
3. Cpałka, K., Rutkowski, L.: Evolutionary learning of flexible neuro-fuzzy structures. In: Recent Advances in Control and Automation, pp. 398–407. Akademicka Oficyna Wydawnicza EXIT (2008)
4. Fletcher, R., Leyffer, S., Toint, P.L.: On the global convergence of a filter-SQP algorithm. SIAM J. Optim. 13, 44–59 (2002)
5. Fletcher, R., Gould, N.I.M., Leyffer, S., Toint, P.L., Wächter, A.: Global convergence of trust-region SQP-filter algorithms for general nonlinear programming. SIAM J. Optimization 13, 635–659 (2002)
6. Fletcher, R.: A Sequential Linear Constraint Programming algorithm for NLP. SIAM Journal of Optimization Vol (3), 772–794
7. Galar, R.: Handicapped Individua in Evolutionary Processes. Biol. Cybern. 53, 1–9 (1985)
8. Galar, R.: Evolutionary Search with Soft Selection. Biol. Cybern. 60, 357–364 (1989)
9. Gong, W., Cai, Z.: A Multiobjective Differential Evolution Algorithm for Constrained Optimization. In: IEEE Congress on Evolutionary Computation (CEC 2008) (2008)
10. Gordián-Rivera, L.-A., Mezura-Montes, E.: A Combination of Specialized Differential Evolution Variants for Constrained Optimization. In: Pavón, J., Duque-Méndez, N.D., Fuentes-Fernández, R. (eds.) IBERAMIA 2012. LNCS, vol. 7637, pp. 261–270. Springer, Heidelberg (2012)
11. Kauthen, J.-P.: The numerical solution of integral-algebraic equations of index 1 by polynomial spline collocation methods. Mathematics of Computation 70(236), 1503–1514 (2000)
12. Kress, R.: Linear Integral Equations. Applied Mathematical Sciences, vol. 82. Springer (1989)
13. Lopez Cruz, I.L., Van Willigenburg, L.G., Van Straten, G.: Efficient Differential Evolution algorithms for multimodal optimal control problems. Applied Soft Computing 3(2), 97–122 (2003) ISSN 1568-4946

14. de Melo, V., Grazieli, L., Costa, C.: Evaluating differential evolution with penalty function to solve constrained engineering problems. Expert Systems with Applications 39, 7860–7863 (2012)
15. Mezura-Montes, E., Coello, C.A.: A Simple Multimembered Evolution Strategy to Solve Constrained Optimization Problems. IEEE Transactions on Evolutionary Computation 9(1), 1–17 (2005)
16. Mezura-Montes, E., Coello Coello, C.A., Tun-Morales, E.I.: Simple Feasibility Rules and Differential Evolution for Constrained Optimization. In: Monroy, R., Arroyo-Figueroa, G., Sucar, L.E., Sossa, H. (eds.) MICAI 2004. LNCS (LNAI), vol. 2972, pp. 707–716. Springer, Heidelberg (2004)
17. Storn, R., Price, K.: Differential evolution – a simple and efficient adaptive scheme for global optimization over continuous spaces. Technical report (1995)
18. Storn, R., Price, K.: Differential evolution – a simple and efficient heuristic for global optimization over continuous spaces. Journal of Global Optimization 11, 341–359 (1997)
19. Price, K., Storn, R., Lampinen, J.,, D.E.: Differential Evolution A Practical Approach to Global Optimization. Springer, Heidelberg (2005)
20. Rafajłowicz, E., Styczeń, K., Rafajłowicz, W.: A modified filter SQP method as a tool for optimal control of nonlinear systems with spatio-temporal dynamics. International Journal of Applied Mathematics and Computer Science 22(2) (2012)
21. Rafajłowicz, E., Rafajłowicz, W.: Fletcher's Filter Methodology as a Soft Selector in Evolutionary Algorithms for Constrained Optimization. In: Rutkowski, L., Korytkowski, M., Scherer, R., Tadeusiewicz, R., Zadeh, L.A., Zurada, J.M. (eds.) EC 2012 and SIDE 2012. LNCS, vol. 7269, pp. 333–341. Springer, Heidelberg (2012)
22. Rafajłowicz, W.: Method of handling constraints in differential evolution using fletcher's filter. In: Rutkowski, L., Korytkowski, M., Scherer, R., Tadeusiewicz, R., Zadeh, L.A., Zurada, J.M. (eds.) ICAISC 2013, Part II. LNCS (LNAI), vol. 7895, pp. 46–55. Springer, Heidelberg (2013)
23. Rocha, A.M.A.C., Costa, M.F.P., Fernandes, E.M.G.P.: An Artificial Fish Swarm Filter-Based Method for Constrained Global Optimization. In: Murgante, B., Gervasi, O., Misra, S., Nedjah, N., Rocha, A.M.A.C., Taniar, D., Apduhan, B.O. (eds.) ICCSA 2012, Part III. LNCS, vol. 7335, pp. 57–71. Springer, Heidelberg (2012)
24. Skowron, M., Styczeń, K.: Evolutionary search for globally optimal constrained stable cycles. Chemical Engineering Science 61(24), 7924–7932 (2006)
25. Skowron, M., Styczeń, K.: Evolutionary search for globally optimal stable multicycles in complex systems with inventory couplings. International Journal of Chemical Engineering (2009)
26. Wang, F.-S., Chiou, J.-P.: Optimal Control and Optimal Time Location Problems of Differential-Algebraic Systems by Differential Evolution. Ind. Eng. Chem. Res. 36(12), 5348–5357 (1997)

Multi-chaotic Differential Evolution: A Preliminary Study

Roman Senkerik[1,*], Michal Pluhacek[1], Ivan Zelinka[2],
Donald Davendra[2], and Zuzana Kominková Oplatková[1]

[1] Tomas Bata University in Zlin, Faculty of Applied Informatics,
Nam T.G. Masaryka 5555, 760 01 Zlin, Czech Republic
{senkerik,pluhacek,oplatkova}@fai.utb.cz
[2] Technical University of Ostrava,
Faculty of Electrical Engineering and Computer Science,
17. listopadu 15,708 33 Ostrava-Poruba, Czech Republic
{donald.davendra,ivan.zelinka}@vsb.cz

Abstract. This research deals with the initial investigations on the concept of a multi-chaos-driven evolutionary algorithm Differential Evolution (DE). This paper is aimed at the embedding and alternating of set of two discrete dissipative chaotic systems in the form of chaos pseudo random number generator for DE. Repeated simulations were performed on the selected test function in higher dimensions. Finally, the obtained results are compared with canonical DE.

Keywords: Differential Evolution, Deterministic chaos, Dissipative systems, Optimization.

1 Introduction

These days the methods based on soft computing such as neural networks, evolutionary algorithms, fuzzy logic, and genetic programming are known as powerful tool for almost any difficult and complex optimization problem. Differential Evolution (DE) [1] is one of the most potent heuristics available.

This paper is aimed at the investigating the novel concept of multi-chaos driven DE. Although a number of DE variants have been recently developed, the focus of this paper is the embedding of chaotic systems in the form of chaos pseudo random number generator (CPRNG) into the DE.

* This work was supported by Grant Agency of the Czech Republic - GACR P103/13/08195S, partially supported by Grants of SGS No. SP2014/159 and SP2014/170, VSB - Technical University of Ostrava, Czech Republic, by the Development of human resources in research and development of latest soft computing methods and their application in practice project, reg. no. CZ.1.07/2.3.00/20.0072 funded by Operational Programme Education for Competitiveness, co-financed by ESF and state budget of the Czech Republic, further was supported by European Regional Development Fund under the project CEBIA-Tech No. CZ.1.05/2.1.00/03.0089 and by Internal Grant Agency of Tomas Bata University under the project No. IGA/FAI/2014/010.

L. Rutkowski et al. (Eds.): ICAISC 2014, Part I, LNAI 8467, pp. 416–427, 2014.

Firstly, the motivation for this research is proposed. The next sections are focused on the description of evolutionary algorithm DE, the concept of chaos driven DE and the used test function. Results and conclusion follow afterwards.

2 Motivation

This research is an extension and continuation of the previous successful initial experiments with chaos driven DE [2], [3] with test functions in higher dimensions.

In this paper the novel initial concept of DE/rand/1/bin strategy driven alternately by two chaotic maps (systems) is introduced. From the previous research it follows, that very promising results were obtained through the utilization of Delayed Logistic, Lozi, Burgers and Tinkerbelt chaotic maps. The last two mentioned chaotic maps have unique properties with connection to DE: strong progress towards global extreme, but weak overall statistical results, like average CF value and std. dev., and tendency to premature stagnation. While through the utilization of the Lozi and Delayed Logistic map the continuously stable and very satisfactory performance of ChaosDE was achieved. The idea is then to connect these two different influences to the performance of DE into the one multi-chaotic concept.

Recent research in chaos driven heuristics has been fueled with the predisposition that unlike stochastic approaches, a chaotic approach is able to bypass local optima stagnation. This one clause is of deep importance to evolutionary algorithms. A chaotic approach generally uses the chaotic map in the place of a pseudo random number generator [4]. This causes the heuristic to map unique regions, since the chaotic map iterates to new regions. The task is then to select a very good chaotic map as the pseudo random number generator.

The initial concept of embedding chaotic dynamics into the evolutionary algorithms is given in [5]. Later, the initial study [6] was focused on the simple embedding of chaotic systems in the form of chaos pseudo random number generator (CPRNG) for DE and SOMA [7] in the task of optimal PID tuning

Several papers have been recently focused on the connection of heuristic and chaotic dynamics either in the form of hybridizing of DE with chaotic searching algorithm [8] or in the form of chaotic mutation factor and dynamically changing weighting and crossover factor in self-adaptive chaos differential evolution (SACDE) [9]. Also the PSO (Particle Swarm Optimization) algorithm with elements of chaos was introduced as CPSO [10] or CPSO combined with chaotic local search [11].

The focus of our research is the pure embedding of chaotic systems in the form of chaos pseudo random number generator for evolutionary algorithms.

This idea was later extended with the successful experiments with chaos driven DE (ChaosDE) [2], [3] with both and complex simple test functions and in the task of chemical reactor geometry optimization [12].

The concept of Chaos DE has proved itself to be a powerful heuristic also in combinatorial problems domain [13].

At the same time the chaos embedded PSO with inertia weigh strategy was closely investigated [14], followed by the introduction of a PSO strategy driven alternately by two chaotic systems [15] and novel chaotic Multiple Choice PSO strategy (Chaos MC-PSO) [16].

The primary aim of this work is not to develop a new type of pseudo random number generator, which should pass many statistical tests, but to try to use and test the implementation of natural chaotic dynamics into evolutionary algorithm as a multi-chaotic pseudo random number generator.

3   Differential Evolution

DE is a population-based optimization method that works on real-number-coded individuals [1]. For each individual $x_{i,G}$ in the current generation G, DE generates a new trial individual $x'_{i,G}$ by adding the weighted difference between two randomly selected individuals $x_{r1,G}$ and $x_{r2,G}$ to a randomly selected third individual $x_{r3,G}$. The resulting individual $x'_{i,G}$ is crossed-over with the original individual$x_{i,G}$. The fitness of the resulting individual, referred to as a perturbed vector $u_{i,G+1}$, is then compared with the fitness of $x_{i,G}$. If the fitness of $u_{i,G+1}$ is greater than the fitness of$x_{i,G}$, then $x_{i,G}$ is replaced with$u_{i,G+1}$; otherwise, $x_{i,G}$ remains in the population as$x_{i,G+1}$. DE is quite robust, fast, and effective, with global optimization ability. It does not require the objective function to be differentiable, and it works well even with noisy and time-dependent objective functions. Please refer to [1], [17] for the detailed description of the used DE-Rand1Bin strategy (1) (both for Chaos DE and Canonical DE) as well as for the complete description of all other strategies.

$$u_{j,i,G+1} = x_{j,r1,G} + F \cdot (x_{j,r2,G} - x_{j,r3,G}) \tag{1}$$

4   The Concept of ChaosDE

The general idea of ChaosDE and CPRNG is to replace the default PRNG with the discrete chaotic map. As the discrete chaotic map is a set of equations with a static start position, we created a random start position of the map, in order to have different start position for different experiments (runs of EA's). This random position is initialized with the default PRNG, as a one-off randomizer. Once the start position of the chaotic map has been obtained, the map generates the next sequence using its current position.

The first possible way is to generate and store a long data sequence (approx. 50-500 thousand numbers) during the evolutionary process initialization and keep the pointer to the actual used value in the memory. In case of the using up of the whole sequence, the new one will be generated with the last known value as the new initial one.

The second approach is that the chaotic map is not re-initialized during the experiment and no long data series is stored, thus it is imperative to keep the current state of the map in memory to obtain the new output values.

As two different types of numbers are required in ChaosDE; real and integers, the modulo operators is used to obtain values between the specified ranges, as given in the following equations (2) and (3):

$$rndreal = mod(abs(rndChaos), 1.0) \tag{2}$$

$$rndint = mod(abs(rndChaos), 1.0) \times Range + 1 \tag{3}$$

Where abs refers to the absolute portion of the chaotic map generated number $rndChaos$, and mod is the modulo operator. $Range$ specifies the value (inclusive) till where the number is to be scaled.

5   Chaotic Maps

This section contains the description of discrete dissipative chaotic maps used as the chaotic pseudo random generators for DE. In this research, direct output iterations of the chaotic maps were used for the generation of real numbers in the process of crossover based on the user defined CR value and for the generation of the integer values used for the selection of individuals. Following chaotic maps were used: Burgers (4), and Lozi map (5).

The Burgers mapping is a discretization of a pair of coupled differential equations which were used by Burgers [18] to illustrate the relevance of the concept of bifurcation to the study of hydrodynamics flows. The map equations are given in (4) with control parameters $a = 0.75$ and $b = 1.75$ as suggested in [19].

$$\begin{aligned} X_{n+1} &= aX_n - Y_n^2 \\ Y_{n+1} &= bY_n + X_nY_n \end{aligned} \tag{4}$$

The Lozi map is a discrete two-dimensional chaotic map. The map equations are given in (5). The parameters used in this work are: $a = 1.7$ and $b = 0.5$ as suggested in [19]. For these values, the system exhibits typical chaotic behavior and with this parameter setting it is used in the most research papers and other literature sources.

$$\begin{aligned} X_{n+1} &= 1 - a\,|X_n| + bY_n \\ Y_{n+1} &= X_n \end{aligned} \tag{5}$$

5.1   Graphical Example – Lozi Map and Burgers Map

The x, y plots of the chaotic maps are depicted in Fig. 1 - left (Lozi map) and Fig. 3 - left (Burgers map). The typical chaotic behavior of the utilized maps, represented by the examples of direct output iterations is depicted in Fig. 1 - right (Lozi map) and Fig. 3 - right (Burgers map).

The illustrative histograms of the distribution of real numbers transferred into the range <0 - 1> generated by means of studied chaotic maps are in Figures 2 and 4.

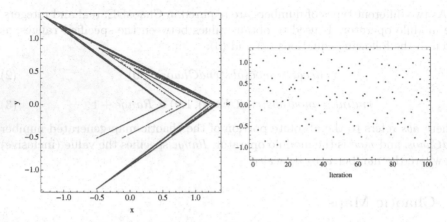

Fig. 1. x, y plot of the Lozi map (left); Iterations of the Lozi map (variable x) (right)

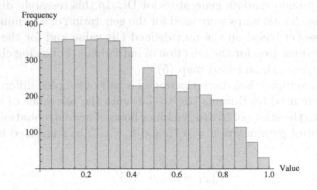

Fig. 2. Histogram of the distribution of real numbers generated by means of the chaotic Lozi map transferred into the range <0 - 1> – 5000 samples

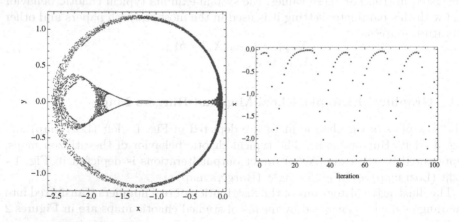

Fig. 3. x, y plot of the Burgers map (left); Iterations of the Burgers map (variable x) (right)

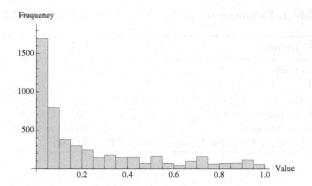

Fig. 4. Histogram of the distribution of real numbers generated by means of the chaotic Burgers map transferred into the range <0 - 1> – 5000 samples

6   Benchmark Function

For the purpose of evolutionary algorithm performance comparison within this initial research, the multimodal Schwefel's test function (6) was selected.

$$f(x) = \sum_{i=1}^{D} -x_i \sin\left(\sqrt{|x_i|}\right) \tag{6}$$

Function minimum:
Position for E_n: $(x_1, x_2 \ldots x_n) = (420.969, 420.969, \ldots, 420.969)$
Value for E_n: $y = -418.983 \cdot Dimension$

7   Results

The novelty of this approach represents the utilization of discrete chaotic maps as the multi-chaotic pseudo random number generator for the DE. In this paper, the canonical DE strategy DERand1Bin and the Multi-Chaos DERand1Bin strategy driven alternately by two different chaotic maps (ChaosDE) were used.

The previous research [2], [3] showed that through the utilization of Burgers and Tinkerbelt maps the unique properties with connection to DE were achieved: strong progress towards global extreme, but weak overall statistical results, like average CF value and std. dev. Whereas through the utilization of the Lozi and Delayed Logistic maps, the continuously stable and very satisfactory performance of ChaosDE was achieved. The idea is then to connect these two different influences to the performance of DE into the one novel multi-chaotic concept. The moment of manual switching over between two chaotic maps as well as the parameter settings for both canonical DE and ChaosDE were obtained analytically based on numerous experiments and simulations (see Table 1)

Experiments were performed in the combined environment of *Wolfram Mathematica* and *C language*, canonical DE therefore used the built-in *C language*

Table 1. Parameter set up for Chaos DE and Canonical DE

Parameter	Value
PopSize	75
F	0.8
CR	0.8
Dimensions	30
Generations	$100 \cdot D = 3000$
Max Cost Function Evaluations (CFE)	225000

pseudo random number generator *Mersenne Twister C* representing traditional pseudorandom number generators in comparisons. All experiments used different initialization, i.e. different initial population was generated within the each run of Canonical or Chaos driven DE.

Within this initial research, one type of experiment was performed. It utilizes the maximum number of generations fixed at 3000 generations. This allowed the possibility to analyze the progress of DE within a limited number of generations and cost function evaluations.

The statistical results of the experiments are shown in Table 2, which represent the simple statistics for cost function values, e.g. average, median, maximum values, standard deviations and minimum values representing the best individual solution for all 50 repeated runs of canonical DE and several versions of ChaosDE and Multi-ChaosDE.

Table 3 compares the progress of several versions of ChaosDE, Multi-ChaosDE and Canonical DE. This table contains the average CF values for the generation No. 750, 1500, 2250 and 3000 from all 50 runs. The bold values within the both Tables 2 and 3 depict the best obtained results. Following versions of Multi-ChaosDE were studied:

– *Burgers-Lozi-Switch-500*: Start with Burgers map CPRNG, switch to the Lozi map CPRNG after 500 generations.
– *Lozi-Burgers-Switch-1500*: Start with Lozi map CPRNG, switch to the Burgers map CPRNG after 1500 generations.

Table 2. Simple results statistics for the Schwefel's function – 30D

DE Version	Avg CF	Median CF	Max CF	Min CF	StdDev
Canonical DE	-5822.8	-5754.4	-5443.23	-6500.44	**226.4365**
Lozi-No-Switch	-11296.9	-11581	-7842.25	-12235.5	879.1985
Burger-No-Switch	-11052.1	-11192.9	-8473.79	-12105	667.7065
Burger-Lozi-Switch-500	-11332.9	-11459.1	-7871.2	**-12486.9**	799.7749
Lozi-Burger-Switch-1500	**-11475.5**	**-11489.6**	**-10354.5**	-12279.7	373.059

Table 3. Comparison of progress towards the minimum for the Schwefel's function

DE Version	Generation No. 750	Generation No. 1500	Generation No. 2250	Generation No. 3000
Canonical DE	-5231.94	-5537.79	-5738.96	-5822.8
Lozi-No-Switch	-5839.69	-7998.35	-9965.25	-11296.9
Burger-No-Switch	-6075.91	**-8854.6**	-10564.1	-11052.1
Burger-Lozi-Switch-500	**-6538.11**	-8658.15	-10356.3	-11332.9
Lozi-Burger-Switch-1500	-5701.57	-7719.37	**-10663.1**	**-11475.5**

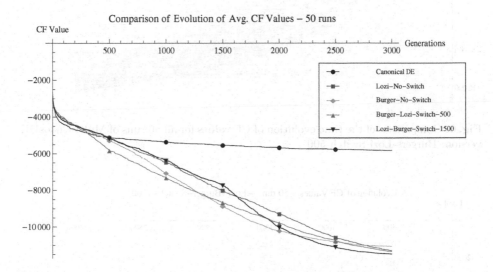

Fig. 5. Comparison of the time evolution of avg. CF values for the all 50 runs of Canonical DE, ChaosDE and Multi-ChaosDE. Schwefel's function, $D = 30$.

The graphical comparison of the time evolution of average CF values for all 50 runs of ChaosDE/Multi-ChaosDE and canonical DERand1Bin strategy is depicted in Fig. 5. Finally the Figures 6 - 8 confirm the robustness of Multi-ChaosDE in finding the best solutions for all 50 runs.

Obtained numerical results given in Tables 2 and 3 and graphical comparisons in Figures 5 - 8 support the claim that all Multi-Chaos/ChaosDE versions have given better overall results in comparison with the canonical DE version. From the presented data it follows, that Multi-Chaos DE versions driven by Lozi/Burgers Map have given the best overall results.

For the *Burgers-Lozi-Switch-500* version the progressive Burgers map CPRNG secured the faster approaching towards the global extreme from the very beginning of evolutionary process. The very fast switch over to the Lozi map based CPRNG helped to avoid the Burgers map based CPRNG weak spots, which are the weak overall statistical results, like average CF value and std. dev.; and

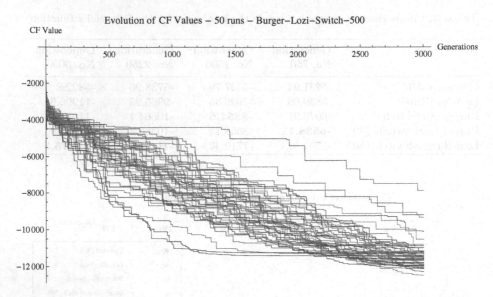

Fig. 6. Comparison of the time evolution of CF values for all 50 runs of Multi-ChaosDE version: Burgers-Lozi-Switch-500

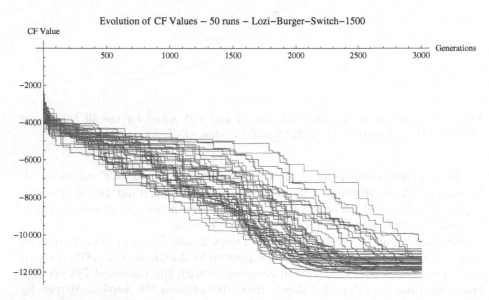

Fig. 7. Comparison of the time evolution of CF values for all 50 runs of Multi-ChaosDE version: Lozi- Burgers -Switch-1500

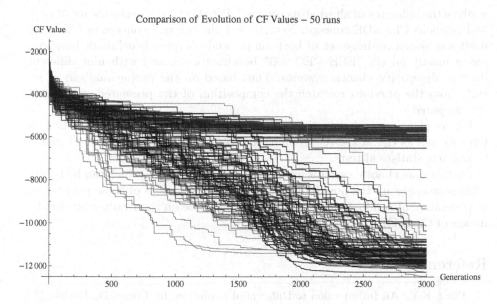

Fig. 8. Comparison of the time evolution of CF values for all 50 runs of canonical DE (blue) and Multi-ChaosDE versions: Burgers-Lozi-Switch-500 (magenta), Lozi-Burgers-Switch-1500 (black)

tendency to stagnation. This version was able to reach the best individual minimum CF value. The initial faster convergence (starting of evolutionary process) and subsequent continuously stable searching process without premature stagnation issues are visible from Fig. 5 (magenta line), Fig. 6 and Fig. 8 (magenta lines).

Through the utilization of *Lozi-Burgers-Switch-1500* version, the strong progress towards global extreme given by Burgers map CPRNG helped to the evolutionary process driven from the start by mans of Lozi map CPRNG to achieve the best avg. CF and median CF values. The moment of switch (at 1500 generations) is clearly visible from Fig. 5 (black line) and Fig. 7 and Fig. 8 (black lines).

8 Conclusions

In this paper, the novel concept of multi-chaos driven DERand1Bin strategy was tested and compared with the canonical DERand1Bin strategy on the selected benchmark function in higher dimension. Based on obtained results, it may be claimed, that the developed Multi-ChaosDE gives considerably better results than other compared heuristics.

Since this was a preliminary study of the novel presented concept, only one single benchmark function in higher dimensions was utilized to test and more deeply analyze the influence of alternating several CPRNGs to the performance of original previous ChaosDE concept. Nevertheless the original concept of ChaosDE itself was tested on huge set of both simple and complex benchmark functions based mostly on the IEEE CEC 2005 benchmark set and with nine different discrete dissipative chaotic systems. Thus based on the deeper analysis of results from the previous research the composition of the presented experiment was prepared.

Future plans are including the testing of combination of different chaotic systems as well as the adaptive switching and obtaining a large number of results to perform statistical tests.

Furthermore chaotic systems have additional parameters, which can by tuned. This issue opens up the possibility of examining the impact of these parameters to generation of random numbers, and thus influence on the results obtained by means of ChaosDE.

References

1. Price, K.V.: An Introduction to Differential Evolution. In: Corne, D., Dorigo, M., Glover, F. (eds.) New Ideas in Optimization, pp. 79–108. McGraw-Hill Ltd. (1999)
2. Senkerik, R., Pluhacek, M., Zelinka, I., Oplatkova, Z.K., Vala, R., Jasek, R.: Performance of Chaos Driven Differential Evolution on Shifted Benchmark Functions Set. In: Herrero, A., et al. (eds.) International Joint Conference SOCO'13-CISIS'13-ICEUTE'13. AISC, vol. 239, pp. 41–50. Springer, Heidelberg (2014)
3. Senkerik, R., Davendra, D., Zelinka, I., Pluhacek, M., Kominkova Oplatkova, Z.: On the Differential Evolution Driven by Selected Discrete Chaotic Systems: Extended Study. In: 19th International Conference on Soft Computing, MENDEL 2013, pp. 137–144 (2013)
4. Aydin, I., Karakose, M., Akin, E.: Chaotic-based hybrid negative selection algorithm and its applications in fault and anomaly detection. Expert Systems with Applications 37(7), 5285–5294 (2010)
5. Caponetto, R., Fortuna, L., Fazzino, S., Xibilia, M.G.: Chaotic sequences to improve the performance of evolutionary algorithms. IEEE Transactions on Evolutionary Computation 7(3), 289–304 (2003)
6. Davendra, D., Zelinka, I., Senkerik, R.: Chaos driven evolutionary algorithms for the task of PID control. Computers & Mathematics with Applications 60(4), 1088–1104 (2010)
7. Zelinka, I.: SOMA — Self-Organizing Migrating Algorithm. In: Onwubolu, G.C., Babu, B.V. (eds.) New Optimization Techniques in Engineering. STUDFUZZ, vol. 141, pp. 167–217. Springer, Heidelberg (2004)
8. Liang, W., Zhang, L., Wang, M.: The chaos differential evolution optimization algorithm and its application to support vector regression machine. Journal of Software 6(7), 1297–1304 (2011)
9. Zhenyu, G., Bo, C., Min, Y., Binggang, C.: Self-Adaptive Chaos Differential Evolution. In: Jiao, L., Wang, L., Gao, X.-B., Liu, J., Wu, F. (eds.) ICNC 2006. LNCS, vol. 4221, pp. 972–975. Springer, Heidelberg (2006)
10. dos Santos Coelho, L., Mariani, V.C.: A novel chaotic particle swarm optimization approach using Henon map and implicit filtering local search for economic load dispatch. Chaos, Solitons & Fractals 39(2), 510–518 (2009)

11. Hong, W.-C.: Chaotic particle swarm optimization algorithm in a support vector regression electric load forecasting model. Energy Conversion and Management 50(1), 105–117 (2009)
12. Senkerik, R., Pluhacek, M., Oplatkova, Z.K., Davendra, D., Zelinka, I.: Investigation on the Differential Evolution driven by selected six chaotic systems in the task of reactor geometry optimization. In: 2013 IEEE Congress on Evolutionary Computation (CEC), June 20-23, pp. 3087–3094 (2013)
13. Davendra, D., Bialic-Davendra, M., Senkerik, R.: Scheduling the Lot-Streaming Flowshop scheduling problem with setup time with the chaos-induced Enhanced Differential Evolution. In: 2013 IEEE Symposium on Differential Evolution (SDE), April 16-19, pp. 119–126 (2013)
14. Pluhacek, M., Senkerik, R., Davendra, D., Kominkova Oplatkova, Z., Zelinka, I.: On the behavior and performance of chaos driven PSO algorithm with inertia weight. Computers & Mathematics with Applications 66(2), 122–134 (2013)
15. Pluhacek, M., Senkerik, R., Zelinka, I., Davendra, D.: Chaos PSO algorithm driven alternately by two different chaotic maps - An initial study. In: 2013 IEEE Congress on Evolutionary Computation (CEC), June 20-23, pp. 2444–2449 (2013)
16. Pluhacek, M., Senkerik, R., Zelinka, I.: Multiple Choice Strategy Based PSO Algorithm with Chaotic Decision Making – A Preliminary Study. In: Herrero, A., et al. (eds.) International Joint Conference SOCO'13-CISIS'13-ICEUTE'13. AISC, vol. 239, pp. 21–30. Springer, Heidelberg (2014)
17. Price, K.V., Storn, R.M., Lampinen, J.A.: Differential Evolution - A Practical Approach to Global Optimization. Natural Computing Series. Springer, Heidelberg (2005)
18. ELabbasy, E., Agiza, H., EL-Metwally, H., Elsadany, A.: Bifurcation Analysis, Chaos and Control in the Burgers Mapping. International Journal of Nonlinear Science 4(3), 171–185 (2007)
19. Sprott, J.C.: Chaos and Time-Series Analysis. Oxford University Press (2003)

Evolutionary Multi-modal Optimization
with the Use of Multi-objective Techniques

Leszek Siwik and Rafał Dreżewski

AGH University of Science and Technology, Department of Computer Science,
Kraków, Poland
{siwik,drezew}@agh.edu.pl

Abstract. When evolutionary algorithms for solving multi-modal optimization problems are applied, the crucial issue to be solved is maintaining population diversity to avoid drifting and focusing individuals around single global optima. A lot of techniques have been used here so far. Simultaneously for last twenty years a lot of effort has been made in the area of evolutionary algorithms for multi-objective optimization. As the result at least several highly efficient algorithms have been proposed such as NSGAII or SPEA2. Obviously, also in this case maintaining of population diversity is crucial but this time, taking the specificity of optimization in the Pareto sense, there are built-in mechanisms to solve this issue effectively. If so, the idea arises of applying of state-of-the-art evolutionary multi-objective optimization algorithms for solving not original multi-modal (but single-objective) optimization task but rather its transformed into multi-objective problem form by introducing additional dispersion-oriented criteria. The goal of this paper is to present some further study in this area.

1 Motivation

One of the most important issue regarding multi-modal optimization is the ability for discovering not only the global but also (as many as possible) local optima (modes). When evolutionary solver is applied it is inseparably connected with keeping population dispersed and not focusing individuals around the global optima. Many techniques responsible for maintaining population diversity have been proposed so far. It is enough to call techniques based on modification of mechanism of selecting individuals for new generation (crowding model), modification of parent selection (fitness sharing, sexual selection), restricted application of selection and/or recombination mechanisms (grouping individuals into sub-populations, introducing environment with some topography etc.) [7] just to mention a few. Each of them however has its own shortcomings and it is not possible to point out a single diversity-maintaining technique giving evidently the best results and to be used in all (or at least in the majority of) cases. What is important their efficiency and the effectiveness depends often on the optimization algorithm used.

For the last thirty years evolutionary multi-objective optimization algorithms (EMOAs) have become more and more popular [4,11]. Historically, one tried

L. Rutkowski et al. (Eds.): ICAISC 2014, Part I, LNAI 8467, pp. 428–439, 2014.
© Springer International Publishing Switzerland 2014

to use classical EAs by combining all objectives in one single objective and repeating algorithm runs with different weights assigned to particular objectives to obtain different non-dominated solutions. The advantage of such an approach is its simplicity, however it is pretty unnatural, slow (since the EA has to be (re)run at least as many times as the number of solutions should be found) and—what is the most important—depending on the definitions of the objective functions (and their combination)—it often turns out that combining objectives with different weights results with the same solution, what makes this approach simply useless.

Also another techniques consisting in redefining multi-objective problem into single-objective one (and then (re)running single-objective algorithms to find consecutive non-dominated solutions, one in single algorithm's run) turned out to be useless in particular cases. It is enough to mention for instance ε—constrains technique which is useless in the case of concave problems.

That is why a lot of effort has been made to develop efficient and effective evolutionary (as general and population-based) algorithms for multi-objective optimization. It has been performed successfully and such algorithms as SPEA-II [20,19] or NSGA-II [14] are nowadays state-of-the-art EMOAs giving a really high-quality results in most cases. Also, agent-based multi-objective evolutionary algorithms (combining agent-based and evolutionary paradigms) were proposed and they proved to be quite effective in some cases (for example in multi-objective portfolio optimization problems) [5,6,8,9].

What is important, when the multi-objective optimization (and algorithms) (in the Pareto sense) are being considered as one of the most important difference in comparison to single objective optimization (algorithms) is the fact that the solution to be found is the whole set of non-dominated alternatives called the Pareto set (or the Pareto frontier in the objective space). The crucial here is the fact that using (weak) non-domination relation instead of simple mutual-comparisons as a mechanisms responsible for distinguishing "better" and "worse" alternatives—EMOAs are dedicated for looking for the whole set of solutions in one single run. One has to remember that the goal of the multi-objective optimization (in the Pareto sense) is to find (as-many-as-possible) non-dominated solutions dispersed over the whole Pareto frontier. Since EMOAs are population-based it is obviously the more so simple and natural but—what is crucial here—they have natural, built-in mechanisms for maintaining population diversity as well as the diversity of the solution itself.

The question thus arises if—in contrast to historical modifications of multi-objective optimization problems into single-objective one(s)—the way for obtaining high-quality solutions of multi-modal optimization tasks is converting multi-modal problems into multi-objective optimization problems by introducing additional objective responsible for maintaining population dispersed and then applying for solving such a modified problem one of the state-of-the-art efficient evolutionary multi-objective optimization algorithms.

Obviously such experiments have already been conducted. It is enough to mention here the work of M. Preuss, G. Rudolph and F. Tumakaka [12] but it still seems to be only a putting a toe into the water and the goal of this paper is to follow this research direction and to make some comparative assessment of several dispersing-oriented objectives introduced as a second objective while converting multi-modal single-objective optimization task into multi-objective optimization problem with the special attention paid to clustering method.

The computing experiments presented in this paper may be treated as preliminary results, planned to be adapted and ported to ParaPhrase[1] agent-based computing platform, which supplies hybrid CPU/GPU computing infrastructure via dedicated virtualisation tools.

2 The Idea of Transformation of Multi-modal into Multi-objective Optimization Problem

Typically, multi-objective (or multi-criteria) optimization problem (MOOP) is formulated as follows ([1,19,4]):

$$MOOP \equiv \begin{cases} Min/Max: & f_l(\bar{x}), \quad l = 1, 2 \ldots, L \\ Taking\ into\ consideration: \\ g_j(\bar{x}) \geq 0, \quad j = 1, 2 \ldots, J \\ h_k(\bar{x}) = 0, \quad k = 1, 2 \ldots, K \\ x_i^{(L)} \leq x_i \leq x_i^{(U)}, \quad i = 1, 2 \ldots, N \end{cases}$$

The set of constraints, both equalities ($h_k(\bar{x})$), as well as inequalities ($g_j(\bar{x})$), and constraints related to the decision variables, i.e. lower bounds ($x_i^{(L)}$) and upper bounds ($x_i^{(U)}$), define so called searching space—feasible alternatives ($\mathcal{D}$). Because of space limitation it is enough to say in this place that in the course of this paper multi-objective optimization in the Pareto sense is considered, so solving of defined problem means determining of all feasible and non-dominated alternatives from the set ($\mathcal{D}$). Such defined set is called Pareto set ($\mathcal{P}$) and in objective space it forms so called Pareto frontier ($\mathcal{PF}$).

Simultaneously, the multi-modal optimization task (assuming minimization) means determining of all $\boldsymbol{x}^+ \in D$ such as $\exists \epsilon > 0 \forall \boldsymbol{x} \in D \parallel \boldsymbol{x} - \boldsymbol{x}^+ \parallel < \epsilon \Rightarrow f(\boldsymbol{x}) \geq \boldsymbol{x}^+$ [2].

So, proposed transformation of multi-modal (but single-objective) into multi-objective optimization problem consists in formulating MOOP with original multi-modal function and dispersing oriented function as the second objective with preserving all original constraints and bounds of course.

$$MOOP \equiv \begin{cases} Min/Max: & f_m(\bar{x}), original\ multi-modal\ function \\ Min/Max: & f_d(\bar{x}), dispersing-oriented\ function \\ Taking\ into\ consideration: \\ g_j(\bar{x}) \geq 0, \quad j = 1, 2 \ldots, J \\ h_k(\bar{x}) = 0, \quad k = 1, 2 \ldots, K \\ x_i^{(L)} \leq x_i \leq x_i^{(U)}, \quad i = 1, 2 \ldots, N \end{cases}$$

---

[1] http://paraphrase-ict.eu

It can be said that such transformation unnecessarily complicates a problem to be solved because it makes multi-objective optimization problem from a single-objective one. However solving multi-modal single-objective problem (finding all global and local optima) is also not an easy task—there were lots of niching techniques for evolutionary algorithms proposed and none of them is simple and perfect. Paradoxically converting such a problem into multi-objective one can lead to constructing simple and efficient techniques for evolutionary algorithms, especially that we utilize well established and very efficient evolutionary multi-objective algorithms.

3   Variants of Dispersion–Oriented Objective

During our experiments following variants of the second objective have been tested: fitness sharing, centroid method, weighted dispersion criteria and clustering.

Fitness sharing is classical niching technique consisting in (artificial) decreasing the value of fitness function according to the (higher) number of direct neighbors of given individual. Obviously there are some issues and decisions to be made (e.g. determining the radius of the neighborhood, determining the distance metrics and making a decision if it is calculated in the objective or in a decision variable space, determining how "density" is calculated and what is its influence on the fitness function value).

Discussion regarding above aspects can be found for instance in [4]. In its most popular version it is described according to the formula $f^{FS}(x_i) = \frac{f(x_i)}{m_i}$, where m_i is the sum of sharing function values defined as $m_i = \sum_{j=1}^{N} sh(d(x_i, x_j))$ and

$$f(x) = \begin{cases} 1 - \left(\frac{d(x_i, x_j)}{\sigma_{sh}}\right)^{\alpha} & , x > 0 \\ 0 & , x = 0 \end{cases} \tag{1}$$

where σ_{sh} is a radius of the niche and α parameter determines the shape of the fitness sharing function (usually equals 1).

Centroid based method is a simple in assumption and easy in implementation method for dispersing the population. The fitness value of the specimen is increased according to its (increasing) distance to the population center of gravity calculated as $\overrightarrow{x_c} = \frac{\sum_{i=0}^{N} \overrightarrow{x_i}}{N}$.

Weighted dispersion criteria technique tries to address one of the most significant problems observed in evolutionary multi-modal optimization: concentration of the whole population (which is usually intensifying over the course of time/iterations) around "strong" individuals, especially individuals located nearby the global optima. As a consequence of this phenomena the loss of the population diversity is observed and the chance for discovering (as many as possible) local optima is lower and lower. So the question is if it is not a good idea while introducing the second objective and converting multi-modal single objective problem into multi-objective optimization problem introducing the second criteria as a function which value would be inversely proportional to the value of the first criteria. In such a way strong individuals (from the first—crucial objective perspective) will not be able to "dominate" and to attract the rest of the population to their neighborhood. Simultaneously those individuals will not be lost by the population since they are "strong" as regards the first objective (so they won't be dominated in the Pareto domination relation). So assuming the first objective as a multi-modal function $F(x)$ with a global optima $M = F(x_{max})$ the second objective $S_{weighted}$ can be defined as $S_{weighted} = \alpha * (F(x_i)/F(x_{max}) * S(x_i)$, where: α is a weighting coefficient, $S(x_i)$ is the original value of dispersing function, $F(x_i)$ and $F(x_{max})$ are current and maximum values of the original (multi-modal) function (i.e. the first objective in fact).

One of interesting and (especially taking presented in section 4 selected preliminary results) promising technique is **clustering**. One of the fundamental question that can be considered is whether any of dispersion-oriented technique (i.e. the second objective after converting multi-modal into multi-objective optimization task) should be applied globally or "locally" i.e. within windows dividing the whole domain into sub-domain(s).When using clustering as a dispersion-oriented technique firstly all clusters are identified and then the fitness of individuals that are located outside or at the borders of the clusters is increased and the fitness of individuals that are located inside clusters is decreased proportionally to their distance from the center of the cluster.

Generally, research on clustering techniques and genetic algorithms was conducted in two areas: using evolutionary algorithms as a clustering technique [10,17,13,3] and using a clustering technique in evolutionary algorithm in order to find multiple solutions of multi-modal (but single criteria) problems [16,15]. We used clustering technique together with evolutionary algorithm as the mechanism of dispersing individuals over the solution space (as the second objective) during solving multi-modal problems converted into multi-objective ones.

For the purposes of making experiments unsupervised k-windows clustering algorithm has been implemented and used [18]. It is using a window(s)-based technique for determining possible clusters. Algorithm initializes a given number of 2-dimensional windows over the set of individuals. Then, it is moving on windows and enlarges them to cover existing clusters. Next, when all moving and enlarging operations have been performed—consolidation is being performed. All overlapping windows are either consolidated or skipped depending on the number of individuals belonging to the overlapped windows. In the consequence, the algorithm is able to reduce reasonably the (large) number of (possible) clusters identified originally at the beginning.

Algorithm consists of two crucial functions: movement and enlargement. The goal of movement function is setting the window as close to the center of the cluster as possible. Movement function is performed iteratively as long as the distance of the center of new window reaches the threshold value Θ_v (set experimentally).

The goal of enlargement operation is to improve the number of individuals belonging to the particular window. The window is being enlarged by Θ_e value in each dimension. Appropriate enlargement is the one assuring improving the number of individuals belonging to the given window with the number higher than Θ_c threshold value. If the number of new individuals belonging to the given window is smaller than Θ_e value then the last step of enlargement function is being withdrawn.

The crucial issue with using clusters is determining the number of clusters covering the whole population in the most appropriate way. In k-window algorithm it is determined by the algorithm itself during its work. To achieve that effectively, relatively the significant number of windows is needed at the beginning. After performing moving and enlarging operation pretty big number of windows are overlapping. So merging function is performed then. To do that—the number of "common" i.e. belonging to overlapped windows individuals is determined and then:

- if it is larger than the threshold value Θ_s windows are treated as parts of the same cluster and the smaller one is being removed;
- otherwise both windows are merged;
- if windows overlap but neither merging nor eliminating threshold is achieved, it is assumed that windows (their individuals) belong to different clusters.

Data: a, Θ_e,Θ_m,Θ_c,Θ_v,k
Result: clusters $c_{11}, c_{12}, \ldots$
begin
   $W \longleftarrow DetermineInitialWindows(k, a)$;
   for $w_j \in W$ **do**
      while *The center or the size change* **do**
         $movement(\Theta_v, w_j)$;
         $enlargement(\Theta_e, \Theta_c, \Theta_v, w_j)$;
      end
   end
   $merge(\Theta_m, \Theta_s, W)$
end

Algorithm 1. Unsupervised k-windows clustering algorithm

There is a pretty big number of parameters influencing significantly the behavior of the algorithm i.e.:

- the ratio between the initial number of windows and the number of individuals in population. It should be relatively high to spread windows among all clusters. During experiments it was set to 10%. (For the population with 1000 individuals it was set to 100 windows);
- the initial size of the window—it was determined experimentally;
- the minimum distance between windows at the beginning. It is important parameter to avoid overlapping windows during initialization;

Data: k,a
Result: a set W of k d − ranges
begin
    initialize k d-ranges windows $w_{m1}, \ldots, w_{mk}$ each of size a;
    select k random points from the dataset and center the d-ranges at these
    points
end

Algorithm 2. DetermineInitialWindows

Data: a, Θ_v,a d-range w
begin
    while *The distance between m and the previous center of w is greater or*
    equal to Θ_v **do**
        find the patterns that lie within the d-range w ;
        calculate the mean m of these patterns ;
        set the center of w equal to m ;
    end
end

Algorithm 3. Operation *movement*

Data: Θ_e,Θ_v,Θ_c,a, d-range w
begin
    while *The increase in number of patterns is* $\geq \Theta_c\%$ *across every* d_i **do**
        for *Each coordinate* d_i **do**
            while *The increase in number of patterns across* d_i *is* $\geq \Theta_c\%$ **do**
                enlarge w across d_i
                $movement(\Theta_v, w)$
            end
        end
    end
end

Algorithm 4. Operation *enlargement*

- the movement threshold (Θ_v)—it defines the minimum distance between the new and the current gravity center of the window during its movement. When this value is not achieved movement operation is finished;
- the enlargement increase ratio (Θ_e)—it is a percentage ratio between the old and the new window size in consecutive steps of enlargement operation. During experiments it was set to 10% for each dimension respectively.
- enlargement stop ratio threshold (Θ_c)—the factor defining the minimum increase of the number of new individuals in the window when enlargement operation is performed. During experiments presented in this paper it was defined as $enlargement\_stop\_threshold = \frac{enlargement\_increase\_ratio}{init\_window\_population\_ratio}$
- merge ratio (Θ_s) is the minimum number of common individuals belonging to two windows to merge them. During experiments it was set to 80%;

Data: Θ_m, Θ_s, a set W of $d - ranges$
begin
    for *Each not marked $d - range$ $w_j \in W$* **do**
        mark w_j with label w_j ;
        if $\exists\ w_i \neq w_j \in W$ *that overlaps with* w_j **then**
            compute the number of points n that lie in the common part of windows ;
            if $n/ \mid w_i \mid \geq \Theta_s$ *and* $\mid w_i \mid < \mid w_j \mid$ **then**
                | **disregard** w_j
            end
            if $0.5(n/ \mid w_j \mid + n/ \mid w_i \mid) \geq \Theta_m$ **then**
                | **mark** all w_j labeled d-ranges in W with label w_j
            end
        end
    end
end

Algorithm 5. Operation *merging*

- merge disregard ratio (Θ_m) is the minimum ratio of common individuals belonging to two windows to remove one of them (the smaller one). During experiments it was set to 90%.

4 Experimental Results

As a multi-modal benchmarks Michalewicz's, Rastrigin's and Schwefel's functions have been used. As a second (dispersion related) objective: fitness sharing, centroids and weighted centroids methods have been applied. As experimental tool jEMO framework has been used[2]. Because of the space limitations only a few experimental results are here presented.

First results obtained without clustering mechanism are presented. In table 1 there are listed the most important parameters of this experiment. As one may see in figure 2 transforming classical multi-modal optimization problem into multi-objective one and applying NSGA-II algorithm for solving such modified problem with centroids as a dispersion-oriented second objective allows for obtaining pretty promising results. They differ of course depending on particular parameters used but generally speaking results are promising.

For comparison in table 2 there are listed parameters of sample experiment where dispersion was applied "locally" i.e. within clusters discovered by described in section 3 k-window clustering algorithm. This time experiment was performed with the use of Michalewicz benchmark and typical obtained results are presented in figure 1. As one may see obtained results are also promising and encouraging for further research.

---

[2] code.google.com/p/jemo/

Table 1. Selected parameters taken in experiment 1

Parameter	Value
Original function	Rastrigin
Distribution function	Centroid
Optimization algorithm	NSGAII
Population size	1000
Number of generations	40
Mutation	Radial mutation
Mutation probability	0.5
Strong mutation probability	0.15
Domain control type	Move to domain border
Specimen repairing	None
Recombination	Radial crossover
Recombination probability	0.5
Domain control type	Move to border
Specimen repairing	None
Selection	Classical tournament
Tournament size ratio	80%
Tournament probability	0.8
Clustering	none

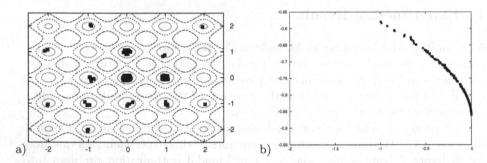

Fig. 1. Results obtained in experiment 1. Found solutions (a) and Pareto frontier (b).

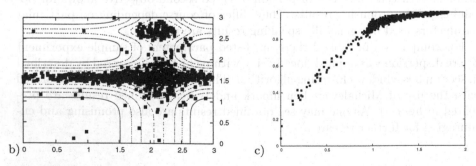

Fig. 2. Results obtained in experiment 2. Found solutions of: (a) multi-modal problem and (b) multi-objective problem

Table 2. Selected parameters taken in experiment 2

Parameter	Value
Original function	Michalewicz
Distribution function	Centroid
Optimization algorithm	NSGAII
Population size	1000
Number of generations	40
Mutation	Radial mutation
Mutation probability	0.5
Strong mutation probability	0.15
Domain control type	Move to domain border
Specimen repairing	None
Recombination	Radial crossover
Recombination probability	0.5
Domain control type	Move to border
Specimen repairing	None
Selection	Classical tournament
Tournament size ratio	80%
Tournament probability	0.8
Clustering	yes
Initial window's size	[0.4][0.4]
Initial number of windows	500
Movement threshold (Θ_v)	0.1
Enlargement increase step	0.08
Enlargement stop ratio threshold (Θ_c)	0.2
Merge ratio (Θ_S)	0.9
Merge disregard ratio (Θ_m)	1

5   Summary and Conclusions

When evolutionary algorithms for solving multi-modal optimization problems
are applied the crucial issue to be solved is maintaining population diversity
to avoid drifting and focusing individuals around single global optima. A lot of
techniques have been proposed and used here so far.

Simultaneously, for the last twenty years a lot of effort has been made in the
area of evolutionary algorithms for multi-objective optimization. As the result
at least several highly efficient algorithms have been proposed such as NSGAII
or SPEA2. Obviously, also in this case maintaining of population diversity is
crucial but this time taking the specificity of optimization in the Pareto sense
there are built-in mechanisms to solve this issue effectively.

If so, the idea arises of applying state-of-the-art evolutionary multi-objective
optimization algorithms for solving not original multi-modal (but single-objective)
optimization task but its transformed into multi-objective problem form by introducing additional dispersion-oriented criteria as it is discussed in section 2.

One of important issues is the definition of the dispersion-oriented criteria. In the course of this paper some of them, i.e. classical fitness sharing, centroids, weighted centroids have been discussed.

On the basis of some observations taken during experiments the idea of applying the second objective not globally but locally within some areas of concentration of individuals arose. To put this idea into practice k-window clustering algorithm has been implemented and applied and then dispersion-oriented mechanisms have been applied not globally but within formed windows.

Because of the space limitations it is impossible to present comprehensive review of obtained results especially that there are many parameters influencing the behavior and effectiveness of the proposed approach. Nevertheless it can be said for sure that preliminary results are promising and encourage for further research in this area.

Acknowledgments. The research presented in the paper was partially supported by the European Commission FP7 through the project *ParaPhrase: Parallel Patterns for Adaptive Heterogeneous Multicore Systems*, under contract no.: 288570 (http://paraphrase-ict.eu) and by Polish Ministry of Science and Higher Education under AGH University of Science and Technology Grant No. 11.11.230.015 (statutory project).

References

1. Abraham, A., Jain, L.C., Goldberg, R.: Evolutionary Multiobjective Optimization Theoretical Advances and Applications. Springer (2005)
2. Byrski, A., Dreżewski, R., Siwik, L., Kisiel-Dorohinicki, M.: Evolutionary multi-agent systems. The Knowledge Engineering Review (to be published, 2014)
3. Chakrabarti, D., Kumar, R., Tomkins, A.: Evolutionary clustering. In: Proceedings of the 12th ACM SIGKDD International Conference on Knowledge Discovery and Data Mining. ACM, New York (2006)
4. Deb, K.: Multi-Objective Optimization using Evolutionary Algorithms. John Wiley & Sons (2008)
5. Dreżewski, R., Obrocki, K., Siwik, L.: Agent-based co-operative co-evolutionary algorithms for multi-objective portfolio optimization. In: Brabazon, A., O'Neill, M., Maringer, D.G. (eds.) Natural Computing in Computational Finance. SCI, vol. 293, pp. 63–84. Springer, Heidelberg (2010)
6. Dreżewski, R., Sepielak, J.: Evolutionary system for generating investment strategies. In: Giacobini, M., et al. (eds.) EvoWorkshops 2008. LNCS, vol. 4974, pp. 83–92. Springer, Heidelberg (2008)
7. Dreżewski, R., Siwik, L.: Techniques for maintaining population diversity in classical and agent-based multi-objective evolutionary algorithms. In: Shi, Y., van Albada, G.D., Dongarra, J., Sloot, P.M.A. (eds.) ICCS 2007, Part II. LNCS, vol. 4488, pp. 904–911. Springer, Heidelberg (2007)
8. Dreżewski, R., Siwik, L.: Agent-based co-operative co-evolutionary algorithm for multi-objective optimization. In: Rutkowski, L., Tadeusiewicz, R., Zadeh, L.A., Zurada, J.M. (eds.) ICAISC 2008. LNCS (LNAI), vol. 5097, pp. 388–397. Springer, Heidelberg (2008)

9. Dreżewski, R., Siwik, L.: Co-evolutionary multi-agent system for portfolio optimization. In: Brabazon, A., O'Neill, M. (eds.) Natural Computing in Computational Finance. SCI, vol. 100, pp. 271–299. Springer, Heidelberg (2008)

10. Hruschka, E.R., Campello, R.J.G.B., Freitas, A.A., de Carvalho, A.C.P.L.F.: A survey of evolutionary algorithms for clustering. IEEE Transactions on Systems, Man, and Cybernetics, Part C, 39(2) (2009)

11. Marler, R., Arora, J.: Survey of multi-objective optimization methods for engineering. Structural and Multidisciplinary Optimization 26(6) (2004)

12. Preuss, M., Rudolph, G., Tumakaka, F.: Solving multimodal problems via multiobjective techniques with application to phase equilibrium detection. In: IEEE Congress on Evolutionary Computation. IEEE (2007)

13. Sarafis, I.A., Trinder, P.W., Zalzala, A.: Towards effective subspace clustering with an evolutionary algorithm. In: Sarker, R., et al. (eds.) Proceedings of the 2003 Congress on Evolutionary Computation, vol. 2. IEEE Press (2003)

14. Srinivas, N., Deb, K.: Multiobjective optimization using nondominated sorting in genetic algorithms. Evolutionary Computation 2(3), 221–248 (1994)

15. Streichert, F., Stein, G., Ulmer, H., Zell, A.: A clustering based niching method for evolutionary algorithms. In: Cantú-Paz, E., et al. (eds.) GECCO 2003. LNCS, vol. 2723, pp. 644–645. Springer, Heidelberg (2003)

16. Tasoulis, D.K., Plagianakos, V.P., Vrahatis, M.N.: Clustering in evolutionary algorithms to efficiently compute simultaneously local and global minima. In: Congress on Evolutionary Computation. IEEE (2005)

17. Tasoulis, D.K., Vrahatis, M.N.: The new window density function for efficient evolutionary unsupervised clustering. In: Congress on Evolutionary Computation. IEEE (2005)

18. Vrahatis, M.N., Boutsinas, B., Alevizos, P., Pavlides, G.: The new k-windows algorithm for improving the k-means clustering algorithm. J. Complex. 18(1) (March 2002)

19. Zitzler, E.: Evolutionary algorithms for multiobjective optimization: methods and applications. PhD thesis, Swiss Federal Institute of Technology, Zurich (1999)

20. Zitzler, E.: Evolutionary algorithms, multiobjective optimization, and applications (September 2003)

Aspects of the Selection
of the Structure and Parameters of Controllers
Using Selected Population Based Algorithms

Jacek Szczypta[1], Krystian Łapa[1], and Zhifei Shao[2]

[1] Częstochowa University of Technology,
Institute of Computational Intelligence, Poland
{jacek.szczypta,krystian.lapa}@iisi.pcz.pl
[2] Nanyang Technological University,
School of Electrical & Electronic Engineering, Singapore
zshao1@ntu.edu.sg

Abstract. In this paper we propose a new approach for selection of the structure and parameters of the control system. Proposed approach is based on the selected population-based algorithms. In this approach we considered a combination of the genetic algorithm (it is used for selection of structure of the control system) fused with one of the following algorithms: evolutionary algorithm, firefly algorithm, gravitational search algorithm, bat algorithm and imperialist competitive algorithm (they are all used for the selection of parameters of the control system). In experimental simulations a typical problem of the control process was used.

1 Introduction

Automatic control is an important issue from scientific and practical point of view (see e.g. [74], [75]). It has a significant impact on the quality and efficiency of industrial processes and human safety. Key issue in process control domain is selection of controller structure. In practice, selection of controller structure is performed by the trial and error method. Moreover, controller structure selection is a process which requires from the designer specific knowledge and experience. In most cases selection of the controller structure is performed from a set of typical structures, then controller parameters are tuned. The selection mentioned earlier is often very time-consuming. In the literature numerous attempts of automatization of control system design are described. In automatization capabilities of computational intelligence are used, such as: neural networks (see e.g. [7]-[9], [28], [30], [33]-[36], [48], [51], [72]), fuzzy system (see e.g. [2]-[6], [16]-[19], [23], [32], [39], [47], [70], [80]-[84]), neuro-fuzzy systems (see e.g. [10]-[14], [31], [43], [44], [46], [53]-[55], [60]-[62], [66]-[69], [71]), evolutionary algorithms (see e.g. [40], [41], [52]), decision trees (see e.g. [29], [49]-[50], [63]-[65]) etc.

In our previous paper we proposed a basic version of the evolutionary algorithm for automatic selection of structure and parameters of control system

L. Rutkowski et al. (Eds.): ICAISC 2014, Part I, LNAI 8467, pp. 440–454, 2014.
© Springer International Publishing Switzerland 2014

consisting simple correction terms (see e.g. [73]). The results obtained in previous examination encouraged us to elaborate new methods using capabilities of population-based algorithms. In this paper four new methods are proposed. Every method was created from combination of genetic algorithm with one of the following algorithm: firefly algorithm (see e.g. [15], [27], [78]), gravitational search algorithm (see e.g. [26], [38], [56], bat algorithm (see e.g. [76], [77], [78]) and imperialist competitive algorithm (see e.g. [1], [42], [79]). Mentioned four algorithms are used for selection of control system parameters, while genetic algorithm is used for the selection of the control system structure. It is important to mention that evolution of parameters and structure is performed concurrently. It is also important that proposed algorithms are dedicated to work with automatic control systems whose structure is built from correction terms. Moreover, the algorithms are based on customizable fitness function evaluating individuals from the population and they cooperate with the models of controller object, which are precise enough. Alternative approaches to nonlinear modelling can be found in [25], [59], [68].

This paper is organised into four sections. Section 2 presents a detailed description of the proposed approach to designing controllers. In Section 3 simulation results are presented. Conclusions are drawn in Section 4.

2   Proposed Approach to Designing Controllers

Key remarks regarding approaches presented in the paper can be stated as follows: **(a)** Fig. 1 presents the controller structure which is initial point for execution of evolutionary algorithm proposed by authors. Controller structure is a result of generalization of typical controllers used in practice: PID controller, cascaded PID controller with feed-forward signals and state-feedback controller. It is important to remark that in generalization any controller can be taken into consideration. **(b)** In Fig. 1 the connections that can be generated during evolution were marked with dashed line. This remark applies to control system structure (see Fig. 1.a) and its basic block (CB). Basic block (CB) consists of proportional term (P), integral term (I) and derivative term (D) (see Fig. 1.b). Signal fb_n, $n=1, \ldots, N$, denotes feedback signal, signal ff_m, $m = 1, \ldots, M$, denotes feedforward signal. **(c)** Selection of the control system structure is performed using genetic algorithm. Selection of the control system parameters is performed using one of the chosen population-based algorithm. Selection of the control system structure and parameters is performed concurrently during evolution process. The evolution is performed on the basis of the knowledge about controlled object and properly defined fitness function. It is important that proposed approach eliminates the need of trial and error selection of the control system. Usage of controlled object model, despite the advantage like elimination of risk of damage of the controlled object, has its disadvantages. Primary disadvantage is need of knowledge about controlled object. Models of the controlled object have to be not only precise enough and have the knowledge about typical operational conditions of the controlled object (representing engine run under

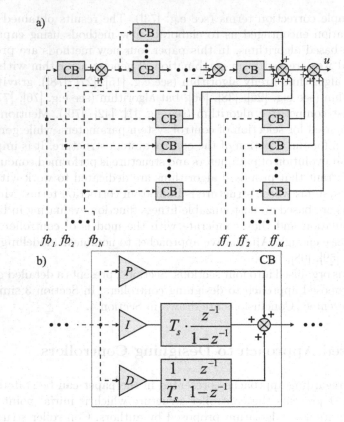

Fig. 1. Initial discrete controller structure (connections that can be obtained in evolution process are marked with continuous line): a) considered, generalized control system, b) CB definition idea (T_s stands for discretization constant in time domain)

load or idle state), but it also have to take into account an unusual operating conditions (e.g., engine short circuit, engine state as a result of surge or overload in supply circuit). It is important that when it is a need to design the control system using classic methods (basing on the designer experience), only typical operating conditions are taken into consideration. Moreover, development of precise model of the controlled object is not currently a big problem (see e.g. [37], [57]).

2.1 Coding of the Structure and Parameters

In proposed method full controller (with its structure and parameters) is encoded in a single chromosome $\mathbf{X}_{ch}$. The chromosome $\mathbf{X}_{ch}$ (further called individual) is described as follows:

$$\mathbf{X}_{ch} = \left\{ \mathbf{X}_{ch}^{\text{par}}, \mathbf{X}_{ch}^{\text{red}} \right\}, \tag{1}$$

where $\mathbf{X}_{ch}^{\mathrm{par}}$ is a chromosome coding correction term parameters, $\mathbf{X}_{ch}^{\mathrm{red}}$ is a chromosome coding connection in general (proposed) structure of the control system presented in Fig. 1. The chromosome $\mathbf{X}_{ch}^{\mathrm{par}}$ is described as follows:

$$\mathbf{X}_{ch}^{\mathrm{par}} = (P_1, I_1, D_1, P_2, I_2, D_2, \ldots) = \left(X_{ch,1}^{\mathrm{par}}, X_{ch,2}^{\mathrm{par}}, \ldots, X_{ch,L}^{\mathrm{par}} \right), \qquad (2)$$

where P_1, I_1, D_1, P_2, I_2, D_2, $\ldots$, denote control system parameters values, $ch = 1, .., Ch$, denotes index of the chromosome in the population, Ch denotes a number of chromosomes in the population, L denotes length of the chromosome $\mathbf{X}_{ch}^{\mathrm{par}}$. The chromosome $\mathbf{X}_{ch}^{\mathrm{red}}$ is described as follows:

$$\mathbf{X}_{ch}^{\mathrm{red}} = \left(X_{ch,1}^{\mathrm{red}}, X_{ch,2}^{\mathrm{red}}, \ldots, X_{ch,L}^{\mathrm{red}} \right), \qquad (3)$$

where every gene $X_{ch,g}^{\mathrm{red}} \in \{0,1\}$, $ch = 1, .., Ch$, $g = 1, .., L$, decides if relevant part of the control system occurs in control process (relevant gene $X_{ch,g}^{\mathrm{red}} = 1$).

2.2 Evolution Process

The proposed approach for selection of the system structure and system parameters is based on fusion between genetic algorithm and one of the specified population-based algorithms. It determines evolution process, in which the following (typical) steps can be shown: initialization of the population, evaluation of the population, checking the stop criterion and presentation of the best individual, selection of the individuals for the use of the specified operators (to assure exploration and exploitation of universe of discourse), population repair, and selection of the individuals for new population (see e.g. [58]).

Genetic algorithm is a well-known method (see e.g. [22], [43], [45], [58]). In our simulations it processes solely chromosomes (3) for selection of the control system structure. On the other hand, population-based algorithms fused with genetic algorithm process exclusively the parameters of the control system encoded in the chromosome (2). The characteristics of the population-based algorithms considered in our work can be described as follows: (a) Firefly algorithm was introduced in 2008 ([78]). In this algorithm every firefly is assumed as unisexual. As a result, every firefly attracts one another. Firefly attractiveness is proportional to its brightness (which depends on fitness function value of individual) and inversely proportional to distance to considered firefly. Dimmer firefly moves to brighter and more attractive one (search space exploitation), the most attractive firefly moves randomly (search space exploration). Main steps of the algorithm are: (1) calculate attractiveness of every firefly on the basis of its fitness value (2) move every firefly to a more attractive one or randomly (3) evaluate fitness of every firefly. Specific parameter for this algorithm is light absorption coefficient. More details for this algorithm can be found in [15], [27], [78]. (b) Gravitational search algorithm was introduced in 2009 ([56]). This algorithm uses assumptions of law of gravity, in which each particle attracts every other particle and the gravitational force between two particles is directly proportional to the product of their masses and inversely proportional to the distance between them. A heavy mass particle has a large effective attraction radius and hence a great intensity of the attraction. Moreover, algorithm is using assumptions of law of motion, in which the current velocity of any mass is equal to the sum of the fraction of its previous velocity and the variation in the velocity. Variation in the velocity or acceleration of any mass is equal to the force acted on the system divided by mass of inertia. Therefore, agents with a higher performance have a greater gravitational mass. The inertia mass is against the motion and make the mass movement slow. Hence, agents with heavy inertia mass move slowly and search the space more locally. In the algorithm, exploration of the search space passes gradually into exploration along with decreasing of gravitational constant. Main steps of the algorithm are: (1) calculation of agent masses (2) calculation of agent acceleration and velocity (3) updating agent positions (4) evaluate fitness of every agent. Specific parameters for this algorithm are: initial value of gravitational constant and gravity decreasing exponential constant. More details can be found in [26], [38], [56]. (c) The bat algorithm was introduced in 2010 ([78]). This algorithm is based on the echolocation behaviour of microbats with varying pulse rates of emission and loudness with purpose to detect and avoid obstacles. In particular in this algorithm the bats can move randomly (exploitation of universe of discourse) and into direction of the best from the bats (based on fitness function value) (exploration of universe of discourse). Consequently, the movement of the best bat determines moves of the whole population. There is the principle for each bat in the population that if it finds a better solution than the solution found in previous steps, its frequency, loudness and pulse emission rate are updated. It allows to control the dynamic behaviour of the swarm of bats, and additionally the balance between exploration and exploitation of the population. Characteristic steps of the algorithm: (1) moving into direction of the best bat, (2) searching area around the best bat, (3) random walk. Characteristic parameters of the algorithm: population size, wavelength f_{min}, wavelength f_{max}, pulse rate, loudness. More details about the bat algorithm can be found in e.g., [76], [77], [78]. (d) Imperialist competitive algorithm was introduced in 2007 ([1]). It was inspired by human social evolution instead of natural genetic evolution. In the initialization process a specified amount of imperialists (best chromosomes from the initial population) is used to create empires (every chromosome is used to create one empire). For every empire a calculated amount of colonies is assigned randomly among rest of the initial population. Main part of the algorithm is to assimilate colonies by imperialist of their empires (moving colonies closer to the imperialist) (exploitation of the space of considerations and its exploration due to a random element in the determination of movement direction). If value of the fitness function of colonies is better than value of the fitness function of imperialist in their imperium - a revolution process takes places (colony became a new imperialist). The second part of the algorithm is the competition of the empires. In each step all empires (based on their power) can take over the weakest colony of the weakest imperium. The empire which lost all its colonies is eliminated from further competition. Characteristic steps of the algorithm: (1) assimilation, (2) revolution, (3) imperialist competition.

Characteristic parameters of the algorithm: number of empires, maximum step of moving into imperialist direction, maximum angle for randomize moving into imperialist direction, weight of colonies power. More details about the imperialist competitive algorithm can be found in e.g., [1], [42], [79].

2.3   Individuals Evaluation

Chromosome evaluation function was set to minimize: RMSE error, oscillations of the controller output signal, controller complexity and overshoot of the control signal. High number of oscillations of the controller output signal is a negative phenomenon, because it tends to excessive use of mechanical control parts and may cause often huge changes of the controller output signal value. This is very important issue, because the overshoot of the control signal is not acceptable in many industrial applications. The chromosome evaluation function is described as follows:

$$ff(\mathbf{X}_{ch}) = \frac{1}{RMSE_{ch} + c_{ch} \cdot w_c + os_{ch} \cdot w_o s + ov_{ch} \cdot w_{ov}}, \tag{4}$$

where $c_{ch} > 0$ denotes the complexity of the controller structure and it is calculated by the formula:

$$c_{ch} = \sum_{g=1}^{L} \mathbf{X}_{ch,g}^{red}, \tag{5}$$

$w_c \in [0, 1]$ denotes a weight factor for the complexity of the controller structure, $os_{ch} \geq 0$ denotes oscillation count of controller output signal (in simulations its value is calculated automatically), $w_o s \in [0, 1]$ denotes a weight for the oscillations factor, $ov_{ch} \geq 0$ denotes value of the greatest overshoot of the controlled s^1 signal and finally $w_{ov} \in [0, 1]$ denotes a weight for the overshoot factor. RMSE error function of the chromosome ch is described by the following formula:

$$RMSE_{ch} = \sqrt{\frac{1}{N} \cdot \sum_{i=1}^{N} \varepsilon_{ch,i}{}^2} = \sqrt{\frac{1}{N} \cdot \sum_{i=1}^{N} \left(s_{ch,i}^* - s_{ch,i}^1\right)^2}, \tag{6}$$

where $i = 1, \ldots, N$, denotes sample index, N denotes the number of samples, $\varepsilon_{ch,i}$ denotes controller tracking error for the sample i, $s_{ch,i}^*$ denotes the value of the reference signal of the controlled value for the sample i, $s_{ch,i}^1$ denotes its current value for the sample i. In our method we maximize the function described by formula (4).

3   Simulations Results

In our simulations a problem of designing controller structure and parameter tuning for double spring-mass-damp object was considered (see Fig. 2). More detail about this model can be found in our previous paper [73]).

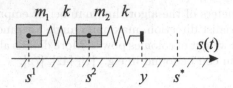

Fig. 2. Simulated spring-mass-damp object

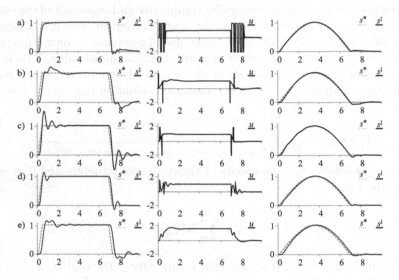

Fig. 3. Signal values s^1, s^* and output signal of the controller y in case of fusion between genetic algorithm with: a) evolutionary algorithm (GA+EA), b) firefly algorithm (GA+FA), c) gravitational search algorithm (GA+GA), d) bat algorithm (GA+BA), e) imperialist competitive algorithm (GA+IA)

Remarks about considering model can be summarized as follows: **(a)** Object parameters values were set as follows: spring constant k was set to 10 N/m, coefficient of friction $\mu = 0.5$, masses $m_1 = m_2 = 0.2$ kg. Initial values of: s^1, v^1, s^2 i v^2 were set to zero. **(b)** Simulation length was set to 10 s, a shape of the reference signal s^* (trapezoid) is presented in Fig. 3, a shape of test signal s^* (sinuous) is presented in Fig. 3. **(c)** Search range for genes coding controller parameter were set as follows: $P = [0,20]$, $I = [0,50]$, $D = [0,5]$. **(d)** Output signal of the controller was limited to the range $y \in (-2,+2)$. **(e)** Quantization resolution for the output signal y of the controller as well as for the position sensor for s^1 and s^2 was set to 10 bit. **(f)** Time step in the simulation was equal to $T = 0.1$ ms, while interval between subsequent controller activations were set to twenty simulation steps.

For simulations an authorial environment (in C# language) was used. Parameters of the algorithms for the calculations were determined as follows: **(a)** Evolutionary algorithm: the number of chromosomes in the population was set to

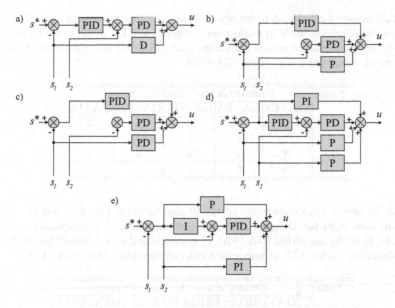

Fig. 4. Structure of the controller obtained in the evolution process in case of fusion between genetic algorithm with: a) evolutionary algorithm (GA+EA), b) firefly algorithm (GA+FA), c) gravitational search algorithm (GA+GA), d) bat algorithm (GA+BA), e) imperialist competitive algorithm (GA+IA)

100, the algorithm performs 10 000 steps (generations), the crossover probability was set as $p_c = 0.8$, the mutation probability was set as $p_m = 0.3$, the mutation intensity was set as $\sigma = 0.3$. **(b)** Firefly algorithm: the number of individuals in the population was set to 100, light absorption coefficient was set to 10. **(c)** Gravitational search algorithm: initial value of the gravitation constant was set to 100, exponential constant of the decreasing gravitation constant was set to 20. **(d)** Bat algorithm: wavelength f_{min} was set to 0, f_{max} was set to 20, pulse rate was set to 0.9 and loudness was set to 0.9. **(e)** Imperialist competitive algorithm: maximum step d for assimilation was set to 2, maxmin angle for random value for assimilation was set to 0.1 rad, weight of the colony for the empires competition was set to 0.2.

Observations obtained from results of the simulations can be summarized as follows: **(a)** Signal values s^1, s^* and output signal of the control y are highly acceptable (see Fig. 3). The smallest oscillations of the signals were obtained by genetic-imperialist and genetic-firefly algorithms (see Fig. 3). The largest oscillations were obtained by the genetic-gravitational algorithm. **(b)** The simplest structure of the system was achieved with the use of the genetic-evolutionary (see e.g. [20], [21], [22], [24]) and genetic-firefly algorithm (see Fig. 4). It is worth to mention that, in every case presented in Fig. 4, the system structure is quite simple (see Table 1), and it does not affect requirements of the fitness function (4) (see Table 2). Obtaining a similarly simple structures using classic algorithms of

Table 1. Number of correction terms obtained in evolution process in case of fusion between genetic algorithm with: a) evolutionary algorithm (GA+EA), b) firefly algorithm (GA+FA), c) gravitational search algorithm (GA+GA), d) bat algorithm (GA+BA), e) imperialist competitive algorithm (GA+IA)

Name	Number of the correction terms				
	GA+ES	GA+FA	GA+GA	GA+BA	GA+IA
P	2	3	3	5	3
I	1	1	1	2	3
D	3	2	3	2	1
All	6	6	7	9	7

Table 2. Values of the components of the fitness function (4) obtained in evolution process in case of fusion between genetic algorithm with: a) evolutionary algorithm (GA+EA), b) firefly algorithm (GA+FA), c) gravitational search algorithm (GA+GA), d) bat algorithm (GA+BA), e) imperialist competitive algorithm (GA+IA)

Name	Parameters of the control systems				
	GA+ES	GA+FA	GA+GA	GA+BA	GA+IA
$RMSE$	0.0625	0.1276	0.1790	0.0901	0.1633
$c_{ch} \cdot w_c$	0.0060	0.000	0.0070	0.0066	0.0047
$z_{ch} \cdot w_z$	0.0350	0.0170	0.0170	0.0299	0.0138
$ov_{ch} \cdot w_{ov}$	0.0001	0.0002	0.0005	0.0014	0.0001
ff	9.6525	6.6312	4.914	7.8125	5.4975

the selection of control systems would be difficult and time consuming. **(c)** The structures and parameters of the control system obtained in the learning process, which was performed on the trapezoid shape of the signal (see Fig. 4), were tested additionally on the sinusoidal shape of the signal (see Fig. 4) and resulted with good performance (generalization).

4   Conclusions

In our work a new approach for selection of the structure and the parameters of the control system was presented. This approach implements a model and allows to choose safe regulation model parameters without need to experiment on real objects. Our method uses a fusion between genetic algorithm (for selection the structure of the control system) and possibilities of specified algorithms: evolutionary algorithm (for comparison), firefly algorithm, gravitational search algorithm, bat algorithm, imperialist competitive algorithm (for selection the parameters of the control system). Obtained (according to fitness function components) simulation results allowed achieve non-complex control systems, characterized by good accuracy, with acceptable infinitesimal oscillations.

Acknowledgement. The project was financed by the National Science Centre (Poland) on the basis of the decision number DEC-2012/05/B/ST7/02138.

References

1. Atashpaz-Gargari, E., Lucas, C.: Imperialist Competitive Algorithm: An algorithm for optimization inspired by imperialistic competition. In: IEEE Congress on Evolutionary Computation, vol. 7, pp. 4661–4666 (2007)
2. Bartczuk, Ł., Dziwiński, P., Starczewski, J.T.: A new method for dealing with unbalanced linguistic term set. In: Rutkowski, L., Korytkowski, M., Scherer, R., Tadeusiewicz, R., Zadeh, L.A., Zurada, J.M. (eds.) ICAISC 2012, Part I. LNCS, vol. 7267, pp. 207–212. Springer, Heidelberg (2012)
3. Bartczuk, Ł., Dziwiński, P., Starczewski, J.T.: New Method for Generation Type-2 Fuzzy Partition for FDT. In: Rutkowski, L., Scherer, R., Tadeusiewicz, R., Zadeh, L.A., Zurada, J.M. (eds.) ICAISC 2010, Part I. LNCS (LNAI), vol. 6113, pp. 275–280. Springer, Heidelberg (2010)
4. Bartczuk, Ł., Przybył, A., Dziwiński, P.: Hybrid state variables - fuzzy logic modelling of nonlinear objects. In: Rutkowski, L., Korytkowski, M., Scherer, R., Tadeusiewicz, R., Zadeh, L.A., Zurada, J.M. (eds.) ICAISC 2013, Part I. LNCS (LNAI), vol. 7894, pp. 227–234. Springer, Heidelberg (2013)
5. Bartczuk, Ł., Rutkowska, D.: A New Version of the Fuzzy-ID3 Algorithm. In: Rutkowski, L., Tadeusiewicz, R., Zadeh, L.A., Żurada, J.M. (eds.) ICAISC 2006. LNCS (LNAI), vol. 4029, pp. 1060–1070. Springer, Heidelberg (2006)
6. Bartczuk, Ł., Rutkowska, D.: Medical Diagnosis with Type-2 Fuzzy Decision Trees. In: Kącki, E., Rudnicki, M., Stempczyńska, J. (eds.) Computers in Medical Activity. AISC, vol. 65, pp. 11–21. Springer, Heidelberg (2009)
7. Bilski, J., Rutkowski, L.: Numerically Robust Learning Algorithms for Feed Forward Neural Networks. In: Advances in Soft Computing - Neural Networks and Soft Computing, pp. 149–154. Physica-Verlag, A Springer-Verlag Company (2003)
8. Bilski, J., Smoląg, J.: Parallel Approach to Learning of the Recurrent Jordan Neural Network. In: Rutkowski, L., Korytkowski, M., Scherer, R., Tadeusiewicz, R., Zadeh, L.A., Zurada, J.M. (eds.) ICAISC 2013, Part I. LNCS (LNAI), vol. 7894, pp. 32–40. Springer, Heidelberg (2013)
9. Bilski, J., Smoląg, J.: Parallel Realisation of the Recurrent Multi Layer Perceptron Learning. In: Rutkowski, L., Korytkowski, M., Scherer, R., Tadeusiewicz, R., Zadeh, L.A., Zurada, J.M. (eds.) ICAISC 2012, Part I. LNCS, vol. 7267, pp. 12–20. Springer, Heidelberg (2012)
10. Cpalka, K.: A Method for Designing Flexible Neuro-fuzzy Systems. In: Rutkowski, L., Tadeusiewicz, R., Zadeh, L.A., Żurada, J.M. (eds.) ICAISC 2006. LNCS (LNAI), vol. 4029, pp. 212–219. Springer, Heidelberg (2006)
11. Cpałka, K.: On evolutionary designing and learning of flexible neuro-fuzzy structures for nonlinear classification. Nonlinear Analysis Series A: Theory, Methods and Applications 71, 1659–1672 (2009)
12. Cpałka, K., Rutkowski, L.: A New Method for Designing and Reduction of Neurofuzzy Systems. In: Proceedings of the 2006 IEEE International Conference on Fuzzy Systems (IEEE World Congress on Computational Intelligence, WCCI 2006), Vancouver, BC, Canada, pp. 8510–8516 (2006)
13. Cpałka, K., Rutkowski, L.: Flexible Takagi-Sugeno Fuzzy Systems. In: Proceedings of the International Joint Conference on Neural Networks 2005, Montreal, Montreal, pp. 1764–1769 (2005)

14. Cpałka, K., Rutkowski, L.: Flexible Takagi Sugeno Neuro-fuzzy Structures for Non-linear Approximation. WSEAS Transactions on Systems 4(9), 1450–1458 (2005)
15. Dos Santos Coelho, L., De Andrade Bernert, D.L., Mariani, V.C.: A chaotic firefly algorithm applied to reliability-redundancy optimization. In: 2011 IEEE Congress on Evolutionary Computation (CEC), pp. 517–521 (2011)
16. Dziwiński, P., Bartczuk, Ł., Starczewski, J.T.: Fully controllable ant colony system for text data clustering. In: Rutkowski, L., Korytkowski, M., Scherer, R., Tadeusiewicz, R., Zadeh, L.A., Zurada, J.M. (eds.) SIDE 2012 and EC 2012. LNCS, vol. 7269, pp. 199–205. Springer, Heidelberg (2012)
17. Dziwiński, P., Rutkowska, D.: Algorithm for generating fuzzy rules for WWW document classification. In: Rutkowski, L., Tadeusiewicz, R., Zadeh, L.A., Żurada, J.M. (eds.) ICAISC 2006. LNCS (LNAI), vol. 4029, pp. 1111–1119. Springer, Heidelberg (2006)
18. Dziwiński, P., Rutkowska, D.: Ant Focused Crawling Algorithm. In: Rutkowski, L., Tadeusiewicz, R., Zadeh, L.A., Zurada, J.M. (eds.) ICAISC 2008. LNCS (LNAI), vol. 5097, pp. 1018–1028. Springer, Heidelberg (2008)
19. Dziwiński, P., Starczewski, J.T., Bartczuk, Ł.: New linguistic hedges in construction of interval type-2 fls. In: Rutkowski, L., Scherer, R., Tadeusiewicz, R., Zadeh, L.A., Zurada, J.M. (eds.) ICAISC 2010, Part II. LNCS (LNAI), vol. 6114, pp. 445–450. Springer, Heidelberg (2010)
20. El-Abd, M.: On the hybridization on the artificial bee colony and particle swarm optimization algorithms. Journal of Artificial Intelligence and Soft Computing Research 2(2), 147–155 (2012)
21. Fogel, D.B.: Evolutionary Computation: Toward a New Philosophy of Machine Intelligence, 3rd edn. IEEE Press, Piscataway (2006)
22. Gabryel, M., Cpałka, K., Rutkowski, L.: Evolutionary strategies for learning of neuro-fuzzy systems. In: I Workshop on Genetic Fuzzy Systems, Granada, pp. 119–123 (2005)
23. Gabryel, M., Korytkowski, M., Scherer, R., Rutkowski, L.: Object Detection by Simple Fuzzy Classifiers Generated by Boosting. In: Rutkowski, L., Korytkowski, M., Scherer, R., Tadeusiewicz, R., Zadeh, L.A., Zurada, J.M. (eds.) ICAISC 2013, Part I. LNCS (LNAI), vol. 7894, pp. 540–547. Springer, Heidelberg (2013)
24. Gabryel, M., Woźniak, M., Nowicki, R.K.: Creating Learning Sets for Control Systems Using an Evolutionary Method. In: Rutkowski, L., Korytkowski, M., Scherer, R., Tadeusiewicz, R., Zadeh, L.A., Zurada, J.M. (eds.) SIDE 2012 and EC 2012. LNCS, vol. 7269, pp. 206–213. Springer, Heidelberg (2012)
25. Greblicki, W., Rutkowska, D., Rutkowski, L.: An orthogonal series estimate of time-varying regression. Annals of the Institute of Statistical Mathematics 35(2), 215–228 (1983)
26. Hassanzadeh, H.R., Rouhani, M.: A Multi-objective Gravitational Search Algorithm. In: Second International Conference on Computational Intelligence, Communication Systems and Networks (CICSyN), pp. 7–12 (2010)
27. Hassanzadeh, T., Meybodi, M.R.: A new hybrid algorithm based on Firefly Algorithm and cellular learning automata. In: The 20th Iranian Conference on Electrical Engineering, pp. 628–633 (2012)
28. Horzyk, A., Tadeusiewicz, R.: Self-Optimizing Neural Networks. In: Yin, F.-L., Wang, J., Guo, C. (eds.) ISNN 2004. LNCS, vol. 3173, pp. 150–155. Springer, Heidelberg (2004)

29. Jaworski, M., Duda, P., Pietruczuk, L.: On fuzzy clustering of data streams with concept drift. In: Rutkowski, L., Korytkowski, M., Scherer, R., Tadeusiewicz, R., Zadeh, L.A., Zurada, J.M. (eds.) ICAISC 2012, Part II. LNCS, vol. 7268, pp. 82–91. Springer, Heidelberg (2012)

30. Jelonkiewicz, J., Przybył, A.: Accuracy improvement of neural network state variable estimator in induction motor drive. In: Rutkowski, L., Tadeusiewicz, R., Zadeh, L.A., Zurada, J.M. (eds.) ICAISC 2008. LNCS (LNAI), vol. 5097, pp. 71–77. Springer, Heidelberg (2008)

31. Korytkowski, M., Nowicki, R., Rutkowski, L., Scherer, R.: AdaBoost Ensemble of DCOG Rough-Neuro-Fuzzy Systems. In: Jędrzejowicz, P., Nguyen, N.T., Hoang, K. (eds.) ICCCI 2011, Part I. LNCS, vol. 6922, pp. 62–71. Springer, Heidelberg (2011)

32. Korytkowski, M., Rutkowski, L., Scherer, R.: On combining backpropagation with boosting. In: Proceedings of the IEEE International Joint Conference on Neural Network (IJCNN), vols.1-10, pp. 1274–1277 (2006)

33. Laskowski, L.: A Novel Continuous Dual Mode Neural Network in Stereo-Matching Process. In: Diamantaras, K., Duch, W., Iliadis, L.S. (eds.) ICANN 2010, Part III. LNCS, vol. 6354, pp. 294–297. Springer, Heidelberg (2010)

34. Laskowski, Ł.: A novel hybrid-maximum neural network in stereo-matching process. Neural Comput. & Applic. 23, 2435–2450 (2013)

35. Laskowski, Ł.: Hybrid-Maximum Neural Network for Depth Analysis from Stereo-Image. In: Rutkowski, L., Scherer, R., Tadeusiewicz, R., Zadeh, L.A., Zurada, J.M. (eds.) ICAISC 2010, Part II. LNCS (LNAI), vol. 6114, pp. 47–55. Springer, Heidelberg (2010)

36. Laskowski, Ł.: Objects Auto-selection from Stereo-Images Realized by Self-Correcting Neural Network. In: Rutkowski, L., Korytkowski, M., Scherer, R., Tadeusiewicz, R., Zadeh, L.A., Zurada, J.M. (eds.) ICAISC 2012, Part I. LNCS (LNAI), vol. 7267, pp. 119–125. Springer, Heidelberg (2012)

37. Leva, A., Papadopoulos, A.V.: Tuning of event-based industrial controllers with simple stability guarantees. Journal of Process Control 23, 1251–1260 (2013)

38. Li, C., Zhou, J., Fu, B., Kou, P., Xiao, J.: T-S Fuzzy Model Identification With a Gravitational Search-Based Hyperplane Clustering Algorithm. IEEE Trans. Fuzzy Systems 20(2), 305–317 (2012)

39. Li, X., Er, M.J., Lim, B.S., Zhou, J.H., Gan, O.P., Rutkowski, L.: Fuzzy Regression Modeling for Tool Performance Prediction and Degradation Detection. International Journal of Neural Systems 20(5), 405–419 (2010)

40. Lobato, F.S., Steffen Jr., V.: A new multi-objective optimization algorithm based on differential evolution and neighborhood exploring evolution strategy. Journal of Artificial Intelligence and Soft Computing Research 1(4), 259–267 (2011)

41. Lobato, F.S., Steffen Jr., V., Silva Neto, A.J.: Solution of singular optimal control problems using the improved differential evolution algorithm. Journal of Artificial Intelligence and Soft Computing Research 1(3), 195–206 (2011)

42. Lucas, C., Nasiri-Gheidari, Z., Tootoonchian, F.: Application of an imperialist competitive algorithm to the design of a linear induction motor. Energy Conversion and Management 51, 1407–1411 (2010)

43. Łapa, K., Przybył, A., Cpałka, K.: A new approach to designing interpretable models of dynamic systems. In: Rutkowski, L., Korytkowski, M., Scherer, R., Tadeusiewicz, R., Zadeh, L.A., Zurada, J.M. (eds.) ICAISC 2013, Part II. LNCS (LNAI), vol. 7895, pp. 523–534. Springer, Heidelberg (2013)

44. Łapa, K., Zalasiński, M., Cpałka, K.: A new method for designing and complexity reduction of neuro-fuzzy systems for nonlinear modelling. In: Rutkowski, L., Korytkowski, M., Scherer, R., Tadeusiewicz, R., Zadeh, L.A., Zurada, J.M. (eds.) ICAISC 2013, Part I. LNCS (LNAI), vol. 7894, pp. 329–344. Springer, Heidelberg (2013)
45. Michalewicz, Z.: Genetic Algorithms + Data Structures = Evolution Programs. Springer (1999)
46. Nowicki, R.: On classification with missing data using rough-neuro-fuzzy systems. International Journal of Applied Mathematics and Computer Science 20(1), 55–67 (2010)
47. Nowicki, R., Scherer, R., Rutkowski, L.: A method for learning of hierarchical fuzzy systems. In: Sincak, P., Vascak, J., Kvasnicka, V., Pospichal, J. (eds.) Intelligent Technologies - Theory and Applications, pp. 124–129. IOS Press (2002)
48. Patan, K., Patan, M.: Optimal training strategies for locally recurrent neural network. Journal of Artificial Intelligence and Soft Computing Research 1(2) (2011)
49. Pietruczuk, L., Duda, P., Jaworski, M.: A new fuzzy classifier for data streams. In: Rutkowski, L., Korytkowski, M., Scherer, R., Tadeusiewicz, R., Zadeh, L.A., Zurada, J.M. (eds.) ICAISC 2012, Part I. LNCS (LNAI), vol. 7267, pp. 318–324. Springer, Heidelberg (2012)
50. Pietruczuk, L., Duda, P., Jaworski, M.: Adaptation of decision trees for handling concept drift. In: Rutkowski, L., Korytkowski, M., Scherer, R., Tadeusiewicz, R., Zadeh, L.A., Zurada, J.M. (eds.) ICAISC 2013, Part I. LNCS (LNAI), vol. 7894, pp. 459–473. Springer, Heidelberg (2013)
51. Pławiak, P., Tadeusiewicz, R.: Approximation of phenol concentration using novel hybrid computational intelligence methods. Applied Mathematics and Computer Science 24(1) (in print, 2014)
52. Prampero, P.S., Attux, R.: Magnetic particle swarm optimization. Journal of Artificial Intelligence and Soft Computing Research 2(1), 59–72 (2012)
53. Przybył, A., Cpałka, K.: A new method to construct of interpretable models of dynamic systems. In: Rutkowski, L., Korytkowski, M., Scherer, R., Tadeusiewicz, R., Zadeh, L.A., Zurada, J.M. (eds.) ICAISC 2012, Part II. LNCS (LNAI), vol. 7268, pp. 697–705. Springer, Heidelberg (2012)
54. Przybył, A., Jelonkiewicz, J.: Genetic algorithm for observer parameters tuning in sensorless induction motor drive. In: Rutkowski, L., Kacprzyk, J. (eds.) Networks and Soft Computing (6th International Conference on Neural Networks and Soft Computing 2002), Zakopane, Poland, pp. 376–381 (2003)
55. Przybył, A., Smoląg, J., Kimla, P.: Distributed Control System Based on Real Time Ethernet for Computer Numerical Controlled Machine Tool (in Polish). Przegląd Elektrotechniczny 86(2), 342–346 (2010)
56. Rashedi, E., Nezamabadi-pour, H., Saryazdi, S.: GSA: A Gravitational Search Algorithm. Information Sciences 179, 2232–2248 (2009)
57. Rasoanarivo, I., Brechet, S., Battiston, A., Nahid-Mobarakeh, B.: Behavioral Analysis of a Boost Converter with High Performance Source Filter and a Fractional-Order PID Controller. In: IEEE Industry Applications Society Annual Meeting (IAS), pp. 1–6 (2012)
58. Rutkowski, L.: Computational Intelligence. Springer (2008)
59. Rutkowski, L.: Multiple Fourier series procedures for extraction of nonlinear regressions from noisy data. IEEE Transactions on Signal Processing 41(10), 3062–3065 (1993)

60. Rutkowski, L., Cpałka, K.: Compromise approach to neuro-fuzzy systems. In: Sincak, P., Vascak, J., Kvasnicka, V., Pospichal, J. (eds.) Intelligent Technologies - Theory and Applications, vol. 76, pp. 85–90. IOS Press (2002)
61. Rutkowski, L., Cpałka, K.: Flexible weighted neuro-fuzzy systems. In: Proceedings of the 9th International Conference on Neural Information Processing (ICONIP 2002), Orchid Country Club, Singapore, CD November 18-22 (2002)
62. Rutkowski, L., Cpałka, K.: Neuro-fuzzy systems derived from quasi-triangular norms. In: Proceedings of the IEEE International Conference on Fuzzy Systems, Budapest, July 26-29, vol. 2, pp. 1031–1036 (2004)
63. Rutkowski, L., Jaworski, M., Pietruczuk, L., Duda, P.: Decision trees for mining data streams based on the gaussian approximation. IEEE Transactions on Knowledge and Data Engineering 26(1), 108–119 (2014)
64. Rutkowski, L., Jaworski, M., Pietruczuk, L., Duda, P.: The CART decision tree for mining data streams. Information Sciences 266, 1–15 (2014)
65. Rutkowski, L., Pietruczuk, L., Duda, P., Jaworski, M.: Decision trees for mining data streams based on the McDiarmid's bound. IEEE Transactions on Knowledge and Data Engineering 25(6), 1272–1279 (2013)
66. Rutkowski, L., Przybył, A., Cpałka, K.: Novel on-line speed profile generation for industrial machine tool based on flexible neuro-fuzzy approximation. IEEE Transactions on Industrial Electronics 59, 1238–1247 (2012)
67. Rutkowski, L., Przybył, A., Cpałka, K., Er, M.J.: Online Speed Profile Generation for Industrial Machine Tool Based on Neuro-fuzzy Approach. In: Rutkowski, L., Scherer, R., Tadeusiewicz, R., Zadeh, L.A., Zurada, J.M. (eds.) ICAISC 2010, Part II. LNCS (LNAI), vol. 6114, pp. 645–650. Springer, Heidelberg (2010)
68. Rutkowski, L., Rafajlowicz, E.: On optimal global rate of convergence of some nonparametric identification procedures. IEEE Transaction on Automatic Control AC-34(10), 1089–1091 (1989)
69. Scherer, R.: Neuro-fuzzy relational systems for nonlinear approximation and prediction. Nonlinear Analysis Series A: Theory, Methods and Applications 71(12), e1420–e1425 (2009)
70. Scherer, R., Rutkowski, L.: Connectionist fuzzy relational systems. In: Halgamuge, S.K., Wang, L. (eds.) 9th International Conference on Neural Information and Processing; 4th Asia-Pacific Conference on Simulated Evolution and Learning; 1st International Conference on Fuzzy Systems and Knowledge Discovery, Computational Intelligence for Modelling and Prediction Book Series, Singapore. SCI, vol. 2, pp. 35–47. Springer, Heidelberg (2005)
71. Starczewski, J., Scherer, R., Korytkowski, M., Nowicki, R.: Modular type-2 neuro-fuzzy systems. In: Wyrzykowski, R., Dongarra, J., Karczewski, K., Wasniewski, J. (eds.) PPAM 2007. LNCS, vol. 4967, pp. 570–578. Springer, Heidelberg (2008)
72. Szaleniec, M., Goclon, J., Witko, M., Tadeusiewicz, R.: Application of artificial neural networks and DFT-based parameters for prediction of reaction kinetics of ethylbenzene dehydrogenase. Journal of Computer-Aided Molecular Design 20(3), 145–157 (2006)
73. Szczypta, J., Przybył, A., Cpałka, K.: Some aspects of evolutionary designing optimal controllers. In: Rutkowski, L., Korytkowski, M., Scherer, R., Tadeusiewicz, R., Zadeh, L.A., Zurada, J.M. (eds.) ICAISC 2013, Part II. LNCS, vol. 7895, pp. 91–100. Springer, Heidelberg (2013)
74. Theodoridis, D.C., Boutalis, Y.S., Christodoulou, M.A.: Robustifying analysis of the direct adaptive control of unknown multivariable nonlinear systems based on a new neuro-fuzzy method. Journal of Artificial Intelligence and Soft Computing Research 1(1), 59–79 (2011)

75. Tran, V.N., Brdys, M.A.: Optimizing control by robustly feasible model predictive control and application to drinking water distribution systems. Journal of Artificial Intelligence and Soft Computing Research 1(1), 43–57 (2011)
76. Tsai, P.W., Pan, J.S., Liao, B.Y., Tsai, M.J., Istanda, V.: Bat algorithm inspired algorithm for solving numerical optimization problems. Applied Mechanics and Materials 148-149, 34–137 (2012)
77. Yang, X.S.: Bat Algorithm for Multi-objective Optimisation. Int. J. Bio-Inspired Computation 3, 267–274 (2011)
78. Yang, X.S.: Nature-Inspired Metaheuristic Algorithms, pp. 80–96, University of Cambridge (2010)
79. Yousefi, M., Mohammadi, H.: Second law based optimization of a plate fin heat exchanger using Imperialist Competitive Algorithm. International Journal of the Physical Sciences 6, 4749–4759 (2011)
80. Zalasiński, M., Cpałka, K.: A new method of on-line signature verification using a flexible fuzzy one-class classifier, pp. 38–53. Academic Publishing House EXIT (2011)
81. Zalasiński, M., Cpałka, K.: New Approach for the On-Line Signature Verification Based on Method of Horizontal Partitioning. In: Rutkowski, L., Korytkowski, M., Scherer, R., Tadeusiewicz, R., Zadeh, L.A., Zurada, J.M. (eds.) ICAISC 2013, Part II. LNCS (LNAI), vol. 7895, pp. 342–350. Springer, Heidelberg (2013)
82. Zalasiński, M., Cpałka, K.: Novel algorithm for the on-line signature verification. In: Rutkowski, L., Korytkowski, M., Scherer, R., Tadeusiewicz, R., Zadeh, L.A., Zurada, J.M. (eds.) ICAISC 2012, Part II. LNCS, vol. 7268, pp. 362–367. Springer, Heidelberg (2012)
83. Zalasiński, M., Cpałka, K.: Novel Algorithm for the On-Line Signature Verification Using Selected Discretization Points Groups. In: Rutkowski, L., Korytkowski, M., Scherer, R., Tadeusiewicz, R., Zadeh, L.A., Zurada, J.M. (eds.) ICAISC 2013, Part I. LNCS (LNAI), vol. 7894, pp. 493–502. Springer, Heidelberg (2013)
84. Zalasiński, M., Łapa, K., Cpałka, K.: New Algorithm for Evolutionary Selection of the Dynamic Signature Global Features. In: Rutkowski, L., Korytkowski, M., Scherer, R., Tadeusiewicz, R., Zadeh, L.A., Zurada, J.M. (eds.) ICAISC 2013, Part II. LNCS, vol. 7895, pp. 113–121. Springer, Heidelberg (2013)

Evolutionary Approach with Multiple Quality Criteria for Controller Design

Jacek Szczypta[1], Andrzej Przybył[1], and Lipo Wang[2]

[1] Częstochowa University of Technology,
Institute of Computational Intelligence, Poland
{jacek.szczypta,andrzej.przybyl}@iisi.pcz.pl
[2] Nanyang Technological University,
School of Electrical & Electronic Engineering, Singapore
elpwang@ntu.edu.sg

Abstract. In the paper we propose a new approach to control system design. The approach is characterized by automated parameters tuning and structure selection of the controller. Structure selection and parameter tuning are performed using evolutionary algorithm and allow accurate control with elimination or minimizing of unfavourable phenomena like overshoot or harmonic distortion. Our method was tested on a model of quarter car active suspension system.

1 Introduction

Automatic control is an important issue from scientific and practical point of view (see e.g. [62]-[63]). In the literature, various approaches to design of parameters and the structure of control systems are considered. More of them are in one of the following groups: **(a) Controllers based on the combination of linear correction terms: P, I, D**. These terms can be coupled as e.g.: PI, PID, PI in cascade, PI with feed-forward (see e.g. [1], [38]), PI or PID with additional low-pass filter (see e.g. [38]), PID with anti-windup and compensation mechanism (see e.g. [47]). In this group controllers based on state-feedback, in which the current state vector (estimated or measured) of the controlled object is used for proportional control (see e.g. [59]), are also included. It is important to remark that the task of controller structure design (i.e. selection of the best configuration of linear correction terms) requires from designer comprehensive knowledge supported by the experience. It should be noted that design of controller structure and tuning of parameters are very time-consuming. **(b) Controllers based on computational intelligence**. In this group, controller structure is not strictly defined. Controller uses neural networks (see e.g. [7]-[10], [27]-[31], [41]-[42], [60]), fuzzy systems (see e.g. [2]-[6], [18]-[21], [25], [32], [40], [57]-[58]), neuro-fuzzy systems (see e.g. [11]-[16], [33], [36]-[37], [52]-[55], [64]-[68]), etc. **(c) Hybrid controllers**. In this group, controller combines approaches from other groups. In hybrid controller we can distinguish correction term and additional supporting mechanism (for example based on an artificial intelligence) for adaptive control (see e.g. [17], [44]-[46], [55]-[56]).

L. Rutkowski et al. (Eds.): ICAISC 2014, Part I, LNAI 8467, pp. 455–467, 2014.
© Springer International Publishing Switzerland 2014

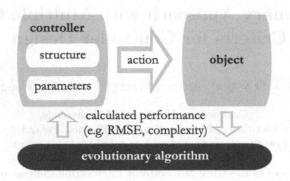

Fig. 1. Idea of the new method for controller design

In this paper a new method for designing control system based on combination of linear correction terms is proposed. Our method is characterized by automation of both operations: structure selection and parameter tuning (see Fig. 1). Concurrent parameter tuning and structure selection is important, because it eliminates mentioned earlier control design problems. Our method also offers strictly, but very flexibly, defined control criteria as a tool for control system tuning, what allows to reach objective expected by its designer.

This paper is organised into four sections. Section 2 presents a detailed description of the new method for controller design. In Section 3 simulation results are presented. Conclusions are drawn in Section 4.

2   Description of the New Method for Designing Optimal Controllers

Presented method gives to designer the freedom of choice of controller blocks (CB) number, connection and definition. In Fig. 2 initial controller structure idea is presented: in Fig. 2.a CB connection idea for the MISO system is presented, in Fig. 2.b CB processing element idea is presented. Dashed lines in Fig. 2.a and in Fig. 2.b denote freedom of connection between CBs and simple correction terms. Existence or lack of connection depends on evolutionary algorithm execution result. Signal fb_n, $n=1, \ldots, N$, denotes feedback signal, signal ff_m, $m = 1, \ldots, M$, denotes feedforward signal. CB connection idea (see Fig. 2.a) is a result of generalisation of PID controller, cascaded PID controller with feedforward signals and state-feedback controller. CB definition idea (see Fig. 2.b) is combination of simple correction terms like P, I and D. There is a possibility to place inside CB other processing elements like finite impulse response filter, infinite response filter, saturation or nonlinear block. Generalised controller structure (CB connection and definition) is initial point of evolutionary algorithm.

In proposed method full controller (with its structure and parameters) is encoded in a single chromosome $\mathbf{X}_{ch}$. Chromosome $\mathbf{X}_{ch}$ is described as follows:

$$\mathbf{X}_{ch} = \left\{ \mathbf{X}_{ch}^{par}, \mathbf{X}_{ch}^{red} \right\}, \tag{1}$$

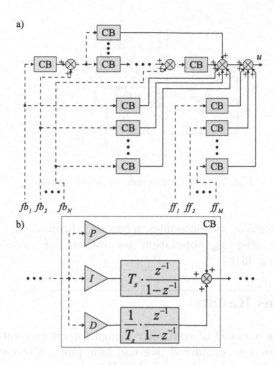

Fig. 2. Initial controller structure idea: a)CB connection idea, b)CB definition idea

where $\mathbf{X}_{ch}^{\mathrm{par}}$ is a chromosome encoding correction term parameters, $\mathbf{X}_{ch}^{\mathrm{red}}$ is a chromosome encoding CB connection. Chromosome $\mathbf{X}_{ch}^{\mathrm{par}}$ is described as follows:

$$\mathbf{X}_{ch}^{\mathrm{par}} = (P_1, I_1, D_1, P_2, I_2, D_2, \ldots) = \left(X_{ch,1}^{\mathrm{par}}, X_{ch,2}^{\mathrm{par}}, \ldots, X_{ch,L}^{\mathrm{par}} \right), \qquad (2)$$

where $P_1, I_1, D_1, \ldots$, denote control system parameter values, $ch = 1, .., Ch$, denotes index of the chromosome in the population, Ch denotes a number of chromosomes in the population, L denotes length of the chromosome $\mathbf{X}_{ch}^{\mathrm{par}}$. Chromosome $\mathbf{X}_{ch}^{\mathrm{red}}$ is described as follows:

$$\mathbf{X}_{ch}^{\mathrm{red}} = \left(X_{ch,1}^{\mathrm{red}}, X_{ch,2}^{\mathrm{red}}, \ldots, X_{ch,L}^{\mathrm{red}} \right), \qquad (3)$$

where every gene $X_{ch,g}^{\mathrm{red}} \in \{0,1\}$, $ch = 1, .., Ch$, $g = 1, .., L$, decides if relevant part of control system occurs in control process (relevant gene $X_{ch,g}^{\mathrm{red}} = 1$).

The steps of the method used in this paper are the same as in typical evolutionary algorithm (see e.g. [12], [22]-[24], [26], [34]-[35], [39], [43], [48]). The evolutionary algorithm is a method of solving problems (mainly optimisation problems) which is based on natural evolution. Evolutionary algorithms are search procedures based on the natural selection and inheritance mechanisms. Method steps are following: chromosomes initialisation, chromosomes evaluation,

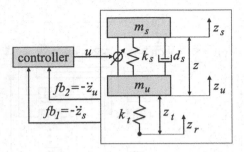

Fig. 3. Active suspension control system

stop condition checking, chromosomes selection, chromosomes crossover, mutation and repair, offspring population generation. For more details see our previous papers, e.g. [61].

3   Simulations Results

In the simulations a model of controller design for quarter car active suspension control system was considered (see e.g. [33], [59]). Alternative approaches to nonlinear modelling can be found in [49]-[51]. Active suspension control system is presented in Fig. 3. Assumed values of the parameters of the model are presented in Table 1. Parameters of active suspension model are following: m_u denotes unsprung mass, m_s denotes sprung mass, k_t denotes tire stiffness, k_s denotes sprung stiffness, d_s denotes sprung damping. Meaning of the rest of the active suspension model parameters is following: z_r denotes road profile, z_t denotes tire compression, z_u denotes displacement of unsprung mass, z denotes suspension travel, z_s denotes displacement of sprung mass. Aim of the controller is to improve the passenger comfort and car handling, etc. We assume that improvement of ride comfort is more important that handling improvement.

In order to create model and perform simulations, following assumptions were taken:

− Controlled object is modelled as follows:

$$\dot{\mathbf{x}} = \mathbf{A}\mathbf{x} + \mathbf{B}\mathbf{u} + \mathbf{f}, \tag{4}$$

where $\mathbf{A}$ is a state matrix in the form:

$$\mathbf{A} = \begin{bmatrix} 0 & 1 & 0 & 0 \\ -\frac{k_s}{m_s} & -\frac{d_s}{m_s} & \frac{k_s}{m_s} & \frac{d_s}{m_s} \\ 0 & 0 & 0 & 1 \\ \frac{k_s}{m_u} & \frac{d_s}{m_s} & -\frac{k_s+k_t}{m_u} & -\frac{d_s}{m_s} \end{bmatrix}, \tag{5}$$

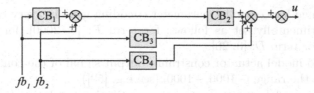

Fig. 4. Initial controller structure for active suspension controller

x is a state vector (initial values of state vector were set to zero) described as follows:

$$\mathbf{x} = \begin{bmatrix} x_1 \\ x_2 \\ x_3 \\ x_4 \end{bmatrix} = \begin{bmatrix} z_s \\ \dot{z}_s \\ z_u \\ \dot{z}_u \end{bmatrix}, \tag{6}$$

B is an input matrix represented by the formula:

$$\mathbf{B} = \begin{bmatrix} 0 & \frac{1}{m_s} & 0 & -\frac{1}{m_u} \end{bmatrix}^{\mathrm{T}}, \tag{7}$$

u is an input vector from controller, **f** is an input vector from kinematic extortion described by the following equation:

$$\mathbf{f} = \begin{bmatrix} 0 & 0 & 0 & -\frac{k_t}{m_u} \end{bmatrix}^{\mathrm{T}} z_r. \tag{8}$$

- The road profile is presented in Fig. 6.a. It represents the typical situations which may occur on the road.

Table 1. Parameters of active suspension control system

name	value	unit
m_u	48.3	kg
m_s	395.3	kg
k_s	30 010	N/m
k_t	340 000	N/m
d_s	1450	Ns/m

- Controlled object was discretized with the first order equation with time step $T = 0.1$ ms as follows: $\mathbf{x}(i+1) = \mathbf{A}_d \cdot \mathbf{x}(i) + \mathbf{B}_d \cdot \mathbf{u}(i) + \mathbf{f}_d$, where $\mathbf{A}_d = \mathbf{I} + \mathbf{A} \cdot T$, $\mathbf{B}_d = \mathbf{B} \cdot T$ and $\mathbf{f}_d = \mathbf{f} \cdot T$.
- Initial controller structure, directly derived from the structure shown in Fig. 2 on the basis on available feedback signals, is shown in Fig. 4 and equipped with four CBs. Every CB is equipped with P, I, D processing elements.
- Feedback signals: fb_1 and fb_2 were set to $-\ddot{z}_s$ and $-\ddot{z}_u$ respectively.

- Search range for controller parameter encoding gene in every control block was experimentally set as follows: for term P: $[0, 2000]$, for term I: $[0, 200000]$, for term D: $[0, 20]$.
- In order to model actuator constrains, output signal of the controller u was limited to the range $[-1000, +1000]$ (see e.g. [59]).
- In order to model sensor constrains, quantisation resolution for the output signal u and feedback signals (fb_1, fb_2) was set to 0.0001.
- Simulation length T was set to 8 seconds. Simulation time step T_s was set to 0.1ms, while interval between subsequent controller activations was set to five simulation steps ($T_r = 5T = 0.5$ ms). This is reasonable value for the implementation of the controller in real microprocessor system.

In order to design controller, following assumptions were taken:

- Fitness function was defined with elements improving operating conditions of genetic algorithm (i.e. accelerating the search of the optimal solution). Those elements are: reference to passive suspension system performance, unification by adding 1 and respectively multiplying by 1000. Fitness function was defined as follows:

$$\text{ff}(\mathbf{X}_{ch}) = \begin{pmatrix} cf_{ch} \cdot w_{cf} + hd_{ch} \cdot w_{hd} + st_{ch} \cdot w_{st} + \\ +cp_{ch} \cdot w_{cp} + os_{ch} \cdot w_{os} + cn_{ch} \cdot w_{cn} \end{pmatrix}, \tag{9}$$

where

- cf_{ch} denotes passenger comfort and was defined as follows:

$$cf_{ch} = (1 + cf_p) - \sqrt{\frac{1}{Z} \cdot \sum_{i=1}^{Z} \ddot{z}_{s,i}^2}, \tag{10}$$

where cf_p denotes, found by experiment, passenger comfort for passive suspension value equal 0.861 (see Table 3), $i = 1, \ldots, Z$, denotes sample index, Z denotes the number of samples and was defined as follows:

$$Z = \frac{T}{T_s}. \tag{11}$$

- w_{cf} denotes weight of cf_{ch} and was set to 5.
- hd_{ch} denotes car handling and was defined as follows:

$$hd_{ch} = (1 + hd_p) - \sqrt{\frac{1}{Z} \cdot \sum_{i=1}^{Z} z_{t,i}^2}, \tag{12}$$

where hd_p denotes, found by experiment, car handling for passive suspension value equal 1.09 (see Table 3).
- w_{hd} denotes weight of hd_{ch} and was set to 1.

$$fb_I \longrightarrow \boxed{\text{PI}} \longrightarrow u$$

Fig. 5. Evolutionary designed controller structure for active suspension system

- st_{ch} denotes suspension travel and was defined as follows:

$$st_{ch} = \left((1 + st_p) - 1000 \cdot \max_{z=1,\dots,Z} \{ \text{abs}(z_i) \} \right), \tag{13}$$

  where st_p denotes, found by experiment, passive system suspension travel value equal 50.9 (see Table 3).
- w_{st} denotes weight of st_{ch} and was set to 0.01.
- cp_{ch} denotes controller structure complexity and was defined as follows:

$$cp_{ch} = \sum_{g=1}^{L} \mathbf{X}_{ch,g}^{\text{red}}. \tag{14}$$

- w_{cp} denotes weight of cp_{ch} and was set to 0.5.
- os_{ch} denotes oscillation of controller output signal and was defined as follows:

$$os_{ch} = \frac{1}{1 + \sum_{i=1}^{Z} \begin{cases} 1 \ \text{for} \ \Delta u_i > 200 \\ 0 \ \ \text{otherwise} \end{cases}}, \tag{15}$$

  where $\Delta u_i = \text{abs}(u(i) - u(i-1))$.
- w_{os} denotes weight of os_{ch} and was set to 0.01.
- cn_{ch} denotes average control force and was defined as follows:

$$cn_{ch} = \frac{1}{1 + \sqrt{\frac{1}{Z} \cdot \sum_{i=1}^{Z} u_i^2}}. \tag{16}$$

- w_{cn} denotes weight of cn_{ch} and was set to 0.1.
- Evolutionary algorithm parameters were set as follows: (a) the number of chromosomes in the population was set to 20, (b) the algorithm performs 10 000 steps (generations), (c) the crossover probability was set as $p_c = 0.8$, (d) the mutation probability was set as $p_m = 0.3$, (e) the mutation intensity was set as $\sigma = 0.3$.

Simulation results can be summarised as follows: **(a)** Goal of significant passenger comfort improvement and slight car handling improvement was achieved (see Table 3). **(b)** Proposed method has automatically selected controller structure for control of quarter car active suspension system (see Fig. 5 and Table 2). **(c)** In simulation two operation modes of suspension system were tested: active and passive (see Fig. 6).

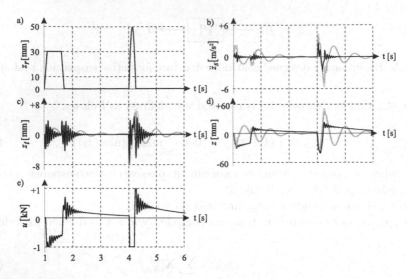

Fig. 6. Simulation results: a) road profile, b) passenger comfort, c) car handling, d) suspension travel, e) actuator force. In b)-d) grey line relates to the passive system and the black line relates to the active system.

Table 2. Parameters of evolutionary designed controller structure

	K_P	K_I	K_D
CB_1	reduced	reduced	reduced
CB_2	reduced	reduced	reduced
CB_3	343	45743	reduced
CB_4	reduced	reduced	reduced

Table 3. Result comparison of evolutionary designed controller structure

name	ff	cf	hd	st
	$[m/s^2]$	[mm]	[mm]	
passive	6.619	0.861	1.09	50.9
evolutionary	9.373	0.273	0.94	41.7

4   Summary

In this paper a new approach to designing controller based on linear correction terms was proposed. During simulation it was possible to select controller structure and tune its parameters including diverse control criteria. Results presented in the paper show that initial controller structure was significantly reduced - by 83% (see Table 2). Proposed method for controller design includes not only control accuracy, but also other control related criteria, e.g. harmonic distortion or overshoot.

Acknowledgement. The project was financed by the National Science Centre (Poland) on the basis of the decision number DEC-2012/05/B/ST7/02138.

References

1. Boiko, I.: Variable-structure PID controller for level process. Control Engineering Practice 21(5), 700–707 (2013)
2. Bartczuk, Ł., Dziwiński, P., Starczewski, J.T.: A new method for dealing with unbalanced linguistic term set. In: Rutkowski, L., Korytkowski, M., Scherer, R., Tadeusiewicz, R., Zadeh, L.A., Zurada, J.M. (eds.) ICAISC 2012, Part I. LNCS, vol. 7267, pp. 207–212. Springer, Heidelberg (2012)
3. Bartczuk, Ł., Dziwiński, P., Starczewski, J.T.: New Method for Generation Type-2 Fuzzy Partition for FDT. In: Rutkowski, L., Scherer, R., Tadeusiewicz, R., Zadeh, L.A., Zurada, J.M. (eds.) ICAISC 2010, Part I. LNCS (LNAI), vol. 6113, pp. 275–280. Springer, Heidelberg (2010)
4. Bartczuk, Ł., Przybył, A., Dziwiński, P.: Hybrid state variables - fuzzy logic modelling of nonlinear objects. In: Rutkowski, L., Korytkowski, M., Scherer, R., Tadeusiewicz, R., Zadeh, L.A., Zurada, J.M. (eds.) ICAISC 2013, Part I. LNCS, vol. 7894, pp. 227–234. Springer, Heidelberg (2013)
5. Bartczuk, Ł., Rutkowska, D.: A New Version of the Fuzzy-ID3 Algorithm. In: Rutkowski, L., Tadeusiewicz, R., Zadeh, L.A., Żurada, J.M. (eds.) ICAISC 2006. LNCS (LNAI), vol. 4029, pp. 1060–1070. Springer, Heidelberg (2006)
6. Bartczuk, Ł., Rutkowska, D.: Medical Diagnosis with Type-2 Fuzzy Decision Trees. In: Kącki, E., Rudnicki, M., Stempczyńska, J. (eds.) Computers in Medical Activity. AISC, vol. 65, pp. 11–21. Springer, Heidelberg (2009)
7. Bilski, J., Rutkowski, L.: Numerically Robust Learning Algorithms for Feed Forward Neural Networks. In: Advances in Soft Computing - Neural Networks and Soft Computing, pp. 149–154. Physica-Verlag, A Springer-Verlag Company (2003)
8. Bilski, J., Smoląg, J.: Parallel Approach to Learning of the Recurrent Jordan Neural Network. In: Rutkowski, L., Korytkowski, M., Scherer, R., Tadeusiewicz, R., Zadeh, L.A., Zurada, J.M. (eds.) ICAISC 2013, Part I. LNCS (LNAI), vol. 7894, pp. 32–40. Springer, Heidelberg (2013)
9. Bilski, J., Smoląg, J.: Parallel Realisation of the Recurrent Elman Neural Network Learning. In: Rutkowski, L., Scherer, R., Tadeusiewicz, R., Zadeh, L.A., Zurada, J.M. (eds.) ICAISC 2010, Part II. LNCS (LNAI), vol. 6114, pp. 19–25. Springer, Heidelberg (2010)
10. Bilski, J., Smoląg, J.: Parallel Realisation of the Recurrent Multi Layer Perceptron Learning. In: Rutkowski, L., Korytkowski, M., Scherer, R., Tadeusiewicz, R., Zadeh, L.A., Zurada, J.M. (eds.) ICAISC 2012, Part I. LNCS (LNAI), vol. 7267, pp. 12–20. Springer, Heidelberg (2012)
11. Cpalka, K.: A Method for Designing Flexible Neuro-fuzzy Systems. In: Rutkowski, L., Tadeusiewicz, R., Zadeh, L.A., Żurada, J.M. (eds.) ICAISC 2006. LNCS (LNAI), vol. 4029, pp. 212–219. Springer, Heidelberg (2006)
12. Cpałka, K.: On evolutionary designing and learning of flexible neuro-fuzzy structures for nonlinear classification. Nonlinear Analysis Series A: Theory, Methods and Applications 71, 1659–1672 (2009)
13. Cpałka, K., Łapa, K., Przybył, A., Zalasiński, M.: A new method for designing neuro-fuzzy systems for nonlinear modelling with interpretability aspects. Neurocomputing (in print, 2014), http://dx.doi.org/10.1016/j.neucom.2013.12.031

14. Cpałka, K., Rutkowski, L.: A New Method for Designing and Reduction of Neuro-fuzzy Systems. In: Proceedings of the 2006 IEEE International Conference on Fuzzy Systems (IEEE World Congress on Computational Intelligence, WCCI 2006), Vancouver, BC, Canada, pp. 8510–8516 (2006)

15. Cpałka, K., Rutkowski, L.: Flexible Takagi-Sugeno Fuzzy Systems. In: Proceedings of the International Joint Conference on Neural Networks 2005, Montreal, pp. 1764–1769 (2005)

16. Cpałka, K., Rutkowski, L.: Flexible Takagi-Sugeno Neuro-fuzzy Structures for Nonlinear Approximation. WSEAS Transactions on Systems 4(9), 1450–1458 (2005)

17. Duana, X.-G., Li, H.-X., Denga, H.: Robustness of fuzzy PID controller due to its inherent saturation. Journal of Process Control 22, 470–476 (2012)

18. Dziwiński, P., Bartczuk, Ł., Starczewski, J.T.: Fully controllable ant colony system for text data clustering. In: Rutkowski, L., Korytkowski, M., Scherer, R., Tadeusiewicz, R., Zadeh, L.A., Zurada, J.M. (eds.) SIDE 2012 and EC 2012. LNCS, vol. 7269, pp. 199–205. Springer, Heidelberg (2012)

19. Dziwiński, P., Rutkowska, D.: Algorithm for generating fuzzy rules for WWW document classification. In: Rutkowski, L., Tadeusiewicz, R., Zadeh, L.A., Żurada, J.M. (eds.) ICAISC 2006. LNCS (LNAI), vol. 4029, pp. 1111–1119. Springer, Heidelberg (2006)

20. Dziwiński, P., Rutkowska, D.: Ant focused crawling algorithm. In: Rutkowski, L., Tadeusiewicz, R., Zadeh, L.A., Zurada, J.M. (eds.) ICAISC 2008. LNCS (LNAI), vol. 5097, pp. 1018–1028. Springer, Heidelberg (2008)

21. Dziwiński, P., Starczewski, J.T., Bartczuk, Ł.: New linguistic hedges in construction of interval type-2 FLS. In: Rutkowski, L., Scherer, R., Tadeusiewicz, R., Zadeh, L.A., Zurada, J.M. (eds.) ICAISC 2010, Part II. LNCS (LNAI), vol. 6114, pp. 445–450. Springer, Heidelberg (2010)

22. El-Abd, M.: On the hybridization on the artificial bee colony and particle swarm optimization algorithms. Journal of Artificial Intelligence and Soft Computing Research 2(2), 147–155 (2012)

23. Fogel, D.B.: Evolutionary Computation: Toward a New Philosophy of Machine Intelligence, 3rd edn. IEEE Press, Piscataway (2006)

24. Gabryel, M., Cpałka, K., Rutkowski, L.: Evolutionary strategies for learning of neuro-fuzzy systems. In: Proceedings of the I Workshop on Genetic Fuzzy Systems, Granada, pp. 119–123 (2005)

25. Gabryel, M., Korytkowski, M., Scherer, R., Rutkowski, L.: Object Detection by Simple Fuzzy Classifiers Generated by Boosting. In: Rutkowski, L., Korytkowski, M., Scherer, R., Tadeusiewicz, R., Zadeh, L.A., Zurada, J.M. (eds.) ICAISC 2013, Part I. LNCS (LNAI), vol. 7894, pp. 540–547. Springer, Heidelberg (2013)

26. Gabryel, M., Woźniak, M., Nowicki, R.K.: Creating Learning Sets for Control Systems Using an Evolutionary Method. In: Rutkowski, L., Korytkowski, M., Scherer, R., Tadeusiewicz, R., Zadeh, L.A., Zurada, J.M. (eds.) EC 2012 and SIDE 2012. LNCS, vol. 7269, pp. 206–213. Springer, Heidelberg (2012)

27. Horzyk, A., Tadeusiewicz, R.: Self-Optimizing Neural Networks. In: Yin, F.-L., Wang, J., Guo, C. (eds.) ISNN 2004. LNCS, vol. 3173, pp. 150–155. Springer, Heidelberg (2004)

28. Jelonkiewicz, J., Przybył, A.: Accuracy improvement of neural network state variable estimator in induction motor drive. In: Rutkowski, L., Tadeusiewicz, R., Zadeh, L.A., Zurada, J.M. (eds.) ICAISC 2008. LNCS (LNAI), vol. 5097, pp. 71–77. Springer, Heidelberg (2008)

29. Korytkowski, M., Rutkowski, L., Scherer, R.: On combining backpropagation with boosting. In: Proceedings of the IEEE International Joint Conference on Neural Network (IJCNN), vols. 1-10, pp. 1274–1277 (2006)
30. Laskowski, Ł.: A novel hybrid-maximum neural network in stereo-matching process. Neural Comput. & Applic. 23, 2435–2450 (2013)
31. Laskowski, Ł.: Objects Auto-selection from Stereo-Images Realised by Self-Correcting Neural Network. In: Rutkowski, L., Korytkowski, M., Scherer, R., Tadeusiewicz, R., Zadeh, L.A., Zurada, J.M. (eds.) ICAISC 2012, Part I. LNCS, vol. 7267, pp. 119–125. Springer, Heidelberg (2012)
32. Li, J., Li, J., Xia, Z.: Delay-dependent generalized H2 control for discrete T-S fuzzy large-scale stochastic systems with mixed delays. International Journal of Applied Mathematics and Computer Science 21(4) (2011)
33. Lin, J., Lian, R.: Intelligent Control of Active Suspension Systems. IEEE Transactions on Industrial Electronics 58(2), 618–628 (2011)
34. Lobato, F.S., Steffen Jr., V.: A new multi-objective optimization algorithm based on differential evolution and neighborhood exploring evolution strategy. Journal of Artificial Intelligence and Soft Computing Research 1(4), 259–267 (2011)
35. Lobato, F.S., Steffen Jr., V., Silva Neto, A.J.: Solution of singular optimal control problems using the improved differential evolution algorithm. Journal of Artificial Intelligence and Soft Computing Research 1(3), 195–206 (2011)
36. Łapa, K., Przybył, A., Cpałka, K.: A new approach to designing interpretable models of dynamic systems. In: Rutkowski, L., Korytkowski, M., Scherer, R., Tadeusiewicz, R., Zadeh, L.A., Zurada, J.M. (eds.) ICAISC 2013, Part II. LNCS (LNAI), vol. 7895, pp. 523–534. Springer, Heidelberg (2013)
37. Łapa, K., Zalasiński, M., Cpałka, K.: A new method for designing and complexity reduction of neuro-fuzzy systems for nonlinear modelling. In: Rutkowski, L., Korytkowski, M., Scherer, R., Tadeusiewicz, R., Zadeh, L.A., Zurada, J.M. (eds.) ICAISC 2013, Part I. LNCS (LNAI), vol. 7894, pp. 329–344. Springer, Heidelberg (2013)
38. Maggio, M., Bonvini, M., Leva, A.: The PID + p controller structure and its contextual autotuning. Journal of Process Control 22, 1237–1245 (2012)
39. Michalewicz, Z.: Genetic Algorithms + Data Structures = Evolution Programs. Springer (1999)
40. Nowicki, R., Scherer, R., Rutkowski, L.: A method for learning of hierarchical fuzzy systems. In: Sincak, P., Vascak, J., Kvasnicka, V., Pospichal, J. (eds.) Intelligent Technologies - Theory and Applications, pp. 124–129. IOS Press (2002)
41. Patan, K., Patan, M.: Optimal training strategies for locally recurrent neural network. Journal of Artificial Intelligence and Soft Computing Research 1(2) (2011)
42. Pławiak, P., Tadeusiewicz, R.: Approximation of phenol concentration using novel hybrid computational intelligence methods. Applied Mathematics and Computer Science 24(1) (in print, 2014)
43. Prampero, P.S., Attux, R.: Magnetic particle swarm optimization. Journal of Artificial Intelligence and Soft Computing Research 2(1), 59–72 (2012)
44. Przybył, A., Cpałka, K.: A new method to construct of interpretable models of dynamic systems. In: Rutkowski, L., Korytkowski, M., Scherer, R., Tadeusiewicz, R., Zadeh, L.A., Zurada, J.M. (eds.) ICAISC 2012, Part II. LNCS (LNAI), vol. 7268, pp. 697–705. Springer, Heidelberg (2012)
45. Przybył, A., Jelonkiewicz, J.: Genetic algorithm for observer parameters tuning in sensorless induction motor drive. In: Rutkowski, L., Kacprzyk, J. (eds.) Neural Networks and Soft Computing (6th International Conference on Neural Networks and Soft Computing 2002), Zakopane, Poland, pp. 376–381 (2003)

46. Przybył, A., Smoląg, J., Kimla, P.: Distributed Control System Based on Real Time Ethernet for Computer Numerical Controlled Machine Tool (in Polish). Przeglad Elektrotechniczny 88(2), 342–346 (2010)
47. Ribića, A.I., Mataušek, M.R.: A dead-time compensating PID controller structure and robust tuning. Journal of Process Control 22, 1340–1349 (2012)
48. Rutkowski, L.: Computational Intelligence. Springer (2008)
49. Rutkowski, L.: Multiple Fourier series procedures for extraction of nonlinear regressions from noisy data. IEEE Transactions on Signal Processing 41(10), 3062–3065 (1993)
50. Rutkowski, L.: Nonparametric identification of quasi-stationary systems. Systems and Control Letters 6, 33–35 (1985)
51. Rutkowski, L.: On Bayes risk consistent pattern recognition procedures in a quasi-stationary environment. IEEE Transactions on Pattern Analysis and Machine Intelligence PAMI-4(1), 84–87 (1982)
52. Rutkowski, L., Cpałka, K.: Compromise approach to neuro-fuzzy systems. In: Sincak, P., Vascak, J., Kvasnicka, V., Pospichal, J. (eds.) Intelligent Technologies - Theory and Applications, vol. 76, pp. 85–90. IOS Press (2002)
53. Rutkowski, L., Cpałka, K.: Flexible weighted neuro-fuzzy systems. In: Proceedings of the 9th International Conference on Neural Information Processing (ICONIP 2002), Orchid Country Club, Singapore, CD, November 18-22 (2002)
54. Rutkowski, L., Cpałka, K.: Neuro-fuzzy systems derived from quasi-triangular norms. In: Proceedings of the IEEE International Conference on Fuzzy Systems, Budapest, July 26-29, vol. 2, pp. 1031–1036 (2004)
55. Rutkowski, L., Przybył, A., Cpałka, K.: Novel on-line speed profile generation for industrial machine tool based on flexible neuro-fuzzy approximation. IEEE Transactions on Industrial Electronics 59, 1238–1247 (2012)
56. Rutkowski, L., Przybył, A., Cpałka, K., Er, M.J.: Online Speed Profile Generation for Industrial Machine Tool Based on Neuro-fuzzy Approach. In: Rutkowski, L., Scherer, R., Tadeusiewicz, R., Zadeh, L.A., Zurada, J.M. (eds.) ICAISC 2010, Part II. LNCS (LNAI), vol. 6114, pp. 645–650. Springer, Heidelberg (2010)
57. Scherer, R.: Neuro-fuzzy relational systems for nonlinear approximation and prediction. Nonlinear Analysis Series A: Theory, Methods and Applications 71(12), e1420–e1425 (2009)
58. Scherer, R., Rutkowski, L.: Connectionist fuzzy relational systems. In: Halgamuge, S.K., Wang, L. (eds.) 9th International Conference on Neural Information and Processing; 4th Asia-Pacific Conference on Simulated Evolution and Learning; 1st International Conference on Fuzzy Systems and Knowledge Discovery, Computational Intelligence for Modelling and Prediction Book Series. SCI, vol. 2, pp. 35–47. Springer, Heidelberg (2005)
59. van der Sande, T.P.J., Gysen, B.L.J., Besselink, I.J.M., Paulides, J.J.H., Lomonova, E.A., Nijmeijer, H.: Robust control of an electromagnetic active suspension system: Simulations and measurements. Mechatronics 23(2) (2013)
60. Szaleniec, M., Goclon, J., Witko, M., Tadeusiewicz, R.: Application of artificial neural networks and DFT-based parameters for prediction of reaction kinetics of ethylbenzene dehydrogenase. Journal of Computer-Aided Molecular Design 20(3), 145–157 (2006)
61. Szczypta, J., Przybył, A., Cpałka, K.: Some aspects of evolutionary designing optimal controllers. In: Rutkowski, L., Korytkowski, M., Scherer, R., Tadeusiewicz, R., Zadeh, L.A., Zurada, J.M. (eds.) ICAISC 2013, Part II. LNCS, vol. 7895, pp. 91–100. Springer, Heidelberg (2013)

62. Theodoridis, D.C., Boutalis, Y.S., Christodoulou, M.A.: Robustifying analysis of the direct adaptive control of unknown multivariable nonlinear systems based on a new neuro-fuzzy method. Journal of Artificial Intelligence and Soft Computing Research 1(1), 59–79 (2011)
63. Tran, V.N., Brdys, M.A.: Optimizing control by robustly feasible model predictive control and application to drinking water distribution systems. Journal of Artificial Intelligence and Soft Computing Research 1(1), 43–57 (2011)
64. Zalasiński, M., Cpałka, K.: A new method of on-line signature verification using a flexible fuzzy one-class classifier, pp. 38–53. Academic Publishing House EXIT (2011)
65. Zalasiński, M., Łapa, K., Cpałka, K.: New Algorithm for Evolutionary Selection of the Dynamic Signature Global Features. In: Rutkowski, L., Korytkowski, M., Scherer, R., Tadeusiewicz, R., Zadeh, L.A., Zurada, J.M. (eds.) ICAISC 2013, Part II. LNCS (LNAI), vol. 7895, pp. 113–121. Springer, Heidelberg (2013)
66. Zalasiński, M., Cpałka, K.: New Approach for the On-Line Signature Verification Based on Method of Horizontal Partitioning. In: Rutkowski, L., Korytkowski, M., Scherer, R., Tadeusiewicz, R., Zadeh, L.A., Zurada, J.M. (eds.) ICAISC 2013, Part II. LNCS (LNAI), vol. 7895, pp. 342–350. Springer, Heidelberg (2013)
67. Zalasiński, M., Cpałka, K.: Novel algorithm for the on-line signature verification. In: Rutkowski, L., Korytkowski, M., Scherer, R., Tadeusiewicz, R., Zadeh, L.A., Zurada, J.M. (eds.) ICAISC 2012, Part II. LNCS (LNAI), vol. 7268, pp. 362–367. Springer, Heidelberg (2012)
68. Zalasiński, M., Cpałka, K.: Novel Algorithm for the On-Line Signature Verification Using Selected Discretization Points Groups. In: Rutkowski, L., Korytkowski, M., Scherer, R., Tadeusiewicz, R., Zadeh, L.A., Zurada, J.M. (eds.) ICAISC 2013, Part I. LNCS (LNAI), vol. 7894, pp. 493–502. Springer, Heidelberg (2013)

Optimization of Router Deployment for Sensor Networks Using Genetic Algorithm

Rony Teguh, Ryo Murakami, and Hajime Igarashi

Graduate School of Information Science and Technology,
Hokkaido University, Japan
ronyteguh@ist.hokudai.ac.jp, murakami@em-si.eng.hokudai.ac.jp,
igarashi@ssi.ist.hokudai.ac.jp

Abstract. This paper presents optimization of router deployment based on genetic algorithm for energy-constrained wireless sensor networks which are used for wildfire monitoring. The router positions are optimized so that the total communication distance is minimized to maximize the lifetime of the sensor network. To consider the real geographical features of the target field, the elevation differences are included in fitness evaluation. It is shown that one can reduce the total communication distance as well as the number of disconnected sensors for both flat and irregular terrains using the present optimization method.

Keywords: Router deployment, Wireless sensor networks, Genetic algorithm, Digital elevation model.

1   Introduction

Development of highly reliable wireless sensor network (WSN) to monitor forest fires has strategic significance for many countries where forest fires occur frequently. It has been shown that WSNs have great potential for wildfire monitoring[1]. A detection system for wildfire in Indonesia using WSNs and UAV has been developed[2, 3]. Hefeeda et al. have proposed data aggregation scheme based on FWI (Fire Weather Index) for WSNs[4]. This scheme can extend the lifetime of WSNs because the data of interest, which can be determined from FWI, are only aggregated. Son et al. have implemented FFSS (Forest-fires Surveillance System) which contains the level risk of forest fires [5].

WSNs consist of sensors, routers and a base-station, which work together to collect data about the status of the target field. The sensors perform periodic measurement of environmental data such as temperature and humidity and send them to the routers or directly to the base station node. The routers collect data from the sensor nodes to send them to the base station. WSNs have several functions such as sensing, data processing and communication, and work as a platform for processing of distributed data collected from wide environment. The sensors in WSNs operate with limited power and wireless communication capability. Especially, energy usage is significant concern in WSNs placed in wild environment since it is difficult to make frequent replacement of batteries in the

L. Rutkowski et al. (Eds.): ICAISC 2014, Part I, LNAI 8467, pp. 468–479, 2014.
© Springer International Publishing Switzerland 2014

sensors. To maximize the lifetime of the energy-constrained WSNs, communication protocols such as LEACH[6] and HEED[7] have been developed in which the cluster heads are autonomously selected to share the energy loss in the sensor nodes. The cluster head collects data from the sensors in its cluster to send them to the base station.

On the other hand, the routers which play a role similar to the cluster heads are a priori determined in Zigbee systems, which we will consider in this paper. It is effective to reduce the communication distance between the sensor nodes and routers to expand the WSN lifetime. In addition, it is expected to reduce the communication errors due to noise by minimizing the distance. While the position of the sensor nodes would be determined from the sensing coverage, the router deployment should be determined so that the communication distance is minimized. Because the communication distance depends on the topology of WSNs, the distance cannot be differentiated with respect to the router positions. It is thus difficult to use gradient-based methods to optimize the router deployment.

In this paper, we propose an optimization method based on genetic algorithm (GA) of the router deployment. The heuristic methods such as simulated annealing, genetic algorithm (GA), immune algorithm and particle swarm [8] have not been applied to optimization of the router deployment in WSNs considering irregular elevation in the target fields.

The proposed optimization method is not only applicable to WSNs for wildfire monitoring but also to WSNs for security and health monitoring, etc. To test the performance of the present method, the router deployment is optimized for flat and irregular terrain. In the latter case, we employ the digital elevation model (DEM) data [9] to consider the realistic geographical features of the target field. The WSN topology will be formed avoiding the occlusion between the nodes.

The paper will be organized as follows: the related works will be described in the next section. Then the optimization problem will be addressed and optimization method will be described detail in the third section. In the fourth section, optimization results for flat and irregular terrains will be shown and discussions on the results will be made. Finally conclusions will be given in the last section.

2   Related Works

Wu et al. have optimized the sensor deployment on planar grid to maximize the detection probability within a given cost using GA[10]. They showed that their method outperforms a greedy sensor placement method. Bari et al. have optimized the data-gathering schedule for the relay nodes, which are equivalent to the routers, using GA[11]. Krishnamachari et al. have optimized the data flow among WSNs to maximize the total information routed to the sink node[12]. They showed that the maximum information which is extracted for a fixed amount of energy decreases as the fairness requirement is reduced. Zhao et al. have discussed optimal deployment of high-powered relay nodes in static heterogeneous sensor networks[13]. The genetic algorithm for integer planning is adopted to optimally deploy the relay nodes so as to obtain the optimal energy efficiency by minimizing the average path length. They consider the Manhattan distance in the optimization because the nodes are placed at the planar grid points.

In this work, we optimize the router deployment for WSNs where the sensors are randomly distributed. We take irregular elevation in the target field which affect communicability into account. We also make an attempt to reduce the number of disconnected sensors outside the communication circles of the routers by including it as a penalty in the objective function.

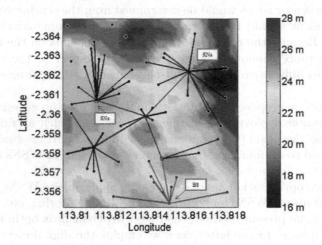

Fig. 1. Wireless sensor network in irregular terrain. The color represents elevation.

3   Model and Numerical Method

3.1   Model of Wireless Sensor Network Model

Let us consider the target field of $D_1 \times D_2$ m^2. Figure 1 shows an example of WSN placed in a field with irregular elevation where $D_1=D_2=1$km. The base station collects all the sensed data from the routers and sensor nodes. It assumed that the base station has unlimited power for its operation. On the other hand, the routers and sensor nodes are assumed to obtain power from the batteries mounted on them so that they are energy constrained. The sensor nodes detect environmental data such as temperature and humidity and send them to the nearest routers or base station.

The routers collect data from the sensor nodes to send them to the base station. Due to the limitation in the power transmission of the routers and sensor nodes, they will use up the energy within the finite duration. It is necessary to maximize their lifetime because the replacement of the batteries is expensive especially when the sensors deployed in deep forest. The aim of this study is to find optimal deployment of the routers which maximizes the lifetime of WSN.

3.2   Optimization Problem

We introduce a grid on the elevation contour map generated from the digital elevation model data [9]. We utilize a linear interpolation to estimate the elevation values at arbitrary points. It is assumed that N sensors are deployed at random location in the geographical map. The router and sensor node have communication radius R_r and R_s inside which they can communicate with other nodes. The optimization problem is defined by

$$F = \frac{1}{\sum\limits_i d_i^2 + P} \to \max, \tag{1}$$

where d_i is the Euclid distance between i-th sensor node and its nearest parent node that is either router or base station. Moreover, P represents the penalty term which is defined by

$$P = nD_1D_2 \tag{2}$$

where n is the number of the disconnected sensor nodes. In the simulation, we test communicability of the nodes, that is, if there is a point whose elevation is above the line connected between two nodes then it is judged that the two nodes cannot communicate with each other. When we consider the flat terrain, there are no obstacles among the nodes. However, when we consider the irregular terrain, the network topology must be constructed taking the communicability into account. The present method can provide optimal network topology for both flat and irregular terrain.

3.3   Real-Coded Genetic Algorithms

In this work, we employ the real-coded genetic algorithms (RGA) for the optimization of router positions, whose algorithm is described below. The gene is composed of the coordinates of M routers, that is $(x_1, x_2, ..., x_M)$, so that the degrees of freedom in the optimization is $2M$. The optimization parameters in RGA are summarized in Table 2. In particular, searching ability of RGA depends on crossover operation largely. In this work, the Blend crossover (BLX-α) is adopted for the crossover operator [14].

1. **Initial population.** Initial population which has a given population size is generated.
2. **Selection.** In this paper, we use roulette wheel selection which implements the proportional selection approach. In roulette wheel selection scheme which resembles survival of the fittest in nature, the chance to be selected for the reproduction of a chromosome is determined by its ratio of fitness value.
3. **Crossover.** The blend-crossover process (α) generates two offspring from two individuals (parents). It randomly picks values that lie between two points that contain the two parents, but may extend equally on either side determined by a user specified parameter .

4. **Mutation.** The coordinates x of the routers are replaced by (pD_1, qD_2) where p and q are independent random numbers whose domain is $[0, 1]$.
5. **Optimal solution and terminal criterion.** The process of fitness computation, selection, crossover, and mutation is executed for a maximum number of iterations. To avoid possible elimination, a parent chromosome with the highest fitness is always copied into the next generation.

4   Simulation Results

We choose the peat forest in Central Kalimantan, Indonesia for a case study of the irregular terrain. The DEM of the location is obtained from the Shuttle Radar Topography Mission (SRTM) FTP site [9]. The elevation ranges from 16m to 28m. We also consider the flat terrain for comparison. In both cases, $D_1=D_2=1$ km. In this model, the sensor and initial router nodes are placed randomly and the latter positions are optimized. We use the same random seed for the optimizations.

Table 1. Simulation parameter

Parameter	Values
Location of base station	113.8185, -2.3610
Number of nodes	50
Number of routers, M	2, 3, 4, 5
Communication radius $R_s=R_r$	50m,100m,200m,400m

Table 2. RGA parameter setting

Parameter	Values
α	1.5
Population size	25
Crossover probability	100%
Mutation probability	20%
Number of generation	100

4.1   Optimization of WSN with Small Communication Radius

We first consider the WSN which has communication radius $R_s = R_r =100$m. The number of routers, M, is set to five unless otherwise specified. Figures 2 and 3 show the optimized WSN deployment for flat and irregular terrain. In both case, there are many disconnected nodes because the maximum covered area $M\pi R_r^2$ is about 15 % of the area of the target field $D_1 D_2$.

We can find that the communication paths are constructed so that there are no obstacles among them in Fig.3. Figure 4 shows the optimization history where

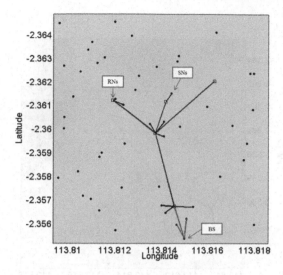

Fig. 2. Optimized topology for flat terrain, $R_s = R_r$=100m, M=5

we find that the fitness is monotonously improved. We also find in Fig.4 that the converged fitness value for the flat terrain is better than that for the irregular terrain. This is due to the fact that the communication paths in the irregular terrain must be formed avoiding the obstacles.

4.2 Optimization of WSN with Large Communication Radius

We increase the communication radius up to 400m. Now the maximum covered area $M\pi R_r^2$ is about 250% of the target area. Figures 5 and 6 show the optimized WSN topologies. There are no disconnected sensor nodes in both cases as expected. We find in Fig.6 that there are no communication paths which go from valley to valley. Figure 7 shows the optimization history, which is similar to Fig. 4. The converged value of the fitness for the flat terrain is larger than that for the irregular terrain as expected.

4.3 Number of Disconnected Sensors

We next consider dependence of the number of disconnected sensor nodes on the communication radius R_r and number of routers M. Figures 8 and 9 show changes in the numbers of disconnected sensor nodes in the WSNs which are optimized by the present method when R_r and M vary, while Figs. 10 and 11 shows them for non-optimized WSN where the routers are randomly deployed.

We can find from these results that $M\pi R_r^2$ must be 200% and 250% at smallest for the flat and irregular terrains to have full connections of the sensors when WSNs are optimized. Note that the latter ratio depends on the terrain; we have to increase the ratio for highly irregular terrains. We can estimate the necessary

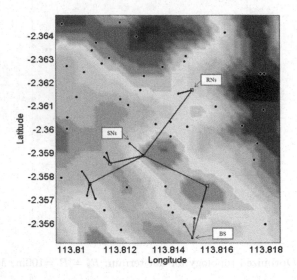

Fig. 3. Optimized topology for irregular terrain $R_s = R_r$=100m, M=5

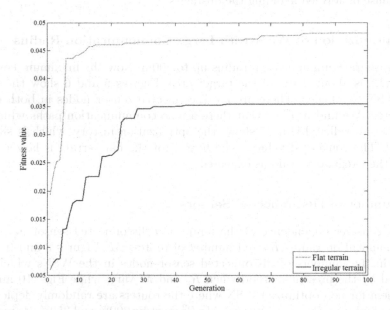

Fig. 4. Optimization history when $R_s = R_r$=100m, M=5

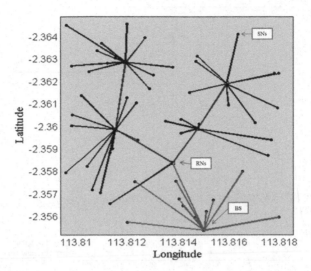

Fig. 5. Optimized topology for flat terrain, $R_s = R_r = 400$m, $M=5$

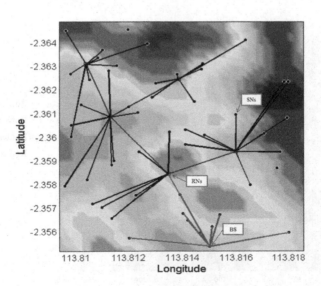

Fig. 6. Optimized topology for irregular terrain $R_s = R_r = 400$m, $M=5$

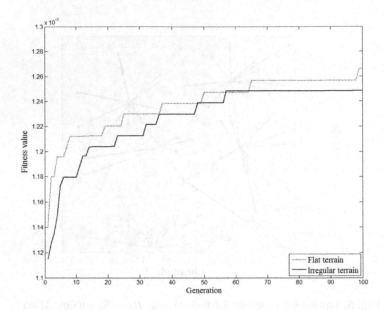

Fig. 7. Optimization history when $R_s = R_r$=400m, M=5

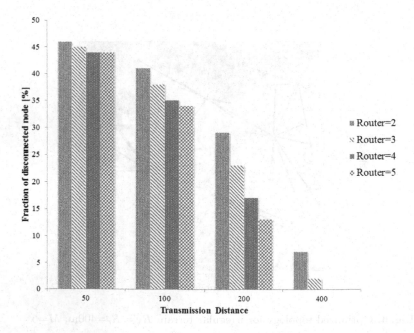

Fig. 8. Number of disconnected sensor nodes for optimized WSN in flat terrain

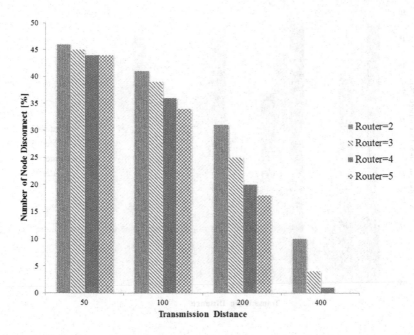

Fig. 9. Number of disconnected sensor nodes for optimized WSN in irregular terrain

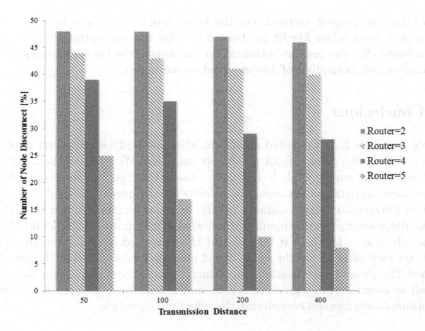

Fig. 10. Number of disconnected sensor nodes for non-optimized WSN in flat terrain

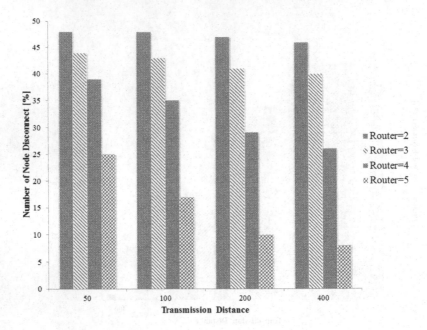

Fig. 11. Number of disconnected sensor nodes for non-optimized WSN in irregular terrain

ratio using the present method. On the other hand, we cannot have the full connections even when $M\pi R_r^2$ is about 250% for the non-optimized WSNs.It is concluded that the present optimization can reduce the total communication distance as well as number of disconnected sensor nodes.

5   Conclusions

In this paper, we have presented an optimization method for the router deployment in WSNs. We employ RGA for the optimization. We consider the irregular elevation in the target field. It has been shown that we can have optimized communication paths which avoid obstacles using the present method.

The total communication distance for the irregular terrain is longer than that for the flat terrain. The maximum covered area $M\pi R_r^2$ must be 200% and 250% of the whole area for the flat terrain and the exampled irregular terrain. The necessary ratio of $M\pi R_r^2$ to the whole target area can be computed by the present method.The present optimization can reduce the total communication distance as well as number of disconnected sensor nodes. In future, we plan to develop the optimization method considering the effect of vegetation.

References

1. Akyildiz, I.F., Su, W., Sankarasubramaniam, Y., Cayirci, E.: Wireless sensor networks: a survey. Computer Networks 38, 393–422 (2002)
2. Teguh, R., Honma, T., Usop, A., Shin, H., Igarashi, H.: Detection and Verification of Potential Peat Fire Using Wireless Sensor Network and UAV. In: International Conference Information Technolgy and Electrical Engineering, pp. 6–10 (2012)
3. Yoon, I., Noh, D.K., Lee, D., Teguh, R., Honma, T., Shin, H.: Reliable Wildfire Monitoring with Sparsely Deployed Wireless Sensor Networks. In: 2012 IEEE 26th Int. Conf. Adv. Inf. Netw. Appl., pp. 460–466 (2012)
4. Hefeeda, M., Bagheri, M.: Wireless Sensor Networks for Early Detection of Forest Fires (2007)
5. Son, B., Her, Y., Kim, J.: A Design and Implementation of Forest-Fires Surveillance System based on Wireless Sensor Networks for South Korea Mountains 6, 124–130 (2006)
6. Heinzelman, W.R., Chandrakasan, A., Balakrishnan, H.: Energy-Efficient Communication Protocol for Wireless Microsensor Networks (2000)
7. Younis, O., Fahmy, S.: HEED A Hybrid, Energy-Efficient, Distributed Clustering Approach for Ad-hoc Sensor Networks 0238294, 1–136.
8. Kulkarni, R.V., Forster, A., Venayagamoorthy, G.K.: Computational Intelligence in Wireless Sensor Networks A Survey 13, 68–96 (2011)
9. http://srtm.csi.cgiar.org/index.asp (2013)
10. Wu, Q., Rao, N.S.V., Du, X., Iyengar, S.S., Vaishnavi, V.K.: On efficient deployment of sensors on planar grid. Comput. Commun. 30, 2721–2734 (2007)
11. Bari, A., Wazed, S., Jaekel, A., Bandyopadhyay, S.: A genetic algorithm based approach for energy efficient routing in two-tiered sensor networks. Ad Hoc Networks 7, 665–676 (2009)
12. Krishnamachari, B., Ord, F.: Analysis of Energy-Efficient, Fair Routing in Wireless Sensor Networks through Non-linear Optimization
13. Zhao, C., Yu, Z., Chen, P.: Optimal Deployment of Nodes Based on Genetic Algorithm in Heterogeneous Sensor Networks. In: 2007 Int. Conf. Wirel. Commun. Netw. Mob. Comput. pp. 2743–2746 (2007)
14. Herrera, F., Lozano, M., Verdegay, J.L.: Tackling Real-Coded Genetic Algorithms: Operators and Tools for Behavioural Analysis, pp. 265–319 (1998)

On Applying Evolutionary Computation Methods to Optimization of Vacation Cycle Costs in Finite-Buffer Queue

Marcin Woźniak[1], Wojciech M. Kempa[1], Marcin Gabryel[2],
Robert K. Nowicki[2], and Zhifei Shao[3]

[1] Institute of Mathematics, Silesian University of Technology,
ul. Kaszubska 23, 44-100 Gliwice, Poland
[2] Institute of Computational Intelligence, Czestochowa University of Technology,
Al. Armii Krajowej 36, 42-200 Czestochowa, Poland
[3] School of Electrical and Electronics Engineering, Nanyang Technological University,
50 Nanyang Avenue, Singapore 639798
{Marcin.Wozniak,Wojciech.Kempa}@polsl.pl,
{Marcin.Gabryel,Robert.Nowicki}@iisi.pcz.pl, zshao1@e.ntu.edu.sg

Abstract. In this paper, problem of positioning and optimization of operation costs for finite-buffer queuing system with exponentially distributed server vacation is investigated. The problem is solved using evolutionary computation methods for independent 2-order hyper exponential input stream of packets and exponential service time distribution. Different scenarios of system operation are analyzed, i.e. different values of parameters of distribution functions describing evolution of the system.

1 Introduction

Queuing model with finite capacity is convenient tool for operation analysis of different computer hardware components used in networking. Analysis of stochastic characteristics of finite-buffer queues is useful in modeling of

- IP router in which queue of packets is connected with buffer of each output interface;
- video (graphic) card with buffer of packets waiting for displaying;
- database servers with queue of requests from remote clients;
- network interface controller (network interface card, LAN adapter) etc.

Moreover, by using queuing models with finite capacities, many other real-life phenomena can be investigated, i.e. manufacturing management or transport optimization.

It is difficult to fit a Poisson process for describing single TCP flow of packets arriving at IP router. Due to typical disturbances of such stream (like burstiness) there are, in fact, two general approaches. We can try to fit one of non-recurrent MAP-type processes describing arrival (input) stream (like MMPP-Markov Modified Poisson Process or BMAP-Batch Markovian Arrival Process),

L. Rutkowski et al. (Eds.): ICAISC 2014, Part I, LNAI 8467, pp. 480–491, 2014.

but parametrization of such processes (basing on IP trace) is difficult. The other possibility is to divide observation horizon on relatively short time intervals in which arrival process is assumed to be recurrent but, of course, inter-arrival times can have different distributions in different interval times. This conclusion is motivation for transient analysis and evolutionary positioning of finite-buffer queue with general independent (GI) input flow of packets. In the paper we deal with transient finite-buffer model with hyper exponential independent input stream of packets and exponential service times. Hyper exponentially distributed server vacation is being initialized immediately after the system becomes empty. During server vacation all arriving packets are buffered in the queue. After vacation, transmission of packets begins normally.

Server vacation is one of tools (in addition to other, like repeated (multiple) vacations or queued wake-up (N-policy) of the server) which can be used in modeling of functioning of node of wireless sensor network (WSN) during energy saving mode (see [10], [11] and [21]). Applying compact-form representation for joint transform of first busy period, first idle time and number of packets transmitted during first busy period (for details see [31]) and fixed values of unit costs of server operation (in busy and idle modes) we solved positioning and cost optimization problem using genetic algorithms (GA) with special evolutionary strategy (ES) for different distributions of server vacation duration in most common scenarios of network operation.

Evolutionary Computation (EC) methods show power of applying computational intelligence (CI) in situations where classic methods may fail. A review of recent advances in CI methods and techniques is presented in [26]. Some aspects of applying reinforcement learning and machine learning methods for AI systems is presented in [27] and [2] respectively. Randomness reduction effect of extreme learning machine in discussed in [3]. Among EC methods one may point GA, ES or heuristic algorithms (HA) as most effective techniques. EC methods help to solve complicated models of differential or integral equations. For example GA or ES find their application in positioning of technical systems (see [25]), creating learning sets for artificial intelligence (AI) control systems (see [5]) or queuing systems (QS) positioning (see [6]). EC is also efficient in analysis or simulation of annealing processes in metallurgy (see [9]). EC methods find application in dynamic, self-generated fuzzy inference systems (see [32]). Computational intelligence help in modeling of networking systems. Source-to-sink distance estimation in wireless sensor networks problem can be solved by CI, please see [19]. While in [20] is presented analysis of peculiar distance estimation methods in wireless sensor networks. Therefore we implemented EC methods to simulate and position $H_2/M/1/N$ queuing model. Optimal values of parameters of probability distributions of inter-arrival, service times, vacation duration and minimal cost of functioning of the system during single vacation cycle are found for different scenarios of system operation. Presented analysis is generalization of the one presented in [4] or [31], where 2-Erlang inter-arrival times were assumed for EC optimization.

Classical linear cost structure of a QS is considered in [29]. To problem of positioning and cost optimization are also devoted [12] and [18]. Queuing models with server vacations are investigated in [7], [8], [23] and [24]. A review of results can be found in [28] and [30]. Representation for joint transform of first busy period, first idle time and number of packets completely served during first busy period in $GI/G/1$-type system with batch arrivals and exponential single server vacation is given in [16] (see also [15]). Transient characteristics of system with single vacations with compound Poisson arrivals, generally distributed service times and infinite buffers can be found in [17] and [14]. In [13] non-stationary behavior of waiting time distribution in a finite-buffer queue with single server vacations is investigated. For all those aspects EC can be efficiently applied using object model and given service restrictions, for details please see [31].

2   Queuing Model

Examined object is a finite-buffer $H_2/M/1/N$-type QS where inter-arrival times are 2-order hyper exponentially distributed random variables with distribution function

$$F(t) = p_1\big(1 - e^{-\lambda_1 t}\big) + p_2\big(1 - e^{-\lambda_2 t}\big), \quad t > 0, \tag{1}$$

where $\lambda_i > 0$ for $i = 1, 2$ and $p_1, p_2 \geq 0$. Distribution of inter-arrival times is mixture of two exponential distributions with parameters λ_1 and λ_2, which are being "chosen" with probabilities p_1 and p_2 respectively. The system capacity is N, i.e. there are $(N - 1)$ places in buffer queue and one for packet in service. System starts working at $t = 0$ with at least one packet present. After busy period the server begins compulsory single vacation which is 2-order hyper exponentially distributed random variable with distribution function

$$V(t) = q_1\big(1 - e^{-\alpha_1 t}\big) + q_2\big(1 - e^{-\alpha_2 t}\big), \quad t > 0, \tag{2}$$

Interpretation of parameters α_i, $i = 1, 2$ and q_1, q_2 is similar to that for λ_i, $i = 1, 2$ and p_1 and p_2. If at the end of vacation there is no packet present in the system, the server is on standby and waits for first arrival to start service process. If there is at least one packet waiting for service in buffer at the end of vacation, the service process starts immediately and new busy period begins. More detailed information of modeling input inter-arrival and vacation processes is presented in [31]. During vacation, the service process is stopped. It is assumed that all inter-arrival times, service times and server vacation are totally independent random variables, where the symbols are

- τ_1 — the first busy period of the system (starting at $t = 0$);
- δ_1 — the first idle time of the system (consisting of the first vacation time v_1 and the first server standby time q_1);
- $h(\tau_1)$ — the number of packets completely served during τ_1;
- $X(t)$ — the number of packets present in the system at time t.

2.1   Auxiliary Results

Let us define only simple equations here. The explicit formula with detailed information for conditional joint characteristic functions of τ_1, δ_1 and $h(\tau_1)$ is presented in [31]. Therefore

$$B_n(s, \varrho, z) = \mathbf{E}\{e^{-s\tau_1 - \varrho\delta_1} z^{h(\tau_1)} \mid X(0) = n\}, \tag{3}$$

where $1 \leq n \leq N$, $s \geq 0$, $\varrho \geq 0$ and $|z| \leq 1$. As defined in [31]

$$a_n(s, z) = \int_0^\infty \frac{(z\mu t)^n}{n!} e^{-(\mu+s)t} dF(t), \quad n \geq 0, \tag{4}$$

$$\Psi_n(s, \varrho, z) = -\frac{(z\mu)^n}{(n-1)!} \Big[\int_0^\infty dF(t) \int_0^t x^{n-1} e^{-(\mu+s)x}$$

$$\times \Big(e^{-\varrho(t-x)} V(t-x) + \int_{t-x}^\infty e^{-\varrho y} dV(y) \Big) dx \Big]. \tag{5}$$

Moreover, sequence $(a_n(s, z))$ in (4) helps to recursively define

$$R_0(s, z) = 0, \quad R_1(s, z) = a_0^{-1}(s, z),$$

$$R_{n+1}(s, z) = R_1(s, z)(R_n(s, z) - \sum_{k=0}^n a_{k+1}(s, z) R_{n-k}(s, z)). \tag{6}$$

With introduced following function

$$f(s) = \int_0^\infty e^{-st} dF(t), \quad s > 0 \tag{7}$$

we finally have components of cost equation

$$D(s, \varrho, z) = \sum_{k=1}^{N-1} a_k(s, z) \sum_{i=2}^{N-k+1} R_{N-k+1-i}(s, z) \Psi_i(s, \varrho, z), \tag{8}$$

$$G(s, \varrho, z) = \Psi_N(s, \varrho, z) + \big(1 - f(\mu+s)\big) \sum_{k=2}^N R_{N-k}(s, z) \Psi_k(s, \varrho, z) \tag{9}$$

and

$$H(s, z) = \big(1 - f(\mu+s)\big) R_{N-1}(s, z) - \sum_{k=1}^{N-1} a_k(s, z) R_{N-k}(s, z). \tag{10}$$

Therefore for $s \geq 0$, $\varrho \geq 0$ and $|z| \leq 1$

$$B_n(s, \varrho, z) = \mathbf{E}\{e^{-s\tau_1 - \varrho\delta_1} z^{h(\tau_1)} \mid X(0) = n\}$$

$$= \frac{D(s, \varrho, z) - G(s, \varrho, z)}{H(s, z)} R_{n-1}(s, z) + \sum_{k=2}^n R_{n-k}(s, z) \Psi_k(s, \varrho, z), \quad 2 \leq n \leq N. \tag{11}$$

where $n \geq 1$ and $a_n(s, z)$, $\Psi_n(s, \varrho, z)$, $D(s, \varrho, z)$, $G(s, \varrho, z)$ and $H(s, z)$ are defined in (4), (5), (8), (9) and (10) respectively (for more details see [4] or [31]).

2.2   Cost Optimization Problem

Model of investigated computation network is described in [31]. However here $F(\cdot)$ and $V(\cdot)$ are implemented as hyper exponential distribution functions to investigate some different aspects of examined phenomena. Therefore in implemented EC system for research was considered computation network system in which inter-arrival times and vacation period have distribution functions defined in (1) and (2), respectively. EC methods were applied to find optimal set of parameters λ_i, p_i, μ and α_i to minimize operation costs $r_n(c_1)$ considered in different variants: under-load, critical load and overload. Here cost optimization problem is defined in

$$r_n(c_1) = \frac{Q_n(c_1)}{\mathbf{E}_n(c_1)} = \frac{r(\tau_1)\mathbf{E}_n\tau_1 + r(\delta_1)\mathbf{E}_n\delta_1}{\mathbf{E}_n\tau_1 + \mathbf{E}_n\delta_1}, \tag{12}$$

where the symbols are: $r(\tau_1)$-fixed unit operation costs during busy period τ_1 and $r(\delta_1)$-idle time δ_1, $\mathbf{E}_n\tau_1$-means of busy period τ_1 and $\mathbf{E}_n\delta_1$-idle time δ_1 on condition that system starts with n packets present.

In this paper we present simulation of queuing model for computational network by EC methods like GA with applied ES. Queuing systems have complicated mathematical models therefore EC calculation is best way to solve cost optimization problem. We present simulation results of $H_2/M/1/N$ finite-buffer queue with single vacation policy. In the research was used dedicated evolutionary simulation system based on mathematical model described in section 2.1 with (μ', λ') ES (for details of applied ES see [1], [6], [4] and [31]). In the research formula (12) represents optimized operation cost. Therefore EC simulation system was searching for best values of $H_2/M/1/N$ queuing model that make it work with lowest costs in specified time unit. Research provide knowledge of proper operation in some possible scenarios to help in tuning and evaluating examined network.

3   Research Results

Research results help to predict possible response time and optimize service cost $r_n(c_1)$. In the research were performed EC experiments in series of 100 samplings. Presented optimal results are average values for each scenario with following assumptions:

- Average service time: $T_{service} = \frac{1}{\mu}$,
- Average time between packages income into the system: $T_{income} = \frac{p_1}{\lambda_1} + \frac{p_2}{\lambda_2}$,
- Average vacation time: $T_{vacation} = \frac{q_1}{\alpha_1} + \frac{q_2}{\alpha_2}$,
- Examined system size: N = buffer size $+1$.

Scenario 1
EC research was performed to find set of parameters for lowest cost of work. In Table 1 are optimum values for all system parameters that affect server work. In computer network we often need to provide service of incoming requests in

Table 1. Optimal parameters μ, λ_i, α_i, p_i, q_i for $i = 1, 2$ and lowest value of (12)

λ_1	λ_2	α_1	α_2	p_1	p_2	q_1	q_2
3.07	2.43	0.97	0.42	1.45	1.20	6.13	5.10
μ	0.56			$r_n(c_1)$	0.32		

	$T_{service}$	T_{income}	$T_{vacation}$
[sec]	1.78	0.97	18.40

predefined time. Therefore parameters of the system must be set in peculiar way. This also affects operation cost, which anyway should be possibly lowest. Therefore we have also tried to simulate and optimize values of parameters in few possible scenarios. Each scenario was defined for special time of service of incoming requests, which represents possible situations of traffic in the system we simulate and optimize. In each scenario there were series of EC optimization experiments and results are given as average values.

Scenario 2
EC simulation was performed for $T_{service} = 1[sec]$, what means that the server is able to service incoming request in $1[sec]$ and lowest possible cost. Research results are shown in Table 2.

Table 2. Optimal parameters μ, λ_i, α_i, p_i, q_i for $i = 1, 2$ and lowest value of (12)

λ_1	λ_2	α_1	α_2	p_1	p_2	q_1	q_2
3.53	4.16	0.83	1.45	0.97	1.37	1.74	3.59
μ	1.00			$r_n(c_1)$	0.35		

	$T_{service}$	T_{income}	$T_{vacation}$
[sec]	1.00	0.60	4.57

Scenario 3
EC simulation was performed for $T_{service} = 2[sec]$, what means that the server is able to service incoming request in $2[sec]$ and lowest possible cost. Research results are shown in Table 3.

Table 3. Optimal parameters μ, λ_i, α_i, p_i, q_i for $i = 1, 2$ and lowest value of (12)

λ_1	λ_2	α_1	α_2	p_1	p_2	q_1	q_2
2.17	2.94	0.62	1.11	0.94	1.35	2.33	9.38
μ	0.5			$r_n(c_1)$	0.33		

	$T_{service}$	T_{income}	$T_{vacation}$
[sec]	2.00	0.89	12.17

Scenario 4

EC simulation was performed for $T_{service} = 0.5[sec]$, what means that the server is able to service incoming request in $0.5[sec]$ and lowest possible cost, what represents fast server machine like those used for business purposes. Research results with system positioning are shown in Table 4.

Table 4. Optimal parameters μ, λ_i, α_i, p_i, q_i for $i = 1, 2$ and lowest value of (12)

λ_1	λ_2	α_1	α_2	p_1	p_2	q_1	q_2
44.21	23.19	106.14	1.52	2.22	1.27	64.77	14.75
μ	2.00			$r_n(c_1)$ 0.30			
	$T_{service}$	T_{income}	$T_{vacation}$				
[sec]	0.5	0.10	10.33				

In the article we present model with description of $T_{service}$ and T_{income}, what can also be very helpful in EC positioning. In real computer networks we often need to position our system for peculiar incoming situations. Therefore we have also simulated traffic in network with some different frequencies of incoming requests. These situations with positioning are presented in following scenarios, where each simulation was performed for only some EC optimized parameters and the others calculated for lowest possible cost of work.

Scenario 5

EC simulation was performed for T_{income} to be (if possible) $1[sec]$, what means that requests are incoming to the server once in every second. Positioning is performed to achieve also lowest possible cost of work. Research results are shown in Table 5.

Table 5. Optimal EC calculated parameters λ_1, λ_2, p_2 and lowest value of (12)

λ_1	λ_2	α_1	α_2	p_1	p_2	q_1	q_2
5.30	5.96	0.89	1.51	3.86	1.38	2.24	3.50
μ	0.54			$r_n(c_1)$ 0.34			
	$T_{service}$	T_{income}	$T_{vacation}$				
[sec]	1.84	1.08	4.82				

Scenario 6

EC simulation was performed for T_{income} to be (if possible) $2[sec]$, what means that requests are incoming to the server once in 2 seconds. Positioning is performed to achieve also lowest possible cost of work. Research results are shown in Table 6.

Table 6. Optimal EC calculated parameters λ_1, λ_2, p_2 and lowest value of (12)

λ_1	λ_2	α_1	α_2	p_1	p_2	q_1	q_2
3.94	4.33	0.84	1.05	6.34	1.82	10.28	7.57
μ	0.25			$r_n(c_1)$	0.31		

	$T_{service}$	T_{income}	$T_{vacation}$
[sec]	3.95	2.03	19.41

Scenario 7

EC simulation was performed for T_{income} to be (if possible) $0.5[sec]$, what means that requests are incoming to the server 2 times in every second. This situation is describing an extensively used networking system. Positioning is performed to achieve also lowest possible cost of work. Research results are shown in Table 7.

Table 7. Optimal EC calculated parameters λ_1, λ_2, p_2 and lowest value of (12)

λ_1	λ_2	α_1	α_2	p_1	p_2	q_1	q_2
26.60	23.90	1.10	0.90	12.18	1.04	5.87	5.26
μ	0.76			$r_n(c_1)$	0.30		

	$T_{service}$	T_{income}	$T_{vacation}$
[sec]	1.32	0.50	11.16

Scenario 8

EC simulation was performed for T_{income} to be (if possible) $1[sec]$, what means that requests are incoming to the server once in every second. Positioning is performed to achieve also lowest possible cost of work. Research results are shown in Table 8.

Table 8. Optimal EC calculated parameters λ_2, p_1, p_2 and lowest value of (12)

λ_1	λ_2	α_1	α_2	p_1	p_2	q_1	q_2
7.27	2.52	1.22	1.63	2.74	1.18	1.76	5.78
μ	0.62			$r_n(c_1)$	0.36		

	$T_{service}$	T_{income}	$T_{vacation}$
[sec]	1.62	0.84	4.99

Scenario 9

EC simulation was performed for T_{income} to be (if possible) $0.5[sec]$, what means that requests are incoming to the server 2 times in every second. This situation is describing an extensively used networking system. Positioning is performed to achieve also lowest possible cost of work. Research results are shown in Table 9.

Table 9. Optimal EC calculated parameters λ_2, p_1, p_2 and lowest value of (12)

λ_1	λ_2	α_1	α_2	p_1	p_2	q_1	q_2
14.59	3.96	1.03	6.34	2.18	0.64	4.48	2.97
μ	2.74			$r_n(c_1)$	0.33		

	$T_{service}$	T_{income}	$T_{vacation}$
[sec]	0.36	0.31	4.83

Scenario 10

EC simulation was performed for T_{income} to be (if possible) 2[sec], what means that requests are incoming to the server once in every 2 seconds. Positioning is performed to achieve also lowest possible cost of work. Research results are shown in Table 10.

Table 10. Optimal EC calculated parameters λ_2, p_1, p_2 and lowest value of (12)

λ_1	λ_2	α_1	α_2	p_1	p_2	q_1	q_2
10.09	2.17	0.99	0.56	3.95	1.68	4.06	6.88
μ	3.74			$r_n(c_1)$	0.20		

	$T_{service}$	T_{income}	$T_{vacation}$
[sec]	0.27	1.16	16.33

3.1 Conclusions

Positioned network model was simulated in situations with predefined time of service or time of income. It reflects situations when traffic in the network is heavy and system must serve many requests. Presented EC research have given results for positioning of simulated system in predefined situations with lowest possible costs of work. Application of EC helps to solve and optimize even very complicated mathematical models, like in this paper. Here the model of service was built and solved using integral, differential and recursive equations, as presented in [4] and [31] in Wolfram Mathematica 9.0. Resulting equations were used for EC simulation and positioning of system parameters in predefined situations of traffic represented in different operation times. EC is powerful tool to solve complicated models where common methods are inefficient. They calculate given criteria functions very fast with appropriate accuracy. Moreover they are simple to implement in different programming languages (here in Java).

4   Final Remarks

In the article, we have examined newly proposed method for QS simulation and positioning (see [4] or [31]). EC methods like GA or ES are useful in simulation or positioning of different types of objects. They help to collect representative samples, which can be used by AI decision support systems. EC methods help to simulate complicated objects and because of EC free design, calculations are possible even in discontinuous spaces. Conducted experiments confirm EC usefulness to simulate examined object in many possible scenarios representing common situations in reality. An important restriction is only to carry out enough simulations to determine the best possible description of the object we simulate. Next research will be performed to prepare and examine implementations of other EC methods, like heuristics or nature inspired algorithms, in positioning of similar objects.

References

1. Eiben, A., Smith, J.: Introduction to Evolutionary Computing. Springer, New York (2003)
2. Er, M., Shao, Z., Wang, N.: A systematic method to guide the choice of ridge parameter in ridge extreme learning machine. In: 10th IEEE International Conference on Control and Automation (ICCA 2013), pp. 852–857. IEEE Conference Publications (2013)
3. Er, M.J., Shao, Z., Wang, N.: A Study on the Randomness Reduction Effect of Extreme Learning Machine with Ridge Regression. In: Guo, C., Hou, Z.-G., Zeng, Z. (eds.) ISNN 2013, Part I. LNCS, vol. 7951, pp. 166–173. Springer, Heidelberg (2013)
4. Gabryel, M., Nowicki, R.K., Woźniak, M., Kempa, W.M.: Genetic cost optimization of the $GI/M/1/N$ finite-buffer queue with a single vacation policy. In: Rutkowski, L., Korytkowski, M., Scherer, R., Tadeusiewicz, R., Zadeh, L.A., Zurada, J.M. (eds.) ICAISC 2013, Part II. LNCS (LNAI), vol. 7895, pp. 12–23. Springer, Heidelberg (2013)
5. Gabryel, M., Woźniak, M., Nowicki, R.K.: Creating learning sets for control systems using an evolutionary method. In: Rutkowski, L., Korytkowski, M., Scherer, R., Tadeusiewicz, R., Zadeh, L.A., Zurada, J.M. (eds.) SIDE 2012 and EC 2012. LNCS, vol. 7269, pp. 206–213. Springer, Heidelberg (2012)
6. Gabryel, M., Rutkowski, L.: Evolutionary designing of logic-type fuzzy systems. In: Rutkowski, L., Scherer, R., Tadeusiewicz, R., Zadeh, L.A., Zurada, J.M. (eds.) ICAISC 2010, Part II. LNCS (LNAI), vol. 6114, pp. 143–148. Springer, Heidelberg (2010)
7. Gupta, U.C., Banik, A.D., Pathak, S.S.: Complete analysis of $MAP/G/1/N$ queue with single (multiple) vacation(s) under limited service discipline. Journal of Applied Mathematics and Stochastic Analysis 3, 353–373 (2005)
8. Gupta, U.C., Sikdar, K.: Computing queue length distributions in $MAP/G/1/N$ queue under single and multiple vacation. Applied Mathematics and Computation 174(2), 1498–1525 (2006)
9. Hetmaniok, E., Słota, D., Zielonka, A., Pleszczyński, M.: Inverse continuous casting problem solved by applying the artificial bee colony algorithm. In: Rutkowski, L., Korytkowski, M., Scherer, R., Tadeusiewicz, R., Zadeh, L.A., Zurada, J.M. (eds.) ICAISC 2013, Part II. LNCS (LNAI), vol. 7895, pp. 431–440. Springer, Heidelberg (2013)

10. Jiang, F.C., Huang, D.-C., Yang, C.-T., Wang, K.-H.: Mitigation techniques for the energy hole problem in sensor networks using N-policy $M/G/1$ queueing models. In: Proceedings of the IET International Conference: Frontier Computing. Theory, Technologies and Applications, Taichung, August 4-6 (2010)

11. Jiang, F.-C., Huang, D.-C., Yang, C.-T., Leu, F.-Y.: Lifetime elongation for wireless sensor network using queue-based approaches. The Journal of Supercomputing 59, 1312–1335 (2012)

12. Kella, O.: Optimal control of the vacation scheme in an $M/G/1$ queue. Operations Research Journal 38(4), 724–728 (1990)

13. Kempa, W.M.: The virtual waiting time in a finite-buffer queue with a single vacation policy. In: Al-Begain, K., Fiems, D., Vincent, J.-M. (eds.) ASMTA 2012. LNCS, vol. 7314, pp. 47–60. Springer, Heidelberg (2012)

14. Kempa, W.M.: On departure process in the batch arrival queue with single vacation and setup time. Annales UMCS Informatica 10(1), 93–102 (2010)

15. Kempa, W.M.: Characteristics of vacation cycle in the batch arrival queuing system with single vacations and exhaustive service. International Journal of Applied Mathematics 23(4), 747–758 (2010)

16. Kempa, W.M.: $GI/G/1/\infty$ batch arrival queuing system with a single exponential vacation. Mathematical Methods of Operations Research 69(1), 81–97 (2009)

17. Kempa, W.M.: Some new results for departure process in the $M^X/G/1$ queuing system with a single vacation and exhaustive service. Stochastic Analysis and Applications 28(1), 26–43 (2009)

18. Lillo, R.E.: Optimal operating policy for an $M/G/1$ exhaustive server-vacation model. Methodology and Computing in Applied Probability 2(2), 153–167 (2000)

19. Ma, D., Er, M., Wang, B., Lim, H.: A novel approach toward source-to-sink distance estimation in wireless sensor networks. IEEE Communications Letters 14(5), 384–386 (2010)

20. Ma, D., Er, M., Wang, B.: Analysis of Hop-Count-Based Source-to-Destination Distance Estimation in Wireless Sensor Networks With Applications in Localization. IEEE T. Vehicular Technology 59(6), 2998–3011 (2010)

21. Mancuso, V., Alouf, S.: Analysis of power saving with continuous connectivity. Computer Networks Journal 56, 2481–2493 (2012)

22. Michalewicz, Z.: Genetic Algorithms + Data Structures = Evolution Programs, 3rd edn. Springer, New York (1996)

23. Niu, Z., Takahashi, Y.: A finite-capacity queue with exhaustive vacation/close-down/setup times and Markovian arrival processes. Queueing Systems 31, 1–23 (1999)

24. Niu, Z., Shu, T., Takahashi, Y.: A vacation queue with setup and close-down times and batch Markovian arrival processes. Performance Evaluation Journal 54(3), 225–248 (2003)

25. Nowak, A., Woźniak, M.: Algorithm for optimization of the active module by the use of genetic algorithm. Acta Mechanica Slovaca 3C, 307–316 (2008)

26. Shao, Z., Er, M.: A review of inverse reinforcement learning theory and recent advances. In: IEEE Congress on Evolutionary Computation (CEC 2012), pp. 1–8. IEEE Conference Publications (2012)

27. Shao, Z., Er, M., Huang, G.: Receding Horizon Cache and Extreme Learning Machine based Reinforcement Learning. In: 12th International Conference on Control Automation Robotics & Vision (ICARCV 2012), pp. 1591–1569. IEEE Conference Publications (2012)

28. Takagi, H.: Queueing Analysis, Vacation and Priority Systems, Finite Systems, vol. 1,2. North-Holland, Amsterdam (1993)

29. Teghem, J.: Control of the service process in a queueing system. European Journal of Operations Research 23, 141–158 (1986)
30. Tian, N., Zhang, Z.G.: Vacation queueing models. Theory and applications. Springer, New York (2006)
31. Woźniak, M., Kempa, W.M., Gabryel, M., Nowicki, R.K.: A finite-buffer queue with single vacation policy - analytical study with evolutionary positioning. International Journal of Applied Mathematics and Computer Science (accepted, 2014)
32. Zhou, Y., Er, M.: An Evolutionary Approach Toward Dynamic Self-Generated Fuzzy Inference Systems. IEEE Transactions on Systems, Man, and Cybernetics, Part B 38(4), 963–969 (2008)

On Convergence of Evolutionary Algorithms Powered by Non-random Generators

Ivan Zelinka[1,*], Donald Davendra[1], Roman Senkerik[2],
Michal Pluhacek[2], and Zuzana Kominková Oplatková[2]

[1] Technical University of Ostrava, Faculty of Electrical Engineering
and Computer Science, 17. listopadu 15,708 33 Ostrava-Poruba, Czech Republic
`ivan.zelinka@vsb.cz, donald.davendra@vsb.cz`
[2] Tomas Bata University in Zlin, Faculty of Applied Informatics, Nam T.G.
Masaryka 5555, 760 01 Zlin, Czech Republic
`{senkerik,pluhacek,oplatkova}@fai.utb.cz`

Abstract. Inherent part of evolutionary algorithms that are based on Darwin theory of evolution and Mendel theory of genetic heritage, are random processes that are used in every evolutionary algorithm like genetic algorithms etc. In this paper we present experiments (based on our previous) of selected evolutionary algorithms and test functions demonstrating impact of non-random generators on performance of the evolutionary algorithms. In our experiments we used differential evolution and SOMA algorithms with functions Griewangk and Rastrigin. We use n periodical deterministic processes (based on deterministic chaos principles) instead of pseudorandom number generators and compare performance of evolutionary algorithms powered by those processes and by pseudorandom number generators. Results presented here has to be understand like numerical demonstration rather than mathematical proofs. Our results (reported sooner and here) suggest hypothesis that certain class of deterministic processes can be used instead of random number generators without lowering the performance of evolutionary algorithms.

Keywords: evolutionary algorithms, non-random generators, pseudorandom generators, deterministic chaos.

* The following grants are acknowledged for the financial support provided for this research: Grant Agency of the Czech Republic - GACR P103/13/08195S, is partially supported by Grant of SGS No. SP2014/42, VSB - Technical University of Ostrava, Czech Republic, by the Development of human resources in research and development of latest soft computing methods and their application in practice project, reg. no. CZ.1.07/2.3.00/20.0072 funded by Operational Programme Education for Competitiveness, co-financed by ESF and state budget of the Czech Republic, further was supported by European Regional Development Fund under the project CEBIA-Tech No. CZ.1.05/2.1.00/03.0089 and by Internal Grant Agency of Tomas Bata University under the project No. IGA/FAI/2014/010.

L. Rutkowski et al. (Eds.): ICAISC 2014, Part I, LNAI 8467, pp. 492–502, 2014.

1 Introduction

The term "chaos" covers a rather broad class of phenomena whose behavior may seem erratic, chaotic at first glance. Till now was chaos observed in many of various systems (including evolutionary one) and in the last few years is also used to replace pseudorandom number generators (PRGNs) in evolutionary algorithms (EAs). Lets mention for example research papers like [4] (a comprehensive overview of mutual intersection between EAs and chaos is discussed here), one of the first use of chaos inside EAs [5], [6] - [8] discussing use of deterministic chaos inside particle swarm algorithm instead of PRGNs, [12] - [13] investigating relations between chaos and randomness or the latest one [14], [15], [11] and [10] using chaos with EAs in applications, amongst the others. A lot of researchers tried to less or more successfully replace PRGNs by different generators, usually based on deterministic chaos. For example research joining deterministic chaos and pseudorandom number generator has been done for example in [12]. Possibility of generation of random or pseudorandom numbers by use of the ultra weak multidimensional coupling of p 1-dimensional dynamical systems is discussed there. Another paper [9] deeply investigate logistic map as a possible pseudo-random number generator and is compared with contemporary pseudo-random number generators. A comparison of logistic map results is made with conventional methods of generating pseudorandom numbers. The approach used to determine the number, delay, and period of the orbits of the logistic map at varying degrees of precision (3 to 23 bits).

Used EAs (we do not discuss here special cases, modified for special experiments) of different kind like genetic algorithms [20], differential evolution [17], particle swarm [21], SOMA [16], scatter search [18], evolutionary strategies [19], etc... do not analyze whether used pseudo-random numbers are really random one and do not use information about its randomness. Random numbers are only simply used. On the other side, as demonstrated in mentioned references, EAs powered by deterministic chaotic systems (DCHS) gives the same or often better performance. Because DCHS can generate periodical series (upon to the final numerical precision) it is obvious that EAs performance shall be from certain numerical precision of DCHS comparable with performance of classical EAs.

This publication is focused on use of n periodic deterministic series (generated by deterministic chaos systems), that are used inside evolutionary algorithms instead of pseudorandom number generator. The first set of proposed experiments here is reported in [1] (periodicity of chaotic systems and its use with differential evolution has been demonstrated on Schwefel function), then in [2] (detail description how periodicity is generated by chaos systems) and in [3] which is extension of the [1] for SOMA algorithm. Also in in [26] is discussed extended version of used of DCHS in EAs. this paper we used differential evolution (DE-Rand1Bin) and SOMA (AllToOne) algorithms with functions Griewangk Rastrigin to more closely demonstrate convergence (based on our previous papers [1], [2], [3] and [26]) of used EAs powered by non-random generators.

2   Experiment Design

Experiments done in this research are based on [2] where it is reported how existence of periodicity generated by deterministic chaos systems depends on numerical precision (numbers behind decimal point) and are using n periodical time series generated by chaotic systems with given numerical precision inside EAs instead of PRGNs. The test functions used for our experiments were: Griewangk (Eq. (1)), (Rastrigin (Eq. (2)). Experiment with each function has been repeated 20× and statistical properties were calculated. Part of them (due to limited space of this paper) are reported in tables and one figure.

$$1 + \sum_{i=1}^{D} \frac{x_i^2}{4000} - \prod_{i=1}^{D} \cos(\frac{x_i}{\sqrt{i}}) \tag{1}$$

$$2D \sum_{i=1}^{D} x_i^2 - 10 \cos(2\pi x_i) \tag{2}$$

In this part the central object of this study is simple logistic equation (Eq. 3). Several experiments were performed and some figures, exhibiting results, were generated, showing how depend periodicity of deterministic chaos system on numerical precision, see for example [1] and extended versions in [2] and [3]. The table 1 show n periodicity of time series generated by deterministic chaos systems. Also another chaotic generators of different mathematical description can be used like Lozi ([2]), Henon, Ikeda or another like for example artificially synthesized and reported in [4].

$$x_{n+1} = A x_n (1 - x_n) \tag{3}$$

The impact of the precision on the dynamics of logistic equation - map is such that mapping function is "converted" to the stepwise mapping function. That is the source of the appearance of many periodic orbits, later on used in our experiments [3].

Our experiments have been set so that periodical deterministic time series based on deterministic chaos generators were used instead of PRNGs. Based on the fact that numerical precision has impact on existence of periodicity in deterministic chaos, we have selected logistic equation, Eq. 3, and data series generated by this equation for numerical precisions from interval [1, 13] with setting $A = 4$, see Tab. 1 which shows minimal and maximal period for current setting and Fig. 1, Fig 2. Algorithms selected for our experiments were differential evolution (DERand1Bin) [17] and SOMA [16].

2.1   Algorithm Setting

Setting of both algorithm is in Tab. 2. Based on this setting and algorithm architecture it is easy to calculate how many times deterministic data series (let call them pseudo-chaotic numbers - PCHNs) generated by DCHS have been

Table 1. Periodicity dependance of Eq. 3 on various numerical precision. Table also shows how many times was used n periodical series by DE and SOMA algorithm (up to precision 13).

Numerical Precision	Minimal Period	Maximal Period	Repeated in DE	Repeated in SOMA
1	4	4	32500	43181
2	2	10	13000	17272
3	10	29	4482	5956
4	15	36	3611	4797
5	67	170	764	1016
6	143	481	270	359
7	421	758	171	227
8	1030	4514	28	38
9	2277	11227	11	15
10	2948	35200	3	4
11	9668	57639	2	2
12	65837	489154	0	0
13	518694	518694	0	0

used in EAs. Tab. 1 summarizes how many times were PCHNs repeatedly used. All experiments were done in Mathematica 9, on MacBook Pro, 2.8 GHz Intel Core 2 Duo. **The main aim was not to compare mutual performance of used algorithms but performance between the same algorithm using PRNGs and PCHN**, that is why we do not use cumber of cost function number evaluations but simply migrations or generations.

Experiments were performed in an environment of Wolfram Mathematica, thus we used the built-in Mathematica software pseudo random number generator. The default Mathematica Software PRNG - extended cellular automaton generator Extended CA with default automatic setting was applied to represent traditional pseudo-random number generator in comparisons, see http://reference. wolfram.com/mathematica/tutorial/RandomNumberGeneration.html.

So in total 3120 (2 algorithms × 2 test functions × 20 repetitions × 13 different numerical precisions) evolutionary experiments has been done. In each experiment was PRNGs used on the start of Eq. 3 to set initial condition $x_{start} \in [0, 1]$. Remaining use of Eq. 3 was PRNGs free, i.e. PRNGs was not further in use. Typical algorithm performance dependance on the precision is depicted on Fig. 3 and Fig. 4. It is visible that both algorithms are sensitive on precision up to 4-8 and then are comparable between themselves as well as between versions with PRNGs and DCHS, see [1], [2] and [3].

3   Results

Here we discusses what impact n periodical time series generated by chaotic systems (with given numerical precision) have inside EAs on its performance and convergence and it is compared with EAs powered by PRGNs.

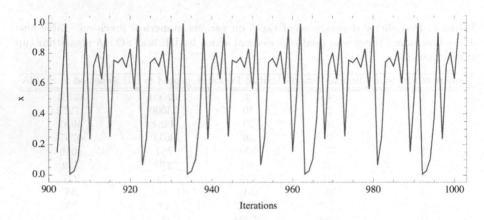

Fig. 1. Periodical time series generated by DCHS (precision = 3) based on Eq. 3 for $A = 4$, see Tab. reftablePeriodAlg.

Table 2. Algorithms setting

DERand1Bin		SOMA AllToAll	
NP	20	PopSize	20
Dimensions	20	Dimensions	20
Generations	500	Migrations	20
F	0.9	PRT	0.1
CR	0.3	PathLength	5
		Step	0.11

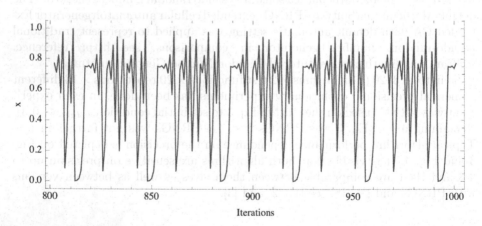

Fig. 2. Periodical time series generated by DCHS (precision = 4) based on Eq. 3 for $A = 4$, see Tab. reftablePeriodAlg.

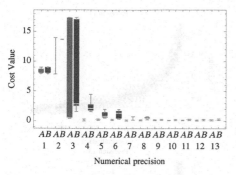

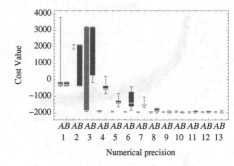

Fig. 3. An example: the performance of DE and SOMA algorithms on Griewangk's function (Eq. (1)) with dependance on precision

Fig. 4. An example: the performance of DE and SOMA algorithms on Rastrigin's function (Eq. (2)) with dependance on precision

Table 3. Summarization of all the best results of DE and SOMA algorithm

	SOMA		DE	
Precision	Griewangk	Rastrigin	Griewangk	Rastrigin
1	7.99999.	-376.187	8.	-376.187
2	7.87547	1852.38	13.6861	2127.76
3	0.291183	-1927.14	1.56746	-1023.23
4	0.120748	-1949.25	1.23773	-920.347
5	**0.0717273**	**-1961.73**	0.437302	-1409.54
6	0.092951	-1965.82	0.274384	-1963.65
7	0.046194	-1990.	**0.150767**	1812.99
8	0.0865711	-1970.78	0.203421	-1994.35
9	0.0765879	-1969.65	0.112012	**-1999.32**
10	0.088343	-1981.46	0.106905	-1995.92
11	0.100957	-1990.46	0.134792	-1999.98
12	0.06444398	-1974.28	0.105057	-1999.98
13	0.0763352	-1971.21	0.16496	-1999.92
PRNGs	0.118099	-1953.17	0.1521	-1998.96

Results based on all experiments are reported in Tab. 3 and for demonstration visualized, see example Fig. 3 and Fig. 4 for total overview. Tables contain the best cost values and figures are selected for demonstration only. Results of the DE and SOMA use are in the Table 3. The classical random case is reported at the bottom of each table. In the figures 5 - 8 is depicted convergence of each algorithm powered by PCHNs and can be easily compared to itself with PRGNs version.

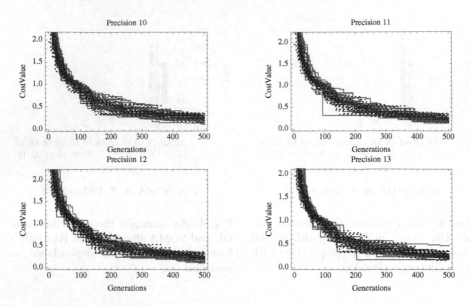

Fig. 5. An example: the performance of DE algorithms on Griewangk's function (Eq. (1)) with dependance on precision.Solid (red) line is the behavior of DE powered by non-random generator, dotted (black) is standard DE with pseudorandom number generator.

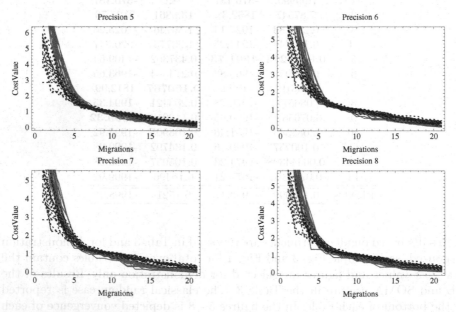

Fig. 6. An example: the performance of SOMA algorithms on Griewangk's function (Eq. (1)) with dependance on precision.Solid (red) line is the behavior of DE powered by non-random generator, dotted (black) is standard DE with pseudorandom number generator.

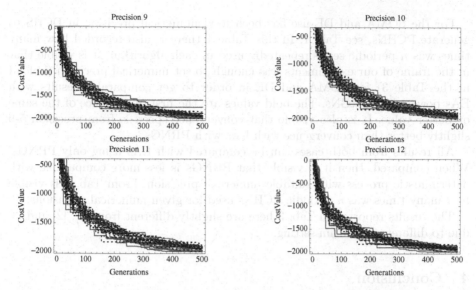

Fig. 7. An example: the performance of DE algorithms on Rastrigin's function (Eq. (2)) with dependance on precision.Solid (red) line is the behavior of DE powered by non-random generator, dotted (black) is standard DE with pseudorandom number generator.

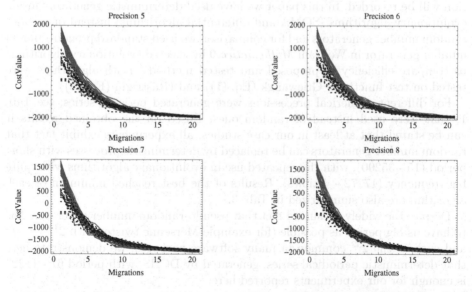

Fig. 8. An example: the performance of SOMA algorithms on Rastrigin's function (Eq. (2)) with dependance on precision.Solid (red) line is the behavior of DE powered by non-random generator, dotted (black) is standard DE with pseudorandom number generator.

For the SOMA and DE use has been used numerical precision in DCHS to generate PCHNs, see Tab. 1. In this Table 1 there is also recorded how many times was n periodic series repeatedly used in each algorithm. It is visible that in the frame of our experiments was enough to set numerical precision (bolded in the Table 3) for SOMA and DE in order to get comparable results with EAs powered by PRGNs. The bold values are the first appearance of the same or better value. It is also visible that convergence speed is from precision 5-9 slightly better than convergence with EAs with PRNGs.

All results from both cases can be compared with EAs using only PRNGs. When compared, then it is visible that PRNGs is less-more comparable with deterministic process with suitable numerical precision. From Tab. 1 is visible how many times was n periodic PCHNs used for given numerical precisions.

The results reported in Tab. 3 here are slightly different from [1], [2] and [3] due to different algorithm setting.

4 Conclusion

The main motivation of the research in this paper is question it is possible to replace random number generators by deterministic periodic processes originated in systems of deterministic chaos and what convergence of EA under investigation will be recorded. In this paper we have used deterministic generators inside evolutionary algorithms (SOMA and differential algorithms) instead of pseudo-random number generators and for comparison we used standard pseudo-random number generator in Wolfram *Mathematica* 9 in selected evolutionary algorithms to compare efficiency of proposed and tested methods. Both algorithms were tested on test functions: Griewangk (Eq. (1)) and (Rastrigin (Eq. (2)).

For different numerical precessions were generated periodic series; see Tab. 1, that were used instead of random ones. Based on the obtained results it can be stated that at least in our case studies, all experiments exhibit fact that random number generators can be replaced by deterministic processes with short period (15 - 35200), with the repeated use in evolutionary algorithms with quite big frequency (17272 - 4 times). Results of the best reached minimum of each algorithm are also summarized in Tab. 3.

Despite the widely presumed fact that pseudo-random number generators has to have as big period as possible (for example Mersenne twister with $2^{19937} - 1$) and such as the 2^{32} common in many software packages, we demonstrate here that deterministic periodical series, generated by DCHS, with period 67 - 11227 is enough for our experiments reported here.

Our further research is focused on more extensive and intensive testing on another algorithms like scatter search [18], evolutionary strategies [19], genetic algorithms [20], [24] or particle swarm [21]. Also novel algorithms will be tested for its performance under our proposed approach in [22], [23] and alternative methods of symbolic regression [25].

It is almost sure that better settings could be found for used algorithms in order to get better results, but as written here, this paper was focused on performance of the same algorithm with different "numerical engine" used to simulate or replace random processes inside evolutionary algorithms.

References

1. Zelinka, I., Senkerik, R., Pluhacek, M.: Do Evolutionary Algorithms Indeed Require Randomness? In: IEEE Congress on Evolutionary Computation, Cancun, Mexico, pp. 2283–2289 (2013)
2. Zelinka, I., Chadli, M., Davendra, D., Senkerik, R., Pluhacek, M., Lampinen, J.: Hidden Periodicity - Chaos Dependance on Numerical Precision. In: Zelinka, I., Chen, G., Rössler, O.E., Snasel, V., Abraham, A. (eds.) Nostradamus 2013: Prediction, Model. & Analysis. AISC, vol. 210, pp. 47–59. Springer, Heidelberg (2013)
3. Zelinka, I., Chadli, M., Davendra, D., Senkerik, R., Pluhacek, M., Lampinen, J.: Do Evolutionary Algorithms Indeed Require Random Numbers? Extended Study. In: Zelinka, I., Chen, G., Rössler, O.E., Snasel, V., Abraham, A. (eds.) Nostradamus 2013: Prediction, Model. & Analysis. AISC, vol. 210, pp. 61–75. Springer, Heidelberg (2013)
4. Zelinka, I., Celikovsky, S., Richter, H., Chen, G.: Evolutionary Algorithms and Chaotic Systems, 550S p. Springer, Germany (2010)
5. Caponetto, R., Fortuna, L., Fazzino, S., Xibilia, M.: Chaotic sequences to improve the performance of evolutionary algorithms. IEEE Trans. Evol. Comput. 7(3), 289–304 (2003)
6. Pluhacek, M., Senkerik, R., Davendra, D., Kominkova Oplatkova, Z., Zelinka, I.: On the behavior and performance of chaos driven PSO algorithm with inertia weight. Computers and Mathematics with Applications 66(2), 122–134 (2013)
7. Pluhacek, M., Budikova, V., Senkerik, R., Oplatkova, Z., Zelinka, I.: Extended Initial Study on the Performance of Enhanced PSO Algorithm with Lozi Chaotic Map. In: Zelinka, I., Snasel, V., Rössler, O.E., Abraham, A., Corchado, E.S. (eds.) Nostradamus: Mod. Meth. of Prediction, Modeling. AISC, vol. 192, pp. 167–177. Springer, Heidelberg (2013)
8. Pluhacek, M., Budikova, V., Senkerik, R., Oplatkova, Z., Zelinka, I.: On the Performance of Enhanced PSO algorithm with Lozi Chaotic Map an Initial Study. In: Proceedings of 18th International Conference on Soft Computing - MENDEL 2012, pp. 40–45 (2012) ISBN 978-80-214-4540-6
9. Persohn, K.J., Povinelli, R.J.: Analyzing logistic map pseudorandom number generators for periodicity induced by finite precision floating-point representation. Chaos, Solitons and Fractals 45, 238–245 (2012)
10. Davendra, D., Zelinka, I., Senkerik, R.: Chaos driven evolutionary algorithms for the task of PID control. Computers and Mathematics with Applications 60(4), 1088–1104 (2010) ISSN 0898-1221
11. Senkerik, R., Davendra, D., Zelinka, I., Oplatkova, Z., Pluhacek, M.: Optimization of the Batch Reactor by Means of Chaos Driven Differential Evolution. In: Snasel, V., Abraham, A., Corchado, E.S. (eds.) SOCO Models in Industrial & Environmental Appl. AISC, vol. 188, pp. 93–102. Springer, Heidelberg (2013)
12. Lozi, R.: Emergence of Randomness from Chaos. International Journal of Bifurcation and Chaos 22(2), 1250021 (2012), doi:10.1142/S0218127412500216
13. Wang, X.-Y., Yang, L.: Design of Pseudo-Random Bit Generator Based On Chaotic Maps. International Journal of Modern Physics B 26(32), 1250208 (9 pages) (2012), doi:10.1142/S0217979212502086

14. Zhang, S.Y., Xingsheng, L.G.: A hybrid co-evolutionary cultural algorithm based on particle swarm optimization for solving global optimization problems. In: International Conference on Life System Modeling and Simulation/International Conference on Intelligent Computing for Sustainable Energy and Environment (LSMS-ICSEE), Wuxi, PEOPLES R CHINA, September 17-20 (2010)

15. Hong, W.-C., Dong, Y., Zhang, W.Y., Chen, L.-Y., Panigrahi, B. K.: Cyclic electric load forecasting by seasonal SVR with chaotic genetic algorithm. International Journal of Electrical Power and Energy Sysytems 44(1), 604–614, doi:10.1016/j.ijepes.2012.08.010

16. Zelinka, I.: SOMA – Self Organizing Migrating Algorithm. In: Babu, B.V., Onwubolu, G. (eds.) New Optimization Techniques in Engineering, pp. 167–218. Springer, New York (2004)

17. Price, K.: An Introduction to Differential Evolution. In: Corne, D., Dorigo, M., Glover, F. (eds.) New Ideas in Optimization, pp. 79–108. McGraw-Hill, London (1999)

18. Glover, F., Laguna, M., Mart, R.: Scatter Search. In: Ghosh, A., Tsutsui, S. (eds.) Advances in Evolutionary Computation: Theory and Applications, pp. 519–537. Springer, New York (2003)

19. Beyer, H.G.: Theory of Evolution Strategies. Springer, New York (2001)

20. Holland, J.H.: Genetic Algorithms. Scientific American, 44–50 (July 1992)

21. Clerc, M.: Particle Swarm Optimization. ISTE Publishing Company (2006) ISBN 1905209045

22. Matousek, R.: HC12: The Principle of CUDA Implementation. In: Matousek (ed.) 16th International Conference on Soft Computing, MENDEL 2010, Brno, pp. 303–308 (2010)

23. Matousek, R., Zampachova, E.: Promising GAHC and HC12 algorithms in global optimization tasks. Journal Optimization Methods & Software 26(3), 405–419 (2011)

24. Matousek, R.: GAHC: Improved Genetic Algorithm. In: Krasnogor, N., Nicosia, G., Pavone, M., Pelta, D. (eds.) Nature Inspired Cooperative Strategies for Optimization (NICSO 2007). SCI, vol. 129, pp. 507–520. Springer, Heidelberg (2008)

25. Zelinka, I., Davendra, D., Senkerik, R., Jasek, R., Oplatkova, Z.: Analytical Programming - a Novel Approach for Evolutionary Synthesis of Symbolic Structures. In: Kita, E. (ed.) Evolutionary Algorithms. InTech (2011), http://www.intechopen.com/books/evolutionary-algorithms/ analytical-programming-a-novel-approach-for-evolutionary-synthesis-of-symbolic-structures, doi:10.5772/16166, ISBN: 978-953-307-171-8

26. Zelinka, I., Senkerik, R., Pluhacek, M.: Evolutionary Algorithms Powered by Nonrandom Processes. In: 19th International Conference on Soft Computing, MENDEL 2013 (2013)

Classification and Estimation

A Semantic Kernel for Text Classification Based on Iterative Higher–Order Relations between Words and Documents

Berna Altinel[1], Murat Can Ganiz[2], and Banu Diri[3]

[1] Department of Computer Engineering, Marmara University, Istanbul, Turkey
berna.altinel@marmara.edu.tr
[2] Department of Computer Engineering, Dogus University, Istanbul, Turkey
mcganiz@dogus.edu.tr
[3] Department of Computer Engineering, Yildiz Technical University, Istanbul, Turkey
banu@ce.yildiz.edu.tr

Abstract. We propose a semantic kernel for Support Vector Machines (SVM) that takes advantage of higher-order relations between the words and between the documents. Conventional approach in text categorization systems is to represent documents as a "Bag of Words" (BOW) in which the relations between the words and their positions are lost. Additionally, traditional machine learning algorithms assume that instances, in our case documents, are independent and identically distributed. This approach simplifies the underlying models, but nevertheless it ignores the semantic connections between words as well as the semantic relations between documents that stem from the words. In this study, we improve the semantic knowledge capture capability of a previous work in [1], which is called χ-Sim Algorithm and use this method in the SVM as a semantic kernel. The proposed approach is evaluated on different benchmark textual datasets. Experiment results show that classification performance improves over the well-known traditional kernels used in the SVM such as the linear kernel (one of the state-of-the-art algorithms for text classification system), the polynomial kernel and the Radial Basis Function (RBF) kernel.

Keywords: machine learning, support vector machine, text classification, higher-order paths, semantic kernel.

1   Introduction

Text categorization is a popular task which aims to label documents via using predefined category labels. There are large amounts of textual data accumulated both in organizations and on the internet especially on social networks, microblogging sites, blogs, forums, new, etc. This huge set of documents continues to increase by the contributions of millions of people every day. Automatically processing and extracting meaning from these increasing amounts of textual data is one of the most important problems for both research and commercial entities. The text classification plays a very important role in several popular and widely used applications such as document

L. Rutkowski et al. (Eds.): ICAISC 2014, Part I, LNAI 8467, pp. 505–517, 2014.
© Springer International Publishing Switzerland 2014

filtering, sentiment classification, information extraction, summarization and question answering.When processing textual data, either in information retrieval or text classification; it is common to use the bag of words (BOW) feature representation. In this approach the documents are represented only by the occurrences or the frequencies of the words or terms independent from their positions in the document. Although this approach is very popular due to its simplicity, it has several drawbacks. First of all, it breaks multi-word expressions into pieces, secondly it treats synonymous words as different terms; and thirdly it treats polysemous words (i.e., words with multiple meanings) as one single component, as it is mentioned in [2]. However, in order to enhance the prediction capabilities of text classification algorithms, it is important to benefit from the semantic relations between the words and even between the documents.

In this study, we introduce a new kernel for Support Vector Machines (SVM) called *Normalized Iterative-Higher-Orders Semantic Kernel* (N-IHOSK) which is based on higher-order paths between documents as well as the terms. Our approach is motivated by the studies of higher-order Naïve Bayes [3], [4] and Higher-Order Smoothing [5], [6] which makes use of the higher-order paths between terms, and recently introduced work of [7] which focus on the higher-order paths between documents. In this study, we improve the semantic knowledge capture capability of a previous work in [1], which is called χ-Sim algorithm and use this method in the SVM as a semantic kernel. Our target is to capture latent semantic information between the terms and between the documents. In our experiments, our proposed framework is compared with other traditional kernel methods for SVM such as linear kernel, polynomial kernel and Radial Basis Function (RBF) kernel. It is important to note that SVM with linear kernel is one the state of the art algorithms for text classification [8], [9]. These traditional kernels can be considered as first-order methods since their context is a single document and they model just the first-order co-occurrences of the terms. However, N-IHOSK can make use of the higher-order paths that include several different terms and documents in the context of the whole dataset. Our experiments running the N-IHOSK on several benchmark datasets show that the classification performance of SVM improves considerably over the first-order kernels.

The remainder of the paper is organized as follows: background information and related work including the SVM, semantic kernels and higher-order paths are summarized in Section 2. Section 3 presents and analyzes the proposed kernel for text classification algorithm. The experiment setup and corresponding results including some discussion points are given in Section 4. Finally, in Section 5 we provide the conclusion and the future work.

2 Background Information and Related Work

2.1 Support Vector Machines for Classification Problem

The SVM in general is a linear classifier which finds the optimal separating hyperplane between the classes. It is possible to use a kernel function in SVM which can map the data into a higher dimensional feature space if it is not possible to find a hyperplane in the original space [8]. We can consider a kernel function as a kind of similarity function, which can give the similarity of data points in the original space. Therefore, defining a suitable kernel is a direct way of finding a good representation of these data points as it is mentioned in [2], [10] and [11]. The SVM algorithm which is first introduced by Vapnik, Guyon and Boser [12] in 1992, has become one of the popular algorithms in real-world-problems producing good accuracies even with high-dimensional and sparse data [8]. Although the SVM is a binary classifier by its nature, it can be used for multi-class categorization using "one-against-the-rest" or "one-against-one" strategies [13]. Because of these benefits the SVM with linear kernel is one of the state of the art algorithms in text classification domain since textual data represented using BOW approach is very high-dimensional and quite sparse. Thus, considering the nature of the text classification (high-dimensional and sparse data), we decided to design a higher-order semantic kernel for SVM.

2.2   Semantic Kernels for Text Classification

According to the definition mentioned in [12], [10], and [2] and [14], any function in the following form (Eq.1) is a valid kernel function.

$$k(d_1, d_2) = \langle \phi(d_1), \phi(d_2) \rangle \tag{1}$$

In Eq.1, d_1 and d_2 are input space vectors and ϕ is a suitable mapping from input space into a feature space.

In [10], Siolas et al. propose a semantic kernel which is based on WordNet [15], which could be seen as a semantic network, for getting the term similarity information. In their work an estimation of two words semantic relation is supplied by WordNet's hierarchical tree structure. The authors in [10] have included this knowledge into the definition of Gaussian kernel. Their results show that the existence of semantic proximity metric increases the classification accuracy in SVM [10]. However, their approach treats multi-word concepts as single terms and does nothing to handle polysemy.

Semantic kernels with super concept declaration were studied in [14]. The aim of their work is to create a kernel algorithm which includes the topological knowledge of their super concept expansion. They apply this mapping with the help of a semantic smoothing matrix Q that is shown to be composed of P and P^T which includes super-concept information about their corpus. The proposed kernel function is given in Eq. 2.

$$k(d_1, d_2) = d_1 \cdot P \cdot P^T \cdot d_2^T \tag{2}$$

Their results show that they get a coherent progress in performance for super-concept semantic smoothing kernels in those cases in which little training data exists or the feature representations are highly sparse [14]. However their experiments were kept introductory and did not use a word sense disambiguation strategy. [14]

Similarly, in [16] the WordNet is used as a semantic information resource. But they ([10], [14] and [16]) stated that the coverage of WordNet is not sufficient and as a result, several following studies focused on information sources of wider coverage such as Wikipedia[1].

---

[1] http://www.wikipedia.org/

Wang et al. [2] combined the background knowledge gathered from Wikipedia into a semantic kernel for enriching the representation of documents. The similarity value between two documents in their kernel function formed as in Eq.3 where S is a semantic matrix which is created as a composition of the contributions from Wikipedia, d_1 and d_2 are term-frequency vectors of documents d_1 and d_2, respectively. This composed S matrix consists of three measures. First of them is a content-based measure which is based on the BOW representation of Wikipedia articles. Second measure is the out-link-category-based measure which gives an information related to the out-link categories of two associative articles [2]. Third measure is a distance measure that is calculated as the length of the shortest path connecting the two categories of two articles belong to, in the acyclic graph schema of Wikipedia's category taxonomy [2].

$$k(d_1, d_2) = d_1 \cdot S \cdot S^T \cdot d_2 \qquad (3)$$

Their method is stated to overcome the shortages of the BOW approach. Their results demonstrate adding semantic knowledge into document representation by means of Wikipedia improves the categorization accuracy.

2.3   Iterative Higher-Order Relations between Words and Documents

Illustration of using the higher-order paths is given in Table 1. There are three documents, d_1, d_2 and d_3 which include sets of terms $\{t_1, t_2\}$, $\{t_3\}$ and $\{t_2, t_3\}$ are depicted. With a classical similarity measure which uses the number of shared terms (e.g. the dot product), the similarity value between documents d_1 and d_2 (in Table 1) is calculated as zero since they do not share any terms. But in fact these two documents are similar to a certain degree through d_3. So using a higher-order approach, it is possible to obtain a similarity value between d_1 and d_2 which is larger than zero. We can explain this phenomenon with the statement that two documents are written about the same topic using two different but semantically closer sets of terms. In this case the terms belonging to each set frequently co-occur in other documents relating to this topic, forming a connection pattern which can be revealed by using second-order paths.

Table 1. Illustration of Higher-Order Paths

D	t_1	t_2	t_3
d_1	1	1	0
d_2	0	0	1
d_3	0	1	1

In our study we are motivated by the work of [4] which uses higher-order paths between terms to exploit latent semantics and by the work of [1] which builds iterative higher-order-paths between documents and terms. In [1], the authors devise an iterative method to learn the similarity matrix between documents using similarity matrix between terms and vice-versa. They build a co-similarity algorithm which is called χ-Sim. The document similarity matrix is generated iteratively using **SR** (a similarity matrix between documents) and **SC** (a similarity matrix between terms). The major steps of their algorithm are described below:

1. Initialize the similarity matrices **SR** (documents) and **SC** (words) with the identity matrix **I**. This is a reasonable starting point since similarity between a document (or a term) and itself equals one and it equals to zero in the other cases. They denote these matrices as SC_0 and SR_0. [1]

2. At each iteration t, they calculate a new similarity matrix between documents SR_t by using the similarity matrix between words SC_{t-1} previously computed. They use the Hadamard product (denoted by "•") in order to multiply their similarity values with normalized weights by the normalization matrix **NR**. [1]

Their SR_t and SC_t formulas are given as

$$SR_t = (D.SC_{(t-1)}.D^T) \bullet NR \quad \text{with} \quad nr_{i,j} = \frac{1}{|d_i|.|d_j|} \tag{4}$$

$$SC_t = (D.SR_{(t-1)}.D^T) \bullet NC \quad \text{with} \quad nc_{i,j} = \frac{1}{|d_i|.|d_j|} \tag{5}$$

where **D** is the document corpus, D^T is the transpose of **D** matrix, **SR** is row (document) similarity matrix, **SC** is column (word) similarity matrix, and **NR** and **NC** are row and column normalization matrices, respectively. They state that they repeat SR_t and SC_t calculations for a limited number of times such as $t=4$ [1].

3   Methodology

In our approach, D_t is the data matrix having r rows (documents) and c columns (words) formed from the training set. In this matrix d_{ij} shows the occurrence frequency of the jth word in the ith document; $d_i = [d_{i1} .. d_{ic}]$ is the row vector representing the document i and $d_j = [d_{1j} ..d_{rj}]$ is the column vector corresponding to word j.

We also tried several term weighting methods. First of them is TF-IDF (Term Frequency- Inverse Document Frequency) which is a statistical measure used to evaluate the importance of a word for a document in a corpus [17]. The formula for TF-IDF is given in Eq. 6.

$$TF - IDF(t,d) = p_{td} \times \log \frac{N}{n} \tag{6}$$

where p_{td} equals the number of times that t occurs in document d, N is the number of documents in the corpus and n is the number of documents that term t occurs. Another weighting approach we tried is from Dumais's research in [19]. In this approach, terms are represented in a document after multiplying by a value that is the global weight of the term in the whole corpus. The local weight of a term t in a document d is calculated as taking the log value of the total frequency of t in d. The global weight of a term is the entropy of that term in the corpus and according to [19] the entropy equals

$$Entropy(t,d) = 1 - \sum_{i=1}^{N} \frac{p_{td} \log(p_{td})}{\log(N)} \quad (7)$$

where N is the number of documents and p_{td} equals the number of times that t occurs in d divided by the total number of times that t occurs.

However, since we get better accuracies for linear kernel with the only TF (Term-Frequency) schema without any weighting, we use TF instead of TF-IDF or Entropy weighting approaches in our experiments for both linear kernel and our algorithm.

We use our term-frequency document corpus for χ-Sim's SC and SR similarity matrix calculations. We calculate up to four iterations. Similar to [1], we calculate SR_0, SC_0, SR_1, SC_1, SR_2, SC_2, SR_3, SC_3, SR_4, SC_4 matrices and after that we use these SC matrices, which contain iterative higher-order relations between terms, into our kernel by using Eq. 8:

$$k_{IHOSK}(d_1, d_2) = d_1 \cdot S.S^T \cdot d_2^T \quad (8)$$

where $K_{IHOSK}(d_1, d_2)$ is the similarity value between documents d_1 and d_2 , S is a semantic matrix which is gathered from the previously mentioned calculations of SC_2 and d_1 and d_2 are term-frequency vectors of the documents. The S is a semantic matrix is based on *iterative higher-order paths* between documents and between terms. This kernel function means that the transformation of a document vector from input space to a feature space can be done by multiplying it with a semantic matrix as given in Eq.9:

$$\phi(d_1) = d_1 \cdot S \quad \text{and} \quad \phi(d_2) = S^T \cdot d_2^T \quad (9)$$

In Eq.9. $\phi(d_1)$ and $\phi(d_2)$ are the transformations of document vectors d_1 and d_2 from their original input space into the feature space as required in the definition of kernel which is mentioned in Section 2.

After performing experiments up to four iterations of SC matrices, we conclude that the best results are obtained with the second iteration matrices (SR_2, SC_2). The following experimental results section reflects the results of our approach using these matrices.

Since we work with textual datasets which are high dimensional and highly sparse, we think that it is possible to benefit from normalization methods which could be applied on the similarity matrices. We experiment with several matrix normalization methods including row-level normalization (dividing each value in a row by the maximum value in that row), column-level normalization (dividing each value in a column by the maximum value in that column), document-length normalization (dividing each term frequency in a row with the corresponding documents length) and several other techniques which are used and explained in [9] (e.g., complement, weight normalization) and also some common methods from the literature which are explained in [18] such as z-score normalization, min-max normalization, etc. We obtained best accuracy results with length normalization which is defined in Eq.10.

$$\forall i, j \in 1...r \quad N\text{-}IHOSK\,(d_i, d_j) = \frac{IHOSK\,(d_i, d_j)}{|d_i|.|d_j|} \tag{10}$$

In Eq. 10, r is the number of documents in our corpus, IHOSK is similarity value between documents d_i and d_j, N-IHOSK is the normalized similarity value of these documents d_i and d_j and $|d_i|$ and $|d_j|$ are the lengths of these documents depending on the number of terms they have, respectively.

Then, we use this kernel function in SVM by plugging in the SMO WEKA's [21] implementation. In other words we built such a kernel function that is directly applicable in Platt's SMO (Sequential Minimal Optimization) [22] learner.

4   Experiment Setup

In order to examine the performance of N-IHOSK in SVM, we run it on several commonly used textual datasets. We use a variant of 20 Newsgroups dataset which is called 20News-18828[2]. This dataset has hierarchical class labels consist of four main groups namely SCIENCE, POLITICS, RELIGION and COMP and a total of 20 groups under them. We use the POLITICS and SCIENCE subsets of 20News-18828 dataset which consist of 3 classes and 4 classes, respectively. These subsets are also used in [3] and [4] for evaluating another higher-order classifiers HONB and HOSVM. We also make our experiments with COMP and RELIGION subsets of 20News-18828 dataset which are composed of 5 classes and 4 classes, respectively. Our third dataset is five-class version of the WebKB[2] dataset, namely WEBKB5, which includes web pages collected from computer science departments of different universities. It is important to note that while 20News-18828 subsets include the same number of documents in each class, WebKB5 dataset has a highly skewed class distribution. Fourth dataset we use is Mini-NewsGroups[3] dataset which has 20 classes. Properties of these datasets are given in Table 2.

We apply stemming and stopword filtering to the datasets. Terms occur less than three times in the documents are filtered. Furthermore, we used Information Gain in order to select most informative 2000 terms. This preprocessing increase the performance of the classifier models by reducing the noise.

In order to observe the behaviors of our semantic kernel under different training set size conditions, we use the following percentage values for training set size; 5%, 10%, 30%, 50%, 70%, 80% and 90%. Remaining documents are used for testing.

---

[2] http:// www.cs.cmu.edu/~textlearning
[3] http://archive.ics.uci.edu/ml/

Table 2. Properties of Datasets

Dataset	#classes	#instances	#features
WEBKB5	5	4,336	12,841
20NewsGroup			
20News-SCIENCE	4	2,000	2,225
20News-POLITICS	3	2,500	2,478
20News-RELIGION	4	1,500	2,125
20News-COMP	5	2,500	2,478
Mini-NewsGroups	20	2,000	12,112

One of the most important parameter of SMO [21] algorithm is misclassification-cost (C) parameter. We performed a series of exhaustive optimization trials on all of our datasets with the values in the set of $\{10^{-2}, 10^{-1}, 1, 10^1, 10^2\}$. For every training-set value of our all datasets we performed these optimization experiments and we selected the best performing value of that training-set of the corresponding dataset. After getting best performing C values for linear kernel which is our baseline algorithm at each training-set value we also use those C values for our proposed kernels of N-IHOSK, too. Optimized C values for each dataset are shown in Table 3.

After running algorithms on 10 random splits for each of the training set percentages with their corresponding optimized C values, we report average of these 10 results as in [4] and [6].   This is a more comprehensive way of well-known classical k-Fold cross validation which divides the data into k sets and train on k-1 of them while the remaining used as   test set. However, the training set size in this approach is fixed (for instance it is %90 in 10-fold cross validation) and we cannot analyze the performance of the algorithm under scarce labeled data conditions. It is prohibitively expensive to obtain large amounts of labeled data in many real world applications and therefore it is important to develop methods that perform better with small training sets.

Table 3. Optimized C Values for Our Datasets

TS %	Optimized C Values for 20News SCIENCE	Optimized C Values for 20News POLITICS	Optimized C Values for WEBKB5	Optimized C Values for MINI-NEWSGROUP
5	1	10^{-1}	1	1
10	1	10^{-1}	1	1
30	1	10^{-1}	1	10^2
50	1	10^{-1}	1	10^2
70	1	1	1	10^2
80	1	1	1	10^2
90	1	10^{-1}	1	10^1

We run our experiments using our experiment framework called Turkuaz which closely uses WEKA [21] library. The main evaluation metric in our experiments is accuracy and in the results tables we also provide standard deviations. Additionally, Students t-Tests for statistical significance are provided. We use $\alpha = 0.05$ significance level which is a commonly used level. In order to highlight the performance differences between baseline algorithms and our approach we report performance gain calculated using the simple formula in Eq. 11;

$$Gain_{N-IHOSK} = \frac{(P_{N-IHOSK} - P_x)}{P_x} \qquad (11)$$

where $P_{N-IHOSK}$ is the accuracy of SMO with N-IHOSK and P_x stands for the accuracy result of the other kernels (linear, polynomial or RBF). The experimental results are demonstrated in Table 4, Table 5, Table 6 and Table 7. These tables include training set percentage (TS), the accuracy results of linear kernel, polynomial kernel, RBF Kernel and N-IHOSK. Also the last columns show the (%) gain of N-IHOSK over linear kernel calculated as in Eq. 11.

5   Experiment Results

According to Table 4, N-IHOSK outperforms our baseline kernel (linear kernel, which is one of the state-of-the-art kernels in text classification [8], [9]) by extensive boundaries in all training set percentages. For instance at training levels 30%, 50% and 70% the accuracies of N-IHOSK are 94.31%, 94.97% and 95.35% while the accuracies of linear kernel are 86.73%, 88.94% and 90.37% ,respectively. The performance gain is obvious at all training set levels. It is important to note that high performance gains are especially visible at low training set levels. For instance at training levels 5%, and 10% N-IHOSK outperforms linear kernel with the gains of 18.64% and 16.25%, respectively. As mentioned above, this performance is of great importance since usually it is difficult and expensive to obtain labeled data in real world applications.

Table 4. Accuracy of Different Kernels on 20News SCIENCE Dataset with Varying Training Set Size

TS %	SMO-linear kernel	SMO-polynomial kernel	SMO-RBF Kernel	SMO-N-IHOSK	Gain
5	70.93±3.89	45.65±3.23	49.16±3.78	84.15±2.87	18.64
10	77.74±3.52	55.77±4.73	51.72±4.64	90.37±0.81	16.25
30	86.73±1.32	70.34±2.43	59.19±1.03	94.31±1.09	8.74
50	88.94±1.16	76.42±0.99	63.60±1.80	94.97±0.90	6.78
70	90.37±0.93	79.57±2.00	66.82±1.97	95.35±0.88	5.51
80	91.25±1.56	81.60±2.13	68.15±1.78	96.23±1.19	5.46
90	91.15±1.73	81.40±2.58	68.45±3.06	96.85±1.70	6.25

Table 5. Accuracy of Different Kernels on 20News POLITICS Dataset with Varying Training Set Size

TS %	SMO-linear kernel	SMO-polynomial kernel	SMO-RBF Kernel	SMO-N-IHOSK	Gain
5	78.33±3.40	56.69±6.79	55.74±6.43	82.27±4.60	5.03
10	84.66±2.09	62.45±6.67	65.33±3.96	88.61±2.1	4.67
30	91.98±1.24	83.30±4.57	80.34±4.05	93.61±1.08	1.77
50	91.21±0.89	89.43±2.03	87.95±2.18	93.55±3.58	2.57
70	92.29±1.22	91.02±1.50	87.84±1.79	93.24±3.08	1.03
80	93.7±0.79	90.77±1.50	88.5±1.12	95.3±1.82	1.71
90	93.69±2.04	92.2±1.81	89.8±2.18	95.8±2.28	2.25

On 20News POLITICS dataset, N-IHOSK gives better accuracies than linear kernel in all of the training levels which can be observable from Table 5.

Very similar situations are observed on the other subgroups of 20NewsGroup, namely RELIGION and COMP. In all training set levels N-IHOSK outputs higher accuracies compare to the baseline kernel. Since we got very similar and parallel outcomes we cannot provide their result-tables based on the reality of the space limitation here.

Same trend can be seen for WEBKB5 dataset which has a highly skewed class distribution. In this dataset again our algorithm N-IHOSK outperforms than all of the kernels including linear kernel, polynomial kernel and RBF Kernel. This can be seen in Table 6.

Table 6. Accuracy of Different Kernels on WEBKB5 Dataset with Varying Training Set Size

TS %	SMO-linear kernel	SMO-polynomial kernel	SMO-RBF Kernel	SMO-N-IHOSK	Gain
5	72.77±1.43	60.63±2.90	49.05±1.39	76.12±1.39	4.60
10	79.12±2.18	78.09±1.22	74.69±2.44	82.41±2.32	4.16
30	86.10±1.52	85.21±1.16	81.67±1.53	88.27±1.62	2.52
50	90.16±1.11	86.61±0.56	85.55±1.41	91.89±1.08	1.92
70	90.60±1.93	87.20±1.52	86.07±1.36	92.31±1.41	1.89
80	91.00±1.45	88.73±1.82	86.57±1.01	93.10±1.77	2.31
90	91.93±2.52	90.00±1.86	88.33±2.34	93.13±1.54	1.31

For us one of the most satisfactory results is observed in Mini-NewsGroups dataset. This dataset has the largest number of classes. Again in all training levels starting from 5% up until 90% N-IHOSK gives higher accuracies than other kernels. This can be seen from Table 7. This is especially obvious at 5% training level; the performance gain of N-IHOSK on linear kernel is 17.79%

Table 7. Accuracy of Different Kernels on Mini-NewsGroups Dataset with Varying Training Set Size

TS %	SMO- linear kernel	SMO- polynomial kernel	SMO- RBF Kernel	SMO- N-IHOSK	Gain
5	52.03±5.95	41.21±1.27	38.61±3.18	61.29±1.03	17.79
10	59.31±4.58	51.31±2.37	50.21±4.48	64.15±0.54	8.16
30	72.61±4.23	68.33±3.23	66.33±4.13	75.51±0.31	4.00
50	76.02±4.24	70.12±3.14	67.06±3.34	79.24±0.31	4.24
70	77.61±2.76	75.80±2.66	70.40±1.26	79.73±0.45	2.73
80	80.70±2.20	76.83±1.20	71.83±2.10	83.05±0.58	2.91
90	83.25±4.05	77.55±4.65	72.15±2.35	85.38±1.28	2.56

The particularly high accuracies of the proposed method on 20News-SCIENCE dataset may be explained with the less average sparsity of the documents of this dataset compare to the other datasets. It is possible that having more terms in documents of this dataset give us the opportunity to generate more higher-order paths between documents.

At small training data levels first-order methods give zero as the similarity of two documents that do not contain common words. But by the use of higher-order paths the similarity between those two instances can be larger than zero. We think that this is the main reason that the difference between N-IHOSK and other first-order kernels (linear kernel. polynomial kernel and RBF Kernel) is most visible at small training levels like 5% and 10%. Through the experiments we observed remarkable gains such as 18.64%, 16.25%, and 17.79% at only using 5% and 10% of the labeled data as training set. This has important implications on real world applications where the labeled data is generally difficult to obtain. In many real world applications serious costs are associated with the labeling of the data.

6   Conclusion

It has been shown that higher-order co-occurrence relations between documents and terms catch "latent semantics" and result higher accuracies in text classification area [1], [3], [20] and [4]. Motivated by these studies, we propose a semantic kernel for the SVM named N-IHOSK. N-IHOSK exploits the semantic information in higher-order paths between documents as well as the higher-order paths between terms based on the methodology in [1]. We have performed detailed experiments on several popular textual datasets and compared N-IHOSK with traditional SVM kernels including state of the art linear kernel for text classification. Experiment results show that N-IHOSK outperforms the linear kernel, polynomial kernel, and RBF in all of our datasets under different training set size conditions. Our results show the usefulness of N-IHOSK as a semantic kernel for SVM in text classification.

As future work, we want to analyze the improved performance of N-IHOSK. Especially, we would like to shed light into if and how our approach implicitly captures semantic information such as synonyms and word sense disambiguation when calculating similarity between documents. Additionally, we plan to get more observations about under what type of conditions N-IHOSK performs better than other algorithms.

Acknowledgments. This work is supported in part by The Scientific and Technological Research Council of Turkey (TÜBİTAK) grant number 111E239. Points of view in this document are those of the authors and do not necessarily represent the official position or policies of the TÜBİTAK.

References

1. Bisson, G., Hussain, F.: Chi-Sim: A New Similarity Measure for the Co-clustering Task. In: Proceedings of the 2008 Seventh International Conference on Machine Learning and Applications, pp. 211–217 (2008)
2. Wang, P., Domeniconi, C.: Building Semantic Kernels for text classification using Wikipedia. In: Proceeding of the 14th ACM SIGKDD International Conference on Knowledge Discovery and Data Mining, pp. 713–721. ACM Press, New York (2008)
3. Ganiz, M.C., Lytkin, N.I., Pottenger, W.M.: Leveraging Higher Order Dependencies between Features for Text Classification. In: Buntine, W., Grobelnik, M., Mladenić, D., Shawe-Taylor, J. (eds.) ECML PKDD 2009, Part I. LNCS, vol. 5781, pp. 375–390. Springer, Heidelberg (2009)
4. Ganiz, M.C., George, C., Pottenger, W.M.: Higher Order Naive Bayes: A Novel Non-IID Approach to Text Classification. IEEE Transactions on Knowledge and Data Engineering 23(7), 1022–1034 (2011)
5. Poyraz, M., Kilimci, Z.H., Ganiz, M.C.: Higher-Order Smoothing: A Novel Semantic Smoothing Method for Text Classification. Journal of Computer Science and Technology (accepted, 2014)
6. Poyraz, M., Kilimci, Z.H., Ganiz, M.C.: A Novel Semantic Smoothing Method Based on Higher Order Paths for Text Classification. In: IEEE International Conference on Data Mining (ICDM), Brussels, Belgium (2012)
7. Altinel, B., Ganiz, M.C., Diri, B.: A Novel Higher-order Semantic Kernel. In: ICECCO 2013 (The 10th International Conference on Electronics Computer and Computation), Ankara, Turkey, November 7-9 (2013)
8. Joachims, T.: Text Categorization with Many Relevant Features. In: Nédellec, C., Rouveirol, C. (eds.) ECML 1998. LNCS, vol. 1398, pp. 137–142. Springer, Heidelberg (1998)
9. Dumais, S., Platt, J., Heckerman, D., Sahami, M.: Inductive learning algorithms and representations for text categorization. In: Proceedings of the Seventh International Conference on Information Retrieval and Knowledge Management (ACM-CIKM 1998), pp. 148–155 (1998)
10. Siolas, G., D'Alche-Buc, F.: Support vectors machines based on a semantic kernel for text Categorization. In: Proceedings of the International Joint Conference on Neural Networks. IEEE Press, Como (2000)
11. Leopold, E., Kindermann, J.: Text Categorization with Support Vector Machines. How to Represent Texts in Input Space? Machine Learning 46, 423–444 (2002)
12. Boser, B.E., Guyon, I.M., Vapnik, V.N.: A Training Algorithm for Optimal Margin Classifier. In: Proc. 5th ACM Workshop, Comput. Learning Theory, Pittsburgh, pp. 144–152 (1992)

13. Hsu, C.W., Lin, C.J.: A Comparison of Methods for Multi-Class Support Vector Machines., 415–425 (2002)
14. Bloehdorn, S., Basili, R., Cammisa, M., Moschitti, A.: Semantic kernels for text classification based on topological measures of feature similarity. In: ICDM 2006: Proceedings of the Sixth International Conference on Data Mining, pp. 808–812 (2006)
15. Miller, G., Beckwith, R., Fellbaum, C., Gross, D., Miller, K.: Five Papers on WordNet. Technical report, Stanford University (1993)
16. Miller, Q., Chen, E., Xiong, H.: A Semantic Term Weighting Scheme for Text Categorization. Journal of Expert Systems with Applications (2011)
17. Salton, G., Buckley, C.: Term-weighting approaches in automatic text retrieval. Information Processing & Management 24(5) (1988)
18. Han, J., Kamber, M., Pei, J.: Data Mining: Concepts and Techniques, 3rd edn. Morgan Kaufmann (2012)
19. Dumais, S.: LSI meets TREC: A status report. In: Hartman, D. (ed.) The First Text Retrieval Conference: NIST Special Publication 500-215, pp. 105–116 (1993)
20. Kontostathis, A., Pottenger, W.M.: A Framework for Understanding LSI Performance. Information Processing & Management, 56–73 (2006)
21. Witten, H.I., Frank, E.: Data Mining: Practical Machine Learning Tools and Techniques with Java Implementations. Morgan Kaufmann (1999)
22. Platt, J.C.: Sequential Minimal Optimization: A Fast Algorithm for Training Support Vector Machines. In: Advances in Kernel Method: Support Vector Learning, pp. 185–208. MIT Press (1998)

Nonparametric Extension
of Regression Functions Outside Domain

Tomasz Galkowski[1] and Miroslaw Pawlak[2]

[1] Institute of Computational Intelligence,
Czestochowa University of Technology, Czestochowa, Poland
tomasz.galkowski@iisi.pcz.pl

[2] Information Technology Institute, University of Social Sciences, Lodz, Poland
Department of Electrical and Computer Engineering
University of Manitoba, Winnipeg, Canada
pawlak@ee.umanitoba.ca

Abstract. The article refers to the problem of regression functions estimation in the points situated near the edges but outside of function domain. We investigate the model $y_i = R(x_i) + \epsilon_i$, $i = 1, 2, \ldots n$, where x_i is assumed to be the set of deterministic inputs, $x_i \in D$, y_i is the set of probabilistic outputs, and ϵ_i is a measurement noise with zero mean and bounded variance. $R(.)$ is a completely unknown function. In the literature the possible ways of finding unknown function are based on the algorithms derived from the Parzen kernel. These algorithms were also applied to estimation of the derivatives of unknown functions. The commonly known disadvantage of the kernel algorithms is that the error of estimation dramatically increases if the point of estimation x is approaching to the left or right bound of interval D. Algorithms on predicting values in the boundary region outside the function domain D are unknown for the author, so far.

The main result of this paper is a new algorithm based on integral version of Parzen methods for local prediction of values of the function R near boundaries in the region outside domain. The results of numerical experiments are presented.

1 Introduction

In literature various nonparametric algorithms have been proposed for modelling and classification in stationary [2-5], [11], [31-32], [38-39], [42-44], quasi-stationary [33], [36] and time-varying [12], [23], [34], [37], [45-46] environments.

The article refers to the problem of regression functions estimation in the points situated near the edges but outside of function domain. We investigate the model of type $y_i = R(x_i) + \epsilon_i$, $i = 1, 2, \ldots n$, where x_i is assumed to be the set of deterministic scalar inputs, $x_i \in D$, y_i is the set of probabilistic outputs, and ϵ_i is a measurement noise with zero mean and bounded variance. $R(.)$ is a completely unknown function. There is no assumption neither on its shape (like e.g. in the spline methods) nor on any mathematical formula depending on a set

L. Rutkowski et al. (Eds.): ICAISC 2014, Part I, LNAI 8467, pp. 518–530, 2014.
© Springer International Publishing Switzerland 2014

of parameters to be found (like in parametric approach). This article considers
an approach known from literature as a nonparametric estimation. One of the
possible approaches of finding unknown function is based on the Parzen kernel
[3], [8-9], [53] or methods derived from orthogonal series [30], [44]. There are
known some works using these algorithms for estimation of function derivatives
as well [9], e.g. for modelling of objects or processes described by spatial differential equations [4], [38]. Let us mention that the Parzen kernel methods are much
more often applied and analysed for estimation of probability density functions
and/or regressions with probabilistic inputs than for deterministic case.

Applications based on above method bring satisfying results when the estimate is taken in the interior of the function $R(.)$ domain, i.e. the error of
estimation dramatically increases if the point of estimation x is approaching to
the left or right bound of interval D in which measurements of R were taken, depending on some smoothing parameter a_n. This phenomenon could be explained
generally by insufficient amount of measurement information in the boundary
regions. Thus the condition (ii) in equation (2) (see Section 2) imposed on the
integral of the kernel function is not satisfied.

There are a lot of efforts to solve the above problem in the boundary regions. The first are taken by Gasser et al. [8-9], followed by Müller [24] and
Schuster [53]. In the last years we may observe that several authors still try to
improve the previous results, e.g. Karunamuni et al. [15-16], Kyung-Joon et al.
[19], Poměnková-Dluhá [29], Chen [1], Hazelton et al. [13], Zhang et al. [58-59].
Original method of estimation of the function values exactly in the edge points
were proposed by Galkowski in [7].

The main result of this paper is an algorithm based on integral version of the
Parzen methods, combined with the work [7] and Taylor's theorem (see e.g. [54]).
It can be used for the estimation of values of function R in the local boundaries
outside the domain D. This method may be applied for local extension and/or
prediction of functions, and could be helpful e.g. in the problem of forecasting energy consumption or many economical issues. The numerical experiment
results have been presented.

2 Preliminaries

Nonparametric algorithms for estimation of unknown function $R(.)$ based on
the Parzen kernel have the form:

$$\hat{R}_n(x) = \frac{1}{a_n} \sum_{i=1}^{n} y_i \int_{D_i} K\left(\frac{x-u}{a_n}\right) du \tag{1}$$

where $K(.)$ is the kernel function described by (2), a_n is a smoothing parameter
depending on the number of observations n. Assume that the measurements
y_i are taken from the interval $D = [0, 1]$. In the experiment the interval D is
partitioned into n disjunctive segments D_i such that $\cup D_i = [0, 1], D_i \cap D_j = \emptyset$

for $i \neq j$. The measurement points x_i are chosen from D_i, i.e.: $x_i \in D_i$. Kernel function should be chosen to satisfy the following conditions:

$$\left.\begin{array}{ll} \text{(i)} & K\left(t\right) = 0, \text{ for } t \notin \left(-\tau, \tau\right), \tau > 0, \\ \text{(ii)} & \int_{-\tau}^{\tau} K\left(t\right) dt = 1 \\ \text{(iii)} & \left|K\left(t\right)\right| < \infty \end{array}\right\} \tag{2}$$

In literature (see e.g. [2] [3] [8]) one may find theorems on convergence of algorithm (1) - in the mean-square sense or with probability 1. One of the standard assumptions of these theorems is that $max\left|D_i\right|$ tends to zero if n tends to infinity. This guarantees an uniform representation of function R in domain D during the measurement experiment - in the presence of noise ϵ_i. Furthermore, we trust that in the set of pairs (x_i, y_i) there is - encoded somehow - the information on properties of function R, like its smoothness, possible trends, etc. Thesis of the theorems on convergence are formulated for the points x in the open interval i.e. $x \in D = (0,1)$. Our aim is at first to propose the estimate of function R in the edge point of the domain D - let it be the right bound $x = 1$ (without loosing the generality of the method for the left bound). This problem is strictly related to the boundary effect studied in literature by a few authors e.g. [21], [24], [58-59]. To solve this problem author applies the original algorithm suggested in previous works [6-7]. In the next section we present a proposition, based on former method for estimation of the extension of function R in the points placed in the near boundary - but behind it $(x > 1)$, i.e. outside the domain interval.

3   The Negative-Mirror-Shifted (NMS) Algorithm for Estimation of Edge Values of Functions

The fundamental problem in forecasting of data outside the interval D is at first to estimate the edge value in the point $x = 1$.

Several works describe methods of improving the boundary phenomenon. Some of them are using artificially expanded set of data e.g. by multinomial extension of function [58-59], or by mirrored reflection of data [21], [53], also by using modified kernel functions in the boundary region [1], [8-9], [15-16], [19]. Mirrored reflection of data is equivalent to assumption that the estimated function has local extreme (minimum or maximum) in the edge point $(x = 0$ or $x = 1)$. Consequently that means that the first derivative of function $R(.)$ is equal to zero in the edge point. Of course, this is a strong limitation of class of considered functions.

The main idea of the procedure is based on using of auxiliary set of points obtained by the special method of reflection of data points relatively to the edges. For better understanding, without loss of generality, at first we shall construct the expansion of function $R(.)$ in the left boundary $(x = 0)$. In the next section algorithm will be used in the analogous way in the opposite boundary $(x = 1)$ of the interval D - right-hand extension is better seen as a "predicted" or "extended" value. The reflection is named "negative" and additionally "shifted" with a properly selected constant. The negative-mirror-shifted (NMS) algorithm is detailed in subsequent part.

Assume that function $R(.)$ is extended beyond the left edge $x = 0$, in the expanded interval [-1,1] by definition as follows:

$$\tilde{R}(x) = \begin{cases} R(x) & \text{for } x \in (0,1] \\ -R(-x) + 2S & \text{for } x \in [-1,0] \end{cases} \tag{3}$$

Let us mention that this expansion is similar to the odd expansion of a function defined in finite interval in order to apply the Fourier series theorem.

The essential problem is to determine the shift value S. Let us define the following loss function:

$$\mathcal{L}(S) = \int\limits_{-1}^{1} \left[\hat{R}_n(x,S) - \tilde{R}(x,S)\right]^2 dx \tag{4}$$

This function is a measure of distance between the expanded regression function $\tilde{R}(x)$ and its estimate $\hat{R}(x)$ taken in the expanded interval [-1,1], where

$$\hat{R}_n(x,S) = \frac{1}{a_n} \sum_{i=-n}^{+n} y_i \int\limits_{D_i} K\left(\frac{x-u}{a_n}\right) du \tag{5}$$

For negative subscripts i we assign

$$y_{-i} = -y_i + 2S, \quad x_{-i} = -x_i \tag{6}$$

and, if $D_i = [d_{i-1}, d_i]$ then $D_{-i} = [-d_i, -d_{i-1}]$.
The problem is to minimize the loss function to find optimal S.

Unfortunately, the function $R(.)$ is unknown so, it is impossible to calculate the value of function (4) at this stage.

Moreover, because we can not use the true (exact) values of $R(.)$, let us use the measurements y_i from experiment. Then the estimates $\hat{R}(x,S)$ should be taken in the points x_i. To assure the independence of the estimate and the observation y_i, we should not put into integral (4) the elements y_i while the estimate $\hat{R}(.)$ is calculated in the corresponding points x_i (i.e. $\hat{R}(x_i)$).

Let us define the auxiliary "skip-one-out" estimator of function $\tilde{R}(.)$:

$$\hat{R}_{n,j}(x,S) = \frac{1}{a_n} \sum_{\substack{i=-n \\ i \neq j}}^{+n} y_i \int\limits_{D_i} K\left(\frac{x-u}{a_n}\right) du \tag{7}$$

Let us replace the integral in (4) by the sum, use the defined above skip-one-out estimator, and substitute the unknown values of $\tilde{R}(x_i,S)$ with the measurements y_i, finally obtaining:

$$\tilde{L}(S) = \sum_{j=1}^{n'} \left[\hat{R}_{n,j}(x_j,S) - y_j\right]^2 \tag{8}$$

where we assume that $n' = n$.

Now the independence of estimator and observation is fulfilled. The problem of finding S is now reduced to the problem of minimizing expression (8) with respect to S. Such technique of using measurement data instead of true - but unknown - values of function is known as a cross-validation method. The expression (8) could be finally rewritten as:

$$\tilde{L}(S) = \sum_{j=1}^{n'} [P_{1j} + 2 \cdot S \cdot P_{2j} - y_j]^2 \tag{9}$$

where

$$P_{1j} = \frac{1}{a_n} \sum_{\substack{i=-n \\ i \neq j}}^{+n} \text{sgn}(i) \cdot y_{|i|} \int_{D_i} K\left(\frac{x_j - u}{a_n}\right) du \tag{10}$$

and

$$P_{2j} = \frac{1}{a_n} \sum_{i=-n}^{-1} \int_{D_i} K\left(\frac{x_j - u}{a_n}\right) du \tag{11}$$

By differentiating expression (9) with respect to S, and by fulfilling condition $\tilde{L}' = 0$ one may obtain the estimate S^*:

$$S^* = \frac{\sum_{j=1}^{n'} (y_j - P_{1j}) \cdot P_{2j}}{2 \sum_{j=1}^{n'} P_{2j}^2} \tag{12}$$

We now apply the estimated value S^* in the negatively mirrored expanded set of measurements:

$$
\begin{aligned}
& [(x_{-n}, (y_{-n} + 2S^*)), (x_{-(n-1)}, (y_{-(n-1)} + 2S^*)), ... \\
& ..., (x_{-1}, (y_{-1} + 2S^*)), (0, S^*), (x_1, y_1), ... \\
& ..., (x_{n-1}, y_{n-1}), (x_n, y_n)]
\end{aligned}
\tag{13}
$$

New estimator of the regression function, working with the expanded data set described by (13), is defined as follows:

$$\hat{R}_n(x) = \frac{1}{a_n} \sum_{i=-n}^{+n} y_i \int_{D_i} K\left(\frac{x - u}{a_n}\right) du \tag{14}$$

It works in the points arbitrarily close to the left edge of interval D.

For the right boundary the main differences in the construction of NMS algorithm will be as follows:

Function $R(.)$ expanded beyond the right edge $x = 1$ is defined as:

$$\tilde{R}(x) = \begin{cases} R(x) & \text{for } x \in (0,1) \\ -R(2-x) + 2S & \text{for } x \in [1,2) \end{cases} \tag{15}$$

Mirrored measurements numbered by index $i = n+1, ..., 2n$ are:

$$y_i = -y_{2n+1-i} + 2S, \quad x_i = 2 - x_{2n+1-i} \tag{16}$$

Finally the estimator of function $R(.)$ based on the expanded data set is:

$$\hat{R}_n(x) = \frac{1}{a_n} \sum_{i=1}^{2n} y_i \int_{D_i} K\left(\frac{x-u}{a_n}\right) du \tag{17}$$

Note that this estimate is valid only in the basic interval $D = [0,1]$.

4   The Algorithm of the Nonparametric Extension of Regression Functions Outside Domain

The problem of prediction of future value and/or local extension of function for the point lying in the near neighbourhood to the fixed point of known function value is one of the classic approximation tasks. There is a great number of publications in many engineering, economical, biological and others fields in which such approximation is needed. The information of currently developed methods and its practical application could be found in e.g. [10], [20], [22-23], [25], [55-56]. In this work we propose a new algorithm helping in prediction of unknown function value outside its domain - generally based on nonparametric methods, which were not applied for this issue, so far.

In previous Section we obtain the tool for estimation of the edge value of unknown regression function. The estimate S^* is obtained by using equation (12). Now we recall the Taylor's theorem of degree 1. If $T(.)$ has the first derivative in the point a then the linear polynomial

$$T_a(x) = T(a) + T'(a)(x - a) + \rho(x, a) \tag{18}$$

is a natural linear approximation in point x near a, $\rho(x, a)$ is the remainder of the Taylor's series. In our proposition this theorem will be applied to estimate the value of regression function outside the domain, behind and near point $x = 1$. Now the estimates of the first derivative of function $R'(.)$ are needed.

4.1   Nonparametric Parzen Kernel Estimation of Function Derivatives

In literature concerning Parzen-Rosenblatt methods there are also positions on estimation of function derivatives. We could cite i.e. works [5], [9], [38]. Without presenting detailed theory we would recall the main result achievable under adequate conditions imposed on function $R(.)$ and sequence a_n in appropriate convergence theorems (see e.g. [5], [9]). The estimator of the derivative of order d of function $R(.)$ has the form:

$$\hat{R}_n^{(d)}(x) = a_n^{-(d+1)} \sum_{i=1}^{n} y_i \int_{D_i} K^{(d)}\left(\frac{x-u}{a_n}\right) du \qquad (19)$$

Now we may apply this equation to estimate the first derivative $(d = 1)$ of regression function $R(.)$ with the procedure described in Section 3, allowing us to do it on the edge point $x = 1$.

4.2   Algorithm of Nonparametric Extension of Function

Having regard to the above considerations we propose the following estimator for the extension of function $R(.)$ in the point $x + \Delta x$, near the x:

$$\hat{R}_n(x+\Delta x, S^*) = a_n^{-1} \sum_{i=1}^{2n} y_i \int_{D_i} K\left(\frac{x-u}{a_n}\right) du + a_n^{-2} \sum_{i=1}^{2n} y_i \int_{D_i} K'\left(\frac{x-u}{a_n}\right) du \cdot \Delta x$$

$$(20)$$

where S^* is the shift component calculated using procedure (12). The result still holds in the points x in the initial interval $D = (0, 1]$ under the assumptions imposed in Section 3.

Finally we can choose the point of estimation behind the endpoint of the interval D). Such approach in practice is equivalent to the problem of determining the extension (or prediction) of the function value outside D, exactly in the point $x = 1 + \Delta x$, for small Δx. The analytical investigation of the error of estimation is not undertaken in this article.

The author has made several testing simulations trying to observe how the algorithm works. One of the remarks is that the estimation of derivatives is much more sensitive to the input data set of measurements than estimator of function itself. This was the reason not to use Taylor's polynomial of higher order than 1. In the next section some figures presenting results of simulations are presented.

5   Simulation Study

Simulation were made using as a model the function $R(x) = 3x(x-0.4)-1$ in the interval $D = [0, 1]$. Choosing simple parabolic function allows us to better see how the algorithm estimates its first derivative - of course it is a linear function. Measurement noise was generated from the normal distribution with zero mean and limited variance. Figure 1. shows function $R(x)$ (continuous line), the set of measurements y_i with additive noise (points marked with +) and the estimates obtained with unmodified algorithm (1) inside the region D (points marked with circles). It is easy to see the boundary effect near the endpoints.

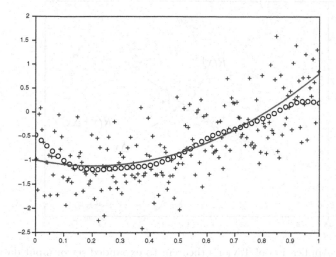

Fig. 1. Regression function $R(x)$ and its nonparametric estimates

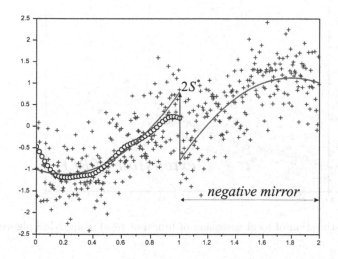

Fig. 2. Illustration of the idea of negative-mirror-shifted (NMS) algorithm

Figure 2. illustrates the idea of the Negative Mirror Shifted (NMS) method, where the constant S^* is calculated from equation (12). The algorithm is applied for the right endpoint $x = 1$, determined from the set of noised measurements. Value of shift estimate is equal $S^* = 0.7758$.

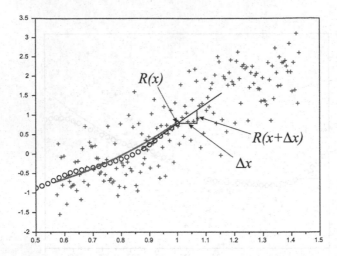

Fig. 3. Application of Taylor's theorem to expanded set of input data

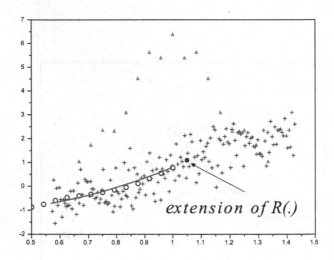

Fig. 4. Estimation of local extension of function $R(x)$ using NMS algorithm

In Figure 3. we can see a diagram presenting the idea of Taylor's theorem for extension of function $R(x)$ at the point $x = 1 + \Delta x$, for small Δx, using expanded by the NMS method set of measurements (magnified in the center of graph). Figure 4. presents the final result of simulation experiment for calculation of estimation of extension of $R(x)$ in the point $x = 1 + \Delta x$, for $\Delta x = 0.05$, applying the equation (18) for the estimation of function $R(1)$ and its first derivative $R'(1)$ at the right endpoint $x = 1$ - based on the NMS method. The first function derivative is marked by triangles. The estimate of the extension $\hat{R}_n(1.05)$ was determined by equation (20) and for given set is equal $\hat{R}_n$ (1.05) = 1.0477 - while the exact value of given parabola $R(x) = 3x(x - 0.4) - 1$ is equal $R(1.05) = 1.0475$. In the graph the local prediction estimate is marked with bold points.

6   Remarks and Extensions

The new algorithm based on the Parzen kernel for estimation of local extension of regression function in deterministic case outside domain has been proposed. By using procedure introduced in [7] with combination of Taylor's theorem it is possible to determine the estimate of the value of unknown function not only exactly in the edge point of domain but also in the neighbourhood near outside domain. The analogous method (NMS) for estimation of function derivatives in the edge point has been proposed. The graphical results of simulation let us to observe that the new algorithm offers a good accuracy. In future research we plan to apply other techniques for nonparametric estimation including neuro-fuzzy structures ([14], [17-18], [27], [47], [51-52]) and decision trees ([28], [48-50]).

References

1. Chen, S.X.: Beta kernel estimators for density functions. Journal of Statistical Planning and Inference 139, 2269–2283 (2009)
2. Galkowski, T., Rutkowski, L.: Nonparametric recovery of multivariate functions with applications to system identification. Proceedings of the IEEE 73, 942–943 (1985)
3. Galkowski, T., Rutkowski, L.: Nonparametric fitting of multivariable functions. IEEE Transactions on Automatic Control AC-31, 785–787 (1986)
4. Galkowski, T.: Nonparametric estimates of parameters in a model of microbial growth process. AMSE Review 8(1), 1–10 (1988)
5. Galkowski, T.: On nonparametric fitting of higher order function derivatives by the kernel method - a simulation study. In: Gutierrez, R., Valderrama, M.J. (eds.) Fifth Int. Symp. Applied Stochastic Models and Data Analysis, Granada, Spain, pp. 230–242 (1991)
6. Galkowski, T.: Nonparametric estimation of boundary values of functions. Archives of Control Science 3(1-2), 85–93 (1994)
7. Gałkowski, T.: Kernel estimation of regression functions in the boundary regions. In: Rutkowski, L., Korytkowski, M., Scherer, R., Tadeusiewicz, R., Zadeh, L.A., Zurada, J.M. (eds.) ICAISC 2013, Part II. LNCS (LNAI), vol. 7895, pp. 158–166. Springer, Heidelberg (2013)
8. Gasser, T., Muller, H.G.: Kernel estimation of regression functions. Lecture Notes in Mathematics, vol. 757, pp. 23–68. Springer, Heidelberg (1979)
9. Gasser, T., Muller, H.G.: Estimating Regression Functions and Their Derivatives by the Kernel Method. Scandinavian Journal of Statistics 11(3), 171–185 (1984)
10. Grbic, R., Kurtagic, D., Sliškovic, D.: Stream water temperature prediction based on Gaussian process regression. Expert Systems with Applications 40, 7407–7414 (2013)
11. Greblicki, W., Rutkowski, L.: Density-free Bayes risk consistency of nonparametric pattern recognition procedures. Proceedings of the IEEE 69(4), 482–483 (1981)

12. Greblicki, W., Rutkowska, D., Rutkowski, L.: An orthogonal series estimate of time-varying regression. Annals of the Institute of Statistical Mathematics 35(2), 215–228 (1983)
13. Hazelton, M.L., Marshall, J.C.: Linear boundary kernels for bivariate density estimation. Statistics and Probability Letters 79, 999–1003 (2009)
14. Jaworski, M., Duda, P., Pietruczuk, L.: On fuzzy clustering of data streams with concept drift. In: Rutkowski, L., Korytkowski, M., Scherer, R., Tadeusiewicz, R., Zadeh, L.A., Zurada, J.M. (eds.) ICAISC 2012, Part II. LNCS (LNAI), vol. 7268, pp. 82–91. Springer, Heidelberg (2012)
15. Karunamuni, R.J., Alberts, T.: On boundary correction in kernel density estimation. Statistical Methodology 2, 191–212 (2005)
16. Karunamuni, R.J., Alberts, T.: A locally adaptive transformation method of boundary correction in kernel density estimation. Journal of Statistical Planning and Inference 136, 2936–2960 (2006)
17. Korytkowski, M., Rutkowski, L., Scherer, R.: On combining backpropagation with boosting. In: IEEE International Joint Conference on Neural Network (IJCNN) Proceedings Vancouver, July 16-21, vols. 1-10, pp. 1274–1277 (2006)
18. Korytkowski, M., Rutkowski, L., Scherer, R.: From Ensemble of Fuzzy Classifiers to Single Fuzzy Rule Base Classifier. In: Rutkowski, L., Tadeusiewicz, R., Zadeh, L.A., Zurada, J.M. (eds.) ICAISC 2008. LNCS (LNAI), vol. 5097, pp. 265–272. Springer, Heidelberg (2008)
19. Kyung-Joon, C., Schucany, W.R.: Nonparametric kernel regression estimation near endpoints. Journal of Statistical Planning and Inference 66, 289–304 (1998)
20. Landberg, L.: Short-term prediction of local wind conditions. Journal of Wind Engineering and Industrial Aerodynamics 89, 235–245 (2001)
21. Marshall, J.C., Hazelton, M.L.: Boundary kernels for adaptive density estimators on regions with irregular boundaries. Journal of Multivariate Analysis 101, 949–963 (2010)
22. Min, W., Wynter, L.: Real-time road traffic prediction with spatio-temporal correlations. Transportation Research Part C 19, 606–616 (2011)
23. Mosallam, A., Medjaher, K., Zerhouni, N.: Nonparametric time series modelling for industrial prognostics and health management. Int. J. Adv. Manuf. Technol. 69, 1685–1699 (2013)
24. Müller, H.G.: Smooth optimum kernel estimators near endpoints. Biometrika 78, 521–530 (1991)
25. Prampero Paulo, S., Romis, A.: Magnetic particle swarm optimization. Journal of Artificial Intelligence and Soft Computing Research 2(1), 59–72 (2012)
26. Parzen, E.: On estimation of a probability density function and mode. Analysis of Mathematical Statistics 33(3), 1065–1076 (1962)
27. Pietruczuk, L., Duda, P., Jaworski, M.: A new fuzzy classifier for data streams. In: Rutkowski, L., Korytkowski, M., Scherer, R., Tadeusiewicz, R., Zadeh, L.A., Zurada, J.M. (eds.) ICAISC 2012, Part I. LNCS (LNAI), vol. 7267, pp. 318–324. Springer, Heidelberg (2012)
28. Pietruczuk, L., Duda, P., Jaworski, M.: Adaptation of decision trees for handling concept drift. In: Rutkowski, L., Korytkowski, M., Scherer, R., Tadeusiewicz, R., Zadeh, L.A., Zurada, J.M. (eds.) ICAISC 2013, Part I. LNCS (LNAI), vol. 7894, pp. 459–473. Springer, Heidelberg (2013)
29. Poměnková-Dluhá, J.: Edge Effects of Gasser-Müller Estimator. Mathematica 15, 307–314 (2004)

30. Rafajlowicz, E.: Nonparametric orthogonal series estimators of regression - A class attaining the optimal convergence in L2. Statistics and Probability Letters 5(3), 219–224 (1987)

31. Rafajlowicz, E., Schwabe, R.: Halton and Hammersley sequences in multivariate nonparametric regression. Statistics and Probability Letters 76(8), 803–812 (2006)

32. Rutkowski, L.: Sequential estimates of probability densities by orthogonal series and their application in pattern classification. IEEE Transactions on Systems, Man, and Cybernetics SMC-10(12), 918–920 (1980)

33. Rutkowski, L.: On Bayes risk consistent pattern recognition procedures in a quasi-stationary environment. IEEE Transactions on Pattern Analysis and Machine Intelligence PAMI-4(1), 84–87 (1982)

34. Rutkowski, L.: On-line identification of time-varying systems by nonparametric techniques. IEEE Transactions on Automatic Control AC-27, 228–230 (1982)

35. Rutkowski, L.: On nonparametric identification with prediction of time-varying systems. IEEE Transactions on Automatic Control AC-29, 58–60 (1984)

36. Rutkowski, L.: Nonparametric identification of quasi-stationary systems. Systems and Control Letters 6, 33–35 (1985)

37. Rutkowski, L.: The real-time identification of time-varying systems by nonparametric algorithms based on Parzen kernels. International Journal of Systems Science 16, 1123–1130 (1985)

38. Rutkowski, L.: A general approach for nonparametric fitting of functions and their derivatives with applications to linear circuits identification. IEEE Transactions Circuits Systems CAS-33, 812–818 (1986)

39. Rutkowski, L.: Sequential pattern recognition procedures derived from multiple Fourier series. Pattern Recognition Letters 8, 213–216 (1988)

40. Rutkowski, L.: An application of multiple Fourier series to identification of multivariable nonstationary systems. International Journal of Systems Science 20(10), 1993–2002 (1989)

41. Rutkowski, L.: Non-parametric learning algorithms in the time-varying environments. Signal Processing 18(2), 129–137 (1989)

42. Rutkowski, L., Rafajlowicz, E.: On optimal global rate of convergence of some nonparametric identification procedures. IEEE Transaction on Automatic Control AC-34(10), 1089–1091 (1989)

43. Rutkowski, L.: Identification of MISO nonlinear regressions in the presence of a wide class of disturbances. IEEE Transactions on Information Theory IT-37, 214–216 (1991)

44. Rutkowski, L.: Multiple Fourier series procedures for extraction of nonlinear regressions from noisy data. IEEE Transactions on Signal Processing 41(10), 3062–3065 (1993)

45. Rutkowski, L.: Adaptive probabilistic neural-networks for pattern classification in time-varying environment. IEEE Trans. Neural Networks 15, 811–827 (2004)

46. Rutkowski, L.: Generalized regression neural networks in time-varying environment. IEEE Trans. Neural Networks 15, 576–596 (2004)

47. Rutkowski, L., Przybyl, A., Cpalka, K.: Novel on-line speed profile generation for industrial machine tool based on flexible neuro-fuzzy approximation. IEEE Transactions on Industrial Electronics 59, 1238–1247 (2012)

48. Rutkowski, L., Pietruczuk, L., Duda, P., Jaworski, M.: Decision trees for mining data streams based on the McDiarmid's bound. IEEE Transactions on Knowledge and Data Engineering 25(6), 1272–1279 (2013)

49. Rutkowski, L., Jaworski, M., Pietruczuk, L., Duda, P.: Decision trees for mining data streams based on the gaussian approximation. IEEE Transactions on Knowledge and Data Engineering 26(1), 108–119 (2014)
50. Rutkowski, L., Jaworski, M., Pietruczuk, L., Duda, P.: The CART decision tree for mining data streams. Information Sciences 266, 1–15 (2014)
51. Starczewski, J., Rutkowski, L.: Interval type 2 neuro-fuzzy systems based on interval consequents. In: Rutkowski, L., Kacprzyk, J. (eds.) Neural Networks and Soft Computing, pp. 570–577. Physica-Verlag, Springer-Verlag Company, Heidelberg, New York (2003)
52. Starczewski, J.T., Rutkowski, L.: Connectionist Structures of Type 2 Fuzzy Inference Systems. In: Wyrzykowski, R., Dongarra, J., Paprzycki, M., Waśniewski, J. (eds.) PPAM 2001. LNCS, vol. 2328, pp. 634–642. Springer, Heidelberg (2002)
53. Schuster, E.F.: Incorporating Support Constraints Into Nonparametric Estimators of Densities. Communications in Statistics, Part A - Theory and Methods 14, 1123–1136 (1985)
54. Strang, G.: Calculus. MIT book, Wellesley-Cambridge Press (1991)
55. Vu Nam, T., Brdys Mietek, A.: Optimizing control by robustly feasible model predictive control and application to drinking water distribution systems. Journal of Artificial Intelligence and Soft Computing Research 1(1), 43–57 (2011)
56. Vilar, J.M., Cao, R., Aneiros, G.: Forecasting next-day electricity demand and price using nonparametric functional methods. Electrical Power and Energy Systems 39, 48–55 (2012)
57. Zhang, J., Tan, Z.: Day-ahead electricity price forecasting using WT, CLSSVM and EGARCH model. Electrical Power and Energy Systems 45, 362–368 (2013)
58. Zhang, S., Karunamuni, R.J.: On kernel density estimation near endpoints. Journal of Statistical Planning and Inference 70, 301–316 (1998)
59. Zhang, S., Karunamuni, R.J.: Deconvolution boundary kernel method in nonparametric density estimation. Journal of Statistical Planning and Inference 139, 2269–2283 (2009)

Nonparametric Function Fitting
in the Presence of Nonstationary Noise

Tomasz Galkowski[1] and Miroslaw Pawlak[2]

[1] Institute of Computational Intelligence,
Czestochowa University of Technology, Czestochowa, Poland
tomasz.galkowski@iisi.pcz.pl
[2] Information Technology Institute, University of Social Sciences, Lodz, Poland
Department of Electrical and Computer Engineering
University of Manitoba, Winnipeg, Canada
pawlak@ee.umanitoba.ca

Abstract. The article refers to the problem of regression functions estimation in the presence of nonstationary noise. We investigate the model $y_i = R(\mathbf{x_i}) + \epsilon_i$, $i = 1, 2, \ldots n$, where x_i is assumed to be the d-dimensional vector, set of deterministic inputs, $\mathbf{x_i} \in S^d$, y_i is the scalar, set of probabilistic outputs, and ϵ_i is a measurement noise with zero mean and variance depending on n. $R(.)$ is a completely unknown function. One of the possible solutions of finding function $R(.)$ is to apply non-parametric methodology - algorithms based on the Parzen kernel or algorithms derived from orthogonal series. The novel result of this article is the analysis of convergence for some class of nonstationarity. We present the conditions when the algorithm of estimation is convergent even when the variance of noise is divergent with number of observations tending to infinity. The results of numerical experiments are presented.

1 Preliminaries and Algorithm

This article is concerned with the systems described by the following equation

$$y_i = R(\mathbf{x_i}) + Z_i, \quad i = 1, ..., n \tag{1}$$

where y_i is the probabilistic scalar output, $\mathbf{x}_i$ is the deterministic d-vector input, Z_i is the random measurement noise. There are two well-known nonparametric algorithms for fitting unknown function $R(.)$ for one- and multi-dimensional case: the Parzen-Rosenblatt methods (see e.g. [1-6], [13]) and methods based on orthogonal series expansions (see e.g. [16] [24-26], [28], [30]), or type-1 and type-2 neuro-fuzzy structures [8-10], [14-15], [33-39]. In non-parametric approach there is no a-priori assumption on mathematical form of unknown function $R(.)$, like in e.g. spline methods or linear regression. In literature one may find the theorems on convergence of mentioned algorithms. The nonstationary situations are investigated more rarely (e.g. [7], [19-20], [27], [31-32]). These algorithm have been applied for identification of some classes of nonlinear dynamical systems (e.g. [12], [21-23], [28-29]).

L. Rutkowski et al. (Eds.): ICAISC 2014, Part I, LNAI 8467, pp. 531–538, 2014.

Consider the d-dimensional space $S_d = \left\{ \mathbf{x} \in [0,1]^d \right\}$. Let $n^{1/d} = N$ be an integer and $p = 1, ..., d$; $i_p = 1, ..., N$. Partition the unit interval $[0,1]$ on the p-th axis into N subsets Δx_{i_p}. Let us define the Cartesian product

$$\Delta x_{i_1} \otimes \Delta x_{i_2} \otimes \cdots \otimes \Delta x_{i_d} = S_{d,i}.$$

Let $S_{d,i} \wedge S_{d,j} = \emptyset$ for $i \neq j$ and $\bigcup_{i=1}^{N} S_{d,i} = S_d$. The inputs $\mathbf{x}_i$ are selected to satisfy $\mathbf{x}_i \in S_{d,i}$. The estimator of multivariate function $R(\mathbf{x})$ in S_d is given by:

$$\hat{R}(\mathbf{x}) = \sum_{i=1}^{N} y_i \int_{S_{d,i}} b_n^{-d} K\left(\frac{x-u}{b_n}\right) du \tag{2}$$

where $\mathbf{1} = [1, ..., 1]$ is $1 \times d$ vector. Function $K(.)$ is chosen as follows:

$$\begin{aligned} K(\mathbf{u}) &= \prod_{m=1}^{d} G(u_m), \quad m = 1, ..., d \\ G(t) &\geq 0 \text{ for } t \in (-L, L), \quad L = const \\ G(t) &= 0 \text{ for } t \notin (-L, L) \\ \int_{-L}^{L} G(t) dt &= 1 \\ \sup &G(t) < \infty \end{aligned} \tag{3}$$

The smoothing parameter b_n is a sequence of positive constants such that

$$b_n \to 0 \text{ as } n \to \infty \tag{4}$$

Note that procedure (2) is not a trivial extension of the one-dimensional Parzen-Rosenblatt algorithm because of the construction of partition of set S_d. In the following we shall denote the length of the interval Δx_{i_p}, $i_p = 1, ..., N$, $p = 1, ..., d$ as $\left| \Delta x_{i_p} \right|$. The main result of this work is concerned with the extension of algorithm (2) to handle non-stationary noise.

2   Convergence Properties

Assume that conditions (3) and (4) are satisfied, $R(.)$ is continuous function in $[0,1]^d$. Suppose that:

$$EZ_i = 0, \quad i = 1, ..., n \tag{5}$$

We shall show that under some conditions estimator (2) is convergent even if the variance of measurement noise is divergent to infinity.

Theorem 1. *(Mean Square Error Convergence): If*

$$EZ_n^2 = \sigma_n^2 = s_n \tag{6}$$

$$\Delta_n = \max_{1 \le i_p \le N} |\Delta x_{i_p}| = O\left(n^{-1/d}\right), \, p = 1, ..., d \tag{7}$$

and

$$s_n n^{-1} b_n^{-d} \to 0 \tag{8}$$

then

$$E\left[\hat{R}_n(\mathbf{x}) - R(\mathbf{x})\right]^2 \to 0 \; if \, n \to \infty \tag{9}$$

for every point $x \in (0,1)^d$.

Proof. Obviously

$$E\left[\hat{R}_n(\mathbf{x}) - R(\mathbf{x})\right]^2 \le \mathrm{var}\hat{R}_n(\mathbf{x}) + 2E\left[\hat{R}_n(\mathbf{x}) - R_n^*(\mathbf{x})\right]^2 + 2[R_n^*(\mathbf{x}) - R(\mathbf{x})]^2 \tag{10}$$

where

$$R_n^*(\mathbf{x}) = \sum_{i=1}^{N} \int_{S_{d,i}} R(u) b_n^{-d} K\left(\frac{x-u}{b_n}\right) du. \tag{11}$$

By the Schwartz inequality we have the following bound for variance:

$$\mathrm{var}\hat{R}_n(\mathbf{x}) = \mathrm{var}\left\{\sum_{i=1}^{N} y_i b_n^{-d} \int_{S_{d,i}} K\left(\frac{x-u}{b_n}\right) du\right\} = \left[\sum_{i=1}^{N} b_n^{-d} \int_{S_{d,i}} K\left(\frac{x-u}{b_n}\right) du\right]^2 \mathrm{var} y_i \le$$

$$\le \sigma_n^2 b_n^{-2d} \sum_{i=1}^{N} \int_{S_{d,i}} K\left(\frac{x-u}{b_n}\right) du \sum_{i=1}^{N} \int_{S_{d,i}} K\left(\frac{x-u}{b_n}\right) du \le$$

$$\le const \cdot s_n n^{-1} b_n^{-d} \sup_w |K(w) dw| \cdot \int_{-1}^{1} K(w) dw \le$$

$$\le const \cdot s_n n^{-1} b_n^{-d} \tag{12}$$

This results from the properties of $K(.)$, (3) and from fact that after substitution $w = \frac{x-u}{b_n}$ we obtain the limits of integral $\left[\frac{-x_p}{b_n}; \frac{1-x_p}{b_n}\right] \supset [-1, 1]$ for sufficiently large n and $x_p \in (0,1)$, $p = 1, ..., d$. For the second term in (10) we have bound

$$\left|E\hat{R}_n(\mathbf{x}) - R_n^*(\mathbf{x})\right| \le \sum_{i=1}^{N} b_n^{-d} \int_{S_{d,i}} |R(x_i) - R(u)| K\left(\frac{x-u}{b_n}\right) du \cdot \mathbf{I}_{\{|x_i-u| \le \varepsilon\}} +$$

$$+ \sum_{i=1}^{N} b_n^{-d} \int_{S_{d,i}} |R(x_i) - R(u)| K\left(\frac{x-u}{b_n}\right) du \cdot \mathbf{I}_{\{|x_i-u| > \varepsilon\}} \le$$

$$\le \sup_{|z-u| \le \varepsilon} |R(z) - R(u)| \int_{-1}^{1} K(w) dw +$$

$$+ 2 \sup_z |R(z)| \sum_{i=1}^{N} b_n^{-d} \int_{S_{d,i}} K\left(\frac{x-u}{b_n}\right) du \cdot \mathbf{I}_{\{|x_i-u| > \varepsilon\}} \tag{13}$$

The first term in the above inequality is arbitrarily small for ε small enough. The second term could be rewrite

$$\sum_{i=1}^{N} b_n^{-d} \int_{S_{d,i}} K\left(\tfrac{x-u}{b_n}\right) du \cdot \mathbf{I}_{\{|x_i-u|>\varepsilon\}} \leq \sum_{i=1}^{N} b_n^{-d} \int_{S_{d,i}} K\left(\tfrac{x-u}{b_n}\right) du \cdot \mathbf{I}_{\{|x_i-u|>\varepsilon-\Delta_n\}} \leq$$
$$\leq \int_{|w|\geq\frac{\varepsilon-\Delta_n}{b_n}} K(w) dw$$

$$(14)$$

Let observe that the above integral tends to zero if $b_n \to \infty$ and ε is small enough.

Convergence of the third term in (10) results from continuity of function $R(.)$ in the point $\mathbf{x}$

$$|R_n^*(\mathbf{x}) - R(\mathbf{x})| = \left| \sum_{i=1}^{N} b_n^{-d} \int_{S_{d,i}} R(u) K\left(\tfrac{x-u}{b_n}\right) du - R(\mathbf{x}) \right| \leq$$
$$\leq \int_{-1}^{1} K(w) |R(x - b_n w) - R(x)| \, dw \to 0 \text{ if } b_n \to 0.$$

$$(15)$$

This completes the proof.

3   Simulation Example

Figure 1. presents an example of simulation of nonparametric function fitting using the Parzen kernel method. This Section refers to the case when the output has a nonstationary additive noise. We assume that the smoothing parameter b_n is of type

$$b_n = O\left(n^{-\alpha}\right), \; \alpha > 0 \qquad (16)$$

Moreover we assume that the sequence s_n is of type

$$s_n = O\left(n^\beta\right), \; \beta > 0 \qquad (17)$$

Assuming $x \in (0,1)^d$, for sufficiently large n we have the bound

$$var \hat{R}_n(\mathbf{x}) \leq C_1 n^{-1+d\alpha+\beta}, \; C_1 = const \qquad (18)$$

This leads to the conclusion that the mean square convergence is assured now by fulfilling the condition

$$d\alpha + \beta - 1 < 0 \qquad (19)$$

The simulations were performed for unidimensional case $d = 1$. We performed series of tests in 50 evenly spaced in $(0,1)$ points, for the number of generated measurements growing up from $n = 150$ to $n = 3500$. The smoothing parameters b_n were chosen according to the formula (16), for $\alpha = 0.43$, whereas the sequence $s_n = n^\beta$, $\beta = 0.2$. As the measure of performance we use the mean square error

$$Err_n = \frac{1}{M} \sqrt{\sum_{m=1}^{M} \left(\hat{R}_n(x_m) - R(x_m)\right)^2} \qquad (20)$$

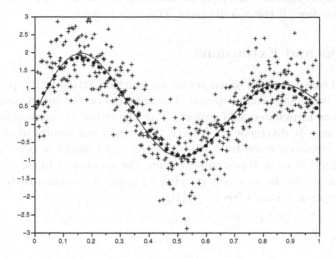

Fig. 1. Example of nonparametric function fitting

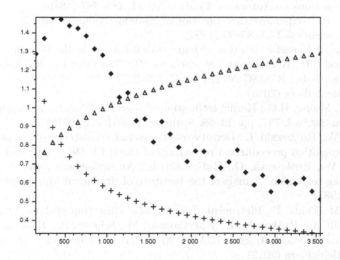

Fig. 2. Mean square error graph for series of simulations

Figure 2. shows graphs of the mean square error Err_n (marked with black diamonds), parameter b_n (marked with pluses) and the variance of the noise bounds s_n (marked with triangles) - according to number n. Note that the graphs were rescaled to obtain better view of their course. The irregularities in the graphs course could arise because of the independent processes of noise generation for each sample set.

The simulations results confirmed the convergence of the mean square error in practical situation, if the conditions of Theorem 1. hold.

4   Remarks and Extensions

The algorithm based on the Parzen kernel for function fitting in the presence of nonstationary noise has been proposed. The theorem on the mean square error convergence was formulated and proved. The algorithm is convergent even if the noise variance is divergent to infinity. The graphical results of simulation showing the calculated error from the series of experiments is presented. We can observe that the error tends to zero when the number of observations n is growing up. In the future research we plan to apply our estimator to optimal control of dynamical systems (see e.g. [11]).

References

1. Galkowski, T., Rutkowski, L.: Nonparametric recovery of multivariate functions with applications to system identification. Proceedings of the IEEE 73, 942–943 (1985)
2. Galkowski, T., Rutkowski, L.: Nonparametric fitting of multivariable functions. IEEE Transactions on Automatic Control AC-31, 785–787 (1986)
3. Galkowski, T.: Nonparametric estimation of boundary values of functions. Archives of Control Science 3(1-2), 85–93 (1994)
4. Gałkowski, T.: Kernel estimation of regression functions in the boundary regions. In: Rutkowski, L., Korytkowski, M., Scherer, R., Tadeusiewicz, R., Zadeh, L.A., Zurada, J.M. (eds.) ICAISC 2013, Part II. LNCS (LNAI), vol. 7895, pp. 158–166. Springer, Heidelberg (2013)
5. Gasser, T., Muller, H.G.: Kernel estimation of regression functions. Lecture Notes in Mathematics, vol. 757, pp. 23–68. Springer, Heidelberg (1979)
6. Greblicki, W., Rutkowski, L.: Density-free Bayes risk consistency of nonparametric pattern recognition procedures. Proceedings of the IEEE 69(4), 482–483 (1981)
7. Greblicki, W., Rutkowska, D., Rutkowski, L.: An orthogonal series estimate of time-varying regression. Annals of the Institute of Statistical Mathematics 35(2), 215–228 (1983)
8. Jaworski, M., Duda, P., Pietruczuk, L.: On fuzzy clustering of data streams with concept drift. In: Rutkowski, L., Korytkowski, M., Scherer, R., Tadeusiewicz, R., Zadeh, L.A., Zurada, J.M. (eds.) ICAISC 2012, Part II. LNCS, vol. 7268, pp. 82–91. Springer, Heidelberg (2012)
9. Korytkowski, M., Rutkowski, L., Scherer, R.: On combining backpropagation with boosting. In: IEEE International Joint Conference on Neural Network (IJCNN) Proceedings, Vancouver, July 16-21, vol. 1-10, pp. 1274–1277 (2006)
10. Korytkowski, M., Rutkowski, L., Scherer, R.: From Ensemble of Fuzzy Classifiers to Single Fuzzy Rule Base Classifier. In: Rutkowski, L., Tadeusiewicz, R., Zadeh, L.A., Zurada, J.M. (eds.) ICAISC 2008. LNCS (LNAI), vol. 5097, pp. 265–272. Springer, Heidelberg (2008)
11. Kroll, A.: On choosing the fuzziness parameter for identifying TS models with multidimensional membership functions. Journal of Artificial Intelligence and Soft Computing Research 1(4), 283–300 (2011)

12. Lobato, F.S., Steffen Jr., V., Neto, A.J.S.: Solution of singular optimal control problems using the improved differential evolution algorithm. Journal of Artificial Intelligence and Soft Computing Research 1(3), 195–206 (2011)

13. Parzen, E.: On estimation of a probability density function and mode. Analysis of Mathematical Statistics 33(3), 1065–1076 (1962)

14. Pietruczuk, L., Duda, P., Jaworski, M.: A new fuzzy classifier for data streams. In: Rutkowski, L., Korytkowski, M., Scherer, R., Tadeusiewicz, R., Zadeh, L.A., Zurada, J.M. (eds.) ICAISC 2012, Part I. LNCS (LNAI), vol. 7267, pp. 318–324. Springer, Heidelberg (2012)

15. Pietruczuk, L., Duda, P., Jaworski, M.: Adaptation of decision trees for handling concept drift. In: Rutkowski, L., Korytkowski, M., Scherer, R., Tadeusiewicz, R., Zadeh, L.A., Zurada, J.M. (eds.) ICAISC 2013, Part I. LNCS (LNAI), vol. 7894, pp. 459–473. Springer, Heidelberg (2013)

16. Rafajlowicz, E.: Nonparametric orthogonal series estimators of regression - A class attaining the optimal convergence in L2. Statistics and Probability Letters 5(3), 219–224 (1987)

17. Rafajlowicz, E., Schwabe, R.: Halton and Hammersley sequences in multivariate nonparametric regression. Statistics and Probability Letters 76(8), 803–812 (2006)

18. Rutkowski, L.: Sequential estimates of probability densities by orthogonal series and their application in pattern classification. IEEE Transactions on Systems, Man, and Cybernetics SMC-10(12), 918–920 (1980)

19. Rutkowski, L.: On Bayes risk consistent pattern recognition procedures in a quasi-stationary environment. IEEE Transactions on Pattern Analysis and Machine Intelligence PAMI-4(1), 84–87 (1982)

20. Rutkowski, L.: On-line identification of time-varying systems by nonparametric techniques. IEEE Transactions on Automatic Control AC-27, 228–230 (1982)

21. Rutkowski, L.: On nonparametric identification with prediction of time-varying systems. IEEE Transactions on Automatic Control AC-29, 58–60 (1984)

22. Rutkowski, L.: Nonparametric identification of quasi-stationary systems. Systems and Control Letters 6, 33–35 (1985)

23. Rutkowski, L.: The real-time identification of time-varying systems by nonparametric algorithms based on Parzen kernels. International Journal of Systems Science 16, 1123–1130 (1985)

24. Rutkowski, L.: A general approach for nonparametric fitting of functions and their derivatives with applications to linear circuits identification. IEEE Transactions on Circuits Systems CAS-33, 812–818 (1986)

25. Rutkowski, L.: Sequential pattern recognition procedures derived from multiple Fourier series. Pattern Recognition Letters 8, 213–216 (1988)

26. Rutkowski, L.: An application of multiple Fourier series to identification of multivariable nonstationary systems. International Journal of Systems Science 20(10), 1993–2002 (1989)

27. Rutkowski, L.: Non-parametric learning algorithms in the time-varying environments. Signal Processing 18(2), 129–137 (1989)

28. Rutkowski, L., Rafajlowicz, E.: On optimal global rate of convergence of some nonparametric identification procedures. IEEE Transaction on Automatic Control AC-34(10), 1089–1091 (1989)

29. Rutkowski, L.: Identification of MISO nonlinear regressions in the presence of a wide class of disturbances. IEEE Transactions on Information Theory IT-37, 214–216 (1991)

30. Rutkowski, L.: Multiple Fourier series procedures for extraction of nonlinear regressions from noisy data. IEEE Transactions on Signal Processing 41(10), 3062–3065 (1993)
31. Rutkowski, L.: Adaptive probabilistic neural-networks for pattern classification in time-varying environment. IEEE Trans. Neural Networks 15, 811–827 (2004)
32. Rutkowski, L.: Generalized regression neural networks in time-varying environment. IEEE Trans. Neural Networks 15, 576–596 (2004)
33. Rutkowski, L., Przybyl, A., Cpalka, K.: Novel on-line speed profile generation for industrial machine tool based on flexible neuro-fuzzy approximation. IEEE Transactions on Industrial Electronics 59, 1238–1247 (2012)
34. Rutkowski, L., Pietruczuk, L., Duda, P., Jaworski, M.: Decision trees for mining data streams based on the McDiarmid's bound. IEEE Transactions on Knowledge and Data Engineering 25(6), 1272–1279 (2013)
35. Rutkowski, L., Jaworski, M., Pietruczuk, L., Duda, P.: Decision trees for mining data streams based on the gaussian approximation. IEEE Transactions on Knowledge and Data Engineering 26(1), 108–119 (2014)
36. Rutkowski, L., Jaworski, M., Pietruczuk, L., Duda, P.: The CART decision tree for mining data streams. Information Sciences 266, 1–15 (2014)
37. Starczewski, J., Rutkowski, L.: Interval type 2 neuro-fuzzy systems based on interval consequents. In: Rutkowski, L., Kacprzyk, J. (eds.) Neural Networks and Soft Computing, pp. 570–577. Physica-Verlag, Springer-Verlag Company, Heidelberg, New York (2003)
38. Starczewski, J.T., Rutkowski, L.: Connectionist Structures of Type 2 Fuzzy Inference Systems. In: Wyrzykowski, R., Dongarra, J., Paprzycki, M., Waśniewski, J. (eds.) PPAM 2001. LNCS, vol. 2328, pp. 634–642. Springer, Heidelberg (2002)
39. Theodoridis, D.C., Boutalis, Y.S., Christodoulou, M.A.: Robustifying analysis of the direct adaptive control of unknown multivariable nonlinear systems based on a new neuro-fuzzy method. Journal of Artificial Intelligence and Soft Computing Research 1(1), 59–79 (2011)

One-Class Classification Decomposition
for Imbalanced Classification
of Breast Cancer Malignancy Data

Bartosz Krawczyk[1], Łukasz Jeleń[2], Adam Krzyżak[3], and Thomas Fevens[3]

[1] Department of Systems and Computer Networks,
Wrocław University of Technology,
Wybrzeże Wyspiańskiego 27, 50-370 Wrocław, Poland
bartosz.krawczyk@pwr.wroc.pl

[2] Institute of Computer Engineering, Control and Robotics,
Wrocław University of Technology,
Wybrzeże Wyspiańskiego 27, 50-370 Wrocław, Poland
lukasz.jelen@pwr.wroc.pl

[3] Department of Computer Science and Software Engineering,
Concordia University,
1455 de Maisonneuve Blvd. West, Montréal, Québec, Canada H3G 1M8
{krzyzak,fevens}@cse.concordia.ca

Abstract. In this paper we address a problem arising from the classification of breast cancer malignancy data. Due to the fact that there is much smaller number of patients which are diagnosed with high malignancy, data sets are prone to have a high imbalance between malignancy classes. To overcome this problem we have applied state-of-the-art methods for imbalanced classification to our data set and demonstrate an improvement in the classification sensitivity. The achieved sensitivity for our data set was recorded at 92.34%.

Keywords: one-class classification, classifier ensemble, pattern recognition, image processing, imbalanced classification, breast cancer, nuclei segmentation.

1   Introduction

Breast cancer is the most often diagnosed type of cancer among middle–age women. Based on the data provided by the National Cancer Registry, there was 16534 diagnosed cases of breast cancer in Poland [1]. The number of diagnosed cases is increasing every year and from 2009 to 2011 there was an increase of 782 cases. Such a large number of diagnoses also suggests a large death rate, which was recorded to be 5437 deaths in 2011 and was larger that in 2009 by 195 cases. Most of these cases could be fully recovered if the diagnosis would be made in the early stage of the disease. This is due to the fact that cancers are vulnerable to treatment in the early stages while in their most advanced stages they are usually almost impossible to treat. Looking at these statistics we can

L. Rutkowski et al. (Eds.): ICAISC 2014, Part I, LNAI 8467, pp. 539–550, 2014.

easily conclude that there is a need for a fast and reliable diagnostic tool that would be able to assist a pathologist during the breast cancer examination. By being able to perform a precise and objective decision, the high death rate can be reduced. This is why we can propose a computerized method for cytological image processing, which can be integrated as part of a diagnosis process [6].

Breast cancer diagnosis is a multi-step process that starts with a simple palpatory examination of a breast. If suspicious masses are found during that examination, a patient is sent to perform a mammography, which is a non–invasive method typically used for screening purposes and not for a precise diagnosis. This tool allows a radiologist to locate possible microcalcifications and other indicators in the breast tissue. If a suspicious region is found, the patient is then sent to a pathologist for a fine needle aspiration biopsy (FNA) examination. This is an invasive method where a small tissue sample (biopsy) is extracted from the suspicious region. Based on the FNA examination a pathologist describes in detail the type of cancer, and its genealogy and malignancy. The determination of the malignancy (i.e., malignancy grading) is essential when predicting the progression of the cancer.

In the literature we can find numerous applications of computer vision approaches to medical images, as described in an extensive survey of computer aided breast cancer classification in [12]. Some more recent research appears in Filipczuk et al. [8]. As described in Section 2, in the data set used for our research into malignancy grading there are more cases with intermediate malignancy than high malignancy. In this paper we present an approach that classifies the malignancy based on the imbalanced data set without sacrificing data. A similar problem was previously addressed in [15], where the highest achieved sensitivity was 88.46%. Here, we were able to obtain the sensitivity as high as 92.34% (see sec. 8.2).

2   Medical Data

For the purpose of this study we have collected a data set of fine needle aspirates that where used for the breast cancer diagnosis. All of the slides were stained with the Haematoxylin and Eosin technique (HE) which yielded purple and black stain for nuclei, shades of pink for cytoplasm and orange/red for red blood cells. These slides where digitalized with Olympus BX 50 microscope with mounted CCD–IRIS camera connected to a PC computer with MultiScan Base 08.98 software at the Department of Pathology of the Medical University of Wrocław, Poland. The resolution of the recorded images was 96 dots per inch (dpi) and their size was 764×572 pixels. The data set is constantly growing and, for the current paper, consists of 341 images. There are two types of images each recorded at different magnifications (see Fig. 1). Images recorded at low magnification ($100 \times$) are used to define features related to the degree of structural differentiation (see Section 4) and images recorded at high magnification ($400 \times$) are used to calculate the features that reflect cells' polymorphy and mitotic count. The description of these features is provided in Section 4.

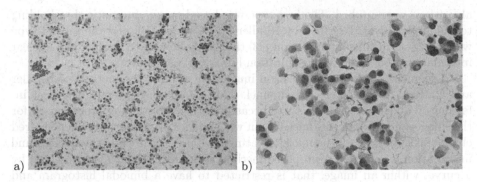

Fig. 1. Example of case images in the data set. a) Low magnification. b) High magnification.

There are 167 low magnification images and 174 images for high magnification. The uneven number of slides is caused by the need to have two or three high magnification images for one low magnification image. From the diagnostic point of view this is caused by the fact that there is more than one suspicious region in the 100× image. In this study images with more than one high magnification per case were treated as separate cases. The images in the data set can also be divided according to the malignancy grade they represent. In this case, we have collected slides of intermediate (G2) and high (G3) malignancy grades. There are 268 images belonging to the G2 class and 73 to the G3 class. The number of images for each malignancy grade shows us the tendency of occurrence of each class. This unbalanced number of cases makes the classification scheme more difficult and was a motivation to perform these studies. The data set does not contain any images of low malignancy cases (G1) due to the fact that these cases are very rare and for the last 5 years there were no such cases at the Department of Pathology and Oncological Cytology. The data set is courtesy of Professor Michał Jeleń, the head of the Department of Pathology and Oncological Cytology at the Wrocław Medical University, Wrocław, Poland.

3   Nuclei Segmentation

In computer vision, segmentation is a very crucial step that influences the feature extraction process and further the classification. Segmentation of the medical data is never an easy task and therefore it is a very active field of research [12, 14]. In our research on malignancy grading, we make use of two kinds of images recorded at different magnifications (see Section 2). Each type of image may require a different segmentation approach depending on the purpose of the segmentation. Low magnification images are needed to extract features based on the topology of nuclei and therefore they can be treated with a simple thresholding. High magnification images will require a more advanced method that will allow for precise nuclear shape representation. They will be used to determine features describing cells' polymorphy. For that reason two types of segmentation algorithms were applied. The first type was based on an automatic thresholding technique that was described by Riddler and Calvard [19] and the second type was a fuzzy c–means segmentation [23] that will allow us to retrieve the nuclear information from fine needle aspiration biopsy (FNA) slides.

To segment the low magnification images we applied the method of Riddler and Calvard to the image red channel. The red channel provides the best information about nuclear structures because during the staining process used for the images in our data set, nuclei stain with shades of purple and when the red channel is extracted all the nuclear features are preserved while the background information is removed. A proposed method seeks a threshold T, represented by a curve, within an image, that is restricted to have a bimodal histogram and the final threshold level is calculated according to the equation $T = (\mu_1 + \mu_2)/2$ where μ_1 and μ_2 are the means of the components separated by T.

For segmentation of nuclei from the high magnification images a method based on a fuzzy approach of Klir and Yuan [13] was applied. According to this algorithm we partition a set of data $X = \{x_1, x_2, ..., x_n\}$ into c clusters with the assumption that $P = \{A_1, A_2, ..., A_c\}$ is known pseudo–partition where A_i is a vector of all memberships of x_k to cluster i. The centers of the c clusters are calculated by the following equation [23]:

$$v_i = \frac{\sum_{k=1}^{n}[A_i(x_k)]^m x_k}{\sum_{k=1}^{n}[A_i(x_k)]^m}, \quad i = 1, 2, ..., c \tag{1}$$

where $m > 1$ is the weight that controls the fuzzy membership. The memberships are defined by equation 2 below if $\|x_k - v_i\|^2 > 0$ for all $i \in \{1, 2, ..., c\}$. If $\|x_k - v_i\|^2 = 0$ for some $i \in I \subseteq \{1, 2, ..., c\}$ the memberships are defined as a nonnegative real number satisfying equation 3 below for $i \in I$.

$$A_i(x_k) = [\sum_{j=1}^{c}(\frac{\|x_k - v_i\|^2}{\|x_k - v_j\|^2})^{\frac{1}{m-1}}]^{-1} \tag{2}$$

$$\sum_{i \in I} A_i(x_k) = 1 \tag{3}$$

The clustering algorithm seeks a set P that minimizes the performance index $J_m(P)$ defined by the following equation:

$$J_m(P) = \sum_{k=1}^{n}\sum_{i=1}^{c}[A_i(x_k)]^m \|x_k - v_i\|^2. \tag{4}$$

The images segmented with the algorithms described in this Section are further used for the determination of features as described in Section 4.

4 Feature Extraction

During the feature extraction step of the classification framework, a so-called feature vector is constructed. This feature vector is then used for classification

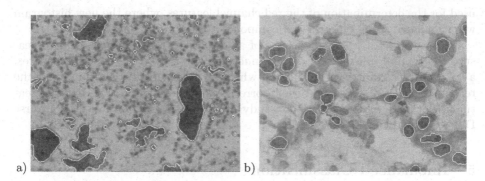

Fig. 2. Illustration of segmentation. a) Low magnification. b) High magnification.

and therefore the proper selection of features is very important. The size of the vector depends on the number of extracted features. Here, we have extracted 33 features, 3 for the low magnification images and 30 for high magnification. For the low magnification images, we have calculated the Area (A_s) which is a total number of nuclei pixels; the Number of Groups (NG) as the number of objects in the segmented image; and Dispersion which is defined as a variation of group areas.

Features extracted from the high magnification images describe features of the nuclei and therefore they are more descriptive in their representation. This led to the definition of additional 30 features that include 8 binary features, 7 moment based features, 5 histogram based features, 5 textural features, and 5 red channel histogram based features, each of which we describe in more detail.

The binary features were calculated based on the binary image ($\mathcal{I}$). A set of nuclei in the image, $N = \{N_1, N_2, ..., N_n\}$, can be defined as a collection of all connected components and the nuclei N_i is a set of pixels that are contained in the extracted nuclei. The binary features include the area of the nucleus (A_i) which is calculated as the sum of all nuclei pixels; perimeter that is a measure of the length of the nuclear envelope; convexity – the ratio of nucleus area and its convex hull; eccentricity that allows us to track how much a segmented nucleus differs from a healthy nucleus; centroid; orientation of the nuclei; and 2 projection features – calculated as a sum of all pixels along rows and columns of the nucleus image [24]. Summation of all the rows provides us with a horizontal projection and summation of all the columns determines the vertical projection.

The second type of extracted features are the moment features. The use of moments is justified by the fact that they allow for the extraction of features that are rotation, scaling and translation (RST) invariant. Based on the normalized central moments, we calculated 7 moment–based features ($\varphi_1 - \varphi_7$) [24].

The image histogram describes the occurrence frequency of intensity values in the image. Features based on the histogram are considered to be statistical features and the histogram is considered to be a probability distribution function of grey level values in the image. In this study we extract 5 statistical features: mean, standard deviation, skew, energy and entropy. These features were also used for the determination of the red channel features, where the new histogram was calculated using only the red component of the RGB image.

The last type of features consists of a set of 5 textural features which measure the texture information of each nucleus [24]. To extract textural features, a co–occurrence matrix is calculated, which provides the information about the relation of pairs of pixels and their corresponding grey levels. The textural features that were extracted in this study are: Energy, Entropy, Inertia, Inverse Difference and Correlation.

5   Imbalanced Classification

A data set is imbalanced if the numbers of objects originating from each of classes is not (approximately) equal. While classifiers are typically evaluated using classification accuracy, this is not appropriate when dealing with imbalanced data, as it will lead to a bias towards the majority class. Consequently, a classifier can display a poor recognition rate for the minority class, while at the same time achieving a high overall accuracy. The uneven distribution of learning examples between classes is however not the sole source of learning difficulties [20]. It has been shown that when sufficient minority samples are available, the difference between the number of training samples itself does not cause a significant drop in recognition rate. However, an uneven class distribution is usually accompanied by other difficulties such as class overlap, small sample size or small data disjuncts.

Various approaches have been suggested to address class imbalance. Among the most effective ones are classifier ensembles or multiple classifier systems (MCSs), which are based on the principle of combining the decisions of several base classifiers. Typically an MCS is combined with a technique dedicated to dealing with imbalanced data [9].

One can distinguish three prominent approaches. i) Over-sampling approaches introduce new, artificial objects on the basis of existing ones, in order to balance the distribution between classes. SMOTEBoost [4] is the most popular examples using SMOTE. IIvotes [3] fuses a rule-based ensemble with a SPIDER pre-processing scheme to achieve a more robust classifier with respect to atypical data distributions in minority classes. ii) Under-sampling ensembles reduce the number of objects in the training set to create an even distribution, and consequently only original samples are used in the training process. The most popular approaches are UnderBagging and Balanced UnderBagging [9]. EasyEnsemble [18] is a hierarchical MCS, as it uses bagging as the primary learning scheme, but for each of the bags AdaBoost is used as the base model. iii) Cost-Sensitive ensembles assign a higher misclassification cost to samples belonging to the minority class in order to boost its recognition rate. Classifiers are constructed in such a way that they minimize the overall misclassification cost, and thus operate in favor of minority objects. Often, this is performed by object weight adjustment in a boosting schema. Recently, a hybrid evolutionary approach for forming cost-sensitive classification forests has been proposed [17].

6   One-Class Classification

A One-Class Classifier (OCC) seeks to distinguish one specific class, known as the target concept from the more broad set of classes (e.g., selecting carrot from vegetables, medical pictures from an extensive image collection, or malicious attacks from Internet activity recordings). The target class is considered as a positive one, while all others are considered as outliers. An OCC may be considered as learning in the absence of counterexamples as the OCC aims at training a classifier using only patterns drawn from the target class distribution. Its main goal is to detect an anomaly or a state other than the one for the target class [22]. It is assumed that only information of the target class is available.

The problem of building MCSs on the basis of one-class classifiers is an area of research that still awaits proper attention. There are some papers dealing with the proposals on how to combine one-class classifiers [25], but most of them are oriented on practical applications, not on theoretical advances.

One-class boundary methods are based on computing the distance between the object x and the description (decision boundary) that encloses the target class ω_T. To apply fusion methods we require the support function of object x for a given class. We propose to use the following heuristic solution:

$$\widehat{F}(x, \omega_T) = \frac{1}{c_1} exp(-d(x|\omega_T)/c_2), \tag{5}$$

which models a Gaussian distribution around the classifier, where $d(x|\omega_T)$ is an Euclidean distance metric between the considered object and a decision boundary, c_1 is the normalization constant, and c_2 is the scale parameter. Parameters c_1 and c_2 should be fitted to the target class distribution.

7   Proposed Approach

In this paper, we propose to decompose the binary problem with a one-class classifier ensemble. To each class a committee of one-class classifiers is assigned and then their individual outputs are combined in order to receive a binary classification decision. Hence, we apply a decomposition of a multi-class data set with one-class classifiers. This raises the question, why use a one-class classifier which does not use information about other classes when such data is available?

This can be explained by the difference in learning paradigms of binary and one-class models. A binary dichotomizer tries to find a decision boundary that will minimize the overall error. Hence in case of an imbalanced problem, such a boundary will be strongly biased towards the majority class and this may result in a poor minority class recognition rate. One-class classifiers try to capture the unique properties of the target class, in order to be able to differentiate it from all other examples. By training two one-class learners – one on the minority and one on the majority class, we achieve a high sensitivity without sacrificing the specificity.

In our previous works, we shown that one-class classifier ensembles can significantly outperform single-model approaches [16]. We have proven that pruning ensembles with the respect to increasing their measure of dissimilarity leads to more accurate OCC systems. We have also introduced several pairwise and non-pairwise diversity measures dedicated to the specific problem of OCC. In this paper, we use one of these measures – One-Class Energy Measure.

Energy approach is an effective measure of fuzziness, successfully implemented in many practical applications such as ECG analysis [5]. Assume that there are L classifiers in the pool, out of which S classifiers can correctly classify a given training object $x_j \in X$ to ω_T. Additionally a threshold $\lambda \in [0,1]$ is introduced. Its role is to filter insignificant degrees of membership that may otherwise contribute to decreasing the stability of the proposed measure. The energy measure is described as follows:

$$DIV_{EN_{oc}}(\Pi^l) = \int_X \sum_{i=1}^{L} f_{\lambda_i}(x)dx, \tag{6}$$

where

$$f_{\lambda_i}(x) = f_i(x) \Leftrightarrow \frac{\sum_{k=1}^{L} \delta(\Psi_{i_k}^M(x), \Psi^*(x))}{L} > \lambda, \tag{7}$$

and $\Psi^*(x)$ denotes a classifier correctly classifying the object x, $\delta(\Psi_{i_k}^M(x), \Psi^*(x))$ is a 0-1 loss function, M stands for M-th class under consideration (when using one-class ensembles for multi-class problems) and $f(x) : [0,1] \to R_+$ is an increasing function in interval [0,1] for $f(0) = 0$.

We propose to select OCC classifiers to the committee according to both the ensemble accuracy and diversity, expecting that this will allow to preserve their advantages while becoming more robust to unwanted properties of models in the pool. To achieve this goal we employ a multi-objective optimization, conducted with the usage of a memetic algorithm (MA) [10].

MAs may be seen as a hybrid solution that tries to blend together concepts from different metaheuristics to gain advantage from combining their strong points. The central philosophy of MAs resolves around the individual improvement plus population cooperation. Unlike traditional Evolutionary Algorithms (EA), MAs are tuned towards exploiting all available knowledge about the problem under study, therefore becoming less random and a more directed search method. The formulation of the so-called No-Free-Lunch Theorem for optimization have proven that the quality of the search algorithm is strictly connected with the amount and quality of the knowledge about the considered problem that is available. Therefore while EA relies on more or less random walking, directed by tuning the mutation and cross-over operation procedures, MA uses the advantages of this highly efficient approach, but improves it with a guided search for finding better solutions in a shorter time.

In this paper we use an MA that is a hybrid approach using both EA and tabu search to exclude re-visiting previously checked points in solution space. Additionally to allow for searching simultaneously for classifiers with high accuracy and diversity we use a multi-objective MA, aiming at maximizing both of these criteria. Let us formulate the multi-objective optimization criterion as:

$$maximize\ g(\Pi^l) = (Acc(\Pi^l) + EN_{oc}(\Pi^l)) \tag{8}$$

where Π^l is the given pool of classifiers that will undergo an ensemble pruning procedure, $Acc(\Pi^l)$ stands for the overall accuracy of the given ensemble and $EN_{oc}(\Pi^l)$ is the diversity of the considered ensemble expressed by the mentioned One-class Energy Measure.

An individual in the MA population represents a classifier ensemble:

$$Ch = [C^{majority}][C^{minority}], \tag{9}$$

where component $C^{majority}$ represents L one-class classifiers at our disposal trained on the majority class; and component $C^{minority}$ represents K one-class classifiers at our disposal trained on the minority class:

$$C = [C_1^{majority}, C_2^{majority}, ..., C_L^{majority}][C_1^{minority}, C_2^{minority}, ..., C_K^{minority}], \tag{10}$$

and is a binary vector with 1s indicating the chosen individual classifiers (i.e., if we have 5 classifiers assigned to each class, then [00101][10010] would indicate that classifiers 3 and 5 are chosen for the minority class and classifiers 1 and 4 for the minority class).

For this MA standard operators for EAs such as individual selection, mutation, cross-over etc. apply. Additionally a tabu search is applied at the end of each iteration to additionally tune the available individuals. The control parameters of the MA algorithm are as follows: N_c (the upper limit of algorithm cycles), N_p (the population quantity), β (the mutation probability), γ (the crossover probability), Δ_m (the mutation range factor), V (the upper limit of algorithm iterations without quality improvement), T (the size of the tabu list) and N_T (the number of cycles for improvement of individuals via the tabu search).

8 Experimental Investigations

The aims of the experimental investigations were to check the quality of the proposed method on a large data set of medical images collected by the authors and to compare the one-class decomposition with state-of-the-art ensembles dedicated to imbalanced classification.

8.1 Set-Up

For the experiment a Support Vector Data Description [21] with a polynomial kernel is used as a base classifier. The pool of classifiers were homogeneous, i.e., consisted of classifiers of the same type. The pool of classifiers was created in a fixed way to allow a proper exploitation of the properties of different classifier selection criteria. It consisted in total of 10 models for each of the classes, build on the basis of a Random Subspace [11] approach with each subspace consisting of 60% of original features.

The Error-Correcting Output Codes (ECOC) [7] framework was used as a classifier fusion block due to its proven efficiency in reconstructing a multi-class task from a set of binary classifiers. ECOC can be easily used for an OCCs ensemble, as we can map the target class as +1 and the unknown, outlier class by -1 [25]. The threshold parameter λ for One-class Energy Measure was set to 0.1 and a hyperbolic tangent was selected as the $f(x)$ function. The parameters used for the weight optimization were set as follows: $N_c = 300$, $N_p = 50$, $\beta = 0.7$, $\gamma = 0.3$, $\Delta_m = 0.2$, $V = 20$, $T = 7$ and $N_T = 15$. These parameters returned the best classification results and were found using a grid-search procedure.

For testing, we used a statistical test to compare the results and judge if their differences were statistically significant. For this purpose, we used a combined 5×2 cv F Test [2], where preprocessing procedures were run independently for each of the folds.

8.2 Results

The results of the experiment are presented in the Table 1. They show the classifiers' sensitivity and specificity. Each classifier has assigned its index number (in the row with classifier names). These indexes correspond with numbers in the *statistical test* row and indicates in comparison with which other tested classification methods (represented by their indexes) the considered classifier is statistically superior.

Table 1. Results of the experiment

	OverBagging[1]	SMOTEBoost[2]	IIVotes[3]	EasyEnsemble[4]	OCC ensemble[5]
Sensitivity	85.23	88.97	90.32	89.03	92.34
Specificity	92.37	91.80	92.10	92.24	94.23
Statistical test	–	1	1, 2, 4	1, 2	1, 2, 3, 4

8.3 Discussion

From the results one may clearly see, that the proposed one-class decomposition ensemble outperforms the other state-of-the-art methods dedicated to the imbalanced classification in a statistically significant way. For reference methods an improved sensitivity is connected with a drop of specificity, as the decision boundary is forced towards the minority class. In case of better specificity, the sensitivity drops as the bias towards the majority class is not reduced enough.

The proposed approach do not suffer from the bias problem, as for each class a separate boundary is constructed. As it is independent from the other class, we do not face the problem of imbalance. Therefore, we have two one-class enclosing boundaries, each being a descriptor of its target class. Reconstructing an original binary problem with ECOC combiner leads to a significantly better results.

Additionally, we improve our method by delegating an ensemble of one-class classifiers. The memetic-based pruning procedure allows for the selection of classifiers with high individual accuracy that are mutually diverse to each other.

This way, we maintain high generalization properties of our ensemble, despite its being trained separately on both classes.

9 Conclusions

In this study a problem of classification of the imbalanced medical data was addressed. In the opening sections it can be noticed that the image processing of such images is not an easy problem either. After successful segmentation and feature extraction we have constructed a 33–element feature vector that was then introduced to the classifier. From the results section one can notice that the problem of uneven classes has been eliminated and the presented methods are suitable for the classification of this type of data. Out of all classifiers it can be easily noticed, as already mentioned in previous section, the one-class decomposition ensemble provided the best results. The highest achieved sensitivity was 92.34%. Looking at the data and the size of the feature vector we can assume that applying a feature selection procedure may lead to a further boost in the sensitivity of our classification. This issue will can be researched further to find the optimal sensitivity level for breast cancer data.

Acknowledgements. Bartosz Krawczyk was supported by The Polish National Science Centre under the grant PRELUDIUM number DEC-2013/09/N/ST6/ 03504. This research was supported in part by the Natural Sciences and Engineering Research Council of Canada.

References

1. National Cancer Registry (December 2013), http://85.128.14.124/krn/ (accessed on December 13, 2013)
2. Alpaydin, E.: Combined 5 x 2 cv F Test for comparing supervised classification learning algorithms. Neural Computation 11(8), 1885–1892 (1999)
3. Błaszczyński, J., Deckert, M., Stefanowski, J., Wilk, S.: Integrating selective preprocessing of imbalanced data with Ivotes ensemble. In: Szczuka, M., Kryszkiewicz, M., Ramanna, S., Jensen, R., Hu, Q. (eds.) RSCTC 2010. LNCS (LNAI), vol. 6086, pp. 148–157. Springer, Heidelberg (2010)
4. Chawla, N.V., Lazarevic, A., Hall, L.O., Bowyer, K.W.: SMOTEBoost: Improving prediction of the minority class in boosting. In: Lavrač, N., Gamberger, D., Todorovski, L., Blockeel, H. (eds.) PKDD 2003. LNCS (LNAI), vol. 2838, pp. 107–119. Springer, Heidelberg (2003)
5. Czogała, E., Łęski, J.: Application of entropy and energy measures of fuzziness to processing of ECG signal. Fuzzy Sets and Systems 97(1), 9–18 (1998)
6. Detyna, J., Jeleń, L., Jeleń, M.: Role of Image Processing in the Cancer Diagnosis. Bio-Algorithms and Med-Systems 7(4), 5–9 (2011)
7. Dietterich, T., Bakiri, G.: Solving multiclass learning problems via error-correcting output codes. J. Artif. Int. Res. 2, 263–286 (1995)
8. Filipczuk, P., Fevens, T., Krzyżak, A., Monczak, R.: Computer-aided breast cancer diagnosis based on the analysis of cytological images of fine needle biopsies. IEEE Transactions on Medical Imaging 32(12), 2169–2178 (2013)

9. Galar, M., Fernández, A., Barrenechea, E., Bustince, H., Herrera, F.: An overview of ensemble methods for binary classifiers in multi-class problems: Experimental study on one-vs-one and one-vs-all schemes. Pattern Recognition 44(8), 1761–1776 (2011)
10. Harman, M., McMinn, P.: A theoretical and empirical study of search-based testing: Local, global, and hybrid search. IEEE Transactions on Software Engineering 36(2), 226–247 (2010)
11. Ho, T.K.: The random subspace method for constructing decision forests. IEEE Trans. Pattern Anal. Mach. Intell. 20, 832–844 (1998)
12. ŁJeleń, Krzyżak, A., Fevens, T., Jeleń, M.: Influence of Pattern Recognition Techniques on Breast Cytology Grading. Scientific Bulletin of Wroclaw School of Applied Informatics 2, 16–23 (2012)
13. Klir, G., Yuan, B.: Fuzzy Sets and Fuzzy Logic: Theory and Applications. Prentice Hall, New Jersey (1995)
14. Kowal, M., Filipczuk, P., Obuchowicz, A., Korbicz, J., Monczak, R.: Computer-aided diagnosis of breast cancer based on fine needle biopsy microscopic images. Computers in Biology and Medicine 43(10), 1563–1572 (2013)
15. Krawczyk, B., Jeleń, Ł., Krzyżak, A., Fevens, T.: Oversampling methods for classification of imbalanced breast cancer malignancy data. In: Bolc, L., Tadeusiewicz, R., Chmielewski, L.J., Wojciechowski, K. (eds.) ICCVG 2012. LNCS, vol. 7594, pp. 483–490. Springer, Heidelberg (2012)
16. Krawczyk, B., Woźniak, M.: Diversity measures for one-class classifier ensembles. Neurocomputing 126, 36–44 (2014)
17. Krawczyk, B., Woźniak, M., Schaefer, G.: Cost-sensitive decision tree ensembles for effective imbalanced classification. Applied Soft Computing 14, Part C, 554–562 (2014)
18. Liu, X., Wu, J., Zhou, Z.: Exploratory undersampling for class-imbalance learning. IEEE Transactions on Systems, Man, and Cybernetics, Part B: Cybernetics 39(2), 539–550 (2009)
19. Ridler, T., Calvard, S.: Picture thresholding using an iterative selection. IEEE Trans. on Systems, Man and Cybernetics 8, 630–632 (1978)
20. Sun, Y., Wong, A.K.C., Kamel, M.S.: Classification of imbalanced data: A review. Inter'l Journal of Pattern Recognition & Artificial Intell. 23(4), 687–719 (2009)
21. Tax, D., Duin, R.: Support vector data description. Machine Learning 54(1), 45–66 (2004)
22. Tax, D., Duin, R.: Characterizing one-class datasets. In: Proceedings of the 16th Annual Symp. of the Pattern Recogn. Assoc. of South Africa, pp. 21–26 (2005)
23. Theera-Umpon, N.: Patch–Based white blood cell nucleus segmentation using fuzzy clustering. ECTI Transactions on Electrical Engineering, Electronics and Communications 3(1), 15–19 (2005)
24. Umbaugh, S.: Computer Imaging: Digital Image Analysis and Processing. CRC Press, New York (2005)
25. Wilk, T., Woźniak, M.: Soft computing methods applied to combination of one-class classifiers. Neurocomputing 75, 185–193 (2012)

Comparison of Tree-Based Ensembles in Application to Censored Data

Malgorzata Kretowska

Faculty of Computer Science
Bialystok University of Technology
Wiejska 45a, 15-351 Bialystok, Poland
e-mail: m.kretowska@pb.edu.pl

Abstract. In the paper the comparison of ensemble based methods applied to censored survival data was conducted. Bagging survival trees, dipolar survival tree ensemble and random forest were taken into consideration. The prediction ability was evaluated by the integrated Brier score, the prediction measure developed for survival data. Two real datasets with different percentage of censored observations were examined.

Keywords: survival tree, ensemble, random forest, censored observation, survival analysis, Brier score.

1 Introduction

Methods for analysis of classification and regression problems are developing to provide faster, more stable and more accurate prediction. The same goal inspires also the researchers working on survival data. Very often new approaches for classification or regression tasks are then adapted to data with incomplete information. Such incomplete information is an integral part of censored data, which contains observations with unknown failure times. For such data we only know how long the observation has not experienced any failure, but the exact failure time remains unknown.

Except statistical methods, which often require many strict assumptions, survival trees and survival ensembles belong to the most common non-parametric methods for survival data analysis. The fast development of survival trees started in the mid-1980s and lasted for the next ten years [3]. The survival ensemble is quite a new branch of analysis of survival data. First methods were proposed in 2004 - bagging survival trees [8] and relative risk forests [10]. The consecutive approaches were proposed by Kretowska [15], Hothorn [9], and Ishwaran [11].

In this paper the comparison of predictive ability of three ensemble methods was conducted. Bagging survival trees [8] and random survival forest [11] are implemented and available in R packages, while dipolar survival tree ensemble [15] was implemented by the author in C++. In order to compare the predictive ability of the models, the integrated Brier score [6] was applied. Experiments were performed on two data sets with different percentage of censored observations. The first data, Veteran's Administration (*VA*) lung cancer study [4], contains

L. Rutkowski et al. (Eds.): ICAISC 2014, Part I, LNAI 8467, pp. 551–560, 2014.

6.5 percent of censored observations, while the other one - malignant melanoma [1] - 72 percent.

The paper consists of six sections. In Section 2 the definition of survival data as well as the survival time distribution functions are presented. Section 3 contains introduction to survival ensemble and more detailed description of three distinguishes ensemble methods. The definition of the integrated Brier score is given in Section 4. Experimental results are presented in Section 5, while Section 6 summarizes the results .

2   Censored Data

Let T^0 denotes the true survival time and C denotes the true censoring time with distribution functions F and G respectively. We observe a random variable $O = (T, \Delta, \mathbf{X})$, where $T = \min(T^0, C)$ is the time to event, $\Delta = I(T \leq C)$ is a censoring indicator and $\mathbf{X} = (X_1, ..., X_N)$ denotes the set of N covariates from a sample space χ. We have a learning sample $L = (\mathbf{x}_i, t_i, \delta_i)$, $i = 1, 2, ..., n$, where $\mathbf{x}_i$ is N-dimensional covariates vector, t_i - survival time and δ_i - failure indicator, which is equal to 0 for censored cases and 1 for uncensored cases.

The distribution of survival time may be described by several functions:

– survival function

$$S(t) = P(T > t) \tag{1}$$

where $P(\bullet)$ means probability, $S(0) = 1$ and $\lim_{t \to \infty} S(t) = 0$
– density function

$$f(t) = \lim_{\Delta t \to 0} \frac{P(t \leq T < t + \Delta t)}{\Delta t} \tag{2}$$

where $f(t)dt$ is the unconditional probability of failure in the infinitesimal interval $(t, t + dt)$.
– hazard function

$$\lambda(t) = \lim_{\Delta t \to 0} \frac{P(t \leq T < t + \Delta t | T \geq t)}{\Delta t} \tag{3}$$

where $\lambda(t)dt$ is the probability of failure in the in infinitesimal interval $(t, t + dt)$, given survival at time t.
– cumulative hazard function

$$\Lambda(t) = \int_0^t \lambda(u)du = -\log S(t) \tag{4}$$

The estimation of survival function $S(t)$ may be done by using the Kaplan-Meier product limit estimator [13], which is calculated on the base of the learning sample L and is denoted by $\hat{S}(t)$:

$$\hat{S}(t) = \prod_{j | t_{(j)} \leq t} \left(\frac{m_j - d_j}{m_j} \right) \tag{5}$$

where $t_{(1)} < t_{(2)} < \ldots < t_{(D)}$ are distinct, ordered survival times from the learning sample L, in which the event of interest occurred, d_j is the number of events at time $t_{(j)}$ and m_j is the number of patients at risk at $t_{(j)}$ (i.e., the number of patients who are alive at $t_{(j)}$ or experience the event of interest at $t_{(j)}$).

The Nelson-Aalen estimator of cumulative hazard function is defined as:

$$H(t) = \sum_{j | t_{(j)} \le t} \frac{d_j}{m_j} \tag{6}$$

The 'patients specific' survival probability function is given by $S(t|\mathbf{x}) = P(T > t | \mathbf{X} = \mathbf{x})$. The conditional survival probability function for the new patient with covariates vector $\mathbf{x}_{new}$ is denoted by $\hat{S}(t|\mathbf{x}_{new})$. Similarly $H(t|\mathbf{x}_{new})$ means a conditional cumulative hazard function.

3 Ensembles of Survival Trees

An ensemble is a set of k single predictors, often trees. Depending on the data, the ensemble may solve classification, regression or survival problems. In case of censored survival data single predictors are usually survival trees, which have the ability to cope with censored observations. Unlike the ensemble for classification and regression problems, the ensemble of survival trees does not return the exact predicted value. The outcome for a given observation is a distribution function of survival time. Thus, analyzing such a function, the time intervals with higher and smaller probability of failure occurrence may be distinguished for the observation.

Each single tree is built on the base of bootstrap sample drawing with replacement from the learning data. A general algorithm of building and using the ensemble is given as follows:

1. Draw k bootstrap samples $(L_1, L_2, \ldots, L_k)$ of size n with replacement from L
2. Induct k single trees T_i based on each bootstrap sample L_i, $i = 1, 2, \ldots, k$
3. Having a new observation $\mathbf{x}_{new}$, drop it down each of k single trees
4. On the base of the results of k single trees, calculate a function $f(t|\mathbf{x}_{new})$, being an outcome of the whole ensemble

Comparing various approaches to building the ensembles, the differences are visible in steps 2 and 4 of the above algorithm.

3.1 Bagging Survival Trees

The approach was proposed by Hothorn *et al.* [8]. The authors did not focus on special splitting criterion for single tree induction. They used a method previously proposed by LeBlanc and Crowley [16] which employed a measure based on Poisson deviance residuals. They presented an original method of calculating the function $f(t|\mathbf{x}_{new})$, which takes a form of aggregated Kaplan-Meier survival function: $\hat{S}_A(t|\mathbf{x}_{new})$. Step 4 is here divided into two parts:

4a Build aggregated sample $L_A(\mathbf{x}_{new}) = \{L_1(\mathbf{x}_{new}); L_2(\mathbf{x}_{new}), \ldots, L_k(\mathbf{x}_{new})\}$, where $L_i(\mathbf{x}_{new})$ is a set of observations from the bootstrap sample L_i that reached the same leaf node of the tree T_i as the observation $\mathbf{x}_{new}$.

4b On the base of aggregated sample $L_A(\mathbf{x}_{new})$, compute the Kaplan-Meier aggregated survival function for a new observation $\mathbf{x}_{new}$: $\hat{S}_A(t|\mathbf{x}_{new})$

3.2 Dipolar Survival Trees Ensemble

Unlike the bagging survival tree, which is an example of univariate tree, the single dipolar survival tree [14] belongs to multivariate approaches. It means that each internal node contains the split which is based not only on one variables (e.g $x_i > c$), but a linear combination of input variables is examined. The test takes the form of a hyperplane: $H(\mathbf{w}, \theta) = \{\mathbf{x} : \mathbf{w}^T\mathbf{x} = \theta\}$. If a given feature vector $\mathbf{x}$ is situated on the positive site of the hyperplane the test returns the value greater or equal to 0, in the other case the test returns the negative value. The values of $\mathbf{w}$ and θ are calculated by the minimization of dipolar criterion function [2].

Dipolar survival trees ensemble [15] is build according to the general rules presented above. Similarly to bagging survival trees, the result of the whole ensemble for a new features vector $\mathbf{x}_{new}$ is calculated as an aggregated survival function $\hat{S}_A(t|\mathbf{x}_{new})$.

3.3 Random Survival Forest

Randon survival forest was proposed by Ishwaran *et al.* [11]. The method differs from the previous ones, both in the induction process and in the way the results are calculated. During the induction process the randomization is injected into each node generation. It means that the best split is not chosen by the analysis of the whole set of available variables but a subset of variables is selected. Then, basing on this subset, the split that maximizes survival difference between two child nodes is chosen.

The results of the whole ensemble is calculated as the average of cumulative hazards functions received for each single tree. Step no. 4 is here divided into three parts:

4a For each survival tree T_i, $i = 1, 2, \ldots, k$, determine a set $L_i(\mathbf{x}_{new})$ containing the covariates vectors from the bootstrap sample L_i which belong to the same leaf node as $\mathbf{x}_{new}$

4b For each set $L_i(\mathbf{x}_{new})$ calculate the Nelson-Aalen estimator of CHF: $H_i^*(t|\mathbf{x}_{new})$, $i = 1, 2, \ldots, k$

4c Calculate the average of CHF to obtain the ensemble CHF:

$$H(t|\mathbf{x}_{new}) = \frac{1}{k}\sum_{i=1}^{k} H_i^*(t|\mathbf{x}_{new}) \tag{7}$$

4   Model Validation

In case of censored survival data where the exact failure time for a given subject may be unknown, the classical validation measures used in regression problems are not applicable. Indexes which are used in survival analysis do not calculate the differences between the given and predicted failure times, they rather use the differences between survival functions [6,5] or the order of predicted and given survival times [7]. The integrated Brier score [6] belongs to the first types of indexes. For a fixed time point t the contribution to the Brier score is divided into three groups:

1. $t_i \leq t$ and $\delta_i = 1$
2. $t_i > t$ and ($\delta_i = 1$ or $\delta_i = 0$)
3. $t_i \leq t$ and $\delta_i = 0$

For the observations belonging to group 1 the failure occurred before t and the event status at t is equal to 0, so in the Brier score we present this as $(0 - \hat{S}(t|\mathbf{x}_i))^2 = \hat{S}(t|\mathbf{x}_i)^2$. The observations of group 2 do not experienced any event at time t, hence the event status at t is equal to 1 and the contribution to the Brier score is: $(1 - \hat{S}(t|\mathbf{x}_i))^2$. The contribution to the Brier score for observation of group 3 can not be calculated, because the event status at t is unknown for them. Since the observations of group 3 do not have any contribution to the Brier score, the loss of information should be compensate by additional weighting of the existing contributions. The observations in group 1 have the weight $\hat{G}(t_i)^{-1}$ and those in group 2 the weight $\hat{G}(t)^{-1}$, where $\hat{G}(t)$ denotes the Kaplan-Meier estimator of the censoring distribution. It is calculated on the base of observations $(t_i, 1 - \delta_i)$. The definition of the Brier score is given as:

$$BS(t) = \frac{1}{n} \sum_{i=1}^{N} (\hat{S}(t|\mathbf{x}_i)^2 I(t_i \leq t \wedge \delta_i = 1)\hat{G}(t_i)^{-1} +$$
$$(1 - \hat{S}(t|\mathbf{x}_i))^2 I(t_i > t)\hat{G}(t)^{-1}) \tag{8}$$

where $I(condition)$ is equal to 1 if the condition is fulfilled, 0 otherwise. The BS equal to 0 means the best prediction.

The integrated Brier score is calculated as:

$$IBS = \frac{1}{max(t_i)} \int_0^{max(t_i)} BS(t)dt \tag{9}$$

5   Experimental Results

The comparison of three ensemble methods in application to censored survival data was conducted. Experimental results were performed on the base of two real data sets with different percentage of censored observations. The value of the integrated Brier score, given in the paper, is the average value of the index calculated for 20 runs of 10-fold cross-validation. The random survival forest (RSF) is implemented in R package 'randomForestSRC' [12]. Since the package uses Harrell's concordance index [7] as a prediction measure, package 'pred' [17] was used to calculate the integrated Brier score. The second aggregation technique is the bagging survival trees method (*BST*) proposed by Hothorn *et al.* [8], which is implemented in 'ipred' package [18].

The first analyzed dataset contains the information from the Veteran's Administration (*VA*) lung cancer study [4]. In this trial, male patients with advanced inoperable tumors were randomized to either standard (69 subjects) or test chemotherapy (68 subjects). Only 9 subjects from 137 were censored. Detailed description of the variables is given in table 1.

Table 1. Description of *VA lung cancer* data

Variable name	Description
Variables assessed at the time of randomization	
Treat	Chemotherapy (0-standard, 1-test)
Cell	Cell type (0-squamous, 1-small, 2-adeno, 3-large)
Prior	Prior therapy (0-no, 1-yes)
KPS	Karnofsky rating
DiagTime	Disease duration
Age	Age
Outcome variables	
Time	Survival time
Status	Failure indicator (0- censored observation, 1- death)

In table 2 the integrated Brier scores (IBS) for *VA lung cancer* data are presented. The experiments were conducted for the ensembles with different number of single trees: 50, 100, 200, 500, 1000. The results for RSF do not depend on the number of single trees, for 100 trees as well as for 1000 trees the IBS equals 0.104. The best results are for bagging survival trees method, for 1000 trees IBS equals 0.098. The most visible influence of the number of trees is for DST ensemble technique. For 50 trees the IBS equals 0.119, then decreasing with increased number of trees, riches the value 0.104 for 1000 trees, what is comparable with the IBS received for RSF.

Table 2. The integrated Brier scores received for *VA lung cancer* data

Number of trees	RSF	BST	DST Ensemble
50	0.105	0.102	0.119
100	0.104	0.101	0.111
200	0.109	0.101	0.108
500	0.103	0.099	0.105
1000	0.104	0.098	0.104

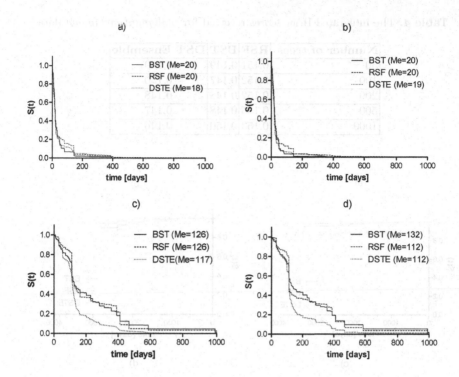

Fig. 1. Survival functions for *VA lung cancer* data a) Treat=0, KPS=20; b)Treat=1, KPS=20; c)Treat=0, KPS=80; d)Treat=1, KPS=80

In figure 1 the survival functions for *VA lung cancer* data are presented. The functions were calculated for patients with standard or test chemotherapy with Karnofsky rating equals 20 or 80. Disease duration and age were fixed as their median values (5 and 62, respectively), Cell and Prior were fixed as 0. For each observation the survival functions received as the results of BST, RSF and DSTE are presented. In figure 1a) and 1b) the functions are quite similar for all the examined methods. The differences exist for functions in figures 1c)

Table 3. Description of *malignant melanoma* data

Variable name	Description
Variables assessed at the time of operation	
Sex	The patients sex (1-male, 0-female)
Age	Age (years)
Thickness	Tumour thickness (cm)
Ulcer	Indicator of ulceration (0-absent, 1-present)
Outcome variables	
Time	Survival time (days)
Status	Failure indicator (0- censored observation, 1- death from melanoma)

Table 4. The integrated Brier scores received for *malignant melanoma* data

Number of trees	RSF	BST	DST Ensemble
50	0.151	0.149	0.149
100	0.152	0.147	0.150
200	0.152	0.148	0.148
500	0.155	0.148	0.147
1000	0.153	0.150	0.146

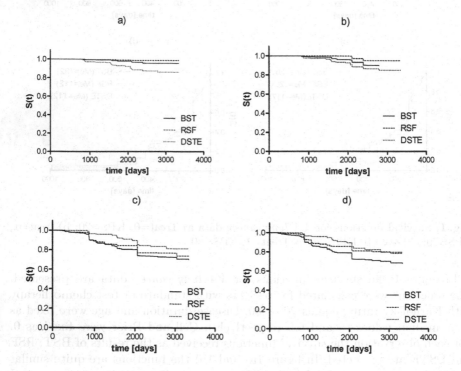

Fig. 2. Survival functions for *malignant melanoma* data a) Sex=0, Thickness=0.97; b) Sex=1, Thickness=0.97; c) Sex=0, Thickness=3.56; d) Sex=1, Thickness=3.56

and 1d). The survival function received for DSTE gives the most pessimistic prediction, especially for time greater than 150 days. Comparing, for example, the probability of survival for 200 days, BST and RSF give the value about 0.4, while for DSTE the probability equals 0.2. Median survival times, also presented in figure 1, are similar for three methods. Analyzing the graphs one could say that the type of treatment does not influence the survival, while Karnofsky rating has a great impact on patients survival.

The other data set contains the information on 205 patients (148 censored cases) with malignant melanoma following radical operation. The data was collected at Odense University Hospital in Denmark by K.T. Drzewiecki [1]. Each patient is described by four variables presented in table 3.

Table 4 presents the integrated Brier scores received for *malignant melanoma* data. The results for RSF do not depend on the number of trees and the integrated Bries scores take the values from the range [0.151; 0.155]. For bagging survival trees the best result is for 100 trees - IBS=0.147, while for 1000 trees IBS equals 0.15. The best results are for DST ensemble and the minimal value of IBS is equal to 0.146 for 1000 trees.

Figure 2 presents survival functions received for *malignant melanoma* data. The influence of sex and tumor thickness was verified. Variable "Thickness" was fixed as its lower and upper quartiles: 0.97 and 3.56, respectively. The experiments were conducted for 54 years old people without ulceration. As we could see, sex do not influence the survival. The differences are visible between figures with different values of Thickness: the prediction is worse for patients with greater tumor thickness. The results received for BST, RSF and DSTE show the main tendency of survival changes in a similar manner, but the exact prediction is slightly different for them.

6 Conclusions

In the paper the prediction ability of tree-based ensemble methods was verified. The analysis covered the results of three techniques: bagging survival trees, random survival forest and dipolar survival tree ensemble. The prediction ability was tested by calculating the integrated Brier score. The analysis was conducted on the base of two medical data sets. The analysis did not show that one method outperformed the results of two others. The best value of the integrated Brier score in case of *VA lung cancer* data was for bagging survival forest, in case of the other data set - *malignant melanoma* - the best result was achieved by dipolar survival tree ensemble.

Acknowledgements. This work was supported by the grant S/WI/2/1013 from Bialystok University of Technology.

References

1. Andersen, P.K., Borgan, O., Gill, R.D.: Statistical Models based on Counting Processes. Springer, New York (1993)
2. Bobrowski, L., Kretowska, M., Kretowski, M.: Design of neural classifying networks by using dipolar criterions. In: Proc. of the Third Conference on Neural Networks and Their Applications, Kule, Poland, pp. 689–694 (1997)
3. Bou-Hamad, I., Larocque, D., Ben-Ameur, H.: A rewiew of survival trees. Statistics Surveys 5, 44–71 (2011)
4. Kalbfleisch, J.D., Prentice, R.L.: The statistical analysis of failure time data. John Wiley & Sons, New York (1980)

5. Gerds, T.A., Cai, T., Schumacher, M.: The performance of risk prediction models. Biometrical Journal 50(4), 457–478 (2008)
6. Graf, E., Schmoor, C., Sauerbrei, W., Schumacher, M.: Assessment and comparison of prognostic classification schemes for survival data. Statistics in Medicine 18, 2529–2545 (1999)
7. Harrell, F.E., Califf, R.M., Pryor, D.B., Lee, K.L., Rosati, R.A.: Evaluating the yield of medical tests. Journal of American Medical Association 247, 2543–2546 (1982)
8. Hothorn, T., Lausen, B., Benner, A., Radespiel-Tröger, M.: Bagging survival trees. Statistics in Medicine 23, 77–91 (2004)
9. Hothorn, T., Buhlmann, P., Dudoit, S., Molinaro, A.M., van der Laan, M.J.: Survival ensembles. Biostatistics 7, 355–373 (2006)
10. Ishwaran, H., Blackstone, E.H., Pothier, C.E., Lauer, M.S.: Relative risk forest for exercise heart rate recovery as a predictor of mortality. Journal of the American Statistical Association 99, 591–600 (2004)
11. Ishwaran, H., Kogalur, U.B., Blackstone, E.H., Lauer, M.S.: Random survival forests. Annals of Applied Statistics 2, 841–860 (2008)
12. Ishwaran, H., Kogalur, U.B.: Random Forests for Survival, Regression and Classification (RF-SRC), R package version 1.3 (2013)
13. Kaplan, E.L., Meier, P.: Nonparametric estimation from incomplete observations. Journal of the American Statistical Association 5, 457–481 (1958)
14. Kretowska, M.: Dipolar regression trees in survival analysis. Biocybernetics and Biomedical Engineering 24(3), 25–33 (2004)
15. Krętowska, M.: Random forest of dipolar trees for survival prediction. In: Rutkowski, L., Tadeusiewicz, R., Zadeh, L.A., Żurada, J.M. (eds.) ICAISC 2006. LNCS (LNAI), vol. 4029, pp. 909–918. Springer, Heidelberg (2006)
16. LeBlanc, M., Crowley, J.: Relative risk trees for censored survival data. Biometrics 48, 411–425 (1993)
17. Mogensen, U.B., Ishwaran, H., Gerds, T.A.: Evaluating Random Forests for Survival Analysis Using Prediction Error Curves. Journal of Statistical Software 50(11), 1–23 (2012), http://www.jstatsoft.org/v50/i11/
18. Peters, A., Hothorn, T.: ipred: Improved Predictors, R package version 0.9-2 (2013), http://CRAN.R-project.org/package=ipred

Advanced Oblique Rule Generating
Based on PCA

Marcin Michalak and Karolina Nurzyńska

Institute of Informatics, Silesian University of Technology, ul. Akademicka 16,
44-100 Gliwice, Poland
{Marcin.Michalak,Karolina.Nurzynska}@polsl.pl

Abstract. In the paper a new algorithm of oblique decision rule induction is presented. It starts from dividing classes into subclasses which is a clustering problem. Then, around each subclass the hyperrectangle is built, which edges are parallel to *PCA* determined directions. Each hyperrectangle represents single decision rule which conditions are hyperplanes containing hyperrectangle sides. In order to simplify the obtained model less important conditions are removed from the rule and then less important variables are also eliminated from the hyperplane equations. The algorithm was applied for real and artificial datasets.

Keywords: machine learning, rules induction, decision systems, Principal Component Analysis, oblique rules, rules pruning.

1   Introduction

Data analysis is a very wide branch of algorithms. There are several ways to organise all algorithms into groups. One of the popular divisions is based on the knowledge of the pattern that we would like to describe. When no pattern is given we say that an unsupervised learning is performed because there is no supervisor: no independent criterion that says whether the results are correct or not. As the example the clustering algorithms can be mentioned. On the other side, there are algorithms that try to describe dependencies between known inputs and known outputs in the data. That they belong to the group of supervised learning techniques, because there is a known reference point. In this group all algorithms of classification and regression must be mentioned.

The other way of data analysis are methods where data division is based on its interpretability. In some situation the predicting model does not explain "why" something happens but only "how". Artificial neural networks are very popular "black boxes" for the classification problem. Teaching the network may give very satisfactory results saying "how" the model behaves. Similar approach present Support Vector Machines in classification or regression. However, it is also very common that we expect the model to describe the analysed process that is given in the interpretable way.

Decision rule induction is a problem of supervised learning that gives interpretable results. Generally, the problem of classification can be mathematically

L. Rutkowski et al. (Eds.): ICAISC 2014, Part I, LNAI 8467, pp. 561–573, 2014.

described as the mapping of the set of objects ($x \in X$) to the finite set of labels (C):

$$f : X \to C$$

This paper presents a new approach to induction of oblique decision rules directly from the data. It is expected that single class can be divided into several smaller subclasses and each of them should generate one decision rule. In this approach subclustering of classes is performed with k−means algorithm and single rule induction is performed with the PCA. Raw results (rules) are then pruned in two aspects: in the first step only the most important conditions in the rule are left and then small coefficients in the rule are trimmed to zero.

The paper is organised as follows: it starts from a short description of decision rules and oblique rules; then the detailed description of all steps of oblique rule induction is presented. Next part contains presentation of results of the comparison of the new algorithm and two other well known methods. The paper ends with a short discussion and some final conclusions and remarks.

2   Related Works

2.1   Decision Rules Generalisation

Decision rule can be considered as the logical formula in the following form:

$$\text{IF } cond_1 \wedge cond_2 \wedge \ldots \wedge cond_n \text{ THEN } class = c$$

where $cond_i$ is a logical expression. This expression is usually one of the following: $a \text{ op } A, \text{op} \in \{=, <, \leq, >, \geq, \in\}$; a is a value of an attribute and A is a constant (or the set, for the "$\in$" operator) and c is one of the labels from the finite set C.

As it was mentioned the main goal of rule induction algorithms is to generate interpretable dependencies. It is also very important for the rule to have the ability of generalisation. Rules that recognise only the object–generator are not considered as interesting. From the other side, the small decrease of model accuracy due to its simplification is allowed. It might be shortening of the rules set or rules itself. This is very common situation when obtained rules are postprocessed [17].

There are several strategies in rules postprocessing. One of the most popular is "from coverage" strategy and its modification. In the beginning the set of rules is ordered with a given ranking. Then the best rule from the raw set to the final result set is moved and the ranking for remaining rules is recalculated, taking into consideration only objects non-covered by rules from the final result set. Iterations are repeated as long as all objects are covered by the final result set.

More advanced methods base on rules shortening or joining. The rule shortening consists of removing elementary conditions or conditions either in the exhaustive searching, the climbing strategy, or some heuristic approach. It is also common to perform the rule shortening as long as the quality of the rule remains on the same level [1].

Rules joining requires at least two decision rules pointing to the same decision class. Two elementary conditions in two rules can be merged in one condition if all other elementary conditions of these rules are the same. The rules joining means that ranges of the same attribute are joined. In the paper [15] the iterative algorithm of this approach is presented. In the paper [9] very similar approach is described: instead of the iterative way, rules are joined before the merging step.

Different approach of rules generalisation is presented in papers [13,18]: the complex elementary conditions in rules premisions are introduced, which are the linear combinations of attributes from elementary conditions of original rules premises.

Rules can also be generalised in such a way that the less important conditions or parameters in the condition are removed with the "from coverage" strategy.

2.2 Oblique Rules

It is a very common limitation of decision rule induction algorithms that they generate only hyper-rectangle shaped rules what causes problem of describing oblique-shaped dependencies. If there is a significant oblique border between two classes it may occur that both of the classes will be described with big number of rules. This remark leads to the definition of oblique criterion of belonging to the class. Let's consider the $k-$dimensional objects. Then the $k-$dimensional separating hyperplane will be given as:

$$H_1 x_1 + H_2 x_2 + \ldots + H_k x_k + H_{k+1} = 0$$

Now, let's define the $k-$dimensional object o and define $H(O)$ as:

$$H(O) = \sum_{i=1}^{k} H_i o_i + H_{k+1}.$$

With this notion the single conditional descriptor for the oblique rule can be defined as one of the following:

$$H(O) < 0, H(O) \leq 0, H(O) > 0, H(O) \geq 0$$

There are also methods to generate this kind of rules from the results of other algorithms like from the oblique decision trees [4,8,12], from linear SVM [2], using the constructive induction [3,19], or directly from the data [11,14].

3   *PCA* Oblique Decision Rules

In order to build a system for oblique decision rules, it is necessary to divide the decision space appropriately. In presented approach, the rules are based on hyperplanes which determine the boundaries for every parameter. The original solution (the *ORG* algorithm [11]) assumed a semi-exhausting search for optimal parameters of separating hyperplanes. There, after some data transformation, the boundaries for every hyperplane parameter were determined. Next, for each combination of parameters (in the parameter range with given step) the rules were evaluated. The performance of this method was satisfactory, however, it was characterised by very high complexity. Moreover, it was noticed that the system does not work well in the situation when a class consists from several disjoint subclasses. Therefore, the *PCA ORG* (called from now as *ORG2.0*) algorithm was introduced [10], which enabled creation of separate hyperplanes for disjoint subclasses. The hyperplanes were calculated basing on the data direction calculated with *PCA*. It improved the overall rules generation, however it was noticed that the system performance diminishes for classes with smaller dimensionality. Hence, this paper deals with the problem of hyperplane definition for class of lower dimensionality.

3.1 *PCA* Overview

Finding the best fitting hyperplanes which divide the class data from the rest of the space is possible when knowing the direction of data scattering. This information can be achieved with principal component analysis (*PCA*) [16]. The *PCA* is a statistical tool that transforms the coordinate system of the data that the new system fits the data scattering direction in the best possible manner. The first principal component reflects the direction in data of highest variance, the second principal component corresponds to the direction, where the second highest variance was noticed, and so on. It may happen that for some directions the variance is equal to zero, because the data might be coplanar. That is the advantage of this method for data dimension reduction, however when only the direction are searched it becomes a disadvantage.

The *PCA* transformation is found using singular value decomposition or the covariance method for a data set X. The data should be normalised with mean value equal to zero. In order to calculate the covariance matrix, C, following formula is applied: $C = XX^T$. The eigenvectors matrix E_{vec} with corresponding eigenvalues vector E_{val} are achieved by solving the equation: $E_{vec}^{-1}CE_{vec} = E_{val}$. In the final step, the E_{vec} should be sorted according to the descending values in E_{val}. This rearrangement sets the most important directions on the top of the eigenvector matrix whereas the less important directions (with lower variation) are on the bottom.

3.2 Disjoint Subclasses Defining

The hyperplanes which are calculated to find the borders of each class are defined by the faces of a hyperrectangle which encloses the class data. Since the class might have a disjoint data or the multidimensional shape of the data might be very complex, the hyperrectangle is defined with some overabundance. Therefore, it was suggested to try to divide the class into some subclasses that assure the most tight fitting of the hyperrectangle to each subclass. It results in more accurate description of class borders.

The class subdivision is based on the k−means algorithm. This is a very easy method which for a given k value divides the data into k subsets providing that each element distance from the class centre is minimised. The drawback is the necessity to know the number of expected subclasses. However, this parameter can be found in adaptive way assuming some given range of search $k_{min} \leq k \leq k_{max}$. In order to estimate the k parameter the k−means algorithm is applied for each k. Then, the error metric is defined as an average distance from each cluster element to its cluster mean. The definition of optimal value considers the smallest possible error value as well as the smallest cluster number.

3.3   Hyperrectangle Estimation

For each subclass the hyperrectangle is calculated with the usage of the PCA method. The faces are determined starting from the highest eigenvalue and terminating on the smallest one. Each eigenvector (eigenvalue) determines two hyperplanes. Their directions are perpendicular to the direction given with eigenvector E_{vec_i} corresponding to its eigenvalue. The exact placement of each plane results from the coefficients of the data point which has the smallest V_{sm} (for the first of two hyperplanes) and greatest V_{gr} (for the second one) value in this direction. The hyperplanes equation corresponding to each eigenvector is given with the formula:

$$H_{low_i} = E_{vec_i} V_{sm}   H_{high_i} = E_{vec_i} V_{gr}$$

When the datasets are divided, it happens that the resultant classes diminishes its dimensionality. In that case the resulting hyperrectangle is created in space with lower dimension, that implores less hyperplanes and complicates the task of oblique rules generation. Therefore, a special routine was designed to add the lacking dimensions. This approach assumes that the lacking hyperplanes should be perpendicular to the existing ones. Although, the data in this direction variation is equal to zero, a constant variation is set to $\varepsilon = 0.0001$ what allows to define two additional faces for each lacking dimension.

Fig. 1 visualizes the examples of the problems concerning a hyperrectangle estimation. The data points are marked with star, cross, and circle symbols. The rectangles reflect the hyperrectangle, the dashed arrows correspond to the eigenvectors. The first example, Fig. 1(a), shows a hyperrectangle estimated for a class, which members are split into several clusters. One can see how inaccurate is the description. On the other hand, Fig. 1(b) depicts the situation when the subclasses were calculated and the hyperrectangle for each of them was created. Here the hyperplanes fit the data very well. This picture presents also the other problem - dimension reduction. In case of the data printed with circles it was possible to calculate only one eigenvector (dashed arrow). However, it was necessary to build the additional faces of hyperrectangle. In order to do so, the epsilon rule was applied as shown on the figure.

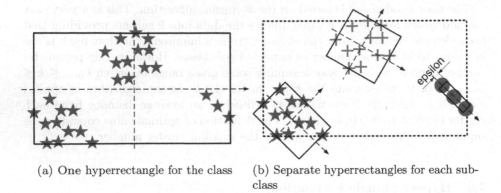

(a) One hyperrectangle for the class   (b) Separate hyperrectangles for each sub-
                                           class

Fig. 1. Example of the necessity of dividing classes to estimate adequate hyperrectangles

3.4 Oblique Rules Induction

Subclass Rule Induction. The single class c is described by a set of hyperplanes. However, for classes with disjoint datasets there exist many hyperrectangles enclosing the data. In order to define the rule describing this class a logical conjunction concerning all the hyperplanes must be generated in the k-dimensional space. Let P be a point corresponding to the currently classified object, then the decision rule R gives the following formula:

$$R: \bigwedge_{i=1}^{k} H_{low_i}(P) \geq 0 \wedge H_{high_i}(P) \geq 0 \rightarrow class = c.$$

Fig. 2 depicts the single oblique rule induction. The data is presented by the dots. The solid lines reflect the hyperplanes calculated on the basis of the hyperrectangle enclosing the data. The faces of the hyperrectangle are perpendicular to the eigenvectors, which directions are marked with dashed lines. One can see that the distance between the parallel faces is minimal. Moreover, each hyperplane has at least one data point that belongs to it.

Orientation of the Hyperplane. The k-dimensional hyperspace $\mathbb{R}^k$ is divided into two separate spaces by each hyperplane. In this approach the hyperplane H is interpreted as a boundary between these two subspaces. It is obvious, that for a given point P one space satisfies the condition $H(P) > 0$, whereas the condition for the other space is $H(P) < 0$. Moreover, it is assumed that the boundary belongs to the first subspace. Hence, it is claimed that the hyperplane H splits the hyperspace into two disjoint spaces:

$$H_+ = \{P \in \mathbb{R}^k : H(P) \geq 0\} \quad \text{and} \quad H_- = \{P \in \mathbb{R}^k : H(P) < 0\}$$

It can be easily noticed that the orientation of the hyperplane H plays an important role in oblique rules definition. Therefore, it is indispensable that for

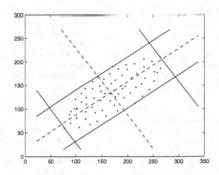

Fig. 2. Visualisation of the single *PCA* oblique rule induction

each hyperplane describing the class boundary the orientation is defined. Having a point Q lying on the correct side of the hyperplane H it is said that $Q \in H_+$. Hence, if there exists a randomly selected point P on the incorrect side of any hyperplane, the coefficients of the equation should be negated.

Rule Generalisation. The raw decision rule is generalised in two ways. Let us assume the linearly separable two-class problem. Setting the $k = 1$ in the step of subclustering classes will give us two decision rules, which accuracies will be 1. Each of them will contain $2d$ oblique descriptors (hyperplanes) where d is the dimensionality of the data. It is obvious that for this kind of data (linearly separable) only one hyperplane is needed. This points out that it is worth to take into consideration the filtration of descriptors. In the presented approach the "from coverage" filtration with the additional parameter α is used. Starting from the empty rule the coverage of each description is evaluated. Then the descriptor with the highest class coverage is added to the rule and removed from the set of considered descriptors. In the following iterations the current rule is extended with every considered descriptor and its coverage is calculated. The process of rule extending ends when the rule coverage is higher then the coverage of the whole raw rule minus the α margin or all descriptors were added to the final rule.

The second step of rule generalisation consists of removing the least significant variables from the hyperplane equation. As *PCA* requires data normalisation we can compare the coefficients of all variables in the hyperplane equation and very small ones regard as needless. It is assumed that significant coefficients are with their absolute value higher than the defined level β.

The Algorithm. The presented algorithm is the extension of the previous version published in [10]. The description of the extended version is presented with pseudocode of two main functions.

```
function PCAORGv2.1(data)
    c_max ← number of classes;
    rules ← ∅;
    for c = 1 to c_max do
        % number of subclasses of the c^th class
        k ← FindK(c^th class);
        % rules generated from c^th class
        c_rules ← ∅;
        for s = 1 to k do
            % find planes...
            [k_pl, cent] ← Planes(s^th subcl, ε);
            % ...and orient them correctly:
            % oriented as H(O) ≥ 0
            k_pl ← OrientPlanes(k_pl, cent);
            k_rl ← GenerateR(k_pl);
            k_rl ← GeneraliseR(k_rl, α, β);
            c_rl ← c_rl ∪ k_rl;
        end for
        rules ← rules ∪ c_rl;
    end for
    Q ← EvaluateR(rules, data);
    return rules, Q;
end function
```

```
function Planes(subclass, ε)
    items ← number of objects in the subclass;
    d ← subclass dimensionality;
    if items = 1 then
        planes ← hyperplanes parallel to axes,
        distant about ε from the item;
        return planes;
    end if
    eigVecs ← PCA(subclass);
    e ← number of eigenvectors;
    planes ← ∅;
    if e < d then
        for i = 1 to e do
            planes ← planes ∪ two planes par-
            allel to the i^th eigenPlane ;
        end for
        for i = e+1 to d do
            planes ← planes ∪ two planes dis-
            tant about ε from the subclass, perpendicular
            to existing planes ;
        end for
    else
        for i = 1 to d do
            planes ← planes ∪ two planes par-
            allel to the i^th eigenPlane ;
        end for
    end if
    return planes;
end function
```

4   Experiments and Results

The new presented algorithm was compared with its predecessor (giving raw results without rules pruning and generalisation) and with two algorithms of decision rule induction from the Weka software: *PART* [7] and *JRIP* (Weka implementation of *RIPPER* [5]). The first comparison was done to prove the ability of rule generalisation without loosing their accuracy.

Experiments were performed on real and artificial data. Real and some of artificial sets come from the benchmark repository [6]. Three artificial datasets come from [18] and each of them contains 1000 objects from two classes. Two two-dimensional sets (named 2d and d2d – double 2d) are almost balanced (562:438 and 534:466 respectively). The third one (3d) is three-dimensional and has two unbalanced classes (835:165). Visualisation of sets is presented on the Fig. 3.

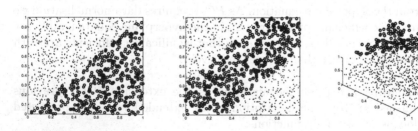

Fig. 3. Visualisation of the synthetic datasets: 2d (left); d2d (center); 3d (right)

The idea of two-dimensional sets is rather easy to interpret. For the third set points from the smaller class are stored in one of the corners of the cube. All points were randomly generated and their coordinates come from the uniform distribution from the range $[0, 1]$.

The first part of experiments were performed to compare the three original versions of Oblique Decision Rule generators (ORG). As the $ORG1.0$ (or just ORG) the algorithm from [11] is considered, the $ORG2.0$ means the first PCA algorithm from [10] and as the $ORG2.1$ the new presented approach is considered. The result of the comparison is presented in the Table 1.

Table 1. Results on real datasets for all versions of algorithm

dataset	accuracy avg (std)			avg. rules number			total number of cond. elem.		
	ORG	ORG2.0	ORG2.1	ORG	ORG2.0	ORG2.1	ORG	ORG2.0	ORG2.1
2d	96.0(1.5)	98.4(1.0)	98.8 (0.98)	2.0	2.0	3.0	3.0	16.0	8.0
d2d	84.3(3.1)	99.0(1.1)	99.3 (0.64)	3.0	2.0	2.0	6.0	16.0	6.0
3d	98.2(1.2)	98.3(1.6)	98.7 (1.27)	2.0	2.0	2.0	2.0	32.0	4.0
iris	94(4.6)	84(8.4)	90.7 (7.42)	3.1	3.0	4.5	5.2	96.0	28.4
balance	92(2.4)	80(4.2)	76.6 (4.7)	6.0	3.0	3.0	12.0	96.0	16.0
Ripley	81(8.4)	65(11.6)	74.4 (10.76)	2.0	6.6	5.2	4.0	28.8	15.0
breast w.	97(1.7)	92(3.0)	89.9 (4.86)	3.0	2.0	2.0	19.0	324.0	36.9

It can be easily observed that for all three artificial datasets the increase of the algorithm version causes the increase of the mean classification accuracy and the decrease of its standard deviation. It is hard to compare the number of conditional descriptors for $ORG1.0$ and $ORG2.X$ as they have different strategies of search. Only the simplification of the model (expressed with the number of elementary conditions) generated by the $ORG2.1$ versus $ORG2.0$ is visible.

As far as the accuracy is concerned the first version of ORG gives the best result on the mentioned data. But it is occupied by the lack of ability of application of this algorithm for more complex (with the higher dimensional) data. The assumed level of the accuracy decrease ($\alpha = 0.05$) is observed for two datasets (balance and breast) but for other two (iris and Ripley) the rule generalisation strategy caused the increase of the mean classification accuracy.

Further experiments were performed in two aspects. In the first aspect only the rule generalisation by condition removing was done assuming $\alpha = 0.05$. In order to observe the influence of removing variables from hyperplanes equations the experiment with the β increase was done (second aspect). β was varied from 0 to 1 with the step 0.01. α remained on the same level as in previous experiments ($\alpha = 0.05$).

The results of the first group of experiment are presented in Table 2. The results of the second group of experiments are presented in the next part of the paper.

Table 2. Comparison of *JRIP*, *PART* and *ORG2.1* results on artificial and benchmark datasets

dataset	accuracy avg (std)			avg. rules number			total number of. cond. elem.		
	PART	*JRIP*	*ORG2.1*	*PART*	*JRIP*	*ORG2.1*	*PART*	*JRIP*	*ORG2.1*
d2d	93.6	95.5	99.3 (0.64)	14	9	3.0	37	18	8.0
3d	94.5	94.8	98.7 (1.27)	13	8	2.0	25	19	6.0
2d	96.3	95.5	98.8 (0.98)	10	10	2.0	22	18	4.0
Ripley	85.6	85.6	74.4(10.76)	5	2	5.2	7	1	15.0
balance	83.5	81.0	76.6(4.70)	47	11	3.0	147	30	16.0
breast w.	95.5	95.6	89.8(4.86)	11	6	2.0	21	10	36.9
iris	94.0	95.3	90.7(7.42)	3	3	4.5	3	4	28.4
vehicle	71.5	69.2	73.9(4.31)	29	16	7.9	108	40	1006.2

4.1 The Model Simplification

In this approach two levels of rule pruning were performed: removing oblique descriptors ("from coverage" strategy) and trimming small coefficients to zero (removing variables from the hyperplane equation). As the pruning level β values from 0 to 1 with the step 0.01 were considered. For each dataset and each β the classification accuracy and the complexity of the model (the total number of elementary conditions) is observed. As it is difficult to present this kind of results in the table, results are presented in charts 4(a)-4(h). The X axis represents the increase of the pruning level. The line (and the left Y axis) is the mean classification accuracy and bars (and the right Y axis) are the average total number of elementary conditions (the model complexity).

4.2 Discussion

The comparison of the following algorithms on synthetic datasets shows two tendencies: the increase of the model accuracy (with the decrease of its standard deviation) and the decrease of the model complexity, understood as the number of elementary conditions. It occurs that for two datasets ("iris" and "Ripley") the generalisation strategy not only simplifies the model but also improves its accuracy. Models of two other datasets are shortened six and almost nine times assuring the decrease of the model accuracy not greater then 5%.

When comparing *ORG2.1* with *PART* and *JRIP* on synthetic oblique data (first three rows in Table 2) it is very easy to notice the ability of data description simplification possible to obtain with the new approach: the smallest number of rules and the smallest number of elementary condition. Unfortunately, it is still hard to state that it gives comparable results, regarding model accuracy, as not oblique rules. The average accuracy is from 4.4% to 11.4% worse for the *ORG2.1*. Only for the "vehicle" dataset the increase of the model accuracy is observed (2.4% and 4.7%).

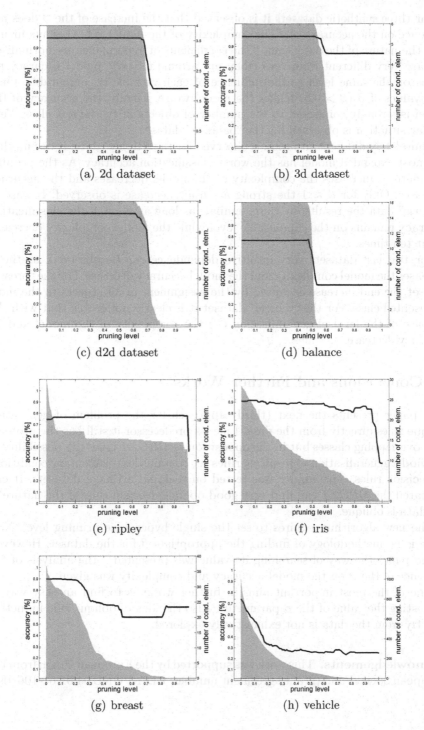

(a) 2d dataset

(b) 3d dataset

(c) d2d dataset

(d) balance

(e) ripley

(f) iris

(g) breast

(h) vehicle

Fig. 4. Influence of level of pruning on classification accuracy and model complexity

For three synthetic datasets it is observed that the increase of the β does not influence on the accuracy and the complexity of the model. This behaviour implies the nature of the data: even if the coefficients of hyperplanes are normalised and are very different from zero (they are around 0.5) the model accuracy remains on the same level as the influence of each variable is comparable. Only high values of β ($\beta > 0.5$) makes the model worse. Finally, the accuracy of the model is strongly connected to the number of objects in the largest class. Very similar situation is observed for the "balance" dataset.

Completely different situation is observed for the "Ripley" data: it occurs that the most expanded model has the worst classification accuracy. As the pruning parameter β increases the complexity of the model decreases and the accuracy increases. Only for $\beta \approx 1$ the strong accuracy decrease is observed. In case of the "iris" data the results are quite similar: as long as $\beta < 0.8$ the classification accuracy remains on the comparable level while the model complexity decreases about ten times.

For two last datasets very intuitive dependence can be observed: as the β increases the model complexity and the model accuracy decrease. For the "breast" dataset the end increase is caused by the assignment of all objects to the most represented class. For the "vehicle" dataset it is clearly noticeable that with the increase of the level of generalisation (β) the complexity of the model and its accuracy decrease.

5   Conclusions and Further Works

This paper presents the next (third) approach for the problem of generating oblique rules directly from the data. Like its predecessor it still has the problem with overlapping classes but in the opposition to $ORG2.1$ gives the possibility of the model generalisation so resulting rules set contains less elementary conditions or decision rules. This ability was tested on real and artificial datasets. It can be stated the $ORG2.1$ can find very good oblique decision rules if the nature of the data is oblique.

The new algorithm requires to set the single hyperplane pruning level. Now there is no methodology of finding the appropriate β for the dataset. However, in the paper the way of searching its value was presented – the analysis of the influence of the β on the model accuracy and complexity was given.

One of the most important aims in further works is to find an easy way of suggesting the value of the β parameter. Also the idea of oblique rule induction directly from the data is not exhaustively explored.

Acknowledgements. This work was supported by the European Union from the European Social Fund (grant agreement number: UDA-POKL.04.01.01-106/09).

References

1. Bazan, J., Szczuka, M.S., Wróblewski, J.: A new version of rough set exploration system. In: Alpigini, J.J., Peters, J.F., Skowron, A., Zhong, N. (eds.) RSCTC 2002. LNCS (LNAI), vol. 2475, pp. 397–404. Springer, Heidelberg (2002)
2. Bennett, K.P., Blue, J.A.: A support vector machine approach to decision trees. In: Proceedings of the International Joint Conference on Neural Networks, pp. 2396–2401 (1998)
3. Bloedorn, E., Michalski, R.S.: Data-Driven Constructive Induction. IEEE Intelligent Systems and Their Application 13(2), 30–37 (1998)
4. Cantu-Paz, E., Kamath, C.: Using evolutionary algorithms to induce oblique decision trees. In: Proc. of Genetic and Evolutionary Computation Conference, pp. 1053–1060 (2000)
5. Cohen, W.W.: Fast effective rule induction. In: Proceedings of the 12th International Conference on Machine Learning, pp. 115–123 (1995)
6. Frank, A., Asuncion, A.: UCI Machine Learning Repository (2010), http://archive.ics.uci.edu/ml
7. Frank, E., Witten, I.H.: Generating Accurate Rule Sets Without Global Optimization. In: Proc. of the 15th International Conference on Machine Learning, pp. 144–151 (1998)
8. Kim, H., Loh, W.-Y.: Classification trees with bivariate linear discriminant node models. Journal of Computational and Graphical Statistics 12, 512–530 (2003)
9. Latkowski, R., Mikołajczyk, M.: Data decomposition and decision rule joining for classification of data with missing values. In: Tsumoto, S., Słowiński, R., Komorowski, J., Grzymała-Busse, J.W. (eds.) RSCTC 2004. LNCS (LNAI), vol. 3066, pp. 254–263. Springer, Heidelberg (2004)
10. Michalak, M., Nurzyńska, K.: PCA Based Oblique Decision Rules Generating. In: Tomassini, M., Antonioni, A., Daolio, F., Buesser, P. (eds.) ICANNGA 2013. LNCS, vol. 7824, pp. 198–207. Springer, Heidelberg (2013)
11. Michalak, M., Sikora, M., Ziarnik, P.: ORG - Oblique Rules Generator. In: Rutkowski, L., Korytkowski, M., Scherer, R., Tadeusiewicz, R., Zadeh, L.A., Zurada, J.M. (eds.) ICAISC 2012, Part II. LNCS (LNAI), vol. 7268, pp. 152–159. Springer, Heidelberg (2012)
12. Murthy, S.K., Kasif, S., Salzberg, S.: A system for induction of oblique decision trees. Journal of Artificial Intelligence Research 2, 1–32 (1994)
13. Pindur, R., Sasmuga, R., Stefanowski, J.: Hyperplane Aggregation of Dominance Decision Rules. Fundamenta Informaticae 61(2), 117–137 (2004)
14. Raś, Z.W., Daradzińska, A., Liu, X.: System ADReD for discovering rules based on hyperplanes. Engineering Applications of Artificial Intelligence 17(4), 401–406 (2004)
15. Sikora, M.: An algorithm for generalization of decision rules by joining. Foundation on Computing and Decision Sciences 30(3), 227–239 (2005)
16. Smith, L.I.: A tutorial on Principal Components Analysis (2002)
17. Sikora, M.: Induction and pruning of classification rules for prediction of microseismic hazards in coal mines. Expert Systems with Applications 38(6), 6748–6758 (2011)
18. Sikora, M., Gudyś, A.: CHIRA – Convex Hull Based Iterative Algorithm of Rules Aggregation. Fundamenta Informaticae 123(2), 143–170 (2011)
19. Ślęzak, D., Wróblewski, J.: Classification Algorithms Based on Linear Combinations of Features. In: Żytkow, J.M., Rauch, J. (eds.) PKDD 1999. LNCS (LNAI), vol. 1704, pp. 548–553. Springer, Heidelberg (1999)

Statistical Assessment
of Signal and Image Symmetries

Miroslaw Pawlak

Electrical and Computer Engineering,
University of Manitoba,
Winnipeg, Canada

Abstract. This paper formulates the problem of assessing the reflection symmetry of a function f observed in the presence of noise. We consider both univariate and bivariate characteristics representing signal and image functions. First the problem of estimating a parameter defining the reflection symmetry is examined. This is followed by the question of testing the given symmetry type. The estimation/detection procedure is based on minimizing the L_2-distance between empirical versions of f and its reflected version. For univariate functions this distance is estimated by the Fourier series type estimate. In the bivariate case we utilize a class of radial series represented by the Zernike functions. It is shown that the symmetry parameter can be recovered with the parametric optimal rate for all functions f of bounded variation.

Keywords: symmetry estimation and detection, noisy data, radial polynomials, limit distributions, semiparametric inference.

1 Introduction

Symmetry plays an important role in signal and image understanding, compression and recognition. In fact, symmetric patterns are common in nature and man-made objects and estimation and detection of a signal/image symmetry can be useful for designing efficient algorithms for object recognition, robotic manipulation, signal and image animation, and signal/image compression [5]. For signals represented by the finite energy waveform $f(t)$ one can define a symmetry class as follows

$$S_1 = \{f \in L_2(D) : f(t) = \tau_\theta f(t), \theta \in \Theta\}, \tag{1}$$

where $\tau_\theta f(t) = f(2\theta - t)$. Here, without loss of generality, Θ is a compact subset of $D = [0, 2\pi]$. Hence, the class S_1 defines all finite energy signals defined on D being symmetric with respect to some $\theta \in \Theta$. In image analysis the bivariate function $f(x, y)$ characterizes the image grey level value at the pixel (x, y). In this case there are only two basic symmetry types, i.e., reflection and rotational symmetries. In this paper we focus on the former type of symmetry. Hence, we say that an image reveals the reflectional symmetry if it belongs to the following class

$$S_2 = \{f \in L_2(D) : f(x, y) = \tau_\theta f(x, y), \theta \in \Theta\}, \tag{2}$$

L. Rutkowski et al. (Eds.): ICAISC 2014, Part I, LNAI 8467, pp. 574–585, 2014.

where

$$\tau_\theta f(x,y) = f(x\cos(2\theta) + y\sin(2\theta), x\sin(2\theta) - y\cos(2\theta))$$

is the reflection of the image $f(x,y)$ with respect to the axis of symmetry defined by the angle $\theta \in \Theta \subset [0, \pi)$. Here D defines the image plane being a compact subset of R^2. Throughout the paper, without the loss of generality, we assume that the center of mass of the image is known and is located at the point $(x,y) = (0,0)$. It is also convenient to express the symmetry constrain in terms of polar coordinates. Hence, let $\tilde{f}(\rho, \varphi) = f(\rho\cos\varphi, \rho\sin\varphi)$ be the version of the image function in polar coordinates. Then, one can easily show that the reflection of the image $f(\rho\cos\varphi, \rho\sin\varphi)$ in a line that makes an angle θ with the x axis is given by $\tau_\theta \tilde{f}(\rho, \varphi) = \tilde{f}(\rho, 2\theta - \varphi)$. The symmetry class in (2) is then defined by the requirement $\tilde{f}(\rho, \varphi) = \tilde{f}(\rho, 2\theta - \varphi)$ and this is fully analogous to (1).

A number of rather ad hoc algorithms have been proposed for automatic estimation, detection and classification of reflectional symmetries for noisy free signals and images see [5] and the references cited therein. Most of the known symmetry detectors utilize the signal/image variability extracted from the derivative of the signal/image function. As such these methods may be very sensitive to noise. Furthermore, the proposed methods assume that the signal/image under examination is symmetric and that they have a certain parametric form. In practice, however, we do not have access to such a knowledge as we merely observe a noisy and digitized version of the original signal/image. In this paper the following signal observational model is used

$$Z_i = f(t_i) + \varepsilon_i, \quad t_i \in D, \quad 1 \leq i \leq n, \tag{3}$$

where the noise process $\{\epsilon_i\}$ is an i.i.d. random sequence with zero mean and finite variance σ_ε^2. We assume that the data are observed on the equally spaced grid with the width Δ, i.e., $t_i - t_{i-1} = \Delta$. Note that $\Delta = 2\pi/n$ and $t_i = i\Delta$. In the case of image data we have the following observation model

$$Z_{i,j} = f(x_i, y_j) + \varepsilon_{i,j}, \quad (x_i, y_j) \in D, \quad 1 \leq i, j \leq n, \tag{4}$$

where the data are observed on a symmetric square grid of edge width Δ, i.e. $x_i - x_{i-1} = y_i - y_{i-1} = \Delta$ and $x_i = -x_{n-i+1}$, $y_i = -y_{n-i+1}$. Note that Δ is of order $1/n$ and the sample size is n^2.

The statistical nature of the observed data and the lack of any a priori knowledge of the shape of underlying signals and images call for formal nonparametric statistical methods for joint estimating and testing the existing symmetry in a signal/image function, see [7] [2], [3] and [1] for some preliminary studies for nonparametric estimation and detection of image symmetries. In this paper we propose a systematic and rigorous statistical approach for joint estimating and testing of the aforementioned reflection symmetry defined in (1), (2). To do so we use the nonparametric orthogonal series estimate utilizing the Fourier series for univariate objects and their natural bivariate extension relying on the concept of radial functions [7], [9]. In the latter case we select the particular radial basis commonly referred to as Zernike functions [4]. The Zernike functions define an orthogonal and rotationally invariant basis of radial functions on the unit disk. As such, the Zernike functions and their corresponding Fourier coefficients (moments) have been extensively used in pattern analysis [6], [7], [9].

Our estimation and test statistics are constructed by expressing the symmetry condition in terms of restrictions on Fourier coefficients of the classical Fourier series (univariate case) or in terms of the Zernike moments for images. The estimation procedure is based on minimizing over $\theta \in \Theta$ the L_2 distance between empirical versions of f and $\tau_\theta f$ defining the symmetry classes in (1) and (2). Hence, f and $\tau_\theta f$ are estimated using truncated Fourier or radial series with empirically determined Fourier coefficients. The inherent symmetry property of Fourier series and the radial Zernike functions results in a particularly simple estimation procedure for θ. In fact, let $\hat{f}_N$ and $\tau_\theta \hat{f}_N$ denote the series estimates of f and $\tau_\theta f$, respectively based on the first N terms of the given orthogonal expansion. Then, we estimate the true parameter θ_0 of the reflection symmetry by

$$\widehat{\theta}_n = argmin_{\theta \in \Theta} \parallel \hat{f}_N - \tau_\theta \hat{f}_N \parallel^2, \tag{5}$$

where $\parallel \cdot \parallel$ is the L_2 norm.

We argue in this paper that the estimate $\widehat{\theta}_n$ converges to θ_0 with the optimal $\sqrt{n}$ rate for all signals/images f that are functions of bounded variation. Further, we establish asymptotic normality of $\widehat{\theta}_n$ assuming additionally that f is Lipschitz continuous. This asymptotic theory holds under the basic assumption that the object f is invariant under some unique reflection, i.e., that there is $\theta_0 \in \Theta$ such that $f = \tau_{\theta_0} f$ as it is defined in (1) and (2).

In the case when the observed object is not symmetric our estimate has an interesting robustness property being converging to the value θ_0 representing the point of symmetry of the closest symmetric object, i.e., θ_0 is characterized by

$$\theta_0 = argmin_{\theta \in \Theta} \parallel f - \tau_\theta f \parallel^2 . \tag{6}$$

The aforementioned estimation problem is closely connected to the problem of symmetry detection based on the concept of the L_2 minimum distance principle. In fact, let us consider the hypothesized classes in (1) and (2), i.e., we wish to test the null hypothesis

$$H_0 : f = \tau_{\theta_0} f \tag{7}$$

for some $\theta_0 \in \Theta$, against the alternative

$$H_a : f \neq \tau_\theta f \tag{8}$$

for all $\theta \in \Theta$. The test statistic for verifying H_0 has the form

$$T_N = \parallel \hat{f}_N - \tau_{\widehat{\theta}_n} \hat{f}_N \parallel^2, \tag{9}$$

where $\widehat{\theta}_n$ is the above introduced estimate with the pointed out robustness property. The minimum distance property of $\widehat{\theta}_n$ suggests the alternative form of T_N, i.e., $T_N = min_{\theta \in \Theta} \parallel \hat{f}_N - \tau_\theta \hat{f}_N \parallel^2$, where for the properly selected truncation parameter N this statistic only needs the numerical minimization with respect to a single variable θ. Furthermore, due to Parseval's formula we can evaluate the norm $\| \widehat{f}_N - \tau_\theta \widehat{f}_N \|^2$ as the sum of the estimated Fourier coefficients. The examined detector is of the form: reject H_0 if $T_N > c_\alpha$, where c_α is a constant controlling the false rejection rate for a pre-specified value $\alpha \in (0,1)$. Hence, the goal is to select the proper value of N such that for a given prescribed value of false rejection rate the detector T_N has the largest possible probability of detection (power). We give the asymptotic distributions of T_N both under the null hypothesis of symmetry as well as under fixed alternatives. The former result is used to construct asymptotic level α tests for lack of symmetry, whereas the latter result can be used to estimate the power of the tests, or to construct tests for validating the approximate symmetry of the signal/image. Our results model the performance of our estimates and tests on the grid which becomes increasingly fine.

2 Nonparametric Function Estimation Using Fourier and Radial Bases

To evaluate the L_2 norm in (5) we will utilize the nonparametric Fourier series estimate of the univariate signal $f(t)$. It is well known that any function $f \in L_2(D)$, defined on $D = [0, 2\pi]$ can be represented by the Fourier series $f(t) = \sum_{k=-\infty}^{\infty} a_k e^{jkt}$, where $a_k = (2\pi)^{-1} \int_D f(t) e^{-jkt} dt$ is the kth Fourier coefficient. A natural nonparametric estimate of $f(t)$ is the following truncated version of the Fourier series

$$\widehat{f}_N(t) = \sum_{|k| \le N} \widehat{a}_k e^{jkt}, \tag{10}$$

where $\widehat{a}_k$ is obtained from the data record in (3) as follows

$$\widehat{a}_k = (2\pi)^{-1} \sum_{l=1}^{n} Z_l e^{-jkt_l} \Delta, \tag{11}$$

where $t_l = l\Delta$, $\Delta = 2\pi/n$. It is known that the estimate $\widehat{f}_N(t)$ converges to $f(t)$, i.e., $\| \widehat{f}_N - f \|^2 \to 0$ as $n \to \infty$ if the truncation parameter N meets the following restrictions $N = N(n) \to \infty$ and $N(n)/n \to 0$. We argue in this paper that the symmetry estimation need not such optimal choice of the truncation parameter N.

Our symmetry class $\mathcal{S}_1$ in (1) requires also estimation of the reflected and shifted version of $f(t)$. First, it is easy to show that the signal $\tau_\theta f(t) = f(2\theta - t)$ has the Fourier representation $\tau_\theta f(t) = \sum_{k=-\infty}^{\infty} b_k e^{jkt}$ with

$$b_k = a_k^* e^{-jk2\theta}, \tag{12}$$

where a_k^* is the conjugate version of a_k. Hence, $\tau_\theta f(t)$ can be estimated by

$$\tau_\theta \widehat{f}_N(t) = \sum_{|k| \le N} \widehat{b}_k e^{jkt}, \tag{13}$$

where $\widehat{b}_k = \widehat{a}_k^* e^{-jk2\theta}$.

The contrast function introduced in (5) for obtaining an estimate of θ and detecting the symmetry in f is

$$\widehat{M}_N(\theta) = \| \hat{f}_N - \tau_\theta \hat{f}_N \|^2 . \tag{14}$$

This criterion results from the fact that for any $f \in L_2(D)$ we have

$$\inf_{g \in S_1} \int_D (f(t) - g(t))^2 dt = 4^{-1} \int_D (f(t) - f(2\theta - t))^2 dt, \tag{15}$$

where the closest symmetric function to f for a given $\theta \in \Theta$ is $g^*(t) = (f(t) + f(2\theta - t))/2$. Minimization of the right-hand-side of (15) with respect to θ gives the closest symmetric function to f within the class of all symmetric functions.

The above facts and due to Parseval's formula allow us to rewrite the contrast function in (14) as follows

$$(2\pi)^{-1} \widehat{M}_N(\theta) = \sum_{|k| \leq N} |\hat{a}_k - \hat{b}_k|^2. \tag{16}$$

The right-hand-side of this formula provides the convenient form of our statistic for both symmetry estimation and detection.

In image analysis it is important to represent an image function in terms of orthogonal bases that can easily incorporate invariance properties of the image. Such bases should be an extension of the Fourier series used above for representing and estimating symmetric functions. In [4] is is shown that a basis that is invariant in form for any rotation of axes must be of the form

$$V_{pq}(x, y) = R_p(\rho)e^{jq\varphi}, \tag{17}$$

where the right-hand-side is expressed in polar coordinates (ρ, φ). Here, $R_p(\rho)$ is a radial orthogonal polynomial of degree p. There are various ways of selecting $R_p(\rho)$ and important examples are Fourier-Mellin, pseudo-Zernike and Zernike radial bases [9], [6], [7]. Among the possible choices for $R_p(\rho)$ there is only one orthogonal set, the set of Zernike functions, for which $R_p(\rho) = R_{pq}(\rho)$ is the radial orthogonal polynomial of degree $p \geq |q|$ such that $p - |q|$ is even [4]. Zernike functions are defined on the unit disk D and allow to represent any $f \in L_2(D)$ as follows

$$f(x, y) = \sum_{p=0}^{\infty} \sum_{q=-p}^{p} \lambda_p^{-1} A_{pq} V_{pq}(x, y), \tag{18}$$

where $\lambda_p = \pi/(p+1)$ is $\|V_{pq}\|^2$. Here and in the following the summation is only taken over the admissible pairs (p, q). The Zernike coefficient (moment) A_{pq} is defined by

$$A_{pq} = \iint_D f(x, y) V_{pq}^*(x, y) \, dx \, dy.$$

Recalling the notation $\tilde{f}(\rho, \varphi)$ we can conventionally express Λ_{pq} in polar coordinates

$$A_{pq} = 2\pi \int_0^1 c_q(\rho) R_{pq}(\rho) \rho \, d\rho, \tag{19}$$

where $c_q(\rho) = \frac{1}{2\pi} \int_0^{2\pi} \tilde{f}(\rho, \varphi) e^{-jq\varphi} \, d\varphi$.

In the following we shall work with a discretized version of the Zernike moments, since we observe the image function f in model (4) only on the discrete grid. Hence, consider the weights

$$w_{pq}(x_i, y_j) = \iint_{\Pi_{ij}} V_{pq}^*(x, y) \, dxdy, \tag{20}$$

where $\Pi_{ij} = \left[x_i - \frac{\Delta}{2}, x_i + \frac{\Delta}{2} \right] \times \left[y_j - \frac{\Delta}{2}, y_j + \frac{\Delta}{2} \right]$ denotes the pixel centered at (x_i, y_j). Consequently, the Zernike moment A_{pq} is estimated by

$$\widehat{A}_{pq} = \sum_{(x_i, y_j) \in D} w_{pq}(x_i, y_j) Z_{i,j}, \tag{21}$$

where the weights are given by (20). A simple approximation for $w_{pq}(x_i, y_j)$ is given by $\Delta^2 V_{pq}^*(x_i, y_j)$. Let us also observe that along the boundary of the disk, some lattice squares are included and some are excluded. When reconstructing f, this gives rise to an additional error, called geometric error in [6], [7]. This will be quantified in our considerations by the factor $\gamma < 1.5$, see [6], [7] for a discussion of this important problem.

As a result, an estimate of the image function $f(x, y)$ is given by

$$\widehat{f}_N(x, y) = \sum_{p=0}^N \sum_{q=-p}^p \lambda_p^{-1} \widehat{A}_{pq} V_{pq}(x, y),$$

where N is a smoothing parameter which determines the number of terms in the truncated Zernike series. The mean integrated square error properties of $\widehat{f}_N(x, y)$ are discussed in [6].

3 Symmetry Estimation

A. Symmetry Estimation in Signals

We begin with the assumption that the signal f is symmetric with respect to the unique value $\theta_0 \in [0, \pi)$. Ignoring the factor 2π in (16) we can write the theoretical version of $\widehat{M}_N(\theta)$ as

$$M_N(\theta) = \sum_{|k| \le N} |a_k - b_k|^2, \tag{22}$$

where $b_k = a_k^* e^{-jk2\theta}$. Clearly, $M_N(\theta_0) = 0$ for all N. An important question for identifying θ_0 is whether the solution of $M_N(\theta) = 0$ yields $\theta = \theta_0$. The following theorem gives the answer to this question.

Theorem 1. *Let $f \in L_2(D)$ be symmetric with respect to unique $\theta_0 \in [0, \pi)$. Then for sufficiently large N, θ_0 is the unique zero of $M_N(\theta)$ if $M_N(\theta)$ contains nonzero a_k's for which the greatest common divisor (gcd) of the k's is 1.*

The proof of this theorem is based on the following representation of $M_N(\theta)$

$$M_N(\theta) = \sum_{|k| \leq N} 2|a_k|^2 (1 - \cos(2\alpha_k + k2\theta)), \qquad (23)$$

where $a_k = |a_k| e^{j\alpha_k}$. This representation provides a useful characterization of θ_0, i.e.,

$$\alpha_k + k\theta_0 = l\pi, \quad l \in Z$$

for all k with $|a_k| \neq 0$. Hence, the form of $M_N(\theta)$ yielding the unique identification of θ_0 is given by

$$M_N(\theta) = \sum_{i=1}^{r} 4|a_{k_i}|^2 (1 - \cos(2\alpha_{k_i} + k_i 2\theta)), \qquad (24)$$

for $k_1, \ldots, k_r$ such that $gcd(k_1, \ldots, k_r) = 1$, $r \leq N$ and $|a_{k_i}| \neq 0$, $i = 1, \ldots, r$. Fig. 1 illustrates the result described in Theorem 1 for a certain function being symmetric with respect to $\theta_0 = \pi$. The contrast function $M_N(\theta)$ is depicted utilizing the terms with $k_1 = 1, k_2 = 3$ and $k_1 = 3, k_2 = 9$. The unique global minimum of $M_N(\theta)$ at θ_0 in the former case is clearly seen. An estimate of θ_0

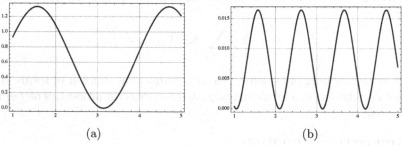

(a)   (b)

Fig. 1. (a) The contrast function $M_N(\theta)$ utilizing the Fourier coefficients a_1 and a_3, (b) The contrast function $M_N(\theta)$ utilizing the Fourier coefficients a_3 and a_9

can be now obtained as the minimizer of $\widehat{M}_N(\theta)$ being the empirical version of $M_N(\theta)$ in (22), i.e., where a_k is replaced by $\widehat{a}_k$. Hence, let

$$\widehat{\theta}_n = \arg \min_{\theta \in [0, \pi)} \widehat{M}_N(\theta) \qquad (25)$$

be the estimate of θ_0. Note that $\widehat{\theta}_n$ depends on the sample size n and the truncation parameter N. The following theorem summarizes the asymptotic properties of $\widehat{\theta}_n$.

Theorem 2. *Let the conditions of Theorem 1 be satisfied. Suppose that f is a function of bounded variation on D. Then, we have*

$$\widehat{\theta}_n = \theta_0 + O_P(n^{-1/2}).$$

Thus, under the above conditions the estimate $\widehat{\theta}_n$ achieves the optimal $\sqrt{n}$ rate for virtually any signal functions. Surprisingly, one need not to select an optimal N but merely to allow N to be large enough such that the conditions of Theorem 1 hold. Furthermore, if $f(t)$ is not symmetric, then $\widehat{\theta}_n$ converges to the value θ_0 being now the point of the symmetry of the closest symmetric object, see (15). Since, however, θ_0 is not a zero of $M_N(\theta)$, therefore Theorem 1 does not hold and the convergence requires now that $N \to \infty$. This robustness property of $\widehat{\theta}_n$ allows us to estimate the closest symmetric function to f, see (15), by

$$\widehat{g}_N^*(t) = (\widehat{f}_N(t) + \widehat{f}_N(2\widehat{\theta}_n - t))/2. \tag{26}$$

Next result gives the asymptotic normality of $\widehat{\theta}_n$ under a slightly stronger assumption on the signal shape. The notation $\overset{\mathcal{L}}{\to}$ stands for the convergence in distribution and $\mathcal{N}(0, \sigma^2)$ denotes the normal law with mean zero and variance σ^2. Moreover, (P) denotes the convergence in probability.

Theorem 3. *Let the conditions of Theorem 1 be satisfied. Suppose that f is Lipschitz continuous. Then, we have*

$$\sqrt{n}(\widehat{\theta}_n - \theta_0) \overset{\mathcal{L}}{\to} \mathcal{N}\left(0, \frac{8\sigma_\varepsilon^2}{M_N^{(2)}(\theta_0)}\right),$$

where $M_N^{(2)}(\theta_0) = 8\sum_{|k| \leq N} k^2 |a_k|^2$ is the second derivative of $M_N(\theta)$ at $\theta = \theta_0$.

The above theorem can be used to design an asymptotic confidence interval for θ_0. This requires estimation of the second derivative of $M_N(\theta_0)$ and noise variance σ_ε^2. We may estimate $M_N^{(2)}(\theta_0)$ by replacing a_k by $\widehat{a}_k$. This gives us a consistent estimate $\widehat{M}_N^{(2)}$ of $M_N^{(2)}(\theta_0)$. On the other hand, σ_ε^2 can be estimated by an estimator based on differences of the observed data $\{Z_i\}$, i.e.,

$$\widehat{\sigma}_\varepsilon^2 = \frac{1}{2(n-1)} \sum_{i=2}^{n} (Z_i - Z_{i-1})^2.$$

It is known that this is the $\sqrt{n}$ consistent estimate of σ_ε^2. Using these estimates, we obtain the following practical confidence interval for θ_0 with the nominal level α.

$$\left[\widehat{\theta}_n - Q_{1-\alpha}\frac{2\sqrt{2}\widehat{\sigma}_\varepsilon}{\sqrt{n}(\widehat{M}_N^{(2)})^{1/2}}, \widehat{\theta}_n + Q_{1-\alpha}\frac{2\sqrt{2}\widehat{\sigma}_\varepsilon}{\sqrt{n}(\widehat{M}_N^{(2)})^{1/2}}\right], \tag{27}$$

where $Q_{1-\alpha}$ is the $1 - \alpha$ quantile of $\mathcal{N}(0, 1)$.

B. Symmetry Estimation in Images

Reflection symmetry estimation for images can be done in the analogous way as for the univariate functions. Let $f \in S_2$ in (2) for some $\theta_0 \in [0, \pi)$. Hence, let $\tau_{\theta_0} \tilde{f}(\rho, \varphi) = \tilde{f}(\rho, 2\theta_0 - \varphi) = \tilde{f}(\rho, \varphi)$ be the unique reflection symmetry requirement imposed on the image f. The invariance property of the Zernike basis (resulting from (19)) yields

$$B_{pq} = e^{-2jq\theta} A_{pq}^*, \tag{28}$$

where B_{pq} is the Zernike moment of $\tilde{f}(\rho, 2\theta - \varphi)$ and A_{pq} is the Zernike moment of f. Owing to this and by Parseval's formula we can form the theoretical contrast function

$$M_N(\theta) = \sum_{p=0}^{N} \lambda_p^{-1} \sum_{|q| \le p} |A_{pq} - e^{-2jq\theta} A_{pq}^*|^2. \tag{29}$$

Similarly as in Theorem 1 the zero of $M_N(\theta)$ uniquely identifies θ_0 if one selects N so large such that the sum defining $M_N(\theta)$ contains nonzero $A_{p_1,q_1}, \ldots, A_{p_r,q_r}$ such that $p_i \le N$, $i = 1, \ldots, r$ and

$$\gcd(q_1, \ldots, q_r) = 1. \tag{30}$$

The estimated contrast function $\widehat{M}_N(\theta)$ is defined as (29) with A_{pq} replaced $\widehat{A}_{pq}$ derived in (21). Consequently, an estimate of θ_0 is defined as

$$\widehat{\theta}_n = \arg \min_{\theta \in [0,\pi)} \widehat{M}_N(\theta).$$

For such defined estimate we have the following counterparts of Theorem 2 and Theorem 3.

Theorem 4. *Suppose that an image function f is of bounded variation on D. Then for sufficiently large N such that the identifiability condition in (30) holds we have*

$$\widehat{\theta}_n = \theta_0 + O_P(\Delta).$$

Note that Δ is of order $1/n$ and n^2 is the sample size.

Theorem 5. *Let the conditions of Theorem 4 be satisfied. Suppose that f is Lipschitz continuous. Then, we have*

$$\Delta^{-1}(\widehat{\theta}_n - \theta_0) \xrightarrow{\mathcal{L}} \mathcal{N}\left(0, \frac{8\sigma_\varepsilon^2}{M_N^{(2)}(\theta_0)}\right),$$

where $M_N^{(2)}(\theta_0) = 8 \sum_{p=0}^{N} \lambda_p^{-1} \sum_{|q| \le p} q^2 |A_{pq}|^2$ is the second derivative of $M_N(\theta)$ at $\theta = \theta_0$.

Analogously as in (27) the result of Theorem 5 allows us to obtain the confidence interval for θ_0.

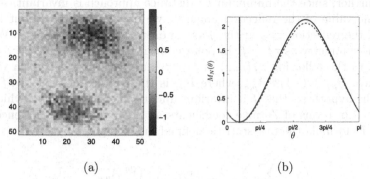

(a)   (b)

Fig. 2. (a) Reflection symmetric noisy image, (b) The contrast functions $M_N(\theta)$ (solid curve) and $\widehat{M}_N(\theta)$ (dashed line) for $N = 7$

Fig. 2 (a) shows an example of the noisy version of the reflection symmetric image of the size 25×25. In Fig. 2 (b) the contrast functions $M_N(\theta)$ and $\widehat{M}_N(\theta)$ for $N = 7$ are depicted. A global minimum of $\widehat{M}_N(\theta)$ defines the estimate $\widehat{\theta}_n$. Fig. 3 (a) shows the noisy version of the image being not reflection symmetric. In Fig. 3 (b) the contrast functions $M_N(\theta)$ and $\widehat{M}_N(\theta)$ for $N = 7$ are depicted. The minimum of $\widehat{M}_N(\theta)$ gives the reflection axis angle $\widehat{\theta}_n$ that defines an estimate of the best symmetric approximation of the image. This optimal symmetric image is estimated by $(\widehat{f}_N + \tau_{\widehat{\theta}_n} \widehat{f}_N)/2$ and is shown in Fig. 3 (c).

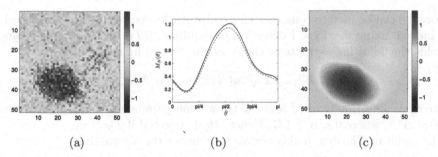

(a)   (b)   (c)

Fig. 3. (a) A noisy image that is not reflection symmetric, (b) The contrast functions $M_N(\theta)$ (solid curve) and $\widehat{M}_N(\theta)$ (dashed line) for $N = 7$, (c) An estimate of the best symmetric approximation of the image

4   Symmetry Detection

In this section we discuss how to test that $f \in L_2(D)$ in the observation models (3), (4) reveal the reflectional symmetry with respect to a certain reflection point/direction θ. We will only focus on the problem of testing symmetry for images. Further, since the minimum L_2-distance approach is invariant, see (9), for the true value of the reflection angle θ_0 we may consider, without loss of generality, the reflection $\tau_{\pi/2}$ at the y-axis, i.e., $\tau_{\pi/2}f(x,y) = f(-x,y)$. We will denote this symmetry as $\tau f = f$. In polar coordinates, the symmetry $\tau f = f$ is equivalent to the following $\tau\tilde{f}(\rho,\varphi) = \tilde{f}(\rho, \pi - \varphi) = \tilde{f}(\rho, \varphi)$. Then, in view of (28) we have $B_{pq} = (-1)^{|q|}A_{p,q}^*$, where B_{pq} is the Zernike moment of τf. Now consider the hypothesis that f is invariant under τ, i.e., $H_0 : f = \tau f$ which can be expressed in terms of Zernike coefficients as $A_{pq} = (-1)^{|q|}A_{p,q}^*$. Hence, due to Parseval's formula the test statistic defined in (9) is given by

$$T_N = \sum_{p=0}^{N} \sum_{q=-p}^{p} \lambda_p^{-1} \left| \widehat{A}_{pq} - (-1)^{|q|}\widehat{A}_{p,q}^* \right|^2.$$

The following result presents the CLT for statistic T_N under the hypothesis H_0 as well as under fixed alternatives. Let $C^2(D)$ denote a class of function possessing two continuous derivatives on D.

Theorem 6. *Under the hypothesis* $H_0 : f = \tau f$, *if* $\Delta \to 0$, $N \to \infty$ *such that* $\Delta N^7 \to 0$, *we have*

$$\frac{T_N - \sigma^2 \Delta^2 a(N)}{\Delta^2 \sqrt{a(N)}} \overset{\mathcal{L}}{\to} \mathcal{N}(0, 8\sigma_\varepsilon^4), \tag{31}$$

where $a(N) = (N+1)(N+2)$.

Under a fixed alternative $H_a : f \neq \tau f$, *suppose that* $f \in C^2(D)$. *If* $\Delta N^5 \to \infty$ *and* $N^{3/2}\Delta^{\gamma-1} \to 0$, *where* $\gamma = 285/208$ *controls the geometric error [6], we have*

$$\Delta^{-1}\left(T_N - \|f - \tau f\|^2\right) \overset{\mathcal{L}}{\to} \mathcal{N}(0, 16\sigma_\varepsilon^2 \|f - \tau f\|^2). \tag{32}$$

Theorem 6 can be used to construct an asymptotic level α test for the hypothesis H_0. Indeed, fixing the Type I detection probability $P\{T_N > c|H_0\}$ to the value α yields the following asymptotic choice of the control limit c

$$c_\alpha = 2Q_{1-\alpha}\Delta^2 \sqrt{2a(N)}\hat{\sigma}_\varepsilon^2 + \Delta^2 a(N)\hat{\sigma}_\varepsilon^2,$$

where $\hat{\sigma}_\varepsilon^2$ is an estimate of σ_ε^2 and the truncation parameter N can be specified as $N = \Delta^{-\alpha}$, where $0 < \alpha < 1/7$. Hence, H_0 is rejected if $T_N > c_\alpha$.

The result of Theorem 6 also reveals that under the alternative

$$T_N \to \| f - \tau f \|^2 \quad (P) \tag{33}$$

as $n \to \infty$. Consequently, we readily obtain that $N^5 \Delta T_N \to \infty$ (P) which implies the following consistency result.

Theorem 7. *Let* $H_a : f \neq \tau f$ *for* $f \in C^2(D)$ *hold. If* $\Delta N^5 \to \infty$ *and* $N^{3/2}\Delta^{\gamma-1} \to 0$, *then as* $\Delta \to 0$

$$P\{N^5 \Delta T_N > c|H_a\} \to 1 \tag{34}$$

for any positive constant $c > 0$.

Hence, the properly normalized decision statistic T_N leads to the testing technique that is able to detect that the null hypothesis is false with the probability approaching to one, i.e., the power of the test tends to one.

Furthermore, let us note that contrary to the symmetry estimation problem the symmetry detection requires the optimal choice of the truncation parameter N.

The condition $\Delta N^7 \to 0$, used under the hypothesis, is rather restrictive, and is due to the only approximate orthogonality of the discretized Zernike polynomials. This condition can be relaxed if we assume a more accurate orthogonal design. In fact, if we have exact discrete orthogonality, then $\Delta N^2 \to 0$ is sufficient for (31) to hold. Under a fixed alternative, the condition $N^{3/2}\Delta^{\gamma-1} \to 0$ is equivalent to $N^{4+\beta}\Delta \to 0$, $\beta = 0.0519\ldots$, so that this condition and $N^5\Delta \to \infty$ can be fulfilled simultaneously.

5   Concluding Remarks

In this paper, we have introduced and examined the unified minimum L_2-distance approach for statistical assessing the signal/image symmetry. The problem of symmetry estimation can be regarded as a semiparametric estimation problem, with θ as the target parameter, and the signal/image function as a nonparametric nuisance component [8]. As such the semiparametric optimality of our estimate of θ remains an open problem. There are numerous ways to refine the results of this paper. This may include the statistical assessment of imperfect symmetries and symmetries that only hold locally.

References

1. Birke, M., Dette, H., Stahjans, K.: Testing symmetry of nonparametric bivariate regression function. J. of Nonparametric Statistics 23, 547–565 (2010)
2. Bissantz, N., Holzmann, H., Pawlak, M.: Testing for image symmetries-with application to confocal microscopy. IEEE Trans. Inf. Theory 55, 1841–1855 (2009)
3. Bissantz, N., Holzmann, H., Pawlak, M.: Improving PSF calibration in confocal microscopic imaging - estimating and exploiting bilateral symmetry. The Annals of Applied Statistics 4, 1871–1891 (2010)
4. Born, M., Wolf, E.: On the circle polynomials of Zernike and related orthogonal sets. Proc. Cambridge Philos. Soc. 50, 40–48 (1954)
5. Liu, Y., Hel-Or, H., Kaplan, C.S., van Gool, L.: Computational Symmetry in Computer Vision and Computer Graphics. Now Publishers, Boston (2010)
6. Pawlak, M., Liao, S.: On the recovery of a function on a circular domain. IEEE Trans. Inf. Theory 48, 2736–2753 (2002)
7. Pawlak, M.: Image Analysis by Moments: Reconstruction and Computational Aspects. Wroclaw University of Technology Press (2006), http://www.dbc.wroc.pl/dlibra/doccontent?id=1432&from=&dirids=1
8. van der Vaart, A.W.: Asymptotic Statistics. Cambridge University Press, Cambridge (1998)
9. Wang, Q., Ronneberger, O., Burkhardt, H.: Rotational invariance based on Fourier analysis in polar and spherical coordinates. IEEE Trans. Pattern Anal. Mach. Intell. 31, 1715–1722 (2009)

Statistical Classifier with Ordered Decisions as an Image Based Controller with Application to Gas Burners

Ewaryst Rafajłowicz[1], Halina Pawlak-Kruczek[2], and Wojciech Rafajłowicz[1]

[1] Institute of Computer Engineering control and Robotics
[2] Institute of Heat Engineering and Fluid Mechanics,
Wrocław University of Technology Wrocław, Poland
ewaryst.rafajlowicz@pwr.wroc.pl

Abstract. We consider a statistical decision problem as a tool for solving control problems with a camera in the loop. The first stage is features extraction from images. Its role is to process images in order to extract features relevant for the control problem. Then, they are fed as inputs to the Bayesian decision problem. At the second stage a loss function, which is a sum of squared deviations of decisions from true decisions is considered. Finally, an approximation of the optimal decision rule is proposed, using a learning sequence of decisions, which – together with feature extracting algorithms – form the control system. The proposed approach is illustrated by a system that is dedicated to control natural gas burners.

Keywords: pattern recognition, ordered labels, control, image processing, flame, burner.

1 Introduction

A camera in a control loop is a very rich source of information, in many cases even too rich. In such a case a control system has to reduce information content. Otherwise, very similar images are considered as different, which may lead to the instability of the control loop. It seems that the Bayes decision theory is a good source of general ideas on how to select proper decisions when an environment is randomly changing (see [5] for fundamentals of general Bayesian decision theory) and [4] or [7] for more specialized pattern recognition setting. However, we have to point out that the Bayes decision theory has two points, which are not compatible with applications in control theory. Namely,

1. the Bayes decision theory is static in the sense that the decision is taken only once (an idea of using classifiers in a nonstationary environment has been proposed in [18], [19]),
2. it assumes that we know all necessary a priori probabilities of an environment states and all probability density functions of states from each class.

L. Rutkowski et al. (Eds.): ICAISC 2014, Part I, LNAI 8467, pp. 586–597, 2014.
© Springer International Publishing Switzerland 2014

In order to apply the Bayesian approach we have to start from assumptions made in 2), but then we have to take a more realistic empirical approach that is based on estimating these quantities from observations. Concerning 1), we have to take into account that

- a decision can be changed when the next image is collected and processed,
- possible reasons for changing decisions include:
  - disturbances in the process under control,
  - a correction of the previous decision, even when disturbances were not present,
  - erroneously interpreted previous frames, resulting in incorrect decisions.
- processing of images should be sufficiently fast in order to ensure proper behavior of the controlled process.

The last point, in turn, requires the extraction of features from images that are relevant for process control. Thus, we arrive to the two stage approach. Namely,

1st stage consists of image acquisition and extraction of relevant features,
2nd stage consists of calculating decisions.

In this paper we assume that the process under control has no long memory. In other words, its dynamics (transient process) can be neglected. If it cannot be ignored, then the proposed approach can be extended, e.g., by assuming that states of the process form a Markov chain, but this generalization is outside the scope of this paper.

We also assume that for a proper process control it suffices to use a finite number, say $l > 1$, of decisions. In other words, we quantize a decision process. The class of decisions can be arbitrarily large (in order to approximate an arbitrary decision function), but it must be finite or at most countable.

In opposite to the classical setting of Bayes problems, in which labels of the decisions are arbitrary and unordered, we consider the problem with decision labels that are linearly ordered. There are practical reasons to take the above point of view. Namely, when decisions are applied to the process under control and we admit some errors in decisions, it is important to attach a larger loss when instead of decision "1" we take decision "4" then if decision "2" (closer to "1") is undertaken. We can assume that $\mathcal{I} \overset{def}{=} \{1, 2, \ldots, I\}$, $I \geq 2$ is the set of labels of our decisions. In practice, decision "1" may mean, apply a force of 10 N to a controlled system, while decisions "2" and "3" correspond to applying forces 15 N and 22 N, respectively. It is only of importance, that 10 N is closer to 15 N, then to 22 N.

As an optimality criterion we take the expectation of the sum of differences between the "true" (mostly desirable) decision label and our decision. We shall prove that the optimal decision rule is extremely simple in this case. Namely, its the a posteriori mean (possibly "rounded" to the nearest decision from the above list).

As the next step, we discuss an empirical version of the controller, i.e., we propose an algorithm, which approximates the optimal decision rule.

It should be mentioned that different orderings were suggested in [20], [13], but they were introduced in the feature space, while here, we consider ordering in the space of labels. In [15] two dimensional class labels were considered and applied to a fault location problem.

2   Decision Problem – Theoretical Setting

Let $Y(t)$ denote an image of the process at time t. $Y(t)$ is an $r \times c$ matrix, where r is the total number of pixels that are stacked in a vector, c is the number of colors, e.g., three in RGB format. Denote by Ω an operator (linear or nonlinear) defined on the above described set of matrices with values in R^d, i.e., $X(t) = \Omega(Y(t))$ is d-dimensional vector. We shall interpret operator Ω as a feature extractor which extracts features relevant to the controlled process and forms a pattern $X(t)$ that is sufficient for proper decision making. The form of operator Ω is problem dependent and not discussed in this section.

2.1   Assumptions

1) For each t, $X(t) \in R^d$ is a random vector, for which a correct decision, denoted as $i(t)$, is an element of I, labeled as $1, 2, \ldots, I$.

2) New pair (X, i) is a random vector representing features and a correct decision i, which is unknown for a new feature vector X to be classified.

3) Probability distribution of (X, i) is unknown, but we also have a learning sequence

$$(X^{(k)} = X(t_k), i^{(k)} = i(t_k)), \quad k = 1, 2, \ldots, n$$

of observed $X^{(k)} \in R^d$ and the corresponding correct decisions $i^{(k)} \in \{1, 2, \ldots, I\}$. We assume that $(X^{(k)}, i^{(k)})$'s are independent, identically distributed random vectors with the same probability distribution as (X, i).

4) Denote by $0 \leq q(i) \leq 1$, a priori probability that for X a correct decision is i, $i = 1, 2, \ldots, I$, $\sum_{i=1}^{I} q(i) = 1$.
5) The next ingredient of the problem setting is a loss function, $L(i, j)$ say, which attaches loss $L(i, j)$ if the correct decision for X is i, while our decision $j \in I$. In this paper we take

$$L(i, j) = (i - j)^2, \quad i, j \in \mathcal{I} \tag{1}$$

as the loss function. It reflects our idea that it is reasonable to attach a larger loss when incorrect decision j is far from the correct one, i.e., i.

Let E_X denotes the expectation w.r.t. X, while $P(i|X)$ is the a posteriori probability that for new feature vector X the correct decision is i. In other words, $P(i|X = x)$ is the conditional probability of the event that i is the correct label of the decision for given vector of features $X = x$.

2.2 Problem Statement

The aim is to find a decision function $\Psi(X)$, which specifies a decision from I for X and such that it minimizes the expected loss given by:

$$R(\Psi) = E_X \left[\sum_{i=1}^{I} (i - \Psi(X))^2 \, P(i|X) \right], \tag{2}$$

In other words, our aim is to minimize the risk $R(\Psi)$, which is our loss that is averaged of all possible feature vectors X, while averaging is done according to the probability distribution of X. In order to ensure correctness of (2), we have to assume that we are looking for minimizer $\Psi^*(x)$, say, in the class of measurable functions.

The above problem statement is a theoretical one, because we do not know $P(i|X)$'s and probability distribution of X. However, it is reasonable to firstly solve problem (2) as if these quantities were known (see the next Section) and then, to estimate $\Psi^*(x)$ from the sequence of past correct decisions. This approach can be named "learning statistically optimal control".

3 From Image Features to Optimal Decision Rule

The outer expectation in (2) is carried out with respect to a nonnegative probability measure corresponding to the distribution of X. Thus, it suffices to minimize the expression in the square brackets in (2) for each vector of feature X separately. In other words, in order to minimize $R(\Psi)$ it suffices to minimize the conditional risk, which is defined as follows

$$r(\psi, x) \stackrel{def}{=} \sum_{i=1}^{I} (i - \psi)^2 \, P(i|X = x) \tag{3}$$

with respect to ψ, which is a real variable, while x is treated as a parameter. Notice that ψ^* which minimizes (3) must depend on x and this dependence is in fact our decision making unit Ψ^*, that can be also described as follow:

$$\Psi^*(x) = \arg\min_{\psi} r(\psi, x) \tag{4}$$

for all $x \in R^d$ in the range of X.

Note that minimizing (4) we have to ensure that $\Psi^*(x)$ is a positive integer form the class of admissible decisions I.

3.1 Optimal Decision Rule

The decision rule $\Psi^*(x)$, which minimizes (3), can be derived in two steps that follows.

Step 1. For fixed x we have to minimize the sum of $(i - \psi)^2$ with weights, which sum up to 1. The best ψ, which is further denoted as $\tilde{\Psi}(x)$, is the a posteriori mean:

$$\tilde{\Psi}(x) = \sum_{i=1}^{I} i\, P(i|X = x) \tag{5}$$

It is worth explaining how formula (5) works in an idealized case. If the range of random vectors (features) X can be divided into disjoint subregions Γ_i, each corresponding to unique decision i, then $P(i|X = x) = 1$ exactly for $x \in \Gamma_i$ and $P(j|X = x) = 0$ for all $j \neq i$. In this case $\tilde{\Psi}(x) = i$ for $x \in \Gamma_i$.

In more realistic cases we have to perform the following step.

Step 2. In order to ensure that our decision is a positive integer we round it as follows:

$$\Psi^*(x) = \text{ROUND}\left(\tilde{\Psi}(x)\right), \tag{6}$$

where $\text{ROUND}(t)$ is an integer, which is closest to t.

Let us assume the existence of probability densities $f(x|i)$, which describes the conditional p.d.f. of X, provided that it corresponds to i-th decision from I. Then, according to the Bayes rule, $P(i|X = x)$ is given by

$$P(i|X = x) = \frac{f(x|i)\, q(i)}{f(x)}, \quad i = 1, 2, \ldots, I, \tag{7}$$

$$f(x) \stackrel{def}{=} \sum_{l=1}^{I} f(x|l)\, q(l), \tag{8}$$

which allows us to express the a posteriori probabilities in terms of probability densities corresponding to i-th and all other decisions and a priori probabilities that i-th decision is appropriate. Reasoning analogously as in the proof of Theorem 1 in [16] the following result can be derived.

Theorem 1. *For linearly ordered decision labels the expected loss (2) is minimized by decision rule (5), (6).*

3.2   Countable Decision Set and Exponential Family of Features

Here we illustrate the above theoretical derivations and simultaneously we shall show that the above theory easily conveys to an infinite but countable set of decisions.

Assume (in this section only) that we have only one feature $x \in [0, \infty)$. Probability densities have the form:

$$f(x|i) = n\, \frac{x^k}{k!}\, exp(-n\, x), \quad x \in [0, \infty), \quad i = 0, 1, \ldots, \tag{9}$$

where $n \geq 1$ is a selected integer. For convenience we have labeled classes from 0. We also assume that a priori probabilities that i-th decision is the proper one are equal to $q_i = (1 - q)\, q^i,\ i = 0, 1, \ldots, 0 < q < 1$. Then,

$$f(x) = \sum_{i=0}^{\infty} f(x|i)\, q_i = n(q-1)\left(-e^{n(q-1)x}\right) \tag{10}$$

while

$$\sum_{i=0}^{\infty} i\, f(x|i)\, q_i = n^2 \left(q^2 - q\right) x \left(-e^{n(q-1)x}\right) \tag{11}$$

Thus, we obtain the optimal decision rule $\Psi^*(x) = \mathrm{ROUND}(n\, q\, x)$.

4   Second Stage – Toward Empirically Tuned Controller

When $P(i|X = x)$ and q_i, $i \in I$ are unknown, one can not apply Thm. 1 directly. The well-established way of circumventing this difficulty consists of the following steps:

1. Collect a learning sequence

$$\mathcal{L}_n = (X^{(k)}, i^{(k)}), \quad k = 1, 2, \ldots, n$$

    that contains pairs: a feature vector $X^{(k)}$ and the corresponding proper decision label $i^{(k)}$ (suggested by experts, which are assumed to provide proper decisions).
2. Estimate $P(i|X = x)$ and q_i, $i \in I$ from $\mathcal{L}_n$
3. Insert the above-mentioned estimates into the optimal decision rule (5), (6) and use it as an approximation of the optimal one.

The above way frequently leads to empirical decision rules that are asymptotically (as $n \to \infty$) as good as the optimal one (in the sense of the expected loss).

Estimators of $f(x|i)$ can be based on orthogonal expansions or the well-known Parzen-Rosenblatt kernel estimator, partitioning estimators and many others (see [6] and [7] for detailed discussions and extensive bibliographies). All these approaches operate directly on the whole learning sequence, which has to be stored and available for each pattern to be recognized. This feature is highly undesirable when one needs to use an empirical decision rule on-line for a process control.

4.1   Empirical Decision Rule

Therefore, we propose simplified estimators of $f(x|i)$'s that do not require the storage of the whole learning sequence in order to make current decision. This goal can be achieved by applying the well known neural nets with radial basis functions.

Denote by $K(t) \geq 0$, $t \in R$ a kernel, which is such that

$$\int_{-\infty}^{\infty} K(t) = 1, \quad \int_{-\infty}^{\infty} t\, K(t) = 0, \quad \int_{-\infty}^{\infty} t^2\, K(t) < \infty$$

Define

$$\mathcal{I}(i) = \{(X^{(k)}, i^{(k)}) : i^{(k)} = i\}.$$

$$\sum_{i=1}^{I} Card(\mathcal{I}(i)) = n,$$

where $Card$ denotes the cardinality of a set. Let $n(i) = Card(\mathcal{I}(i))$ denote the number of decisions with the label i in the learning sequence.

The simplest task is estimating a priori probability that a decision has label i. It suffices to set

$$\hat{q}(i) = \frac{n(i)}{n}, i = 1, 2, \ldots, I \tag{12}$$

as the estimator of $q(i)$.

As estimators $\hat{f}(x|i)$ of $f(x|i)$ we take the following RBF net:

$$\hat{f}(x|i) = \frac{1}{J(i) \, h^d(n(i), i)} \sum_{j=1}^{J(i)} K\left(\frac{\|x - C_i^{(j)}\|}{h(n(i), i)}\right), \quad i = 1, 2, \ldots, I, \tag{13}$$

where
- $C_i^{(j)} \in R^d$, $j = 1, 2, \ldots, J(i)$ are centers of RBF's for estimating $f(x|i)$,
- $h(n(i), i)$ is i-th smoothing parameter that depends on $n(i)$,
- $\|.\|$ is a norm in R^d.

We refer the reader to rich bibliography and recent results on RBF's contained in [2], [4], [15], [16], [18], [19], [21], [22], [13], [10]. Define the second, composite, RBF net as follows:

$$\hat{f}(x) = \sum_{i=1}^{I} \hat{q}_i \, \hat{f}(x|i). \tag{14}$$

It consists of RBF nets (13) with weights $\hat{q}_i$.

In (13) and (14) the role of the learning sequence is not directly visible. It is "hidden" in selecting centers $C_i^{(j)} \in R^d$. Firstly, we select those $(X^{(k)}, i^{(k)})$'s that are contained in $\mathcal{I}(i)$ for given i. Then, they serve for selecting $C_i^{(j)}$ $j = 1, 2, \ldots J(i)$ for the same i. We omit the discussion on selecting centers, since it is well covered in the available literature.

Define the estimators $\hat{p}(i, x)$ of $P(i|X = x)$ as follows

$$\hat{p}(i, x) = \frac{\hat{q}_i \, \hat{f}(x|i)}{\hat{f}(x)}, \tag{15}$$

Now, as the empirical decision rule $\hat{\Psi}$ we take

$$\hat{\Psi}(x) = \text{ROUND}\left[\frac{1}{\hat{f}(x)} \sum_{i=1}^{I} i \, \hat{q}_i \, \hat{f}(x|i)\right]. \tag{16}$$

4.2 Important Special Case

Training controllers (16) with $\hat{f}(x|i)$ given by (13) usually requires a long learning sequence. In many cases one can simplify (13) by setting $J(i) = 1, i = 1,, 2, \ldots I$ and properly selecting $K(.)$ and $C_i^{(1)}$ (further we use a simplified notation simplified, namely C_i).

Then, (16) can be rewritten as follows:

$$\hat{\Psi}(x) = \text{ROUND} \left[\frac{\sum_{i=1}^{I} i \, \hat{q}_i \, h^{-d}(n(i), i) \, K\left(\frac{||x - C_i||}{h(n(i), i)}\right)}{\sum_{i=1}^{I} \hat{q}_i \, h^{-d}(n(i), i) \, K\left(\frac{||x - C_i||}{h(n(i), i)}\right)} \right] \tag{17}$$

5 Example – A Control System for a Natural Gas Burner

In [11], [12], [1] monitoring gas burners by cameras have been discussed. As far as we know, a control system based on a camera in the loop has been proposed only in [14]. In this paper, a decision unit is based on learning an artificial neural network. Our approach is based on (17), which can be interpreted as an RBF net, but it differs from the one considered in [14] in that the structure of the decision unit is the empirical version of the optimal decisions. Thus, also its structure has some optimality advantages.

It is worth explaining why we need to control burners that are fed by a natural gas. The reason is that natural gas contains varying amounts of methane and in order to get a flame having reasonable properties we have to control the air supply rate.

Our two-stage approach is sketched in Fig. 2 (left panel), where fat lines are paths of a video stream, while thin lines are paths of transmitting signals varying in time only.

5.1 Extraction of Features from Flames

As mentioned in the Introduction, we propose the two-stage approach. The first stage consists of features extraction from a current flame. Algorithms dedicated to feature extraction and state recognition will be developed elsewhere. Here we use relatively simple features of flames. Namely, **color** i.e., the content of yellow and blue parts of the flame (see Fig. 1) and **shape of the flame** that can indicate laminar or turbulent flow of the gas and air mixture (compare images in the bottom row of Fig. 1).

At each image in Fig.1 one can notice a rotameter with its float indicating the air flow rate. The air flow rate is our input signal to the burner. Thus, the model of our system to be controlled is very simple. It consists of an input signal $u(t)$, which represents the air flow rate at time t. The flow rate is scaled from 0 (the lowest rotameter position, which corresponds to flow rate 3.5 m^3/h) to 100% (maximal air flow rate). The outputs of our system consists of two variables, namely,

– $x_1(t)$ – the percentage of the blue color in the flame at time t,
– $x_2(t)$ – the percentage of the flame height, in which the flame burns in the laminar way, i.e., it does not contain a turbulent flow.

Fig. 1 explains the meaning of $x_1(t)$ and $x_2(t)$. The flame in upper left panel contains almost no blue color ($x_1(t) = 5\%$, say) and almost all the flame shape is turbulent ($x_2(t)$ close to zero). Upper right and lower left panels show flames with more blue color and more parts with laminar shape of the flame, i.e., $x_1(t)$ and $x_2(t)$ are larger. Finally, the flame in lower right panel contains about $x_1(t) = 50$-60% of blue color and about $x_2(t) = 50$-60% of the flame length burns in the laminar way. The flame in lower right panel of Fig. 1 is considered as the reference

Fig. 1. Flames (rotated to save space corresponding to different air flow rates that are measured by the rotameter shown at the bottom of each figure

image, i.e., the one that we would like to keep by increasing or decreasing the air flow rate independently of the methane content in a natural gas. that is supplied to the burner. One can select slightly different proportions as desired x_1^* and x_2^*, taking into account that if more air can mix with the gas before combustion, the flame burns providing a higher temperature, which results in more blue color in it. On the other hand, a smaller air supply rate leads to an incomplete reaction that appears as a light yellow flame, which is cooler.

Analyzing the intense reactions zone of flame, the fuel undergoes pyrolysis initially, as evidenced by the presence in the area of soot and compounds C2 and CH, as manifested by a yellow color of the flame zone. Next there is an intensive zone of the oxidation reaction as the oxygen concentration increases, as evidenced by the initial absence of visible light radiation, and then the blue color of the area. This area is characterized by the highest concentrations of radicals and the highest temperature.

5.2   Control Unit

At the second stage, vectors of extracted features $x_1(t)$ and $x_2(t)$ are supplied to a control unit, where a control action, denoted as $\hat{\Psi}(x(t))$, is calculated as follows.

Table 1. Interpretation of decisions and their a priori probabilities

$$C = \begin{bmatrix} 0.1 & 0.2 \\ 0.3 & 0.4 \\ 0.5 & 0.5 \\ 0.7 & 0.6 \\ 0.9 & 0.9 \end{bmatrix}$$

Dec.	Interpretation	prior q_i
dec1	increase $u(t)$ by 40%	0.1
dec2	increase $u(t)$ by 20%	0.2
dec3	keep previous $u(t)$	0.4
dec4	decrease $u(t)$ by 20%	0.2
dec5	decrease $u(t)$ by 40%	0.1

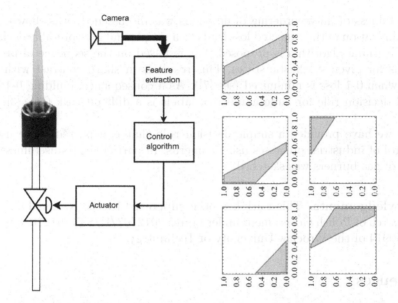

Fig. 2. Estimated optimal decision regions in Example 2 for $h = 0.005$

Consider (17) with $I = 5$ decisions, each based on $x(t) = [x_1(t),\, x_2(t)]$ and $K(.)$ being the Gaussian kernel. Matrix of centers C is selected as shown in Tab. 1 (left table).

Positions of centers correspond to the above-mentioned interpretation of $x_1(t)$, $x_2(t)$, where the row $[0.5,\,] 0.5]$ reflects the desired state x_1^* and x_2^*.

Interpretation of decisions and a priori probabilities of selecting them are shown in Tab. 1 (right table). In other words, the image based controller works as follows:

$$u(t) = u(t-1) - (\hat{\Psi}(x(t)) - 3)\, 20\%, \tag{18}$$

where $u(t-1)$ is our previous decision (it should be replaced by $u(t-\Delta)$ if the time interval between decisions is $\Delta > 0$). Finally, $u(t)$ is sent to an actuator that changes position of a valve that controls the air flow rate.

We do not present the results on selecting smoothing parameters $h(n(i), i)$, $i = 1, 2, \ldots, I$, referring the reader to [17], in which it was demonstrated that in this case $h = 0.005$ provides acceptable results. For simplicity we set all $h(n(i), i)$'s to be equal to each other. This common value will be denoted by h.

Summarizing, in Figure 2 (right panel) decision regions in the feature space are shown. We provide this version in order to stress that having decision regions one can implement the empirical decision rule as a fast controller, provided that also feature extraction is sufficiently fast.

6   Conclusions

The usefulness of linear ordering of decisions was discussed. It was shown that the minimization of the expected loss leads to a simple and interpretable decision rule. A learning algorithm is proposed that is based on the sequence of proper decisions for given stochastic states. This result is in sharp contrast with the results when 0-1 loss is minimized (see [7]). As a consequence, building 0-1 loss optimal decision rule for large number of labels is a difficult task (see, [3], [8], [9]).

Here we have provided a simple decision rule that is expected to be useful in control of industrial processes using cameras. In particular, its usefulness for control of gas burners was sketched.

Acknowledgements. This work has been supported by the National Council for Research of Polish Government under grant: 2012/07/B/ST7/01216, internal code 350914 of the Wrocław University of Technology.

References

1. Bheemul, H.C., Lu, G., Yan, Y.: Three-dimensional visualization and quantitative characterization of gaseous flames. Meas. Sci. Technol. 13, 1643–1650 (2002)
2. Bors, A.G., Pitas, I.: Median Radial Basis Function Neural Network. IEEE Trans. on Neural Networks I, 1351–1364 (1996)
3. Allwein, A., Schapire, R., Singer, Y.: Reducing Multiclass to binary: A Unifying approach for Margin classifiers. J. Machine Learning Research 1, 113–141 (2000)
4. Bishop, C.: Neural Networks for Pattern Recognition. Oxford Univ. Press (1995)
5. de Groot, M.H.: Optimal Statistical Decisions. Wiley, New Jersey (2004)
6. Devroye, L., Györfi, L.: Nonparametric Density Estimation. The L_1 View. Wiley, New York (1985)
7. Devroye, L., Györfi, L., Lugosi, G.: Probabilistic Theory of Pattern Recognition. Springer, New York (1996)
8. Dietterich, T., Bakiri, G.: Solving Multiclass Learning Problems via Error-Correcting Output Codes. J. Artificial Intelligence Research 2, 263–286 (1995)
9. Hastie, T., Tibshirani, R.: Classification by Pairwise Coupling. The Annals of Statistics 26, 451–471 (1998)
10. Karayiannis, N.B., Randolph-Gips, M.M.: On the Construction and Training of Reformulated Radial Basis Function Neural Networks. IEEE Trans. on Neural Networks 14, 835–846 (2003)

11. Kotyra, A., Wójcik, W.: Application of image flame features to assesment of combustion process. PAK 55, 117–121 (2009) (in Polish)
12. Wójcik, W., Kotyra, A.: Combustion diagnosis by image processing. Photonics Letters of Poland 1(1), 40–42 (2009)
13. Krzyżak, A., Skubalska-Rafajłowicz, E.: Combining Space-Filling Curves and Radial Basis Function Networks. In: Rutkowski, L., Siekmann, J.H., Tadeusiewicz, R., Zadeh, L.A. (eds.) ICAISC 2004. LNCS (LNAI), vol. 3070, pp. 229–234. Springer, Heidelberg (2004)
14. Lu, G., Yan, Y., Huang, Y., Reed, A.: An intelligent vision system for monitoring and control of combustion flames. Meas Control 32, 164–168 (1999)
15. Rafajłowicz, E.: RBF nets in faults localization. In: Rutkowski, L., Tadeusiewicz, R., Zadeh, L.A., Żurada, J.M. (eds.) ICAISC 2006. LNCS (LNAI), vol. 4029, pp. 113–122. Springer, Heidelberg (2006)
16. Rafajłowicz, E., Krzyżak, A.: Pattern recognition with ordered labels. Nonlinear Analysis, Theory, Methods & Applications. Series A, Theory and Methods 17(12), 1437–1441 (2009)
17. Rafajłowicz, E.: Two stage control algorithm for industrial processes using camera. Bayesian theoretic approach, Preprint Institute of Computer Eng., control and Robotics (2013)
18. Rutkowski, L.: Adaptive Probabilistic Neural Networks for Pattern Classification in Time-Varying Environment. IEEE Trans. Neural Networks 15(4), 811–827 (2004)
19. Rutkowski, L.: Generalized Regression Neural Networks in Time-Varying Environment. IEEE Trans. Neural Networks 15(3), 576–596 (2004)
20. Skubalska-Rafajłowicz, E.: Pattern Recognition Algorithms Based on Space-Filling Curves and Orthogonal Expansions. IEEE Trans. Information Theory 47, 1915–1927 (2001)
21. Skubalska-Rafajłowicz, E.: RBF Neural Network for Probability Density Function Estimation and Detecting Changes in Multivariate Processes. In: Rutkowski, L., Tadeusiewicz, R., Zadeh, L.A., Żurada, J.M. (eds.) ICAISC 2006. LNCS (LNAI), vol. 4029, pp. 133–141. Springer, Heidelberg (2006)
22. Xu, L., Krzyżak, A., Yuille, A.: On Radial Basis Function Nets and Kernel Regression: Statistical Consistency, Convergence Rates and Receptive Field Size. Neural Networks 4, 609–628 (1994)

Crop Classification Using Different Color Spaces and RBF Neural Networks

Guillermo Sandoval, Roberto A. Vazquez, Paulina Garcia, and Jose Ambrosio

Intelligent Systems Group, Faculty of Engineering, La Salle University
Benjamin Franklin 47, Condesa, Mexico, DF, 06140
ravem@lasallistas.org.mx

Abstract. Agricultural activities could represent an important sector for the economy of certain countries. In order to maintain control of this sector, it is necessary to schedule censuses on a regular basis, which represents an enormous cost. In recent years, different techniques have been proposed with the objective of reducing the cost and improving automation, these cover from Personal Digital Assistants usage to satellite image processing. In this paper, we described a methodology to perform a crop classification task over satellite images based on the Gray Level Co-Occurrence Matrix (GLCM) and Radial Basis Function (RBF) neural network. Furthermore, we study how different color spaces could be applied to analyze satellite images. To test the accuracy of the proposal, we apply the methodology over a region and we present a comparison by evaluating the efficiency using three color spaces and different distance classifiers.

Keywords: Crop classification, Gray Level Co-Occurrence Matrix, Radial Basis Funtion Neural Network.

1   Introduction

Remote sensing is a field in which aerial sensors are employed to obtain information of the earths surface, and then a numerous amount of techniques are used to identify objects among that information.

In some countries, agriculture is one of their principal economic activities. Mexican agricultural sector employs about 5.2% of the active working population. This is why it is important to generate statistics by a census. A census provides a data set which allows to know several variables concerning to the production volume, crop identification, location and all attributes conforming their study. Thanks to this information it is possible to characterize the agricultural sector structure and performance.

Automation in censuses has gained popularity in recent years, aimed to be more agile and accurate. For that reason, satellite image processing as a method for crop classification using remote sensing is a good option considering cost, data actualization frequency and the possibility of becoming the process more comprehensive. The crop classification problem has been around approximately

L. Rutkowski et al. (Eds.): ICAISC 2014, Part I, LNAI 8467, pp. 598–609, 2014.

since 1972 with studies such as [8] and government initiatives in the United States.

The problem of crop classification can be dissected in three essential steps: the selection of the information source, the feature extraction process and the classification process. Nowadays, there are a lot of applications using satellite image in order to obtain crop characteristics. Different commercial companies provide these satellite images which are multispectral. Spectral bands range change from company to company. Usually, only some bands are used depending the application. For example, in order to obtain the biomass and carbon stock estimation of brazilian coffee crops GeoEye-1 satellite images was utilized with RED, GREEN and NIR bands [9].

Images used in remote sensing can be of different natures depending on the sensor employed to acquire the information. One of these sensors is the Synthetic Aperture Radar (SAR), which captures dielectric characteristics of objects such as their structure (size, shape and orientation). In [14] for instance a two band approach is presented, using band C and L a success of 80 and 78% is achieved when considered separately, and an 84% when both bands are combined. Another study working with SAR is [7], where an uncommon SAR band, named X, is used reaching an 84% of correct classification without any kind of image preprocessing. The main disadvantage of this kind of images though, is they describe crops in a very specific stage and in order to show good results it is commonly needed to include multitemporal information, as shown in [12] and [15].

Previous studies have tackled the feature extraction stage using texture descriptors as a mechanism to identify the class or crop to which one given pixel or region belongs. One of most cited textural descriptors is the Gray Level Co-Occurrence Matrix (GLCM), presented in [16], where the authors obtained a 60.72% of success in the classification of crops. In [11] GLCM was used as a secondary discrimination method and made the success rate to increase from 71.2% to 83% when it was included in the process of differentiating between residential districts, parking lots, highways, commercial districts, etc. in SAR images.

As for the classification algorithms, the authors in [13] have proposed the approach of comparing a parametric with a non-parametric classifier previously shown in other studies. For example, the Radial Basis Function Neural Network (RBFNN) has been used for crop classification in [2], but only as a mean of performance comparison against Support Vector Machines (SVM) in a study classifying crops in Hyper-spectral images.

On the other hand, an assortment applications apply different color spaces, for example in [4], where the authors use HSL space for apple classification with satisfactory results. Another interesting example is described in [10], where the authors use a L*u*v* model along with clustering data for wood segmentation in vineyards; the proposed methodology allows a better classification rate working with images taken in different climate conditions and natural lightening issues. There exists an application in the wine growing area, which implements L*a*b* model, as well as CMYK space, for leaves and bunches identification [3]. Although there are several applications of different color spaces, their use has not been explored in crop classification due to satellite and hyper-spectral images focus on NIR bands.

In this paper, we present an approach which focuses on satellite images obtained from the visible electromagnetic spectrum, composed of only three bands commonly known as the red, blue and green channels. These images are cheaper than others compared with images that use channels out of the visible electromagnetic spectrum. Our main objective is to reduce the requirements imposed on the characteristics of the information used for the classification process even if some difficulties related to changes in lightness are present during image processing. For solving these difficulties different color spaces have been evaluated. After applying a color space transformation, the Gray Level Co-Occurrence Matrix (GLCM) was used as a texture descriptor in the pre-processing phase. Then, with the information obtained, a Radial Basis Function (RBF) neural network was trained for classifying different crops. The accuracy of the proposal is tested over a region of Mexico where five different crops were detected.

2   Color Spaces

Several color spaces has been designed in the last years. Among the most popular, we could mention RGB, CIEXYZ, HSV, HSI, HSL, CMYK, YIQ, CIEL*a*b*, CIEL*u*v, SCH and LCH. Every color space has certain characteristics about the manner the color is measured into a geometric space. In this paper, we compare the behavior of RGB, XYZ, HSV, HSI and HSL color spaces in the task of crop classification.

2.1   CIEXYZ

The XYZ color space is the first mathematically defined color spaces created by the International Commission on Illumination (CIE) in 1931. It is a linear transformation of RGB color space. The standardized transformation is given by (1).

$$\begin{bmatrix} X \\ Y \\ Z \end{bmatrix} = \begin{bmatrix} 0.49018626 & 0.30987954 & 0.19993420 \\ 0.17701522 & 0.81232418 & 0.01066060 \\ 0.00000000 & 0.01007720 & 0.98992280 \end{bmatrix} \begin{bmatrix} R \\ G \\ B \end{bmatrix}. \tag{1}$$

2.2   HSI

HSI is a color space that measures the color within three components: Hue, Saturation and Intensity. Where Hue is an angular measure respecting the red axis as it can be seen on (2). Saturation is the proximity of a color point to the white point reference $W = (\frac{1}{3}, \frac{1}{3}, \frac{1}{3})$ as seen on (4) and intensity is defined as the average of the components A, B and C, see (5).

$$\theta = \cos^{-1} \left(\frac{(R - G) + (R - B)}{2\sqrt{(R - G)^2 + (R - B)(G - B)}} \right). \tag{2}$$

If $\theta > 180$ then (3) is applied.

$$H = 360 - \theta \tag{3}$$

$$S = 1 - \frac{3}{R + G + B} \min(R, G, B) \tag{4}$$

$$I = \frac{1}{3}(R + G + B) \tag{5}$$

2.3 HSV and HSL

HSL, HSV, and related models can be derived via geometric strategies. HSV has almost the same characteristics than HSI, except for the Value (V) component showed in (6), which correspond to the normalization of the highest value of the RGB channels.

$$V = \frac{1}{255} \max(R, G, B) \tag{6}$$

For the case of HSL, where, Luminance (L) is calculated as shown in (7).

$$L = \frac{\min(R, G, B) + \max(R, G, B)}{2} \tag{7}$$

3 Co-Occurrence Matrix

The Gray Level Co-Occurrence Matrix (GLCM), introduced in 1973 by Haralick et al. [20] is a textural measure that describes some properties about the spatial distribution of the gray levels in an image. This square matrix measure how often a pixel value known as the reference pixel with the intensity value i occurs in a specific relationship to a pixel value known as the neighbor pixel with the intensity value j. The spatial relationship between two pixels can be specified with different offsets and angles, for example between a pixel and its immediate neighbor to its right.

To build a Co-Occurrence Matrix from a region of a images, it is necessary to define a neighborhood relationship and window size. With this information, we proceed to create a two dimensional histogram; a squared matrix with the quantification of the image as length. Each of the cells of this histogram is filled with the occurrence count of the given pixel relationship, so if we have that in the analyzed window theres a pixel with a value of 42 and the neighbor pixel has value of 3 then the value of the histograms cell (42,3) would have to be incremented by one.

Once the whole histogram has been calculated, it needs to be transformed into probabilities; the probability that a given relationship exists is computed by (8).

$$\mathbf{P}_{ij} = \frac{\mathbf{V}_{ij}}{\sum_{i,j=0}^{N-1} \mathbf{V}_{ij}} \tag{8}$$

where each element of matrix $\mathbf{V}_{ij}$ is the number of occurrences of the pair of pixel with value i and a pixel with value j which are at a distance d relative to each other.

After compute the probability that a given relationship exits, it is possible to calculate a set of 8 properties describing characteristics of the evaluated region such as contrast, dissimilarity, homogeneity, angular second moment (ASM), entropy, energy, average and standard deviation. The result is a vector of eight characteristics describing a region of the desired size. Using (9), (10), (11), (12) and (13), the contrast, dissimilarity, homogeneity, angular second moment (ASM), entropy, energy characteristics over a specific region can be computed.

$$c_1 = \sum_{i,j=0}^{N-1} \mathbf{P}_{ij} \left(i - j\right)^2 \tag{9}$$

$$c_2 = \sum_{i,j=0}^{N-1} \mathbf{P}_{ij} \left|i - j\right|^2 \tag{10}$$

$$c_3 = \sum_{i,j=0}^{N-1} \frac{\mathbf{P}_{ij}}{1 + (i - j)^2} \tag{11}$$

$$c_4 = \sum_{i,j=0}^{N-1} \mathbf{P}_{ij}^2 \tag{12}$$

$$c_5 = \sum_{i,j=0}^{N-1} \mathbf{P}_{ij} \left(-In\mathbf{P}_{ij}\right) \tag{13}$$

4   Radial Basis Function Neural Network

In this section, we present a Radial Basis Function Neural Network (RBFNN) classification algorithm. RBFNN were introduced into the neural network literature by Broomhead and Lowe which is motivated by the locally tuned response observed in biologic neurons [18]. RBFNN are a class of neural networks such that RBF are included in a neuron layer, thus the problem space is transformed from the original vector space to a new one, where the patterns are expressed in terms of their belonging to the RBF neurons.

The behavior of this kind of network is similar to the Multilayer Perceptron, since there is a set of layers joint together by weighted edges. To better understand how a RBFNN work a common topology of these type of networks is presented in 1. A typical RBFNN is composed of an input layer, a hidden layer and an output layer.

Neurons in the input layer do not have an activation function, all these neurons do is to propagate the input value to the next neuron layer. Along with this, weights W_{ij} going from the input layer to the hidden layer have all a value of 1.

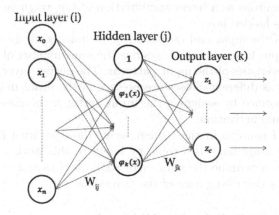

Fig. 1. Common RBFNN topology

This merely means each input vector is presented horizontally to each neuron in the hidden layer.

Neurons in the hidden layer have an RBF activation function, typically a Gaussian function, although there are other possibilities. According to [18],the RBF network has to perform a mapping from a continuous input space $\mathbb{R}^d$ into a finite set of classes $Y = \{1, \ldots, L\}$, where L is the number of classes. In the training phase, the parameters of the network are determined from a finite training set defined as in (14)

$$S = \left\{ (\mathbf{x}^\mu, y^\mu) \,|\, \mathbf{x}^\mu \in \mathbb{R}^d, y^\mu \in Y, \mu = 1, \ldots, M \right\} \tag{14}$$

where each feature vector $\mathbf{x}^\mu$ is labeled with its class membership y^μ.

In the recall phase, further unlabeled observations $\mathbf{x} \in \mathbb{R}^d$ are presented to the network which estimates their class memberships $y \in Y$. The number of output units corresponds to the number of classes, and the classmemberships $y \in Y$ are encoded through a 1-of-L coding into a binary vector $\mathbf{z} \in \{0, 1\}^L$ through the relation $\mathbf{z}_i^\mu = 1$ iff $y^\mu = i$.

Using the 1-of-L encoding scheme an RBF network with K basis functions is performing a mapping as:

$$F_i(\mathbf{x}) = \sum_{j=1}^{K} w_{ij} h\left(\|\mathbf{x} - \mathbf{c}_j\| \right), i = 1, \ldots, L \tag{15}$$

where $h\left(\|\mathbf{x} - \mathbf{c}_j\| \right) = exp\left(-\|\mathbf{x} - \mathbf{c}_j\|^2 / 2\sigma^2 \right)$ is a Gaussian function with peak at center $\mathbf{c}^\mu \in \mathbb{R}^d$.

Outputs from the hidden layer represent how much the given pattern belongs to the given Gaussian function present in the neuron. These outputs are forwarded to the output layer, while forwarded these values are weighted with w_{jk}. Neurons from the output layer have a linear activation function, leaving the output of these neurons as a linear combination of the weighted inputs coming from the previous hidden layer.

The number of the input and output layer neurons is rarely a theme of discussion, as the input layer almost always has the same number of neurons as the number of characteristics of the input patterns. The output layer commonly has as many neurons as different classes are present in the problem data set. Categorization is performed by assigning the input vector $\mathbf{x}$ the class of the output unit with maximum activation.

The number of neurons in the hidden layer, the ones with RBF activation functions, on the other hand is a topic by itself. In this work an unsupervised method is used to determine the number of RBF neurons and at the same time the parameters for describing each of the Gaussians.

4.1 Algorithm for Defining the Hidden Layer

It is worth however to notice that is not the version of the Gaussian function used in the RBFNN presented in this paper. A more accurate version of what is really used is computed with (16).

$$\varphi(x) = e^{-\beta \|x - \mu\|^2} \tag{16}$$

From (16), it can be observed the whole $\frac{1}{\sigma\sqrt{2\pi}}$ coefficient is removed. This term normally controls the height of the Gaussian bell, but in this case the height of the bell will be controlled by the output neurons and the weighted edges W_{jk}, which will be adjusted during the training phase.

The second change to the original Gaussian function is the coefficient $\frac{1}{2\sigma^2}$ has been replaced by a β constant. The replaced term usually is in charge of the width of the Gaussian bell. But the β parameter can have the same effect.

Having defined what does the RBF look like it is possible to proceed to find how many Gaussian functions are needed and what their parameters are. To find how many neurons are required in the hidden layer the unsupervised algorithm of KMeans is used. The training data set is separated into subsets of single classes which are used to find clusters using KMeans. From each subset (each composed of single classes) a number N of clusters is obtained, and from each of these clusters a center can be identified. The centers of these clusters are used as the parameter M of the Gaussian functions in the hidden layer. These means that for each cluster identified for each class in the training data set a neuron in the hidden layer is created.

The β parameter can be obtained from the distance of each pattern to the center of the cluster as can be seen in equation (17).

$$\beta = \frac{1}{2\sigma^2} \tag{17}$$

4.2 Algorithm for Adjusting the Weights

Once the topology of the neural network has been completely defined the next step is to train it. The training process consists of presenting the patterns in the input layer and adjusting the weights connecting the hidden and output layer so the output is the closest to the desired class.

It is expected the outputs are not the closest to the desired class, but in order to improve this a process of adjusting the weights W_{jk} is performed. This adjustment is done by using a gradient descent algorithm as shown in equation (18).

$$W_{jk} = W_{jk} + \alpha * \varphi * \xi \tag{18}$$

Where φ is the output of the hidden layer, α is a learning rate constant and ξ is given by the equation (19), where δ is the desired output and ζ is the actual output.

$$\xi = \delta - \zeta \tag{19}$$

5   Methodology

In the present study, the data used for performing the experiments was obtained from the Internet maps service Google Earth. The images contain data from the visible part of the electromagnetic spectrum. This in contrast with traditional research projects where either multi-spectral, hyper-spectral or Synthetic Aperture Radar images are used.

The image obtained from the maps service was manually segmented, by visual inspection, into distinct classes defining polygons in the image. Each one of these polygons belonged to a single class which made easier the feature extraction process. Once segmented the region, the image was transformed into a different color space.

For obtaining characteristics that describe the data in the image, the feature extraction algorithm known as Co-Occurrence Matrix was used. This algorithm provides descriptors representing textural information in the image. Using the mentioned algorithm a database was created.

The classification process, for which the results are presented in the experimentation section, was carried on using a RBFNN. The RBFNN topology was determined by using the algorithm for selecting the number of neurons in the hidden layer presented previously in this paper.

6   Experimental Results

To evaluate the accuracy of the proposed methodology, a test region was defined. In Figure 2, a scaled version of the data used through this study is shown. The original size of the image is 8000 pixels wide and 8000 pixels height. This image was cropped from a bigger image of size 20000 pixels in each dimension. These images was taken from the northwest region of Mexico, a region very active from an agriculture point of view.

From this image, five classes were identified and a set of polygons over each of these classes were drawn in the image. These polygons made the feature

Fig. 2. Scaled image used for the experiments shown in the present study

extraction task easier to perform. From this information we built five datasets, each one evaluated with a different color space for the experiment. Each dataset is composed of 2752 patterns with 24 features (eight features for each space color channel).

To validate the accuracy of the proposed method, 30 experiments over each dataset were performed. It is important to notice that, for every experiment two subsets were randomly generated from each dataset. The 50% of the samples compose the training subset, and the remain the testing subset.

The topology of the RBFNN was composed of three layers. The hidden layer is composed of 16 neurons; finally, the output layer is composed of five linear neurons. The learning rate was set to 0.001 and the RBFNN was trained during 1000 epochs.

In Table 1, the average accuracy of the proposed methodology using the RBFNN as a classification device is shown.

Table 1. Results of the experiment with 5 crop classes with the RBFNN classifier

Color Space	Training Recognition Rate	Testing Recognition Rate
RGB	0.8629	0.8409
HSI	0.9179	0.9049
HSL	0.9158	0.8977
HSV	0.9198	0.9022
XYZ	0.8337	0.8084

As can be observed, the results obtained during training and testing phases are greater than 80%. For the case of the RGB color space, the results are near of 85%. The XYZ color space provides a worse accuracy than RGB color space; however, the obtained results were acceptable. Furthermore, the accuracy of the proposed methodology increased when it was combined with HSI, HSL or HSV color spaces. In general, the recognition rate for these color spaces was greater than 90%. These color spaces allow the methodology to be applied with images that contain data from the visible part of the electromagnetic spectrum, even if they present some illumination changes.

In addition to these experiments, the accuracy of the proposed methodology was compared against different distance classifiers. The next three distance classifiers were compared: Euclidean, Cityblock, Minkowski, Chebychev. This distances are documented in the MathWorks Documentation Center [17].

Table 2. Average accuracy obtained with the classification method for the crop classification problem

Dataset	Euclidean Classifier		Cityblock Classifier		Chebychev Classifier	
	Tr. cr.	Te. cr.	Tr. cr.	Te. cr.	Tr. cr.	Te. cr.
RGB	0.7515	0.7477	0.7358	0.7364	0.7700	0.7704
HSI	0.8753	0.8715	0.8662	0.8686	0.8281	0.8274
HSL	0.8507	0.8433	0.8384	0.8370	0.8069	0.8089
HSV	0.8745	0.8732	0.8632	0.8597	0.8254	0.8246
XYZ	0.7377	0.7380	0.7273	0.7276	0.7509	0.7534

Tr. cr = Training classification rate, Te. cr. = Testing classification rate.

As can be observed, the accuracy of the methodology diminished when the RBFNN was replaced with the distance classifiers. The best results were obtained with the euclidean distance classifier combined with the HSI, HSL, HSV color spaces; however, the accuracy was not greater than 90% as with the RBFNN.

After evaluate these results, we observe that is possible to perform crop classification tasks with satellite images that contain data from the visible part of the electromagnetic spectrum.

7 Conclusions

In this paper, we presented a methodology to perform a crop classification task over satellite images that contain data from the visible part of the electromagnetic spectrum. During the experiments, it was shown that the Gray Level Co-Occurrence Matrix (GLCM) is a useful descriptor for performing crop classification tasks. Furthermore, the combination of this descriptor with a Radial Basis Function (RBF) neural network provides highly acceptable results, even when distance classifiers are used.

Moreover, we study how different color spaces could be applied to analyze satellite images. During the experimental results, we also observed that HSI, HSL and HSV color spaces provide a better accuracy than RGB and XYZ color spaces, reaching an accuracy of 90%.

These preliminary results suggest that the methodology could be applied to different crop classification tasks using satellite images that contain data from the visible part of the electromagnetic spectrum and multi- and hyper-spectral images.

Nowadays, we are evaluating different feature extraction technique combined with different types of neural networks including spiking neural networks [19].

Acknowledgments. The authors would like to thank CONACYT-INEGI and Universidad La Salle for the economic support under grant number 187637, I-065/12 and I-061/12, respectively. Guillermo Sandoval thanks to the CONACYT-INEGI for the scholarship provided through the project number 187637.

References

1. Bauer, M.E., Cipra, J.E., Anuta, P.E., Etheridge, J.B.: Identification and area estimation of agricultural crops by computer classification of LANDSAT MSS data. Remote Sensing of Environment 8, 77–92 (1979)
2. Camps-Valls, G., et al.: Support Vector Machines for Crop Classification Using Hyperspectral Data. In: Perales, F.J., Campilho, A.C., Pérez, N., Sanfeliu, A. (eds.) IbPRIA 2003. LNCS, vol. 2652, pp. 134–141. Springer, Heidelberg (2003)
3. Correa, C.: Image processing for identification of grape and foliage using techniques of unsupervised classification. In: IV University Students Congress on Science, Technology and Agricultural Engineering, pp. 53–56 (2011) (in Spanish)
4. D'Amato, J.P., García-Bauza, C., Vénere, M., Clausse, A.: Image processing for mass classification based fruit color (2007), Available in web and pdf format: http://www.pladema.net/cgarcia/publications/JIDIS-2007.pdf
5. El Hajj, M., Bégué, A., Guillaume, S., Martiné, J.F.: Integrating SPOT-5 time series, crop growth modeling and expert knowledge for monitoring agricultural practices. The case of sugarcane harvest on Reunion Island. Remote Sensing of Environment 113, 2052–2061 (2009)
6. Grace, K., Husak, G.J., Harrison, L., Pedreros, D., Machaelsen, J.: Using high resolution satellite imagery to estimate cropped area in Guatemala and Haiti. Applied Geography 32, 433–440 (2012)
7. McNairn, H., Shang, J., Champagne, C., Jiao, X.: TerraSAR-X and RADARSAT-2 for crop classification and acreage estimation. In: 2009 IEEE International Geoscience and Remote Sensing Symposium, IGARSS 2009, pp. II-898–II-901 (2009)
8. Nagy, G., Tolaba, J.: Nonsupervised Crop Classification through Airborne Multispectral Observations. IBM Journal of Research and Develop 16(2), 138–153 (1972)
9. Pereira Coltri, P., Zullo, J., Ribeiro do Valle Goncalves, R., Romani, L.A.S., Pinto, H.S.: Coffee Crop's Biomass and Carbon Stock Estimation With Usage of High Resolution Satellites Images. IEEE Journal of Selected Topics in Applied Earth Observations and Remote Sensing 6, 1786–1795 (2013)
10. Pérez, D.S., Bromberg, F.: Image segmentation in vineyards for wine autonomous measurement variables. In: XVIII Argentine Congress of Computer Science (2012) (in Spanish)
11. Pingxiang, L., Shenghui, F.: SAR Image Classification Based on Its Texture Features. Geo-Spatial Information Science 6(3), 16–19 (2003)
12. Schotten, C.G.J., Van Rooy, W.W.L., Janssen, L.L.F.: Assessment of the capabilities of multi-temporal ERS-1 SAR data to discriminate between agricultural crops. International Journal of Remote Sensing 16(14), 2619–2637 (1995)

13. Sheikho, K.M., et al.: Crops classification using multiple Landsat data; a case study in arid lands. In: 1998 IEEE International Geoscience and Remote Sensing Symposium Proceedings, IGARSS 1998, vol. 2, pp. 794–797 (1998)
14. Skriver, H.: Crop Classification by Multitemporal C- and L-Band Single- and Dual-Polarization and Fully Polarimetric SAR. IEEE Transactions on Geoscience and Remote Sensing 50(6), 2138–2149 (2012)
15. Skriver, H., et al.: Crop classification using short-revisit multitemporal SAR data. IEEE J. of Sel. Topics in App. Earth Obs. and Remote Sensing 4(2), 423–431 (2011)
16. Yi, C., Pan, Y., Zhang, J.: An Integrated Approach to Agricultural Crop Classification Using SPOT5 HRV Images. IFIP Advances in Information and Communication Technology 8, 677–684 (2008)
17. MathWorks Documentation Center: pdist function consulted (August, 2013), http://www.mathworks.com/help/stats/pdist.html
18. Schwenker, F., Kestler, H., Palm, G.: Three learning phases for radial-basis-function networks. Neural Networks 14, 439–458 (2001)
19. Vazquez, R.A., Sandoval, G., Ambrosio, J.: How to Generate the Input Current for Exciting a Spiking Neural Model Using the Cuckoo Search Algorithm. In: Yang, X.-S. (ed.) Cuckoo Search and Firefly Algorithm. SCI, vol. 516, pp. 155–178. Springer, Heidelberg (2014)
20. Haralick, R.M., Shanmugam, K., Dinstein, I.: Textural Features for Image Classification. IEEE Trans. on Systems, Man and Cybernetics 3(6), 610–621 (1973)

Small Sample Size in High Dimensional Space - Minimum Distance Based Classification

Ewa Skubalska-Rafajłowicz

Institute of Computer Engineering, Automatics and Robotics,
Department of Electronics, Wrocław University of Technology, Poland
ewa.rafajlowicz@pwr.wroc.pl

Abstract. In this paper we present some new results concerning classification in small sample and high dimensional case. We discuss geometric properties of data structures in high dimensions. It is known that such data form in high dimension an almost regular simplex, even if covariance structure of data is not unity. We restrict our attention to two class discrimination problems. It is assumed that observations from two classes are distributed as multivariate normal with a common covariance matrix. We develop consequences of our findings that in high dimensions N Gaussian random points generate a sample covariance matrix estimate which has similar properties as a covariance matrix of normal distribution obtained by random projection onto subspace of dimensionality N. Namely, eigenvalues of both covariance matrices follow the same distribution. We examine classification results obtained for minimum distance classifiers with dimensionality reduction based on PC analysis of a singular sample covariance matrix and a reduction obtained using normal random projections. Simulation studies are provided which confirm the theoretical analysis.

Keywords: small sample, classification in high dimensions, eigenvalues of a sample covariance matrix, maximum likelihood ratio, normal random projection, minimum distance rule.

1 Introduction

Analysis of high-dimension low-sample size classification is one of most important problems both from theoretical and practical point of view. It often happens that the dimension d of data vectors is larger than the sample size N and this case is referred to as small sample size, high dimensional data. Microarrays, medical imaging, text recognition, finance and chemometrics are examples of such classification problems. On the other hand we know that in practice, statistical methods based on very small sample sizes might not be reliable. Many results in this area have been obtained in the asymptotic setting, when both dimension d of the vector observations and the size of the data sample N is very large, with d possibly much larger than N [2], [19], [4]. It is assumed that d and N grow at the same rate, i.e. $d/N \to \gamma$ as $d \to \infty$ [19]. Others focus their attention on

L. Rutkowski et al. (Eds.): ICAISC 2014, Part I, LNAI 8467, pp. 610–621, 2014.

the case that dimension d increases while the sample size N is fixed [1], [8], [10], [9]. In [13] and [8] it was observed that data in high dimensions form an almost regular simplex and distances between $N < d$ random points are very close to $c\sqrt{(2d)}$.

Here we restrict our attention to two class discrimination problems. It is assumed that observations from two classes are distributed as multivariate normal with a common covariance matrix. We assume that the number of available samples equals N and consists of independent vector observations from both classes, N_0 and N_1, respectively.

Using the very popular Fisher classifier LDA (linear discrimination analysis) [5], [21], [16], [19] when the data are from the normal distribution with a common covariance matrix: $X_l \sim N(m_l, \Sigma)$ for $l = 0, 1$, we can estimate a single, pooled covariance matrix as an estimate of the common covariance matrix:

$$S = \frac{1}{N-2} \left(\sum_{j=1}^{N_0} (X_{0j} - \bar{X}_0)(X_{0j} - \bar{X}_0)^T + \sum_{j=1}^{N_1} (X_{1j} - \bar{X}_1)(X_{1j} - \bar{X}_1)^T \right),$$

where

$$\bar{X}_0 = \sum_{j=1}^{N_0} X_{0j}, \quad \bar{X}_1 = \sum_{j=1}^{N_1} X_{1j},$$

and $N = N_0 + N_1$.

The Fisher classification rule is based on

$$D(X) = (X - M)S^{-1}(\bar{X}_0 - \bar{X}_1), \tag{1}$$

where $M = (\bar{X}_0 + \bar{X}_1)/2$. If $D(X) > 0$ classify X to class C_0 (labeled by 0), otherwise classify X to class C_1 (labeled by 1).

The maximum likelihood ratio (MLR) rule [11], [19] classifies X to the class C_0 if

$$\frac{N_0 + 1}{N_0} (X - \bar{X}_0)^T S^{-1} (X - \bar{X}_0) \leq \frac{N_1 + 1}{N_1} (X - \bar{X}_1)^T S^{-1} (X - \bar{X}_1). \tag{2}$$

The MLR rule can be also used when covariances in the both classes differ. Firstly, one estimates the covariance matrix of each class, based on samples known to belong to each class. Then, given a new sample X, one computes the squared Mahalanobis distance [12] to each class, i.e.,

$$(X - \bar{X}_l)^T S_l^{-1} (X - \bar{X}_l), \quad l = 0, 1$$

and classifies the new point as belonging to that class for which the (weighted by $\frac{Nl+1}{Nl}$) Mahalanobis distance is minimal. It is well known [22] (and easy to show) that the MLR rule coincides with the Fisher method when numbers of samples from both classes are equal to each other, i.e., $N_0 = N_1$. Mahalanobis distance is also closely related to Hotelling's T-square distribution used for multivariate statistical testing [15]. It is, however, hard to implement the covariance based

classification methods when dimensionality is high due to the difficulty of estimating the unknown covariance matrix. Even if number of samples N is greater
than the dimension of the data it is advisable to reduce dimensionality due to
some near zero eigenvalues of S. Thus, it is proposed to drop zero or near zero
eigenvalues of S.

If the number of data samples is smaller than the dimension of the data space,
the sample based estimate of the covariance matrix is singular with probability
one. Srivastava [19] has proposed a sample-squared distance between the two
groups, using the Moore–Penrose pseudoinverse of the singular sample covariance
matrix S.

The Moore–Penrose pseudoinverse of a matrix A is unique and is defined as
matrix A^+ satisfying the following four properties:

- $AA^+A = A$,
- $A^+AA^+ = A^+$
- $(AA^+)^T = AA^+$,
- $(A^+A)^T = A^+A$

The sample covariance matrix S is a symmetric positive semidefinite matrix.
Thus, it can be written as

$$S = QDQ^T,$$

where D is diagonal with the positive eigenvalues of S, and $Q \in R^{d \times N}$ is orthogonal and consists of N eigenvectors of S connected to the positive eigenvalues of
S. This orthogonal decomposition is often called principal components analysis
(PCA). The sample covariance matrix provides the conventional estimator of
principal component analysis (PCA) through the eigenvalue-eigenvector decomposition. For the covariance or correlation matrix, the eigenvectors correspond
to principal components and the eigenvalues to the variance explained by the
principal components. The MoorePenrose inverse of S is defined by

$$S^+ = QD^{-1}Q^T,$$

where $d - N$ principal components directions connected to zero (or close to
zero) eigenvalues are removed. For numerical matrices computations of their
pseudoinverses are based on singular value decomposition (SVD) [7].

In this paper we will show why in many cases it is more effective to use unit
diagonal matrix I and the Euclidean distance instead of Mahalanobis distance
based on the pseudoinverse of the sample covariance matrix S^+ in the context of
small sample and high dimension classification problems. The analysis is followed
by some simulation experiments which indicate that the same phenomena one
can observe also in a relatively small dimension in comparison to many practical
high dimensional problems. The most important condition is that the number
of samples is smaller than the dimension of the data.

The starting point of the paper is the observation that in high dimensions
N Gaussian random points generate a sample covariance matrix estimate which

has similar properties as a covariance matrix of normal distribution obtained by random projection onto subspace of dimensionality N. Namely, eigenvalues of both covariance matrices follow the same distribution. This property explains why PC analysis of singular sample covariance matrix (for $N < d$) leads to the similar results as dimensionality reduction made at random.

The next section describes geometric properties of small sample data in high dimensions. Section 3 is concentrated on properties of both mentioned earlier dimensionality reduction methods. Section 4. shows some simulation results which explain and confirm proposals and conclusions developed in the previous sections. In Section 5 we summarize the provided theoretical and simulation results.

2   Geometric Structure of Data in High Dimensions

It is well known that high dimensional data concentrates close to the surface of a hypersphere. For example, if samples are drawn according to multidimensional normal distribution in a high-dimensional space, the center region where the value of the density function is largest is empty and almost all samples are located close to the sphere of radius $\sqrt{(Trace(\Sigma))} = c\sqrt{(d)}$ (for detailed assumptions see [8] or [1], [6]). Figure 1 (left panel) illustrates this phenomenon, where diagram of the ordered lengths of 100 iid random observations taken from normal distribution $N_d(0, I)$ of dimensionality $d = 20000$ is depicted. Furthermore, as is indicated in [8], [3], the data in high dimension form an almost regular simplex. The distances between random points are very close to $c\sqrt{(2d)}$. Figure 1, right panel depicts a diagram of the Euclidean distances between the same set of 100 points. Mean Euclidean distance between these points (iid normal $N_d(0, 1)$, for $d = 20000$) equals 199.69 with standard deviation 0.78.

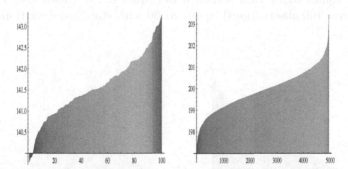

Fig. 1. Left) Diagram of the length of 20000 dimensional random vectors generated independently according to multivariate normal distribution (100 samples). Right) Diagram of the Euclidean distances between the same set of points.

This means that the variability of the small sample of high-dimensional data is contained only in the random rotation of this simplex. For random vector X being the multivariate Gaussian distribution with identity covariance matrix I it is known that $||X||^2$ has χ^2 distribution with d degree of freedom and furthermore $||X||$ follows χ distribution with the same degree of freedom. The mean of χ distribution is

$$\sqrt{(2)}\frac{\Gamma[(d+1)/2]}{\Gamma[d/2]}$$

and $\mu = E||X|| \to \sqrt{(d)}$ as $d \to \infty$ and its variance equals $d - \mu^2$.

In general the Euclidean norm of a multivariate normally distributed random vector follows a noncentral χ distribution.

Ahn et al [1] have shown, using asymptotic properties of sample covariance matrices, that the conditions for forming by a small data sample a regular simplex are rather mild. More precisely, they have shown, that if eigenvalues of the true covariance matrix Σ are all distinct and positive

$$\lambda_1 > \lambda_2 > \ldots > \lambda_d > 0,$$

and if

$$\frac{\sum_{i=1}^{d} \lambda_i^2}{(\sum_{i=1}^{d} \lambda_i)^2} \to 0 \qquad (3)$$

as $d \to \infty$, then the nonzero eigenvalues of the sample covariance matrix behave as if they are from diagonal matrix $\frac{Trace(\Sigma)}{N} I_N$.

The similar phenomenon one can obtain for a uniform distribution. Figure 2 shows a diagram of the lengths of 20000 dimensional random vectors generated independently according to the uniform distribution from $[0,1]^d$ cube (100 samples) and of the Euclidean distances between the same set of points. Mean Euclidean distance between 100 points iid uniform from unit cube $[0,1]^d$, for $d = 20000$ equals 57.74 with standard deviation 0.236. Mean vector's length (averaged over 100 observations) equals 81.60 with standard deviation equal to 0.236.

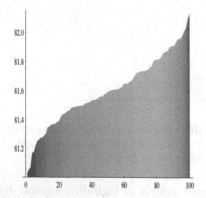 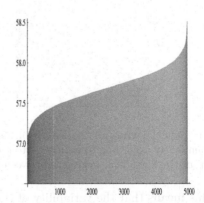

Fig. 2. Left) Diagram of the lengths of 20000 dimensional random vectors generated independently according to the uniform distribution from $[0,1]^d$ cube (100 samples). Right) Diagram of the Euclidean distances between the same set of points.

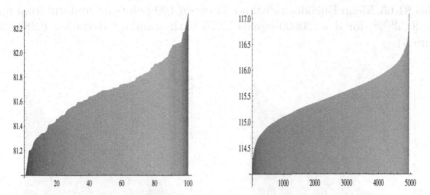

Fig. 3. Left) Diagram of the lengths of 20000 dimensional random vectors generated independently according to the uniform distribution from $[-1, 1]^d$ cube (100 samples). Right) Diagram of the Euclidean distances between the same set of points.

Further examples are given in Figures 3, 4 and 5.

Mean Euclidean distance between 100 points iid uniform unit cube $[-1, 1]^d$, for $d = 20000$ equals 115.49 with standard deviation 0.473. Mean vector's length (averaged over 100 observations) equals 81.64 with standard deviation equal to 0.236 (see Figure 3).

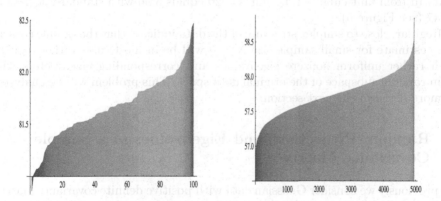

Fig. 4. Diagram of the normalized lengths of 20000 dimensional random vectors generated independently according to the uniform distribution from $[0, \lambda_i^{0.5}]^d$ cube (100 samples). Right) Diagram of the Euclidean distances between the same set of points with scaling factor $1/\sqrt{(\sum \lambda_i^2/d)}$ with $\lambda_i^2 = i$.

Mean vector's length (averaged over 100 observations) equals 8165 with standard deviation equal to 30.28. The adequate mean with rescaling factor

$$1/\sqrt{\left(\sum \lambda_i^2/d\right)} \approx 100$$

equals 81.65. Mean Euclidean distance between 100 points iid uniform from unit cube $[0, i^{0.5}]^d$, for $d = 20000$ equals 57.73 with standard deviation 0.284 (see Figure 4).

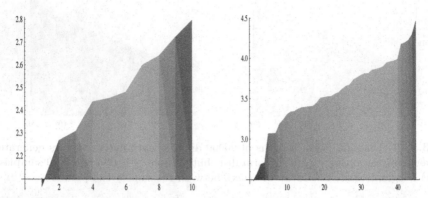

Fig. 5. Left) Diagram of the lengths of 20 dimensional random vectors generated independently according to the uniform distribution from $[-1, 1]^d$ cube (10 samples). Right) Diagram of the Euclidean distances between the same set of points.

Even if a dimension of data is relatively small, the random observations form a rather regular structure. The mean Euclidean distance between 10 points iid uniform from unit cube $[-1, 1]^d$, for $d = 20$ equals 3.56 with standard deviation 0.447 (see Figure 5).

Regular, close to simplex structure of the data indicate that the sample covariance estimate for small sample size $N < d$ will be in most cases rather regular with rather uniform nonzero eigenvalues and corresponding eigenvectors will form random subspace of the original data space. This problem will be analyzed in more detail in the next section.

3   Random Projections and Eigenvalues of a Sample Covariance Matrix

As previously we consider Gaussian data with positive definite covariance matrix Σ, i.e., such that its eigenvalues are all distinct and strictly positive

$$\lambda_1 > \lambda_2 > \ldots > \lambda_d > 0.$$

Suppose we have a data matrix $Y \in R^{d \times N}$, where $N \leq d$. For the sake of simplicity we will assume that the class means are known. Let's say that $m_0 = 0$ and $m_1 = \mu$. Thus, without loss of generality we can assume that each column of Y is iid normal $N_d(0, \Sigma)$, since every observation from the class labeled by 1, let say X, is replaced by $X - \mu$.

It is well known [7] that the nonzero eigenvalues of $S = YY^T/N$ are also the eigenvalues of $Y^T Y/N$. Srivastava observed [19] that if columns of $d \times N$ matrix

Y are independent identically distributed observations of normal random vector $\sim N_d(0, \Sigma)$ then the eigenvalues of $Y^T Y$ have the same distribution as the eigenvalues of

$$U^T \Sigma U,$$

where $U \in R^{d \times N}$ is a random matrix with entries iid $N(0, 1)$ (see also [1]).

When number of samples N is smaller than a dimension of a data, then randomly chosen vector observations Y and vector 0 span a random subspace of the original data space of dimensionality N. If means are not given and should be estimated from data N centered vectors span (with probability one) $N - 1$ dimensional space.

The same effect of choosing random subspace of the original space one can obtain using normal random projections [20], [17], [18], [3].

Let $Z \in R^{d \times N}$ be a random matrix with entries iid $N(0, 1)$. We can project matrix of observations onto N dimensional subspace using transformation $V = Z^T Y$.

Each column of matrix $V \in R^{N \times N}$ is iid zero mean normal random vector with covariance matrix $Z^T \Sigma Z$. A normal random projection with projection matrix Z transforms $N_d(0, \Sigma)$ distribution onto $N_N(0, Z^T \Sigma Z)$. Thus, instead of $x^T S^+ x$ we can analyze a random quadratic form in normal variables $N_N(0, Z^T \Sigma Z)$:

$$(Z^T x)^T (Z^T S Z)^{-1} (Z^T x). \tag{4}$$

It is easy to show that matrix Z can be decomposed into $Z = R\tilde{Q}$, where

$$\tilde{Q} \in St(d, N) = \{A \in R^{d \times N} : A^T A = I_N\}$$

consists of N columns of rotation matrix obtained from Z by the Gram–Schmidt orthogonalization process and $R \in R^{N \times N}$ is an adequate scaling matrix. So, (4) equals

$$x^T \tilde{Q} (\tilde{Q} S \tilde{Q}^T)^{-1} \tilde{Q}^T x. \tag{5}$$

This formula is very similar to the previous one, proposed by Srivastava [19], i.e.,

$$x^T Q D^{-1} Q^T x, \tag{6}$$

where $Q^T x$ follows the normal distribution with zero mean and the covariance matrix $Q^T \Sigma Q$, and where D is random with respect to the matrix of learning samples Y.

The precise connections between (6) and (5) are still open question. However it is known, that the mean value of

$$\tilde{Q} (\tilde{Q} S \tilde{Q}^T)^{-1} \tilde{Q}^T$$

with respect to $\tilde{Q}$ (taken uniformly, i.e., according to the Haar measure on the compact Stiefel manifold $St(d, N)$) is equal to a pseudoinverse of S [14]. It is hard, for the numerical reasons, to apply this property in practice.

Notice that eigenvalues of covariance matrix $Z^T \Sigma Z$ of a normal distribution $N_N(0, Z^T \Sigma Z)$ obtained after random normal projection have the same distribution as nonzero eigenvalues of YY^T. This property is not asymptotic and it holds for every $N < d$.

In the next section we will show experimentally that using only one N dimensional projection at a time leads to the same mean classification error as the method MLR proposed by Srivastava when results are averaged over many different learning samples.

4   Numerical Results

We had performed the following experiment. A two class Gaussian problem was examined with different numbers of learning samples in dimensions $d = 20$. The classes differ in the mean, i.e., $m_0 = (0, \ldots, 0)^T$ and $m_1 = (1, \ldots, 1)^T$. Eigenvalues of the common covariance matrix equal $1, 2, \ldots, 20$. It is easy to check that such covariance structure fulfills assumption (3). For simplicity, we have also assumed that there are available $N_0 = N_1$ samples from both classes $N_0 = N_1 = 5$, 8, 10, 20, 40, 100, 200. 100 different learning samples were drawn and both methods were performed on 2×10000 testing samples (10000 for each class). Class means are also estimated from the data.

Figure 6 demonstrates a comparison of averaged classification accuracy obtained using different classification methods, namely: Srivastava modification of the MLR rule and the MLR rule applied to randomly projected data (using normal random projections) onto subspaces of dimension $k = 5$, 10 and 20. When the number of samples was greater than the dimension of the problem, the original version of the MLR rule was used and a pseudoinverse was replaced by the inverse of the sample covariance matrix estimate. For projection of dimensionality $k = 20$ which is in fact nonsingular the eigenvalues of the sample covariance matrix were almost the same. Small differences occur due to numerical errors. For $N_0 = N_1 = 5$ one of the estimated covariance matrices has the following nonzero eigenvalues:

$$\{56.8024, 41.7466, 30.6846, 28.181, 15.2784, 12.4807, 5.73685, 3.17399\}$$

and the trace of these covariance matrices equals ≈ 194.1. When the dimension of a projection was lower than 20, the eigenvalues of the estimated covariance matrix were more spread. For example, for $k = 10$ (and the same learning sample) we have obtained the following set of nonzero eigenvalues:

$$\{49.1553, 39.4426, 31.963, 13.7017, 9.29589, 3.33462, 1.41191, 0.115814\}.$$

Using unity covariance matrix I instead of estimated ones, i.e., the minimum Euclidean distance classification rule (MEDC), results in $0.61 - -0.0.74$ mean classification accuracy. The true covariance matrix allows to obtain accuracy changing from 0.684425 (means are estimated from only 5 samples) to 0.82 (for $N_0 = N_1 = 200$). These results indicate that for small data samples estimation of the covariance matrix was useless.

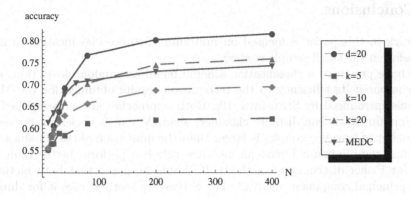

Fig. 6. Averaged classification accuracy for two 20-dimensional Gaussian classes and different number of learning samples $N = N_0 + N_1$. $N = 10, 16, 20, \ldots, 400$.

Figure 7 shows magnified part of Figure 6, which contains results obtained when number of samples N was smaller than the dimension d. This figure demonstrates that both dimension reduction methods give the same mean recognition errors providing that the dimension of the random projection is larger than the number of samples.

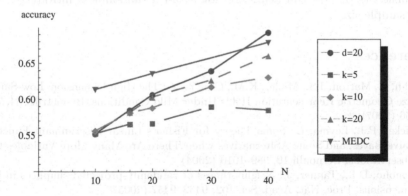

Fig. 7. Averaged classification accuracy for two 20-dimensional Gaussian classes and different number of learning samples $N = N_0 + N_1$. $N = 10, 16, 20, 30, 40$.

The similar behavior we have observed for $d = 80$ and $N_0 = N_1 = 30$. As previously the class means were $m_0 = (0, \ldots, 0)^T$ and $m_1 = (1, \ldots, 1)^T$ and eigenvalues of the common covariance matrix equal $1, 2, \ldots, 80$. The averaged classification accuracy was equal to 0.579 for Srivastava's method and equals 0.583 for random projection of dimensionality $k = 60$. Using I (unity) covariance matrix, i.e. MEDC rule, allows us to obtain better results of classification with accuracy 0.63.

5   Conclusions

The work in this paper is focused on minimum distance classification in high dimension in the small sample context.

We have presented a classification scheme based on random projections and have compared its efficiency to the recognition results obtained for the MLR type rule introduced by Srivastava [19]. Both approaches are outperformed by the minimum Euclidean distance classifier, when $N < d$. It is clear that even if the number of learning samples is larger than the dimension of the classification problems, the minimum Euclidean distance rule can perform better than the MLR (or Fisher discriminant method). It should be noted that both methods apply principal component analysis. The Srivastava method uses it for dimensionality reduction. The random projection method starts from reducing the dimension of the problem. It allows us to diminish computational costs for PCA. If small values of principal components occur, it is possible to reduce further the dimension of the data.

It is an open question how large should be the learning sample in high dimension taking into account the regular structure of data in high dimension. In other words one may ask where is the transition point between spherical and non-spherical structure of data when a covariance matrix is not unity.

Another important problem is how to test classification results in a low sample size context. It is known that in such a case the cross validation methods are very unstable [1]. We can definitely not avoid a randomness introduced by a small sample size.

References

1. Ahn, J., Marron, J.S., Müller, K.M., Chi, Y.-Y.: The High Dimension. Low-Sample Size Geometric Representation Holds Under Mild Conditions. Biometrika 94, 760–766 (2007)
2. Bickel, P.J., Levina, E.: Some Theory for Fisher's Linear Discriminant Function, Naive Bayes, and Some ASlternatives when There Are Many More Variables than Observations. Bernoulli 10, 989–1010 (2004)
3. Donoho, D.L., Tanner, J.: Neighborliness of randomly-projected simplices in high dimensions. Proc. Nat. Acad. Sci. 102, 9452–9457 (2005)
4. Fan, J., Fan, Y., Wu, Y.: High-dimensional Classification. In: Cai, T.T., Shen, X. (eds.) High-dimensional Data Analysis. Frontiers of Statistics, vol. 2, pp. 3–37. World Scientific, Singapore (2011)
5. Fisher, R.A.: The Use of Multiple Measurements in Taxonomic Problems. Ann. Eugenics 7, 179–188 (1936)
6. Fukunaga, K.: Introduction to Statistical Pattern Recognition, 2nd edn. Academic Press, San Diego (1990)
7. Golub, G., Van Loan, C.F.: Matrix Computations. The Johns Hopkins University Press, Baltimore (1996)
8. Hall, P., Marron, J.S., Neeman, A.: Geometric Representation of High-Dimension Low-Sample Size Data. Journal of the Royal Statistical Society, Ser. B 67, 427–444 (2005)

9. Jung, S., Senb, A., Marron, J.S.: Boundary Behavior in High Dimension, Low Sample Size Asymptotics of PCA. Journal of Multivariate Analysis 109, 190–203 (2012)

10. Jung, S., Marron, J.S.: PCA Consistency in High Dimension, Low Sample Size Context. Ann. Statist. 37, 4104–4130 (2009)

11. Kiefer, J., Schwartz, R.: Admissible Bayes Character of $T^2 - -R^2$ and Other Fully Invariant Tests for Classical Multivariate Normal Problems. Ann. Math. Statist. 36, 747–770 (1965)

12. Mahalanobis, P.C.: On the Generalised Distance in Statistics. Proceedings of the National Institute of Sciences of India 2, 49–55 (1936)

13. Marron, J.S., Todd, M.J., Ahn, J.: Distance-Weighted Discrimination. Journal of the American Statistical Association 102, 1267–1271 (2007)

14. Marzetta, T.L., Tucci, G.H., Simon, S.H.: A Random Matrix-Theoretic Approach to Handling Singular Covariance Estimates. IEEE Transactions on Information Theory 57, 6256–6271 (2011)

15. Rao, C.R.: Linear Statistical Inference and Its Applications, 2nd edn. Wiley, New York (1973)

16. Saranadasa, H.: Asymptotic Expansion of the Misclassification Probabilities of D- and A-criteria for Discrimination from the Two High dimensional Populations Using the Theory of Large Dimensional Metrices. J. Multivariate Anal. 46, 154–174 (1993)

17. Skubalska-Rafajłowicz, E.: Clustering of Data and Nearest Neighbors Search for Pattern Recognition with Dimensionality Reduction Using Random Projections. In: Rutkowski, L., Scherer, R., Tadeusiewicz, R., Zadeh, L.A., Zurada, J.M. (eds.) ICAISC 2010, Part I. LNCS, vol. 6113, pp. 462–470. Springer, Heidelberg (2010)

18. Skubalska-Rafajowicz, E.: Random Projections and Hotelling's T^2 Statistics for Change Detection in High–dimensional Data Streams. International Journal of Applied Mathematics and Computer Science 23, 447–461 (2013)

19. Srivastava, M.S.: Minimum Distance Classification Rules for High Dimensional Data. Journal of Multivariate Analysis 97, 2057–2070 (2006)

20. Vempala, S.: The Random Projection Method. American Mathematical Society, Providence (2004)

21. Wald, A.: On the statistical problem arising in the classification of an individual into one of two groups. Ann. Math. Statist. 15, 145–162 (1944)

22. Wasserman, L.: All of Statistics: A Concise Course in Statistical Inference. Springer, New York (2004)

Failures Prediction in the Cold Forging Process Using Machine Learning Methods

Tomasz Żabiński[1], Tomasz Mączka[1], Jacek Kluska[1], Maciej Kusy[1],
Zbigniew Hajduk[1], and Sławomir Prucnal[2]

[1] Faculty of Electrical and Computer Engineering, Rzeszów University of Technology,
35-959 Rzeszów, Powstańców Warszawy 12, Poland
{tomz,tmaczka,jacklu,mkusy,zh}@prz.edu.pl
[2] Faculty of Mechanical Engineering and Aeronautics,
Rzeszów University of Technology,
35-959 Rzeszów, Powstańców Warszawy 12, Poland
spktmiop@prz.edu.pl

Abstract. In this paper, single correct and three defective states for the cold headed fasteners production technological process are detected. Computational intelligence methods are used for this purpose: single decision tree, probabilistic neural network, support vector machine, multi-layer perceptron, linear discriminant analysis and K–Means clustering. The predictor variables are taken in time and frequency domain. The row data sets consist of sampled signals of the real process collected in fasteners manufacturing company. The prediction ability determined by 10-fold cross validation is investigated by means of accuracy, sensitivity and specificity. The results show the superiority of probabilistic neural network and support vector machine classifiers. The average accuracy is over 98%.

Keywords: cold headed fasteners, cold forging process, computational intelligence methods, accuracy, sensitivity, specificity.

1 Introduction

The industrial platform for production processes monitoring is created in cooperation between Rzeszów University of Technology (Department of Computer and Control Engineering), ŻBIK company and Green Forge Innovation Cluster [2] [3] [4]. The main assumption of the project is to design a relevant solution for metal processing industry, which enables an iterative implementation of Intelligent Manufacturing System (IMS) concept [4]. Additionaly it determines the selection of extensible hardware platform, as well as preparation of software modules open for communication purposes. The goal for the base version of the platform is to monitor machines and operators work, as well as to trace production orders realization and support auxiliary services, e.g. maintenance, transport. Up to now, the platform has been successfully deployed in four manufacturing companies in Poland (Subcarpathia province). The most important testbed has been continuously working in a fasteners manufacturing company

L. Rutkowski et al. (Eds.): ICAISC 2014, Part I, LNAI 8467, pp. 622–633, 2014.
© Springer International Publishing Switzerland 2014

since 2009 [1] [2] [3]. Further descriptions in this paper will be referred to the testbed.

The hardware platform consists of modern industrial automation equipment used at shop-floor level, as well as typical computers and mobile data collectors. For data acquisition and communication purposes, appropriate devices are installed on the factory floor, i.e. Programmable Automation Controllers (PACs) with touchable screens. There is a separate PAC with input and output modules installed for each machine. Dedicated software, that works on PAC, performs diverse tasks simultaneously, both in real-time and in a general purpose operating system layer. The PAC's real-time software (PLC - Programmable Logic Controller level) automatically acquires data concerning machine states on the basis of electrical signals from machine control systems. The application for Windows CE operating system provides Human System Interface (HSI) [3] for machine operator. It also communicates with PLC level, peripheral devices (e.g. barcode reader, electronic caliper, etc.) and with the server layer. Ethernet is used for communication between PACs and the server. Mobile data collectors are also included in the platform to collect data from technological processes which are not equipped with PACs or from auxiliary processes. The collectors communicate with the main server using 802.11 g wireless network. PCs with touchable screens are also used as extended operator interface, e.g. for browsing technical documentation.

In the server layer the GlassFish application server is hosting business logic components, as well as World Wide Web (WWW) applications for system end users, i.e. production management board. Data is stored in PostgreSQL database server and web services are used for communication with devices on a factory floor. The hardware structure of the platform is shown in Fig. 1.

The platform functionality can be divided into a few areas [3] [4]. The first one, covered by Efficiency module, is related to monitoring machines and operators' work. The monitoring is performed on the basis of binary signals acquired from machines control systems and data inputted by human operators via HSI. The second module, named Start-Stop-End (SSE), registers the flow of production orders between operations defined in the production technology. As the result, products genealogy can be traced. Maintenance module currently supports the process of signaling and reporting progress of fixing machines failures. There are also other modules which support: scheduling production orders, quality control procedures and communication between factory and its cooperating companies.

Currently, 70 machines and 6 production processes are covered by the system in the fasteners manufacturing company [1]. Since May 2009, over 24 million of events have been registered in the Efficiency module. It is planned to include additional 37 machines in the system in 2014.

The base platform version has been recently extended for processes and machines condition monitoring. It is an important extension for Maintenance module. In order to perform condition monitoring there is a necessity to register an additional set of binary and analog parameters. The base version of the platform

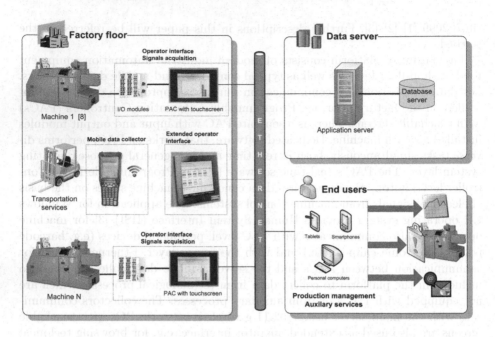

Fig. 1. Hardware structure of IMS platform

supports only acquisition of binary parameters. The main purpose of the extension is to enable analog parameters registration.

Due to this reason, modifications in the software layer of the system are implemented (Fig. 2). In the real-time software level of PAC, a separate task for reading data from analog input terminals is added. An analog signal connected to a single input terminal is treated as a separate measurement channel. Signals values from input terminals are temporarily stored in memory circular buffers. A single record in the buffer contains: channel identifier, analog signal values and timestamp. The application which runs under operating system of PAC reads data from PLC buffers using Automation Device Specification (ADS) [7] protocol. It serializes data into a form of byte-array and sends it to the server application using Transmission Control Protocol (TCP) sockets via the Ethernet network. The in-memory buffer mechanism is implemented to prevent data loss during periods of troubles with the network communication. The server application receives data from PACs and stores it as Comma Separated Values (CSV) text files on a hard drive.

In the hardware layer, it is necessary to choose analog input modules compatible with the electrical standards for particular signals.

A sampling interval for a particular signal is a result of PLC task cycle time and the type of analog input module. The lowest standard value of PLC task cycle time for chosen hardware solution is 1 ms. However, computational power of PAC, taking into account other running tasks and applications, can limit this value. On the other hand, one of two types of analog input modules can be chosen: module without oversampling (single probe per one PLC cycle) or module

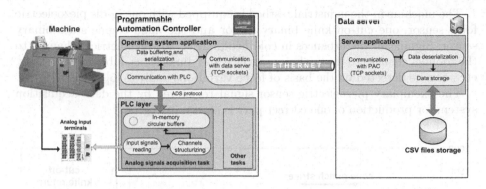

Fig. 2. Software structure of IMS platform for analog parameter acquisition

with oversampling (N probes per one PLC cycle, where N is an oversampling factor). Currently, modules with oversampling factor $N = 100$ are available, therefore sampling interval of $10\mu s$ can be achieved.

The main objective of this paper is to show how we can effectively use machine learning methods in prediction of some failures in the cold forging technological process on the basis of data registered by IMS platform.

This paper is composed of the following sections. Section 2 describes the cold forging process and data acquisition system. In Section 3, the computational intelligence methods used in this research are discussed. Section 4 shows the results. Finally, in Section 5, the conclusions are formulated.

2 Cold Forging Process and Data Acquisition System

Cold forging (cold heading) is a high speed and efficient bulk metal forming process in which a force is used to create a destination workpiece shape at a room temperature. During the process, a bulk of metal is placed within a die and a punch is pressed into the workpiece. As a result, the workpiece takes the form of the punch and the die. In contrast to machining, the cold forging process makes very efficient use of material, producing little or no scrap. Modern machines, called coldformers, are very efficient and can produce hundreds of pieces per minute. Although originally cold forging was used to create heads for fasteners, currently many kinds of parts, even with complex shapes, can be produced by cold forging.

Experiments described in the paper are conducted in the manufacturing company which produces cold headed fasteners [1]. The experiments are performed on a typical one-die, two-punch coldformer machine. Two different punches (cone punch, 2-nd punch) are used, one after the other, to create a correct geometry of a fastener head. At first, a bulk of metal (wire) is automatically fed into the machine from a large coil. Next, a precise length of the wire is cut off by the machine's built-in cut-off knife. In the next phase, the first strike makes an initial shape of the head, then a shifting mechanism replaces the cone punch with the 2-nd punch. The second strike makes the final shape of the head. After the second strike, the piece is pushed out of the die.

The machine in the industrial testbed is equipped with one in-die piezoelectric force sensor, one cut-off knife binary sensor and the main engine state binary sensor. Significant disturbances in cold heading, i.e. any geometrical changes to the tooling, changes to the workpiece surface and dimensions, lubrication defects, etc., can be detected on the basis of force variations analysis [5] [6].

The exemplary piezoelectric sensor signal registered by the data acquisition system for production of one correct part is shown in Fig. 3.

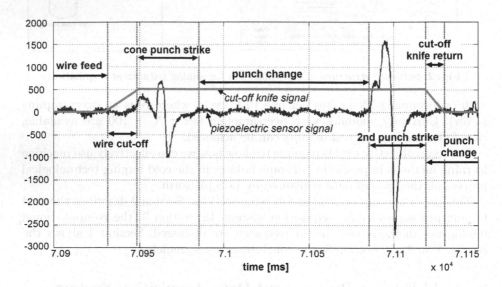

Fig. 3. Raw piezoelectric sensor signal for production of one correct part: force signal and cut-off knife scaled signal

During the experiments, data from the sensor are collected using IMS platform described in Section 1. A dedicated PAC controller and an analog input module with oversampling (EL3702) from Beckhoff [7] is used for piezoelectric sensor signal acquisition. PAC is responsible for signal acquisition and communication with the server application. Collected data are stored on the separate hard drive connected to the main server.

The sampling interval is configured to be as short as possible ($10\mu s$), taking into account computational power of PAC and oversampling feature of the analog input module.

Four different experiments are conducted in the testbed:

- correct part (new tools, quality control test passed),
- defective cone punch,
- defective 2-nd punch,
- no 2-nd punch.

The piezoelectric sensor signals patterns for the experiments are compared in Fig. 4.

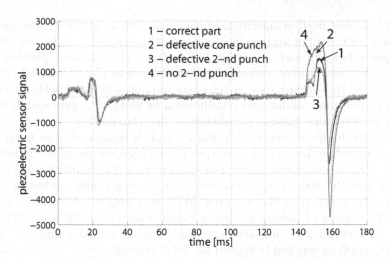

Fig. 4. The piezoelectric sensor signals patterns for the experiments: 1 – correct part, 2 – defective cone punch , 3 – defective 2-nd punch, 4 – no 2-nd punch

In the analog data acquisition system, the same model of PAC as in the IMS platform is applied. The system is integrated with the platform and has been collecting data constantly since June 2013. Currently, additional output of a typical industrial process monitoring device installed in the testbed is registered. The output signalizes an incorrect process run and can be used in the future to evaluate the correctness of the condition monitoring system integrated with the IMS platform.

3   Computational Intelligence Methods Used in the Study

In this research we use the following classification algorithms: single decision tree (SDT), probabilistic neural network (PNN), support vector machine (SVM), multilayer perceptron (MLP), linear discriminant analysis (LDA) and K–Means clustering (K–Means). All the models are well described in the literature, e.g. in [9]. Therefore, only the short description is here presented.

SDT is a data classifier and a decision model originally described in [10]. The algorithm of SDT searches for all possible variables and values in order to find the best split – the question that splits the data into two parts until some stopping criterion is satisfied. In this study, Gini algorithm is applied to split variables, maximum tree levels are set to 6.

PNN is a feedforward model proposed by Specht [11]. It is a direct implementation of Bayes classifier. The network is composed of four layers: an input layer, a pattern layer, a summation layer, and an output layer. The neurons in the pattern layer are activated by the radial basis transfer function which depends on the smoothing parameter (sigma). The appropriate choice of sigma influences the prediction ability of the model. We use single sigma for each attribute and class. The conjugate gradient method is applied to train PNN.

SVM is a classification algorithm which constructs an optimal separating hypersurface for the input vectors with associated class labels ± 1. The equation of this hypersurface is found by solving the quadratic programming problem. Two types of SVM algorithms are considered in this work: C-SVM model [12] and ν-SVM model [13]. In each case, radial basis and polynomial kernel functions are utilized to perform training and classification of SVM. The grid search is used in order to determine optimal parameters of this classifier.

MLP is the feedforward neural network [14]. It is composed of an input layer, a number of hidden layers and an output layer. The neurons in the hidden and output layer are activated by some transfer functions. The number of hidden layers along with the number of hidden neurons is an open problem which is usually solved experimentally. In this research, MLP with single hidden layer is simulated. The number of hidden neurons is taken from the set $\{2, 3, \ldots, 20\}$. Both hidden and output layer are activated using logistic transfer function. Scaled conjugate gradient method is applied for MLP training.

LDA is a statistical algorithm which classifies objects into mutually exclusive and exhaustive groups based on a set of object's features. It was originally developed by Fisher [15]. The algorithm finds a linear transformation (discriminant function) of the input variables that yields a new set of transformed values.

K–Means method (K–Means) is a clustering algorithm used to group records based on similarity of values for a set of input fields [16]. The basic idea is to try to discover k clusters, such that the records within each cluster are similar to each other and distinct from records in other clusters. The grouping process relies on the iterative minimization of the sum of squared distances computed between input data and the cluster center. In the experiments, k is taken from the interval $\{2, 3, \ldots, 200\}$.

4   Results

The classification is performed for 530 signals which belong to four classes listed in Section 2 and shown in Fig. 4. In particular, there are: 133 signals of class "correct part" (labeled henceforth as 1), 131 signals of class "defective cone punch" and "defective 2-nd punch" (labeled henceforth as 2 and 3, respectively) and 135 signals of class "no 2-nd punch" (labeled henceforth as 4).

Tables 1–6 show the classification results represented in form of accuracy (Acc), sensitivity (Spe) and specificity (Spe) computed using 10-fold cross validation procedure for SDT, PNN, SVM, MLP, LDA and K–Means algorithms. The results are shown for all 530 signals with:

(a) 256 attributes representing the values of measured force signal from the piezoelectric sensor in successive 256 discrete instances of time $\{1, 2, \ldots, 256\}$;
(b) 3 attributes extracted from the set $\{1, 2, \ldots, 256\}$ using the algorithm which determines the importance of variables;
(c) single attribute found after applying discrete Fourier transform to the input signals.

Thus, first two above analyses are performed in time domain (TD). The last one is determined in frequency domain (FD). In case of (a), all attributes are involved in the classification. In case (b), the computation of the importance of particular input variables from the set $\{1, 2, \ldots, 256\}$ is carried out by means of DTREG software [17] and analysis of sensitivity. As the result, the most important features are extracted which constitute the set $\{4, 48, 57\}$. In case (c), after Fourier transform, we observe single dominating peak in the power spectral density (PSD). Maximum value of PSD is chosen as the single predictor for classification as mentioned above.

Table 1. The accuracy, sensitivity and specificity determined by SDT in the classification of considered types of signals

Classes	256 attributes (TD)			3 attributes (TD)			1 attribute (FD)		
	Acc	Sen	Spe	Acc	Sen	Spe	Acc	Sen	Spe
1	97.36	94.74	98.24	98.30	96.24	98.99	93.40	91.73	93.95
2	97.92	94.66	99.00	98.87	99.24	98.75	95.85	92.37	96.99
3	99.06	96.95	99.75	99.43	98.47	99.75	96.98	92.37	98.50
4	96.98	96.30	97.22	98.87	97.04	99.49	96.04	88.15	98.73

Table 2. The accuracy, sensitivity and specificity determined by PNN in the classification of considered types of signals

Classes	256 attributes (TD)			3 attributes (TD)			1 attribute (FD)		
	Acc	Sen	Spe	Acc	Sen	Spe	Acc	Sen	Spe
1	95.85	93.23	96.73	99.06	98.50	99.24	96.04	92.48	97.23
2	97.55	93.13	99.00	99.06	98.47	99.25	94.91	92.37	95.74
3	97.17	89.31	99.75	99.62	99.24	99.75	97.17	93.13	98.50
4	93.21	91.85	93.67	99.25	97.78	99.75	95.66	89.63	97.72

Table 3. The accuracy, sensitivity and specificity determined by SVM in the classification of considered types of signals

Classes	256 attributes (TD)			3 attributes (TD)			1 attribute (FD)		
	Acc	Sen	Spe	Acc	Sen	Spe	Acc	Sen	Spe
1	98.68	96.24	99.50	98.87	97.74	99.24	95.85	85.71	99.24
2	99.25	98.47	99.50	99.06	98.47	99.25	93.96	96.95	92.98
3	99.06	96.95	99.75	99.25	97.71	99.75	96.60	93.13	97.74
4	97.74	97.78	97.72	98.68	97.78	98.99	96.60	90.37	98.73

Table 4. The accuracy, sensitivity and specificity determined by MLP in the classification of considered types of signals

Classes	256 attributes (TD)			3 attributes (TD)			1 attribute (FD)		
	Acc	Sen	Spe	Acc	Sen	Spe	Acc	Sen	Spe
1	97.17	96.99	97.23	97.74	96.99	97.98	96.04	85.71	99.50
2	98.68	97.71	99.00	98.68	97.71	99.00	93.96	98.47	92.48
3	98.49	94.66	99.75	98.87	96.95	99.50	96.79	93.13	97.99
4	97.36	94.07	98.48	97.92	94.81	98.99	96.98	90.37	99.24

Table 5. The accuracy, sensitivity and specificity determined by LDA in the classification of considered types of signals

Classes	256 attributes (TD)			3 attributes (TD)			1 attribute (FD)		
	Acc	Sen	Spe	Acc	Sen	Spe	Acc	Sen	Spe
1	97.74	96.24	98.24	97.36	99.25	96.73	95.28	85.71	98.49
2	97.36	95.42	97.99	98.11	94.66	99.25	93.21	95.42	92.48
3	98.11	95.42	99.00	98.87	96.95	99.50	97.17	93.13	98.50
4	97.36	94.07	98.48	98.11	94.07	99.49	96.60	90.37	98.73

Table 6. The accuracy, sensitivity and specificity determined by K–Means in the classification of considered types of signals

Classes	256 attributes (TD)			3 attributes (TD)			1 attribute (FD)		
	Acc	Sen	Spe	Acc	Sen	Spe	Acc	Sen	Spe
1	97.55	95.49	98.24	98.49	97.74	98.74	95.28	85.71	98.49
2	97.36	98.47	96.99	99.06	98.47	99.25	95.47	95.42	95.49
3	97.74	93.89	99.00	98.68	96.95	99.25	96.42	93.13	97.49
4	98.30	94.07	99.75	98.87	97.04	99.49	95.47	91.11	96.96

The results in Tables 1–6 can be summarized as follows:

In the classification of signals that consist of 256 attributes one can observe that:

- for the class 1: the highest *Acc* is found for SVM (98.68%), the highest *Sen* is determined for MLP (96.99%) and the highest *Spe* is computed for SVM (99.50%);
- for the class 2: the highest *Acc* is found for SVM (99.25%), the highest *Sen* is determined for SVM and K–Means (98.47%) and the highest *Spe* is computed for SVM (99.50%);

- for the class 3: the highest *Acc* is found for SDT and SVM (99.06%), the highest *Sen* is determined for SDT and SVM (96.95%) and the highest *Spe* is computed for SDT, PNN, SVM and MLP (99.75%);
- for the class 4: the highest *Acc* is found for K–Means (98.30%), the highest *Sen* is determined for SVM (97.78%) and the highest *Spe* is computed for K–Means (99.75%).

In the classification of signals that posses 3 features we notice that:

- for the class 1: the highest *Acc* is found for PNN (99.06%), the highest *Sen* is determined for LDA (99.25%) and the highest *Spe* is computed for PNN and SVM (99.24%);
- for the class 2: the highest *Acc* is found for PNN, SVM and K–Means (99.06%), the highest *Sen* is determined for SDT (99.24%) and the highest *Spe* is computed for PNN, SVM, LDA and K–Means (99.25%);
- for the class 3: the highest *Acc* is found for PNN (99.62%), the highest *Sen* is determined for PNN (99.24%) and the highest *Spe* is computed for SDT, PNN and SVM (99.75%);
- for the class 4: the highest *Acc* is found for PNN (99.25%), the highest *Sen* is determined for PNN and SVM (97.78%) and the highest *Spe* is computed for PNN (99.75%).

In the classification of signals that are composed of a single variable, it can be shown that:

- for the class 1: the highest *Acc* is found for PNN and MLP (96.04%), the highest *Sen* is determined for PNN (92.48%) and the highest *Spe* is computed for MLP (99.50%);
- for the class 2: the highest *Acc* is found for SDT (95.85%), the highest *Sen* is determined for MLP (98.47%) and the highest *Spe* is computed for SDT (96.99%);
- for the class 3: the highest *Acc* is found for PNN and LDA (97.17%), the highest *Sen* is determined for PNN, SVM, MLP, LDA and K–Means (93.13%) and the highest *Spe* is computed for SDT, PNN and LDA (98.50%);
- for the class 4: the highest *Acc* is found for MLP (96.98%), the highest *Sen* is determined for K–Means (91.11%) and the highest *Spe* is computed for MLP (99.24%).

5 Conclusions

In this article, we identified one correct (normal) and three defective states of the technological process for the production of cold headed fasteners. For this purpose, we applied six methods of computational intelligence. As shown, PNN and SVM were the classifiers which provided the best prediction ability determined by 10-fold cross validation. Namely, PNN achieved the highest accuracy, sensitivity and specificity six, four and six times, respectively. In case of SVM, the highest accuracy, sensitivity and specificity was obtained four, five and six times, respectively. The smallest number of best classification results was found for LDA, MLP and K–Means models.

Regardless the number of predictors, we used the same settings for all the algorithms. Therefore, the obtained results can be fairly compared. In case of SDT, PNN and K–Means, the reduction of original 256 attributes down to 3 features improved the prediction ability of these models. For the remaining algorithms (SVM, MLP and LDA), the improvement in the classification ability was not observed.

It is worth noting that the representation of the input parameters by means of the single feature in the frequency domain slightly decreased the prediction ability of the compared classifiers.

Due to limited space of the article, we only provided the results of a selected fragment of the technological process for the cold headed fasteners production, i.e. "2nd punch strike" period. For another fragment, called "cone punch strike", we obtained slightly worse results, namely, the values for the three considered indicators (Acc, Sen, Spe) were on average lower by about 4%. We believe that the results will help us to build an early warning system, that will be able to detect faults (classes 2, 3 and 4) on-line. Our studies show that in order to achieve this objective in the real-time system, the implementation of PNN or SVM algorithms is worth considering.

The results of the presented research will be used in the prediction of process failures in the production of thinwalled aircraft engine components.

Acknowledgements. This research was partially supported by the Grant INNO-TECH–K2/IN2/41/182370/NCBR/13 from the National Centre for Research and Development in Poland and by U–235/DS/2013.

References

1. Gaweł Zakład Produkcji Śrub, http://www.gzps.pl/
2. Mączka, T., Żabiński, T., Kluska, J.: Computational Intelligence application in fasteners manufacturing. In: Proceedings of 13th IEEE International Symposium on Computational Intelligence and Informatics (CINTI), Budapest, pp. 335–340 (2012)
3. Żabiński, T., Mączka, T.: Implementation of Human-System Interface for Manufacturing Organizations. In: Hippe, Z.S., Kulikowski, J.L., Mroczek, T. (eds.) Human – Computer Systems Interaction: Backgrounds and Applications 2. AISC, vol. 98, pp. 13–31. Springer, Heidelberg (2012)
4. Mączka, T., Żabiński, T.: Platform for Intelligent Manufacturing Systems with elements of knowledge discovery. In: Manufacturing System, pp. 183–204. InTech, Croatia (2012)
5. Kong, L.X., Nahavandi, S.: On-line tool condition monitoring and control system in forging process. Journal of Materials Processing Technology 125-126, 464–470 (2002)

6. Rolfe, B., Frayman, Y., Hodgson, P., Webb, G.I.: Fault Detection in a Cold Forging Process Through Feature Extraction with a Neural Network. In: Proceedings of the IASTED International Conference on Artificial Intelligence and Applications (AIA), Benalmdena, Spain, pp. 155–159 (2002)
7. Beckhoff Information System, http://infosys.beckhoff.com/
8. Carlo Salvi 332 DL machine (1 Die 2 Blow Headers), http://www.carlosalvi.it
9. Wu, X., Kumar, V., Quinlan, J.R., et al.: Top 10 algorithms in data mining. Knowledge Information Systems 14, 1–37 (2008)
10. Breiman, L., Friedman, J.H., Olshen, R.A., Stone, C.J.: Classification and regression trees. Wadsworth, Belmont (1984)
11. Specht, D.F.: Probabilistic neural networks. Neural Networks 3, 109–118 (1990)
12. Vapnik, V.: The Nature of Statistical Learning Theory. Springer, New York (1995)
13. Schölkopf, B., Smola, A.J., Williamson, R.C., Bartlett, P.L.: New support vector algorithms. Neural Computation 12, 1207–1245 (2000)
14. Rumelhart, D., McClelland, J.: Parallel Distributed Processing. MIT Press, Cambridge (1986)
15. Fisher, R.A.: The Use of Multiple Measurements in Taxonomic Problems. Annals of Eugenics 7(2), 179–188 (1936)
16. Hartigan, J.A., Wong, M.A.: A k-means clustering algorithm. Journal of the Royal Statistical Society - Series C (Applied Statistics) 1, 100–108 (1979)
17. Sherrod, P.H.: DTREG predictive modelling software, http://www.dtreg.com

Computer Vision, Image
and Speech Analysis

An Approach for Imperfection Propagation: Application to Land Cover Change Prediction

Amine Bouatay[1], Wadii Boulila[1,2], and Imed Riadh Farah[1,2]

[1] Laboratoire RIADI, Ecole Nationale des Sciences de l'Informatique
Campus Universitaire de la Manouba, 2010 la Manouba, Tunisie
[2] TELECOM-Bretagne, LaboratoireITI
Technopole Brest Iroise CS83818, 29238 Brest Cedex, France

Abstract. We propose an approach that propagates imperfection throughout a model of land cover change prediction. The proposed approach is based on Polynomial Collocation method. The proposed approach estimates the imperfection in the output of the prediction model from the imperfection in its inputs. It incorporates two steps:
1. Computing membership functions for input variables for the model of land cover change prediction, and
2. Propagating imperfections of input variables throughout this model and determining the effect of these imperfection in the model. A probabilistic collocation method is used to propagate imperfection.

Experimental results show the effectiveness of the proposed approach in improving both computation time and prediction of the land cover change of the Saint-Denis region, Reunion Island.

Keywords: imperfection propagation, land cover change prediction, probabilistic collocation method, satellite images, membership functions.

1 Introduction

Predicting land cover change provides an important knowledge that is useful for decision management. However, this prediction is often marred by several types of imperfections that affect the accuracy of decisions. In literature, most works attempt to resolve this problem. These works disregard the imperfection related to the input of their models and its propagation through their models. To bridge this research gap, we propose a methodology that propagates imperfection throughout the model of land cover change prediction. We are interested in random imperfections. A probabilistic collocation method is used to propagate imperfection as it is a computationally efficient method for performing imperfection propagation on large complex models. A comparison with the traditional Monte Carlo simulation showed good performances of the proposed approach.

2 Related Works

In the current paper, we focus in studying probabilistic uncertainty propagation methods. Probabilistic methods have the advantage of being simple to represent.

L. Rutkowski et al. (Eds.): ICAISC 2014, Part I, LNAI 8467, pp. 637–648, 2014.
© Springer International Publishing Switzerland 2014

They have no restrictions on incoming attributes. The probability distribution functions defining their attributes are assumed to be known.

Among probabilistic methods, we can list Monte Carlo method (MC). It is a very common statistical and probabilistic method for propagating uncertainty. It is based on calculating a large number of times. However, MC has two problems: the computation time and complexity. In literature, many methods have been developed to reduce the computational effort.

Another probabilistic method is Galerkin Polynomial Chaos method (GPC) [5][2]. It is an intrusive uncertainty propagation method. Intrusive means that the uncertainty propagation method requires modifying model in which uncertainty propagation method will be applied.

Non-intrusive polynomial chaos methods (NIPCM) are proposed to overcome the model modification problem as presented in [6] [13][16]. These methods use model as a black-box. Both GPC and NIPCM methods use sampling to estimate coefficients of the polynomial chaos expansion.

3   Proposed Approach

Figure 1 describes the proposed approach to propagate imperfection through the model of land cover change prediction. The first step consists of estimating the probability distribution of input parameters. Then, these distribution are propagated through a model of land cover change prediction presented in [2].

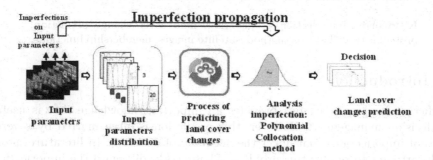

Fig. 1. The proposed approach to study the propagation of imperfection throughout the land cover change prediction model with collocation method

3.1   Review of the Module for Land Cover Change Prediction

In previous works [2],[3],[4], we presented an approach to predict land cover change. In order to better understand the process of land cover change prediction, let suppose that an object is extracted from a satellite image acquired at a date t using previous work [4].This object can be a lake, vegetation zone, urban area, etc. Five features are considered for this object which are: the radiometry, geometry, texture, spatial relations, and acquisition context. Each feature is described through a set of attributes $Ai(1 < i < N)$. We note by a state the set of attribute values computed for the object at a given date.

The prediction process is divided into the three main steps. It starts by a similarity measurement step to find similar states (in the object database) to a query state (representing the query object at a given date). The second step is composed by three sub-steps: (1) finding the corresponding model for the state, (2) finding all forthcoming states in the model (states having dates superior to the date of the retrieved state), and (3) for each forthcoming date, build the spatiotemporal change tree for the retrieved state. The third step is to construct the spatiotemporal change for the query state. Interested readers can refer to [2],[3].

The module for the prediction of land cover changes allows taking into account imperfection related to the prediction process. However, the propagation of the input imperfection through this module is not considered.

3.2   Probabilistic Collocation Method (PCM)

The analysis proceeds through the steps as presented in [11],[8]. In our case, the model to be analyzed has 20 parameters. The steps of the collocation approach are illustrated in Figure 2. First, the parameters must be identified and their distribution of uncertainty must be determined. The determination of the distribution may either be based on the designer's experience, or be based on statistical data. Second, the orthogonal polynomials distributions determined for the previous step must be derived. If the approximation of the response of the model should be of the order p, orthogonal polynomials up to order p+1 must be determined. Third, a polynomial expression is generated to represent the performance or output variable based on orthogonal polynomials of random variables $(\xi_{i_1}, .., \xi_{i_p})$.

This is called the extension of polynomial chaos. Since the model is a black box, we can use a linear approximation in the first estimate.

$$Y' = y_0 + \sum_{i_1=1}^{n} y_1 \Gamma_1(\xi_{i_1}) + \sum_{i_1=1}^{n} \sum_{i_2=1}^{i_1} y_2 \Gamma_2(\xi_{i_1}, \xi_{i_2}) +$$

$$\sum_{i_1=1}^{n} \sum_{i_2=1}^{i_1} \sum_{i_3=1}^{i_2} y_3 \Gamma_3(\xi_{i_1}, \xi_{i_2}, \xi_{i_3}) +$$

$$\sum_{i_1=1}^{n} \sum_{i_2=1}^{i_1} \sum_{i_3=1}^{i_2} \sum_{i_4=1}^{i_3} y_4 \Gamma_4(\xi_{i_1}, \xi_{i_2}, \xi_{i_3}, \xi_{i_4}) + ... \tag{1}$$

Where y_i are deterministic coefficients to be estimated, the $\Gamma p(\xi_{i_1}, .., \xi_{i_p})$ denote the multidimensional Hermite polynomials of degree p, and $\xi = (\xi_{i_1}, .., \xi_{i_p})$ is the set of random variables associated with reduced centered Gaussian variables that are used to represent input uncertainty.

The random inputs and outputs are approximated by the PC expansions. These expansions contain unknown coefficients of the outputs which are calculated by solving a linear system of equations that uses a selected number of

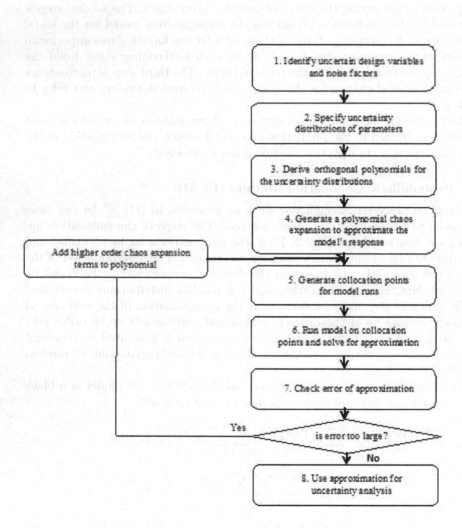

Fig. 2. Diagram of the polynomial collocation method to study the propagation of imperfection throughout the land cover change prediction model proposed by [14]

collocations points. For a problem with n random variables, the total number of deterministic solutions required is:

$$T = \frac{(p+n)!}{p!n!} \tag{2}$$

where p is the PC order.

For example: if n=2 and p=2 then T=6, so:

$$Y' = y_0 + y_1 \Gamma_1(\xi_1) + y_2 \Gamma_1(\xi_2) + y_3 \Gamma_2(\xi_1,\xi_1) + y_4 \Gamma_2(\xi_1,\xi_2) + y_5 \Gamma_2(\xi_2,\xi_2) \tag{3}$$

Collocation points can be selected from a number of methods. In this study, the roots of the higher order polynomials were chosen as collocation points. The roots of orthogonal polynomials are always real and distinct, and always lie in the interval of support of the distribution.

Specifically, the N+1 roots of the $(N+1)^{th}$ order polynomial corresponding to each parameter y_k are used to define the collocation points. Because these roots help to define the high probability region of each input parameter, we obtain an approximation of Y that is particularly good within the most probable range of values of the input parameters. Moreover, the roots of the $(N+2)^{th}$ order polynomials are used to define another set of collocation points that can be used to estimate the error of the approximation which, again, takes account of the actual probability distribution of the parameters.

After, we run the model for each of the input sets, and we have as a result the corresponding y_i. Then, by replacing each ξ_i, in the approximation of the approximation, we can solve the three simultaneous equations for the unknowns: $y_0, y_1, y_2, y_3, \ldots$.

Before using the approximation, we need to check the error. We need to test the quality of the adjustment. For this, a little more executions of simulations are needed, and we compare the model results with the results of approximation. We need more collocation points. In this work, we use the method of [14]. These points are obtained from the next orders of the orthogonal polynomial, because if the errors are too large, and we need a higher order approximation, we already have the solutions of the model and we need to solve the approximation.

For each of these sets of input, we solve the real model Y through the approximation of Y_i^p. Then, the error term for each e_{App} is calculated as follows:

$$e_{App} = \frac{\sqrt{\frac{1}{T}| \sum_{i=1}^{T} (Y_i^{p+1} - Y_i^p)|}}{\frac{1}{T} \sum_{i=1}^{T} Y_i^p} \tag{4}$$

Where T is the number of terms in the approximation Y_i^P, equivalent to the number of collocation points. $Y_i^{(P+1)}$ is the value of Y for collocation points for a $(p+1)^{th}$ polynomial order approximation. Y_i^P is the value of Y at the collocation points for a for a $(p+1)^{th}$ polynomial order approximation using a pth polynomial order approximation.

Since the error is large, we have to add higher order terms to try to get a better approximation. Then we need to check the error for this approximation. We repeat this step and steps 4, 5 and 6 until you find a good approximation.

Once we found a pretty good approximation, we can use it in the prediction of land cover changes. Such a complex model can be reasonably approximated by a simple polynomial.

4   Experimental Results

Experiments are made on the Saint-Denis region capital of the Reunion Island. The region is located in the north-eastern in the Indian Ocean, east of Madagascar.

Figure 3 depicts a satellite image acquired on June 18, 2008. This image is conducted on SPOT5 satellite images and belong to the Kalideos[1] database set up by the CNES[2] .

Fig. 3. Satellite image acquired on June 18, 2008

4.1   Validation of the Proposed Approach

In the current study, we are concerned by predicting urban changes. Let us consider that an urban object is extracted after a segmentation of the image in Figure 3 using previous work [4]. 20 attributes $A_{i(i=1..20)}$ are considered to describe the urban object work [4]. These attributes represent the input of the proposed approach.

The first step in the proposed methodology is to estimate the membership function for the urban attributes. These attributes are random attributes and they can bere presented by probability distributions. Next, we derive a set of orthogonal polynomials for each of these distributions.

In the proposed approach, urban attributes are represented by a normal distribution $N(\mu, \sigma)$ with a mean of μ, and a standard deviation of σ. The Hermite

---

[1] http://kalideos.cnes.fr

[2] *Centre National d'Etudes Spatiales.*

polynomials are a set of polynomials which are orthogonal to the standard normal distribution. This allows using the same set of orthogonal polynomials for all Gaussian distributions, instead of deriving the orthogonal polynomials for each specific distribution.

Collocation points are selected from the roots of orthogonal polynomials of next higher order for each uncertain parameter.In the current example, we need 21 collocation points. The goal is to find a good approximation in these point with the smallest number of simulations. Collocation points are selected from the roots of orthogonal polynomials of next higher order (n +1) for each uncertain parameter, as mentioned in [14] and [7]. We run the model for each collocation point for the approximation of Y at the order p and p+1. The approximation can be used only when the values between the two orders p and p+1 are below a certain threshold.

In our case, 1*st* order, 2*nd* order and 3*rd* order PCM models were evaluated. An error of 47.5% is found for the first order. In order to reduce this error, we pass to the second and third orders.

Figure 4.a describes the reduction of the approximation error by increasing the order of the polynomial chaos approximation. Figure 4.b shows the reduction of the error rate by increasing the polynomial order. By observing the two curves in Figure 3, we can choose the order 3 as an approximation order for our polynomial.

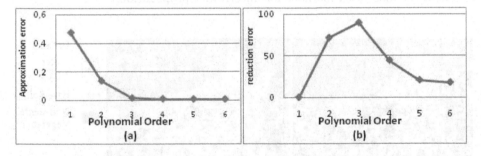

Fig. 4. Approximation error variation (a) and the global error reduction (b) according to the polynomial order

Figure 5 shows that for the propagation of imperfection based chaos polynomial improves the calculated prediction rate. The average rate of predicting changes for the urban area passes from 70.76% to 71.01% to 71.07% respectively when the polynomial order passes from order 1 to order 2 and then to order 3.

After identifying the order of the PCM (in our case the order is 3), we return to the probability distributions for the input parameters. Then, we determine the optimal values of these parameters corresponding to the order 3. These values are finally incorporated into the model presented in [2].

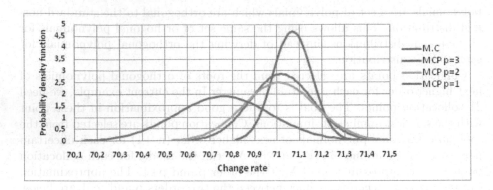

Fig. 5. Comparison of MC results and MCP with an order equal to 1, 2 and 3

4.2   Evaluation of the Proposed Approach

In order to evaluate the proposed approach in improving land cover change prediction, we apply the proposed propagation method and the Monte Carlo method to the prediction model presented in [2]. Then, we compare the proposed prediction changes to the MC ones. In literature, Monte Carlo method is considered as one of the most used methods for uncertainty propagation.

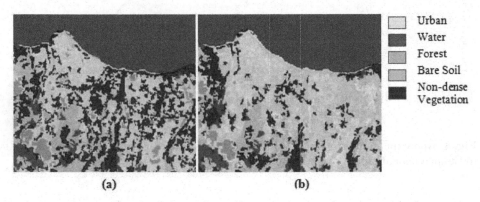

(a)   (b)

Fig. 6. Land cover change prediction for obtained by the approach of collocation (a) and Monte Carlo (b) for the date 2012

Figure 6 depicts the prediction images at the date 2012 obtained after the application of the proposed approach (Fig. 6.a) and Monte Carlo method (Fig. 6.b). In the current example, we use MCP with an order equal to 3. Prediction changes between MCP and MC are compared according to an image presenting the same region and acquired at the date 2012.

Table 1 depicts the error calculated between proposed and real urban changes. As we note, when applying the two approaches to the prediction model presented

Table 1. Error for the prediction of urban changes between MCP with an order equal to 3 and MC between 2008 and 2012

Approach	Prediction change rate
Monte Carlo Approach	0.79
Proposed Approach	0.72

in [2], the proposed approach provides a better results than the MC method in predicting urban changes. This shows the effectiveness of our approach and its performance in reducing the imperfection related to the prediction process.

Table 2 illustrates the percentage of change of the five objects (forest, water, bare soil, non-dense vegetation and urban). Land cover changes between 2008 and 2012 are computed for the method presented in [2] (model without applying the imperfection propagation process), the MC and MCP with an order equal to 3 and compared to real changes. Results show that applying an imperfection propagation process to the land cover change model improves the prediction results. It helps reducing the influence of the propagation of imperfection throughout the prediction model.

Table 2. Comparison of percentage changes between 2008 and 2012 for the [2] method, collocation approach and Monte Carlo approach

	Forest	Water	Bare soil	Non dense vegetation	Urban
Method proposed by [2]	69.80%	2.89%	66.43%	31.71%	40.15%
Monte Carlo approach	71.02%	3.42%	65.45%	32.98%	41.52%
MCP with an order=3	71.07%	3.52%	65.39%	33.25%	41.65%
Real	71.09%	3.61%	65.31%	33.80%	41.74%

In order to better evaluate performances of the polynomial collocation method, 20 experiments are performed. Twenty different periods are considered. Predicted land cover changes for these 20 periods are estimated through the proposed approach. Then, real urban changes are evaluated based on images representing the same dates in each period.

The Table 3, we note that of the 20 areas studied we have good results compared to the Monte Carlo approach. Indeed, the proposed approach results are better in improving land cover changes for 14 regions.

In addition to the improvement of the land cover changes prediction, we decide to evaluate the performance of the proposed approach in term of processing time

Table 3. Error prediction land cover changes for the proposed approach and the Monte Carlo approach for 20 period tests

	R1	R2	R3	R4	R5	R6	R7	R8	R9	R10
M.C	0,36	0,344	0,386	0,268	0,305	0,381	0,407	0,372	0,295	0,345
P.C.M	0,351	0,312	0,368	0,273	0,291	0,369	0,401	0,36	0,311	0,34

	R11	R12	R13	R14	R15	R16	R17	R18	R19	R20
M.C	0,352	0,395	0,421	0,412	0,329	0,412	0,457	0,343	0,361	0,392
P.C.M	0,354	0,389	0,422	0,409	0,334	0,375	0,426	0,331	0,329	0,385

Table 4. Comparison of computation time between the approaches: Monte Carlo and collocation method

Approach	Poly. Order	N.Total work	Total time work
Collocation method	1	27	54sec
without sensitivity	2	378	756=12min 36sec
analysis	3	3654	7308=2h 1min 48sec
N=20	4	27405	15h 13min
	5	169911	94h 23min
Monte Carlo	-	10000	20000 = 6h 15min
method	-	100000	200000= 55h33min

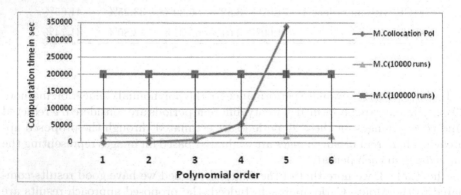

Fig. 7. Convergence of computing time for three methods: Monte Carlo and Polynomial Collocation method

Table 4 provides a comparison of computation time for two methods: Monte Carlo approach and collocation approach (the proposed approach). The calculations are performed on a Dell i7- 2670QM (2.2 GHz 6MB cache and 6GB of RAM).In Figure 7, we plotted the evolution of the computation time of the three methods tested according to the order of the polynomial chaos expansion. As we note, applying the MCP with an order less than 4 gives better computation time than the MC method.

5   Conclusion

This paper presents a methodology for propagating imperfection throughout a model for land cover change prediction. An approach based on Polynomial Collocation method is presented.

The proposed approach is based on computing membership functions for input features for a given land cover type. Then, these membership functions are propagated through the land cover prediction model.

Our approach was compared on efficiency to Monte Carlo's simulation. The comparison depicts that the proposed approach helps reducing the effect of imperfection related to the model of land cover change prediction. This allows obtaining more reliable decisions about prediction changes.

A big advantage of the PCM is that it is non-intrusive, which means that the existing deterministic solvers can be used. It reduces the number of operations and the computing time.

However, the number of variables is a major problem for PCM method. When this number increases the application of the method becomes more difficult. This problem will be will also be addressed in future studies.

References

[1] Babuska, I., Nobile, F., Tempone, R.: A stochastic collocation method for elliptic partial differential equations with random input data. SIAM Journal on Numerical Analysis 123(1), 1005–1034 (2007)

[2] Boulila, W., Farah, I.R., Ettabaa, K.S., Solaiman, B., Ben Ghézala, H.: A data mining based approach to predict Spatio-temporal changes in satellite images. International Journal of Applied Earth 13(3), 386–395 (2011)

[3] Boulila, W., Farah, I.R., Ettabaa, K.S., Solaiman, B.: Combining decision fusion and uncertainty propagation to improve land cover change prediction insatellite image databases. Journal of Multimedia Processing and Technologies 2(3), 127–139 (2011)

[4] Boulila, W., Farah, I.R.: S.Ettabaa K., Solaiman B., Ben Ghézala H.: Spatiotemporal modeling for knowledge discovery in satellite image databases. In: CORIA 2010: Conference en Recherche d'Information et Applications, Sousse, pp. 35–49 (2010)

[5] Ghanem, R.G., Spanos, P.D.: Stochastic Finite Elements: A Spectral Approach. Springer (1991)

[6] Hosder, S., Walters, R.W., Perez, R.: A non-intrusive polynomial chaos method for uncertainty propagation in CFD simulations. In: Proceedings of the 44th AIAA Aerospace Sciences Meeting, vol. 14, pp. 10649–10667 (2006)

[7] Isukapalli, S.S.: Uncertainty Analysis of Transport-Transformation Models. PhD Thesis, The State University of New Jersey (1999)

[8] Knopp, J.S., Blodgett, M.P., Cherry, M.R.: Probabilistic collocation method for NDE problems with uncertain parameters with arbitrary distributions, Air Force Research Laboratory Materials and Manufacturing Directorate,Wright-Patterson Air Force Base, Air Force Materiel Command, United States Air Force (2011)

[9] Loeven, G.J.A., Witteveen, J.A.S., Bijlz, H.: Probabilistic Collocation: An Efficient Non- Intrusive Approach For Arbitrarily Distributed Parametric Uncertainties. In: 45th AIAA Aerospace Sciences Meeting and Exhibit, Reno, Nevad, January 8-11 (2007)

[10] Matteoli, S., Veracini, T., Diani, M., Corsini, G.: Models and Methods forAutomated Background Density in Hyperspectral Anomaly Detection. IEEE Transactions on Geosciences and Remote Sensing 51(5), 2837–2852 (2013)

[11] Tatang, M., Pan, W., Prinn, R., McRae, G.: An efficient method for parametric uncertainty analysis of numerical geophysical models. J. Geophys. 102(18), 21925–21932 (1997)

[12] Walter, L., Randeu, M., Kozu, T., Shimomai, T., Schönhuber, M., Hashiguchi, H.: Estimation of raindrop size distribution parameters by maximum likelihood and L-moment methods: Effect of discretization. Atmospheric Research 112, 1–11 (2012)

[13] Walters, R.W., Huyse, L.: Stochastic methods for fluid mechanics - an introduction.Technical Report in preparation, ICASE, NASA Langley Research Center, Hampton, VA (2001)

[14] Webster, M., Tatang, M.A., McRae, G.J.: Application of the Probabilistic Collocation Method for an Uncertainty Analysis of a simple Ocean Model, MIT Joint Program on the Science and Policy of Global Change, Cambridge, Ma (1996)

[15] Webster, M., Calbo, J., Pan, W., Prinn, R.G., McRae, G.J.: Parameterization of urban sub-grid scale processes in global atmospheric chemistry models (1997)

[16] Wiener, N.: The homogeneous chaos. American Journal of Mathematics 60(13), 897–936 (1938)

[17] Xiu, D., Karniadakis, G.E.: The Wiener-Askey polynomial chaos for stochastic differential equations. SIAM J. Sci. Comput. 24(2), 619–644 (2002)

Large-Scale Region-Based Multimedia Retrieval
for Solar Images

Juan M. Banda and Rafal A. Angryk

Montana State University, Georgia State University, USA
juan.banda@cs.montana.edu, angryk@gsu.edu

Abstract. In this paper we present an extensive analysis into our task of
expanding our Solar Dynamics Observatory (SDO) content-based image-
retrieval (CBIR) system query capabilities with region-based search features. In this first-of-its-kind functionality, for solar physics, we will be
taking advantage of pre-computed image descriptors in order to generate region-based histogram-like signatures from our training set of previously identified solar events. With these signatures we then retrieve
new similar solar events solely based on these scale and rotation invariant signatures. In this paper we present our proposed methodology and
our extensive experimental setup with retrieval results. Our multimedia
retrieval mechanism will be extensively tested with multiple variants of
our signatures, multiple similarity measures, and finally validated using
classification algorithms.

Keywords: Multimedia Indexing and Retrieval, Content-based
Retrieval.

1 Introduction

With over 70,000 solar images being sent to Earth on a daily basis by NASAs
Solar Dynamics Observatory (SDO) mission, most traditional solar image analysis techniques have been rendered obsolete. This is evidence that solar physics
has now entered a new era of big data mining [1]. While individual systems have
been developed for the SDO mission to help identify particular solar events
(flares, filaments, sigmoids, active regions, etc.) as indicated in [2], our approach has been to develop a more generalized event finding system capable
of finding multiple events at once using data mining techniques. Reaching a
milestone, called the SDO Content-Based Image Retrieval (CBIR) system, we
have utilized machine learning and information retrieval methodologies to provide an all-purpose tool capable of identifying solar events solely on their visual
characteristics [3–7]. A currently working version of said system is available at
http://cbsir.cs.montana.edu/sdocbir.

The most critical limitation of our current system is that it searches for similar
images in a full-disk manner (entire image as the query). With our methodology
initially introduced in [8], we have proceeded to expand the querying capabilities
to integrate region-of-interest based querying (outlined in Figure 1) to provide

L. Rutkowski et al. (Eds.): ICAISC 2014, Part I, LNAI 8467, pp. 649–661, 2014.

solar physics researchers with a highly-refined search of particular regions of interest in solar images. In order to develop our approach, we will use pre-existing solar event labels taken from the Heliophysics Event Knowledgebase (HEK) (and its respective Feature Finding Team (FFT) modules) to build standard image signatures for each identified solar event. Our image signatures are scale-and-rotation invariant in order to allow us to query the extensive SDO dataset, and other solar datasets, using images or image segments of any size, type, and resolution covering any location on the sun.

The overall organization of this paper is as follows: after some background information (Section 2), we will introduce our dataset (Section 3) and provide a detailed outline of our methodology (Section 4). In Section 5 we present our multiple experimental scenarios with results and some discussion. Finally, in Section 6 we will highlight our general conclusions and the best performing experiments, and in Section 7 we conclude the paper with an outline of our future work.

2   Background

Massive image repositories are becoming more readily available for science applications as new technology and instruments evolve. One of the main issues of such large image repositories is to be able to query them in an effective manner. Most widely-used image search engines rely on comparing meta-data or textual tags associated with the images [9]. Through the years, a number of content-based image retrieval (CBIR) systems have facilitated these general purpose querying tasks. Some systems, as Photobook [10] from MIT, allow users to retrieve images based on several different image features by reducing said images to a smaller set of perceptually relevant coefficients and then computing basic similarities between them. Other available software systems are based on low-level image features, such as Candid [11], Chabot [12] and QBIC [13] from IBM. These systems rely on features such as shape, color, or texture in a complete-image manner, not particular areas of interest. Only Blobworld [14], developed by University of California - Berkeley, is an example of a system based on finding coherent image regions that are related to objects.

In our previous work, we have presented our steps into discovering image parameters and segmenting strategies that work for solar image data [4], and we have analyzed dissimilarity measures [7] and dimensionality reduction strategies to reduce numerosity for our solar data [3]. We then have tested multiple indexing and retrieval mechanisms in order to create a working solar image CBIR system. During our work we have released a framework to create general-purpose CBIR systems [15] to facilitate this task for other researchers. This paper presents our work into expanding said system capabilities to include region-based querying, a task that is not as usual (but much needed) for CBIR systems. In the following sections we present our signature image description generation and multiple experimental evaluations to fulfill this ambitious objective. For a more descriptive state-of-the-art and solar image analysis perspective, please visit our previous work [3-8].

The general standard practice in solar physics was to rely on experts to hand-label images - a task that is unfeasible now. Thus, this implies the need for an automated system that allows researchers to perform this analysis in a scalable and more feasible way. In the literature, histogram based query methods are often utilized to facilitate the feature comparison among pixels (and descriptors) in the region of interest. Our approach is motivated by the interrelation among pixels in particular regions of interest. The benefits of our approach is that the descriptors generated are invariant under rotation, translation and scaling, thus allowing us to compare against regions of interest from different format images and images scaled to bigger or smaller sizes, particularly useful for researchers using solar event images from other solar missions.

3 Dataset

In this paper, we utilized solar images from the Atmospheric Imaging Assembly (AIA) module of the SDO mission. This AIA module captures eight high-resolution (4096-by-4096 pixels) images every 10 seconds (more information on this can be found at [2, 16]). Using the work of Schuh et al. [17], our SDO test dataset was constructed. This dataset spans a six-month period of data containing around 15,000 images in two wavebands that feature 24,000 event instances of six different event types, which are listed in Table 1.

Table 1. Dataset Events and Labels

Label	Event Type
AR	Active Region
CH	Coronal Hole
FL	Flare
SG	Sigmoid

In the next section we will describe the image parameter extraction from the SDO dataset images in detail. These parameters will be used to construct our descriptor signatures for retrieval.

4 Methodology

4.1 Feature Extraction

Our image data from Section 3 is presented in a pre-processed form and then each image is segmented into a 64-by-64 grid of cells. Then ten image parameters are extracted from each cell. In the work performed by Banda and Angryk [4, 5], many possible parameters were tested for solar images based on factors such as computational expense and classification accuracy, but it was observed that only the ten parameters selected were sufficient for the task. The ten image parameters that we chose to use for characterization of solar images are: entropy, fractal dimension, the mean intensity, the third and fourth moments, relative smoothness, the standard deviation of the intensity, Tamura contrast, Tamura directionality and uniformity. These image parameters and corresponding formulas are listed in Table 2.

Table 2. Image Parameters Used

Label	Image Parameter	Formula
P1	Entropy	$E = -\sum\limits_{i=0}^{L-1} p(z_i) \log_2 p(z_i)$
P2	Fractal Dimension	$D_0 = \lim\limits_{\epsilon \to 0} \frac{logN(\epsilon)}{log\frac{1}{\epsilon}}$
P3	Mean	$m = \frac{1}{K} \sum\limits_{j=1}^{K} z_j$
P4	3rd Moment (Skewness)	$\mu_3 = \sum\limits_{i=0}^{L-1} (z_i - m)^3 p(z_i)$
P5	4th Moment (Kurtosis)	$\mu_4 = \sum\limits_{i=0}^{L-1} (z_i - m)^4 p(z_i)$
P6	Relative Smoothness	$R = 1 - \frac{1}{1+\sigma^2}$
P7	Standard Deviation	$\sigma = \sqrt{\frac{1}{k} \sum\limits_{j=1}^{k} (z_j - m)^2}$
P8	Tamura Contrast	*Tamura, Mori and Yamawaki [18]
P9	Tamura Directionality	*Tamura, Mori and Yamawaki [18]
P10	Uniformity	$U = \sum\limits_{i=0}^{L-1} p^2(z_i)$

z represents an image cell, z_i is the i-th gray level, m is the mean, $p(z_i)$ denotes the gray scale histogram of the i-th gray level in the cell. z_j is the value of each pixel of the image, and j will go up to K where K is the number of pixels.

Please take into consideration that we selected each event and wavelength based on what the current SDO Feature Finding Team (FFT) modules use to identify the particular events as indicated in [2]. We selected these four different types of events reported on AIA data for which the FFT modules provide boundary outlines (chain codes) for them. With our configuration, we are now able to build a training set of properly identified regions of interest for our selected the images.

4.2   Descriptor Generation

Considered as the critical step in this work, our region-based retrieval is built on the descriptor signatures. Said signature generation utilizes pre-existing solar event label reported by FFT modules matched to the images in dataset [17]. This allows our descriptor signature to be represented by a histogram-like structure with ten bins (for the basic case), one for each extracted image parameter based on the average value of the image cells contained within said events boundary. We describe this signature calculation procedure in Algorithm 1 (as previously published in [8]. In our procedure we match each event to its corresponding cells in our grid and then normalize the values of each parameter, on each selected cell, with respect to the whole training dataset. We finally average the values of all cells of the same parameter type creating a histogram bin for each averaged value. Immediately after each descriptor signature is calculated, we will have one ten-dimensional (for the general case) descriptor signature representing every reported event. With this step we achieve considerable dimensionality reduction when compared to our previous approaches, were we had over 40 thousand dimensions as we compared whole images against each other as described in [3].

Algorithm 1. *Steps for calculating descriptor signatures*

1: Calculate the maximum $Max(P_i)$ and minimum value $Min(P_i)$ of each of the 10 parameters, for all cells in the dataset. Where P_i is the i-th image parameter value.
2: Match the boundary outline of each event to the corresponding image cells. For each cell, find the parameter values.
3: Min-Max normalize each parameter value using: $P_i = \frac{P_i - Min(P_i)}{Max(P_i) - Min(P_i)}$
4: Take the average of each parameter and use it as a bin, in a histogram representing a given event.

4.3   Distance Measures

In order to match similar region-based solar events, we are going to compare the descriptor signatures in a pair-wise manner. These sorted results will be the nearest neighbor's lists for each event we analyze. In order to provide a comprehensive analysis of different distance measures and how they would affect our retrieval results, we selected 13 different measures. These distance measures used to compare signatures are critical for a comprehensive query retrieval analysis. For example, the cosine distance measures similarity based on the cosine of the angle between two vectors, while the Euclidean distance calculates the pair-wise distance between two elements. We have kept our list considerably reasonable since we do not want to add too much computational costs or any factor that would considerably slowdown our retrieval. Each of the measures selected are widely used in other content-based image analyses as we can see in [6, 19, 20]. Each measure used is listed in Table 3, for the particular formula or a more complete explanation of each measure we refer the reader to [7].

4.4   Retrieval Evaluation

In order to provide a clear and concise explanation on how we evaluate retrieval precision, we present Algorithm 2.

Table 3. Distance Measures

Label	Distance Name
D1	Euclidean
D2	Standarized Euclidean
D3	Mahalanobis
D4	City Block
D5	Chebychev
D6	Cosine
D7	Correlation
D8	Spearman
D9	Hausdorff
D10	Jensen-Shannon divergence (JSD)
D11	χ^2 Distance
D12	Kullback-Leibler divergence (KLD) A-B
D13	Kullback-Leibler divergence (KLD) B-A

In Euclidean distance x_s and x_t are the values of histogram bins. In cosine distance, the cosine of the angle between histogram bins x_s and x_t is calculated. In the rest of measures, A and B are a pair of histograms.

Algorithm 2. *Retrieval precision calculation*

1: Let E_i be the number of instances for the ith event type.
2: Calculate the top E_i nearest-neighbors of each event.
3: Determine how many of them are of the ith event type, called true positives (TP).
4: Divide TP over E_i and multiply by 100. This results in the final accuracy percentage for that particular event.

In all our experiments we calculated all possible nearest neighbors for each event in the dataset and calculated the retrieval precision using these numbers. We theorize that if we adjust the number of nearest neighbors extracted, we could increase our accuracy results this is something we will explore in the future and is not part of the scope of this paper.

4.5   Validation Through Classification

In order to present our classification analysis, we used the WEKA data mining package. Using this package we selected three of the most popular classification algorithms: Naive Bayes, Random Forest, and Support Vector Machines (SVM). These selected classifiers have been shown to produce solid results for solar data in the past [4–6]. Naive Bayes and SVM (linear kernel) are our linear classifiers and to provide a broader scope, we also selected our decision tree-based classifier: Random Forest, which is very fast to train and highly effective for numerical data. The SVM classifier, while expensive to train, is one of the most popular in the literature due to its typically better performance than the rest. All classification experiments have been run five times using 10-fold cross validation, we presented the averaged results.

5   Experiments and Results

5.1   Base-line Results

In this section we will present our initial base-line results for our three classification algorithms and our retrieval scenario. These results are intended to be used as a baseline comparison since most of the changes and different scenarios tested in the following sections are designed to improve upon them and/or aggregate some of them. Please note the classification results are presented to validate our retrieval experiments and not much time went into improving them by fine-tuning the individual classifier options.

As we can see in Figure 1, we are performing adequately in finding the multiple solar events on our dataset, with over 70% on average for at least 3 different events. This Figure also shows how comparable our retrieval methodology is to a classification environment, allowing us to use our retrieval mechanism with the confidence that is performing up to par with more advanced and costlier classification algorithms that required labeled data to be trained.

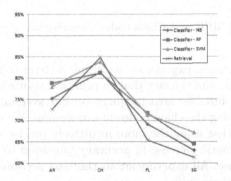

Fig. 1. Baseline classification accuracy and retrieval precision results for our Solar dataset

5.2   Bounding Boxes Versus Chain-Codes

Our dataset includes two different types of labels: Maximal Bounding Boxes (MBR) and chain-codes. MBRs provide a rectangular area that fully encompasses the solar event (Figure 2a). A chain-code will provide a pixel outline of the exact solar event area as reported by the HEK (Figure 2b). While intuitively chain-codes should provide the better (and more precise) area of interest, we present Figure 2 as a comparison between the two labeling methods.

As it is shown in Figure 3, the difference between MBR and Chain Codes, in terms of classification accuracy and retrieval precision is less than one percent.

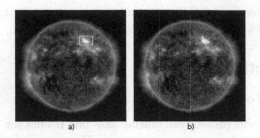

Fig. 2. Solar image with an MBR defined on a), and a chain-code on b)

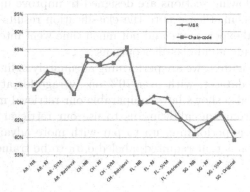

Fig. 3. Comparison of MBR and Chain-codes Classification Accuracy and Retrieval Precision

If we add the computation expense of matching a chain code to a set of corresponding image labels, and the fact that in practical terms the user will be able to select a bounding-box like area to query on our system, we have validated our decision of not using the chain codes in our system. We did not find enough evidence to support that using the more intuitively precise chain codes will actually provide a dramatic increase in accuracy/precision to justify their added computational expense. All experiments in the next sections will be performed using MBRs of our labels only.

5.3   Multiple Distance Measure Experiments

Having shown that Euclidean distance is not always the best fit to find similarity in our solar data [7, 21], we will extend our retrieval analysis to use more than ten dissimilarity measures listed on Table 2. Expanding on our initial work [8], we have selected measures that range from Minkowski-based metrics, histogram-based measures, and measures that use different selection criteria (Mahalanobis, Chebyshev, etc). In order to observe these distance measures in action and see how they affect our retrieval results, we present Figure 4, note that we only present retrieval results and not classification accuracy results due to the fact that we do not want to adapt the similarity/distance functions in the classifiers to use our different distance measures (this is not the scope of our work).

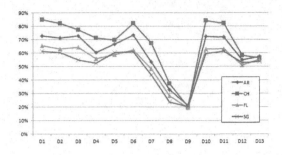

Fig. 4. Retrieval Precision Results for the different distance measures

As seen in Figure 4, there best performing results are on average using the Euclidean distance (D1). We do have other measures coming very close (D10 and D6) but the improvements/advantages are minimal. On the other side, we do have some measures that perform quite badly (D8 and D9) were we almost drop 50% of accuracy by using this. This is due to the fact that, as we have shown in the past [7], they are not well suited for our image parameters. Also to note, the histogram-based measures (D9 to D13) do not perform well in our experiments with only one of them (D10 or JSD) being comparable to the Euclidean distance. With the added computation overheard of some of the measures like D12 and D13 and even for D10, we do not have any considerable precision results to justify using any other measure than Euclidean distance. The remainder of our retrieval experiments will use this distance.

5.4   Three-Number Summary Experiments

In order to try to better capture the distribution of our selected region of interest when querying our repository, we will use a Five-Number summary[22] type of approach labeled as the Three-Number summary (3NS). In order to avoid computationally intense operations (if our region-of-interest is large), we will avoid using the median, lower quartile, and upper quartile. Instead we will just use the sample minimum, maximum and the average. Our 10-dimensional signature will now grow to a 10 by 3 dimensional signature representing the region of interest. Figure 5 shows the retrieval experiments using this complementary information.

In a very surprising result, we showed that for our best performing distance measure the Three-Number approach is actually a lot worse than just using our original average value of all the cells. We theorize that this is due to the fact that the max and min actually create bigger differences between our signature vectors thus making them harder to differentiate than by only using the average value of the parameters in the region of interest. With the 3NS signature vector being bigger to store and more computationally complex to evaluate, we are quite relieved that our original simple approach provides the best results and allows us to keep our computational expense to a minimum.

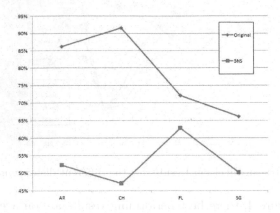

Fig. 5. Retrieval Precision comparison between original average descriptor and 3-Number Summary (3NS)

5.5   Retrieval Area Experiments

After extensively experimenting with most aspects of our region-based retrieval, we are still not exploring the last avenue we have: do we divide our region of interest by our grid cells or should we treat it as a whole cell? This is an interesting question since we are averaging the values of all image cells up until now, maybe using one complete big cell instead will provide better or similar results.

While this might add computational overhead since we need to calculate the 10 image parameters for the arbitrary sized region on the fly, rather than just matching the cells that we have stored on our database, we still think it is a good avenue to explore. This approach will also allow us to test our approach when a user submits a zoomed in image or an image of a different solar mission, greatly enhancing the functionality of our system and benefiting the overall user experience. In case the selected region of interest is too big, we will also add a four cell comparison into our analysis, this means that we will be dividing the selected region in 4 cells rather than just one (or matching it to our pre-existing grid), Figure 6 contains our retrieval results.

In our experiment we have shown that we are able to have very similar retrieval precision results when using four and even one cells to extract our parameters from the selected region of interest. This leads to considerable processing time savings when allowing users to upload their own images to query. This also reduces the computational overhead of matching large selected regions of interest to their equivalent cells in our gridding methodology. These findings are one of the most important results of this work, since we have shown that regions of interest can easily be identified by a single image descriptor and we have no need to use multiple cells to describe them.

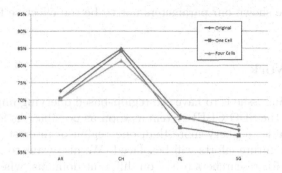

Fig. 6. Retrieval Precision for Original, one cell, and four cell experiments

6 Conclusions

As we have shown through exhaustive experimentation in this work, we have been able to successfully develop a methodology that allows us to add region-based querying to our existing SDO CBIR system. In our experimental evaluation we validated our signature generation using traditional classification algorithms and demonstrated we can transfer these signatures into a traditional image retrieval context without loss of retrieval precision / classification accuracy (Sec. 5.1). We then demonstrated that using chain-codes does not provide any significant advantage to our signatures, and the increases in retrieval precision / classification accuracy are negible considering the added computational expense of matching the chain-code to our grid cells (Sec. 5.2). In our experiments we have concluded that Euclidean is the best distance measure to evaluate similarity based on our image signatures, and performed extensive experimentation in order to show this (Sec. 5.3). Once we had a distance measure selected, we opted to test several aggregation methods for our region of interest cells and observed that our intuitive choice of averaging parameter values for the cells shown to be the best performing and most straightforward to compare against our massive repository (Sec. 5.5). Lastly, in order to provide a fast and efficient region-selection for user submitted queries, we experimented with several parameter extraction methods (standard, one-cell, and four-cell) and observed very little performance variations. This allows us to be able to switch between using our cell matching, or the one and four cell approaches depending on the size of the query region in order to speed up query processing on our server. All the findings of each step have carried over to the next one, allowing the benefits to transfer through our experiments and preparing our final approach to be implemented into the live system.

In general, since we can use this approach for our parameters effectively, the same methodology can transfer to the medical domain (as shown in [23]). We can theorize that said approach would work very well for images with fuzzy objects and very well defined foregrounds. However, we can surely say that this approach will not be efficient for natural scene images with non-dominant objects in the scene, as we have shown our parameters not to be too effective for said type of images.

7 Future Work

The initial pressing issue is to have the region-based querying implemented into a new version of the SDO CBIR system as soon as possible. As for future work, we want to be able to query more than one region of interest at a time, and this is where our future efforts will be placed. We also want to make our technology available for researchers to try on different domains, where our selected image parameters are applicable. Future extensions would involve making our methodology available as part of imageFARMER to be tested and analyzed on different sets of image parameters and allowing it to be seamlessly implemented on research CBIR systems developed by said software package. We encourage researchers that want our code and functionality to contact us for a pre-release version of this code and inform us of the application and results they are achieving with our methodology.

References

1. Banda, J.M., Schuh, M.A., Angryk, R.A., Pillai, K.G., McInerney, P.: Big data new frontiers: Mining, search and management of massive repositories of solar image data and solar events. In: Catania, B., Cerquitelli, T., Chiusano, S., Guerrini, G., Kämpf, M., Kemper, A., Novikov, B., Palpanas, T., Pokorny, J., Vakali, A. (eds.) New Trends in Databases and Information Systems. AISC, vol. 241, pp. 151–158. Springer, Heidelberg (2014)
2. Martens, P., Attrill, G., Davey, A., Engell, A., et al.: Computer vision for the solar dynamics observatory (sdo). Solar Physics 275, 79–113 (2012)
3. Banda, J., Angryk, R., Martens, P.: On dimensionality reduction for indexing and retrieval of large-scale solar image data. Solar Physics 283, 113–141 (2013)
4. Banda, J., Angryk, R.: An experimental evaluation of popular image parameters for monochromatic solar image categorization. In: 23rd Inter. FLAIRS Conf., pp. 380–385 (2010)
5. Banda, J., Angryk, R.: On the effectiveness of fuzzy clustering as a data discretization technique for large-scale classification of solar images. In: Proceedings of the 18th IEEE International Conference on Fuzzy System, pp. 2019–2024 (2009)
6. Banda, J., Angryk, R.: Selection of image parameters as the first step towards creating a cbir system for the solar dynamics observatory. In: Digital Image Computing: Techniques and Applications (DICTA), pp. 528–534 (2010)
7. Banda, J., Angryk, R., Martens, P.: Steps toward a large-scale solar image data analysis to differentiate solar phenomena. Solar Physics, 1–28 (2013)
8. Banda, J., Liu, C., Angryk, R.: Region-based querying using descriptor signatures for solar physics. In: 2013 IEEE International Conference on Data Mining Workshops (ICDMW 2013) Astroinformatics Workshop (2013)
9. Chakravarti, R., Meng, X.: A study of color histogram based image retrieval. In: Sixth International Conference on Information Technology: New Generations, pp. 1323–1328 (2009)

10. Pentland, A., Picard, R., Sclaroff, S.: Photobook: Content-based manipulation of image databases. International Journal of Computer Vision 18(3), 233–254 (1996)
11. Ogle, V., Stonebraker, M.: Chabot: Retrieval from a relational database of images. Computer, 40–48 (1995)
12. Kelly, P., Cannon, T., Hush, D.: Query by image example: the comparison algorithm for navigating digital image databases approach. In: Storage and Retrieval for Image and Video Databases, pp. 238–248 (1995)
13. Flickner, M., Sawhney, H.T.: Query by image and video content: The qbic system. Computer 28(9), 23–32 (1995)
14. Carson, C., Thomas, M., et al.: Blobworld: A system for region-based image indexing and retrieval. In: Visual Information and Information Systems, pp. 509–517 (1999)
15. Banda, J., Anrgyk, R., Martens, P.: Imagefarmer introducing a framework for the creation of large-scale content-based image retrieval systems. International Journal of Computer Applications 79(13), 8–13
16. Lemen, J., Title, A., Akin, D.T.: The atmospheric imaging assembly (aia) on the solar dynamics observatory (sdo). Solar Physics 275(1-2), 17–40 (2012)
17. Schuh, M., Angryk, R., Pillai, K., Banda, J., Martens, P.: A large-scale solar image dataset with labeled event regions. In: 20th IEEE Int. Conf. on Image Processing (ICIP), pp. 4349–4353 (2013)
18. Tamura, H., Mori, S., Yamawaki, T.: Textural features corresponding to visual perception. IEEE Transactions on Systems, Man and Cybernetics 8(6), 460–473 (1978)
19. Cao, W., Shi, Z., Feng, J.: Traffic image classification method based on fractal dimension. In: 5th IEEE International Conference on Cognitive Informatics, pp. 903–907 (2006)
20. Devendran, V., Thiagarajan, H., Wahi, A.: Svm based hybrid moment features for natural scene categorization. In: International Conference on Computational Science and Engineering, pp. 356–361 (2009)
21. Banda, J.M., Schuh, M.A., Wylie, T., McInerney, P., Angryk, R.A.: When too similar is bad: A practical example of the solar dynamics observatory content-based image-retrieval system. In: Catania, B., Cerquitelli, T., Chiusano, S., Guerrini, G., Kämpf, M., Kemper, A., Novikov, B., Palpanas, T., Pokorny, J., Vakali, A. (eds.) New Trends in Databases and Information Systems. AISC, vol. 241, pp. 87–95. Springer, Heidelberg (2014)
22. Hoaglin, D., Mosteller, F., Tukey, J.: Understanding robust and exploratory data analysis (1983)
23. Banda, J., Angryk, R., Martens, P.: On the surprisingly accurate transfer of image parameters between medical and solar images. In: 18th IEEE Int. Conf. on Image Processing, pp. 3669–3672 (2011)

Three-Dimensional Urban-Type Scene Representation in Vision System of Unmanned Flying Vehicles

Andrzej Bielecki[1], Tomasz Buratowski[2], and Piotr Śmigielski[3]

[1] AGH University of Science and Technology,
Faculty of Electrical Engineering, Automation,
Computer Science and Biomedical Engineering,
Chair of Applied Computer Science,
Al. Mickiewicza 30, 30-059 Cracow, Poland
[2] AGH University of Science and Technology,
Faculty of Mechanical Engineering and Robotics,
Chair of Robotics and Mechatronics,
Al. Mickiewicza 30, 30-059 Cracow, Poland
[3] Asseco Poland S.A.
Podwale 3, 31-118 Cracow, Poland
{bielecki,tburatow}@agh.edu.pl, smigielski.piotr@gmail.com

Abstract. In this paper a vision system for autonomous flying agents is considered in the context of industrial inspection tasks performed by unmanned aerial vehicles. A syntactic algorithm of a three-dimensional scene representation is proposed. The algorithm of creating three-dimensional single object representation has been tested by using artificial data. It has turned out to be effective.

Keywords: autonomous flying agents, structure projection, 3D scene representation.

1 Introduction

The unmanned autonomous flying robots, in order to operate effectively, are equipped with sensors that are used to collect information about surrounding environment [6,8]. Beside the need to collect mission-specific data such information enables the unmanned autonomous agent to find a collision-free path between obstacles. Another typical challenge for the mobile agents is to identify their location in space [4]. Therefore, vision systems play crucial role in various types of robots [11,12]. In two previous papers the algorithm of two-dimensional scene analysis was worked out [2,3]. The algorithm described there was based on syntactic methods. It was the first stage in creating a visual-based system for an autonomous flying agent system of the urban-type scene representation, analysis and understanding in the context of navigation possibilities. The algorithm of three-dimensional objects representation, which is presented in this

L. Rutkowski et al. (Eds.): ICAISC 2014, Part I, LNAI 8467, pp. 662–671, 2014.
© Springer International Publishing Switzerland 2014

paper, is the continuation of studies presented in [2,3] and is the second stage of the unmanned autonomous vehicle vision system creation.

2   The Problem Foundation

Let us consider an UAV which is aimed at performing an inspection of an urban object - building, chimney, bridge, tower etc. The robot is autonomous one. It has to plan out the trajectory from the starting point to the mission area, then to analyze the mission scene - to locate the recognized object and to plan out the performing of the inspection task in the context of the structure of the investigated object and the scene properties. The agent's memory contains the map which is given a priori, for instance as a preprocessed satellite image of an urban environment. The robot is equipped with the mobile camera which is able to point to the ground in order to take the pictures of the surface that it flies above. The map that the robot carries presents the buildings extracted from the base satellite image. The problem of preprocessing which, beside other problems, consists of object extraction from the image, is out of the scope of this paper. By referring to the given two-dimensional map and the two-dimensional image from its senses - camera, radar - the agent orients itself in the environment, also by using other pieces of information, for instance GPS. More precisely, in order to find its location on the map the robot takes successive pictures of the ground below. Then it compares the extracted shape of the building from the picture and locate it in the bigger map. The method of the objects recognition has to be rotation and scale invariant as the pictures of the ground are taken from different altitudes and various directions of the robot's flight. This problem belongs to the group of tasks that consist in recognition and representing polygonal-type objects by a robot sensory systems. The method is extended with the recognition of the group of buildings. Then, the robot descends in order to explore the environment directly by using camera and sensors. This allows the agent to create the three-dimensional representation of the environment. Then, the environment should be understood and the desired object should be found. Thus, the studies can be divided in the following stages:

1. Creation a single, two-dimensional object representation, based on the camera image taken from high height.
2. Creation of two-dimensional scene representation based on the high height camera image. Then, the videoed scene should be recognized as a fragment of the previously given map. The single desired object should be recognized.
3. Creation of a representation of the three-dimensional scene, based on the worked out two-dimensional scene representation. The two-dimensional representation allows us to locate the buildings. When their localization is known, the robot can investigate individual objects in order to create their three-dimensional representation.
4. Understanding the three-dimensional scene.

The points 1 and 2 were the topics of the papers [2,3]. The point 3 is the topic of this paper.

The algorithm described in following sections requires the examined structure (building) to be of some class in order to obtain fully precise representation. Basically, the structure has to have capability of being represented as a sum, result of substraction or multiplication of some number of basic construction elements: rectangular prism and pyramid.

3 The Problem Solution

To satisfy the requirements described in previous sections authors propose a method of obtaining a 3-dimensional vector representation of urban structures.

The general idea is to construct the set of walls in 3-dimensional space that will represent boundaries of a building. To enrich the representation and make it more informative, suggested method also creates representation of *holes* in the examined structure. To create 3-dimensional representation authors propose the method based on the idea of composing the solid from projections that consists of photographed and vectorised sides of a building.

Input to this method is composed of a set of vectorised pictures of a structure. In such picture each element (either building projection or wall *feature*) is represented by the sequence of points in Euclidean space $((x_1, y_1), (x_2, y_2), ..., (x_n, y_n))$ - where $(x_1, y_1) = (x_n, y_n)$ as the sequence represents a closed solid. Description of the method of obtaining vectorised picture, based on bordering algorithm, can be found in [2,3]. Three of the pictures from this collection will be treated as projections and will be used to obtain 3-dimensional representation of the examined structure's boundaries. Rest of the pictures will be used to reveal a specific features of the building. A feature can be either window, indepth or a *hole* piercing through the structure. The examples in this paper are limited to the case of *holes*.

The set of vectorised pictures used as an input to the algorithm has to undergo specific restrictions:

1. All pictures, from which vector representation is obtained, have to be taken from the distance from which the overall shape of the building is revealed. The idea is to avoid any distortion or high influence of perspective
2. One picture has to show the top side of the examined building $[i, j]$)
3. Two of the pictures have to be taken from two sides with angle of 90° between them. One should be taken aiming towards the longest dimension revealed on the picture of the top side. Second one has to be taken aiming at the side of the building (in the examples the right side of the building was taken into account)
4. In order to reveal the features of the walls (*holes*), the input set has to include pictures of half of the *external* side walls of the building ($\lceil n/2 \rceil$ - where n is the number of external walls). To be specific, the building has to be photographed aiming (horizontally) towards half of the sides represented by the convex hull of the top side shape (see Fig.1)

The method of obtaining the representation mentioned above can be separated into two steps:

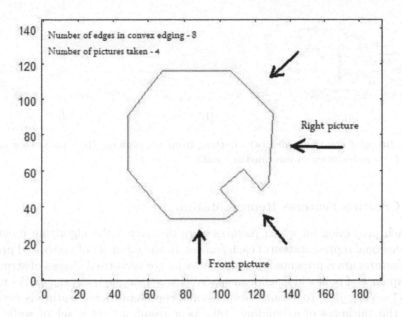

Fig. 1. Vectorised top side of a building showing directions from which the rest of the pictures should be taken

1. Creating 3-dimensional representation of the structure boundaries.
2. Creating representation of walls' features that consist of *holes* in the examined walls of the building.

3.1   Creating 3-Dimensional Representation

In the algorithm of obtaining 3-dimensional boundaries representation of the structure three vectorised pictures are taken into account - top side, front side and right side picture. This algorithm can be divided into three parts. In each part one building projection is taken as *reference* and two other projections are treated as *models*, part of which will be cut and transformed using the *reference* to obtain final walls in 3-dimensional space.

Each of the three parts of the algorithm can be described in following steps:

1. Get two succeeding point from reference projection: $A = (x_i, y_i)$, $B = (x_{i+1}, y_{i+1})$, $i \in 1, ..., n - 1$. Such pair is called *reference segment*
2. *reference segment* is used to cut parts from two other projections and translate obtained sequences of points as shown in Fig.2a, Fig.2b.
3. Obtained walls lie on the same plane, perpendicular to reference wall (right in presented example), which inclination is defined by the *reference segment*. Final step consists in calculating common part of walls (see Fig.2c)

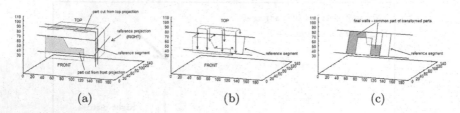

(a)   (b)   (c)

Fig. 2. Steps of creating walls, (a) - cutting from projections, (b) - projecting onto a plane, (c) - intersection of intermediate walls

3.2   Creating Features Representation

For each projection on which *features* were discovered the algorithm creates a 3-dimensional representation of each *feature*. In the input set of vectorised projections *features* are represented in similar way as are vectorised shapes of structure - as sequence of points in Euclidean space $((x_1, y_1), (x_2, y_2), ..., (x_m, y_m))$ - where $(x_1, y_1) = (x_m, y_m)$. To obtain 3-dimensional representation a feature is swept along the thickness of a building [13]. As a result we get a set of walls that represent inside walls of a hole in a building. The idea of this method is depicted in Fig.3.

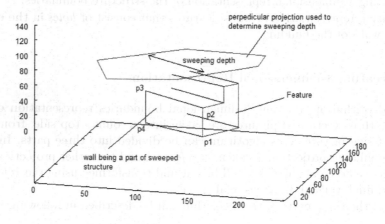

Fig. 3. Process of feature sweeping

4   Sample Applications

In this section three test cases are presented. In each case vectorised projections are shown along with the resulting 3-dimensional representation of the building structure with *features* (if there were any). In presented tests vectorised projections were obtained basing on photographed paintings of buildings sides. As a vectorisation algorithm is not included in the scope of this paper, only first test case is provided with the mentioned photographs to give a notion of how vector representation was obtained.

Example 1. Triumphal Arch Structure

In the first test case the shape of building resembles a triumphal arch with two ledges protruding out from the base shape. Note that vectorised shapes in Fig.5 were scaled and shifted with respect to those in Fig.4 in order to locate properly corresponding vectors from different pictures for the algorithm of composing the structure from projections. The created representation is shown in Fig.6.

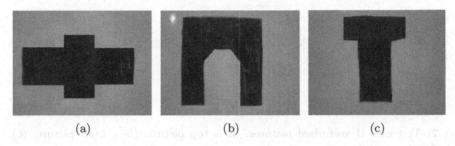

(a) (b) (c)

Fig. 4. Raw photographs of the structure, (a) - top picture, (b) - front picture, (c) - right picture

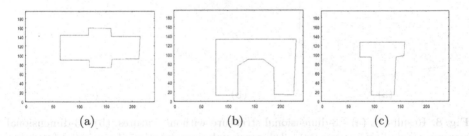

(a) (b) (c)

Fig. 5. Test case I vectorised pictures, (a) - top picture, (b) - front picture, (c) - right picture

Example 2. Structure with Features on Each Side

This test scenario shows the structure with every wall having at least one hole. The top view, front view and right-hand view are presented in Fig.7. The results show the complexity of the final 3-dimensional structure involving sweeped features - see Fig.8.

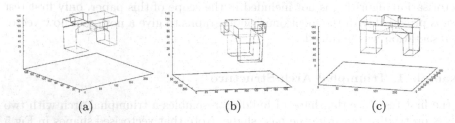

(a)   (b)   (c)

Fig. 6. Results I - view from different angle

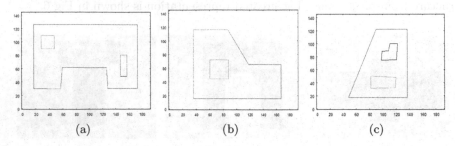

(a)   (b)   (c)

Fig. 7. Test case II vectorised pictures, (a) - top picture, (b) - front picture, (c) - right-hand picture

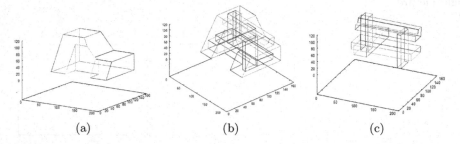

(a)   (b)   (c)

Fig. 8. Results II, (a) - 3-dimensional structure without features, (b) - 3-dimensional structure including features, (c) - 3-dimensional representation of separated features

Example 3. Structure with Features in Multiple Side Walls

In this case each of the side walls of the building has a hole piercing through whole structure. As the building has eight side walls, four ones has to be photographed and processed in order to reveal the holes. The views of the object are presented in Fig.9 - the top view with marked sides from which other pictures were taken and views of four walls: front view, 45° angle view, right-hand view and 135° angle view. In Fig.10 the three-dimensional representation of the object is shown. There is presented the three-dimensional structure without features, including features and the three-dimensional representation that shows crossing of the swept features inside the building structure.

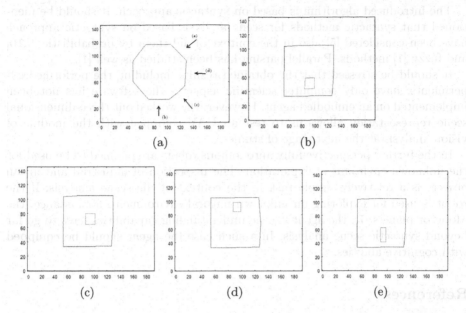

Fig. 9. Test case III vectorised pictures, (a) - top picture with marked sides from which other pictures were taken, (b) - front picture, (c) - 45° angle picture (d) - right picture, (e) 135° angle picture

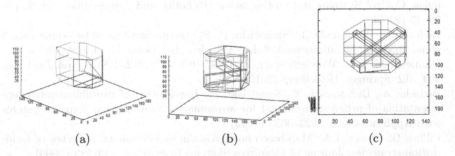

Fig. 10. Results III, (a) - 3-dimensional structure without features, (b) - 3-dimensional structure including features, (c) - 3-dimensional representation showing crossing of the swept features inside building structure

5   Concluding Remarks

In this paper the algorithm, based on syntactic methods for a single three-dimensional object representation, has been presented directly. However, it should be stressed, that the composition of the presented algorithm and the one described in [2,3] gives us the three-dimensional urban-type scene representation. The mentioned combination is trivial - the three-dimensional object should only be assigned to the proper unit of the structure describing the two-dimensional scene that corresponds to the satellite view.

The introduced algorithm is based on syntactic approach. It should be mentioned that syntactic methods for scene analysis based on syntactic approach have been considered [5] also in the context of aid them by probabilistic [9,10] and fuzzy [1] methods. Parallel parsing has been studied as well [1].

It should be stressed that the obtained results, including the performed experiments, have only computer scientific aspect - the software has not been implemented on an embodied agent. However, the worked out three-dimensional scene representation allows us to test an UAV equipped with the module of vision analysis at the next stage of studies.

In the further perspective fully autonomous robots are planned to be used for the unknown environment exploration. The inspection of industrial and urban objects is a relatively simple task in the context of the scene analysis. If the robot is used for exploring un unknown natural environment, for instance, the Moon or planets [7], the agent's scene understanding capabilities have to go far beyond syntactic scene analysis. In a such case the agent should be equipped with cognitive abilities.

References

1. Bielecka, M., Skomorowski, M., Bielecki, A.: Fuzzy syntactic approach to pattern recognition and scene analysis. In: Proceedings of the 4th International Conference on Informatics in Control, Automatics and Robotics ICINCO 2007, ICSO Intelligent Control Systems and Optimization, Robotics and Automation, vol. 1, pp. 29–35 (2007)
2. Bielecki, A., Buratowski, T., Śmigielski, P.: Syntactic algorithm of two-dimensional scene analysis for unmanned flying vehicles. In: Bolc, L., Tadeusiewicz, R., Chmielewski, L.J., Wojciechowski, K. (eds.) ICCVG 2012. LNCS, vol. 7594, pp. 304–312. Springer, Heidelberg (2012)
3. Bielecki, A., Buratowski, T., Śmigielski, P.: Recognition of two-dimensional representation of urban environment for autonomous flying agents. Expert Systems with Applications 40, 3623–3633 (2013)
4. Filliat, D., Mayer, J.A.: Map-based navigation in mobile robots. A review of localization strategies. Journal of Cognitive Systems Research 4, 243–283 (2003)
5. Flasiński, M.: On the parsing of deterministic graph languages for syntactic pattern recognition. Pattern Recognition 26, 1–16 (1993)
6. Muratet, L., Doncieux, S., Briere, Y., Meyer, J.A.: A contribution to vision-based autonomous helicopter flight in urban environments. Robotics and Autonomous Systems 50, 195–229 (2005)
7. Pederson, L., Kortencamp, D., Wettergreen, D., Nourbakhsh, I.: A survey of space robotics. In: Proceedings of the 7th International Symposium on Artificial Intelligence, Robotics, and Automation in Space, Munich, Germany (2003)
8. Sinopoli, B., Micheli, M., Donato, G., Koo, T.J.: Vision based navigation for an unmanned aerial vehicle. In: Proceedings of the International Conference on Robotics and Automation ICRA, vol. 2, pp. 1757–1764 (2001)

9. Skomorowski, M.: Use of random graph parsing for scene labeling by probabilistic relaxation. Pattern Recognition Letters 20, 949–956 (1999)
10. Skomorowski, M.: Syntactic recognition of syntactic patterns by means of random graph parsing. Pattern Recognition Letters 28, 572–581 (2006)
11. Tadeusiewicz, R.: Vision Systems of Industrial Robots. WNT, Warszawa (1992)
12. Tadeusiewicz, R.: A visual navigation system for a mobile robot with limited computational requirements. Problemy Eksploatacji 4, 205–218 (2008)
13. Tadeusiewicz, R., Flasiński, M.: Pattern Recognition. Polish Scientific Publishers PWN, Warsaw (1991)

Classification of Dynamic Sequences of 3D Point Clouds

Michał Cholewa and Przemysław Sporysz

Institute of Theoretical and Applied Informatics, Polish Academy of Sciences, Poland

Abstract. The subject of this article is 3D action recognition in point cloud sequences. A popular approach to classification of point clouds is the Bag-of-Words method, which classifies histograms of spatial features (as described e.g. by Toldo et al. in "The bag of words approach for retrieval and categorization of 3D objects", 2010). This approach is, however, less effective when applied to action recognition of similar agents (e.g. humans). We will compare a simple HMM-based classifier with the well known Bag-of-Words scheme method, within sensible parameters for 3D point clouds close range acquisition methods. We then show that the dynamic classifier performs better when applied to action recognition of objects of the same type.

1 Introduction

With rapid development and popularization of commercial 3D image capturing devices, the obtained scene data are often not images, but 3-dimensional clouds of points. This does not only allow better 3D scene reconstruction, but also a far more precise image analysis. With higher availability of 3D scanners (such as KINECT), the acquired point clouds have become a common type of data.

There has been a significant increase in need for techniques of analysis of 3D data. The problems that arose include filling the areas a scanner was unable to track, object reconstruction or classification methods adjusted for 3D point clouds. Those problems require a new set of tools that handle 3-dimensional data.

Point clouds are now a vastly researched topic both from the perspective of scene reconstruction and classification (see [1–4]). While classification schemes for 2D work on 2D snapshots, or sequences of such snapshots, with 3D images it is clear they have to be improved to meet the new type of datasets. There are now several effective approaches to analysis of both static and dynamic sequences of point clouds (e.g. [4] or [5]).

One of the most popular approaches is adapting the Bag-of-Words scheme, which classifies objects using histograms of local features. This approach is successfully applied to a static scene in [1, 2]. This scheme, however, while highly successful in a static scene and in differentiating between various objects, proves less effective when applied to classification of actions performed by relatively similar objects (e.g. human action recognition). It is also usually a time-consuming technique.

L. Rutkowski et al. (Eds.): ICAISC 2014, Part I, LNAI 8467, pp. 672–683, 2014.

In this article, we consider motion sequences, describing dynamic actions performed by 3D objects. We build a classification framework, containing the Hidden Markov Model (HMM) using two simple feature sequences – the size of an ellipsoid containing an object and the length of vectors from the centre of mass to extreme points.

We compare this framework with the Bag-of-Words selecting and classifying static features of each frame (as described e.g. in [1], [4]) of the sequence and combining those results into a global classification.

In our experiments, the constructed system gives better results (better classification effectiveness) than the reference technique. We show this by testing each of them against real-life 3D sequence data and comparing their effectiveness.

This article is organized as follows: in Section 2 we discuss related work in the subject of both 3D point clouds classification and motion classifiers for images. In Section 3 we describe basic techniques we will use in the experiments, namely HMMs and the Bag-of-Words model, in Section 4 we discuss the theoretical foundations of our approach then we follow to Section 5.1 to discuss the used data. Finally we present the experiments and their results in Section 5.

2 Related Work

3D point cloud classification has been widely researched since this type of data has become commonly used and easily obtained, especially now, when acceptable quality sensors for point clouds acquisition are commercially available.

The Bag-of-Words method, as a system adapted from text classifiers is often used as an approach focusing mainly on classification of unordered sets of features. The selection of those features varies, depending on expected use of the classifier. In [2], Wu and Lin utilized the scheme to efficiently detect objects in a point cloud scene. The Bag-of-Words scheme was also successfully used for facial expression recognition by Xu and Mordohai in [6] who used histograms of gradients as features for the classifier.

Toldo et al. in [4] proposed a multi-dictionary Bag-of-Words classifier, that uses various different feature sets, such as density of points within regions or shape index in the analysed region. They also handled the problem of parameters by using several instances of a dictionary used paralelly before obtaining the final feature set. Their work addresses the problem of relative location of visual words, which is usually not an issue in the Bag-of-Words approach as it mainly focuses on the mere presence of certain features. The same problem was addressed in [3], where Li et al. proposed an advanced version of the usual scheme, by including elements of relative position of detected features. Feature selection mostly focuses on local object-perspective descriptors of particular points. Johnson, A.E. and Martial in [1] used spin images of salient points as the features, the same was applied by Wu in [2]. Toldo et al. in [4] used salient points as seeds for regions to be used as the features while Głomb and Romaszewski in [7] proposed another approach, involving translation of 3D mesh fragments directly to symbols from a learned alphabet.

Motion classification was researched separately, though some methods were similar those applied applied to its static counterpart. A number of works refers to various approaches from the field of 2D vision, such as Zhang and Wang in [8] who analysed noisy information from traffic scene cameras or [9] which contains an analysis of cheetah habitats made in order to recognize individuals by motion characteristics. It also extends to 3D data methods included in [10], where Li and Fukui proposed an approach to view-invariant human dynamic action recognition based on the Hidden Markov Model.

3D information in motion recognition is obtained in various ways, which leads to different input data. The most commonly used one is motion capture. Authors of [11] use a combination of Gaussian Mixture Modelling and SVD to extract and classify features of human behaviour, achieving high effectiveness rates. Barbič et al. in [12] focused on the problem of data segmentation, detecting transition from one motion pattern to another.

3D point clouds have recently become popular means of presenting 3D data, mostly because they are easier to obtain with available equipment of various types. Such equipment includes LiDARs, 3D sensors similar to KINECT and others. Wei et al. in [13] segment and classify point clouds for LiDAR data on traffic by utilizing 3D features such as point shape information and spatial edges. Their work was further developed in [14]. LiDAR data is also analysed by Steinhauser et al. in [5], in which the authors use gradient bounding to determine the classification of points on the road.

3   Preliminaries

In our framework we will use a well-known and widely applied method for action classification – the Hidden Markov Model, which is a tool of probabilistic modelling of time sequences. We will test it against the Bag-of-Words scheme, a classification method which was first used for text analysis and then extended to visual data.

In this section we will describe some basics of their construction and use. For a more detailed description, please refer to such works as [15] or [4]. We will assume the following:

The set $O = O_t \cup O_c$ will be a set of point cloud sequences, where O_t will represent the training dataset and O_c – the test dataset. Each sequence $\mathcal{O} \in O$ contains l point clouds $\mathcal{O}_i, i = 1, \dots, l$. Each sequence $\mathcal{O}$ belongs to one of the $c = 1, \dots, C$ classes. The class that $\mathcal{O}$ belongs to will be denoted as $Cl(\mathcal{O})$.

3.1   Hidden Markov Model (HMM)

The Hidden Markov Model is a stochastic tool for modelling time sequences. The HMM

$$\lambda = \{S, T, \pi, \mathcal{L}, E\} \tag{1}$$

where $S = \{S_1, \dots, S_n\}$ is a set of states, $T \in \mathbb{R}^{n \times n}$ -a stochastic transition matrix, $\mathcal{L}$ is an alphabet of symbols, π is the probability vector representing the starting state distribution, and E - n-dimensional vector of emission distributions for each state.

Given HMM λ and the sequence of features $f_d(\mathcal{O})$, one can compute the log likelihood $\log(P(f_d(\mathcal{O})|\lambda))$, the logarithm of probability of $f_d(\mathcal{O})$ having been generated by λ. This can be done e.g. with Forward Algorithm [15]. Given a set of HMMs $\{\lambda_i\}_{i=1}^m$ we can use the likelihood to determine the most probable HMM associated with the sequence as

$$\operatorname{argmax}_i \log(P(f_d(\mathcal{O})|\lambda_i)) \ . \tag{2}$$

3.2   Bag-of-Words Scheme

The Bag-of-Words model was designed for documents classification, but its use has been extended to visual data to aid with image categorization, such as texture recognition and content-based image retrieval. More recently it has been introduced to 3D data classification. We use the very same approach as [2], which describes a point cloud as an unordered set of features.

The classification scheme assigns histograms of features to objects (e.g. texts are presented as histograms of features f_s which are usually a specified word or sequence of words). Those histograms are compared to class patterns allowing classification by the Naive Bayes classifier.

The Bag-of-Words approach in our case first of all consists of generating a set of features $f_s(\mathcal{O})$ from each sequence $\mathcal{O} \in O_t$. This global set of features $\{f_s(\mathcal{O})\}_{\mathcal{O} \in O_t}$ is then clusterized into the pre-defined number of clusters K. This clustering will be referred to as the *visual dictionary* $D(O_t)$.

Finally, for each sequence $\mathcal{O} \in O_t$, a histogram $H(f_s(\mathcal{O}))$ of features is constructed, which is then used to train the Naive Bayes classifier.

4   Approaches

Each sequence $\mathcal{O} \in O$ consists of l static point clouds $\{\mathcal{O}_i\}_{i=1,...,l}$, representing a 3D snapshot of an object performing an action. Let then C be the number of classes.

The goal of this approach is to correctly classify sequences $\mathcal{O} \in O_c$ of point clouds representing an object's movement during a specified action to one of C pre-defined classes (e.g. 'Human squatting'), based on an analysis of sequences from the training set $o \in O_t$.

To achieve this we will construct a combined classifier based on weighted votes of two HMM classifiers γ_e^d and γ_s^d distinguishing the dynamics of two feature sets. We will also describe the combination of Bag-of-Words classifiers $\{\gamma_i^s\}_{i=1}^l$ (as used in [1, 2]) which we will use as a reference.

4.1   Combined HMMs Approach

This approach combines two Hidden Markov Models γ_e^d and γ_s^d, each analysing the dynamics of simple features. Their results are then used as input to the combined classifier (γ^c) which produces the final classification based on weighted voting of those partials results.

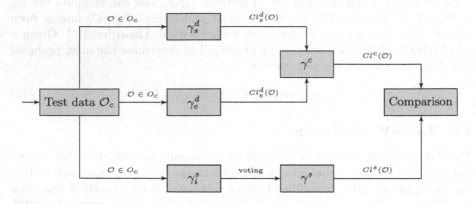

Dynamic Classifiers γ_e^d and γ_s^d. Classification of motion patterns bases on the Hidden Markov Model (HMM), which is a commonly used method for modelling time sequences.

HMMs $\lambda_c^x, x \in \{e, s\}$ are built, each trained with sequences from a specific class $c \in C$. The sequence $\mathcal{O} \in O_c$ is analysed by each of them and classification depends on the resulting table $\gamma_x^d(\mathcal{O}), x \in \{s, e\}$.

Feature set: ellipsoid (γ_e^d). The first set of features we will use will be the size of an ellipsoid containing six points with the maximum and minimum coordinates (which we will refer to as *extreme points*). This produces a sequence of three dimensional vectors, illustrating size dynamics of the object's 3D "frame".

In our approach we will use the length of three main axes of an ellipsoidal hull containing all the extreme points of the point cloud $\mathcal{O}_i$ as a sequence of features $f_e^d(\mathcal{O})$. By *extreme points* of the point cloud $\mathcal{O}_i$, $F(\mathcal{O}_i)$ we understand six points with the highest and the lowest x, y and z coordinates.

$$F(\mathcal{O}_i) = \left\{ p_\theta^j \right\}_{j \in \{0,1,2\}, \theta \in \{\min(\cdot), \max(\cdot)\}} , \qquad (3)$$

so $p_\theta^j = \{(p[0], p[1], p[2]) \in \mathcal{O}_i : p[j] = \theta_{x \in \mathcal{O}_i} x[j]\}$.

Feature sequence $f_e^d(\mathcal{O})$ will be a sequence of l 3-dimensional vectors, describing the dynamics of objects' size changes over time.

Feature set: extreme points (γ_s^d). Another set will illustrate the position of the centre of mass of a point cloud as referred to the extreme points, by showing six real numbers representing the distance between the centre and each of the six extreme points. This produces information on an object's behaviour within the frame calculated by use of the ellipsoid feature.

The sequence of features $f_s^d(\mathcal{O})$ will contain the lengths of segments from the centre of mass of the point cloud

$$\rho = \sum_{x \in \mathcal{O}_i} \frac{x}{|\{x \in \mathcal{O}_i\}|} \tag{4}$$

to the extreme points $F(\mathcal{O}_i)$ of the point cloud $\mathcal{O}_i$.

$$f_s^d(\mathcal{O}) = \{[|\rho - p_1|, \ldots, |\rho - p_6|]^T\}_{i=1,\ldots,l} \quad \text{if } p_k \in F(\mathcal{O}_i). \tag{5}$$

Feature sequence $f_s^d(\mathcal{O})$ will be a sequence of l 6-dimensional vectors representing positioning of a point cloud's centre between extreme point coordinates.

Classification. Each dynamic classifier (containing C HMMs) will separately try to recognize the class of a given object, according to the dynamics of its feature set. Those will be used as partials for the combined classifier.

We use two classifiers, each consisting of a set of Gaussian HMMs $\lambda_c^x, c = 1, \ldots, C, x \in \{s, e\}$ of s_n states, where C is the number of classes.

Each HMM λ_c accepts input of a sequence $f_x^d(\mathcal{O}), x \in \{s, e\}$ of feature vectors. It returns a score $\log(P(f_x^d(\mathcal{O})|\lambda_x^c))$.

Let

$$O_t^c = \{\mathcal{O} \in O_t : Cl(\mathcal{O}) = c\} \tag{6}$$

be a set of all training sequences of class c. Then each HMM λ_x^c is trained with sequences from $f_x^d(\mathcal{O})_{\mathcal{O} \in O_t^c}$.

For classification of an unknown sequence $\mathcal{O} \in O_c$ we calculate $\log(P(\mathcal{O}|\lambda_x^i))$. The result of classification

$$\gamma_x^d(\mathcal{O}) = \{\log(P(f_x^d(\mathcal{O})|\lambda_x^c))\}_{c=1,\ldots,C} \tag{7}$$

is a sequence of log likelihoods of sequence $f_x^d(\mathcal{O})$ being generated by $\lambda_x^c, c = 1, \ldots, C$. Additionally, γ_x^d classifies sequence $\mathcal{O}$ as

$$Cl_x^d(\mathcal{O}) = \text{argmax}_{c=1,\ldots,C} \log\left(P(f_x^d(\mathcal{O})|\lambda_x^c)\right) \tag{8}$$

Combined Classifier (γ^c). We combine the dynamic classifiers using voting with dynamic weights of each vote. To accomplish this, we first measure the effectiveness of two γ_s^d and γ_e^d against each class, by calculating

$$E_c(\gamma_x^d) = \frac{T_c(\gamma_x^d)}{A_c(\gamma_x^d)}, x \in \{s, e\}, c = 1, \ldots, C \tag{9}$$

where $T_c(\gamma_x^d)$ is the number of correct classifications of objects of class c by γ_x^d and $A_c(\gamma_x^d)$ is the total number of classifications of objects as class c by classifier γ_x^d.

$$T_c(\gamma_x^d) = |\{\mathcal{O} \in O_t : Cl(\mathcal{O}) = c \wedge Cl_x^d(\mathcal{O}) = c\}| \tag{10}$$

$$A_c(\gamma_x^d) = |\{\mathcal{O} \in O_t : Cl_x^d(\mathcal{O}) = c\}| \tag{11}$$

In other words $E_c(\gamma_x^d) \in \langle 0, 1 \rangle$ measures the trustworthiness of classification of sequence $\mathcal{O}$ as class c by γ_x^d.

After this, we associate γ_s^d and γ_e^d with vectors $\{E_c^{d_s}\}_{c=1}^C, \{E_c^{d_e}\}_{c=1}^C$ which will be used as weights of votes of those two classifiers.

Then, for each $\mathcal{O} \in O_c$ we assume

$$Cl^c(\mathcal{O}) = \operatorname{argmax}\left\{ Cl_e^d(\mathcal{O}) E_{Cl_e^d(\mathcal{O})}^{d_e}, Cl_s^d(\mathcal{O}) E_{Cl_s^d(\mathcal{O})}^{d_s} \right\}. \tag{12}$$

4.2   Bag-of-Words Classifier γ^s

We will use the Bag-of-Words approach, as described in [1, 2], as a reference classification of sequence $\mathcal{O} \in O_c$. As described in 3.2, the approach analyses the features of each point cloud $\mathcal{O}_i, i = 1, 2, \ldots, l$ from sequence $\mathcal{O} \in O_c$, constructing a histogram of its visual words $H(\mathcal{O})$, according to a visual dictionary $D(O_t)$ created by use of all training sequences $\mathcal{O} \in O_t$.

The $H(\mathcal{O})$ histogram is an input to the Naive Bayes classifier, which returns the classification result $\gamma^s(\mathcal{O})$. The classifications of individual frames $\mathcal{O}_i$ are then combined to obtain a sequence classification.

Feature Extraction. To extract features from a 3D point cloud $\mathcal{O}_i$, we use its salient points – a term we associate with points with the highest value of the shape index. We use r of the highest shape indexes to determine the salient points. The image features are spin images of those points similar to those presented in [2].

Definition 1. *Shape index of point p, $SI(p)$ is a value which determines if point p lies on the sharp surface and has details around it. For point p it is calculated as*

$$SI(p) = \frac{2}{\pi} \tan^{-1}\left(\frac{\kappa_1 + \kappa_2}{\kappa_1 - \kappa_2} \right), \kappa_1 \neq \kappa_2 \tag{13}$$

where κ_1, κ_2 are principal curvatures of point p.

What immediately follows

Definition 2. *We will call point p of the point cloud o_i, a salient point in o_i with range r or, simply speaking, a salient point if $SI(p)$ is among r of the highest $SI(p) \forall_{p \in o_i}$*

It is easy to see that saliency of a point strongly depends on point cloud $\mathcal{O}_i$. We will also denote the set of all salient points of point cloud $\mathcal{O}_i$ with range r as $SP(\mathcal{O}_i, r)$. For each point $p \in SP(\mathcal{O}_i, r)$ we will then calculate its *spin image*.

The spin image is a surface representation technique used for analysing 3D scenes. The main advantage of spin images is that it shifts perspective from viewer-oriented (based on the observer's viewpoint) to object-oriented (fixed on the surface of an object). This allows description of an object in a view-independent manner, i.e. not changeable when the viewpoint changes.

For the training set of objects O_t, the visual vocabulary for the Bag-of-Words approach is constructed by clustering the spin images of all salient points in $\{f_s(\mathcal{O})\}_{\mathcal{O} \in O_t}$ into K clusters. For that we use K-means++ clustering. This clustering will form the *visual dictionary* $D(O_t)$.

The Bag-of-Words classifier is constructed as l Bag-of-Words frame classifiers $\gamma_i^s, i = 1, \ldots, l$, one for each frame.

Classification of a Single Frame. For each $\mathcal{O} \in O_t$, a histogram $H(f_s(\mathcal{O}))$ of its features (spin images of salient points) is constructed. Those features are used to train the Naive Bayes classifier.

To classify a frame of sequence $\mathcal{O}_i, \mathcal{O} \in O_c$, we calculate its salient points and their spin images, then assign them to clusters according to $D(O_t)$ and construct $H(f_s(\mathcal{O}))$. Then we use the Naive Bayes classifier to obtain its classification

$$\gamma_i^s(\mathcal{O}_i) = \left\{ P(c|H(f_s(\mathcal{O}_i))) \right\}_{c=1,\ldots,C}. \tag{14}$$

Additionally, γ_i^s classifies $\mathcal{O}_i$ as

$$Cl_i^s(\mathcal{O}_i) = \text{argmax}_{c=1,\ldots,C} \{ P(c|H(f_s(\mathcal{O}_i))) \} \tag{15}$$

Classification of a Sequence. To classify sequence $\mathcal{O} \in O_c$, we classify each frame of the sequence $\mathcal{O}_i$ with γ_i^s, obtaining an l- long sequence of classifications $S = \{Cl_i^s(\mathcal{O}_i)\}$. The classification of sequence $\mathcal{O}$ is

$$Cl^s(\mathcal{O}) = \text{argmax}_{c=1,\ldots,C} \{ S_k : S_k = c, k = 1, \ldots, l \}. \tag{16}$$

5 Experiments

Our goal was to compare a classifier combining two sets of features in the HMM model and a combination of classifications of individual frames of a sequence using the Bag-of-Words approach, which analyses only static features. To do this, we have performed the following experiment:

1. We trained all three classifiers $\gamma^s, \gamma_e^d, \gamma_s^d$ and the resulting γ^c with all sequences $\mathcal{O} \in O_t$
2. We used γ^s, γ^c to classify all sequences $\mathcal{O} \in O_c$

For the experiment we set parameters $l = 7, C = 11, n = 12, \Phi \in \{0.002, 0.02, 0.1\}$, $P^s = 0.1, P_{sh} \in \{2, 3\}, P_{sc} = \{0, 0.2\}$.

By the experiment result for classifier $\gamma^x(O_c), x \in \{s, d_e, d_s, c\}$ we will understand

1. Classifier's effectiveness on set O_c,

$$E(O_c) = \frac{|\{\mathcal{O} \in O_c : Cl(\mathcal{O}) = Cl^x(\mathcal{O})\}|}{|O_c|} \tag{17}$$

2. Classifier's confusion matrix $T^x(O_c) = [t_{ij}]_{i,j=1,\ldots C}$ where

$$t_{ij} = |\{\mathcal{O} \in O_c : Cl(\mathcal{O}) = i \wedge Cl^x(\mathcal{O}) = j\}| \tag{18}$$

5.1 Dataset

For our experiments we had chosen datasets provided by

1. "Mesh Data from Deformation Transfer for Triangle Meshes" by Robert W. Sumner and Jovan Popovic (available in [16]) - which contains sequences of objects in different motion patterns (from "pose", to "gallop" for animals, "collapse")
2. Articulated Mesh Animation from Multi-view Silhouettes, by Daniel Vlasic, Ilya Baran, Wojciech Matusik, Jovan Popović (available in [17]) - containing 3D clouds of people performing such activities as dancing, marching or jumping.

From those two datasets we have selected $C = 11$ unique classes, 3 of animal actions and 8 of human actions. This was done to allow us to observe the Bag-of-Words classifier's effectiveness in action recognition of objects of the same type.

5.2 Data Preparation

From each dataset element d, we generate sequences $\mathcal{O}$ in the following way:

1. Each frame $d_i \in d$ is randomly sparsed to P^s of its original vertices.
2. Sequence $\mathcal{O}$ is randomly reduced to l point clouds
3. Each vertex $v \in \mathcal{O}_i, i = 1, \ldots, l$ is then shifted and scaled with shift and scale operators, calculated for every $\mathcal{O}$ in the following way:
   (a) Shifted using formula $v_{\text{shift}} = v + P_{sh}r_1$, where $r_1 \in \mathbb{R}^3$ is uniformly distributed random vector and $r[i] \in \langle -0.5, 0.5 \rangle, i = 1, 2, 3$.
   (b) $v_{\text{scaled}} = (1 + P_{sc})r_2 v$, where $r_2 \in \langle -0.5, 0.5 \rangle$ is uniformly distributed random variable.
4. Finally $v \in \mathcal{O}_i, i = 1, \ldots, l$ is distorted by adding a normally distributed noise ϕ bound by parameter Φ, where

$$\Phi = \sup \left| \frac{\phi(v)}{v} - 1 \right| \tag{19}$$

Thus, experiment parameters are: l – length of the sequence, $s \in \langle 0, 1 \rangle$ – sparsing of each frame, P_{sh} as shift operator, P_{sc} as scaling operator and distortion Φ.

5.3 Results

The results of the experiments are shown in Table 1. What we can easily observe is that the effectiveness of the combined classifier based on HMMs outmatches the Bag-of-Words classification. Most classes we use are humans, therefore the Bag-of-Words scheme has significant problems with distinguishing them from one another. Overall, the static classifier based on Bag-of-Words provided results which can be perceived as expected. What we can also observe is the spike

Table 1. Correct classification by class (for 40 objects of each class in the test set) and overall scores achieved by classifiers for various sets of parameters

Data	1	2	3	4	5	6	7	8	9	10	11	Overall $E(\mathcal{O}_C)$
$P_{sh} = 3.0$		$P_{sc} = 0.2$		$\Phi = 0.1$								
γ^s	11	18	14	22	13	15	8	7	27	33	36	0.4204
γ_e^d	25	31	37	24	29	20	30	16	39	40	40	0.7272
γ_g^d	9	32	26	27	35	32	35	24	40	40	40	0.7522
γ^c	13	33	30	25	30	23	31	16	39	40	40	0.7477
$P_{sh} = 3.0$		$P_{sc} = 0.2$		$\Phi = 0.02$								
γ^s	10	7	11	11	14	22	16	9	36	23	40	0.4522
γ_e^d	25	35	34	30	35	18	36	24	40	40	40	0.8133
γ_g^d	24	36	35	32	38	23	33	15	38	40	40	0.7977
γ^c	25	35	35	31	39	20	34	14	40	40	40	0.8022
$P_{sh} = 3.0$		$P_{sc} = 0.2$		$\Phi = 0.002$								
γ^s	11	7	23	8	5	7	11	22	32	35	26	0.4250
γ_e^d	24	21	26	30	27	21	31	26	40	39	40	0.7386
γ_g^d	16	29	24	34	28	28	31	19	39	40	40	0.7455
γ^c	0	20	40	30	30	20	30	10	40	40	40	0.7295
$P_{sh} = 3.0$		$P_{sc} = 0.0$		$\Phi = 0.1$								
γ^s	10	11	23	8	10	8	14	14	28	22	30	0.4046
γ_e^d	30	35	39	27	35	20	30	27	40	40	40	0.825
γ_g^d	32	37	39	39	40	34	38	28	40	40	40	0.9182
γ^c	31	35	40	27	35	23	30	30	40	40	40	0.8431
$P_{sh} = 3.0$		$P_{sc} = 0.0$		$\Phi = 0.02$								
γ^s	7	6	15	10	9	7	15	14	32	30	38	0.4159
γ_e^d	17	39	28	27	30	22	20	25	36	39	40	0.7340
γ_g^d	24	35	22	36	38	21	32	31	40	40	40	0.8136
γ^c	17	36	24	30	39	21	24	20	38	40	40	0.7613
$P_{sh} = 3.0$		$P_{sc} = 0.0$		$\Phi = 0.002$								
γ^s	25	15	20	20	25	5	5	10	40	30	40	0.5341
γ_e^d	39	40	37	38	40	39	39	38	40	40	40	0.9772
γ_g^d	40	40	40	40	39	33	40	37	40	28	40	0.9477
γ^c	40	40	40	40	40	35	40	35	40	40	40	0.9659
$P_{sh} = 2.0$		$P_{sc} = 0.2$		$\Phi = 0.1$								
γ^s	8	9	16	12	7	17	18	9	30	22	36	0.4409
γ_e^d	26	32	28	27	24	12	24	19	37	39	40	0.7000
γ_g^d	11	25	5	19	33	9	27	9	34	34	40	0.5204
γ^c	11	26	6	19	25	10	25	10	30	35	40	0.5386
$P_{sh} = 2.0$		$P_{sc} = 0.2$		$\Phi = 0.02$								
γ^s	12	16	22	12	11	9	22	8	36	26	40	0.4841
γ_e^d	28	31	26	29	30	23	20	22	40	40	40	0.7477
γ_g^d	16	36	19	19	21	15	34	31	36	40	40	0.7159
γ^c	17	35	26	25	27	25	20	35	30	40	40	0.7136
$P_{sh} = 2.0$		$P_{sc} = 0.2$		$\Phi = 0.002$								
γ^s	6	13	10	22	8	9	3	3	40	17	40	0.3411
γ_e^d	23	27	39	32	36	29	26	30	40	40	40	0.8227
γ_g^d	23	35	36	34	28	17	40	21	40	36	40	0.8
γ^c	20	31	32	34	30	30	20	23	40	36	40	0.7705
$P_{sh} = 2.0$		$P_{sc} = 0.0$		$\Phi = 0.1$								
γ^s	14	13	29	12	9	14	14	17	40	30	39	0.4017
γ_e^d	18	23	36	30	31	30	25	25	37	40	40	0.7613
γ_g^d	31	36	29	39	38	18	32	15	35	40	40	0.7954
γ^c	30	30	40	30	40	10	40	20	40	40	40	0.7954
$P_{sh} = 2.0$		$P_{sc} = 0.0$		$\Phi = 0.02$								
γ^s	13	11	26	14	13	15	19	3	40	10	35	0.4803
γ_e^d	39	37	40	40	40	36	31	38	40	40	40	0.9568
γ_g^d	34	39	37	40	39	33	37	35	32	40	40	0.9227
γ^c	38	34	39	30	38	10	36	40	40	39	8	0.9613
$P_{sh} = 2.0$		$P_{sc} = 0.0$		$\Phi = 0.002$								
γ^s	20	14	35	13	12	16	15	13	40	25	35	0.4142
γ_e^d	37	40	38	38	38	37	37	37	40	40	40	0.9590
γ_g^d	31	40	39	31	39	29	40	36	40	40	40	0.9022
γ^c	33	40	39	34	38	30	37	36	40	40	40	0.9113

of γ^s Bag-of-Words classifier's effectiveness when dealing with classes that are not human (9, 10, 11), which shows that when applied to actions of various object types, the Bag-of-Words scheme works quite efficiently. Both HMM-based classifiers γ_s^d and γ_e^d seem to obtain better results, since dynamics is the main distinguishing property of analysed sequences.

What was found surprising was that applying the voting procedure to the results of γ_i^s partial Bag-of-Words classifiers did not significantly increase their effectiveness, and γ^s did not yield significant advantage over γ_i^s (even though it is clearly visible).

Another thing worth noting is the effectiveness of γ^c which seems to not improve the results of partial classifiers γ_e^d and γ_s^d. It is, however, an important stabilizing element, and while it is indeed usually worse than the best of partial classifications, it plays an important role in correcting problems of the one with worse results. Since the experiments prove that it remains unknown which element of the pair of γ_e^d and γ_s^d works better in an arbitrary case, the correction value of γ^c is not to be underestimated.

6   Conclusion

This article presents an approach to classification based on the HMM scheme and on combining two sets of features – one describing the size dynamics of an object while performing an action and the other – positioning of the centre within an object. This method is compared to the popular Bag-of-Words scheme, which is often used for classification of point clouds. As we see in the experiment results, the combined system achieves better results than a combination of Bag-of-Words classifiers. One of the interesting results is that the obtained classifier is relatively resistant to both scaling and shifting the image, as well as significant distortion in analysed point clouds. We believe that this research on action recognition on point clouds can be further improved by selecting additional sets of features to enter the combined classifier as a weighted vote.

In view of proliferation of 3D imaging, the proposed method potentially has a broad range of applications.

Acknowledgements. The work of M. Cholewa and P. Sporysz was partially supported by the Polish Ministry of Science and Higher Education, National Science Centre project N N516 405137 'Representation of dynamic 3D scenes using the Atomic Shapes Network model'.

References

1. Johnson, A., Martial, H.: Using spin-images for efficient object recognition in cluttered 3-d scenes. IEEE Transactions on Pattern Analysis and Machine Intelligence 21(5), 433–449 (1999)
2. Wu, C.C., Lin, S.F.: Efficient model detection in point cloud data based on bag of words classification. Journal of Computational Information Systems 7(12), 4170–4177 (2011)

3. Li, X., Godil, A., Wagan, A.: Spatially enhanced bags of words for 3d shape retrieval. In: Bebis, G., Boyle, R., Parvin, B., Koracin, D., Remagnino, P., Porikli, F., Peters, J., Klosowski, J., Arns, L., Chun, Y.K., Rhyne, T.-M., Monroe, L. (eds.) ISVC 2008, Part I. LNCS, vol. 5358, pp. 349–358. Springer, Heidelberg (2008)
4. Toldo, R., Castellani, U., Fusiello, A.: The bag of words approach for retrieval and categorization of 3d objects. Vis. Comput. 26(10), 1257–1268 (2010)
5. Steinhauser, D., Ruepp, O., Burschka, D.: Motion segmentation and scene classification from 3d lidar data. In: Proceeding of IEEE Intelligent Vehicles Symposium, pp. 398–403 (2008)
6. Xu, L., Mordohai, P.: Automatic facial expression recognition using bags of motion words. In: Proceeding of British Machine Vision Conference (2010)
7. Romaszewski, M., Głomb, P.: 3D mesh approximation using vector quantization. In: Kurzynski, M., Wozniak, M. (eds.) Computer Recognition Systems 3. AISC, vol. 57, pp. 71–78. Springer, Heidelberg (2009)
8. Zhang, Z., Wang, Y.: Automatic object classification using motion blob based local feature fusion for traffic scene surveillance. Frontiers of Computer Science 6(5)
9. Grunewalder, S., Broekhuis, F., Macdonald, D., Wilson, A., McNutt, J., Shawe-Taylor, J., Hailes, S.: Movement activity based classification of animal behaviour with an application to data from cheetah (acinonyx jubatus). PLoS ONE 7(11), e49120 (2012)
10. Li, X., Fukui, K.: View-invariant human action recognition based on factorization and hmms. In: Proceeding of IAPR Conference on Machine Vision Applications, pp. 2207–2230 (2007)
11. Jin, Y., Prabhakaran, B.: Semantic quantization of 3d human motion capture data through spatial-temporal feature extraction. In: Satoh, S., Nack, F., Etoh, M. (eds.) MMM 2008. LNCS, vol. 4903, pp. 318–328. Springer, Heidelberg (2008)
12. Barbič, J., Safonova, A., Pan, J.Y., Faloutsos, C., Hodgins, J.K., Pollard, N.S.: Segmenting motion capture data into distinct behaviors. In: Proceedings of Graphics Interface, GI 2004, pp. 185–194. Canadian Human-Computer Communications Society (2004)
13. Wei, Y., Hinz, S., Stilla, U.: 3D object-based classification for vehicle extraction from airborne lidar data by combining point shape information with spatial edge. In: Workshop on Pattern Recognition in Remote Sensing (PRRS), 2010 IAPR, pp. 1–4 (2010)
14. Wei, Y., Stilla, U.: Comparison of two methods for vehicle extraction from airborne lidar data toward motion analysis. Geoscience and Remote Sensing Letters 8(4), 607–611 (2011)
15. Rabiner, L.: A tutorial on hidden markov models and selected applications in speech recognition. Proceedings of the IEEE 77(2), 257–286 (1989)
16. Sumner, R., Popovic, J.: Mesh data from deformation transfer for triangle meshes
17. Vlasic, D., Baran, I., Matusik, W., Popovic, J.: Articulated mesh animation from multi-view silhouettes

Texture Image Classification
with Improved Weber Local Descriptor

Hassan Dawood, Hussain Dawood, and Ping Guo*

Image Processing and Pattern Recognition Laboratory, Beijing Normal University,
Beijing 100875, China
{hasandawod,hussaindawood2002}@yahoo.com, pguo@ieee.org

Abstract. Texture features play an important role in image texture classification. Inspired by Weber's law, Weber Local Descriptor (WLD) has been proposed for image texture classification. Orientation component in Weber Local Descriptor is the gradient of an image, which does not properly represent the local spatial information of an image. In this paper for orientation component, we propose to compute the histogram of gradient instead of the gradient of an image. The gradient of an image is computed, then image is divided in to small spatial regions named as cells and histogram of each cell is obtained. We have tested our proposed scheme on publically available texture datasets named as Brodatz and KTH-TIPS2-a, which shows that our proposed method can achieve significant improvement as compared to the state-of-the-art method like Local Binary Pattern, Local Phase Quantization and Weber Local Descriptor.

Keywords: Weber Local descriptor, Histogram of Gradient, Image Texture Classification.

1 Introduction

Texture image classification has been an active research topic in computer vision and image processing. It is used in many applications like object-based image coding [1], image retrieval and remote sensing[2], Medical image analysis and image retrieval [3]. With the increment of the texture image classification applications, plenty of work has been done by researchers in last two decades.

For local features number of methods have been proposed. These local descriptors are categorized into two classes that are sparse descriptor and dense descriptor. The dense local descriptor extracts the features pixel by pixel from given image. The typical examples of dense descriptor are Local Binary Pattern (LBP) [4], Local Phase Quantization (LPQ) [5], Weber Local Descriptor (WLD)[6] and Gabor wavelet[7]. The sparse descriptor first detects the interest points in given image then samples a local patch and describes its invariant features. The most popular examples of sparse descriptors are scale invariant feature transform (SIFT) [8] and histogram of oriented gradients (HOG) [9].

---

* Corresponding author.

L. Rutkowski et al. (Eds.): ICAISC 2014, Part I, LNAI 8467, pp. 684–692, 2014.

Ojalaet et al. [4] proposed a method for texture image classification named as LBP. This method recognizes the certain local binary patterns, termed as "uniform". It is the basic property of local image texture. LBP has a drawback of losing global spatial information. A new texture descriptor named as LBP variance (LBPV) has been proposed to characterize the local contrast information into one dimensional LBP histogram. There is no need of quantization and training [10]. A complete modeling of the local binary pattern (LBP) operator is proposed by Guo et al. named as completed-LBP (C_LBP) [11] in which local region is represented by its central pixel and a local difference sign-magnitude transform (LDSMT) collectively. The central pixels represent the image gray level which is converted into binary value named as CLBP-Center (C_LBPC). The LDSMT have two parts, one is CLBP-Sign (C_LBPS) and other is CLBP-Magnitude (C_LBPM).

A Monogenic-LBP (M-LBP) [12] is used to integrate the traditional Local Binary Pattern (LBP) operator with the other two rotation invariant measures: the local phase and the local surface type. These are computed by the 1st-order and 2nd-order Riesz transforms, respectively. Soo and Kang [13] proposed the feature extraction method by using wavelet packet frame decomposition and the Gaussian-mixture-based classifier to assign each pixel to the class. Each subnet of the classifier is modeled by a Gaussian mixture model and each texture image is assigned to the class to which pixels of the image most belong. Zhang et al. [14] proposed a new method to estimate the dominant orientations of textures using Gabor filters, where it's modified version is used to fit the multi-orientation cases. The discrete wavelet transform is used as a feature extraction tool and nearest neighbor method is used for classification.

Some statistical methods that are insensitive to blur, have been used for texture image classification, however these methods are not rotation invariant, like Gabor filtering [7], wavelet frames [15], wavelet transform [16] and co-occurrence matrix method [17]. Weijer and Schmid proposed a blur robust descriptor based on color constancy [19]. Ojansivu et al. [5] proposed a descriptor for texture image classification named as Local Phase Quantization (LPQ), in which short-time Fourier Transform (STFT) is used to extract the image features. Dawood et al. [19] proposed a method in which they consider the contrast information in spatial domain and the phase information in frequency domain of the image. They have used the joint histogram of the two complementary features, Local Phase Quantization (LPQ) and the contrast of the image.

Chen et al. [6] proposed a Weber Local Descriptor (WLD) for texture image classification, which consists of two components: orientation and differential excitation. Where the orientation is the gradient orientation of the current pixel and differential excitation component is the function of the ratio between two terms, one is relative intensity differences and other is intensity of the current pixel. A hybrid approach that combines the WLD with contrast information is proposed by Dawood et al. [20] in which, the histograms of WLD and contrast information are computed independently and then combined to get the robust descriptor. The orientation component in the WLD is the gradient orientation of the current pixel. The computed features from orientation component, blur the texture of an image, which leads to misclassification of images.

To overcome the aforementioned problem, we have proposed to compute the gradient over an image. Then gradient image is divided into small spatial regions "cells" and the histogram is computed for all small cells. In order to obtain the neighbouring pixel information differential excitation is used with histogram of gradients. Experiments conducted on Brodatz and KTHTIPS2-a datasets show that our proposed method performs well in term of classification as compared to the state-of-the-art feature extraction methods like LBP[4], LPQ [5],and WLD [6] itself. Support Vector Machine (SVM) is used for the classification task.

The rest of this paper is organized as follows: In section 2, a brief introduction of Differential excitation and gradients. In section 3, our proposed method is described. The detailed experiments are presented in section 4, and finally we provide the conclusions in section 5.

2   Related Work

In this section, we will briefly review the differential excitation and Histogram of gradient.

2.1   Differential Excitation

Jian [21] stated that the ratio of the increment threshold to the background intensity is a constant which is known as weber law, it can be expressed as

$$\Delta I/I = k,$$

where ΔI represents the increment threshold (just noticeable difference for discrimination), I represents the initial stimulus intensity, and k signifies that the proportion on the left side of the equation remains constant despite variations in the I term. The fraction $\Delta I/I$ is known as the Weber fraction.

In WLD [6], differential excitation $\xi(x_c)$ of a current pixel x_c is calculated. The differences between the center point and its neighbors is calculated by using filter f_{00}.

$$x_s = \begin{bmatrix} x_1 & x_2 & x_3 \\ x_8 & x_c & x_4 \\ x_7 & x_6 & x_5 \end{bmatrix}$$

$$f_{00} = \begin{bmatrix} +1 & +1 & +1 \\ +1 & -8 & +1 \\ +1 & +1 & +1 \end{bmatrix}$$

$$f_{01} = \begin{bmatrix} 0 & 0 & 0 \\ 0 & +1 & 0 \\ 0 & 0 & 0 \end{bmatrix}$$

$$v_s^{00} = \sum_{i=0}^{p-1}(\Delta x) = \sum_{i=0}^{p\ 1}(x_i - x_c) \tag{1}$$

where $x_i (i = 0, 1, ..., p-1)$ denotes the ith neighbour of x_c and p is the number of neighbours. Following the hints in Weber's law, by combining the two filters f_{00} and f_{00}, the ratio of the differences to the intensity can be computed. The output v_s^{01} is the original obtained image.

$$G_{ratio}(x_c) = \frac{v_s^{00}}{v_s^{01}} \tag{2}$$

The differential of the current pixel $\xi(x_c)$ is computed as

$$\xi(x_c) = arctan\left[\frac{v_s^{00}}{v_s^{01}}\right] = arctan\left[\sum_{i=0}^{p-1}\left(\frac{x_i - x_c}{x_c}\right)\right] \tag{3}$$

If the intensities of the neighbouring pixels is smaller than the current pixel, the value of the differential excitation will be negative. From this, we can see that instead of using the absolute value of $\xi(x)$ the more discriminating information is preserved. Intuitively, if $\xi(x)$ is positive, then the surroundings are lighter than the current pixel. if $\xi(x)$ is negative, it simulates the case that the surroundings are darker than the current pixel. $\xi(x_c)$ is defined in the range of $[-\pi/2, \pi/2]$.

2.2   Histogram of Gradient

By computing the gradient of an image, we can observe that the image is changing rapidly. Gradient of an image has two kind of information, one is magnitude and other is direction of the gradient. Magnitude gives the information of how rapidly the image is changing and direction of the gradient tells us direction image is changing more rapidly. The gradient of the image $f(x, y)$ at location (x, y) is defined as

$$\nabla f = \begin{bmatrix} G_x \\ G_y \end{bmatrix} = \begin{bmatrix} \frac{\partial f}{\partial x} \\ \frac{\partial f}{\partial y} \end{bmatrix} \tag{4}$$

We can detect the edges in image by computing the magnitude of the vector,

$$\nabla f = mag(\nabla f) = \left[\frac{G_x^2}{G_y^2}\right]^{1/2} \tag{5}$$

And the direction of gradient can be computed as

$$\alpha(x, y) = tan^{-1}\left[\frac{G_y}{G_x}\right] \tag{6}$$

Where the angle is measured with respect to x-axis and the edge direction at (x, y) is perpendicular to the direction of the gradient vector at the point.

3   Proposed Method

Fig. 1 shows flowchart of our proposed method. Differential excitation and gradient of an image is computed independently. Dense texture feature for the gradient image is obtained by partitioning the image into small spatial regions and histogram is obtained for these spatial regions.

The shape and appearance of local object in an image is represented by local intensity gradients or edge directions. The gradient is calculated over the complete image, which gives complete information about the edges. Then image is divided into small spatial cells, and histograms are calculated over those cells. The overlapping of cells is used to make it more distinctive and powerful for identifying the edges, which provides the edge orientations and gradient directions over the pixels of the cell. After getting the histograms from each cell, image is formed from these histograms. Gradient of image provide the information that how fast image is changing, however it does not define the relationship among the neighboring pixels. So, we use the differential excitation to get the relative intensity difference of a current pixel and its neighbor's. Finally, the differential excitation and gradient information is concatenated.

2D histogram of differential excitation and gradient orientation is computed as follows:

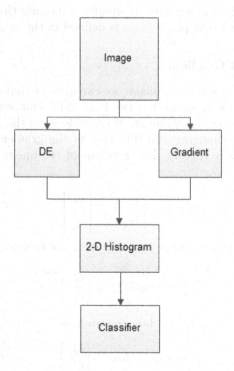

Fig. 1. Flowchart of proposed method

1. Compute the differential excitation and gradient of each pixel in cell.
2. Quantize the gradient information into 8 dominant orientations. Map the differential excitation into 256 bins by[22].
3. Compute the histogram of each gradient orientation by accumulating the differential excitation showing the same gradient orientation.
4. Cut the histograms of each gradient orientation into M=6 segmentation obtained from step 3.
5. Assign the Weight to each segmented area as in [6].
6. Concatenate eight segmentations from eight dominant orientations into one histogram. We can get 6 histograms.
7. Concatenate these M=6 histograms into one histogram, which is the final histogram.

4   Results and Discussion

The experiments have been conducted on two datsets: Brodatz [4] and KTH-TIPS2-a [7]. Brodatz data set contains 2,048 sample images. There are total 32 texture categories with 64 samples in each category. Some examples of Brodatz textures used in our experiments are shown in Fig. 2. First row has the images of size 256x256 pixels having 256 gray levels. The KTH-TIPS2-a database contains 4 physical, planar samples of each of 11 materials under varying illumination, pose and scale. Some examples from each sample are shown in Fig. 2 (second row) .The KTH-TIPS2-a texture dataset contains 11 texture classes with 4,395

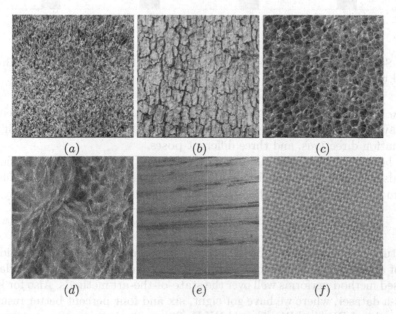

Fig. 2. Some examples of images from data set KTH-TIPS2-a (first row) and Brodatz (second row)

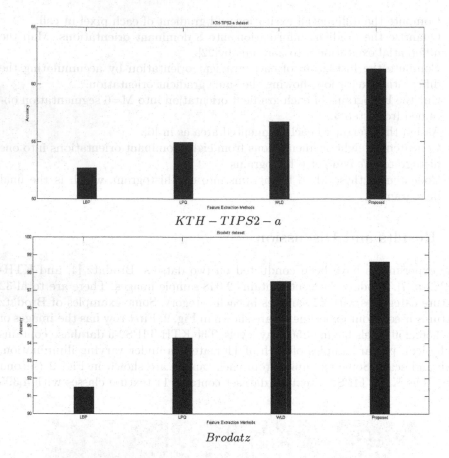

$$KTH - TIPS2 - a$$

$$Brodatz$$

Fig. 3. Some examples of images from data set KTH-TIPS2-a (first row) and Brodatz (second row)

images. The images are 200x200 pixels in size, and they are transformed into 256 gray levels. The database contains images at 9 scales, under four different illumination directions, and three different poses.

We have compared our method with state-of-the-art texture classification methods like LBP [4], Local Phase Quantization (LPQ) [5] and WLD [6]. The performance of proposed method has been evaluated in terms of accuracy,

$$Accuracy = \text{correctly classified images/total number of images.}$$

Texture classification is a basic problem in computer vision with a wide variety of applications [23]. From Fig. 3, we can observe that for Brodatz dataset proposed method performs well over the state-of-the-art methods. Also for KTH-TIPS2-a dataset, where we have got eight, six and four percent better results as compared to LBP [4], LPQ [5], and WLD [23] respectively.

For the verification of our proposed method, experiments have been conducted ten times with randomly selected training and testing images. The neighbour's values of LBP and LPQ has been used as in [4]. The correlation coefficient of LPQ set to $\rho = 0.9$ in the experiments.

In WLD, the histogram of an image is obtained after computing the gradient orientation of an image, which leads to lack of information in small spatial regions while computing the histogram of complete image for classification. In proposed method after computing the gradient information of the image, image is divided into small spatial regions. Then the histogram of those small spatial regions is computed, which defines the texture of the image at cell level effectively. At cell level, information of edges is more compact, so it obtains strong local contrast information and reduces the blurring. In WLD, the computation of the gradient of an image did not cater the information of edges effectively, the local contrast information is not sufficient and also blurs the edges of an image, results into decrease the texture recognition rate.

5 Conclusion

In this paper, an improvement of Weber's Local Descriptor has been proposed. Orientation component of WLD has been computed by using Histogram of gradient of an image. At first, the image is partitioned into small spatial regions and then histogram is calculated. By applying the histogram of gradient on small spatial regions, the compact information of image texture is obtained. SVM classifier is used for the classification. Our proposed method outperforms over the state-of-the-art methods like LBP, LPQ and WLD in term of classification accuracy.

Acknowledgments. The research work described in this paper was fully supported by the grants from the National Natural Science Foundation of China (61375045) and Beijing Natural Science Foundation (4142030). Prof. Ping Guo is the author to whom all correspondence should be addressed.

References

1. Qiang, J., John, E., Eric, C.: Texture analysis for classification of cervix lesions. IEEE Transactions on Medical Imaging 19(11), 1144–1149 (2000)
2. Anys, H., He, D.C.: Evaluation of textural and multipolarization radar features for crop classification. IEEE Transactions on Geoscience and Remote Sensing 33(5), 1170–1181 (1995)
3. Nanni, L., Lumini, A., Brahnam, S.: Local binary patterns variants as texture descriptors for medical image analysis. Artificial Intelligence in Medicine 49(2), 117–125 (2010)
4. Ojala, T., Pietikainen, M., Maenpaa, T.: Multiresolution gray-scale and rotation invariant texture classification with local binary patterns. IEEE Transactions on Pattern Analysis and Machine Intelligence 24(7), 971–987 (2002)

5. Ojansivu, V., Heikkilä, J.: Blur insensitive texture classification using local phase quantization. In: Elmoataz, A., Lezoray, O., Nouboud, F., Mammass, D. (eds.) ICISP 2008 2008. LNCS, vol. 5099, pp. 236–243. Springer, Heidelberg (2008)
6. Chen, J., Shan, S., He, C., Zhao, G., Pietikainen, M., Chen, X., Gao, W.: WLD: A robust local image descriptor. IEEE Transactions on Pattern Analysis and Machine Intelligence 32(9), 1705–1720 (2010)
7. Manjunath, B.S., Ma, W.Y.: Texture features for browsing and retrieval of image data. IEEE Transactions on Pattern Analysis and Machine Intelligence 18(8), 837–842 (1996)
8. Lowe, D.G.: Distinctive image features from scale-invariant keypoints. International Journal of Computer Vision 60(2), 91–110 (2004)
9. Dalal, N., Triggs, B.: Histograms of oriented gradients for human detection. In: IEEE Computer Society Conference on Computer Vision and Pattern Recognition, vol. 1, pp. 886–893 (2005)
10. Guo, Z., Zhang, L., Zhang, D.: Rotation invariant texture classification using LBP variance (LBPV) with global matching. Pattern Recognition 43(3), 706–719 (2010)
11. Guo, Z., Zhang, L., Zhang, D.: A completed modeling of local binary pattern operator for texture classification. IEEE Transactions on Image Processing 19(6), 1657–1663 (2010)
12. Zhang, L., Zhang, L., Guo, Z., Zhang, D.: Monogenic-LBP: A new approach for rotation invariant texture classification. In: 17th IEEE International Conference on Image Processing (ICIP), pp. 2677–2680 (2010)
13. Kim, S.C., Kang, T.J.: Texture classification and segmentation using wavelet packet frame and Gaussian mixture model. Pattern Recognition 40(4), 1207–1221 (2007)
14. Zhang, J., Mai, X., Wu, X.: Rotation invariant texture classification with dominant orientation estimation based on Gabor filters. In: IEEE International Conference on Computer Science and Automation Engineering (CSAE), vol. 1, pp. 606–609 (2011)
15. Unser, M.: Texture classification and segmentation using wavelet frames. IEEE Transactions on Image Processing 4(11), 1549–1560 (1995)
16. Laine, A., Fan, J.: Texture classification by wavelet packet signatures. IEEE Transactions on Pattern Analysis and Machine Intelligence 15(11), 1186–1191 (1993)
17. Haralick, R.M., Shanmugam, K., Dinstein, I.H.: Textural features for image classification. IEEE Transactions on Systems Man and Cybernetics 6, 610–621 (1973)
18. Van De Weijer, J., Schmid, C.: Blur robust and color constant image description. In: IEEE International Conference on Image Processing (ICIP), pp. 993–996 (2006)
19. Dawood, H., Dawood, H., Guo, P.: Combining the contrast information with LPQ for texture classification. In: 6th International Conference on Sciences of Electronics Technologies of Information and Telecommunications (SETIT), pp. 380–385 (2012)
20. Dawood, H., Dawood, H., Guo, P.: Combining the contrast information with WLD for texture classification. In: IEEE International Conference on Computer Science and Automation Engineering (CSAE), vol. 3, pp. 203–207 (2012)
21. Jain, A.K.: Fundamentals of digital image processing, vol. 3. Prentice-Hall, Englewood Cliffs (1989)
22. Ojala, T., Valkealahti, K., Oja, E., Pietikakinen, M.: A comparative study of texture measures with classification based on featured distributions of signed gray-level differences. Pattern Recognition 34, 727–739 (2001)
23. Chen, C.H.: Handbook of pattern recognition and computer vision. World Scientific (2009)

Different Orderings and Visual Sequence Alignment Algorithms for Image Classification

Paweł Drozda, Krzysztof Sopyła, and Przemysław Górecki

Department of Mathematics and Computer Sciences,
University of Warmia and Mazury, Olsztyn, Poland
{pdrozda,pgorecki}@matman.uwm.edu.pl, ksopyla@uwm.edu.pl

Abstract. This paper presents a successful connection of different sequence alignment algorithms with Bag of Visual Words concept for image classification. In particular, sequences were created on the basis of dense SIFT descriptors, for which different types of sequence orderings were proposed. Then, the similarities between images were calculated with two different sequence alignment algorithms. Finally, the SVM algorithm was proposed as a classifier. The obtained results showed that both sequence alignment algorithms obtain very similar results and that the type of ordering affects the accuracy very slightly.

Keywords: Dense SIFT, Sequence Ordering, Sequence Alignment Algorithms, Classification, SVM.

1 Introduction

The process of classification is one of the most frequently approached problems of the machine learning field. The main aim of classification for the considered object is to choose one of the predefined categories, which contains the most similar elements to the queried one. The similarities between objects are calculated on the basis of the set of object descriptors and in this paper, the visual features of images are taken into account. We can distinguish global visual features like color, edges, texture or shapes and local key point descriptors like SIFT [18], SURF [2] or MSER [8]. After calculating object similarities, the classification training is performed. There have been proposed a large variety of solutions for classification which use different algorithms from many computer science fields. In particular, in [16], [14], [15] authors proposed Rough-Neuro-Fuzzy Systems to perform classification, in [10], [23] the Neural Networks are used while SVM and its many variants were introduced in [25], [3], [11] or [6].

This paper extends the work undertaken in [7], where a novel method was proposed, which combines the sequence alignment algorithm from the domain of biology with content based image retrieval. In particular, similarly to [7] we used dense version of SIFT as a local descriptor [18] and the Bag of Visual Words concept for Visual Dictionary creation. As image representation we created a sequence of visual words ordered in four different ways: vertical, horizontal, Z ordering and

L. Rutkowski et al. (Eds.): ICAISC 2014, Part I, LNAI 8467, pp. 693–702, 2014.
© Springer International Publishing Switzerland 2014

Hilbert ordering. We introduced these orderings to verify sensitivity of classification accuracy on different arrangement of sequence elements, which describe the geometrical relationships between SIFT descriptors. For the obtained sequences we used Smith - Waterman Local Sequence Alignment Algorithm [24] to calculate the similarities between all pairs of images and we compared it with the results obtained for the Needleman - Wunsch Global Sequence Alignment Algorithm [21]. Finally, we used SVM algorithm for the classification process with 5-fold cross validation. The obtained results indicate that in all cases the classification accuracy reaches high level (from 95% to 99%) regardless the sequence alignment algorithm, type of normalization or ordering choice. In SVM classification only the grid size for the dense SIFT descriptor slightly affects accuracy.

The paper is organized as follows. The second section presents successful solutions in CBIR domain which use spatial dependencies. Moreover, first attempts of bridging sequence alignment with BoVW are highlighted. In section 3 we describe the whole classification process with the use of sequence alignment algorithms in detail. Section 4 is devoted to experiments comparing different orderings as well as global and local sequence alignment algorithms. The last section concludes the paper.

2   State of the Art

The main Bag of Visual Words (BoVW) idea is to represent visual objects using feature vectors similarly to Information Retrieval domain. One issue still open is finding such image descriptors that are able to grasp the visual difference of images in machine learning problems. These descriptors should be invariant to different image changes, such as: rotation, illumination, scale or translation. To the authors knowledge, in the group of leading descriptors we can distinguish MSER[8], SIFT[18], SURF[2] and ASIFT[19,26]. It should be noted that using a vector of the descriptors as an image representation may not be sufficient, since images are characterized by high impact of spatial information. It has been shown in [22] that humans and computers perform equally when recognizing jumbled images, where global spatial information is discarded. In contrast, current algorithms fall short if global information is present, which is the case for the vast majority of computer vision problems.

A lot of effort has been devoted to the development of efficient image representations that capture global information in the image. For example, in [17] a spatial pyramid of image keypoints is proposed. In this approach, the image is partitioned recursively into finer subregions, and for each subregion an orderless histogram of visual words is computed. A similar approach was presented in [4] where PHOG image descriptor was proposed. In particular, an image is recursively subdivided into a 4 subregions, as in a quadtree. For each subregion at each level of the quadtree, the HOG vector is computed and the PHOG descriptor for entire image is created by concatenating individual HOG vectors. Authors of [5] took different approach by projecting local features to different directions or points, so that a series of ordered bag-of-features are obtained. The projections were designed to capture the invariance to object transformations (translation, scaling, rotation). Successively, a final bag-of-features is generated from the projected bag-of-features by a using boosting-like method. In [27], Geometry-Preserving Visual Phrases (GVP) are proposed which are defined as a number Visual Words in a certain spatial layout, which are common for the two given images. GVP are identified in the offset space and are capable of modeling local and long range spatial information.

The first successful implementation of sequence alignment into content based image retrieval was made be Hung-sik et al [12], [13], where authors used the BLAST algorithm [1]. They represent image features as proteins and DNA alphabets for sequence alignment. It significantly limits the ability to use the algorithm, since protein alphabet has only 23 letters and DNA only 4. Moreover, the authors proposed a similarity matrix only with 1 for equal elements and -1 for different, which does not reflect the differences between different image features. The second work [7] overcomes these restrictions where Needleman - Wunsch algorithm with a k-NN classifier is implemented. The similarity matrix is based on distances between visual words from the created dictionary. The dictionary can contain any number of elements.

This paper extends the work undertaken in [7]. The second sequence alignment Smith Waterman algorithm was implemented, which searches for the best local alignments. We also proposed different types of sequence orderings to study their impact on classification accuracy. Moreover, we performed classification process with the use of the SVM classifier, which is considered as one of the best classification algorithm.

3   Classification with Sequence Alignment

This section presents the main contribution of this paper. In particular, the image classification process based on Sequence Alignment algorithms and SVM classifier is described in detail. There are proposed two different Sequence Alignment methods: Needleman Wunsch Global Sequence Alignment and Smith Waterman Local Sequence Alignment. As a classifier kernel we used the similarity matrix obtained in previous phase.

3.1   Sequences of Visual Words

As a representation of the image, we decided to use one of the best and most frequently used descriptors for visual objects, which is the SIFT. Many studies have shown a very good adaptation of the SIFT to the classification process as well as its resistance against various image changes and image distortion. More specifically, there has been applied the dense version of the SIFT, in which each of the processed image is divided into square areas with pre-defined size and for each of these areas the SIFT descriptor is calculated. It should be noted that the cells, for which the contrast of descriptors are very low, are eliminated. It is done in order to exclude the background area and to examine only the object from the picture. On the basis of the obtained descriptors the k - visual word dictionary is created. It is done with the use of the k-means algorithm, where the value k indicates the number of visual words in the dictionary. Each cluster generated by k-means corresponds to one visual word from the dictionary and for each cell descriptor on the image, the most similar visual word is assigned. In this manner the visual word representation is created. The whole process is illustrated in figure 1.

(a) Original Shoe

(b) Shoe with SIFT descriptors on a dense grid

(c) Shoe with assigned visual words, vocabulary size 50

Fig. 1. Procedure of creating sequences

For such grid image representation we create four different sequences for sequence alignment algorithms to verify if the order of visual words in the sequence has any impact on classification accuracy. In particular, the following orderings are proposed:

a) Vertical - the visual words are sequenced row by row from left to right.
b) Horizontal - the visual words are sequenced column by column from top to bottom.
c) Z ordering - ordering is based on the letter Z. For details see [20].
d) Hilbert ordering - a continuous fractal space-filling curve. For details see [9].

3.2 Sequence Alignment Algorithms

Having obtained the sequences for all images from the dataset, one of the sequence alignment algorithm is executed in order to compute similarities between each pair of images. In DNA sequencing both algorithms are provided with a pre-defined similarity matrix, which is inapplicable for our purposes. For this reason we compute the similarity of visual words on the basis of k-means clusters. In particular, the similarity between two visual words is given by the Euclidean distance between two corresponding clusters. These distances are normalized to the set $< -1; 1 >$ where -1 indicates the maximum possible distance while the value 1 is for distance 0.

The sequence alignment derives from the biological domain where the main task was two find alignments between DNA, protein or nucleotide sequences. In this paper we evaluate two different algorithms from which the first, the Needleman Wunsch algorithm, finds the best possible global alignment for two sequences. This algorithm is given by the following recursive formula:

$$F_{i0} = p * i, \quad i \in \{0, ..., n\}, j = 0$$
$$F_{0j} = p * j, \quad i = 0, \ j \in \{0, ..., n\} \tag{1}$$
$$F_{ij} = \max(F_{i-1,j-1} + S(A_i, B_j), F_{i,j-1} + p, F_{i-1,j} + p).$$

where F_{ij} is the similarity score, $S(A_i, B_j)$ is a similarity between visual words A_i and B_j and p is defined as the penalty parameter and is subtracted from the similarity score when a gap appears in the alignment. The final score is equal to F_{nm}, where n and m are lengths of the sentences.

The Smith Waterman is the second of the introduced algorithms. Instead of finding the best global alignment it searches for local similar regions of two sequences for all possible sub-sequence lengths and optimizes the similarity measure. The following formula illustrates the work-flow of the algorithm:

$$H_{i0} = 0, \quad i \in \{0, ..., n\}, j = 0$$
$$H_{0j} = 0, \quad i = 0, \ j \in \{0, ..., n\} \tag{2}$$
$$H_{ij} = \max(0, H_{i-1,j-1} + S(A_i, B_j), H_{i,j-1} + p, H_{i-1,j} + p).$$

where H_{ij} is a similarity score for sub-sequences $A_0...A_i$ and $B_0...B_j$, while p and $S(A_i, B_j)$ are defined in the same way as for the Needleman Wunsch algorithm.

The main difference between these algorithms lies in the final score. The Needleman Wunsch finds always the best possible alignment while Smith Waterman finds local alignment which is close to optimal, but not necessary the best globally. The second difference concerns the time of algorithm execution. Global alignment is significantly more computationally intensive.

The final step involves the SVM classification with 5-fold cross-validation. As the SVM kernel, the matrix of sequence alignment similarities is used. It was observed that similarities highly depend on the sequence length and therefore two different normalizations were performed. First, the similarity was divided by sum of sequence lengths. It is illustrated by the formula:

$$Sim_{A,B} = \frac{Sim_{A,B}}{(length(A) + length(B))}, \tag{3}$$

The second normalization is given by:

$$Sim_{A,B} = \frac{Sim_{A,B}}{(length(A)} * \frac{Sim_{A,B}}{length(B))}. \tag{4}$$

Next section provides an evaluation of the proposed solution and discusses experimental results.

4 Experiment Results

This section evaluates the proposed methods for image classification. To be precise, we compare SVM classification accuracy for different sequence alignment algorithms as well as verify the impact of different sequence orderings on image classification accuracy. As sequence alignment algorithms, we implemented the Needleman Wunsch global sequence alignment algorithm and the Smith Waterman local sequence alignment algorithm. To investigate the importance of sequence arrangement we proposed four different orderings: vertical, horizontal, Hilbert and Z order. Moreover, for each combination of algorithm and order we used different sizes of visual dictionary, which is $k = 200, 500, 1000, 2000$. We chose such dictionary sizes since in the previous work [7] we proved that the dictionary size under 200 significantly decreases the accuracy of classification. Finally, we tested our method over two grid sizes: 16 and 32 pixels, since the detailed experiments investigating the impact of grid size on classification accuracy were provided in [7] and the penalty parameter p was set to 0.1, since changes of p have a slight impact on the precision of classification.

For experiments, we provided a dataset of 200 shoe images, which was divided into 5 distinctive categories(20, 29, 34, 58 and 59 images). Figure 2 presents exemplary elements of each category.

Tables 1, 2, 3 and 4 summarize the obtained results, each table for different orderings. In all tables the sign − means no normalization, the normalization defined in equation 3 is labeled $N1$ and $N2$ represents normalization given by formula 4.

In all cases, the differences between the Needleman - Wunsch and the Smith - Waterman algorithms in accuracy are very small or even non-existent. The maximal reported difference between these two methods reaches 1%, which proves that with the use of the SVM as a classifier, the choice between the global and local sequence alignment algorithms has no impact on classification accuracy. When considering various types of ordering, we can observe that the obtained accuracies for horizontal and vertical orderings are slightly higher (from 0.5% to 2%) than for Z and Hilbert orderings, which shows that the ordering does not affect classification effectiveness.

The biggest differences in accuracy, reaching up to 4%, can be perceived for different values of the grid size parameter. Despite the fact that in almost every case the results achieved for the denser grid are better, the differences are so slight that it does not significantly affect classification accuracy.

When comparing this paper with the previous work [7], it should be noted that in every case the obtained results for the SVM classifier are better than for the k-NN. It can be seen precisely for grid size equal to 32, where the SVM reaches 99% for horizontal ordering, while the best reported accuracy for the k-NN classifier is 92%.

(a)   (b)   (c)   (d)

(e)

Fig. 2. Sample images from each of 5 shoe categories (a-e)

Table 1. SVM Classification Accuracy for Vertical Ordering

Vocab. size	Vertical Ordering											
	N-W algorithm						S-W algorithm					
	16			32			16			32		
	-	N1	N2	-	N1	N2	-	N1	N2	-	N1	N2
200	0.985	0.99	0.99	0.965	0.965	0.965	0.985	0.99	0.99	0.965	0.96	0.965
500	0.99	0.99	0.995	0.975	0.975	0.97	0.99	0.99	0.995	0.97	0.975	0.96
1000	0.99	0.99	0.99	0.975	0.975	0.975	0.99	0.995	0.995	0.975	0.97	0.975
2000	0.99	0.99	0.995	0.975	0.975	0.975	0.99	0.995	0.995	0.975	0.97	0.98

Table 2. SVM Classification Accuracy for Horizontal Ordering

Vocab. size	Horizontal Ordering											
	N-W algorithm						S-W algorithm					
	16			32			16			32		
	-	N1	N2	-	N1	N2	-	N1	N2	-	N1	N2
200	0.99	0.99	0.99	0.975	0.975	0.97	0.99	0.99	0.99	0.96	0.965	0.96
500	0.99	0.985	0.99	0.99	0.99	0.99	0.99	0.985	0.985	0.97	0.97	0.97
1000	0.995	0.99	0.995	0.98	0.98	0.98	0.995	0.99	0.99	0.985	0.985	0.985
2000	0.99	0.995	0.995	0.98	0.98	0.98	0.995	0.995	0.995	0.98	0.98	0.98

Table 3. SVM Classification Accuracy for Hilbert Ordering

Vocab. size	Hilbert Ordering											
	N-W algorithm						S-W algorithm					
	16			32			16			32		
	-	N1	N2	-	N1	N2	-	N1	N2	-	N1	N2
200	0.98	0.98	0.98	0.965	0.965	0.965	0.975	0.98	0.98	0.965	0.965	0.965
500	0.98	0.98	0.98	0.975	0.975	0.975	0.98	0.98	0.98	0.98	0.975	0.98
1000	0.985	0.98	0.98	0.98	0.975	0.97	0.985	0.98	0.98	0.98	0.975	0.98
2000	0.985	0.985	0.985	0.965	0.955	0.955	0.985	0.985	0.985	0.955	0.95	0.96

Table 4. SVM Classification Accuracy for Z Ordering

Vocab. size	Z Ordering											
	N-W algorithm						S-W algorithm					
	16			32			16			32		
	-	N1	N2	-	N1	N2	-	N1	N2	-	N1	N2
200	0.985	0.985	0.985	0.95	0.97	0.975	0.985	0.985	0.985	0.96	0.96	0.955
500	0.985	0.98	0.98	0.975	0.97	0.975	0.985	0.98	0.98	0.955	0.96	0.97
1000	0.985	0.985	0.985	0.95	0.96	0.975	0.985	0.985	0.985	0.95	0.975	0.965
2000	0.98	0.98	0.98	0.97	0.97	0.98	0.98	0.98	0.98	0.96	0.96	0.95

5   Conclusion and Future Work

This paper compares different sequence alignment algorithms and different sequence orderings for image classification tasks. The obtained results, which vary between 95% and 99.5% indicate that for the SVM classifier the choice of the sequence alignment algorithm as well as ordering has very little impact on accuracy. Moreover, it was observed that the SVM reaches significantly better results than the k-NN presented in [7]. The experiments have proven that bridging sequence alignment with content based image retrieval domains can be promising for image classification.

As the next step in our research in this field, we plan to test our findings over the state of the art imaginary datasets. We will also evaluate time of the algorithm execution. Moreover, we are going to implement other, faster sequence alignment algorithms (FASTA, BLAST).

Acknowledgments. The research has been supported by grant N N516 480940 from The National Science Center of the Republic of Poland and by grant 1309-802 from Ministry of Science and Higher Education of the Republic of Poland. We would like to thank Geox and Salomon companies for providing a set of shoe images for scientific purposes.

References

1. Altschul, S., Gish, W., Miller, W., Myers, E., Lipman, D.: Basic local alignment search tool. Journal of Molecular Biology 215, 403–410 (1990)
2. Bay, H., Tuytelaars, T., Van Gool, L.: SURF: Speeded up robust features. In: Leonardis, A., Bischof, H., Pinz, A. (eds.) ECCV 2006, Part I. LNCS, vol. 3951, pp. 404–417. Springer, Heidelberg (2006)
3. Bordes, A., Bottou, L., Gallinari, P.: SGD-QN: Careful Quasi-Newton Stochastic Gradient Descent. Journal of Machine Learning Research 10, 1737–1754 (2009)
4. Bosch, A., Zisserman, A., Muñoz, X.: Representing shape with a spatial pyramid kernel. In: CIVR, pp. 401–408 (2007)
5. Cao, Y., Wang, C., Li, Z., Zhang, L., Zhang, L.: Spatial-bag-of-features. In: CVPR, pp. 3352–3359 (2010)

6. Chang, C.C., Lin, C.J.: LIBSVM: a library for support vector machines (2001), software available at, http://www.csie.ntu.edu.tw/~cjlin/libsvm
7. Drozda, P., Górecki, P., Sopyla, K., Artiemjew, P.: Visual words sequence alignment for image classification. In: ICCI*CC, pp. 397–402. IEEE (2013)
8. Extremal, M.S., Matas, J., Chum, O., Urban, M., Pajdla, T.: Robust wide baseline stereo from. In: British Machine Vision Conference, pp. 384–393 (2002)
9. Hamilton, C.H., Rau-Chaplin, A.: Compact hilbert indices: Space-filling curves for domains with unequal side lengths. Inf. Process. Lett. 105(5), 155–163 (2008)
10. Huang, K., Yan, H.: Off-line signature verification based on geometric feature extraction and neural network classification. Pattern Recognition 30 (1997)
11. Joachims, T.: Training linear svms in linear time. In: Proceedings of the 12th ACM SIGKDD International Conference on Knowledge Discovery and Data Mining, KDD 2006, pp. 217–226. ACM, New York (2006), http://doi.acm.org/10.1145/1150402.1150429
12. Sik Kim, H., Chang, H.W., Liu, H., Lee, J., Lee, D.: Bim: Image matching using biological gene sequence alignment. In: ICIP, pp. 205–208. IEEE (2009)
13. Kim, H.S., Chang, H.W., Lee, J., Lee, D.: Basil: effective near-duplicate image detection using gene sequence alignment. In: Gurrin, C., He, Y., Kazai, G., Kruschwitz, U., Little, S., Roelleke, T., Rüger, S., van Rijsbergen, K. (eds.) ECIR 2010. LNCS, vol. 5993, pp. 229–240. Springer, Heidelberg (2010), http://dx.doi.org/10.1007/978-3-642-12275-0_22
14. Korytkowski, M., Nowicki, R., Rutkowski, L., Scherer, R.: Adaboost ensemble of dcog rough neuro fuzzy systems. In: Jędrzejowicz, P., Nguyen, N.T., Hoang, K. (eds.) ICCCI 2011, Part I. LNCS, vol. 6922, pp. 62–71. Springer, Heidelberg (2011)
15. Korytkowski, M., Nowicki, R., Scherer, R.: Neuro-fuzzy rough classifier ensemble. In: Alippi, C., Polycarpou, M., Panayiotou, C., Ellinas, G. (eds.) ICANN 2009, Part I. LNCS, vol. 5768, pp. 817–823. Springer, Heidelberg (2009)
16. Korytkowski, M., Nowicki, R., Scherer, R., Rutkowski, L.: Ensemble of rough-neuro-fuzzy systems for classification with missing features. In: 2008 IEEE International Conference on Fuzzy Systems (FUZZ 2008), pp. 1745–1750 (2008)
17. Lazebnik, S., Schmid, C., Ponce, J.: Beyond bags of features: Spatial pyramid matching for recognizing natural scene categories. In: Proceedings of the 2006 IEEE Computer Society Conference on Computer Vision and Pattern Recognition, CVPR 2006, vol. 2, pp. 2169–2178. IEEE Computer Society, Washington, DC (2006), http://dx.doi.org/10.1109/CVPR.2006.68
18. Lowe, D.G.: Distinctive image features from scale-invariant keypoints. Int. J. Comput. Vision 60, 91–110 (2004)
19. Morel, J.M., Yu, G.: Asift: A new framework for fully affine invariant image comparison. SIAM J. Img. Sci. 2(2), 438–469 (2009), http://dx.doi.org/10.1137/080732730
20. Morton: A computer oriented geodetic data base and a new technique in file sequencing. Tech. Rep. Ottawa, Ontario, Canada (1966)
21. Needleman, S.B., Wunsch, C.D.: A general method applicable to the search for similarities in the amino acid sequence of two proteins. Journal of Molecular Biology 48(3), 443–453 (1970)
22. Parikh, D.: Recognizing jumbled images: The role of local and global information in image classification. In: ICCV, pp. 519–526 (2011)
23. Richard, M.D., Lippmann, R.P.: Neural Network Classifiers Estimate Bayesian a posteriori Probabilities. Neural Computation 3(4), 461–483 (1991), http://dx.doi.org/10.1162/neco.1991.3.4.461

24. Smith, T., Waterman, M.: Identification of common molecular subsequences. Journal of Molecular Biology 147(1), 195–197 (1981), http://www.sciencedirect.com/science/article/pii/0022283681900875
25. Sopyła, K., Drozda, P., Górecki, P.: SVM with CUDA accelerated kernels for big sparse problems. In: Rutkowski, L., Korytkowski, M., Scherer, R., Tadeusiewicz, R., Zadeh, L.A., Zurada, J.M. (eds.) ICAISC 2012, Part I. LNCS, vol. 7267, pp. 439–447. Springer, Heidelberg (2012)
26. Yu, G., Morel, J.M.: ASIFT: An Algorithm for Fully Affine Invariant Comparison. Image Processing on Line 2011 (2011)
27. Zhang, Y., Jia, Z., Chen, T.: Image retrieval with geometry-preserving visual phrases. In: CVPR, pp. 809–816 (2011)

Surface Mixture Models for the Optimization of Object Boundary Representation

Przemysław Głomb and Arkadiusz Sochan

Multimedia Systems Division,
Institute of Theoretical and Applied Informatics,
Polish Academy of Sciences,
Bałtycka 5, 44-100 Gliwice, Poland
przemg@iitis.pl

Abstract. We explore an original approach to represent boundaries of objects based on mixture of densities in parametrized submanifolds embedded in $\mathbb{R}^n$. This method combines representation of boundary by 'patchwork' of surfaces and traditional mixture models to represent point distributions within the surfaces. Specifically, this method could be used for lossy compression/storage of point clouds, with significant data compression factor. We present method description and experiments with scanned objects.

Keywords: Point Cloud representation, Mixture Model, surface fitting, part based representation, graphical models, Point Cloud compression.

1 Introduction

Methods for representing imaged objects form the base of computer vision. Both 2D planar images and 3D scanned scenes require digital representation. One of the most popular ways to represent objects and scenes, recently growing in applications like robotic vision, are point clouds (PC). A PC is an unordered set of points, or vertices, coordinates sometimes accompanied by a color or normal information. Usually a single PC is a result of scanning some scene with 3D scanner, using techniques like time-of-flight or infra-red structured light.

Various technical conditions influence and limit precision of the acquisition process, hence a PC can be viewed as a noisy sample of an object's boundary. On the other hand, it can oversample a simple object geometry, as it does not consider the shape of the underlying surface; local object structure is often smooth and this fact is often exploited [1,2] for efficient 3D data processing. Considering the probabilistic characteristics of the acquisition process (a single scan viewed as a realization of a random process) and smoothness constraints, we propose to represent the boundary as a parametrized point distribution. To account for smoothness constraints, we consider first the surface corresponding to local vertex neighbourhood; then a distribution of points is approximated within a submanifold defined by that surface. To represent the probabilities we use a widely known and effective method for capturing unknown distributions, the

L. Rutkowski et al. (Eds.): ICAISC 2014, Part I, LNAI 8467, pp. 703–714, 2014.

Mixture Models (MM). Owning to the fact that the proposed approach amounts to 'mixing' surface fragments, we name it 'Surface Mixture Models' (SMM).

We explore this representation with experiments. We use simple quadric surface for local neighbourhood approximation, as they can effectively represent elements of real-life 3D objects [3]. We model point probabilities with Gaussian Mixture Models, with number of components established with Bayesian Information Criteria. We propose an algorithm for converting a PC to SMM, and investigate it's performance on database scans of several physical objects. We investigate errors (RMSE and Hausdorff) in this process, and analyse compression factor, as SMM requires much less coefficients to represent a given shape. We finish experiments section with general discussion of quantitative and qualitative results.

2   Related Work

A traditional area of applications of object description methods are 3D Computer Graphics (CG) and Computer Aided Design (CAD), where techniques to represent 3D models form the foundation of the discipline. Two main approaches have been: used Constructive Solid Geometry (CSG), and Boundary Representation (BREP). With BREP, models are represented as boundaries defined with vertices, edges and faces. Triangular meshes are by far most common, although Non-uniform rational basis spline (NURBS) [4] are used for precise modeling of complex parts (e.g. turbine blades).

The use of surfaces in vision has been supported from theoretical research on foundations of psychophysics, e.g. [6] and recently discovered evidence for specific neural circuit for surface representation in the brain at various stages of visual processing pathway ([7, chap. 1]). Estimated surfaces have been successfully applied to 3D vision processing tasks, e.g. in robot perception [1]. Of many possible function types, quadric surfaces have been many times reported as well performing tool; in particular, [3] reports that arbitrary shapes can be represented by quadric primitives, [8] notes that the quadric fitting was found best performing for estimation of local surface geometry, [9] uses quadrics to effectively estimate geometric properties, and number of others (see e.g. [10], [2]) report successful application.

As 3D data acquisition often is viewed as probabilistic in character, stochastic methods have been successfully employed for 3D representation. In [11], standard approach of representing with octrees has been combined with probabilistic occupancy model, resulting in highly effective representation of 3D environment that can be easily extended when additional data is available. A changing structure of 3D robot working area has been modelled using Gaussian Mixture Models [12] which allows for representation of acquired 3D space data and efficient novelty detection. A probabilistic likelihood map framework [13] has been proposed for resampling and merging a set of scans in presence of noise.

Segmentation and description of 3D objects in parts has been long advocated as natural from semantic point of view (see i.e. functional relation between parts

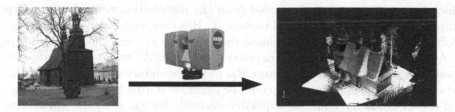

Fig. 1. Illustration of 3D digitalization process

[14] and the 'geon' approach [6]). A very interesting approach to describe shapes with multiscale local descriptor, the 'surflets' is presented in [15], where piecewise constant functions are used within a tree (e.g. an octree) framework. In another approach [16], a set of basic shapes combined with efficient RANSAC-based algorithm is used to provide total or partial decomposition of a point cloud.

3 Surface Mixture Models

Imagine the process of 3D digitalization of a physical object (Fig. 1). Using a 3D scanner, we can acquire positions of selected points from object surface. Our method deals with representation of such scans of objects' boundaries. We present the model, algorithm for its recovery, and evaluation procedure.

3.1 The Model

Scanning process works on the physical boundary of the object. We represent it as a surface $\mathcal{S}$ defined by some unknown function $f(\cdot)$, embedded in $\mathbb{R}^3$:

$$\mathcal{S} = \{\mathbf{x} \in \mathbb{R}^3 \mid \mathbf{x} = f(\mathbf{u}) \text{ with } \mathbf{u} \in \mathcal{R} \subset \mathbb{R}^2\}. \tag{1}$$

Note that in this formulation the scanning process samples points $\mathbf{u}$ from object surface. We can approximate this behavior by drawing a sequence of values from random variable U with range $\mathcal{R}$ and unknown distribution $P(U = \mathbf{u})$. This distribution is dependent on object geometry and position/rotation in scanner coordinate system. In a similar way, we can represent the acquired points $\mathbf{x}$ as values from random variable that is a function of U, or $X = f(U)$. If scanner errors are considered, the points have an added noise component, $\mathbf{x} = f(\mathbf{u}) + \mathbf{e}$. X is no longer a function, but still dependent on U, a fact that can be represented by a simple belief network (see Fig. 2a)

$$p(X = \mathbf{x}) = p(X = \mathbf{x}|U = \mathbf{u})p(U = \mathbf{u}) \tag{2}$$

The scanning result is a set of m points (also called the 'point cloud'):

$$\mathcal{X} = \{\mathbf{x}_1, \ldots, \mathbf{x}_n\}, \ \mathbf{x}_i \in \mathbb{R}^3, \tag{3}$$

which we can view as being sampled from the distribution defined above. The simplest way to store scan data is to store $\mathcal{X}$. However, one can view the storage problem as an attempt to approximate and save both $f(\cdot)$ and the distribution of U. Advantages of such approach (in relation to storing $\mathcal{X}$) would be to reduce the number of coefficient needed to store the object boundary data, thus achieving data compression; scanning noise could be excluded during the estimation stage, and object geometry would be explicitly available for e.g. semantic application like similarity search. One possible disadvantage would be that any reproduction of the original $\mathcal{X}$ is performed by sampling from a distribution (akin to scanning again), so $\mathcal{X}$ won't be recovered exactly. Also, the nature of the recovery process is necessarily approximate. In short, a method for storing shape and distribution could produce lossy compression algorithm for point clouds.

As both $f(\cdot)$ and $P(U = \mathbf{u})$ can be complex and thus difficult to represent in whole, our approach is to use a number of simpler surfaces $f_i(\cdot)$, suitably parametrized by position, orientation and shape and corresponding elemental distributions U_i, that can be approximated e.g. by Mixture Models. The scanning model presented above is extended with a random index I (discrete random variable that selects the surface and distribution to use), producing in noise free case

$$X = f(U) =_d f_I(U_I) = \sum_i f_i(U_i)\mathbb{1}_{\{I=i\}} \tag{4}$$

where $=_d$ denotes equality in distributions. With noise included, the describing belief network changes to (see Fig. 2b)

$$p(X = \mathbf{x}) = p(X = \mathbf{x}|U_i = \mathbf{u})p(U_i = \mathbf{u}|I = i)p(I = i). \tag{5}$$

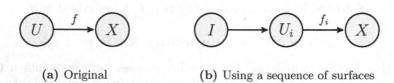

(a) Original   (b) Using a sequence of surfaces

Fig. 2. Belief networks representing the scanning process

Aside from the change in parameters, the model is applicable in the same way as before. Recovering the approximate $\mathcal{X}$ is done by sampling from the distribution, while model recovery from $\mathcal{X}$ involves estimating individual sequence of (f_i, U_i). As this model is conceptually similar to traditional Mixture Models, but involves mixing surfaces and points on surfaces, hence the name 'Surface Mixture Models'.

3.2　The Model Recovery

The basic model recovery can be outlined as follows:

1. Decide on the class of surfaces and distributions model to use and select corresponding parameter recovery algorithm.
2. Partition the input point cloud $\mathcal{X}$ into individual parts or regions and perform recovery of surface and distribution parameters.
3. Optionally, optimize the model e.g. by iteratively alternating the steps of partition and parameter recovery.

Our starting point, besides focusing on local description, was the concept of fitting predefined model to an object fragment, with estimation of model parameters independently of position and orientation [17]. There exists a number of options for parametric surface representations. While many classes could be used here, we use quadrics, due to their potential for modelling diverse shapes with relatively few parameters. Various algorithms for their parameters' recovery exist, however with most general ones the estimation process is computationally intensive, e.g. [18] method that involves two levels of iteration. Since our objective is to model simple geometry of the small local region, we restrict the quadric shape and propose an algorithm to compensate for that restriction. We start with approximation of local point cloud $\mathcal{X}_j$ with a plane, using moment matrix approach [19]:

$$M \triangleq \begin{bmatrix} m_{xx} & m_{xy} & m_{xz} \\ m_{yx} & m_{yy} & m_{yz} \\ m_{zx} & m_{zy} & m_{zz} \end{bmatrix} \tag{6}$$

$$m_{xy} = \frac{1}{n_j} \sum_{i=1}^{n_j} (x_i - \bar{x})(y_i - \bar{y}) \quad \mathbf{x}_i = \begin{bmatrix} x_i \\ y_i \\ z_i \end{bmatrix}. \tag{7}$$

where $\bar{\mathbf{x}} = \begin{bmatrix} \bar{x}, \bar{y}, \bar{z} \end{bmatrix}^{\top}$ is the local centroid. The normal vector $\mathbf{n}$ is obtained by decomposing matrix M with SVD and choosing singular vector corresponding to the smallest singular value. We then translate the local vertex cloud by $-\bar{\mathbf{x}}$ and rotate by the angle between $\mathbf{n}$ and versor $\mathbf{k} = \begin{bmatrix} 0, 0, 1 \end{bmatrix}^{\top}$ (rotation matrix R) before fitting the surface coefficients. An algorithm for estimating rotation matrix R given two vectors [20] is applied at this stage to improve effectiveness. We use surface equation in the form

$$f(x, y, z) = a_0 + a_1 x^2 + a_2 xy + a_3 y^2 - z \tag{8}$$

The coefficient vector $\mathbf{a} = \begin{bmatrix} a_0, a_1, a_2, a_3 \end{bmatrix}^{\top}$ is established as a solution to overdetermined homogeneous linear equation set, again by using SVD decomposition and choosing singular vector corresponding to the smallest singular value.

Given the center point $\bar{\mathbf{x}}$, rotation matrix R, and surface coefficients $\mathbf{a}$, we can compute images of $\mathcal{X} = \{\mathbf{x}_i\}$ in the surface parameters plane, $\mathcal{U} = \{\mathbf{u}_i\}$, $\mathbf{u}_i \in \mathbb{R}^2$. We model this distribution of points in parameter space $\mathcal{U}$ with a Mixture Model [21]

$$P(U = \mathbf{u}) = \sum_{i=1}^{n_m} w_i h(U = \mathbf{u} | \lambda_i) \tag{9}$$

where $h(\cdot)$ is a suitable distribution, e.g. a Gaussian $h_i = \mathcal{N}(\boldsymbol{\mu}_i; \Sigma_i)$, λ_i are the distribution parameters, and w_i a normalizing weight with $\sum_i w_i = 1$. The distribution modelling uses standard EM (Expectation-Maximization) approach. To identify best number of mixtures n_m for each region, a standard approach with minimizing the Bayesian Information Criterion is used. Relative number of points in regions is used to construct the distribution of region labels (the independent I variable).

While the algorithm presented is conceptually straightforward and simple to implement, it's drawbacks are limited degrees of freedom for describing diverse shapes. Rather that include a more complex surface type, we propose a region growing segmentation to keep the regions within the surface/mixture describing ability. The proposed algorithm is defined as follows:

1. Split initial point set $\mathcal{X}$ into disjoint regions with small number of points each.
2. Estimate surface and mixture parameters for each region.
3. Prepare list of region pairs (i, j) for neighbouring regions.
4. Sort the list based on norm of coefficient vector $\|\mathbf{a}_i - \mathbf{a}_j\|$, where i and j are regions from the pair.
5. For the top n_p items from the sorted list, estimate the parameters from region constructed from merging i with j.
6. Replace pair with the smallest error from step 5 with a single merged region.
7. If minimum number of regions is achieved, or last merging error is above threshold, stop; else go to 3.

The selection of top n_p in step 5 is an optimization, based on initial experiments; excludes very few cases where surfaces can be joined with small error, while at the same time greatly reduces candidates to merge (and corresponding number of calculations to be made).

3.3 Error and Performance Measure

We measure errors of the representation in two cases:

1. Surface representation error. We can compare the distances of points on the fitted surfaces in the regions, to their original values. This describes the fidelity of representation of surface component of our model. We denote this by $\mathcal{X} \to \mathcal{U} \to \mathcal{X}'$. As this preserves point correspondence, root-mean-square error (RMSE) is used

$$\epsilon_{\mathrm{R}} = \sqrt{\frac{1}{m} \sum_{i=1}^{m} \|\mathbf{x}_i - \mathbf{x}_i'\|^2} \tag{10}$$

2. Full representation error. Here, the points in $\mathcal{X}'$ are sampled back from the cached distribution; as this removes 1:1 correspondence of points, a point set

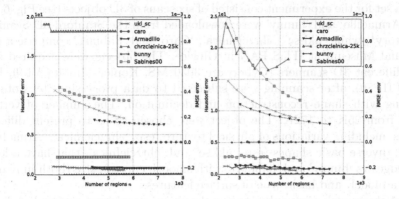

Fig. 3. Surface representation errors (RMSE, ϵ_R, dotted lines and Hausdorff ϵ_H, solid lines) for different objects with varying number of regions. This corresponds to the error component of approximation of the point cloud with surfaces. Left plot corresponds to experiment 'A', right to 'C' (see text).

measure is appropriate here. We denote this situation by $\mathcal{X} \to \mathcal{U} \to p(\mathbf{u}) \to \mathcal{U}' \to \mathcal{X}'$ and use the Hausdorff distance

$$\epsilon_H = \max\{ \sup_{\mathbf{x}' \in \mathcal{X}'} \inf_{\mathbf{x} \in \mathcal{X}} \|\mathbf{x} - \mathbf{x}'\|, \sup_{\mathbf{x} \in \mathcal{X}} \inf_{\mathbf{x}' \in \mathcal{X}'} \|\mathbf{x} - \mathbf{x}'\| \} \qquad (11)$$

Besides quantifying error, our performance measure is the estimated compression factor, describing potential space gains on using proposed representation. We use the fraction of count of coefficients needed to represent this model, which is

$$c = \frac{n_s}{n_o} \qquad n_o = 3n \qquad n_s = 10n_r + 5 \sum_{i=1}^{n_r} n_{m_i} \qquad (12)$$

where n_o denotes the number of coefficients needed to represent original 3D point set; n is the number of points in the original PC; n_r is the number of regions; n_{m_i} denotes number of mixture components at region i; while n_s denotes the total number of SMM model coefficients (for each region: center point $d = 3$, rotation angles $d = 3$, surface coefficients $d = 4$, distribution parameters: mean $d = 2$ and covariance matrix $d = 3$ for each distribution). The c can be viewed as percentage fraction, the lower the better.

4   Experiments

In this section we present the results of an empirical investigation of the proposed representation. The objective of performed experiments was to quantitatively measure and qualitatively investigate the performance of the representation; introduced errors and compression ratio.

Data set for the experiment consisted of six scans of 3D objects (see Fig. 6, top row). 'Armadillo' and 'bunny' were downloaded from the Stanford 3D Scanning Repository[1], while 'ukl_sc', 'chrzcielnica', 'Caro' and 'Sabines' comprise a part of Virtual Museum at IITiS PAN in Gliwice. The objects were acquired with three different 3D scanners (Cyberware 3030 MS, Konica-Minolta VI-9i, Faro LS 880 HE80), after scanning were subjected to data processing steps of scan matching with shape reconstruction and decimation. The number of vertices ranged from 25K to 172K. The object were chosen so as to present different features, including variations of physical texture (esp. 'chrzcielnica', 'Armadillo', 'Caro'), diverse basic shapes (esp. 'ukl_sc' and 'chrzcielnica', that have a lot of sharp edges vs 'bunny' and 'Sabines', with smooth curves), size (both in real life and as a model) and basic type of surface features.

All of the models were subjected to the same experiment protocol. A list of approximate number of regions was defined as $n_r \in \{3000, 2900, \ldots, 200, 100\}$. For each n_r value, number of points per region was decided as $n_p = \frac{n}{n_r}$. Then initial segmentation was created by randomly picking out region center point and points around it up to n_p. Actual number of regions for each n_r thus varies with object geometry and n. Value $n_r = 3000$, producing smallest number of points per region, produce most detailed representation (smallest errors and worst compression ratio). Initialization (initial point split) was performed by randomly separating input point set into disjoint regions. Each model was used in two experiments:

1. Experiment 'A', where only one initialization was performed ($n_r = 3000$), then regions were merged one at a time using proposed algorithm.
2. Experiment 'C', where for each n_r value separate initialization was performed;

The purpose of different experiments were to evaluate the iterative merging algorithm described in Sec. 3.2. and also to observe how representation errors grow with region size.

Quantitative results of experiments are presented on Fig. 3, 4 and 5. Fig. 3 presents surface approximation errors: RMSE and Hausdorff errors for case 1 (see Sec. 3.3–distance between input points and their images on the surface). Fig. 4 presents Hausdorff errors between input points and randomized from the representation. In the latter case number of points was constrained to original number of vertices in region, to enhance the readability of representation fidelity. Error bars are signify minimum and maximum error over the course of $n = 5$ trials. Compression ratios are presented on Fig. 5. Left plots correspond to experiment 'A', right to 'C'.

Qualitiative results are presented on Fig. 6. Objects are arranged in columns, in rows are presented: enlarged sample fragment from original point cloud; surfaces fitted at $n_r = 3000$, corresponding to $c \approx 0.3$; samples randomized from representation at $n_r = 3000, 2000, 1000$, corresponding to $c \approx 0.3, 0.1, 0.01$.

---

[1] http://graphics.stanford.edu/data/3Dscanrep/

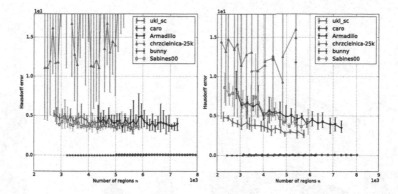

Fig. 4. Full representation errors (Hausdorff, ϵ_H) for different objects with varying number of regions. Left plot corresponds to experiment 'A', right to 'C' (see text).

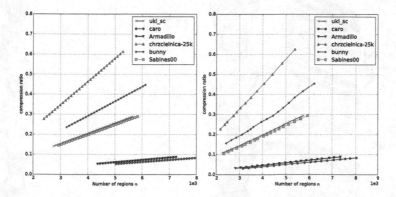

Fig. 5. Compression ratio c with varying number of regions. The value c measures the fraction of the number of coefficients needed to store the model, in relation to original point cloud. Left plot corresponds to experiment 'A', right to 'C' (see text).

The results confirm the validity of the method. While representation change (from original PC to SMM) introduces some errors at the start, the performance drop with successive merging steps is very small. Smooth objects, where sampling (point) density is higher than feature density ('ukl_sc', 'Armadillo', 'bunny', 'Sabines') can be represented with high fidelity with only 10% or less of initial number of coefficients. The case of slightly undersampled objects ('caro', 'chrzcielnica') is more problematic, as even in initial situation regions are too rich in features to be well represented by simple quadric surfaces, which leads to observable errors. Even in this case, after small precision loss, mostly in details in surface texture, the shape is well preserved throughout the n_r range.

Additional experiments were prepared to confirm that for all objects, the high precision representation is possible that preserves space gains in terms of compression factor. Precise rate-distortion optimization (and individual best value

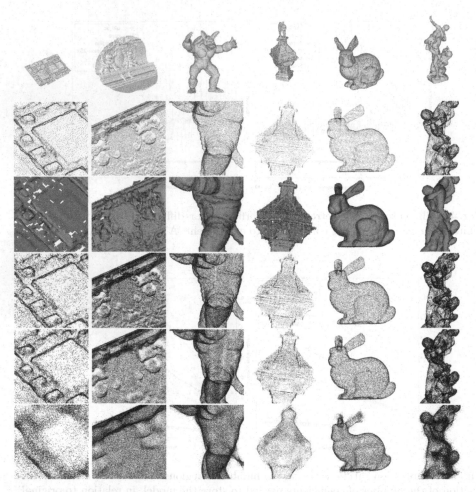

Fig. 6. Visualization of point clouds. Different objects in columns, in rows: object image; close up of fragment of original point set; surfaces fitted at $c \approx 0.3$; close up of points at $c \approx 0.3, 0.1, 0.01$. Last row requires only $\approx 1\%$ of number of coefficients to store in relation to original point cloud. See text.

of n_r) depends on individual application. As a possible extension, more advanced initial partition steps were considered (using K-Means and 'mini-batch' K-Means), but were found not to improve the performance. For given number of regions, different initial random splits did not introduce a noticeable change to the results. The only drawback observed was the occasional generation of outliers, especially near sharp corners. This is a result of using mixtures of Gaussians to approximate highly non-Gaussian distribution.

5   Conclusions

This paper presents an original approach to represent 3D scans of real-life objects. The algorithm produces a lossy representation of initial point cloud, effective in terms of compression factor. The basic principle applied combines local quadric surface fitting and modelling of distributions of point projections on the surface. Recovering point cloud from the representation can be quickly done by sampling from cached distribution.

Beyond efficient storage, the method has various interesting properties. It explicitly stores local object geometry, approximated with quadric surfaces. This facilitates various processing tasks, e.g. subsampling, part matching, or semantic map applications. The constrained nature of used surfaces and fitting process could in many cases lead to denoising performed at the time of estimation. The method also could be used for hole filling/inpainting applications. Representing shapes as a distribution can lead to new approaches for measuring similarity of 3D shapes, by using distribution distances. The only problems observed relate to occasional outliers and the necessity to set the number of regions individually for an object, based on its feature detail to number of samples ratio.

Acknowlegements. The work of P. Głomb has been partially supported by the Polish Ministry of Science and Higher Education project N N516 440738 'Active creation of environment model using 3D scanner and autonomous robot'. Work of A. Sochan was partially supported by Polish Ministry of Science and Higher Education project N N516 405137 'Representation of dynamic 3D scenes using the Atomic Shapes Network model' (National Science Centre DEC-2011/03/D/ST6 /03753).

References

1. Biegelbauer, G., Vincze, M., Wohlkinger, W.: Model-based 3D object detection. Machine Vision and Applications 21(4), 497–516 (2010)
2. Luchowski, L.: Segmenting 3D mesh images of the human face by local quadric parametrization. In: XI Conference "Medical Informatics & Technologies" (2006)
3. Guo, B.: Representation of arbitrary shapes using implicit quadrics. The Visual Computer 9, 267–277 (1993)
4. Farin, G.: Curves and Surfaces for CAGD, 5th edn. A Practical Guide. Morgan Kaufmann (2001)
5. Catmull, E., Clark, J.: Recursively generated B-spline surfaces on arbitrary topological meshes. Computer-Aided Design 10(6), 350–355 (1978)
6. Biederman, I.: Recognition-by-Components: A Theory of Human Image Understanding. Psychological Review 94, 115–147 (1987)
7. Tyler, C.W. (ed.): Computer Vision: From Surfaces to 3D Objects. Chapman and Hall/CRC (2011)
8. McIvor, A.M., Valkenburg, R.J.: A comparison of local surface geometry estimation methods. Machine Vision and Applications 10, 17–26 (1997)

9. Li, X.: Geometric property estimation from 3D range data points aided by local quadric surface fitting. In: Ninth International Conference on Computer Aided Design and Computer Graphics (CAD/CG 2005) (2005)
10. Xie, H., Wang, J., Hua, J., Qin, H., Kaufman, A.: Piecewise C^1 continuous surface reconstruction of noisy point clouds via local implicit quadric regression. In: Proceedings of the 14th IEEE Visualization 2003 (VIS 2003), p. 13 (2003)
11. Wurm, K.M., Hornung, A., Bennewitz, M., Stachniss, C., Burgard, W.: OctoMap: A probabilistic, flexible, and compact 3D map representation for robotic systems. In: Proc. of the ICRA 2010 Workshop on Best Practice in 3D Perception and Modeling for Mobile Manipulation (2010)
12. Núñez, P., Drews, P., Bandera, A., Rocha, R., Campos, M., Dias, J.: Change detection in 3d environments based on gaussian mixture model and robust structural matching for autonomous robotic applications. In: 2010 IEEE/RSJ International Conference on Intelligent Robots and Systems (IROS), pp. 2633–2638 (2010)
13. Pauly, M., Mitra, N.J., Guibas, L.: Uncertainty and variability in point cloud surface data. In: Symposium on Point-Based Graphics, pp. 77–84 (2004)
14. Rivlin, E., Dickinson, S.J., Rosenfeld, A.: Recognition by functional parts. Computer Vision and Image Understanding 62(2), 164–176 (1995)
15. Chandrasekaran, V., Wakin, M.B., Baron, D., Baraniuk, R.G.: Representation and compression of multi-dimensional piecewise functions using surflets. IEEE Transactions on Information Theory 55(1), 374–400 (2009)
16. Schnabel, R., Wahl, R., Klein, R.: Efficient ransac for point-cloud shape detection. Computer Graphics Forum 26(2), 214–226 (2007)
17. Dickinson, S.J., Metaxas, D., Pentland, A.: The role of model-based segmentation in the recovery of volumetric parts from range data. IEEE Transactions On Pattern Analysis And Machine Intelligence 19(3), 259–267 (1997)
18. Ahn, S.J.: Least Squares Orthogonal Distance Fitting of Curves and Surfaces in Space. Springer (2004)
19. Beer, F.P., Johnston, E.R.: Vector Mechanics for Engineers: Dynamics. McGraw-Hill International (1977)
20. Möller, T., Hughes, J.: Efficiently building a matrix to rotate one vector to another. Journal of Graphics Tools 4(4), 1–4 (1999)
21. Titterington, D.M., Smith, A.F.M., Makov, U.E.: Statistical Analysis of Finite Mixture Distributions. Wiley (1985)

Video Compression Algorithm
Based on Neural Network Structures

Michal Knop[1], Robert Cierniak[1,*], and Nimit Shah[2]

[1] Institute of Computational Intelligence, Czestochowa University of Technology,
Armii Krajowej 36, 42-200 Czestochowa, Poland
cierniak@kik.pcz.czest.pl
[2] Department of Electrical Engineering
M. S. University of Baroda, Vadodara, India

Abstract. The presented here paper describes a new approach to the video compression problem. Our method uses the neural network image compression algorithm which is based on the predictive vector quantization (PVQ). In this method
of image compression two different neural network structures are exploited in the
following elements of the proposed system: a competitive neural networks quantizer and a neuronal predictor. For the image compression based on this approach
it is important to correctly detect scene changes in order to improve performance
of the algorithm. We describe the image correlation method and discuss its effectiveness.

1 Introduction

Multimedia data transmission is widely spread nowadays. Most of the applications require effective data compression in order to lower the required bandwidth or storage
space. Various techniques of the data coding achieve this goal by reducing data redun-
dancy. In most of the algorithms and codecs a spatial compensation of images as well
as movement compensation in time is used. Video compression codecs can be found in
such applications as:

1. various video services over the satellite, cable, and land based transmission channels (e.g., using H.222.0 / MPEG-2 systems [1]);
2. by wire and wireless real-time video conference services (e.g., using H.32x [2] or
   Session Initiation Protocol (SIP) [3]);
3. Internet or local area network (LAN) video streaming [4];
4. storage formats (e.g., digital versatile disk (DVD), digital camcorders, and personal
   video recorders) [5].

Currently, many image compression standards are used. The most popular are JPEG
and MPEG. They differ in the level of compression as well as application. JPEG and
JPEG2000 standards are used for image compression with an adjustable compression
rate. There is a whole family of international compression standards of audiovisual data

---

* Corresponding author.

L. Rutkowski et al. (Eds.): ICAISC 2014, Part I, LNAI 8467, pp. 715–724, 2014.
© Springer International Publishing Switzerland 2014

combined in the MPEG standard, which is described in more details in literature (see e.g. [6]). The best known members are MPEG-1, MPEG-2, and MPEG-4. We used a PVQ (Predictive Vector Quantization) algorithm in our work to compress a video sequence. It combines a VQ (Vector Quantization) [7], [8] and DPCM (Differential Pulse Code Modulation). More information on the techniques can be found in sources [9], [10], [11]. To detect a scene change we used image correlation method. Then we can change necessary parameters of the predictor and the codebook.

2   Video Compression Algorithm

The design of the compression algorithm described here is based on the existing algorithm described in [9–11]. Selected algorithm due to neural network features presents better adjustment to a frame and gives better compression. The extension includes a scene change detection algorithm, which is based on the correlation between frames. The diagram below (see Fig. 1) shows the proposed algorithm.

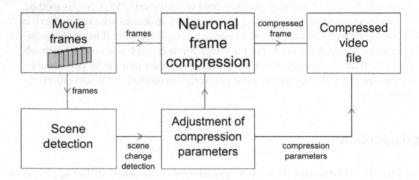

Fig. 1. Video compression algorithm

2.1   Neuronal Image Compression Algorithm

In the literature several methods for image compression have been proposed. Among them the vector quantization (VQ) technique has emerged as an effective tool in this area of research [12]. A special approach to image compression combines the VQ technique with traditional (scalar) differential pulse code modulation (DPCM) leading to the predictive vector quantization (PVQ). In this paper, we develop a methodology where the vector quantizer will be based on competitive neural network, whereas the predictor will be designed as the nonlinear neural network.

We assume that an image is represented by an $N_1 \times N_2$ array of pixels $\mathbf{X} = [x_{n_1,n_2}]$; $n_1 = 1, 2, \ldots, N_1$, $n_2 = 1, 2, \ldots, N_2$. The image is portioned into contiguous small blocks $\mathbf{Y}(k_1,k_2) = [y_{m_1,m_2}(k_1,k_2)]$ of the dimension $M_1 \times M_2$; $m_1 = 1, 2, \ldots, M_1$, $m_2 = 1, 2, \ldots, M_2$:

$$\mathbf{Y}(k_1,k_2) = \begin{bmatrix} y_{1,1}(k_1,k_2) & \cdots & y_{1,M_2}(k_1,k_2) \\ \vdots & \ddots & \vdots \\ y_{M_1,1}(k_1,k_2) & \cdots & y_{M_1,M_2}(k_1,k_2) \end{bmatrix}, \qquad (1)$$

where we identify: $k_1 = 1, 2, \ldots, K_1 = \frac{N_1}{M_1}$, $k_2 = 1, 2, \ldots, K_2 = \frac{N_2}{M_2}$.

The arrays (1) will be represented by the corresponding vectors

$$\mathbf{V}(k_1, k_2) = [v_1(k_1, k_2), \ldots, v_L(k_1, k_2)]^T, \qquad (2)$$

where: $L = M_1 \cdot M_2$, $v_1(k_1, k_2) = y_{1,1}(k_1, k_2)$, $v_L(k_1, k_2) = y_{M_1, M_2}(k_1, k_2)$. It means that the original image is represented by $\frac{N_1 \cdot N_2}{L}$ vectors $\mathbf{V}(k_1, k_2)$. The successive input vectors to the encoder $\mathbf{V}(t)$; $t = 1, 2, \ldots, K_1 \cdot K_2$ correspond to vectors $\mathbf{V}(k_1, k_2)$ in the line-by-line order.

The general architecture of the predictive vector quantization algorithm (PVQ) is depicted in Fig.2. This architecture is a straightforward vector extension of the traditional (scalar) differential pulse code modulation (DPCM) scheme (see e.g. [9, 10]).

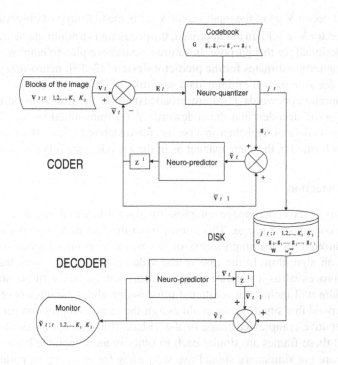

Fig. 2. The architecture of the image compression algorithm

The block diagram of the PVQ algorithm consists of the following elements: encoder and decoder, each containing an identical neural-predictor, codebook and neural vector quantizer. The successive input vectors $\mathbf{V}(t)$ are introduced to the encoder. The differences $\mathbf{E}(t) = [e_1(t), e_2(t), \ldots, e_L(t)]^T$ given by the equation

$$\mathbf{E}(t) = \mathbf{V}(t) - \overline{\mathbf{V}}(t) \qquad (3)$$

are formed, where: $\overline{\mathbf{V}}(t) = [\bar{v}_1(t), \bar{v}_2(t), \ldots, \bar{v}_L(t)]^T$ is the predictor of $\mathbf{V}(t)$. Statistically, the differences $\mathbf{E}(t)$ require fewer quantization bits than the original subimages $\mathbf{V}(t)$. The next step is vector quantization of $\mathbf{E}(t)$ using the set of reproduction vectors

$\mathbf{G} = [\mathbf{g}_0, \mathbf{g}_1, ..., \mathbf{g}_J]$ (codebook), where $\mathbf{g}_j = [g_{1j}, g_{2j}, ..., g_{qj}]^T$ (codewords). For every L-dimensional difference vector $\mathbf{E}(t)$, the distortion (usually the mean square error) between $\mathbf{E}(t)$ and every codeword $\mathbf{g}_j, j = 0, 1, ..., J-1$ is determined. The codeword $\mathbf{g}_{j^0}(t)$ is selected as the representation vector for $\mathbf{E}(t)$ if

$$d_{j^0} = \min_{0 \leq j \leq J} d_j, \tag{4}$$

where we can take a measure d in expression (4) as e.g. the Euclidean distance. When adding the prediction vector $\overline{\mathbf{V}}(t)$ to the quantized difference vector $\mathbf{g}_{j^0}(t)$ we get the reconstructed approximation $\widetilde{\mathbf{V}}(t)$ of the original input vector $\mathbf{V}(t)$, i.e.

$$\widetilde{\mathbf{V}}(t) = \overline{\mathbf{V}}(t) + \mathbf{g}_{j^0}(t). \tag{5}$$

The predicted vector $\overline{\mathbf{V}}(t)$ of the input vector $\mathbf{V}(t)$ is made from past observation of reconstructed vector $\widetilde{\mathbf{V}}(t-1)$. In our approach, the predictor is a nonlinear neural network specifically designed for this purpose. In future research we plan to employ orthogonal series nonparametric estimates for the predictor design [13–15], neuro-fuzzy predictor [16–19], and decision trees for mining data streams [20–25].

The appropriate codewords $j^0(t)$ are broadcasted via the transmission channel to the decoder. In the decoder, first the codewords $j^0(t)$ transmitted by the channel are decoded using codebook and then inverse vector-quantized. Next, the reconstructed vector $\widetilde{\mathbf{V}}(t)$ is formed in the same manner as in the encoder (see relation (4)).

2.2 Scene Detection

The parameters of the neural image compression algorithm are strictly determined basing on given compressed image. This comes from the fact that these parameters are established through the learning process of the neural networks applied in this neural compression algorithm. In the case of the video compression, every frame of the film will be processed as a separate image. Unfortunately, that a file containing our compressed film will include an additional information about parameters of this compression. To avoid this situation, we could assign the same compression parameters to several consecutive compressed frame of the video. This concept is based on the assumption that these frames are similar each to other in an acceptable level. Clearly, if these frames are not similar we should use separately for every frame parameters determined for a given frame. For instance, we observed this situation when a change of the scene in the film is encountered. In our concept, we will try to detect the key frame which separates neighboring scenes. Thanks to this idea, we save a space in the file containing compressed film, assigning the same parameters to all frames from a given scene, and we improve quality of the compressed film giving different compression parameters for significantly different frames.

In this context, the scene detection is a crucial problem. Among many other approaches [26–28], the methods based on the correlation coefficient are worth consideration. Correlation coefficient is the number indicating the level of the linear ratio between two random variables. Cuts, gradual transitions, and motion can be distinguished in the video frames using this parameter. For the cuts, the difference between the two frames is large, and the correlation of these frames is low. For a gradual transition, pixel values of two adjacent frames are different, but are similar in the edges and textures, so the correlation in the spatial domain is high [29]. A histogram of brightness changes slightly for motion scenes that take place on the same background. However, for scenes of gradual transition or cuts, it changes gradually or abruptly.

Differences between objects motion in the scene and the scene change can be obtained by comparison of the key frames with subsequent frames. The key frame histogram H_{kf} can be defined as:

$$H_{kf}(r_k) = n_k, \tag{6}$$

where r_k is the k-th level of brightness, n_k is the number of pixels in frame of the brightness level r_k.

For N frames in the video, we calculate the histogram H_i, i = 2,3, ..., N. The correlation between H_{kf} and H_i can be defined as:

$$corr(H_{kf}, H_i) = \frac{\sum_{j=0}^{m}(H_{kf}(j) - h_{kf})(H_i(j) - h_i)}{\sqrt{\sum_{j=0}^{m}(H_{kf}(j) - h_{kf})^2 \sum_{j=0}^{m}(H_i(j) - h_i)^2}}, \tag{7}$$

where m is the number of brightness scale levels r_k; h_{kf}, h_i are mean values of H_{kf} and H_i [30], respectively, and can be defined as:

$$h_i = \frac{1}{m} \sum_{j=0}^{m} H_i(j). \tag{8}$$

Then, the correlation value computed from Eq. (7) is compared with a threshold. If the correlation value is lower than the assumed threshold, the algorithm determines a new key frame. A diagram of the proposed scene change detection algorithm is shown in Fig. 3.

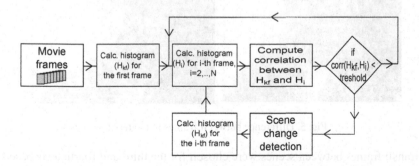

Fig. 3. Scene change detection algorithm

3   Experimental Results

The efficiency of the algorithm was tested on a set of frames extracted directly from a video file of a 576x416 resolution with 256 levels of gray. Four tests were conducted.

In the first and second tests, the frames were compressed within single scene (Fig. 4). In the first test the frames were compressed with a separate codebook and predictor for each of the frames (Fig. 5). For the second test, a single codebook and predictor were used for all frames (Fig. 6).

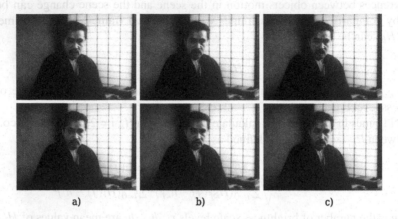

a)   b)   c)

Fig. 4. Original sequence (a); compressed sequence: test 1 (b); compressed sequence: test 2 (c)

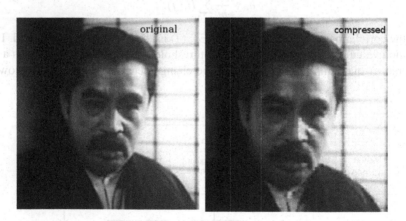

Fig. 5. Difference between frames in the test 1

A transit frames between scenes were chosen for the third and fourth tests based on the scene change detection algorithm (Fig. 7). In this algorithm each frame is compared with the keyframe. When the new scene is detected the algorithm marks a new keyframe (see Fig. 8).

In the test 3 the same codebook and predictor were used before and after the scene change. As the results show, this approach is insufficient in case of a major scene change (Fig.9). For the fourth test, the scene transition was detected and separate codebooks and predictors were created for frames before and after the scene transition (Fig.10).

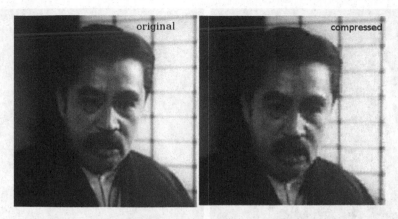

Fig. 6. Difference between frames in the test 2

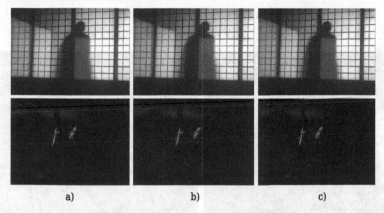

a)   b)   c)

Fig. 7. Original sequence (a); compressed sequence: test 3 (b); compressed sequence: test 4 (c)

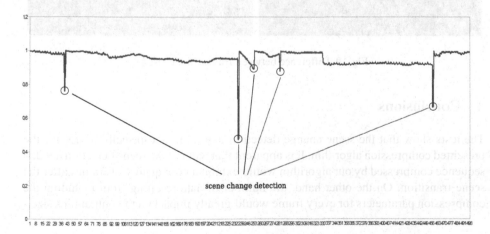

scene change detection

Fig. 8. Scene change detection

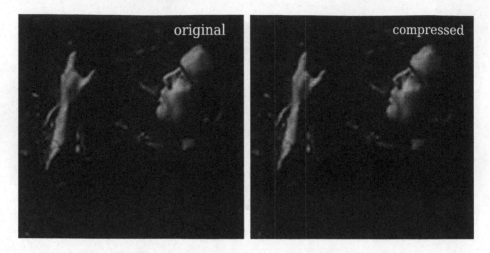

Fig. 9. Difference between frames in the test 3

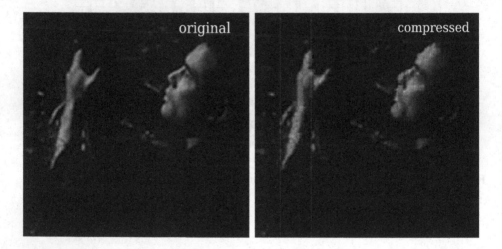

Fig. 10. Difference between frames in the test 4

4   Conclusions

The tests show that the scene change detection algorithm is especially useful for the presented compression algorithm. It is apparent that without the scene detection a video sequence compressed by our algorithm would exhibit a poor quality of frames after the scene transition. On the other hand, the number of data resulting from including the compression parameters for every frame would greatly impact on the output files size.

References

1. Generic coding of moving pictures and associated audio information–Part 1: Systems. Int. Telecommun. Union-Telecommun. (ITU-T), Recommendation H.222.0, MPEG-2 Systems (1994)
2. Narrow-band visual telephone systems and terminal equipment. Int. Telecommun. Union-Telecommun. (ITU-T), Recommendation H.320 (1999)
3. Rosenberg, J., Schulzrinne, H., Camarillo, G., Johnston, A., Peterson, J., Sparks, R., Handley, M., Schooler, E.: SIP: Session initiation protocol. Internet Eng. Task Force (IETF). Request for Comments (RFC), vol. 3261 (2002)
4. Schulzrinne, H., Casner, S., Frederick, R., Jacobson, V.: RTP: A transport protocol for real-time applications. Internet Eng. Task Force (IETF). Request for Comments (RFC), vol. 1889 (1996)
5. Sullivan, G.J., Wiegand, T.: Video compression – from concepts to the H.264/AVC standard. Proceedings of the IEEE 93, 18–31 (2005)
6. Clarke, R.J.: Digital compression of still images and video. Academic Press, London (1995)
7. Gray, R.: Vector quantization. IEEE ASSP Magazine 1, 4–29 (1984)
8. Gersho, A., Gray, R.M.: Vector quantization and signal compression. Kluwer Academic Publishers (1992)
9. Rutkowski, L., Cierniak, R.: Image compression by competitive learning neural networks and predictive vector quantization. International Journal of Applied Mathematics and Computer Science 18, 147–157 (1996)
10. Cierniak, R., Rutkowski, L.: On image compression by competitive neural networks and optimal linear predictors. Signal Processing: Image Communication 15, 559–565 (2000)
11. Cierniak, R.: An image compression algorithm based on neural networks. In: Rutkowski, L., Siekmann, J.H., Tadeusiewicz, R., Zadeh, L.A. (eds.) ICAISC 2004. LNCS (LNAI), vol. 3070, pp. 706–711. Springer, Heidelberg (2004)
12. Fowler, J.E., Carbonara, M.R., Ahalt, S.C.: Image coding using differential vector quantization. IEEE Transactions on Circuits and Systems for Video Technology 3, 350–367 (1993)
13. Rutkowski, L.: A general approach for nonparametric fitting of functions and their derivatives with applications to linear circuits identification. IEEE Transactions Circuits Systems CAS-33, 812–818 (1986)
14. Rutkowski, L.: Identification of MISO nonlinear regressions in the presence of a wide class of disturbances. IEEE Transactions on Information Theory IT-37, 214–216 (1991)
15. Greblicki, W., Rutkowska, D., Rutkowski, L.: An orthogonal series estimate of time-varying regression. Annals of the Institute of Statistical Mathematics 35, 215–228 (1983)
16. Korytkowski, M., Rutkowski, L., Scherer, R.: From ensemble of fuzzy classifiers to single fuzzy rule base classifier. In: Rutkowski, L., Tadeusiewicz, R., Zadeh, L.A., Zurada, J.M. (eds.) ICAISC 2008. LNCS (LNAI), vol. 5097, pp. 265–272. Springer, Heidelberg (2008)
17. Rutkowski, L., Przybyl, A., Cpalka, K.: Novel on-line speed profile generation for industrial machine tool based on flexible neuro-fuzzy approximation. IEEE Transactions on Industrial Electronics 59, 1238–1247 (2012)
18. Korytkowski, M., Rutkowski, L., Scherer, R.: On combining backpropagation with boosting. In: IEEE International Joint Conference on Neural Network (IJCNN) Proceedings, Vancouver, July 16-21, vols. 1-10, pp. 1274–1277 (2006)
19. Greenfield, S., Chiclana, F.: Type-reduction of the discretized interval type-2 fuzzy set: approaching the continuous case through progressively finer discretization. Journal of Artificial Intelligence and Soft Computing Research 1, 193 (2011)

20. Pietruczuk, L., Duda, P., Jaworski, M.: A new fuzzy classifier for data streams. In: Rutkowski, L., Korytkowski, M., Scherer, R., Tadeusiewicz, R., Zadeh, L.A., Zurada, J.M. (eds.) ICAISC 2012, Part I. LNCS (LNAI), vol. 7267, pp. 318–324. Springer, Heidelberg (2012)
21. Jaworski, M., Duda, P., Pietruczuk, L.: On fuzzy clustering of data streams with concept drift. In: Rutkowski, L., Korytkowski, M., Scherer, R., Tadeusiewicz, R., Zadeh, L.A., Zurada, J.M. (eds.) ICAISC 2012, Part II. LNCS (LNAI), vol. 7268, pp. 82–91. Springer, Heidelberg (2012)
22. Rutkowski, L., Pietruczuk, L., Duda, P., Jaworski, M.: Decision trees for mining data streams based on the McDiarmid's bound. IEEE Transactions on Knowledge and Data Engineering 25, 1272–1279 (2013)
23. Pietruczuk, L., Duda, P., Jaworski, M.: Adaptation of decision trees for handling concept drift. In: Rutkowski, L., Korytkowski, M., Scherer, R., Tadeusiewicz, R., Zadeh, L.A., Zurada, J.M. (eds.) ICAISC 2013, Part I. LNCS (LNAI), vol. 7894, pp. 459–473. Springer, Heidelberg (2013)
24. Rutkowski, L., Jaworski, M., Pietruczuk, L., Duda, P.: Decision trees for mining data streams based on the gaussian approximation. IEEE Transactions on Knowledge and Data Engineering 26, 108–119 (2014)
25. Rutkowski, L., Jaworski, M., Pietruczuk, L., Duda, P.: The CART decision tree for mining data streams. Information Sciences 266, 1–15 (2014)
26. Chen, L., Feris, R., Turk, M.: Efficient partial shape matching using Smith-Waterman algorithm. In: IEEE Computer Society Conference on Computer Vision and Pattern Recognition Workshops, CVPRW, pp. 1–6 (2008)
27. Adhikari, P., Gargote, N., Digge, J., Hogade, B.G.: Abrupt scene change detection. World Academy of Science, Engineering and Technology 18, 687–692 (2008)
28. Seeling, P.: Scene change detection for uncompressed video. In: Technological Developments in Education and Automation, pp. 11–14 (2010)
29. Li, Z., Liu, G.: A novel scene change detection algorithm based on the 3D wavelet transform. In: IEEE International Conference on Image Processing, ICIP, pp. 1536–1539 (2008)
30. Radwan, N.I., Salem, N.M., El Adawy, M.I.: Histogram correlation for video scene change detection. In: Wyld, D.C., Zizka, J., Nagamalai, D. (eds.) Advances in Computer Science, Engineering & Applications. AISC, vol. 166, pp. 765–773. Springer, Heidelberg (2012)

A New Image Reconstruction
from Projections Algorithm

Anna Lorent[1], Robert Cierniak[1], Piotr Dobosz[1], and Olga Rebrova[2]

[1] Institute of Computational Intelligence, Czestochowa University of Technology,
Armii Krajowej 36, 42-200 Czestochowa, Poland
cierniak@kik.pcz.czest.pl
[2] The Russian National Research Medical University,
Department of Medical Cybernetics and Informatics, Moscow, Russia

Abstract. In this paper we propose a new iterative algorithm for image reconstruction from projections problem. The reconstruction problem is reformulated as a system of linear equations with a Toeplitz-block-Toeplitz coefficient matrix. The structure of the matrix enables us to use efficient methods for solving the system. We investigate the use of gradient methods benefiting from fast FFT-based matrix-vector multiplication for minimizing the quadratic form objective function. We present and compare simulation results for the algorithm with different methods for step size selection.

1 Introduction

Computed Tomography (CT) is a widely used imaging technique enabling a non-invasive inspection of the inside of an object. The key scientific problem emerging with regard to that technique is developing new, efficient algorithms for image reconstruction from projections. In the present paper we concentrate on the applications of CT in the discipline of medicine. It presents more challenges than industrial CT, because of the detrimental influence of the x-ray radiation on the human body, which needs to be taken into consideration.

The most widely used image reconstruction methods are algebraic reconstruction techniques (ART) and analytical reconstruction methods, e.g. filtered back-projection method (FBP) [1]. Also neural networks, especially recurrent Hopfield-type networks, extensively used for numerous image processing tasks (see e.g. [2,3,4,5]), find their application in image reconstruction (see e.g. [6,7]). In recent years methods based on the statistical models of the projection acquisition process are becoming increasingly popular.

In this paper we propose a new analytical, iterative algorithm based on the approach described in papers [7,8,9,10].

2 Reconstruction Algorithm

The input to every reconstruction from projections algorithm consists of projections $\bar{p}(s, \Psi)$ acquired from a scanner of a given geometry from which it is

L. Rutkowski et al. (Eds.): ICAISC 2014, Part I, LNAI 8467, pp. 725–732, 2014.

possible to determine the unknown distribution of the attenuation coefficient $\mu(i,j)$ at the cross section of the body.

We derive our approach assuming the parallel beam scanner geometry, but it should be noted that it is possible to adapt it to different geometries, e.g. fan-beam projections data, with rebinning techniques.

The first step of the reconstruction algorithm is the backprojection operation described by the formula

$$\tilde{\mu}(i,j) \cong \Delta_\alpha \sum_{\psi=0}^{\Psi-1} \hat{p}(s_{ij}, \psi\Delta_\alpha), \tag{1}$$

where $s_{ij} = i\Delta_s \cos\psi\Delta_\alpha + j\Delta_s \sin\psi\Delta_\alpha$ defines the position of a pixel (i,j) in the coordinate system of the screen and $\psi\Delta_\alpha$ specifies the projection angle.

Because of the discrete nature of the projections data $\hat{p}$, measured with a raster Δ_s, performed during the backprojection operation, it is very unlikely for any ray to pass exactly through a given point (i,j). The remedy for this is the use of the interpolation function $int\,(\cdot)$ to specify how other pixels affect the given pixel (i,j),

$$\bar{p}(s_{ij}, \psi\Delta_\alpha) \cong \Delta_s \sum_{l} \hat{p}(l\Delta_s, \psi\Delta_\alpha) \cdot int\,(s_{ij} - l\Delta_s), \tag{2}$$

As shown in [9], [10] the above relations make it possible to formulate the image after backprojection $\hat{\mu}$ as a convolution of the original image with a geometrical distortion term h.

$$\tilde{\mu}(i,j) = \sum_{\hat{i}=0}^{N-1} \sum_{\hat{j}=0}^{N-1} \mu^*(\hat{i},\hat{j})h(i-\hat{i}, j-\hat{j}) \tag{3}$$

where $\mu^*(i,j)$ is the unknown image that we attempt to reconstruct and the coefficients h are defined as

$$h(\Delta i, \Delta j) = \Delta_\alpha (\Delta_s)^2 \cdot \sum_{\psi=0}^{\Psi-1} int\,(\Delta i\Delta_s \cos\psi\Delta_\alpha + \Delta j\Delta_s \sin\psi\Delta_\alpha), \tag{4}$$

where $\Delta i = i - \hat{i}$, $\Delta j = j - \hat{j}$.

Equation (3) can be written in a matrix form as

$$\tilde{\mu} = \mathbf{H}\mu^* \tag{5}$$

where the relation between the elements of the coefficient matrix $\mathbf{H}$ and coefficients h is as follows

$$\mathbf{H}_{i \cdot N+j, \hat{i} \cdot N+\hat{j}} = h(i-\hat{i}, j-\hat{j}) \tag{6}$$

Image reconstruction algorithm can thus be formulated as solving the system of linear equations (5) for μ^*.

Matrix $\mathbf{H}$ is invertible, symmetric and positive definite which makes it possible to find the exact solution of the system. Also, as a deconvolution matrix of the two dimensional signal, it exhibits a Toeplitz-block-Toeplitz structure. This structure is characterized by identical blocks on each descending diagonal of the matrix. Each of those blocks is in turn a Toeplitz (diagonally constant) matrix. The structure of 256×256 matrix $\mathbf{H}$ can be seen in Fig. 1.

Moreover, the condition number of $\mathbf{H}$ is low enough to make it possible to allow for finding a reliable solution of the system (5) without the need of regularization. The relation between the condition number of $\mathbf{H}$ and its size is presented in Fig. 2. For $2^{20} \times 2^{20}$ matrix, used for reconstruction of 1024×1024 image, the condition number $\kappa(\mathbf{H})$ will be approximately 2500. It means that for those dimensions we can lose up to 3 decimal digits of accuracy, which for our purposes constitutes a reliable solution.

However, the majority of direct methods for solving linear systems cannot be used for this reconstruction problem, because the size of matrix $\mathbf{H}$ is too large. Reconstruction of the $N \times N$ image requires the coefficient matrix $\mathbf{H}$ of size $N^2 \times N^2$. It means that 1024×1024 image reconstruction results in a 1048576×1048576 linear system. Such a matrix with double precision elements needs 8TB of memory and it can be easily seen that the problem would quickly become intractable.

It is possible to avoid this problem by utilizing the special structure of the matrix $\mathbf{H}$ and solving the system with a method that benefits from it. One of possible methods suitable for our problem is a gradient descent method which, with the efficient method for computing matrix-vector products, is a simple and effective algorithm for solving the problem at hand.

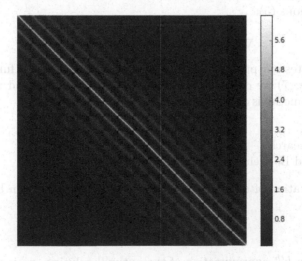

Fig. 1. 256×256 coefficient matrix $\mathbf{H}$

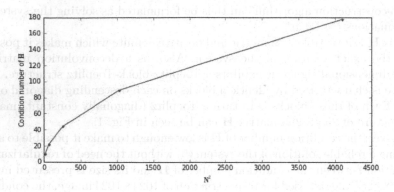

Fig. 2. Condition number of the $N^2 \times N^2$ coefficient matrix $\mathbf{H}$ used for $N \times N$ image reconstruction

2.1   Solving of the Linear System

Taking into consideration the fact that matrix $\mathbf{H}$ is symmetric and positive-definite it is possible to formulate the objective function as a following strictly convex quadratic form

$$L(\mu^*) = \mu^{*T}\mathbf{H}\mu^* - \tilde{\mu}^T\mu^* \tag{7}$$

For the symmetric $\mathbf{H}$ the gradient of (7) can be written as

$$\nabla L(\mu^*) = \mathbf{H}\mu^* - \tilde{\mu} \tag{8}$$

As can be easily seen the minimum of (7) is the solution of our original system of linear equations (5).

$$\nabla L = \mathbf{H}\mu^* - \tilde{\mu} = 0 \implies \mathbf{H}\mu^* = \tilde{\mu} \tag{9}$$

This reformulates our problem as minimization of the objective function (7).

To minimize (7) we chose the gradient descent algorithm and we compared three different methods for selecting the step size α, namely:

– constant α,
– exact line search,
– Barzilai and Borwein method (BB method)

A single iteration of a general gradient descent algorithm can be written as follows

$$\mu^*_{k+1} = \mu^*_k - \alpha_k \mathbf{g}_k \tag{10}$$

where μ^*_k is the kth approximation of the optimal solution, α_k is a step size in the kth iteration and $\mathbf{g}_k = \nabla L(\mu^*_k)$.

The gradient descent method in which α_k is determined with exact line search is also known as the Steepest Descent method. The step size is chosen so as to minimize the objective function value along the direction of the gradient at a given point.

$$\alpha_k^{SD} = \arg\min_{\alpha} L(\mu_k^* - \alpha \mathbf{g}_k) \tag{11}$$

$$\alpha_k^{SD} = \frac{\mathbf{g}_k^T \mathbf{g}_k}{\mathbf{g}_k^T \mathbf{H} \mathbf{g}_k} \tag{12}$$

The method proposed by Barzilai and Borwein in [11] is an efficient algorithm for determining the step size for gradient method taking into consideration the result of the previous iteration and approximating the secant equation. It is computationally inexpensive in comparison with the exact line search, since the procedure of step size determination does not require a matrix-vector multiplication.

$$\alpha_k^{BB} = \arg\min_{\alpha} \| \Delta\mu_k^* - \alpha \Delta\mathbf{g}_k \| \tag{13}$$

where $\Delta\mu_{\mathbf{k}}^* = \mu^*{}_k - \mu^*{}_{k-1}$ and $\Delta\mathbf{g}_k = \mathbf{g}_k - \mathbf{g}_{k-1}$
The minimization of (13) results in the following formula for α_k

$$\alpha_k^{BB} = \frac{\Delta\mathbf{g}_k^T \Delta\mu_k^*}{\Delta\mathbf{g}_k^T \Delta\mathbf{g}_k} \tag{14}$$

For the gradient method as described above it is not required that the matrix H should be explicitly stored in memory. The algorithm needs to be provided only with a procedure performing matrix-vector multiplication.

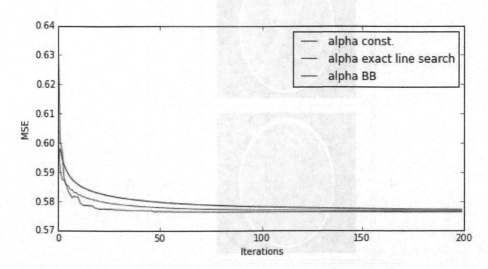

Fig. 3. The MSE value as a function of the number of iterations

Table 1. Simulation results after 200 iterations for gradient descent with different methods for step size α selection a) original image b) constant α c) α determined with exact line search d) α determined with the BB method

	Image	MSE	Time
a)		—	—
b)		0.5771	173s
c)		0.5766	310s
d)		0.5763	192s

Table 2. Intermediate simulation results for step size selection with the BB method

	a)	b)	c)
Iter.:	10	20	30
MSE:	0.5815	0.5776	0.5770

It greatly simplifies our reconstruction problem because the structure of H makes it possible to write such an operation as a convolution of a given vector with a vector of coefficients h (4). This in turn enables us to use FFT and perform the efficient convolution in the frequency domain, since convolution in the time or space domain can be computed as multiplication in the frequency domain.

$$\tilde{\mu} = \mathcal{F}^{-1}\{\mathcal{F}\{\mathbf{h}\} \cdot \mathcal{F}\{\mu^*\}\} \tag{15}$$

Computational complexity of such a matrix-vector multiplication is then $O(M \log_2 M)$ for the $M \times M$ matrix.

3 Experimental Results

To test the presented approach we performed computer simulations reconstructing a mathematical model of the human head - the Shepp-Logan phantom. The size of the reconstructed image was 1024×1024 pixels. Three different methods for selecting the step size α for gradient descent method were compared: a) constant α, b) α determined with the exact line search and c) α determined with the BB method as described above. For a constant α we chose the value 0.00018 which proved to be the largest value guaranteeing the convergence of the algorithm.

The algorithm was implemented sequentially and executed on the 3.2 GHz AMD Phenom machine.

The results for different methods after 200 iterations can be seen in Table 1 together with the original Shepp-Logan phantom. The behaviour of the MSE metric with respect to the number of iterations of the algorithm was shown in Fig. 3. Intermediate reconstruction results for the algorithm using the BB method are shown in Table 2.

4   Conclusions

As can be seen in Fig. 3 and Table 1 gradient methods with adaptive step size significantly outperform the algorithm with a constant step size. The largest rate of convergence is achieved for algorithm c), i.e. with the BB method for step size selection and the smallest for the algorithm a) with constant α.

It is worth noting that in case of the algorithm c) the number of iterations required for obtaining the image quality that is satisfactory for the human expert is as low as 30 iterations.

The running time of a single iteration is approximately one second for the sequential implementation of the algorithm which, in this setting, makes the reconstruction process reasonably fast. However the algorithm can be easily parallelized and implemented for GPU which will result in a very significant decrease in the reconstruction time allowing for a nearly real-time performance.

References

1. Cierniak, R.: X-Ray Computed Tomography in Biomedical Engineering. Springer, London (2011)
2. Laskowski, Ł.: Hybrid-maximum neural network for depth analysis from stereo-image. In: Rutkowski, L., Scherer, R., Tadeusiewicz, R., Zadeh, L.A., Zurada, J.M. (eds.) ICAISC 2010, Part II. LNCS, vol. 6114, pp. 47–55. Springer, Heidelberg (2010)
3. Laskowski, Ł.: A novel continuous dual mode neural network in stereo-matching process. In: Diamantaras, K., Duch, W., Iliadis, L.S. (eds.) ICANN 2010, Part III. LNCS (LNAI), vol. 6354, pp. 294–297. Springer, Heidelberg (2010)
4. Laskowski, Ł.: Objects auto-selection from stereo-images realised by self-correcting neural network. In: Rutkowski, L., Korytkowski, M., Scherer, R., Tadeusiewicz, R., Zadeh, L.A., Zurada, J.M. (eds.) ICAISC 2012, Part I. LNCS (LNAI), vol. 7267, pp. 119–125. Springer, Heidelberg (2012)
5. Laskowski, Ł.: A novel hybrid-maximum neural network in stereo-matching process. Neural Computing and Applications 23(7-8), 2435–2450 (2013)
6. Cichocki, A., Unbehauen, R., Lendl, M., Weinzierl, K.: Neural networks for linear inverse problems with incomplete data especially in application to signal and image reconstruction. Neurocomputing 8, 7–41 (1995)
7. Cierniak, R.: A 2D approach to tomographic image reconstruction using a Hopfield-type neural network. International Journal Artificial Intelligence in Medicine 43, 113–125 (2008)
8. Cierniak, R.: A new approach to image reconstruction from projections problem using a recurrent neural network. Applied Mathematics and Computer Science 18, 147–157 (2008)
9. Cierniak, R.: A novel approach to image reconstruction problem from fan-beam projections using recurrent neural network. In: Rutkowski, L., Tadeusiewicz, R., Zadeh, L.A., Zurada, J.M. (eds.) ICAISC 2008. LNCS (LNAI), vol. 5097, pp. 752–761. Springer, Heidelberg (2008)
10. Cierniak, R.: New neural network algorithm for image reconstruction from fan-beam projections. Neurocomputing 72, 3238–3244 (2009)
11. Barzilai, J., Borwein, J.M.: Two point step size gradient method. IMA J. Numer. Anal. 8, 141–148 (1988)

Discovering Multi-sense Features from Images Using Random Indexing

Haïfa Nakouri[1] and Mohamed Limam[1,2]

[1] Institut Supérieur de Gestion, LARODEC Laboratory
University of Tunis, Tunisia
[2] Dhofar University, Oman
nakouri.hayfa@gmail.com, mohamed.limam@isg.rnu.tn

Abstract. Random Indexing is a recent technique for dimensionality reduction while creating Word Space model from a given text. The present work explores the possible application of Random Indexing in discovering feature semantics from image data. The features appearing in the image database are plotted onto a multi-dimensional Feature Space using Random Indexing. The geometric distance between features is used as an indicative of their contextual similarity. Clustering by Committee method is used to aggregate similar features. In this paper, we show that the Feature Space model based on Random Indexing can be used effectively to constellate similar features. The proposed clustering approach has been applied to the Corel databases and motivating results have obtained.

1 Introduction

Most of the image analysis approaches consider each image as a whole, represented by a D-dimensional vector. However, the user's query is often just one part of the query image (i.e. a region in the image that has an obvious semantic meaning). Therefore, rather than viewing each image as a whole, it is more reasonable to view it as a set of semantic regions of features. In this context, we consider an image feature as a relevant semantic region of an image that can summarize the whole or a part of the context of the image.

In this work, we propose the Feature Space model similarly to the Word Space model [10] that has long been used for semantic indexing of text. The key idea of a Feature Space model is to assign a vector to each feature in the high dimensional vector space, whose relative directions are assumed to indicate semantic similarities or similar representations of the features. However, high dimensionality of the semantic space of features, sparseness of the data and large sized data sets are the major drawbacks of the Feature Space model.

Random Indexing (RI) [5, 9] is an approach developed to cope with the problem of high dimensionality in the Word Space model. It is an incremental approach proposed as an alternative to Latent Semantic Indexing (LSI) [6]. To the best of our knowledge, no Random Indexing approaches have been used to deal with image features in the Feature Space model especially for similar semantics

L. Rutkowski et al. (Eds.): ICAISC 2014, Part I, LNAI 8467, pp. 733–744, 2014.

discovery between features in image data sets. In this paper we aim to show that a Feature Space model constructed using Random Indexing can be used efficiently to cluster features, which in turn can be used to identify the representation or the context of the feature. In a Feature Space model, the geometric distance between the features is an indicative of their semantic similarity. The interesting point in RI is that it enables finding relevant image documents even if they do not contain the query key features and the whole procedure is incremental and automatic. The fact that RI does not require an exact match to return useful results fits perfectly with the scenario of feature image clustering. Assume that there is a query image of a 'cat' in the grass and the user is interested in finding all images in the database that contain a 'cat'. It is obviously not a good idea to use exact match since no 'cat' image would have exactly the same low-level features with the query image itself. Hence, in the context of our work, if we consider an image as a document, the 'cat' object is then one of the words in the document. The only difference is that the 'cat' object is not a word but a multidimensional feature vector. The objective of using the *context vectors* computed on the language data is to map the features onto the Feature Space.

We used the Clustering by Committee (CBC) [8] method to agglomerate similar features and each constellation represents a context of images. In this work, we attempt to show that the Feature Space model based on Random Indexing can be used efficiently to cluster features, which in turn can be used to approximate the contexts represented by a feature.

The rest of this paper is organized as follows. Sect. 2 introduces the Feature Space model and the Random Indexing approach. Sect. 3 presents the proposed feature clustering process based on Random Indexing. Sect. 4 presents the experimental results of the proposed work.

2   Vector-Based Feature Analysis Using Random Indexing

Basically, vector-based semantic analysis is a technology for extracting semantically similar terms from textual data by observing the distribution and collocation of terms in text. The result of running a vector-based semantic analysis on a text collection can be used to find correspondences across terms. The meaning or representation of a term is interpreted by the context it is used in. By analogy to the Word Space model which is a spacial representation of word meaning, we consider a Feature Space model as a spacial representation of feature meaning.

2.1   Feature Space Model

In this model, the complete features of any image (containing n features) can be represented in a n-dimensional space in which each feature occupies a specific point in the space, and has a vector associated with it defining its meaning. The features are placed on the Feature Space model according to their distributional properties in the image, such that:

1. The features that are used within similar group of features (i.e. in a similar context) should be placed nearer to each other.
2. The features that lie closer to each other in the Feature Space represent the same context. Meanwhile, the features that lie farther from each other in the Feature Space model are dissimilar in their representation.

2.2   The Feature Space Model and Random Indexing

Random Indexing (RI) is based on Kanerva's work [4] on sparse distributed memory. It was proposed by Karlgren and Sahlgren [5, 9] and was originally used as a text mining technique. It is a word-occurrence based approach to statistical semantics. RI uses statistical approximations of the full word-occurrences data to achieve dimensionality reduction. Besides, it is an incremental vector space model that is computationally less demanding. The Random Indexing model reduces dimensionality by, instead of giving each word a whole dimension, it gives them a random vector with less dimensionality than the total number of words in the text. Thus, RI results in a much quicker time and fewer required dimensions.

Random Indexing used sparse, high-dimensional random *index vectors* to represent image features. Sparsity ensures that the chance of any two arbitrary index vectors having an overlapping meaning (i.e. a cosine similarity [10] that is non-zero) is very low. Given that each feature has been assigned a random *index vector*, features similarities can be calculated by computing a feature-context co-occurrence matrix. Each row in the matrix represents a feature and the feature vectors are of the same dimensionality as are the random vectors assigned to images. Each time a feature is found in an image, that image's random *index vector* is added to the row of the feature in question. In this way, features are represented in the matrix by high-dimensional semantic *context vectors* which contain trances of each context the feature has been observed in.

This technique is akin to Latent Semantic Analysis (LSA) of Indexing (LSI) [6], except that no dimension reduction (e.g. Singular Value Decomposition (SVD)) is needed to reduce the dimensions of the co-occurrence matrix, since the dimensionality of the random *index vectors* is smaller than the number of images in the training data. This makes the technique more efficient that the LSI methods, since SVD is a computationally demanding operation. The technique is also easier to scale and more flexible as regards unexpected data than are methods which rely on dimension reduction. A new image does not require a larger matrix but will simply be assigned a new random *index vector* of the same dimensionality as the preceding ones and a new term requires no more than a row in the matrix.

The size of the context used to accumulate feature-image matrix may range from just few features on each side of the focus feature to the entire image data consisting of more than hundred features [9].

In the context of our work, the context of a feature image is understood as the visual surrounding of a feature. For instance, an "umbrella" and "surf board" are two features representing the context "beach".

A context vector thus obtained can be used to represent the distributional information of the feature into the geometrical space. This is similar to each feature being assigned a unique unary vector of dimension d, called *index vector*. The *context vector* for a feature can be obtained by summing up the *index vectors* of the features on the either side of it. In other words, all the features representing the same context should have approximately equal *context vectors*.

Random Indexing accumulates *context vectors* to form the Feature Space model in a two step process.

1. Each feature in the image is assigned a unique and randomly generated d-dimensional vector called the *index vector*. Each feature is also assigned an initially empty *context vector* which has the same dimensionality (d) as the *index vector*. These *index vectors* are sparse, high dimensional, and ternary (i.e. 1, -1, 0). In other words, the dimensionality (d) is in the order of hundreds, and that they consist of all small numbers (ϵ) of randomly distributed $+1$ and -1, with the remaining elements of the vector to 0. In our work, we allocate each elements as follows:

$$\begin{cases} +1 \text{ for the probability } (\epsilon/2)/d \\ 0 \text{ for the probability } (d-\epsilon)/d \\ -1 \text{ for the probability } (\epsilon/2)/d \end{cases}$$

2. The *context vectors* are then accumulated by advancing through the image data set one feature taken at time, and then adding the context's *index vector* to the focus feature's *context vector*. When the entire data is processed, the d-dimensional *context vectors* are effectively the sum of the feature's contexts. *Context vectors* are produced by scanning through the images. As scanning the image data, each time a feature occurs in a context, that context's d-dimensional *index vector* is added to the *context vector* of the feature. This way, features are represented by d-dimensional *context vectors* that are the sum of the *index vectors* of all the contexts in which the feature appears.

In further experiments, we used Random Indexing to index aligned features and extract semantically similar features across image documents.

3 Feature Clustering

Figure 1 illustrates the overall procedure of the feature clustering process based on Random Indexing. The clustering procedure is based on three steps: data preprocessing, modelling the Feature Space using Random Indexing and the feature clustering. More details are outlined in this Section.

3.1 Data Preprocessing

The preprocessing phase consists in the feature extraction from images. To this end, we first need to perform an image segmentation and then extract the relevant features. In our experiment, we choose to use the conventional Blob-world [1] as our image segmentation method. Figure 2 shows an example of segmented images using the Blob-world method and the extracted features.

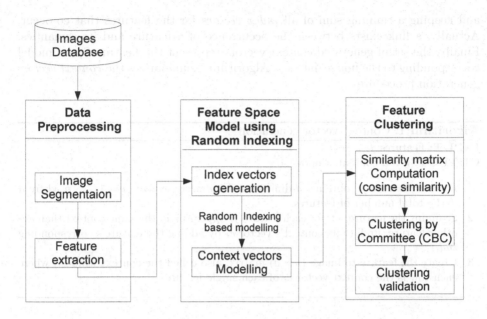

Fig. 1. Feature clustering approach based on Random Indexing

Fig. 2. Examples of segmented images

3.2 Feature Space Model Using Random Indexing

Once all relevant features are extracted, further analysis should be done to find common contexts between features and create a proper context model for the features clustering. Feature semantics are computed by scanning the features set and keeping a running sum of all *index vectors* for the features that co-occur. Actually, a link exists between the occurrence of a feature and its semantics. Finally, the set of generated context vectors represent the Feature Space model corresponding to the image data set. Algorithm 1 summarizes the *context vectors* generation procedure.

Algorithm 1. Context vector generation

INPUT: Features f_i, $i = 1, \ldots, n$.
OUTPUT: $n \times d$ context window A.

1. For each feature f_i, obtain a d-dimensional *index vector* $ind_i, i = 1, \ldots, n$ where n is the total number of features.
2. Scanning the feature set, for each feature f_i appearing in the same context than another feature, update its context's vector c_i by adding the feature's corresponding ind_i.
3. Create the feature-to image $(n \times d)$ matrix, also called the context window, where each row is the context vector c_i of each single feature.

3.3   Similarity Measure in the Feature Space Model

Basically, *context vectors* give the location of the word in the Word Space. Similarly, we can assume that *context vectors* give the location of the feature in the Feature Space model. In order to determine how similar the features are in the context, a similarity measure has to be defined. Various schemes e.g. scalar product or vector, Euclidean distance, Minkowski metrics [9], are used to compute similarity between vectors corresponding to the features. However, the cosine distance [9] might make sense for these data because it would ignore absolute sizes of the measurements, and only consider their relative sizes. Thus, two flowers that were different sizes, but which had similarly shaped petals and sepals, might not be close with respect to squared Euclidean distance, but would be close with respect to cosine distance. We have used cosine of the angles between pairs of vectors x_i and y_i , $i = 1, \ldots, n$ of the context window A generated with Random Indexing to compute normalized vector similarity. The cosine angle between two vectors x and y is defined as:

$$sim_\propto(x, y) = \frac{xy}{abs(x)abs(x)} = \frac{\sum_{i=1}^n x_i y_i}{\sqrt{(\sum_{i=1}^n x_i^2)}\sqrt{(\sum_{i=1}^n y_i^2)}} \tag{1}$$

The cosine measure is the most frequently used similarity metric in vector space research. The advantage of the cosine metric over other metrics is that it provides a fixed measure of similarity, which ranges from 1 (for identical vectors) to 0 (for orthogonal vectors) and -1 (for vectors pointing in the opposite directions). Moreover, it is comparatively efficient to compute. Hence, a similarity index between different features is defined, and a similarity matrix is generated from the features appearing in the images data set. Each cell of the similarity matrix contains the numerical value of the similarity between any pair of features.

3.4 Clustering by Committee

Clustering by Committee (CBC) [8] has been basically designed for Natural Language Processing purposes. the hard version of CBC , in which a word is assigned to exactly one cluster, is typically used for document retrieval. We use a soft version of CBC in feature sense/context disambiguation. The advantage thus is that it allows fuzzy clustering, and thereby, the features are assigned to more than one cluster. CBC consists of three phases:

Phase I: Generation of similarity matrix A similarity index, using the cosine metric, is defined between features. Then, a similarity matrix generated from the features appearing in the image data set, in which each cell contains the numerical value of the similarity between each pair of features.

Phase II: Formation of committees The second phase of the clustering algorithm takes in as input the list of features to be clustered and the similarity matrix. It recursively finds tight clusters called committees, scattered in the similarity space. Each committee can be thought of as the representation of a context or a sense. Each committee is assigned a centroid vector which is the average of the vectors of the features contained by them. The algorithm tries to form as many committees as possible on the condition that each newly formed committee is not very similar to any existing committee (i.e. the similarity should not exceed a given threshold θ_1). If the condition is violated, the committee is discarded. The similarity between two committee is computed by determining the cosine metric between the centroid vectors of the respective committees. Next, it identifies the residue features that are not covered by any committee. A committee is said to cover a feature if the feature's similarity to the centroid of the committee exceeds some high similarity threshold (i.e. greater than another given threshold θ_2). The algorithm than attempts to find recursively more committees among the residue features. The output of the algorithm is the union of all committees found in each recursive step. Committees are the cores of the clusters to which features are successfully added in Phase III as explained below. The committees do not change after their formation.

Phase III: Assigning a feature to its most similar committee In the final phase of the algorithm, each feature is assigned to its most similar cluster. The feature is assigned to a cluster if its similarity to the committee that forms the core of the cluster exceeds a given threshold γ. The cluster now represents the context the feature has been used in. Once a feature has been assigned to a cluster, the centroid of the committee is subtracted from the context vector of the feature. This enables the algorithm to find the less frequent context of the feature.

Once a feature is assigned to its most similar cluster, the centroid of the committee is subtracted from the context vector of the concerned feature. The context vector of the feature is the sum of all the contexts the feature may have appeared in the data set. If one of the contexts is removed from the context vector of the feature, the similarity of the features with other committees increases thus allowing the algorithm to discover other less frequent senses of the feature.

Algorithm 2. Soft Clustering By Committee Algorithm

---

1. **Phase 1**
   Let F be the list of unique features (n) in the data sets
   Let S be the similarity matrix $(n \times n)$
   Assign values to S_{ij} by computing the cosine metric between E_i and E_j

2. **Phase 2**
   Let S be the symmetric matrix generated from Phase 1 Let F be the set of features to be clustered Let C be the list of committees.
   $discover - committees(S, F, \theta_1, \theta_2)$
   { for each feature $f \in F$ { cluster features for S using average link clustering }
   for each discovered cluster c { Compute $avgsim(c)$ // average pairwise similarity between features in c
   Compute score: $|c| \times avgsim(c)$ // $|c|$ is the number of features in c }
   Store the highest-scoring cluster in a list L
   Store the clusters in L in descending order of their scores
        Let C be a list of Committees.
   For each cluster $c \in L$ {
   compute the centroid of c
   c's similarity to the centroid of each committee previously added to C is below a threshold θ_1, add c to C. }
        if L is empty, return C. else {
   for each element $f \in F$ { if e's similarity to every committee in C is below threshold θ_2, add e to a list of residues R } If R is empty, return c
   else $discover - committees(S, R, \theta_1, \theta_2)$ } }

3. **Phase 3**
   Let X be a list of clusters initially empty
   Let c be the list of Committees from phase 2
   while S is not empty { Let $c \in S$ be the most similar committee to e
   if the $similarity(e, c) < \gamma$, exit the loop
   if c is not similar to any cluster in C {
   assign e to C
   remove from e the centroid vector of c }
   remove c from S }

---

4   Experiments

4.1   The Training Dataset

In this work, we used the Corel database [7] for training and constructing our Feature Space model. The Corel image database contains close to $60,000$ general purpose photographs. A large portion of images in the database are scene photographs. The rest includes man-made objects with smooth background, fractals, texture patches, synthetic graphs, drawings, etc. This database was categorized into 599 semantic concepts. Each concept/category/context, containing roughly 100 images, e.g. 'landscape', 'mountain', 'ice', 'lake', 'space', 'planet', 'star'. For clarification, general-purpose photographs refer to pictures taken in daily life in contrast to special domain such as medical or satellite images.

4.2 Clustering Validity Measures

In order to evaluate the performance of the proposed clustering algorithm, we use the CS index [3] that computes the ratio of *Compactness* and *Separation*. A common measure of *Compactness* is the intra-cluster variance within a cluster, named *Comp*:

$$Comp = \frac{1}{k} \sum_{i=1}^{k} \parallel \gamma(C_i) \parallel, \tag{2}$$

where $\gamma(X)$ represents the variance of data set X. *Separation* is computed by the average of distances between the centers of different clusters:

$$Sep = \frac{1}{k} \sum \parallel z_i - z_j \parallel^2, \qquad i = 1, 2, \ldots, k-1, \qquad j = i+1, \ldots, k \tag{3}$$

It is clear that if the data set contains compact and well separated clusters, the distance between the clusters is expected to be large and the diameter of the clusters is expected to be small. Thus, cluster results can be compared by taking the ratio between *Comp* and *Sep*:

$$CS = \frac{Comp}{Sep}. \tag{4}$$

Based on the definition of CS, we can conclude that a small value of CS indicates compact and well-separated clusters. CS reaches its best score at 0 and worst value at 1. Therefore, the smaller it is the better the clusters are formed.

4.3 Parameter Settings

We experimented the impact of some key parameters and assigned initial values to them.

Dimensionality: in order to evaluate the effects of varying dimensionality on the performance of Random Indexing in our work, we computed the values of CS with d ranging from 100 to 600. The performance measures are reported using average values over 5 different turns. Figure 3 depicts the results and shows that for $d = 300$ we get the smallest CS value. Therefore, we choose $d = 300$ as the dimension of the *index vectors* for Random Indexing, which is way less than the original $D = 1000$ (corresponding to total number of images in the data set).

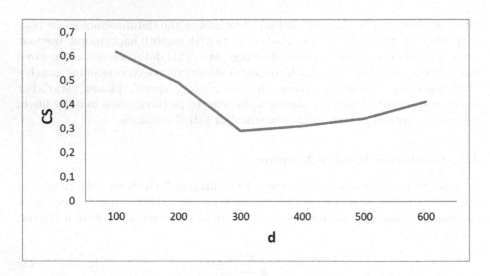

Fig. 3. The impact of different d values to RI-based feature clustering

Sparsity of the index vectors: another parameter is crucial for the quality of our indexing is the number of +1, and −1 in the index vectors ϵ. We use $\epsilon = 10$ as proposed in [2].

4.4   Clustering Results

As indicated above, the data consists of 59900 features and 599 contexts. For the clustering results, most of the predicted clusters corresponding to the 599 different contexts have been correctly formed and Table 1 shows some of the formed clusters/contexts and their assigned features. Note that some of the features belong to more than one cluster, assuming that they are used in more than one context.

Table 1. Some of the features and their discovered contexts

Description of the feature	clusters/Contexts
Beach umbrella	beach, ocean, people
Horse	**context 1**: horse, grass, animal **context 2**: rural, people, animal, horse, landscape, grass
The Colosseum	**context 1**: Italy, Europe, historical building **context 2**: landmark, historical building, landscape
London bus	**context 1**: London, historical building, sky, water, people **context 2**: bus, man-made, car

We report the rest of the results using three other validation criteria: precision, recall and the F-measure. These three measures are widely used in pattern recognition and information retrieval. According to our evaluation context, we slightly changed the definitions: *Precision* of a feature is defined as the ratio of the correct clusters to the total number of clusters it is assigned to. The precision (P) of a the algorithm is the average precision of all features. *Recall* of a feature is defined as the ratio of the correct clusters of the feature and the total number of contexts the feature is used in the data set. The recall (R) of the algorithm is the average recall of the features. P and R range between 0 and 1. The F-measure (F) is the combination result of precision and recall and is given by:

$$F = \frac{2RP}{R + P}. \tag{5}$$

The F-measure reaches its best value at 1 and worst score at 0. As stated in [10], if the value of θ_1 increases, the clustering becomes more and only features with very high similarity index are clustered, cause the F-measures to decrease when θ_1 increases. For all context/sense discovery, a feature element is assigned to a cluster if its similarity to the cluster exceeds a threshold γ. We tested the clustering with a fixed $\gamma = 0.5$ and different values of θ_1 varying from 0.25 and 0.45 with the features examples showed in Table 1 and the best F-measure of these 4 examples is obtained with $\theta_1 = 0.4$. The value of γ does not affect the first sense returned by the CBC algorithm for each feature because each feature is initially assigned to its most similar cluster. We also experimented with different values of γ ranging from 0.3 and 0.6 and $\theta_1 = 0.4$. With lower γ value, features are assigned to more clusters causing a decrease in precision and then in the F-measure. Nevertheless, at higher values of γ, the recall reduces given that the algorithm ignores some relevant senses/contexts of features and hence a decrease in F-measure is noticed. For the same examples showed in Table 1, the best F-measure is obtained for $\gamma = 0.45$. On the other hand, we fix $\theta_2 = 0.5$.

For the fixed values of θ_1, θ_2 and γ, Table 2 shows that the best results of the proposed measures are given for dimension $d = 300$: the smallest Compactness Separation ($CS = 0.294$) and accordingly the largest F-measure ($F = 0.710$). The best formed clusters (e.g. with the least CS index) cause a decrease in precision and hence in F-measure. It can be observed from the results that Random Indexing can improve the quality of features clustering and allows the construction of a high quality Feature Space model. For all context discoveries, a feature is assigned to a cluster if its closer to this cluster's center. Thus, a feature is assigned to its most similar context. Nevertheless, we can notice that some category of images is better classified than others. For instance, 'The Colosseum' feature is used in two contexts: '*Italy, Europe, historical building*' and '*landmark, historical building, landscape*' contexts. Thus, the context/sense of 'The Colosseum' can be clearly defined. However, a feature like 'Flower' is used in 32 different contexts such as '*plant, flower, grass*' and '*plant, art, flower, indoor*', which means that a 'Flower' and a 'Painted Bird' features are related with a very small similarity index. Hence, this causes a poor clustering of features for some category of images.

Table 2. Results of RI-based clustering for values $\theta_1 = 0.4$, $\theta_2 = 0.5$ and $\gamma = 0.45$

Dimension	d=200				d=300				d=400			
Validation Measure	CS	P	R	F	CS	P	R	F	CS	P	R	F
RI-Clustering	0.49	0.534	0.378	0.442	0.29	0.817	0.628	0.710	0.31	0.617	0.514	0.560

5 Conclusion

In this paper, we have used a Random Indexing based approach, mergerd with the Clustering by Committee technique to discover feature semantics from images. The approach works efficiently on the Corel database. At present, we do not focus on computational complexity. We intent to perform a computational analysis for the proposed algorithm in further works.

Acknowledgements. We wish to thank Pr. James Z. Wang from The Pennsylvania State University for providing us with Corel database.

References

[1] Carson, C., Belongie, S., Greenspan, H., Malik, J.: Blobworld: Image Segmentation Using Expectation-Maximization and Its Application to Image Querying. IEEE Trans. on Pattern Analysis and Machine Intelligence 24(8), 1026–1038 (2002)

[2] Gorman, J., Curran, J.R.: Random Indexing using Statistical Weight Functions. In: Proceedings of EMNLP 2006, pp. 457–464 (2006)

[3] Halkidi, M., Vazirgiannis, M., Batistakis, Y.: Quality Scheme Assessment in the Clustering Process. In: Zighed, D.A., Komorowski, J., Żytkow, J.M. (eds.) PKDD 2000. LNCS (LNAI), vol. 1910, pp. 265–276. Springer, Heidelberg (2000)

[4] Kanerva, P.: Sparse Distributed Memory and Related Models. Associative Neural Memories 26, 50–76 (1993)

[5] Karlgren, J., Sahlgren, M.: From words to understanding. In: Uesaka, Y., Kanerva, P., Asoh, H. (eds.) Foundations of Real-world Understanding, vol. 26, pp. 294–308 (2001)

[6] Landauer, T.K., Foltz, P.W., Laham, D.: An Introduction to Latent Semantic Analysis. In: 45th Annual Computer Personnel Research Conference. ACM (2004)

[7] Müller, H., Marchand-Maillet, S., Pun, T.: The Truth about Corel - Evaluation in Image Retrieval. In: Lew, M., Sebe, N., Eakins, J.P. (eds.) CIVR 2002. LNCS, vol. 2383, pp. 38–49. Springer, Heidelberg (2002)

[8] Pantel, P., Lee, D.: Discovering Word Senses from Text. In: Proceedings of ACM SIGKDD Conference on Knowledge Discovery and Data Mining, pp. 613–619 (2002)

[9] Sahlgren, M.: An Introduction to Random Indexing. In: Methods and Applications of Semantic Indexing Workshop at the 7th International Conference on Terminology and Knowledge Engineering, TKE (2005)

[10] Sahlgren, M.: The Word-Space Model: Using Distributional Analysis to Represent Syntagmatic and Paradigmatic Relations Between Words in High-Dimensional Vector Spaces. Ph.D. dissertation, Department of Linguistics, Stockholm University (2006)

Recognition of Signed Expressions Using Symbolic Aggregate Approximation

Mariusz Oszust and Marian Wysocki

Department of Computer and Control Engineering,
Rzeszow University of Technology,
W. Pola 2, 35-959 Rzeszow, Poland
{marosz,mwysocki}@kia.prz.edu.pl
http://www.kia.prz.edu.pl

Abstract. Complexity of sign language recognition system grows with growing word vocabulary. Therefore it is advisable to use units smaller than words. Such elements, called subunits, resemble phonemes in spoken language. They are concatenated to form word models. We propose a data–driven procedure for finding subunits in time series representing signed expressions. The procedure consists in: (i) transformation of video material to time series describing hand movements, (ii) using Piecewise Aggregate Approximation (PAA) coefficients to represent subunits, and (iii) applying Symbolic Aggregate Approximation (SAX), which is based on PAA, to obtain appropriate symbolic description. Signed words represented by strings of SAX symbols are classified using nearest neighbour method with Dynamic Time Warping (DTW) technique. We compare the approach with whole–word recognition by presenting ten–fold cross–validation tests on a Polish sign language (PSL) corpus of 30 words. Recognition of new words using small number of examples is also considered. The experiments show superiority of the SAX based approach.

Keywords: Sign Language Recognition, Piecewise Aggregate Approximation, Symbolic Aggregate Approximation, Dynamic Time Warping.

1 Introduction

Development of gesture–based human–computer interfaces recently become a popular trend due to the need of providing tools for more natural ways for giving commands. It is also very important for the society of hearing impaired people in helping them to overcome communication barriers of daily life. All gestures, starting with a simple hand movement and ending with complex, mutual hands' interaction, should be unequivocally interpreted. In order to make a system correctly recognising hand gestures one must go through many steps, and at each choose an approach, which affects the results. The first step is acquisition of observed gestures, and here the use of computer vision seems to be one of the most attractive possibilities due to resemblance to human ability to see. After recording a video material decision how to track hands must be made. In many approaches skin colour regions are found on images and tracked [1, 2].

L. Rutkowski et al. (Eds.): ICAISC 2014, Part I, LNAI 8467, pp. 745–756, 2014.

Kinect sensor [3] is an example of an active depth camera, which is insensitive to most problems with scene lightning, which make skin colour tracking solutions troublesome in changing light conditions. The sensor applies range camera technology developed by PrimeSense [4], can interpret specific gestures by using an infrared (IR) projector and a camera to track body movements of individuals in three dimensions. Software development kit (SDK) attached to the camera allows to obtain so-called *skeletal image*, which contains 3D position of 20 most important body joints (or parts) connected together and forming a kind of a skeleton. Moreover, it offers 3D information of every observed pixel transforming the sensor to a depth camera. In the literature there are only a few works applying Kinect to dynamic sign language gestures recognition. They use the skeletal data [5–7] or utilise Kinect as the depth camera [8, 9].

Hidden Markov Models (HMMs) [10], neural networks [11] or applying the nearest neighbour approach with Dynamic Time Warping (DTW) [2] are common, and state of the art, classifiers applied to sign language recognition. These solutions use whole–word models approach, i.e. one word model represents one sign. In order to provide better performance, especially with large sign vocabulary [12] or provide more robust gesture representation, signs are modelled using smaller units than words (*subunits*), which resembles modelling speech by means of phonemes. Subunit models are concatenated to form sign models [13]. In [10] HMMs and an iterative process of data-driven extraction of subunits were applied. Two state HMMs representing subunits were concatenated to model single signs. The boundaries of subunits result from the alignment of appropriate feature vector sequence to the states by the Viterbi algorithm. In work [14] the subunit–based classifier for selecting discriminative features was designed, but in this, also data–driven, solution adding new words to the vocabulary will result in creation of the new classifier and losing previous knowledge of subunits. Han et. al in [1] define subunits' boundaries using hand motion discontinuity and adapting temporal clustering by DTW to merge similar time series segments. Finally a code book of possible exemplar trajectories was created. The code book of symbols representing subunits was also obtained in our previous work [2]. Here a data–driven procedure divided time series of signed expressions into subsequences, which form homogeneous groups. Time series cut points were found using evolutionary algorithm optimising a quality of resulted clustering. That solution could be seen as an idea of changing time series into strings of symbols, in which symbol denotes subunit.

Since all these solutions are data–driven, it means, that a different set of learning data or even different run of the algorithm can produce a new set of subunits and a new code book. This observation leads us to search in a direction of a technique, in which time series will be unequivocally (i.e. always in the same manner, disregarding other time series influence) transformed into smaller units and then such units will obtain symbolic representation. Symbolic Aggregate Approximation (SAX) [15, 16] is time series representation, it consists in calculating Piecewise Aggregate Approximation (PAA) [17] coefficients and then mapping them to symbols.

SAX was successfully applied to human action recognition [18] and obtained comparable accuracy on publicly available datasets to related works. In work [19] indexed version of SAX was applied to create and select simple gestures distinguishable from users' normal movements.

The main contribution of our paper is that it presents experimental comparison of two approaches to recognition: one using whole–word model and the other based on subunits obtained using SAX. Both methods are applied for two different sets of features: one based on Kinect's skeletal images and the other using a description of hands extracted as skin coloured regions. All experiments are performed on real Polish sign language (PSL) 30 words corpus.

The rest of the paper is organised as follows. Section 2 gives preliminary information concerning PSL and our gesture dataset. Features used for recognition are discussed in Section 3. Section 4 is focused on subunits extraction method. Recognition results are shown and compared in Section 5. Section 6 concludes the paper and indicates future directions.

2 PSL Words Corpus

Number of people in Poland with hearing impairment, their relatives or supervisors according to Polish Association of the Deaf [20] reaches 400 thousands. They form a community with difficult communication problems, especially in public places.

Sign language is the language of deaf people communicated by their deaf parents [21]. It, similarly to the spoken language, has it's own grammar and words (signs). PSL signs are static or dynamic and mostly two-handed [22]. During gesture performance hands often touch each other or appear against the background of the face. Hand can occur in 32 possible orientations (32 one-handed and 1024 two-handed), but about 180 are utilised daily [22]. One can distinguish 37 places of articulation, i.e. the position of the hands in a specific place against the body or in relation to each other - 17 against or near the face, 18 against the chest, and 2 in against the lower half of the body. Each of these locations may be offset to some extent from the body, while the portion of them (26) is in contact with the body. Because the hand's configuration, its orientation and the position is related to static gestures or define a hand shape at the start of a dynamic gesture, and most of the gestures (98%) in sign language gestures are dynamic, one must also take into account the movement of the hand. Hand during gesture performance changes its positions, orientations and configurations. Sign gestures are both sequential and simultaneous [10]. Sequentiality indicates that the order of shown hand shapes and places of execution is important. Simultaneity means that during gesture performance the features (e.g. hand position and shape) can be changed in parallel, although not necessarily in synchrony.

Research on subunits in PSL undertaken by linguistics is on the stage of recognising so-called *minimal pairs* of gesture components (configuration, orientation, position, and movement) [21]. Change of such component in a gesture will be followed by change of its meaning. Lack of general knowledge how to break down signs into subunits additionally supports motivation for data–driven approaches.

In cooperation with PSL interpreter we selected 30 common words that can be used at the doctors': *obtain, write, bed, must, to rest, operation, meninges, analysis, examine, be, want, cotton, tooth, inflammation, healthy, ill, lie down, translucence, come, rescue, family, hearing, tablet, where, and, how much, other, cost, blood,* and *drop.* Since interpreters often take part in medical examination, the patient's privacy is obviously not sufficiently preserved and the future purpose of our system addresses this problem. Each word was performed 10 times by the PSL interpreter, the data have been registered with the rate of 30 frames/s using Kinect TCP software [23].

3   Feature Extraction

Developers of Kinect based interfaces have access to colour and depth information of observed scene with the resolution of 640×480 through the SDK. Skeletal images of two tracked people consisting of 3D points estimating the joints of arms and legs, the position of the head, hands and spine. Although known Kinect's tracking drawbacks [24] for gesture recognition we used 6 points representing right and left hand, wrist and elbow ($6 \times 3 = 18$ features in total). Since hand shape plays important role in sign language, we proposed a set of features describing hand, which rely on Kinect's depth stream and apart from 3D position of the hand, which is only available in a case of using the skeletal image. Hands are detected on colour images as skin coloured regions analysing RGB components [25], i.e. sets of contiguous pixels in the skin colour forming region taking into consideration the depth image. Pixels are assigned to the same region if a depth difference between them is smaller than a threshold. This procedure allows to distinguish occluding objects. If more than three objects (left, right hand and face) are found procedure utilises knowledge from previous frame of the video recording. The following hand features are calculated: the gravity centre with respect to the gravity centre of the face and depth difference between mean depth of the hand and the face, area, compactness, eccentricity, and orientation of the hand. Four features represent hand shape description, and three its location. Feature selection was motivated by linguistic directions, i.e. every sign language gesture can be analysed by specifying at least three components [22, 26]: (i) the place of the body against which the sign is made, (ii) the shape of a hand or hands, (iii) the movement of a hand or hands.

Exemplary execution of the word *analysis* (*analysis_4*) is shown on Fig. 1, depth images with left and right hands and face are marked with colours, skeleton is also shown (from left to right, from top to bottom). It is worth noticing that skeletal image sometimes does not fit to the body posture.

Time series of the horizontal placement of the gravity centre of the right hand with respect to the gravity centre of the face for executions of the word *analysis* are shown on Fig. 2.

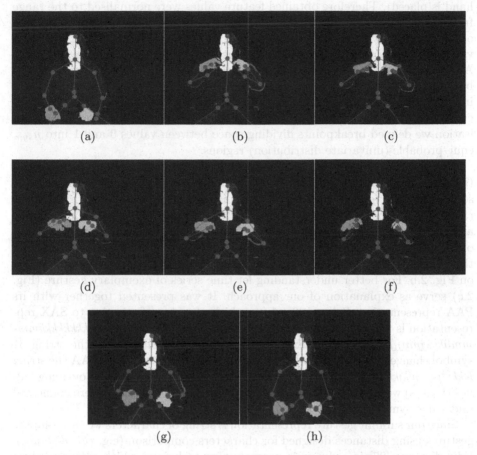

Fig. 1. Exemplary images from execution of sign *analysis* with hands and face identified. Colour pixels are aligned with pixels from the depth camera. Right hand, left hand, face and skeleton are coloured: green, orange, white and red (respectively).

4   Subunits Obtained with Symbolic Aggregate Approximation

SAX [15] is time series representation that reduces the dimensionality (length) and lower bounds the distance functions. Lower bounding guarantees that the distance between two SAX vectors (strings of symbols) is smaller than, or equal to, the distance between these two vectors in the original space. It is advised to normalise time series to have mean of zero and a standard deviation of one (*zscore*) to meaningful comparison of them without offset or different amplitudes. It is important for shape mining, but zscoring time series representing sign language expressions can distort information carried by their amplitudes (e.g. the same hand movement can have different meaning depending on where hand is placed). Therefore obtained feature values were normalised to the range from zero to one. The SAX is performed in three following steps: (i) division of time series into n_{seg} segments of equal length, (ii) calculation of the mean value of every obtained segment, (iii) creating a vector of Piecewise Aggregate Approximation (PAA) coefficients (means) and assigning symbols to them. Number of symbols (n_{sym}) is a parameter indicating how the time series values are inserted into n_{sym} equi-probable regions. Region is an area under a Gaussan curve between breakpoints b_i and b_{i+1} equal to $1/n_{sym}$. Due to applied normalisation we defined breakpoints dividing space between values 0 and 1 into n_{sym} equi–probable (univariate distribution) regions.

Time series have different lengths thus decision how many PAA coefficients (n_{seg}) should be produced is not trivial. Therefore we transformed a given time series into SAX representation without dimensionality reduction with PAA and calculated number of symbol changes. Obtained value was incremented by one and assigned to n_{seg}. Fig. 2.a shows time series of the horizontal placement of the gravity centre of the right hand with respect to the gravity centre of the face of ten executions of word *analysis*, their PAA representations are shown on Fig. 2.b. For better understanding let time series of exemplary gesture (Fig. 2.c) serve as explanation of our approach. It was presented together with its PAA representation. It has 109 values, which after transformation to SAX representation is written as: *lllkllkkkkkkkkkkkkkkkklllllmmmnnnnnmlllkjijjjkkkkkkkkkmm-mmllkkkjjiiiijjjjkkklmmmnnnnlkkjjjjjjjjjjkklmmmmmmmmmlllllllk*. In the string 31 symbol changes are detected what gives $n_{seg} = 32$. After applying PAA the string *lkkkkllmnmkjkkllkjijlmnkjjklmmll* is obtained. As one can see some outlying values (letters) were omitted and other, similar to their neighbours, were connected under one symbol.

Since our subunit gesture representation is string of characters we can compare gestures using distances designed for characters comparison (e.g. *edit distance*). Edit distance [27] is a dynamic programming technique which calculates how many changes are needed to transform one string of characters into the other. It treats each character equally, and since obtained symbols can be ordered because their corresponding breakpoints can be ordered, we applied dynamic time warping (DTW) for their comparison. Dynamic time warping is a technique for time series comparison with different length [27]. In DTW two time series are aligned to minimise their difference. A matrix containing Euclidean distances between each pair of data values is created and then, using dynamic programming, path across the matrix is computed. Warping path indicate how to transform compared time series in order to make them have equal length. After lengthening Euclidean distance between them is reported as the *DTW distance*. In many solutions DTW processing multidimensional time series treats attributes together and use multidimensional Euclidean distance to calculate the matrix. Since we are processing 14 or 18 dimensional time series representing gestures we decided to compute DTW for each feature separately and finally sum DTW values as a distance between two gestures. It yielded better recognition results than the approach with features processed together.

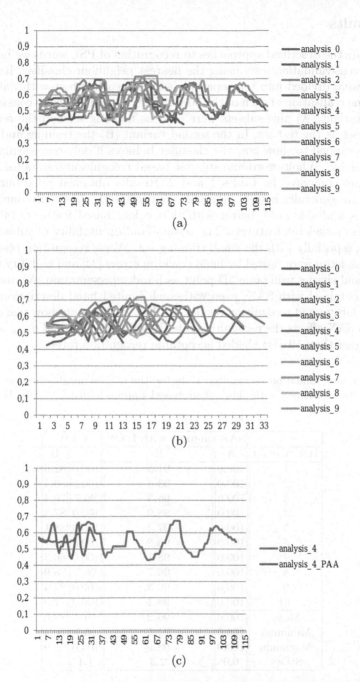

Fig. 2. Ten executions of the word *analysis*: the horizontal placement of the gravity centre of the right hand with respect to the gravity centre of the face (a), their PAA representations (b), and exemplary execution (*analysis_4*) with its PAA representation (c)

5   Results

To compare the described approaches to recognition of PSL words we performed ten-fold cross-validation tests using the nearest neighbour classifier. Respective datasets were divided into ten separable subsets, each subset with data representing one realisation of each of the 30 words. Two variants were considered. In the first variant (A) nine subsets were used as training set and the remaining, tenth subset as the test set. In the second variant (B) the training and the test set were swapped to show how the classifier behaves if only one learning example is available. Whole–word and subunit based recognition results for different features are compared in Tables 1 and 2. Results obtained by subunit-based classifier are generally better, especially in variant B, when only one learning example is available (13% better with skin colour based features, 14% better with Kinect's skeleton features). The results confirm usability of subunit based approach, especially with the small training set. Worse recognition results with Kinect's skeleton were caused by hand tracking errors [24] and inability to differentiate hand shapes using one 3D point as hand representation. As one can see subunits obtained with SAX, even with such limited hand description allowed to obtain fairly good recognition results. On Fig. 3 we present how size of the alphabet in SAX affects the recognition rate. Results in tables had $n_{sym} = 20$, but values higher than 10 also yielded acceptable recognition rates.

Table 1. Cross–validation recognition tests for the nearest neighbour classifier with feature vectors obtained with skin colour based approach ($n_{sym} = 20$). Results are given in %.

Test, Variant	SAX subunits with DTW		DTW	
	A	B	A	B
1	100.0	91.5	100.0	82.6
2	100.0	93.3	100.0	80.4
3	100.0	96.3	96.7	70.4
4	100.0	98.9	100.0	87.4
5	100.0	97.4	100.0	88.1
6	100.0	95.2	100.0	83.7
7	100.0	98.1	100.0	86.3
8	100.0	96.7	96.7	88.9
9	100.0	96.3	100.0	84.4
10	100.0	98.1	100.0	77.8
Mean	100.0	96.2	99.3	83.0
Minimum	100.0	91.5	96.7	70.4
Maximum	100.0	98.9	100.0	88.9
StDev	0.0	2.3	1.4	5.7

It is worth considering a situation, in which some new words are recognised on the basis of small set of examples. Such scenario lays behind motivation for using subunit–based approach in extending word vocabulary. We used the same dataset as before. Instead of preparing new data we randomly chose one word

Table 2. Cross–validation recognition tests for the nearest neighbour classifier with Kinect skeletal data features ($n_{sym} = 20$). Results are given in %.

Test, Variant	SAX subunits with DTW		DTW	
	A	B	A	B
1	90.0	80.4	90.0	63.0
2	90.0	81.9	90.0	67.4
3	90.0	81.5	90.0	58.5
4	100.0	86.7	96.7	71.9
5	100.0	88.5	100.0	75.6
6	100.0	85.6	93.3	70.0
7	100.0	90.7	96.7	71.5
8	100.0	90.7	96.7	78.1
9	93.3	84.8	100.0	70.7
10	100.0	86.7	86.7	60.4
Mean	96.3	85.7	94.0	68.7
Minimum	90.0	80.4	86.7	58.5
Maximum	100.0	90.7	100.0	78.1
StDev	4.8	3.7	4.7	6.4

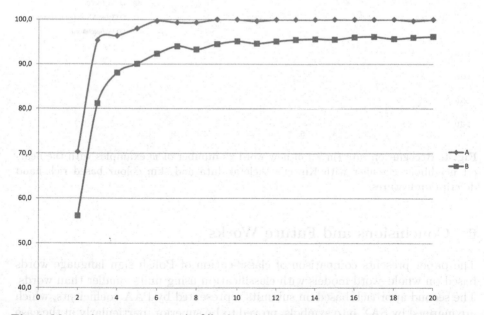

Fig. 3. Mean of recognition rate (in %) of ten A and B cross-validation tests for different number of symbols (2-20) with skin colour based features

(since then called *new*) from the dataset and omitted it from the process of determining subunits. A small number w of examples of each new word was used to create subunit–based models of these words. Remaining $10 - w$ examples of the new word were used for testing. This experiment has been repeated 100 times, each time with a randomly chosen new word and randomly chosen its example. We repeated the experiment with whole–word models and nearest neighbour classifier based on DTW distance. Figure 4 shows mean values of recognition rates in relation to the number w of examples. As we can see, a relatively small number of examples enables good recognition. Subunit based approach obtained considerably better recognition rate due to more robust representation, which tends to filtrate outlying data values and gathering them under one symbol. What is interesting, our subunit-based solution yielded outstanding results with richer hand description. In the case with skeletal image results of the classifier are generally worse than those obtained with richer hand description.

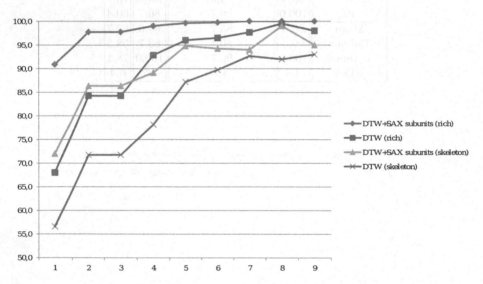

Fig. 4. Recognition rate (in %) of new word vs number of w examples with the nearest neighbour classifier with Kinect's skeletal data and skin colour based rich hand description features

6   Conclusions and Future Works

The paper presents comparison of classification of Polish sign language words based on whole–word models with classification using units smaller than words. The second approach based on subunits represented by PAA coefficients, which are mapped by SAX into symbols, proved to be superior, particularly in the case where only one learning example was available. Two sets of features obtained with Kinect sensor were considered: (i) features based on Kinect's skeletal image and (ii) features describing hands as skin coloured regions. In the second case Kinect's ability to extract person body from the background and to distinguish partially occluded, skin coloured objects on the basis of depth information has been used. Due to better hand description proposed features led to better recognition results. Future works will concern experiments with larger vocabulary including words and sentences. Indexed version of SAX [19] seems to be a promising approach to gesture spotting problem, in which place of a word appearance in longer expression has to be detected.

References

1. Han, J.W., Awad, G., Sutherland, A.: Modelling and Segmenting Subunits for Sign Language Recognition based on Hand Motion Analysis. Pattern Recognition Letters 30(6), 623–633 (2009)
2. Oszust, M., Wysocki, M.: Modelling and Recognition of Signed Expressions Using Subunits Obtained by Data–Driven Approach. In: Ramsay, A., Agre, G. (eds.) AIMSA 2012. LNCS, vol. 7557, pp. 315–324. Springer, Heidelberg (2012)
3. Shotton, J., Fitzgibbon, A., Cook, M., Sharp, T., Finocchio, M., Moore, R., Kipman, A., Blake, A.: Real-time Human Pose Recognition in Parts from Single Depth Images. In: IEEE Computer Vision and Pattern Recognition, pp. 1297–1304 (2011)
4. Primesense, http://www.primesense.com/casestudies/kinect/
5. Capilla, D.: Sign Language Translator using Microsoft Kinect XBOX 360. MSc Thesis Department of Electrical Engineering and Computer Science Computer Vision Lab University of Tennessee, Knoxville (2012)
6. Lang, S., Block, M., Rojas, R.: Sign Language Recognition Using Kinect. In: Rutkowski, L., Korytkowski, M., Scherer, R., Tadeusiewicz, R., Zadeh, L.A., Zurada, J.M. (eds.) ICAISC 2012, Part I. LNCS, vol. 7267, pp. 394–402. Springer, Heidelberg (2012)
7. Zafrulla, Z., Brashear, H., Starner, T., Hamilton, H., Presti, P.: American Sign Language Recognition with the Kinect. In: ICMI, pp. 279–286 (2011)
8. Suarez, J., Murphy, R.R.: Hand Gesture Recognition with Depth Images: a Review, pp. 411–417. IEEE Press (2012)
9. Uebersax, D., Gall, J., den Bergh, M.V., Gool, L.J.V.: Real-time Sign Language Letter and Word Recognition from Depth Data. In: ICCV Workshops, pp. 383–390. IEEE Press (2011)
10. Kraiss, K.F.: Advanced Man-machine Interaction. Springer, Berlin (2006)
11. Zahedi, M., Manashty, A.R.: Robust Sign Language Recognition System using ToF Depth Cameras. Computing Research Repository - CORR, abs/1105.0 (2011)
12. Cooper, H.: Sign Language Recognition: Generalising to More Complex Corpora. Centre for Vision Speech and Signal Processing, PhD thesis. University of Surrey (2010)
13. Agris, U., Zieren, J., Canzler, U., Bauer, B., Kraiss, K.F.: Recent Developments in Visual Sign Language Recognition. Universal Access in the Information Society 6(4), 323–362 (2008)
14. Ong, E.J., Cooper, H., Pugeault, N., Bowden, R.: Sign Language Recognition using Sequential Pattern Trees. In: IEEE Computer Vision and Pattern Recognition, pp. 2200–2207 (2012)
15. Keogh, E., Lin, J.: Hot Sax: Efficiently Finding the most Unusual Time Series Subsequence. In: 5th IEEE International Conference on Data Mining, pp. 226–233 (2005)

16. Lin, J., Keogh, E., Wei, L., Lonardi, S.: Experiencing SAX: a Novel Symbolic Representation of Time Series. Data Mining and Knowledge Discovery 15(2), 107–144 (2007)
17. Keogh, E., Chakrabarti, K., Pazzani, M., Mehrotra, S.: Dimensionality Reduction for Fast Similarity Search in Large Time Series Databases. Knowledge and Information Systems 3(3), 263–286 (2001)
18. Junejo, I.N., Al Aghbari, Z.: Using SAX Representation for Human Action Recognition. Journal of Visual Communication and Image Representation 23(6), 853–861 (2012)
19. Kohlsdorf, D.K.H., Starner, T.E.: MAGIC Summoning: Towards Automatic Suggesting and Testing of Gestures with Low Probability of False Positives During Use. Journal of Machine Learning Research 14, 209–242 (2013)
20. Polish Association of the Deaf, http://pzg.pl
21. Tomaszewski, P.: Visual phonology of Polish Sign Language. Publishing House Matrix (2010) (in Polish)
22. Hendzel, J.: Polish Sign Language Dictionary. Publishing House Pojezierze (1986) (in Polish)
23. Lakaemper, R.: KinectTCP. Temple University, https://sites.google.com/a/temple.edu/kinecttcp/
24. Obdrzalek, S., Kurillo, G., Ofli, F., Bajcsy, R., Seto, E., Jimison, H., Pavel, M.: Accuracy and Robustness of Kinect Pose Estimation in the Context of Coaching of Elderly Population. In: IEEE Annual International Conference on Engineering in Medicine and Biology Society (EMBC), pp. 1188–1193 (2012)
25. Vezhnevets, V., Sazonov, V., Andreeva, A.: A survey on Pixel-Based Skin Color Detection Techniques. In: GraphiCon, pp. 85–92 (2003)
26. Stokoe, W.C.: Sign Language Structure: an Outline of the Visual Communication Systems of the American Deaf. Journal of Deaf Studies and Deaf Education (1960, 2005)
27. Xu, R., Wunsch, D.: Clustering. Wiley-IEEE Press (2009)

Dimensionality Reduction of Dynamic Animations Using HO-SVD

Michał Romaszewski, Piotr Gawron, and Sebastian Opozda

Institute of Theoretical and Applied Informatics, Polish Academy of Sciences
ul. Bałtycka 5, 44-100 Gliwice, Poland
{michal,gawron,sebastian}@iitis.pl

Abstract. This work presents an analysis of Higher Order Singular Value Decomposition (HO-SVD) applied to reduction of dimensionality of 3D mesh animations. Compression error is measured using three metrics (MSE, Hausdorff, MSDM). Results are compared with a method based on Principal Component Analysis (PCA) and presented on a set of animations with typical mesh deformations.

1 Introduction

The goal of this paper is to provide an analysis of Higher Order Singular Value Decomposition [1] (HO-SVD) applied to reduction of dimensionality of dynamic animations. The paper includes an estimation of lossy reconstruction quality using three error metrics and a comparison with a method based on Principal Component Analysis (PCA).

A compression algorithm usually consist of elements including compensation of motion (like in [2]), reduction of dimensionality and entropy encoding [3]. In this work we will concentrate on HO-SVD-based dimensionality reduction with only a simplified approach to frame aligning.

HO-SVD is a multi-linear generalization of Singular Value Decomposition. It has been shown (e.g. in [4]) that HO-SVD is an efficient method for dimensionality reduction of data represented as tensors, also called N-way arrays. Consecutive frames of a 3D animation can naturally be represented as a 3-mode tensor (a data cube), by stacking arrays of their vertices.

When using PCA-based compression, dimensionality reduction is often applied to animation frames (e.g. [5], [6]), reducing their number to a sequence of significant key-frames. On the contrary, HO-SVD allows for multidimensional reduction of the data tensor. In our experiment we truncated the number of components obtained through tensor decomposition, associated with mesh vertices and animation frames. Reduction of components associated with 3D coordinates of vertices is not advised since it results in a significant loss of information and low quality of reconstructed data.

For estimation of reconstruction quality we used three metrics. The Mean Squared Error (MSE) and the Hausdorff distance are both widely used for measuring 3D mesh distortions. Additionally, we decided to include a perceptual

L. Rutkowski et al. (Eds.): ICAISC 2014, Part I, LNAI 8467, pp. 757–768, 2014.

method, the Mesh Structural Distortion Measure (MSDM), since according to
[7], it correlates well with human perception of errors in 3D data. An example of
a distortion resulting from a lossy reconstruction of an animation using HO-SVD
is presented in Fig.1.

The article is organised as follows. In the two following subsections, the related
work and HO-SVD decomposition are presented. Definitions and methodology
of our experiments are presented in Section 2. Obtained results can be found in
Section 3, while a summary is presented in Section 4.

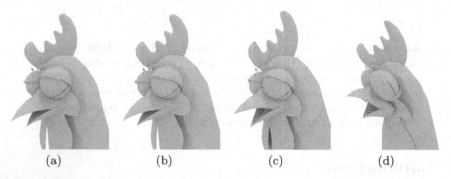

| (a) | (b) | (c) | (d) |

Fig. 1. A fragment of a reconstructed animation sequence for *Chicken* animation. Panel
(a) presents an original model, in further panels the data tensor is compressed to (b):
5.1%, (c): 2.1%, and (d): 1.1% of its original size.

1.1   Related Work

Due to their amount, data generated by using 3D scanners or animation software require effective compression methods for their storage, transmission, and
processing. Particularly, compression of dynamic animations is a subject to intensive research. A dimensionality reduction for 3D animations using PCA was
introduced in [5] and refined in [6], where authors performed motion clustering
on an animation and applied PCA to its subsegments. PCA-based compression
solutions are presented in [8] and [9] while [2] and [10] employ information about
mesh connectivity.

Higher Order Singular Value Decomposition (HO-SVD) may be treated as a
natural extension of PCA for high-dimensional data. A survey of tensor properties as well as the description of higher-order tensor decomposition is provided
in [11]. Tensor decomposition was successfully applied to compression and classification of images [12], face recognition [13] or watermarking of videos [14]. In
[15] HO-SVD was applied to Level-of-Detail reduction in animation of human
crowds. [16] presented the decomposition of a motion tensor and applied it for animation dimensionality reduction, denoising and gap filling. In [17], an approach
based on tensor decomposition and scalable hierarchical volume representation
of spatial data is used for fast 3D visualization.

1.2 Higher Order Singular Value Decomposition

Higher Order Singular Value Decomposition, also called Tucker decomposition, is a generalisation of SVD from matrices to tensors (N-way arrays). In this section we recall basic facts about tensors and HO-SVD. We follow conventions presented in [11].

To describe this decomposition, first we will recall basic notions regarding operations on tensors. Let a tensor

$$\mathcal{T} = \{t_{i_1,i_2,\ldots,i_n}\}_{i_1,i_2,\ldots,i_n=0}^{I_1-1,I_2-1,\ldots,I_N-1} \in \mathbb{R}^{I_1,I_2,\ldots,I_N} \tag{1}$$

be given — we say that this tensor has n modes. Each of the indices corresponds to one of the modes $i.e.$ i_l to mode l.

By $multiplication$ of tensor $\mathcal{T}$ by matrix $\mathbf{U} = \{u_{i_l d}\}_{i_l,d=0}^{I_l-1,D} \in \mathbb{R}^{I_l,D}$ in mode l we define tensor $\mathcal{T}' \in \mathbb{R}^{I_1,\ldots,I_{l-1},D,I_{l+1},\ldots,I_N}$, such that:

$$\mathcal{T}' = (\mathcal{T} \times_l \mathbf{U})_{i_1\ldots i_{l-1}d\,i_{l+1}\ldots i_N} = \sum_{i_l=0}^{I_l-1} t_{i_1 i_2 \ldots i_l \ldots i_N} u_{i_l d}. \tag{2}$$

By $unfolding$ tensor $\mathcal{T}$ in mode l we define matrix $\mathbf{T}_{(l)}$ such that

$$(\mathbf{T}_{(l)})_{i,j} = t_{i_1\ldots i_{l-1}j\,i_{l+1}\ldots i_N}, \tag{3}$$

where $i = 1 + \sum_{\substack{k=1 \\ l\neq l}}^{N}(i_k - 1)J_k$ and $J_k = \prod_{\substack{m=1 \\ m\neq l}}^{k-1} I_m$.

Given tensor $\mathcal{T}$, defined as in Eq. (1), a new $sub\text{-}tensor$ $\mathcal{T}_{i_n=\alpha}$ can be created according to the equation with the following elements:

$$\mathcal{T}_{i_l=\alpha} = \{t_{i_1 i_2 \ldots i_{l-1} i_{l+1} \ldots i_n}\}_{i_1=0,i_2=0,\ldots,i_l=\alpha,\ldots,i_n=0}^{I_1-1,I_2-1,\ldots,\alpha,\ldots,I_N-1} \in \mathbb{R}^{I_1,I_2,\ldots,1,\ldots,I_N}. \tag{4}$$

The $scalar\ product$ $\langle \mathcal{A}, \mathcal{B} \rangle$ of tensors $\mathcal{A}, \mathcal{B} \in \mathbb{R}^{I_1,I_2,\ldots,I_N}$ is defined as

$$\langle \mathcal{A}, \mathcal{B} \rangle = \sum_{i_1=0}^{I_1-1} \sum_{i_2=0}^{I_2-1} \cdots \sum_{i_N=0}^{I_N-1} b_{i_1,i_2,\ldots,i_n} a_{i_1,i_2,\ldots,i_n}. \tag{5}$$

We say that if scalar product of tensors equals 0, then they are orthogonal.

The $Frobenius\ norm$ of tensor $\mathcal{T}$ is given by $||\mathcal{T}|| = \sqrt{\langle \mathcal{T}, \mathcal{T} \rangle}$.

Given tensor $\mathcal{T}$, in order to find its HO-SVD, in the form of the so called Tucker operator $[\![\mathcal{C}; \mathbf{U}^{(1)}, \ldots, \mathbf{U}^{(N)}]\!]$, such that $\mathcal{C} \in \mathbb{R}^{I_1,\ldots,I_N}$ and $\mathbf{U}^{(k)} \in \mathbb{R}^{I_k,I_k}$ are orthogonal matrices, Algorithm 1 can be used.

Tensor $\mathcal{C}$ is called the core tensor and has the following useful properties. Reconstruction: $\mathcal{T} = \mathcal{C} \times_1 \mathbf{U}^{(1)} \times_2 \mathbf{U}^{(2)} \times_3 \ldots \times_N \mathbf{U}^{(N)}$, where $\mathbf{U}^{(i)}$ are orthogonal matrices. Orthogonality: $\langle \mathcal{C}_{i_l=\alpha}, \mathcal{C}_{i_l=\beta} \rangle = 0$ for all possible values of l, α and β, such that $\alpha \neq \beta$. Order of sub-tensor norms: $||\mathcal{C}_{i_n=1}|| \leq ||\mathcal{C}_{i_n=2}|| \leq \ldots \leq ||\mathcal{C}_{i_n=I_n}||$ for all n.

Therefore, informally, one can say that larger magnitudes of a core tensor are denoted by low values of indices. This property is the basis for the development of compression algorithms based on HO-SVD.

Input: Data Tensor $\mathcal{T}$
Output: Tucker operator $[\![C; \mathbf{U}^{(1)}, \ldots, \mathbf{U}^{(N)}]\!]$
for $k \in \{1, \ldots, N\}$ **do**
$\quad | \quad \mathbf{U}^{(k)} = $ left singular vectors of $T_{(k)}$ in unfolding k;
end
$C = \mathcal{T} \times_1 \mathbf{U}^{(1)T} \times_2 \mathbf{U}^{(2)T} \ldots \times_N \mathbf{U}^{(N)T}$;
return $[\![C; \mathbf{U}^{(1)}, \ldots, \mathbf{U}^{(N)}]\!]$;

Algorithm 1: HO-SVD algorithm

Formally $\tilde{\mathcal{T}} = \tilde{\mathcal{C}} \times_1 \tilde{\mathbf{U}}^{(1)} \times_2 \tilde{\mathbf{U}}^{(2)} \times_3 \ldots \times_N \tilde{\mathbf{U}}^{(N)}$, where

$$\tilde{\mathcal{C}} = \{c_{i_1,i_2,\ldots,i_n}\}_{i_1,i_2,\ldots,i_n=0}^{R_1-1,R_2-1,\ldots,R_N-1} \in \mathbb{R}^{R_1,R_2,\ldots,R_N} \tag{6}$$

is a truncated tensor in such a way that in each mode l indices span from 0 to $R_l - 1 \leq I_l - 1$ and $\tilde{\mathbf{U}}^{(l)} \in \mathbb{R}^{R_l, I_l}$ matrices whose columns are orthonormal and rows form orthonormal basis in respective vector spaces.

Given $(R_l)_{l=1}^N$ one can form tensor $\tilde{\mathcal{T}}$ that approximates tensor $\mathcal{T}$ in the sense of their euclidean distance $||\tilde{\mathcal{T}} - \mathcal{T}||$. This approximation can be exploited to form lossy compression algorithms of signals that are indexed by more than two indices. It should by noted that the choice of $(R_l)_{l=1}^N$ in a given application is non-obvious and depends on the properties of processed signals.

2   Method

Our experiments aim to assess the effectiveness of HO-SVD for reduction of dimensionality of 3D animations. We will present results using multiple error metrics and compare them to a method based on PCA.

2.1   Input Data

Three-dimensional mesh will be treated as a $K \times J$ matrix $\mathbf{M}$, with mesh vertices $\mathbf{v}_i \in \mathbb{R}^J, i \in \{0, \ldots, K-1\}$ as rows, together with a set of triangle faces $\mathfrak{G}$ defined as three element tuples of vertex indices. We denote $J = 3$ as the number of spatial dimensions. An animation consists of F successive frames enumerated with k, each containing a mesh $\mathbf{M}_k, k \in \{0, \ldots, F-1\}$, with the same topology, but different coordinates of vertices. Therefore, input data can form tensor $\mathcal{T} = t_{i,j,k} \in \mathbb{R}^{K,J,F}$ while meshes $\mathbf{M}_k$, following the notation in [11], form frontal slices $\mathcal{T}_{::i}$. A pair $(\mathcal{T}, \mathfrak{G})$ contains all available information about the animation. We apply compression only to $\mathcal{T}$, a set of faces $\mathfrak{G}$ is used only for data visualization.

2.2   Dimensionality Reduction Testing Procedure

Steps of the procedure aimed at calculating the quality of mesh reconstruction include: estimation and removal of rigid motion from an animation, performing HO-SVD dimensionality reduction and its reconstruction and determining reconstruction quality.

2.3   Rigid Motion Estimation

The first step of the algorithm follows the idea from [5] and applies a simple rigid normalization of a dynamic animation. If a set of faces $\mathfrak{G}$ of mesh $\mathbf{M}$ is constant through the animation, mesh state in frame i, can be described by the sum of changes applied to $\mathbf{M}$ in each frame: $\mathbf{M}_i = \sum_{j=1}^{i}(\mathbf{M}_j - \mathbf{M}_{j-1}) = \sum_{j=1}^{i} \Delta\mathbf{M}_j$. Assuming that animation is represented in homogeneous coordinates, the difference between two consecutive frames $\Delta\mathbf{M}_j = \mathbf{D}_j \mathbf{R}_j^T$, where $\mathbf{R}_j$ is a rigid transformation between frames, and $\mathbf{D}_j$ corresponds to deformation of mesh vertices. Therefore $\mathbf{M}_i = \sum_j \mathbf{D}_j \mathbf{R}_j^T$, where $\mathbf{R}_j$ is a rigid transformation between frames 0 and j.

The output of this step is sequence $\mathfrak{R} = (\mathbf{R}_1, \ldots, \mathbf{R}_F)$ of transformation matrices between frame 0 and all consecutive ones, as well as a new, transformed data tensor $\mathcal{X} : \forall_i \mathcal{X}_{::i} = \mathcal{T}_{::i} \mathbf{R}_i^T$.

2.4   Higher Order Singular Value Decomposition

For the purpose of our compression algorithm, data tensor $\mathcal{X}$ containing normalised animation frames is decomposed using HO-SVD. The resulting Tucker operator $[\![C; \mathbf{U}^{(1)}, \mathbf{U}^{(2)}, \mathbf{U}^{(3)}]\!]$ is passed to further steps of the algorithm.

2.5   Dimensionality Reduction and Reconstruction

Vertices of a 3D mesh form $K \times J$ matrix $\mathbf{M}$, where $J = 3$. The number of memory units required to store or transmit an animation of F frames, not considering a set of faces $\mathfrak{G}$, may be expressed as $S = K \times F \times J \times d_s$, where d_s is the size of a single floating-point variable, e.g. $d_s = 4$ bytes. HO-SVD allows to reduce the amount of memory required to store an animation, by decomposing data tensor $\mathcal{T}$ and storing only the truncated Tucker operator $[\![\tilde{C}; \tilde{U}^{(1)}, \tilde{U}^{(2)}, \tilde{U}^{(3)}]\!]$. Theoretically there are three compression parameters, corresponding to J dimensions of $\mathcal{T}$. However, since the reduction of mode-2 components heavily impacts the quality of the reconstructed mesh, we will only consider the reduction of K mode-1 and F mode-3 components. The amount of data required to store the Tucker operator $[\![C; \mathbf{U}^{(1)}, \mathbf{U}^{(2)}, \mathbf{U}^{(3)}]\!]$ equals $S^{(\mathrm{hosvd})} = (v \times K + J^2 + f \times F + v \times J \times f) \times d_s$, where v corresponds to the number of mode-1 and f to mode-3 components kept. Therefore

$$CR^{(\mathrm{hosvd})} = \frac{S^{(\mathrm{hosvd})}}{S} = \frac{v \times K + J^2 + f \times F + f \times F + v \times J \times f}{K \times F \times J}.$$

For visualization of results, space savings (SS) will be used in place of compression rate, defined as $SS = (1 - CR)100\%$, so $SS = 99\%$ denotes only 1% of data remaining after compression.

In addition, we need to store a set of transformation matrices $\mathfrak{R}$, obtained during the first step of the algorithm. Its size is $S^{(\mathfrak{R})} = 12 \times F$, and it will be included in our results.

2.6   HO-SVD Compression Parameter Estimation

Application of HO-SVD for 3D mesh compression requires choosing the proportion of preserved components for each mode, resulting in the required CR. Mode-1 components correspond to spatial information (vertices) and mode-3 to temporal information (frames). If we denote the number of preserved mode-1 components as v and the number of mode-3 components as f, $\frac{v}{f}$ is the Vertices-To-Frames ratio (VTF). In our experiments we obtain VTF by searching for a pair $(v_{\min}, f_{\min})$ that gives the lowest reconstruction error for selected CR.

2.7   Reconstruction Error

Reconstruction errors were measured by using two standard metrics:

- Mean Squared Error: $d_{\mathrm{MSE}}(\mathbf{v}, \mathbf{v}') = \frac{1}{n} \sum_{i=1}^{n} (\mathbf{v}' - \mathbf{v})^2$, where $\mathbf{v}$ is the original data vector and $\mathbf{v}'$ is its reconstruction.
- Hausdorff distance: $d_{\mathrm{H}}(\mathfrak{A}, \mathfrak{B}) = \max\{\sup_{x \in \mathfrak{A}} \inf_{y \in \mathfrak{B}} d_e(x, y), \sup_{y \in \mathfrak{A}} \inf_{x \in \mathfrak{B}} d_e(x, y)\}$, where $\mathfrak{A}$ is the original, $\mathfrak{B}$ – a reconstructed data set and d_e denotes the euclidean distance.

Since these metrics may not correspond well with human perception of quality for 3D objects, an additional, perceptual metric called Mesh Structural Distortion Measure (MSDM) described in [7] was applied. This metric compares two shapes based on differences of curvature statistics (mean, variance, covariance) over their corresponding local windows. A global measure between the two meshes is then defined by the Minkowski sum of the distances over local windows. Since the metric compares static meshes, the final result for dynamic sequence is averaged between animation frames.

2.8   Comparison of HO-SVD and PCA Application for 3D Animation Compression

In order to verify the performance of HO-SVD, we compared it with a simple method of 3D animation dimensionality reduction. Following the idea from [5] we performed experiments using PCA.

Principal Component Analysis [18] may be defined as follows. Let $\mathbf{X} = [\mathbf{x}_1, \mathbf{x}_2 \ldots, \mathbf{x}_L]$ be a data matrix, where $\mathbf{x}_i \in \mathbb{R}^p$ are data vectors with zero empirical mean. The associated covariance matrix is given by $\mathbf{E} = \mathbf{X}\mathbf{X}^T$. By performing eigenvalue decomposition of $\mathbf{E} = \mathbf{O}\mathbf{D}\mathbf{O}^T$ such that eigenvalues $\lambda_i, i = 1, .., p$ of $\mathbf{D}$ are ordered in a descending order $\lambda_1 \geq \lambda_2 \geq \ldots \geq \lambda_p > 0$, one obtains the sequence of principal components $[\mathbf{o}_1, \mathbf{o}_2, \ldots, \mathbf{o}_p]$ which are columns of $\mathbf{O}$. One can form a feature vector $\mathbf{y}$ of dimension $p' \leq p$ by calculating $\mathbf{y} = [\mathbf{o}_1, \mathbf{o}_2, \ldots, \mathbf{o}_{p'}]^T \mathbf{x}$.

In order to apply PCA, tensor $\mathcal{T} = t_{i,j,k} \in \mathbb{R}^{F,J,K}$ must be unfolded according to Eq. (3). Therefore mode-1 unfolding is performed so the data is flattened row by row to form matrix $\mathbf{X}_{\mathcal{T}} \in \mathbb{R}^{F,J \times K}$.

Compression is performed by storing only a limited number of principal components of $\mathbf{F}$. When reconstructing matrix $\mathbf{X}$, the dimension of the desired feature vector p' equals the number of principal components $\mathbf{y} = [\mathbf{o}_1, \mathbf{o}_2, \ldots, \mathbf{o}_{p'}]^T \mathbf{x}$ used for its calculation and is the only parameter. The ratio of reduction depends on number f' of the key-frames left. The compression rate for an animation of a 3D mesh using PCA can be expressed as: $CR^{(\text{pca})} = \frac{(V \times J + F) \times f' \times d_s}{S}$

3   Results

Presentation of results is performed by using a set of well-known 3D animations, summarised in Table 1. *Chicken* and *Gallop* are artificial sequences of moving animal models. *Collapse* uses the same model as *Gallop* but the applied deformation is an elastic, non-rigid transformation. *Samba, Jumping, Bouncing* are motion capture animations of moving and dancing humans.

Table 1. An overview of animations used for visualization of results

Name	Referenced as	Vertices	Frames	Description
Chicken Crossing[a]	*Chicken*	3030	400	animation
Horse Gallop[b]	*Gallop*	8431	48	animation
Horse Collapse	*Collapse*	8431	48	animation
Samba[c]	*Samba*	9971	174	motion capture sequence
Jumping	*Jumping*	10002	149	motion capture sequence
Bouncing	*Bouncing*	10002	174	motion capture sequence

[a] *Chicken* animation was published by Jed Lengyel (http://jedwork.com/jed)
[b] *Gallop* and *Collapse* animations, described in [19], were obtained from the website of Doug L. James and Christopher D. Twigg (http://graphics.cs.cmu.edu/projects/sma).
[c] Motion capture sequences were obtained from the website of Daniel Vlasic (http://people.csail.mit.edu/drdaniel/mesh_animation).

The impact of proportion of mode-1 and mode-3 (VTF ratio) is presented in Fig. 2. The reconstruction error drops sharply as the number of components grows. For high SS values, mode-3 components, associated with animated frames, tend to be more important than mode-1 ones, associated with mesh vertices.

Frames from reconstructed animations are presented in Fig. 3 (*Chicken*), Fig. 4 (*Gallop*) and Fig. 5 (*Samba*). Observable deformations for artificial animated meshes (*Chicken, Gallop*) are almost unnoticeable for $SS \sim 90\%$ and only minor ones are present for $SS \sim 95\%$. For motion capture sequences (*Samba, Jumping, Bouncing*), major deformations are present for $SS \sim 95\%$, and only minor ones for $SS \sim 85\%$, with unnoticeable distortions for $SS \sim 70\%$. Reconstruction errors are higher for the *Collapse* mesh, as its animation is hard to describe using rigid transformations. Major deformations are observable for

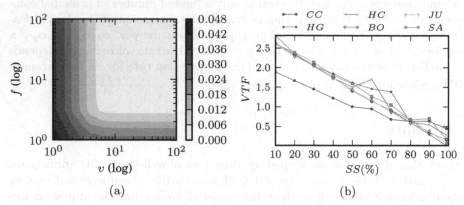

(a)   (b)

Fig. 2. An impact of HO-SVD parameter selection on MSE reconstruction for the *Chicken* animation. Panel (a) presents the reconstruction error as a function of the number of mode-1 (v) and mode-3 (f) components. Note that the distortion drops sharply with only a few first components. Panel (b) presents Vertices-to-Frame ratio as a function of SS.

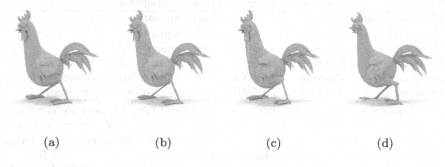

(a)   (b)   (c)   (d)

Fig. 3. Visualization of a reconstructed model for *Chicken*. (a): original, (b): SS=94.8%, (c): SS=97.8%, (d): SS=98.8%.

(a)   (b)   (c)   (d)

Fig. 4. Visualization of a reconstructed model for *Collapse*. (a): original, (b): SS=69.9%, (c): SS=84.9%, (d): SS=97.9%.

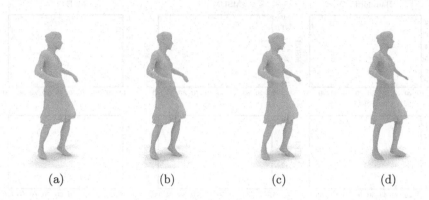

(a)   (b)   (c)   (d)

Fig. 5. Visualization of a reconstructed model for *Samba*. (a): original, (b): SS=89.9%, (c): SS=94.9%, (b): SS=97.9%.

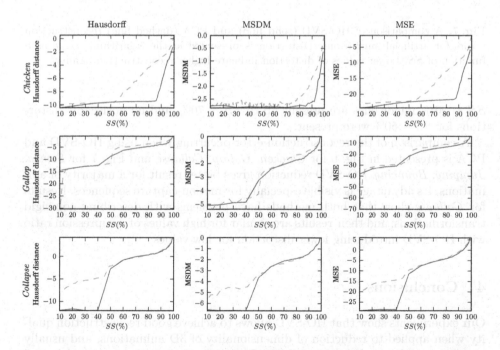

Fig. 6. A comparison of HO-SVD (solid line) and PCA (dashed line) reconstruction errors for artificial animations. Distortion is presented in the logarithmic scale as a function of *SS*. Lower values of distortion indicate higher reconstruction quality.

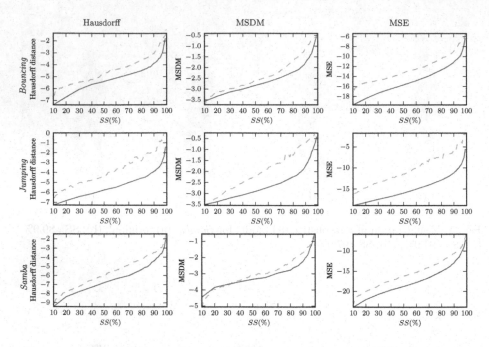

Fig. 7. A comparison of HO-SVD (solid line) and PCA (dashed line) reconstruction errors for artificial animations. Distortion is presented in the logarithmic scale as a function of SS. Lower values of distortion indicate higher reconstruction quality.

$SS \sim 90\%$, minor ones are present up to $SS \sim 70\%$, and no noticeable distortions for $SS \sim 50\%$ were present.

A comparison of the reconstruction error occurring when using HO-SVD and PCA is presented in Fig. 6 for *Chicken, Gallop, Collapse* and Fig. 7 for *Samba, Jumping, Bouncing.* HO-SVD reduction gives better result for a majority of animations. Its advantage is visible especially for motion-capture sequences. Results for *Collapse* show that both methods have problems with describing non-rigid transformations, and their results are similar for high values of compression ratio with HO-SVD introducing lower distortion for low values.

4 Conclusions

Our experiments show that HO-SVD allows to achieve good reconstruction quality when applied to reduction of dimensionality of 3D animations, and usually outperforms the application of PCA. For most of the animated models and motion-capture sequences, $SS \sim 90\%$ produces a reconstruction similar to the original, especially when lower Level-of-Detail is required.

The reconstruction error can be measured by using objective metrics, which allows reliable control over compression parameters. Parameters related to the proportion of preserved components in each mode, after performing data decomposition, can be found by using the simple heuristic approach.

Acknowledgements. This work has been partially supported by the Polish Ministry of Science and Higher Education projects: M. Romaszewski by NN516405137, P. Gawron by NN516481840, and S. Opozda by NN516482340.

References

[1] De Lathauwer, L., De Moor, B., Vandewalle, J.: A multilinear singular value decomposition. SIAM Journal on Matrix Analysis and Applications 21(4), 1253–1278 (2000)

[2] Ibarria, L., Rossignac, J.: Dynapack: space-time compression of the 3D animations of triangle meshes with fixed connectivity. In: Proceedings of the 2003 ACM SIGGRAPH/Eurographics Symposium on Computer Animation, pp. 126–135. Eurographics Association (2003)

[3] Sayood, K.: Introduction to data compression. Access Online via Elsevier (2012)

[4] Inoue, K., Urahama, K.: DSVD: a tensor-based image compression and recognition method. In: IEEE International Symposium on Circuits and Systems, ISCAS 2005, vol. 6, pp. 6308–6311 (2005)

[5] Alexa, M., Müller, W.: Representing Animations by Principal Components. Computer Graphics Forum 19(3), 411–418 (2000)

[6] Sattler, M., Sarlette, R., Klein, R.: Simple and efficient compression of animation sequences. In: Proceedings of the 2005 ACM SIGGRAPH/Eurographics Symposium on Computer Animation, SCA 2005, pp. 209–217. ACM, New York (2005)

[7] Lavoué, G., Drelie Gelasca, E., Dupont, F., Baskurt, A., Ebrahimi, T.: Perceptually driven 3D distance metrics with application to watermarking. In: SPIE Applications of Digital Image Processing XXIX (August 2006)

[8] Karni, Z., Gotsman, C.: Compression of soft-body animation sequences. Computers & Graphics 28(1), 25–34 (2004)

[9] Váša, L., Skala, V.: Cobra: Compression of the basis for pca represented animations. Computer Graphics Forum 28, 1529–1540 (2009)

[10] Váša, L., Skala, V.: Geometry-driven local neighbourhood based predictors for dynamic mesh compression. Computer Graphics Forum 29, 1921–1933 (2010)

[11] Kolda, T.G., Bader, B.W.: Tensor Decompositions and Applications. SIAM Review 51(3), 455–500 (2009)

[12] Shashua, A., Levin, A.: Linear image coding for regression and classification using the tensor-rank principle. In: Proceedings of the 2001 IEEE Computer Society Conference on Computer Vision and Pattern Recognition, CVPR 2001, vol. 1, p. I-42. IEEE (2001)

[13] Wang, H., Ahuja, N.: Facial expression decomposition. In: Proceedings of the Ninth IEEE International Conference on Computer Vision, vol. 2, pp. 958–965 (2003)

[14] Abdallah, E.E., Hamza, A.B., Bhattacharya, P.: MPEG video watermarking using tensor singular value decomposition. In: Kamel, M.S., Campilho, A. (eds.) ICIAR 2007. LNCS, vol. 4633, pp. 772–783. Springer, Heidelberg (2007)

[15] Mukai, T., Kuriyama, S.: Multilinear Motion Synthesis with Level-of-Detail Controls. In: 15th Pacific Conference on Computer Graphics and Applications, PG 2007, pp. 9–17 (2007)

[16] Akhter, I., Simon, T., Khan, S., Matthews, I., Sheikh, Y.: Bilinear spatiotemporal basis models. ACM Transactions on Graphics 31(2), 17:1–17:12 (2012)

[17] Suter, S.K., Makhynia, M., Pajarola, R.: Tamresh–tensor approximation multiresolution hierarchy for interactive volume visualization. Computer Graphics Forum 32, 151–160 (2013)

[18] Jolliffe, I.: Principal Component Analysis, 2nd edn. Springer (2002)

[19] James, D.L., Twigg, C.D.: Skinning Mesh Animations. ACM Trans. Graph. 24, 399–407 (2005)

Intelligent Methods
in Databases

Big Data Paradigm Developed in Volunteer Grid System with Genetic Programming Scheduler

Jerzy Balicki, Waldemar Korłub, Julian Szymanski, and Marcin Zakidalski

Faculty of Telecommunications, Electronics and Informatics,
Gdansk University of Technology, Gdask, Poland
{balicki,julian.szymanski}@eti.pg.gda.pl, waldemar.korlub@pg.gda.pl,
mzakidalski@gmail.com

Abstract. Artificial intelligence techniques are capable to handle a large amount of information collected over the web. In this paper, big data paradigm has been studied in volunteer and grid system called Comcute that is optimized by a genetic programming scheduler. This scheduler can optimize load balancing and resource cost. Genetic programming optimizer has been applied for finding the Pareto solu-tions. Finally, some results from numerical experiments have been shown.

Keywords: big data, volunteer computing, genetic programming.

1   Introduction

It is estimated that 2.5 exabytes of digital data are captured per day. A collection of large data sets requires some advanced database management tools based on artificial intelligence techniques to allow decision making, discovery and process optimization. Especially, big data sharing is a scientific and practical challenge due to some rapid progresses in finance, business as well as web banking. It is worth to mention that large data sets are gathered by ubiquitous smartphones, tablets, and wireless sensor networks with cameras or microphones. In result, the data store capacity has approximately doubled every three years since the 1980s. Moreover, data storage and also their visualization, analysis and search are still considered as an open problem to solve, too [17].

Massively parallel software on thousands of servers is required and that is why big data (an acronym BD) is not convenient to most relational database management systems. In such systems as desktop statistics and visualization packages, sizes of data are beyond the capability of commonly used tools within a tolerable elapsed time. A single big data set consists of terabytes of data and it can increase to achieve many petabytes for one volume. What is more, progress in speed of data in and out gives an opportunity to take advantage for big data development. Another criterion is wide variety data that is related to a huge range of data types and sources. Above four criteria: high volume, extraordinary velocity, great data variety, and veracity create the 4Vs model for big data description [20].

L. Rutkowski et al. (Eds.): ICAISC 2014, Part I, LNAI 8467, pp. 771–782, 2014.

We can distinguish some differences between big data and business intelligence as regards data use. Some nonlinear system identification methods and inductive statistics are applied for BD to deduce causal effects, nonlinear relationships. We can use regressions to discover dependencies and to find behaviors and predictions. On the other hand, some descriptive statistics can be developed for business intelligence to identify quantity effects or trends.

Genetic programming starts from a goal to be achieved and then it creates an application autonomously without explicitly programming [14]. To some extent, it replies the question that has been formulated by Arthur Samuel - a founder of machine learning - "How can computers be made to do what needs to be done, without being told exactly how to do it?" [18]. This paradigm uses the principle of selection, crossover and mutation to obtain a population of programs. It has been successfully applied to some problems from different fields [15]. Especially, multi-criterion genetic programming (MGP) can determine the Pareto-optimal solutions [2].

In this paper, MGP has been applied as a multi-objective scheduler for efficient using big data by volunteer grids. This scheduler optimizes both a workload of a bottleneck computer and the cost of the system. Moreover, an immunological system based procedure has been applied to handle admissible solutions. Finally, some outcomes for numerical experiments have been presented.

2   Multiagent Approach to Big Data Acquisition and Mining

Big data introduces a lot of issue in terms of data acquisition, storing and mining. Data is often gathered from multiple sources, which may be heterogeneous and spread geographically across the world. Moreover, the collected data may be stored in multiple geographically spread facilities as well due to sheer requirement of storage capacity, which cannot be fulfilled by a single outpost. Like in every distributed system, possibilities of communication loss and node downtime are undeniable and such occurrences need to be handled by software involved in data mining. This problem is even more important in case of mobile settings (e.g. mo-bile sources of data) as availability of data depends on time in such environments. Because of that, connection losses are no longer an anomaly they become a given trait of the system [5].

Multiagent systems are well suited for big data acquisition because of traits, which are commonly assigned to agents. The most important is mobility, which means the ability to move between different facilities. By doing that agents can get closer to the source of data or closer to the data they are about to process. It reduces bandwidth requirements and delays caused by network communication over long distances [5].

The ability to react upon sudden changes of the environment and to act proactively are other important traits, which an agent can take advantage of to improve data mining efficiency. Those traits provide foundation for handling changes in availability of data sources or collected data. Proactivity and autonomy translate to capability of an agent to set its own goals and act upon them

without external influence or control. An agent can proactively decide to move
to another set of data or initiate communication with other agents when it sees
it feasible. It is especially important in case of big data mining, as the expected
results of the extraction of deeply concealed knowledge from the data set, which
is processed, cannot be pre-determined. This means that appropriate actions
and intermediate goals of the knowledge extraction cannot be predetermined as
well, so the agent needs to decide what to do on its own.

Other useful traits of agents include abilities to communicate and negotiate.
In agent-based data mining system it is possible to distinguish different roles
and groups of tasks that constitute the whole mining process [12]. Individual
roles can be then assigned to agents. Through communication and negotiation
working groups of agents can be established, each of them containing agents with
a unified incentive to fulfill goals of their group.

Agent-based approach can improve efficiency of data mining compared to centralized approaches [23]. It was applied in different domains showing promising
results for further research, e.g banking and finance domain [16] or resource
allocation in distributed environments [5].

3   Genetic Programming and Immunological Systems

Genetic programming permits discovering a game playing strategy and can be
applied in optimal control, planning and sequence induction [14]. Fig. 1 shows
an example of a tree as a model of the computer program performance. This tree
is equivalent to the parse tree that most compilers (parsers) construct internally
from a computer program source. A parse tree consists of branches and nodes:
a root node, a branch node, and a leaf node. A parent node is one which has at
least one other node linked by a branch under it. A child node is one which has
at least one node directly above it to which it is linked by a branch of the tree.

The size of the parse tree is limited by the number of nodes or by the number
of the tree levels. Nodes in the parse tree are divided on functional nodes and
terminal ones. A functional node represents the procedure randomly chosen from
the primary defined set of functions:

$$\mathcal{F} = \{f_1, \ldots, f_n, \ldots, f_N\} \ . \tag{1}$$

Each function should be able to accept, as its arguments, any value and data
type that may possible be returned by the other procedure [14]. Moreover, each
procedure should be able to accept any value and data type that may possible
be assumed by any terminal in the terminal set:

$$\mathcal{T} = \{a_1, \ldots, a_m, \ldots, a_M\} \ . \tag{2}$$

So, each function should be well defined for any arrangement of arguments
that it may come across. Furthermore, the solution to the problem should be
expressed by the combination of the procedures from the set of functions and
the arguments from the set of terminals. For example, $\mathcal{F} = \{\text{AND}, \text{NOT}\}$ is
sufficient to express any Boolean function.

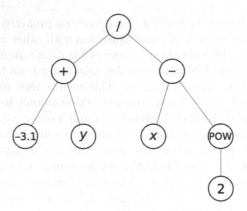

Fig. 1. An example of a parse tree as a chromosome of an genetic algorithm

The biological immune system has distributed elements as well as some features of artificial intelligence like an adaptation, learning, using memory, and associative retrieval of information in recognition [11]. Especially, the negative selection algorithm (NSA) can be applied for change detection because it uses the discrimination rule to classify some trespassers [10]. Detectors can be randomly generated to reduce those detectors that are not capable of recognizing themselves. However, detectors capable to distinguish intruders are kept to defense an organism. In the NSA, detection is performed probabilistically [3].

An antigen can support an antibody generation by stimulation a reaction against squatters. Besides, some positive viruses and bacteria cooperate with antigens [13]. An antibody (an immunoglobulin) is a large Y-shaped protein capable to recognize and deactivate external objects as negative bacteria and viruses [22]. It is worth to underline that the NSA can manage constraints in an evolutionary algorithm by dividing the population in two assemblies [6]. Antigens belong to the feasible solution sub-population, and "antibodies" – to the infeasible one.

The initial fitness for all antibodies in the current infeasible subpopulation is equal to zero. Next, a randomly selected antigen G^- from the feasible subpopulation is compared to the some chosen antibodies. After that, the match measure S between G^- and the antibody B^- is calculated due to the similarity at the genotype level. This measure of genotype similarity for the chromosome integer coding is, as follows [1]:

$$S(G^-, B^-) = \sum_{m=1}^{M} |G_m^- - B_m^-| \, , \tag{3}$$

where:
M – the length of the solution,
G_m^- - value of the antigen at position m, $m = \overline{1, M}$,
B_m^- - value of the antibody at position m, $m = \overline{1, M}$.

The negative selection can be modeled by an evolutionary algorithm, which prefers infeasible solutions that are similar to randomly chosen feasible one in the current population. We assume that all random choices of antigens are based on the uniform distribution.

The situation is different in the case of antibodies. If the fitness of the selected winner is increased by adding the amount of the similarity measure, then an antibody may pass over because of the relatively small value of assessment (3). On the other hand, some constraints may be satisfied by this alternative. What is more, if a constraint is exceeded and the others are not, the value of a similarity measure may be lower for some cases. One of two similar solutions, in genotype sense, may not satisfy this constraint and another may satisfy it.

4   An Extended NSA*

To avoid above disadvantages, some similarity measures can be developed from the state of an antibody B^- to the state of the selected antigen G^-, as below:

$$f_n(B^-, G^-) = \begin{cases} g_k(B^-) - g_k(G^-), k = \overline{1,K}, n = k, \\ |h_l(B^-)|, l = \overline{1,L}, n = K+l, \end{cases} n = \overline{1,N}, N = K+L \quad (4)$$

where
$g_k(x) \leq 0, k = \overline{1,K},$
$h_l(x) = 0, l = \overline{1,L}.$

The distance $f_n(B^-, G^-)$ between B^- and G^- is supposed to be minimized for all constraint indexes n. If $f_n(B^-, G^-) < f_n(C^-, G^-)$, then B^- ought to be preferred to C^- due to the nth constraint. Moreover, if B^- is characterized by all shorter distances to the antigen than the antibody C^-, then B^- should be preferred for all constraints. However, some situations may occur when B^- is characterized by the shorter distances for some constraints and C^- is marked by the shorter distances for the others. In this case, it is difficult to select an antibody. So, a ranking procedure can be applied to calculate fitness of antibodies and then to select the winner.

In a ranking procedure, distances between the chosen antigen and some antibodies are calculated due to their ranks [2]. If B^- is characterized by the rank $r(B^-)$ such that $1 \leq r(B^-) \leq r_{\max}$, then the increment of the fitness function is estimated, as below:

$$\Delta f(B^-) = r_{\max} - r(B^-) + 1 . \quad (5)$$

Subsequently, some fitness values of selected antibodies are increased by their given increments. Then antibodies are returned to the current population and this process is repeated typically three times the number of antibodies. Each time, a randomly chosen antigen is compared to the same subset of antibodies.

Afterwards, a new population is constructed by selection, crossover and mutation without calculations of fitness. That process is repeated until a convergence of population emerges or until a maximal number of iterations is exceeded. At the end, the final population as outcomes from the negative selection algorithm is re-turned to the external evolutionary algorithm.

5   Optimization Model for Volunteer Grid

In the grid and volunteer computing systems like BOINC or Comcute, some scientific projects are transformed to a set of the calculation tasks that are executed concurrently by volunteer computers with a support of some levels of the middle-ware modules. A society of scientists can use these systems for extensive distributed calculations in some research projects. The 24-hour average performance of the most popular volunteer system BOINC is 8.186 TeraFLOPS. Moreover, the number of active volunteers can be estimated as 238,412, and also 388,929 computers process data [4].

In the Comcute system, an application for the Collatz hypothesis verification and another one for finding the 49th Mersenne number were applied to prove the intense human interactions, scalability and high performance [7].

In the architecture of the volunteer grid Comcute (Fig. 2), we can distinguish the Z-layer where the system client defines new tasks, starts instances of previously defined tasks, tracks statuses of running tasks and fetches results for completed tasks. On the other hand, the W-server layer supervises execution of tasks. For each task instance, a subset of W-servers is arranged that partitions the task among its members. The tasks pass input data packets for the task instance to connected S-servers beneath them as well as collect and merge results obtained from the S-layer. S-server is a distribution server that is exposed to clients who fetch execution code and subsequent data packets and return results for these data packets. I-client level is an untrusted layer of volunteers fetching and returning results to the system.

To test the ability of the MGP with NSA* for handling constraints, we consider a multi-criterion optimisation problem for task assignment in a distributed computer system [2]. Especially, MGP can minimize $Z_{\max}$ – the workload of a bottleneck computer and C – the cost of machines, concurrently.

A set of parallel tasks $\{T_1, \ldots, T_v, \ldots, T_V\}$ communicated with each other is considered among the coherent computer network with hosts located at the processing nodes from the given set $W = \{w_1, \ldots, w_i, \ldots, w_I\}$. Let the task T_v be executed on some hosts taken from the set of available sorts $\Pi = \{\pi_1, \ldots, \pi_j, \ldots, \pi_J\}$. The over-head execution time of the task T_v by the computer π_j is represented by an item t_{vj}.

The first criterion is a total host cost, as follows:

$$C(x) = \sum_{i=1}^{I} \sum_{j=1}^{J} \kappa_j x_{ij}^{\pi} \tag{6}$$

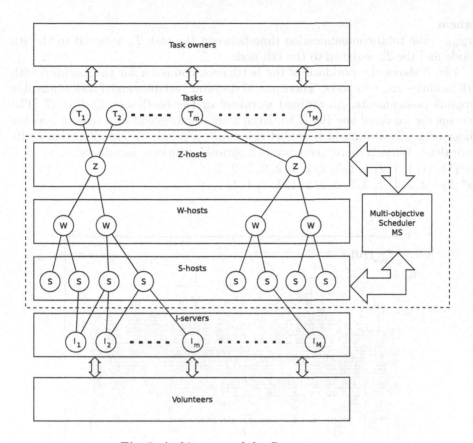

Fig. 2. Architecture of the Comcute system

where
$$x = \left[x_{11}^m, \ldots, x_{vi}^m, \ldots, x_{VI}^m, x_{11}^\pi, \ldots, x_{ij}^\pi, \ldots, x_{IJ}^\pi\right]^T,$$

$$x_{ij}^\pi = \begin{cases} 1 & \text{if } \pi_j \text{ is assigned to the } w_i, \\ 0 & \text{otherwise,} \end{cases}$$

$$x_{vi}^m = \begin{cases} 1 & \text{if task } T_v \text{ is assigned to the } w_i, \\ 0 & \text{otherwise,} \end{cases}$$

κ_j – the cost of the host π_j.

Another criterion is $Z_{\max}$ – a workload of the bottleneck host that is supposed to be minimized. It is provided by the subsequent formula:

$$Z_{\max}(x) = \max_{i \in \overline{1, I}} \left\{ \sum_{j=1}^J \sum_{v=1}^V t_{vj} x_{vi}^m x_{ij}^\pi + \sum_{v=1}^V \sum_{\substack{u=1 \\ u \neq v}}^V \sum_{i=1}^I \sum_{\substack{k=1 \\ k \neq i}}^I \tau_{vuik} x_{vi}^m x_{uk}^m \right\} , \quad (7)$$

where
τ_{vuik} – the total communication time between the task T_v assigned to the ith node and the T_u assigned to the kth node.

Fig. 3 shows the workload of the bottleneck computer for the instance with 15 modules and two hosts. There are 30 decision variables and 7.394 admissible module assignments. An optimal workload of the bottleneck host is 47 [TU] versus the maximal one 102 [TU]. Even a small movement of a task to another host or a substitution of host sort can cause a relatively big alteration of its workload. What is more, there are two optimal solutions, as follows:

x*(1)=[1, 1, 1, 1, 1, 1, 1, 2, 2, 1, 2, 2, 2, 2, 2]
x*(2)=[2, 2, 1, 1, 2, 2, 2, 2, 2, 1, 1, 1, 1, 1, 1]

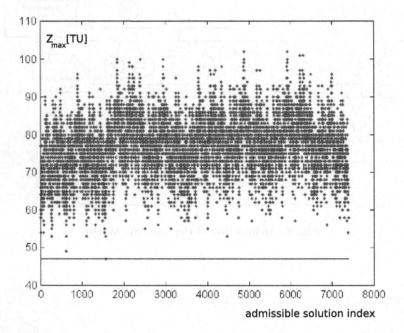

Fig. 3. Workload of the bottleneck computer for generated solutions

A host is supposed to be equipped with necessary capacities of resources. Let the memories $z_1, \ldots, z_r, \ldots, z_R$ be available in the volunteer system and let d_{jr} be the capacity of memory z_r in the host π_j. We assume the task Tv holds c_{vr} units of memory z_r during a program execution. The host memory limit cannot be exceeded in the ith node, as bellow:

$$\sum_{v=1}^{V} c_{vr} x_{vi}^m \leq \sum_{j=1}^{J} d_{jr} x_{ij}^\pi, i = \overline{1,I}, r = \overline{1,R} \ . \tag{8}$$

Let π_j be distributed independently according to the exponential distribution with rate λ_j. Hosts and tasks like Z, W or S can be allocated to nodes to guarantee the required reliability R, as below [1]:

$$\prod_{v=1}^{V} \prod_{i=1}^{I} \prod_{j=1}^{J} \exp\left(-\lambda_j t_{vj} x_{vi}^m x_{ij}^\pi\right) \leq R_{\min} . \qquad (9)$$

Let $(\boldsymbol{X}, F, P)$ be the multi-criterion optimization question for finding the representation of Pareto-optimal solutions [6]. It can be established, as follows:

1. $\boldsymbol{X}$ - an admissible solution set

$$\boldsymbol{X} = \{x \in \boldsymbol{B}^{I(V+J)} \mid \sum_{v=1}^{V} c_{vr} x_{vi}^m \leq \sum_{j=1}^{J} d_{jr} x_{ij}^\pi, i = \overline{1,I}, r = \overline{1,R};$$

$$\prod_{v=1}^{V} \prod_{i=1}^{I} \prod_{j=1}^{J} \exp\left(-\lambda_j t_{vj} x_{vi}^m x_{ij}^\pi\right) \leq R_{\min}; \sum_{i=1}^{I} x_{vi}^m = 1, v = \overline{1,V};$$

$$\sum_{j=1}^{J} x_{ij}^\pi = 1, i = \overline{1,I}\}$$

where: $\boldsymbol{B} = \{0,1\}$,
2. F - a vector quality criterion

$$F : \boldsymbol{X} \to \boldsymbol{R}^2 \qquad (10)$$

where:
$\boldsymbol{R}$ – the set of real numbers,
$F(x) = [Z_{\max}(x), C(x)]^T$ for $x \in \boldsymbol{X}$,
$Z_{\max}(x)$ and $C(x)$ are calculated by (7) and (6) respectively.
3. P - the Pareto relation [8].

To solve this problem we can apply the Strength Pareto Evolutionary Algorithm SPEA [24] or the Adaptive Multi-Criterion Evolutionary Algorithm with Tabu Mutation AMEA+ [1]. Moreover, some scheduling algorithms based on tabu search studied in [21] can be combined with an evolutionary approach.

In AMEA+, a tabu search procedure was applied as the second mutation operator to decrease the workload of the bottleneck computer. Moreover, we introduced the NSA* to improve the quality of obtained solutions and the evolutionary algorithm was denoted as AMEA*.

6 Numerical Experiments

For the instance with 15 tasks, 4 nodes, and 5 computer sorts, there are 80 binary decision variables. An average level of convergence to the Pareto set is 17.7% for the MGP* and 17.4% for the AMEA*. A maximal level is 28.5% for the MGP* and 29.6% for the AMEA*. For this instance the average number of optimal solutions is 19.5% for the MGP* and 21.1% for the AMEA*. Fig. 4 6 shows the process of finding efficient task assignment by MGP* for the cut obtained from the evaluation space according to the cost criterion C and the workload of the bottleneck computer Z_{max}. An average level of convergence to the Pareto set, an maximal level, and the average number of optimal solutions become worse, when the number of task, number of nodes, and number of computer types increase. An average level is 37.7% for the MGP* versus 35,7% for the AMEA*, if the instance includes 50 tasks, 4 nodes, 5 computer types and also 220 binary decision variables.

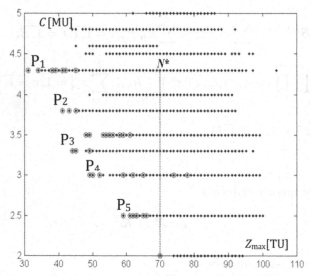

Fig. 4. Pareto front determined by GMP*

Concluding Remarks

Multi-objective genetic programming is relatively new paradigm of artificial intelligence that can be used for finding Pareto-optimal solutions. A computer program as a chromosome gives possibility to represent knowledge that is specific to the problem in more intelligent way than the data structure.

Our future works will focus on testing the other sets of procedures and terminals to find the Pareto-optimal task assignments for different criteria and constraints. Initial numerical experiments confirmed that sub-optimal in Pareto sense task assignments can be found by genetic programming. That approach permits for obtaining comparable quality outcomes to advanced evolutionary algorithm. Us-ing volunteer model of computations based on our Comcute system we plan implement large scale text classifier [9]. This task will allow us to evaluate the proposed architecture for real life tasks. Also the implementation will served as a proof of concept of an easy integration model for distributed computational nodes.

References

1. Balicki, J.: Immune Systems in Multi-criterion Evolutionary Algorithm for Task Assignments in Distributed Computer System. In: Szczepaniak, P.S., Kacprzyk, J., Niewiadomski, A. (eds.) AWIC 2005. LNCS (LNAI), vol. 3528, pp. 51–56. Springer, Heidelberg (2005)
2. Balicki, J.: Multicriterion Genetic Programming for Trajectory Planning of Underwater Vehicle. Int. Journal of Computer Science and Network Security 6, 1–6 (2006)
3. Bernaschi, M., Castiglione, F., Succi, S.: A High Performance Simulator of the Immune System. Future Generation Computer System 15, 333–342 (2006)
4. BOINC. Open-source software for volunteer and grid computing, http://boinc.berkeley.edu/ (accessed January 25, 2014)
5. Cao, L., Gorodetsky, V., Mitkas, P.A.: Agent Mining: The Synergy of Agents and Data Mining. IEEE Intelligent Systems 24(3), 64–72 (2009)
6. Coello Coello, C.A., Van Veldhuizen, D.A., Lamont, G.B.: Evolutionary Algorithms for Solving Multi-Objective Problems. Kluwer Academic Publishers, New York (2002)
7. Comcute. Volunteer grid at Gdask University of Technology, http://comcute.eti.pg.gda.pl/ (accessed January 25, 2014)
8. Deb, K.: Multi-Objective Optimization using Evolutionary Algorithms. John Wiley & Sons, Chichester (2001)
9. Draszawka, K., Szymanski, J.: Thresholding strategies for large scale multi-label text classifier. In: Proceedings of Human System Interaction IEEE (2013)
10. Forrest, S., Perelson, A.S.: Genetic Algorithms and the Immune System. In: Schwefel, H.-P., Männer, R. (eds.) PPSN 1990. LNCS, vol. 496, pp. 320–325. Springer, Heidelberg (1991)
11. Jerne, N.K.: Idiotypic Networks and Other Preconceived Ideas. Immunological Revue 79, 5–25 (1984)
12. Khan, D.: CAKE Classifying, Associating and Knowledge DiscovEry - An Approach for Distributed Data Mining (DDM) Using PArallel Data Mining Agents (PADMAs). In: IEEE/WIC/ACM International Conference on Web Intelligence and Intelligent Agent Technology, vol. 3, pp. 596–601 (2008)
13. Kim, J., Bentley, P.J.: Immune Memory in the Dynamic Clonal Selection Algorithm. In: Proc. the First Int. Conference on Artificial Immune Systems, Canterbury, Australia, pp. 57–65 (2002)
14. Koza, J.R.: Genetic Programming: On the Programming of Computers by Means of Natural Selection. The MIT Press, Cambridge (1992)
15. Koza, J.R., Keane, M.A., Streeter, M.J., Mydlowec, W., Yu, J., Lanza, G.: Genetic programming IV. Routine Human-Competitive Machine Intelligence. Kluwer Academic Publishers, New York (2003)
16. Li, H.X., Chosler, R.: Application of Multilayered Multi-Agent Data Mining Architecture to Bank Domain. In: International Conference on Wireless Communications, Networking and Mobile Computing, WiCom 2007, pp. 6721–6724 (2007)
17. O'Leary, D.E.: Artificial Intelligence and Big Data. IEEE Intelligent Systems 28(2), 96–99 (2013)
18. Samuel, A.L.: Programming Computers to Play Games. Advances in Computers 1, 165–192 (1960)
19. Sheble, G.B., Britting, K.: Refined Genetic Algorithm Economic Dispatch Example. IEEE Transactions on Power Systems 10, 117–124 (1995)

20. Snijders, C., Matzat, U., Reips, U.D.: Big Data: Big gaps of knowledge in the field of Internet. International Journal of Internet Science 7, 1–5 (2012)
21. Weglarz, J., Nabrzyski, J., Schopf, J.: Grid Resource Management: State of the Art and Future Trends. Kluwer Academic Publishers, Boston (2003)
22. Wierzchon, S.T.: Immune-based Recommender System. In: Hryniewicz, O., Kacprzyk, J., Koronacki, J., Wierzchon, S.T. (eds.) Issues in Intelligent Systems. Paradigms, pp. 341–356. Exit, Warsaw (2005)
23. Zhou, D., Rao, W., Lv, F.A.: Multi-Agent Distributed Data Mining Model Based on Algorithm Analysis and Task Prediction. In: 2nd International Conference on Information Engineering and Computer Science, pp. 1–4 (2010)
24. Zitzler, E., Deb, K., Thiele, L.: Comparison of Multiobjective Evolutionary Algorithms: Empirical Results. Evolutionary Computation 8, 173–195 (2000)

Novel Algorithm for Translation
from Image Content to Semantic Form

Janusz Rygał[1], Jakub Romanowski[1], Rafał Scherer[1], and Sohrab Ferdowsi[2]

[1] Institute of Computational Intelligence, Częstochowa University of Technology
al. Armii Krajowej 36, 42-200 Częstochowa, Poland
{janusz.rygal,jakub.romanowski,rafal.scherer}@iisi.pcz.pl
http://iisi.pcz.pl
[2] University of Geneva, Computer Science Department,
7 Route de Drize, Geneva, Switzerland
http://sip.unige.ch

Abstract. In this paper we present a new algorithm for translating visual information into a semantic form. In our approach we try to combine these two separate areas of computer since into one process. The main goal is to achieve very good performance at searching for similar images. In this paper we explain in details the design of the translation algorithm which is only one part of the whole process, but the most important one. This module is some kind of interface between information in the form of digital image and the information represented by lexems. We will also concisely demonstrate the structure of the whole SIA (Semantic Image Analysis) project.

Keywords: semantic translation, image transformation, semantic image analysis, CBIR.

1 Introduction

Nowadays we are surrounded by the immensity of information. Because of computers and power of digital processing we are able to analyze more and more information in a shorter period of time. Humans are already very good at searching and analyzing information in a textual form, everyone of us is familiar with using popular Internet search engines. In the area of digital image processing we are still far away from the quality and effectiveness of text retrieval. Translation of the information in the form of digital image into text is one of the most important parts of the SIA project [25]. To enable semantic analysis [25] on the data representing the image we have to convert it into text and this conversion has to be a deterministic and stable process [19]. Before we were ready to establish our translation algorithm we had had to prepare the whole preprocessing module, which is responsible for filtering out some unimportant information and noises from the image and fetching the most important one [3][13][14][21][24][27]. Fetched data are translated by our translation formula and saved in the database in the form of the vector of lexems. Our approach is designed to be applied on

L. Rutkowski et al. (Eds.): ICAISC 2014, Part I, LNAI 8467, pp. 783–792, 2014.

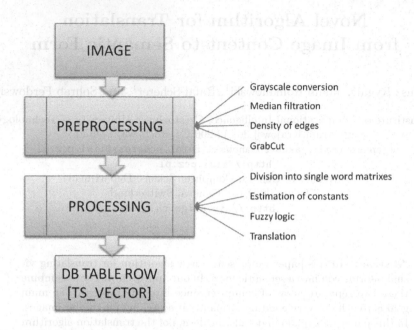

Fig. 1. Simplified structure of the conversion process used by the proposed approach

every kind of images but it could be specialized to process only specific classes of image objects [4] or to images with specific features [1][9][10][26] which may be classified by multiple methods [5][6][7][8][16][17][20][22].

2   Image Processing Algorithm

As we see in Fig. 1, the whole process of the image conversion into the semantic form consists in two general parts – preprocessing and processing. Results of our research concerning each preprocessing step have been already described in [24][27]. In this paper we are focused on our latest research about the translation algorithms. This part of the process is also divided into stages what is described in following subsections.

2.1   Division into Single Word Matrixes

The output from the preprocessing part is the grayscale image with marked important parts, which were selected as significant areas of the image [2][15]. Relying on the information enclosed in that image, we need first to select the ROI (Region Of Interest), which is a rectangle containing the significant areas of the image and then restrict that rectangle by searching for a shape which is the best pattern for areas representing the important parts of an image. The selected shape has to be divided into areas, which we called SWM (Single Word

Matrix). The question was how large these matrixes have to be. In our approach we assumed that the number of rows and columns of the SWM will be equal to 5% of the height and width of the selected ROI. Thanks to this operation we can keep our process robust for images containing the same objects in a different scale.

2.2 Estimation of Constants

In the result, each SWM has to be represented by a single word, so we had to find a method to convert a matrix of pixels into one word. What was very important, this algorithm had to be stable, that means that conversion of the matrix representing the same part of the image has to be always transformed into the same word. Because of that we employed markers, which represent the constant properties of that area. In the current implementation we used the following markers:

1. Percentage amount of edges contained by the matrix,
2. Average value of the intensity of pixels contained by the matrix.

At the beginning of the research we decided that this part has to be generic, which means, that adding new markers has to be feasible. That is why in the next planed phase of our project we can combine diverse markers to achieve the best selectivity of similar images.

2.3 Fuzzy Logic

We used fuzzy logic mechanisms by conversion the values of single SWM represented by array of markers. To each marker we assigned some number of levels, to this levels we round every marker value to reduce diversity and the number of possible combinations.

2.4 Translation

To translate the values of markers into single word, we used an English dictionary. Each array of markers, which represents the single SWM is converted by the SHA-1 algorithm into a hash code. Then the algorithm searches in the dictionary if there exists already a word to which this hash code was exactly assigned, if yes then the SWM becomes this word, if not, then to this value of hash code is assigned the next free word from the dictionary. The whole image is represented by the row of single word matrixes separated by the space characters.

3 Structure of the Conversion Mechanism

In this paragraph we present each step of the conversion. Description of each step is connected with the input and output information, so the order of presentation

Fig. 2. Original test image

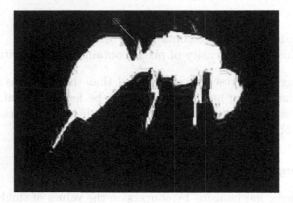

Fig. 3. Image representing the result of the preprocessing phase

is very important. The original test image is shown in Fig. 2. As already mentioned, in this paper we are focused on the processing part of the approach. The resulting image at the output of the preprocessing part is presented in Fig. 3. Now we present the steps of the algorithm:

1. In the first step we have to divide the selected ROI into SWMs. The number of rows and columns is equal to 5% of the height and width of the selected ROI. Fig. 4 presents the image with marked ROI divided into single word matrixes.

2. In the next part of the conversion we have to filter out these matrixes, which do not contain any pixels which were marked as the significant and important information. In our approach it is performed by finding the maximum value of intensity of pixels included into matrix, when this maximum is equal 255, then the whole matrix is selected as important one. Fig. 5 shows only these matrixes, which were marked as containing significant information and were selected for further computation.

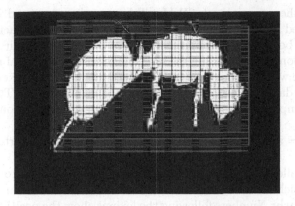

Fig. 4. Image representing the ROI divided into single word matrixes

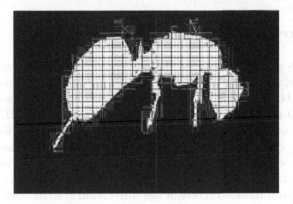

Fig. 5. Image representing selection of important single word matrixes

3. Having selected list of SWMs we are ready to compute constant markers for every matrix. Our algorithm was designed in such a way that adding new markers is an easy and fast action, but in this situation we need to compute values for every image in the database. In the current implementation we used the percentage value of edges in the matrix and average intensity of pixels. Thus, for one SWM these values can take values as follows:
   - Percentage value of edges: 22
   - Average value of intensity: 120
4. When we have already estimated values of constant markers for every SWM, we have to compute the hashcode, which is going to be the representation of these values. For this computation we use a SHA1 algorithm, e.g.:
   SHA1(22,120) = 2311516461361441305020396432261951401781561133132386
5. In the next step we need to find a word which will be the representation of our hash code, if our hash code already exists in the database, then we will take the word which is assigned to this hash code, otherwise we will take the first one without assigned a word.

At the end of the process, each SWM will have assigned a word. All the words will be combined into a single text, separated by the space characters. Such prepared text will be the textual representation of the image. But it is not the last step of conversion, during adding the new image with the textual representation to the database we call a trigger which converts the text into lexems. The name of this form of data in PostgreSql database system is TS_VECTOR. Below we present an example of the structure with this form of information:

TS_VECTOR = airfar 127 aisl 289 alarmist 346 albedo 304 alert 201,217

We see words followed by certain numbers. These words are not ordinary words, but lexems, which are normalized words to make different variants of the same word look similarly. Numbers following the lexems show the position of the lexem occurrence.

4 Structure of the Research Environment

For our research we have developed the next version of the software which is responsible for the whole SIA [25] process. In this paper we are focused on the processing part, so the following information concerns only this phase. Our software called CBIR 4.0 is divided into server and database layers. CBIR 4.0 software was written using C# .NET 4.0 and PostgreSQL 9.0 technologies. In addition, for the purposes of image processing we use Emgu.CV-2.3.0 library. Because the end result of the conversion mechanism is a database item, it is worth to describe in details the database structure and functionalities. In Fig. 6 we presented the main part of the database structure of the conversion system. As we see in Fig. 6, the most important tables in the database are table "DICTIONARY" and table "IMAGE". Table "DICTIONARY" contains 109.583 rows, which represent single words in English language (obtained from the SIL Organisation, available at http://www.sil.org). Each item with filled field "HASHCODE" is already assigned to specific values of constant markers. Data from this table are strongly used and updated during the conversion of images into semantic form. Table "IMAGE" contains of course already transformed images, the most important field of the table is "TSV_BODY", which contains data representing digital image in the form of TS_VECTOR, which is the sorted list of lexems. Database table "IMAGE" together with the trigger, the trigger function and the GIN index create the independent fast text engine construction (PostgreSQL 9.1.2 Documentation, available at http://www.postgresql.org/). By each update or insert on the table "IMAGE" the trigger is started, which calls the trigger function, while the main task of this function is to convert data into TS_VECTOR and save them in silent mode inside table in the field "TSV_BODY".

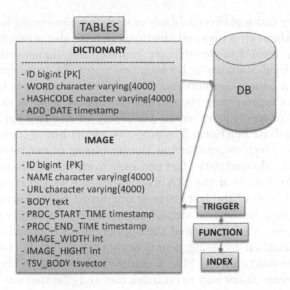

Fig. 6. The most important parts of the database structure

5   Experimental Results

For tests of our algorithm and system we chose a set of images representing different types of objects. Several of them represent different objects but of the same type [12]. For example there are multiple images representing ants in various scale, on diverse background and with other coexisting objects. By performing these tests we wanted to check following properties of our approach: determinism, performance and structure of converted data. Presented statistics and properties describe our test on 100 of test images from Caltech 101 images data base. Total number of words generated in dictionary is 109.583 with number of distinct words used for conversion the first 100 images in amount of 5.536. During conversion of first 100 images there were used 28.835 words. Average size of processed images is 232 pixels height and 294 pixels width and disk size of table containing 100 converted images in number 1264 kB. Average time used for the whole process of conversion is 2686 ms.

It is worth to mention that we also tested that the same image converted twice gives the same results. With this test we proved the deterministic behavior of our algorithm. More than 90% of time used for conversion is the preprocessing phase, the GrabCut algorithm is the the slowest part of the process.

6   Conclusions

With this paper we proved that the idea of conversion of images from pixels into words is not only an idea but the real way to combine two important branches of computer science. Because of usage of fast text search engine we obtained the possibility of very fast and effective analysis of data representing images. Because of advanced database structure and functions we have also possibility of applying fuzzy logic on the level of single table row, representing single words. It is possible to establish the level of similarity between two words. By extending the function we can achieve a connection between similarities of two words to similarity of constant markers representing the single word matrix what is an exact area of the image. This property gives us the possibility of effective applying fast text search engine analytic functions. The proposed algorithm of translation fulfilled all requirements, which we specified at the beginning of our research. The new approach is stable, deterministic, fast and easy to extend, these properties allow us to look in the future of the SIA with promising expectations. As already mentioned this is one of the last parts of our broad SIA project, but also the most important one. In the next step of our research we will develop new search and rank functions. Also we noticed the opportunity to expand our algorithms of SWMs classification by using neural networks [11][18][23] but it is one of additional functionality of the SIA. Our novel algorithm of translation is an important milestone on our way to establish fast and effective way to find similar images to the one given on the input. Our alfa tests already provided satisfying results and we hope that in a short period of time we will be ready to publish results of the whole SIA mechanism.

Acknowledgements. The project was funded by the National Center for Science under decision number DEC-2011/01/D/ST6/06957.

References

1. Bazarganigilani, M.: Optimized image feature selection using pairwise classifiers. Journal of Artificial Intelligence and Soft Computing Research 1(2), 147–153 (2011)
2. Blake, A., Rother, C., Brown, M., Perez, P., Torr, P.: Interactive image segmentation using an adaptive GMMRF model. In: Pajdla, T., Matas, J(G.) (eds.) ECCV 2004. LNCS, vol. 3021, pp. 428–441. Springer, Heidelberg (2004)
3. Canny, J.: A computational approach to edge detection. IEEE Trans. Pattern Anal. Mach. Intell. 8(6), 679–698 (1986)
4. Chang, Y., Wang, Y., Chen, C., Ricanek, K.: Improved image-based automatic gender classification by feature selection. Journal of Artificial Intelligence and Soft Computing Research 1(3), 241–253 (2011)
5. Cpalka, K., Rutkowski, L.: Flexible takagi-sugeno fuzzy systems. In: Proceedings of the 2005 IEEE International Joint Conference on Neural Networks, IJCNN 2005, vol. 3, pp. 1764–1769 (July 2005)
6. Cpalka, K., Rutkowski, L.: A new method for designing and reduction of neuro-fuzzy systems. In: 2006 IEEE International Conference on Fuzzy Systems, pp. 1851–1857 (2006)
7. Cpalka, K.: A new method for design and reduction of neuro-fuzzy classification systems. IEEE Transactions on Neural Networks 20(4), 701–714 (2009)
8. Cpalka, K., Rutkowski, L.: Flexible takagi sugeno neuro-fuzzy structures for nonlinear approximation. WSEAS Transactions on Systems 4(9), 1450–1458 (2005)

9. Drozda, P., Górecki, P., Sopyla, K., Artiemjew, P.: Visual words sequence alignment for image classification. In: ICCI*CC, pp. 397–402. IEEE (2013)
10. Drozda, P., Sopyła, K., Górecki, P.: Online crowdsource system supporting ground truth datasets creation. In: Rutkowski, L., Korytkowski, M., Scherer, R., Tadeusiewicz, R., Zadeh, L.A., Zurada, J.M. (eds.) ICAISC 2013, Part I. LNCS (LNAI), vol. 7894, pp. 532–539. Springer, Heidelberg (2013)
11. Duda, P., Jaworski, M., Pietruczuk, L., Scherer, R., Korytkowski, M., Gabryel, M.: On the application of fourier series density estimation for image classification based on feature description. In: Proceedings of the 8th International Conference on Knowledge, Information and Creativity Support Systems, Krakow, Poland, November 7-9, pp. 81–91 (2013)
12. Fei-Fei, L., Fergus, R., Perona, P.: Learning generative visual models from few training examples. In: IEEE Proc. CVPR Workshop on Generative-Model Based Vision (2004)
13. Gonzalez, R.C., Woods, R.E.: Digital Image Processing, 3rd edn. Prentice-Hall, Inc., Upper Saddle River (2006)
14. Hocenski, Z., Vasilic, S., Hocenski, V.: Improved canny edge detector in ceramic tiles defect detection. In: IECON 2006 - 32nd Annual Conference on IEEE Industrial Electronics, pp. 3328–3331 (November 2006)
15. Mai, F., Hung, Y.S., Zhong, H., Sze, W.F.: A hierarchical approach for fast and robust ellipse extraction. Pattern Recogn. 41(8), 2512–2524 (2008)
16. Nowicki, R.: Rough-neuro-fuzzy system with micog defuzzification. In: 2006 IEEE International Conference on Fuzzy Systems, pp. 1958–1965 (2006)
17. Nowicki, R.: On classification with missing data using rough-neuro-fuzzy systems. International Journal of Applied Mathematics and Computer Science 20(1), 55–67 (2010)
18. Nowicki, R., Rutkowski, L.: Soft techniques for bayesian classification. In: Neural Networks and Soft Computing, pp. 537–544. Springer (2003)
19. Zhang, N., Watanabe, T.: Text-transformed image classification based on data compression. In: Gaol, F.L. (ed.) Recent Progress in DEIT, Vol. 1. LNEE, vol. 156, pp. 365–370. Springer, Heidelberg (2013)
20. Przybył, A., Cpałka, K.: A new method to construct of interpretable models of dynamic systems. In: Rutkowski, L., Korytkowski, M., Scherer, R., Tadeusiewicz, R., Zadeh, L.A., Zurada, J.M. (eds.) ICAISC 2012, Part II. LNCS (LNAI), vol. 7268, pp. 697–705. Springer, Heidelberg (2012)
21. Rui-ling, D., Qing-xiang, L., Yu-he, L.: Summary of image edge detection. Optical Technique 3, 415–419 (2005)
22. Rutkowski, L., Cpalka, K.: Neuro-fuzzy systems derived from quasi-triangular norms. In: Proceedings of the 2004 IEEE International Conference on Fuzzy Systems, vol. 2, pp. 1031–1036 (July 2004)
23. Rutkowski, L.: Non-parametric learning algorithms in time-varying environments. Signal Processing 18(2), 129–137 (1989)
24. Rygał, J., Najgebauer, P., Romanowski, J., Scherer, R.: Extraction of objects from images using density of edges as basis for grabCut algorithm. In: Rutkowski, L., Korytkowski, M., Scherer, R., Tadeusiewicz, R., Zadeh, L.A., Zurada, J.M. (eds.) ICAISC 2013, Part I. LNCS (LNAI), vol. 7894, pp. 613–623. Springer, Heidelberg (2013)

25. Rygał, J., Najgebauer, P., Nowak, T., Romanowski, J., Gabryel, M., Scherer, R.: Properties and structure of fast text search engine in context of semantic image analysis. In: Rutkowski, L., Korytkowski, M., Scherer, R., Tadeusiewicz, R., Zadeh, L.A., Zurada, J.M. (eds.) ICAISC 2012, Part I. LNCS (LNAI), vol. 7267, pp. 592–599. Springer, Heidelberg (2012)
26. Sopyła, K., Drozda, P., Górecki, P.: SVM with CUDA accelerated kernels for big sparse problems. In: Rutkowski, L., Korytkowski, M., Scherer, R., Tadeusiewicz, R., Zadeh, L.A., Zurada, J.M. (eds.) ICAISC 2012, Part I. LNCS (LNAI), vol. 7267, pp. 439–447. Springer, Heidelberg (2012)
27. Tabolt, J.F., Xu, X.: Implementing grabcut (2006)

Recommendations and Object Discovery in Graph Databases Using Path Semantic Analysis

Lukasz Strobin and Adam Niewiadomski

Insitute of Information Technology
Lodz University of Technology
ul. Wólczańska 215, 90-924 Lodz, Poland
800337@edu.p.lodz.pl, adam.niewiadomski@p.lodz.pl

Abstract. This paper presents a novel approach to recommendation systems based on graph databases (e.g. LinkedData). Graph databases contain large amounts of heterogeneous and interlinked data from many sources, hence different algorithms to analyze these data are necessary. Moreover, it must be said that these properties of collected data make it impossible to store them in a relational data model. As for now, there are few methods of intelligent data exploration from graph databases.

In this paper, we propose new methods of discovering, searching and recommending objects in a graph database. The proposed methods can be applied to many domains or semantics, e.g. books, movies, etc. Paths in the graph (sequences of graph edges) have weights assigned, on the base of a training set according to their semantic importance. Recommended objects (vertices of the graph) may be found by analysing existing paths and where they lead to. Additionally, the method is able to determine if a found object belongs to a given problem from the point of view of a chosen semantics, hence only objects intuitively linked one to each other, are recommended. The proposed method is verified in two case studies, using an open graph database.

1 Introduction

This paper presents a new method of exploring graph databases. The graph data model differs from the most known relational model by Codd (1970). In a graph database, objects are stored in vertices of the graph, and edges (hence, as the consequence, paths) of the graph are models of "links" or "connections" between the objects described by vertices. These links or connections are determined within a given semantics which implies some similarity of given vertices. Recommendations and new objects discovering are based mostly on similarity of vertices, and the similarity is determined via analysis of paths connecting the vertices. The proposed approach is based on semantic analysis of paths using training sets. Paths found as important from the point of view of a given semantics are used to search the database and to discover new objects, possibly linked to objects already found. The proposed approach is able to face many

L. Rutkowski et al. (Eds.): ICAISC 2014, Part I, LNAI 8467, pp. 793–804, 2014.

problems related to graph data– incompleteness of data, unordered data, noised or heterogeneous data[1].

An example of a graph database is given in Fig. 1. As it is seen, this model of data, apart from vertices (objects) and edges (relations), enables dealing with additional abstraction layer: paths understood as sequences of edges between vertices. For example, vertex $V3$ is connected to vertex $V4$ with a path $V3$-$I6$-$V1$-$I5$-$V4$. Such links between data objects are not possible to be shown if a relational database is used.

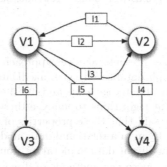

Fig. 1. A sample graph database with vertices $V1, \ldots, V4$ and edges $I1, \ldots, I6$. Paths are sequences of edges, e.g. $I3$-$I1$-$I6$

More and more data is easily available over the Internet in the form of graph databases, cf. [1, 2]. Therefore, new exploration algorithms should be designed to enable knowledge discovery from graph databases. It must emphasized that such data are not only sets of objects and relations (edges), but links between them are modeled – in the larger abstraction layer – with paths. That is why we focus mostly on path analysis in graph databases. Analysis of paths provides us with information and knowledge impossible or very difficult to be discovered from traditional datasets.

Some of recent research on path analysis in graph databases [3–5]) is mostly focused on evaluating semantic similarity. These methods are applied to recommendations, since by analyzing large amounts of data available over the Internet, recommendations can be made without the need of expensive item-tagging by experts [6–8].

However, generating recommendations in graph databases (e.g. LinkedData) is not a simple or straightforward task. The property that make these databases interesting is that they contain large amounts of data related to different semantics (topics, domains, contexts). This is an opposite to a typical approach, where relational databases contain data closely related to a specific domain.

---

[1] By heterogeneous we mean data from different sources, with different properties, and about different subjects.

The method for path analysis proposed in this paper is an original approach to address problems of recommending and searching data in path analysis. Using a training set, the paths that are relevant to a particular semantics are being found and applied to search new objects related to provided set. These links are then used for generating recommendations in a particular domain, e.g. in music, movies, books, etc. The rest of the paper is organized as follows: Section 2 contains an overview of path analysis methods in the recent literature. An original method of path analysis with respect to as specific semantics is introduced in Section 3. Section 4 presents details of generating recommendations from data stored in a graph database. Two case studies for two different semantics are presented in Section 5. Finally, the paper is concluded in Section 6.

2 An Overview of Path Analysis Methods

The authors of [9–11] propose various methods of evaluating semantic similarity based on path analysis in graph databases. However, these methods compute the similarity of two given graph vertices (with analysis of paths that connect them), but do not provide means of searching for other obejcts in the databases. The main advantage of the proposed methods is that based on initial analysis relevant paths are found, which can be used to search the database (see Section 3).

The simplest method of path analysis is to calculate the similarity as a function of a length of a shortest path between two analyzed objects (vertices). However such a simple analysis is not relevant to the characteristics of graph database, in particular, to their ability of storing information on semantic similarity, i.e. if two vertices belong to the same domain or not.

In many graph databases, this assumption does not hold, since evaluating semantic similarity must differentiate if there is only one or more paths of the same length for the same pair of vertices.

Another approach of evaluating semantic similarity is described in [2]. It is based on the number of short paths between two objects. In its expanded form (see [12]) paths are also weighted with real numbers to provide additional information on the similarity evaluated. Weights assigned to paths are related to the frequency of their occurrence – if a certain path occurs (is used) rarely, it is regarded as more important, and its weight is larger.

A method of determining informativeness of a path is also shown in [10]. The authors propose to analyze and to rank paths using various heuristics originating from information theory. Using these measures, paths between objects (vertices) are ranked as more or less informative. Yet another approach of path analysis is presented in [5]. The authors propose to assign weights to particular edges of a graph database, and to evaluate similarity by summing weights on paths connecting two objects. The major drawback of this approach is the necessity of assigning weights to edges manually by a human.

3 Evaluating Semantics-Specific Path Weights

The main focus of the proposed method is to determine which paths between vertices of graph database are important for a particular problem domain, i.e. in a given semantics. In contrary to existing approaches with manual assignment of weights to paths (e.g. [5]), we propose to use a training set, and evaluate weights in an adaptive way. The most important information that has to be given to a system is: *in what kind of relationship between vertices we are interested in?*. The training set is composed of pairs of objects, and values of their semantic similarity.

3.1 Evaluating Semantic Similarity of Vertices Using Path Weights

The main goal of the proposed method is to find and distinguish relevant and not relevant paths, and use them to evaluate semantic similarity of vertices. Thus, we propose a function of similarity based on paths connecting the vertices, presented in (1).

$$Sim(x,y) = \frac{\sum_{i=1}^{|P_{x,y}|} w(p_i)}{|P_{x,y}|} \tag{1}$$

where: $P_{x,y}$ denotes the set of all paths between vertices x and y, $|P_{x,y}|$ denotes the number of elements in set P (number of paths), p_i denotes a particular path - *ith* element of P, $w(p) \in [0,1]$ denotes the weight assigned to path, $i = 1, ..., |P_{x,y}|$ The method of finding weights of paths $w(p_i)$ is presented in Section 3.2.

Illustrative Example. Assume, a music recommendation system is to be built. Consider a graph database D, and three bands (vertices in D): A, B and C. Now we have to instruct the system which connections are important to us, and which are not. Say we are interested in connections that exist between bands A and B, but not in connections that exisit between A and C. Let us denote the set of paths between vertices A and B by $P_{A,B}$. Paths that are common to A-B and A-C ($P_{A,B} \cap P_{A,C}$) are regarded as unimportant (since their presence does not indicate that bands are related). On the other hand, paths that exist only between A and B, but not between A and C ($P_{A,B} \backslash P_{A,C}$) are regarded as important, since their presence indicates that bands are related in a way that we are interested in. Our method is a way to determine which paths are important, and how much.

Hence the information required for performing the analysis is a set of pairs of objects and their associated similarity. From the practical point of view, obtaining this information may be straightforward - after user specifies the objects (e.g. musical artists) he is interested in, he may be asked to choose a most and least similar objects from the list. Another possibility would be to use the training set given for a particular domain (e.q. music) by different user (or users).

3.2   Determining Path Weights

This section describes the process of finding the proper weight of paths $(w(p))$ based on the provided training set.

Fuzzy Relation Training Set. The training set is a set of pairs with the information that they are related or not. Hence, it is a binary relation. However, a classic bi-valued relation is not sufficient to express more values of similarity than 0 and 1. Therefore, we propose a training set which is a fuzzy relation representing similarity between two objects/vertices. The fuzzy relation links objects from set X – the set of all vertices in a graph database D:

$$U = \{\langle \langle x, y \rangle, \mu_U(x, y) \rangle : x, y \in X\} \tag{2}$$

where $\mu_U(x, y) \colon X \times X \to [0, 1]$ is the membership function of U representing values of semantic similarity between vertices x and y.

Evaluating Path Weights from the Training Set. Path weights are evaluated based on the analysis of the training set provided by the user. We analyze which paths connect objects that are highly related, and which paths connect objects that are not related.

Consider a database $\mathcal{D}$ and training set U. Each element (denoted U_i) of the training set describes the similarity between two vertices, x_i and y_i ($i = 1, ..., |U|$). Between these two vertices there exist a set of paths, denoted P_i. Each element of P_i, so each path connecting x_i and y_i, is assigned a weight which we denote w_i.

A path is a sequence of graph edges, and we say that two paths are the same, iff they are composed of a sequence of the same graph edges. In a graph database, the notion of *edge* is different that in case of a graph - we consider two edges in a graph database as equal if they have the same label.

Hence, it is possible that a number of the same paths exist in set P_i. Also, the same path may exists in in path sets P for different elements of the training set U (so it is possible that $P_i \cap P_j \neq \emptyset, i \neq j$). Hence, each path p may have more than one w_i associated with it.

In order to calculate the total weight of path p we propose to simply calculate an average of all weights associated to it. Function for calculating $w(p)$ is given in (3).

$$w(p) = \frac{\sum_{i=1}^{|U|} w_i(p) * n_{p_i}}{\sum_{i=1}^{|U|} n_{p_i}} \tag{3}$$

where: U denotes the training set, $|U|$ denotes the number of elements in the training set, $i = 1..|U|$, $w_i(p)$ denotes the weight associated to path p by the i-th member of U (so the $\mu(x_i, y_i)$ from (2)), $n_i(p)$ denotes the number of paths of type p that exist between pair of vertices (x_i, y_i) (so in the path set P_i)

4   Generating Recommendations Using Path Weights

After the analysis described in Section 3 , we have a set of paths and weights associated with them. These weights may used to evaluate semantic similarity between graph vertices, or may be used to search the database.There are two types of recommendations that have to be clearly differentiated: recommending from a known set of vertices, and discovering (that is searching) vertices based on found paths.

An important distinction is that in the first case we have to know which objects (from the domain at hand) a given database contains. While this is obvious in case of relational databases (in which in most cases tables are prepared especially for recommendations), it may become problematic in case of multi-pupose heterogeneous open graph databases. To select all objects from a given domain we have to rely on an ontology or some set of properties. For example, authors in [13] selected movies from DBPedia using a complex SPARQL query (which returned 1682 movies). The disadvantage of such approach is the possibility of missing (or wrong) data, necessity for knowledge of how the data is represented in the database (i.e. an ontology class for a given domain). In our approach based on searching the graph database (using found paths) this preprocessing is not necessary, paths are followed whereever they lead to. Graph nature of the data is directly leveraged, on contrary to most methods were data originating from graph is flattened to a different data structure and processed using non-graph algorithms.

A second step for (content-based) recommendation is ewaluation of similarity between a user object (or a set of objects, possibly with a grade) and all the other obejcts that may be recommended. In our proposed method based on searching the databases this is also not required. There is no need to look at every object and ewaluate the similarity. Links are followed from the user objects, in which way candidate objects are discovered (which are a small subset of whole domain). In the movie recommendation example that follows, a condidate set (where paths led to) consists usually of about 50 of 1682 movies, which shows clearly how much the problem domain is reduced.

Recommending from a Known Set of Objects. A set of objects (graph vertices) from which the recommendations are generated is given beforehand. We denote this set as T. Recommendations are based on a set of of items (also graph vertices) a user is interested in. We call this vertex set $USER\_SET$. Note that this set can be derived from the training set - the set of all x in U (see (2)).

To generate recommendations, for every vertex in T a vertex weight is calculated (denoted as $w(T_i)$). Vertex weight is a sum of its similarity (see (1)) to all elements from the input set ($USER\_SET$). Hence vertices most similar to the ones provided in the $USER\_SET$ will have the highest weight. Equation for calculating vertex weight is given in (4).

$$w(T_i) = \sum_{j=1}^{|USER\_SET|} Sim(T_i, v_j) \tag{4}$$

where: T is the set from which the recommendations are generated, $USER\_SET$ is the set of graph vertices important for a user, $Sim(T_i, v_j)$ is the semantic similarity (see (1)) between i-th element of set T and j-th vertex from set $USER\_SET$, $j = 1..|USER\_SET|$

After calculating the vertex weight for all elements of T, n vertices (n is a number of recommendations that is desired) from set T with the highest vertex weight are recommended.

Discovering New Objects. This approach to recommendation system is based on searching the graph database using paths found in the training phase.

However, in a heterogeneous database, these paths may lead to objects that are not related to the desired domain. For example, in case of music recommendation system, these paths may lead to objects that are not related to music. Since our goal is to do recommendation using provided input set, is it also desired to compute the vertex domain from the training set. In order to do this, we analyze the properties of the vertex, which we denote $properties(v)$.

We denote a set of properties that form a type definition by T_U, where U indicates that the type is defined for a particular training set U, and may be different for each training set U. Also, this type defnition is different for each database.

$$T_U = \{property_1, property_2, ..., property_n\} \tag{5}$$

And example of a type definition for music domain (rock music in particular) for DBPedia database is given in Section 5.1.

The question is: which properties an object has to have to be regarded as a member of a given type? The simplest answer to this question is that we take properties that are common to all elements in a training set, so that: $T_D = properties(v_1) \cap properties(v_2) \cap ... \cap properties(v_i)$, where $properties(v)$ is the property set of a vertex v.

However, we also have to take into account the fact that data from graph databases may be incomplete, hence only one vertex that does not have a particular property would make it disappear from the type definition. We propose that properties that exist in most of the vertices in a training set (so the threshold equals 50%) should be included in the type definition T_U from (5).

During the discovery of vertices we check if an object is of the desired type, by comparing its properties to the property set T_U. Type compatibility is defined in (6) (used in Algorithm 1).

$$c_{T_U}(v) = \frac{|properties(v) \cap T_U|}{|T_U|} \tag{6}$$

where: T_U is the type definition, so a set of properties, $properties(v)$ are properties of vertex v

The more properties a new vertex has in common with the properties that form type definition (defined in (5)), the higher the type compatibility.

In order to find new objects the set of paths and their weights is used (found in Section 3). We sort the obtained path set according to their weight. In the algorithm below, we denote the path set as PATHS. For recommendations, user also has to provide vertex set as a recommendation base (so a set that describes user taste). In the algorithm below, this set is denoted as USER_SET.

A path anchored in a given vertex leads to a set of other vertices, and the value for each of these vertices is increased by $w(p)$ (path weight) multiplied by the type compatibility of a vertex (see next paragraph and (6)). This means that if an important path ($w(p)$ close to 1) leads us to a vertex with similar type ($c_{T_U}(v)$ close to 1, see (6)), the recommendation measure for this vertex is increased significantly. After repeating this operation for some most important paths, values for certain vertices continue increasing. The most related vertices are recommended. This process is described in Algorithm 1.

Algorithm 1. Vertex discovery based on path weights

> **for** $p \in PATHS$ **do**
> > **for** $u \in USER\_SET$ **do**
> > > $u \xrightarrow{p} vertices$ { see to which vertices path p lead to}
> > > **for** $v \in vertices$ **do**
> > > > $w(v) = w(v) + w(p) * c_{T_U}(v)$ { increase the weight of vertex v by path weight times type compatibility (see (6)}
> > > **end for**
> > **end for**
> > **if** w(v) > threshold **then**
> > > recommend vertex v
> > **end if**
> **end for**

---

5 Experimental Evaluation

In this section, we present the complete process of applying the proposed path analysis method. We focus of the problem of recommending objects based on new object discovery, because in such scenario our method presents most of its merits.

5.1 Music Recommendation Using DBPedia

Used training set composed of the following elements:
U = {⟨ Metallica, Megadeth, 1.0 ⟩,⟨ Metallica, Lady Gaga, 0.0 ⟩,⟨ Iron Maiden, Slayer, 1.0 ⟩, ⟨ Iron Maiden, Eminem, 0.0 ⟩}

Table 1. The most informative paths found for music semantics

path length	path	weight of path $w(p)$
2	$associatedBand - associatedBand$	1
	$associatedMusicalArtist-$	1
	$-associatedMusicalArtist$	
	$genre - genre$	1
	$bandMember - formerBandMember$	1
	$artist - artist$	0.78
	$22 - rdf - syntax - ns\#type$ -	0.4
	...	
3	$background - background$	1
	$-formerBandMember$	
	$associatedMusicalArtist-$	1
	$currentMembers - associatedActs$	
	$hometown-$	0.9
	$hometown - associatedActs$	
	...	

It is important to emphasise the importance of the not related elements in the training set (Metallica - Lady Gaga and Iron Maiden - Eminem). In the graph database, many links may exists between these objects, since they represent the same type. For example, in DBPedia all musical artists are connected with the following paths (for readability, we abbreviate the names):

$$wikiPageUsesTemplate \rightarrow Template : Refend \leftarrow wikiPageUsesTemplate$$
$$wordnet\_type \rightarrow synset - musician - noun - 1 \leftarrow wordnet\_type$$
$$ontology/background \rightarrow "group\_or\_band"@en \leftarrow ontology/background$$

There are many such links between all musical artists. Adidtionally, some links are shared between most objects in the database (for example the fact that both objects are 'Things'). Hence, these not related input pairs are used to separate such uninformative links are largely informative links.

Using (3), we have obtained the most informative paths that can be used for recommendation. A small subset of these links is shown in the Table 1:

The type definition obtained for this training set U is composed of a large set of properties, below we present just some of them.

T_U = { Thing, Agent, Band, Organisation, Music Group, AmericanHardRock-MusicalGroups, Category:Musical quartets, Category:American hard rock musical groups, Category:Elektra Records artists, Category:Grammy Award-winning artists}

Using these paths we have searched the graph according to algorithm 1, where USER_PATHS are two elements from the provided training set - Metallica and Megadeth. Computed recommendation is shown in the Table 2.

Another important advantage of the proposed method is that the speed and precision of the recommendation process can be adjusted. If fast recommendations are

Table 2. Recommended musical artists (input bands: Metallica,Iron Maiden)

Band	Vertex weight $w(v)$ (see Algorithm 1)	type compatibility $c_{T_U}(v)$
Ozzy_Osbourne	81.2	0.97
Anthrax	49	0.97
Black_Sabbath	45	0.99
ASAP	43	0.95
Samson	38	0.91
System_of_a_Down	35	0.87
...		

required, we may just take a couple of important paths, preferably short. If we wish to search deeper in the graph, or nothing is discovered using short paths, we may use the longer paths.

Additionally, using the calibration obtained for the provided training set, we may also compute more recommendation. Results of the experiments shown below prove that the calibration for a given domain can be reused. Therefore, it is not necessary for every user to provide a full training set - if the system already has calibration data for a particular domain, we may use previously obtained path weights for new recommendations.

1. Input Bands: Eminem, 2Pac, 50Cent
   Recommendations: Dr.Dre, Snoop Dogg, Obie Trice, Busta Rhymes, Game, Xzibit, G-Unit, Nate Dogg
2. Input Bands: Rihanna, Lady Gaga, Shakira
   Recommendations: Akon, Nicki Minaj, T-Pain, Usher, Beyonce, Pitbull, Christina Aguilera, Chris Brown

5.2 Movies Recommendation Using DBPedia

Second experiment we conducted concerned movies recommendation. We used the following training set:
U = {⟨ Terminator, RoboCop, 1.0 ⟩, ⟨ Terminator, Annie Hall, 0.0 ⟩, ⟨ Reservoir Dogs, Goodfellas, 1.0 ⟩, ⟨ Reservoir Dogs, Clerks, 0.0 ⟩ }

Obtained most relevant paths are shown in Table 3. Compared to Table 1, we see a lot of differences. It is clear that the database has no information about direct associations, which proves that paths have to be computed for each problem domain separately.

Table 4 and points below show computed recommendations.

1. Input Movies: Toy Story, Shrek
   Recommendations: Shrek the Third, Shrek Forever After, The Road to El Dorado, Over the Hedge, Ratatouille, Wreck-It Ralph, Antz, Happy Feet Two, How to Train Your Dragon

Table 3. The most informative paths found for the movie semantics

path length	path	weight of path $w(p)$
2	$starring - starring$	0.44
	$type - type$	0.55
3	$subject - broader - subject$	1
	$director - type - type$	0.62
	$type - type - producer$	0.58
	$type - type - country$	0.48
	$writer - type - type$	0.45
	...	

Table 4. Recommended movies (input movies: Terminator, Reservoir Dogs)

Movie	Vertex weight $w(v)$ (see Algorithm 1)	type compatibility $c_{T_U}(v)$
Jackie Brown	4.01	0.98
Confessions of a Dangerous Mind	3.23	0.93
Sin City	3.12	0.96
The Lookout	2.67	0.91
Quick Change	2.33	0.88
Payback	2.23	0.94
Memento	1.78	0.87
...		

6 Conclusions

In this paper, we have presented a new method of generating recommendations using path semantic analysis in graph databases. Graph databases contain various data that are unordered, noised or heterogeneous. Hence, methods for exploration of such data are different than in case of relational databases. In graph database we take into account vertices and edges of the graph, but also paths (sequences of edges) must be analyzed. The analysis of paths includes weights assignment, and the weights describe how a given path is important from the point of view of a given semantics, e.g. music or movies.

We show that the proposed method is able to find paths for two main purposes: for determining semantic similarity between existing vertices of a graph and for searching graph databases for recommendations generating. Using our approach, there is no need to prepare a list of vertices which are sorted according to their similarity to a given object set, because these objects are discovered during the graph search process. By leveraging the fact that the data is a graph, the problem size is greatly reduced - in case of movies in DBPedia from 1682 to about 50. This feature makes the method – in comparison to those presented in the literature, see Section 2 – more efficient and computationally less costly. In addition, since the database may contain many types of objects, we have shown how to select objects that are relevant to a given semantics. Experimental evaluation proved that it suffices to perform calibration only once for a given recommendation domain, and there is no need to create a full training set each time. All experiments were conducted using an on-line DBPedia endpoint. In this experiment set up method scalability and performance could not be precisiely measured. Setting up a local instances of a graph databases and performing a thorough analysis is left for future work.

References

1. Bizer, C., Heath, T., Berners-Lee, T.: Linked Data - The Story So Far. International Journal on Semantic Web and Information Systems (IJSWIS) 5(3), 1–22 (2009)
2. Passant, A.: Measuring Semantic Distance on Linking Data and Using it for Resources Recommendations (2010)
3. Euzenat, J., Shvaiko, P.: Ontology Matching. Springer-Verlag New York, Inc., Secaucus (2007)
4. Rada, R., Mili, H., Bicknell, E., Blettner, M.: Development and application of a metric on semantic nets. IEEE Transactions on Systems, Man, and Cybernetics 19(1), 17–30 (1989)
5. Leal, J.P., Rodrigues, V., Queirós, R.: Computing semantic relatedness using dbpedia. In: Simões, A., Queirós, R., da Cruz, D.C. (eds.) SLATE. OASICS, vol. 21, pp. 133–147. Schloss Dagstuhl - Leibniz-Zentrum fuer Informatik (2012)
6. Passant, A.: dbrec — music recommendations using dBpedia. In: Patel-Schneider, P.F., Pan, Y., Hitzler, P., Mika, P., Zhang, L., Pan, J.Z., Horrocks, I., Glimm, B. (eds.) ISWC 2010, Part II. LNCS, vol. 6497, pp. 209–224. Springer, Heidelberg (2010)
7. Celma, O.: Music Recommendation and Discovery: The Long Tail, Long Fail, and Long Play in the Digital Music Space, 1st edn. Springer Publishing Company, Incorporated (2010)
8. Harispe, S., Ranwez, S., Janaqi, S., Montmain, J.: Semantic measures based on RDF projections: Application to content-based recommendation systems. In: Meersman, R., Panetto, H., Dillon, T., Eder, J., Bellahsene, Z., Ritter, N., De Leenheer, P., Dou, D. (eds.) OTM 2013. LNCS, vol. 8185, pp. 606–615. Springer, Heidelberg (2013)
9. Anyanwu, K., Sheth, A.P.: The ρ operator: Discovering and ranking associations on the semantic web. SIGMOD Record 31(4), 42–47 (2002)
10. Thushar, A.K.: An RDF Approach for Discovering the Relevant Semantic Associations in a Social Network. In: 16th International Conference on Advanced Computing and Communications, ADCOM 2008 (2008)
11. Sun, Y., Han, J., Yan, X., Yu, P.S., Wu, T.: Pathsim: Meta path-based top-k similarity search in heterogeneous information networks. In: VLDB 2011 (2011)
12. Zhong, J., Zhu, H., Li, J., Yu, Y.: Conceptual graph matching for semantic search. In: Priss, U., Corbett, D.R., Angelova, G. (eds.) ICCS 2002. LNCS (LNAI), vol. 2393, pp. 92–106. Springer, Heidelberg (2002)
13. Di Noia, T., Mirizzi, R., Ostuni, V.C., Romito, D., Zanker, M.: Linked open data to support content-based recommender systems. In: Proceedings of the 8th International Conference on Semantic Systems, I-SEMANTICS 2012, pp. 1–8. ACM, New York (2012)

Belief Propagation during Data Integration in a P2P Network

Piotr Szwed

AGH University of Technology, Kraków, Poland
pszwed@agh.edu.pl

Abstract. We examine properties of a peer to peer network comprising several agents that store various types of local data and exchange them through established communication channels. We propose a communication model applicable to a developed platform for data integration between various security agencies and we focus on analysis of consequences of established channels, e.g. an unintended information leakage or a presence of data silos that can be an impediment for cooperation. To detect such situations efficiently, we do not concentrate on exchanged data itself, but on a belief related to known classes of data. In the analyses we use a model, in which communications and belief states are expressed as matrix operations of linear algebra. We show that applying this model we can efficiently reason about the data that can potentially be exchanged between agents not linked directly and about the ranges, which can be reached by the data during communication flows.

Keywords: peer to peer network, data integration, belief revision, linear algebra.

1 Introduction

We analyze properties of a peer to peer network comprising several agents that store various types of local data and exchange it through established communication channels.

The presented considerations stem from a practical problem related to specification and design of a platform enabling data integration based on secure exchange of information between various security and law enforcement agencies in Poland. The project is conducted within the Polish Platform for Homeland Security.

An operational concept of the system is presented in Fig. 1. Several organizations $(A_1 \ldots A_n)$ are responsible for collecting data and keeping them in local repositories. The information exchange between participants is subject to various restrictions having their origins in law regulations or bilateral contracts. Typically, they specify which data object(or its part) and in which situation can be provided for a given requester. In many cases getting access to data requires following a certain workflow in which one institution issues a formal request for information and obtains either positive or negative response.

L. Rutkowski et al. (Eds.): ICAISC 2014, Part I, LNAI 8467, pp. 805–816, 2014.

The main goal of the designed integration platform is to automate the communication process, while respecting strictly the security and confidentiality requirements, as well as the defined rules for information exchange.

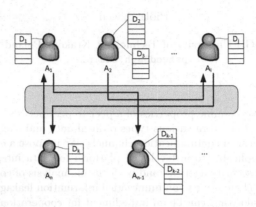

Fig. 1. An operational concept of a platform for secure exchange of information

Setting up the platform in a real environment brings up two problems. The first has rather technical implications. If an agent participates in an information exchange, appropriate interfaces, e.g. web services, should be implemented at its side. These interfaces reference data types that are either sent or received. Hence, an agent should be aware of types of objects that can reach him after flowing through the network (including readiness to accept incomplete records).

The second problem is related to the consequences of rules specifying information flows. A set of communication channels established between participants may result in unintended information leakage or, on the other side, create information silos or islands that can be an impediment for cooperation between security agencies.

To solve those problems efficiently, we do not focus on exchanged data itself, but on types of data (classes) that an agent is aware of. Moreover, it is assumed that all data types belong to a global schema (ontology) and potential problems related to definition of mappings between local ontologies and the global one can be at this stage ignored. Hence, a statement that an agent A_i *knows* a class D_j can be treated as a part of global belief state, which may be changed due to defined information flows. In the analyses we use a relatively simple, yet computationally efficient model, in which belief states and their updates are expressed as matrix operations of linear algebra. We show that this model allows for reasoning about the data, which can potentially be exchanged between agents not linked directly and about ranges the data may reach during the communication flows.

The paper is organized as follows: next Section 2 discusses various approaches to data integration with a special focus on application to crime and intelligence support, as well as on models for P2P integration approach. It is followed by

Section 3, which discusses the model of communication and integration based on linear algebra. Formal tools enabling reasoning are defined in Section 4. An example of a communication system is discussed in Section 5. Section 6 provides concluding remarks.

2 Related Works

Integration of data from heterogeneous data sources is an intensively researched topic stimulated by growing demand from various domains. They include business IT systems, which challenge the problem of interoperability between legacy systems after company mergers or acquisitions, bioinformatics [1], coordination of military systems [2], as well as crime and intelligence analysis [3].

The last domain encounters specific problems related to strict rules of data ownership and privacy, legal regulations pertaining to data exchange, as well as various impediments including lack of agreement between agencies responsible for collecting, storing and disseminating criminal intelligence [4]. In consequence, national or multinational security agencies often develop local repositories [5] and dedicated data integration and analysis tools, e.g. Coplink in USA [6] or recently LINK in Poland [7].

Basically, two approaches to the problem of data integration can be applied. The first assumes migration of data from heterogeneous sources to a central repository or a warehouse that can be queried referencing the terms in defined a common schema. Nevertheless, solutions based on such architecture often occurs too costly, moreover, they suffer from problems with data freshness and synchronization between local sources and the warehouse. In many situations they are also unfeasible and this is obviously the case for the considered application in the security domain.

The second approach consists in building a platform allowing to query the data in local repositories maintained by independent agents, e.g. company branches or institutions. Integration architectures within this approach fall into two categories: they are either centralized or peer to peer (P2P) [8].

A centralized architecture relies on a mediator service [9] providing a uniform interface to integrated data sources and referencing a global schema (or ontology). Within this setting, the most discussed architectural decision is related to the method of mapping between local and global schemas. It may follow either *Global as View* (GaV) or *Local as View* (LaV) approach [10]. In GaV every entity in a global schema is assigned with a set of mapping from local schemas. In LaV each local schema is treated as a view of the global one.

In a P2P architecture [11,12] each peer represents an autonomous information system with a local schema and the data integration is usually achieved by defining separate mapping between pairs of agents. However, P2P systems may also use a global ontology approach [13].

Epistemic logic [14] is a formal language that can be used to describe state of communicating agents; it was used by Calvanese et al. [12] to define semantcis of P2P data integration systems. A multi-agent modal logic capable of representing communications among agents was proposed by Pacuit and Parikh [15]. Liau showed in [16] that belief reasoning, revision and fusion can be interpreted as operations of matrix algebra.

This paper owns the most to the work [17] by Tojo, who proposed a linear algebra model describing belief updates in a network of communicating agents. We adapted this model to enable reasoning about types of data being exchanged among agents under the assumption that their schema belongs to or can be mapped to a global ontology.

3 Model of Communication System

We analyze a system comprised of a set of agents $A = \{A_1 \ldots A_n\}$ linked by channels $c_1, \ldots c_m$. Agents may store and exchange various data objects. The number of classes (types) of objects that can be used within the system is finite. Hence, they can be enumerated as $D_1, \ldots D_k$. Let us denote $D = \{D_1, \ldots D_k\}$

Each agent A_i can store objects belonging to a set of classes $D_{A_i} \subseteq D$. It may, however, expose only a part of its data. The restriction rules may concern both particular classes and particular objects. Moreover, they can be established individually for each bilateral communication within a pair of agents Nevertheless, in this work we are focused on modeling restrictions related to classes.

A communication channel is described as a tuple $c = (A_i, D_s, A_j, D_r)$, where A_i is a sender, D_s is a class of sent data, A_j is a receiver and D_r is a class of received data. Hence, a data object o of class D_s while being transmitted by a channel n can be transformed to an object o' belonging to D_r.

3.1 Classes

Let $\mathcal{A}$ is a global set of attributes (relations) and $\mathcal{V}$ a set of values. Let $v \colon \mathcal{A} \to 2^{\mathcal{V}}$ be a function that assigns to an attribute $a \in \mathcal{A}$ a set of values.

Definition 1. *A class is defined as a tuple $D = (\mathcal{A}_c, v_c)$, where $\mathcal{A}_c \subset \mathcal{A}$ and $v_c \subset v$ satisfies: $\forall a \in \mathcal{A}_c \colon a \in \operatorname{dom} v_c \wedge v_c(a) \subset v(a)$.*

Speaking informally, a class is defined by giving a set of its attributes $\mathcal{A}_c$ and possible attribute values.

Following Definition 1 an object o belonging to a class D can be interpreted as a valuation function $v_o \colon \mathcal{A} \to 2^{\mathcal{V}}$, satisfying: $\forall a \in \operatorname{dom} v_o \colon v_o(a) \subset v(a)$ and $\forall a \in \mathcal{A}_c \colon a \in \operatorname{dom} v_o \wedge v_o(a) \subset v_c(a)$.

Definition 2. *A class $D_1 = (\mathcal{A}_1, v_1)$ subsumes (is more general than) $D_2 = (\mathcal{A}_2, v_2)$, what is denoted by $D_1 \sqsupseteq D_2$ if $\mathcal{A}_1 \subset \mathcal{A}_2$ and $\forall a \in \mathcal{A}_1 \colon v_1(a) \supset v_2(a)$.*

A child class may introduce additional attributes or restrict values of attributes appearing in its supperclass. The definition allows to classify an object based on valuation of attributes.

To give some examples: *Person $\sqsupseteq$ PersonWithAddress*, provided that *Person $= (\{forename, surname, age\}, \{(forename \to string), (surname \to$*

$string), (age \rightarrow [0, \infty]\})$ and $PersonWithAddress = (\{forename, surname, address\}, \{(forename \rightarrow string), (surname \rightarrow string), (age \rightarrow [0, \infty]), (address \rightarrow string)\})$.

Another example is $Person \sqsupseteq Adolescent$, where $Adolescent = (\{forename, surname, age\}, \{(forename \rightarrow string), (surname \rightarrow string), (age \rightarrow [12, 18]\})$.

3.2 Upcasting

If a condition $D_1 \sqsupseteq D_2$ holds, then an object o_2 of the class D_2 can be *upcast* to the class D_1.

Let us assume that o_2 is described by a valuation function v_2. The upcast object o_1 should satisfy: $v_1 = v_2 \setminus \{(a, v_2(a)) : a \in \mathcal{A}_2 \setminus \mathcal{A}_1\}$. Upcasting allows to view an object of a child class D_2 as belonging to its parent class D_1. The upcasting operation removes a number of attributes from the mapping v_2. It should be mentioned, that the sets of admissible attribute values, which are restricted in child classes, do not need to be changed while upcasting.

Let $D = \{D_1, \ldots, D_n\}$ be a set of classes, and $\sqsupseteq$ is a subsumption relation. The relation $\sqsupseteq$ is a transitive closure if $\forall (D_i, D_j), (D_j, D_k) \in \sqsupseteq : (D_i, D_k) \in \sqsupseteq$.

Technically, a closure is stored by $n \times n$ matrix of boolean values $U = [u_{ij}]$ called the *upcast matrix*. The value of an element u_{ij} is set to T if $C_i \sqsupseteq C_j$ and F otherwise. If H is a matrix showing direct taxonomic relations (direct subsumption), then $U = H^*$.

3.3 Definition of a Communication System

Let $c = (A_i, D_s, A_j, D_r)$ be a communication channel between two agents. We limit our considerations to *upcasting channels*, i.e. channels satisfying $D_r \sqsupseteq D_s$. Such assumption can be justified as follows: while an object is sent through a channel it is not likely that its content will be extended, e.g. by setting additional attributes. Rather an opposite direction is to be taken. Some attributes may be hidden and removed due to legal restrictions related to information access.

To summarize the discussed concepts we give below the definition of a communication system.

Definition 3. *A communication system is defined as* $\Gamma = (A, D, \sqsupseteq, C)$, *where A is a set of agents, D a set of data types (classes), $\sqsupseteq$ is a subsumption relation and $C \subset A \times D \times A \times D$) is a set of communication channels. It is assumed that all channels are upcasting, i.e. the following condition holds:* $\forall (A_i, D_m, A_j, D_n) \in C : D_n \sqsupseteq D_m$.

4 Reasoning

In this section we reformulate definition of the communication system in terms of linear algebra, as well as we provide formal tools enabling reasoning about its properties.

4.1 System State

The state of the system is described as an assignment of sets of classes to agents. We do not focus on the data items that are known to an agents, but rather on classes of objects which they store.

We assume that sets of classes D and agents A are ordered. System state is a $|D| \times |A|$ matrix $S = [s_j^i]$. Its element s_j^i is equal to T (true) if an agent A_j is aware of the existence of a class D_i.

4.2 Communication and Belief Propagation

The set of channels $C \subset A \times D \times A \times D$ is encoded as 4-dimensional matrix $E = [e_{ki}^{lj}]$ of size $|D| \times |A| \times |A| \times |D|$ containing boolean values T and F.

$$e_{ki}^{lj} = \begin{cases} T, & \text{if } (A_i, D_j, A_k, D_l) \in C \\ T, & \text{if } l = i \text{ and } k = j \\ F, & \text{otherwise} \end{cases} \tag{1}$$

It can be observed that elements at diagonals $l = i$ and $k = j$ are set to T. They play the role of identity matrix I, hence each matrix E can be decomposed into $E' + I$, where E' describes the true communications and I guarantees that agents preserve the information gained.

Belief propagation is described by a state equation (2), where $S(m)$ and $S(m+1)$ denote successive states and $\circ$ is an operator that takes on input a 4D and a 2D boolean matrix and yields a 2D matrix, whose elements are calculated according to formula (3). In each step agents propagate information on classes of stored data to their neighbors. They also keep information on classes they know.

Following the Einstein convention for tensors we omit conjunction and disjunction in the subsequent formulas defining matrix operators.

$$S(m+1) = E \circ S(m) \tag{2}$$

$$s_k^l(m+1) = \bigvee_i \bigwedge_j e_{ki}^{lj} s_j^i(m) \tag{3}$$

4.3 Reachable State

Applying the equation (2) multiple times we obtain a sequence of states.

Proposition 1. *The sequence of states $\sigma = S(0), S(1), \dots, S(n), \dots$, where $S(i+1) = E \circ S(i)$ converges.*

Proof. From (1) the matrix E can be expressed as sum of $(E' + I)$, hence for any i: $S(i+1) = E' \circ S(i) + S(i)$, thus σ is nondecreasing. As each state S_i is bounded above by a matrix S_{max} having all elements equal to T (true), the sequence σ converges.

Consequences of Proposition 1 are the following: if we assume, what an agent knows, i.e. which types of data it stores, we may conclude how far this information can be propagated in the network. This allows for detecting information silos or islands of belief.

4.4 Closure of a Communication Graph

Let us define and operator $\otimes$ that multiplies two communication matrices E and G. The resulting matrix $F = E \otimes G$ id given by formula (4).

$$f_{mn}^{kl} = e_{ij}^{kl} g_{mn}^{ji} \tag{4}$$

Each i-th element $S(i)$ of the sequence σ can be expressed applying the operator $\otimes$ as $(E \otimes E \otimes \ldots E) \circ S(0)$, where E component appear i times. This can be denoted shortly as: $S(i) = E^i \circ S(0)$

Proposition 2. *The sequence $\epsilon = E, E^2, \ldots E^i \ldots$ converges.*

Proof. Observe that $E^i \otimes E$ can be expressed as $(E'' + I) \otimes (E' + I) = E'' \otimes E' + E'' + E' + I$, hence the sequence ϵ is nondecreasing, it is also bounded above, thus converges.

As a consequence of Proposition 2, the E^* matrix can be interpreted as a transitive closure of the communication graph. To give an example, if there exist two channels $c_{12} = (A_1, D_1, A_2, D_2)$ and $c_{23} = (A_2, D_2, A_3, D_3)$ represented as appropriate elements in E, the matrix E^* contains an element corresponding to the derived channel $c_{13} = (A_1, D_1, A_3, D_3)$ being a shortcut from A_1 to A_3. Such derived channels can be identified by examination of $E^* - E$.

4.5 Channel and Class Matching

Let us consider a situation where agents A_i and A_j are linked by a channel $n = (A_i, C_s, A_j, C_r)$ and the agent A_i is aware of a class C_{s2} satisfying $C_s \sqsupseteq C_{s2}$. The channel specification does not match directly the class C_{s2}, hence objects of this class cannot be transmitted trough the channel. However, they can be upcast to C_s (by removing extra attributes appearing in C_{s2}) and then sent.

Following this observation, we introduce additional component to the state equation (2), namely the upcast matrix U.

$$S(m + 1) = E \circ (U S(m)) \tag{5}$$

The formula (5) can be rewritten as (6), where $\odot$ operator is defined by (7).

$$S(m + 1) = (E \odot U) \circ S(m) \tag{6}$$

$$f_{mj}^{kl} = e_{mi}^{kl} u_j^i \tag{7}$$

Let us observe that an upcast operation can be also applied on arrival of data through a channel, i.e. on left side of the state equation (2). With a set of introduced operators it can be defined as (8).

$$S(m + 1) = ((I \odot U) \otimes E) \circ S(m) \tag{8}$$

From now we will omit operators in presented formulas assuming that appropriate operator can be selected based on types of operands. It should be noted that the data structures supporting E, S and U matrices and operators given by (3), (4) and (7) were implemented in a prototype software that was used to analyze the example presented in the next section.

5   Example

An example of a system comprising five agents linked by communication channels is given in Fig. 2. Agents $A_1 \ldots A_5$ are marked as circles, whereas channels as rectangles. Each channel is attributed with two class names: the first is a class of objects that are sent, the second class of objects received. The hierarchy of classes referenced on the diagram is shown in Fig. 3. As it can be checked, all channels are upcasting channels, i.e. classes on output subsume classes on input.

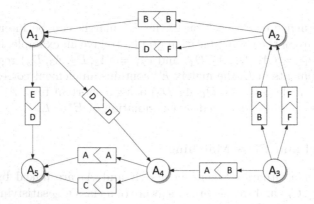

Fig. 2. Five agents $A_1 \ldots A_5$ linked by communication channels

The upcast matrix for the class hierarchy in Fig. 3 is given by (9). As we are not capable of presenting communication matrices, we will rather enumerate the channels they define.

$$U = \begin{pmatrix} T & T & F & F & F & F \\ F & T & F & F & F & F \\ F & F & T & T & T & T \\ F & F & F & T & T & T \\ F & F & F & F & T & F \\ F & F & F & F & F & T \end{pmatrix} \tag{9}$$

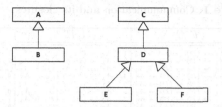

Fig. 3. Example of a class hierarchy

5.1 Closures of Communication Graph

In order to reason about possible communications we calculate closures of the communication graph. Table 1 gives the communication channels for E^*, E^*U, UE^* and $(EU)^*$. The initial setting defines 9 channels. The first column related to E^* gives 17 information flows, that are obtained by direct class matching (without upcasting). The second applies upcasting on the right side. The third column corresponds to UE^* (upcasting objects on arrival) and the fourth applies upcasting each time the objects are sent. For the considered example E^*U fits the best intuition, how the communication is performed. Calculation of the closure $(EU)^*$ yields channels that apply upcasting on arrival, e.g. $A_1 \to (D) \to (C) \to A_4$, whereas the initial channel specification is $A_1 \to (D) \to (D) \to A_4$. This can be explained by analysis of formula (10) showing the expanded chain of matrix multiplications for $(EU)^*$. It can be observed, that actually for each communication, apart the last one, upcasting on reception of data occurs.

$$(EU)^* = EUEU \ldots E(UEU) \ldots EU \tag{10}$$

Regardless of the closure applied, its analysis yields valuable information about possible information flows. Returning back to the problem origins, each implemented channel (described by E) is defined according to law regulations or bilateral contracts. In the case where E^* and E differs, e.g. the channel $A_3 \to (B) \to (B) \to A_1$ exists in E^* and not in E, a contract between A_3 and A_1 can be proposed to shorten the communication path.

An interesting problem that can be examined is a possible specification of *forbidden* communication channels. Such restriction may stem from legal regulations. For example, if a channel $A_3 \to (F) \to (C) \to A_4$ is forbidden (c.f. Fig. 2), its presence in $(EU)^*$ can be considered a possibility of an unintended information leakage violating current law regulations.

5.2 State Reachability

Another property that can be examined is state reachability. For the analysis an initial state S_0 defining, which classes are known by the agents is required. Then, the state equation (2) or (5) can be applied multiple times giving information about the data types that the agents eventually should be aware of. An alternative method consists in calculating directly E^*US_0 or $(EU)^*S_0$.

Table 1. Commnunication and its closures

E^*	E^*U	UE^*	$(EU)^*$
1. $A_1 \to (D) \to (D) \to A_4$	1. $A_1 \to (D) \to (D) \to A_4$	1. $A_1 \to (D) \to (C) \to A_4$	1. $A_1 \to (D) \to (C) \to A_4$
2. $A_1 \to (D) \to (C) \to A_5$	2. $A_1 \to (D) \to (C) \to A_5$	2. $A_1 \to (D) \to (D) \to A_4$	2. $A_1 \to (D) \to (D) \to A_4$
3. $A_1 \to (E) \to (D) \to A_5$	3. $A_1 \to (E) \to (D) \to A_4$	3. $A_1 \to (D) \to (C) \to A_5$	3. $A_1 \to (D) \to (C) \to A_5$
4. $A_2 \to (B) \to (B) \to A_1$	4. $A_1 \to (E) \to (C) \to A_5$	4. $A_1 \to (E) \to (C) \to A_5$	4. $A_1 \to (E) \to (C) \to A_4$
5. $A_2 \to (F) \to (D) \to A_1$	5. $A_1 \to (E) \to (D) \to A_5$	5. $A_1 \to (E) \to (D) \to A_5$	5. $A_1 \to (E) \to (D) \to A_4$
6. $A_2 \to (F) \to (D) \to A_4$	6. $A_1 \to (F) \to (D) \to A_4$	6. $A_2 \to (B) \to (A) \to A_1$	6. $A_1 \to (E) \to (C) \to A_5$
7. $A_2 \to (F) \to (C) \to A_5$	7. $A_1 \to (F) \to (C) \to A_5$	7. $A_2 \to (B) \to (B) \to A_1$	7. $A_1 \to (E) \to (D) \to A_5$
8. $A_3 \to (B) \to (B) \to A_1$	8. $A_2 \to (B) \to (B) \to A_1$	8. $A_2 \to (F) \to (C) \to A_1$	8. $A_1 \to (F) \to (C) \to A_4$
9. $A_3 \to (B) \to (B) \to A_2$	9. $A_2 \to (F) \to (D) \to A_1$	9. $A_2 \to (F) \to (D) \to A_1$	9. $A_1 \to (F) \to (D) \to A_4$
10. $A_3 \to (B) \to (A) \to A_4$	10. $A_2 \to (F) \to (D) \to A_4$	10. $A_2 \to (F) \to (C) \to A_4$	10. $A_1 \to (F) \to (C) \to A_5$
11. $A_3 \to (B) \to (A) \to A_5$	11. $A_2 \to (F) \to (C) \to A_5$	11. $A_2 \to (F) \to (C) \to A_5$	11. $A_2 \to (B) \to (A) \to A_1$
12. $A_3 \to (F) \to (D) \to A_1$	12. $A_3 \to (B) \to (B) \to A_1$	12. $A_2 \to (F) \to (C) \to A_5$	12. $A_2 \to (B) \to (B) \to A_1$
13. $A_3 \to (F) \to (F) \to A_2$	13. $A_3 \to (B) \to (B) \to A_2$	13. $A_3 \to (B) \to (A) \to A_1$	13. $A_2 \to (F) \to (C) \to A_1$
14. $A_3 \to (F) \to (D) \to A_4$	14. $A_3 \to (B) \to (A) \to A_4$	14. $A_3 \to (B) \to (B) \to A_1$	14. $A_2 \to (F) \to (D) \to A_1$
15. $A_3 \to (F) \to (C) \to A_5$	15. $A_3 \to (B) \to (A) \to A_5$	15. $A_3 \to (B) \to (A) \to A_2$	15. $A_2 \to (F) \to (C) \to A_4$
16. $A_4 \to (A) \to (A) \to A_5$	16. $A_3 \to (F) \to (D) \to A_1$	16. $A_3 \to (B) \to (B) \to A_2$	16. $A_2 \to (F) \to (D) \to A_4$
17. $A_4 \to (D) \to (C) \to A_5$	17. $A_3 \to (F) \to (F) \to A_2$	17. $A_3 \to (B) \to (A) \to A_4$	17. $A_2 \to (F) \to (C) \to A_5$
	18. $A_3 \to (F) \to (D) \to A_4$	18. $A_3 \to (B) \to (A) \to A_5$	18. $A_3 \to (B) \to (A) \to A_1$
	19. $A_3 \to (F) \to (C) \to A_5$	19. $A_3 \to (F) \to (C) \to A_1$	19. $A_3 \to (B) \to (B) \to A_1$
	20. $A_4 \to (A) \to (A) \to A_5$	20. $A_3 \to (F) \to (D) \to A_1$	20. $A_3 \to (B) \to (A) \to A_2$
	21. $A_4 \to (B) \to (A) \to A_5$	21. $A_3 \to (F) \to (C) \to A_2$	21. $A_3 \to (B) \to (B) \to A_2$
	22. $A_4 \to (D) \to (C) \to A_5$	22. $A_3 \to (F) \to (D) \to A_2$	22. $A_3 \to (B) \to (A) \to A_4$
	23. $A_4 \to (E) \to (C) \to A_5$	23. $A_3 \to (F) \to (F) \to A_2$	23. $A_3 \to (B) \to (A) \to A_5$
	24. $A_4 \to (F) \to (C) \to A_5$	24. $A_3 \to (F) \to (C) \to A_4$	24. $A_3 \to (F) \to (C) \to A_1$
		25. $A_3 \to (F) \to (D) \to A_4$	25. $A_3 \to (F) \to (D) \to A_1$
		26. $A_3 \to (F) \to (C) \to A_5$	26. $A_3 \to (F) \to (C) \to A_2$
		27. $A_4 \to (A) \to (A) \to A_5$	27. $A_3 \to (F) \to (D) \to A_2$
		28. $A_4 \to (D) \to (C) \to A_5$	28. $A_3 \to (F) \to (F) \to A_2$
			29. $A_3 \to (F) \to (C) \to A_4$
			30. $A_3 \to (F) \to (D) \to A_4$
			31. $A_3 \to (F) \to (C) \to A_5$
			32. $A_4 \to (A) \to (A) \to A_5$
			33. $A_4 \to (B) \to (A) \to A_5$
			34. $A_4 \to (D) \to (C) \to A_5$
			35. $A_4 \to (E) \to (C) \to A_5$
			36. $A_4 \to (F) \to (C) \to A_5$

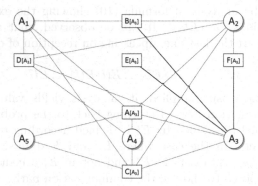

Fig. 4. Reachable state from A_3 for $(EU)^*$

Probably, the most valuable result can be obtained by analyzing a state that can be reached assuming that only one agent is aware of several classes (e.g. related to the data that are stored in its local database). Hence, the reachable state describes the range, which information originating from a given agent can reach.

Fig. 4 shows reachable states that can be computed applying $(EU)^*$. Classes are marked as rectangles and are connected by edges with agents, who know them. In the initial state S_0 agent A_3 knows classes from the set $\{E, F, B\}$. The initial assignment is marked with the continuous bold lines.

It can be observed, that A_3 does not share information of type E with anyone, i.e. behaves like a silo with respect to E, further, data objects of type F can reach only A_2 and for B the information is shared with A_1 and A_2.

The analysis of reachable states may indicate several clusters of agents, each of them assigned with a certain class D_i. Hence, no data object belonging to classes in D_i may leave the cluster, which constitutes in this way an island of belief. Presence of islands may indicate a serious obstacle for integration of activities of various security agencies.

6 Conclusions

The main contributions of this work are an extension of Tojo's model of belief update with the concept of upcasting operations and an idea of its application to reason about a P2P data integration platform within the security domain.

Introduction of upcasting channels was indispensable to model schema mapping and partial information hiding during data transmission. As a distinction is made between types of data that are sent and received, 4-dimensional tensors were used to model communications. A new element of the model is also the idea of applying upcasting operation before transmission (technically implemented by an upcast matrix) to match a channel specification.

Mapping the concept of upcasting back to the Tojo's belief revision model related to logic propositions, we may consider an atomic proposition p as a statement: an agent A knows (stores objects of) the class P. Hence, if a class Q subsumes P, then such knowledge can be specified by an axiom $p \Rightarrow q$, which should be globally satisfied by an underlying semantic model.

Although the formal tools used for analysis of communications between agents are relatively simple, they occurred surprisingly very efficient and computationally feasible. The size of the presented example is small, hence, it is possible to reason about its properties by hand. As a real use case for the developed platform, we may expect few dozen agents storing data belonging to about ten categories, that can be further divided into about fifty subclasses. Even if the expected structure of communication is rather sparse, we find that for systems of such size, a manual analysis of their properties would be virtually impossible. Hence, models and tools supporting automated analysis can be considered a very useful aid during the deployment and the validation.

Acknowledgments. This work is supported by the National Centre for Research and Development (NCBiR) under Grant No. O ROB 0021 01/ID 21/2.

References

1. Caragea, D., Pathak, J., Bao, J., Silvescu, A., Andorf, C., Dobbs, D., Honavar, V.: Information integration and knowledge acquisition from semantically heterogeneous biological data sources. In: Ludäscher, B., Raschid, L. (eds.) DILS 2005. LNCS (LNBI), vol. 3615, pp. 175–190. Springer, Heidelberg (2005)

2. Tolk, A., Muguira, J.A.: The levels of conceptual interoperability model. In: Proceedings of the 2003 Fall Simulation Interoperability Workshop, vol. 7. Citeseer (2003)
3. Chen, H., Wang, F.Y.: Guest editors' introduction: Artificial intelligence for homeland security. IEEE Intelligent Systems 20(5), 12–16 (2005)
4. Parliamentary Joint Committee on Law Enforcement: Inquiry into the gathering and use of criminal intelligence. Commonwealth of Australia (May 2013)
5. Ruść, T., Orzechowski, T., Korus, P., Grega, M., Leszczuk, M., et al.: Preliminary report on police and prosecutor repositories and access procedures. Deliverable D5.1, INDECT Consortium (June 2010)
6. Hauck, R., Atabakhsb, H., Ongvasith, P., Gupta, H., Chen, H.: Using Coplink to analyze criminal-justice data. Computer 35(3), 30–37 (2002)
7. Dajda, J., Dębski, R., Kisiel-Dorohinicki, M., Piętak, K.: Multi-domain data integration for criminal intelligence. In: Gruca, A., Czachórski, T., Kozielski, S. (eds.) Man-Machine Interactions 3. AISC, vol. 242, pp. 345–352. Springer, Heidelberg (2014)
8. Cruz, I.F., Xiao, H.: Ontology driven data integration in heterogeneous networks. In: Tolk, A., Jain, L. (eds.) Complex Systems in Knowledge-based Environments: Theory, Models and Applications. SCI, vol. 168, pp. 75–98. Springer, Heidelberg (2009)
9. Hull, R., Zhou, G.: A framework for supporting data integration using the materialized and virtual approaches, vol. 25. ACM (1996)
10. Lenzerini, M.: Data integration: A theoretical perspective. In: Proceedings of the Twenty-first ACM SIGMOD-SIGACT-SIGART Symposium on Principles of Database Systems, pp. 233–246. ACM (2002)
11. Arenas, M., Kantere, V., Kementsietsidis, A., Kiringa, I., Miller, R.J., Mylopoulos, J.: The hyperion project: from data integration to data coordination. ACM SIGMOD Record 32(3), 53–58 (2003)
12. Calvanese, D., Damaggio, E., De Giacomo, G., Lenzerini, M., Rosati, R.: Semantic data integration in P2P systems. In: Aberer, K., Koubarakis, M., Kalogeraki, V. (eds.) DBISP2P 2003. LNCS, vol. 2944, pp. 77–90. Springer, Heidelberg (2004)
13. Cruz, I.F., Xiao, H., Hsu, F.: Peer-to-peer semantic integration of XML and RDF data sources. In: Moro, G., Bergamaschi, S., Aberer, K. (eds.) AP2PC 2004. LNCS (LNAI), vol. 3601, pp. 108–119. Springer, Heidelberg (2005)
14. Gochet, P., Gribomont, P.: Epistemic logic. In: Gabbay, D.M., Woods, J. (eds.) Logic and the Modalities in the Twentieth Century. Handbook of the History of Logic, vol. 7, pp. 99–195. North-Holland (2006)
15. Pacuit, E., Parikh, R.: Reasoning about communication graphs. Interactive Logic 1, 135–157 (2007)
16. Liau, C.-J.: Belief reasoning, revision and fusion by matrix algebra. In: Tsumoto, S., Słowiński, R., Komorowski, J., Grzymała-Busse, J.W. (eds.) RSCTC 2004. LNCS (LNAI), vol. 3066, pp. 133–142. Springer, Heidelberg (2004)
17. Tojo, S.: Collective belief revision in linear algebra. In: Ganzha, M., Maciaszek, L., Paprzycki, M. (eds.) Proceedings of the 2013 Federated Conference on Computer Science and Information Systems, pp. 175–178. IEEE (2013)

Author Index

Printed in the United States
By Bookmasters